NAVIGATOR SERIES

2000+ PROBLEMS

JEE Main & Advanced

Thermodynamics & Waves

PRADEEP BENIWAL
IIT Kharagpur

arihant
SUCCESS AND NOTHING LESS

arihant
SUCCESS AND NOTHING LESS

ARIHANT PRAKASHAN (Series), MEERUT

Administrative & Production Offices

Regd. Office
'Ramchhaya' 4577/15, Agarwal Road, Darya Ganj, New Delhi -110002
Tele: 011- 47630600, 43518550

Head Office
Kalindi, TP Nagar, Meerut (UP) - 250002
Tel: 0121-7156203, 7156204

Sales & Support Offices
Agra, Ahmedabad, Bengaluru, Bareilly, Chennai, Delhi, Guwahati, Hyderabad, Jaipur, Jhansi, Kolkata, Lucknow, Nagpur & Pune.

PRICE : ₹470.00

PO No : TXT-XX-XXXXXXX-X-XX

Published by Arihant Publications (India) Ltd.

For further information about the books published by Arihant, log on to www.arihantbooks.com or e-mail at info@arihantbooks.com

Follow us on

PREFACE

Physics is a subject that requires a lot of practice to master it and the best way to practice Physics is to solve more & more problems right from the beginner's level to the most complex ones. That's why the search for a good Physics Problems book has always been the top notch task of each good student.

During the last 15 Years while teaching & mentoring thousands of students preparing for JEE Main, JEE Advanced, KVPY, Olympiads etc. I always felt the need of such a book that can offer quality problems of Physics for all the topics of different chapters. There are many problems books available in the market but unfortunately none of them serve the purpose perfectly.

To fulfil the need of a good Physics Problems book, I have prepared the book **JEE Navigator Thermodynamics & Waves.** All the problems given in this book are arranged conceptually and systematically in order to test the conceptual understanding & analytical ability of the students.

All the problems given in each chapter of this book have been developed with the utmost care and arranged in a way to enhance the problem-solving skills of the students & to boost their confidence to tackle complex JEE Problems.

The Points given below will help you to learn the basic structure of the book;

- Each chapter is divided into three major heads; **Level 1 'Starter Level', Level 2 'JEE Main Level' & Level 3 'JEE Advanced Level'.**
- **Level 1 'Starter Level'** consists of preliminary questions that test basic concepts. After completing this level student will have a solid understanding of fundamentals of the chapter necessary to solve the problems.
- **Level 2 'JEE Main Level'** has single choice correct questions and numerical value questions aimed especially for JEE Main.
- **Level 3 'JEE Advanced Level'** consists of various types of questions; MCQ with one or more than one correct answer, Comprehension Based Questions, Match the Columns and Numerical Value Questions as per the latest JEE Advanced Pattern.
- The problems given in JEE Advanced Level are made to be conceptually challenging resulting in practical and relevant practice for JEE Advanced.
- **Past Exams' Questions** of JEE Main & JEE Advanced are also covered in each chapter.
- Detailed solutions to all the problems have been provided at the end of every chapter just to help the students in case they stuck somewhere while solving some questions.

At the end, I can say confidently that if you rigorously practice the problems given in this book, then surely you will get an edge in Physics and will increase your chance of getting good JEE Score.

However, I have taken the utmost care while writing this book but if any error or whatsoever has skipped my attention, then please bring it to my notice so that it can be rectified. I would also like to appeal all my fellow Physics Teachers to have a look at the book and share their valuable suggestions for its further improvement.

Pradeep Beniwal
B.Tech, IIT Kharagpur
problemsinphysics@yahoo.com

CONTENTS

CHAPTER~01

THERMAL EXPANSION

LEVEL 01 Starter Level

1.1 Temperature

1 Temperature of a patient is 40°C. Find the temperature on Fahrenheit scale and Kelvin scale.

2 The temperature of an iron piece is heated from 30°C to 90°C. What is the change in its temperature on the Fahrenheit scale and on the Kelvin scale?

3 At what temperature is the Fahrenheit scale reading equal to twice of Celsius?

4 The upper and lower fixed points of a faulty thermometer are 5°C and 105°C. If the thermometer reads 25° C, what is the actual temperature?

5 The pressures of the gas in a constant volume gas thermometer are 80 cm, 90 cm and 100 cm of mercury at the ice point, the steam point and in a heated wax bath, respectively. Find the temperature of the wax bath.

6 A platinum resistance thermometer reads 0° when its resistance is 80 Ω and 100° when its resistance is 90Ω. Find the temperature at the platinum scale at which the resistance is 86Ω.

1.2 Thermal Expansion

1 A small ring having small gap is shown in figure. On heating, what will happen to the size of gap?

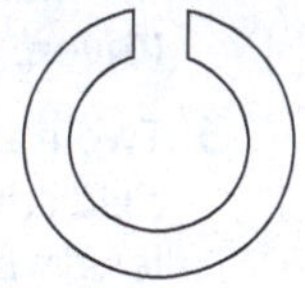

2. A rectangular plate has a circular cavity as shown in the figure. If we increase its temperature, then which dimension will increase in following figure?

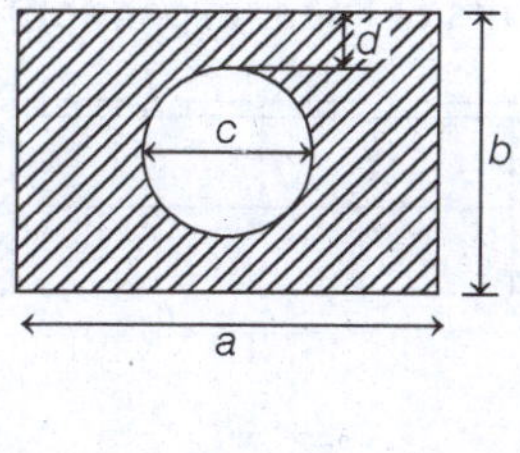

1.3 Linear Expansion

1 A concrete slab has a length of 10 m on a winter night when the temperature is 0°C. Find the length of the slab on a summer day when the temperature is 35°C. (Coefficient of linear expansion of concrete is 1.0×10^{-5} /°C.)

2 The length of a metal rod at 0°C is 0.5 m. When it is heated, its length increases by 2.7 mm. What will be the final temperature of rod? (Coefficient of linear expansion of metal = 90×10^{-6} /°C)

3 The length of each steel rail is 10 m in winter. The coefficient of linear expansion of steel is 0.000012/°C and the temperature increases by 15°C in summer. What is the gap to be left between the rails?

4 What is the percentage change in length of 1m iron rod, if its temperature changes by 100°C? (α for iron is 2×10^{-5} /°C).

5 A steel ring of 3.000 inches inside diameter at 20° C is to be heated and slipped over a brass shaft measuring 3.002 inches in diameter at 20°C. To what temperature should ring be heated? ($\alpha_{steel} = 1.2 \times 10^{-5}$ /°C).

6 An iron tyre is to be fitted onto a wooden wheel 1.0 m in diameter. The diameter of the tyre is 6 mm smaller than that of wheel. What is the minimum temperature rise to which the tyre should be heated?
(Coefficient of volume expansion of iron is 3.6×10^{-5} /°C).

7 What length of brass and iron at 0°C must be used, if the difference between their lengths is always 0.2 m? (The value of α for brass and iron are 18×10^{-6} /°C and 12×10^{-6} /°C respectively.)

8 An iron rod of length 50 cm is joined at an end to copper rod of length 100 cm at 20°C. Find the length of the system at 100°C and average coefficient of linear expansion of the system.
($\alpha_{iron} = 12 \times 10^{-6}$ /°C and $\alpha_{copper} = 17 \times 10^{-6}$ /°C.)

9 An aluminium plate fixed in a horizontal position has a hole of diameter 2.000 cm. A steel sphere of diameter 2.005 cm rests on this hole. All the lengths refer to a temperature of 10°C. The temperature of the entire system is slowly increased. At what temperature will the ball fall down? (Coefficient of linear expansion of aluminium is 23×10^{-6} /°C and that of steel is 11×10^{-6} /°C.)

1.4 Variation of Time Period of Simple Pendulum with Temperature

1 A pendulum clock consists of an iron rod connected to a small, heavy bob. If it is designed to keep correct time at 20°C, how fast or slow will it go in 24 hours at 40°C? (Coefficient of linear expansion of iron $= 1.2 \times 10^{-6}$ /°C.)

2 A pendulum clock having copper rod keeps correct time at 20°C. It gains 15 seconds per day, if cooled to 0°C. Calculate the coefficient of linear expansion of copper.

3 A clock with a metallic pendulum is 5 s fast each day at a temperature of 15°C and 10 s slow each day at a temperature of 30°C. Find the temperature at which the clock will show correct time and the coefficient of linear expansion of the metal of the pendulum metal.

1.5 Effect of Temperature on Measurement with Scale

1 A steel ruler exactly 20 cm long is graduated to give correct measurements at 20°C.

(a) Will it give readings that are too long or too short at lower temperatures?

(b) What will be the actual length of the ruler when it is used in the desert at a temperature of 40°C? ($\alpha_{steel} = 1.2 \times 10^{-5}$ /°C).

2 A meter scale made of steel is calibrated at 20°C to give correct reading. Find the distance between 50 cm mark and 51 cm mark, if the scale is used at 10°C. (Coefficient of linear expansion of steel is 1.1×10^{-5} /°C.)

3 A surveyor's 30 m steel tape is correct at a temperature of 20°C. The distance between two points, as measured by this tape on a day when the temperature is 35°C, is 26 m. What is the true distance between the points? ($\alpha_{steel} = 1.2 \times 10^{-5}$ /°C)

4 A meter scale is made of steel and measures correct length at 16°C. What will be the percentage error, if the scale is used

(a) on a summer day when temperature is 46°C and

(b) on a winter day when the temperature is 6°C? (Coefficient of linear expansion of steel $= 11 \times 10^{-6}$ /°C)

1.6 Thermal Stress and Strain

1 A steel rod of length 1 m rests on a smooth horizontal base. If it is heated from 0°C to 100°C, what is the longitudinal strain developed?

2 A steel rod is clamped at its two ends and rests on a fixed horizontal base. The rod is in natural length at 20°C. Find the longitudinal strain developed in the rod, if the temperature rises to 50°C. (Coefficient of linear expansion of steel $= 1.2 \times 10^{-5}$ /°C.)

3 A steel wire of cross-sectional area 0.5 mm^2 is held between two fixed supports. If the wire is just taut at 20°C, determine the tension when the temperature falls to 0°C. (Coefficient of linear expansion of steel is 1.2×10^{-5} /°C and its Young's modulus is 2.0×10^{11} N/m^2.)

4 An iron ring measuring 15.00 cm in diameter is to be shrunk on a pulley which is 15.05 cm in diameter. All measurements refer to the room temperature 20°C. To what minimum temperature should the ring be heated to make the job possible? Calculate the strain developed in the ring when it comes to the room temperature. (Coefficient of linear expansion of iron $= 12 \times 10^{-6}$ /°C.)

5 A mass of 2 kg is suspended from a fixed point by a wire of length 3 m and diameter 0.5 mm. Initially the wire is just unstretched, the mass resting on a fixed support. By how much must the temperature fall, if the mass is to be entirely supported by the wire? (Given, Y for wire = 206 GPa, $\alpha = 11 \times 10^{-6}$ °C)

6 Two metal rods are fixed end to end between two rigid supports as shown in figure. Each rod is of length L and area of cross-section is A. When the system is heated up, determine the condition when the junction between rods does not shift. (Y_1 and Y_2 are Young's modulus of materials of rods, α_1 and α_2 are coefficients of linear expansion)

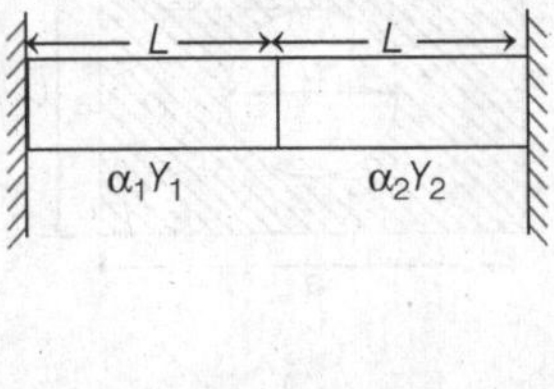

1.7 Bimetallic Strip

1 In figure which strip brass or steel have higher coefficient of linear expansion?

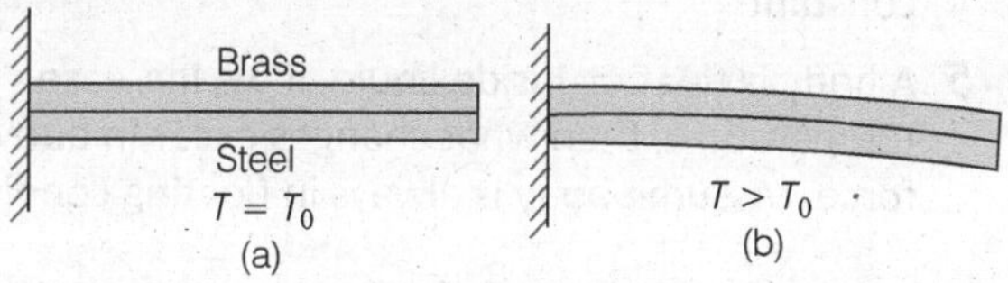

2 A copper and a tungsten plate having a thickness $\delta = 2$ mm each are riveted together, so that at 0°C they form a flat bimetallic plate. Find the average radius of curvature of this plate at $t = 200°$ C. (Coefficients of linear expansion for copper and tungsten are $\alpha_c = 1.7 \times 10^{-5} K^{-1}$ and $\alpha_t = 0.4 \times 10^{-5} K^{-1}$)

1.8 Areal Expansion

1 A plane lamina has area 2 m^2 at 10°C, then what will be its area at 110°C? (Coefficient of superficial expansion is 2×10^{-5} /°C)

2 The coefficient of linear expansion of a metal is 1×10^{-5} /°C. What will be the percentage increase in area of a square plate of that metal, when it is heated through 100°C?

1.9. Volume Expansion

1 A crystal has a coefficient of linear expansion 12×10^{-6} /°C in one direction and 244×10^{-6} /°C in every direction at right angles to it. Then, what is the coefficient of cubical expansion of crystal?

2 A metal plate of area 1.2 m^2 increases its area by $2.4 \times 10^{-4} m^2$ when it is heated from 0°C to 100°C. What is the coefficient of cubical expansion of the metal?

3 The volume occupied by a thin-wall brass vessel and the volume of a solid brass sphere are the same and equal to 1000 cm^3 at 0°C. How much will the volume of the vessel and that of the sphere change upon heating to 20°C? (The coefficient of linear expansion of brass is $\alpha = 1.9 \times 10^{-5}$ /°C)

4 An aluminium sphere of 20 cm diameter is heated from 0°C to 100°C. Find the change in its volume. (Given, Coefficient of linear expansion for aluminium $\alpha_{Al} = 23 \times 10^{-6}$ /°C)

5 If percentage change in length is 1% with change in temperature of a cuboid object ($l \times 2l \times 3l$), then what is percentage change in its area and volume?

1.10 Apparent Expansion of Liquid

1 The coefficient of real expansion of a liquid is 7×10^{-4} /°C. The coefficient of linear expansion of the vessel is 1×10^{-5} /° C. What will be the coefficient of apparent expansion of the liquid?

2 When a liquid in a glass vessel is heated, its coefficient of apparent expansion is 10.3×10^{-4} /°C. Same liquid when heated in a metallic vessel, its coefficient of apparent expansion is 10.06×10^{-4} /° C. What will be the coefficient of linear expansion of metal? ($\alpha_{glass} = 9 \times 10^{-6}$ /°C)

3 A 250 cm^3 glass bottle is completely filled with water at 50°C. The bottle and water are heated to 60° C. How much water runs over, if

(a) the expansion of the bottle is neglected

(b) the expansion of the bottle is included?

(Coefficient of areal expansion of glass $\beta = 1.2 \times 10^{-5}$ /°C and $\gamma_{water} = 60 \times 10^{-5}$ /°C)

4 A glass vessel of volume 100 cm^3 is filled with mercury and is heated from 25°C to 75°C. What volume of mercury will overflow? (Coefficient of linear expansion of glass = 1.8×10^{-6} /°C and coefficient of volume expansion of mercury is 1.8×10^{-4} /°C.)

5 The volume of glass vessel is 1000 cc at 20°C. What volume of mercury should be poured into it at this temperature, so that the volume of the remaining space does not change with temperature? (Coefficient of cubical expansion of mercury and glass are 1.8×10^{-4} /°C and 9.0×10^{-6} /°C, respectively.)

1.11 Variation of Density with Temperature

1 The density of a liquid at 100°C is 8.0 gm/ cm^3 and at 0°C is 8.4 g/cm^3, what is the coefficient of cubical expansion of the liquid?

2 The density of water at 0°C is 0.998 g/cm^3 and at 4°C is 1.000 g / cm^3. Calculate the average coefficient of volume expansion of water in the temperature range 0 to 4°C.

3 The coefficient of volume expansion of glycerine is 49×10^{-5} /°C. What is the fractional change in its density for 30°C rise in temperature?

1.12 Variation of Buoyancy with Temperature

1 The loss of weight of a solid immersed in a liquid at 0°C is ΔW_0. If α and β are the volume coefficients of expansion of the solid and the liquid respectively, then what is the loss of weight at t°C approximately?

2 A block floats in water at 4°C, so that 0.984 of its height is under water. At what temperature of water will the block just sink in water? Neglect expansion of block. (γ_R for water $= 2.1 \times 10^{-4}$ /°C).

3 The densities of wood and benzene at 0°C are 880 kg/m^3 and 900 kg/m^3, respectively. The coefficients of volume expansion are 1.2×10^{-3} /°C for wood and 1.5×10^{-3} /°C for benzene. At what temperature will a piece of wood just sink in benzene?

4 A solid floats in a liquid at 20°C with 75% of it immersed. When the liquid is heated to 100°C, the same solid floats with 80% of it immersed in the liquid. Calculate the coefficient of expansion of the liquid. Assume the volume off the solid to be constant.

5 A body is floating inside liquid, if we increase temperature, then what changes occur in buoyancy force. (Assume body is always in floating condition)

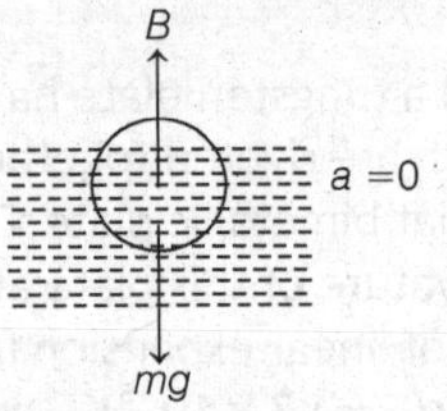

6 In previous question discuss the case when body moves downward, upwards and remains at same position when we increase temperature.
γ_L = Coefficient of volume expansion of liquid,
α_s = Coefficient of linear expansion of body

LEVEL 02 JEE Main Level

Single Choice Correct Type Questions

1 A faulty thermometer reads freezing point and boiling point of water as $-5°$C and 95°C, respectively. What is the correct value of temperature as it reads 60°C on faulty thermometer?

(a) 60°C (b) 65°C
(c) 64°C (d) 62°C

2 On an X temperature scale, water freezes at $-125.0°X$ and boils at $375.0°X$. On a Y temperature scale, water freezes at $-70.0°Y$ and boils at $-30.0°Y$. The value of temperature on X-scale equal to the temperature of $50.0°Y$ on Y-scale is

(a) 455.0°X
(b) -125.0°X
(c) 1375.0°X
(d) 1500.0°X

3 The temperature T on a thermometric scale is defined in terms of a property K by the relation $T = a \ln K + b$ where a and b are constants. The values of K is found to be 2 and 8 at the ice point and steam point, respectively. Temperature corresponding to $K = 4$ is

(a) 50°C (b) 37.5°C
(c) 26°C (d) 12.5°C

4 The temperature coefficient of resistance of a conductor varies as $\alpha(T) = 3T^2 + 2T$. If R_0 is resistance at $T = 0$ and R be resistance at T, then

(a) $R = R_0(6T + 2)$
(b) $R = 2R_0(3 + 2T)$
(c) $R = R_0(1 + T^2 + T^3)$
(d) $R = R_0(1 - T + T^2 + T^3)$

5 A uniform circular disc with the hole lies over a smooth horizontal surface, C is centre of the disc and A is a point on the rim of the disc as shown. As the temperature is increased,

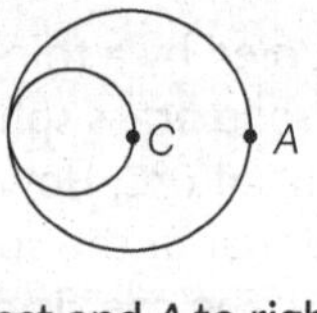

(a) C remains at rest and A to right
(b) Both A and C move to right
(c) Both remain at rest
(d) C moves to left and A to right

6 A square plate has three circular holes of same radius, so that centre of each hole is equidistant from the centre of the square plate. A Δ ABC can be formed by joining the centres of the holes as shown in the figure. The plate is placed on a frictionless horizontal surface. If we increase the temperature, then

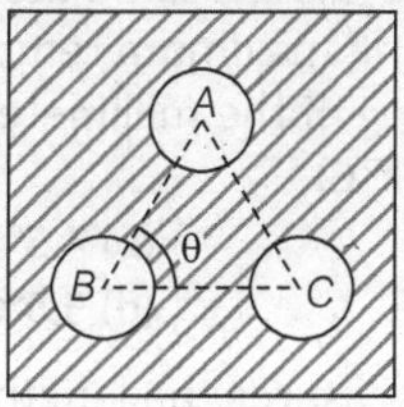

(a) each side of the triangle will increase and the angle θ will remain same

(b) each side of the triangle will remain same and the angle θ will increase

(c) sides of the triangle as well as θ will increase

(d) sides of the triangle as well as θ will remain same

7 A circular hole in an aluminium plate is 2.54 cm in diameter at 0 °C. What is the diameter when the temperature of the plate is raised to 100°C ? (Given, $\alpha_{Al} = 2.3 \times 10^{-5}$ /°C)

(a) 2.4558 cm (b) 2.5458 cm
(c) 1.4558 cm (d) 1.5458 cm

8 An iron tyre of diameter 2 m is to be fitted on to a wooden wheel of diameter 2.01 m. The temperature to which the tyre must be heated, if $\alpha = 11 \times 10^{-6}$ /°C and room temperature is 20°C, will be

(a) 474.5°C (b) 490.5°C
(c) 440.5°C (d) 460.5°C

9 A steel rod is 4.000 cm in diameter at 30°C. A brass ring has an interior diameter of 3.992 cm at 30°C. In order that the ring just slides onto the steel rod, the common temperature of the two should be nearly

($\alpha_{steel} = 11 \times 10^{-6}$ /°C and $\alpha_{brass} = 19 \times 10^{-6}$ /°C)

(a) 200°C (b) 250 °C
(c) 280 °C (d) 400 °C

10 The gap between any two rails, each of length l laid on a railway track equals x at 27°C. When the temperature rises to 40°C, the gap closes up. The coefficient of linear expansion of the material of the rail is α. The length l of a rail at 27° C will be

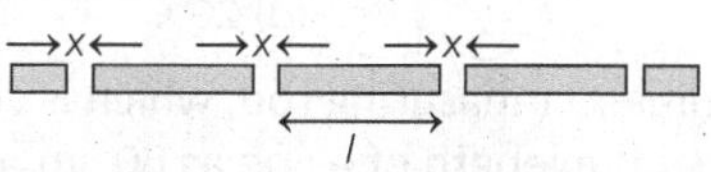

(a) $\frac{x}{26\alpha}$ (b) $\frac{2x}{13\alpha}$
(c) $\frac{x}{13\alpha}$ (d) none of these

11 A meter washer has a hole of diameter d_1 and external diameter d_2, where $d_2 = 3d_1$. On heating, d_2 increases by 0.3%. Then, d_1 will

(a) decrease by 0.1%
(b) decrease by 0.3%
(c) increase by 0.1%
(d) increase by 0.3%

12 The variation of lengths of two metal rods A and B with change in temperature is shown in figure. The ratio of $\frac{\alpha_A}{\alpha_B}$ is

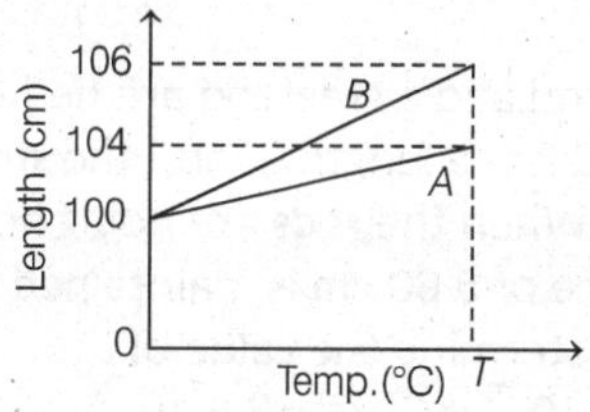

(a) $\frac{3}{2}$ (b) $\frac{2}{3}$
(c) $\frac{4}{3}$ (d) $\frac{3}{4}$

13 A rod of length 20 cm is made of metal A. It expands by 0.075 cm when its temperature is raised from 0°C to 100°C. Another rod of a different metal B having the same length expands by 0.045 cm for the same change in temperature. A third rod of the same length is composed of two parts one of metal A and the other of metal B. This rod expands by 0.060 cm for the same change in temperature. The portion made of metal A has the length

(a) 20 cm (b) 10 cm
(c) 15 cm (d) 18 cm

14 A rod of length 2 m at 0°C and having expansion coefficient $\alpha = (3x + 2) \times 10^{-6}$ /° C, where x is the distance (in cm) from one end of rod. The length of rod at 20°C is

(a) 2.124 m (b) 3.24 m
(c) 2.0120 m (d) 3.124 m

15 Two rods of length l_1 and l_2 are made of materials whose coefficient of linear expansion are α_1 and α_2. If difference between two lengths is independent of temperature, then

(a) $\frac{l_1}{l_2} = \frac{\alpha_1}{\alpha_2}$ (b) $\frac{l_1}{l_2} = \frac{\alpha_2}{\alpha_1}$
(c) $l_2^2\alpha_1 = l_1^2\alpha_2$ (d) $\frac{\alpha_1^2}{l_1} = \frac{\alpha_2^2}{l_2}$

16 A composite bar of length $L = L_1 + L_2$ is made up from a rod of material 1 and of length L_1 attached to a rod of material 2 and of length L_2 as shown. If α_1 and α_2 are their respective coefficients of linear expansion, then equivalent coefficient of linear expansion for the composite rod is

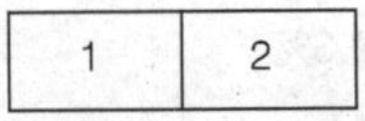

(a) $\frac{\alpha_1 L_2 + \alpha_2 L_1}{L}$ (b) $\frac{\alpha_1 L_2 + \alpha_2 L_2}{L}$

(c) $\frac{\alpha_1 L_1 + \alpha_2 L_2}{L}$ (d) $\frac{\alpha_1 \alpha_2 (L_1^2 + L_2)}{(\alpha_1 L_1 + \alpha_2 L_2)}$

17 A copper rod and a steel rod are heated. At 0°C, the copper rod has a length L_C and the steel one has a length L_S. When the rods are being heated or cooled, a difference of 5.00 cm is maintained between their lengths. Determine the value of L_C.
($\alpha_{Cu} = 5 \times 10^{-5}$ /°C, $\alpha_s = 2 \times 10^{-5}$ /°C.)

(a) 3.33 cm (b) 5 cm (c) 8.33 cm (d) 15 cm

18 If I is the moment of inertia of a solid body, the change in I corresponding to a small change in temperature ΔT is

(a) $\alpha I \Delta T$ (b) $\frac{1}{2}\alpha I \Delta T$ (c) $2\alpha I \Delta T$ (d) $3\alpha I \Delta T$

19 A solid sphere of radius r and coefficient of linear expansion α rotates about an axis passing through its centre in absence of any external torque. What should be the change in temperature, so that its angular velocity increases by 1%?

(a) $\frac{1}{100\alpha}$ increase (b) $\frac{1}{200\alpha}$ increase

(c) $\frac{1}{100\alpha}$ decrease (d) $\frac{1}{200\alpha}$ decrease

20 A uniform solid brass sphere is rotating with angular speed ω_0 about a diameter. If its temperature is now increased by 100°C, what will be its new angular speed? (Given, $\alpha_B = 2.0 \times 10^{-5}$ /°C)

(a) $\frac{\omega_0}{1 - 0.002}$ (b) $\frac{\omega_0}{1 + 0.002}$

(c) $\frac{\omega_0}{1 + 0.004}$ (d) $\frac{\omega_0}{1 - 0.004}$

21 A steel tape gives correct measurement at 20°C. A piece of wood is being measured with the steel tape at 0°C. The reading is 25 cm on the tape, the real length of the given piece of wood must be

(a) 25 cm (b) > 25 cm

(c) < 25 cm (d) can not say

22 A steel scale is to be prepared such that the millimeter intervals are to be accurate within 6×10^{-5} mm. The maximum temperature variation during the ruling of the millimeter marks is
($\alpha = 12 \times 10^{-6}$ /°C)

(a) 4.0°C (b) 4.5°C

(c) 5.0°C (d) 5.5°C

23 A steel scale measures the length of a copper rod as l_0 when both are at 20°C, which is the calibration temperature for the scale. The scale reading when both are at 40°C, is

(a) $(1 + 20\alpha_c) l_0$ (b) $(1 + 20\alpha_s) l_0$

(c) $\left(\frac{1 + 20\alpha_s}{1 + 20\alpha_c}\right) l_0$ (d) $\left(\frac{1 + 20\alpha_c}{1 + 20\alpha_s}\right) l_0$

24 A surveyor's 30 m steel tape is correct at 68°F. On a hot day the tape has expanded to 30.02 m. On that day, the tape indicates a distance of 15.02 m between two points. The distance between these points is approximately.

(a) 15.00 m
(b) 15.01 m
(c) 15.03 m
(d) 15.04 m

25 A bar measured with a Vernier caliper is found to be 180 mm long. The temperature during the measurement is 10°C. What will be the measurement error, if the scale of the Vernier caliper has been graduated at a temperature of 20°C? ($\alpha = 1.1 \times 10^{-5}$ °C^{-1}. Assume that the length of the bar does not change)

(a) 1.98×10^{-1} mm
(b) 1.98×10^{-2} mm
(c) 1.98×10^{-3} mm
(d) 1.98×10^{-4} mm

26 A metal tape is calibrated at 30°C. It gave the measurement 1000 m at a lesser temperature. It is found that the error in measurement is 2.5 cm. The temperature at which the measurement is made is ($\alpha = 10^{-6}$ /°C).

(a) 5°C (b) 10°C

(c) 15°C (d) 20°C

27 An aluminium measuring rod, which is correct at 5°C measures the length of a line as 80 cm at 45°C. If thermal coefficient of linear expansion of aluminium is 2.50×10^{-5} /°C, the correct length of the line is

(a) 80.08 cm (b) 79.92 cm

(c) 81.12 cm (d) 79.62 cm

28 Figure shows the action of a switch by a bimetallic strip. If α_1 and α_2 are coefficients of thermal expansion of metal 1 and metal 2, respectively.

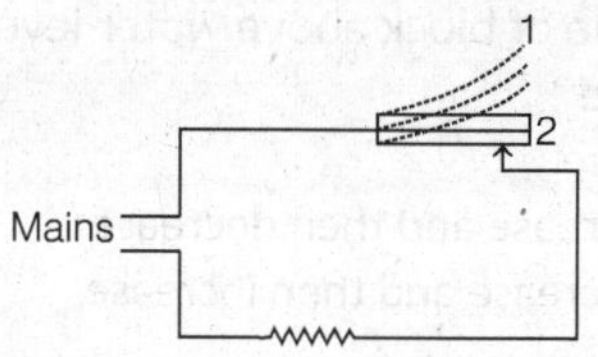

(a) $\alpha_1 < \alpha_2$ (b) $\alpha_1 > \alpha_2$
(c) $\alpha_1 > \alpha_2$, if the current in circuit is clockwise
(d) None of the above

29 A pendulum clock having time period of 2 s keeps correct time at 25°C. The pendulum is made of brass whose coefficient of linear expansion is 0.000019/°C. How many seconds in a day will it gain, if the temperature falls to 0°C?
(a) 0.000475 s (b) 15.00 s
(c) 20.52 s (d) 0.00475 s

30 A clock with a metallic pendulum gains 6 s each day when the temperature is 20°C and loses 6 s when the temperature is 40°C. Find the coefficient of linear expansion of the metal.
(a) $1.4 \times 10^{-5}\,°C^{-1}$ (b) $1.4 \times 10^{-6}\,°C^{-1}$
(c) $1.4 \times 10^{-4}\,°C^{-1}$ (d) $0.4 \times 10^{-6}\,°C^{-1}$

31 A thin copper wire of length l increases in length by 1% when heated from 20°C to 70°C. If a thin copper plate of length $3l$ and breadth $2l$ is heated from 20°C to 70°C, then percentage increase in its area will be
(a) 3% (b) 2% (c) 7% (d) 5%

32 Imagine a hypothetical material whose average temperature coefficient of linear expansion is 0.1 /°C. Find the fractional increase in the area of a thin square plate of above material when temperature increases by 10°C.
(a) 1 (b) 2 (c) 3 (d) None of these

33 Figures shows the expansion of a 2 m long metal rod with temperature. The volume expansion coefficient of the metal is

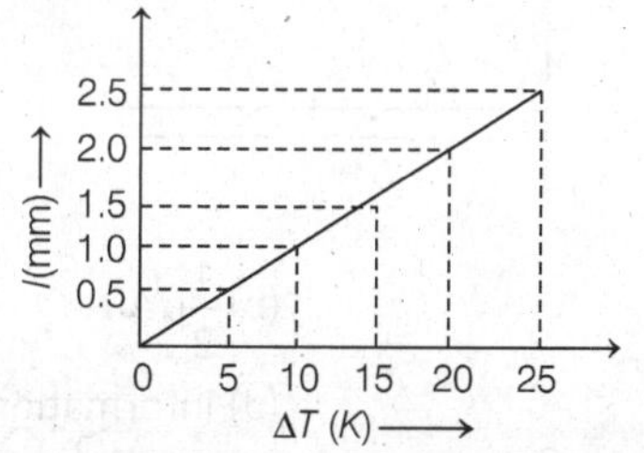

(a) $3 \times 10^{-4}\,K^{-1}$ (b) $1.5 \times 10^{-4}\,K^{-1}$
(c) $3 \times 10^{-5}\,K^{-1}$ (d) $1.5 \times 10^{-5}\,K^{-1}$

34 The coefficient of linear expansion of crystal in one direction is α_1 and that in every direction perpendicular to it α_2. The coefficient of cubical expansion is
(a) $\alpha_1 + \alpha_2$ (b) $2\alpha_1 + \alpha_2$
(c) $\alpha_1 + 2\alpha_2$ (d) None of these

35 The coefficient of apparent expansion of a liquid in a copper vessel is C and in a silver vessel is S. The coefficient of volume expansion of copper is γ_c. What is the coefficient of linear expansion of silver?
(a) $\dfrac{(C + \gamma_c + S)}{3}$ (b) $\dfrac{(C - \gamma_c + S)}{3}$
(c) $\dfrac{(C + \gamma_c - S)}{3}$ (d) $\dfrac{(C - \gamma_c - S)}{3}$

36 The absolute coefficient of expansion of a liquid is 7 times that the volume coefficient of expansion of the vessel. Then, the ratio of absolute and apparent expansion of the liquid is
(a) $\dfrac{1}{7}$ (b) $\dfrac{7}{6}$
(c) $\dfrac{6}{7}$ (d) None of these

37 A container is filled with water at 4°C. At one time the temperature is increased by few degrees above 4°C and at another time it is decreased by few degrees below 4°C. One shall observe that
(a) the level remains constant in each case
(b) water overflows in both the cases
(c) water overflows in the latter case, while comes down in the previous case
(d) in previous case water overflows while in later case its levels comes down

38 An open vessel is filled completely with oil which has same coefficient of volume expansion as that of the vessel. On heating both oil and vessel,
(a) the vessel can contain more volume and more mass of oil
(b) the vessel can contain same volume and same mass of oil
(c) the vessel can contain same volume but more mass of oil
(d) the vessel can contain more volume but same mass of oil

39 A glass flask of volume one litre at 0°C is filled, level full of mercury at this temperature. The flask and mercury are now heated to 100°C. How much mercury will spill out if coefficient of volume expansion of mercury is $1.82 \times 10^{-4}\,/°C$ and linear expansion of glass is $0.1 \times 10^{-4}\,/°C$, respectively?
(a) 21.2 cc (b) 15.2 cc (c) 1.52 cc (d) 2.12 cc

40 A glass flask contains some mercury at room temperature. It is found that at different temperatures the volume of air inside the flask remains the same. If the volume of mercury in the flask is 300 cm^3, then volume of the flask is (Given that coefficient of volume expansion of mercury and coefficient of linear expansion of glass are $1.8 \times 10^{-4} {}^\circ C^{-1}$ and $19 \times 10^{-6} {}^\circ C^{-1}$, respectively)
(a) 4500 cm^3 (b) 450 cm^3
(c) 2000 cm^3 (d) 6000 cm^3

41 A thin walled cylindrical metal vessel of linear coefficient of expansion $10^{-3} {}^\circ C^{-1}$ contains benzene of volume expansion coefficient $1.8 \times 10^{-4} {}^\circ C^{-1}$. If the vessel and its contents are now heated by 10°C, then the pressure due to the liquid at the bottom.
(a) Increases by 2% (b) Decreases by 1%
(c) Decreases by 2% (d) Remains unchanged

42 The density of steel at 0°C is 8.0 g/cc. At what temperature is density lesser by 0.1%? Coefficient of linear thermal linear expansion of steel is 10^{-5} /°C
(a) 37.2°C (b) 33.3°C
(c) 55.4°C (d) 40.2°C

43 The density of water at 20°C is 998 kgm^{-3} and at 40°C, it is 992 kgm^{-3}. The coefficient of cubical (volume) expansion of water is nearest to
(a) 2×10^{-4} /°C (b) 4×10^{-4} /°C
(c) 6×10^{-4} /°C (d) 3×10^{-4} /°C

44 A vertical column 50 cm long at 50°C balances another column of same liquid 60 cm long at 100°C. The coefficient of absolute expansion of the liquid is
(a) 0.005/°C (b) 0.0005 /°C
(c) 0.002/°C (d) 0.0002/°C

45 A U-tube filled with a liquid of volumetric expansion coefficient 10^{-5} /°C lies in a vertical plane. The height of liquid column in the left vertical limb is 100 cm. The liquid in the left vertical limb is maintained at a temperature = 0°C while the liquid in the right limb is maintained at a temperature = 100°C. The difference in levels in the two limbs is
(a) 0.1 cm (b) 0.2 cm
(c) 0.2 mm (d) zero

46 A metal ball immersed in Alcohol weighs W_1 at 0°C and W_2 at 50°C. The coefficient of cubical expansion of the metal γ_m is less than that of alcohol γ_{Al}. Assuming that density of metal is large compared to that of alcohol, it can be shown that
(a) $W_1 > W_2$ (b) $W_1 = W_2$
(c) $W_1 < W_2$ (d) any of (a), (b) or (c)

47 A block of wood is floating in water at 0°C. The temperature of only water is slowly raised from 0°C to 10°C. With the rise in temperature of the water, the volume of block above water level will
(a) increase
(b) decrease
(c) first increase and then decrease
(d) first decrease and then increase

48 A solid ball is completely immersed in a liquid. The coefficients of volume expansion of the ball and liquid are 3×10^{-6} and 8×10^{-6}/°C, respectively. The percentage change in upthrust when the temperature is increased by 100 °C is
(a) 0.5 % (b) 0.11 % (c) 1.1 % (d) 0.05 %

49 At 4°C, 0.98 of the volume of a body is immersed in water. The temperature at which the entire body gets immersed in water is (neglect the expansion of the body) ($\gamma_W = 3.3 \times 10^{-4} K^{-1}$)
(a) 40.8°C (b) 65.8°C
(c) 60.6°C (d) 58.8°C

50 A sphere of diameter 7 cm and mass 266.5 gm floats in a bath of a liquid. As the temperature is raised, the sphere just begins to sink at a temperature of 35°C. If the density of a liquid at 0°C is 1.527 gm/cc, then neglecting the expansion of the sphere, the coefficient of cubical expansion of the liquid is
(a) 8.278×10^{-4} /°C (b) 8.278×10^{-5} /°C
(c) 8.278×10^{-6} /°C (d) 8.278×10^{-3} /°C

51 A piece of metal weighs 46 g in air. When immersed in a liquid of specific gravity 1.24 at 27°C, it weighs 30 g. When the temperature of liquid is raised to 42°C, the metal piece weighs 30.5 g. Specific gravity of liquid at 42°C is 1.20. The coefficient of linear expansion of metal is
(a) 2.31×10^{-5} /°C (b) 6.7×10^{-5} /°C
(c) 4.46×10^{-5} /°C (d) none of these

52 In the given figure a rod is free at one end and other end is fixed. When we change the temperature of rod by $\Delta\theta$, then strain produced in the rod will be

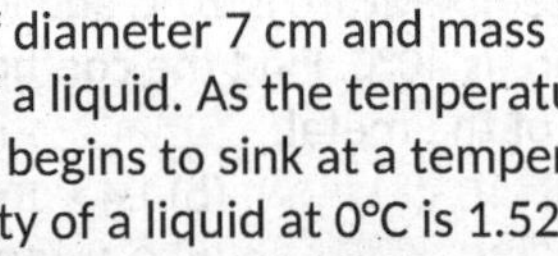

(a) $\alpha\Delta\theta$ (b) $\frac{1}{2}\alpha\Delta\theta$
(c) zero (d) information incomplete

53 A steel rod of length 1 m is heated from 25°C to 75°C keeping its length constant. The longitudinal strain developed in the rod is (Given, Coefficient of linear expansion of steel = 12×10^{-6} /°C

(a) 6×10^{-6} (b) -6×10^{-5} (c) -6×10^{-4} (d) zero

54 A metallic rod 1 cm long with a square cross-section is heated through t°C. If Young's modulus of elasticity of the metal is E and the mean coefficient of linear expansion is α per degree Celsius, then the compressional force required to prevent the rod from expanding along its length is
(Neglect the change of cross-sectional area)

(a) $EA\alpha t$ (b) $\dfrac{EA\alpha t}{1+\alpha t}$ (c) $\dfrac{EA\alpha t}{1-\alpha t}$ (d) $\dfrac{E}{\alpha t}$

55 A thin steel ring of inner diameter 40 cm and cross-sectional area 1 mm^2, is heated until it easily slides on a rigid cylinder of diameter 40.05 cm. When the ring cools down, the tension in the ring will be (for steel, $\alpha = 10^{-5}$ /°C, $Y = 200$ GPa)

(a) 1000 N (b) 500 N (c) 250 N (d) 100 N

56 The bulk modulus of copper is 1.4×10^{11} Pa and the coefficient of linear expansion is 1.7×10^{-5} C°$^{-1}$. What hydrostatic pressure is necessary to prevent a copper block from expanding when its temperature is increased from 20°C to 30°C?

(a) 6.0×10^5 Pa (b) 7.1×10^7 Pa
(c) 5.2×10^6 Pa (d) 40 atm

Numerical Value Questions

1 A rod has variable coefficient of linear expansion $\alpha = \dfrac{x}{5000}$. Length of the rod is 1 m. Determine increase in length of the rod (in cm) on increasing temperature of the rod by 100°C.

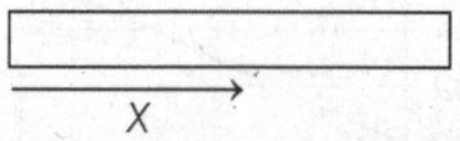

2 The length of sections AB and EF is l_1 in the figure, and their coefficient of thermal expansion is same $\alpha_1 = 2 \times 10^{-5}$ /°C. The length of section CD is l_2 and its expansion coefficient is $\alpha_2 = 1 \times 10^{-5}$ /°C. What must be the ratio $\dfrac{l_2}{l_1}$ to ensure that distance AF remains the same at all temperatures?
(Points A, B, E and F reside on the same line.)

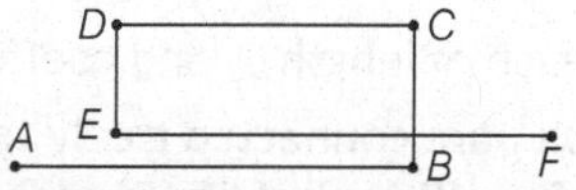

3 A thermostatted chamber at small height h above earth's surface maintained at 30°C has a clock fitted in it with an uncompensated pendulum. The clock designer correctly designs it for height h, but for temperature of 20°C. If this chamber is taken to earth's surface, the clock in it would click correct time at 30°C. Earth's radius is R. If the coefficient of linear expansion of material of pendulum is $\dfrac{h}{nR}$, then find n.

4 A thermometer has a spherical bulb having 1 cm^3 of mercury. A long cylindrical capillary tube is connected to spherical bulb. Volumetric coefficient of expansion of mercury is 1.8×10^{-4} K^{-1}; crossection area of capillary is 1.8×10^{-4} cm^2. Ignoring expansion of glass, how far apart (in cm) on the stem are marks indicating 1K temperature change?

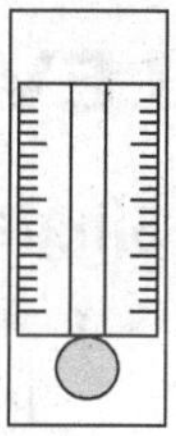

5 A glass vessel is partially filled with mercury and when both are heated together, the volume of the unfilled part of vessel remain constant at all temperature. Find the initial volume of mercury (in cm^3), if the empty part measures 34 cm^3.
(Given, $\alpha_{vessel} = 9 \times 10^{-6}$ /°C; $\gamma_{Hg} = 18 \times 10^{-5}$ /°C)

6 A thermometer has stem of internal diameter 0.8 mm and contains 0.07 g of a liquid. The liquid level in the thermometer rises by 11.9 mm when the temperature changes from 0°C to 40°C. If the coefficient of cubical expansion of the liquid is 1.75×10^{-n} °C^{-1}, then find n.
($\gamma_{glass} = 1 \times 10^{-5}$ /°C; density of liquid at 0°C = 0.82 g/cm^3)

7 A sphere made of polymer is floating on the surface of water, which is at a temperature of 20°C and 1% of the volume of the sphere is above the water. To what temperature (in °C) must the water be heated in order to submerge the polymer sphere completely? (Take, coefficient of linear expansion of the polymer 2.30×10^{-5} /°C and coefficient of volume expansion of water 3.19×10^{-4} /°C.)

8 A steel wire of length 2 m and cross-sectional area = 2 mm^2 is fixed between two rigid supports. If wire is stretched and tied firmly between two rigid supports, at a temperature = 20°C. At this moment, the tension in the wire is 200 N. At what temperature (in °C) will the tension become zero?
(Given, $Y = 200$ GPa, $\alpha = 10^{-5}$ /°C)

9 Two rods of different materials but of equal cross-section and length (1.0 m each) are joined to make a rod of length 2.0 m. The metal of one rod has coefficient of linear thermal expansion 10^{-5} /°C and Young's modulus 3×10^{10} N/m^2. The other metal has the values 2×10^{-5} /°C and 10^{10} N/m^2, respectively. If the pressure which must be applied to the ends of the composite rod to prevent its expansion when the temperature is raised by 100°C is $n\times10^7$ N/m^2, then find n.

10 A rod PQ of length $l=1$ m is pivoted at an end P and is freely rotating in a horizontal plane at an angular speed ω about a vertical axis passing through P. If coefficient of linear expansion of material of rod is $\alpha=2\times10^{-4}$ /°C, then calculate percentage change in its angular speed (in multiple of 10^{-1}), if the temperature of system is increased by $\Delta T=10$°C.

LEVEL 03 JEE Advanced Level

Single Choice Correct Questions

1 The figure below shows four isotropic solids having positive coefficient of thermal expansion. A student predicts that on heating the solid, following things can happen. Mark True (T) or False (F) for comments made by the student.

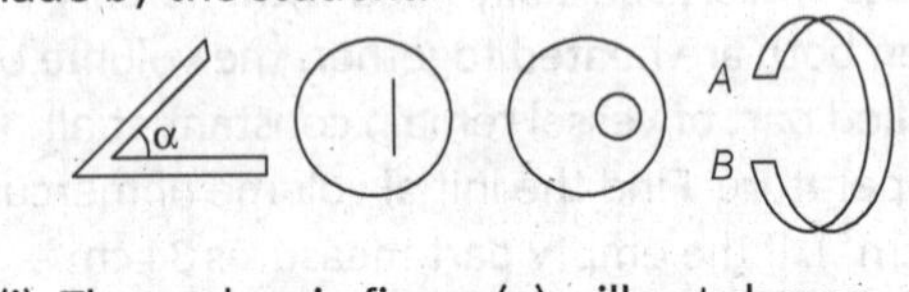

(i) The angle α in figure (a) will not change.
(ii) The length of line in figure (b) will decrease.
(iii) The radius of inner hole will decrease.
(iv) The distance AB will increase.

(a) T F F T (b) F T T F
(c) T T T T (d) F F T F

2 The coefficient of linear expansion α of the material of a rod of length L_0 varies with absolute temperature as $\alpha=aT-bT^2$, where a and b are constants. The linear expansion of the rod when heated from T_1 to $T_2=2T_1$ is

(a) $\left(\frac{3}{2}aT_1^2-\frac{7b}{3}T_1^3\right)L_0$ (b) $\left(4a-\frac{7b}{3}\right)T_1L_0$
(c) $\left(2aT_1^2-\frac{7b}{3}T_1^3\right)L_0$ (d) None of these

3 The coefficient of thermal expansion of a rod is temperature dependent and is given by the formula $\alpha=aT$, where a is a positive constant and T in °C. If the length of the rod is l at temperature 0°C, then the temperature at which the length will be $2l$ is

(a) $\sqrt{\frac{\ln 2}{a}}$ (b) $\sqrt{\frac{\ln 4}{a}}$ (c) $\frac{1}{\alpha}$ (d) $\frac{2}{\alpha}$

4 A steel tape is placed around the earth at the equator when the temperature is 10°C. What will be the clearance between the tape and the ground (assumed to be uniform), if the temperature of the tape rises to 40°C? Neglect expansion of the earth. Radius of earth at equator is 6400 km and $\alpha_{steel}=1.2\times10^{-5}\text{K}^{-1}$

(a) 2.3 m (b) 2.1 m
(c) 2.3 km (d) 230 m

5 An iron ball (coefficient of linear expansion $=1.2\times10^{-5}$ /°C) has a diameter of 6 cm and is 0.010 mm too large to pass through a hole in a brass plate (coefficient of linear expansion $=1.9\times10^{-5}$ /°C) when the ball and the plate are both at a temperature of 30°C. At what common temperature of the ball and the plate will the ball just pass through the hole in the plate?

(a) 23.8°C (b) 53.8°C
(c) 42.5°C (d) 63.5°C

6 The variation of lengths of two metal rods A and B with change in temperature is shown in Figure. The coefficients of linear expansion α_A for the metal A and the temperature T will be (Given, $\alpha_B=9\times10^{-6}$ /°C)

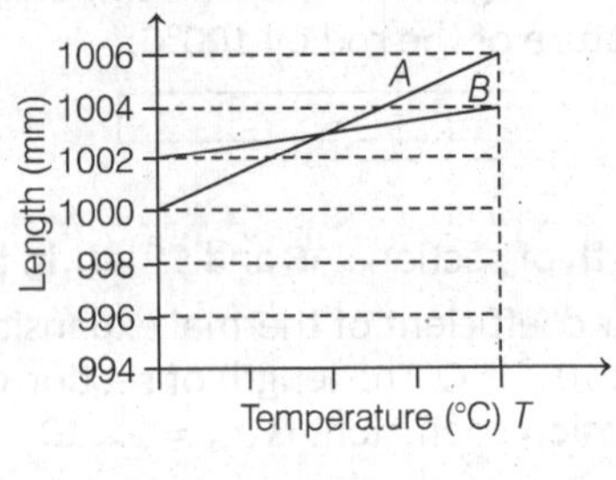

(a) $\alpha_A=3\times10^{-6}$ /°C, 500°C
(b) $\alpha_A=3\times10^{-6}$ /°C, 222.22°C
(c) $\alpha_A=27\times10^{-6}$ /°C, 500°C
(d) $\alpha_A=27\times10^{-6}$ /°C, 222.22°C

7 Two rods each of length L_2 and coefficient of linear expansion α_2 are connected freely to a third rod of length L_1 of coefficient of linear expansion α_1 to form an isosceles triangle. The arrangement is supported on the knife edge at the mid-point of L_1 which is horizontal. The apex of the isosceles triangle is to remain at a constant distance from the knife edge, if

(a) $\frac{L_1}{L_2} = \frac{\alpha_2}{\alpha_1}$ (b) $\frac{L_1}{L_2} = \sqrt{\frac{\alpha_2}{\alpha_1}}$

(c) $\frac{L_1}{L_2} = 2\frac{\alpha_2}{\alpha_1}$ (d) $\frac{L_1}{L_2} = 2\sqrt{\frac{\alpha_2}{\alpha_1}}$

8 A thin circular metal disc of radius 500.0 mm is set rotating about a central axis normal to its plane. Upon raising its temperature gradually, the radius increases to 507.5 mm. The percentage change in the rotational kinetic energy will be

(a) 1.5 % (b) – 1.5% (c) 3% (d) – 3%

9 Two uniform rods of equal lengths (l_0) and equal masses have coefficient of linear expansion α and 2α are placed in contact on a smooth horizontal surface as shown. The temperature of system is $\theta°$C. Now the temperature is increased by $\Delta\theta°$C. The junction of the rods will shift from its initial position by

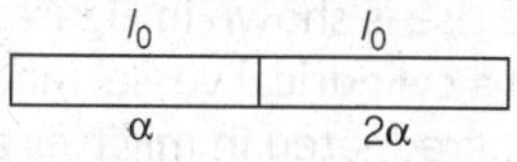

(a) $\frac{l_0\alpha\Delta\theta}{2}$ (b) $\frac{l_0\alpha\Delta\theta}{3}$

(c) $\frac{l_0\alpha\Delta\theta}{4}$ (d) $\frac{l_0\alpha\Delta\theta}{6}$

10 Figure shows the graphs of elongation versus temperature for two different metals. If these are employed to form a straight bimetallic strip of thickness 6 cm and heated, it bends in the form of an arc, the radius of curvature changing with temperature approximately as shown in the figure. The linear expansivities of the two metals are

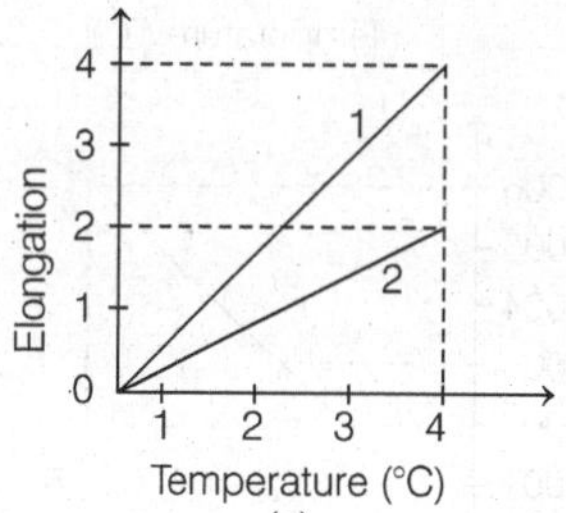

(a)

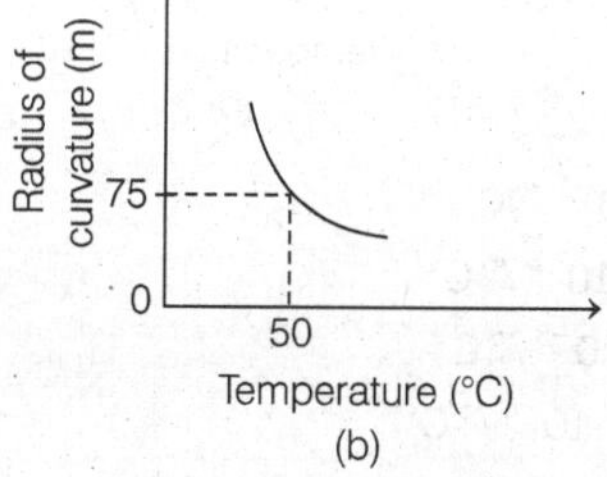

(b)

(a) 24×10^{-6} /°C and 12×10^{-6} /°C

(b) 20×10^{-6} /°C and 10×10^{-6} /°C

(c) 18×10^{-6} /°C and 9×10^{-6} /°C

(d) 16×10^{-6} /°C and 8×10^{-6} /°C

11 The coefficients of thermal expansion of steel and a metal X are respectively 12×10^{-6} /°C and 2×10^{-6} /°C. At 40°C, the side of a cube of metal X was measured using a steel vernier callipers. The reading was 100 mm. Assuming that the calibration of the vernier was done at 0°C, then the actual length of the side of the cube at 0°C will be

(a) > 100 mm

(b) < 100 mm

(c) = 100 mm

(d) data insufficient to conclude

12 A steel scale is calibrated at 0°C to measure accurately. If this scale measures the length of a wooden rod at 0°C and 20°C as 10 cm and 9.975 cm respectively, find the scale reading at 50°C, by this scale

(a) 9.9425 cm (b) 9.9375 cm

(c) 10.0625 cm (d) 9.875 cm

13 A glass rod when measured with a zinc scale, both being at 30°C, appears to be of length 100 cm. If the scale shows correct reading at 0°C, then the true length of glass rod at 30°C and 0°C are

$(\alpha_{glass} = 8 \times 10^{-6}\,°C^{-1}, \alpha_{zinc} = 26 \times 10^{-6} K^{-1})$

(a) 100.054 cm, 100.054 cm

(b) 100.078 cm, 100.078 cm

(c) 100.078 cm, 100.054 cm

(d) 100.054 cm, 100.078 cm

14 Arrangement of three metallic rods riveted to each other is as shown in figure. α_{Al} is the coefficient of linear expansion for aluminium and α_S (when $\alpha_{Al} > \alpha_S$) for steel. The arrangement is heated, then

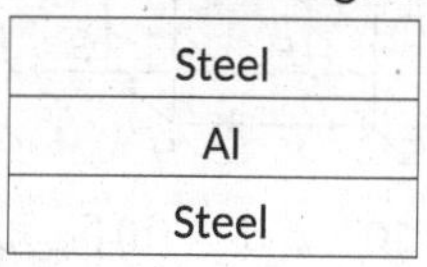

(a) Tensile stress is developed in the aluminium rod.

(b) Compressive stress is developed in the aluminium rod

(c) No stress is developed in the aluminium rod

(d) Data is incomplete

15 A wire having cross-sectional area S is attached to wall on one side and a block of mass M on the other side which is placed on a horizontal surface having coefficient of friction μ as shown. Material of wire has coefficient of thermal expansion α and Young's modulus Y. At initial temperature there is no stress in the wire. Now, the wire is cooled. At what decrease in temperature the block will begin to move?

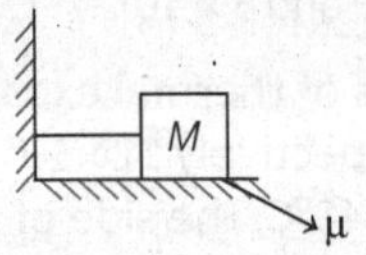

(a) $\frac{\mu Mg}{\alpha YS}$ (b) $\frac{2\mu Mg}{\alpha YS}$
(c) $\frac{\mu Mg}{2\alpha YS}$ (d) None of these

16 Two fine steel wires, fastened between the projections of a heavy brass bar, are just taut when the whole system is at 0°C. What is the tensile stress in the steel wires when the temperature of the system is raised by 200°C?

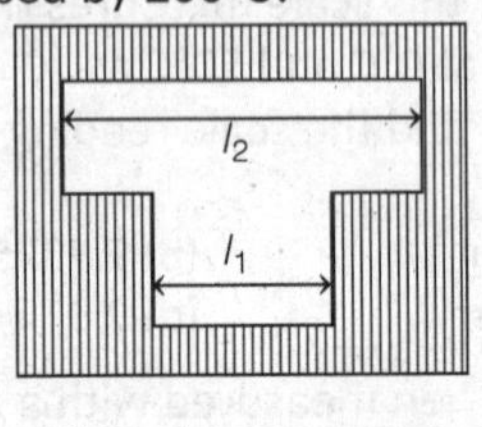

($\alpha_{brass} = 2 \times 10^{-5} \text{°C}^{-1}, \alpha_{steel} = 1.2 \times 10^{-5} \text{°C}^{-1}$, $Y_{steel} = 200 \text{ GNm}^{-2}$)
(a) 3.2 Nm^{-2} (b) $3.2 \times 10^8 \text{ Nm}^{-2}$
(c) $32 \times 10^8 \text{ Nm}^{-2}$ (d) 0.48 Nm^{-2}

17 A cuboid $ABCDEFGH$ is anisotropic with $\alpha_x = 1 \times 10^{-5}$ /°C, $\alpha_y = 2 \times 10^{-5}$ /°C, $\alpha_z = 3 \times 10^{-5}$ /°C.
Coefficient of superficial expansion of faces can be

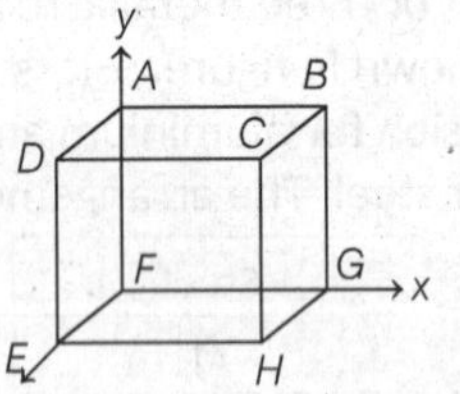

(a) $\beta_{ABCD} = 5 \times 10^{-5}$ /°C (b) $\beta_{BCGH} = 4 \times 10^{-5}$ /°C
(c) $\beta_{CDEH} = 3 \times 10^{-5}$ /°C (d) $\beta_{EFGH} = 2 \times 10^{-5}$ /°C

18 The volume of 0.5 kg of liquid water over the temperature range from 0°C to 50°C fits reasonably well to the polynomial function
$V = 0.500 - (4 \times 10^{-5})T + (5 \times 10^{-6})T^2$,
where volume is measured in cubic meters and T is temperature in degree celsius. The volume expansion coefficient for liquid water at 20°C is
(a) 1.2×10^{-4} /°C (b) 3.2×10^{-4} /°C
(c) 0.9×10^{-4} /°C (d) 7.2×10^{-4} /°C

19 In a vertical U-tube containing a liquid, the two arms are maintained at different temperatures, t_1 and t_2. The liquid columns in the two arms have heights l_1 and l_2, respectively. The coefficient of volume expansion of the liquid is equal to

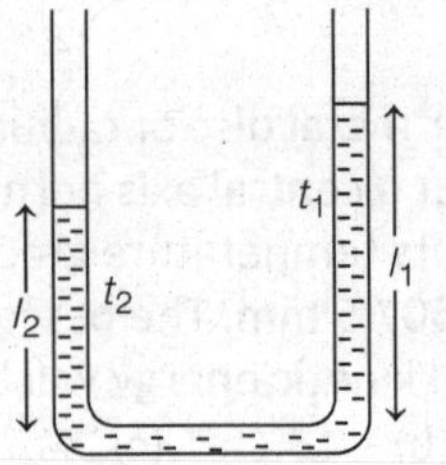

(a) $\frac{l_1 - l_2}{l_2 t_1 - l_1 t_2}$ (b) $\frac{l_1 - l_2}{l_1 t_1 - l_2 t_2}$
(c) $\frac{l_1 + l_2}{l_2 t_1 + l_1 t_2}$ (d) $\frac{l_1 + l_2}{l_1 t_1 + l_2 t_2}$

20 The graph of elongation of rod of a substance A with temperature rise is shown in Figure. A liquid B contained in a cylindrical vessel made up of substance A, graduated in millitres at 0°C is heated gradually. The readings of the liquid level in the vessel corresponding to different temperatures are shown in the figure. The real volume expansivity of liquid is

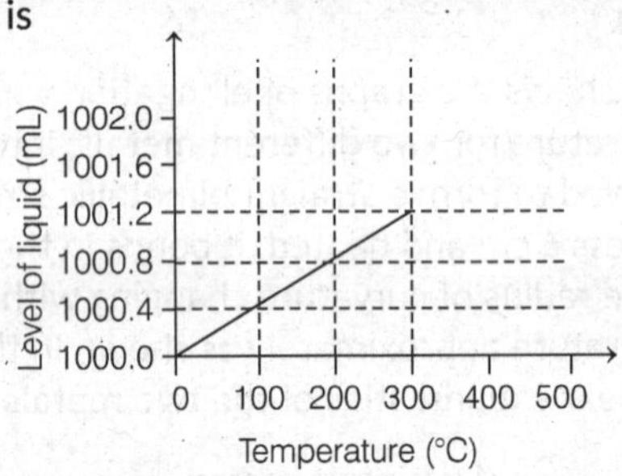

(a)

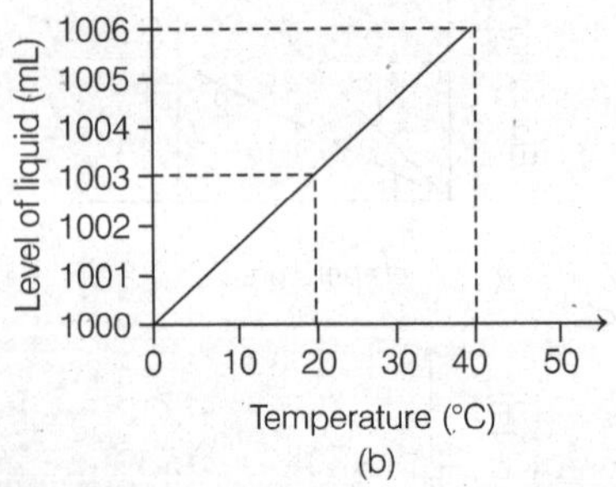

(b)

(a) 2.7×10^{-5} /°C
(b) 15.4×10^{-6} /°C
(c) 16.2×10^{-5} /°C
(d) 151.2×10^{-6} /°C

21 A container of capacity 700 mL is filled with two immiscible liquids of volume 200 mL and 500 mL with respective volume expansivities as 1.4×10^{-5} /°C and 2.1×10^{-5} /°C. During the heating of the vessel, it is observed that neither any liquid overflows nor any empty space is created. The volume expansivity of the container is

(a) 1.9×10^{-5} /°C (b) 1.9×10^{-6} /°C
(c) 1.6×10^{-5} /°C (d) 1.6×10^{-6} /°C

22 A thread of liquid is in a uniform capillary tube of length L, as measured by a ruler. The temperature of the tube and thread of liquid is raised by ΔT. If γ be the coefficient of volume expansion of the liquid and α be the coefficient of linear expansion of the material of the tube, then the increase ΔL in the length of the thread, again measured by the ruler will be

(a) $\Delta L = L(\gamma - \alpha)\,\Delta T$ (b) $\Delta L = L(\gamma - 2\alpha)\Delta T$
(c) $\Delta L = L(\gamma - 3\alpha)\Delta T$ (d) $\Delta L = L\,\gamma\,\Delta T$

23 A glass cylinder container $m_0 = 100$ g of mercury at a temperature of $t_0 = 0$°C. When temperature becomes $t_1 = 20$°C, the cylinder contains $m_1 = 99.7$ g of mercury. The coefficient of volume expansion of mercury $\gamma_{Hg} = 18 \times 10^{-5}$ /°C. Assume that the temperature of the mercury is equal to that of the cylinder. The coefficient of linear expansion of glass α is

(a) 10^{-5} /°C (b) 2×10^{-5} /°C
(c) 3×10^{-5} /°C (d) 6×10^{-5} /°C

24 The volume of the bulb of a mercury thermometer at 0°C is V_0 and cross-section of the capillary is A_0. The coefficient of linear expansion of glass is α_g per °C and the cubical expansion of mercury γ_m per °C. If the mercury just fills the bulb at 0°C, what is the length of mercury column in capillary at T°C?

(a) $\dfrac{V_0T(\gamma_m + 3\alpha_g)}{A_0(1 + 2\alpha_g T)}$

(b) $\dfrac{V_0T(\gamma_m - 3\alpha_g)}{A_0(1 + 2\alpha_g T)}$

(c) $\dfrac{V_0T(\gamma_m + 2\alpha_g)}{A_0(1 + 3\alpha_g T)}$

(d) $\dfrac{V_0T(\gamma_m - 2\alpha_g)}{A_0(1 + 3\alpha_g T)}$

25 Three immiscible liquids are filled in a container as shown. The base area of the container is A and coefficient of cubical expansion of the material of the container is $\dfrac{3\gamma}{2}$ while the coefficient of cubical expansion of the liquids are shown in the figure. The temperature of the system is increased by ΔT. The volume of the liquid flown out of the container is

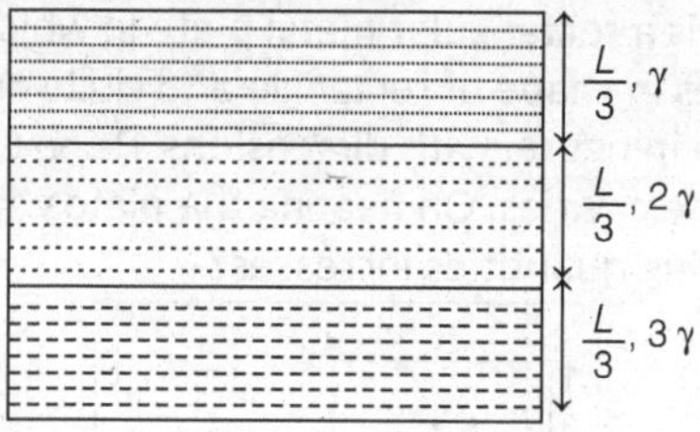

(a) $\dfrac{AL\gamma\Delta T}{3}$ (b) $AL\gamma\Delta T$
(c) $\dfrac{2AL\gamma\Delta T}{3}$ (d) $\dfrac{AL\gamma\Delta T}{2}$

26 A hollow steel sphere ,weighing 200 kg is floating on water. A weight of 10 kg is to be placed on it in order to submerge it at a temperature of 20°C. Now, the weight that should be decreased when temperature increases to 25°C is
(Given $\gamma_{water} = 1.5 \times 10^{-4}\,°C^{-1}$, $\alpha_{steel} = 1 \times 10^{-5}\,°C^{-1}$)

(a) 126 g (b) 252 g
(c) 53 g (d) 500 g

27 A platinum sphere floats in mercury. Find the percentage change in the fraction of volume of sphere immersed in mercury when the temperature is raised by 80°C (volume expansivity of mercury is 182×10^{-6} /°C and linear expansivity of platinum is 9×10^{-6} /°C.

(a) 1.24% (b) 1.38%
(c) 2.48% (d) 2.76%

28 A solid whose volume does not change with temperature floats in a liquid. For two different temperatures t_1 and t_2 of the liquid, fractions f_1 and f_2 of the volume of the solid remain submerged in the liquid. The coefficient of volume expansion of the liquid is equal to

(a) $\dfrac{f_1 - f_2}{f_2t_1 - f_1t_2}$ (b) $\dfrac{f_1 - f_2}{f_1t_1 - f_2t_2}$
(c) $\dfrac{f_1 + f_2}{f_2t_1 - f_1t_2}$ (d) $\dfrac{f_1 + f_2}{f_1t_1 + f_2t_2}$

29 A flask of mercury is sealed off at 20°C and is completely filled with mercury. If the bulk modulus for mercury is 2500 MPa and the coefficient of volume expansion of mercury is 1.82×10^{-4} /°C and the expansion of glass is ignored, then pressure of mercury within the flask at 100°C will be

(a) 100 MPa (b) 72 MPa
(c) 36 MPa (d) 24 MPa

Multiple Choice(s) Correct Type Questions

1 There is a rectangular metal plate in which two cavities in shape of rectangle and circle are made, as shown in figure, with dimensions. P and Q are centres of these cavities. On heating the plate which of the following quantities increases?

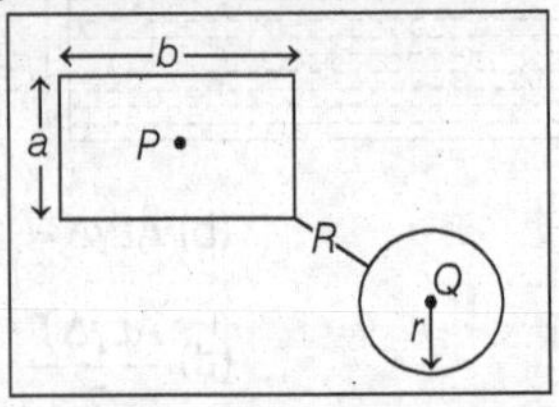

(a) πr^2 (b) ab (c) R (d) b

2 A thin cylindrical metal rod is bent into a ring with a small gap as shown in figure. On heating the system

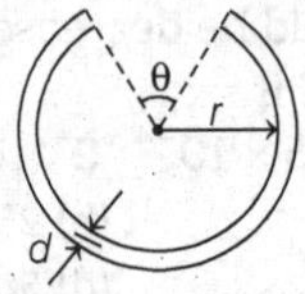

(a) θ decreases, r and d increase
(b) θ increases
(c) d and r increase
(d) θ is constant,

3 Due to thermal expansion, with rise in temperature
(a) metallic scale reading becomes lesser than true value (α of the metal is greater than α of the object)
(b) Pendulum clock becomes slower
(c) A floating body sinks a little more (assuming temperature of liquid remains unchanged)
(d) The apparent weight of a body in a liquid may decrease (assuming temperature of liquid remains unchanged)

4 Two rods of length L_1 and L_2 are made of materials of co-efficients of linear expansions α_1 and α_2, respectively such that $L_1\alpha_1 = L_2\alpha_2$. The temperature of the rods is increased by ΔT and correspondingly the change in their respective lengths are ΔL_1 and ΔL_2
(a) $\Delta L_1 \neq \Delta L_2$
(b) $\Delta L_1 = \Delta L_2$
(c) the difference in the lengths $(L_1 - L_2)$ is constant and is independent of rise of temperature
(d) data is insufficient to arrive at a conclusion

5 A uniform cylinder of steel of mass M, radius R is placed on frictionless bearings and set to rotate about its vertical axis with angular velocity ω_0. After the cylinder has reached the specified state of rotation it is heated without any mechanical contact from temperature T_0 to $T_0 + \Delta T$. If $\frac{\Delta I}{I}$ is the fractional change in moment of inertia of the cylinder and $\frac{\Delta\omega}{\omega}$ be the fractional change in the angular velocity of the cylinder and α be the coefficient of linear expansion, then
(a) $\frac{\Delta I}{I} = \frac{2\Delta R}{R}$ (b) $\frac{\Delta I}{I} = \frac{\Delta\omega}{\omega}$
(c) $\frac{\Delta\omega}{\omega} = -2\alpha\,\Delta T$ (d) $\frac{\Delta I}{I} = -\frac{2\Delta R}{R}$.

6 A clock is calibrated at a temperature of 20 °C. Assume that the pendulum is a thin brass rod of negligible mass with a heavy bob attached to the end ($\alpha_{brass} = 19 \times 10^{-6}$ /K)
(a) On a hot day at 30°C, the clock gains 8.2 s
(b) On a hot day at 30°C, the clock loses 8.2 s
(c) On a cold day at 10°C, the clock gains 8.2 s
(d) On a cold day at 10°C, the clock loses 8.2 s

7 A bimetallic strip is formed out of two identical strips, one of copper and other of brass. The coefficients of linear expansion of the two metals are α_C and α_B. On heating, the temperature of the strip goes up by ΔT and the strip bends to form an arc of radius of curvature R. Then, R is
(a) proportional to ΔT
(b) inversely proportional to ΔT
(c) proportional to $|\alpha_B - \alpha_C|$
(d) inversely proportional to $|\alpha_B - \alpha_C|$

8 When the temperature of a copper coin is raised by 80 °C, its diameter increases by 0.2%
(a) Percentage rise in the area of a face 0.4%
(b) Percentage rise in the thickness 0.4%
(c) Percentage rise in the volume is 0.6%
(d) Coefficient of linear expansion of copper is 0.25×10^{-4} /° C.

9 A vessel is partly filled with liquid. When the vessel is cooled to a lower temperature, the space in the vessel unoccupied by the liquid remains constant. Then, the volume of the liquid (V_L), volume of the vessel (V_V), the coefficient of cubical expansion of the material of the vessel (γ_V) and of the liquid (γ_L) are related as
(a) $\gamma_L > \gamma_V$ (b) $\gamma_L < \gamma_V$
(c) $\frac{\gamma_V}{\gamma_L} = \frac{V_V}{V_L}$ (d) $\frac{\gamma_V}{\gamma_L} = \frac{V_L}{V_V}$

Comprehension Based Questions

Comprehension-1

A copper collar is to fit tightly about a steel shaft that has a diameter of 6 cm at 20°C. The inside diameter of the copper collar at that temperature is 5.98 cm.

1 To what temperature must the copper collar be raised, so that it will just slip on the steel shaft, assuming the steel shaft remains at 20°C? $(\alpha_{copper} = 17 \times 10^{-6}/°C)$

(a) 324°C (b) 21.7°C

(c) 217°C (d) 32.4°C

2 The tensile stress in the copper collar when its temperature returns to 20°C is $(Y = 11 \times 10^{10} N/m^2)$

(a) $1.34 \times 10^5 N/m^2$ (b) $3.68 \times 10^{-12} N/m^2$

(c) $3.68 \times 10^8 N/m^2$ (d) $1.34 \times 10^{-12} N/m^2$

3 If the breaking stress of copper is $230 \times 10^6 N/m^2$ at what temperature will the copper collar break as it cools?

(a) 20°C (b) 47°C (c) 94°C (d) 217°C

Comprehension-2

At 20°C, a liquid is filled upto 10 cm height in a container of glass of length 20 cm and cross-sectional area 100 cm^2. Scale is marked on the surface of container. This scale gives correct reading at 20°C.
(Given $\gamma_L = 5 \times 10^{-5} K^{-1}, \alpha_{glass} = 1 \times 10^{-5} °C^{-1}$)

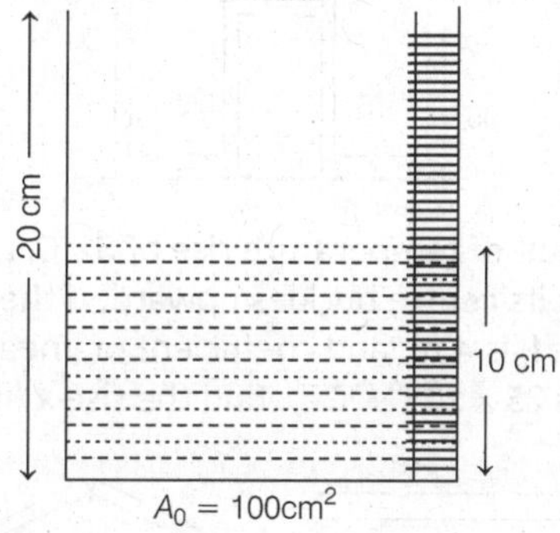

4. The volume of liquid at 40°C is

(a) 1002 cc (b) 1001 cc

(c) 1003 cc (d) 1000.5 cc

5. The actual height of liquid at 40°C is

(a) 10.01 cm (b) 10.006 cm

(c) 10.6 cm (d) 10.1 cm

6. The reading of scale at 40°C is

(a) 10.01 cm (b) 10.004 cm

(c) 10.006 cm (d) 10.04 cm

Comprehension-3

Two steel rods and an aluminium rod of equal length L and equal cross-section area are rigidly joined as shown in figure. All the rods are in a state of zero tension at 0°C. Temperature of the system is increased by ΔT. Coefficient of linear expansion of aluminium and steel are respectively α_A and α_S $(\alpha_A > \alpha_S)$, Young's modulus for aluminium and steel are respectively Y_A and Y_S.

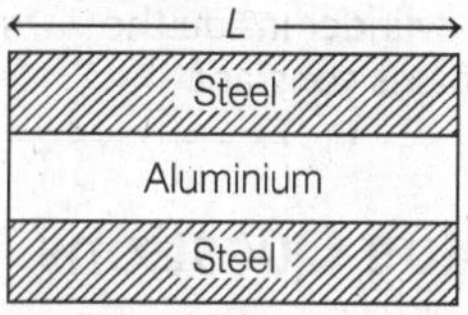

7 The value of stress developed in the aluminium rod is

(a) $\dfrac{(\alpha_A - \alpha_S)\Delta T}{\dfrac{1}{Y_A} + \dfrac{1}{2Y_S}}$ (b) $\dfrac{(\alpha_A - \alpha_S)\Delta T}{\dfrac{2}{Y_A} + \dfrac{1}{Y_S}}$

(c) $\dfrac{(\alpha_A - \alpha_S)\Delta T}{\dfrac{1}{Y_A} + \dfrac{2}{Y_S}}$ (d) $\dfrac{(\alpha_A - \alpha_S)\Delta T}{\dfrac{1}{2Y_A} + \dfrac{1}{Y_S}}$

8 Change in the length of aluminium rod is

(a) $L\Delta T\left[\dfrac{2\alpha_A Y_A + \alpha_S Y_S}{2Y_A + Y_S}\right]$ (b) $L\Delta T\left[\dfrac{\alpha_A Y_A + 2\alpha_S Y_S}{2Y_A + Y_S}\right]$

(c) $L\Delta T\left[\dfrac{\alpha_A Y_A + 2\alpha_S Y_S}{Y_A + 2Y_S}\right]$ (d) $L\Delta T\left[\dfrac{\alpha_A Y_A - \alpha_S Y_S}{Y_A + Y_S}\right]$

Match the Columns Questions

1 A piece of metal of density ρ_1 floats on mercury of density ρ_2. The coefficients of expansion of the metal and mercury are γ_1 and γ_2, respectively. The temperatures of both mercury and metal are increased by ΔT. Then, match the following:

Column I		Column II
A. If $\gamma_2 > \gamma_1$	p.	No effect on fraction of solid submerged in mercury
B. If $\gamma_2 = \gamma_1$	q.	fraction of the volume of metal submerged in mercury increases
C. If $\gamma_2 < \gamma_1$	r.	the solid sinks
	s.	the solid lifts up

2 A cylindrical isotropic solid of coefficient of linear expansion α and density ρ floats in a liquid of coefficient of volume expansion γ and density d as shown in the diagram.

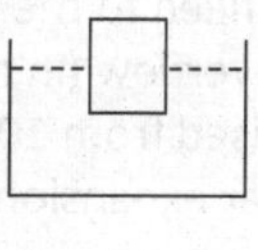

Column I		Column II
A. Volume of cylinder inside the liquid remains constant	p.	$\gamma = 0$
B. Volume of cylinder outside the liquid remains constant	q.	$\gamma = 2\alpha$
C. Height of cylinder outside the liquid remains constant	r.	$\gamma = 3\alpha\frac{d}{\rho}$
D. Height of cylinder inside the liquid remains constant	s.	$\gamma = \left(2\alpha + \alpha\frac{d}{\rho}\right)$

Numerical Value Questions

1 Three aluminium rods of equal length form an equilateral triangle *ABC*. Taking *O* (mid-point of rod *BC*) as the origin. If the increase in *Y*-coordinate of center of mass per unit change in temperature of the system is $n \times 10^{-6}$ m/°C, then find *n*. Assume the length of the each rod is 2 m, and $\alpha_{Al} = 4\sqrt{3} \times 10^{-6}$ /°C.

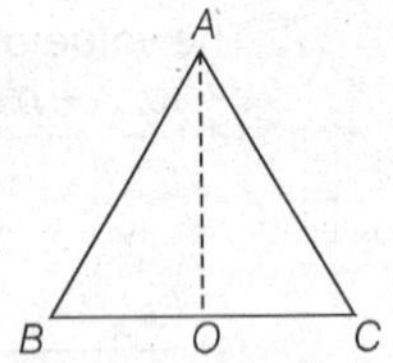

2 A simple seconds pendulum is constructed out of a very thin string of thermal coefficient of linear expansion $\alpha = 20 \times 10^{-4}$ /°C and a heavy particle attached to one end. The free end of the string is suspended from the ceiling of an elevator at rest. The pendulum keeps correct time at 0°C. When the temperature rises to 50°C, the elevator operator of mass 60 kg being a student of Physics accelerates the elevator vertically, to have the pendulum correct time. What is the apparent weight (in kg) of the operator when the pendulum keeps correct time at 50°C?

3 Two liquids having coefficients of volume expansion $\gamma_1 = 1.2 \times 10^{-4}$ /°C and $\gamma_2 = 1.5 \times 10^{-4}$ /°C are filled in a large container having heights $h_1 = 10$ cm and $h_2 = 10$ cm, respectively as shown. The container has coefficient of linear expansion $\alpha_c = 1 \times 10^{-5}$ °/C. Determine the height (in cm) of container for which the empty volume in the container is independent of temperature.

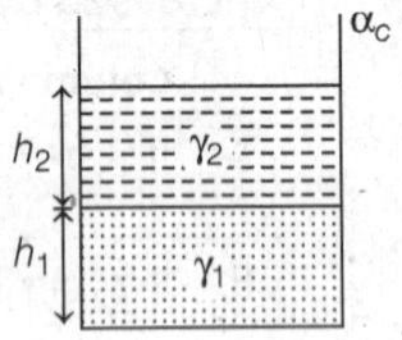

4 A flask of volume 2 liter, containing a piece of iron, volume 1 dm^3, is filled to the brim with water. How much water will overflow (in mm^3), if the temperature is raised from 10°C to 60°C? (The coefficient of linear expansion of iron is 12×10^{-6} /°C, that of glass 8×10^{-6} /°C and the coefficient of volume expansion of water is 1.8×10^{-4} /°C)

5 A composite rod is made by joining two rods of different material but of the same cross-section. At 35°C, the composite rod is 100 cm in length, out of which the length of the first rod is 40 cm. At 135°C, the length of the composite rod increases by 2.1mm. When the composite rod is not allowed to expand by holding it between two rigid walls, it is found that the lengths of the two constituents do not change with rise in temperature. Young's modulus of the first rod is 1.2×10^{11} dyne / cm^2 and its coeficient of linear expansion is 1.5×10^{-5} /°C. If the Young's modulus of the second rod is $n \times 10^9$ dyne / cm^2, then what is the value *n*?

6 The apparatus shown in the figure consists of four glass columns connected by horizontal sections. The height of two central columns *B* and *C* are 49 cm each. The two outer columns *A* and *D* are open to the atmosphere. *A* and *C* are maintained at a temperature of 95° C, while the columns *B* and *D* are maintained at 5°C. The height of the liquid in *A* and *D* measured from the base line are 52.8 cm and 51 cm, respectively. If the coefficient of thermal expansion of the liquid is 2×10^{-n}, then find *n*

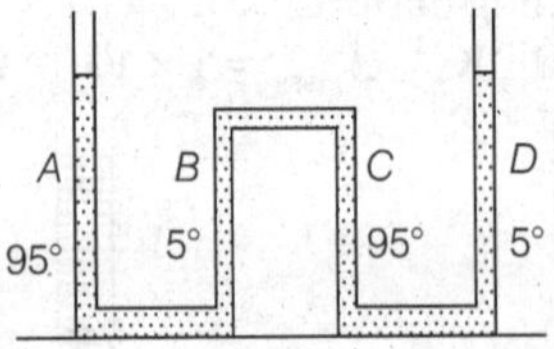

7 As a result of temperature rise of 32°C, a bar with a crack at its centre buckles upward. If the fixed distance l_0 is 4 m, and coefficient of linear expansion of bar is 25×10^{-6} /°C^{-1}, find the rise *x* (in cm) of the centre.

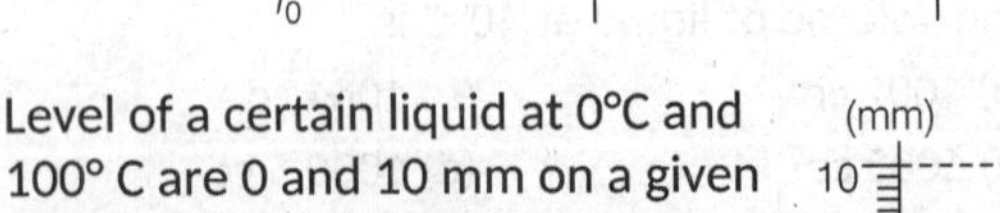

8 Level of a certain liquid at 0°C and 100° C are 0 and 10 mm on a given fixed scale (as shown in figure). Coefficient of volume expansion of this liquid varies with temperature as $\gamma = \gamma_0\left(1 + \frac{T}{100}\right)$ (where *T* in °C).

Find the level (in mm) of liquid at 48°C. Round off the answer to the nearest integer.

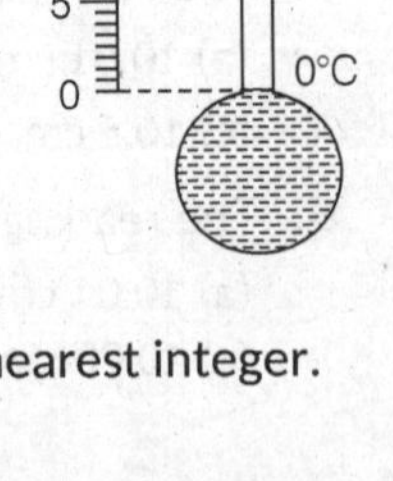

Previous Year's Questions

JEE Main

1 A steel rod of length 1 m and cross-sectional area 10 m is heated from 0°C to 200°C without beint allowed to extend or bend. The compressive tension produced in the rod is .... $\times 10^4$ N. (Given Young's modulus of steel $= 2 \times 10^{11}$ Nm^{-2} coefficient of linear expansion $= 10^{-5}$ K^{-1}) **[2023, 8 April Shift-II]**

2 A hole is drilled in a metal sheet. At 27°C, the diameter of hole is 5 cm. When the sheet is heated to 177°C, the change in the diameter of hole is $d \times 10^{-3}$ cm. The value of d will be .... if coefficient of linear expansion of the metal is 1.6×10^{-5}/°C. **[2023, 24 Jan Shift-I]**

3 On a temperature scale X, the boiling point of water is 65°X and the freezing point is – 15° X. Assume that the X scale is linear. The equivalent temperature corresponding to – 95° X on the Farenheit scale would be **[2023, 11 April Shift-I]**

(a) – 148°F (b) – 112°F
(c) – 48°F (d) – 63°F

4 The graph between two temperature scales P and Q is shown in the figure. Between upper fixed point and lower fixed point, there are 150 equal divisions of scale P and 100 divisions on scale Q. The relationship for conversion between the two scales is given by **[2023, 25 Jan Shift-II]**

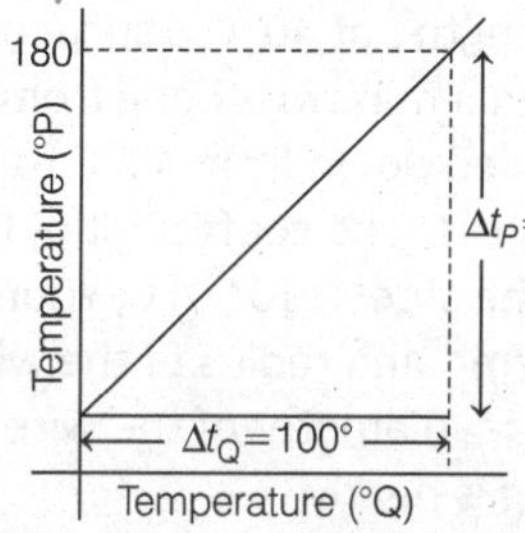

(a) $\frac{t_P}{180} - \frac{t_Q - 40}{100}$ (b) $\frac{t_Q}{100} = \frac{t_P - 30}{150}$

(c) $\frac{t_Q}{150} = \frac{t_P - 180}{100}$ (d) $\frac{t_P}{100} = \frac{t_Q - 180}{150}$

5 A solid metallic cube having total surface area 24 m^2 is uniformly heated. If its temperature is increased by 10°C, calculate the increase in volume of the cube (Given, $\alpha = 5.0 \times 10^{-4}$ °C^{-1}) **[2022, 25 June Shift-II]**

(a) 2.4×10^6 cm^3
(b) 1.2×10^5 cm^3
(c) 6.0×10^4 cm^3
(d) 4.8×10^5 cm^3

6 A unit scale is to be prepared whose length does not change with temperature and remains 20 cm, using a bimetallic strip made of brass and iron each of different length. The length of both components would change in such a way that difference between their lengths remains constant. If length of brass is 40 cm and length of iron will be .... cm $\{a_{iron} = 1.2 \times 10^{-5} K^{-1}$ and $\alpha_{brass} = 1.8 \times 10^{-5}$ K^{-1}) **[2022, 25 July Shift-I]**

7 The area of cross-section of a railway track is 0.01 m^2. The temperature variation is 10° C. Coefficient of linear expansion of material of track is 10^{-5} /° C. The energy stored per metre in the track is ......J/m. (Young's modulus of material of track is 10^{11} Nm^{-2}) **[2021, 22 July Shift-II]**

8 A bimetallic strip consists of metals A and B. It is mounted rigidly as shown. The metal A has higher coefficient of expansion compared to that of metal B. When the bimetallic strip is placed in a cold bath, it will **[2021, 16 March Shift-II]**

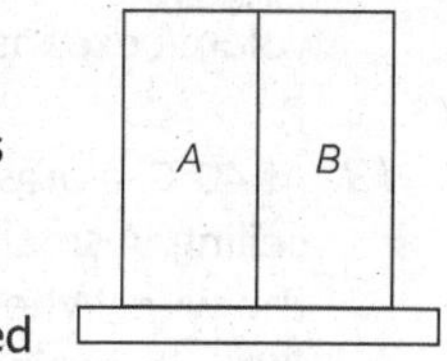

(a) bend towards the right
(b) not bend but shrink
(c) Neither bend nor shrink
(d) bend towards the left

9 Each side of a box made of metal sheet in cubic shape is a at room temperature T, the coefficient of linear expansion of the metal sheet is α. The metal sheet is heated uniformly, by a small temperature ΔT, so that its new temperature is $T + \Delta T$. Calculate the increase in the volume of the metal box. **[2021, 24 Feb Shift-I]**

(a) $4\pi a^3 \alpha \Delta T$ (b) $4a^3 \alpha \Delta T$

(c) $\frac{4}{3}\pi a^3 \alpha \Delta T$ (d) $3a^3 \alpha \Delta T$

10 Given below are two slalements: one is labelled as Assertion A and the other is labelled as Reason R.

Assertion A When a rod lying freely is heated, no thermal stress is developed in it.

Reason R On heating, the length of the rod increases.

In the light of the above statements, choose the correct answer from the options given below. **[2021, 25 Feb Shift-I]**

(a) A is true but R is false.
(b) Both A and R are true and R is the correct explanation of A.
(c) Both A and R are true but R is not the correct explanation of A.
(d) A is false but R is true.

11 Two different wires having lengths L_1 and L_2 and respective temperature coefficients of linear expansion α_1 and α_2, are joined end-to-end. Then the effective temperature coefficient of linear expansion is **[2020, 5 Sep Shift-II]**

(a) $\frac{\alpha_1 L_1 + \alpha_2 L_2}{L_1 + L_2}$ (b) $2\sqrt{\alpha_1 \alpha_2}$

(c) $\frac{\alpha_1 + \alpha_2}{2}$ (d) $4\frac{\alpha_1 \alpha_2}{\alpha_1 + \alpha_2}\frac{L_2 L_1}{(L_2 + L_1)^2}$

12 A bakelite beaker has volume capacity of 500 cc at 30°C. When it is partially filled with V_m volume (at 30°C) of mercury, it is found that the unfilled volume of the beaker remains constant as temperature is varied. If $\gamma_{(\text{beaker})} = 6 \times 10^{-6}\ °C^{-1}$ and $\gamma_{(\text{mercury})} = 1.5 \times 10^{-4}\ °C^{-1}$, where γ is the coefficient of volume expansion, then V_m (in cc) is close to .... **[2020, 3 Sep Shift-I]**

13 At 40°C, a brass wire of 1 mm radius is hung from the ceiling. A small mass, M is hung from the free end of the wire. When the wire is cooled down from 40°C to 20°C, it regains its original length of 0.2 m. The value of M is close to (coefficient of linear expansion and Young's modulus of brass are 10^{-5}°C and 10^{11} N/m^2 respectively, $g = 10$ ms^{-2}) **[2019, 12 April Shift-1]**

(a) 1.5 kg (b) 9 kg

(c) 0.5 kg (d) 0.9 kg

14 A uniform cylindrical rod of length L and radius r, is made from a material whose Young's modulus of elasticity equals Y. When this rod is heated by temperature T and simultaneously subjected to a net longitudinal compressional force F, its length remains unchanged. The coefficient of volume expansion, of the material of the rod, is (nearly) equal to **[2019, 12 April Shift-II]**

(a) $\frac{9F}{(\pi r^2 YT)}$ (b) $\frac{F}{(3\pi r^2 YT)}$ (c) $\frac{6F}{(\pi r^2 YT)}$ (d) $\frac{3F}{(\pi r^2 YT)}$

15 A rod of length L at room temperature and uniform area of cross-section A, is made of a metal having coefficient of linear expansion α/°C. It is observed that an external compressive force F, is applied on each of its ends, prevents any change in the length of the rod, when its temperature rises by ΔTK. Young's modulus Y, for this metal is **[2019, 9 Jan Shift-I]**

(a) $\frac{2F}{A\alpha\Delta T}$ (b) $\frac{F}{A\alpha\Delta T}$

(c) $\frac{F}{2A\alpha\Delta T}$ (d) $\frac{F}{A\alpha(\Delta T - 273)}$

16 Two rods A and B of identical dimensions are at temperature 30°C. If A is heated upto 180°C and B upto T°C, then new lengths are the same. If the ratio of the coefficients of linear expansion of A and B is 4 : 3, then the value of T is **[2019, 11 Jan Shift-II]**

(a) 230°C (b) 270°C

(c) 200°C (d) 250°C

17 A thermometer graduated according to a linear scale reads a value x_0, when in contact with boiling water and $x_0/3$, when in contact with ice. What is the temperature of an object in °C, if this thermometer in the contact with the object reads $x_0/2$? **[2019, 11 Jan Shift-II]**

(a) 35 (b) 60

(c) 40 (d) 25

JEE Advanced

1 Steel wire of length L at 40°C is suspended from the ceiling and then a mass m is hung from its free end. The wire is cooled down from 40°C to 30°C to regain its original length L. The coefficient of linear thermal expansion of the steel is 10^{-5}/°C, Young's modulus of steel is 10^{11} N/m^2 and radius of the wire is 1 mm. Assume that $L >>$ diameter of the wire. Then the value of m in kg is nearly. **(Adv. 2011)**

Answer Key

Level 1

1.1 Temperature

1. 104°F, 313K 2. 108° F, 60 K 3. 160° C 4. 20° C
5. 200°C 6. 60°

1.2 Thermal Expansion

1. Gap will also increase
2. All dimensions a, b, c and d will increase

1.3 Linear Expansion

1. 10.0035 m 2. 60°C 3. 0.0018m 4. 0.2%
5. $\theta = 75.6$°C 6. 167°C 7. 0.4 m and 0.6 m
8. 150.184 cm, $\alpha_{avg} = 15.3 \times 10^{-6}$/°C 9. 219°C

1.4 Variation of Time Period of Simple Pendulum with Temperature

1. 1.04 s 2. 1.7×10^{-5}/°C 3. 20°C, 2.31×10^{-5}°C

1.5 Effect of Temperature on Measurement with Scale

1. (a) readings that are too long (b) 20.0048 cm
2. 0.99989 cm
3. 26.00468 m
4. (a) –0.033% (b) + 0.011%

1.6 Thermal Stress and Strain

1. 0
2. 3.6×10^{-4}
3. 24 N
4. 298°C, 3.33×10^{-3}
5. 44°C
6. $\alpha_1 Y_1 = \alpha_2 Y_2$

1.7 Bimetallic Strip

1. Brass Strip
2. $R = 0.769$ m

1.8 Areal Expansion

1. $2.004\ m^2$
2. 0.2%

1.9 Volume Expansion

1. 5×10^{-4}/°C
2. 3×10^{-6}/°C
3. $1.14\ cm^3$ for both
4. 28.9 cc
5. 2% and 3% respectively

1.10 Apparent Expansion of Liquid

1. 6.7×10^{-4}/°C
2. 17×10^{-6}/°C
3. (a) $1.50\ cm^3$ (b) $1.455\ cm^3$
4. $\Delta V = 0.87\ cm^3$
5. $V_m = 50$ cc

1.11 Variation of Density with Temperature

1. 5×10^{-4}/°C
2. -5×10^{-4} /°C
3. 0.0147

1.12 Variation of Buoyancy with Temperature

1. $\Delta W_0 (1 + (\alpha - \beta)t)$
2. 81.43°C
3. 83°C
4. 8.33×10^{-4}/°C
5. Buoyancy force remains constant.
6. **Case I :** Body moves downward, if $\gamma_L > 3\alpha_S$

   Case II : Body moves upwards, if $\gamma_L < 3\alpha_S$

   Case III : Body remains at same position, if $\gamma_L = 3\alpha_S$

Level 2

Single Choice Correct Questions

1. (b)	2. (c)	3. (a)	4. (c)	5. (d)
6. (a)	7. (b)	8. (a)	9. (c)	10. (c)
11. (d)	12. (b)	13. (b)	14. (c)	15. (b)
16. (c)	17. (a)	18. (c)	19. (d)	20. (c)
21. (c)	22. (c)	23. (d)	24. (c)	25. (b)
26. (a)	27. (a)	28. (a)	29. (c)	30. (a)
31. (b)	32. (d)	33. (b)	34. (c)	35. (c)
36. (b)	37. (b)	38. (d)	39. (b)	40. (c)
41. (c)	42. (b)	43. (d)	44. (a)	45. (a)
46. (c)	47. (c)	48. (d)	49. (b)	50. (a)
51. (a)	52. (c)	53. (c)	54. (b)	55. (c)
56. (b)				

Numerical Value Questions

1. 1	2. 4	3. 5	4. 1	5. 6
6. 3	7. 60	8. 70	9. 2.25	10. 4

Level 3

Single Choice Correct Questions

1. (a)	2. (a)	3. (b)	4. (c)	5. (b)
6. (d)	7. (d)	8. (d)	9. (c)	10. (d)
11. (a)	12. (b)	13. (c)	14. (b)	15. (a)
16. (b)	17. (c)	18. (b)	19. (a)	20. (c)
21. (a)	22. (b)	23. (a)	24. (b)	25. (d)
26. (a)	27. (a)	28. (a)	29. (c)	

Multiple Choice(s) Correct Questions

1. (abcd)	2. (cd)	3. (abd)	4. (bc)	5. (ac)
6. (bc)	7. (bd)	8. (acd)	9. (ad)	

Comprehension Based Questions

1. (c)	2. (c)	3. (c)	4. (b)	5. (b)
6. (b)	7. (a)	8. (c)		

Match the Column Questions

1. $A \rightarrow (q); B \rightarrow (p); C \rightarrow (s)$
2. $A \rightarrow (p); B \rightarrow (r); C \rightarrow (s); D \rightarrow (q)$

Numerical Value Questions

1. 4	2. 66	3. 90	4. 8.4	5. 72
6. 4	7. 8	8. 4		

Previous Year's Questions

JEE Main

1. (4)	2. (12)	3. (a)	4. (b)	5. (b)
6. (60)	7. (5)	8. (d)	9. (d)	10. (c)
11. (a)	12. (20)	13. (b)	14. (d)	15. (b)
16. (a)	17. (d)			

JEE Advanced

1. (3)

SOLUTIONS

Level-1

1.1 Temperature

1. $\frac{T_C - 0}{100} = \frac{T_F - 32}{180} = \frac{T_K - 273}{100}$

$\Rightarrow \frac{40 - 0}{100} = \frac{T_F - 32}{180} = \frac{T_K - 273}{100}$

$\Rightarrow T_F = 104°\text{F and } T_K = 313\text{ K}$

2. $\frac{\Delta T_C}{100} = \frac{\Delta T_F}{180} = \frac{\Delta T_K}{100}$

$\Rightarrow \frac{90 - 30}{100} = \frac{\Delta T_F}{180} = \frac{\Delta T_K}{100}$

$\Rightarrow \Delta T_F = 108°\text{F and } \Delta T_K = 60\text{K}$

3. $\frac{T_C - 0}{100} = \frac{T_F - 32}{180}$

$\Rightarrow \frac{x - 0}{100} = \frac{2x - 32}{180}$

$\Rightarrow x = 160°\text{ C}$

4. $\frac{T_C - 0}{100} = \frac{T - T_1}{T_2 - T_1}$

$\Rightarrow \frac{T_C - 0}{100} = \frac{25 - 5}{105 - 5}$

$\Rightarrow T_C = 20°\text{ C}$

5. $\frac{T_C - 0}{100} = \frac{p - p_1}{p_2 - p_1}$

$\Rightarrow \frac{T_C - 0}{100} = \frac{100 - 80}{90 - 80}$

$\Rightarrow T_C = 200°\text{ C}$

6. $\frac{T - T_1}{T_2 - T_1} = \frac{R - R_1}{R_2 - R_1}$

$\Rightarrow \frac{T - 0}{100 - 0} = \frac{86 - 80}{90 - 80}$

$\Rightarrow T = 60°\text{ C}$

1.2 Thermal Expansion

1. Gap will also increase as distance between any two points on the object increases on heating.
2. All dimensions will increase.

1.3 Linear Expansion

1. $l = l_0(1 + \alpha\Delta T)$

$= 10(1 + 1.0 \times 10^{-5} \times 35)$

$= 10.0035\text{ m}$

2. $\Delta l = l\alpha\Delta T$

$\Rightarrow 2.7 \times 10^{-3} = 0.5 \times 90 \times 10^{-6} \times (T - 0)$

$\Rightarrow T = 60°\text{ C}$

3. $\Delta l = l\alpha\Delta T$

$= 10 \times 0.000012 \times 15 = 0.0018\text{ m}$

4. % change in length $= \frac{\Delta l}{l} \times 100$

$= \alpha\Delta T \times 100$

$= 2 \times 10^{-5} \times 100 \times 100$

$= 0.2\%$

5. $\Delta l = \alpha l\Delta T$

$\Rightarrow 3.002 - 3.000 = 1.2 \times 10^{-5} \times 3.000 \times (T - 20)$

$\Rightarrow T = 75.6°\text{ C}$

6. $\Delta l = \alpha l\Delta T$

$\Rightarrow 6 \times 10^{-3} = 3.6 \times 10^{-5} \times 1.0 \times \Delta T$

$\Rightarrow \Delta T = 167°\text{ C}$

7. $l'_2 - l'_1 = l_2 - l_1$

$\Rightarrow l_2(1 + \alpha_2\Delta T) - l_1(1 + \alpha_1\Delta T) = l_2 - l_1$

$\Rightarrow l_1\alpha_1 = l_2\alpha_2$

$\Rightarrow l_1(18 \times 10^{-6}) = l_2(12 \times 10^{-6})$

$\Rightarrow 3l_1 = 2l_2$ ...(i)

$l_2 - l_1 = 0.2\text{ m}$ ...(ii)

Solving Eqs. (i) and (ii), we get

$l_1 = 0.4\text{ m and } l_2 = 0.6\text{ m}$

8. $\Delta l = \alpha_1 l_1\Delta T + \alpha_2 l_2\Delta T$

$= 12 \times 10^{-6} \times 50 \times 80 + 17 \times 10^{-6} \times 100 \times 80$

$= 0.184\text{ cm}$

Final length of system = 150 + 0.184 = 150.184 cm

$\alpha_{avg} = \frac{\Delta l}{l\Delta T} = \frac{0.184}{150 \times 80} = 15.3 \times 10^{-6}/°\text{C}$

9. Final diameter of ball = Final diameter of hole

$\Rightarrow 2.005\,(1 + 11 \times 10^{-6}\,(\Delta T))$

$= 2.000\,(1 + 23 \times 10^{-6}\,(\Delta T))$

$\Rightarrow \Delta T = 209°\text{ C}$

Final temperature = 209 + 10 = 219°C

1.4 Variation of Time Period of Simple Pendulum with Temperature

1. $\Delta t = \frac{1}{2}\alpha\Delta\theta t$

$= \frac{1}{2} \times 1.2 \times 10^{-6} \times (40 - 20) \times 24 \times 3600 = 1.04\text{ s}$

2. $\Delta t = \frac{1}{2}\alpha\Delta\theta t$

$\Rightarrow \quad 15 = \frac{1}{2}\alpha(20-0)\times 24\times 3600$

$\Rightarrow \quad \alpha = 1.7\times 10^{-5}/°C$

3. $\Delta t = \frac{1}{2}\alpha\Delta\theta t$

$\Rightarrow \quad 5 = \frac{1}{2}\alpha(T-15)\times 24\times 3600 \quad$ ...(i)

and $\quad 10 = \frac{1}{2}\alpha(30-T)\times 24\times 3600 \quad$ ...(ii)

Solving Eqs. (i) and (ii), we get

$T = 20°C$ and $\alpha = 2.31\times 10^{-5}/°C$

1.5 Effect of Temperature on Measurement with Scale

1. (a) At lower temperature, division size on the scale will decrease. So, it will give readings that are too long.

(b) $l = l_0(1+\alpha\Delta T) = 20(1+1.2\times 10^{-5}\times(40-20))$

$= 20.0048$ cm

2. $l = l_0(1+\alpha\Delta T) = 1(1+1.1\times 10^{-5}(10-20))$

$= 0.99989$ cm

3. Measured distance = True distance $(1-\alpha_s\Delta T)$

$\Rightarrow$ 26 = True distance $(1-1.2\times 10^{-5}\times(35-20))$

$\Rightarrow$ True distance = 26.00468 m

4. (a) Percentage error $= -\alpha_s\Delta T\times 100$

$= -11\times 10^{-6}(46-16)\times 100 = -0.033\%$

(b) Percentage error $= -\alpha_s\Delta T\times 100$

$= -11\times 10^{-6}(6-16)\times 100 = +0.011\%$

1.6 Thermal Stress and Strain

1. In absence of external force, no strain or stress will be created as the rod is free to move.

2. Strain $= \alpha\Delta T = 1.2\times 10^{-5}\times(50-20) = 3.6\times 10^{-4}$

3. $F = AY\alpha\Delta T = 0.5\times 10^{-6}\times 2.0\times 10^{11}\times 1.2\times 10^{-5}\times(20-0)$

$= 24$ N

4. $l = l_0(1+\alpha\Delta T)$

$\Rightarrow \quad 15.05 = 15.00(1+12\times 10^{-6}(T-20))$

$\Rightarrow \quad T = 298°C$

Strain developed $= \frac{l_2-l_1}{l_1} = \frac{15.05-15.00}{15.00} = 3.33\times 10^{-3}$

5. $F = AY\alpha\Delta T = mg$

$\Rightarrow 3.14(0.25\times 10^{-3})^2\times 206\times 10^9\times 11\times 10^{-6}\Delta T = 2\times 9.8$

$\Rightarrow \quad \Delta T = 44°C$

6. $F_1 = F_2$

$\Rightarrow \quad A_1Y_1\alpha_1\Delta T = A_2Y_2\alpha_2\Delta T$

$\Rightarrow \quad \alpha_1Y_1 = \alpha_2Y_2 \quad [\because A_1 = A_2]$

1.7 Bimetallic Strip

1. Material with higher coefficient of linear expansion lies on the convex side of the bimetallic strip.

2. $R = \frac{t}{(\alpha_1-\alpha_2)\Delta\theta} = \frac{2\times 10^{-3}}{(1.7\times 10^{-5}-0.4\times 10^{-5})(200-0)}$

$= 0.769$ m

1.8 Areal Expansion

1. $A' = A(1+\beta\Delta T) = 2(1+2\times 10^{-5}\times(110-10)) = 2.004\text{ m}^2$

2. Percentage increase in area $= \frac{\Delta A}{A}\times 100$

$= \beta\Delta T\times 100 = 2\alpha\Delta T\times 100$

$= 2\times 1\times 10^{-5}\times 100\times 100$

$= 0.2\%$

1.9 Volume Expansion

1. $\gamma = \alpha_1+\alpha_2+\alpha_2 = 12\times 10^{-6}+244\times 10^{-6}+244\times 10^{-6}$

$= 5\times 10^{-4}/°C$

2. $\Delta A = \beta A\Delta T$

$\Rightarrow \quad 2.4\times 10^{-4} = \beta\times 1.2\times 100$

$\Rightarrow \quad \beta = 2\times 10^{-6}/°C$

$\gamma = \frac{3\beta}{2} = \frac{3}{2}\times 2\times 10^{-6} = 3\times 10^{-6}/°C$

3. For each of them,

$\Delta V = \gamma V\Delta T = 3\alpha V\Delta T$

$= 3\times 1.9\times 10^{-5}\times 1000\times 20 = 1.14\text{ cm}^3$

4. $\Delta V = \gamma V\Delta T = 3\alpha V\Delta T$

$= 3\times 23\times 10^{-6}\times\left(\frac{4}{3}\times 3.14\times(10)^3\right)(100-0) = 28.9$ cc

5. Percentage change in length $= \alpha\Delta T\times 100 = 1$

Percentage change in area $= \beta\Delta T\times 100$

$= 2(\alpha\Delta T\times 100) = 2(1\%) = 2\%$

Percentage change in volume $= \gamma\Delta T\times 100$

$= 3(\alpha\Delta T\times 100) = 3(1\%) = 3\%$

1.10 Apparent Expansion of Liquid

1. $\gamma_{app} = \gamma_{liquid} - \gamma_{vessel}$

$= 7\times 10^{-4} - 3\times 1\times 10^{-5}$

$= 6.7\times 10^{-4}/°C$

2. When liquid is in glass vessel,

$\gamma_{app} = \gamma_{liquid} - \gamma_{glass}$

$\Rightarrow \quad 10.3\times 10^{-4} = \gamma_{liquid} - 3\times 9\times 10^{-6}$

$\Rightarrow \quad \gamma_{liquid} = 10.57\times 10^{-4}/°C$

When liquid is in metallic vessel,

$\gamma_{app} = \gamma_{liquid} - \gamma_{metal}$

$\Rightarrow \quad 10.06\times10^{-4} = 10.57\times10^{-4} - 3\alpha_{metal}$

$\Rightarrow \quad \gamma_{metal} = 17\times10^{-6}/^\circ C$

3. (a) $\Delta V = \gamma_{liquid} V\Delta T = 60\times10^{-5}\times250\times(60-50) = 1.50\text{ cm}^3$

(b) $\Delta V = \gamma_{app} V\Delta T = (\gamma_{liquid} - \gamma_{glass}) V\Delta T$

$= \left(60\times10^{-5} - \frac{3}{2}\times1.2\times10^{-5}\right)250(60-50)$

$= 1.455\text{ cm}^3$

4. $\Delta V = \gamma_{app} V\Delta T = (1.8\times10^{-4} - 3\times1.8\times10^{-6})\,100(75-25)$

$= 0.87\text{ cm}^3$

5. Let, the volume of mercury poured be V.

Empty volume $= 1000 - V$

At new temperature,

Empty volume $= 1000(1+9\times10^{-6}\Delta T) - V(1+1.8\times10^{-4}\Delta T)$

Empty volume remains constant at all temperatures

$1000(1+9\times10^{-6}\Delta T) - V(1+1.8\times10^{-4}\Delta T) = 1000 - V$

$\Rightarrow \quad V = 50\text{ cc}$

1.11 Variation of Density with Temperature

1. $\rho = \dfrac{\rho_0}{1+\gamma\Delta T}$

$\Rightarrow \quad 8.0 = \dfrac{8.4}{1+\gamma(100-0)}$

$\Rightarrow \quad \gamma = 5\times10^{-4}/^\circ C$

2. $\rho = \dfrac{\rho_0}{1+\gamma\Delta T}$

$\Rightarrow \quad 1.000 = \dfrac{0.998}{1+\gamma(4-0)}$

$\Rightarrow \quad \gamma = -5\times10^{-4}/^\circ C$

3. Fractional change in density $= \gamma\Delta T$

$= 49\times10^{-5}\times(30-0)$

$= 0.0147$

1.12 Variation of Buoyancy with Temperature

1. Loss in weight of solid in a liquid is equal to buoyant force.

At 0°C, $\Delta W_0 = \rho_L V_S g$

At t°C,

$\Delta W = \left(\dfrac{\rho_L}{1+\beta t}\right) V_S(1+\alpha t)\, g$

$= \Delta W_0(1+\alpha t)(1-\beta t)$

$= \Delta W_0(1+(\alpha-\beta)t)$

2. At 4°C, $\dfrac{\rho_S}{\rho_W} = 0.984$

$\Rightarrow \quad \rho_S = 0.984\rho_W$

For the block to sink in water,

$\rho'_W = \rho_S$

$\Rightarrow \quad \dfrac{\rho_W}{1+\gamma\Delta T} = 0.984\rho_W$

$\Rightarrow \quad \Delta T = 77.43^\circ C$

New temperature = 77.43 + 4 = 81.43°C

3. For the piece of wood to just sink in benzene,

$\rho_{wood} = \rho_{benzene}$

$\Rightarrow \quad \dfrac{880}{1+1.2\times10^{-3}T} = \dfrac{900}{1+1.5\times10^{-3}T}$

$\Rightarrow \quad T = 83^\circ C$

4. At 20°C, $\dfrac{\rho_S}{\rho_L} = \dfrac{75}{100}$

$\Rightarrow \quad \rho_S = 0.75\rho_L$

At 100°C, $\dfrac{\rho_S}{\rho'_L} = \dfrac{80}{100}$

$\Rightarrow \quad \dfrac{0.75\rho_L}{\left(\dfrac{\rho_L}{1+\gamma(100-20)}\right)} = 0.8$

$\Rightarrow \quad \gamma = 8.33\times10^{-4}/^\circ C$

5. Body is in equilibrium. So, $mg = B$ and gravitational force does not change with temperature. So, buoyancy force remains constant.

6. Fraction submerged $= f_1 = \dfrac{\rho_S}{\rho_L}$

When temperature is increased,

New fraction submerged $= f_2 = \dfrac{\rho'_S}{\rho'_L}$

$= \dfrac{\left(\dfrac{\rho_S}{1+3\alpha_S\Delta T}\right)}{\left(\dfrac{\rho_L}{1+\gamma_L\Delta T}\right)} = \dfrac{f_1(1+\gamma_L\Delta T)}{1+3\alpha_S\Delta T}$

Case I If $\gamma_L > 3\alpha_S \Rightarrow f_2 > f_1$

$\Rightarrow$ Body moves downward

Case-II If $\gamma_L < 3\alpha_S \Rightarrow f_2 < f_1$

$\Rightarrow$ Body moves upward

Case III If $\gamma_L = 3\alpha_S \Rightarrow f_2 = f_1$

$\Rightarrow$ Body remains at same position

Level-2

Single Choice Correct Questions

1. $\dfrac{T_C - 0}{100} = \dfrac{T - T_1}{T_2 - T_1}$

$\Rightarrow \quad \dfrac{T_C - 0}{100} = \dfrac{60-(-5)}{95-(-5)}$

$\Rightarrow \quad T_C = 65^\circ C$

2. $\frac{T_X - T_1}{T_2 - T_1} = \frac{T_Y - T_1'}{T_2' - T_1'}$

$\Rightarrow \quad \frac{T_X - (-125)}{375 - (-125)} = \frac{50 - (-70)}{-30 - (-70)}$

$\Rightarrow \quad T_X = 1375.0° X$

3. $\frac{T_C - 0}{100} = \frac{T - T_1}{T_2 - T_1}$

$\Rightarrow \quad \frac{T_C - 0}{100} = \frac{(a \ln 4 + b) - (a \ln 2 + b)}{(a \ln 8 + b) - (a \ln 2 + b)}$

$\Rightarrow \quad T_C = 50° C$

4. $\alpha = \frac{1}{R_0} \frac{dR}{dT}$

$\Rightarrow \quad 3T^2 + 2T = \frac{1}{R_0} \frac{dR}{dT}$

$\Rightarrow \quad \int_{R_0}^{R} dR = R_0 \int_0^T (3T^2 + 2T)\, dT$

$\Rightarrow \quad R - R_0 = R_0(T^3 + T^2)$

$\Rightarrow \quad R = R_0(1 + T^2 + T^3)$

5. Distance between C and A will increase as temperature is increased. Since, there is no external force on the disc, centre of mass will remain at rest. Centre of mass lies between C and A. To keep centre of mass stationary, C moves to left and A to right.

6. (a)

7. $d = d_0(1 + \alpha \Delta T) = 2.54(1 + 2.3 \times 10^{-5} \times 100)$

$= 2.5458$ cm

8. $d = d_0(1 + \alpha \Delta T)$

$\Rightarrow \quad 2.01 = 2(1 + 11 \times 10^{-6}(T - 20))$

$\Rightarrow \quad T = 474.5° C$

9. $d_{rod} = d_{ring}$

$\Rightarrow 4.000(1 + 11 \times 10^{-6}(T - 30)) = 3.992(1 + 19 \times 10^{-6}(T - 30))$

$\Rightarrow \quad T = 280° C$

10. $\Delta l = \alpha l_0 \Delta T$

$\Rightarrow \quad x = \alpha l\,(40 - 27) \Rightarrow l = \frac{x}{13\alpha}$

11. % increase in length $= \alpha \Delta T \times 100$

So, percentage increase in d_1 and d_2 will be same.

12. $\alpha = \frac{\Delta l}{l \Delta T}$

$\alpha_A = \frac{104 - 100}{100(T - 0)}$ and $\alpha_B = \frac{106 - 100}{100(T - 0)}$

$\therefore \quad \frac{\alpha_A}{\alpha_B} = \frac{2}{3}$

13. $\Delta l = \alpha l \Delta T$

For metal A,

$0.075 = \alpha_A (20)(100 - 0)$

$\Rightarrow \quad \alpha_A = 3.75 \times 10^{-5} /° C$

For metal B,

$0.045 = \alpha_B (20)(100 - 0)$

$\Rightarrow \quad \alpha_B = 2.25 \times 10^{-5} /° C$

For third rod,

$\Delta l = \alpha_A l_A \Delta T + \alpha_B l_B \Delta T$

$\Rightarrow \quad 0.060 = 3.75 \times 10^{-5} \times l_A (100 - 0)$

$+ 2.25 \times 10^{-5} \times (20 - l_A)(100 - 0)$

$\Rightarrow \quad l_A = 10$ cm

14. $\Delta l = \left(\int \alpha\, dx\right) \Delta T$

$\Rightarrow \quad l - 200 = \left(\int_0^{200} (3x + 2) \times 10^{-6} dx\right)(20 - 0)$

$\Rightarrow \quad l - 200 = \left[\frac{3x^2}{2} + 2x\right]_0^{200} (20 \times 10^{-6})$

$\Rightarrow \quad l = 201.20 \text{ cm} = 2.0120 \text{ m}$

15. $\Delta l_1 = \Delta l_2$

$\Rightarrow \quad l_1 \alpha_1 \Delta T = l_2 \alpha_2 \Delta T$

$\Rightarrow \quad \frac{l_1}{l_2} = \frac{\alpha_2}{\alpha_1}$

16. $\Delta L = \Delta L_1 + \Delta L_2 = \alpha_1 L_1 \Delta T + \alpha_2 L_2 \Delta T$

$\alpha_{eq} = \frac{\Delta L}{L \Delta T} = \frac{\alpha_1 L_1 \Delta T + \alpha_2 L_2 \Delta T}{L(\Delta T)} = \frac{\alpha_1 L_1 + \alpha_2 L_2}{L}$

17. $\Delta L_C = \Delta L_S$

$\Rightarrow \quad \alpha_C L_C \Delta T = \alpha_S L_S \Delta T$

$\Rightarrow \quad \frac{L_C}{L_S} = \frac{\alpha_S}{\alpha_C} = \frac{2 \times 10^{-5}}{5 \times 10^{-5}}$

$\Rightarrow \quad L_S = \frac{5L_C}{2}$

Also, $\quad L_S - L_C = 5$

$\Rightarrow \quad \frac{5L_C}{2} - L_C = 5$

$\Rightarrow \quad L_C = 3.33$ cm

18. $I = mL^2$

$\Rightarrow \quad \frac{\Delta I}{I} = 2 \frac{\Delta L}{L}$

$\Rightarrow \quad \frac{\Delta I}{I} = 2\alpha \Delta T$

$\Rightarrow \quad \Delta I = 2\alpha I \Delta T$

19. $I\omega = \text{constant}$

$\Rightarrow \quad \frac{2}{5} mR^2 \omega = \text{constant}$

$\Rightarrow \quad 2\frac{\Delta R}{R} + \frac{\Delta \omega}{\omega} = 0$

$\Rightarrow \quad 2(\alpha \Delta T) + \frac{1}{100} = 0$

$\Rightarrow \quad \Delta T = -\frac{1}{200\alpha} = \frac{1}{200\alpha}$ decrease

20. $I_0\omega_0 = I\omega$

$\Rightarrow \quad \frac{2}{5}mR_0^2\omega_0 = \frac{2}{5}mR^2\omega$

$\Rightarrow \quad R_0^2\omega_0 = (R_0(1+\alpha\Delta T))^2\omega$

$\Rightarrow \quad \omega = \frac{\omega_0}{1+2\alpha\Delta T}$

$= \frac{\omega_0}{1+2(2.0\times10^{-5})100} = \frac{\omega_0}{1+0.004}$

21. Measured value is greater than actual value at lesser temperature. Measured value is 25 cm at 0°C. So, the real length must be less than 25 cm.

22. $\Delta l = \alpha l \Delta T$

$\Rightarrow \quad 6\times10^{-5} = 12\times10^{-6}\times1\times\Delta T$

$\Rightarrow \quad \Delta T = 5°\text{C}$

23. $l_0(1+\alpha_C\Delta T) = l_1(1+\alpha_S\Delta T)$

$\Rightarrow \quad l_1 = \left(\frac{1+\alpha_C(40-20)}{1+\alpha_S(40-20)}\right)l_0 = \left(\frac{1+20\alpha_C}{1+20\alpha_S}\right)l_0$

24. Error in measurement for 30 m steel tape

$= 30.02 - 30 = 0.02$ m

Error in measurement for 15 m (approx.) steel tape

$= \frac{0.02}{2} = 0.01$ m

Actual distance = Measured distance + error

= 15.02 + 0.01 = 15.03 m

25. $\Delta l = \alpha l \Delta T = 1.1\times10^{-5}\times180\times(20-10)$

$= 1.98\times10^{-2}$ mm

26. $\Delta l = \alpha l \Delta T$

$\Rightarrow \quad 2.5\times10^{-2} = 10^{-6}\times1000\times(30-T)$

$\Rightarrow \quad T = 5°\text{C}$

27. Measured value = Actual value $(1-\alpha_S\Delta T)$

$\Rightarrow$ 80 = Actual value $(1-2.50\times10^{-5}(45-5))$

$\Rightarrow$ Actual value = 80.08 cm

28. When a bimetallic strip is heated, metal with higher α lies on the convex side.

$\therefore \quad \alpha_1 < \alpha_2$

29. $\Delta t = \frac{1}{2}\alpha\Delta\theta t = \frac{1}{2}\times0.000019\times(25-0)\times24\times3600 = 20.52$ s

30. $\Delta t = \frac{1}{2}\alpha\Delta\theta t$

At 20°C,

$6 = \frac{1}{2}\alpha(T-20)(24\times3600)$ ...(i)

At 40°C,

$6 = \frac{1}{2}\alpha(40-T)(24\times3600)$ ...(ii)

Solving Eqs. (i) and (ii), we get

$\alpha = 1.4\times10^{-5}\,°\text{C}^{-1}$

31. Percentage increase in length $= \frac{\Delta l}{l}\times100$

$= \alpha\Delta T\times100 = 1\%$

Percentage increase in area $= \frac{\Delta A}{A}\times100 = 2\alpha\Delta T\times100$

$= 2\,(1\%) = 2\%$

32. $dA = \beta A dT$

$\Rightarrow \quad \int_{A_0}^{A}\frac{dA}{A} = 2\alpha\int_{T_0}^{T}dT$

$\Rightarrow \quad \ln\left(\frac{A}{A_0}\right) = 2\alpha\Delta T$

$\Rightarrow \quad A = A_0e^{2\alpha\Delta T}$

Fractional increase in area $= \frac{A-A_0}{A_0} = e^{2\alpha\Delta T} - 1$

$= e^{2(0.1)(10)} - 1 = e^2 - 1 = 6.39$

33. $\alpha = \frac{\Delta l}{l\Delta T} = \frac{\text{Slope of graph}}{l}$

$= \frac{1\times10^{-3}/10}{2} = 5\times10^{-5}\,\text{K}^{-1}$

$\gamma = 3\alpha = 1.5\times10^{-4}\,\text{K}^{-1}$

34. $\gamma = \alpha_1+\alpha_2+\alpha_3 = \alpha_1+\alpha_2+\alpha_2 = \alpha_1+2\alpha_2$

35. When liquid is in copper vessel,

$\gamma_{app} = \gamma_{liquid} - \gamma_{vessel}$

$\Rightarrow \quad C = \gamma_{liquid} - \gamma_C$

$\Rightarrow \quad \gamma_{liquid} = C + \gamma_C$

When liquid is in silver vessel,

$\gamma_{app} = \gamma_{liquid} - \gamma_{vessel}$

$\Rightarrow \quad S = (C+\gamma_C) - 3\alpha_{silver}$

$\Rightarrow \quad \alpha_{silver} = \frac{C+\gamma_C-S}{3}$

36. $\gamma_L = 7\gamma_S$

$\gamma_{app} = \gamma_L - \gamma_S = 7\gamma_S - \gamma_S = 6\gamma_S$

$\therefore \quad \frac{\gamma_L}{\gamma_{app}} = \frac{7\gamma_S}{6\gamma_S} = \frac{7}{6}$

37. Density of water is maximum at 4°C. So, when temperature is increased or decreased from 4°C, density of water decreases. So, water overflows in both the cases.

38. Since, the coefficient of expansion of both oil and vessel is same, as the temperature increases, volume of both oil and vessel increase by same amount without any overflow of oil. Hence, more volume of oil is now being contained. However, the vessel is always completely filled, never empty by any fraction. Hence, the mass of oil containable remains the same.

39. $\Delta V = \gamma_{app}V\Delta T$

$= (\gamma_{Hg} - \gamma_{glass})V\Delta T$

$= (1.82\times10^{-4} - 3\times0.1\times10^{-4})(1000)(100-0)$

= 15.2 cc

40. Let, volume of flask be V.

Volume of air $= V - 300$

$$= V(1 + 3\times 9\times 10^{-6}\Delta T) - 300(1 + 1.8\times 10^{-4}\Delta T)$$

$$\Rightarrow \quad V = 2000\text{ cm}^3$$

41. $p = \dfrac{mg}{A} \Rightarrow \dfrac{\Delta p}{p} = -\dfrac{\Delta A}{A}$

$$\Rightarrow \frac{\Delta p}{p}\times 100 = -2\alpha\Delta T\times 100$$

$$= -2\times 10^{-3}\times 10\times 100$$

$$= -2\%$$

42. $\rho = \rho_0(1 - 3\alpha\Delta T)$

$$\frac{\Delta\rho}{\rho}\times 100 = -3\alpha\Delta T\times 100$$

$$\Rightarrow \quad -0.1 = -3\times 10^{-5}(T - 0)\times 100$$

$$\Rightarrow \quad T = 33.33^\circ\text{ C}$$

43. $\gamma = -\dfrac{\Delta\rho}{\rho\Delta T}$

$$= -\frac{992 - 998}{998(40 - 20)} \simeq 3\times 10^{-4}/^\circ\text{C}$$

44. $\rho_1 g h_1 = \rho_2 g h_2$

$$\Rightarrow \left(\frac{\rho_0}{1 + \gamma\,\theta_1}\right) g h_1 = \left(\frac{\rho_0}{1 + \gamma\,\theta_2}\right) g h_2$$

$$\Rightarrow \frac{h_1}{h_2} = \frac{1 + \gamma\,\theta_1}{1 + \gamma\,\theta_2}$$

$$\Rightarrow \gamma = \frac{h_2 - h_1}{h_1\theta_2 - h_2\theta_1} = \frac{60 - 50}{50\times 100 - 60\times 50} = 0.005/^\circ\text{C}$$

45. $\rho_1 g h_1 = \rho_2 g h_2$

$$\Rightarrow \quad \rho_0(h_1) = \left(\frac{\rho_0}{1 + \gamma\Delta T}\right) h_2$$

$$\Rightarrow \quad h_2 = h_1(1 + \gamma\Delta T)$$

$$\Delta h = h_2 - h_1 = h_1\gamma\Delta T$$

$$= 100\times 10^{-5}\times 100 = 0.1\text{ cm}$$

46. $F_B' = F_B\left(\dfrac{1 + \gamma_m\Delta T}{1 + \gamma_{Al}\Delta T}\right)$

$$\Rightarrow \quad F_B' < F_B \qquad \because [\gamma_m < \gamma_{Al}]$$

Apparent weight $= mg - F_B$

As buoyant force decreases, apparent weight increases.

$$\therefore \quad W_1 < W_2$$

47. Fraction in air $= 1 - \dfrac{\rho_S}{\rho_W}$

Density of water is maximum at 4°C. As temperature is raised from 0°C to 10°C, density of water first increases and then decreases. Therefore, volume of block above water level will first increase and then decrease.

48. $B = \rho_L V_S g$

$$\Rightarrow \quad \frac{\Delta B}{B} = \frac{\Delta\rho_L}{\rho_L} + \frac{\Delta V_S}{V_S}$$

$$= -\gamma_L\Delta T + \gamma_S\Delta T$$

Percentage change in upthrust $= \dfrac{\Delta B}{B}\times 100$

$$= (\gamma_S - \gamma_L)\,\Delta T\times 100$$

$$= (3\times 10^{-6} - 8\times 10^{-6})\times 100\times 100$$

$$= -0.05\%$$

49. At 4°C,

Fraction submerged $= \dfrac{\rho_S}{\rho_W} = 0.98$

$$\Rightarrow \quad \rho_S = 0.98\rho_W$$

For the body to get completely immersed in water,

$$\rho_S = \rho'_W$$

$$\Rightarrow \quad 0.98\rho_W = \frac{\rho_W}{1 + 3.3\times 10^{-4}(T - 4)}$$

$$\Rightarrow \quad T = 65.8^\circ\text{ C}$$

50. Density of sphere $= \dfrac{\text{Mass}}{\text{Volume}}$

$$= \frac{266.5}{\frac{4}{3}\pi\,(3.5)^3} = 1.484\text{ g/cc}$$

For the sphere to just sink at 35°C,

$$\rho_{sphere} = \rho_{liquid}$$

$$\Rightarrow \quad 1.484 = \frac{1.527}{1 + \gamma\,(35 - 0)}$$

$$\Rightarrow \quad \gamma = 8.278\times 10^{-4}/^\circ\text{C}$$

51. Buoyant force = Loss in weight

At 27°C, $B = 46\text{ g} - 30\text{ g}$

$$\Rightarrow \quad 1.24V\text{ g} = 16\text{ g}$$

$$\Rightarrow \quad V = \frac{16}{1.24}\text{ cm}^3$$

At 42°C, $B = 46\text{ g} - 30.5\text{ g}$

$$\Rightarrow \quad 1.20\times\frac{16}{1.24}(1 + 3\alpha\,(42 - 27))\text{ g} = 15.5\text{ g}$$

$$\Rightarrow \quad \alpha = 2.31\times 10^{-5}/^\circ\text{C}$$

52. As the rod will expand freely, there will not be any strain produced in the rod.

53. Longitudinal strain $= \alpha\Delta T$

$$= 12\times 10^{-6}\times(75 - 25)$$

$$= 6\times 10^{-4}$$

Strain will be negative as the rod is in compressed state.

54. Strain $= \dfrac{l_2 - l_1}{l_1} = \dfrac{l_1 - l_1(1 + \alpha\Delta T)}{l_1(1 + \alpha\Delta T)} = \dfrac{-\alpha\Delta T}{1 + \alpha\Delta T}$

$$Y = \frac{\text{Stress}}{\text{Strain}}$$

$$\Rightarrow \quad E = \frac{F/A}{\frac{\alpha\Delta T}{1+\alpha\Delta T}}$$

$$\Rightarrow \quad F = \frac{AE\alpha\Delta T}{1+\alpha\Delta T} = \frac{AE\alpha t}{1+\alpha t}$$

55. Strain $= \frac{\Delta l}{l} = \frac{40.05 - 40}{40} = 1.25 \times 10^{-3}$

$$Y = \frac{\text{Stress}}{\text{Strain}}$$

$$\Rightarrow 200 \times 10^9 = \frac{\frac{F}{1\times10^{-6}}}{1.25\times10^{-3}}$$

$$\Rightarrow \quad F = 250\text{ N}$$

56. $p = B\left(\frac{\Delta V}{V}\right) = B(3\alpha\Delta T)$

$$= 1.4\times10^{11}\times3\times1.7\times10^{-5}\times(30-20)$$

$$= 7.1\times10^7\text{ Pa}$$

Numerical Value Questions

1. $\Delta l = \left(\int \alpha dx\right)\Delta T = \left(\int_0^1 \frac{x}{5000}dx\right)100$

$$= \frac{1}{50}\left[\frac{x^2}{2}\right]_0^1 = \frac{1}{100}\text{ m} = 1\text{ cm}$$

2. $AF = AB + EF - CD = 2l_1 - l_2$

At new temperature,

$$AF = 2l_1(1+\alpha_1\Delta T) - l_2(1+\alpha_2\Delta T)$$

Distance AF remains same at all temperatures.

$$2l_1 - l_2 = 2l_1(1+\alpha_1\Delta T) - l_2(1+\alpha_2\Delta T)$$

$$\Rightarrow \quad \frac{l_2}{l_1} = \frac{2\alpha_1}{\alpha_2} = \frac{2(2\times10^{-5})}{1\times10^{-5}} = 4$$

3. Time period at h at 20°C = Time period at ground at 30°C

$$2\pi\sqrt{\frac{l}{g\left(1-\frac{2h}{R}\right)}} = 2\pi\sqrt{\frac{l(1+\alpha\Delta\theta)}{g}}$$

$$\Rightarrow \quad \left(1-\frac{2h}{R}\right)^{-1} = 1+\alpha\Delta\theta$$

$$\Rightarrow \quad 1+\frac{2h}{R} = 1+\alpha\Delta\theta$$

$$\Rightarrow \quad \alpha = \frac{2h}{\Delta\theta R} = \frac{2h}{(30-20)R} = \frac{h}{5R}$$

$\therefore \quad n = 5$

4. $\Delta V = \gamma V\Delta T$

$$\Rightarrow \quad A\Delta h = \gamma V\Delta T$$

$$\Rightarrow (1.8\times10^{-4})\,\Delta h = 1.8\times10^{-4}\times1\times1$$

$$\Rightarrow \quad \Delta h = 1\text{ cm}$$

5. Let initial volume of mercury = x

$\therefore$ Volume of glass vessel = $x + 34$

At new temperature,

$$(x+34)(1+3\times9\times10^{-6}\Delta T)$$
$$-x(1+18\times10^{-5}\Delta T) = 34$$

$$\Rightarrow \quad \frac{x+34}{x} = \frac{20}{3}$$

$$\Rightarrow x = 6\text{ cm}^3$$

6. Apparent expansion of mercury $= \pi(0.04)^2(1.19)$

$$= 5.98\times10^{-3}\text{ cm}^3$$

Volume of mercury $= \frac{0.07}{0.82} = 0.0853\text{ cm}^3$

$$\Delta V = \gamma_{app}V\Delta T$$

$$\Rightarrow \quad 5.98\times10^{-3} = (\gamma - 1\times10^{-5})(0.0853)(40-0)$$

$$\Rightarrow \quad \gamma = 1.75\times10^{-3}/°\text{C}$$

$\therefore \quad n = 3$

7. At 20°C, Fraction submerged $= \frac{\rho_S}{\rho_W} = 1 - \frac{1}{100}$

$$\Rightarrow \quad \frac{\rho_S}{\rho_W} = \frac{99}{100}$$

To submerge the sphere completely in water,

$$\rho'_S = \rho'_W$$

$$\Rightarrow \quad \frac{\rho_S}{1+3\times2.30\times10^{-5}(T-20)} = \frac{\rho_W}{1+3.19\times10^{-4}(T-20)}$$

$$\Rightarrow \quad \frac{\rho_S}{\rho_W} = \frac{1+6.9\times10^{-5}(T-20)}{1+3.19\times10^{-4}(T-20)} = \frac{99}{100}$$

$$\Rightarrow \quad T = 60°\text{ C}$$

8. $F = AY\alpha\Delta T$

$$\Rightarrow 200 = 2\times10^{-6}\times200\times10^9\times10^{-5}\times(T-20)$$

$$\Rightarrow \quad T = 70°\text{ C}$$

9. Let, first rod extends by ΔL and second rod compressed by ΔL.

$$F_1 = F_2$$

$$\Rightarrow \quad \frac{AY_1(L\alpha_1\Delta T - \Delta L)}{L} = \frac{AY_2}{L}(L\alpha_2\Delta T + \Delta L)$$

$$\Rightarrow \quad \Delta L = \frac{L\Delta T\,(Y_1\alpha_1 - Y_2\alpha_2)}{Y_1+Y_2}$$

Substituting value of ΔL, we get

$$F_1 = F_2 = \frac{Y_1Y_2A\Delta T}{Y_1+Y_2}(\alpha_1+\alpha_2)$$

$$\therefore \quad p = \frac{F_1}{A} = \frac{Y_1Y_2\Delta T}{Y_1+Y_2}(\alpha_1+\alpha_2)$$

$$= 2.25\times10^7\text{ N/m}^2$$

10. $L = \left(\frac{ml^2}{3}\right)\omega$

$$\Rightarrow \quad \frac{\Delta L}{L} = 2\frac{\Delta l}{l} + \frac{\Delta\omega}{\omega}$$

$$\Rightarrow \quad 0 = 2(\alpha \Delta T) + \frac{\Delta \omega}{\omega}$$

$$\Rightarrow \quad \frac{\Delta \omega}{\omega} \times 100 = -2\alpha \Delta T \times 100$$

$$= -2 \times 2 \times 10^{-4} \times 10 \times 100 = -4 \times 10^{-1}\%$$

So, answer will be 4.

Level 3

1. (a)

2. $\Delta L = L_0 \int \alpha dT = L_0 \int_{T_1}^{2T_1} (aT - bT^2)\, dT$

$$= \left(\frac{3}{2} aT_1^2 - \frac{7b}{3} T_1^3\right) L_0$$

3. $dl = \alpha l dT$

$$\Rightarrow \quad \int_l^{2l} \frac{dl}{l} = \int_0^T aT\, dT$$

$$\Rightarrow \quad [\ln l]_l^{2l} = a\left[\frac{T^2}{2}\right]_0^T$$

$$\Rightarrow \quad \ln 2 = \frac{aT^2}{2}$$

$$\Rightarrow \quad T = \sqrt{\frac{\ln 4}{a}}$$

4. $\Delta R = \alpha R \Delta T$

$$= 1.2 \times 10^{-5} \times 6400 \times (40 - 10) = 2.3 \text{ km}$$

5. Let, the common temperature be T.

For the ball to just pass through the hole,

$$d_{\text{ball}} = d_{\text{hole}}$$

$$\Rightarrow \quad 6(1 + 1.2 \times 10^{-5}(T - 30))$$

$$= 5.999(1 + 1.9 \times 10^{-5}(T - 30))$$

$$\Rightarrow \quad T = 53.8° \text{C}$$

6. Slope of line $A = \frac{1006 - 1000}{T} = \frac{\Delta L}{\Delta T} = L\alpha_A$

$$\Rightarrow \quad \frac{6}{T} = 1000\alpha_A \quad \text{...(i)}$$

Slope of line $B = \frac{1004 - 1002}{T} = L\alpha_B$

$$\Rightarrow \quad \frac{2}{T} = 1002\alpha_B \quad \text{...(ii)}$$

From Eqs. (i) and (ii), we get

$$3 = \frac{1000\alpha_A}{1002\alpha_B}$$

$$\Rightarrow \quad \alpha_A = 3\alpha_B = 3(9 \times 10^{-6}) = 27 \times 10^{-6}/°\text{C}$$

From Eqs. (i),

$$\frac{6}{T} = 1000 \times 27 \times 10^{-6}$$

$$\Rightarrow \quad T = 222.22° \text{C}$$

7. Before expansion, $CD = \sqrt{L_2^2 - \left(\frac{L_1}{2}\right)^2}$

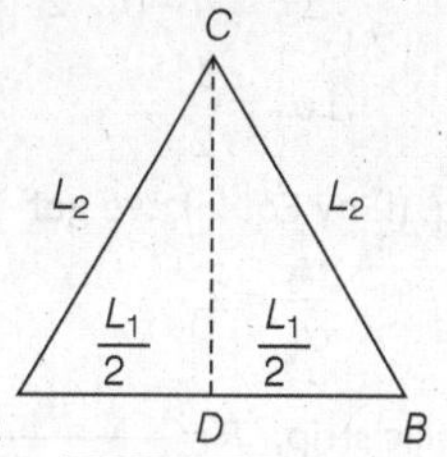

After expansion, $CD = \sqrt{(L_2(1 + \alpha_2 \Delta T))^2 - \left(\frac{L_1}{2}(1 + \alpha_1 \Delta T)\right)^2}$

Distance CD remains constant,

$$\sqrt{L_2^2 - \frac{L_1^2}{4}} = \sqrt{(L_2(1 + \alpha_2 \Delta T))^2 - \frac{L_1^2}{4}(1 + \alpha_1 \Delta T)^2}$$

$$\Rightarrow \quad L_2^2 - \frac{L_1^2}{4} = L_2^2(1 + 2\alpha_2 \Delta T) - \frac{L_1^2}{4}(1 + 2\alpha_1 \Delta T)$$

$$\Rightarrow \quad \frac{L_1^2}{4}(2\alpha_1 \Delta T) = L_2^2(2\alpha_2 \Delta T)$$

$$\Rightarrow \quad \frac{L_1}{L_2} = 2\sqrt{\frac{\alpha_2}{\alpha_1}}$$

8. $\frac{\Delta R}{R} \times 100 = \frac{507.5 - 500.0}{500.0} \times 100 = 1.5\%$

$$K = \frac{L^2}{2I} = \frac{L^2}{2\left(\frac{1}{2} mR^2\right)} \quad \Rightarrow \quad K = \frac{L^2}{mR^2}$$

$$\therefore \quad \frac{\Delta K}{K} \times 100 = -2\frac{\Delta R}{R} \times 100 = -2(1.5\%) = -3\%$$

9. Elongation in the left rod $= \Delta l = l_0 \alpha \Delta \theta$

Elongation in the right rod $= 2\Delta l = 2l_0 \alpha \Delta \theta$

Since, the centre of mass of two rod system will not shift, the junction will shift by x as shown.

Taking moment of mass about original centre of mass C,

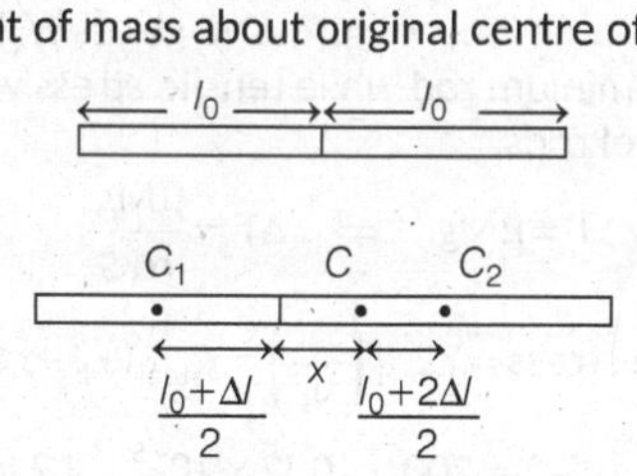

$$m \times \left(\frac{l_0 + \Delta l}{2} + x\right) = m\left(\frac{l_0 + 2\Delta l}{2} - x\right)$$

Solving, we get

$$x = \frac{\Delta l}{4} = \frac{l_0 \alpha \Delta \theta}{4}$$

10. For metal 1,

$$\text{Slope} = \frac{\Delta L}{\Delta T} = \frac{4 - 0}{4 - 0} = 1$$

$$\Rightarrow \quad L\alpha_1 = 1 \quad \text{...(i)}$$

For metal 2,

$$\text{Slope} = \frac{\Delta L}{\Delta T} = \frac{2-0}{4-0} = \frac{1}{2}$$

$$\Rightarrow \quad L\alpha_2 = \frac{1}{2} \quad \text{...(ii)}$$

Dividing Eq. (i) by Eq. (ii), we get

$$\frac{\alpha_1}{\alpha_2} = 2 \quad \text{...(iii)}$$

For bimetallic strip, $R = \dfrac{t}{(\alpha_1 - \alpha_2)\,\Delta T}$

$$\Rightarrow \quad 75 = \frac{3\times 10^{-2}}{(\alpha_1 - \alpha_2)\,50}$$

$$\Rightarrow \quad \alpha_1 - \alpha_2 = 8\times 10^{-6}/^\circ C \quad \text{...(iv)}$$

Solving Eqs. (iii) and (iv), we get

$$\alpha_1 = 16\times 10^{-6}/^\circ C \quad \text{and} \quad \alpha_2 = 8\times 10^{-6}/^\circ C$$

11. Since, the scale expands more than the object, actual length will be greater than the measured length.

12. At 20°C,

Measured value = Actual value $(1 - \alpha_S \Delta T)$

$$\Rightarrow \quad 9.975 = 10(1 - \alpha_S(20-0))$$

$$\Rightarrow \quad \alpha_S = 1.25\times 10^{-4}/^\circ C$$

At 50°C,

Measured value $= 10(1 - 1.25\times 10^{-4}(50-0)) = 9.9375$ cm

13. $MV = AV(1 + (\alpha_0 - \alpha_S)\,\Delta T)$

$\Rightarrow 100 = AV(1 + (8\times 10^{-6} - 26\times 10^{-6})(30-0))$

$\Rightarrow$ Actual value = 100.054 cm

So, the true length of rod at 0°C = 100.054 cm

For rod at 30°C,

True length $= l(1 + \alpha_0 \Delta T) = 100.054\,(1 + 8\times 10^{-6}\times 30)$

$= 100.078$ cm

14. Aluminium expands more than steel but their final lengths will be same. So, compressive stress will be developed in the aluminium rod while tensile stress will be developed in the steel rods.

15. $F = SY\alpha\Delta T = \mu Mg \quad \Rightarrow \quad \Delta T = \dfrac{\mu Mg}{\alpha YS}$

16. Tensile stress $= Y_{\text{steel}}\left(\dfrac{\Delta l}{l}\right) = Y_{\text{steel}}(\alpha_b - \alpha_s)\,\Delta T$

$$= 200\times 10^9 (2\times 10^{-5} - 1.2\times 10^{-5})(200)$$

$$= 3.2\times 10^8 \text{ Nm}^{-2}$$

17. $\beta_{ABCD} = \alpha_X = \alpha_Z = 4\times 10^{-5}/^\circ C$

$\beta_{BCGH} = \alpha_Y + \alpha_Z = 5\times 10^{-5}/^\circ C$

$\beta_{CDEH} = \alpha_X + \alpha_Y = 3\times 10^{-5}/^\circ C$

$\beta_{EFGH} = \alpha_X + \alpha_Z = 4\times 10^{-5}/^\circ C$

18. $\gamma = \dfrac{1}{V}\dfrac{dV}{dT} = \dfrac{-4\times 10^{-5} + 10\times 10^{-6}T}{0.500 - (4\times 10^{-5})T + (5\times 10^{-6})T^2}$

At 20°C, $\gamma = 3.2\times 10^{-4}/^\circ C$

19. $p_1 = p_2 \quad \Rightarrow \quad \rho_1 g h_1 = \rho_2 g h_2$

$$\Rightarrow \quad \left(\frac{\rho_0}{1+\gamma t_1}\right) l_1 = \left(\frac{\rho_0}{1+\gamma t_2}\right) l_2$$

$$\Rightarrow \quad \gamma = \frac{l_1 - l_2}{l_2 t_1 - l_1 t_2}$$

20. From figure (a),

$$\text{Slope} = \frac{\Delta L}{\Delta T} = \frac{1001.2 - 1000}{300 - 0} = 4\times 10^{-3}\text{ mm}/^\circ C$$

Also, $\dfrac{\Delta L}{\Delta T} = L\alpha$

$$\Rightarrow \quad 4\times 10^{-3} = 1000\alpha \quad \Rightarrow \quad \alpha = 4\times 10^{-6}/^\circ C$$

From figure (b),

$$\text{Slope} = \frac{\Delta V_a}{\Delta T} = \frac{1003 - 1000}{20 - 0} = \frac{3}{20}\text{ mL}/^\circ C$$

Also, $\dfrac{\Delta V_a}{\Delta T} = V\gamma_a$

$$\Rightarrow \quad \frac{3}{20} = 1000\gamma_a \quad \Rightarrow \quad \gamma_a = 150\times 10^{-6}/^\circ C$$

$$\gamma_a = \gamma_{\text{liquid}} - \gamma_{\text{vessel}}$$

$$\Rightarrow 150\times 10^{-6} = \gamma_{\text{liquid}} - 3(4\times 10^{-6})$$

$$\Rightarrow \quad \gamma_{\text{liquid}} = 16.2\times 10^{-5}/^\circ C$$

21. $\gamma_C V_C \Delta T = \gamma_1 V_1 \Delta T + \gamma_2 V_2 \Delta T$

$$\Rightarrow \quad \gamma_C = \frac{\gamma_1 V_1 + \gamma_2 V_2}{V_C} = \frac{1.4\times 10^{-5}\times 200 + 2.1\times 10^{-5}\times 500}{700}$$

$$= 1.9\times 10^{-5}/^\circ C$$

22. New volume of liquid $= AL(1 + \gamma\Delta T)$

New cross-section area $= A(1 + 2\alpha\Delta T)$

New height $= L' = \dfrac{AL(1+\gamma\Delta T)}{A(1+2\alpha\Delta T)} = L(1 + (\gamma - 2\alpha)\,\Delta T)$

$$\therefore \quad \Delta L = L' - L = L(\gamma - 2\alpha)\,\Delta T$$

23. Initial volume of container $= \dfrac{100}{\rho_0}$

Final volume of container $= \dfrac{99.7}{\rho} = \dfrac{99.7}{\left(\dfrac{\rho_0}{1+\gamma_{\text{Hg}}(20)}\right)}$

$$= \frac{99.7}{\rho_0}(1 + \gamma_{\text{Hg}}(20))$$

For container,

$$V = V_0(1 + \gamma_{\text{glass}}\Delta T)$$

$$\Rightarrow \quad \frac{99.7}{\rho_0}(1 + \gamma_{\text{Hg}}(20)) = \frac{100}{\rho_0}(1 + \gamma_{\text{glass}}(20))$$

$$\Rightarrow \quad \gamma_{\text{glass}} = \frac{99.7(1 + 18\times 10^{-5}\times 20) - 100}{100\times 20}$$

$$= 2.946\times 10^{-5}/^\circ C$$

$$\therefore \quad \alpha_{\text{glass}} = \frac{\gamma_{\text{glass}}}{3} \simeq 10^{-5}/^\circ C$$

24. Apparent expansion in mercury $= V_0(\gamma_m - 3\alpha_g)T$

Final area of cross-section of capillary $= A_0(1 + 2\alpha_g T)$

Length of mercury column in capillary $= \dfrac{V_0(\gamma_m - 3\alpha_g)T}{A_0(1 + 2\alpha_g T)}$

25. Volume of liquid overflown

$$= A\left(\frac{L}{3}\right)\left(3\gamma - \frac{3\gamma}{2}\right)\Delta T + A\left(\frac{L}{3}\right)\left(2\gamma - \frac{3\gamma}{2}\right)\Delta T + A\left(\frac{L}{3}\right)\left(\gamma - \frac{3\gamma}{2}\right)\Delta T$$

$$= \frac{AL\gamma\Delta T}{2}$$

26. At 20°C, $(200 + 10)\,g = \rho_\omega V g$ ...(i)

At 25°C, $(200 + 10 - \Delta m)\,g$

$$= \left(\frac{\rho_\omega}{1 + 1.5 \times 10^{-4}(5)}\right) V(1 + 3 \times 1 \times 10^{-5}(5))\,g \quad ...(ii)$$

Dividing Eq. (ii) by Eq. (i), we get

$$\frac{210 - \Delta m}{210} = \frac{1 + 15 \times 10^{-5}}{1 + 7.5 \times 10^{-4}}$$

$$\Rightarrow \frac{210 - \Delta m}{210} = (1 + 15 \times 10^{-5})(1 - 7.5 \times 10^{-4})$$

$$\Rightarrow 1 - \frac{\Delta m}{210} = 1 - 6 \times 10^{-4}$$

$$\Rightarrow \Delta m = 126 \times 10^{-3}\text{ kg} = 126\text{ g}$$

27. $f_1 = \dfrac{\rho_S}{\rho_L}$

$$f_2 = \frac{\rho'_S}{\rho'_L} = \frac{\left(\dfrac{\rho_S}{1 + \gamma_S \Delta T}\right)}{\left(\dfrac{\rho_L}{1 + \gamma_L \Delta T}\right)} = f_1\left(\frac{1 + \gamma_L \Delta T}{1 + \gamma_S \Delta T}\right)$$

Percentage change in fraction immersed

$$= \frac{f_2 - f_1}{f_1} \times 100 = \left(\frac{1 + \gamma_L \Delta T}{1 + \gamma_S \Delta T} - 1\right) \times 100$$

$$= \frac{(\gamma_L - \gamma_S)\,\Delta T}{1 + \gamma_S \Delta T} \times 100$$

$$= \frac{(182 \times 10^{-6} - 3 \times 9 \times 10^{-6})\,80}{1 + 3 \times 9 \times 10^{-6} \times 80} \times 100 = 1.24\%$$

28. Density of liquid at temperature $t_1 = \dfrac{\rho_0}{1 + \gamma t_1}$

Density of liquid at temperature $t_2 = \dfrac{\rho_0}{1 + \gamma t_2}$

$$f_1 = \frac{\rho_S}{\rho_L} = \frac{\rho_S(1 + \gamma t_1)}{\rho_0}$$

$$f_2 = \frac{\rho_S}{\rho'_L} = \frac{\rho_S(1 + \gamma t_2)}{\rho_0}$$

$$\therefore \frac{f_1}{f_2} = \frac{1 + \gamma t_1}{1 + \gamma t_2} \Rightarrow \gamma = \frac{f_1 - f_2}{f_2 t_1 - f_1 t_2}$$

29. $B = \dfrac{p}{\dfrac{\Delta V}{V}}$

$$\Rightarrow p = B\left(\frac{\Delta V}{V}\right) = B\gamma\Delta T$$

$$= 2500 \times 10^6 \times 1.82 \times 10^{-4} \times (100 - 20)) = 36.4\text{ MPa}$$

Multiple Choice(s) Correct Questions

1. Distance between any two points on an object increases when it is heated up.

2. d and r increase while θ remains constant.

3. (a, b, d)

4. $\Delta L_1 = L_1\alpha_1\Delta T$ and $\Delta L_2 = L_2\alpha_2\Delta T$

$\Delta L_1 = \Delta L_2$ $[\because L_1\alpha_1 = L_2\alpha_2]$

$L'_1 - L'_2 = (L_1 + \Delta L_1) - (L_2 + \Delta L_2)$

$= L_1 - L_2$ $\because [\Delta L_1 = \Delta L_2]$

So, the difference in the lengths is constant and is independent of rise of temperature.

5. In absence of external torque, angular momentum is conserved.

$$L = I\omega = \text{constant}$$

$$\Rightarrow \frac{\Delta I}{I} + \frac{\Delta\omega}{\omega} = 0 \Rightarrow \frac{\Delta I}{I} = -\frac{\Delta\omega}{\omega}$$

$$I = \frac{MR^2}{2} \Rightarrow \frac{\Delta I}{I} = 2\frac{\Delta R}{R}$$

$$\therefore \frac{\Delta\omega}{\omega} = -2\frac{\Delta R}{R} = -2\alpha\Delta T$$

6. $\Delta t = \dfrac{1}{2}\alpha\Delta\theta t$

At 30°C, $\Delta t = \dfrac{1}{2} \times 19 \times 10^{-6} \times (30 - 20) \times 24 \times 3600 = 8.2\text{ s}$

At 10°C, $\Delta t = \dfrac{1}{2} \times 19 \times 10^{-6} \times (20 - 10) \times 24 \times 3600 = 8.2\text{ s}$

∴ On a hot day at 30°C, the clock loses 8.2 s and on a cold day at 10°C, the clock gains 8.2 s.

7. $R = \dfrac{t}{|\alpha_B - \alpha_C|\,\Delta T}$

$\therefore R \propto \dfrac{1}{\Delta T}$ and $R \propto \dfrac{1}{|\alpha_B - \alpha_C|}$

8. $\dfrac{\Delta d}{d} \times 100 = 0.2\%$

$$\Rightarrow \alpha\Delta T \times 100 = 0.2$$

$$\Rightarrow \alpha\,(80) \times 100 = 0.2$$

$$\Rightarrow \alpha = 0.25 \times 10^{-4}/^\circ\text{C}$$

$$\frac{\Delta A}{A} \times 100 = 2\alpha\Delta T \times 100 = 2(0.2) = 0.4\%$$

$$\frac{\Delta V}{V} \times 100 = 3\alpha\Delta T \times 100 = 3(0.2) = 0.6\%$$

9. $\Delta V_V = \Delta V_L$

$\Rightarrow \quad \gamma_V V_V \Delta T = \gamma_L V_L \Delta T$

$\Rightarrow \quad \dfrac{\gamma_V}{\gamma_L} = \dfrac{V_L}{V_V}$

Since, $V_V > V_L \Rightarrow \gamma_L > \gamma_V$

Comprehension Based Questions

1. $l = l_0(1+\alpha\Delta T)$

$\Rightarrow \quad 6 = 5.98(1+17\times10^{-6}(T-20))$

$\Rightarrow \quad T = 217°\text{C}$

2. Tensile stress $= Y\alpha\Delta T$

$= 11\times10^{10}\times17\times10^{-6}\times(217-20)$

$= 3.68\times10^{8}\ \text{N/m}^2$

3. Breaking stress $= 230\times10^6$

$\Rightarrow \quad Y\alpha\Delta T = 230\times10^6$

$\Rightarrow \quad 11\times10^{10}\times17\times10^{-6}\times(217-T) = 230\times10^6$

$\Rightarrow \quad T = 94°\text{C}$

4. $V = V_0(1+\gamma_L\Delta T) = (100)(10)(1+5\times10^{-5}(40-20)$

$= 1001$ cc

5. Cross-sectional area of vessel at 40°C,

$A = A_0(1+2\alpha_g\Delta T) = 100(1+2\times1\times10^{-5}\times(40-20)$

$= 100.04\ \text{cm}^2$

Actual height of liquid $= \dfrac{\text{Volume}}{\text{Area}} = \dfrac{1001}{100.04} = 10.006$ cm

6. Measured value $=$ Actual value $(1-\alpha_g\Delta T)$

$= 10.006(1-1\times10^{-5}\times20)$

$= 10.004\ \text{cm}^2$

7. As the co-efficient of linear expansion of aluminium is greater than that of steel, aluminium has tendency to expand more than steel. But system will reach to common length and hence, compressive stress will be developed in the aluminium rod and tensile stress in the steel rods.

Net change in the length of aluminium rod,

$$\Delta l = \Delta l_{\text{thermal}} - \Delta l_{\text{stress}} = L\alpha_A\Delta T - \frac{\sigma L}{Y_A} \quad \text{...(i)}$$

where, σ is the stress developed in aluminium rod.

Net external force on the system is zero and hence, force applied by aluminium rod will be equal to force experienced by steel rods. The force applied by aluminium rod is equally shared by both steel rods. As area of cross-section of rods are same hence, stress developed in the steel rod should be equal to half the stress developed in aluminium rod.

Net change in length of a steel rod,

$$\Delta l = \Delta l_{\text{thermal}} + \Delta l_{\text{stress}}$$

$$\Rightarrow \quad \Delta l = L\alpha_S\Delta T + \frac{\sigma L}{2Y_S} \quad \text{...(ii)}$$

From Eqs. (i) and (ii), we get

$$L\alpha_A\Delta T - \frac{\sigma L}{Y_A} = L\alpha_S\Delta T + \frac{\sigma L}{2Y_S}$$

$$\Rightarrow \quad \sigma L\left[\frac{1}{Y_A} + \frac{1}{2Y_S}\right] = L\Delta T(\alpha_A - \alpha_S)$$

$$\Rightarrow \quad \sigma = \frac{(\alpha_A-\alpha_S)\Delta T}{\dfrac{1}{Y_A}+\dfrac{1}{2Y_S}}$$

8. Substituting value of σ in Eqs. (i),

$$\Delta l = L\alpha_A\Delta T - \frac{(\alpha_A-\alpha_S)\Delta T}{\dfrac{1}{Y_A}+\dfrac{1}{2Y_S}}\left(\frac{L}{Y_A}\right)$$

$$= L\Delta T\left[\alpha_A - \frac{2Y_S(\alpha_A-\alpha_S)}{2Y_S+Y_A}\right]$$

$$= L\Delta T\left[\frac{\alpha_A Y_A + 2\alpha_S Y_S}{Y_A+2Y_S}\right]$$

Match the Columns Questions

1. Fraction submerged, $f = \dfrac{\text{Density of metal}}{\text{Density of mercury}}$

$\therefore \quad f_1 = \dfrac{\rho_1}{\rho_2}$

When temperature is increased by ΔT,

$$f_2 = \frac{\rho'_1}{\rho'_2} = \frac{\left(\dfrac{\rho_1}{1+\gamma_1\Delta T}\right)}{\left(\dfrac{\rho_2}{1+\gamma_2\Delta T}\right)} = f_1\left(\frac{1+\gamma_2\Delta T}{1+\gamma_1\Delta T}\right)$$

(A) If $\gamma_2 > \gamma_1 \Rightarrow f_2 > f_1$

i.e., fraction of the volume of metal submerged in mercury increases.

(B) If $\gamma_2 = \gamma_2 \Rightarrow f_2 = f_1$

i.e., no effect on fraction of solid submerged in mercury.

(C) If $\gamma_2 < \gamma_1 \Rightarrow f_2 < f_1$

i.e., the solid lifts up.

2. (A) Condition for floatation, $B = mg$

$\Rightarrow \quad dV_d g = mg \Rightarrow V_d = \dfrac{m}{d}$

V_d remains constant, if $d =$ constant *i.e.*, $\gamma = 0$

(B) $V_{\text{out}} = V_S - V_d = \dfrac{m}{\rho} - \dfrac{m}{d}$

As temperature is increased,

$$V'_{\text{out}} = \frac{m}{\rho'} - \frac{m}{d'} = \frac{m(1+3\alpha\Delta T)}{\rho} - \frac{m(1+\gamma\Delta T)}{d}$$

$$V'_{\text{out}} = V_{\text{out}}$$

$$\Rightarrow \quad \frac{m(1+3\alpha\Delta T)}{\rho} - \frac{m(1+\gamma\Delta T)}{d} = \frac{m}{\rho} - \frac{m}{d}$$

$$\Rightarrow \quad \frac{3\alpha}{\rho} - \frac{\gamma}{d} = 0$$

$$\Rightarrow \quad \gamma = 3\alpha \frac{d}{\rho}$$

(C) $Ah_{in}d = A(h_{in} + h_{out})\rho = M$

$$\Rightarrow \quad h_{in} + h_{out} = \frac{M}{A\rho} \quad \text{...(i)}$$

and $$h_{in} = \frac{M}{Ad} \quad \text{...(ii)}$$

Subtracting Eq. (ii) from Eq. (i), we get

$$h_{out} = \frac{M}{A\rho} - \frac{M}{Ad}$$

As temperature is increased,

$$h'_{out} = \frac{M(1+3\alpha\Delta T)}{A(1+2\alpha\Delta T)\rho} - \frac{M(1+\gamma\Delta T)}{A(1+2\alpha\Delta T)\,d}$$

$$h'_{out} = h_{out}$$

$$\Rightarrow \quad \frac{M(1+3\alpha\Delta T)}{A(1+2\alpha\Delta T)\rho} - \frac{M(1+\gamma\Delta T)}{A(1+2\alpha\Delta T)\,d} = \frac{M}{A\rho} - \frac{M}{Ad}$$

$$\Rightarrow \quad \gamma = 2\alpha + \alpha\left(\frac{d}{\rho}\right)$$

(D) $$h_{in} = \frac{M}{Ad}$$

$$h'_{in} = \frac{M(1+\gamma\Delta T)}{A(1+2\alpha\Delta T)\,d} = \frac{M}{Ad}(1+(\gamma-2\alpha)\,\Delta T)$$

$$h'_{in} = h_{in}$$

$$\Rightarrow \quad \frac{M}{Ad}(1+(\gamma-2\alpha)\,\Delta T) = \frac{M}{Ad}$$

$$\Rightarrow \quad \gamma = 2\alpha$$

Numerical Value Questions

1. $$y_{cm} = \frac{1}{3}\left(\frac{\sqrt{3}}{2}a\right) = \frac{a}{2\sqrt{3}}$$

$$\Delta y_{cm} = \frac{\Delta a}{2\sqrt{3}} = \frac{\alpha a \Delta T}{2\sqrt{3}}$$

$$\Rightarrow \quad \frac{\Delta y_{cm}}{\Delta T} = \frac{\alpha a}{2\sqrt{3}} = \frac{4\sqrt{3}\times 10^{-6}\times 2}{2\sqrt{3}} = 4\times 10^{-6}\ \text{m/}^\circ\text{C}$$

2. $$T = 2\pi\sqrt{\frac{l}{g}} = 2\pi\sqrt{\frac{l(1+\alpha\Delta\theta)}{g+a}}$$

$$\Rightarrow \quad a = g\alpha\Delta\theta = 10\times 20\times 10^{-4}\times(50-0) = 1\ \text{m/s}^2$$

$$W_{app} = \frac{m(g+a)}{g} = \frac{60(10+1)}{10} = 66\ \text{kg}$$

3. $\Delta V_{container} = \Delta V_1 + \Delta V_2$

$$\Rightarrow \quad (Ah)(3\alpha_C)\,\Delta T = (Ah_1)\,\gamma_1\Delta T + (Ah_2)\,\gamma_2\Delta T$$

$$\Rightarrow \quad h = \frac{h_1\gamma_1 + h_2\gamma_2}{3\alpha_C} = \frac{10(1.2\times 10^{-4}) + 10(1.5\times 10^{-4})}{3(1\times 10^{-5})}$$

$$= 90\ \text{cm}$$

4. $\Delta V_{overflown} = \Delta V_{water} + \Delta V_{iron} - \Delta V_{flask}$

$$= (1000)(1.8\times 10^{-4})\,50 + (1000)(3\times 12\times 10^{-6})\,50 - (2000)(3\times 8\times 10^{-6})\,50$$

$$= 8.4\ \text{mm}^3$$

5. $\Delta l_1 + \Delta l_2 = \Delta l$

$$\Rightarrow \quad l_1\alpha_1\Delta T + l_2\alpha_2\Delta T = \Delta l$$

$$\Rightarrow \quad 40(1.5\times 10^{-5})(135-35) + 60\alpha_2(135-35) = 2.1\times 10^{-1}$$

$$\Rightarrow \quad \alpha_2 = 2.5\times 10^{-5}/^\circ\text{C}$$

Condition for not shifting of junction,

$$F_1 = F_2$$

$$\Rightarrow \quad AY_1\alpha_1\Delta T = AY_2\alpha_2\Delta T$$

$$\Rightarrow \quad Y_2 = \frac{\alpha_1 Y_1}{\alpha_2} = \frac{1.5\times 10^{-5}\times 1.2\times 10^{11}}{2.5\times 10^{-5}}$$

$$= 72\times 10^9\ \text{dyne/cm}^2$$

So, $n = 72$

6. Applying Pascal's law from column A to column D,

$$p_0 + \rho_A g h_A - \rho_B g h_B + \rho_C g h_C - \rho_D g h_D = p_0$$

$$\Rightarrow \quad \rho_{95}h_A - \rho_5 h_B + \rho_{95}h_C - \rho_5 h_D = 0$$

$$\Rightarrow \quad \frac{\rho_{95}}{\rho_5} = \frac{h_B + h_D}{h_A + h_C}$$

$$\Rightarrow \quad \frac{\left(\dfrac{\rho_0}{1+95\gamma}\right)}{\left(\dfrac{\rho_0}{1+5\gamma}\right)} = \frac{49+51}{52.8+49}$$

$$\Rightarrow \quad \frac{1+5\gamma}{1+95\gamma} = \frac{100}{101.8}$$

$$\Rightarrow \quad \gamma = 2\times 10^{-4}/^\circ\text{C}$$

7. Final length $= 2\sqrt{\left(\frac{l_0}{2}\right)^2 + x^2} = 2\sqrt{4+x^2}$

$$\Delta l = l_2 - l_1 = 2(4+x^2)^{1/2} - 4$$

$$= 4\left(1+\frac{x^2}{4}\right)^{1/2} - 4 = 4\left(1+\frac{1}{2}\left(\frac{x^2}{4}\right)\right) - 4 = \frac{x^2}{2}$$

Also, $\Delta l = \alpha l \Delta T$

$$\Rightarrow \quad \frac{x^2}{2} = 25\times 10^{-6}\times 4\times 32$$

$$\Rightarrow \quad x = 8\times 10^{-2}\ \text{m} = 8\ \text{cm}$$

8. $dV = Adx$

$$\Rightarrow \quad V_0\gamma_0\left(1+\frac{T}{100}\right)dT = Adx$$

$$\Rightarrow \quad V_0\gamma_0\int_0^{100}\left(1+\frac{T}{100}\right)dT = A\int_0^{10} dx$$

$$\Rightarrow \quad V_0\gamma_0\left[100 + \frac{(100)^2}{2(100)}\right] = A\times 10$$

$$\Rightarrow \quad V_0\gamma_0\times 150 = A\times 10 \quad \text{...(i)}$$

$$V_0\gamma_0 \int_0^{48}\left(1+\frac{T}{100}\right)dT = A\int_0^x dx$$

$$\Rightarrow \quad V_0\gamma_0\left[48+\frac{(48)^2}{2(100)}\right] = A\times x \qquad \text{...(ii)}$$

From Eqs. (i) and (ii), we get

$$x = 3.968\text{ mm} \simeq 4\text{ mm}$$

Previous Year's Questions

JEE Main

1. We know that,

$$F = YA \propto \Delta T$$

$$\Rightarrow \quad F = 2\times10^{11}\times10^{-4}\times10^{-5}\times200 = 4\times10^{4}\text{ N}$$

$$\therefore \quad x = 4$$

2. Change in diameter is given by

$$\Delta d = d_0\,\alpha\,\Delta T = d\times10^{-3}$$

Given, $d_0 = 5\times10^{-2}$ m

$$\alpha = 1.6\times10^{-5}/^\circ\text{C}$$

$$\Delta T = (177-27)^\circ\text{ C} = 150^\circ\text{C}$$

$$\therefore \quad \Delta d = 5\times10^{-2}\times1.6\times10^{-5}\times150$$

$$= 1200\times10^{-7} = 12\times10^{-5}\text{ m}$$

$$= 12\times10^{-3}\text{cm} = d\times10^{-3}\text{cm}$$

So, $d = 12$

3. $$\frac{X_T - X_L}{X_H - X_L} = \frac{T_F - 32}{212-32}$$

$$\Rightarrow \frac{-95-(-15^\circ)}{65-(-15^\circ)} = \frac{T_F-32}{180}$$

$$\Rightarrow \frac{-80^\circ}{80} = \frac{T_F-32}{180}$$

$$\Rightarrow -180 = T_F - 32$$

$$\Rightarrow T_F = -180+32$$

$$\Rightarrow T_F = -148^\circ\text{F}$$

4. In the given graph, for scale P
Lower fixed point = 30°
Upper fixed point = 180°
and for the scale Q,
Lower fixed point (LFP) = 0°
Upper fixed point = 100°
∵ The relationship between the two scals P and Q is given by

$$\frac{T_P - (\text{LFP})_P}{\text{Number of divisions on scale P}} = \frac{T_Q - (\text{LFP})_Q}{\text{Number of divisions on scale Q}}$$

$$\Rightarrow \frac{T_P-30}{150} = \frac{T_Q-0}{100}$$

$$\Rightarrow \frac{T_P-30}{150} = \frac{T_Q}{100}$$

5. Given, $A = 24\text{ m}^2$

$\Delta T = 10\,^\circ\text{C}, \alpha = 5.0\times10^{-4}\,^\circ\text{C}^{-1}$.

We know, $\gamma = 3\alpha = 3\times5\times10^{-4} = 1.5\times10^{-3}\,^\circ\text{C}^{-1}$

Since, total surface area of cube,

$$6a^2 = 24$$

$$\Rightarrow \quad a = 2\text{ m}$$

∴ Volume of cube, $V = a^3 = 2^3 = 8\text{ m}^3$

$$\because \quad \Delta V = \gamma V\Delta T = 1.5\times10^{-3}\times8\times10$$

$$= 1.2\times10^{5}\text{ cm}^3$$

6. As given,

$$\alpha_{\text{iron}} = 1.2\times10^{-5}\text{ K}^{-1},$$

$$\alpha_{\text{brass}} = 1.8\times10^{-5}\text{ K}^{-1}$$

$$l_{\text{iron}} - l_{\text{brass}} = K \qquad \text{...(i)}$$

$$l_{0(\text{iron})}(1+\alpha_{\text{iron}}\Delta T) - l_{0(\text{brass})}(1+\alpha_{\text{brass}}\Delta T) = K$$

$$\text{So, } l_{0(\text{iron})} - l_{0(\text{brass})} + l_{0_{\text{iron}}}\alpha_{\text{iron}}\Delta T - l_{0_{\text{brass}}}\alpha_{\text{brass}}\Delta T = K$$

$$K + (l_{0(\text{iron})}\times\alpha_{\text{iron}} - l_{0(\text{brass})}\alpha_{\text{brass}})\ \Delta T = K$$

$$\alpha_{\text{iron}}\times l_{0(\text{iron})} = \alpha_{\text{brass}}\times l_{0(\text{brass})}$$

$$1.2\times10^{-5}\times l_{0(\text{iron})} = 1.8\times10^{-5}\times l_{0(\text{brass})}$$

$$2l_{0(\text{iron})} = 3\times40, l_{0(\text{iron})} = 60\text{ cm}$$

7. Given,

$$A = 0.01\text{ m}^2, \alpha = 10^{-5}/^\circ\text{C},$$

$$Y = 10^{11}\text{ N/m}^2$$

As, Energy stored in a stretched wire

$$= \frac{Y}{2}\times(\text{Strain})^2\times\text{Area}\times\text{length}$$

$$\frac{\text{Energy}}{\text{Length}} = \frac{Y}{2}\times\left(\frac{\Delta l}{l}\right)^2\times A = \frac{Y}{2}A\times(\alpha\cdot\Delta T)^2$$

$$= \frac{10^{11}}{2}\times0.01(10^{-5}\times10)^2$$

$$= 5\text{ J/m} \qquad (\because \Delta l = l\alpha\,\Delta T)$$

The energy stored per metre in the track is 5 J/m.

8. Given, $\alpha_A > \alpha_B$

$$\Delta l = l_0 \propto \Delta T$$

Thus, $\Delta l_A > \Delta l_B$ In (for equal, ΔT and l_0)

∴ The bimetallic strip will bend towards left.

It can be shown as below.

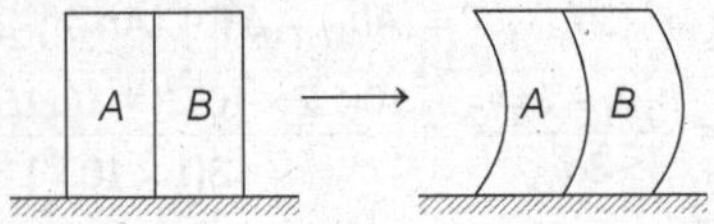

9. We know that $\gamma = 3\alpha$ ...(i)

and $\frac{\Delta V}{V} = \gamma \Delta T \Rightarrow \frac{\Delta V}{V} = 3\alpha\Delta T$ [From Eq. (i)]

$\Delta V = 3a^3\alpha\Delta T$ [$\because$ volume of cube= a^3]

10. If a rod is fixed between true supports, it will have thermal stress. In the given situation there will be no thermal stress because the rod is free to expand due to increase in temperature.

11. Let α be the effective temperature coefficient of linear expansion.

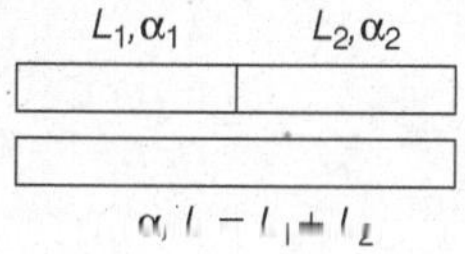

Therefore,

$$\Delta L = \Delta L_1 + \Delta L_2$$

$$\Rightarrow L\alpha\Delta T = L_1\alpha_1\Delta T + L_2\alpha_2\Delta T \quad (\because L = L_1 + L_2)$$

$$\therefore (L_1 + L_2)\alpha\,\Delta T = \Delta T\,(L_1\alpha_1 + L_2\alpha_2)$$

$$\Rightarrow \alpha = \frac{L_1\alpha_1 + L_2\alpha_2}{L_1 + L_2}$$

Hence, correct option is (a).

12. Volume of empty part

= Volume of beaker – Volume of mercury

Since given that there is no change in unfilled volume of the beaker with the varying temperature.

So, change in volume of beaker

= change in volume of mercury

$$\Rightarrow V_b\gamma_b\Delta T = V_m\gamma_m\Delta T$$

$$\Rightarrow V_b\gamma_b = V_m\gamma_m$$

$$\Rightarrow V_m = \frac{V_b\gamma_b}{\gamma_m} = \frac{500 \times 6 \times 10^{-6}}{1.5 \times 10^{-4}}$$

$$= 20\text{ cm}^3 = 20\text{ cc}$$

13. Extension due to the weight will be equal to contraction by cooling.

$$Y = \frac{Mg/A}{\Delta l/l} \Rightarrow \Delta l = \frac{Mgl}{AY}$$

Also, $\Delta l = l\alpha\Delta T \Rightarrow l\alpha\Delta T = \frac{Mgl}{AY}$

$$\Rightarrow M = \frac{\alpha\Delta TAY}{g} = \frac{10^{-5} \times 10^{11} \times 20 \times \pi \times (10^{-3})^2}{10}$$

$$\therefore M = 2\pi\text{ kg} = 6.28\text{ kg}$$

Value of M will be close to 9 kg as per options.

14. For the given question,

$$\therefore (\text{Stress})_{\text{Compressive}} = (\text{Stress})_{\text{Thermal}}$$

$$\frac{F}{A} = Y\alpha T$$

$$\Rightarrow \frac{F}{\pi r^2} = Y\alpha T$$

Where, symbols have their usual meaning

$$\therefore \alpha = \frac{F}{\pi r^2 YT}$$

$\because$ Coefficient of volume expansion,

$$\gamma = 3\alpha$$

$$\therefore \gamma = \frac{3F}{\pi r^2 YT}$$

15. As the temperature of rod rises,

Extension in the rod, $\Delta L = L\alpha\Delta T$

Young's modulus of the rod, $Y = \frac{F/A}{\Delta L/L}$

$$Y = \frac{F \times L}{A\Delta L} = \frac{F}{A\alpha\Delta T}$$

16. Let initial length of identical rods is l_0. Thermal expansion due to heating is

$$\Delta l = l_0.\alpha(\Delta T) = l_0\,\alpha\,(T_2 - T_1)$$

So, change in length of rods are

$$\Delta l_1 = l_0\,\alpha_1(180 - 30)$$

$$\Delta l_2 = l_0\alpha_2(T - 30)$$

Because new lengths are same, that means

i.e. $\Delta l_1 = \Delta l_2$

$$\Rightarrow l_0\,\alpha_1\,(180 - 30) = l_0\,\alpha_2\,(T - 30)$$

or $\frac{\alpha_1}{\alpha_2} = \frac{(T - 30)}{150}$

Given, $\alpha_1 : \alpha_2 = 4:3$

$$\therefore \frac{T - 30}{150} = \frac{4}{3} \text{ or } T = 200 + 30 = 230°\text{C}$$

17. By principle of thermometry for any liner temperature scale,

$$\frac{T - T_{\text{LFP}}}{T_{\text{UFP}} - T_{\text{LFP}}} = a \quad \text{(constant)}$$

Where, symbols have their usual meaning, we have

$$\frac{T - 0°\text{C}}{100°\text{C} - 0°\text{C}} = \frac{\frac{X_0}{2} - \frac{X_0}{3}}{X_0 - \frac{X_0}{3}}$$

or $\frac{T}{100} = \frac{1}{4}$ or $T = 25°\text{C}$

JEE Advanced

1. $\Delta l_1 = \frac{FL}{AY} = \frac{mgL}{\pi r^2 Y}$ = Increase in length

$\Delta l_2 = L\alpha\,\Delta\theta$ = Decrease in length.

To regain its original length, $\Delta l_1 = \Delta l_2$

$$\therefore \frac{mgL}{\pi r^2 Y} = L\alpha\,\Delta\theta$$

$$\Rightarrow m = \left(\frac{r^2 Y\alpha\,\Delta\theta}{g}\right)$$

Substituting the values we get, $m \simeq 3$ kg

$\therefore$ Answer is 3.

CHAPTER~02

CALORIMETRY

LEVEL 01 Starter Level

2.1 Specific Heat and Heat Capacity

1 When 300 J of heat is added to 25 g of sample of a material, its temperature rises from 25°C to 45°C. What are the thermal capacity of the sample and specific heat of the material?

2 Two spheres A and B have diameters in the ratio 1 : 2, densities in the ratio 2: 1 and specific heats in the ratio 1 : 3, find the ratio of their thermal capacities.

3 A bullet of mass 5 g moving with speed 400 m/s strikes a target and stops. Then, calculate rise of temperature of bullet. Assuming all the loss in kinetic energy is converted into heat energy of bullet and its specific heat is 500J / kg °C

4 An iron block of mass 2 kg, falls from a height 10 m. After colliding with the ground, it loses 25% of its energy to surroundings. Then, find the temperature rise of the block. (Take, specific heat of iron 500 J/kg °C)

5 A copper cube of mass 200 g slides down on a rough inclined plane of inclination 37° at a constant speed. Assume, that any loss in mechanical energy goes into the copper block as thermal energy. Find the increase in the temperature of the block as it slides down 60 cm.
(Specific heat capacity of copper = 420 J/kg-K.)

6 A paddle wheel is connected with a block of mass 10 kg as shown in figure. The wheel is completely immersed in liquid of heat capacity 4000 J/°C. The container is adiabatic. For the time interval in which block goes down 2 m slowly, calculate

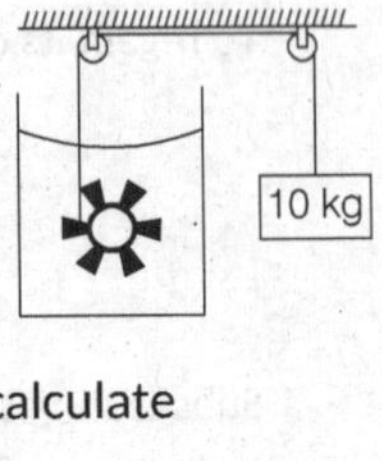

(a) heat supplied to the liquid
(b) work done on the liquid
(c) rise in the temperature of the liquid
Neglect the heat capacity of the container and the paddle. ($g = 10 \text{ m}/\text{s}^2$)

7 A 2100 W continuous flow geyser (instant geyser) has water inlet temperature of 10°C while the water flows out at the rate of 20 g/s. What must be the outlet temperature of water?

8 An electrically heated coil is immersed in a calorimeter containing 360 g of water at 10°C. The coil consumes energy at the rate of 90 W. The water equivalent of calorimeter and coil is 40 g. What will be the temperature of water after 10 min?

9 The specific heat of metal at low temperature varies as $s = aT^3$, where a is a constant and T is the absolute temperature. What is the amount of heat energy needed to raise 2 g of metal from $T = 1$ K and $T = 2$K?

2.2 Latent Heat

1 How much heat must be added to a 3 kg block of ice at – 22°C to change it to water at 18°C ? (Take, specific heat of ice = 0.5 cal/g°C, specific heat of water = 1 cal/g°C, latent heat of fusion = 80 cal/g.)

2 How much heat is required to convert 8.0 gm of ice at −15° C to steam at 100°C?
(Given, s_{ice} = 0.5 cal/g°C, L_f = 80 cal/g and L_v = 540 cal/g and s_{water} = 1 cal/g°C)

3 Find the amount of heat released, if 1 kg steam at 200°C is converted into – 20°C ice.

4 A solid material is supplied with heat at a constant rate. The temperature of the material is changing with the heat input as shown in figure. Study the graph carefully and answer the following questions.
(a) What do the horizontal regions AB and CD represent?

(b) If $CD = 2BA$, what do you infer?

(c) What does slope of line DE represent?

(d) The slope of $OA >$ the slope of BC. What does this indicate?

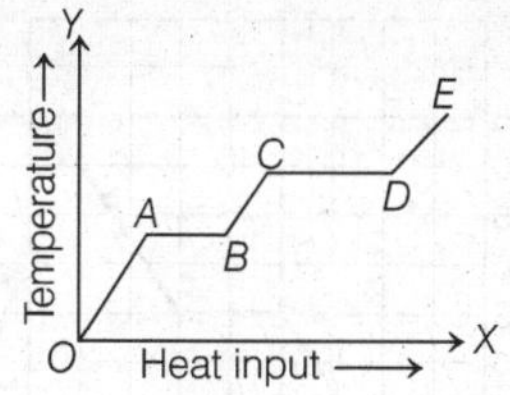

2.3 Law of Mixture

1 3 kg water at 80°C is mixed with 2 kg of water at 30°C. Find temperature of the mixture in equilibrium.

2 The temperature of three different liquids A, B and C are 10°C, 15° C and 20°C respectively. The temperature when A and B are mixed is 13°C and when B and C are mixed, it is 16°C. What will be the temperature when A and C are mixed?

3 100 kg solid iron at 730°C is cooled by immersing into vessel filled by water at 30° C. In the process, final temperature of water is 80°C. How much was mass of water? (Neglect vaporisation)

$s_{water} = 4200\ J/kg°C$, $s_{iron} = 420\ J/kg°C$

4 200 g of water at 98° C is mixed with 206 g of milk at 30°C contained in a brass vessel of water equivalent 8 g and the temperature of the mixture is 64°C. Find the specific heat of milk.

5 If three different liquids of different masses, specific heats and temperature are mixed with each other, then what is the temperature mixture at thermal equilibrium?

$m_1, s_1, T_1 \rightarrow$ Specification for liquid 1,

$m_2, s_2, T_2 \rightarrow$ Specification for liquid 2,

$m_3, s_3, T_3 \rightarrow$ Specification for liquid 3

2.4 Phase Change in Mixing

1 40 g of water at 60°C is poured on a large block of ice at 0°C. What is the mass of ice that melts?

2 How many grams of ice at – 14°C is needed to cool 200 g of water from 25°C to 10°C ?
($s_{ice} = 0.5$ cal /g°C and L_f for ice = 80 cal/g)

3 Steam is passed into 54 g of water at 30°C till the temperature of mixture becomes 90°C. If the latent heat of steam is 536 cal /g, what will be the mass of the mixture?

4 1 kg ice at – 10°C is mixed with 1 kg water at 100°C. Then, find equilibrium temperature and mixture content.

5. 1 kg ice at – 20°C is mixed with 1 kg water at 50°C. Then, find equilibrium temperature and mixture content.

6 1 kg ice at – 20°C is mixed with 1 kg steam at 200°C. Then, find equilibrium temperature and mixture content.

LEVEL 02 JEE Main Level

Single Choice Correct Questions

1 The ratio of mass densities of the two bodies is 3 : 4 and the ratio of their specific heats is 4 : 3. Then, the ratio of their thermal capacities for unit volume is

(a) 9 : 16 (b) 3 : 6
(c) 1 : 1 (d) 16 : 9

2 In a container of negligible heat capacity 100 g of a liquid at 20°C is heated. Specific heat of the liquid varies with temperature given as
$s = (100T + 500) J/kg°C$, where T is in °C. Find the amount of heat required to raise the temperature of the liquid to 40°C.

(a) 5000 J (b) 6000 J
(c) 7000 J (d) 8000 J

3 A lead bullet just melts when stopped by an obstacle. Assuming that 25% of heat is absorbed by the obstacle, find the minimum velocity of the bullet if its initial temperature is 27°C (Melting point of lead = 327°C, specific heat of lead = 0.03 cal / g ° C, latent heat of fusion of lead = 6 cal/g, 1 cal = 4.2 J)

(a) 250 m/s
(b) 375 m/s
(c) 410 m/s
(d) 450 m/s

4 If the height of Niagra fall is 50 m, the difference between the temperatures of water at the top and the bottom of the fall is

(a) 117°C (b) 11.7°C
(c) 1.17°C (d) 0.117°C

5 An electrical steam generator has rated power 1000 W and heat converting efficiency = 0.9. Water enters the inlet at 20°C and steam comes out from the outlet at 100°C. Latent heat of steam = 2250 J/g. What mass of water enters the device per second?
(a) 1.2 g (b) 0.5 g
(c) 0.35 g (d) 0.39 g

6 A body of mass 25 kg is dragged on a rough horizontal floor for one hour with a speed of 2 km/h. The coefficient of friction between the body and the surface in contact is 0.5 and half the heat produced is absorbed by the body. If specific heat of body is $0.1\ \text{cal/g}^{-1}(°\text{C})^{-1}$, then the rise in temperature of body is
(a) 50°C (b) 23.8°C
(c) 100°C (d) 11.9°C

7 A piece of ice of mass 50 kg is pushed with a velocity of 5 m/s along a horizontal surface. As a result of friction between the piece and the surface, the piece stops after travelling 25 m. The ice melted in this process is (assume complete heat is given to ice)
(a) 50 kg (b) 50 g
(c) 7.86 g (d) 1.86 g

8 A stationary object at 4°C weighing 3.5 kg falls from a height of 2000 m on a snow mountain at 0°C. If the temperature of the object just before hitting the snow is 0°C and the object comes to rest immediately $(g = 10\ \text{m/s}^2)$ and latent heat of ice is 3.5×10^5 J/kg, then the object will melt
(a) 2 g of ice (b) 20 g of ice
(c) 200 g of ice (d) 2 kg of ice

9 How much heat must be supplied to convert 1 kg ice at – 10° C to steam at 100°C?
(a) 725 kal (b) 720 kcal
(c) 730 kcal (d) 735 kcal

10 10 g of ice at 0°C is kept in a calorimeter of water equivalent 10 g. How much heat should be supplied to the apparatus to evaporate the water thus formed? (Neglect loss of heat)
(a) 6200 cal (b) 7200 cal
(c) 13600 cal (d) 8200 cal

11 A refrigerator converts 100g of water at 25°C into ice at – 10°C in one hour and 50 min. The quantity of heat removed per minute is
(Specific heat of ice = 0.5 cal / g °C, latent heat of fusion = 80 cal/g)
(a) 50 cal (b) 100 cal
(c) 200 cal (d) 75 cal

12 The graph shown in the figure represents change in the temperature of 5 kg of a substance as it absorbs heat at a constant rate of 42 kJ min^{-1}. The latent heat of vaporisation of the substance is

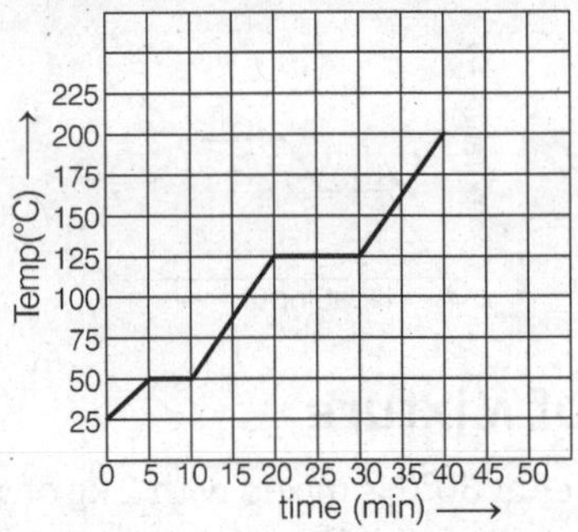

(a) 630 kJ kg^{-1} (b) 126 kJ kg^{-1}
(c) 84 kJ kg^{-1} (d) 12.6 kJ kg^{-1}

13 The temperature of a body rises by 44°C when a certain amount of heat is given to it. The same heat when supplied to 22 g of ice at – 80°C, raises its temperature by 16°C. The water equivalent of the body is [Given, $s_{\text{water}} = 1$ cal /g °C and $L_f = 80$ cal/g, $s_{\text{ice}} = 0.5$ cal/g°C]
(a) 25 g (b) 46 g (c) 80 g (d) 100 g

14 It takes 10 min for an electric kettle to heat a certain quantity of water from 0°C to 100°C. If it takes 54 min to convert this water at 100°C into steam, then latent heat of steam is
(a) 580 cal/g (b) 560 cal/g
(c) 540 cal/g (d) 520 cal/g

15 A substance of mass *m* kg requires a power input of *P* watts to remain in the molten state at its melting point. When the power is turned off, the sample completely solidifies in time *t* s. What is the latent heat of fusion of the substance?
(a) $\frac{Pm}{t}$ (b) $\frac{Pt}{m}$ (c) $\frac{m}{Pt}$ (d) $\frac{t}{Pm}$

16 A metal vessel of negligible heat capacity contains 0.5 kg of water (of specific heat capacity 4200 J kg^{-1}K^{-1}). It is heated from 15°C to 85°C by 750 W immersion heater in 4 min. The average loss of heat in watts to the surroundings from the vessel during this time is nearly
(a) 70 (b) 123 (c) 138 (d) 212

17 Heat is being supplied at constant rate to a sphere of ice which is melting at the rate of 0.1 g/s. It melts completely in 100 s. The rate of rise of temperature there after will be (assume no loss of heat)
(a) 0.8 °C/s (b) 5.4 °C/s
(c) 3.6 °C/s (d) will change with time

18 An aluminium container of mass 100 g contains 200 g of ice at – 20°C. Heat is added to the system at the rate of 100 cal/s. The temperature of the system after 4 min will be (specific heat of ice = 0.5 cal/g °C and $L = 80$ cal/g, specific heat of Al = 0.2 cal/g °C)
(a) 40.5°C (b) 25.5°C
(c) 30.3°C (d) 35.0°C

19 A liquid of mass m and specific heat C is heated to a temperature T. Another liquid of mass $m/2$ and specific heat $2C$ is heated to a temperature $2T$. If these two liquids are mixed, the resulting temperature of the mixture is
(a) (2/3) T (b) (8/5) T
(c) (3/5) T (d) (3/2) T

20 Two liquids A and B are at 30°C and 20°C. When mixed in equal masses, the temperature of the mixture is found to be 26°C. The ratio of specific heats of A and B is
(a) 3 : 2 (b) 2 : 3
(c) 1 : 1 (d) 4 : 3

21 A calorimeter contains 0.2 kg of water at 30°C. 0.1 kg of water at 60°C is added to it, the mixture is well stirred and the resulting temperature is found to be 35°C. The thermal capacity of the calorimeter is
(a) 6300 J/°C (b) 1260 J/°C
(c) 4200 J/°C (d) None of these

22 20 g of boiling water is poured into an ice-cold brass vessel (specific heat 0.1 cal/g °C) of mass 100 g. The resulting temperature is
(a) 66.66°C (b) 6.66°C
(c) 0.66°C (d) 50°C

23 A beaker contains 200 g of water. The heat capacity of the beaker is equal to that of 20 g of water. The initial temperature of water in the beaker is 20°C. If 440 g of hot water at 92°C is poured in it, the final temperature, neglecting radiation loss, will be nearest to
(a) 58°C (b) 68°C
(c) 73°C (d) 78°C

24 A brass ball of mass 100 g is heated to 100°C and then dropped into 200 g of turpentine in a calorimeter at 15°C. The final temperature is found to be 23°C. Take specific heat of brass as 0.09 cal/g-°C and water equivalent of calorimeter as 4 g. The specific heat of turpentine is
(a) 0.41 cal/g°C
(b) 0.82 cal/g°C
(c) 1.23 cal/g°C
(d) 1.64 cal/g°C

25 A ball of thermal capacity 10 cal/°C is heated to the temperature of furnace. It is then transferred into a vessel containing water. The water equivalent of vessel and the contents is 200 g. The temperature of the vessel and its contents rises from 10°C to 40°C. What is the temperature of furnace?
(a) 640°C (b) 64°C (c) 600°C (d) 100°C

26 Equal masses of three liquids A, B and C have temperatures 10°C, 25°C and 40°C respectively. If A and B are mixed, the mixture has a temperature of 15°C. If B and C are mixed, the mixture has a temperature of 30°C. If A and C are mixed, the mixture will have a temperature of
(a) 16°C (b) 20°C (c) 25°C (d) 29°C

27 A block of mass 2.5 kg is heated to temperature of 500°C and placed on a large ice block. What is the maximum amount of ice that can melt? Specific heat for the body = 0.1 cal/g°C.
(a) 1 kg (b) 1.6 kg (c) 2 kg (d) 2.6 kg

28 10 g of ice at 0°C is mixed with m g of water at 50°C. What is minimum value of m, so that ice melts completely? ($L_f = 80$ cal/g and $s_w = 1$ cal/g °C)
(a) 32 g (b) 20 g (c) 40 g (d) 16 g

29 1 kg of ice at 0°C is mixed with 1 kg of water at 75°C. The final temperature of the mixture is
(a) 0°C (b) 40°C
(c) 50°C (d) 60°C

30 10 g of ice cubes at 0°C are released in a tumbler containing water (water equivalent 55 g) at 40°C. Assuming that negligible heat is taken from the surrounding, the temperature of water in the tumbler becomes nearly ($L = 80$ cal/g)
(a) 31°C (b) 22°C
(c) 19°C (d) 15°C

31 1 kg of ice at – 10°C is mixed with 4.4 kg of water at 30°C. The final temperature of mixture is (specific heat of ice is 2100 J/kg/K)
(a) 2.3° C (b) 4.4° C
(c) 5.3° C (d) 8.7° C

32 10 g of ice at – 20°C is dropped into a calorimeter containing 10 g of water at 10°C. The specific heat of water is twice that of ice. Neglect heat capacity of the calorimeter. When equilibrium is reached, the calorimeter will contain
(a) 10 g ice and 10 g of water
(b) 20 g of water
(c) 5 g ice and 15 g of water
(d) 20 g ice

33 50 g of ice at 0°C are put into 125 g of water at 20°C in a calorimeter of negligible heat capacity. When the system has reached equilibrium, how much of the ice remains? (latent heat of fusion of water $L_f = 80$ cal/g, specific heat of water $c = 1$ cal/g °C).

(a) 19 g (b) 48 g (c) 31 g (d) 0 g

34 A copper calorimeter of mass 60 g contains 400 g of water at 38°C. When 158 g of ice is added, the temperature falls to 5°C. The latent heat of fusion of ice will be, if the specific heat of calorimeter is 0.1 cal/g°C will be

(a) 79.2 cal/g (b) 79.4 cal/g
(c) 79.8 cal/g (d) 80.8 cal/g

35 A calorimeter (of water equivalent 50 g) contains 250 g of water and 50 g of ice at 0°C, 30 g of water at 80°C is added to it. The final condition of the system will be [$s_{water} = 1$ cal/g °C, $L_f = 80$ cal/g]

(a) temperature of the system will be 4.2°C.
(b) temperature of the system will still be 0°C and the entire ice will melt
(c) the temperature will be 0°C and half of ice will melt
(d) the temperature will be 0°C and 20 g of ice will be left.

36 If 100 g of ice at 0°C is mixed with 100 g of boiling water at 100°C, which of the following graphs would best represent the temperature *versus* time of the two components of the mixture?

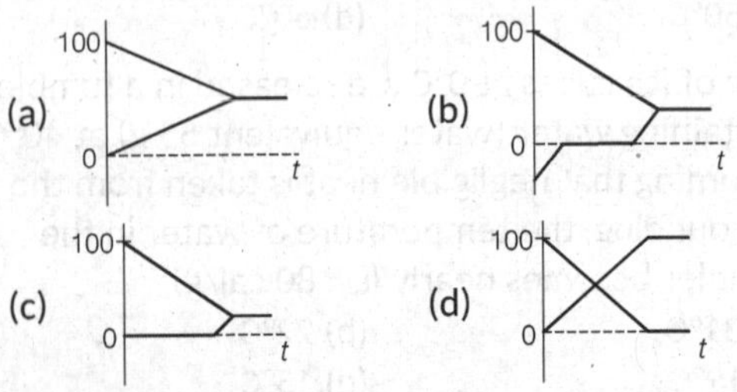

37 1 g of steam at 100°C and an equal mass of ice at 0°C are mixed. The temperature of the mixture in steady state will be [Latent heat of steam = 540 cal g^{-1} and latent heat of ice = 80 cal/g]

(a) 50°C (b) 100°C
(c) 67°C (d) None of these

38 5 g of steam at 100°C is passed into 6 g of ice at 0°C. If the latent heats of steam and ice in cal per g are 540 and 80 respectively, then the final temperature is

(a) 0°C (b) 100°C (c) 50°C (d) 30°C

39 In the above question, the mixture contains

(a) 11 g of water (b) 8 g of water
(c) 6 g of water (d) 5 g of water

40 50 g of steam at 100°C is passed into 250 g of ice at 0°C. Find the resultant temperature (Latent heat of steam is 540 cal/g , latent heat of ice is 80 cal/g and specific heat of water is 1 cal/g °C)

(a) 40°C (b) 30°C (c) 20°C (d) 10°C

41 Steam is passed into 22 g of water at 20°C. The mass of water that will be present when the water acquires a temperature of 90°C (Latent heat of steam is 540 cal/g) is

(a) 24.8 g (b) 24 g (c) 36.6 g (d) 30.0 g

42 A vessel contains 100 g of ice at 0°C. Now steam is passed into the vessel to melt ice. Neglecting the thermal capacity of the vessel, find the mass of water in the vessel when all ice melts into water.

(a) 12.5 g (b) 100 g (c) 112.5 g (d) 125 g

Numerical Value Questions

1 The specific heat of a substance varies with temperature according to $c = 0.2 + 0.16\,T + 0.024T^2$ with T in °C and c is cal/g-°C. Find the energy (in cal) required to raise the temperature of 2 g substance from 0° to 5°C.

2 A block of ice (0°C) is dropped under uniform gravity. During fall, because of air resistance 70% of the loss in gravitational potential energy is converted to heat. Due to this, the ice melts completely by the instant it reaches the ground. Take, $g = 10$ m/s^2, latent heat of fusion for ice = 80 cal/g and mechanical equivalent of heat is 4.2 J/cal. Find the initial height (in km) from which the block was dropped.

3 A 50 g lead bullet (specific heat 0.020 cal/g) is initially at 30°C. It is fired vertically upward with a speed 84 m/s. On returning to the starting level, it strikes a slab of ice at 0°C. How much ice (in mg) is melted? Assume no loss of heat. Latent heat of ice 80 cal/g. (Mechanical equivalent of heat = 4.2 J/cal)

4 An aluminium container of mass 100 g contains 200 g of ice at −20°C. Heat is added to the system at a rate of 250 cal/s. What is the temperature (in °C) of the system after 100 s?
Specific heat capacity of ice = 0.5 cal / g °C,
specific heat capacity of aluminium = 0.2 cal / g °C,
specific heat capacity of water = 1 cal / g °C and
latent heat of fusion of ice = 80 cal / g.

5 A thermos contains 140 g coffee at 80°C. To cool it, we drop two 10 g ice cubes at 0°C into thermos. Ice cubes are at 0°C initially. What is the final temperature of the coffee (in °C), if its specific heat capacity is same as that of water.

6 50 g of ice at 0°C is mixed with 200 g of water at 0°C. 6 kcal heat is given to system [Ice + water]. Find the temperature (in °C) of the system.

7 The temperature of 100 g of water is to be raised from 24° C to 90° C by adding steam to it. Calculate the mass of the steam (in g) required for this purpose.

8 Two empty identical calorimeters are initially at 20°C. When we pour some water at 80°C into one of them, the temperature of this water reduces to 60°C. If this water (which is now at 60°C) is completely transferred to the second calorimeter (still at 20°C), the final temperature of water is $\frac{n}{3}$ °C, then find the value of n.

9 A conducting tube is passing through a bath. A liquid at temperature 90°C and specific heat s is entering at one end of tube. Rate of flow of liquid is 1 kg/s and exit temperature is 50°C. In bath another liquid having specific heat 2s and inlet temperature 20°C is entering at a rate of 2 kg/s. Find the exit temperature of liquid (in °C) coming out of the bath. (assume steady state condition)

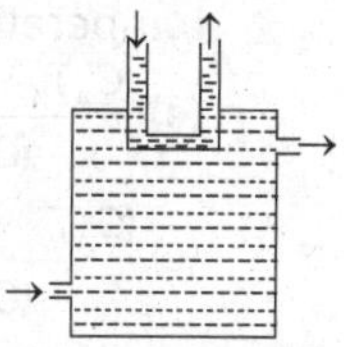

10 The specific gravity of ice is 0.92. A metal of mass 10 g at 100°C is immersed in a mixture of ice and water and the volume of mixture is found to be reduced by 0.1 cm^3 without change of temperatures. Assume the specific gravity of water at 0°C to be unity and the latent heat of fusion of ice to be 80 cal/g. If the specific heat of metal is $n \times 10^{-3}$ cal / g° C, then find the value of n.

11 A heating curve has been plotted for a solid object as shown in the figure. If the mass of the object is 200 g, then latent heat of vaporisation for the material of the object is $n \times 10^6$ J/kg. If power supplied to the object is constant and equal to 1 kW, then find the value of n.

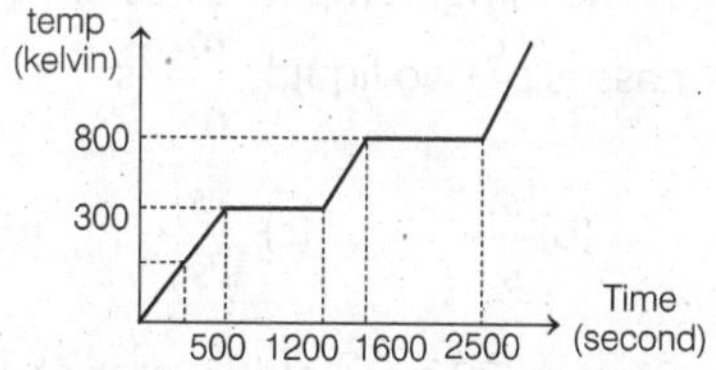

12 A calorimeter whose water equivalent is 50 g contains 400 g of water and 100 g ice at 0°C. What will be the final temperature (in °C), if 50 g of steam at 100°C is admitted to the calorimeter? Given, L_f ice = 80 cal/g, L_v of water = 540 cal/g, $s_{ice} = 0.5$ cal / gK, $s_{water} = 1.0$ cal / gK

LEVEL 03 JEE Advanced Level

Single Choice Correct Questions

1 Four spheres A, B, C and D have their radii in arithmetic progression and the specific heat capacities of their substances are in geometric progression. If the ratios of heat capacities of D and B to that of C and A are as 8:27, the ratio of masses of B and A is (assume same density for all spheres)

(a) 8:1 (b) 4:1
(c) 1:8 (d) 1:4

2 A hollow sphere of mass M and radius R is rotating with an angular frequency ω. It suddenly stops rotating and 75% of the KE is converted into heat energy. If s is the specific heat of the material of the sphere, the rise of temperature of the sphere is

(a) $\frac{R^2\omega^2}{4s}$ (b) $\frac{3R^2\omega^2}{20s}$
(c) $\frac{R^2\omega^2}{4Js}$ (d) $\frac{2R^2\omega^2}{3s}$

3 There are two identical spheres, (I) hangs by thermally insulated wire and (II) is placed on thermally insulated stand as shown. Same amount of heat is supplied to the spheres. Which will suffer greater rise in temperature?

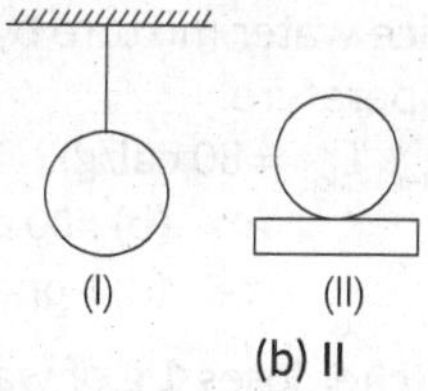

(a) I (b) II
(c) both same (d) Cannot be predicted

4 In two experiments with a continuous flow calorimeter to determine the specific heat capacity of a liquid, an input power of 60 W produced a rise of 10 K in the liquid. When the power was doubled, the same temperature rise was achieved by making the rate of flow of liquid three times faster. The power lost to the surroundings in each case was

(a) 20 W (b) 30 W (c) 40 W (d) 120 W

5 A mass m of lead shot is placed at the bottom of a vertical cardboard cylinder that is 1.5 m long and closed at both ends. The cylinder is suddenly inverted, so that the shot falls 1.5 m. If this process is repeated quickly 100 times, assuming no heat is dissipated or lost, the temperature of the shot will increase by (specific heat of lead = 0.03 cal/g°C)

(a) 0°C (b) 5°C (c) 7.3°C (d) 11.7°C

6 A thermally insulated vessel contains two liquids A and B with initial temperatures T_1 and T_2 and specific heats s_1 and s_2 respectively. They are separated by a non-conducting piston. When the partition is removed the final equilibrium temperature is average of the initial temperatures of the liquids. The ratio of masses of two liquids $\frac{m_1}{m_2}$ is

(a) $\frac{s_2}{s_1}$ (b) $\frac{s_1}{s_2}$ (c) $\sqrt{\frac{s_1}{s_2}}$ (d) $\sqrt{\frac{s_2}{s_1}}$

7 In a calorimeter, 20 g of liquid water at 100°C is mixed with 50 g of steam at 100°C. The system is allowed to come to equilibrium. Assuming that heat exchanged between the calorimeter and the surroundings can be ignored, which of the following best describes the net energy exchange between the steam and the liquid during the process of coming to equilibrium?

(a) There is no net energy exchange

(b) Energy is transferred from the steam to the liquid, vaporising some of the liquid

(c) Energy is transferred from the steam to the liquid until all of the liquid vaporises

(d) Energy is transferred from the liquid to the steam, condensing some steam

8 Find the amount of heat supplied to decrease the volume of an ice water mixture by 1 cm^3 without any change in temperature.

($\rho_{ice} = 0.9\,\rho_{water}$, $L_{ice} = 80$ cal/g).

(a) 360 cal (b) 500 cal

(c) 720 cal (d) None of these

9 An earthen pitcher loses 1 g of water per minute due to evaporation. If the water equivalent of pitcher is 0.5 kg and the pitcher contains 9.5 kg of water, calculate the time required for the water in the pitcher to cool to 28°C from its original temperature of 30°C. Neglect radiation effects. Latent heat of vaporisation of water in this range of temperature is 580 cal/g and specific heat of water is 1 kcal/kg°C

(a) 38.6 min (b) 30.5 min

(c) 34.5 min (d) 41.2 min

10 Water at 0°C was heated until it started to boil and then until it all changed to steam. The times required are: time to heat water from 0°C to 100°C = 5 min time to change boiling water to steam = 28 min Specific heat of water c_w = 4.2 J/g. If the flame supplied heat at a constant rate, the specific latent heat of vaporisation of water is (neglecting heat losses, container etc.)

(a) 534 J/g (b) 17.9 J/g

(c) 2352 J/g (d) 3342 J/g

11 Solid A, with mass M, is at its melting point T_A. It is placed in thermal contact with solid B, with heat capacity C_B and initially at temperature $T_B (T_B > T_A)$. The combination is thermally isolated. A has latent heat of fusion L and when it has melted has heat capacity C_A. If A completely melts, the final temperature of both A and B is

(a) $\frac{(C_A T_A + C_B T_B - ML)}{(C_A + C_B)}$ (b) $\frac{(C_A T_A - C_B T_B + ML)}{(C_A + C_B)}$

(c) $\frac{(C_A T_A - C_B T_B - ML)}{(C_A + C_B)}$ (d) $\frac{(C_A T_A + C_B T_B + ML)}{(C_A - C_B)}$

12 Some steam at 100°C is passed into 1.1 kg of water contained in a calorimeter of water equivalent 0.02 kg at 15°C, so that the temperature of the calorimeter and its contents rises to 80°C. What is the mass of steam condensing?

(a) 0.130 kg (b) 0.065 kg

(c) 0.260 kg (d) 0.135 kg

13 A thermally insulated vessel contains some water at 0°C. The vessel is connected to a vacuum pump to pump out water vapour. This results in some water getting frozen. It is given, Latent heat of vaporisation of water at 0°C $= 21 \times 10^5$ J/kg and latent heat of freezing of water $= 3.36 \times 10^5$ J/kg. The maximum percentage amount of water that will be solidified in this manner will be

(a) 86.2% (b) 33.6%

(c) 21% (d) 24.36%

14 Ice at 0°C is added to 200 g of water initially at 70°C in a vacuum flask. When 50 g of ice has been added and has all melted, the temperature of flask and contents is 40°C. When a further 80 g of ice is added and has all melted, the temperature of whole becomes 10°C. Neglecting heat lost to surroundings, the latent heat of fusion of ice is

(a) 80 cal/g

(b) 90 cal/g

(c) 70 cal/g

(d) 540 cal/g

15 A volume of 120 mL of drink (half alcohol + half water by mass) originally at a temperature of 25°C is cooled by adding 20 g ice at 0°C. If all the ice melts, the final temperature of the drink is
(Density of drink = 0.833 g/cc, specific heat of alcohol = 0.6 cal/g/°C)
(a) 4°C (b) 5°C (c) 0°C (d) 6°C

16 A metal ball of specific gravity 4.5 and specific heat 0.1 cal/g °C is placed on a large slab of ice at 0°C. When ball's temperature become 0°C, then half of the ball sinks in the ice. The initial temperature of the ball is (Latent heat capacity of ice = 80 cal/g, specific gravity of ice = 0.9)
(a) 100 °C (b) 90 °C (c) 80 °C (d) 70 °C

17 In an industrial process 10 kg of water per hour is to be heated from 20°C to 80°C. To do this steam at 200°C is passed from a boiler into a copper coil immersed in water. The steam condenses in the coil and is returned to the boiler as water at 90°C. How many kilograms of steam is required per hour? (specific heat of steam = 0.5 cal/g°C, Latent heat of vaporisation = 540 cal/g)
(a) 1 g (b) 1 kg
(c) 10 g (d) 10 kg

18 Two solid objects of the same mass are supplied with heat at the same rate $\frac{\Delta Q}{\Delta t}$. The temperature of the first object with latent heat L_1 and specific heat capacity c_1 changes according to graph 1 on the diagram. The temperature of the second object with latent heat L_2 and specific heat capacity c_2 changes according to graph 2 on the diagram. Based on what is shown on the graph, the latent heats L_1 and L_2 and the specific heat capacities c_1 and c_2 in solid state obey which of the following relationships?

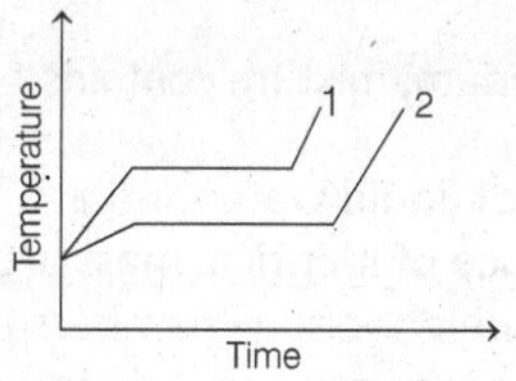

(a) $L_1 < L_2, c_1 < c_2$ (b) $L_1 < L_2, c_1 > c_2$
(c) $L_2 < L_1, c_1 > c_2$ (d) $L_2 < L_1, c_2 > c_1$

19 A cooking vessel on a slow burner contains 5 kg of water and an unknown mass of ice in equilibrium at 0°C at time $t = 0$. The temperature of the mixture is measured at various times and the result is plotted as shown in Figure. During the first 50 min, the mixture remains at 0°C. From 50 min to 60 min, the temperature increases to 2°C. Neglecting the heat capacity of the vessel, the initial mass of the ice is

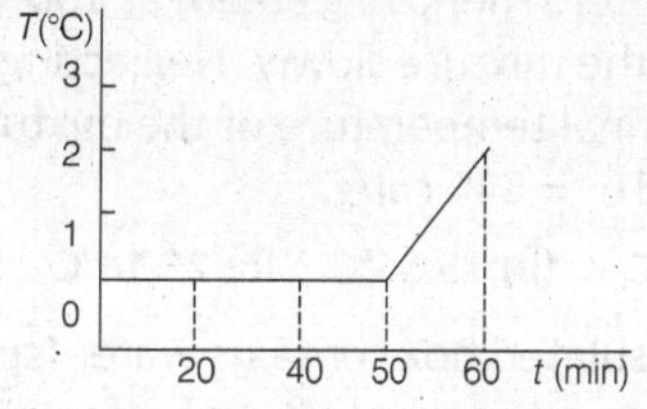

(a) 10/7 kg (b) 5/7 kg (c) 5/4 kg (d) 5/8 kg

20 A vessel contains M g of water at a certain temperature and water at certain other temperature is passed into it at a constant rate of m g/s. The variation of temperature of the mixture with time is shown in Figure. The value of M and m are, respectively (the heat exchanged after a long time is 800 cal)

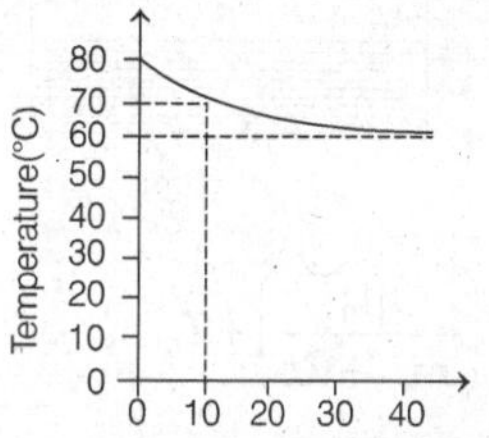

(a) 40 and 2 (b) 40 and 4
(c) 20 and 4 (d) 20 and 2

21 The temperature θ *versus* heat transfer Q plot for two substances A and B is given in the figure. If some quantity of substance A in liquid phase at temperature 30°C is mixed with substance B in liquid phase at 20°C, then the temperature of the mixture will be.
(Given, that boiling point for substance A is more than 30°C) .

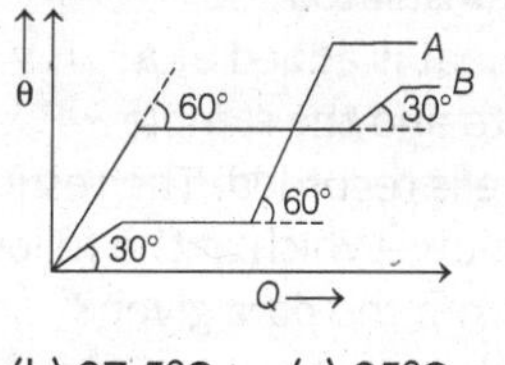

(a) 22.5°C (b) 27.5°C (c) 25°C (d) 20°C

22 A calorimeter contains 400 g of water at temperature of 5°C. Then, 200 g of water at a temperature of 10°C and 400 g of ice at a temperature of – 60° C are added. What is the final amount of ice in the mixture?
(Specific heat of ice = 0.5 cal/g°C.)
(a) 200 g (b) 300 g
(c) 500 g (d) 600 g

23 100 g of water at 20°C is kept in a calorimeter of water equivalent 200 g. 40 g of ice at – 20°C is added to the water. Then, 10 g steam at 100°C is bubbled through the mixture slowly. Neglecting any heat loss find the final temperature of the mixture. $L_f = 80$ cal/g and $L_v = 540$ cal/g.

(a) 5.34°C (b) 15.55°C (c) 25.14°C (d) 35.45°C

24 A well insulated box contains water (specific heat = c and very large conductivity) of mass m_0 and temperature T_0 at time $t = 0$. If heat is being added to it uniformly at a constant rate $\frac{dQ}{dt} = R$ and water is leaking from it at a constant rate $\frac{dm}{dt} = \lambda$, then the temperature of the water at time $t\left(t < \frac{m_0}{\lambda}\right)$ will be

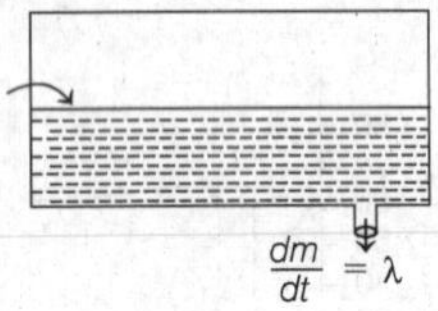

(a) $T = \frac{R}{2\lambda c} \ln\left(\frac{m_0}{m_0 - \lambda t}\right) + T_0$

(b) $T = \frac{R}{\lambda c} \ln\left(\frac{m_0}{m_0 - \lambda t}\right) + T_0$

(c) $T = \frac{R}{\lambda c} e^{(m_0 - \lambda t)}$

(d) $T = \frac{R}{2\lambda c} e^{(m_0 - \lambda t)}$

Multiple Choice(s) Correct Questions

1 A sample of a pure compound is contained in a closed, well-insulated container. Heat is added at a constant rate and the sample temperature is recorded. The resulting data is sketched below. Which of the following conclusions is justified from the data given?

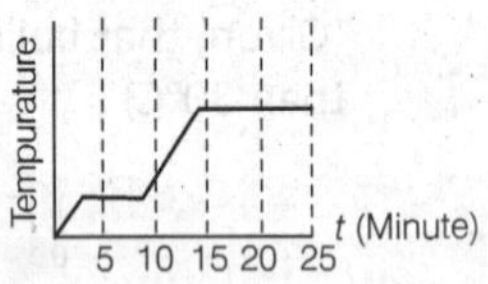

(a) The sample boiled
(b) The latent heat of fusion is greater than the latent heat of vaporisation
(c) At 5 min the sample was mixture of solid and liquid
(d) At 20 min the solid was all liquid

2 The water equivalent of a copper calorimeter is 4.5 g. If the specific heat of copper is 0.09 cal/g°C,
(a) mass of the calorimeter is 0.5 kg
(b) thermal capacity of the calorimeter is 4.5 cal/°C
(c) heat required to raise the temperature of the calorimeter by 8°C will be 36 cal
(d) heat required to melt 15 g of ice placed in the calorimeter will be 1200 cal

3 During the melting of a slab of ice at 273 K at the atmospheric pressure,
(a) positive work is done by the ice-water system on the atmosphere.
(b) positive work is done on the ice-water system by the atmosphere.
(c) the internal energy of the ice-water system increases.
(d) the internal energy of the ice-water system decreases.

4 When m g of water at 10°C is mixed with m g of ice at 0°C, which of the following statements are false?
(a) The temperature of the system will be given by the equation $m \times 80 + m \times 1 \times (T - 0) = m \times 1 \times (10 - T)$
(b) Whole of ice will melt and temperature will be more than 0°C but lesser than 10°C
(c) Whole of ice will melt and temperature will be 0°C
(d) Whole of ice will not melt and temperature will be 0°C

5 During heat exchange, temperature of a solid mass does not change. In this process, heat
(a) is not being supplied to the mass
(b) is not being taken out from the mass
(c) may have been supplied to the mass
(d) may have been taken out from the mass

6 5 kg of steam at 100°C is mixed with 10 kg of ice at 0°C. Choose correct alternative/s.
(Given, $s_{water} = 1$ cal/g°C, $L_f = 80$ cal/g, $L_v = 540$ cal/g)
(a) Equilibrium temperature of mixture is 160°C.
(b) Equilibrium temperature of mixture is 100°C.
(c) At equilibrium, mixture contains $13\frac{1}{3}$ kg of water.
(d) At equilibrium, mixture contains $1\frac{2}{3}$ kg of steam.

7 A sample A of liquid water and a sample B of ice of identical mass are kept in two neighboring chambers in an otherwise insulated container. The chambers can exchange heat with each other. The graph of temperatures of the two chambers is plotted with time. $S_{ice} = \frac{S_{water}}{2}$.

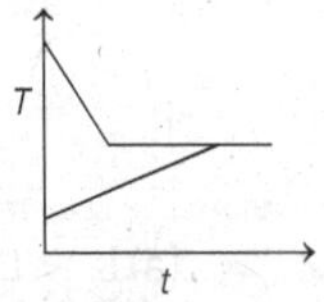

(a) Finally the contents in sample A is water.
(b) Equilibrium temperature is freezing point of water.
(c) Ice melts partly.
(d) Finally the contents in sample B is ice only.

8 In a heat insulated vessel there is tap water of 15°C. We place in it n ice cubes of – 15°C taken out of the deep-freezer. $S_{ice} = \frac{S_{water}}{2}$. Each ice cube has same mass as mass of water in vessel.

(a) If $n = 1$, some ice will melt

(b) If $n = 1$, some water will freeze.

(c) If $n = 2$, some water will freeze

(d) If $n = 2$, final temperature is 0°C

Comprehension Based Questions

Comprehension-1

Heat is given to equal amount of two bodies at the same rate. The variation of temperature with time is as shown in figure.

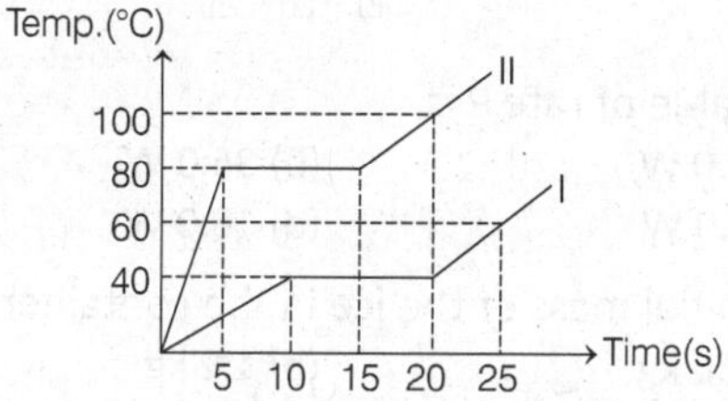

1 The ratio of melting points of body I and body II is

(a) $\frac{1}{2}$ (b) $\frac{2}{1}$ (c) $\frac{5}{3}$ (d) $\frac{3}{5}$

2 The ratio of specific heats of body I and body II is

(a) $\frac{1}{4}$ (b) $\frac{4}{1}$ (c) $\frac{8}{1}$ (d) $\frac{1}{8}$

3 The ratio of latent heats of body I and body II is

(a) 1 (b) $\frac{2}{1}$ (c) $\frac{1}{4}$ (d) $\frac{4}{1}$

Comprehension-2

In a small pan of heat capacity 300J/°C, we pour 0.5 L water and we put this pan on a stove, heating it at a constant rate. The temperature of the water is plotted in figure (a) against time. There were no heat losses. Then, we removed the water from pan and cooled the pan back to 0°C. We poured 0.7 kg alcohol and heat it at the same constant rate. The temperature time graph is plotted in figure (b).

Density of water = 1 kg/L, specific heat capacity of water = 4200 J/kg°C,

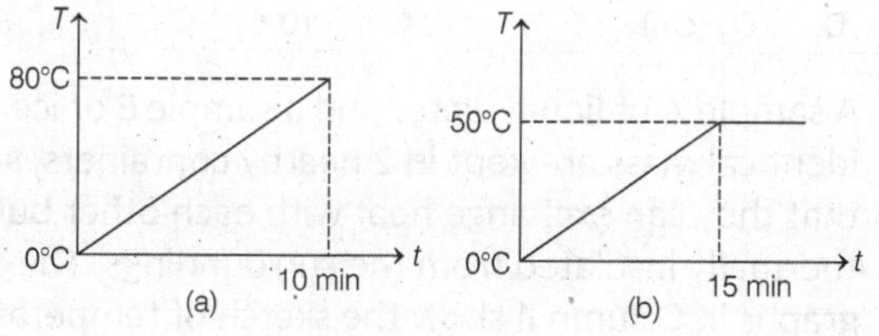

4 The specific heat capacity of alcohol is

(a) 7200 J/kg°C (b) 7800 J/kg°C

(c) 7500 J/kg°C (d) None of these

5 Half of the alcohol evaporates in 22 min from $t = 0$. What is the specific latent heat of vaporisation of alcohol?

(a) 4.24×10^5 J/kg (b) 3.6×10^5 J/kg

(c) 3.84×10^5 J/kg (d) None of these

Comprehension-3

A calorimeter of mass m contains an equal mass of water in it. The temperature of the water and calorimeter is t_2. A block of ice of mass m and temperature $t_3 < 0°C$ is gently dropped into the calorimeter. Let C_1, C_2 and C_3 be the specific heats of calorimeter, water and ice respectively and L be the latent heat of ice.

6 The whole mixture in the calorimeter becomes ice if

(a) $C_1t_2 + C_2t_2 + L + C_3t_3 > 0$

(b) $C_1t_2 + C_2t_2 + L + C_3t_3 < 0$

(c) $C_1t_2 + C_2t_2 - L + C_3t_3 > 0$

(d) $C_1t_2 + C_2t_2 - L - C_3t_3 < 0$

7 The whole mixture in the calorimeter becomes water if

(a) $(C_1 + C_2)t_2 - C_3t_3 + L > 0$

(b) $(C_1 + C_2)t_2 + C_3t_3 + L > 0$

(c) $(C_1 + C_2)t_2 - C_3t_3 - L > 0$

(d) $(C_1 + C_2)t_2 + C_3t_3 - L > 0$

8 Water equivalent of calorimeter is

(a) mC_1 (b) $\frac{mC_1}{C_2}$

(c) $\frac{mC_2}{C_1}$ (d) None of these

Comprehension-4

The figure below shows a plot of temperature *versus* heat energy supplied to 1.00 kg of some substance. The substance has melting point of – 10.0°C and is a gas at temperatures above 20.0°C.

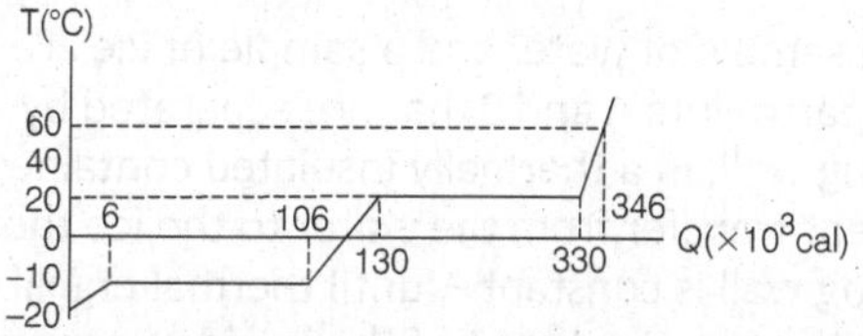

9 The latent heat of fusion for the substance is

(a) 100 cal/g (b) 200 cal/g

(c) 300 cal/g (d) 400 cal/g

10 If the substance is heated at a constant rate $\frac{dQ}{dt}$

(a) the time taken for the temperature to increase from – 20 °C to 10°C is the same as the time taken for the temperature to increase from 10°C to 40 °C
(b) the time taken for the temperature to increase from – 20 °C to 10 °C is less than the time taken for the temperature to increase from 10°C to 40°C
(c) the time taken for the temperature to increase from – 20 °C to 10°C is more than the time taken for the temperature to increase from 10°C to 40 °C
(d) None of these

11 Compare the specific heat capacity of the substance in solid, liquid and gaseous state

(a) $s_{liquid} > s_{Solid} > s_{gas}$
(b) $s_{liquid} > s_{gas} > s_{solid}$
(c) $s_{solid} > s_{liquid} > s_{gas}$
(d) $s_{gas} > s_{liquid} > s_{solid}$

Comprehension-5

In a container of negligible heat capacity, 200 g ice at 0°C and 100 g steam at 100°C are added to 200 g of water that has temperature 55°C. Assume no heat is lost to the surroundings and the pressure in the container is constant 1.0 atm.($L_f = 80$ cal/g, $L_v = 540$ cal/g, $s_w = 1$ cal/g °C)

12 What is the final temperature of the system ?

(a) 48°C (b) 72°C
(c) 94°C (d) 100°C

13 At the final temperature, mass of the total water present in the system, is

(a) 472.6 g (b) 483.3 g
(c) 493.6 g (d) 500 g

14 Amount of the steam left in the system, is equal to

(a) 16.7 g
(b) 12.0 g
(c) 8.4 g
(d) 0 g, as there is no steam left

Comprehension-6

A 0.60 kg sample of water and a sample of ice are placed in two compartments *A* and *B* that are separated by a conducting wall, in a thermally insulated container. The rate of heat transfer from the water to the ice though the conducting wall is constant *P*, until thermal equilibrium is reached. The temperature *T* of the liquid water and the ice are given in graph as functions of time *t*. Temperature of the compartments remain homogeneous during whole heat transfer process.

Given specific heat of ice = 2100 J/kg K,

specific heat of water = 4200 J/kg K

Latent heat of fusion of ice = 3.3×10^5 J / kg

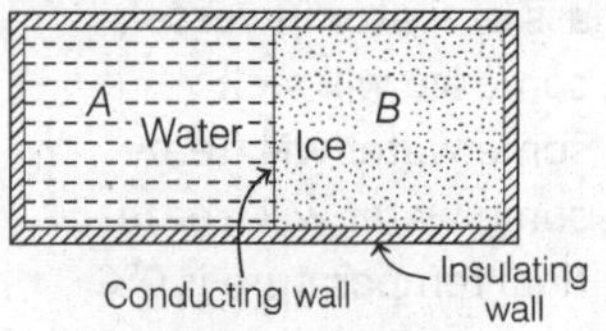

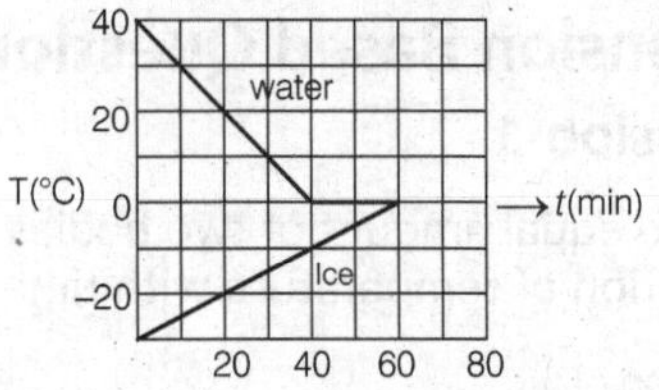

15 The value of rate *P* is

(a) 42.0 W (b) 36.0 W
(c) 21.0 W (d) 18.0 W

16 The initial mass of the ice in the container is equal to

(a) 0.36 kg (b) 1.2 kg
(c) 2.4 kg (d) 3.6 kg

17 The mass of the ice formed due to conversion from the water till thermal equilibrium is reached, is equal to

(a) 0.12 kg (b) 0.15 kg
(c) 0.25 kg (d) 0.40 kg

Match the Columns Questions

1 Figure shows the temperature variation when heat is added continuously to a specimen of ice (1 g) at – 20 °C. Specific heat of ice is 0.53 cal/g °C.

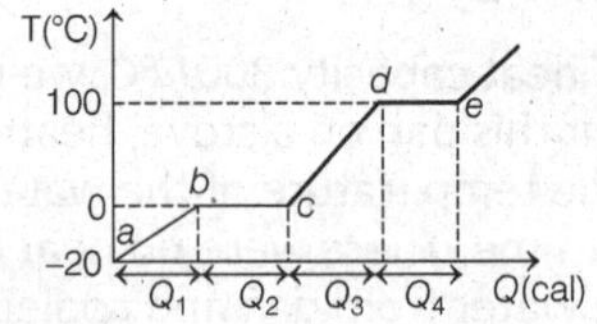

	Column I		Column II
A.	Q_1 (cal)	p.	80
B.	Q_2 (cal)	q.	539
C.	Q_3 (cal)	r.	100
D.	Q_4 (cal)	s.	10.6

2 A sample *A* of liquid water and a sample *B* of ice of identical mass are kept in 2 nearby containers, so that they can exchange heat with each other but are thermally insulated from the surroundings. The graphs in Column II show the sketch of temperature

T of samples *versus* time t. Match with appropriate description in Column I.

Column I	Column II
A. Equilibrium temperature is above melting point of ice	p. 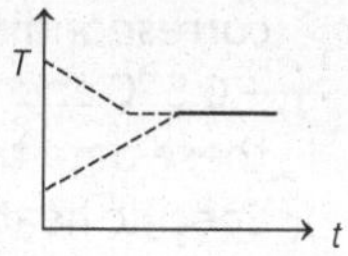
B. At least some of water freezes	q. 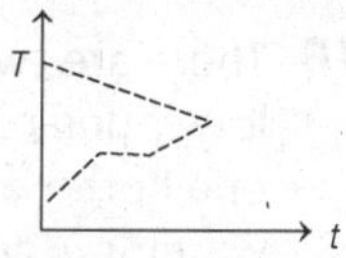
C. The graph is impossible	r. 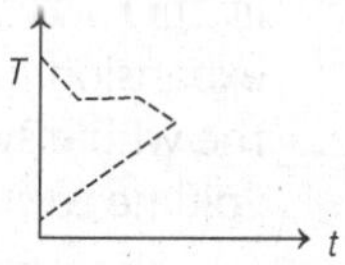
	s. 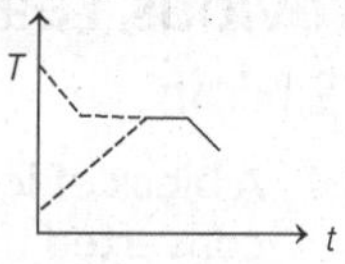

3 Match the column

Column I	Column II
A. Final mixture contains water only	p. 5g of ice at – 20° C is mixed with 25g of water at 30°C
B. Final mixture contains both ice and water	q. 5g of ice at – 20° C is mixed with 18g of water at 25°C
C. Final mixture's temperature is 0°C	r. 5g of ice at – 20° C is mixed with 10g of water at 25°C
D. Final temperature of mixture is 10°C	s. 50g of ice at – 20° C is mixed with 5g of water at 20°C
	t. 5 g of water at 0°C is mixed with 2.5g of water at 30°C

4 A calorimeter of water equivalent 1 kg contains 10 kg of ice and 10 kg of water in thermal equilibrium. The atmospheric temperature is 15° below freezing point due to which the calorimeter loses heat. As a result ice is formed inside the calorimeter at a rate of 10.8 g per second. To try to compensate for this heat loss, steam at 100°C is supplied to the calorimeter at a rate of r. ($L_v = 540$ cal/g, $L_f = 80$ cal/g, specific heat of water = 1 cal/g °C.) Column-I gives the value of r and Column II gives the situation just after the introduction of steam.

Column I	Column II
A. $r = 1.6$ g/s	p. Amount of ice in calorimeter increases.
B. $r = 1.35$ g/s	q. Amount of water in calorimeter increases.
C. $r = 1.2$ g/s	r. Amount of ice remains constant at 10 kg.
D. $r = 1$ g/s	s. Amount of water remains constant at 10 kg.
	t. Amount of ice in calorimeter decreases.

Numerical value questions

1 We throw a lead sphere of mass 600 g at 90°C and a steel sphere of mass 100 g at 60°C into water at 74°C. The lead sphere cools by as many degrees as the steel sphere gains. What was the mass of water (in g)?
Take, $s_{lead} = 127$ J/kg°C, $s_{steel} = 454$ J/kg°C, $s_{water} = 4200$ J/kg°C.

2 An insulated container of negligible heat capacity contains 620 g of ice at – 10 °C. What mass (in g) of steam at 100 °C must be added such that the final equilibrium state of the system is all water at 20°C? Specific heat capacity of ice = 0.5 cal/g/°C. Latent heat of steam = 540 cal g^{-1} and latent heat of ice = 80 cal/g.

3 Two cylinders of equal masses, one made of material A and the other of material B, are heated to 50°C and placed on two large blocks of ice at 0°C. If both the cylinders have the same height, find the ratio $\left(\frac{h_A}{h_B}\right)$ of their maximum depth of penetration in the ice. Assume that no heat is lost to the surroundings and change in gravitational potential energy is not considered.
$s_A = 0.2$ calg^{-1}°C^{-1},
$\rho_A = 4$ g cm^{-3},
$s_B = 0.1$ cal g^{-1}°C^{-1}, $\rho_B = 2$ g cm^{-3}

4 An ice block of mass 120 g with a shot of lead of mass $m = 2$ g frozen in the centre, floats on water, at temperature 0°C, in a closed tank. How much heat(in cal) should be transferred to the ice if we want the block to start sinking? The density of lead is 12 g/cm^3, the density of ice 0.9 g/cm^3, its heat of fusion 80 cal/g.

5 We want to cool down 15 L of 80°C water to 20°C by putting 0°C ice into it. What minimum volume (in L) should the vessel have to prevent the water from overflowing at the rim? (Latent heat of fusion of ice is 80 cal/g)

6 A copper ring has a diameter of exactly 25 mm at its temperature of 0°C. An aluminium sphere has a diameter of exactly 25.04 mm at its temperature of 100°C. The sphere is placed on top of the ring and two are allowed to come to thermal equilibrium, no heat being lost to the surrounding. The sphere just passes through the ring at the equilibrium temperature. Find the ratio $\frac{10m_{sphere}}{m_{ring}}$

(Given, $\alpha_{Cu} = 6.96 \times 10^{-6}/°C$, $\alpha_{Al} = 2.5 \times 10^{-5}/°C$, specific heat of Cu = 0.092 cal / g °C and specific heat of Al = 0.230 cal/g°C)

7 A calorimeter of water equivalent 18 g contain a liquid of mass 100 g at 30°C. Specific heat capacity of the liquid is $s = \frac{1}{2}\left(1 + \frac{\theta}{500}\right)$ cal/g °C, where θ is temperature in degree Celsius. m g of ice at − 20 °C is put in the calorimeter such that final temperature of the mixture and calorimeter is 10°C. Specific heat capacity of water $s_w = 1$ cal/g-°C, specific heat capacity of ice = 0.5 cal/g-°C. Latent heat of fusion = 80 cal/g. There is no loss of heat to surrounding. Find the value of *m*.

8 A container (water equivalent of container is negligible) contains 50 gm of water at 0°C. If *H* amount of heat is extracted per second from water and keeping the spray closed, then whole water freezes in 10 s. If spray is also working and sprays the water with 2 g/s at 0°C, then water freezes in t_1 s keeping the rate of extraction of heat from water same. Then calculate $6t_1$.
(Latent heat capacity of ice = 80 cal/g)

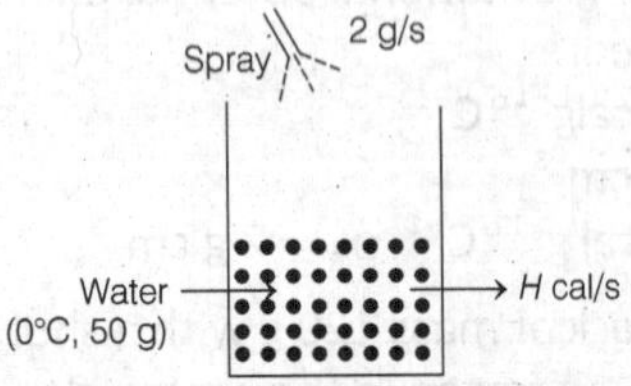

9 An experimenter collected 6.7 kg wet snow from street at a temperature of 0°C, placed it in the freezer and started measuring its temperature at regular intervals, recording data (the first record was made immediately after the start of the experiment). Subsequently, however, the file has been corrupted, so it could only read the temperature values corresponding to the tenth and eleventh records − 0.5 °C and − 4°C, respectively. Determine from these data the mass of water (in kg) in wet snow. Specific heat of ice = 2.1×10^3 J / kg °C, latent heat of ice = 3.35×10^5 J / kg.

10 There are two layers of water in a calorimeter, the lower one colder at temperature 30°C and the upper one hotter at temperature 60°C. The mass of lower water is m and volume is V. The mass of upper water is 2 m and volume is 2 V. The coefficient of volume expansion for water is γ. When the temperature of the whole system becomes equal, the ratio of new volume to the old volume is

Previous Year's Questions

JEE Main

1 A block of ice at −10°C is slowly heated and converted to steam at 100°C. Which of the following curves represent the phenomenon qualitatively?
[2024, 30 Jan Shift-II]

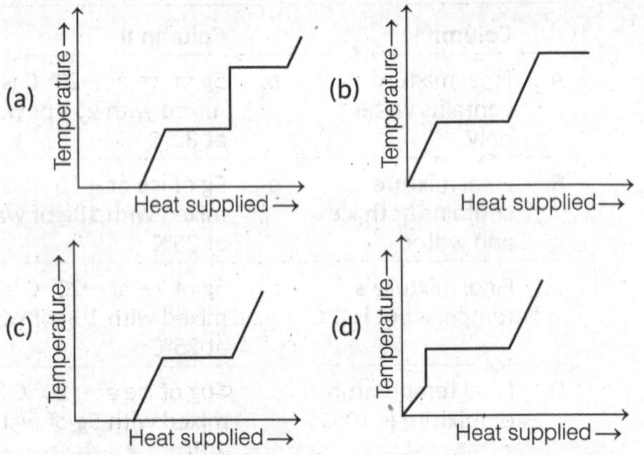

2 Heat energy of 184 kJ is given to ice of mass 600 g at − 12°C. Specific heat of ice is 2222.3 J $kg^{-1}°C^{-1}$ and latent heat of ice is 336 kJ kg^{-1}. **[2023, 29 Jan Shift-II]**

A. Final temperature of system will be 0°C.
B. Final temperature of the system will be greater than 0°C
C. The final system will have a mixture of ice and water in the ratio of 5 : 1.
D. The final system will have a mixture of ice and water in the ratio of 1: 5.
E. The final system will have water only.

Choose the correct answer from the options given below.

(a) A and C Only (b) A and D Only
(c) B and D Only (d) A and E Only

3 A block of ice of mass 120 g at temperature 0°C is put in 300 g of water at 25°C. The x g of ice melts as the temperature of the water reaches 0°C. The value of x is ....

[Use specific heat capacity of water $= 4200\ \text{J kg}^{-1}\ \text{K}^{-1}$,
Latent heat of ice $= 3.5 \times 10^5\ \text{J kg}^{-1}$]
[2022, 25 July Shift-II]

4 A geyser heats water flowing at a rate of 2.0 kg per minute from 30°C to 70°C. If geyser operates on a gas burner, the rate of combustion of fuel will be .... g min^{-1}

[Heat of combustion $= 8 \times 10^3\ \text{Jg}^{-1}$]
Specific heat of water $= 4.2\ \text{Jg}^{-1}\ {}^\circ\text{C}^{-1}$]
[2022, 26 June Shift-II]

5 A 100 g of iron nail is hit by a 1.5 kg hammer striking at a velocity of $60\ \text{ms}^{-1}$. What will be the rise in the temperature of the nail if one-fourth of energy of the hammer goes into heating the nail?

[Specific heat capacity of iron $= 0.42\ \text{Jg}^{-1}\ {}^\circ\text{C}^{-1}$]
[2022, 24 June Shift-II]

(a) 675°C (b) 1600°C (c) 16.07°C (d) 6.75°C

6 A copper block of mass 5.0 kg is heated to a temperature of 500°C and is placed on a large ice block. What is the maximum amount of ice that can melt? [Specific heat of copper, $0.39\ \text{Jg}^{-1}{}^\circ\text{C}^{-1}$ and latent heat of fusion of water, $335\ \text{J g}^{-1}$]
[2022, 25 June Shift-II]

(a) 1.5 kg (b) 5.8 kg (c) 2.9 kg (d) 3.8 kg

7 A lead bullet penetrates into a solid objected and melts. Assuming that 40% of its kinetic energy is used to heat it, the initial speed of bullet is

(Given, initial temperature of the bullet $= 127^\circ\text{C}$,
Melting point of the bullet $= 327^\circ\text{C}$,
Latent heat of fusion of lead $= 2.5 \times 10^4\ \text{J kg}^{-1}$)
Specific heat capacity of lead = 12.5 J/kg K)
[2022, 27 June Shift-II]

(a) $125\ \text{m s}^{-1}$ (b) $500\ \text{m s}^{-1}$
(c) $250\ \text{m s}^{-1}$ (d) $600\ \text{m s}^{-1}$

8 The height of victoria falls is 63 m. What is the difference in temperature of water at the top and at the bottom of fall ?

[Given, 1 cal = 4.2 J and specific heat of water $= 1\ \text{cal g}^{-1}{}^\circ\text{C}^{-1}$]
[2021, 27 Aug Shift-II]

(a) 0.147°C (b) 14.76°C
(c) 1.476°C (d) 0.014°C

9 The temperature of equal masses of three different liquids x, y and z are 10°C, 20°C and 30°C, respectively. The temperature of mixture when x is mixed with y is 16°C and that when y is mixed with z is 26°C. The temperature of mixture when x and z are mixed will be **[2021, 26 Aug Shift-II]**

(a) 28.32°C
(b) 25.62°C
(c) 23.84°C
(d) 20.28°C

10 Two different metal bodies A and B of equal mass are heated at a uniform rate under similar conditions. The variation of temperature of the bodies is graphically represented as shown in the figure. The ratio of specific heat capacities is **[2021, 25 July Shift-I]**

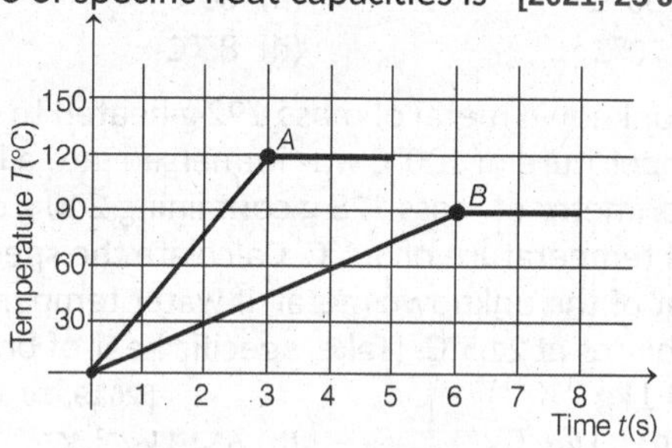

(a) $\frac{8}{3}$ (b) $\frac{3}{8}$
(c) $\frac{3}{4}$ (d) $\frac{4}{3}$

11 M grams of steam at 100°C is mixed with 200 g of ice at its melting point in a thermally insulated container. If it produces liquid water at 40°C [heat of vaporisation of water is 540 cal/g and heat of fusion of ice is 80 cal/g], the value of M is .... .
[2020, 7 Jan Shift-II]

12 A bullet of mass 5 g, travelling with a speed of 210 m/s, strikes a fixed wooden target. One-half of its kinetic energy is converted into heat in the bullet while the other half is converted into heat in the wood. The rise of temperature of the bullet, if the specific heat of its material is $0.030\ \text{cal g}^{-1}{}^\circ\text{C}^{-1}$, is close to **[2020, 5 Sep Shift-I]**

(a) 87.5° C (b) 83.3° C
(c) 119.2° C (d) 38.4° C

13 The specific heat of water $= 4200\ \text{J kg}^{-1}\text{K}^{-1}$ and the latent heat of ice $= 3.4 \times 10^5\ \text{J kg}^{-1}$. 100 g of ice at 0°C is placed in 200 g of water at 25°C. The amount of ice that will melt as the temperature of water reaches 0°C is close to (in grams) **[2020, 4 Sep Shift-I]**

(a) 63.8 (b) 69.3 (c) 64.6 (d) 61.7

14 When M_1 gram of ice at $-10°C$ (specific heat $= 0.5 \text{ cal g}^{-1}°C^{-1}$) is added to M_2 gram of water at 50°C, finally no ice is left and the water is at 0°C. The value of latent heat of ice, in cal g^{-1} is **[2019, 12 April Shift-I]**

(a) $\frac{50M_2}{M_1} - 5$ (b) $\frac{50M_1}{M_2} - 50$

(c) $\frac{50M_2}{M_1}$ (d) $\frac{5M_2}{M_1} - 5$

15 When 100 g of a liquid A at 100°C is added to 50 g of a liquid B at temperature 75°C, the temperature of the mixture becomes 90°C. The temperature of the mixture, if 100 g of liquid A at 100°C is added to 50 g of liquid B at 50°C will be **[2019, 11 Jan Shift-II]**

(a) 60°C (b) 80°C

(c) 70°C (d) 85°C

16 An unknown metal of mass 192 g heated to a temperature of 100°C was immersed into a brass calorimeter of mass 128 g containing 240 g of water at a temperature of 8.4°C. Calculate the specific heat of the unknown metal, if water temperature stabilises at 21.5°C. (Take, specific heat of brass is $394 \text{ J kg}^{-1}\text{K}^{-1}$) **[2019, 10 Jan Shift-II]**

(a) $916 \text{ J kg}^{-1} \text{ K}^{-1}$ (b) $654 \text{ J kg}^{-1} \text{ K}^{-1}$

(c) $1232 \text{ J kg}^{-1} \text{ K}^{-1}$ (d) $458 \text{ J kg}^{-1} \text{ K}^{-1}$

17 Ice at $-20°C$ is added to 50 g of water at 40°C. When the temperature of the mixture reaches 0°C, it is found that 20 g of ice is still unmelted. The amount of ice added to the water was close to (Take, specific heat of water $= 4.2$ J/g/°C specific heat of ice $= 2.1$ J/g/°C and heat of fusion of water at 0°C $= 334$ J/g) **[2019, 11 Jan Shift-I]**

(a) 40 g (b) 50 g (c) 60 g (d) 100 g

18 A metal ball of mass 0.1 kg is heated upto 500°C and dropped into a vessel of heat capacity 800 JK^{-1} and containing 0.5 kg water. The initial temperature of water and vessel is 30°C. What is the approximate percentage increment in the temperature of the water? [Take, specific heat capacities of water and metal are respectively $4200 \text{ Jkg}^{-1}\text{K}^{-1}$ and $400 \text{ Jkg}^{-1}\text{K}^{-1}$] **[2019, 11 Jan Shift-II]**

(a) 25% (b) 15% (c) 30% (d) 20%

19 A massless spring ($k = 800$ N/m), attached with a mass (500 g) is completely immersed in 1 kg of water. The spring is stretched by 2 cm and released, so that it starts vibrating. What would be the order of magnitude of the change in the temperature of water when ihe vibrations stop completely? (Assume that the water container and spring receive negligible heat and specific heat of mass = 400 J/kg K, specific heat of water = 4184 J/kg K) **[2019, 9 April Shift-II]**

(a) 10^{-4} K (b) 10^{-3} K (c) 10^{-1} K (d) 10^{-5} K

JEE Advanced

1 A water cooler of storage capacity 120 litres can cool water at a constant rate of P watts. In a closed circulation system (as shown schematically in the figure), the water from the cooler is used to cool an external device that generates constantly 3 kW of heat (thermal load). The temperature of water fed into the device cannot exceed 30°C and the entire stored 120 litres of water is initially cooled to 10°C. The entire system is thermally insulated. The minimum value of P (in watts) for which the device can be operated for 3 hours is **(2016 Adv.)**

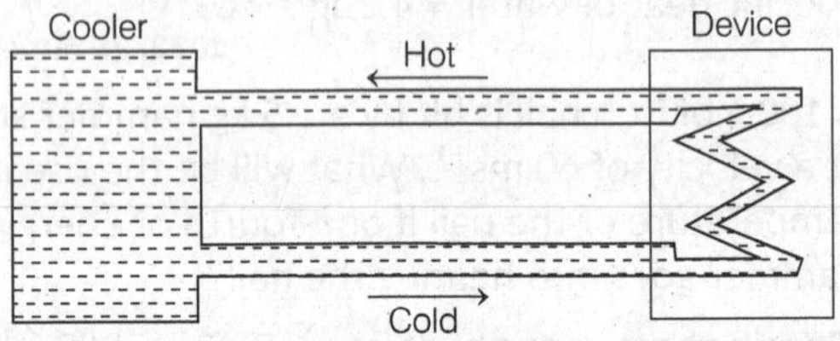

(Specific heat of water is $4.2 \text{ kJ kg}^{-1}\text{K}^{-1}$ and the density of water is 1000 kg m^{-3})

(a) 1600 (b) 2067

(c) 2533 (d) 3933

2. The figure below shows the variation of specific heat capacity (C) of a solid as a function of temperature (T). The temperature is increased continuously from 0 to 500 K at a constant rate. Ignoring any volume change, the following statement(s) is (are) correct to reasonable approximation. **(2013 Adv.)**

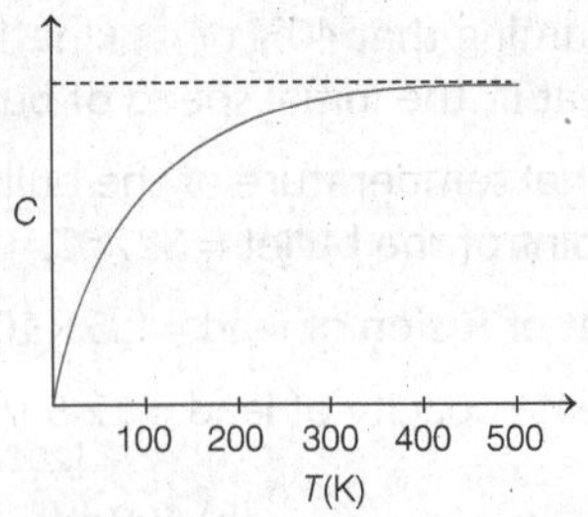

(a) the rate at which heat is absorbed in the range 0-100 K varies linearly with temperature T

(b) heat absorbed in increasing the temperature from 0-100 K is less than the heat required for increasing the temperature from 400-500 K

(c) there is no change in the rate of heat absorbtion in the range 400-500 K

(d) the rate of heat absorption increases in the range 200-300 K

Answer Key

Level 1

2.1 Specific Heat and Heat Capacity

1. 15 J/°C, 600 J/kg-°C
2. 1 : 12
3. 160° C
4. 0.05 °C
5. 8.6×10^{-3} °C
6. (a) 0 (b) 200 J (c) 0.05 °C
7. 35°C
8. 42.14°C
9. $15a/2$

2.2 Latent Heat

1. 327 kcal
2. 5820 cal
3. 780 kcal
4. (a) *AB*: Conversion from solid to liquid state, *CD*: Conversion from liquid to vapours
   (b) $L_v = 2L_f$
   (c) Reciprocal of heat capacity
   (d) Specific heat of liquid is greater than that of specific heat of solid.

2.3 Law of Mixture

1. 60°C
2. 140/11 °C
3. 130 kg
4. 0.93 cal/g°C
5. $\dfrac{m_1s_1T_1 + m_2s_2T_2 + m_3s_3T_3}{m_1s_1 + m_2s_2 + m_3s_3}$

2.4 Phase Change in Mixing

1. 30 g
2. 31 gm
3. 60 g(approx)
4. 7.5 °C, 2 kg water
5. (1.5 kg water + 0.5 kg ice) and temperature is 0°C
6. 100°C, mass of steam = 20/27 kg, mass of water = 34/27 kg

Level 2

Single Choice Correct Questions

1.	(c)	2.	(c)	3.	(c)	4.	(d)	5.	(c)
6.	(d)	7.	(d)	8.	(c)	9.	(a)	10.	(d)
11.	(b)	12.	(c)	13.	(b)	14.	(c)	15.	(b)
16.	(c)	17.	(a)	18.	(b)	19.	(d)	20.	(a)
21.	(b)	22.	(a)	23.	(b)	24.	(a)	25.	(a)
26.	(a)	27.	(b)	28.	(d)	29.	(a)	30.	(b)
31.	(d)	32.	(a)	33.	(a)	34.	(c)	35.	(d)
36.	(c)	37.	(b)	38.	(b)	39.	(b)	40.	(a)
41.	(a)	42.	(a)						

Numerical Value Questions

1. 8	2. 48	3. 900	4. 30	5. 60
6. 8	7. 12	8. 140	9. 30	10. 92
11. 4.5	12. 40			

Level 3

Single Choice Correct Questions

1.	(a)	2.	(a)	3.	(a)	4.	(b)	5.	(d)
6.	(a)	7.	(a)	8.	(c)	9.	(c)	10.	(c)
11.	(a)	12.	(a)	13.	(a)	14.	(b)	15.	(a)
16.	(c)	17.	(b)	18.	(a)	19.	(b)	20.	(b)
21.	(a)	22.	(c)	23.	(c)	24.	(b)		

Multiple Choice(s) Correct Questions

1. (ac)	2. (bcd)	3. (bc)	4. (abc)	5. (cd)
6. (bcd)	7. (bd)	8. (ad)		

Comprehension Based Questions

1.	(a)	2.	(b)	3.	(a)	4.	(b)	5.	(c)
6.	(b)	7.	(d)	8.	(b)	9.	(a)	10.	(b)
11.	(a)	12.	(d)	13.	(b)	14.	(a)	15.	(a)
16.	(c)	17.	(b)						

Match the Column Questions

1. (A) $\rightarrow$ s, (B) $\rightarrow$ p, (C) $\rightarrow$ r, (D) $\rightarrow$ q
2. (A) $\rightarrow$ q ; (B) $\rightarrow$ p, r ; (C) $\rightarrow$ s
3. (A) $\rightarrow$ p,q,t; (B) $\rightarrow$ r; (C) $\rightarrow$ q,r,s; (D) $\rightarrow$ p,t
4. (A) $\rightarrow$ q, t ; (B) $\rightarrow$ q, r ; (C) $\rightarrow$ p, s ; (D) $\rightarrow$ p

Numerical Value Questions

1. 110	2. 105	3. 4	4. 8280	5. 24
6. 4	7. 14	8. 100	9. 1.45	10. 1

Previous Year's Questions

JEE Main

1.	(b)	2.	(b)	3.	(90)	4.	(42)	5.	(c)
6.	(c)	7.	(b)	8.	(a)	9.	(c)	10.	(b)
11.	(40)	12.	(a)	13.	(d)	14.	(a)	15.	(b)
16.	(a)	17.	(a)	18.	(d)	19.	(d)		

JEE Advanced

1. (b)
2. (b, c, d)

SOLUTIONS

Level-1

2.1 Specific Heat and Heat Capacity

1. $\Delta T = T_2 - T_1 = 45 - 25 = 20° C$

Thermal capacity $= \frac{\Delta Q}{\Delta T} = \frac{300}{20} = 15$ J/°C

Specific heat $= \frac{\Delta Q}{m\Delta T} = \frac{300}{0.025 \times 20} = 600$ J/kg-°C

2. Mass = Density × Volume

$$m = \rho\left(\frac{4}{3}\pi r^3\right)$$

$$\therefore \quad \frac{m_1}{m_2} = \left(\frac{\rho_1}{\rho_2}\right)\left(\frac{r_1}{r_2}\right)^3 = \left(\frac{2}{1}\right)\left(\frac{1}{2}\right)^3 = \frac{1}{4}$$

Thermal capacity, $C = ms$

$$\therefore \quad \frac{C_1}{C_2} = \left(\frac{m_1}{m_2}\right)\left(\frac{s_1}{s_2}\right) = \left(\frac{1}{4}\right)\left(\frac{1}{3}\right) = 1:12$$

3. $\frac{1}{2}mv^2 = ms\Delta T$

$$\Rightarrow \quad \Delta T = \frac{v^2}{2s} = \frac{(400)^2}{2(500)} = 160° C$$

4. $ms\Delta T = \frac{25}{100} mgh$

$$\Rightarrow \quad \Delta T = \frac{gh}{4s} = \frac{10 \times 10}{4 \times 500} = 0.05°C$$

5. $\Sigma F = ma$

$\Rightarrow \quad mg \sin 37° - f_K = m(0)$

$\Rightarrow \quad f_K = mg \sin 37° = 0.2 \times 10 \times 0.6 = 1.2$ N

Work done by friction $= Fs \cos\theta = 1.2\,(0.6) \cos 180°$

$= -0.72$ J

$Q = ms\Delta T$

$\Rightarrow \quad 0.72 = 0.2 \times 420 \times \Delta T$

$\Rightarrow \quad \Delta T = 8.6 \times 10^{-3}\,°C$

6. (a) No heat is supplied to the liquid.

(b) Work done on liquid = Loss in potential energy of 10 kg block

$= mgh = 10 \times 10 \times 2 = 200$ J

(c) $Q = C\Delta T$

$\Rightarrow \quad 200 = 4000\Delta T$

$\Rightarrow \quad \Delta T = 0.05°$ C

7. $\frac{dQ}{dT} = \frac{dm}{dt} s\Delta T$

$\Rightarrow \quad 2100 = 20 \times 4.2 \times (T - 10)$

$\Rightarrow \quad T = 35°$ C

8. $Q = pt = 90 \times 10 \times 60 = 54000$ J

$Q = ms\Delta T$

$\Rightarrow \quad 54000 = (360 + 40) \times 10^{-3} \times 4200 \times (T - 10)$

$\Rightarrow \quad T = 42.14°$ C

9. $Q = m\int s\,dT = 2\int_1^2 aT^3 dT$

$$= 2a\left[\frac{T^4}{4}\right]_1^2 = \frac{15a}{2}$$

2.2 Latent Heat

1. 3kg ice −22°C $\xrightarrow{Q_1}$ 3kg ice 0°C $\xrightarrow{Q_2}$ 3kg water 0°C $\xrightarrow{Q_3}$ 3kg water 18°C

$Q_1 = m_{ice}s_{ice}\Delta T$

$= 3 \times 0.5 \times [0 - (-22)] = 33$ kcal

$Q_2 = mL_f = 3 \times 80 = 240$ kcal

$Q_3 = m_w s_w \Delta T$

$= 3 \times 1 \times (18 - 0) = 54$ kcal

$Q = Q_1 + Q_2 + Q_3 = 327$ kcal

2. 8g ice −15°C $\xrightarrow{Q_1}$ 8g ice 0°C $\xrightarrow{Q_2}$ 8g water 0°C $\xrightarrow{Q_3}$ 8g water 100°C $\xrightarrow{Q_4}$ 8g steam 100°C

$Q_1 = m_{ice}s_{ice}\Delta T$

$= 8 \times 0.5 \times [0 - (-15)] = 60$ cal

$Q_2 = mL_f = 8 \times 80 = 640$ cal

$Q_3 = m_w s_w \Delta T$

$= 8 \times 1 \times (100 - 0) = 800$ cal

$Q_4 = mL_v = 8 \times 540 = 4320$ cal

$Q = Q_1 + Q_2 + Q_3 + Q_4 = 5820$ cal

3. 1kg Steam 200°C $\xrightarrow{Q_1}$ 1kg Steam 100°C $\xrightarrow{Q_2}$ 1kg Water 100°C $\xrightarrow{Q_3}$ 1kg Water 0°C $\xrightarrow{Q_4}$ 1kg Ice 0°C $\xrightarrow{Q_5}$ 1kg Ice −20°C

$Q_1 = m_{steam}s_{steam}\Delta T$

$= 1 \times 0.5 \times (200 - 100) = 50$ kcal

$Q_2 = mL_v = 1 \times 540 = 540$ kcal

$Q_3 = m_w s_w \Delta T$

$= 1 \times 1 \times (100 - 0) = 100$ kcal

$Q_4 = mL_f = 1 \times 80 = 80$ kcal

$Q_5 = m_{ice}s_{ice}\Delta T$

$= 1 \times 0.5 \times [0 - (-20)] = 10$ kcal

$Q = Q_1 + Q_2 + Q_3 + Q_4 + Q_5$

$= 780$ kcal

4. (a) In horizontal portions *AB* and *CD*, temperature remains constant. Hence these portions show change of state.

AB : Conversion from solid to liquid state

CD : Conversion from liquid to vapours

(b) $CD = 2AB \Rightarrow Q_{CD} = 2Q_{AB}$

$\Rightarrow \quad mL_v = 2mL_f$

$\Rightarrow \quad L_v = 2L_f$

(c) Slope of $DE = \dfrac{\Delta T}{\Delta Q} = \dfrac{1}{ms} = \dfrac{1}{\text{Thermal capacity}}$

$\therefore$ Slope of line DE represents reciprocal of heat capacity.

(d) Slope of $OA >$ Slope of BC,

$\Rightarrow \quad \left(\dfrac{\Delta T}{\Delta Q}\right)_{OA} > \left(\dfrac{\Delta T}{\Delta Q}\right)_{BC}$

$\Rightarrow \quad \dfrac{1}{ms_{\text{solid}}} > \dfrac{1}{ms_{\text{liquid}}}$

$\Rightarrow \quad s_{\text{liquid}} > s_{\text{solid}}$

The specific heat of liquid is greater than that of specific heat of solid.

2.3 Law of Mixture

1. Heat lost by 3 kg water = Heat gained by 2 kg water

$\Rightarrow 3 \times 1 \times (80 - T) = 2 \times 1 \times (T - 30)$

$\Rightarrow \quad T = 60°\,C$

2. When A and B are mixed,

$m_A s_A (13 - 10) = m_B s_B (15 - 13)$

$\Rightarrow \quad 3m_A s_A = 2m_B s_B$ ...(i)

When B and C are mixed,

$m_B s_B (16 - 15) = m_C s_C (20 - 16)$

$\Rightarrow \quad m_B s_B = 4m_C s_C$ ...(ii)

From Eqs. (i) and (ii), we get

$m_A s_A = \dfrac{8}{3} m_C s_C$

When A and C are mixed,

$m_A s_A (T - 10) = m_C s_C (20 - T)$

$\Rightarrow \quad \dfrac{8}{3} m_C s_C (T - 10) = m_C s_C (20 - T)$

$\Rightarrow \quad T = \dfrac{140}{11}\,°C$

3. Heat lost by iron = Heat gained by water

$\Rightarrow \quad 100 \times 420 \times (730 - 80) = m \times 4200 \times (80 - 30)$

$\Rightarrow \quad m = 130 \text{ kg}$

4. Heat lost by water = Heat gained by milk + Heat gained by vessel

$\Rightarrow \quad 200 \times 1 \times (98 - 64)$

$= 206 s_{\text{milk}} (64 - 30) + 8 \times 1 \times (64 - 30)$

$\Rightarrow s_{\text{milk}} = 0.93 \text{ cal/g°C}$

5. Let the equilibrium temperature be T.

Net heat lost by the system = 0

$\Rightarrow \quad m_1 s_1 (T_1 - T) + m_2 s_2 (T_2 - T) + m_3 s_3 (T_3 - T) = 0$

$\Rightarrow \quad T = \dfrac{m_1 s_1 T_1 + m_2 s_2 T_2 + m_3 s_3 T_3}{m_1 s_1 + m_2 s_2 + m_3 s_3}$

2.4 Phase Change in Mixing

1. Heat lost by water = Heat taken by ice from melting

$m_w s_w \Delta T = m_{\text{ice}} L_f$

$\Rightarrow 40 \times 1 \times (60 - 0) = m_{\text{ice}}(80)$

$\Rightarrow \quad m_{\text{ice}} = 30 \text{ g}$

2. Heat consumed by ice = Heat supplied by water

$\Rightarrow \quad m_{\text{ice}} s_{\text{ice}} \Delta T + m_{\text{ice}} L_f + m_{\text{ice}} s_w \Delta T = m_w s_w \Delta T$

$\Rightarrow \quad m(0.5)[0 - (-14)] + m(80) + m(1)(10 - 0)$

$= 200 \times 1 \times (25 - 10)$

$\Rightarrow \quad m = 31 \text{ g}$

3. Let mass of steam condensed = m g

Heat supplied by steam = Heat consumed by water

$\Rightarrow \quad m \times L_v + m s_w \Delta T = m_w s_w \Delta T$

$\Rightarrow \quad m \times 536 + m \times 1 \times (100 - 90) = 54 \times 1 \times (90 - 30)$

$\Rightarrow \quad m = 5.93 \text{ g} \simeq 6 \text{ g}$

Mass of mixture = 54 + 6 = 60 g

4. 1kg ice −10°C $\xrightarrow{Q_1}$ 1kg ice 0°C $\xrightarrow{Q_2}$ 1kg water 0°C

$Q_1 = m_{\text{ice}} s_{\text{ice}} \Delta T$

$= 1 \times 0.5 \times [0 - (-10)] = 5 \text{ kcal}$

$Q_2 = mL_f = 1 \times 80 = 80 \text{ kcal}$

So, heat required by 1kg ice at −10°C to become water at 0°C = 5 + 80 = 85 kcal

1kg water 100°C $\xrightarrow{Q_3}$ 1kg water 0°C

$Q_3 = m_w s_w \Delta T$

$= 1 \times 1 \times (100 - 0) = 100 \text{ kcal}$

So, heat lost by 1 kg water at 100°C to become water at 0°C = 100 kcal

As $Q_3 > Q_1 + Q_2$, so remaining heat (100 − 85 = 15 kcal) will increase temperature of 2 kg of water at 0°C to final temperature lets say T.

$Q = ms\Delta T$

$\Rightarrow \quad 15 = 2 \times 1 \times (T - 0)$

$\Rightarrow \quad T = 7.5°C$

5. 1kg water 50°C $\xrightarrow{Q_1}$ 1kg water 0°C

Heat lost by 1kg water at 50°C to become water at 0°C,

$Q_1 = 1 \times 1 \times (50 - 0) = 50 \text{ kcal}$

Heat needed by 1 kg ice at −20°C to become water at 0°C,

$$Q_2 = 1\times 0.5\times[0-(-20)]+1\times 80 = 90 \text{ kcal}$$

As $Q_1 < Q_2$, the whole ice will not melt. It will be ice-water mixture and temperature will be 0°C.

$$\underset{-20^\circ C}{\underset{\text{ice}}{1\text{kg}}} \xrightarrow{10 \text{ Kcal}} \underset{0^\circ C}{\underset{\text{ice}}{1\text{kg}}} \xrightarrow{40 \text{ Kcal}} \underset{0^\circ C}{\underset{\text{water}}{m\text{kg}}} + \underset{0^\circ C}{\underset{\text{ice}}{(1-m)\text{kg}}}$$

Heat available for melting ice $= 50 - 10 = 40$ kcal

$$Q = mL_f \Rightarrow 40 = m(80)$$

$$\Rightarrow \quad m = 0.5 \text{ kg}$$

So. we will have 1.5 kg water and 0.5 kg ice at 0°C.

6. Heat consumed by 1 kg ice at –20°C to become 1 kg water at 100°C,

$$Q_1 = 1\times 0.5\times 20 + 1\times 80 + 1\times 1\times 100 = 190 \text{ kcal}$$

Heat supplied by 1 kg steam at 200°C to become water at 100°C,

$$Q_2 = 1\times 0.5\times(200-100)+1\times 540 = 590 \text{ kcal}$$

As $Q_1 < Q_2$, the entire steam will not condense.
It will be steam-water mixture at 100°C.

$$\underset{200^\circ C}{\underset{\text{Steam}}{1\text{kg}}} \xrightarrow{50 \text{ Kcal}} \underset{100^\circ C}{\underset{\text{Steam}}{1\text{kg}}} \longrightarrow \underset{100^\circ C}{\underset{\text{Water}}{m\text{kg}}} + \underset{100^\circ C}{\underset{\text{Steam}}{(1-m)\text{kg}}}$$

For condensation of steam, $Q = mL_v$

$$\Rightarrow \quad 190 - 50 = m(540)$$

$$\Rightarrow \quad m = \frac{7}{27} \text{ kg}$$

$$\text{Mass of steam} = 1 - \frac{7}{27} = \frac{20}{27} \text{ kg}$$

$$\text{Mass of water} = 1 + \frac{7}{27} = \frac{34}{27} \text{ kg}$$

Level–2

Single Choice Correct Questions

1. $m = \rho V$

$$\therefore \quad \frac{m_1}{m_2} = \frac{\rho_1}{\rho_2} = \frac{3}{4} \qquad \text{[For unit volume]}$$

$$C = ms$$

$$\therefore \quad \frac{C_1}{C_2} = \left(\frac{m_1}{m_2}\right)\left(\frac{s_1}{s_2}\right) = \left(\frac{3}{4}\right)\left(\frac{4}{3}\right) = 1:1$$

2. $Q = m\int s\,dT = 0.1\int_{20}^{40}(100T + 500)\,dT$

$$= 10\left[\frac{T^2}{2} + 5T\right]_{20}^{40}$$

$$= 10\left[\frac{(40)^2-(20)^2}{2} + 5(40-20)\right] = 7000 \text{ J}$$

3. $\frac{75}{100}\left(\frac{1}{2}mv^2\right) = ms\Delta T + mL_f$

$$\Rightarrow \quad \frac{3}{8}v^2 = 0.03\times 4200\times(327-27)+6\times 4200$$

$$\Rightarrow \quad v = 409.88 \text{ m/s} \simeq 410 \text{ m/s}$$

4. $ms\Delta T = mgh$

$$\Rightarrow \Delta T = \frac{gh}{s} = \frac{9.8\times 50}{4200} = 0.117^\circ C$$

5. $\frac{dQ}{dt} = \frac{dm}{dt}s_w\Delta T + \frac{dm}{dt}L_v$

$$\Rightarrow 1000\times 0.9 = \frac{dm}{dt}\times 4.2\times(100-20) + \frac{dm}{dt}\times 2250$$

$$\Rightarrow \quad \frac{dm}{dt} = 0.35 \text{ g/s}$$

6. Distance = Speed × Time

$$= 2\times 1 = 2 \text{ km} = 2000 \text{ m}$$

Heat produced $= (\mu mg)\,s$

$$= (0.5\times 25\times 10)\,(2000) = 2.5\times 10^5 \text{ J}$$

$$Q = ms\Delta T$$

$$\Rightarrow \frac{1}{2}\times 2.5\times 10^5 = 25\times 0.1\times 4200\times \Delta T$$

$$\Rightarrow \quad \Delta T = 11.9^\circ C$$

7. $\frac{1}{2}mv^2 = m_{ice}L_f$

$$\Rightarrow \frac{1}{2}\times 50\times 5^2 = m_{ice}(80\times 4200)$$

$$\Rightarrow \quad m_{ice} = 0.00186 \text{ kg} = 1.86 \text{ g}$$

8. $m_{ice}L_f = mgh$

$$\Rightarrow m_{ice}(3.5\times 10^5) = 3.5\times 10\times 2000$$

$$\Rightarrow \quad m_{ice} = 0.2 \text{ kg} = 200 \text{ g}$$

9. $Q = ms_{ice}\Delta T + mL_f + ms_w\Delta T + mL_v$

$$= 1\times 0.5\times[0-(-10)] + 1\times 80 + 1\times 1\times 100 + 1\times 540$$

$$= 725 \text{ kcal}$$

10. $Q = Q_{ice} + Q_{calorimeter}$

$$= (10\times 80 + 10\times 1\times(100-0) + 10\times 540) + [10\times 1\times(100-0)]$$

$$= 8200 \text{ cal}$$

11. $Q = 100\times 1\times(25-0) + 100\times 80 + 100\times 0.5\times[0-(-10)]$

$$= 11000 \text{ cal}$$

$$\text{Heat removed per minute} = \frac{Q}{t} = \frac{11000 \text{ cal}}{110 \text{ min}} = 100 \text{ cal/min}$$

12. Vaporisation takes place from $t = 20$ min to $t = 30$ min i.e., 10 min interval.

$$Q = mL_v \Rightarrow 42\times 10 = 5L_v$$

$$\Rightarrow \quad L_v = 84 \text{ kJ/kg}$$

13.

$$\underset{-8^\circ C}{\underset{\text{ice}}{22\text{g}}} \longrightarrow \underset{0^\circ C}{\underset{\text{ice}}{22\text{g}}} \longrightarrow \underset{0^\circ C}{\underset{\text{water}}{22\text{g}}} + \underset{8^\circ C}{\underset{\text{water}}{22\text{g}}}$$

$$Q = ms_{ice}\Delta T + mL_f + ms_w\Delta T$$

$$= 22\times 0.5\times[0-(-8)] + 22\times 80 + 22\times 1\times(8-0)$$

$$= 2024 \text{ cal}$$

For the body, $Q = m_w s_w \Delta T$

$$\Rightarrow \quad 2024 = m_w\times 1\times 44$$

$\Rightarrow \quad m_w = 46 \text{ g}$

14. Let power of kettle be P.

$$Q = P \times (10 \text{ min}) = m \times 1 \times (100 - 0) \quad \text{...(i)}$$

$$Q = P \times (54 \text{ min}) = mL_v \quad \text{...(ii)}$$

From Eqs. (i) and (ii), we get

$$L_v = 540 \text{ cal/g}$$

15. In the molten state,

Power input = Power lost to surroundings $= P$

When the power is turned off,

Heat lost $= P \times t = mL_f$

$$\Rightarrow \quad L_f = \frac{Pt}{m}$$

16. $Q = ms\Delta T = 0.5 \times 4200 \times (85 - 15) = 1.47 \times 10^5$ J

Average power consumed $= \dfrac{1.47 \times 10^5}{240} = 612.5$ W

Average power loss $= 750 - 612.5 = 137.5 \text{ W} \simeq 138 \text{W}$

17. $\dfrac{dQ}{dt} = \dfrac{dm}{dt} L_f = 0.1 \times 80 = 8$ cal/s

$m = 0.1 \times 100 = 10$ g

$$\frac{dQ}{dt} = mS\frac{dT}{dt}$$

$$\Rightarrow \quad 8 = 10 \times 1 \times \frac{dT}{dt}$$

$$\Rightarrow \quad \frac{dT}{dt} = 0.8^\circ \text{C/s}$$

18. Heat added $= 100 \times 4 \times 60 = 24000$ cal

Let final temperature be T.

Heat consumed by container

$= 100 \times 0.2 \times [T - (-20)]$

Heat consumed by ice

$= 200 \times 0.5 \times (0 - [-20]) + 200 \times 80 + 200 \times 1 \times (T - 0)$

Total heat consumed = 24000

$\Rightarrow 20(T + 20) + 2000 + 16000 + 200T = 24000$

$$\Rightarrow \quad T = 25.5^\circ \text{C}$$

19. Heat gained = Heat lost

$$\Rightarrow mC(T' - T) = \left(\frac{m}{2}\right)(2C)(2T - T')$$

$$\Rightarrow \quad T' = \frac{3T}{2}$$

20. Heat lost = Heat gained

$$\Rightarrow \quad ms_A(30 - 26) = ms_B(26 - 20)$$

$$\Rightarrow \quad \frac{s_A}{s_B} = \frac{3}{2}$$

21. Heat lost = Heat gained

$\Rightarrow 0.1 \times 4200 \times (60 - 35)$

$= 0.2 \times 4200 \times (35 - 30) + C(35 - 30)$

$$\Rightarrow \quad C = 1260 \text{ J/°C}$$

22. Heat lost by boiling water = Heat gained by brass vessel

$$\Rightarrow \quad 20 \times 1 \times (100 - T) = 100 \times 0.1 \times (T - 0)$$

$$\Rightarrow \quad T = 66.66^\circ \text{C}$$

23. Heat lost = Heat gained

$$\Rightarrow \quad 440 \times 1 \times (92 - T) = (200 + 20) \times 1 \times (T - 20)$$

$$\Rightarrow \quad T = 68^\circ \text{C}$$

24. Heat lost = Heat gained

$\Rightarrow \quad 100 \times 0.09 \times (100 - 23)$

$= 200 \times s \times (23 - 15) + 4 \times 1 \times (23 - 15)$

$$\Rightarrow \quad s = 0.41 \text{ cal/g-°C}$$

25. Heat lost = Heat gained

$\Rightarrow 10 \times (T - 40) = 200 \times 1 \times (40 - 10)$

$$\Rightarrow \quad T = 640^\circ \text{C}$$

26. Heat gained = Heat lost

When A and B are mixed,

$$ms_A(15 - 10) = ms_B(25 - 15)$$

$$\Rightarrow \quad s_A = 2s_B \quad \text{...(i)}$$

When B and C are mixed,

$$ms_B(30 - 25) = ms_C(40 - 30)$$

$$\Rightarrow \quad s_B = 2s_C \quad \text{...(ii)}$$

From Eqs. (i) and (ii), we get

$$s_A = 4s_C$$

When A and C are mixed,

$$ms_A(T - 10) = ms_C(40 - T)$$

$$\Rightarrow \quad 4(T - 10) = 40 - T$$

$$\Rightarrow \quad T = 16^\circ \text{C}$$

27. $ms\Delta T = m_{ice}L_f$

$$\Rightarrow \quad 2.5 \times 0.1 \times (500 - 0) = m_{ice} \times 80$$

$$\Rightarrow \quad m_{ice} = 1.6 \text{ kg}$$

28. $ms\Delta T = m_{ice}L_f$

$$\Rightarrow \quad m \times 1 \times (50 - 0) = 10 \times 80$$

$$\Rightarrow \quad m = 16 \text{ g}$$

29. Heat released by 1 kg water at 75°C to become water at 0°C,

$$Q_1 = ms\Delta T$$

$$= 1 \times 1 \times (75 - 0) = 75 \text{ cal}$$

Heat required by 1 kg ice at 0°C to become 1 kg water at 0°C,

$$Q_2 = mL_f = 1 \times 80 = 80 \text{ cal}$$

Since $Q_1 < Q_2$, ice will not melt completely. It will be ice-water mixture at 0°C.

30. Heat released by 55 g water at 40°C to become water at 8°C,

$$Q_1 = ms\Delta T = 55 \times 1 \times (40 - 0) = 2200 \text{ cal}$$

Heat required by 10 g ice at 0°C to become water at 0°C,

$$Q_2 = mL_f = 10 \times 80 = 800 \text{ cal}$$

Since $Q_1 > Q_2$, ice will melt completely.

For 55 + 10 = 65 g of water at 0°C,

$$Q = ms\Delta T$$

$$\Rightarrow \quad 2200 - 800 = 65 \times 1 \times (T - 0)$$

$$\Rightarrow \quad T = 21.53°\text{C} \simeq 22°\text{C}$$

31. Heat released by 4.4 kg of water at 30°C to become water at 0°C,

$$Q_1 = ms\Delta T = 4.4 \times 1 \times (30 - 0) = 132 \text{ kcal}$$

Heat required by 1 kg ice at –10°C to become 1 kg water at 0°C,

$$Q_2 = mS\Delta T + mL_f$$

$$= 1 \times 0.5 \times [0 - (-10)] + 1 \times 80 = 85 \text{ kcal}$$

Since $Q_1 > Q_2$, ice will melt completely.

For 4.4 + 1 = 5.4 kg of water at 0°C,

$$Q = ms\Delta T$$

$$\Rightarrow 132 - 85 = 5.4 \times 1 \times (T - 0)$$

$$\Rightarrow \quad T = 8.7°\text{C}$$

32. Heat released by 10 g of water at 10°C to become water at 0°C,

$$Q_1 = ms\Delta T = 10 \times 1 \times (10 - 0) = 100 \text{ cal}$$

Heat required by 10 g of ice at –20°C to become ice at 0°C,

$$Q_2 = ms\Delta T$$

$$= 10 \times 0.5 \times [0 - (-20)] = 100 \text{ cal}$$

Since $Q_1 = Q_2$, no ice will melt. The calorimeter will contain 10 g ice and 10 g of water.

33. Heat released by 125 g of water at 20°C to become water at 0°C,

$$Q_1 = ms\Delta T = 125 \times 1 \times (20 - 0) = 2500 \text{ cal}$$

For melting of ice,

$$Q = mL_f$$

$$\Rightarrow \quad 2500 = m(80)$$

$$\Rightarrow \quad m = 31 \text{ g}$$

Amount of ice remaining = 50 – 31 = 19g

34. Heat lost by calorimeter = $ms\Delta T$

$$= 60 \times 0.1 \times (38 - 5) = 198 \text{ cal}$$

Heat lost by water = $ms\Delta T$

$$= 400 \times 1 \times (38 - 5) = 13200 \text{ cal}$$

Heat consumed by ice = $mL_f + ms\Delta T$

$$= 158 \times L_f + 158 \times 1 \times (5 - 0)$$

$$\therefore 198 + 13200 = 158L_f + 158 \times 1 \times (5 - 0)$$

$$\Rightarrow \quad L_f = 79.8 \text{ cal/g}$$

35. Heat released by 30 g of water at 80°C to become water at 0°C,

$$Q_1 = ms\Delta T = 30 \times 1 \times (80 - 0) = 2400 \text{ cal}$$

Heat required by 50 g of ice at 0°C to become 50g of water at 0°C,

$$Q_2 = mL_f = 50 \times 80 = 4000 \text{ cal}$$

Since, $Q_1 < Q_2$, ice will not melt completely. It will be ice-water mixture at 0°C.

For melting of ice, $Q = mL_f$

$$\Rightarrow \quad 2400 = m(80)$$

$$\Rightarrow \quad m = 30 \text{ g}$$

Amount of ice left = 50 – 30 = 20 g

36. Heat released by 100 g of water at 100°C to become water at 0°C,

$$Q_1 = ms\Delta T = 100 \times 1 \times (100 - 0) = 10000 \text{ cal}$$

Heat required by 100 g of ice at 0°C to become water at 0°C,

$$Q_2 = mL_f = 100 \times 80 = 8000 \text{ cal}$$

Since $Q_1 > Q_2$, all ice will melt. We will have 200 g water at 0°C with 2000 cal of heat remaining.

$$Q = ms\Delta T$$

$$\Rightarrow \quad 2000 = 200 \times 1 \times (T - 0)$$

$$\Rightarrow \quad T = 10°\text{C}$$

So, finally we will have 200 g of water at 10°C.

The above situation is best represented by graph (c).

37. Heat released by 1 g steam at 100°C to become 1 g water at 100°C,

$$Q_1 = mL_v = 1 \times 540 = 540 \text{ cal}$$

Heat required by 1 g ice at 0°C to become 1 g water at 100°C,

$$Q_2 = mL_f + ms\Delta T$$

$$= 1 \times 80 + 1 \times 1 \times 100 = 180 \text{ cal}$$

Since $Q_2 < Q_1$, the entire steam will not condense. It will be steam-water mixture at 100°C.

38. Heat released by 5 g of steam at 100°C to become 5 g of water at 100°C,

$$Q_1 = mL_v = 5 \times 540 = 2700 \text{ cal}$$

Heat required by 6 g ice at 0°C to become 6 g of water 100°C,

$$Q_2 = mL_f + ms\Delta T$$

$$= 6 \times 80 + 6 \times 1 \times 100 = 1080 \text{ cal}$$

Since $Q_1 < Q_2$, the entire steam will not condense. It will be steam-water mixture at 100°C.

39. For condensation of steam,

$$Q = mL_v$$

$$\Rightarrow \quad 1080 = m(540)$$

$$\Rightarrow \quad m = 2 \text{ g}$$

Amount of water in the mixture = 6 + 2 = 8 g

40. Heat released by 50 g of steam 100°C to become 50 g of water at 0°C,

$$Q_1 = mL_v + ms\Delta T$$

$$= 50 \times 540 + 50 \times 1 \times (100 - 0)$$

$$= 32000 \text{ cal}$$

Heat required by 250 g of ice at 0°C to become 250 g of water at 0°C,

$$Q_2 = mL_f = 250 \times 80 = 20000 \text{ cal}$$

For 50 + 250 = 300 g of water at 0°C,

$$Q = ms\Delta T$$

$\Rightarrow$ $32000 - 20000 = 300 \times 1 \times (T - 0)$

$\Rightarrow$ $T = 40°C$

41. Let the amount of steam condensed be m g.

Heat lost = Heat gained

$m \times 540 + m \times 1 \times (100 - 90) = 22 \times 1 \times (90 - 20)$

$\Rightarrow$ $m = 2.8$ g

Mass of water = 22 + 2.8 = 24.8 g

42. Let the amount of steam condensed be m g.

Heat lost = Heat gained

$\Rightarrow$ $m \times 540 + m \times 1 \times (100 - 0) = 100 \times 80$

$\Rightarrow$ $m = 12.5$ g

Mass of water = 100 + 12.5 = 112.5 g

Numerical Value Questions

1. $Q = m \int C dT$

$= 2 \int_0^5 (0.2 + 0.16T + 0.024T^2)\, dT$

$= 2 \left[0.2T + \frac{0.16T^2}{2} + \frac{0.024T^3}{3} \right]_0^5$

= 8 cal

2. $L_f = 80$ kcal/kg $= 80 \times 4.2 \times 10^3$ J/kg

$mL_f = \frac{70}{100} mgh$

$\Rightarrow$ $L_f = \frac{70}{100} gh$

$\Rightarrow$ $80 \times 4.2 \times 10^3 = \frac{70}{100} \times 10 \times h$

$\Rightarrow h = 48 \times 10^3$ m = 48 km

3. Heat produced due to kinetic energy

$= \frac{1}{2} \times (50 \times 10^{-3}) \times (84)^2$

= 176.4 J

$= \frac{176.4}{4.2}$ cal = 42 cal

Heat given by bullet due to temperature fall

$= ms\Delta T$

$= 50 \times 0.02 \times (30 - 0) = 30$ cal

Total heat given by bullet = 42 + 30 = 72 cal

For melting of ice, $Q = mL_f$

$\Rightarrow$ $72 = m(80)$

$\Rightarrow$ $m = 0.9$ g = 900 mg

4. Heat added to system = 250 × 100 = 25000 cal

Heat required by 200 g of ice at –20°C to become 200 g of water at 0°C,

$Q = ms\Delta T + mL_f$

$= 200 \times 0.5 \times [0 - (-20)] + 200 \times 80$

= 18000 cal

Heat required by aluminium container to reach 0°C,

$Q = ms\Delta T$

$= 100 \times 0.2 \times [0 - (-20)] = 400$ cal

Remaining heat = 25000 – 18000 – 400 = 6600 cal

Let final temperature of the system be T.

$Q = m_1 s_1 \Delta T + m_2 s_2 \Delta T$

$\Rightarrow$ $6600 = 200 \times 1 \times (T - 0) + 100 \times 0.2 \times (T - 0)$

$\Rightarrow$ $T = 30°C$

5. Heat released by 140 g coffee at 80°C to become coffee at 0°C,

$Q_1 = ms\Delta T = 140 \times 1 \times (80 - 0) = 11200$ cal

Heat required by 20 g ice at 0°C to become 20 g water at 0°C,

$Q_2 = mL_f = 20 \times 80 = 1600$ cal

Since $Q_1 > Q_2$, the whole ice will melt.

For 140 + 20 = 160 g water at 0°C,

$Q = ms\Delta T$

$\Rightarrow$ $11200 - 1600 = 160 \times 1 \times (T - 0)$

$\Rightarrow$ $T = 60°C$

6. Heat required by 50 g of ice at 0°C to become 50 g of water at 0°C,

$Q = mL_f = 50 \times 80 = 4000$ cal

Remaining heat = 6000 – 4000 = 2000 cal

$Q = ms\Delta T$

$\Rightarrow$ $2000 = (50 + 250) \times 1 \times (T - 0)$

$\Rightarrow$ $T = 8°C$

7. Let the amount of steam condensed be m g.

$m \times 540 + m \times 1 \times (100 - 90)$

$= 100 \times 1 \times (90 - 24)$

$\Rightarrow$ $m = 12$ g

8. Let water equivalent of each calorimeter be m_w.

Heat lost by water = Heat gained by calorimeter

$\Rightarrow$ $m \times 1 \times (80 - 60) = m_w \times 1 \times (60 - 20)$

$\Rightarrow$ $m_w = \frac{m}{2}$

When water at 60°C is added to the second calorimeter

$m \times 1 \times (60 - T) = m_w \times 1 \times (T - 20)$

$\Rightarrow$ $m(60 - T) = \frac{m}{2}(T - 20)$

$\Rightarrow$ $T = \frac{140}{3}°C$

So, $n = 140$

9. $\frac{dQ_1}{dt} = \frac{dQ_2}{dt}$

$\Rightarrow$ $\frac{dm_1}{dt} s_1 \Delta T_1 = \frac{dm_2}{dt} s_2 \Delta T_2$

$\Rightarrow$ $1 \times s \times (90 - 50) = 2 \times 2s \times (T - 20)$

$\Rightarrow$ $T = 30°C$

10. Let the amount of ice melted by m g.

Change in volume $= \frac{m}{0.92} - \frac{m}{1}$

$\Rightarrow \quad 0.1 = \frac{m}{0.92} - \frac{m}{1} \Rightarrow m = 1.15$ g

Heat lost by metal = Heat consumed by ice

$\Rightarrow \quad 10 \times s \times (100 - 0) = 1.15 \times 80$

$\Rightarrow \quad s = 92 \times 10^{-3}$ cal/g °C

So, $n = 92$

11. Time for which vaporisation takes place

$= 2500 - 1600 = 900$ s

Heat supplied for vaporisation = Power × Time

$= 1 \times 10^3 \times 900 = 9 \times 10^5$ J

Latent heat of vaporisation $= \frac{Q}{m}$

$= \frac{9 \times 10^5}{0.2} = 4.5 \times 10^6$ J/kg

So, $n = 4.5$

12. Heat released by 50 g of steam at 100°C to become 50 g water at 0°C,

$Q_1 = mL_v + ms\Delta T = 50 \times 540 + 50 \times 1 \times (100 - 0)$

$= 32000$ cal

Heat consumed by 100 g of ice at 0°C to become 100 g of water at 0°C,

$Q_2 = mL_f = 100 \times 80 = 8000$ cal

Remaining heat $= 32000 - 8000 = 24000$ cal

$Q = ms\Delta T$

$\Rightarrow 24000 = (50 + 400 + 100 + 50) \times 1 \times (T - 0)$

$\Rightarrow \quad T = 40°$ C

Level-3

Single Choice Correct Questions

1. Let the radii of the spheres be $R, R + a, R + 2a$ and $R + 3a$, where a is a constant.

Let the specific heat capacities be s, sr, sr^2 and sr^3, where r is another constant.

$$\left(\frac{\text{Heat capacity of } D}{\text{Heat capacity of } B}\right) : \left(\frac{\text{Heat capacity of } C}{\text{Heat capacity of } A}\right) = 8:27$$

$$\Rightarrow \left(\frac{(R+3a)^3\, sr^3}{(R+a)^3\, sr}\right) : \left(\frac{(R+2a)^3\, sr^2}{R^3 s}\right) = 8:27$$

$$\Rightarrow \frac{R+3a}{R+a} : \frac{R+2a}{R} = 2:3$$

$$\Rightarrow \quad R = a$$

$$\frac{m_B}{m_A} = \frac{\rho \frac{4}{3}\pi (R+a)^3}{\rho \frac{4}{3}\pi R^3} = \frac{8}{1}$$

2. Rotational kinetic energy $= \frac{1}{2} I\omega^2$

$$= \frac{1}{2}\left(\frac{2}{3}MR^2\right)\omega^2 = \frac{1}{3}MR^2\omega^2$$

$$Q = ms\Delta T$$

$$\Rightarrow \frac{75}{100}\left(\frac{1}{3}MR^2\omega^2\right) = Ms\Delta T$$

$$\Rightarrow \quad \Delta T = \frac{R^2\omega^2}{4S}$$

3. Part of heat given to II is used up in doing work against gravitational force. So, temperature of I will be slightly higher.

4. Let power lost to the surroundings be P.

Net power $= \frac{dm}{dt} s\Delta T$

In first case,

$$60 - P = \frac{dm}{dt} s(10) \quad \text{...(i)}$$

In second case,

$$120 - P = \left(3\frac{dm}{dt}\right) s(10) \quad \text{...(ii)}$$

From Eqs. (i) and (ii), we get

$P = 30$ W

5. Gravitational potential energy is converted into thermal energy which is absorbed by the lead shot.

$ms\Delta T = 100mgh$

$$\Rightarrow \quad \Delta T = \frac{100gh}{S} = \frac{100 \times 9.8 \times 1.5}{0.03 \times 4200} = 11.7°\text{C}$$

6. $T = \frac{T_1 + T_2}{2}$

Heat lost = Heat gained

$$\Rightarrow \quad m_1 s_1\left(T_1 - \frac{T_1 + T_2}{2}\right) = m_2 s_2\left(\frac{T_1 + T_2}{2} - T_2\right)$$

$$\Rightarrow \quad \frac{m_1}{m_2} = \frac{s_2}{s_1}$$

7. No net energy exchange as the temperature difference is zero.

8. Let the amount of ice melted $= m$ g

Volume of m g of ice $= \frac{m}{0.9}$

Volume of m g of water $= \frac{m}{1}$

Decrease in volume $= \frac{m}{0.9} - \frac{m}{1} = 1$

$\Rightarrow \quad m = 9$ g

$Q = mL_f = 9 \times 80 = 720$ cal

9. Heat released by pitcher and water $= ms\Delta T$

$= (0.5 + 9.5)(1)(30 - 28)$

$= 20$ kcal

Heat observed for evaporation per minute $= mL_v$

$= 1 \times 580 = 580$ cal

Time taken $= \dfrac{20 \times 10^3}{580} = 34.5$ min

10. Heat supplied = Power × Time

$P \times (5\text{ min}) = m \times 4.2 \times (100 - 0)$ ...(i)

$P \times (28\text{ min}) = mL_v$ ...(ii)

From Eqs. (i) and (ii), we get

$L_v = 2352$ J/g

11. Heat released by B in going from temperature T_B to T_A,

$Q_1 = C_B(T_B - T_A)$

Heat absorbed by A for melting,

$Q_2 = ML$

Remaining heat $= Q_1 - Q_2 = C_B(T_B - T_A) - ML$

Let final temperature of $(A + B)$ system be T.

$Q = C_A \Delta T_A + C_B \Delta T_B$

$\Rightarrow C_B(T_B - T_A) - ML = C_A(T - T_A) + C_B(T - T_A)$

$\Rightarrow \quad T = \dfrac{C_A T_A + C_B T_B - ML}{C_A + C_B}$

12. Let the amount of steam condensed $= m$

Heat lost by steam = Heat gained by calorimeter and water

$\Rightarrow m \times 540 + m \times 1 \times (100 - 80) = (1.1 + 0.02) \times 1 \times (80 - 15)$

$\Rightarrow \quad m = 0.130$ kg

13. As the system is thermally isolated, the heat required for vaporisation is extracted from the water itself. Since the water in the vessel is at 0°C, this results in part of the water getting frozen.

Let x be the maximum fraction of water that solidifies and $(1 - x)$ is the fraction that gets vaporized.

At 0°C, $\quad m_i L_f = m_S L_v$

$\Rightarrow \quad x \times 3.36 \times 10^5 = (1 - x) \times 21 \times 10^5$

$\Rightarrow \quad x = 0.862$ or 86.2%

14. Let water equivalent of flask $= W$

Heat consumed by ice = Heat released by water and flask

$50L_f + 50 \times 1 \times (40 - 0)$

$= (200 + W) \times 1 \times (70 - 40)$ ...(i)

When further 80 g of ice is added,

$80L_f + 80 \times 1 \times (10 - 0)$

$= (200 + 50 + W) \times 1 \times (40 - 10)$ ...(ii)

Solving Eqs. (i) and (ii), we get

$L_f = 90$ cal/g

15. Mass of drink = Density × Volume

$= 0.833 \times 120 = 100$ g

∴ Mass of water = Mass of alcohol = 50 g

Heat released by the drink in cooling from 25°C to 0°C,

$Q_1 = 50 \times 1 \times (25 - 0) + 50 \times 0.6 \times (25 - 0) = 2000$ cal

Heat required by ice for melting,

$Q_2 = 20 \times 80 = 1600$ cal

Remaining heat $= 2000 - 1600 = 400$ cal

Let final temperature of the system be T.

$Q = m_w s_w \Delta T + m_{Al} s_{Al} \Delta T$

$\Rightarrow \quad 400 = (50 + 20) \times 1 \times (T - 0) + 50 \times 0.6 \times (T - 0)$

$\Rightarrow \quad T = 4°\text{C}$

16. Let volume of metal ball $= V$

As half of the ball sinks in the ice, volume of ice melted will be $\dfrac{V}{2}$.

Heat released by ball = Heat required for melting ice

$\Rightarrow \quad (4.5 \times V) \times 0.1 \times (T - 0) = \left(0.9 \times \dfrac{V}{2}\right) \times 80$

$\Rightarrow \quad T = 80°\text{C}$

17. Heat released by steam = Heat consumed by water

$\Rightarrow m \times 0.5 \times (200 - 100) + m \times 540 + m \times 1 \times (100 - 90)$

$= 10 \times 1 \times 60$

$\Rightarrow \quad m = 1$ kg

18. Let heat be supplied at constant rate $= P$

$Q = P\Delta T = mL$

$\Rightarrow \quad L \propto \Delta t$

$\Rightarrow L \propto$ length of horizontal line

$\therefore \quad L_2 > L_1$

In solid state, $P = mC\dfrac{dT}{dt}$

$\Rightarrow \quad C \propto \dfrac{1}{\left(\dfrac{dT}{dt}\right)} \Rightarrow C \propto \dfrac{1}{\text{Slope}}$

$(\text{Slope})_1 > (\text{Slope})_2 \Rightarrow C_1 < C_2$

19. Let heat be supplied at constant rate $= P$

For first 50 min

$P \times (50\text{ min}) = m_{ice} \times 80$ ...(i)

From 50 min to 60 min,

$P \times (10\text{ min}) = (5 + m_{ice}) \times 1 \times (2 - 0)$ ...(ii)

From Eqs. (i) and (ii), we get

$5 = \dfrac{40m_{ice}}{5 + m_{ice}}$

$\Rightarrow \quad m_{ice} = \dfrac{5}{7}$ kg

20. Evidently the initial temperature of the water in the vessel (M g) is 80°C. The temperature of the water passed into it is 60°C as the final temperature of the mixture tends to attain a value of 60°C.

For the first 10 seconds duration,

Heat lost by hot body = Heat gained by cold body

$\Rightarrow \quad M \times 1 \times (80 - 70) = (m \times 10) \times 1 \times (70 - 60)$

$\Rightarrow \quad \dfrac{M}{m} = 10$

Since the heat exchanged after a long time is 800 cal.

Heat lost by M g = 800 cal

$\Rightarrow \quad M \times 1 \times (80-60) = 800$

$\Rightarrow \quad M = 40$ g

$\therefore \quad m = \frac{40}{10} = 4$ g

21. $dQ = Cd\theta \quad \Rightarrow \quad C \propto \frac{dQ}{d\theta}$

$\Rightarrow \quad C \propto \frac{1}{\text{Slope}}$

$\therefore \quad C_A = \frac{1}{\tan 60°} = \frac{1}{\sqrt{3}}$

and $\quad C_B = \frac{1}{\tan 30°} = \sqrt{3}$

Heat lost by A = Heat gained by B

$\Rightarrow \quad C_A(30-T) = C_B(T-20)$

$\Rightarrow \quad \frac{1}{\sqrt{2}}(30-T) = \sqrt{3}(T-20)$

$\Rightarrow \quad T = 22.5°$ C

22. Heat released by water in cooling to 0°C,

$Q_1 = 400 \times 1 \times (5-0) + 200 \times 1 \times (10-0) = 4000$ cal

Heat required by 400 g ice at -60°C to become 400 g ice at 0°C,

$Q_2 = 400 \times 0.5 \times [0-(-60)] = 12000$ cal

Since $Q_1 < Q_2$, water will not start freezing

$Q = mL_f$

$\Rightarrow \quad 12000 - 4000 = m(80)$

$\Rightarrow \quad m = 100$ g

$\therefore$ Final amount of ice = 400 + 100 = 500 g

23. Heat released by 10 g steam at 100°C to become 10 g water at 0°C,

$Q_1 = 10 \times 540 + 10 \times 1 \times (100-0) = 6400$ cal

Heat released by 300 g water at 20°C to become 300 g water at 0°C,

$Q_2 = 300 \times 1 \times (20-0) = 6000$ cal

Heat required by 40 g ice at –20°C to become 40 g water at 0°C,

$Q_3 = 40 \times 0.5 \times [0-(-20)] + 40 \times 80 = 3600$ cal

Remaining heat $= Q_1 + Q_2 - Q_3$

$= 6400 + 6000 - 3600 = 8800$ cal

Let final temperature of (10 + 300 + 40 = 350 g) of water = T

$Q = ms\Delta T$

$\Rightarrow \quad 8800 = 350 \times 1 \times (T-0)$

$\Rightarrow \quad T = 25.14°$ C

24. $\frac{dQ}{dt} = mC\frac{dT}{dt}$

$\Rightarrow \quad R = (m_0 - \lambda t)C\frac{dT}{dt}$

$\Rightarrow \quad \int_{T_0}^{T} dT = \frac{R}{C}\int_0^t \frac{dt}{m_0 - \lambda t}$

$\Rightarrow \quad T - T_0 = \frac{R}{C(-\lambda)}[\ln(m_0 - \lambda t)]_0^t$

$\Rightarrow \quad T - T_0 = -\frac{R}{\lambda C}\ln\left(\frac{m_0 - \lambda t}{m_0}\right)$

$\Rightarrow \quad T = T_0 + \frac{R}{\lambda C}\ln\left(\frac{m_0}{m_0 - \lambda t}\right)$

Multiple Choice(s) Correct Questions

1. (a, c)

2. (a) $\quad ms = m_w s_w$

$\Rightarrow m(0.09) = 4.5 \times 1$

$\Rightarrow \quad m = 50$ g = 0.05 kg

(b) Thermal capacity $= m_w s_w$

$= 4.5 \times 1 = 4.5$ cal/°C

(c) $Q = C\Delta T = 4.5 \times 8 = 36$ cal

(d) $Q = mL_f = 15 \times 80 = 1200$ cal

3. When ice melts into water, volume decreases. So, positive work is done by the atmosphere.

(c) $\Delta U = \Delta Q + \Delta W_{\text{by atmosphere}}$

During melting, heat is supplied.

$\therefore \quad \Delta Q > 0$

$\Rightarrow \quad \Delta U > 0 \quad [\because \Delta W > 0]$

So, the internal energy of the ice-water system increases.

4. Heat released by m g of water at 10°C to become m g of water at 0°C,

$Q_1 = m \times 1 \times (10-0)$

Heat required by m g of ice at 0°C to become m g of water at 0°C,

$Q_2 = m \times 80$

As $Q_1 < Q_2$, the whole of ice will not melt and it will be ice-water mixture at 0°C.

5. During melting, heat is supplied and temperature of solid doesn't change.

(b) During freezing, heat is taken out and temperature of solid doesn't change.

6. Heat released by 5 kg of steam at 100°C to become 5 kg of water at 100°C,

$Q_1 = 5 \times 540 = 2700$ kcal

Heat required by 10 kg of ice at 0°C to become 10 kg of water at 100°C,

$Q_2 = 10 \times 80 + 10 \times 1 \times (100-0) = 1800$ kcal

As $Q_2 < Q_1$, the whole steam will not condense and it will be water-steam mixture at 100°C.

For condensation of steam,

$Q = mL_v$

$\Rightarrow \quad 1800 = m(540)$

$$\Rightarrow \quad m = \frac{10}{3}\text{ kg}$$

$$\text{Amount of water} = 10 + \frac{10}{3} = 13\frac{1}{3}\text{ kg}$$

$$\text{Amount of steam} = 5 - \frac{10}{3} = 1\frac{2}{3}\text{ kg}$$

7.

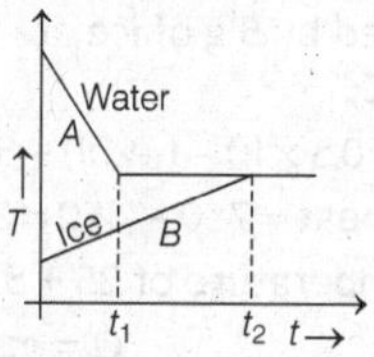

At $t = t_1$, water in sample A drops to freezing point of water and ice in sample B is still at temperature below freezing point of water.

From $t = t_1$ to $t = t_2$, water in sample A starts freezing and heat released by this increases temperature of ice in B to the freezing point of water.

8. (a) If $n = 1$,

$$Q_1 = ms_w(15 - 0) = ms_w(15)$$

$$Q_2 = ms_{ice}(0 - (-15)) = m\left(\frac{s_w}{2}\right)15$$

As $Q_1 > Q_2$, heat released by water will melt some ice.

(d) If $n = 2$,

$$Q_1 = ms_w(15 - 0) = ms_w(15)$$

$$Q_2 = 2ms_{ice}(0 - (-15))$$

$$= 2m\left(\frac{s_w}{2}\right)(15) = ms_w(15)$$

As $Q_1 = Q_2$, heat released by water is just enough to take ice to 0°C. No ice will melt.

Final temperature is 0°C.

Comprehension Based Questions

1. $$\frac{\text{Melting point of body I}}{\text{Melting point of body II}} = \frac{40}{80} = \frac{1}{2}$$

2. Specific heat $\propto \dfrac{1}{\text{Slope}}$

$$\frac{\text{Specific heat of body I}}{\text{Specific heat of body II}} = \frac{(\text{Slope})_{II}}{(\text{Slope})_{I}}$$

$$= \frac{80/5}{40/10} = \frac{4}{1}$$

3. Let heat be supplied at constant rate $= P$

$$Q = P \times \Delta t = mL \quad \Rightarrow \quad L \propto \Delta t$$

$\Rightarrow L \propto$ length of horizontal line

$$\therefore \quad \frac{L_I}{L_{II}} = \frac{20 - 10}{15 - 5} = 1$$

4. $$\frac{dQ}{dt} = (C + ms)\frac{dT}{dt}$$

For water, $$\frac{dQ}{dt} = (300 + 0.5 \times 4200)\left(\frac{80 - 0}{10 - 0}\right) \quad \text{...(i)}$$

For alcohol,

$$\frac{dQ}{dt} = (300 + 0.7 \times s)\left(\frac{50 - 0}{15 - 0}\right) \quad \text{...(ii)}$$

Solving Eqs. (i) and (ii), we get

$$s = 7800 \text{ J/kg-°C}$$

5. $$\frac{dQ}{dt} = (300 + 0.5 \times 4200)8 = 19200 \text{ J/min}$$

Time taken by half of the alcohol to vapourise

$$= 22 - 15 = 7\text{ min}$$

For vaporisation,

$$Q = mL_v$$

$$\Rightarrow \quad 19200 \times 7 = \left(\frac{0.7}{2}\right)L_v$$

$$\Rightarrow \quad L_v = 3.84 \times 10^5 \text{ J/kg}$$

6. Heat released by calorimeter and water when water becomes ice,

$$Q_1 = mC_1(t_2 - 0) + mC_2(t_2 - 0) + mL$$

Heat absorbed by ice at temperature t_3 to reach temperature 0°C,

$$Q_2 = mC_3(0 - t_3)$$

For the whole mixture in calorimeter to become ice,

$$Q_1 < Q_2$$

$$\Rightarrow \quad mC_1t_2 + mC_2t_2 + mL < -mC_3t_3$$

$$\Rightarrow \quad C_1t_2 + C_2t_2 + L + C_3t_3 < 0$$

7. Heat released by calorimeter and water in reaching 0°C,

$$Q_1 = mC_1(t_2 - 0) + mC_2(t_2 - 0)$$

Heat absorbed by ice at temperature t_3 to become water at 0°C,

$$Q_2 = mC_3(0 - t_3) + mL$$

For the whole mixture to become water

$$Q_1 > Q_2$$

$$\Rightarrow \quad mC_1t_2 + mC_2t_2 > -mC_3t_3 + mL$$

$$\Rightarrow \quad (C_1 + C_2)t_2 + C_3t_3 - L > 0$$

8. $$mC_1 = m_wC_2 \quad \Rightarrow \quad m_w = \frac{mC_1}{C_2}$$

9. Heat supplied for melting

$$= 106 \times 10^3 - 6 \times 10^3 = 100 \times 10^3 \text{ cal}$$

$$L_f = \frac{Q}{m} = \frac{100 \times 10^3}{10^3} = 100 \text{ cal/g}$$

10. $$\text{Time taken} = \frac{\text{Heat supplied}}{\text{Heating rate}}$$

When temperature increases from −20°C to 10°C,

$$t_1 = \frac{\left(\frac{106 + 130}{2} - 6\right) \times 10^3}{\left(\frac{dQ}{dt}\right)} = \frac{112 \times 10^3}{\left(\frac{dQ}{dt}\right)}$$

When temperature increases from 10°C to 40°C

$$t_2 = \frac{\left(\frac{330+346}{2} - \frac{106+130}{2}\right)\times 10^3}{\left(\frac{dQ}{dt}\right)} = \frac{220\times 10^3}{\left(\frac{dQ}{dt}\right)}$$

$\therefore \quad t_1 < t_2$

11. $\Delta Q = ms\Delta T \Rightarrow s = \frac{\Delta Q}{\Delta t}$

$$s_{solid} = \frac{6-0}{-10-(-20)} = 0.6$$

$$s_{liquid} = \frac{130-106}{20-(-10)} = 0.8$$

$$s_{gas} = \frac{346-330}{60-20} = 0.4$$

$\therefore s_{liquid} > s_{solid} > s_{gas}$

12. Heat required by 200 g ice at 0°C to become 200 g water at 100°C,

$$Q_1 = 200\times 80 + 200\times 1\times(100-0) = 36000 \text{ cal}$$

Heat required by 200 g water at 55°C to become 200 g water at 100°C,

$$Q_2 = 200\times 1\times(100-55) = 9000 \text{ cal}$$

Heat released by 100 g steam at 100°C to become 100 g water at 100°C,

$$Q_3 = 100\times 540 = 54000 \text{ cal}$$

As total heat required is less than the total heat released, the entire steam will not condense. It will be steam-water mixture at 100°C.

13. For condensation of steam,

$$Q = mL_v$$

$\Rightarrow 36000 + 9000 = m(540)$

$\Rightarrow \quad m = 83.3 \text{ g}$

Total mass of water $= 200 + 200 + 83.3 = 483.3$ g

14. Amount of steam left $= 100 - 83.3 = 16.7$ g

15. Heat released by water in first 40 min,

$$Q = ms\Delta T = 0.6\times 4200\times(40-0)$$

$$P = \frac{Q}{t} = \frac{0.6\times 4200\times 40}{40\times 60} = 42.0 \text{ W}$$

16. Ice goes from −30°C to 0°C in 60 min

$$Q = ms\Delta T$$

$\Rightarrow 42\times 60\times 60 = m\times 2100\times(0-(-30))$

$\Rightarrow \quad m = 2.4 \text{ kg}$

17. Water freezes from 40 min to 60 min interval

$$Q = mL_f$$

$\Rightarrow 42\times 20\times 60 = m\times 3.3\times 10^5$

$\Rightarrow \quad m = 0.15 \text{ kg}$

Match the Columns Questions

1. (A) $Q_1 = ms\Delta T = 1\times 0.53\times[0-(-20)] = 10.6$ cal

(B) $Q_2 = mL_f = 1\times 80 = 80$ cal

(C) $Q_3 = ms\Delta T = 1\times 1\times(100-0) = 100$ cal

(D) $Q_4 = mL_v = 1\times 539 = 539$ cal

2. A-Q, B-P, R, C-S

3. (p) Heat released by 25 g of water at 30°C to become 25 g of water at 0°C,

$$Q_1 = 25\times 1\times(30-0) = 750 \text{ cal}$$

Heat required by 5 g of ice at −20°C to become 5 g of water at 0°C,

$$Q_2 = 5\times 0.5\times(0-(-20)) + 5\times 80 = 450 \text{ cal}$$

Remaining heat $= 750 - 450 = 300$ cal

Let final temperature of 25 + 5 = 30 g of water be T.

$$Q = ms\Delta T$$

$\Rightarrow \quad 300 = 30\times 1\times(T-0)$

$\Rightarrow \quad T = 10°\text{C}$

(q) $Q_1 = 18\times 1\times(25-0) = 450$ cal

$Q_2 = 450$ cal

As $Q_1 = Q_2$, heat released by water is just enough to melt all the ice. The final mixture contains water only at 0°C.

(r) $Q_1 = 10\times 1\times(25-0) = 250$ cal

$Q_2 = 450$ cal

As $Q_1 < Q_2$, all ice will not melt. It will ice-water mixture at 0°C.

(s) Heat released by 5 g of water at 20°C to become 5 g of water at 0°C,

$$Q_1 = 5\times 1\times(20-0) = 100 \text{ cal}$$

Heat required by 50 g of ice at −20°C to become 50 g of ice at 0°C,

$$Q_2 = 50\times 0.5\times[0-(-20)] = 500 \text{ cal}$$

As $Q_1 < Q_2$, water will now start freezing.

$$Q = mL_f \Rightarrow 500 - 100 = m(80)$$

$\Rightarrow \quad m = 5$ g

So, all water will freeze into ice and temperature of mixture will be 0°C.

(t) Heat lost = Heat gained

$\Rightarrow 2.5\times 1\times(30-T) = 5\times 1\times(T-0)$

$\Rightarrow \quad T = 10°\text{C}$

4. Rate of heat loss $= \frac{dm}{dt}L_f = 10.8\times 80 = 864$ cal/s

(A) Rate of heat supplied by converting steam to water at 0°C

$$= \frac{dm}{dt}L_v + \frac{dm}{dt}s\Delta T$$

$$= 1.6\times 540 + 1.6\times 1\times(100-0)$$

$$= 1024 \text{ cal/s}$$

$\therefore$ Additional ice will melt.

(B) Rate of heat supplied by converting steam to water at 0°C

$$= 1.35\times 540 + 1.35\times 1\times(100-0) = 864 \text{ cal/s}$$

$\therefore$ No additional ice will melt or water will fuse.

(C) Rate of heat supplied by converting steam of ice at 0°C

$= 1.2 \times 540 + 1.2 \times 1 \times (100 - 0) + 1.2 \times 80$

= 864 cal/s

∴ No additional ice will melt or water will fuse.

(D) Additional water will fuse.

Numerical Value Questions

1. $90° - T = T - 60° \Rightarrow T = 75°$

Heat lost by lead sphere

$= 0.6 \times 127 \times (90 - 75) = 1143$ J

Heat gained by steel sphere

$= 0.1 \times 454 \times (75 - 60) = 681$ J

Heat gained by water $= m_w \times 4200 \times (75 - 74)$

From energy conservation,

$$1143 = 681 + m_w \times 4200 \times 1$$

$\Rightarrow m_w = 0.11$ kg = 110 g

2. Heat required by 620 g ice at –10°C to become 620 g water at 20°C,

$$Q_1 = 620 \times 0.5 \times [0 - (-10)] + 620 \times 80 + 620 \times 1 \times (20 - 0)$$

= 65100 cal

Heat released by *m* g of steam at 100°C to become *m* g of water at 20°C,

$$Q_2 = m \times 540 + m \times 1 \times (100 - 20) = 620\ m$$

$Q_1 = Q_2 \Rightarrow 65100 = 620$ m

$\Rightarrow m = 105$ g

3. Heat released by cylinder in dropping to 0°C will go into melting ice.

$$\rho_A s_A (50 - 0) = (\rho_{ice} A h_A) L_f \quad ...(i)$$

$$\rho_B s_B (50 - 0) = (\rho_{ice} A h_B) L_f \quad ...(ii)$$

From Eqs. (i) and (ii), we get

$$\frac{h_A}{h_B} = \frac{\rho_A s_A}{\rho_B s_B} = \frac{4 \times 0.2}{2 \times 0.1} = 4$$

4. Let the amount of ice melted by *x* g.

For the block to just sink,

$$B = mg$$

$$\Rightarrow 1 \times \left(\frac{120 - x}{0.9} + \frac{2}{12}\right) g = (120 - x + 2)\ g$$

$\Rightarrow x = 103.5$ g

Heat required $= mL_f = 103.5 \times 80 = 8280$ cal

5. Heat released by 15 kg of water at 80°C to become 15 kg of water at 20°C,

$$Q_1 = ms\Delta T$$

$$= 15 \times 1 \times (80 - 20) = 900 \text{ kcal}$$

Heat required by *m* kg of ice at 0°C to become *m* kg of water at 20°C,

$$Q_2 = mL_f + ms\Delta T$$

$$= m \times 80 + m \times 1 \times (20 - 0)$$

$$= m \times 100$$

From energy conservation,

$$Q_1 = Q_2$$

$\Rightarrow m \times 100 = 900$

$\Rightarrow m = 9$ kg

So, 9 kg of ice will form 9 kg of water or 9 L of water.

Minimum volume of vessel = 15 + 9 = 24 L

6. For the sphere to just pass through the ring,

$$d_{ring} = d_{sphere}$$

$$\Rightarrow 25[1 + 6.96 \times 10^6 (T - 0)]$$

$$= 25.04[1 - 2.5 \times 10^{-5}(100 - T)]$$

$\Rightarrow T = 50°$ C

Heat lost by sphere = Heat gained by ring

$$\Rightarrow m_{sphere} \times 0.230 \times (100 - 50)$$

$$= m_{ring} \times 0.092 \times (50 - 0)$$

$$\Rightarrow \frac{m_{sphere}}{m_{ring}} = 0.4$$

$$\therefore \frac{10 m_{sphere}}{m_{ring}} = 4$$

7. Heat lost by calorimeter $= ms\Delta T$

$= 18 \times 1 \times (30 - 10) = 360$ cal

Heat lost by liquid $= m \int s d\theta$

$$= 100 \int_{10}^{30} \frac{1}{2}\left(1 + \frac{\theta}{500}\right) d\theta$$

$$= 50 \left[\theta + \frac{\theta^2}{1000}\right]_{10}^{30} = 1040 \text{ cal}$$

Heat required by *m* g of ice at –10°C to become *m* g of water at 10°C,

$$Q = m \times 0.5 \times [0 - (-20)] + m \times 80 + m \times 1 \times (10 - 0)$$

= 100 m

From energy conservation,

$$100m = 1040 + 360$$

$\Rightarrow m = 14$ g

8. $\dfrac{dQ}{dt} = \dfrac{dm}{dt} L_f$

$$\Rightarrow H = \left(\frac{50 - 0}{10 - 0}\right) 80 = 400 \text{ cal/s}$$

If the water is sprayed at a rate 2 g/s,

$$Q = mL_f = (50 + 2t_1) 80$$

$$\text{Time taken} = \frac{\text{Heat extracted}}{\text{Heat extraction rate}}$$

$$\Rightarrow t_1 = \frac{(50 + 2t_1) 80}{400}$$

$$\Rightarrow t_1 = \frac{50}{3} \text{ s}$$

$$\therefore 6t_1 = 6\left(\frac{50}{3}\right) = 100$$

9. Let mass of water in snow = m kg
Rate of heat extraction = R
Time interval between successive records = t
Upto 10th record,
$$Q = mL_f + ms_{ice}\Delta T$$
$$\Rightarrow R \times 10t = m \times 3.35 \times 10^5 + 6.7 \times 2.1 \times 10^3 \times [0-(-0.5)] \quad ...(i)$$
Between 10th and 11th record,
$$\Rightarrow R \times t = 6.7 \times 2.1 \times 10^3 \times [-0.5-(-4)] \quad ...(ii)$$
From Eqs. (i) and (ii), we get
$$m = 1.45 \text{ kg}$$

10. Heat lost by upper layer = Heat gained by lower layer
$$\Rightarrow 2m \times 1 \times (60-T) = m \times 1 \times (T-30)$$
$$\Rightarrow T = 50°\text{C}$$
$$\Delta V = V_1\gamma_1\Delta T + V_2\gamma_2\Delta T$$
$$= V\gamma(50-30) + 2V\gamma(50-60) = 0$$
$$\therefore \frac{V_{final}}{V_{initial}} = 1$$

Previous Year's Questions

JEE Main

1.

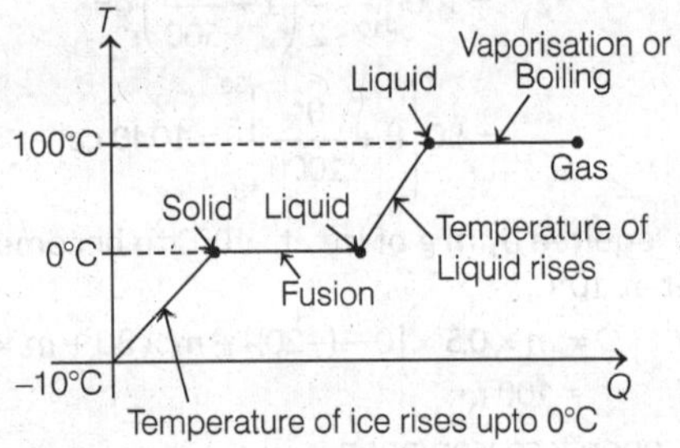

2.

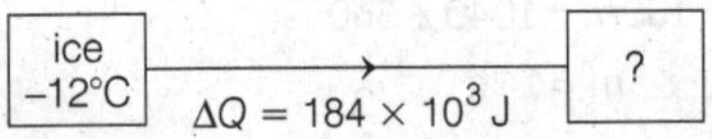

First ice absorbs heat and it's temperature rises to 0°C.
Now using, $\Delta Q = mc\Delta T$
We have,
$$\Delta Q = (600 \times 10^{-3})(2222.3)(12)$$
$$= 16000.56 \text{ J} \approx 16 \text{ kJ}$$
Now, ice at 0°C starts melting. Let m kg of ice melts due to remaining heat.
Heat available = 184 − 16 = 168 kJ.
Now using,
$$\Delta Q = mL, \text{ we have}$$
$$168 = m(336)$$
$$\Rightarrow m = 0.5 \text{ kg} = 500 \text{ g}$$
As out of 600 g of ice, 500 g is converted into water, final mixture contains 100 g ice and 500 g water.

3. Given,
$$m_{ice} = 120 \text{ g} = 0.12 \text{ kg},$$
$$T_{ice} = 0°\text{C}$$
$$m_{water} = 300 \text{ g} = 0.3 \text{ kg},$$
$$T_w = 25°\text{C}$$
$$c_w = 4200 \text{ J/kg/K},$$
$$L_{ice} = 3.5 \times 10^5 \text{ J/kg}$$
Heat lost by water
$$H_1 = m_{water} \times c_w \times \Delta T = 0.3 \times 4200 \times (25-0),$$
$$H_1 = 31500 \text{ J}$$
Heat gain by x gram ice $H_2 = \frac{x \times L}{1000}$
$$= \frac{x}{1000} \times 3.5 \times 10^5 = 350x$$
According to calorimetry law, $31500 = 350x$
$\therefore$ Total heat gained by body, $x = 90$

4. According to the question,
$$\frac{\Delta Q}{\Delta t} = \frac{m}{\Delta t} \cdot s\Delta T = m' \times \text{Heat of combustion}$$
$$\frac{2}{60} \times 4.2 \times 10^3 \times (70-30) = m' \times 8 \times 10^3 \times 10^3$$
$$m' = \frac{2 \times 4.2 \times 10^3 \times 40}{60 \times 8 \times 10^3 \times 10^3} \text{ kg/s}$$
$$m' = \frac{2 \times 4.2 \times 10^3 \times 40 \times 10^3 \times 60}{60 \times 8 \times 10^3 \times 10^3} \text{ g/min; } m' = 42 \text{ g/min}$$

5. Mass of iron ball,
$$m_1 = 100 \text{ g} = 0.1 \text{ kg}$$
Mass of hammer, $m_2 = 1.5$ kg
$$v = 60 \text{ m/s}, s = 0.42 \text{Jg}^{-1}\,°\text{C}^{-1}$$
$$= 420 \text{ J kg}^{-1}\,°\text{C}^{-1}$$
According to question,
$$\frac{\text{Total kinetic energy of hammer}}{4} = \text{Heat energy gain by nail}$$
$$\Rightarrow \frac{1}{4}\left[\frac{1}{2}m_2v^2\right] = m_1 s\Delta T$$
$$\Rightarrow \frac{1}{4}\left[\frac{1}{2} \times 1.5 \times 60^2\right] = 0.1 \times 420 \times \Delta T$$
$$\Rightarrow \Delta T = \frac{675}{42} = 16.07\,°\text{C}$$

6. Given, $m = 5$ kg
$$T_1 = 500°\text{C and}$$
$$T_2 = 0°\text{C (Placed in the ice block)}$$
$$Sc_u = 0.39 \text{ Jg}^{-1}\,°\text{C}^{-1} = 0.39 \times 10^3 \text{ Jkg}^{-1}\,°\text{C}^{-1}$$
$\therefore$ Heat given by the block,
$$\Delta Q = ms\Delta T$$
$$= 5 \times 0.39 \times 10^3 \times (500-0)$$
$$= 9.75 \times 10^5 \text{ J}$$
Heat taken by ice to melt m kg of ice

$$Q_2 = mL_f$$
$$Q_2 = m \times 335 \times 10^3$$
$$[\because L_f = 335 \text{ Jg}^{-1} = 335 \times 10^3 \text{Jkg}^{-1}]$$

Hence, according to principle of calorimetry,

$$Q_2 = Q_1$$
$$m \times 335 \times 10^3 = 9.75 \times 10^5$$
$$m = \frac{9.75 \times 10^5}{335 \times 10^3} = 2.91 \text{ kg} \simeq 2.9 \text{ kg}$$

7. Let the mass fo the bullet be m.

Heat needed to increace the temperature of the bullet from 127° C to 327° C, $Q_1 = ms\Delta T$

$$= m \times 125 \text{ J/kg K} \times (600 - 400) \text{ K}$$
$$= m \times 2.5 \times 10^4 \text{ Jkg}^{-1}$$

Heat needed to melt the bullet,

$$Q_2 = mL = m \times 2.5 \times 10^4 \text{ Jkg}^{-1}$$

The net heat needed to melt the bullet,

$$Q = Q_1 + Q_2 = m \times (2.5 + 2.5) \times 10^4 \text{ Jkg}^{-1}$$

Let v be the initial speed of the bullet, then 40% of its kinetic energy will be equal to the heat Q.

$$\therefore \frac{2}{5} \times \frac{1}{2} mv^2 = m \times 5 \times 10^4$$

or $\quad v^2 = 25 \times 10^4$

or $\quad v = 500 \text{ ms}^{-1}$

8. Given, $H = 63$ m

$$g = 9.8 \text{ ms}^{-2}$$

Specific heat of water,

$$s = 1 \text{ cal g}^{-1} \text{ C}^{-1} = 4.2 \times 10^3 \text{ J kg}^{-1} \text{ C}^{-1}$$

Since, energy, $E = mgH = ms\Delta T$

$$\therefore \quad \Delta T = \frac{gH}{s} = \frac{9.8 \times 63}{4.2 \times 10^3} = 0.147° \text{C}$$

9. Given, i.e. $m_x = m_y = m_z = m$

Temperature of mixture of liquids x and y, $T_1 = 16°$ C

Temperature of mixture of liquids y and z, $T_2 = 26°$ C

While mixing the liquids x and y

Thus,

Heat gained by liquid x = Heat lost by liquid y

$$ms_x (T_1 - 10) = ms_y (20 - T_1)$$
$$\Rightarrow \quad s_x (16 - 10) = s_y (20 - 16)$$
$$\Rightarrow \quad \frac{s_x}{s_y} = \frac{2}{3} \quad \text{...(i)}$$

Similarly, for liquid y and z,

$\therefore$ Heat gained by liquid y = Heat lost by liquid z

$$ms_y (T_2 - 20) = ms_z (30 - T_2)$$
$$\Rightarrow \quad s_y (26 - 20) = s_z (30 - 26)$$
$$\Rightarrow \quad \frac{s_y}{s_z} = \frac{2}{3} \quad \text{...(ii)}$$

Multiply Eq. (i) by Eq. (ii), we get

$$\frac{s_x}{s_z} = \frac{4}{9}$$

Consider the mixing of liquids x and z, let the temperature of mixture be T_3.

$\therefore$ Heat gained by liquid x = Heat lost by liquid z

$$ms_x (T_3 - 10) = ms_z (30 - T_3)$$
$$\Rightarrow \quad s_x (T_3 - 10) = s_z (30 - T_3)$$
$$\Rightarrow \quad \frac{s_x}{s_z} = \frac{30 - T_3}{T_3 - 10}$$
$$\Rightarrow \quad \frac{4}{9} = \frac{30 - T_3}{T_3 - 10}$$
$$\Rightarrow \quad 4T_3 - 40 = 270 - 9T_3 \Rightarrow T_3 = 23.84° \text{C}$$

10. Given, $m_A = m_B = m$ (Let)

As we know that

$$\Delta Q / \Delta t = ms \, \Delta T / \Delta t$$

Since, $\left(\frac{\Delta Q}{\Delta t}\right)_A = \left(\frac{\Delta Q}{\Delta t}\right)_B$

$$\Rightarrow \quad ms_A \left(\frac{\Delta T}{t}\right)_A = ms_B \left(\frac{\Delta T}{t}\right)_B$$
$$\Rightarrow \quad \frac{s_A}{s_B} = \frac{\left(\frac{\Delta T}{t}\right)_B}{\left(\frac{\Delta T}{t}\right)_A} = \frac{\frac{90}{6}}{\frac{120}{3}} = \frac{3}{2 \times 4} = \frac{3}{8}$$

11. M grams of steam at 100° C is mixed with 200 g of ice at 0°C and mixture obtained is at 40°C.

Using the principle of energy conservation, we get

$$\Rightarrow M_{\text{steam}} \times L_V + M_{\text{steam}} \times s_W \times \Delta T$$
$$= M_{\text{ice}} \times L_f + M_{\text{ice}} \times s_W \times \Delta T$$
$$\Rightarrow M \times 540 + M \times 1 \times (100 - 40)$$
$$= 200 \times 80 + 200 \times 1 \times (40 - 0)$$
$$\Rightarrow \quad M \times 600 = 24000$$
$$\Rightarrow \quad M = 40 \text{ g}$$

12. We know that,

for bullet $\Delta Q = (ms\Delta T)_{\text{bullet}}$ ...(i)

$$\Delta Q = ms\Delta T$$

Given $\quad \Delta Q = \frac{1}{2}\left(\frac{1}{2} mv^2\right)$ ...(ii)

From Eqs. (i) and (ii), we get

$$(ms\Delta T)_{\text{bullet}} = \frac{1}{2}\left(\frac{1}{2} mv^2\right)$$
$$\Rightarrow \quad \Delta T = \frac{v^2}{4s}$$

Since, $\quad s = 0.030$ cal/g° C

and $\quad v = 210$ m/s

On putting values,

$$\Delta T = \frac{(210)^2}{4 \times 4.2 \times 0.03 \times 1000} = 87.5\,^\circ C$$

Hence, correct option is (a).

13. Let the mass of ice which gets melted be m_i. Now,

Heat lost by water = Heat gained by ice

$\Rightarrow \quad m_w c_w \Delta T_w = m_i L_i$

$\Rightarrow \quad \frac{200}{1000} \times 4200 \times (25-0) = m_i \times 3.4 \times 10^5$

$\Rightarrow \quad 21000 = m_i \times 3.4 \times 10^5$

$\Rightarrow \quad m_i = \frac{21000}{3.4 \times 10^5} = 0.0617\text{ kg} = 61.7\text{ g}$

Hence, correct option is (d).

14. Heat given by water is (specific heat of water is 1 cal $g^{-1}\,^\circ C^{-1}$)

$(\Delta H)_{water} = M_2 \times 1 \times (50-0) = 50M_2$ ...(i)

Heat taken by ice is

$(\Delta H)_{ice} = M_1 \times 0.5 \times [0-(-10)] + M_1 \times L_{ice}$

$\Rightarrow \quad (\Delta H)_{ice} = 5M_1 + M_1 L_{ice}$ ...(ii)

Comparing Eqs. (i) and (ii), we get

$(\Delta H)_{water} = (\Delta H)_{ice}$

$\therefore \quad 50M_2 = 5M_1 + M_1 L_{ice}$

$\Rightarrow \quad L_{ice} = \frac{50M_2 - 5M_1}{M_1}$

$\Rightarrow \quad L_{ice} = 50\frac{M_2}{M_1} - 5$

15. In first case, according to principle of calorimetry,

heat lost by liquid A = heat gained by liquid B

or $\quad m_A S_A \Delta T_A = m_B S_B \Delta T_B$

$\Rightarrow 100 \times S_A(100-90) = 50 \times S_B(90-75)$

$\Rightarrow \quad 1000 S_A = 50 \times 15 S_B$

or $\quad 4S_A = 3S_B$ ...(i)

Similarly, in second case,

$100 \times S_A(100-T) = 50 \times S_B(T-50)$

where, T = Final temperature of the mixture.

$\Rightarrow \quad 4S_A(100-T) = 2S_B(T-50)$

Using Eq. (i),

$3S_B(100-T) = 2S_B(T-50)$

or $\quad 300 - 3T = 2T - 100$

or $\quad 5T = 400$ or $T = 80°C$

16. Let specific heat of unknown metal is s and heat lost by this metal is ΔQ.

Heat lost

$\Delta Q = ms\Delta T$ ... (i)

For unknown metal, $m = 192$ g and

$\Delta T = (100-21.5)\,°C$

$\therefore \quad \Delta Q' = 192(100-21.5) \times s$ ...(ii)

Now, this heat is gained by the calorimeter and water inside it.

As, heat gained by calorimeter can be calculated by Eq. (i).

So, for brass specific heat,

$s = 394\text{ J kg}^{-1}\text{ K}^{-1}$ (given)

$= 0.394\text{ J g}^{-1}\text{ K}^{-1}$

Mass of calorimeter, $m = 128$ g

$\Delta T = (21.5 - 8.4)\,°C$

So, using Eq. (i) for calorimeter, heat gained by brass

$\Delta Q_1 = 128 \times 0.394 \times (21.5-8.4)$ ...(iii)

Heat gained by water

$\Delta Q_2 = ms_w \Delta T$

$m = 240$g,

$S_w = 4.18\text{ J g}^{-1}\text{K}^{-1}$,

$\Delta T = (21.5-8.4)°C$

$\Delta Q_2 = 240 \times 4.18 \times (21.5-8.4)$ ...(iv)

Now, according to the principle of calorimeter,

$\Delta Q' = \Delta Q_1 + \Delta Q_2$

Using Eqs. (ii), (iii) and (iv), we get

$\Rightarrow \quad = 192(100-21.5) \times s$

$= 128 \times 0.394 \times (21.5-8.4) + 240 \times 4.18 \times (21.5-8.4)$

$\Rightarrow$ $15072\,s = 660.65 + 13142$

$\Rightarrow$ $s = 0.916\text{ J g}^{-1}\text{ K}^{-1}$

or $s = 916\text{ J kg}^{-1}\text{ K}^{-1}$.

17. Let amount of ice be x g.

According to the principle of calorimeter, heat lost by water = heat gained by ice

Here, heat lost by water,

$\Delta Q = ms_{water}\,\Delta T$

Substituting the given values, we get

$\Delta Q = 50 \times 4.2 \times 40$

Heat gained by ice,

$\Delta Q = x\, s_{ice}\,\Delta T + (x-20)L$

$= x \times 2.1 \times 20 + (x-20) \times 334$

$= 20\,x \times 2.1 + 334x - 6680$

$\therefore$ $20\,x \times 2.1 + 334x - 6680 = 50 \times 4.2 \times 40$

$42x + 334x - 6680 = 8400$

$\Rightarrow$ $376\,x = 15080$ or $x = 40.10$ g

$x \approx 40$ g

18. Using heat lost or gained without change in state is $\Delta Q = ms\Delta T$,

Let final temperature of ball be T.

Then heat lost by ball is,

$\Delta Q = 0.1 \times 400(500-T)$ ...(i)

This lost heat by ball (ΔQ) is gained by water and vessel (ΔQ_2) and given as

$\therefore \quad \Delta Q_1 = 0.5 \times 4200(T-30)$

and $\quad \Delta Q_2$ = heat capacity $\times \Delta T = 800 \times (T-30)$

According to principle of calorimetry, total heat lost = total heat gained

$\Rightarrow 0.1 \times 400(500-T) = 0.5 \times 4200(T-30) + 800(T-30)$

$$\Rightarrow \quad (500 - T) = \frac{(2100 + 800)(T - 30)}{40}$$

$$\Rightarrow \quad 500 - T = 72.5(T - 30)$$

$$\Rightarrow \quad 500 + 2175 = 72.5T$$

or $\quad T = 36.39$ K

So, percentage increment in temperature of water

$$= \frac{36.39 - 30}{30} \times 100 \approx 20\%$$

19. Applying the principle of energy

$$\frac{1}{2}kx^2 = (m_1s_1 + m_2s_2)\,\Delta T,$$

$$\Delta T = \frac{kx^2}{2(m_1s_1 + m_2s_2)} = \frac{800 \times 4 \times 10^{-4}}{2(500 \times 10^{-3} \times 400 + 1 \times 4184)}$$

$$= 3.6 \times 10^{-5}\ \text{K}$$

JEE Advanced

1. Heat generated in device in 3 h

$$= \text{time} \times \text{power} = 3 \times 3600 \times 3 \times 10^3 = 324 \times 10^5\ \text{J}$$

Heat used to heat water

$$= ms\,\Delta\theta = 120 \times 1 \times 4.2 \times 10^3 \times 20\text{J}$$

Heat absorbed by coolant

$$= Pt = 324 \times 10^5 - 120 \times 1 \times 4.2 \times 10^3 \times 20\ \text{J}$$

$$Pt = (325 - 100.8) \times 10^5\ \text{J}$$

$$P = \frac{223.2 \times 10^8}{3 \times 3600} = 2067\ \text{W}$$

2. $Q = mCT \quad \Rightarrow \quad \frac{dQ}{dt} = mc\frac{dT}{dt}$

$$R = \text{rate of absortion of heat} = \frac{dQ}{dt} \propto C$$

(i) In the range, $0 - 100$ K, C increases, so R increases but not linearly.

(ii) $\Delta Q = mC\Delta T$ as C is more in (400 K -500 K) then (0 – 100 K) so heat is increasing

(iii) C remains constant so there no change in R from (400 K – 500 K)

(iv) C is increases so R increases in range(200 K - 300 K)

CHAPTER~03

Conduction

LEVEL 01 Starter Level

3.1 Conduction at Steady State

1 A uniform slab of dimension 10 cm $\times$ 10 cm $\times$ 1 cm is kept between two heat reservoirs at temperatures 10°C and 90°C. The larger surface areas touch the reservoirs. The thermal conductivity of the material is 0.80 W/m-°C. Find the amount of heat flowing through the slab per second.

2 One face of an aluminium cube of edge 2 m is maintained at 100°C and the opposite face is maintained at 0°C. All other surfaces are covered by adiabatic walls. Find the amount of heat flowing through the cube in 5 s. (Thermal conductivity of aluminium is 209 W/m-°C)

3 One end of a brass rod 2 m long and having 1 cm radius is maintained at 250°C. When the steady state is reached, the rate of heat flow across any cross-section of 0.5 cal s^{-1}. What is the temperature of the other end? $K = 0.26$ cal s^{-1} cm^{-1} $°C^{-1}$.

4 Steam at 373 K is passed through a tube of radius 10 cm and length 2 m. The thickness of the tube is 5 mm and thermal conductivity of the material is 390 $Wm^{-1}K^{-1}$, calculate the heat lost per second. The outside temperature is 0°C.

5 A room is maintained at 20°C by a heater of power 2 kW. The temperature is uniform throughout the room and the heat is transmitted through a glass window of area 1 m^2 and thickness 0.2 cm. Calculate the temperature outside.Thermal conductivity of glass is 0.84 W/m-°C.

6 Water is boiled in a container having a bottom of surface area 25 cm^2, thickness 1.0 mm and thermal conductivity 50 W/m-°C. 100 g of water is converted into steam per minute in the steady state after the boiling starts. Assuming that no heat is lost to the atmosphere, calculate the temperature of the lower surface of the bottom. Latent heat of vaporisation of water = 2.26×10^6 J/kg.

7 One end of a steel rod ($K = 42$ J/m-s-°C) of length 1.0 m is kept in ice at 0°C and the other end is kept in boiling water at 100°C. The area of cross-section of the rod is 0.04 cm^2. Assuming no heat loss to the atmosphere, find the mass of the ice melting per second. Latent heat of fusion of ice = 3.36×10^5 J/kg.

8 An icebox almost completely filled with ice at 0°C is dipped into a large volume of water at 20°C. The box has walls of surface area 2400 cm^2, thickness 2.0 mm and thermal conductivity 0.06 W/m-°C. Calculate the rate at which the ice melts in the box. Latent heat of fusion of ice = 3.4×10^5 J/kg.

9 A pitcher with 1 mm thick porous walls contains 10 kg of water. Water comes to its outer surface and evaporates at the rate of 0.1 g/s. The surface area of the pitcher (one side) = 200 cm^2. The room temperature = 42°C, latent heat of vaporisation = 2.27×10^6 J/kg and the thermal conductivity of the porous walls = 0.80 J/m-s-°C. Calculate the temperature of water in the pitcher, when it attains a constant value.

10 A container of negligible heat capacity contains 1 kg of water. It is connected by a steel rod ($K = 46$ W/m-°C) of length 10 m and area of cross-section 10 cm^2 to a large steam chamber which is maintained at 100°C. If initial temperature of water is 0°C, find the time after which it becomes 50°C.

(Neglect heat capacity of steel rod and assume no loss of heat to surroundings)

(Take, specific heat of water = 4180 J/kg °C)

3.2 Temperature Gradient

1 The left end of a copper rod (length = 20 cm, area of cross-section = 0.20 cm^2) is maintained at 80°C and

the right end is maintained at 20°C. Neglecting any loss of heat through radiation, find

(a) the temperature gradient

(b) the temperature at a point 12 cm from the left end

2 A metal rod of cross-sectional area 1.0 cm^2 is being heated at one end. At one time, the temperature gradient is 5.0°C/cm at cross-section A and is 2.6°C/cm at cross-section B. Calculate the rate at which the temperature is increasing in the part AB of the rod. The heat capacity of the part AB = 0.40 J/°C, thermal conductivity of the material of rod = 200 W/m-°C. Neglect any loss of heat to the atmosphere.

3 Two ends of a conducting rod of varying cross-section are maintained at 200°C and 0°C, respectively. In steady state, compare

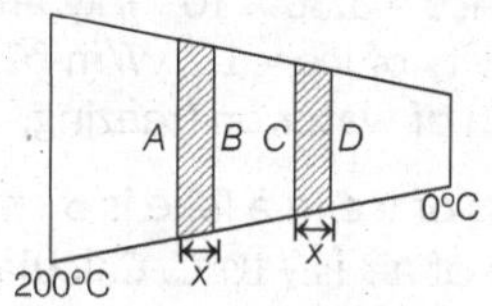

(a) heat currents through AB and CD

(b) compare temperature differences across AB and CD

4 A rod of length L with sides fully insulated is of a material whose thermal conductivity varies with temperature at $K = \frac{\alpha}{T}$, where α is constant. The ends of the rod are kept at temperature T_1 and T_2. Find the temperature T at x, where x is the distance from the end whose temperature is T_1.

3.3 Kirchhoff's Junction Law

1 Three identical rods of length 1 m each, having cross-section area of 1 cm^2 each and made of aluminium, copper and steel, respectively are maintained at temperatures of 12°C, 4°C and 50°C, respectively at their separate ends. Find the temperature of their common junction.

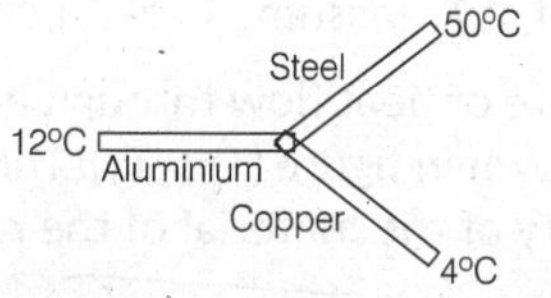

[K_{Cu} = 400 W/m-K, K_{Al} = 200 W/m-K, K_{steel} = 50 W/m-K]

2 A rod CD of thermal resistance 5.0 K/W is joined at the middle of an identical rod AB as shown in figure. The ends A, B and D are maintained at 100°C, 0°C and 25°C, respectively. Find the heat current in CD.

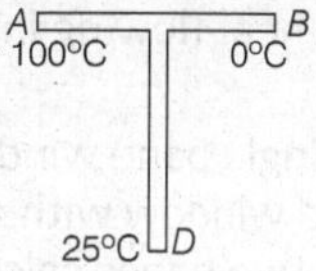

3 Figure shows a steel rod joined to a brass rod. Each of the rods has length of 31 cm and area of cross-section 0.20 cm^2. The junction is maintained at a constant temperature 50°C and the two ends are maintained at 100°C. Calculate the amount of heat taken out from the cold junction in 10 min after the steady state is reached. The thermal conductivities are K_{steel} = 46 W/m-°C and K_{brass} = 109 W/m-°C.

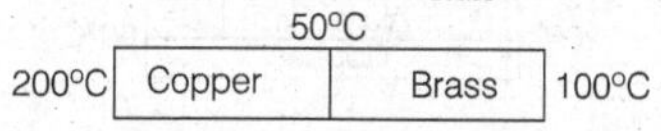

4 The coefficient of thermal conductivity of copper is nine times that of steel. In the composite cylindrical bar shown in the figure, what will be the temperature at the junction of copper and steel?

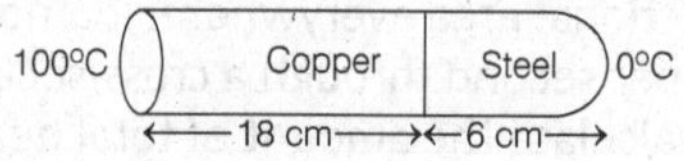

3.4 Combination of Rods

1 A composite rod made of three rods of equal length and cross-section as shown in the figure. The thermal conductivities of the materials of the rods are $K/2$, $5K$ and K, respectively. The end A and end B are at constant temperatures. All heat entering the face A goes out of the end B there being no loss of heat from the sides of the bar. Find the effective thermal conductivity of the bar.

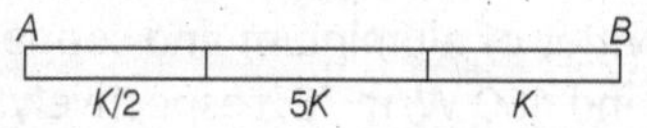

2 A bar of length 40 cm and uniform cross-section 5 cm^2 consists of two halves, AB of copper and BC of iron welded at B. The end A is maintained at 200°C and C at 0°C. The sides are thermally insulated. Find the rate of heat-flow along the bar in the steady state.

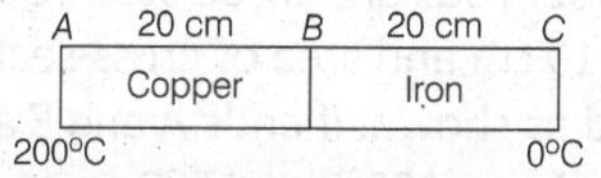

K for Cu and Fe are 0.9 and 0.1 cal/s-cm-°C), respectively.

3 A room has a window fixed with a pane of area $1.2\ m^2$. The glass has thickness 2.2 mm. If the temperature outside the room is 36°C and the temperature inside is 26°C

(a) calculate the heat flowing into the room every hour.

(b) If the same single pane window is replaced by double paned window with an air gap of 0.50 cm between the two panes calculate the heat flowing into the room every hour.

$K_{glass} = 0.80$ W/m-K, $K_{air} = 0.0234$ W/m-K

4 An aluminium rod and a copper rod of equal length 1.0 m and cross-sectional area $1\ cm^2$ are welded together as shown in figure. One end is kept at a temperature of 20°C and the other at 60°C. Calculate the amount of heat taken out per second from the hot end.

Thermal conductivity of aluminium = 200 W/m-°C and of copper = 400 W/m-°C.

5 Consider the situation shown in figure. The frame is made of the same material and has a uniform cross-sectional area everywhere. If amount of heat flowing per second through a cross-section of part A is 60 J, calculate the amount of total heat taken out per second from the end at 50°C.

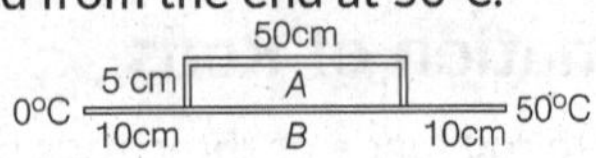

6 The three rods shown in figure have identical geometrical dimensions. Heat flows from the hot end at a rate of 40 W in the arrangement shown in figure.

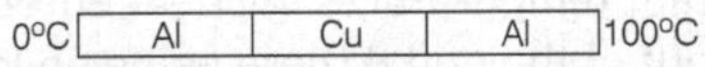

Find the rates of heat flow when the same three rods are joined in the following arrangements. Thermal conductivities of aluminium and copper are 200 W/m-°C and 400 W/m-°C, respectively.

(a) 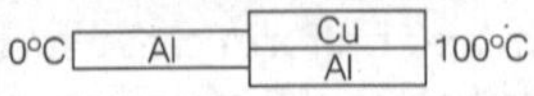

(b) 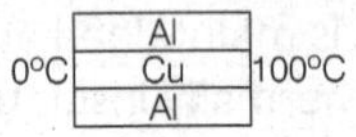

7 Three copper rods and three steel rods each of length $l = 10$ cm and area of cross-section $1\ cm^2$ are connected as shown. If ends A and E are maintained at temperatures 125°C and 0°C respectively, calculate the amount of heat flowing per second from the hot to cold junction.

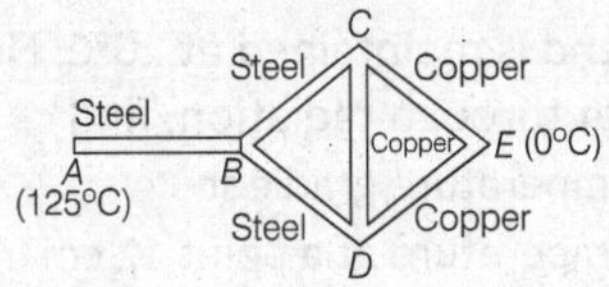

$[K_{cu} = 400$ W/m-K, $K_{steel} = 50$ W/m-K$]$

3.5 Formation of Ice on Lake

1 On a winter day when the atmospheric temperature drops to −10°C, ice forms on the surface of a lake.

(a) Calculate the rate of increase of thickness of the ice when 10 cm of ice is already formed.

(b) Calculate the total time taken in forming 10 cm of ice.

Assume that the temperature of the entire water reaches 0°C before the ice starts forming. Density of water = 1000 kg/m^3, latent heat of fusion of ice = 3.36×10^5 J/kg and thermal conductivity of ice = 1.7 W/m-°C. Neglect the expansion of water on freezing.

2 The thickness of ice in a lake is 5 cm and the temperature of air is −10°C. Calculate the time required for the thickness of ice to be doubled. Constants for ice are : conductivity = 0.004 cal s^{-1}cm^{-1}°C^{-1}, density = 0.92 g/cm^3, latent heat = 80 cal/g.

3.6 Conduction in Non-linear Conductors at Steady State

1 Two thin concentric shells made of copper with radius R_1 and R_2 $(R_2 > R_1)$ have a material of thermal conductivity K filled between them. The inner and outer spheres are maintained at temperatures T_1 and T_2 $(T_1 > T_2)$, respectively. Find the amount of heat flowing radially from the inner sphere to the outer sphere per second.

2 A hollow tube has a length l, inner radius R_1 and outer radius R_2. The material has thermal conductivity K. Find the heat flowing through the walls of the tube per second, if the inside of the tube is maintained at temperature T_1 and the outside is maintained at T_2 [assume $T_2 > T_1$].

3 Find the rate of heat flow through a cross-section of the rod shown in figure $(T_1 > T_2)$. Thermal conductivity of the material of the rod is K.

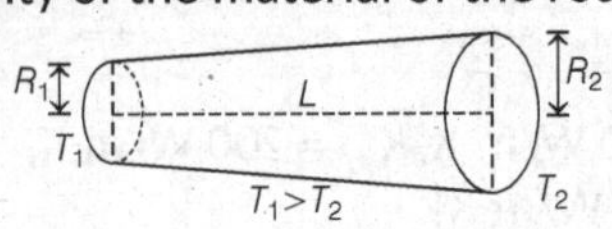

LEVEL 02 \\ JEE Main Level

Single Choice Correct Questions

1 The ends of two rods of different materials with their thermal conductivities, radii of cross-sections and lengths all in the ratio 1 : 2 are maintained at the same temperature difference. If the rate of flow of heat in the larger rod is 4 cal/s, that in the shorter rod will be

(a) 1 cal/s (b) 2 cal/s
(c) 8 cal/s (d) 16 cal/s

2 A metallic rod of cross-sectional area 9.0 cm^2 and length 0.54 m, with the surface insulated to prevent heat loss, has one end immersed in boiling water and the other in ice-water mixture. The heat conducted through the rod melts the ice at the rate of 1 g for every 33 s. The thermal conductivity of the rod is

(a) 330 $Wm^{-1}K^{-1}$ (b) 61 $Wm^{-1}K^{-1}$
(c) 600 $Wm^{-1}K^{-1}$ (d) 33 $Wm^{-1}K^{-1}$

3 A cylindrical rod with one end in a steam chamber and the other end in ice results in melting of 0.1 g of ice per second. If the rod is replaced by another with half the length and double the radius of the first and if the thermal conductivity of material of second rod is 1/4 that of first, the rate at which ice melts is

(a) 3.2 g/s (b) 1.6 g/s
(c) 0.2 g/s (d) 0.1 g/s

4 The ends of a meter stick are maintained at 100°C and 20°C. One end of a rod is maintained at 40°C. Where should its other end be touched on the meter stick, so that there is no heat current in the rod in steady state?

(a) 25 cm from cold end
(b) 40 cm from cold end
(c) 75 cm from cold end
(d) 60 cm from cold end

5 Three rods made of the same material and having same cross-sectional area but different lengths 10 cm, 20 cm and 30 cm are joined as shown. The temperature of the joint is

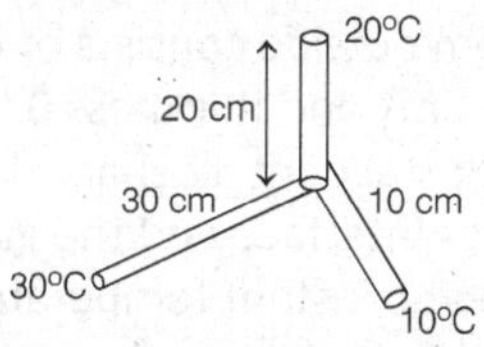

(a) 20°C (b) 23.7°C
(c) 16.4°C (d) 18.2°C

6 Three conducting rods of same material and cross-section are shown in figure. Temperatures of A, D and C are maintained at 20°C, 90°C and 0°C. The ratio of lengths of BD and BC, if there is no heat flow in AB is

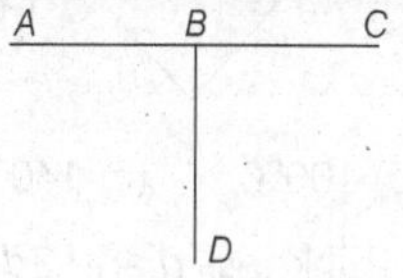

(a) 2/7 (b) 7/2
(c) 9/2 (d) 2/9

7 Heat is conducted across a composite block of two slabs of thickness d and $2d$. Their thermal conductivities are $2k$ and k, respectively. All the heat entering the face AB leaves from the face CD. The temperature of the junction EF of the two slabs is

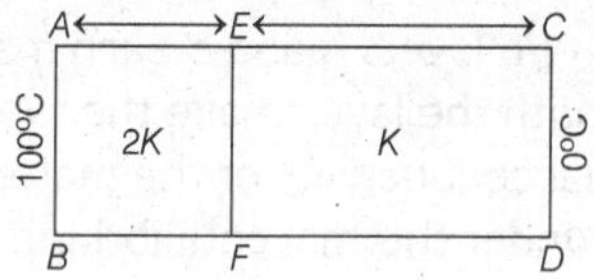

(a) 20°C (b) 50°C
(c) 60°C (d) 80°C

8 A composite metal bar of uniform section is made up of length 25 cm of copper, 10 cm of nickel and 15 cm of aluminium. Each part being in perfect thermal contact with the adjoining part. The copper end of the composite rod is maintained at 100°C and the aluminium end at 0°C. The whole rod is covered with belt, so that there is no heat loss occurs at the sides. If $K_{Cu} = 2K_{Al}$ and $K_{Al} = 3K_{Ni}$, then what will be the temperature of Cu-Ni and Ni-Al junctions, respectively?

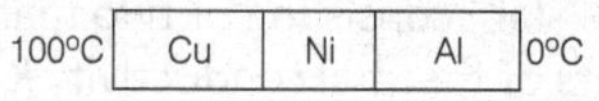

(a) 78.3° and 26.1°C (b) 83.33°C and 20°C
(c) 50°C and 30°C (d) 30°C and 50°C

9 Two rods shown in figure have identical geometrical dimensions. They are in contact with two heat bath at temperature 100°C and 0°C. The temperature of the junction is 65°C. Find the temperature of the junction if the rods are interchanged.

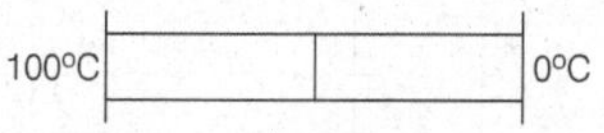

(a) 65°C (b) 35°C
(c) 40°C (d) 100/3°C

10 Six identical conducting rods are joined as shown in figure. Points *A* and *D* are maintained at temperature of 200°C and 20°C, respectively. The temperature of junction *B* will be

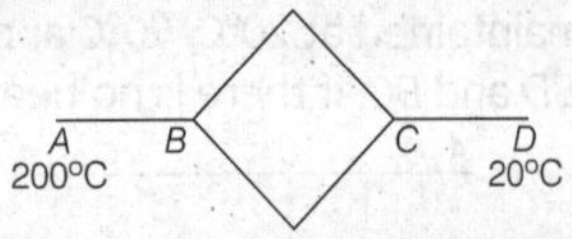

(a) 120°C (b) 100°C (c) 140°C (d) 80°C

11 Two sheets of thickness *d* and 3*d*, are touching each other. The temperature just outside the thinner sheet side is *A* and on the side of the thicker sheet is *C*. The interface temperature is *B*. *A*, *B* and *C* are in arithmetic progressing, the ratio of thermal conductivity of thinner sheet and thicker sheet is

(a) 1 : 3 (b) 3 : 1
(c) 2 : 3 (d) 1 : 9

12 A wall has two layers *A* and *B* each made of different material, both the layers have the same thickness. The thermal conductivity of the material *A* is thrice that of *B*. Under thermal equilibrium, the temperature difference across the wall *B* is 36°C. The temperature difference across the wall *A* is

(a) 6°C (b) 12°C (c) 108°C (d) 72°C

13 Three identical metal rods *A*, *B* and *C* are placed end to end and a temperature difference is maintained between the free ends of *A* and *C*. If the thermal conductivity of $B(K_B)$ is twice that of $C(K_C)$ and half that of $A(K_A)$, then the effective thermal conductivity of the system will be

(a) $K_A/7$ (b) $6K_B/7$
(c) $6K_A/7$ (d) None of these

14 The temperature of the two outer surfaces of a composite slab, consisting of two materials having coefficients of thermal conductivity *K* and 2*K* and thickness *x* and 4*x*, respectively are T_2 and T_1 $(T_2 > T_1)$. The rate of heat transfer through the slab, in the steady state is $\left(\frac{A(T_2 - T_1)K}{x}\right) f$, with *f* equal to

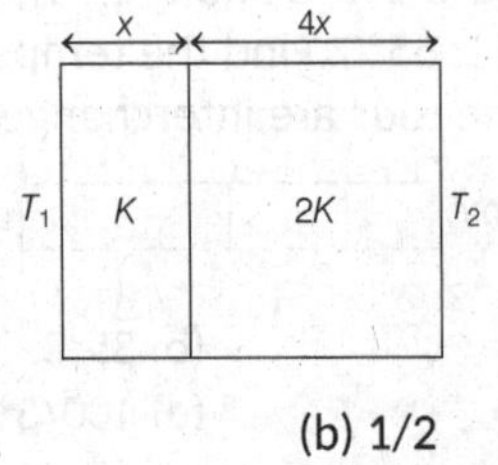

(a) 1 (b) 1/2
(c) 2/3 (d) 1/3

15 The container *A* is constantly maintained at 100°C and insulated container *B* of the figure initially contains ice at 0°C. Different rods are used to connect them. For a rod made of copper, it takes 30 min for the ice to melt and for a rod of steel of same cross-section taken in different experiment it takes 60 min for ice to melt. When these rods are simultaneously connected in parallel, the ice melts in

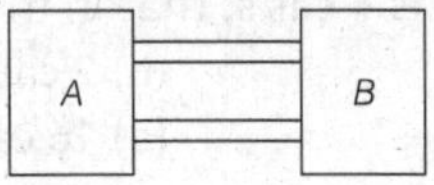

(a) 15 min (b) 20 min (c) 45 min (d) 90 min

16 Rate of heat flow through two conducting rods of identical dimensions having thermal conductivities K_1 and K_2 are Q_1 and Q_2, when their ends are maintained at the same difference temperature individually. When the two rods are joined in series with their ends maintained at the same temperature difference (as shown in the figure), the rate of heat flow will be

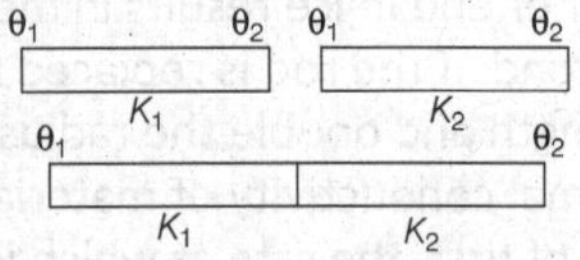

(a) $\frac{Q_1 + Q_2}{2}$ (b) $(K_1Q_1 + K_2Q_2)$

(c) $\frac{K_1Q_1 + K_2Q_2}{K_1 + K_2}$ (d) $\frac{Q_1Q_2}{Q_1 + Q_2}$

17 Two identical square rods of metal are welded end to end as shown in figure (a), 20 cal of heat flows through it in 4 min. If the rods are welded as shown in figure (b), the same amount of heat will flow through the rods in

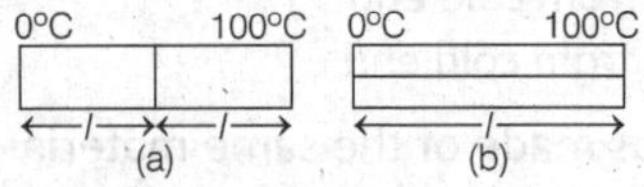

(a) 1 min (b) 2 min (c) 4 min (d) 16 min

18 A double-pane window used for insulating a room thermally from outside consists of two glass sheets each of area 1 m^2 and thickness 0.01 m separated by a 0.05 m thick stagnant air space. In the steady state, the room glass interface and the glass-outdoor interface are at constant temperatures of 27°C and 0°C, respectively. Calculate the rate of heat flow through the window plane. Given, thermal conductivities of glass and air as 0.8 and 0.08 Wm^{-1}K^{-1}, respectively.

(a) 25 W (b) 35.5 W (c) 41.6 W (d) 78.7 W

19 Three rods of identical cross-section area and made from the same material form the sides of an isosceles triangle *ABC*, right angled at *B*. The points *A* and *C* are maintained at temperatures *T* and $\sqrt{2}T$, respectively. In the steady state, the temperature of the point *B* is T_B. Assuming that only heat conduction takes place, the ratio T_B/T is equal to

(a) $\frac{2}{\sqrt{2}-1}$ (b) $\frac{1+\sqrt{2}}{2}$ (c) $\sqrt{2}-1$ (d) $\sqrt{2}+1$

20 The temperature drop through each layer of a two layer furnace wall is shown in figure. Assume that the external temperature T_1 and T_3 are maintained constant and $T_1 > T_0$. If the thickness of the layers x_1 and x_2 are the same, which of the following statements is correct?

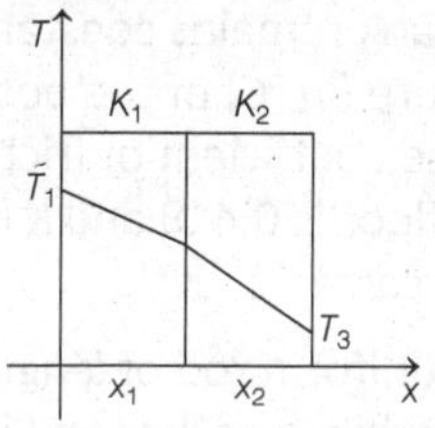

(a) $K_1 > K_2$

(b) $K_1 < K_2$

(c) $K_1 = K_2$ but heat flow through material (1) is larger, than through (2)

(d) $K_1 = K_2$ but heat flow through material (1) is less than that through (2)

21 A boiler is made up of a copper plate 2.4 mm thick with an inside coating of a 0.2 mm thick layer of tin. The surface area exposed to gases at 700°C is 400 cm^2. The amount of steam that could be generated per hour at atmospheric pressure is ($K_{Cu} = 0.9$ and $K_{tin} = 0.15$ cal/cm/s/°C and $L_{steam} = 540$ cal/g)

(a) 5000 kg (b) 1000 kg (c) 4000 kg (d) 200 kg

22 Five rods having thermal conductivities K_1, K_2, K_3, K_4 and K_5 are arranged as shown. The points *A* and *B* are maintained at different temperature such that no thermal current flows through the central rod.

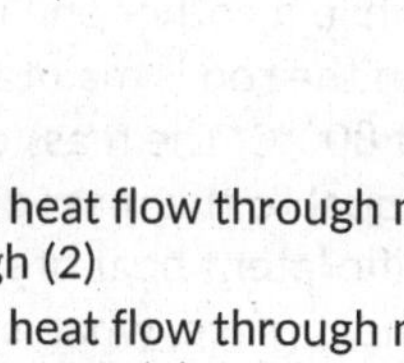

(a) $K_1K_4 = K_2K_3$ (b) $K_1 = K_3, K_2 = K_4$

(c) $K_1K_3 = K_2K_4$ (d) $\frac{K_1}{K_4} = \frac{K_3}{K_2}$

23 *A* and *B* are two points on a uniform metal ring whose centre is *C*. The angle $ACB = \theta$, *A* and *B* are maintained at two different constants temperatures. When $\theta = 180°$, the rate of total heat flow from *A* to *B* is 1.2 W. When $\theta = 90°$, this rate will be

(a) 0.6 W (b) 0.9 W (c) 1.6 W (d) 1.8 W

24 Two rods (one semi-circular and other straight) of same material and of same cross-sectional area are joined as shown in figure. The points *A* and *B* are maintained at different temperatures. The ratio of the heat transferred through a cross-section of a semi-circular rod to the heat transferred through a cross-section of the straight rod in a given time is

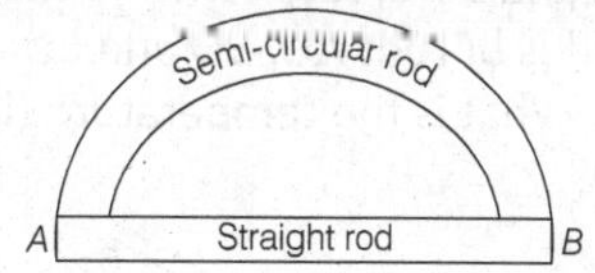

(a) $2:\pi$ (b) $1:2$ (c) $\pi:2$ (d) $3:2$

25 The diameter of a rod is given by $d = d_0(1+ax)$, where *a* is a constant and *x* is the distance from one end. If the thermal conductivity of the material is *K*, what is the thermal resistance of the rod if length is *l*.

(a) $\frac{1}{K\pi d_0^2}$ (b) $\frac{4l}{K\pi d_0^2(al+1)}$

(c) $\frac{2l}{K\pi d_0^2(al+1)^2}$ (d) $\frac{2l}{K\pi d_0^2(al+1)}$

26 A composite cylinder is made of two different materials *A* and *B* of thermal conductivities K_A and K_B. The dimensions of the cylinder are as shown in the figure. The thermal resistance of the cylinder between the two end faces is

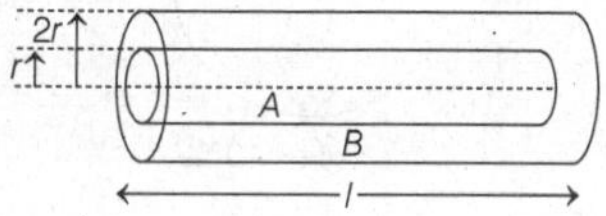

(a) $\frac{l}{\pi r^2(K_A + 3K_B)}$ (b) $\frac{l}{\pi r^2}\left(\frac{1}{K_A} + \frac{3}{K_B}\right)$

(c) $\frac{l}{\pi r^2}\left(\frac{1}{K_A} + \frac{4}{K_B}\right)$ (d) $\frac{l}{\pi r^2(K_A + 4K_B)}$

27 Ice starts forming in a lake with water at 0°C when the atmospheric temperature is −10°C. If the time taken for the first 1 cm of ice to be formed is 7 h, then the time taken for the thickness of ice to change from 1 cm to 2 cm is

(a) 7 h (b) 14 h

(c) 21 h (d) 3.5 h

28 The thickness of ice in a lake is 5 cm and the atmospheric temperature is $-10°C$. Calculate the time required for the thickness of ice to grow to 7 cm. Thermal conductivity of ice $= 4 \times 10^{-3}$ cal/cm-s-°C, density of ice $= 0.92$ g/cm^3 and latent heat of fusion of ice = 80 cal/g

(a) 3.53 h (b) 6.13 h (c) 9.33 h (d) 15.23 h

Numerical Value Questions

1 Three rods *AO*, *BO* and *CO* having equal lengths and equal area of cross-section are connected as shown in the figure. The temperature of ends *A*, *B* and *C* are 30°C, 60°C and 90°C, respectively. The thermal conductivities of rods *AO*, *BO* and *CO* are in the ratio of 1 : 2 : 3. What is the temperature (in °C) of junction *O*?

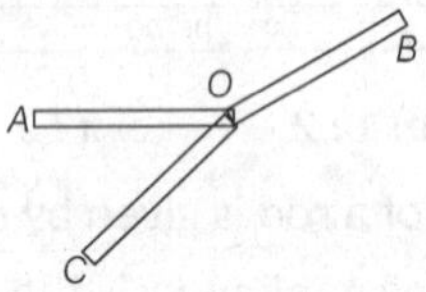

2 A uniform rod of cross-section area a ($= 0.20$ cm^2) is bent to form a ring. Length of rod (= 60 cm). Three points on this ring namely, *A*, *B* and *C* are maintained at temperature 80°C, 80°C, 110°C. The thermal conductivity of the material of the ring is K ($= 385$ W/m-°C). Neglect any loss of heat through lateral side. Assume arc length $AB = BC = CA$. Let the sum of modulus of heat current (in watt) through all the three branches be α. Find 100α.

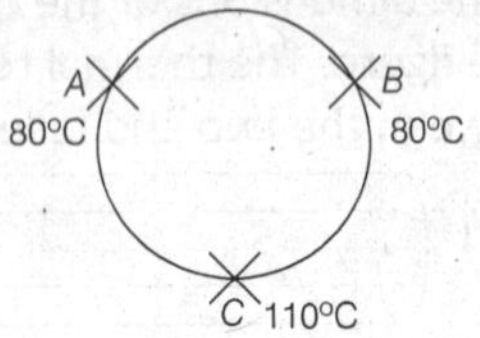

3 Two different rods *A* and *B* are kept as shown in figure. The variation of temperature of different cross-sections with distance is plotted in a graph shown in figure. What is the ratio of thermal conductivities of *B* and *A*?

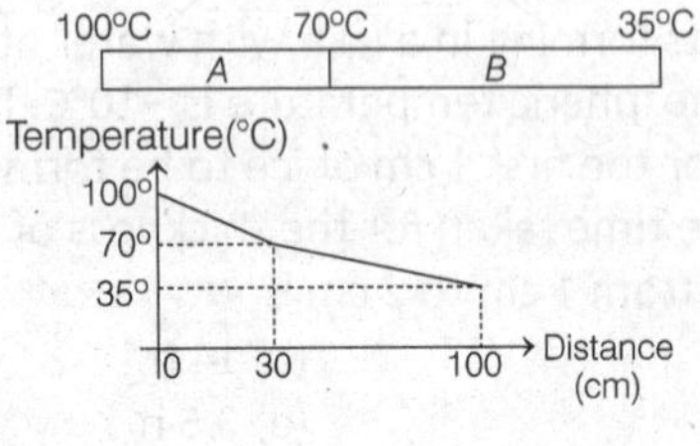

4 A lagged stick of cross-section area 1 cm^2 and length 1 m is initially at a temperature of 0°C. It is then kept between 2 reservoirs of temperature 100°C and 0°C. Specific heat capacity is 10 J/kg°C and linear mass density is 2 kg/m. Find the total heat (in kJ) absorbed by the rod to reach steady state.

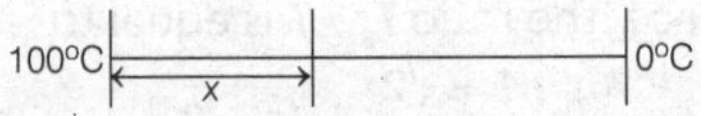

5 A flat bottomed metal tank of water is dragged along a horizontal floor at the rate of 20 m/s. The tank is of mass 20 kg and contains 980 kg of water and all the heat produced in the dragging is conducted to the water through the bottom plate of the tank. If the bottom plate has an effective area of conduction 1 m^2 and the thickness 5 cm and the temperature of water in the tank remains constant at 50°C, calculate the temperature (in °C) of the bottom surface of the tank. Given the coefficient of friction between the tank and the floor is 0.418 and K for the material of the tank is 25 cal m^{-1}s^{-1}K^{-1}.

6 One end of a uniform rod of length 18 m is placed in boiling water while its other end is placed in melting ice. A point *P* on the rod is maintained at a constant temperature of 800°C. The mass of steam produced per second is equal to the mass of ice melted per second. If specific latent heat of steam is 7 times the specific latent heat of ice, what is the distance (in m) of *P* from the steam chamber?

7 One end of a uniform brass rod 20 cm long and 10 cm^2 cross-sectional area is kept at 100°C. The other end is in perfect thermal contact with another rod of identical cross-section and length 9 cm. The free end of this rod is kept in melting ice and when the composite rod is well lagged and steady state has been reached, it is found that 360 gm of ice melt per hour. Given that the thermal conductivity of brass is 0.25 cal/s/cm/°C and $L = 80$ cal/g. If the thermal conductivity of the rod is k cal/s/cm/°C, then find the value of k.

8 For a temperature difference $\Delta T = 20°C$, one slab of material conducts 60 W/m^2, another of same shape conducts 30 W/m^2. What is the rate of heat flow (in W/m^2) when the slabs are placed side by side with same $\Delta T = 20°C$.

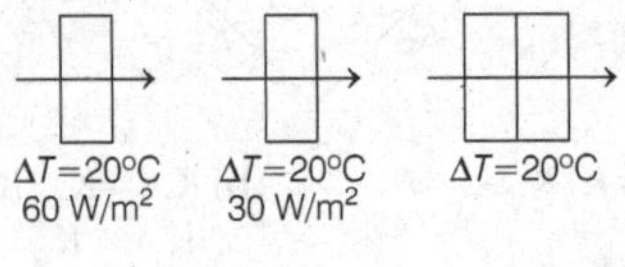

9 In a 10 m deep lake, the bottom is at a constant temperature of 4°C. The air temperature is constant at −4°C. The thermal conductivity of ice is 3 times that of water. Neglecting the expansion of water on freezing, the maximum thickness (in m) of ice will be ....

10 A hollow metallic sphere of radius 20 cm surrounds a concentric metallic sphere of radius 5 cm. The space between the two spheres is filled with a non-metallic material. The inner and outer spheres are maintained at 50°C and 10°C, respectively and it is found that 160πJ of heat passes radially from the inner sphere to the outer sphere per second. Find the thermal conductivity (in W/m-°C) of the material between the spheres.

LEVEL 03 \ JEE Advanced Level

1 The ends of copper rod of length 1 m and area of cross-section 1 cm^2 are maintained at 0°C and 100°C. At the centre of the rod there is a source of heat of power 25 W. Thermal conductivity of copper is 400 W/m-K. In steady state, the temperature at the section on rod at which source is supplying heat, will be
(a) 150.50°C (b) 325.75°C (c) 206.25°C (d) 126.25°C

2 The only possibility of heat flow in a thermo flask is through a cork which is 75 cm^2 in area and 5 cm thick. Its thermal conductivity is 0.0075 cal/cm-s-°C. The outside temperature is 40°C and latent heat of ice is 80 cal/g. Time taken by 500 g of ice at 0°C in the flask to melt into water at 0°C is

(a) 2.47 h (b) 4.27 h (c) 7.42 h (d) 4.72 h

3 Two thin walled spheres of different materials, one with double the radius and one-fourth wall thickness of the other, are filled with ice. If the time taken for complete melting of ice in the sphere of larger radius is 25 min and that for smaller one is 16 min, the ratio of thermal conductivities of the materials of larger sphere to the smaller sphere is
(a) 4 : 5 (b) 25 : 1 (c) 1 : 25 (d) 8 : 25

4 A rod of negligible heat capacity has length 40 cm, area of cross-section 1.0 cm^2 and thermal conductivity 100 W/m-°C. The temperature of one end is maintained at 0°C and that of the other end is slowly and linearly varied from 0°C to 60°C in 10 min. Assuming, no loss of heat through the sides find the total heat transmitted through the rod in these 10 min.
(a) 250 J (b) 350 J (c) 450 J (d) 550 J

5 A metal ball (having thermally insulated surface) of large conductivity and heat capacity = 10 J/K is welded to a thin rod of length 20 cm, thermal conductivity 50 W/m-K and cross-section area 1 cm^2. The other end of the rod is in contact with a lot of ice at 0°C. The initial temperature of ball is 100°C. If no heat is lost from the surface of the rod, the temperature of ball is 50°C after a time
(a) 10.51 min
(b) 4.62 min
(c) 6.78 min
(d) more than 15 min

6 Twelve conducting rods form the sides of a uniform cube of side l. If in steady state, B and H ends of the rod are at 100°C and 0°C, find the temperature of the junction A.

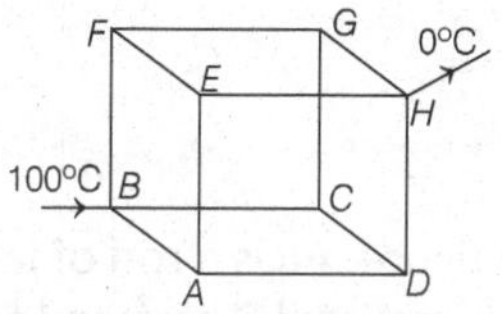

(a) 80°C (b) 60°C (c) 40°C (d) 70°C

7 Two sheets of thickness d and $2d$ and same area are touching each other on their face. Temperature T_A, T_B, T_C shown are in geometric progression with common ratio $r = 2$. Then, ratio of thermal conductivity of thinner and thicker sheet is

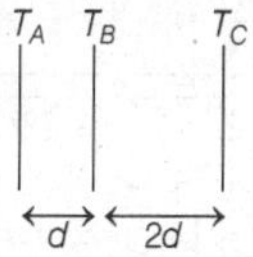

(a) 1 (b) 2
(c) 3 (d) 4

8 Three rods of same dimensions are arranged as shown in figure. They have thermal conductivities K_1, K_2 and K_3. The points P and Q are maintained at different temperatures for the heat to flow at the same rate along PQR and PQ. Which of the following options is correct?

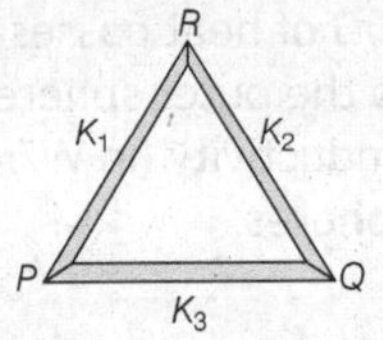

(a) $K_3 = \frac{1}{2}(K_1 + K_2)$ (b) $K_3 = K_1 + K_2$

(c) $K_3 = \frac{K_1 K_2}{K_1 + K_2}$ (d) $K_3 = 2(K_1 + K_2)$

9 Two rods of same length and cross-sectional area are joined in series. Thermal conductivity of the rods are in ratio of 2 : 1. The ends are maintained at temperatures θ_A and θ_B as shown with $\theta_A > \theta_B$ and sides are thermally insulated. Which of the following graph represents temperature gradient $\left(\frac{dT}{dx}\right)$ against x in steady state?

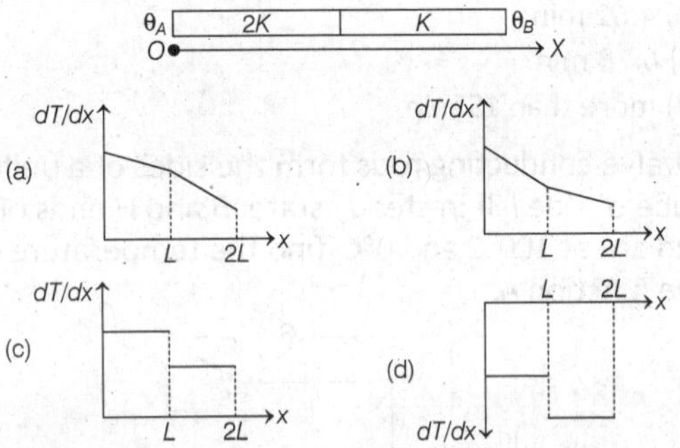

10 As shown in figure, AB is a rod of length 30 cm and area of cross-section 1.0 cm^2 and thermal conductivity 336 SI units. The ends A and B are maintained at temperatures 20°C and 40°C, respectively. A point C of this rod is connected to a box D, containing ice at 0°C, through a highly conducting wire of negligible heat capacity. The rate at which ice melts in the box is

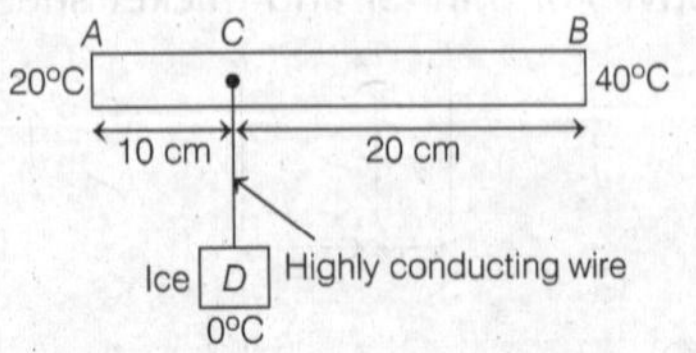

(Assume latent heat of fusion for ice $L_f = 80$ cal/g)

(a) 84 mg/s (b) 84 mg/s

(c) 20 mg/s (d) 40 mg/s

11 Three rods AB, BC and BD of same length l and cross-section A are arranged as shown. The end D is immersed in ice whose mass is 440 g and is at 0°C. The end C is maintained at 100°C. Heat is supplied at constant rate of 200 cal/s. Thermal conductivities of AB, BC and BD are K, $2K$ and $K/2$, respectively. Time after which whole ice will melt is

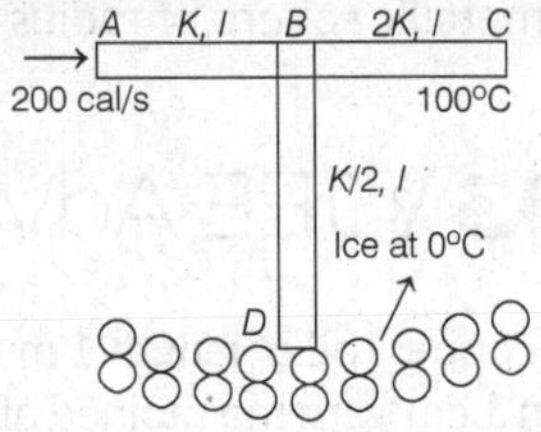

($K = 100$ cal/m-s-°C, $A = 10$ cm^2, $l = 1$ m)

(a) 400 s (b) 600 s

(c) 700 s (d) 800 s

12 A ring consisting of two parts ADB and ACB of same conductivity k carries an amount of heat H. The ADB part is now replaced with another metal keeping the temperatures T_1 and T_2 constant. The heat carried increases to $2H$. What should be the conductivity of the new ADB part? Given, $\frac{ACB}{ADB} = 3$

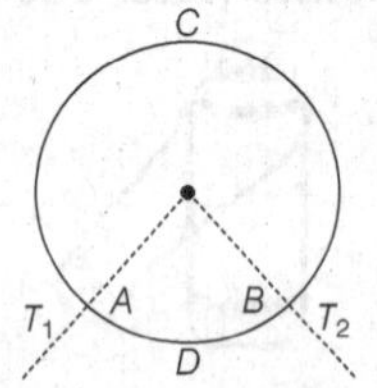

(a) $7k/3$ (b) $2k$

(c) $5k/2$ (d) $3k$

13 An electric heater is used in a room of total wall area 137 m^2 to maintain a temperature of +20°C inside it, when the outside temperature is −10°C. The walls have three different layers materials. The innermost layer is of wood of thickness 2.5 cm, the middle layer of the cement of thickness 1.0 cm and the outermost layer is of brick of thickness 25.0 cm. Find the power of the electric heater. Assume that there is no heat loss through the floor and the ceiling. The thermal conductivities of wood, cement and brick are 0.125, 1.5 and 1.0 W/m/°C, respectively.

(a) 5 kW (b) 9 kW

(c) 15 kW (d) 27 kW

14 Two models of a window pane are made. In one model, two identical glass panes of thickness 3 mm are separated with an air gap of 3 mm. This composite system is fixed in the window of a room. The other model consists of a single glass pane of thickness 6 mm, the temperature difference being the same as for the first model. The ratio of the heat flow for the double pane to that for the single pane is

($K_{glass} = 2.5 \times 10^{-4}$ cal/s-m°C and $K_{air} = 6.2 \times 10^{-6}$ cal/s-m°C)

(a) 1/20
(b) 1/70
(c) 31/1312
(d) 31/656

15 A closed cubical box is made of a perfectly insulating material walls of thickness 8 cm and the only way for heat to enter or leave the box is through two solid metallic cylindrical plugs, each of cross-sectional area 12 cm^2 and length 8 cm, fixed in the opposite walls of the box. The outer surface *A* on one plug is maintained at 100°C while the outer surface *B* of the other plug is maintained at 4°C. The thermal conductivity of the material of each plug is 0.5 cal/°C/cm. A source of energy generating 36 cal/s is enclosed inside the box. Assuming the temperature to be the same at all points on the inner surface, the equilibrium temperature of the inner surface of the box is

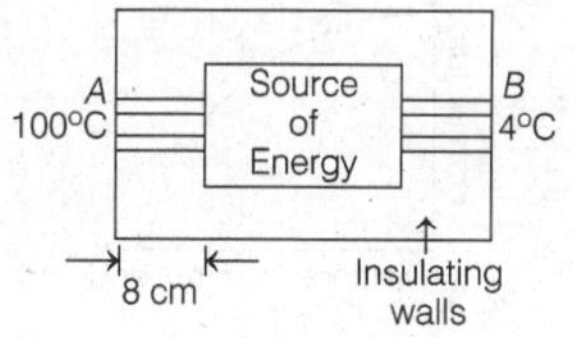

(a) 62°C
(b) 46°C
(c) 76°C
(d) 52°C

16 The temperature at the interface for steady flow of heat through the slab, if heat conductivity of first slab of length *l* is K_0 and is uniform every where but the conductivity of second slab of length 2*l* varies with the distance *x* measured from the interface according to the law $K = K_0\left(1 + \frac{x}{l}\right)$ is

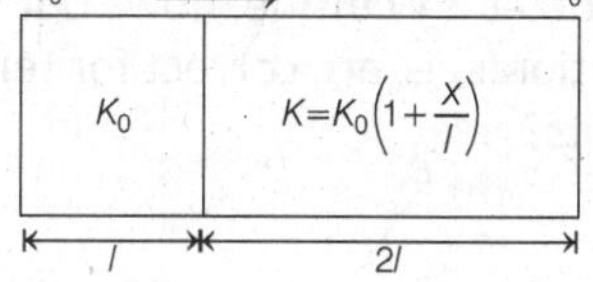

(The temperature at the boundaries of the composite slab are $2T_0$ and T_0)

(a) $\left(\frac{2\ln 2 + 1}{\ln 2 + 1}\right)T_0$
(b) $\left(\frac{2\ln 3 + 1}{\ln 3 + 1}\right)T_0$
(c) $\left(\frac{2\ln 3 + 1}{\ln 3 - 1}\right)T_0$
(d) $\left(\frac{4\ln 3 + 1}{\ln 3 + 1}\right)T_0$

17 An irregular rod of same uniform material as shown in figure is conducting heat at a steady rate. The temperature gradient at various sections *versus* area of cross-section graph will be

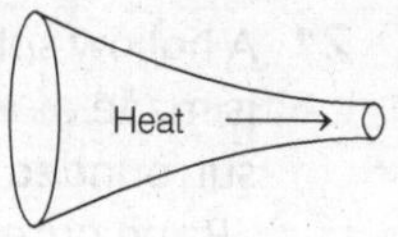

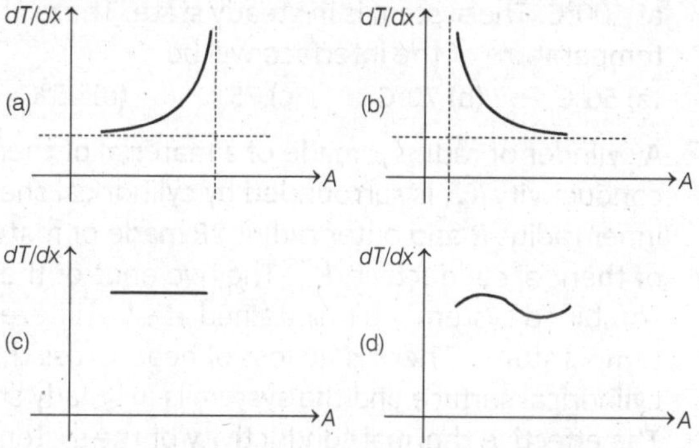

18 A rod of length *l* and cross-section area *A* has a variable thermal conductivity given by $K = \alpha T$, where α is a positive constant and *T* is temperature in Kelvin. Two ends of the rod are maintained at temperatures T_1 and T_2 ($T_1 > T_2$). Heat current flowing through the rod will be

(a) $\frac{A\alpha\,(T_1^2 - T_2^2)}{3l}$
(b) $\frac{A\alpha\,(T_1^2 + T_2^2)}{l}$
(c) $\frac{A\alpha\,(T_1^2 + T_2^2)}{3l}$
(d) $\frac{A\alpha\,(T_1^2 - T_2^2)}{2l}$

19 A long rod has one end at 0°C and other end at a high temperature. The coefficient of thermal conductivity varies with distance from the low temperature end as $K = K_0(1 + \alpha x)$, where $K_0 = 10^{+2}$ SI unit and $\alpha = 1\,\text{m}^{-1}$. At what distance from the first end the temperature will be 100°C? The area of cross-section is 1 cm^2 and rate of heat conduction is 1 W.

(a) 2.7 m
(b) 1.7 m
(c) 3 m
(d) 1.5 m

20 Figure shows a rod of variable cross-section area. Two ends of rod are maintained at different temperatures. Let radius of cross-section, where temperature is arithmetic mean of temperatures at two ends be *r*. Then, *r*

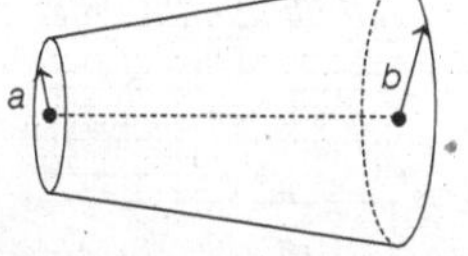

(a) is equal to arithmetic mean of *a* and *b*
(b) is equal to geometric mean of *a* and *b*
(c) is equal to harmonic mean of *a* and *b*
(d) depends upon length of rod *a* and *b*

21 A hollow sphere of inner radius R and outer radius $2R$ is made of a material of thermal conductivity K. It is surrounded by another hollow sphere of inner radius $2R$ and outer radius $3R$ made of same material of thermal conductivity K. The inside of smaller sphere is maintained at 0°C and the outside of bigger sphere at 100°C. The system is in steady state. The temperature of the interface will be

(a) 50°C (b) 70°C (c) 75°C (d) 45°C

22 A cylinder of radius R made of a material of thermal conductivity K_1, is surrounded by cylindrical shell of inner radius R and outer radius $2R$ made of material of thermal conductivity K_2. The two ends of the combined system are maintained at two different temperatures. There is no loss of heat across the cylindrical surface and the system is in steady state. The effective thermal conductivity of the system is

(a) $K_1 + K_2$ (b) $\dfrac{K_1 K_2}{K_1 + K_2}$ (c) $\dfrac{K_1 + 3K_2}{4}$ (d) $\dfrac{3K_1 + K_2}{4}$

Multiple Choice(s) Correct Questions

1 The two ends of a uniform lagged rod of thermal conductivity K are maintained at different but constant temperatures. The temperature gradient at any point on the rod is $\dfrac{d\theta}{dl}$ (equal to the difference in temperature per unit length). The heat flow per unit time per unit cross-section of the rod is I

(a) $\dfrac{d\theta}{dl}$ is the same for all points on the rod

(b) I will decrease as we move from higher to lower temperature

(c) $I = K \cdot \dfrac{d\theta}{dl}$

(d) All the above options are incorrect

2 Consider the shown case of a freezing lake due to negative environmental temperature (–θ° C). Thickness (x) of ice layer is small in comparison to depth of lake. Rate of increase in x will be greater

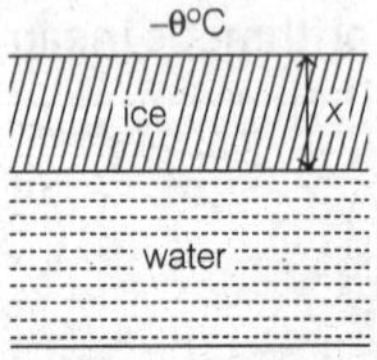

(a) if environmental temperature increases

(b) for larger thickness of ice layer

(c) if environmental temperature decreases

(d) for smaller thickness of ice layer

3 The temperature drop through a two layer furnace wall is 900°C. Each layer is of equal area of cross-section. Which of the following action(s) will result in lowering the temperature θ of the interface?

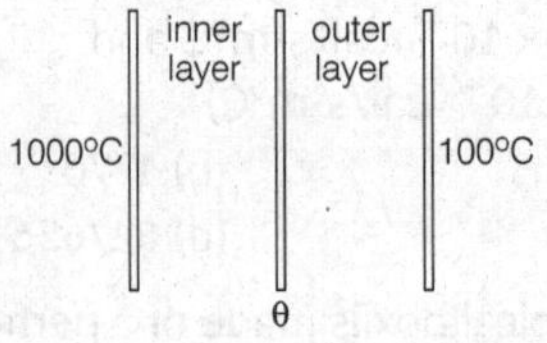

(a) By increasing the thermal conductivity of outer layer.

(b) By increasing the thermal conductivity of inner layer.

(c) By increasing thickness of outer layer.

(d) By increasing thickness of inner layer.

4 The ends of a long homogeneous bar are maintained at different temperatures and there is no loss of heat from the sides of the bar due to conduction or radiation. The graph of temperature against distance of the bar when it has attained steady state is shown here. The graph shows

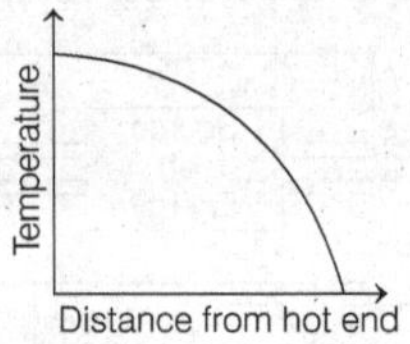

(a) the temperature gradient is not constant

(b) the bar has uniform cross-sectional area

(c) the cross-sectional area of the bar increases as the distance from the hot end increases

(d) the cross-sectional area of the bar decreases at the distance from the hot end increases

5 Four identical rods which have thermally insulated lateral surfaces are joined at point A. Points B, C, D and E are connected to large reservoirs. If heat flows into the junction from point B at rate of 1 W and from point C at 3 W inside, flows out from D at 5 W, which relation(s) is/are correct for temperature of these points?

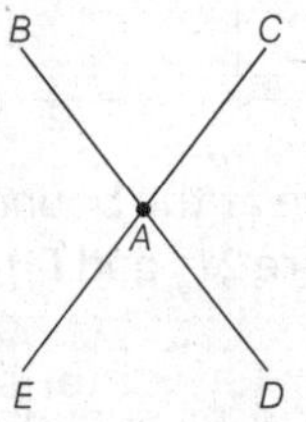

(a) $T_A < T_E$ (b) $T_B = T_C$

(c) $T_C > T_D$ (d) $T_B = T_E$

6 Seven identical rods of material of thermal conductivity K are connected as shown in figure. All the rods are of the identical length l and cross-sectional area A. If the one end A is kept at 100°C and the other end B kept at 0°C, what would be the temperature of the junctions C, D and E (θ_C, θ_D and θ_E) in the steady state?

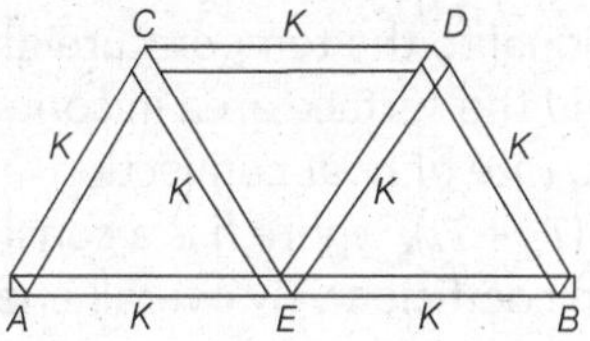

(a) $\theta_C > \theta_E > \theta_D$

(b) $\theta_E = 50°C$ and $\theta_D = 37.5°C$

(c) $\theta_E = 50°C, \theta_C = 62.5°C$ and $\theta_D = 37.5°C$

(d) $\theta_E = 50°C, \theta_C = 60°C$ and $\theta_D = 40°C$

7 A circular ring (centre O) of radius a, and of uniform cross-section is made up of three different metallic rods AB, BC and CA (joined together at the points A, B and C in pairs) of thermal conductivities α_1, α_2 and α_3, respectively (see diagram). The junctions A, B and C are maintained at the temperatures 100°, 50° and 0°C, respectively. All the rods are of equal lengths and cross-sections. Under steady state conditions, assume that no heat is lost from the sides of the rods. Let Q_1, Q_2 and Q_3 be the rates of transmission of heat along the three rods AB, BC and CA. Then,

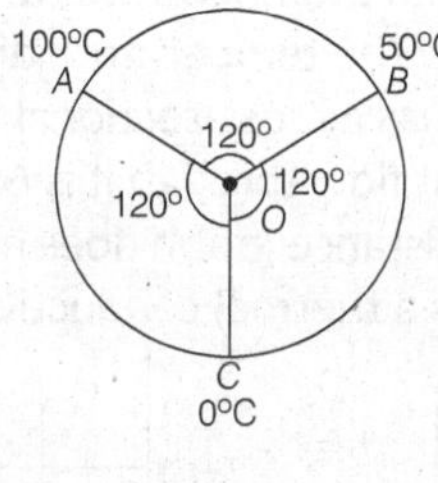

(a) $Q_1 = Q_2 = Q_3$ and all are transmitted in the clockwise sense

(b) Q_1 and Q_2 flow in clockwise sense and Q_3 in the anti-clockwise sense

(c) $Q_1 : Q_2 : Q_3 :: \alpha_1 : \alpha_2 : 2\alpha_3$

(d) $\dfrac{Q_1}{\alpha_1} + \dfrac{Q_2}{\alpha_2} = \dfrac{Q_3}{\alpha_3}$

8 A 100 cm long cylindrical flask with inner and outer diameter 2 cm and 4 cm respectively is completely filled with ice as shown in the figure. The constant temperature outside the flask is 40°C.

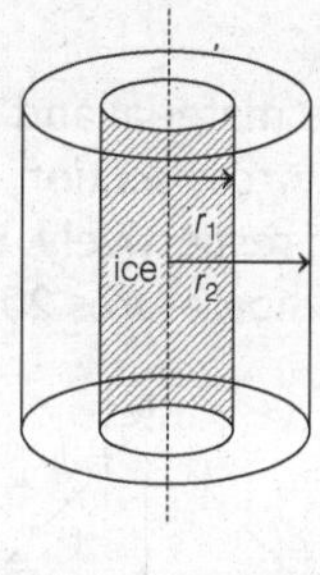

(Thermal conductivity of the flask is 0.693 W/m°C, $L_{ice} = 80$ cal/gm and ln 2 = 0.693).

(a) Rate of heat flow from outside to the flask is 80π J/s.

(b) The rate at which ice melts is $\dfrac{\pi}{4200}$ kg/s.

(c) The rate at which ice melts is 100π kg/s.

(d) Rate of heat flow from outside to flask is 40π J/s.

Comprehension Based Questions

Comprehension-1

Two rods A and B of same cross-sectional area A connected between a source ($T_1 = 100°C$) and a sink ($T_2 = 0°C$) as shown in figure. The rods are laterally insulated.

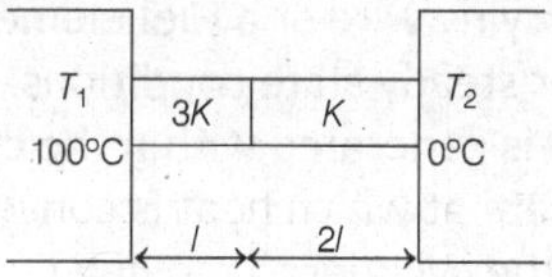

1 The ratio of the thermal resistance of the rods is

(a) $\dfrac{R_A}{R_B} = \dfrac{1}{6}$ (b) $\dfrac{R_A}{R_B} = 6$

(c) $\dfrac{R_A}{R_B} = \dfrac{3}{2}$ (d) $\dfrac{R_A}{R_B} = \dfrac{2}{3}$

2 If T_A and T_B are the temperature drops across the rods A and B, then

(a) $\dfrac{T_A}{T_B} = \dfrac{6}{1}$ (b) $\dfrac{T_A}{T_B} = \dfrac{1}{6}$

(c) $\dfrac{T_A}{T_B} = \dfrac{3}{2}$ (d) $\dfrac{T_A}{T_B} = \dfrac{2}{3}$

3 If G_A and G_B are the temperature gradients across the rods A and B, then

(a) $\dfrac{G_A}{G_B} = \dfrac{3}{1}$ (b) $\dfrac{G_A}{G_B} = \dfrac{1}{3}$

(c) $\dfrac{G_A}{G_B} = \dfrac{3}{4}$ (d) $\dfrac{G_A}{G_B} = \dfrac{4}{3}$

Comprehension-2

Five rods of same material and same length are joined as shown. Cross-section of rods *ab*, *ad* and *bc* are *A*, 2*A* and 3*A*, respectively. Ends *a* and *c* are maintained at temperatures 200 C° and 0°C, respectively.

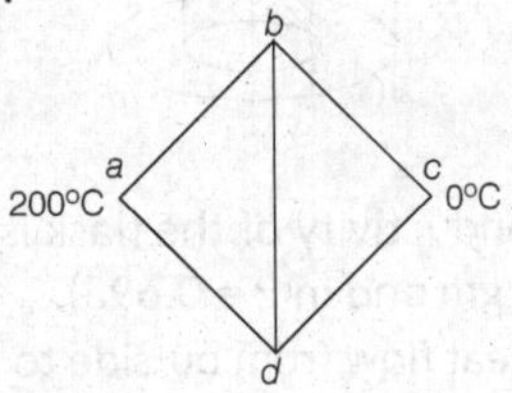

4 For what cross-section *x* of rod *dc* there will be no heat flow through rod *bd*?
(a) 4 A (b) 2 A (c) 6 A (d) 9 A

5 If *x* has the value calculated in above question, then temperature of junction *b* or *d* is
(a) 50°C (b) 100°C (c) 90°C (d) 150°C

Comprehension-3

Heat generation may occur in a variety of radial geometries. Consider a long, solid cylinder as shown in the figure, which could represent a current-carrying wire or a fuel element in a nuclear reactor. For steady state conditions, the rate at which heat is generated within the cylinder must equal the rate at which heat is convected from the surface of the cylinder to moving fluid. This condition allows the surface temperature to be maintained at a fixed value of T_S.

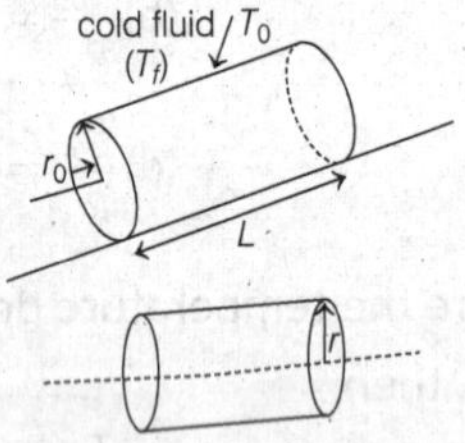

To determine the temperature distribution in the cylinder, we begin with energy conservation principle. Consider a cylindrical section of radius *r*. The rate at which energy is generated $\dot{q} = dQ/dt$ within the given volume is conducted radially outward.

$$\therefore \ \dot{q}\pi r^2 l = -K2\pi r l \frac{dT}{dr}$$

where, $\dot{q}$ is the energy generated per unit time per unit volume, *K* is the thermal conductivity and $\frac{dT}{dr}$ is the temperature gradient at radius *r*.

If $\dot{q}$ is constant $T(r) = -\frac{\dot{q}}{4k}r^2 + C$

At $r = r_0$, $T(r_0) = T_S$

Therefore, $T(r) = \frac{\dot{q}}{4k} r_0^2 \left(1 - \frac{r^2}{r_0^2}\right) + T_s$

The rate of heat convected to the surrounding fluid (at temperature T_f) by the surface at temperature T_s is proportional to the temperature difference $(T_S - T_f)$ and the surface area in contact with the fluid. Thus, rate of heat convection $= h(2\pi r_0 L)(T_s - T_f)$, where *h* is a constant called heat convection coefficient. By overall energy balance,

$\dot{q}(\pi r_0^2 L) = h(2\pi r_0 l)(T_s - T_f)$

$\Rightarrow T_s = T_f + \frac{\dot{q} r_0}{2h}$

6 In the above passage, the ratio of temperature gradient at $r = r_0/2$ and $r = r_0$ is
(a) 1 (b) 1/4 (c) 1/2 (d) 1/8

7 In the given passage, the difference in temperature at the axis and surface of the cylinder is
(a) $\frac{\dot{q}r_0^2}{4k}$ (b) $\frac{\dot{q}r_0^2}{k}$ (c) $\frac{\dot{q}r_0^2}{2k}$ (d) $\frac{2\dot{q}r_0}{k}$

8 The dimension of heat convection coefficient is
(a) $[ML^2T^{-1}\theta^{-1}]$ (b) $[ML^0T^{-3}\theta^{-1}]$
(c) $[ML^2T^{-2}\theta^{-1}]$ (d) $[ML^4T^{-2}\theta^{-1}]$

Comprehension-4

The figure shows a cross-section of a double glass unit and a graph of the temperatures at different points within the unit. The temperature difference across the unit is 13 K. It has a cross-sectional area of 1.3 m^2 and the rate of heat flow through it is 65 W. The temperature distance graph does not change with time. Glass has a thermal conductivity of 1 W/mK.

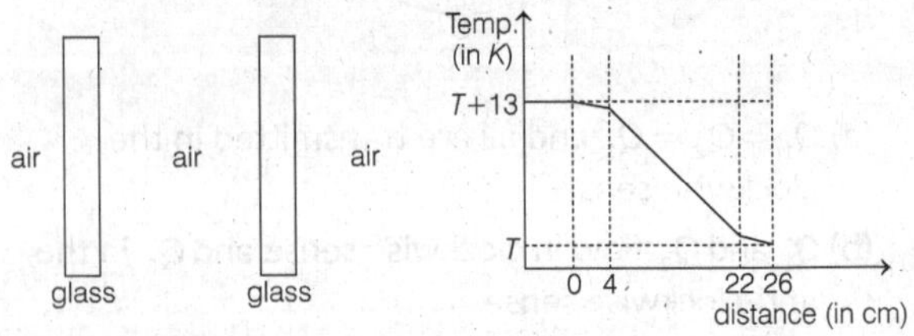

9 Select the correct statement
(a) The unit is in steady state and in thermal equilibrium
(b) The unit is in steady state but not in thermal equilibrium
(c) The unit is not in steady state but is in thermal equilibrium
(d) The unit is neither in steady state nor in thermal equilibrium

10 The thermal conductivity of air is

(a) $\frac{1}{10}$ W/mK (b) $\frac{1}{12}$ W/mK

(c) $\frac{1}{14}$ W/mK (d) $\frac{1}{18}$ W/mK

Match the Columns

1 Four rods of material X and three rods of material Y are connected as shown in figure. All the rods are of identical lengths are cross-sectional area. Given, thermal resistance of rod of material X, $R_X = R$ and thermal conductivities of materials are related by relation $K_Y = 2K_X$.

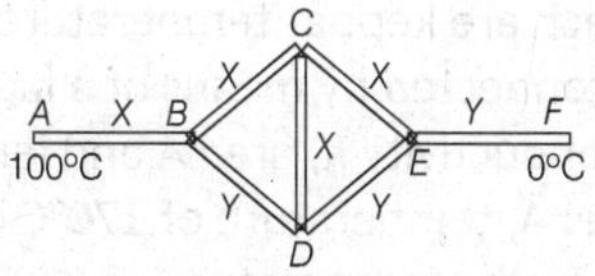

	Column I		Column II
(A)	Thermal resistance between B and E	(p)	$\frac{500}{13}$°C
(B)	Thermal resistance between A and F	(q)	$\frac{700}{13}$°C
(C)	Temperature of junction B	(r)	$\frac{2R}{3}$
(D)	Temperature of junction D	(s)	$\frac{13R}{6}$

2 A copper rod (initially at room temperature 20°C) of non-uniform cross-section is placed between a steam chamber at 100°C and ice-water chamber at 0°C. A and B are cross-sections as shown in figure. Then, match the statements in Column I with results in Column II using comparing only between cross-section A and B. (The mathematical expressions in Column I have usual meaning in heat transfer)

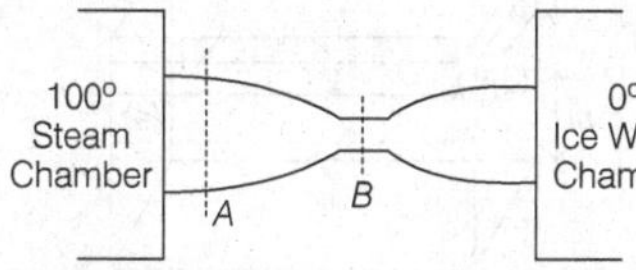

	Column I		Column II
(A)	Initially rate of heat flow $\left(\frac{dQ}{dt}\right)$ will be	(p)	Maximum at section A
(B)	At steady state, rate of heat flow $\left(\frac{dQ}{dt}\right)$ will be	(q)	Maximum at section B
(C)	At steady state, temperature gradient $\left\lvert\left(\frac{dT}{dx}\right)\right\rvert$ will be	(r)	Minimum at section B
(D)	At steady state, rate of change of temperature $\left(\frac{dT}{dt}\right)$ at a certain point will be	(s)	Same for all sections

3 In Column I, certain situations are depicted where steam at 100°C is used to melt ice at 0°C by means of a conducting body which is insulated to prevent heat losses to surrounding. Match the numerical value of question asked in each entry to the corresponding entry in Column II. Symbols have usual meaning.

	Column I		Column II
(A)	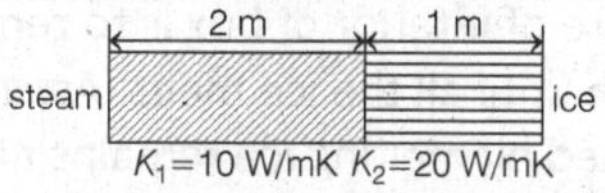 Find temperature of interface of two rods in °C.	(p)	10
(B)	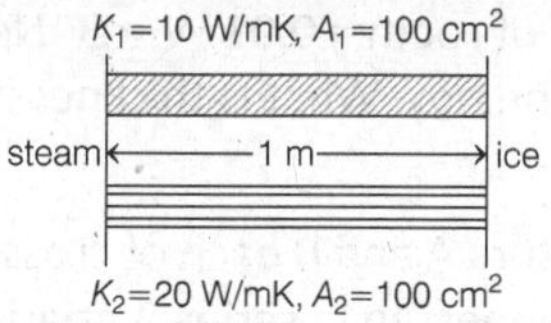 Find total rate of heat transfer through the two rods in SI units.	(q)	20
(C)	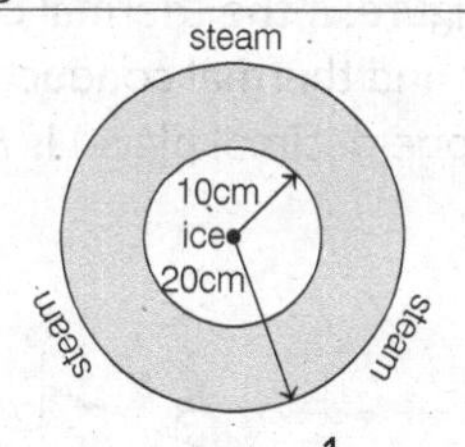 Hollow sphere of $K = \frac{1}{32\pi}$ W/mK. Find thermal resistance in SI units.	(r)	30
(D)	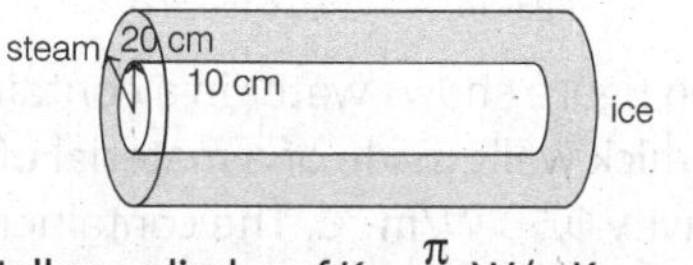 Hollow cylinder of $K = \frac{\pi}{10}$ W/mK. Find temperature gradients in SI units.	(s)	40

Numerical Value Questions

1 A rod is initially at a uniform temperature of 0°C throughout, One end is kept at 0°C and the other is brought into contact with a steam bath at 100°C. The surface of the rod is isolated, so that heat can flow only lengthwise along rod. The cross-sectional area of the rod is 2.5 cm^2, its length 120 cm, its thermal conductivity is 400 W/m-K, its density is 2×10^4 kg/m^3 and its specific heat is 520 J/kg-K. Consider a short cylindrical element of the rod 1 cm in length. If temperature gradient at the cooler end of this element is 140 °C/m and average temperature of the element is rising at 0.250°C/s, what is the temperature gradient (in °C/m) at the other end of the element?

2 A block of ice, mass 24 kg, is placed inside a closed cubical box having dimension 1 m. Water from melting ice collects in the bottom of box. The ice block is at 0°C and outside temperature is 15°C. Temperature of interior of box is to remain at 5°C for exactly 24 h until all the ice melts. Assume that liquid water formed by melting ice remains at 0°C, heat conduction takes place from all the surfaces. Latent heat of fusion of water = 360 kJ/kg Thermal conductivity of room = 0.01 W/mK. Neglect heat capacity of the box. What is thickness (in mm) of the box?

3 Two conductors *A* and *B* each of cross-section area 5 cm^2 are connected in series. Variation of temperature (in °C) along the length (in cm) is as shown in the figure. If the thermal conductivity of *A* is 200 J/m-s °C and thermal conductivity of *B* (in J/m-s °C upto one decimal place) is *K*, then find $\sqrt{\frac{K}{8\sqrt{3}}}$.

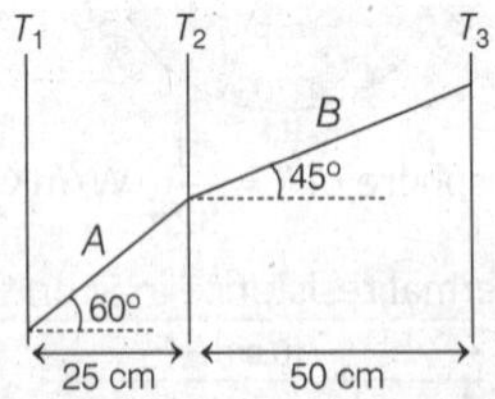

4 The given figure shows water in a container having 2.0 mm thick walls made of a material of thermal conductivity 0.50 W/m-°C. The container is kept in a melting-ice bath at 0°C. The total surface area in contact with water is 0.05 m^2. A wheel is clamped inside the water and is coupled to a block of mass *M* as shown in the figure. As the block goes down, the wheel rotates. It is found that after some time a steady state is reached in which the block goes down with a constant speed of 10 cm/s and the temperature of the water remains constant at 1.0°C. Find the mass *M* (in kg) of the block. Assume that the heat flows out of the water only through the walls in contact. (Take, $g = 10\ m/s^2$).

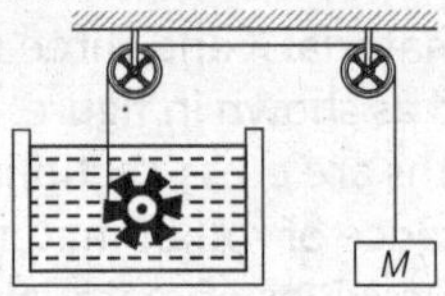

5 Two thermally insulated vessel filled with water of mass *m* each are kept at temperature 30°C and 10°C. They are connected by means of a lagged rod of thermal conductivity *K*, area *A* and length *L*. At *L*/4 from vessel A, temperature of 170°C is maintained. What will be the temperature of *B* (in °C) when water in *A* starts boiling? Assume no heat loss to the surrounding. (Take, $2^{1/3} = 5/4$)

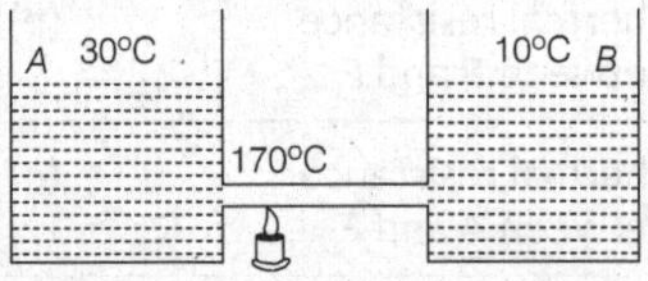

6 An arrangement consisting of slabs is shown in the figure. When system is placed in situation (a) with temperature difference maintained between (1) and (2), equivalent thermal conductivity of system is *K* and when system is changed to situation (b) and temperature difference is maintained between (3) and (4), then equivalent thermal conductivity increases by 20%. Find number of slabs in the arrangement.

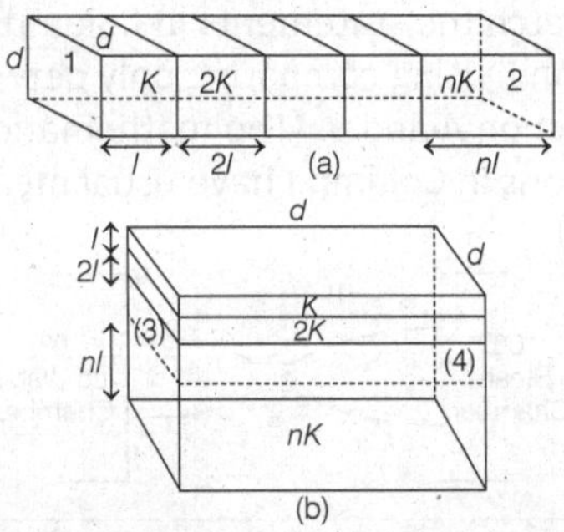

7 A composite rod is made from stainless steel and iron and has a length of 0.5 m. The cross-section of this composite rod consists of a square within a circle. The square is 1 cm on a side. $K_{steel} = 14$ W/m°C, $K_{iron} = 80$ W/m°C. One end of the rod is at

78°C and other end is in melting ice. Find the amount of ice melted in 7 min (in g).

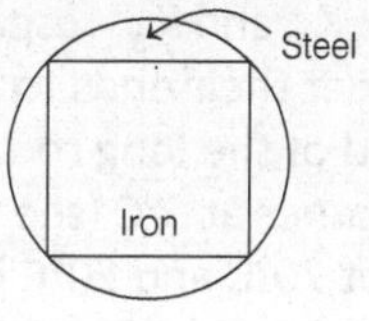

(Take $\pi = 22/7$).

8 After the warm days, a sharp frost hit a lake and its surface got covered with ice. One day after the cold snap; the ice thickness was $d_1 = 2$ cm. Some ship builders want to take weights on the opposite shore of the lake. But for security reasons ice thickness of at least $d_2 = 10$ cm is needed. How many days after moment of frost is it possible to transport the goods, if the temperature of surrounding does not change?

9 A 2 m long wire of resistance 10 Ω and radius 0.5 mm is coated with plastic of thickness 0.5 mm. A current of 2 A flows through the wire. If the temperature difference across the plastic insulation in steady state is $\frac{n \ln 2}{\pi}$ °C, then find the value of n. Thermal conductivity of plastic is 0.005 J/s-m°C.

10 A hollow spherical conducting shell of inner radius $R_1 = 0.25$ m and outer radius $R_2 = 0.50$ m in placed inside a heat reservoir of temperature $T_\theta = 1000°C$. The shell is initially filled with at 0°C. The thermal conductivity of the material is $k = \frac{10^2}{4\pi}$ W/m-K and its heat capacity is negligible. The time required to raise the temperature of water to 100°C is $1100K \ln\left(\frac{10}{9}\right)$ s. Find K. (Take, specific heat of water $s = 4.2$ kJ/kg°C, density of water $d_w = 1000 \text{ kg/m}^3$, $\pi = \frac{22}{7}$)

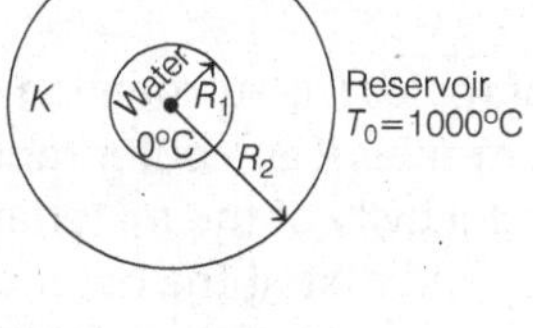

Previous Year's Questions

JEE Main

1 Two plates A and B have thermal conductivities 84 $Wm^{-1}K^{-1}$ and 126 $Wm^{-1}K^{-1}$ respectively. They have same surface area and same thickness. They are placed in contact along their surfaces. If the temperatures of the outer surfaces of A and B are kept at 100°C and 0°C respectively, then the temperature of the surface of contact in steady state is .... °C. **[2023, 13 April Shift-II]**

2 As per the given figure, two plates A and B of thermal conductivity K and $2K$ are joined together to form a compound plate. The thickness of plates are 4.0 cm and 2.5 cm, respectively and the area of cross-section is 120 cm^2 for each plate. The equivalent thermal conductivity of the compound plate is $\left(1 + \frac{5}{\alpha}\right)K$, then the value of α will be __________. **[2022, 29 June Shift-I]**

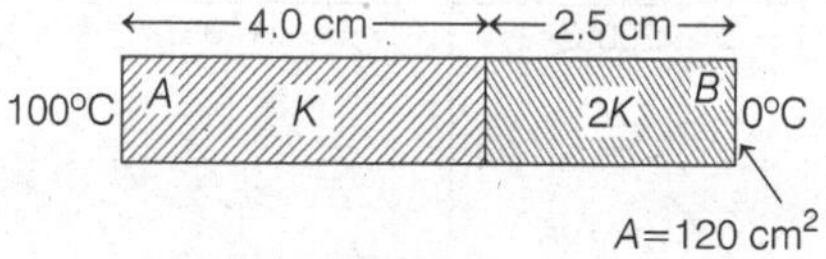

3 An ice cube of dimensions 60 cm × 50 cm × 20 cm is placed in an insulation box of wall thickness 1 cm. The box keeping the ice cube at 0°C of temperature is brought to a room of temperature 40°C. The rate of melting of ice is approximately (Latent heat of fusion of ice is 3.4×10^5 J kg^{-1} and thermal conducting of insulation wall is 0.05 $Wm^{-1}°C^{-1}$) **[2022, 26 July Shift-II]**

(a) 61×10^{-3} kg s^{-1}
(b) 61×10^{-5} kg s^{-1}
(c) 208 kg s^{-1}
(d) 30×10^{-5} kg s^{-1}

4 If K_1 and K_2 are the thermal conductivities, L_1 and L_2 are the lengths and A_1 and A_2 are the cross-sectional areas of steel and copper rods respectively, such that $\frac{K_2}{K_1} = 9$, $\frac{A_1}{A_2} = 2$, $L_1/L_2 = 2$. Then, for the arrangement as shown in the figure, the value of temperature T of the steel-copper junction in the steady state will be **[2022, 27 July Shift-I]**

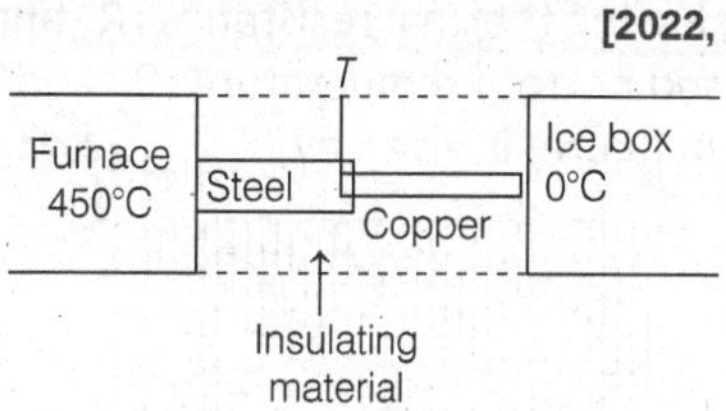

(a) 18°C (b) 14°C
(c) 45°C (d) 150°C

5 Two metallic blocks M_1 and M_2 of same area of cross-section are connected to each other (as shown in figure). If the thermal conductivity of M_2 is K, then the thermal conductivity of M_1 will be :[Assume steady state heat conduction] **[2022, 24 June Shift-I]**

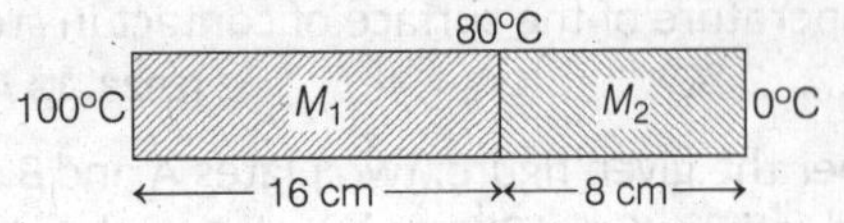

(a) $10\,K$ (b) $8\,K$ (c) $12.5\,K$ (d) $2\,K$

6 A rod CD of thermal resistance 10.0 kW^{-1} is joined at the middle of an identical rod AB as shown in figure. The end A, B and D are maintained at 200°C, 100°C and 125°C respectively. The heat current in CD is P watt. The value of P is .... **[2021, 27 Aug Shift-I]**

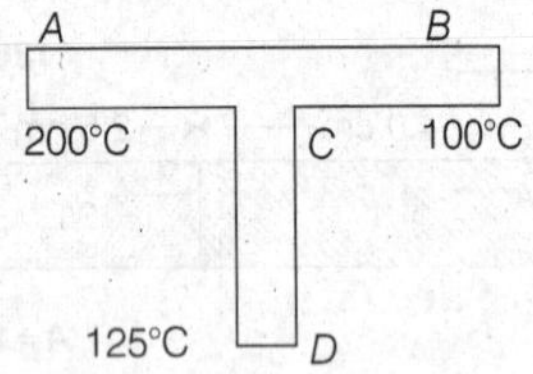

7 Two thin metallic spherical shells of radii r_1 and r_2 $(r_1 < r_2)$ are placed with their centres coinciding. A material of thermal conductivity K is filled in the space between the shells. The inner shell is maintained at temperature θ_1 and the outer shell at temperature $\theta_2\,(\theta_1 < \theta_2)$. The rate at which heat flows radially through the material is **[2021, 31 Aug Shift-II]**

(a) $\dfrac{4\pi K r_1 r_2 (\theta_2 - \theta_1)}{r_2 - r_1}$ (b) $\dfrac{\pi r_1 r_2 (\theta_2 - \theta_1)}{r_2 - r_1}$

(c) $\dfrac{K(\theta_2 - \theta_1)}{r_2 - r_1}$ (d) $\dfrac{K(\theta_2 - \theta_1)(r_2 - r_1)}{4\pi r_1 r_2}$

8 Two identical metal wires of thermal conductivities K_1 and K_2 respectively are connected in series. The effective thermal conductivity of the combination is **[2021, 17 March Shift-I]**

(a) $\dfrac{2K_1 K_2}{K_1 + K_2}$ (b) $\dfrac{K_1 + K_2}{2K_1 K_2}$ (c) $\dfrac{K_1 + K_2}{K_1 K_2}$ (d) $\dfrac{K_1 K_2}{K_1 + K_2}$

9 The temperature θ at the junction of two insulating sheets, having thermal resistances R_1 and R_2 as well as top and bottom temperatures θ_1 and θ_2 (as shown in figure) is given by **[2021, 26 Feb Shift-I]**

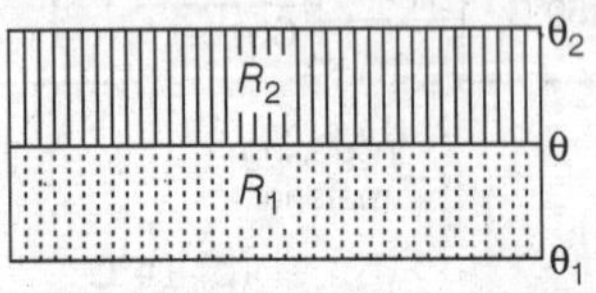

(a) $\dfrac{\theta_2 R_2 - \theta_1 R_1}{R_2 - R_1}$ (b) $\dfrac{\theta_1 R_2 - \theta_2 R_1}{R_2 - R_1}$

(c) $\dfrac{\theta_1 R_2 + \theta_2 R_1}{R_1 + R_2}$ (d) $\dfrac{\theta_1 R_1 + \theta_2 R_2}{R_1 + R_2}$

10 Three rods of identical cross-section and lengths are made of three different materials of thermal conductivity K_1, K_2 and K_3, respectively. They are joined together at their ends to make a long rod (see figure). One end of the long rod is maintained at 100°C and the other at 0°C (see figure). If the joints of the rod are at 70°C and 20°C in steady state and there is no loss of energy from the surface of the rod, the correct relationship between K_1, K_2 and K_3 is **[2020, 6 Sep Shift-II]**

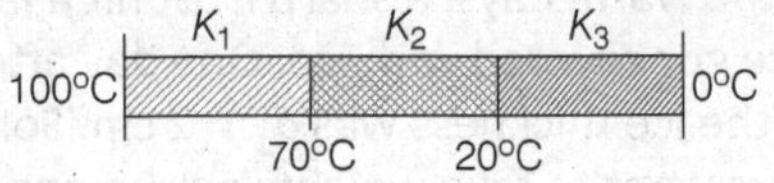

(a) $K_1 : K_3 = 2:3; K_2 : K_3 = 2:5$

(b) $K_1 < K_2 < K_3$

(c) $K_1 : K_2 = 5:2; K_1 : K_3 = 3:5$

(d) $K_1 > K_2 > K_3$

11 Two materials having coefficients of thermal conductivity '$3K$' and 'K' and thickness 'd' and '$3d$' respectively, are joined to form a slab. The temperatures of the outer surfaces are 'θ_2' and 'θ_1' respectively, $(\theta_2 > \theta_1)$. The temperature at the interface is **[2019, 9 April Shift-II]**

(a) $\dfrac{\theta_2 + \theta_1}{2}$ (b) $\dfrac{\theta_1}{3} + \dfrac{2\theta_2}{3}$

(c) $\dfrac{\theta_1}{6} + \dfrac{5\theta_2}{6}$ (d) $\dfrac{\theta_1}{10} + \dfrac{9\theta_2}{10}$

12 A heat source at $T = 10^3$ K is connected to another heat reservoir at $T = 10^2$ K by a copper slab which is 1 m thick. Given that the thermal conductivity of copper is 0.1 $WK^{-1}m^{-1}$, the energy flux through it in the steady state is **[2019, 10 Jan Shift-I]**

(a) 90 Wm^{-2}

(b) 65 Wm^{-2}

(c) 120 Wm^{-2}

(d) 200 Wm^{-2}

13 A cylinder of radius R is surrounded by a cylindrical shell of inner radius R and outer radius $2R$. The thermal conductivity of the material of the inner cylinder is K_1 and that of the outer cylinder is K_2. Assuming no loss of heat, the effective thermal conductivity of the system for heat flowing along the length of the cylinder is **[2019, 12 Jan Shift-I]**

(a) $\dfrac{K_1 + K_2}{2}$ (b) $\dfrac{K_1 + 3K_2}{4}$

(c) $\dfrac{2K_1 + 3K_2}{5}$ (d) $K_1 + K_2$

JEE Advanced

1. Two conducting cylinders of equal length but different radii are connected in series between two heat baths kept at temperatures $T_1 = 300\text{K}$ and $T_2 = 100$ K, as shown in the figure. The radius of the bigger cylinder is twice that of the smaller one and the thermal conductivities of the materials of the smaller and the larger cylinders are K_1 and K_2, respectively. If the temperature at the junction of the cylinders in the steady state is 200K, then $K_1/K_2 =$.......... . **(2018 Adv.)**

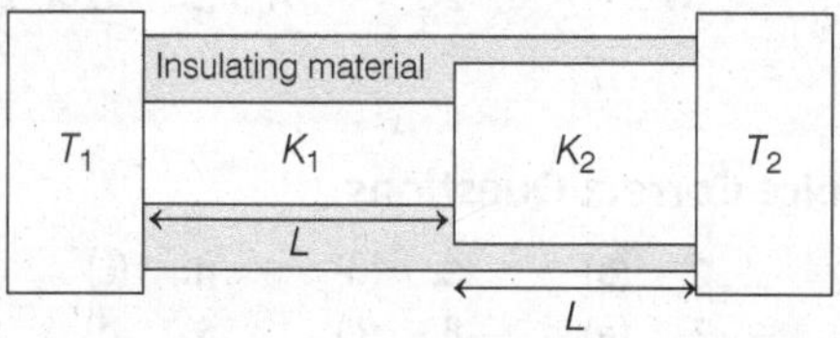

2. The ends Q and R of two thin wires, PQ and RS, are soldered (joined) together. Initially, each of the wire has a length of 1 m at 10°C. Now, the end P is maintained at 10°C, while the end S is heated and maintained at 400°C. The system is thermally insulated from its surroundings. If the thermal conductivity of wire PQ is twice that of the wire RS and the coefficient of linear thermal expansion of PQ is $1.2\times 10^{-5}\ \text{K}^{-1}$, the change in length of the wire PQ is **(2016 Adv.)**

(a) 0.78 mm
(b) 0.90 mm
(c) 1.56 mm
(d) 2.34 mm

3. Two rectangular blocks, having indentical dimensions, can be arranged either in configuration I or in configuration II as shown in the figure. One of the blocks has thermal conductivity K and the other $2K$. The temperature difference between the ends along the X-axis is the same in both the configurations. It takes 9s to transport a certain amount of heat from the hot end to the cold end in the configuration I. The time to transport the same amount of heat in the configuration II is **(2013 Adv.)**

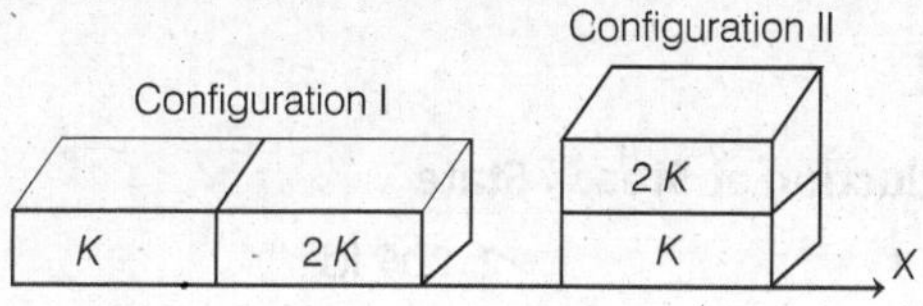

(a) 2.0 s
(b) 3.0 s
(c) 4.5 s
(d) 6.0 s

4. A composite block is made of slabs A, B, C, D and E of different thermal conductivities (given in terms of a constant K) and sizes (given in terms of length, L) as shown in the figure. All slabs are of same width. Heat Q flows only from left to right through the blocks. Then, in steady state **(2011 Adv.)**

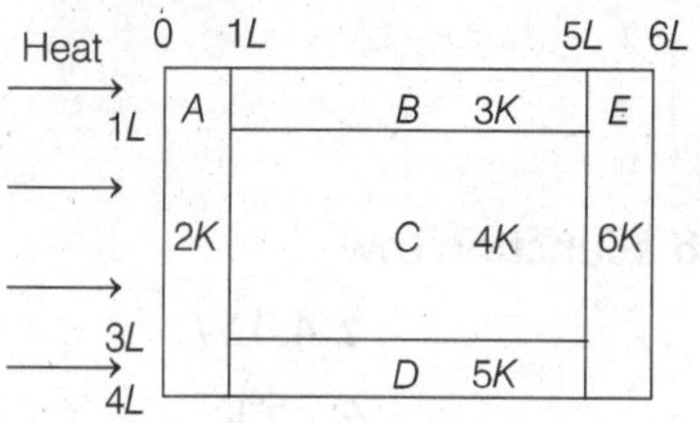

(a) heat flow through A and E slabs are same
(b) heat flow through slab E is maximum
(c) temperature difference across slab E is smallest
(d) heat flow through C = heat flow through B + heat flow through D

5. A metal rod AB of length $10x$ has its one end A in ice at 0°C and the other end B in water at 100°C. If a point P on the rod is maintained at 400°C, then it is found that equal amounts of water and ice evaporate and melt per unit time. The latent heat of evaporation of water is 540 calg^{-1} and latent heat of melting of ice is 80 calg^{-1}. If the point P is at a distance of λx from the ice end A, find the value of λ. (Neglect any heat loss to the surrounding.) **(2009 Adv.)**

Answer Key

Level 1

3.1 Conduction at Steady State

1. 64 J
2. 209 kJ
3. 127.5°C
4. 98×10^5 J
5. 15.24°C
6. 130°C
7. 5×10^{-5} g/s
8. 1.5 kg/h
9. 28°C
10. 6.3×10^5 s = 175 h

3.2 Temperature Gradient

1. (a) 3°C/cm (b) 44°C
2. 12°C/s
3. (a) equal heat currents (b) $(\Delta T)_{AB} < (\Delta T)_{CD}$
4. $T_1 \left(\frac{T_2}{T_1}\right)^{x/L}$

3.3 Kirchhoff's Junction Law

1. 10°C
2. 4.0 W
3. 300 J
4. 75°C

3.4 Combination of Rods

1. 15K / 16
2. 4.5 cal/s
3. 1.57×10^7 J (b) 1.97×10^5 J
4. 2.36 J
5. 132 J
6. (a) 75 W (b) 400 W
7. 4 W

3.5 Formation of Ice on Lake

1. (a) 5.0×10^{-7} m/s, (b) 27.5 h
2. 69000 seconds = 19.1 h

3.6 Conduction in Non-linear Conductors at Steady State

1. $\frac{4\pi K(T_1 - T_2) R_1 R_2}{(R_2 - R_1)}$
2. $\frac{2\pi Kl(T_2 - T_1)}{\ln (R_2 / R_1)}$
3. $\frac{K\pi R_1 R_2 (T_1 - T_2)}{L}$

Level 2

Single Choice Correct Questions

1. (a)	2. (b)	3. (c)	4. (a)	5. (c)
6. (b)	7. (d)	8. (a)	9. (b)	10. (c)
11. (a)	12. (b)	13. (b)	14. (d)	15. (b)
16. (d)	17. (a)	18. (c)	19. (b)	20. (a)
21. (c)	22. (a)	23. (c)	24. (a)	25. (b)
26. (a)	27. (c)	28. (b)		

Numerical Value Questions

1. 70	2. 231	3. 2	4. 1	5. 90
6. 2	7. 0.2	8. 20	9. 7.5	10. 15

Level 3

Single Choice Correct Questions

1. (c)	2. (a)	3. (d)	4. (c)	5. (b)
6. (b)	7. (a)	8. (c)	9. (d)	10. (d)
11. (d)	12. (a)	13. (b)	14. (d)	15. (c)
16. (b)	17. (b)	18. (d)	19. (b)	20. (c)
21. (c)	22. (c)			

Multiple Choice(s) Correct Questions

1. (ac)	2. (cd)	3. (ad)	4. (ad)	5. (acd)
6. (ac)	7. (bcd)	8. (ab)		

Comprehension Based Questions

1. (a)	2. (b)	3. (b)	4. (c)	5. (a)
6. (c)	7. (a)	8. (b)	9. (b)	10. (c)

Match the Columns Questions

1. A-r B-s C-q D-p
2. A-p, r; B-s; C-q; D-s
3. A-q, B-r, C-s, D-p

Numerical Value Questions

1. 205	2. 6	3. 5	4. 12.5	5. 42
6. 4	7. 1.716	8. 25	9. 2000	10. 5

Previous Year's Questions

JEE Main

1. (40)	2. (21)	3. (b)	4. (c)	5. (b)
6. (2)	7. (a)	8. (a)	9. (c)	10. (a)
11. (d)	12. (a)	13. (b)		

JEE Advanced

1. (4)	2. (a)	3. (a)	4. (a,c,d)	5. (9)

SOLUTIONS

Level-1

3.1 Conduction at Steady State

1. $\frac{dQ}{dt} = \frac{KA(T_1 - T_2)}{L}$

$= \frac{0.8 \times (10 \times 10^{-2})^2 (90 - 10)}{1 \times 10^{-2}} = 64 \text{ J/s}$

2. $i = \frac{dQ}{dt} = \frac{KA(T_1 - T_2)}{L} = \frac{209 \times 2^2 \times (100 - 0)}{2} = 418 \times 10^2 \text{ J/s}$

$Q = i \times t = 418 \times 10^2 \times 5 = 209 \text{ kJ}$

3. $\frac{dQ}{dt} = \frac{KA(T_1 - T_2)}{L}$

$\Rightarrow \quad 0.5 = \frac{0.26 \times 3.14 \times (1)^2 (250 - T_2)}{200}$

$\Rightarrow \quad T_2 = 127.5° \text{ C}$

4. $\frac{dQ}{dt} = \frac{KA(T_1 - T_2)}{L} = \frac{390 \times (2 \times 3.14 \times 0.1 \times 2) \times (373 - 273)}{5 \times 10^{-3}}$

$= 98 \times 10^5 \text{ J/s}$

5. Power of heater = Heat current due to conduction

$\Rightarrow \quad 2 \times 10^3 = \frac{0.84 \times 1 \times (20 - T_2)}{0.2 \times 10^{-2}}$

$\Rightarrow \quad T_2 = 15.24° \text{ C}$

6. $\frac{dQ}{dt} = \frac{KA(T_1 - T_2)}{L} = \frac{dm}{dt} L_v$

$\Rightarrow \quad \frac{50 \times 25 \times 10^{-4} \times (T_1 - 100)}{1 \times 10^{-3}} = \frac{0.1}{60} \times 2.26 \times 10^6$

$\Rightarrow \quad T_1 = 130° \text{ C}$

7. $\frac{dQ}{dt} = \frac{KA(T_1 - T_2)}{L} = \frac{dm}{dt} L_f$

$\Rightarrow \quad \frac{42 \times 0.04 \times 10^{-4} \times (100 - 0)}{1} = \frac{dm}{dt} \times 3.36 \times 10^5$

$\Rightarrow \quad \frac{dm}{dt} = 5 \times 10^{-8} \text{ kg/s} = 5 \times 10^{-5} \text{ g/s}$

8. $\frac{dQ}{dt} = \frac{KA(T_1 - T_2)}{L} = \frac{dm}{dt} L_f$

$\Rightarrow \quad \frac{0.06 \times 2400 \times 10^{-4} \times (20 - 0)}{2 \times 10^{-3}} = \frac{dm}{dt} \times 3.4 \times 10^5$

$\Rightarrow \quad \frac{dm}{dt} = 4.2 \times 10^{-4} \text{ kg/s} = 1.5 \text{ kg/h}$

9. $\frac{dQ}{dt} = \frac{KA(T_1 - T_2)}{L} = \frac{dm}{dt} L_v$

$\Rightarrow \quad \frac{0.8 \times 200 \times 10^{-4} \times (42 - T_2)}{1 \times 10^{-3}} = 0.1 \times 10^{-3} \times 2.27 \times 10^6$

$\Rightarrow \quad T_2 = 28° \text{ C}$

10. Let, temperature of water at time t be T.

$\frac{dQ}{dt} = \frac{KA(100 - T)}{L} = mS\frac{dT}{dt}$

$\Rightarrow \quad \frac{mSL}{KA} \int_0^{50} \frac{dT}{100 - T} = \int_0^t dt$

$\Rightarrow \quad \frac{mSL}{KA} \frac{1}{(-1)} [\ln(100 - T)]_0^{50} = [t]_0^t$

$\Rightarrow \quad t = \frac{mSL \ln 2}{KA} = \frac{1 \times 4180 \times 10 \times 0.693}{46 \times 10 \times 10^{-4}}$

$= 6.3 \times 10^5 \text{ s} = 175 \text{ h}$

3.2 Temperature Gradient

1. (a) $\frac{dT}{dx} = \frac{T_1 - T_2}{L} = \frac{80 - 20}{20} = 3° \text{C/cm}$

(b) $\frac{dT}{dx} = 3° \text{C/cm}$

$\Rightarrow \quad \frac{80 - T}{12} = 3 \quad \Rightarrow \quad T = 44° \text{ C}$

2. $KA\left[\frac{dT}{dx}\right]_A - KA\left[\frac{dT}{dx}\right]_B = C\frac{dT}{dt}$

$\Rightarrow 200 \times 1 \times 10^{-4}\left(\frac{5}{10^{-2}} - \frac{2.6}{10^{-2}}\right) = 0.4\frac{dT}{dt}$

$\Rightarrow \quad \frac{dT}{dt} = 12° \text{ C/s}$

3. (a) Heat currents will be equal.

(b) $i = KA\frac{dT}{dx} = \text{constant} \quad \Rightarrow \quad \frac{dT}{dx} \propto \frac{1}{A}$

So, temperature difference will be larger, where cross-section is narrower.

$\therefore \quad (\Delta T)_{AB} < (\Delta T)_{CD}$

4. $i = -KA\frac{dT}{dx}$

$\Rightarrow \quad i = -\frac{\alpha}{T} A \frac{dT}{dx}$

$\Rightarrow \quad \int_{T_1}^{T} \frac{dT}{T} = -\frac{i}{\alpha A}\int_0^x dx$

$\Rightarrow \quad [\ln T]_{T_1}^{T} = -\frac{i}{\alpha A}[x]_0^x$

$\Rightarrow \quad \ln\left(\frac{T}{T_1}\right) = -\frac{ix}{\alpha A}$

When $\quad x = L, T = T_2$

$\Rightarrow \quad \ln\left(\frac{T_2}{T_1}\right) = -\frac{iL}{\alpha A}$

$\Rightarrow \quad \frac{i}{\alpha A} = -\frac{1}{L}\ln\left(\frac{T_2}{T_1}\right)$

Substituting value of $\frac{i}{\alpha A}$,

$$\ln\left(\frac{T}{T_1}\right) = \left(\frac{1}{L}\ln\left(\frac{T_2}{T_1}\right)\right)x$$

$$\Rightarrow \quad T = T_1\left(\frac{T_2}{T_1}\right)^{x/L}$$

3.3 Kirchhoff's Junction Law

1.

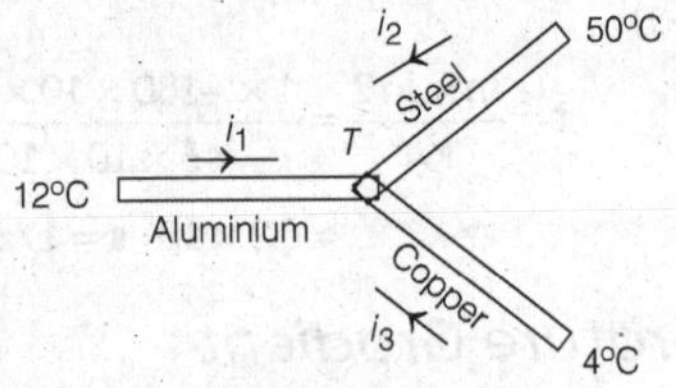

Let, temperature of junction be T.

Applying Kirchhoff's junction law,

$$i_1 + i_2 + i_3 = 0$$

$$\Rightarrow \frac{12 - T}{\left(\frac{1}{200 \times 1 \times 10^{-4}}\right)} + \frac{50 - T}{\left(\frac{1}{50 \times 1 \times 10^{-4}}\right)} + \frac{4 - T}{\left(\frac{1}{400 \times 1 \times 10^{-4}}\right)} = 0$$

$$\Rightarrow 4(12 - T) + 50 - T + 8(4 - T) = 0$$

$$\Rightarrow \quad T = 10^\circ\ C$$

2.

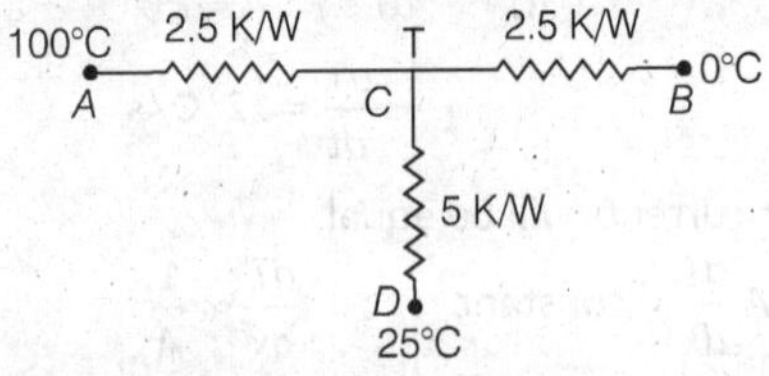

Let, temperature of junction C be T.

Applying Kirchhoff's junction law,

$$\frac{100 - T}{2.5} + \frac{0 - T}{2.5} + \frac{25 - T}{5} = 0 \quad \Rightarrow \quad T = 45^\circ\ C$$

Heat current in $CD = \frac{45 - 25}{5} = 4$ W

3. $$i = i_1 + i_2 = \frac{100 - 50}{\left(\frac{0.31}{46 \times 0.2 \times 10^{-4}}\right)} + \frac{100 - 50}{\left(\frac{0.31}{109 \times 0.2 \times 10^{-4}}\right)} = 0.5 \text{ J/s}$$

$$Q = i \times t = 0.5 \times 10 \times 60 = 300 \text{ J}$$

4. Let, temperature of junction be T.

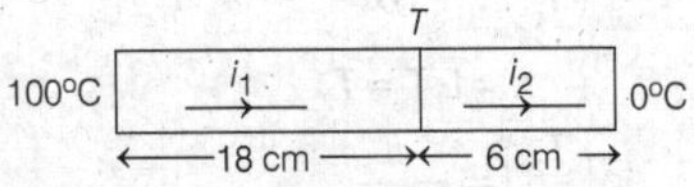

$$i_1 = i_2$$

$$\Rightarrow \quad \frac{100 - T}{\left(\frac{18}{9KA}\right)} = \frac{T - 0}{\left(\frac{6}{KA}\right)} \quad \Rightarrow \quad T = 75^\circ\text{C}$$

3.4 Combination of Rods

1. For series combination of rods,

$$R_{eq} = R_1 + R_2 + R_3$$

$$\Rightarrow \quad \frac{3L}{K_{eff}A} = \frac{L}{\left(\frac{K}{2}\right)A} + \frac{L}{5KA} + \frac{L}{KA}$$

$$\Rightarrow \quad K_{eff} = \frac{15}{16}K$$

2. $$R_{eq} = R_1 + R_2 = \frac{20}{0.9 \times 5} + \frac{20}{0.1 \times 5} = \frac{400}{9}\ ^\circ\text{C/cal-s}$$

$$i = \frac{T_A - T_C}{R_{eq}} = \frac{200 - 0}{\left(\frac{400}{9}\right)} = 4.5 \text{ cal/s}$$

3. (a) $$R = \frac{L}{KA} = \frac{2.2 \times 10^{-3}}{0.8 \times 1.2} = 2.29 \times 10^{-3}\ ^\circ\text{C/W}$$

$$i = \frac{T_1 - T_2}{R} = \frac{36 - 26}{2.29 \times 10^{-3}} = 4.37 \times 10^3 \text{ J/s}$$

$$Q = i \times t = 4.37 \times 10^3 \times 3600 = 1.57 \times 10^7 \text{J}$$

(b) $$R_{eq} = 2R_1 + R_2 = 2 \times 2.29 \times 10^{-3} + \frac{0.5 \times 10^{-2}}{0.0234 \times 1.2}$$

$$= 182.64 \times 10^{-3}\ ^\circ\text{C/W}$$

$$i = \frac{T_1 - T_2}{R_{eq}} = \frac{36 - 26}{182.64 \times 10^{-3}} = 54.75 \text{ W}$$

$$Q = i \times t = 54.75 \times 3600 = 1.97 \times 10^5 \text{J}$$

4. $$R_{Cu} = \frac{1}{400 \times 1 \times 10^{-4}} = 25^\circ \text{ C/W}$$

$$R_{Al} = \frac{1}{200 \times 1 \times 10^{-4}} = 50^\circ \text{ C/W}$$

$$R_{eq} = \frac{R_{Cu}R_{Al}}{R_{Cu} + R_{Al}} = \frac{50 \times 25}{50 + 25} = \frac{50}{3}\ ^\circ\text{C/W}$$

$$i = \frac{T_1 - T_2}{R_{eq}} = \frac{60 - 20}{50/3} = 2.4 \text{ J/s}$$

5.

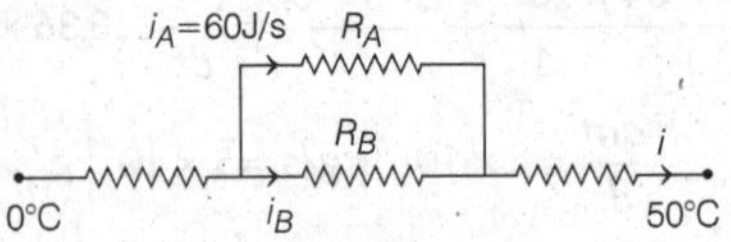

$$R = \frac{L}{KA} \quad \Rightarrow \quad R \propto L$$

$$\frac{i_A}{i_B} = \frac{R_B}{R_A} = \frac{l_B}{l_A}$$

$$\Rightarrow \quad \frac{60}{i_B} = \frac{50}{5 + 50 + 5} \quad \Rightarrow \quad i_B = 72 \text{ J/s}$$

$$i = i_A + i_B = 60 + 72 = 132 \text{ J/s}$$

6. Let, resistance of Al rod be R_1 and copper rod be R_2.

$$i = \frac{T_1 - T_2}{R_{eq}}$$

$$\Rightarrow \quad 40 = \frac{100 - 0}{2R_1 + R_2}$$

$$\Rightarrow \quad 40 = \frac{100}{2\left(\frac{L}{200A}\right)+\left(\frac{L}{400A}\right)}$$

$$\Rightarrow \quad \frac{L}{A} = 200\,\text{m}^{-1}$$

$$\therefore \quad R_1 = \frac{L}{K_{Al}A} = \frac{200}{200} = 1°\,\text{C/W}$$

$$R_2 = \frac{L}{K_{Cu}A} = \frac{200}{400} = 0.5°\,\text{C/W}$$

(a)

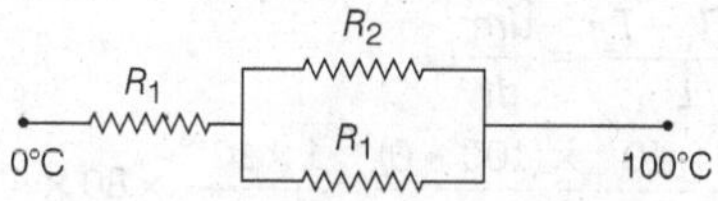

$$R_{eq} = R_1 + \frac{R_1R_2}{R_1+R_2} = 1 + \frac{1(0.5)}{1+0.5} = \frac{4}{3}°\,\text{C/W}$$

$$i = \frac{T_1 - T_2}{R_{eq}} = \frac{100-0}{(4/3)} = 75\,\text{W}$$

(b)

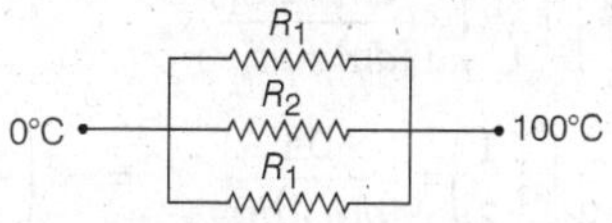

$$\frac{1}{R_{eq}} = \frac{1}{R_1} + \frac{1}{R_2} + \frac{1}{R_1}$$

$$\Rightarrow \quad \frac{1}{R_{eq}} = \frac{1}{1} + \frac{1}{0.5} + \frac{1}{1}$$

$$\Rightarrow \quad R_{eq} = 0.25°\,\text{C/W}$$

$$i = \frac{T_1 - T_2}{R_{eq}} = \frac{100-0}{0.25} = 400\,\text{W}$$

7. $R_1 = \frac{l}{K_{steel}A} = \frac{0.1}{50 \times 1 \times 10^{-4}} = 20°\,\text{C/W}$

$$R_2 = \frac{l}{K_{Cu}A} = \frac{0.1}{400 \times 1 \times 10^{-4}} = 2.5°\,\text{C/W}$$

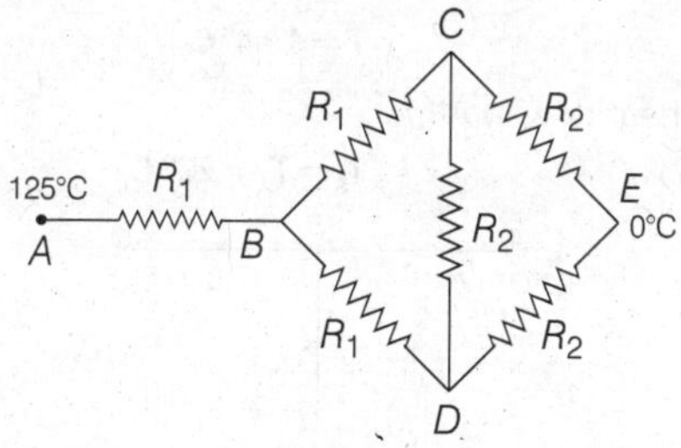

This is a balanced Wheatstone bridge. So, we can remove the rod *CD*.

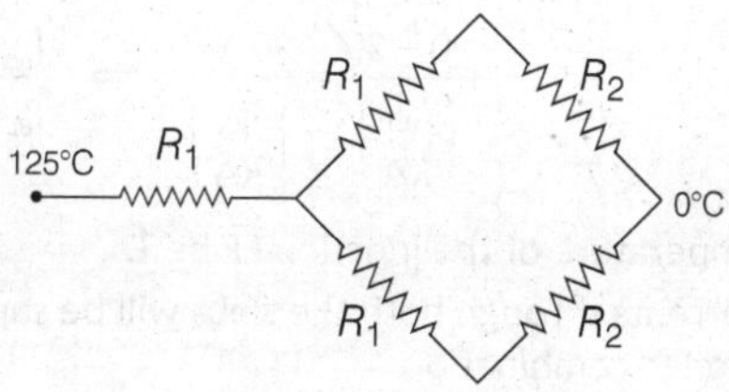

$$R_{eq} = R_1 + \frac{R_1 + R_2}{2} = \frac{3R_1 + R_2}{2}$$

$$= \frac{3(20) + 2.5}{2} = \frac{125}{4}°\,\text{C/W}$$

$$i = \frac{T_1 - T_2}{R_{eq}} = \frac{125 - 0}{125/4} = 4\,\text{W}$$

3.5 Formation of Ice on Lake

1. (a) $\frac{dQ}{dt} = \frac{dm}{dt}L_f = \frac{K_{ice}A(0-(-\theta))}{x}$

$$\Rightarrow \quad \frac{d}{dt}(\rho_w Ax)L_f = \frac{K_{ice}A\theta}{x}$$

$$\Rightarrow \quad \frac{dx}{dt} = \frac{K_{ice}\theta}{\rho_w L_f x} = \frac{1.7 \times 10}{1000 \times 3.36 \times 10^5 \times 0.1}$$

$$= 5.0 \times 10^{-7}\,\text{m/s}$$

(b) $\frac{dx}{dt} = \frac{K_{ice}\theta}{\rho_w L_f x}$

$$\Rightarrow \quad \int_0^t dt = \frac{\rho_w L_f}{K_{ice}\theta}\int_0^{0.1} x\,dx$$

$$\Rightarrow \quad t = \frac{1000 \times 3.36 \times 10^5}{1.7 \times 10}\left[\frac{x^2}{2}\right]_0^{0.1}$$

$$= 9.88 \times 10^4\,\text{s} = 27.5\,\text{h}$$

2. $\frac{dx}{dt} = \frac{K\theta}{\rho L_f x}$

$$\Rightarrow \quad \int_0^t dt = \frac{\rho L_f}{K\theta}\int_5^{10} x\,dx$$

$$\Rightarrow \quad t = \frac{0.92 \times 80}{0.004 \times 10}\left[\frac{x^2}{2}\right]_5^{10} = 69000\,\text{s} = 19.1\,\text{h}$$

3.6 Conduction in Non-Linear Conductors at Steady State

1. Lets, take an elemental spherical shell of radius *r* and thickness *dr*.

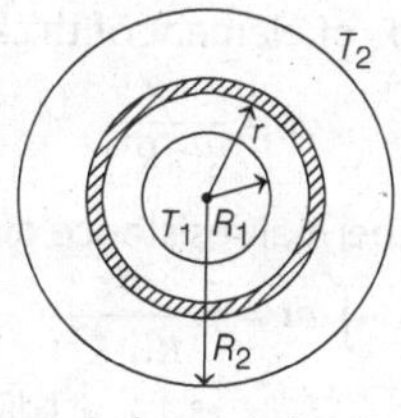

Thermal resistance of elemental spherical shell,

$$dR = \frac{dr}{K(4\pi r^2)}$$

For finding total thermal resistance,

$$\int dR = \int_{R_1}^{R_2} \frac{dr}{K(4\pi r^2)}$$

$$\Rightarrow \quad R = \frac{1}{4\pi K}\left[-\frac{1}{r}\right]_{R_1}^{R_2} = \frac{1}{4\pi K}\left[\frac{1}{R_1} - \frac{1}{R_2}\right]$$

Heat current, $i = \frac{T_1 - T_2}{R} = \frac{4\pi K(T_1 - T_2)R_1R_2}{R_2 - R_1}$

2. Lets, take an elemental cylindrical shell of radius r and thickness dr.

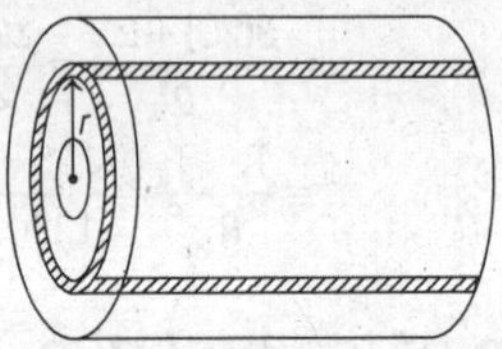

Thermal resistance of elemental cylindrical shell,

$$dR = \frac{dr}{K(2\pi rl)}$$

For finding total thermal resistance,

$$\int dR = \int_{R_1}^{R_2} \frac{dr}{K(2\pi rl)}$$

$$\Rightarrow \quad R = \frac{1}{2\pi Kl} \ln\left(\frac{R_2}{R_1}\right)$$

Heat current, $$i = \frac{T_2 - T_1}{R} = \frac{2\pi Kl(T_2 - T_1)}{\ln\left(\frac{R_2}{R_1}\right)}$$

3. Lets, take an element of width dx at a distance x from left end as shown in figure.

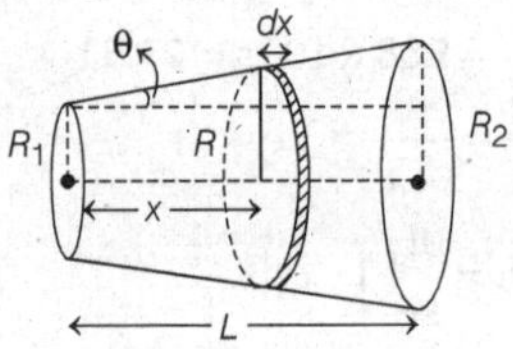

$$\tan\theta = \frac{R - R_1}{x} = \frac{R_2 - R_1}{L}$$

$$\Rightarrow \quad R = \left(\frac{R_2 - R_1}{L}\right)x + R_1$$

$$\Rightarrow \quad dR = \left(\frac{R_2 - R_1}{L}\right)dx$$

Thermal resistance of element of thickness dx,

$$dr = \frac{dx}{K(\pi R^2)}$$

For finding total thermal resistance of the rod,

$$\int dr = \int \frac{dx}{K(\pi R^2)}$$

$$\Rightarrow \quad r = \int_{R_1}^{R_2} \frac{LdR}{K(R_2 - R_1)\pi R^2}$$

$$\left[\because dx = \left(\frac{L}{R_2 - R_1}\right)dR\right]$$

$$\Rightarrow \quad r = \frac{L}{K\pi(R_2 - R_1)}\left[-\frac{1}{R}\right]_{R_1}^{R_2}$$

$$\Rightarrow \quad r = \frac{L}{K\pi R_1 R_2}$$

Rate of heat flow $= \dfrac{T_1 - T_2}{r} = \dfrac{(T_1 - T_2)K\pi R_1 R_2}{L}$

Level-2

Single Choice Correct Questions

1. $i = \dfrac{KA\Delta T}{L} = \dfrac{K\pi r^2 \Delta T}{L}$

$$\therefore \quad \frac{i_1}{i_2} = \left(\frac{K_1}{K_2}\right)\left(\frac{r_1}{r_2}\right)^2\left(\frac{L_2}{L_1}\right)$$

$$\Rightarrow \quad \frac{i_1}{4} = \left(\frac{1}{2}\right)\left(\frac{1}{2}\right)^2\left(\frac{2}{1}\right) \quad \Rightarrow \quad i_1 = 1 \text{ cal/s}$$

2. $\dfrac{dQ}{dt} = \dfrac{KA(T_1 - T_2)}{L} = \dfrac{dm}{dt}L_f$

$$\Rightarrow \quad \frac{K \times 9 \times 10^{-4} \times (100 - 0)}{0.54} = \frac{1 \times 10^{-3}}{33} \times 80 \times 4200$$

$$\Rightarrow \quad K = 61 \text{ Wm}^{-1}\text{K}^{-1}$$

3. $\dfrac{dQ}{dt} = \dfrac{K(\pi r^2)(T_1 - T_2)}{L} = \dfrac{dm}{dt}L_f$

$$\Rightarrow \quad \left(\frac{K_1}{K_2}\right)\left(\frac{r_1}{r_2}\right)^2\left(\frac{L_2}{L_1}\right) = \frac{(dm/dt)_1}{(dm/dt)_2}$$

$$\Rightarrow \quad \left(\frac{4}{1}\right)\left(\frac{1}{2}\right)^2\left(\frac{1}{2}\right) = \frac{0.1}{(dm/dt)_2} \quad \Rightarrow \quad \left(\frac{dm}{dt}\right)_2 = 0.2 \text{ g/s}$$

4. For the metre stick,

$$\frac{dT}{dx} = \frac{T_1 - T_2}{L} = \frac{100 - 20}{100} = 0.8° \text{ C/cm}$$

For no heat current, the other end of the rod should also be at 40°C.

$$\frac{dT}{dx} = \frac{40 - 20}{x} = 0.8 \quad \Rightarrow \quad x = 25 \text{ cm}$$

5. Let, temperature of the joint be T.

$$i_1 + i_2 + i_3 = 0$$

$$\Rightarrow \quad \frac{10 - T}{\left(\frac{10}{KA}\right)} + \frac{20 - T}{\left(\frac{20}{KA}\right)} + \frac{30 - T}{\left(\frac{30}{KA}\right)} = 0$$

$$\Rightarrow \quad T = 16.4° \text{ C}$$

6. For no heat flow in AB,

$$T_B = T_A = 20° \text{ C}$$

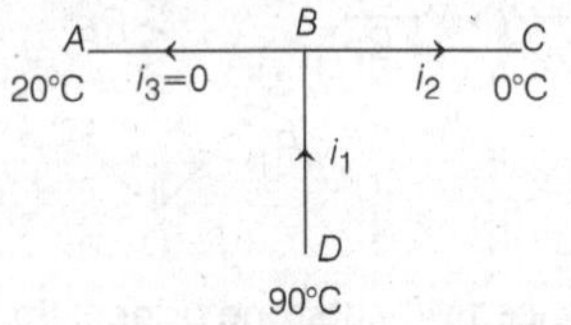

$$i_1 = i_2$$

$$\Rightarrow \quad \frac{90 - 20}{\left(\frac{l_{BD}}{KA}\right)} = \frac{20 - 0}{\left(\frac{l_{BC}}{KA}\right)} \quad \Rightarrow \quad \frac{l_{BD}}{l_{BC}} = \frac{7}{2}$$

7. Let, temperature of the junction EF be T.

Heat currents through both the slabs will be same as they are in series combination.

$$i_1 = i_2$$

$$\Rightarrow \quad \frac{100-T}{\left(\frac{d}{(2K)A}\right)} = \frac{T-0}{\left(\frac{2d}{KA}\right)} \Rightarrow T = 80^\circ C$$

8.

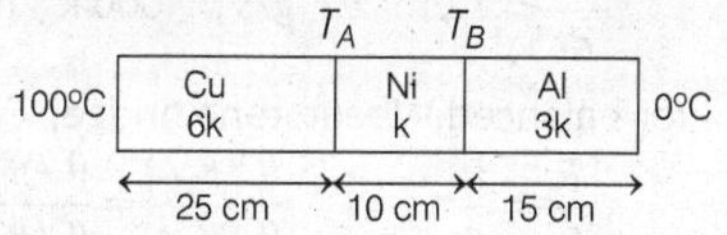

Let, temperature of the two junctions be T_A and T_B.

For the composite rod,

$$i = \frac{T_1 - T_2}{R}$$

$$\Rightarrow \quad i = \frac{100-0}{\frac{25}{6KA} + \frac{10}{KA} + \frac{15}{3KA}} = \frac{120KA}{23}$$

For the copper rod,

$$i = \frac{T_1 - T_2}{R_{Cu}}$$

$$\Rightarrow \quad \frac{120KA}{23} = \frac{100 - T_A}{\left(\frac{25}{6KA}\right)} \Rightarrow T_A = 78.3^\circ C$$

For the aluminium rod,

$$i = \frac{T_1 - T_2}{R_{Al}}$$

$$\Rightarrow \quad \frac{120KA}{23} = \frac{T_B - 0}{\left(\frac{15}{3KA}\right)} \Rightarrow T_B = 26.1^\circ C$$

9.

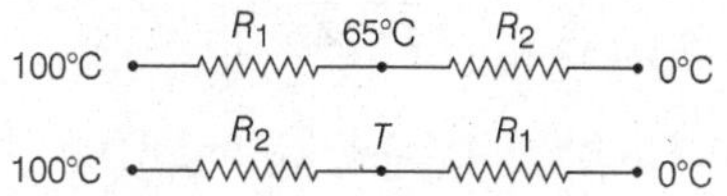

$$i = \frac{100-65}{R_1} = \frac{65-0}{R_2}$$

$$\Rightarrow \quad \frac{R_1}{R_2} = \frac{7}{13}$$

When the rods are interchanged,

$$i' = \frac{100-T}{R_2} = \frac{T-0}{R_1}$$

$$\Rightarrow \quad \frac{100-T}{T} = \frac{R_2}{R_1} = \frac{13}{7} \Rightarrow T = 35^\circ C$$

10.

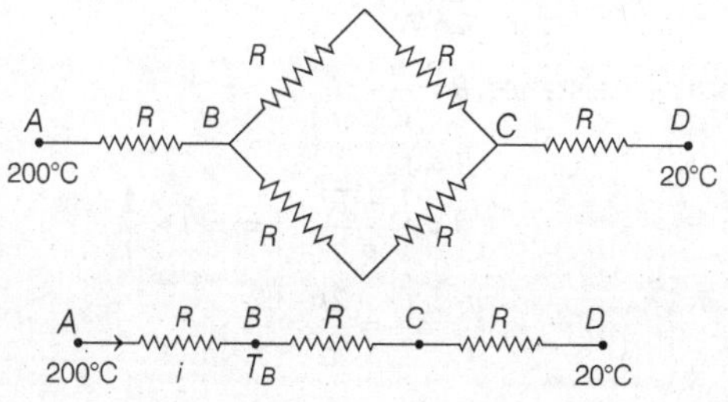

$$i = \frac{200-20}{3R} = \frac{200-T_B}{R}$$

$$\Rightarrow \quad T_B = 140^\circ C$$

11. A, B and C are in A.P.

$$\Rightarrow \quad B - A = C - B$$

$$i_1 = i_2$$

$$\Rightarrow \quad \frac{B-A}{\left(\frac{d}{K_1 A}\right)} = \frac{C-B}{\left(\frac{3d}{K_2 A}\right)} \Rightarrow \frac{K_1}{K_2} = 1:3$$

12. $i_A = i_B$

$$\Rightarrow \quad \frac{(\Delta T)_A}{\left(\frac{d}{(3K)A}\right)} = \frac{36}{\left(\frac{d}{KA}\right)}$$

$$\Rightarrow \quad (\Delta T)_A = 12^\circ C$$

13.

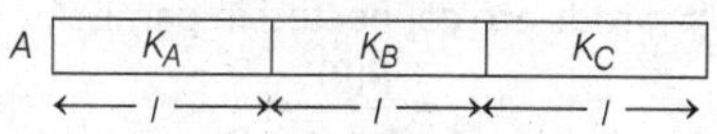

$$R_{eq} = R_A + R_B + R_C$$

$$\Rightarrow \quad \frac{3l}{K_{eff}A} = \frac{l}{K_A A} + \frac{l}{K_B A} + \frac{l}{K_C A}$$

$$\Rightarrow \quad \frac{3}{K_{eff}} = \frac{1}{2K_B} + \frac{1}{K_B} + \frac{1}{(K_B/2)}$$

$$\Rightarrow \quad K_{eff} = \frac{6K_B}{7}$$

14. $R_{eq} = R_1 + R_2 = \dfrac{x}{KA} + \dfrac{4x}{2KA} + \dfrac{3x}{KA}$

$$\text{Rate of heat transfer} = \frac{T_2 - T_1}{R_{eq}} = \frac{T_2 - T_1}{\left(\frac{3x}{KA}\right)} = \left(\frac{A(T_2 - T_1)K}{x}\right)\frac{1}{3}$$

$$\therefore \quad f = \frac{1}{3}$$

15. $\dfrac{\Delta Q}{\Delta t} = \dfrac{T_1 - T_2}{R} = \dfrac{\Delta m}{\Delta t} L_f$

For copper rod, $\dfrac{100-0}{R_1} = \left(\dfrac{\Delta m}{30}\right) L_f$

For steel rod, $\dfrac{100-0}{R_2} = \left(\dfrac{\Delta m}{60}\right) L_f$

When both rods are connected in parallel,

$$\frac{100-0}{R_{eq}} = \left(\frac{\Delta m}{\Delta t}\right) L_f$$

$$\frac{1}{R_{eq}} = \frac{1}{R_1} + \frac{1}{R_2}$$

$$\Rightarrow \quad \frac{100-0}{R_{eq}} = \frac{100-0}{R_1} + \frac{100-0}{R_2}$$

$$\Rightarrow \quad \frac{1}{\Delta t} = \frac{1}{30} + \frac{1}{60}$$

$$\Rightarrow \quad \Delta t = 20 \text{ min}$$

16. $Q_1 = \dfrac{\theta_1 - \theta_2}{R_1} \Rightarrow R_1 = \dfrac{\theta_1 - \theta_2}{Q_1}$

$Q_2 = \dfrac{\theta_1 - \theta_2}{R_2} \Rightarrow R_2 = \dfrac{\theta_1 - \theta_2}{Q_2}$

When both the rods are connected in series,

$$R_{eq} = R_1 + R_2$$

$$\Rightarrow \quad \frac{\theta_1 - \theta_2}{Q} = \frac{\theta_1 - \theta_2}{Q_1} + \frac{\theta_1 - \theta_2}{Q_2}$$

$$\Rightarrow \quad Q = \frac{Q_1 Q_2}{Q_1 + Q_2}$$

17. Let, thermal resistance of each rod be R.

In figure (a), rods are connected in series,

$$\therefore \quad R_{eq} = R + R = 2R$$

$$\frac{\Delta Q}{\Delta t} = \frac{100 - 0}{2R} = \frac{20 \text{ cal}}{4 \text{ min}} \quad \text{...(i)}$$

In figure (b), rods are connected in parallel,

$$\therefore \quad R_{eq} = \frac{R(R)}{R + R} = \frac{R}{2}$$

$$\frac{\Delta Q}{\Delta t} = \frac{100 - 0}{R/2} = \frac{20 \text{ cal}}{t} \quad \text{...(ii)}$$

Solving Eqs. (i) and (ii), we get

$$t = 1 \text{ min}$$

18. $R_{eq} = 2R_{glass} + R_{air} = \dfrac{2(0.01)}{0.8 \times 1} + \dfrac{0.05}{0.08 \times 1} = 0.65° \text{ C/W}$

Rate of heat flow $= \dfrac{T_1 - T_2}{R_{eq}} = \dfrac{27 - 0}{0.65} = 41.6 \text{ W}$

19.

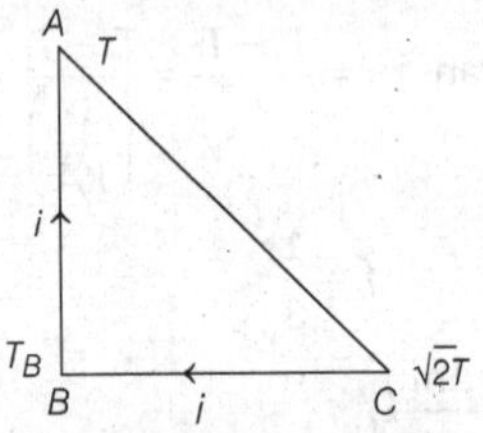

$$R_{AB} = R_{BC} = R$$

$$i = \frac{\sqrt{2}T - T_B}{R} = \frac{T_B - T}{R}$$

$$\Rightarrow \quad \frac{T_B}{T} = \frac{1 + \sqrt{2}}{2}$$

20. $i_H = KA \dfrac{dT}{dx}$

Heat current is same through both the layers.

$\Rightarrow K \propto \dfrac{1}{\left(\dfrac{dT}{dx}\right)} \quad \Rightarrow K \propto \dfrac{1}{\text{Slope}}$

$(\text{Slope})_1 < (\text{Slope})_2 \quad \Rightarrow \quad K_1 > K_2$

21. $R_{eq} = R_1 + R_2 = \dfrac{0.24}{0.9 \times 400} + \dfrac{0.02}{0.15 + 400} = 0.001°\text{C/cal/s}$

$$\frac{dQ}{dt} = \frac{T_1 - T_2}{R_{eq}} = \frac{dm}{dt} L_v$$

$$\Rightarrow \quad \frac{700 - 100}{0.001} = \frac{dm}{dt}(540)$$

$$\Rightarrow \quad \frac{dm}{dt} = 1.11 \times 10^3 \text{ g/s} = 4000 \text{ kg/h}$$

22. Condition for balanced Wheatstone bridge,

$$\frac{R_1}{R_2} = \frac{R_3}{R_4} \Rightarrow \frac{(l/K_1A)}{(l/K_2A)} = \frac{(l/K_3A)}{(l/K_4A)}$$

$$\Rightarrow \quad K_1K_4 = K_2K_3$$

23. Let resistance of metal ring be R.

When $\theta = 180°$,

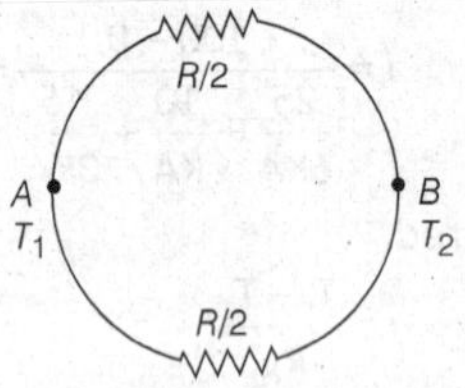

$$R_{eq} = \frac{(R/2)(R/2)}{\frac{R}{2} + \frac{R}{2}} = \frac{R}{4}$$

Rate of heat flow $= \dfrac{T_1 - T_2}{R_{eq}}$

$$\Rightarrow \quad 1.2 = \frac{T_1 - T_2}{R/4} \quad \text{...(i)}$$

When $\theta = 90°$

$$R_{eq} = \frac{(R/4)(3R/4)}{\frac{R}{4} + \frac{3R}{4}} = \frac{3R}{16}$$

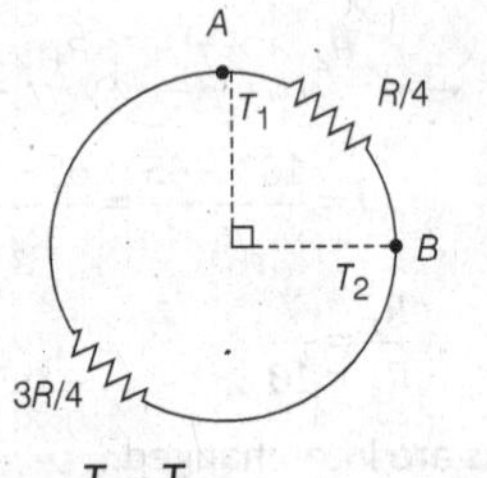

Rate of heat flow $= \dfrac{T_1 - T_2}{R_{eq}}$

$$i = \frac{T_1 - T_2}{3R/16} \quad \text{...(ii)}$$

Solving Eqs. (i) and (ii), we get

$$i = 1.6 \text{ W}$$

24. Thermal resistance, $R = \dfrac{l}{KA}$

$$\therefore \quad R \propto l$$

$$i = \frac{T_1 - T_2}{R} \quad \Rightarrow \quad i \propto \frac{1}{l}$$

$$\therefore \quad \frac{i_1}{i_2} = \frac{l_2}{l_1} = \frac{2r}{\pi r} = \frac{2}{\pi}$$

25. Let us take an element of width dx at a distance x from one end as shown in figure.

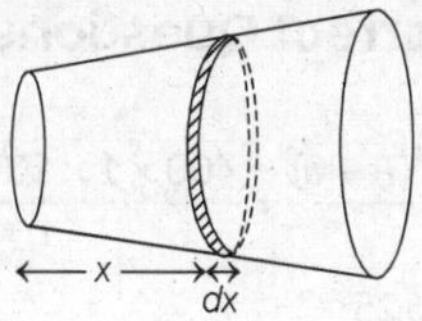

Thermal resistance of this element,

$$dR = \frac{dx}{K\pi\left(\frac{d_0}{2}(1+ax)\right)^2} = \frac{4dx}{K\pi d_0^2(1+ax)^2}$$

For finding thermal resistance of rod,

$$\int dR = \frac{4}{K\pi d_0^2}\int_0^l \frac{dx}{(1+ax)^2}$$

$$\Rightarrow \quad R = \frac{4}{K\pi d_0^2}\frac{1}{a}\left[-\frac{1}{(1+ax)}\right]_0^l = \frac{4l}{K\pi d_0^2(al+1)}$$

26.
$$R_A = \frac{l}{K_A(\pi r^2)},$$

$$R_B = \frac{l}{K_B(\pi(2r)^2 - \pi r^2)} = \frac{l}{3K_B\pi r^2}$$

$$\frac{1}{R_{eq}} = \frac{1}{R_A} + \frac{1}{R_B}$$

$$\Rightarrow \quad \frac{1}{R_{eq}} = \frac{K_A(\pi r^2)}{l} + \frac{3K_B(\pi r^2)}{l}$$

$$\Rightarrow \quad R_{eq} = \frac{l}{\pi r^2(K_A + 3K_B)}$$

27.
$$t \propto x_f^2 - x_i^2$$

$$\Rightarrow \quad \frac{t_1}{t_2} = \frac{2^2 - 1^2}{1^2 - 0^2}$$

$$\Rightarrow \quad \frac{t_1}{7} = 3 \quad \Rightarrow \quad t_1 = 21\text{ h}$$

28.
$$\frac{dx}{dt} = \frac{K\theta}{\rho L_f x}$$

$$\Rightarrow \quad \int_0^t dt = \frac{\rho L_f}{K\theta}\int_5^7 x\,dx$$

$$\Rightarrow \quad t = \frac{0.92 \times 80}{4 \times 10^{-3} \times 10}\left[\frac{x^2}{2}\right]_5^7$$

$$= 22080\text{ s} = 6.13\text{ h}$$

Numerical Value Questions

1. Let, temperature of junction O be T.

Applying Kirchhoff's junction law,

$$i_1 + i_2 + i_3 = 0$$

$$\Rightarrow \frac{T-30}{\left(\frac{l}{KA}\right)} + \frac{T-60}{\left(\frac{l}{2KA}\right)} + \frac{T-90}{\left(\frac{l}{3KA}\right)} = 0$$

$$\Rightarrow \quad T = 70^\circ\text{ C}$$

2.
$$l_{AB} = l_{BC} = l_{CA} = 20\text{ cm}$$

$$R_{AB} = R_{BC} = R_{CA} = R$$

$$R = \frac{l}{KA} = \frac{0.2}{385 \times 0.2 \times 10^{-4}} = \frac{2000}{77}\,^\circ\text{C/W}$$

$$i_{AB} + i_{CA} + i_{CB} = \frac{80-80}{R} + \frac{110-80}{R} + \frac{110-80}{R}$$

$$= \frac{60}{(2000/77)} = 2.31\text{ W}$$

$$\therefore \quad 100\alpha = 100 \times 2.31 = 231$$

3. $i = KA\dfrac{dT}{dx} = \text{constant}$

$$\Rightarrow \quad K \propto \frac{1}{\frac{dT}{dx}} \propto \frac{1}{\text{Slope}}$$

$$\therefore \quad \frac{K_B}{K_A} = \frac{(\text{Slope})_A}{(\text{Slope})_B} = \frac{\frac{100-70}{30-0}}{\frac{70-35}{100-30}} = 2$$

4.

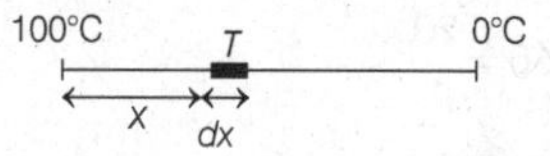

$$\text{Temperature gradient} = \frac{100-0}{1} = \frac{100-T}{x}$$

$$\Rightarrow \quad T = 100(1-x)$$

Heat absorbed by dx element,

$$dQ = msdT$$

$$\Rightarrow \quad dQ = (\lambda dx)\, s(T-0)$$

$$\Rightarrow \quad \int dQ = \int_0^1 (2dx)\,10(100(1-x))$$

$$\Rightarrow \quad Q = 2000\int_0^1 (1-x)\,dx$$

$$= 2000\left[x - \frac{x^2}{2}\right]_0^1 = 1000\text{ J}$$

5. $\dfrac{dQ}{dt} = (\mu\, mg)\, v = \dfrac{KA(T_1 - T_2)}{L}$

$$\Rightarrow 0.418 \times (980 + 20) \times 10 \times 20$$

$$= \frac{25 \times 4.18 \times 1 \times (T-50)}{5 \times 10^{-2}}$$

$$\Rightarrow \quad T = 90^\circ\text{ C}$$

6.

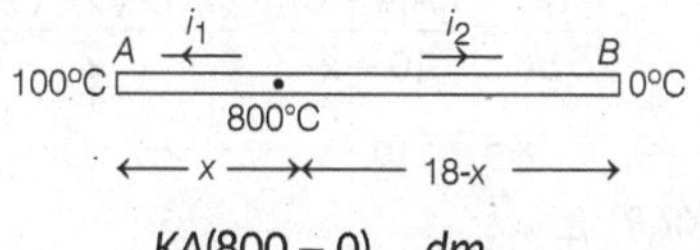

$$i_2 = \frac{KA(800-0)}{18-x} = \frac{dm}{dt}L_f \qquad \text{...(i)}$$

$$i_1 = \frac{KA(800-100)}{x} = \frac{dm}{dt}L_v \qquad \text{...(ii)}$$

Dividing Eqs. (ii) by (i), we get

$$\frac{L_v}{L_f} = \frac{7(18-x)}{8x}$$

$$\Rightarrow \quad 7 = \frac{7(18-x)}{8x} \quad \Rightarrow \quad x = 2\text{ m}$$

7. $\frac{dQ}{dt} = \frac{dm}{dt} L_f = \frac{360}{3600} \times 80 = 8\text{ cal/s}$

Also, $\frac{dQ}{dt} = \frac{T_1 - T_2}{R_{eq}}$

$$\Rightarrow \quad 8 = \frac{100-0}{R_{eq}}$$

$$\Rightarrow \quad R_{eq} = 12.5°\text{ C/cal/s}$$

$$R_{eq} = R_1 + R_2$$

$$\Rightarrow \quad 12.5 = \frac{20}{0.25 \times 10} + \frac{9}{K \times 10}$$

$$\Rightarrow \quad K = 0.2\text{ cal/s/cm/°C}$$

8. For first slab, $i_1 = \frac{T_1 - T_2}{R_1}$

$$\Rightarrow \quad 60 = \frac{20}{R_1}$$

$$\Rightarrow \quad R_1 = \frac{1}{3}\text{°C/W/m}^2$$

For second slab, $i_2 = \frac{T_1 - T_2}{R_2}$

$$\Rightarrow \quad 30 = \frac{20}{R_2} \quad \Rightarrow \quad R_2 = \frac{2}{3}\text{°C/W/m}^2$$

When both slabs are placed side by side,

$$R_{eq} = R_1 + R_2$$

$$= \frac{1}{3} + \frac{2}{3} = 1°\text{ C / W / m}^2$$

$$\therefore \quad i = \frac{T_1 - T_2}{R_{eq}} = \frac{20}{1} = 20\text{ W / m}^2$$

9.

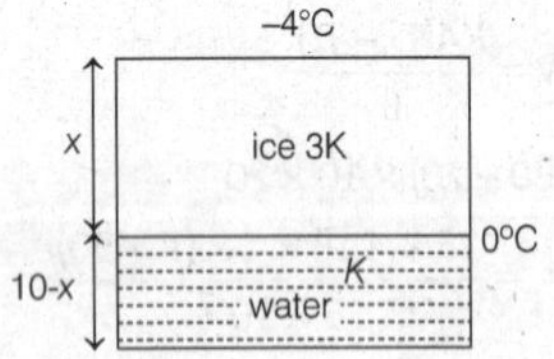

In steady state,

$$\frac{dQ}{dt} = \frac{KA(4-0)}{10-x} = \frac{(3K)\,A(0-(-4))}{x}$$

$$\Rightarrow \quad x = 7.5\text{ m}$$

10. $\frac{dQ}{dt} = \frac{4\pi K R_1 R_2}{R_2 - R_1}(T_1 - T_2)$

$$\Rightarrow \quad 160\pi = \frac{4\pi K(0.05)(0.2)(50-10)}{0.2-0.05}$$

$$\Rightarrow \quad K = 15\text{ W/m-°C}$$

Level-3

Single Choice Correct Questions

1. $i_1 + i_2 = 25$

$$\Rightarrow \quad \frac{400 \times 1 \times 10^{-4}(T-0)}{0.5} + \frac{400 \times 1 \times 10^{-4}(T-100)}{0.5} = 25$$

$$\Rightarrow \quad T = 206.25°\text{ C}$$

2. $\frac{dQ}{dt} = \frac{KA(T_1 - T_2)}{L} = \frac{\Delta m}{\Delta t} L_f$

$$\Rightarrow \quad \frac{0.0075 \times 75 \times (40-0)}{5} = \frac{500}{\Delta t} \times 800$$

$$\Rightarrow \quad \Delta t = 8888.8\text{ s} = 2.47\text{ h}$$

3. $\frac{dQ}{dt} = \frac{KA(T_1 - T_2)}{x} = \frac{\Delta m}{\Delta t} L_f$

$$\Rightarrow \quad \frac{K(4\pi r^2)(T_1 - T_2)}{x} = \frac{\rho\left(\frac{4}{3}\pi r^3\right)}{\Delta t} L_f$$

$$\Rightarrow \quad \Delta t \propto \frac{xr}{K}$$

$$\therefore \quad \frac{\Delta t_1}{\Delta t_2} = \left(\frac{x_1}{x_2}\right)\left(\frac{r_1}{r_2}\right)\left(\frac{K_2}{K_1}\right)$$

$$\Rightarrow \quad \frac{25}{16} = \left(\frac{1}{4}\right)\left(\frac{2}{1}\right)\left(\frac{K_2}{K_1}\right)$$

$$\Rightarrow \quad \frac{K_1}{K_2} = 8:25$$

4. $T = \left(\frac{60-0}{600}\right)t = \frac{t}{10}$

$$\frac{dQ}{dt} = \frac{KA(T_1 - T_2)}{L}$$

$$\Rightarrow \quad \frac{dQ}{dt} = \frac{100 \times 1 \times 10^{-4}}{40 \times 10^{-2}}\left(\frac{t}{10} - 0\right)$$

$$\Rightarrow \quad \int dQ = \frac{1}{400}\int_0^{600} t\,dt$$

$$\Rightarrow \quad Q = \frac{1}{400}\left[\frac{t^2}{2}\right]_0^{600} = 450\text{ J}$$

5. Let temperature of ball at time t be T.

$$\frac{dQ}{dt} = \frac{KA(T-0)}{L} = -C\frac{dT}{dt}$$

$$\Rightarrow \quad \int_0^t dt = -\frac{LC}{KA}\int_{100}^{50}\frac{dT}{T}$$

$$\Rightarrow \quad t = \frac{LC \ln 2}{KA}$$

$$= \frac{0.2 \times 10 \times 0.693}{50 \times 1 \times 10^{-4}}$$

$$= 277.2\text{ s} = 4.62\text{ min}$$

6. Let thermal resistance of each rod $= R$

For cube, $R_{eq} = \frac{5R}{6}$

$$i = \frac{100-0}{R_{eq}} = \frac{100-0}{5R/6} = \frac{120}{R}$$

$$i_{AB} = i_{BC} = i_{BF} = \frac{i}{3}$$

$\therefore$ $$i_{AB} = \frac{100-T_A}{R} = \frac{1}{3}\left(\frac{120}{R}\right)$$

$\Rightarrow$ $$T_A = 60^\circ \text{C}$$

7. Let T_A, T_B and T_C be $T, 2T, 4T$, respectively.

$$i_1 = i_2$$

$\Rightarrow$ $$\frac{K_1A(T_B - T_A)}{d} = \frac{K_2A(T_C - T_B)}{2d}$$

$\Rightarrow$ $$K_1(2T - T) = K_2\left(\frac{4T - 2T}{2}\right)$$

$\Rightarrow$ $$\frac{K_1}{K_2} = 1$$

8. $$i_1 = i_2$$

$\Rightarrow$ $$R_1 + R_2 = R_3$$

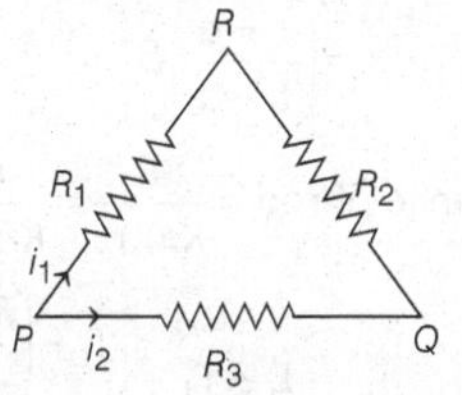

$\Rightarrow$ $$\frac{l}{K_1A} + \frac{l}{K_2A} = \frac{l}{K_3A}$$

$\Rightarrow$ $$K_3 = \frac{K_1K_2}{K_1 + K_2}$$

9. $i = -KA\dfrac{dT}{dx}$ = constant

$\Rightarrow$ $$\frac{dT}{dx} \propto -\frac{1}{K}$$

$$K_1 = 2K_2$$

$\Rightarrow$ $$\left(\frac{dT}{dx}\right)_1 = \frac{1}{2}\left(\frac{dT}{dx}\right)_2$$

$\therefore$ Temperature gradient is constant for a rod. Temperature gradient of first rod is half of temperature gradient of second rod.

10. $i_1 + i_2 = \dfrac{dQ}{dt}$

$\Rightarrow$ $$\frac{KA(T_A - T_C)}{L_1} + \frac{KA(T_B - T_C)}{L_2} = \frac{dm}{dt}L_f$$

$\Rightarrow$ $$\frac{336 \times 1 \times 10^{-4}(20-0)}{0.1} + \frac{336 \times 10^{-4}(40-0)}{0.2}$$

$$= \frac{dm}{dt} \times 80 \times 4200$$

$\Rightarrow$ $$\frac{dm}{dt} = 4 \times 10^{-5} \text{ kg/s} = 40 \text{ mg/s}$$

11. $$R_{BC} = \frac{l}{2KA} = \frac{1}{2 \times 100 \times 10 \times 10^{-4}} = 5$$

$$R_{BD} = \frac{l}{(K/2)A} = 20$$

Let, temperature of junction B be T_B.

Applying Kirchhoff's junction law,

$$i_{AB} + i_{CB} = i_{BD}$$

$\Rightarrow$ $$200 + \frac{100 - T_B}{5} = \frac{T_B - 0}{20}$$

$\Rightarrow$ $$T_B = 880^\circ \text{C}$$

$\therefore$ $$i_{BD} = \frac{880-0}{20} = 44 \text{ cal/s}$$

$$i_{BD} = \frac{\Delta m}{\Delta t}L_f$$

$\Rightarrow$ $$44 = \frac{440}{\Delta t} \times 80 \quad \Rightarrow \quad \Delta t = 800 \text{ s}$$

12. $$H = \frac{T_1 - T_2}{R_{eq}} = \frac{T_1 - T_2}{(3R/4)} \qquad \text{...(i)}$$

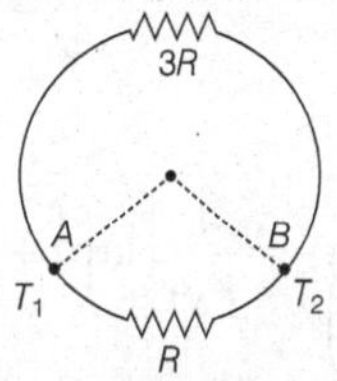

$$2H = \frac{T_1 - T_2}{R'_{eq}} = \frac{T_1 - T_2}{\left(\frac{(3R)R'}{3R + R'}\right)} \qquad \text{...(ii)}$$

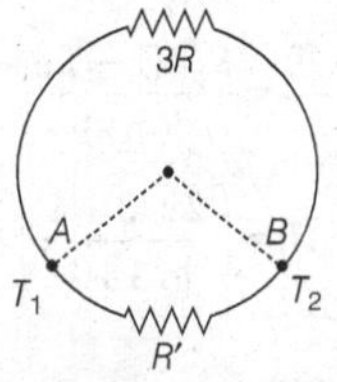

Solving Eqs. (i) and (ii), we get

$$R' = \frac{3R}{7}$$

$$R \propto \frac{1}{K} \quad \Rightarrow \quad \frac{R'}{R} = \frac{K}{K'}$$

$\Rightarrow$ $$K' = \frac{7K}{3}$$

13. $$R_{eq} = R_{wood} + R_{cement} + R_{brick}$$

$$= \frac{2.5 \times 10^{-2}}{0.125 \times 137} + \frac{1 \times 10^{-2}}{1.5 \times 137} + \frac{25 \times 10^{-2}}{1 \times 137}$$

$$= \frac{10}{3} \times 10^{-3} \,^\circ\text{C/W}$$

$$P = \frac{T_1 - T_2}{R_{eq}} = \frac{20-(-10)}{\frac{10}{3} \times 10^{-3}} = 9 \text{ kW}$$

14. $R_1 = 2R_{glass} + R_{air} = 2\left(\dfrac{3\,mm}{K_{glass}A}\right) + \dfrac{3\,mm}{K_{air}A}$

$$R_2 = R_{glass} = \frac{(6\,mm)}{K_{glass}A}$$

$$\frac{i_1}{i_2} = \frac{R_2}{R_1} = \frac{2K_{air}}{K_{glass} + 2K_{air}}$$

$$= \frac{2 \times 6.2 \times 10^{-6}}{2.5 \times 10^{-4} + 2 \times 6.2 \times 10^{-6}} = \frac{31}{656}$$

15. Let, temperature of the inner surface be T.

$$R_{plug} = \frac{l}{KA} = \frac{8}{0.5 \times 12} = \frac{4}{3}\,°C/cal/s$$

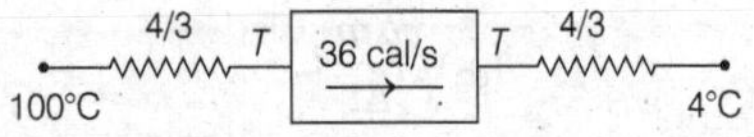

In the steady state,

$$\frac{100 - T}{4/3} + 36 = \frac{T - 4}{4/3}$$

$$\Rightarrow \quad T = 76°\,C$$

16. $R_1 = \dfrac{l}{K_0 A}$

$$R_2 = \int_0^{2l} \frac{dx}{K_0\left(1 + \frac{x}{l}\right)A} = \frac{l}{K_0 A}\left[\ln\left(1 + \frac{x}{l}\right)\right]_0^{2l} = \frac{l(\ln 3)}{K_0 A}$$

Let, temperature of interface be T.

$$i_1 = i_2$$

$$\Rightarrow \quad \frac{2T_0 - T}{R_1} = \frac{T - T_0}{R_2}$$

$$\Rightarrow \quad \frac{K_0 A(2T_0 - T)}{l} = \frac{K_0 A(T - T_0)}{l(\ln 3)}$$

$$\Rightarrow \quad T = \left(\frac{2\ln 3 + 1}{\ln 3 + 1}\right)T_0$$

17. $i = -KA\dfrac{dT}{dx} = \text{constant}$

$$\Rightarrow \quad \frac{dT}{dx} \propto \frac{1}{A}$$

$\therefore \dfrac{dT}{dx}$ *versus* A graph will be rectangular hyperbola.

18. $i = -KA\dfrac{dT}{dx}$

$$\Rightarrow \quad i = -\alpha TA\frac{dT}{dx}$$

$$\Rightarrow \quad i\int_0^l dx = -\alpha A\int_{T_1}^{T_2} T\,dT$$

$$\Rightarrow \quad i\,[x]_0^l = -\alpha A\left[\frac{T^2}{2}\right]_{T_1}^{T_2}$$

$$\Rightarrow \quad i = \frac{A\alpha\,(T_1^2 - T_2^2)}{2l}$$

19. $R = \displaystyle\int_0^x \frac{dx}{100(1 + x) \times 1 \times 10^{-4}} = 100\ln(1 + x)$

$$i = \frac{T_1 - T_2}{R}$$

$$\Rightarrow \quad 1 = \frac{100 - 0}{100\ln(1 + x)}$$

$$\Rightarrow \quad \ln(1 + x) = 1$$

$$\Rightarrow \quad 1 + x = e$$

$$\Rightarrow \quad x = e - 1 = 2.7 - 1 = 1.7\,m$$

20.

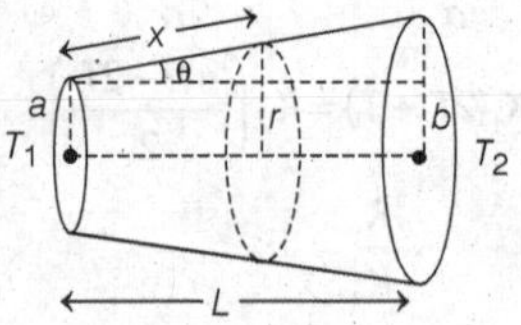

$$\tan\theta = \frac{r - a}{x} = \frac{b - a}{L}$$

$$\Rightarrow \quad x = \left(\frac{r - a}{b - a}\right)L$$

$$\text{Thermal resistance of rod} = \frac{L}{K\pi r_1 r_2} = \frac{L}{K\pi ab}$$

$$i = \frac{T_1 - T_2}{\left(\frac{L}{K\pi ab}\right)} = \frac{T_1 - \left(\frac{T_1 + T_2}{2}\right)}{\left(\frac{x}{K\pi ar}\right)}$$

$$\Rightarrow \quad \frac{2x}{r} = \frac{L}{b}$$

$$\Rightarrow \quad \frac{2}{r}\left(\frac{r - a}{b - a}\right)L = \frac{L}{b}$$

$$\Rightarrow \quad r = \frac{2ab}{a + b}$$

$\therefore r$ is equal to harmonic mean of a and b.

21. $R_1 = \displaystyle\int_R^{2R} \frac{dx}{K(4\pi x^2)} = \frac{1}{8\pi KR}$

$$R_2 = \int_{2R}^{3R} \frac{dx}{K(4\pi x^2)} = \frac{1}{24\pi KR}$$

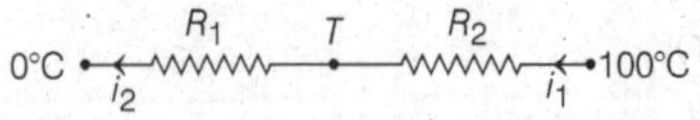

$$i_1 = i_2 \quad \Rightarrow \quad \frac{100 - T}{R_2} = \frac{T - 0}{R_1}$$

$$\Rightarrow \quad \frac{100 - T}{T} = \frac{1}{3}$$

$$\Rightarrow \quad T = 75°\,C$$

22. Thermal resistance of cylinder $= \dfrac{L}{K_1(\pi R^2)}$

Thermal resistance of cylindrical shell

$$= \frac{L}{K_2\pi[(2R)^2 - R^2]} = \frac{L}{K_2(3\pi R^2)}$$

$$\frac{1}{R_{eq}} = \frac{1}{R_1} + \frac{1}{R_2}$$

$$\Rightarrow \frac{1}{\left[\dfrac{L}{K_{eff}\pi(2R)^2}\right]} = \frac{1}{\left[\dfrac{L}{K_1(\pi R^2)}\right]} + \frac{1}{\left[\dfrac{L}{K_2(3\pi R^2)}\right]}$$

$$\Rightarrow \quad K_{eff} = \frac{K_1 + 3K_2}{4}$$

Multiple Choice(s) Correct Questions

1. $i = KA\dfrac{d\theta}{dl}$

   Since, *i*, *K* and *A* are constants, $\dfrac{d\theta}{dl}$ is same for all points on the rod.

$$\frac{i}{A} = I = K\frac{d\theta}{dl}$$

2. $\dfrac{dQ}{dt} = \dfrac{KA[0-(-\theta)]}{x} = \dfrac{dm}{dt}L_f$

$$\Rightarrow \frac{KA\theta}{x} = \frac{d}{dt}(\rho A x)L_f$$

$$\Rightarrow \frac{dx}{dt} = \frac{K\theta}{\rho L_f x}$$

$$\therefore \quad \frac{dx}{dt} \propto \theta \text{ and } \frac{dx}{dt} \propto \frac{1}{x}$$

3. $i_i = i_2$

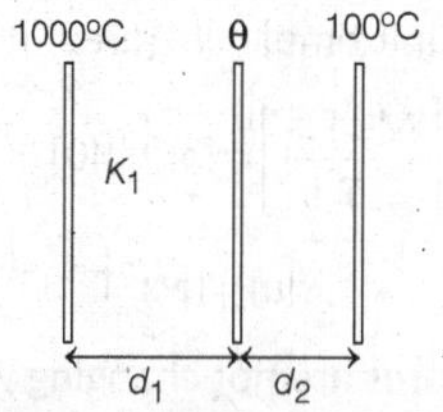

$$\Rightarrow \frac{1000-\theta}{\left(\dfrac{d_1}{K_1A}\right)} = \frac{\theta - 100}{\left(\dfrac{d_2}{K_2A}\right)}$$

$$\Rightarrow 1000 - \theta = \frac{\theta - 100}{\dfrac{K_1d_2}{K_2d_1}}$$

$$\Rightarrow \quad \theta = 1000 - \frac{900}{1 + \dfrac{K_1d_2}{K_2d_1}}$$

So, θ can be lowered by increasing K_2 and d_1.

4. Temperature gradient $= \dfrac{dT}{dx}$ = Slope of graph

   Temperature gradient is not constant as slope is not constant.

$$i = -KA\frac{dT}{dx} = \text{constant}$$

$$\Rightarrow \quad A \propto \frac{1}{\left(\dfrac{dT}{dx}\right)} \quad \Rightarrow \quad A \propto \frac{1}{\text{Slope}}$$

As distance from the hot end increases, slope also increases. Therefore, cross-sectional area of the bar decreases.

5.

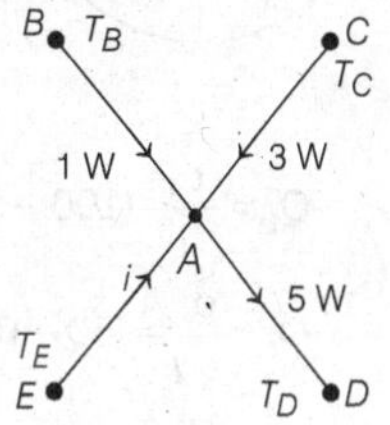

Applying Kirchhoff's junction law,

$$i + 1 + 3 - 5 = 0$$

$$\Rightarrow \quad i = 1\,\text{W}$$

$T_A < T_E$ as heat current flows from *E* to *A*.

$$i_C = \frac{T_C - T_A}{R} = 3$$

$$\Rightarrow \quad T_C = T_A + 3R$$

$$i_D = \frac{T_A - T_D}{R} = 5$$

$$\Rightarrow \quad T_D = T_A - 5R$$

$$\therefore \quad T_C > T_D$$

$$\frac{T_B - T_A}{R} = \frac{T_E - T_A}{R} = 1 \quad \Rightarrow \quad T_B = T_E$$

6. Let thermal resistance of each rod be *R*.

   Due to input-output symmetry, junction at *E* can be broken as shown.

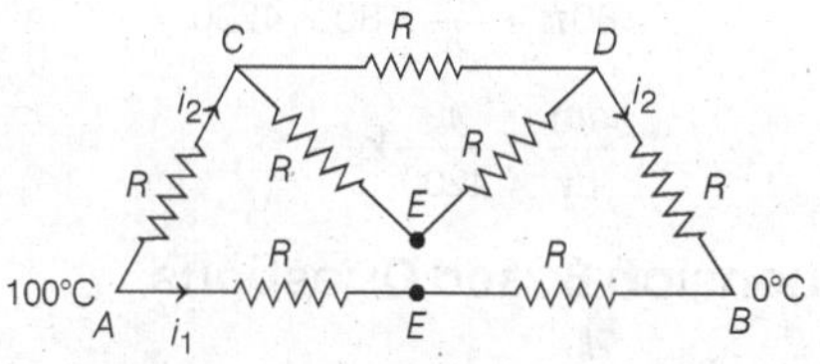

$$i_1 = \frac{100 - \theta_E}{R} = \frac{\theta_E - 0}{R}$$

$$\Rightarrow \quad \theta_E = 50°\text{C}$$

$$i_2 = \frac{100 - 0}{R + \dfrac{(2R)R}{2R + R} + R} = \frac{100 - \theta_C}{R}$$

$$\Rightarrow \quad \theta_C = 62.5°\text{C}$$

$$i_2 = \frac{100 - \theta_C}{R} = \frac{\theta_D - 0}{R}$$

$$\Rightarrow \quad \theta_D = 37.5°\text{C}$$

Also, $\theta_C > \theta_E > \theta_D$

7. Heat always flows from high temperature to low temperature, so Q_1 and Q_2 flow in clockwise sense and Q_3 in anti-clockwise sense.

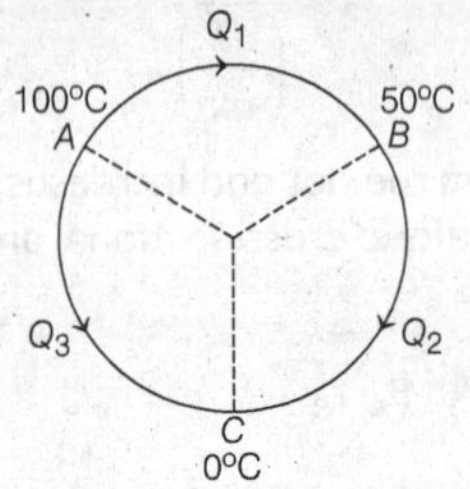

$$Q_1 = \frac{\alpha_1 A}{l}(100-50)$$

$$Q_2 = \frac{\alpha_2 A}{l}(50-0)$$

$$Q_3 = \frac{\alpha_3 A}{l}(100-0)$$

$\therefore \quad Q_1 : Q_2 : Q_3 = \alpha_1 : \alpha_2 : 2\alpha_3$

Also, $\quad \dfrac{Q_1}{\alpha_1} + \dfrac{Q_2}{\alpha_2} = \dfrac{Q_3}{\alpha_3}$

8. Thermal resistance,

$$R = \int_{r_1}^{r_2} \frac{dx}{K(2\pi r l)} = \frac{1}{2\pi K l} \ln\left(\frac{r_2}{r_1}\right)$$

$$\frac{dQ}{dt} = \frac{T_1 - T_2}{R} = \frac{2\pi K l (T_1 - T_2)}{\ln\left(\frac{r_2}{r_1}\right)}$$

$$= \frac{2\pi \times 0.693 \times 1 \times (40-0)}{\ln 2}$$

$$= 80\pi \text{ J/s}$$

$$\frac{dQ}{dt} = \frac{dm}{dt} L_f$$

$\Rightarrow \quad 80\pi = \dfrac{dm}{dt} \times 80 \times 4200$

$\Rightarrow \quad \dfrac{dm}{dt} = \dfrac{\pi}{4200}$ kg/s

Comprehension Based Questions

1. $R_A = \dfrac{l}{3KA}, \quad R_B = \dfrac{2l}{KA}$

$\therefore \quad \dfrac{R_A}{R_B} = \dfrac{1}{6}$

2. $i_1 = i_2 \quad \Rightarrow \quad \dfrac{T_A}{R_A} = \dfrac{T_B}{R_B}$

$\Rightarrow \quad \dfrac{T_A}{T_B} = \dfrac{R_A}{R_B} = \dfrac{1}{6}$

3. $G_A = \dfrac{T_A}{l}, \quad G_B = \dfrac{T_B}{2l}$

$\therefore \quad \dfrac{G_A}{G_B} = 2\left(\dfrac{T_A}{T_B}\right) = 2\left(\dfrac{1}{6}\right) = \dfrac{1}{3}$

4. $R_{ab} = \dfrac{l}{KA}, \quad R_{bc} = \dfrac{l}{K(3A)},$

$$R_{dc} = \frac{l}{Kx}, R_{ad} = \frac{l}{K(2A)}$$

Condition for balanced Wheatstone bridge,

$$\frac{R_{ab}}{R_{bc}} = \frac{R_{ad}}{R_{dc}}$$

$\Rightarrow \quad \dfrac{l/KA}{l/3KA} = \dfrac{l/2KA}{l/Kx}$

$\Rightarrow \quad x = 6A$

5. $i_{ab} = i_{bc}$

$\Rightarrow \quad \dfrac{200-T}{(l/KA)} = \dfrac{T-0}{(l/3KA)}$

$\Rightarrow \quad T = 50°\text{C}$

6. $\dfrac{dT}{dr} \propto r$

$\therefore$ Ratio of temperature gradients $= \dfrac{r_1}{r_2} = \dfrac{r_0/2}{r} = \dfrac{1}{2}$

7. $T(r) = \dfrac{\dot{q}}{4K} r_0^2 \left(1 - \dfrac{r^2}{r_0^2}\right) + T_s$

For temperature at the axis,

$$r = 0 \quad \Rightarrow \quad T(0) = \frac{\dot{q} r_0^2}{4K} + T_s$$

$\therefore \quad T(0) - T(r_0) = \dfrac{\dot{q} r_0^2}{4K}$

8. $\dot{q}(\pi r_0^2 L) = h(2\pi r_0 l)(T_s - T_f)$

$\Rightarrow$ [Energy per unit time] = [h] [area] [temperature]

$\Rightarrow \quad \left[\dfrac{ML^2T^{-2}}{T}\right] = [h][L^2][\theta]$

$\Rightarrow \quad [h] = [ML^0T^{-3}\theta^{-1}]$

9. Since temperatures are not changing with time, the unit is in steady state but not in thermal equilibrium.

10. $R = 2R_{\text{glass}} + R_{\text{air}} = 2\left(\dfrac{4 \times 10^{-3}}{1 \times 1.3}\right) + \dfrac{18 \times 10^{-3}}{K_{\text{air}} \times 1.3}$

$$i = \frac{\Delta T}{R} \quad \Rightarrow \quad 65 = \frac{13}{R}$$

$\Rightarrow \quad R = \dfrac{1}{5}$ °C/W

$\therefore \quad R = \dfrac{8 \times 10^{-3}}{1.3} + \dfrac{18 \times 10^{-3}}{K_{\text{air}} \times 1.3} = \dfrac{1}{5}$

$\Rightarrow \quad K_{\text{air}} = \dfrac{1}{14}$ W/mK

Match the Columns

1. $R_X = R = \dfrac{l}{K_X A},$

$$R_Y = \frac{l}{K_Y A} = \frac{l}{2K_X A} = \frac{R}{2}$$

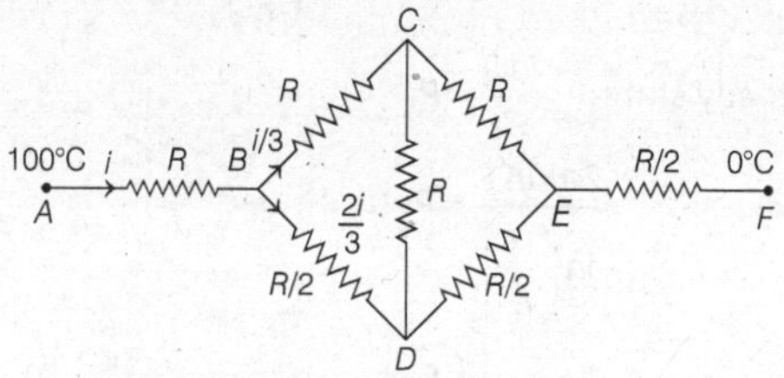

This is a balanced Wheatstone bridge. So, rod between C and D can be removed.

(A) $R_{BE} = \frac{(2R)R}{2R+R} = \frac{2R}{3}$

(B) $R_{AF} = R + \frac{2R}{3} + \frac{R}{2} = \frac{13R}{6}$

(C) $i = \frac{100-0}{13R/6} = \frac{100-T_B}{R} \Rightarrow T_B = \frac{700}{13}°C$

(D) For rod BD,

$$\frac{2i}{3} = \frac{T_B - T_D}{R/2}$$

$$\Rightarrow \frac{2}{3}\left(\frac{100-0}{13R/6}\right) = \frac{\frac{700}{13} - T_D}{R/2}$$

$$\Rightarrow \quad T_D = \frac{500}{13}°C$$

2. (A) Initially temperature difference is greatest at A and also area is more at A. So, the rate of heat flow is maximum at A and minimum at B.

(B) At steady state, rate of heat flow is same at all sections as no heat is being absorbed by any section.

(c) At steady state,

$$i = -KA\frac{dT}{dx} = \text{constant}$$

$$\Rightarrow \quad \left|\frac{dT}{dx}\right| \propto \frac{1}{A}$$

(D) At steady state, temperatures do not change with time. So, $\frac{dT}{dt} = 0$ at all sections.

3. (A) $i_1 = i_2$

$$\Rightarrow \quad \frac{10A(100-T)}{2} = \frac{20A(T-0)}{1}$$

$$\Rightarrow \quad T = 20° C$$

(B) $R_1 = \frac{l_1}{K_1 A_1} = \frac{1}{10 \times 100 \times 10^{-4}} = 10° C/W$

$$R_2 = \frac{l_2}{K_2 A_2} = \frac{1}{20 \times 100 \times 10^{-4}} = 5° C/W$$

$$R_{eq} = \frac{R_1 R_2}{R_1 + R_2} = \frac{10(5)}{10+5} = \frac{10}{3}° C/W$$

$$i = \frac{T_1 - T_2}{R_{eq}} = \frac{100-0}{10/3} = 30 \text{ W}$$

(C) $R = \int_{r_1}^{r_2} \frac{dx}{K(4\pi x^2)} = \frac{1}{4\pi K}\left[\frac{1}{r_1} - \frac{1}{r_2}\right]$

$$= \frac{1}{4\pi\left(\frac{1}{32\pi}\right)}\left[\frac{1}{0.1} - \frac{1}{0.2}\right] = 40°C/W$$

(D) Temperature gradient $= \frac{T_1 - T_2}{L} = \frac{100-0}{10} = 10° C/m$

Numerical Value Questions

1. Mass of element $= \rho A l = 2 \times 10^4 \times 2.5 \times 10^{-4} \times 1 \times 10^{-2}$

$$= 0.05 \text{ kg}$$

$$\frac{dQ}{dt} = KA\left[\left(\frac{dT}{dx}\right)_1 - \left(\frac{dT}{dx}\right)_2\right] = ms\frac{dT}{dt}$$

$$\Rightarrow 400 \times 2.5 \times 10^{-4}\left[\left(\frac{dT}{dx}\right)_1 - 140\right] = 0.05 \times 520 \times 0.250$$

$$\Rightarrow \quad \left(\frac{dT}{dx}\right)_1 = 205° C/m$$

2. $\frac{dQ}{dt} = \frac{KA(T_1 - T_2)}{L} = \frac{\Delta m}{\Delta T} L_f$

$$\Rightarrow \frac{0.01 \times 6(1)^2 \times (15-5)}{L} = \left(\frac{24}{24 \times 3600}\right) \times 360 \times 10^3$$

$$\Rightarrow \quad L = 6 \times 10^{-3} \text{ m} = 6 \text{ mm}$$

3. $i_1 = i_2$

$$\Rightarrow \quad K_A A\left(\frac{dT}{dx}\right)_A = K_B A\left(\frac{dT}{dx}\right)_B$$

$$\Rightarrow \quad 200(\tan 60°) = K_B(\tan 45°)$$

$$\Rightarrow \quad K_B = 200\sqrt{3}$$

$$\therefore \quad \sqrt{\frac{K_B}{8\sqrt{3}}} = 5$$

4. $\frac{dQ}{dt} = \frac{KA(T_1 - T_2)}{L}$,

$$\frac{dU}{dt} = Mg\frac{dh}{dt} = Mgv$$

In steady state,

$$\frac{dQ}{dt} = \frac{dU}{dt}$$

$$\Rightarrow \quad \frac{KA(T_1 - T_2)}{L} = Mgv$$

$$\Rightarrow \quad M = \frac{KA(T_1 - T_2)}{gLv} = \frac{0.5 \times 0.05 \times (1-0)}{10 \times 2 \times 10^{-3} \times 0.1} = 12.5 \text{ kg}$$

5. For A,

$$\frac{dQ}{dt} = \frac{KA(170-T)}{(L/4)} = ms\frac{dT}{dt}$$

$$\int_0^t dt = \frac{msL}{4KA}\int_{30°C}^{100°C}\frac{dT}{170-T}$$

$$\Rightarrow \quad t = \frac{msL}{4KA}\ln\left(\frac{170-30}{170-100}\right) = \frac{msL}{4KA}\ln 2$$

For B,

$$\frac{dQ}{dt}=\frac{KA(170-T)}{(3L/4)}=ms\frac{dT}{dt}$$

$$\Rightarrow \int_{10}^{T_B}\frac{dT}{170-T}=\frac{4KA}{3msL}\int_0^t dt$$

$$\Rightarrow \ln\left(\frac{170-10}{170-T_B}\right)=\frac{4KA}{3msL}\left(\frac{msL}{4KA}\right)\ln 2$$

$$\Rightarrow T_B=170-\frac{160}{2^{1/3}}=170-\frac{160}{5/4}=42^\circ\text{C}$$

6. In situation (a),

$$R_{eq}=R_1+R_2+R_3+\ldots+R_n$$

$$\Rightarrow \frac{l+2l+3l+\ldots+nl}{KA}=\frac{l}{kA}+\frac{2l}{2kA}+\frac{3l}{3kA}+\ldots+\frac{nl}{nkA}$$

$$\Rightarrow \frac{n(n+1)}{2k}=\frac{n}{k} \Rightarrow K=\left(\frac{n+1}{2}\right)k$$

In situation (b),

$$\frac{1}{R_{eq}}=\frac{1}{R_1}+\frac{1}{R_2}+\frac{1}{R_3}+\ldots+\frac{1}{R_n}$$

$$\Rightarrow \frac{K'(l+2l+\ldots+nl)\,d}{d}=\frac{k(ld)}{d}+\frac{2k(2ld)}{d}+\ldots+\frac{nk(nld)}{d}$$

$$\Rightarrow \frac{K'n(n+1)}{2}=\frac{n(n+1)(2n+1)}{6}k$$

$$\Rightarrow K'=\left(\frac{2n+1}{3}\right)k$$

Given, $K'=1.2K$

$$\Rightarrow \left(\frac{2n+1}{3}\right)k=1.2\left(\frac{n+1}{2}\right)k \Rightarrow n=4$$

7. $R_{iron}=\frac{l}{KA}=\frac{0.5}{80\times(1\times10^{-2})^2}=62.5^\circ$ C/W

$$R_{steel}=\frac{l}{KA}=\frac{0.5}{14\left[\pi\left(\frac{0.01}{\sqrt{2}}\right)^2-(0.01)^2\right]}=625^\circ\text{ C/W}$$

$$R_{eq}=\frac{R_{iron}R_{steel}}{R_{iron}+R_{steel}}=\frac{625}{11}{}^\circ\text{C/W}$$

$$\frac{dQ}{dt}=\frac{T_1-T_2}{R_{eq}}=\frac{\Delta m}{\Delta t}L_f$$

$$\Rightarrow \frac{78-0}{625/11}=\frac{\Delta m}{7\times60}\times336 \Rightarrow \Delta m=1.716\text{ g}$$

8. $t\propto d^2$

$$\therefore \frac{t_1}{t_2}=\left(\frac{d_1}{d_2}\right)^2$$

$$\Rightarrow \frac{1}{t_2}=\left(\frac{2}{10}\right)^2 \Rightarrow t_2=25\text{ days}$$

9. $P=i^2R=(2)^2(10)=40$ W

Thermal resistance, $R_{eq}=\int_{r_1}^{r_2}\frac{dx}{K(2\pi xl)}=\frac{1}{2\pi Kl}\ln\left(\frac{r_2}{r_1}\right)$

Rate of heat flow, $\frac{dQ}{dt}=\frac{\Delta T}{R_{eq}}=\frac{2\pi Kl\Delta T}{\ln\left(\frac{r_2}{r_1}\right)}$

In steady state, $\frac{dQ}{dt}=P$

$$\Rightarrow \frac{2\pi Kl\Delta T}{\ln\left(\frac{r_2}{r_1}\right)}=P$$

$$\Rightarrow \Delta T=\frac{P\ln\left(\frac{r_2}{r_1}\right)}{2\pi Kl}=\frac{40\ln 2}{2\pi(0.005)2}=\frac{2000\ln 2}{\pi}{}^\circ\text{C}$$

$$\therefore n=2000$$

10. Thermal resistance,

$$R_{eq}=\int_{R_1}^{R_2}\frac{dx}{K(4\pi x^2)}=\frac{1}{4\pi K}\left[\frac{1}{R_1}-\frac{1}{R_2}\right]=0.02^\circ\text{C/W}$$

Mass of water $=\rho_w\left(\frac{4}{3}\pi R_1^3\right)=\frac{125}{6}\pi$ kg

$$\frac{dQ}{dt}=\frac{1000-T}{0.02}=\left(\frac{125\pi}{6}\right)(4200)\frac{dT}{dt}$$

$$\int dt=5500\int_0^{100}\frac{dT}{1000-T}$$

$$\Rightarrow t=5500\ln\left(\frac{10}{9}\right)$$

$$\therefore K=5$$

Previous Year's Questions

JEE Main

1. Let the temperature of contact surface is T then,

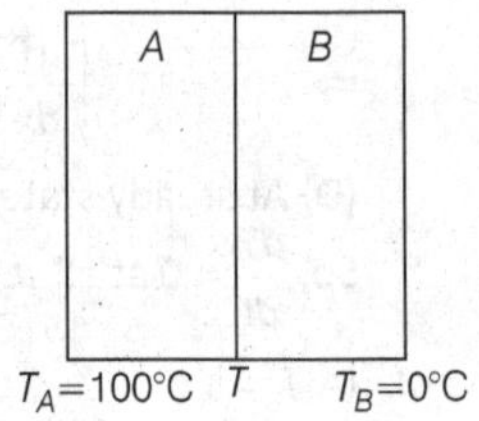

$$\frac{K_AA(T_A-T)}{L}=\frac{K_BA(T-T_B)}{L}$$

$$\Rightarrow 84(100-T)=126(T-0)$$

$$\Rightarrow 8400-84T=126T$$

$$\Rightarrow 8400=210T$$

$$\Rightarrow T=\frac{8400}{210}=40^\circ\text{ C}$$

2. The given figure for two plates A and B is given as

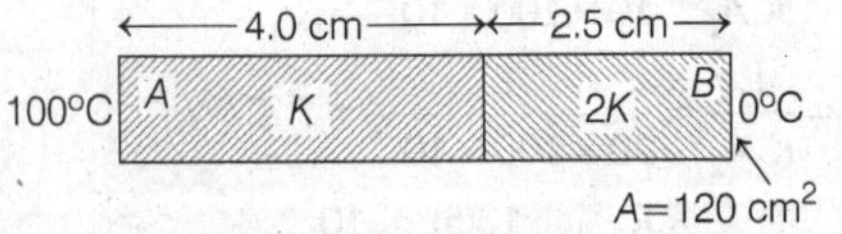

For series combination, $R_{seris}=R_1+R_2+\ldots$

$$\Rightarrow \frac{l_1+l_2+\ldots}{K_{eq}A}=\frac{l_1}{K_1A}+\frac{l_2}{K_2A}+\ldots$$

$\Rightarrow$ For two slabs of same area, we have

$$\frac{l_1 + l_2}{K_{eq}} = \frac{l_1}{K_1} + \frac{l_2}{K_2}$$

Here, $l_1 = 4$ cm,

$K_1 = K$

$l_2 = 2.5$ cm and $K_2 = 2K$

So, $\frac{4 + 2.5}{K_{eq}} = \frac{4}{K} + \frac{2.5}{2K}$

$$\Rightarrow \frac{6.5}{K_{eq}} = \frac{10.5}{2K}$$

or $K_{eq} = \frac{13K}{10.5} = \frac{26}{21}K = \left(1 + \frac{5}{21}\right)K = \left(1 + \frac{5}{\alpha}\right)K$ (given)

$\alpha = 21$

3. Thickness of wall of insulation box,

$$l = 1 \text{ cm} = 1 \times 10^{-2} \text{ m}$$

$$T_1 = 0, T_2 = 40° \text{ C}$$

Latent heat of fusion of ice,

$$L_f = 3.4 \times 10^5 \text{ Jkg}^{-1}$$

Thermal conductivity,

$$k = 0.05 \text{ Wm}^{-1}{}^\circ\text{C}^{-1}$$

$$= 5 \times 10^{-2} \text{Wm}^{-1}{}^\circ\text{C}^{-1}$$

Area, $A = 2(0.6 \times 0.5 + 0.5 \times 0.2 + 0.2 \times 0.6) = 1.04 \text{ m}^2$

We know that, rate of flow of heat

$$\frac{\Delta Q}{\Delta t} = \frac{kA(T_2 - T_1)}{l}$$

$$\Rightarrow \frac{mL_f}{\Delta t} = \frac{kA(T_2 - T_1)}{l} \quad [\because Q = mL]$$

$$\Rightarrow \frac{m}{\Delta t} = \frac{kA(T_2 - T_1)}{lL_f} = \frac{5 \times 10^{-2} \times 1.04(40 - 0)}{1 \times 10^{-2} \times 3.4 \times 10^5}$$

$$= 61 \times 10^{-5} \text{ kg/s}$$

4. Given, for steel and copper rods,

$$\frac{K_2}{K_1} = 9, \frac{A_1}{A_2} = 2, \frac{L_1}{L_2} = 2$$

From the diagram given in question, for steel rod

$$\frac{dQ}{dt} = K_1 A_1 \frac{(450 - T)}{L_1} \quad \text{...(i)}$$

and for copper rod,

$$\frac{dQ}{dt} = K_2 A_2 \frac{(T - 0)}{L_2} \quad \text{...(ii)}$$

Dividing Eq. (i) by Eq. (ii), we get

$$1 = \frac{K_1}{K_2} \frac{A_1}{A_2} \left(\frac{450 - T}{T}\right) \frac{L_2}{L_1}$$

$$\Rightarrow \frac{450 - T}{T} = \frac{K_2}{K_1} \cdot \frac{A_2}{A_1} \cdot \frac{L_1}{L_2}$$

$$\Rightarrow \frac{450}{T} - 1 = 9 \times \frac{1}{2} \times 2 \Rightarrow \frac{450}{T} = 9 + 1$$

$$\Rightarrow T = \frac{450}{10} = 45° \text{ C}$$

5. Since, both blocks M_1 and M_2 are connected in series, hence rate of heat flow through block M_1 = rate of heat flow through block M_2

$$\Rightarrow \frac{K_1 A(\Delta T_1)}{l_1} = \frac{K_2 A(\Delta T_2)}{l_2}$$

$$\Rightarrow \frac{K_1 \Delta T_1}{l_1} = \frac{K_2 \Delta T_2}{l_2}$$

$$\Rightarrow \frac{K_1(100 - 80)}{16 \times 10^{-2}} = \frac{K_2(80 - 0)}{8 \times 10^{-2}}$$

$$\Rightarrow \frac{20K_1}{2} = 80K_2$$

$$\Rightarrow K_1 = 8K_2 = 8K \quad [\because K_2 = K \text{ given}]$$

6. Given, thermal resistances

$$R_{AB} = R_{CD} = 10.0 \text{ kW}^{-1}$$

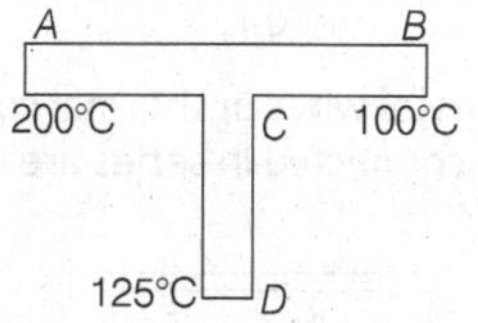

As, C is mid-point of AB, and as we know

$$R \propto \text{length}$$

$$R_{AC} = R_{BC} = 5 \text{ kW}^{-1}$$

Now, we know that heat current is given as

$$\frac{Q}{t} = \frac{\Delta T}{R}$$

Let temperature of point C as T.

Consider at point C heat is coming in from A and going out at point B and D.

Therefore, we can write,

$$\frac{T_A - T}{R_{AC}} = \frac{T - T_D}{R_{CD}} = \frac{T - T_B}{R_{BC}}$$

$$\Rightarrow \frac{200 - T}{5} = \frac{T - 125}{10} + \frac{T - 100}{5}$$

$$\Rightarrow 400 - 2T = T - 125 + 2T - 200$$

$$5T = 725°\text{C}$$

$$\Rightarrow T = 145°\text{C}$$

The heat current in CD is

$$I_{CD} = \frac{T - T_D}{R_{CD}} = \frac{145 - 125}{10} = \frac{20}{10} = 2 \text{ W}$$

Thus, the value of P is 2.

7. Given that, r_1 and r_2 be the radii of inner and outer shells.

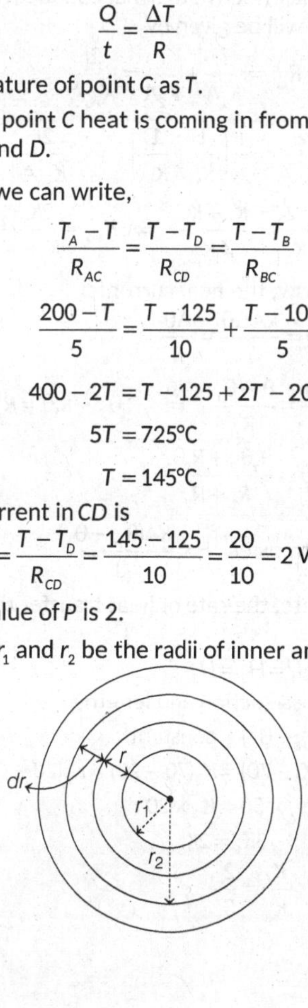

A material of thermal conductivity (K) is filled between region.

Consider an elementary sphere of radius r and thickness dr.

Now, thermal resistance of elementary sphere $dR = \dfrac{dr}{K 4\pi r^2}$

[$\because$ Inner surface area, $A = 4\pi r^2$]

So, total thermal resistance,

$$R = \int dR = \int_{r_1}^{r_2} \frac{dr}{4\pi K r^2} = -\frac{1}{4\pi K}\left[\frac{1}{r}\right]_{r_1}^{r_2}$$

$$R = \frac{r_2 - r_1}{4\pi K r_1 r_2}$$

Hence, heat current (or the rate of flow of heat)

$$\frac{dQ}{dt} = \frac{\Delta\theta}{R} = \frac{(\theta_2 - \theta_1)}{\dfrac{(r_2 - r_1)}{4\pi K r_1 r_2}} = \frac{4\pi K r_1 r_2 (\theta_2 - \theta_1)}{r_2 - r_1}$$

8. Two identical metal wires of thermal conductivities K_1 and K_2 respectively connected in series are represented as follows

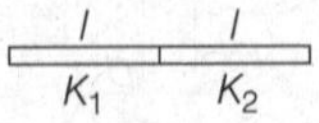

The above figure can also be represented as

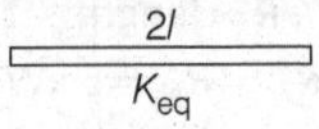

Therefore, the effective thermal conductivity of the combination will be given by

$$R_{\text{eff}} = \frac{l}{K_1 A} + \frac{l}{K_2 A} = \frac{2l}{K_{eq} A}$$

$$\Rightarrow \quad \frac{2l}{K_{eq} A} = \frac{l}{A}\left(\frac{1}{K_1} + \frac{1}{K_2}\right) \Rightarrow \frac{2l}{K_{eq} A} = \frac{l}{A}\left(\frac{K_1 + K_2}{K_1 K_2}\right)$$

$$\Rightarrow \quad \frac{2}{K_{eq}} = \frac{K_1 + K_2}{K_1 K_2} \Rightarrow K_{eq} = \frac{2K_1 K_2}{K_1 + K_2}$$

9. Since, we know, the heat currents,

$$\therefore \quad Q = \frac{kA\Delta\theta}{l} = \frac{\Delta\theta}{R} \qquad \left(\because R = \frac{l}{kA}\right)$$

$$\Rightarrow \quad \frac{\theta_2 - \theta}{R_2} = \frac{\theta - \theta_1}{R_1} \Rightarrow R_1\theta_2 - R_1\theta = R_2\theta - R_2\theta_1$$

$$\Rightarrow \quad \theta = \frac{R_1\theta_2 + R_2\theta_1}{R_1 + R_2}$$

10. Rate of heat transfer, $H = \dfrac{KA(\theta_H - \theta_L)}{L}$

At steady state, the rate of heat transfer through each rod is same.

i.e., $H_1 = H_2 = H_3$

For same cross-section and lengths,

$$K \times (\theta_H - \theta_L) = \text{constant}$$

$$K_1(100 - 70) = K_2(70 - 20) = K_3(20 - 0)$$

$$K_1 \times 30 = K_2 \times 50 = K_3 \times 20$$

$$3K_1 = 2K_3$$

$$\frac{K_1}{K_3} = \frac{2}{3}$$

or $\quad K_1 : K_3 = 2 : 3 \quad$ or $\quad 5K_2 = 2K_3$

or $\quad \dfrac{K_2}{K_3} = \dfrac{2}{5} \quad$ or $\quad K_2 : K_3 = 2 : 5$

11. Let interface temperature in steady state conduction be θ, then assuming no heat loss through sides;

$$\begin{pmatrix}\text{Rate of heat}\\ \text{flow through}\\ \text{first slab}\end{pmatrix} = \begin{pmatrix}\text{Rate of heat}\\ \text{flow through}\\ \text{second slab}\end{pmatrix}$$

$$\Rightarrow \quad \frac{(3K)A(\theta_2 - \theta)}{d} = \frac{KA(\theta - \theta_1)}{3d}$$

$$\Rightarrow \quad 9(\theta_2 - \theta) = \theta - \theta_1 \Rightarrow 9\theta_2 + \theta_1 = 10\theta$$

$$\Rightarrow \quad \theta = \frac{9}{10}\theta_2 + \frac{1}{10}\theta_1$$

12. Energy flux is the rate of heat flow per unit area through the rod.

Also, rate of flow of heat per unit time through a material of area of cross-section A and thermal conductivity k between the temperatures T_1 and T_2 ($T_1 > T_2$) is given as,

$$\frac{\Delta Q}{\Delta t} = \frac{kA(T_1 - T_2)}{l} \qquad \text{... (i)}$$

Energy flux using Eq. (i), we get

$$= \frac{1}{A} \cdot \frac{\Delta Q}{\Delta t} = \frac{k(T_1 - T_2)}{l}$$

Here, $k = 0.1\ \text{W K}^{-1}\text{m}^{-1}, l = 1\ \text{m}$

$T_1 = 1000\ \text{K}$ and $T_2 = 100\ \text{K}$

$$\therefore \text{Energy flux} = \frac{0.1(1000 - 100)}{1} = 90\ \text{Wm}^{-2}$$

13. Both the given cylinders are in parallel as heat flow is given along length. In parallel, equivalent thermal conductivity of system is

$$K_{eq} = \frac{K_1 A_1 + K_2 A_2}{A_1 + A_2}$$

So, in given system

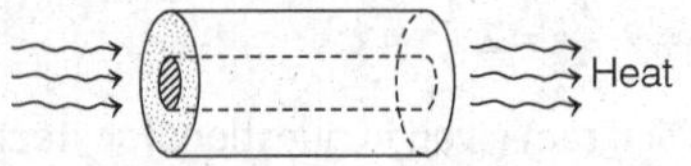

$$K_{eq} = \frac{K_1(\pi R^2) + K_2[\pi(2R)^2 - \pi R^2]}{(\pi R^2) + (4\pi R^2 - \pi R^2)}$$

or $\quad K_{eq} = \dfrac{K_1 + 3K_2}{4}$

JEE Advanced

1. Rate of heat flow will be same,

$$\therefore \quad \frac{300 - 200}{R_1} = \frac{200 - 100}{R_2} \qquad \left(\text{as } H = \frac{dQ}{dt} = \frac{T \cdot D}{R}\right)$$

$$\therefore \quad R_1 = R_2 \Rightarrow \frac{L_1}{K_1 A_1} = \frac{L_2}{K_2 A_2}$$

$$\Rightarrow \quad \frac{K_1}{K_2} = \frac{A_2}{A_1} = 4$$

2.

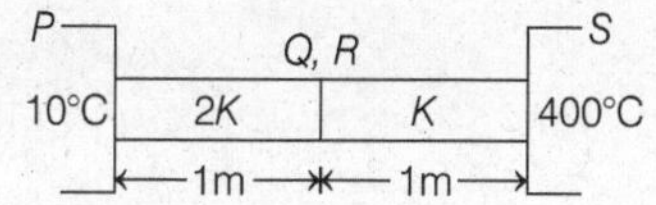

Rate of heat flow from P to Q

$$\frac{dQ}{dt} = \frac{2KA(T-10)}{1}$$

Rate of heat flow from Q to S

$$\frac{dQ}{dt} = \frac{KA(400-T)}{1}$$

At steady state rate of heat flow is same

$$\therefore \quad \frac{2KA(T-10)}{1} = KA(400-T)$$

or $\quad 2T - 20 = 400 - T$ or $3T = 420$

$$\therefore \quad T = 140^\circ C$$

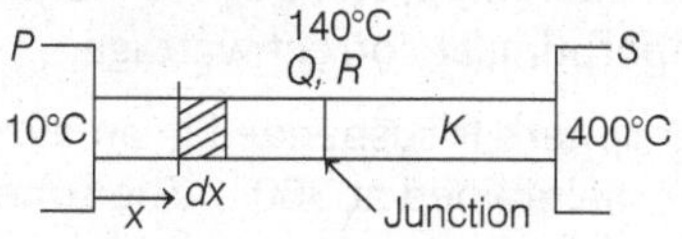

Temperature of junction is 140° C

Temperature at a distance x from end P is

$$T_x = (130x + 10)^\circ C$$

Change in length dx is suppose dy

Then, $dy = \alpha dx\,(T_x - 10)$

$$\int_0^{\Delta y} dy = \int_0^1 \alpha dx\,(130x + 10 - 10)$$

$$\Delta y = \left[\frac{\alpha x^2}{2} \times 130\right]_0^1; \quad \Delta y = 1.2 \times 10^{-5} \times 65$$

$$\Delta y = 78.0 \times 10^{-5} \text{ m} = 0.78 \text{ mm}$$

3. $R_{\text{I}} = R_1 + R_2 = \left(\frac{l}{KA}\right) + \left(\frac{l}{2KA}\right) = \frac{3}{2}\left(\frac{l}{KA}\right)$

$$\frac{1}{R_{\text{II}}} = \frac{1}{R_1} + \frac{1}{R_2} = \frac{KA}{l} + \frac{2KA}{l} \text{ or } R_{\text{II}} = \frac{l}{3KA} = \frac{R_{\text{I}}}{4.5}$$

Since, thermal resistance R_{II} is 4.5 times less than thermal resistance R_{I}.

$$\therefore \quad t_{\text{II}} = \frac{t_{\text{I}}}{4.5} = \frac{9}{4.5} \text{ s} = 2 \text{ s}$$

4. Thermal resistance $R = \frac{l}{KA}$

$$\therefore \quad R_A = \frac{L}{(2K)(4Lw)} \qquad \text{(Here } w = \text{width)}$$

$$= \frac{1}{8Kw},$$

$$R_B = \frac{4L}{3K\,(Lw)} = \frac{4}{3Kw} \Rightarrow R_C = \frac{4L}{(4K)\,(2Lw)} = \frac{1}{2Kw}$$

$$R_D = \frac{4L}{(5K)\,(Lw)} = \frac{4}{5Kw} \Rightarrow R_E = \frac{L}{(6K)\,(Lw)} = \frac{1}{6Kw}$$

$$R_A : R_B : R_C : R_D : R_E = 15 : 160 : 60 : 96 : 12$$

So, let us write, $R_A = 15\,R$, $R_B = 160\,R$ etc and draw a simple electrical circuit as shown in figure

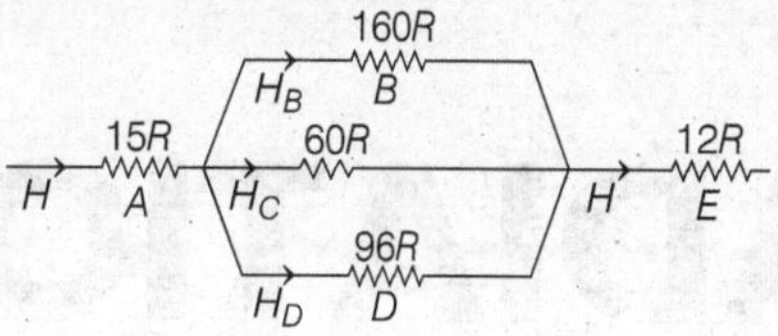

H = Heat current = Rate of heat flow.

$$H_A = H_E = H \qquad \text{(let)}$$

In parallel current distributes in inverse ratio of resistance.

$$\therefore \quad H_B : H_C : H_D = \frac{1}{R_B} : \frac{1}{R_C} : \frac{1}{R_D} = \frac{1}{160} : \frac{1}{60} : \frac{1}{96} = 9 : 24 : 15$$

$$\therefore \quad H_B = \left(\frac{9}{9+24+15}\right) H = \frac{3}{16} H$$

$$H_C = \left(\frac{24}{9+24+15}\right) H = \frac{1}{2} H$$

and $\quad H_D = \left(\frac{15}{9+24+15}\right) H = \frac{5}{16} H$

$$H_C = H_B + H_D$$

Temperature difference (let us call it T)

= (Heat current) × (Thermal resistance)

$$T_A = H_A R_A = (H)(15R) = 15\,HR$$

$$T_B = H_B R_B = \left(\frac{3}{16} H\right)(160\,R) = 30\,HR$$

$$T_C = H_C R_C = \left(\frac{1}{2} H\right)(60\,R) = 30HR$$

$$T_D = H_D R_D = \left(\frac{5}{16} H\right)(96\,R) = 30\,HR$$

$$T_E = H_E R_E = (H)\,(12\,R) = 12\,HR$$

Here, T_E is minimum. Therefore option (c) is also correct.

∴ Correct options are (a), (c) and (d).

5.

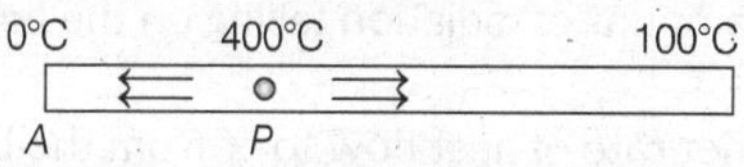

Heat will flow both sides from point P.

$$\Rightarrow \left(\frac{dQ}{dt}\right)_{\text{calorimetry}} = \left(\frac{dQ}{dt}\right)_{\text{conduction}}$$

$$L_1 \frac{dm_1}{dt} = \left(\frac{\text{Temperature difference}}{\text{Thermal resistance}}\right)_1 = \frac{400}{(\lambda x)/kA} \qquad \text{...(i)}$$

Similarly,

$$L_1 \frac{dm_2}{dt} = \frac{400-100}{(100-\lambda)x/kA} \qquad \text{...(ii)}$$

In above two equations, $\frac{dm_1}{dt} = \frac{dm_2}{dt}$ (given)

$$L_1 = 80 \text{ calg}^{-1} \text{ and } L_2 = 540 \text{ calg}^{-1}$$

Solving these two equations, we get $\lambda = 9$.

CHAPTER~04

RADIATION

LEVEL 01 Starter Level

4.1 Stefan-Boltzmann's Law

1 If the rate of emission of radiation of a black body at 0°C is E, then what will be the rate of emission of radiation of this body at 273°C?

2 Find the temperature of an oven if it radiates 8.28 cal per second through an opening, whose area is 6.1 cm^2. Assume that the radiation is close to that of a blackbody.

3 Assume that the total surface area of a human body is 1.6 m^2 and that it radiates like an ideal radiator. Calculate the amount of energy radiated per second by the body if the body temperature is 37° C. Stefan constant $\sigma = 6.0 \times 10^{-8} W/m^2\text{-}K^4$

4 Calculate the amount of heat radiated per second by a body of surface area 12 cm^2 kept in thermal equilibrium in a room at temperature 27°C. The emissivity of the surface = 0.80 and $\sigma = 6.0 \times 10^{-8} W/m^2\text{-}K^4$.

5 A spherical ball of surface area 20 cm^2 absorbs any radiation that falls on it. It is suspended in a closed box maintained at 57°C.
(a) Find the amount of radiation falling on the ball per second.
(b) Find the net rate of heat flow to or from the ball at an instant when its temperature is 2270°C. Stefan constant = $6.0 \times 10^{-8} W/m^2\text{-}K^4$.

6 A body of emissivity (e = 0.75), surface area of 300 cm^2 and temperature 227°C is kept in a room at temperature 27°C. Calculate the initial value of net power emitted by the body.

7 A blackbody of surface area 100 cm^2 is placed inside an enclosure. The enclosure has a constant temperature 27°C and the blackbody is maintained at 327°C by heating it electrically. What electric power is needed to maintain the temperature? $\sigma = 6.0 \times 10^{-8} W/m^2\text{-}K^4$.

8 A 100W bulb has tungsten filament of total length 1.0 m and radius 4×10^{-5} m. The emissivity of the filament is 0.8 and $\sigma = 6.0 \times 10^{-8} W/m^2\text{-}K^4$. Calculate the temperature of the filament when the bulb is operating at correct wattage.

9 A copper sphere is suspended in an evacuated chamber maintained at 300 K. The sphere is maintained at a constant temperature of 500 K by heating it electrically. A total of 210W of electric power is needed to do it. When the surface of the copper sphere is completely blackened, 700 W is needed to maintain the same temperature of the sphere. Calculate the emissivity of copper.

10 The rate at which the radiant energy reaches the surface of earth from the sun is about 1.4 kW/m^2. The distance from earth to the sun is about 1.5×10^{11} m, and the radius of sun is about 7×10^8 m.
(a) What is the rate of radiation of energy, per unit area, from the sun's surface?
(b) If the sun radiates as an ideal blackbody, what is the temperature of its surface?

4.2 Rate of Cooling

1 A cubical block of mass 1.0 kg and edge 5.0 cm is heated to 227°C. It is kept in an evacuated chamber maintained at 27°C. Assuming that the block emits radiation like a blackbody, find the rate at which the temperature of the block will decrease initially. Specific heat capacity of the material of the block is 400 J/kg-K.

2 Two solids spheres are heated to the same temperature and allowed to cool under identical conditions. Compare:
(a) initial rates of loss of heat, and
(b) initial rates of fall of temperature
Assume that all the surfaces have the same emissivity and ratios of their radii, specific heats and densities are respectively $1:\alpha$, $1:\beta$ and $1:\gamma$.

4.3 Newton's Law of Cooling

1 A body at temperature 40°C is kept in a surrounding of constant temperature 20°C. It is observed that its temperature falls to 35°C in 10 min. Find how much more time will it take for the body to attain a temperature of 30°C?

2 A body cools down from 50°C to 45°C in 5 min and to 40°C in another 7 min. Find the temperature of the surrounding.

3 A body cools in 7 min from 60°C to 40°C. What will be its temperature after the next 7 min? The temperature of surroundings is 10°C.

4 A calorimeter contains 50 g of water at 50°C. The temperature falls to 45°C in 10 min. When the calorimeter contains 100 g of water at 50°C, it takes 18 min for the temperature to become 45°C. Find the water equivalent of the calorimeter.

5 A calorimeter of negligible heat capacity contains 100 cc of water at 40°C. The water cools to 35°C in 5 min. The water is now replaced by K-oil of equal volume at 40°C. Find the time taken for the temperature to become 35°C under similar conditions. Specific heat capacities of water and K-oil are 4200 J/kg-K and 2100 J/kg-K respectively. Density of K-oil = 800 kg/m^3.

4.4 Wien's Displacement Law

1 If a black body is radiating at $T = 1650$ K, at what wavelength is the intensity maximum?

2 Estimate the temperature at which a body may appear blue or red. The values of λ_{mean} for these are 5000 Å and 7500 Å, respectively. [Given Wien's constant $b = 0.3$ cmK]

3 Solar radiation is found to have an intensity maximum near the wavelength range of 470 nm. Assuming the surface of sun to be perfectly absorbing ($a = 1$), calculate the temperature of solar surface.

4 A hot blackbody emits the energy at the rate of 16 J m^{-2} s^{-1} and its most intense radiation corresponds to 20000 Å. When the temperature of this body is further increased and its most intense radiation corresponds to 10000 Å, then find the value of energy radiated in Jm^{-2} s^{-1}.

5 The plots of intensity *versus* wavelength for three black bodies at temperatures T_1, T_2 and T_3 respectively are shown in figure. How their temperatures are related?

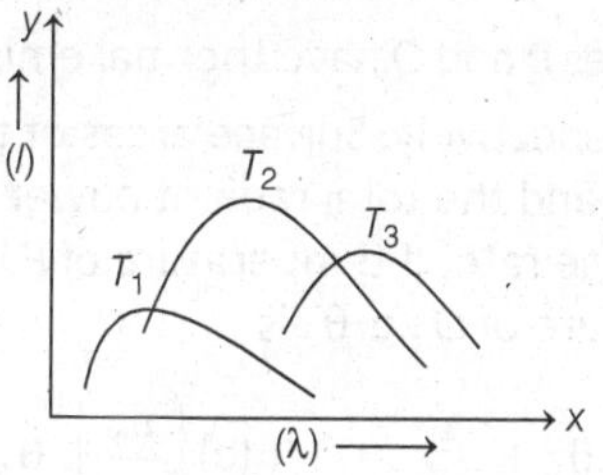

6 The spectra of radiation emitted by two distant stars are shown below. What is the ratio of the surface temperature of star *A* to that of star *B*, $T_A : T_B$, approximately?

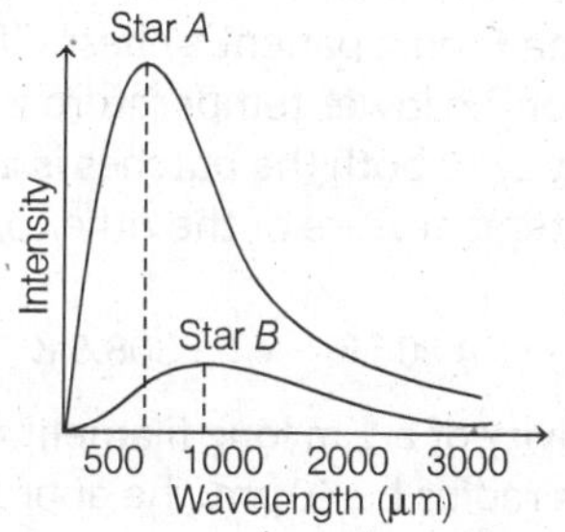

LEVEL 02 JEE Main Level

Single Choice Correct Questions

1 At 0°C a body emits
(a) no radiation
(b) electromagnetic radiation of single wavelength
(c) electromagnetic radiation of all wavelengths that are emitted by it at room temperature
(d) electromagnetic radiation of fewer wavelengths than that are emitted by it at room temperature

2 A black body radiates heat energy at the rate of 2×10^5 J / s / m^2 at temperature 127°C. The temperature of the black body, at which the rate of heat radiation is 32×10^5 J / s / m^2, is
(a) 273°C
(b) 527°C
(c) 873°C
(d) 927°C

3 The emissive power of a blackbody at $T = 300$ K is $100\ W/m^2$. Consider a body B of area $A = 10m^2$, coefficient of reflectivity $r = 0.3$ and coefficient of transmission $t = 0.5$. Its temperature is 300 K. Then, which of the following is incorrect?
(a) The emissive power of B is $20\ W/m^2$
(b) The emissive power of B is $200\ W/m^2$.
(c) The power emitted by B is 200 W
(d) The emissivity of B is 0.2

4 A spherical black body with a radius of 12 cm radiates 450 W power at 500 K. If the radius were halved and the temperature doubled, the power radiated would be
(a) 225 W (b) 450 W
(c) 900 W (d) 1800 W

5 Two bodies P and Q have thermal emissivities of ε_P and ε_Q respectively. Surface areas of these bodies are same and the total radiant power is also emitted at the same rate. If temperature of P is θ_P K, then temperature of Q i.e. θ_Q is
(a) $\left(\frac{\varepsilon_Q}{\varepsilon_P}\right)^{\frac{1}{4}}\theta_P$ (b) $\left(\frac{\varepsilon_P}{\varepsilon_Q}\right)^{\frac{1}{4}}\theta_P$
(c) $\left(\frac{\varepsilon_Q}{\varepsilon_P}\right)^{\frac{1}{4}}\frac{1}{\theta_P}$ (d) $\left(\frac{\varepsilon_Q}{\varepsilon_P}\right)^{4}\theta_P$

6 The rates of heat radiation from two patches of skin each of area S, on a patient's chest differ by 2%. If the patch of the lower temperature is at 300 K and the emissivity of both the patches is assumed to be unity, the temperature of the other patch is closest to
(a) 301.5 K (b) 306 K (c) 308.5 K (d) 312 K

7 The emissivity of a 1 m long filament of a 100 W bulb is 0.4. If its radius be 40 μm, the approximate temperature at which it operates at correct rating is
(a) 625 K (b) 815 K
(c) 1025 K (d) 2100 K

8 Two identical solid spheres have the same constant temperature. One of the spheres is cut into two identical pieces. These two hemispheres are then separated. The intact sphere radiates an energy Q during a given time interval at temperature T_0. During the same interval, the two hemisphere radiate at total energy Q' at temperature T_0. Emissivity of all the surfaces is same. The ratio Q'/Q has value
(a) 0.50 (b) 0.75
(c) 2.0 (d) 1.5

9 A black metal foil is warmed by radiation from a small sphere at temperature T and at a distance d. It is found that the power received by the foil is P. If both the temperature and distance are doubled, the power received by the foil will be
(a) $16P$ (b) $4P$ (c) $2P$ (d) P

10 If the surface temperature of the sun and its mass were to remain constant and its radius were to increase by a factor of 2, the equilibrium temperature of a planet (T_P) would
(a) decrease by a factor of 2
(b) increase by a factor of $\sqrt{2}$
(c) increase by a factor of $2^{\frac{3}{2}}$
(d) increase by a factor of 4

11 A planet is at an average distance d from the sun and its average surface temperature is T. Assume that the planet receives energy only from sun and loses energy only through radiation, from surface. Neglect atmospheric effects. Temperature T is propotional to
(a) d^2 (b) $d^{\frac{-1}{2}}$ (c) $d^{\frac{1}{2}}$ (d) $d^{\frac{1}{4}}$

12 The solar constant of earth is 2 cal/min- cm^2. If distance of mercury planet from sun is 0.4 times the distance of earth from the sun, then solar constant of mercury planet will be
(a) 12.5 cal/min-cm^2 (b) 25 cal/min-cm^2
(c) 0.32 cal/min-cm^2 (d) 2 cal/min-cm^2

13 A spherical tungsten piece of radius 1.0 cm is suspended in an evacuated chamber maintained at 300 K. The piece is maintained at 1000 K by heating it electrically. Find the rate at which the electrical energy must be supplied. The emissivity of tungsten is 0.30 and Stefan's constant (σ) is $6.0 \times 10^{-8}\ W/m^2\text{-}K^4$.
(a) 16 W (b) 18 W
(c) 20 W (d) 22 W

14 If a body (coated black) at 600K surrounded by atmosphere at 300K has cooling rate r_0, the same body at 900K, surrounded by the same atmosphere, will have the cooling rate close to
(a) $\frac{16\ r_0}{3}$ (b) $\frac{81 r_0}{16}$ (c) $16r_0$ (d) $4r_0$

15 Four spheres A, B, C and D of different metals but of same radius are kept at same temperature. The ratio of their densities and specific heats are 2 : 3 : 5 : 1 and 3 : 6 : 2 : 4. Which sphere will show the fastest rate of cooling(initially)?
(a) A (b) B (c) C (d) D

16 Two metallic spheres S_1 and S_1 are made of the same material and have got identical surface finish. The mass of S_1 is thrice that of S_2. Both the spheres are heated to the same high temperature and placed in the same room having lower temperature but are thermally insulated from each other. The ratio of the initial rate of cooling of S_1 to that S_2 is

(a) $\frac{1}{3}$ (b) $\frac{1}{\sqrt{3}}$ (c) $\frac{\sqrt{3}}{1}$ (d) $\left(\frac{1}{3}\right)^{\frac{1}{3}}$

17 A solid sphere of copper of radius R and a hollow sphere of the same material of inner radius r and outer radius R are heated to the same temperature and allowed to cool in the same environment. Hollow sphere

(a) will cool faster than solid sphere
(b) will cool slower than solid sphere
(c) will cool at the same rate as the solid sphere
(d) data is not sufficient to decide

18 Which of the following laws state that good absorbers of heat are also good emitters?

(a) Stefan's law (b) Wien's law
(c) Prevost's theory (d) Kirchhoff's law

19 A metallic sphere having radius 0.08 m and mass m = 10 kg is heated to a temperature of 227°C and suspended inside a box whose walls are at a temperature of 27°C. The maximum rate at which its temperature will fall is: (Take e = 1, Stefan's constant $\sigma = 5.8 \times 10^{-8}\ Wm^{-2}K^{-4}$ and specific heat of the metal $s = 90$ cal/kg/°C, $J = 4.2$ J/cal).

(a) 0.055 °C/s (b) 0.066 °C/s
(c) 0.044 °C/s (d) 0.03 °C/s

20 Match the following:

	List I		List II
(A)	Thermal resistance	(i)	$[MT^{-3}\theta^{-4}]$
(B)	Stefan's constant	(ii)	$[M^{-1}L^{-2}T^{3}\theta]$
(C)	Wien's constant	(iii)	$[ML^2T^{-3}]$
(D)	Heat current	(iv)	$[L\theta]$

(a) A-(ii) B - (i), C-(iv), D-(iii)
(b) A - (iii), B-(iv), C-(i), D-(ii)
(c) A-(i), B-(iii), C-(ii), D-(iv)
(d) A-(iv), B-(ii), C-(iii), D-(i)

21 A blackbody, initially at temperature T, cools to temperature $(T/2)$ in time Δt in surrounding which is near absolute zero. It will cool further to a temperature $(T/4)$ in additional time

(a) $8\Delta t$ (b) $7\Delta t$ (c) $9\Delta t$ (d) None

22 The temperature θ of "cup of coffee" in a "BARISTA" restaurant was plotted as a function of time. Which of the following curves may represent the plot?

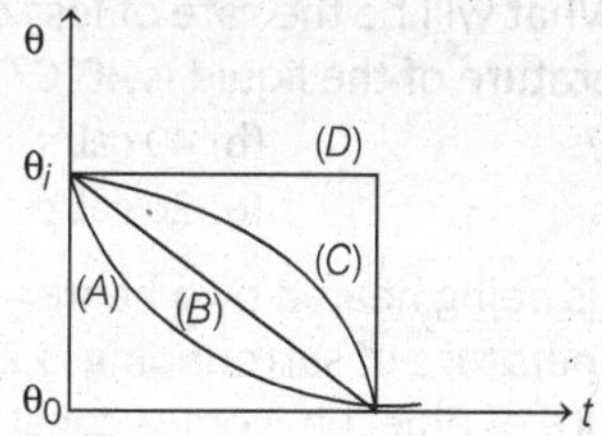

(a) Curve *A* (b) Curve *B*
(c) Curve *C* (d) Curve *D*

23 Temperature of a body θ is slightly more than the temperature of the surrounding θ_0. Its rate of cooling R *versus* temperature of body θ is plotted. Its shape would be

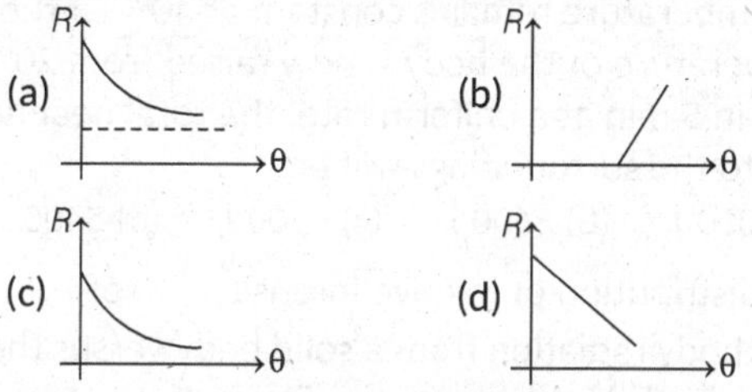

24 The temperature of a body falls from 52°C to 36°C in 10 min when placed in a surrounding of constant temperature 20°C. What will be the temperature of the body after another 10 min? (Use Newton's law of cooling)

(a) 28°C (b) 20°C (c) 32°C (d) 24°C

25 The temperature of a body falls from 40°C to 36°C in 4 min when placed in a surrounding of constant temperature 20°C. Its temperature falls further from 36°C to 32°C in the same surrounding in time (Use approximation in Newton's law of cooling)

(a) 5.1 min (b) 6 min (c) 6.5 min (d) 6.8 min

26 A black body calorimeter filled with hot water cools from 60°C to 50°C in 4 min and 40°C to 30°C in 8 min. The approximate temperature of surrounding is

(a) 10°C (b) 15°C (c) 20°C (d) 25°C

27 A polished metal with rough black spot on it is heated to about 1400 K and quickly taken to a dark room, which one of the following statements will be true?

(a) the spot will appear brighter than the plate
(b) The spot will appear darker than the plate
(c) The spot and plate will be equally bright
(d) The spot and plate will not be visible in dark

28 Liquid is filled in a vessel which is kept in a room with temperature 20°C. When the temperature of the liquid is 80°C, then it loses heat at the rate of 60 cal/s. What will be the rate of loss of heat when the temperature of the liquid is 40°C?

(a) 180 cal/s (b) 40 cal/s
(c) 30 cal/s (d) 20 cal/s

29 An object is being heated by a heater supplying 60 W heat. Temperature of surrounding is 20°C and the temperature of object becomes constant at 50°C. Now the heater is switched off. What is the rate at which the object will lose heat when its temperature has dropped to 30°C ?

(a) 20 W (b) 30 W (c) 40 W (d) 60 W

30 When a body is placed in surroundings at a constant temperature of 20°C, and heated by a 10W heater, its temperature remains constant at 40°C. If the temperature of the body is now raised from 20°C to 80°C in 5 min at a uniform rate, the total heat it will lose to the surroundings will be

(a) 3000 J (b) 3600 J (c) 4500 J (d) 5400 J

31 The distribution of relative intensity $I(\lambda)$ of blackbody radiation from a solid body *versus* the wavelength λ is shown in the figure. If the Wien displacement law constant is 2.9×10^{-3} mK, what is the approximate temperature of the object?

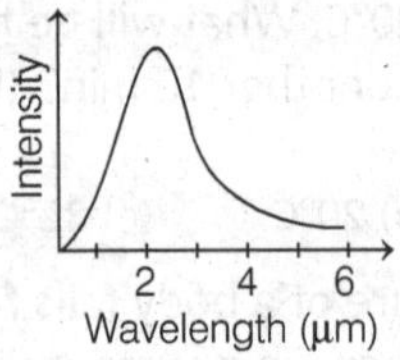

(a) 50 K (b) 250 K (c) 1450 K (d) 6250 K

32 The intensity of radiation emitted by the Sun has its maximum value at a wavelength of 510 nm and that emitted by the North star has the maximum value at 350 nm. If these stars behave like black bodies, then the ratio of the surface temperature of the sun and the North star is

(a) 1.46 (b) 0.69 (c) 1.21 (d) 0.83

33 The power radiated by a blackbody is P and it radiates maximum energy around the wavelength λ_0. If the temperature of the blackbody is now changed, so that it radiates maximum energy around wavelength $\frac{2\lambda_0}{3}$, the power radiated by it will increase by a factor is

(a) $\frac{4}{3}$ (b) $\frac{16}{9}$ (c) $\frac{81}{16}$ (d) $\frac{256}{81}$

34 The power emitted per unit area of a black body is $R\ \mathrm{W/m^2}$. At what wavelength will the power radiated by the black body be maximum? Stefan's constant $=\sigma$ and Wien's constant $= b$.

(a) $\lambda=\left(\frac{b\sigma}{R}\right)^{\frac{1}{4}}$ (b) $\lambda=\left(\frac{b}{R}\right)^{\frac{1}{4}}$

(c) $\lambda=\left(\frac{bR}{\sigma}\right)^{\frac{1}{4}}$ (d) $\lambda=b\left(\frac{\sigma}{R}\right)^{\frac{1}{4}}$

35 In solar radiation, the intensity of radiation is maximum around the wavelength λ. If R is the radius of the sun and c is the velocity of light, the mass lost by the sun per second is proportional to

(a) $\frac{R^2}{\lambda^4c^2}$ (b) $\frac{R^2}{\lambda^2c^2}$ (c) $\frac{R^3}{\lambda^4c^3}$ (d) $\frac{R^3}{\lambda^4c^2}$

36 Identify the graph which correctly represents the spectral intensity *versus* wavelength graph at two temperatures T' and T $(T < T')$?

(a)
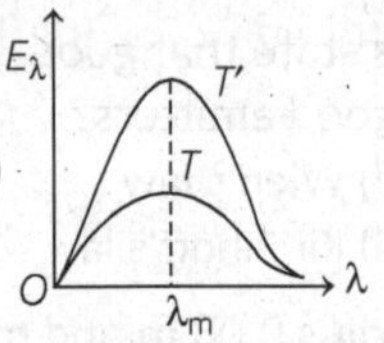

(b)
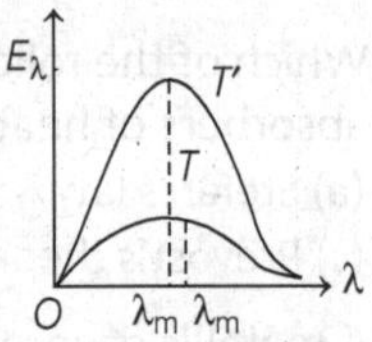

(c)
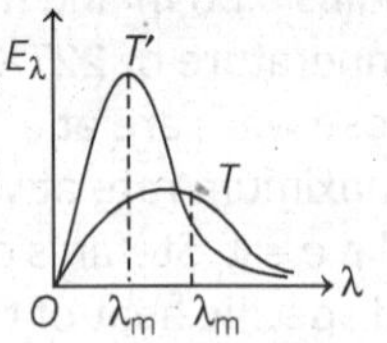

(d) None of these

37 Let the wavelength at which the spectral emissive power of a black body (at a temperature T) is maximum, be denoted by λ_{max}. As the temperature of the body is increased by 1 K, λ_{max} decreases by 1 percent. The temperature T of the black body is

(a) 100 K (b) 200 K
(c) 400 K (d) 288 K

38 The spectral emissive power E_λ for a body at temperature T_1 is plotted against the wavelength and area under the curve is found to be A. At a different temperature T_2, the area is found to be $81A$. Then, $\frac{\lambda_1}{\lambda_2}=$

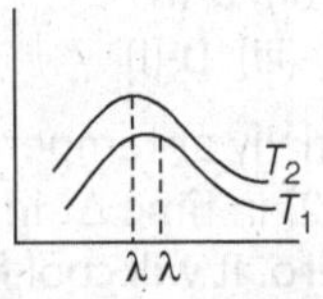

(a) 3 (b) $\frac{1}{3}$ (c) $\frac{1}{\sqrt{3}}$ (d) 3

Numerical Value Questions

1 A solid copper sphere cools at the rate of 2.8°C per minute, when its temperature is 127°C. Find the rate (in °C/min) at which another solid copper sphere of twice the radius lose its temperature at 327°C, if in both the cases, the room temperature is maintained at 27°C.

2 A room is heated by a radiator that has a constant temperature T (unknown). When the outside temperature is 260 K, the room temperature is 300 K. However, when the outside temperature drops to 240 K, the room temperature is only 290 K. Estimate the radiator temperature T (in K).

3 A lizard of mass 4g is warming itself in the bright sunlight. Its surface area is 4.2 cm^2, but its body casts a shadow of area 1.4 cm^2 on a piece of paper held perpendicular to sun rays. The intensity of sun rays at earth is 1000 W/m^2. Assume that specific heat capacity of lizard is same as that of water and its body behaves like a black body, also neglect the radiation from the lizard's body. How long (in minutes) must lizard lie in sun in order to raise its temperature by 5°C? Specific heat capacity of water is 4200 J/kg°C.

4 The filament of an incandescent lamp of power 64 W is made of Tungsten. The operation temperature of the lamp is 2000K. Consider the filament a black body and find its radius (in mm).
[Given : $\sigma = 6 \times 10^{-8}$ W / m^2 and length of filament is $\frac{10}{3\pi}$ cm]

5 A person of surface area 1.75 m^2 is lying out in the sunlight to get sun bath. If the intensity of the incident sunlight is 7×10^2 W / m^2, at what rate must heat be lost (in watt) by the person in order to maintain a constant body temperature? Assume the effective area of skin exposed to the Sun is 40% of the total surface area and that internal metabolic processes contribute another 90W for an inactive person. Emissivity of the body is 0.6.

6 A body cools from 50°C to 49.90°C in 5 s. It cools from 40°C to 39.9°C in t s. Assuming Newton's law of cooling to be valid and temperature of surroundings at 30°C, value of $t/5$ will be?

7 Emissivity e is a property of surface. Suppose for a surface emissivity e varies with Kelvin temperature T as $e = CT$ (C is a constant). If energy emission rate at temperature 600 K from the surface is 160W, what will be the energy emission rate (in W) at 300 K?

LEVEL 03 JEE Advanced Level

Single Choice Correct Questions

1 The rectangular surface of area 8 cm × 4 cm of a black body at a temperature of 127°C emits energy at the rate of E per second. If the length and breadth of the surface are each reduced to half of the initial value and the temperature is raised to 327°C, the rate of emission of energy will become

(a) $\frac{3}{8}E$ (b) $\frac{81}{16}E$

(c) $\frac{9}{16}E$ (d) $\frac{81}{64}E$

2 The radiation emitted by a star A is 10000 times that of the sun. If the surface temperatures of the sun and star are 6000 K and 2000 K, respectively. The ratio of the radii of the star and the sun is

(a) 300:1

(b) 600:1

(c) 900:1

(d) 1200:1

3 A sphere with diameter of 80 cm is held at a temperature of 227°C and is radiating energy. If the intensity of the radiation detected at a distance of 2.0 m from the sphere's centre is 100 W/m^2, what is the emissivity of the sphere? Stefan constant $\sigma = 6 \times 10^{-8}$ W/m^2-K^4.

(a) $\frac{1}{4}$ (b) $\frac{1}{3}$ (c) $\frac{2}{3}$ (d) $\frac{3}{4}$

4 Solar constant is 1370 W/m^2. 70% of the light incident on the earth is absorbed by the earth and the earth's average temperature is 288 K. The effective emissivity of the earth is

(a) 0.2 (b) 0.4 (c) 0.6 (d) 1

5 A cylindrical rod of length 1 m is fitted between a large ice chamber at 0°C and an evacuated chamber maintained at 27°C as shown in figure. Only small portions of the rod are inside the chambers and the rest is thermally insulated from the surrounding. The cross-section going into the evacuated chamber is blackened, so that it completely absorbs any radiation falling on it. The temperature of the

blackened end is 17°C when steady state is reached. Stefan constant $\sigma = 6 \times 10^{-8} W/m^2\text{-}K^4$. Find the thermal conductivity of the material of the rod. ($29^4 = 707281$)

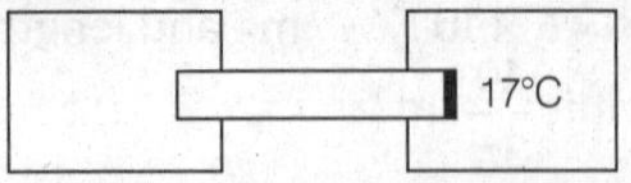

(a) 3.6 W / m - °C (b) 2.4 W / m - °C
(c) 1.2 W / m - °C (d) 4.8 W / m - °C

6 Liquid helium is stored at its boiling point (4.2 K) in a spherical can, separated by a vacuum space from a surrounding shield which is maintained at the temperature of liquid nitrogen (77 K). If a can is 0.1m in radius and is blacked on the outside so that it acts as a blackbody, how much helium boils away per hour? (Latent heat of vapourization is 21 kJ/kg)

(a) 43 g/h (b) 43 kg/h
(c) 4.3 g/h (d) 43×10^{-3} g/h

7 Two plates identical in size, one of black and rough surface (B_1) and the other smooth and polished (A_2) are interconnected by a thin horizontal pipe with a mercury pellet at the centre. Two more plates A_1 (identical to A_2) and B_2 (identical to B_1) are heated to the same temperature and placed closed to the plates B_1, and A_2 as shown in figure. The mercury pellet

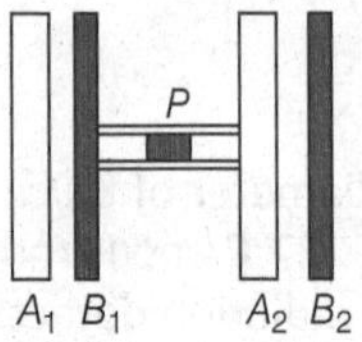

(a) moves to the right
(b) moves to the left
(c) remains stationary
(d) starts oscillating left and right

8 The graph, shown in the adjacent diagram, represents the variation of temperature T of two bodies, x and y having same surface area, with time t due to the emission of radiation. Find the correct relation between the emissivity and absorptivity power of the two bodies.

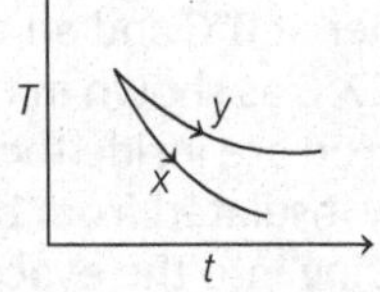

(a) $E_x > E_y$ and $a_x < a_y$ (b) $E_x < E_y$ and $a_x > a_y$
(c) $E_x > E_y$ and $a_x > a_y$ (d) $E_x < E_y$ and $a_x < a_y$

9 A solid copper sphere (density ρ and specific heat capacity c) of radius r at an initial temperature 200K is suspended inside a chamber whose walls are at almost 0 K. The time required (in μs) for the temperature of the sphere to drop to 100 K is

(a) $\frac{72}{7}\frac{r\rho c}{\sigma}$ (b) $\frac{7}{72}\frac{r\rho c}{\sigma}$
(c) $\frac{27}{7}\frac{r\rho c}{\sigma}$ (d) $\frac{7}{27}\frac{r\rho c}{\sigma}$

10 A and B are two isolated spheres kept in close proximity, so that they can exchange energy by radiation. The two spheres have identical physical dimensions but the surface of A behaves like a perfectly blackbody while the surface of B reflects 20% of all the radiations it receives. They are isolated from all other sources of radiation.

(a) If they are in thermal equilibrium and exchange equal amounts of radiation per second, then they will be at same absolute temperature, $T_A = T_B$.
(b) If they are in thermal equilibrium and exchange equal amounts of radiation per second, then $T_A = (0.8)^{\frac{1}{4}} T_B$.
(c) If they are not in thermal equilibrium and are each at $t = 0$ at the same temperature $T_A = T_B = T$, then the sphere A will lose thermal energy and B will gain thermal energy.
(d) If they are not in thermal equilibrium and are each at t = 0 at the same temperature $T_A = T_B = T$, then the sphere A will gain thermal energy and B will lose thermal energy.

11 A sphere and a cube of same material and same total surface area are placed in the same evacuated space turn by turn after they are heated to the same temperature. Find the ratio of their rates of cooling in the enclosure.

(a) $\sqrt{\frac{\pi}{6}} : 1$ (b) $\sqrt{\frac{\pi}{3}} : 1$ (c) $\frac{\pi}{\sqrt{6}} : 1$ (d) $\frac{\pi}{\sqrt{3}} : 1$

12 There are two thin spheres A and B of the same material and same thickness. They behave like black bodies. Radius of A is double that of B and both have same temperature T. When A and B are kept in a room of temperature T_0 ($<T$), the ratio of their rates of cooling is (assume negligible heat exchange between A and B).

(a) 2 : 1 (b) 1 : 1
(c) 4 : 1 (d) 8 : 1

13 A solid copper cube of edge 1 cm is suspended in an evacuated enclosure. Its temperature is found to fall from 100°C to 99°C in 100 s. Another solid copper cube of edge 2 cm, with similar surface nature, is suspended in a similar manner. The time required for this cube to cool from 100°C to 99°C will be approximately.

(a) 25 s (b) 50 s (c) 200 s (d) 400 s

14 250 g of water and equal volume of alcohol of mass 200 g are replaced successively in the same calorimeter and cool from 60°C to 55°C in 130 s and 67 s, respectively. If the water equivalent of the calorimeter is 10 g, then the specific heat of alcohol in cal/g- °C is

(a) 1.30 (b) 0.67
(c) 0.62 (d) 0.985

15 A body cools in a surrounding which is at a constant temperature of θ_0. Assume that it obeys Newton's law of cooling. Its temperature θ is plotted against time t. Tangents are drawn to the curve at the points $P(\theta = \theta_2)$ and $Q(\theta = \theta_1)$. These tangents meet the time axis at angles of ϕ_2 and ϕ_1 as shown, then

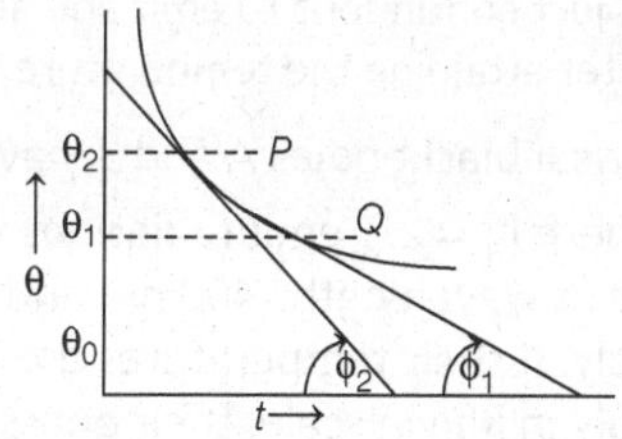

(a) $\frac{\tan\phi_2}{\tan\phi_1} = \frac{\theta_1 - \theta_0}{\theta_2 - \theta_0}$ (b) $\frac{\tan\phi_2}{\tan\phi_1} = \frac{\theta_2 - \theta_0}{\theta_1 - \theta_0}$

(c) $\frac{\tan\phi_1}{\tan\phi_2} = \frac{\theta_1}{\theta_2}$ (d) $\frac{\tan\phi_1}{\tan\phi_2} = \frac{\theta_2}{\theta_1}$

16 A system receives heat continuously at the rate of 10 W. The temperature of the system becomes constant at 70°C when the temperature of the surroundings is 30°C. After the heater is switched off, the system cools from 50°C to 49.9°C in 1 min. The heat capacity of the system is

(a) 1000 J/°C (b) 1500 J/°C
(c) 3000 J/°C (d) None of these

17 A black body is at a temperature of 2880 K. The energy of radiation emitted by this object with wavelength between 499 nm and 500 nm is U_1, between 999 nm and 1000 nm is U_2 and between 1499 nm and 1500 nm is U_3. Wien's constant $b = 2.88 \times 10^6$ nm-K, Then

(a) $U_1 = 0$ (b) $U_3 = 0$ (c) $U_1 = U_2$ (d) $U_2 > U_1$

18 Two spherical bodies A (radius 6 cm) and B (radius 18 cm) are at temperature T_1 and T_2, respectively. The maximum intensity in the emission spectrum of A is at 500 nm and in that of B is at 1500 nm. Considering them to be black bodies, what will be the ratio of the rate of total energy radiated by A to that of B?

(a) 9 (b) 9.5 (c) 8 (d) 8.5

19 Three discs, A, B and C having radii 2 m, 4 m and 6 m, respectively are coated with carbon black on their outer surfaces. The wavelengths corresponding to maximum intensities are 300 nm, 400 nm and 500 nm, respectively. The power radiated by them are Q_A, Q_B and Q_C, respectively.

(a) Q_A is maximum (b) Q_B is maximum
(c) Q_C is maximum (d) $Q_A = Q_B = Q_C$

20 Three bodies A, B and C have equal surface area and thermal emissivities in the ratio $e_A : e_B : e_C = 1 : \frac{1}{2} : \frac{1}{4}$. All the three bodies are radiating at same rate. Their wavelength corresponding to maximum intensity are λ_A, λ_B and λ_C, respectively and their temperatures are T_A, T_B and T_C on kelvin scale, then select the incorrect statement.

(a) $\sqrt{T_A T_C} = T_B$
(b) $\sqrt{\lambda_A \lambda_C} = \lambda_B$
(c) $\sqrt{e_A T_A}\sqrt{e_C T_C} = e_B T_B$
(d) $\sqrt{e_A \lambda_A T_A \cdot e_B \lambda_B T_B} = e_C \lambda_C T_C$

21 A copper sphere is suspended in an evacuated chamber maintained at 300 K. The sphere is maintained at a constant temperature of 500 K by heating it electrically. A total of 300 W of electric power is needed to do it. When half of the surface of the copper sphere is completely blackened, 600 W is needed to maintain the same temperature of the sphere. Calculate the emissivity of copper.

(a) $\frac{1}{2}$ (b) $\frac{1}{3}$ (c) $\frac{2}{3}$ (d) $\frac{3}{4}$

22 Two identical metallic sheets each behaves like a black body are kept parallel to each other with small separation between them in vacuum. Thermal energy is generated at a constant rate P in one of the sheets by passing electricity in it. In steady state, temperature of the other sheet is found to be constant at 300K. Find the value of P.
Given, area of the plates $A = 2\ \text{m}^2$ and $\sigma = 6.0 \times 10^{-8}\ \text{W/m}^2\text{-K}^4$

(a) 1944 W (b) 1458 W (c) 2916 W (d) 3888 W

Multiple Choice(s) Correct Questions

1 Two metallic sphere A and B are made of same material and have got identical surface finish. The mass of sphere A is four times that of B. Both the spheres are heated to the same temperature and placed in a room having lower temperature but thermally insulated from each other.

(a) The ratio of heat loss of A to that of B is $2^{\frac{4}{3}}$.

(b) The ratio of heat loss of A to that of B is $2^{\frac{2}{3}}$.

(c) The ratio of the initial rate of cooling of A to that of B is $2^{\frac{-2}{3}}$.

(d) The ratio of the initial rate of cooling of A to that of B is $2^{\frac{-4}{3}}$.

2 A metal cylinder of mass 0.5 kg is heated electrically by a 12 W heater in a room at 15°C. The cylinder temperature rises uniformly to 25°C in 5 min and finally becomes constant at 45°C. Assuming that the rate of heat loss is proportional to the excess temperature over the surroundings

(a) The rate of loss of heat of the cylinder to surrounding at 20°C is 2 W.

(b) The rate of loss of heat of the cylinder to surrounding at 45°C is 2 W.

(c) Specific heat capacity of metal is $\dfrac{240}{\ln\left(\frac{3}{2}\right)}$ J/kg°C.

(d) None of the above

3 A polished metallic piece and a black painted wooden piece are kept in open in bright sun for a long time.

(a) The wooden piece will absorb less heat than the metallic piece

(b) The wooden piece will have a lower temperature than the metallic piece

(c) If touched, the metallic piece will be felt hotter than the wooden piece

(d) When the two pieces are removed from the open to a cold room, the wooden piece will lose heat at a faster rate than the metallic piece

4 In a dark room with ambient temperature T_0, a black body is kept at a temperature T. Keeping the temperature of the black body constant (at T), sun rays are allowed to fall on the black body through a hole in the roof of the dark room. Assuming that there is no change in the ambient temperature of the room, which of the following statement is/are correct?

(a) The quantity of radiation absorbed by the black body in unit time will increase

(b) Since emissivity = absorptivity, hence the quantity of radiation emitted by black body in unit time will increase

(c) Black body radiates more energy in unit time in the visible spectrum

(d) The reflected energy in unit time by the black body remains same

5 Two identical objects A and B are at temperature T_A and T_B, respectively. Both objects are placed in a room with perfectly absorbing walls maintained at a temperature $T(T_A > T > T_B)$. The objects A and B attain the temperature T eventually. Select the correct statements from the following

(a) A only emits radiation, while B only absorbs it until both attain the temperature T.

(b) A loses more heat by radiation than it absorbs, while B absorbs more radiation than it emits, until they attain the temperature T.

(c) Both A and B only absorb radiation, but do not emit it, until they attain the temperature T.

(d) Each object continuous to emit and absorb radiation even after attaining the temperature T.

6 Two spherical blackbodies A and B, having radii r_A and r_B, where $r_B = 2r_A$ emit radiations with peak intensities at wavelengths 400 nm and 800 nm, respectively. If their temperatures are T_A and T_B, respectively in Kelvin scale, their emissive powers are E_A and E_B and energies emitted per second are P_A and P_B, then

(a) $\dfrac{T_A}{T_B} = 2$ (b) $\dfrac{P_A}{P_B} = 4$

(c) $\dfrac{E_A}{E_B} = 8$ (d) $\dfrac{E_A}{E_B} = 4$

7 Two bodies A and B have thermal emissivities of 0.01 and 0.81, respectively. The outer surface areas of the two bodies are same. The two bodies radiate energy at the same rate. The wavelength λ_B, corresponding to the maximum spectral radiancy in the radiation from B, is shifted from the wavelength corresponding to the maximum spectral radiancy in the radiation from A by 1.00 μm. If the temperature of A is 5802 K,

(a) the temperature of B is 1934 K

(b) $\lambda_B = 1.5$ μm

(c) the temperature of B is 11604 K

(d) the temperature of B is 2901 K

8 Which of the following graph(s) shows the correct variation in intensity of heat radiations by black body and wavelength/frequency at a fixed temperature?

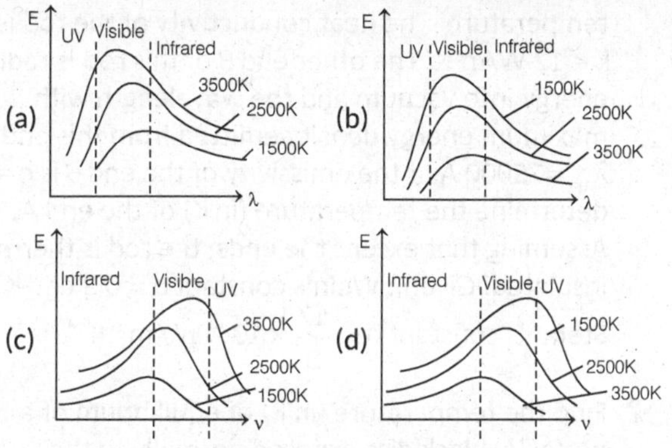

Comprehension Based Questions

Comprehension-1

A metal ball of mass 2 kg is heated by means of a 100W heater in a room at 25°C. The temperature of the ball becomes steady at 60°C.

1 Find the rate of loss of heat to the surrounding when the ball is at 60°C.

(a) 40 W (b) 60 W
(c) 80 W (D) 100 W

2 Assuming Newton's law of cooling, calculate the rate of loss of heat to the surrounding when the ball is at 39°C.

(a) 40 W (b) 60 W
(c) 80 W (d) 100 W

3 Assume that the temperature of the ball rises uniformly from 25°C to 39°C in 2 minutes. Find the total loss of heat to the surrounding during this period.

(a) 960 J (b) 1260 J
(c) 1860 J (d) 2400 J

Comprehension-2

A metal block of heat capacity 90 J/°C placed in a room at 25°C is heated electrically. The heater is switched OFF when the temperature reaches 35°C. The temperature of the block rises at the rate of 2°C/s just after the heater is switched ON and falls at the rate of 0.2 °C/s just after the heater is switched OFF. Assume Newton's law of cooling to hold.

4 Find the power of the heater.

(a) 140 W (b) 160 W
(c) 180 W (d) 200 W

5 Find the power radiated by the block just after the heater is switched OFF.

(a) 16 W (b) 18 W
(c) 20 W (d) 22 W

6 Find the power radiated by the block when the temperature of the block is 30°C

(a) 6 W (b) 9 W
(c) 12 W (d) 10 W

Comprehension-3

A body cools in a surrounding of constant temperature 30°C. Its heat capacity is 2 J/°C. Initial temperature of the body is 40°C. Assume, Newton's law of cooling is valid. The body cools to 36°C in 10 min.

7 In further 10 min, it will cool from 36°C to

(a) 34.8°C (b) 32.1°C
(c) 32.8°C (d) 33.6°C

8 The temperature of the body in °C denoted by θ, the variation of θ *versus* time *t* is best denoted as

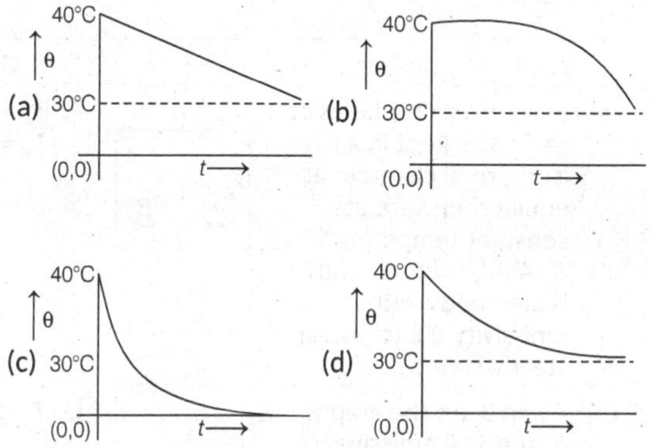

9 When the body temperature has reached 36°C, it is heated again, so that it reaches to 40°C in 10 min. Assume that the rate of loss of heat at 38°C is the average rate of loss for the given time. The total heat required from a heater by the body is

(a) 7.2 J (b) 0.728 J
(c) 16 J (d) 32 J

Match the Columns Questions

1 Match the following :

	List I		List II
(a)	Specific heat	p.	$[MLT^{-3}\theta^{-1}]$
(b)	Coefficient of thermal conductivity	q.	$[MT^{-3}\theta^{-4}]$
(c)	Boltzmann constant	r.	$[L^2T^{-2}\theta^{-1}]$
(d)	Stefan's constant	s.	$[ML^2T^{-2}\theta^{-1}]$

2 A black body has surface temperature T_b initially at time $t = 0$, that is less than surrounding constant temperature T_0. On the vertical axis of the graph shown has either power radiated/absorbed or net power radiated/absorbed as a function of time t by the ball. Correctly match the curves marked in the graph : (Assume Newton's law of cooling)

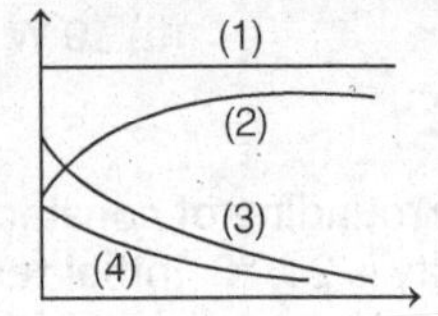

List I	List II
(a) Power emitted as a function of time	p. 1
(b) Power absorbed as a function of time	q. 2
(c) Net power emitted as a function of time	r. 3
	s. 4

3

List I		List II
(a) A and B are 2 spheres of same size kept in an isothermal chamber at equilibrium kept at constant temperature T_0. A is blackbody and B is grey body with emissivity 0.8 (consider steady state)	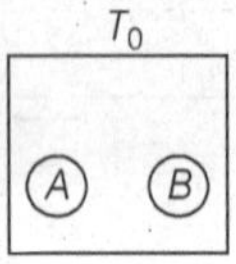	P. $T_A > T_B$ or $T_A = T_B$
(b) A and B are the graphs of spectral emissive powers E_λ vs wavelength of two black bodies A and B of same surface area	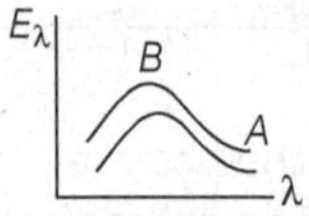	Q. $T_A < T_B$
(c) A is a solid sphere and B is a thick spherical shell. A is connected to a power source. Surfaces of A and B are perfect blackbodies. (Consider steady state)	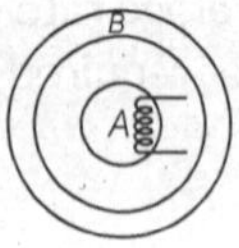	R. Heat energy radiated by A is greater than B.
(d) (1) and (2) are large black body surfaces maintained at temperature T_1 and T_2, respectively. A and B are large plates with emissivity $e = 1$. (Consider steady state only, $T_1 > T_2$)	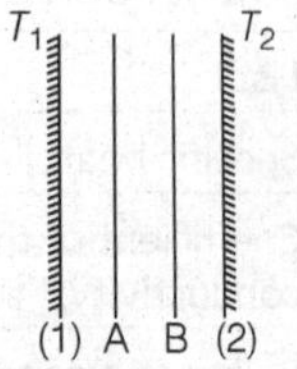	S. Heat energy radiated by B is greater than A.

Numerical Value Questions

1 End A of a rod AB of length $L = 1.5$ m and of uniform cross-sectional area is maintained at some constant temperature. The heat conductivity of the rod is $k = 17$ W/m-K. The other end B of this rod is radiating energy into vacuum and the wavelength with maximum energy density emitted from this end is $\lambda_0 = 75000$ Å. If the emissivity of the end B is e = 1, determine the temperature (in K) of the end A. Assuming that except the ends, the rod is thermally insulated. Given : Wein's constant $b = 0.3$ cm-K and Stefan's constant $\sigma = \frac{17}{3} \times 10^{-8}\ \text{W/m}^{-2}\text{K}^{-4}$.

2 Find the temperature (in K) of equilibrium of a perfectly black disc exposed normally to the Sun's ray on the surface of Earth. Imagine that it has a non-conducting backing, so that it can radiate only to hemisphere of space. Assume, temperature of surface of Sun = 6200 K, radius of sun $= 7.35 \times 10^8$ m, distance between the sun and the earth $= 1.5 \times 10^{11}$ m. Stefan's constant $= 5.7 \times 10^{-8}\ \text{W/m}^2\text{-K}^4$.

3 A wire of length 1.0 m and radius 10^{-3} m is carrying a heavy current and is assumed to radiate as a black body. At equilibrium temperature of wire is 900 K, while that of the surroundings is 300 K. The resistivity of the material of the wire at 300 K is $\pi^2 \times 10^{-8}\ \Omega$-m and its temperature coefficient of resistance is 7.8×10^{-3} /°C. Find the current (in A) in the wire. [$\sigma \cong 5.68 \times 10^{-8}\ \text{W/m}^2\text{K}^4$].

4 The shell of a space station is a blackened sphere in which a temperature $T = 500$ K is maintained due to operation of appliances of the station. Find the temperature (in K) of the shell, if the station is enveloped by a thin spherical, black screen of nearly the same radius as the radius of the shell.

(Given $2^{\frac{1}{4}} = 1.2$)

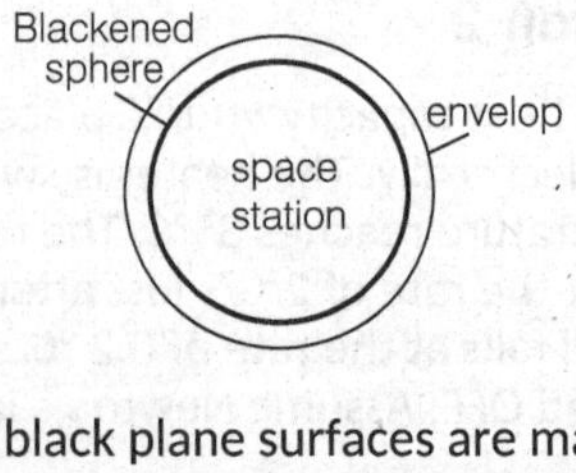

5 Two large black plane surfaces are maintained at constant temperatures T_1 and T_2 $(T_1 > T_2)$. Two thin black plates A and B are placed between the two surfaces and in parallel to the given plates. After sometime, steady conditions are obtained.

By what factor, is the steady heat flow increased due to the removal of black plates?

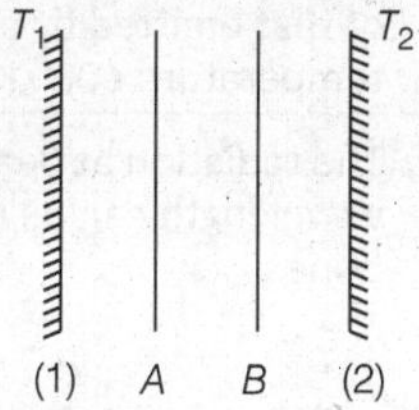

6 A small sphere (emissivity = 0.9, radius = r_1) is located at the centre of a spherical asbestos shell (thickness = 5.0 cm, outer radius = r_2). The thickness of the shell is small compared to the inner and outer radii of the shell. The temperature of the small sphere is 800 K, while the temperature of the inner surface of the shell is 600 K. The temperature of small sphere is maintained constant. Assuming that $\frac{r_2}{r_1} = 10.0$ and ignoring any air inside the shell, find the temperature (in K) of the outer surface of the shell.
(Take $K_{\text{asbestos}} = 0.085\ \text{W/m}^\circ\text{C}$,
$\sigma = \frac{17}{3} \times 10^{-8}\ \text{W/m}^2\text{K}^4$)

7 An astronomer observed with his telescope two stars, *A* and *B*. Star *A* has a spectral peak at 3500 Å and star *B* has a spectral peak at 7000 Å. If they appear equally bright (emitting equal energy per unit time) what is the ratio of radius of star *B* to that of *A*?

8 A highly conducting solid sphere of radius *R*, density ρ and specific heat *s* is placed in an evacuated chamber. A parallel beam of thermal radiation of uniform intensity *I* is incident on its surface. Assuming the surface of sphere is perfectly black and its temperature at $t = 0$ to be equal to T_0, find the maximum temperature of sphere in Kelvin. Given $\sigma = 5.6 \times 10^{-8}$ in SI unit and $I = 358.4$ SI unit.

Previous Year's Questions

JEE Main

1 A body cools from 60°C to 40°C in 6 minutes. If temperature of surroundings is 10 °C. Then, after the next 6 minutes, its temperature will be .... °C.
[2023, 29 Jan Shift-I]

2 A body cools in 7 minutes from 60°C to 40°C. The temperature of the surrounding is 10°C. The temperature of the body after the next 7 minutes will be **[2023, 6 April Shift-II]**
(a) 32°C (b) 30°C (c) 34°C (d) 28°C

3 A body cools from 80°C to 60°C in 5 minutes. The temperature of the surrounding is 20°C. The time it takes to cool from 60°C to 40°C is **[2023, 12 April Shift-I]**
(a) 450 s (b) 420 s (c) 500 s (d) $\frac{25}{3}$ s

4 A bowl filled with very hot soup cools from 98°C to 86°C in 2 minutes when the room temperature is 22°C. How long it will take to cool from 75°C to 69°C?
[2023, 25 Jan Shift-I]
(a) 1 min (b) 1.4 mins
(c) 2 min (d) 0.5 min

5 In an experiment to verify Newton's law of cooling, a graph is plotted between, the temperature difference (ΔT) of the water and surroundings and time as shown in figure. The initial temperature of water is taken as 80° C. The value of t_2 as mentioned in the graph will be .... **[2022, 24 June Shift-II]**

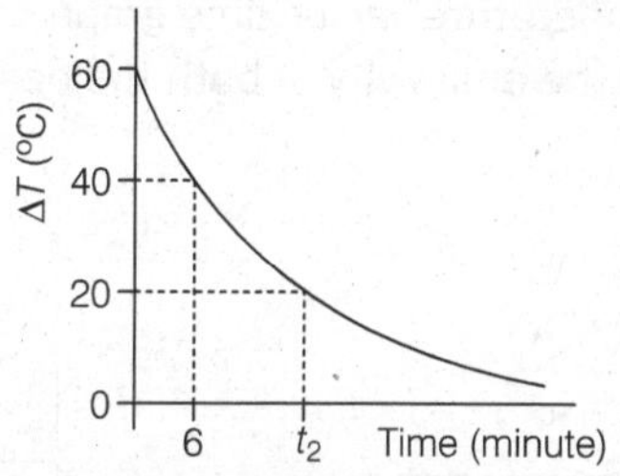

6 Read the following statements.
A. When small temperature difference between a liquid and its surrounding is doubled, the rate of loss of heat of the liquid becomes twice.
B. Two bodies *P* and *Q* having equal surface areas are maintained at temperature 10°C and 20°C. The thermal radiation emitted in a given time by *P* and *Q* are in the ratio 1 : 1.15.
C. A carnot engine working between 100 K and 400 K has an efficiency of 75%.
D. When small temperature difference between a liquid and its surrounding is quadrupled, the rate of loss of heat of the liquid becomes twice.

Choose the correct answer from the options given below. **[2022, 27 July Shift-I]**
(a) A, B and C only
(b) A and B only
(c) A and C only
(d) B, C and D only

7 In 5 min, a body cools from 75°C to 65°C at room temperature of 25°C. The temperature of body at the end of next 5 min is .... °C.
[2021, 22 July Shift-II]

8 A body takes 4 min to cool from 61° C to 59°C. If the temperature of the surroundings is 30°C, then the time taken by the body to cool from 51°C to 49° C is **[2021, 27 July Shift-I]**

(a) 4 min (b) 3 min (c) 8 min (d) 6 min

9 A metallic sphere cools from 50°C to 40°C in 300 s. If atmospheric temperature around is 20°C, then the sphere's temperature after the next 5 min will be close to **[2020, 3 Sep Shift-II]**

(a) 31°C (b) 35°C
(c) 28°C (d) 33°C

10 Two identical beakers *A* and *B* contain equal volumes of two different liquids at 60°C each and left to cool down. Liquid in *A* has density of 8×10^2 kg / m^3 and specific heat of 2000 J kg^{-1}K^{-1} while liquid in *B* has density of 10^3 kg m^{-3} and specific heat of 4000 J kg^{-1}K^{-1}. Which of the following best describes their temperature *versus* time graph schematically? (Assume the emissivity of both the beakers to be the same) **[2019, 8 April Shift-I]**

(a)
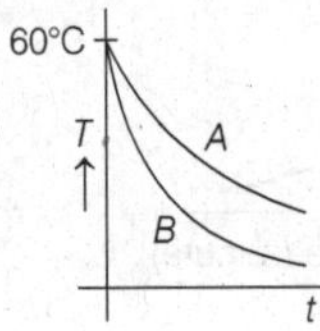

(b)
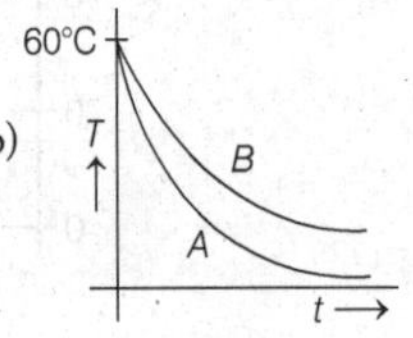

(c)
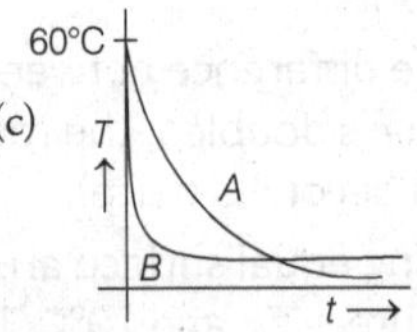

(d)
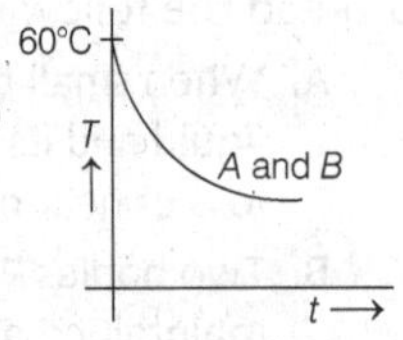

JEE Advanced

1 Match the temperature of a black body given in List-I with an appropriate statement in List-II and choose the correct option.
(Given Wien's constant as 2.9×10^{-3} m-K and $\frac{hc}{e} = 1.24\times10^{-6}$ V-m) **(2023 Adv.)**

List-I	List-II
(P) 2000 K	(1) The radiation at peak wavelength can lead to emission of photoelectrons from a metal of work function 4 eV.
(Q) 3000 K	(2) The radiation at peak wavelength is visible to human eye.
(R) 5000 K	(3) The radiation at peak emission wavelength will result in the widest central maximum of a single slit diffraction.
(S) 10000 K	(4) The power emitted per unit area is 1/16 of that emitted by a blackbody at temperature 6000 K.
	(5) The radiation at peak emission wavelength can be used to image human bones.

	P	Q	R	S		P	Q	R	S
(a)	3	5	2	3	(b)	3	2	4	1
(c)	3	4	2	1	(d)	1	2	5	3

2 A small object is placed at the centre of a large evacuated hollow spherical container. Assume that, the container is maintained at 0 K. At time $t = 0$, the temperature of the object is 200 K. The temperature of the object becomes 100 K at $t = t_1$ and 50 K at $t = t_2$. Assume the object and the container to be ideal black bodies. The heat capacity of the object does not depend on temperature.

The ratio (t_2/t_1) is ______. **(2021 Adv.)**

3 A container with 1 kg of water in it is kept in sunlight, which causes the water to get warmer than the surroundings. The average energy per unit time per unit area received due to the sunlight is 700 Wm^{-2} and it is absorbed by the water over an effective area of 0.05 m^2. Assuming that the heat loss from the water to the surroundings is governed by Newton's law of cooling, the difference (in °C) in the temperature of water and the surroundings after a long time will be ______. (Ignore effect of the container and take constant for Newton's law of cooling = 0.001 s^{-1}, Heat capacity of water = 4200 Jkg^{-1} K^{-1}) **(2020 Adv.)**

4 A human body has a surface area of approximately 1 m^2. The normal body temperature is 10K above the surrounding room temperature T_0. Take the room temperature to be $T_0 = 300$ K. For $T_0 = 300$ K, the value of $\sigma T_0^4 = 460$ Wm^{-2} (where σ is the Stefan Boltzmann constant). Which of the following options is/are correct? **(2017 Adv.)**

(a) If the body temperature rises significantly, then the peak in the spectrum of electromagnetic radiation emitted by the body would shift to longer wavelengths

(b) If the surrounding temperature reduces by a small amount $\Delta T_0 << T_0$, then to maintain the same body temperature the same (living) human being needs to radiate $\Delta W = 4\sigma T_0^3 \Delta T_0$ more energy per unit time

(c) The amount of energy radiated by the body in 1s is close to 60 J

(d) Reducing the exposed surface area of the body (e.g. by curling up) allows humans to maintain the same body temperature while reducing the energy lost by radiation

5 A metal is heated in a furnace where a sensor is kept above the metal surface to read the power radiated (P) by the metal. The sensor has a scale that displays $\log_2(P/P_0)$, where P_0 is a constant. When the metal surface is at a temperature of 487°C, the sensor shows a value 1. Assume that the emissivity of the metallic surface remains constant. What is the value displayed by the sensor when the temperature of the metal surface is raised to 2767°C? **(2016 Adv.)**

6 Two spherical stars A and B emit black body radiation. The radius of A is 400 times that of B and A emits 10^4 times the power emitted from B. The ratio $\left(\frac{\lambda_A}{\lambda_B}\right)$ of their wavelengths λ_A and λ_B at which the peaks occur in their respective radiation curves is **(2015 Adv.)**

Answer Key

Level 1

4.1 Stefan-Boltzmann Law

1. 16 E 2. 1000 K 3. 887 J
4. 0.42 J 5. (a) 1.4 J, (b) 4.58 W from the ball
6. 69.4 W 7. 73 W 8. 1700 K
9. 0.3 10. (a) 6.43×10^7 W/m^2 (b) 5803 K

4.2 Rate of Cooling

1. 0.12°C/s 2. (a) $1 : \alpha^2$ (b) $\alpha\beta\gamma : 1$

4.3 Newton's Law of Cooling

1. 14 min 2. 300°C 3. 28°C 4. 12.5 g
5. 2 min

4.4 Wien's Displacement Law

1. 1.8 μm 2. 6×10^3 K, 4×10^3K
3. ≈6000 k 4. 256 Jm^{-2}s^{-1} 5. $T_1 > T_3 > T_2$
6. 2 : 1

Level 2

Single Choice Correct Questions

1. (c)	2. (b)	3. (b)	4. (d)	5. (b)
6. (a)	7. (d)	8. (d)	9. (b)	10. (b)
11. (b)	12. (a)	13. (d)	14. (a)	15. (d)
16. (d)	17. (a)	18. (d)	19. (b)	20. (a)
21. (a)	22. (a)	23. (b)	24. (a)	25. (a)
26. (b)	27. (a)	28. (d)	29. (a)	30. (c)
31. (c)	32. (b)	33. (c)	34. (d)	35. (a)
36. (b)	37. (a)	38. (a)		

Numerical Value Questions

1. 9.72 2. 340 3. 10 4. 1
5. 384 6. 2 7. 5

Level 3

Single Choice Correct Questions

1. (d)	2. (c)	3. (c)	4. (c)	5. (a)
6. (a)	7. (c)	8. (c)	9. (b)	10. (a)
11. (a)	12. (b)	13. (c)	14. (c)	15. (b)
16. (c)	17. (d)	18. (a)	19. (b)	20. (d)
21. (b)	22. (c)			

Multiple Choice(s) Correct Questions

1. (a, c) 2. (a, c) 3. (c, d)
4. (a, b, c, d) 5. (b, d) 6. (a, b) 7. (a, b)
8. (a, c)

Comprehension Based Questions

1. (d) 2. (a) 3. (d) 4. (c)
5. (b) 6. (b) 7. (d) 8. (d)
9. (c)

Match the Columns Questions

1. a → r; b → p; c → s; d → q 2. a → q; b → p; c → s
3. a → pr; b → qs; c → pr; d → p

Numerical Value Questions

1. 528 2. 434 3. 36 4. 600
5. 3 6. 516 7. 4 8. 200

Previous Year's Questions

JEE Main

1. (28)	2. (d)	3. (c)	4. (b)	5. (16)
6. (a)	7. (57)	8. (d)	9. (d)	10. (b)

JEE Advanced

1. (c)	2. (9)	3. (8.33)	4. (b, c, d)	5. (9)
6. (2)				

SOLUTIONS

Level–01

4.1 Stefan-Boltzmann's Law

1. $E = \sigma T^4$

At 0°C, $E = \sigma (273)^4$

At 273°C, $E' = \sigma (546)^4$

$\therefore \quad \frac{E'}{E} = 16 \Rightarrow E' = 16E$

2. $E = \sigma T^4$

$\Rightarrow \quad \frac{8.28 \times 4.2}{6.1 \times 10^{-4}} = 5.67 \times 10^{-8} T^4 \Rightarrow T = 1000 \text{ K}$

3. $\frac{dQ}{dt} = Ae\sigma T^4 = 1.6 \times 1 \times 6 \times 10^{-8} \times (310)^4 = 887 \text{ J}$

4. $\frac{dQ}{dt} = Ae\sigma T^4 = 12 \times 10^{-4} \times 0.8 \times 6 \times 10^{-8} \times (300)^4 = 0.47 \text{ J/s}$

5. (a) $\frac{dQ}{dt} = Aa\sigma T_s^4 = 20 \times 10^{-4} \times 1 \times 6 \times 10^{-8} \times (330)^4 = 1.4 \text{ J/s}$

(b) Net power loss $= Ae\sigma (T^4 - T_s^4)$

$= 20 \times 10^{-4} \times 1 \times 6 \times 10^{-8} ((500)^4 - (330)^4)$

$= 6.08$ W from the ball

6. $P_{net} = Ae\sigma (T^4 - T_s^4)$

$= 300 \times 10^{-4} \times 0.75 \times 5.67 \times 10^{-8}((500)^4 - (300)^4)$

$= 69.4 \text{ W}$

7. Power of heater = Net power loss

$= Ae\sigma (T^4 - T_s^4)$

$= 100 \times 10^{-4} \times 1 \times 6 \times 10^{-8}(600)^4 - (300)^4)$

$= 73 \text{ W}$

8. $P_R = Ae\sigma T^4$

$\Rightarrow \quad 100 = (2\pi \times 4 \times 10^{-5} \times 1) \times 0.8 \times 6 \times 10^{-8} \times T^4$

$\Rightarrow \quad T = 1700 \text{ K}$

9. $P = Ae\sigma (T^4 - T_s^4)$

$210 = Ae\sigma ((500)^4 - (300)^4)$ ...(i)

$700 = A(1)\sigma [(500)^4 - (300)^4]$ ...(ii)

Dividing Eq. (i) by Eq. (ii), we get

$e = \frac{210}{700} = 0.3$

10. (a) Let power emitted by the sun be P.

Intensity at earth's surface $= \frac{P}{4\pi d^2} = 1.4 \times 10^3$

$\Rightarrow \quad \frac{P}{4 \times 3.14 \times (1.5 \times 10^{11})^2} = 1.4 \times 10^3$

$\Rightarrow \quad P = 3.96 \times 10^{26} \text{ W}$

Rate of radiation per unit area $= \frac{P}{4\pi r^2}$

$= \frac{3.96 \times 10^{26}}{4 \times 3.14 \times (7 \times 10^8)^2}$

$= 6.43 \times 10^7 \text{ W/m}^2$

(b) $E = \sigma T^4$

$\Rightarrow \quad T = \left(\frac{E}{\sigma}\right)^{1/4} = \left(\frac{6.43 \times 10^7}{5.67 \times 10^{-8}}\right)^{1/4} = 5803 \text{ K}$

4.2 Rate of Cooling

1. $-ms\frac{dT}{dt} = Ae\sigma (T^4 - T_s^4)$

$\Rightarrow \frac{dT}{dt} = -\frac{Ae\sigma (T^4 - T_s^4)}{ms}$

$= -\frac{6 \times (5 \times 10^{-2})^2 \times 1 \times 5.67 \times 10^{-8} \times ((500)^4 - (300)^4)}{1 \times 400}$

$= -0.12\text{°C/s}$

2. (a) $P = Ae\sigma (T^4 - T_s^4) = (4\pi r^2) e\sigma (T^4 - T_s^4)$

$\therefore \quad P \propto r^2$

$\Rightarrow \quad \frac{P_1}{P_2} = \left(\frac{r_1}{r_2}\right)^2 = \left(\frac{1}{\alpha}\right)^2 = 1 : \alpha^2$

(b) $-ms\frac{dT}{dt} = Ae\sigma (T^4 - T_s^4)$

$\Rightarrow \quad -\frac{dT}{dt} = \frac{Ae\sigma}{ms}(T^4 - T_s^4) = \frac{4\pi r^2 e\sigma (T^4 - T_s^4)}{\rho\left(\frac{4}{3}\pi r^3\right)s}$

Rate of cooling $= -\frac{dT}{dt} = R$

$\therefore \quad R \propto \frac{1}{\rho r s}$

$\Rightarrow \quad \frac{R_1}{R_2} = \left(\frac{\rho_2}{\rho_1}\right)\left(\frac{r_2}{r_1}\right)\left(\frac{s_2}{s_1}\right) = \alpha\beta\gamma : 1$

4.3 Newton's Law of Cooling

1. $40\text{°C} \xrightarrow{10\text{min}} 35\text{°C}$

$\left\langle \frac{d\theta}{dt} \right\rangle = -K(\langle\theta\rangle - \theta_0)$

$\Rightarrow \quad \frac{35 - 40}{10 \text{ min}} = -K\left(\frac{40 + 35}{2} - 20\right)$ ...(i)

$35\text{°C} \xrightarrow{t} 30\text{°C}$

$\frac{30 - 35}{t} = -K\left(\frac{35 + 30}{2} - 20\right)$ ...(ii)

Solving Eqs. (i) and (ii), we get

$t = 14 \text{ min}$

2. $<\frac{d\theta}{dt}> = -K(<\theta> - \theta_0)$

$50°C \xrightarrow{5\,min} 45°C$

$$\frac{45-50}{5\,min} = -K\left(\frac{50+45}{2} - \theta_0\right) \quad ...(i)$$

$45°C \xrightarrow{7\,min} 40°C$

$$\frac{40-45}{7\,min} = -K\left(\frac{45+40}{2} - \theta_0\right) \quad ...(ii)$$

Solving Eq. (i) and (ii), we get

$$\theta_0 = 30°\,C$$

3. $60°C \xrightarrow{7\,min} 40°C$

$$<\frac{d\theta}{dt}> = -K(<\theta> - \theta_0)$$

$$\Rightarrow \frac{40-60}{7} = -K\left(\frac{60+40}{2} - 10\right) \quad ...(i)$$

$40°C \xrightarrow{7\,min} \theta$

$$\Rightarrow \frac{\theta-40}{7} = -K\left(\frac{40+\theta}{2} - 10\right) \quad ...(ii)$$

Solving Eqs. (i) and (ii), we get

$$\theta = 28°C$$

4. Let water equivalent of calorimeter be *W*.

$$ms\frac{d\theta}{dt} = -K(\theta - \theta_0)$$

$$\Rightarrow t \propto m \Rightarrow \frac{t_1}{t_2} = \frac{m_1}{m_2}$$

$$\Rightarrow \frac{10}{18} = \frac{50+W}{100+W} \Rightarrow W = 12.5\text{ g}$$

5. $-ms\frac{dT}{dt} = K(T - T_s)$

$$\Rightarrow t \propto ms$$

$$\Rightarrow \frac{t_1}{t_2} = \left(\frac{\rho_1}{\rho_2}\right)\left(\frac{s_1}{s_2}\right) \quad [\because m = \rho V]$$

$$\Rightarrow \frac{5}{t_2} = \left(\frac{1000}{800}\right)\left(\frac{4200}{2100}\right)$$

$$\Rightarrow t_2 = 2\text{ min}$$

4.4 Wien's Displacement Law

1. $\lambda T = b \Rightarrow \lambda = \frac{b}{T} = \frac{2.9\times10^{-3}}{1650} = 1.8\,\mu m$

2. $\lambda T = b \Rightarrow T = \frac{b}{\lambda}$

For red, $T = \frac{0.3\times10^{-2}}{5000\times10^{-10}} = 6\times10^3 K$

For blue, $T = \frac{0.3\times10^{-2}}{7500\times10^{-10}} = 4\times10^3 K$

3. $\lambda T = b \Rightarrow T = \frac{b}{\lambda} = \frac{3\times10^{-3}}{470\times10^{-9}} \simeq 6000\,K$

4. $\lambda_1 T_1 = \lambda_2 T_2$

$$\Rightarrow \frac{T_2}{T_1} = \frac{\lambda_1}{\lambda_2} = \frac{20000}{10000}$$

$$\Rightarrow \frac{T_2}{T_1} = 2$$

$$E = \sigma T^4$$

$$\Rightarrow \frac{E_1}{E_2} = \left(\frac{T_1}{T_2}\right)^4 \Rightarrow \frac{16}{E_2} = \left(\frac{1}{2}\right)^4$$

$$\Rightarrow E_2 = 256\text{ Jm}^{-2}\text{s}^{-1}$$

5. $\lambda T = b \Rightarrow T \propto \frac{1}{\lambda}$

Since, $\lambda_2 > \lambda_3 > \lambda_1$

$$\Rightarrow T_1 > T_3 > T_2$$

6. $\lambda T = b \Rightarrow T \propto \frac{1}{\lambda}$

$$\therefore \frac{T_A}{T_B} = \frac{\lambda_B}{\lambda_A} = \frac{1000}{500} = 2:1$$

Level-2

Single Choice Correct Questions

1. (c)

2.

$$\frac{E_1}{E_2} = \left(\frac{T_1}{T_2}\right)^4$$

$$\Rightarrow \frac{2\times10^5}{32\times10^5} = \left(\frac{400}{T_2}\right)^4 \Rightarrow T_2 = 800\text{ K or }527°C$$

3.

$$a + r + t = 1$$

$$\Rightarrow a + 0.3 + 0.5 = 1 \Rightarrow a = 0.2$$

$$a = e = 0.2$$

From Kirchhoff's law,

$$\frac{E_{blackbody}}{a_{blackbody}} = \frac{E_{body}}{a_{body}}$$

$$\Rightarrow \frac{100}{1} = \frac{E_B}{0.2} \Rightarrow E_B = 20\text{ W/m}^2$$

Power emitted by $B = EA = 20\times10 = 200\text{ W}$

4. $P = Ae\sigma T^4 = 4\pi r^2 e\sigma T^4$

$$\therefore \frac{P_1}{P_2} = \left(\frac{r_1}{r_2}\right)^2\left(\frac{T_1}{T_2}\right)^4$$

$$\Rightarrow \frac{450}{P_2} = \left(\frac{12}{6}\right)^2\left(\frac{500}{1000}\right)^4 \Rightarrow P_2 = 1800\text{ W}$$

5. $P = Ae\sigma T^4 \Rightarrow T \propto \frac{1}{e^{1/4}}$

$$\therefore \frac{T_2}{T_1} = \left(\frac{e_1}{e_2}\right)^{1/4}$$

$$\Rightarrow \quad \frac{\theta_Q}{\theta_P} = \left(\frac{\varepsilon_P}{\varepsilon_Q}\right)^{1/4} \Rightarrow \theta_Q = \left(\frac{\varepsilon_P}{\varepsilon_Q}\right)^{1/4} \theta_P$$

6. $P = Ae\sigma T^4 \Rightarrow \frac{\Delta P}{P} = 4\frac{\Delta T}{T}$

$$\Rightarrow \frac{\Delta P}{P} \times 100 = 4\left(\frac{\Delta T}{T} \times 100\right)$$

$$\Rightarrow 2 = 4\left(\frac{\Delta T}{300} \times 100\right) \Rightarrow \Delta T = 1.5 \text{ K}$$

∴ Temperature of other patch = 300 + 1.5 = 301.5 K

7. $P = Ae\sigma T^4 \Rightarrow P = (2\pi rl)\, e\sigma T^4$

$\Rightarrow 100 = (2 \times 3.14 \times 40 \times 10^{-6} \times 1) \times 0.4 \times 5.67 \times 10^{-8} \times T^4$

$\Rightarrow T \simeq 2100 \text{ K}$

8. $Q \propto A$

$$\Rightarrow \frac{Q'}{Q} = \frac{A'}{A} = \frac{(2\pi R^2 + \pi R^2) \times 2}{4\pi R^2} = 1.5$$

9. Power received $= \frac{Ae\sigma T^4}{4\pi d^2}$

$$\therefore \frac{P_1}{P_2} = \left(\frac{T_1}{T_2}\right)^4 \left(\frac{d_2}{d_1}\right)^2$$

$$\Rightarrow \frac{P}{P_2} = \left(\frac{1}{2}\right)^4 \left(\frac{2}{1}\right)^2 \Rightarrow P_2 = 4P$$

10. $T_P^4 \propto r^2 \Rightarrow T_P \propto \sqrt{r}$

11. Power received $= \frac{Ae\sigma T_s^4}{4\pi d^2}$

$$\Rightarrow T_P^4 \propto \frac{1}{d^2} \Rightarrow T_P \propto d^{-1/2}$$

12. $S \propto \frac{1}{d^2} \Rightarrow \frac{S_1}{S_2} = \left(\frac{d_2}{d_1}\right)^2$

$$\Rightarrow \frac{2}{S_2} = \left(\frac{0.4d}{d}\right)^2$$

$\Rightarrow S_2 = 12.5 \text{ cal / min - cm}^2$

13. Power supplied = Net power loss

$= Ae\sigma(T^4 - T_s^4)$

$= 4 \times 3.14 \times (0.01)^2 \times 0.3 \times 6 \times 10^{-8} \times ((1000)^4 - (300)^4)$

$= 22$ W

14. $-ms\frac{dT}{dt} = Ae\sigma(T^4 - T_s^4)$

Cooling rate $= R = -\frac{dT}{dt}$

$\therefore R \propto T^4 - T_s^4$

$$\Rightarrow \frac{R_1}{R_2} = \frac{T_1^4 - T_s^4}{T_2^2 - T_s^4}$$

$$\Rightarrow \frac{r_0}{R_2} = \frac{(600)^4 - (300)^4}{(900)^4 - (300)^4} \Rightarrow R_2 = \frac{16r_0}{3}$$

15. $-ms\frac{dT}{dt} = Ae\sigma(T^4 - T_s^4)$

$$\Rightarrow -\left(\rho\frac{4}{3}\pi r^3\right)s\frac{dT}{dt} = (4\pi r^2)\, e\sigma(T^4 - T_s^4)$$

$\Rightarrow$ Rate of cooling $= -\frac{dT}{dt} \propto \frac{1}{\rho s}$

$$\therefore R_A : R_B : R_C : R_D = \frac{1}{2(3)} : \frac{1}{3(6)} : \frac{1}{5(2)} : \frac{1}{1(4)}$$

So, rate of cooling will be maximum for sphere *D*.

16. $m = \rho\left(\frac{4}{3}\pi r^3\right) \Rightarrow \frac{m_1}{m_2} = \left(\frac{r_1}{r_2}\right)^3$

$$\Rightarrow \frac{r_1}{r_2} = \left(\frac{m_1}{m_2}\right)^{1/3} = (3)^{1/3}$$

$$R = -\frac{dT}{dt} = \frac{Ae\sigma(T^4 - T_s^4)}{ms} = \frac{(4\pi r^2)\, e\sigma(T^4 - T_s^4)}{\rho\left(\frac{4}{3}\pi r^3\right)s}$$

$$\therefore \frac{R_1}{R_2} = \left(\frac{r_2}{r_1}\right)^{1/3} = \left(\frac{1}{3}\right)^{1/3}$$

17. $-\frac{dT}{dt} = \frac{Ae\sigma(T^4 - T_s^4)}{ms} = \frac{(4\pi R^2)\, e\sigma(T^4 - T_s^4)}{ms}$

∴ Rate of cooling $\propto \frac{1}{m}$

Since, hollow sphere has lesser mass, it will cool faster than solid sphere.

18. (d)

19. $-\frac{dT}{dt} = \frac{Ae\sigma(T^4 - T_s^4)}{ms}$

$$= \frac{4 \times 3.14 \times (0.08)^2 \times 1 \times 5.8 \times 10^{-8}((500)^4 - (300)^4)}{10 \times 90 \times 4.2}$$

$= 0.067$°C/s

20. (a)

21. $-ms\frac{dT}{dt} = Ae\sigma(T^4 - 0^4)$

$$\Rightarrow -\frac{dT}{dt} \propto T^4 \Rightarrow -\int T^{-4}dT \propto \int dt$$

$$\Rightarrow \Delta t \propto \frac{1}{T_2^3} - \frac{1}{T_1^3}$$

$$\therefore \frac{\Delta t}{\Delta t'} = \frac{\frac{1}{(T/2)^3} - \frac{1}{T^3}}{\frac{1}{(T/4)^3} - \frac{1}{(T/2)^3}} \Rightarrow \Delta t' = 8\,\Delta t$$

22. $\theta = \theta_0 + (\theta_i - \theta_0)\, e^{-kt}$

So, temperature decreases exponentially with time.

23. Rate of cooling $= -\frac{d\theta}{dt} = K(\theta - \theta_0)$

So, *R versus* θ graph will be straight line with positive slope.

24. $\ln\left(\frac{T_f - T_s}{T_i - T_s}\right) = -Kt$

$52°C \xrightarrow{10 \text{min}} 36°C$

$$\ln\left(\frac{36-20}{52-20}\right) = -K(10) \quad \text{...(i)}$$

$36°C \xrightarrow{10 \text{min}} T$

$$\ln\left(\frac{T-20}{36-20}\right) = -K(10) \quad \text{...(ii)}$$

Solving Eqs. (i) and (ii), we get

$$T = 28° C$$

25. $\left\langle \frac{d\theta}{dt} \right\rangle = -K(\langle\theta\rangle - \theta_0)$

$40°C \xrightarrow{4 \text{min}} 36°C$

$$\frac{36-40}{4} = -K\left(\frac{40+36}{2} - 20\right) \Rightarrow K = \frac{1}{18}$$

$36°C \xrightarrow{t} 32°C$

$$\frac{32-36}{t} = -\frac{1}{18}\left(\frac{36+32}{2} - 20\right)$$

$\Rightarrow \quad t = 5.1 \text{ min}$

26. $\left\langle \frac{d\theta}{dt} \right\rangle = -K(\langle\theta\rangle - \theta_0)$

$60°C \xrightarrow{4 \text{min}} 50°C$

$$\frac{50-60}{4} = -K\left(\frac{60+50}{2} - \theta_0\right) \quad \text{...(i)}$$

$40°C \xrightarrow{8 \text{min}} 30°C$

$$\frac{30-40}{8} = -K\left(\frac{40+30}{2} - \theta_0\right) \quad \text{...(ii)}$$

Solving Eqs. (i) and (ii), we get

$$\theta_0 = 15°C$$

27. On heating, the black spot will absorb maximum radiation while the polished part reflects most of the radiation. Therefore, when the plate is taken to a dark room, the spot will emit more radiations than the rest of the plate surface. Hence, it will appear brighter than the plate surface.

28. $$\frac{dQ}{dt} \propto \theta - \theta_0$$

$$\Rightarrow \quad \frac{\frac{dQ}{dt}}{60} = \frac{40-20}{80-20} \Rightarrow \frac{dQ}{dt} = 20 \text{ cal/s}$$

29. At steady state,

Power lost to surroundings = Power of heater

$\Rightarrow \quad K(50-20) = 60 \Rightarrow K = 2$

When temperature drops to 30°C,

Power lost $= K(\theta - \theta_0) = 2(30-20) = 20$ W

30. Power lost to surroundings = Power of heater

$\Rightarrow \quad K(40-20) = 10 \Rightarrow K = 0.5$

Temperature increases 20°C to 80°C in 5 min at a uniform rate,

$$T = \left(\frac{80-20}{300}\right)t + 20$$

$$\Rightarrow \quad T = \frac{t}{5} + 20$$

Heat lost to surroundings $= \int K(T - T_0)\, dt$

$$= \int_0^{300} 0.5\left(\frac{t}{5} + 20 - 20\right) dt = 4500 \text{ J}$$

31. From graph, wavelength corresponding to most intense radiation is $2\,\mu$m.

$$\lambda T = b$$

$$\Rightarrow \quad T = \frac{b}{\lambda} = \frac{2.9 \times 10^{-3}}{2 \times 10^{-6}} = 1450 \text{ K}$$

32. $\lambda T = b$

$$\Rightarrow \quad \frac{T_1}{T_2} = \frac{\lambda_2}{\lambda_1} = \frac{350}{510} = 0.69$$

33. $\lambda_0 T_0 = \lambda T$

$$\Rightarrow \quad \frac{T}{T_0} = \frac{\lambda_0}{\lambda} = \frac{\lambda_0}{2\lambda_0/3} = \frac{3}{2}$$

$$P \propto T^4$$

$$\Rightarrow \quad \frac{P}{P_0} = \left(\frac{T}{T_0}\right)^4 \Rightarrow \frac{P}{P_0} = \left(\frac{3}{2}\right)^4$$

$$\Rightarrow \quad P = \frac{81}{16} P_0$$

34. $E = \sigma T^4 \Rightarrow R = \sigma T^4$

$$\Rightarrow \quad T = \left(\frac{R}{\sigma}\right)^{1/4}$$

$$\lambda_m T = b \Rightarrow \lambda_m = \frac{b}{T} = b\left(\frac{\sigma}{R}\right)^{1/4}$$

35. $E = mc^2$

$$\Rightarrow \quad \frac{dE}{dt} = \frac{dm}{dt} c^2$$

$$\lambda T = b \Rightarrow T = \frac{b}{\lambda}$$

$$P = Ae\sigma T^4$$

$$\Rightarrow \quad \frac{dm}{dt} c^2 = (4\pi R^2)(1)\sigma\left(\frac{b}{\lambda}\right)^4$$

$$\Rightarrow \quad \frac{dm}{dt} = \frac{R^2}{\lambda^4 c^2}$$

36. As temperature increases, spectral intensity corresponding to all wavelengths increases but the wavelength with maximum spectral intensity decreases according to Wein's displacement law.

37. $\lambda_{max} T = b$

$$\Rightarrow \quad \frac{\Delta T}{T} = -\frac{\Delta\lambda}{\lambda}$$

$$\Rightarrow \quad \frac{\Delta T}{T} \times 100 = -\left(\frac{\Delta\lambda}{\lambda} \times 100\right)$$

$$\Rightarrow \quad \frac{1}{T} \times 100 = -(-1) \Rightarrow T = 100 \text{ K}$$

38. Area under the curve $= \int E_\lambda d\lambda = E$

Also, $E = \sigma T^4$

$\therefore \quad A \propto T^4$

$\Rightarrow \quad \frac{A_1}{A_2} = \left(\frac{T_1}{T_2}\right)^4 \Rightarrow \frac{A}{81A} = \left(\frac{T_1}{T_2}\right)^4$

$\Rightarrow \quad \frac{T_1}{T_2} = \frac{1}{3}$

$\lambda T = b \Rightarrow \frac{\lambda_1}{\lambda_2} = \frac{T_2}{T_1} = 3$

Numerical Value Questions

1. $R = -\frac{dT}{dt} = \frac{Ae\sigma}{mS}(T^4 - T_s^4) = \frac{(4\pi r^2)\, e\sigma\, (T^4 - T_s^4)}{\rho\left(\frac{4}{3}\pi r^3\right)s}$

$\therefore \quad R \propto \frac{T^4 - T_s^4}{r}$

$\Rightarrow \quad \frac{R_1}{R_2} = \left(\frac{T_1^4 - T_s^4}{T_2^4 - T_s^4}\right)\left(\frac{r_2}{r_1}\right)$

$\Rightarrow \quad \frac{2.8}{R_2} = \left(\frac{(400)^4 - (300)^4}{(600)^4 - (300)^4}\right)\left(\frac{2r}{r}\right)$

$\Rightarrow \quad R_2 = 9.72°\text{C/min}$

2. The rate of the heat transfer is approximately proportional to the temperature difference, between radiator and room as well as between the room and the outside. The corresponding proportionality constants can be denoted as C (radiator-room) and D (room-outside). Then, initially,

$C(T - 300) = D(300 - 260)$ ...(i)

For the second set of temperatures,

$C(T - 290) = D(290 - 240)$ ...(ii)

Solving Eqs. (i) and (ii), we get

$T = 340$ K

3. Power received $= EA = 1000 \times (1.4 \times 10^{-4}) = 0.14$ W

Power absorbed $= 0.14$ W $[\because a = 1]$

$Q = mS\,\Delta T$

$\Rightarrow \quad 0.14 \times t = 4 \times 10^{-3} \times 4200 \times 5$

$\Rightarrow \quad t = 600$ s or 10 min

4. $P = Ae\sigma T^4 = (2\pi r l)\, e\sigma T^4$

$\Rightarrow \quad 64 = 2\pi r\left(\frac{10}{3\pi} \times 10^{-2}(1)(6 \times 10^{-8})(2000)^4\right)$

$\Rightarrow \quad r = 1 \times 10^{-3}$ m $= 1$ mm

5. $a = e = 0.6$

Power absorbed $= aEA$

$= 0.6 \times 7 \times 10^2 \times \left(\frac{40}{100} \times 1.75\right) = 294$ W

Power lost $= 294 + 90 = 384$ W

6. $\frac{d\theta}{dt} = -K(\theta - \theta_0)$

$50°\text{C} \xrightarrow{5s} 49.9°\text{C}$

$\Rightarrow \quad \frac{49.9 - 50}{5} = -K(50 - 30)$

$\Rightarrow \quad K = 1 \times 10^{-3}$

$40°\text{C} \xrightarrow{t} 39.9°\text{C}$

$\Rightarrow \quad \frac{39.9 - 40}{t} = -1 \times 10^{-3}(40 - 30) \Rightarrow t = 10$ s

$\therefore \quad \frac{t}{5} = 2$

7. $P = Ae\sigma T^4 = A(CT)\sigma T^4$

$\therefore \quad P \propto T^5$

$\Rightarrow \quad \frac{P_1}{P_2} = \left(\frac{T_1}{T_2}\right)^5 \Rightarrow \frac{160}{P_2} = \left(\frac{600}{300}\right)^5$

$\Rightarrow \quad P_2 = 5$ W

Level-3

Single Choice Correct Questions

1. $E = Ae\sigma T^4$

$\therefore \quad \frac{E_1}{E_2} = \left(\frac{A_1}{A_2}\right)\left(\frac{T_1}{T_2}\right)^4$

$\Rightarrow \quad \frac{E}{E_2} = \left(\frac{A}{A/4}\right)\left(\frac{400}{600}\right)^4 \Rightarrow E_2 = \frac{81E}{64}$

2. $P = Ae\sigma T^4 = (4\pi r^2)\, e\sigma T^4$

$\therefore \quad \frac{P_1}{P_2} = \left(\frac{r_1}{r_2}\right)^2\left(\frac{T_1}{T_2}\right)^4$

$\Rightarrow \quad 10000 = \left(\frac{r_1}{r_2}\right)^2\left(\frac{2000}{6000}\right)^4$

$\Rightarrow \quad \frac{r_1}{r_2} = 900:1$

3. $I = \frac{P}{4\pi d^2} = \frac{Ae\sigma T^4}{4\pi d^2} = \frac{4\pi r^2 e\sigma T^4}{4\pi d^2} = \frac{r^2 e\sigma T^4}{d^2}$

$\therefore \quad 100 = \frac{(0.4)^2 \times e \times 6 \times 10^{-8} \times (500)^4}{(2)^2}$

$\Rightarrow \quad e = \frac{2}{3}$

4. Power absorbed = Power emitted

$\Rightarrow \quad 1370 \times \pi R^2 \times \frac{70}{100} = (4\pi R^2)\, e(5.67 \times 10^{-8})(288)^4$

$\Rightarrow \quad e \simeq 0.6$

5. In steady state,

$\frac{dQ}{dt} = \frac{KA(T_2 - T_1)}{L} = Ae\sigma\,(T_s^4 - T_2^4)$

$$\Rightarrow \frac{K(290-273)}{1} = (1)(6\times10^{-8})((300)^4-(290)^4)$$

$$\Rightarrow \quad K = 3.6 \text{ W/m-°C}$$

6. $$\frac{dQ}{dt} = Ae\sigma(T_s^4 - T^4) = \frac{dm}{dt}L_v$$

$$\Rightarrow \frac{dm}{dt} = \frac{4\pi r^2 e\sigma(T_s^4 - T^4)}{L_v}$$

$$= \frac{4\times3.14\times(0.1)^2\times1\times5.67\times10^{-8}}{21\times10^3}((77)^4-(4.2)^4)$$

$$= 0.0119 \text{ g/s} = 43 \text{ g/h}$$

7. Smooth and polished plates are poor radiators of heat. Hence, heat coming out from A is small, even though B being a black and rough plate is a good absorber. Effectively the heat coming to the left of pellet P is small. Black and rough plates are good radiations of heat. Hence, plate B_2 radiates heat to a satisfactory level, however plate A_2 being smooth and polished, is a bad absorber. Effectively the heat coming to the right of P is also small.

8. It follows from the figure that the temperature of body x falls more rapidly with time than that of body y. Hence, $E_x > E_y$. Also a good emitter of radiation is also a good absorber of radiation (Kirchhoff's law).
Hence, $a_x > a_y$

9. $$-ms\frac{dT}{dt} = Ae\sigma(T^4 - 0^4)$$

$$\Rightarrow -\frac{dT}{dt} = \frac{4\pi r^2\sigma T^4}{\left(\rho\frac{4}{3}\pi r^3\right)C}$$

$$\Rightarrow \int_0^t dt = -\frac{r\rho C}{3\sigma}\int_{200}^{100} T^{-4}dT$$

$$\Rightarrow t = \frac{7}{72}\frac{r\rho C}{\sigma}\mu s$$

10. Since, they are in thermal equilibrium, the temperatures must necessarily be equal.

11. Let radius of sphere be r and edge of cube be a,

$$4\pi r^2 = 6a^2$$

$$\Rightarrow \frac{r}{a} = \left(\frac{3}{2\pi}\right)^{1/2}$$

$$m_1 = \rho\left(\frac{4}{3}\pi r^3\right),\ m_2 = \rho a^3$$

$$\therefore \frac{m_1}{m_2} = \frac{4\pi}{3}\left(\frac{r}{a}\right)^3 = \frac{4\pi}{3}\left(\frac{3}{2\pi}\right)^{3/2} = \sqrt{\frac{6}{\pi}}$$

$$R = \text{Rate of cooling} = -\frac{dT}{dt} = \frac{Ae\sigma(T^4 - T_s^4)}{ms}$$

$$\therefore \frac{R_1}{R_2} = \frac{m_2}{m_1} = \sqrt{\frac{\pi}{6}} : 1$$

12. $$R = -\frac{dT}{dt} = \frac{Ae\sigma(T^4 - T_0^4)}{ms} = \frac{Ae\sigma(T^4 - T_0^4)}{(\rho At)s}$$

$$\therefore \frac{R_1}{R_2} = 1:1$$

13. $$-\frac{dT}{dt} = \frac{Ae\sigma(T^4 - T_0^4)}{ms} = \frac{(6a^2)e\sigma(T^4 - T_0^4)}{(\rho a^3)s}$$

For the same fall in temperature,

$$dt \propto a$$

$$\therefore \frac{\Delta t_2}{\Delta t_1} = \frac{a_2}{a_1} \Rightarrow \frac{\Delta t_2}{100} = \frac{2}{1}$$

$$\Rightarrow \Delta t_2 = 200 \text{ s}$$

14. Rate of loss of heat in the two cases will be equal.

Rate of heat loss in first case $= \dfrac{(250+10)\times1\times5}{130}$

Rate of heat loss in second case $= \dfrac{(200s+10)\times5}{67}$

$$\therefore \frac{(250+10)\times1\times5}{130} = \frac{(200\,s+10)\times5}{67}$$

$$\Rightarrow s = 0.62$$

15. Rate of cooling $= -\dfrac{d\theta}{dt} = \tan\phi = K(\theta-\theta_0)$

$$\therefore \frac{\tan\phi_2}{\tan\phi_1} = \frac{\theta_2-\theta_0}{\theta_1-\theta_0}$$

16. In steady state,

Power lost to surroundings = Power of heater

$$\Rightarrow K(70-30) = 10$$

$$\Rightarrow K = 0.25$$

After the heater is switched off,

$$-C\frac{dT}{dt} = K(T - T_0)$$

$$\Rightarrow -C\left(\frac{49.9-50}{60}\right) = 0.25\,(50-30)$$

$$\Rightarrow C = 3000 \text{ J/°C}$$

17. $$\lambda_m T = b$$

$$\Rightarrow \lambda_m = \frac{b}{T} = \frac{2.88\times10^6}{2880} = 1000 \text{ nm}$$

The black body radiates maximum energy around

$$\lambda_m = 1000 \text{ nm}$$

$\therefore U_2$ is greater than U_1 or U_3.

Also, energy is radiated at all wavelengths.

$$\therefore U_1, U_3 \neq 0$$

18. $$\lambda \propto \frac{1}{T}$$

$$\Rightarrow \frac{T_A}{T_B} = \frac{\lambda_B}{\lambda_A} = \frac{1500}{500} = 3$$

$$P = Ae\sigma T^4 = (4\pi r^2)e\sigma T^4$$

$$\therefore \frac{P_A}{P_B} = \left(\frac{r_A}{r_B}\right)^2\left(\frac{T_A}{T_B}\right)^4 = \left(\frac{6}{18}\right)^2\left(\frac{3}{1}\right)^4 = 9:1$$

19. For a thin disc emitting from both surfaces,

$$A = 2\pi R^2$$

$$Q = Ae\sigma T^4 = (2\pi R^2)\, e\sigma \left(\frac{b}{\lambda_m}\right)^4$$

$$\Rightarrow \quad Q \propto \frac{R^2}{\lambda^4}$$

$$\therefore Q_A : Q_B : Q_C = \frac{R_A^2}{\lambda_A^4} : \frac{R_B^2}{\lambda_B^4} : \frac{R_C^2}{\lambda_C^4} = \frac{2^2}{(300)^4} : \frac{4^2}{(400)^4} : \frac{6^2}{(500)^4}$$

$$= 49 : 62.5 : 57$$

So, Q_B is maximum.

20. For the same power of radiation,

$$P_A = P_B = P_C$$

$$\Rightarrow \quad Ae_A\sigma T_A^4 = Ae_B\sigma T_B^4 = Ae_C\sigma T_C^4$$

$$\Rightarrow \quad T_A^4 = \frac{1}{2}T_B^4 = \frac{1}{4}T_C^4$$

$$\Rightarrow \quad T_A = \frac{T_B}{2^{1/4}} = \frac{T_C}{4^{1/4}} \quad \Rightarrow T_B = \sqrt{T_A T_C}$$

$$\lambda \propto \frac{1}{T}$$

$$\Rightarrow \quad \lambda_B = \sqrt{\lambda_A \lambda_C}$$

Also, $\sqrt{e_A T_A e_C T_C} = e_B T_B$

21. In steady state,

$$P_{loss} = P_{heater}$$

$$(4\pi r^2)\, e\sigma\, ((500)^4 - (300)^4) = 300 \quad \text{...(i)}$$

When half of sphere is blackened,

$$(2\pi r^2)\, e\sigma\, ((500)^4 - (300)^4) + (2\pi r^2)(1)\sigma\, ((500)^4 - (300)^4) = 600$$

$$\Rightarrow \quad (2\pi r^2)(1+e)\sigma\, ((500)^4 - (300)^4) = 600 \quad \text{...(ii)}$$

Dividing Eq. (i) by Eq. (ii),

$$\frac{2e}{1+e} = \frac{1}{2} \quad \Rightarrow \quad e = \frac{1}{3}$$

22. Steady state condition of sheet A,

$$P + \sigma A T_2^4 = \sigma (2A) T_1^4 \quad \text{...(i)}$$

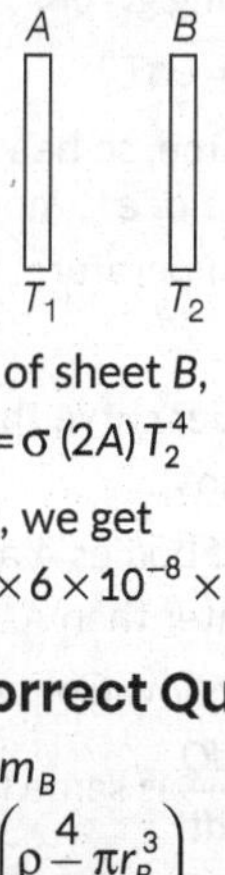

Steady state condition of sheet B,

$$\sigma A T_1^4 = \sigma (2A) T_2^4 \quad \text{...(ii)}$$

From Eq. (i) and Eq. (ii), we get

$$P = 3\sigma A T_2^4 = 3 \times 6 \times 10^{-8} \times 2 \times (300)^4 = 2916 \text{ W}$$

Multiple Choice(s) Correct Questions

1.

$$m_A = 4m_B$$

$$\Rightarrow \quad \rho\left(\frac{4}{3}\pi r_A^3\right) = 4\left(\rho \frac{4}{3}\pi r_B^3\right)$$

$$\Rightarrow \quad \frac{r_A}{r_B} = 2^{2/3}$$

Heat loss rate $= P = Ae\sigma\,(T^4 - T_s^4) = (4\pi r^2)\, e\sigma\,(T^4 - T_s^4)$

$$\therefore \quad \frac{P_A}{P_B} = \left(\frac{r_A}{r_B}\right)^2 = 2^{4/3}$$

Initial rate of cooling $= R = \dfrac{Ae\sigma\,(T^4 - T_s^4)}{ms}$

$$= \frac{(4\pi r^2)\, e\sigma\,(T^4 - T_s^4)}{ms}$$

$$\therefore \quad \frac{R_A}{R_B} = \left(\frac{r_A}{r_B}\right)^2 \left(\frac{m_B}{m_A}\right) = (2^{2/3})^2 \left(\frac{1}{4}\right) = 2^{-2/3}$$

2. $ms\dfrac{dT}{dt} = 12 - K(T - 15)$

At 45°C, $\dfrac{dT}{dt} = 0$

$$\Rightarrow \quad 0 = 12 - K(45 - 15) \quad \Rightarrow \quad K = 0.4 \text{ W/°C}$$

Rate of heat loss $= K(T - 15) = 0.4(T - 15)$

At 20°C, Rate of heat loss $= 0.4(20 - 15) = 2$ W

At 45°C, Rate of heat loss $= 0.4(45 - 15) = 12$ W

$$ms\frac{dT}{dt} = 12 - 0.4(T - 15)$$

$$\Rightarrow \quad ms\int_{15}^{25} \frac{5\,dT}{90 - 2T} = \int_0^{300} dt$$

$$\Rightarrow \quad s = \frac{240}{\ln\left(\frac{3}{2}\right)} \text{ J/kg°C}$$

3. Metal is better conductor of heat than wood. Hence, from metallic piece more heat is conducted into the body than from a wooden piece.

Black painted wooden piece will act as a black body. It will absorb more heat as compared to a polished metallic piece when placed in open in bright sun. Now, according to Kirchhoff's law, a good absorber is also a good emitter. Hence, wooden piece will lose heat at a faster rate than the metallic piece.

4. (a,b,c,d)

5. (b) Since, $T_A > T$, A radiates heat larger than it absorbs heat. Since, $T_B < T$, B absorbs heat larger than it radiates. This process goes on until both A and B reach the temperature T.

(d) After reaching thermal equilibrium, both bodies radiate and absorb at the same rate.

6. $T \propto \dfrac{1}{\lambda} \quad \Rightarrow \quad \dfrac{T_A}{T_B} = \dfrac{\lambda_B}{\lambda_A} = \dfrac{800}{400} = 2$

$$P = (4\pi r^2)\, e\sigma T^4$$

$$\Rightarrow \quad \frac{P_A}{P_B} = \left(\frac{r_A}{r_B}\right)^2 \left(\frac{T_A}{T_B}\right)^4 = \left(\frac{1}{2}\right)^2 \left(\frac{2}{1}\right)^4 = 4$$

$$E = \sigma T^4$$

$$\Rightarrow \quad \frac{E_A}{E_B} = \left(\frac{T_A}{T_B}\right)^4 = (2)^4 = 16$$

7. $P_A = P_B$

$\Rightarrow Ae_A\sigma T_A^4 = Ae_B\sigma T_B^4$

$\Rightarrow (0.01)T_A^4 = (0.81)T_B^4$

$$\Rightarrow \quad T_B = \frac{T_A}{3} = \frac{5802}{3} = 1934\text{ K}$$

$$\lambda_A T_A = \lambda_B T_B$$

$$\Rightarrow \quad \frac{\lambda_A}{\lambda_B} = \frac{T_B}{T_A} = \frac{1}{3} \quad \Rightarrow \quad \lambda_A = \frac{\lambda_B}{3}$$

Also, $\lambda_B - \lambda_A = 1\,\mu\text{m}$

$$\Rightarrow \quad \lambda_B - \frac{\lambda_B}{3} = 1\,\mu\text{m} \quad \Rightarrow \quad \lambda_B = 1.5\,\mu\text{m}$$

8. $\lambda_m T = b \quad \Rightarrow \quad \lambda_m \propto \frac{1}{T}$ or $v_m \propto T$

Comprehension Based Questions

1. $$ms\frac{dT}{dt} = 100 - P_{\text{Loss}}$$

At 60°C, $\frac{dT}{dt} = 0$

$$\Rightarrow \quad P_{\text{Loss}} = 100\text{ W}$$

2. $$P_{\text{Loss}} = K(T - T_s)$$

At 60°C, $100 = K(60 - 25)$

$$\Rightarrow \quad K = \frac{20}{7}\text{W/°C}$$

At 39°C, $P_{\text{Loss}} = \frac{20}{7}(39 - 25) = 40\text{ W}$

3. $T = \left(\frac{39-25}{120}\right)t + 25 = \frac{7}{60}t + 25$

$$P_{\text{Loss}} = \frac{dQ}{dt} = \frac{20}{7}(T - 25)$$

$$\Rightarrow \quad \int dQ = \int_0^{120} \frac{20}{7}\left(\frac{7}{60}\right)t\,dt$$

$$\Rightarrow \quad Q = \frac{1}{3}\left[\frac{t^2}{2}\right]_0^{120} = 2400\text{ J}$$

4. $$C\frac{dT}{dt} = P_{\text{heater}} - P_{\text{loss}}$$

$$\Rightarrow \quad 90\frac{dT}{dt} = P_{\text{heater}} - K(T - 25)$$

Just after the heater is switched ON,

$$\Rightarrow \quad 90(2) = P_{\text{heater}} - 0$$

$$\Rightarrow \quad P_{\text{heater}} = 180\text{ W}$$

5. $$90\frac{dT}{dt} = 180 - P_{\text{loss}}$$

Just after the heater is switched OFF,

$$90(-0.2) = 0 - P_{\text{loss}}$$

$$\Rightarrow \quad P_{\text{loss}} = 18\text{ W}$$

6. At 35°C, $P_{\text{loss}} = K(35 - 25) = 18$

$$\Rightarrow \quad K = 1.8\text{ W/°C}$$

At 30°C, $P_{\text{loss}} = K(30 - 25) = 1.8 \times 5 = 9\text{ W}$

7. $\ln\left(\frac{\theta - \theta_0}{\theta_i - \theta_0}\right) = -Kt$

$$40°\text{C} \xrightarrow{10\text{min}} 36°\text{C}$$

$$\ln\left(\frac{36-30}{40-30}\right) = -K(10) \qquad \text{...(i)}$$

$$36°\text{C} \xrightarrow{10\text{min}} \theta$$

$$\ln\left(\frac{\theta-30}{36-30}\right) = -K(10) \qquad \text{...(ii)}$$

Solving Eq. (i) and Eq. (ii), we get

$$\theta = 33.6°\text{C}$$

8. $\theta = \theta_0 + (\theta_i - \theta_0)e^{-Kt}$

9. $\frac{40-36}{10} = K(38 - 30) \Rightarrow K = \frac{1}{20}$

Rate of heat loss at 38°C

$$= CK(38 - 30) = 2 \times \frac{1}{20} \times 8 = 0.8\text{ J/min}$$

Heat loss in 10 minutes $= 0.8 \times 10 = 8$ J

Total heat required $= C\Delta\theta +$ Heat loss

$$= 2 \times (40 - 36) + 8 = 16\text{ J}$$

Match the Columns Questions

1. A-R, B-P, C-S, D-Q

2. (A) Initially temperature of body is less and finally it will attain equilibrium temperature, i.e. of the surrounding, thus the graph will be exponentially increasing.

(B) Power is absorbed from surrounding and that is constant. Thus, power absorbed will be constant. Thus, the graph will be constant.

(C) Finally temperature of body will be that of surrounding. Thus, net power emitted will be zero finally. Thus, an exponentially decaying graph.

3. (A) Emissive power $= e\sigma T^4$

Area of A and B is same, so heat energy radiated will be more for which value of e is more.

(B) On increasing temperature, peak of graph shifts left.

So, $T_B > T_A$

B has more area under curve than A. So, emissive power of B will be greater than A.

Since surface area of bodies A and B are same, heat energy radiated by B is greater than A.

(C) Direction of heat flow from A to B, so $T_A > T_B$

(D) At steady state $\frac{dQ}{dt}$ is same for all but direction of heat flow from T_1 to T_2, so $T_A > T_B$.

Numerical Value Questions

1. For end B, $\lambda T = b$

$$\Rightarrow \quad T_B = \frac{b}{\lambda} = \frac{0.3 \times 10^{-2}}{75000 \times 10^{-10}} = 400\,\text{K}$$

In steady state,

$$\frac{dQ}{dt} = \frac{KA(T_A - T_B)}{L} = Ae\sigma T_B^4$$

$$\Rightarrow \quad \frac{17 \times (T_A - 400)}{1.5} = 1 \times \frac{17}{3} \times 10^{-8} \times (400)^4$$

$$\Rightarrow \quad T_A = 528\,\text{K}$$

2. Intensity at the Earth's surface,

$$I = \frac{P_{\text{sun}}}{4\pi d^2} = \frac{(4\pi R_s^2)(1)\sigma T_s^4}{4\pi d^2} = \frac{\sigma R_s^2 T_s^4}{d^2}$$

Power absorbed by disc $= aIA = 1 \times \dfrac{\sigma R_s^2 T_s^4}{d^2} \times \pi r_d^2$

In steady state for disc,

Power absorbed = Power radiated

$$\Rightarrow \quad \frac{\sigma R_s^2 T_s^4}{d^2} \times \pi r_d^2 = (\pi r_d^2) \times 1 \times \sigma T_d^4$$

$$\Rightarrow \quad T_d = \left(\frac{R_s}{d}\right)^{1/2} T_s = \left(\frac{7.35 \times 10^8}{1.5 \times 10^{11}}\right)^{1/2} \times 6200$$

$$= 434\,\text{K}$$

3. $i^2 R = A_{\text{surface}} e\sigma (T^4 - T_s^4)$

$$\Rightarrow i^2 \left(\frac{\rho_0 (1 + \alpha \Delta T) L}{\pi r^2}\right) = (2\pi r L)\, e\sigma (T^4 - T_s^4)$$

$$\Rightarrow i = \sqrt{\frac{2\pi^2 r^3 e\sigma (T^4 - T_s^4)}{\rho_0 (1 + \alpha \Delta T)}}$$

$$= \sqrt{\frac{2\pi^2 (10^{-3})^3 \times 1 \times 5.68 \times 10^{-8}((900)^4 - (300)^4)}{\pi^2 \times 10^{-8}(1 + 7.8 \times 10^{-3} \times 600)}} = 36\,\text{A}$$

4. In steady state,

Generated power = Radiated power

$$\Rightarrow \quad P = (4\pi R^2)(1)\sigma T^4$$

After the space station is enveloped by a thin spherical black screen, let the temperature of space station be T_1. Temperature of screen must be equal to T since, the total amount of energy liberated per unit time remains unchanged.

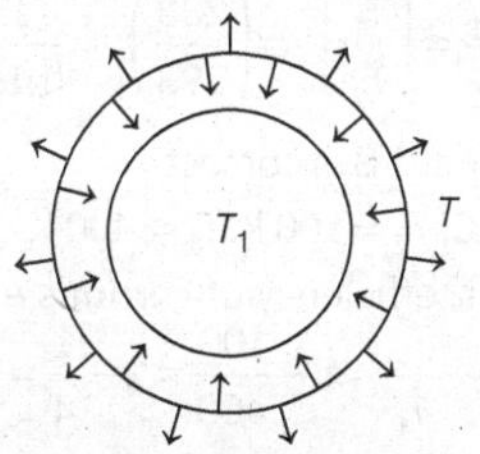

Generated power = Radiated power

$$\Rightarrow \quad P = (4\pi R^2)(1)\sigma (T_1^4 - T^4)$$

$$\therefore \quad (4\pi R^2)(1)\sigma T^4 = (4\pi R^2)(1)\sigma (T_1^4 - T^4)$$

$$\Rightarrow \quad T_1 = 2^{1/4} T = 1.2 \times 500 = 600\,\text{K}$$

5. Let the temperatures of A and B be T_3 and T_4, respectively.

In the steady state,

$$Q = A\sigma (T_1^4 - T_3^4) = A\sigma (T_3^4 - T_4^4) = A\sigma (T_4^4 - T_2^4)$$

In the absence of plates,

$$Q_0 = A\sigma (T_1^4 - T_2^4)$$

$$= A\sigma (T_1^4 - T_3^4) + A\sigma (T_3^4 - T_4^4) + A\sigma (T_4^4 - T_2^4)$$

$$= Q + Q + Q = 3Q$$

$$\therefore \quad \frac{Q_0}{Q} = 3$$

6. $$\frac{dQ}{dt} = (4\pi r_1^2)\, e\sigma ((800)^4 - (600)^4) = \frac{K(4\pi r_2^2)(600 - T)}{t}$$

$$\Rightarrow \quad 0.9 \times \frac{17}{3} \times 10^{-8}((800)^4 - (600)^4) = \frac{0.085(10)^2 (600 - T)}{5 \times 10^{-2}}$$

$$\Rightarrow \quad T = 516\,\text{K}$$

7. $T = \dfrac{b}{\lambda}, \quad P = Ae\sigma T^4 = (4\pi r^2) e\sigma \left(\dfrac{b}{\lambda}\right)^4$

$$P_A = P_B$$

$$\Rightarrow (4\pi r_A^2)(1)\sigma \left(\frac{b}{\lambda_A}\right)^4 = (4\pi r_B^2)(1)\sigma \left(\frac{b}{\lambda_B}\right)^4$$

$$\Rightarrow \quad \frac{r_B}{r_A} = \left(\frac{\lambda_B}{\lambda_A}\right)^2 = \left(\frac{7000}{3500}\right)^2 = 4$$

8. Power absorbed by sphere $= aI(\pi R^2) = I(\pi R^2)$

Power radiated by sphere $= (4\pi R^2) e\sigma T^4 = (4\sigma T^4)\pi R^2$

Net power absorbed $= \pi R^2 (I - 4\sigma T^4)$

$$\Rightarrow \quad mS \frac{dT}{dt} = \pi R^2 (I - 4\sigma T^4)$$

For maximum temperature, $\dfrac{dT}{dt} = 0$

$$\Rightarrow \quad T = \left(\frac{I}{4\sigma}\right)^{1/4} = 200\,\text{K}$$

Previous Year's Questions

JEE Main

1. According to Newton's law of cooling.

$$\frac{\theta_1 - \theta_2}{t} = K \cdot \left(\frac{\theta_1 + \theta_2}{2} - \theta\right)$$

Here, θ_1 and θ_2 are initial and final temperatures of body,

θ = temperature of surroundings

t = time duration

K = constant

Now, from conditions given in question, we have

$$\frac{60 - 40}{6} = K \cdot \left(\frac{60 + 40}{2} - 10\right) \quad \text{(From Ist situation)}$$

$\Rightarrow \quad 20 = 6K \times 40$

$\Rightarrow \quad K = 1/12$

And $\dfrac{40-\theta_2}{6} = \dfrac{1}{12}\left(\dfrac{40+\theta_2}{2} - 10\right)$ (From IInd situation)

$\Rightarrow 2(40-\theta_2) = \dfrac{20+\theta_2}{2}$

$\Rightarrow \quad \theta_2 = 28°\text{C}$

2. Using Newton's law of cooling,

$$\frac{T_i - T_f}{t} = k\left(\frac{T_i + T_f}{2} - T_s\right)$$

Case-I $\dfrac{60-40}{7} = k\left[\dfrac{60+40}{2} - 10\right]$

$\Rightarrow \quad \dfrac{20}{7} = k[40]$ ...(i)

Case-II $\dfrac{40-T}{7} = k\left(\dfrac{40+T}{2} - 10\right)$

$\dfrac{40-T}{7} = k\left[\dfrac{20+T}{2}\right]$ ...(ii)

Dividing Eq. (ii) by Eq. (i)

$$\frac{40-T}{20} = \frac{20+T}{40\times 2}$$

$$160 - 4T = 20 + T$$

$$5T = 140$$

$$T = 28°\text{C}$$

3. Given, initial temperature,

$$T_i = 80°\text{C}$$

Final temperature, $T_f = 60°\text{C}$

Time taken, $t = 5\,\text{min}$

According to question;

$\dfrac{80-60}{5} = k(70-20)$ ... (i)

and $\dfrac{60-40}{t} = k(50-20)$ ... (ii)

From Eqs. (i) and (ii), we get

$$\frac{4t}{20} = \frac{50}{30}$$

$\Rightarrow \quad t = \dfrac{25}{3}\,\text{min} = 500\,\text{s}$

4. Given, room temperature,

$$T_0 = 22°\text{C}$$

In first case, $T_1 = 98°\text{C}, T_2 = 86°\text{C}$

$$t = 2\,\text{min} = 120\,\text{s}$$

According to Newton's law of cooling,

$$mc\frac{T_1 - T_2}{t} = K\left(\frac{T_1 + T_2}{2} - T_0\right)$$

$\Rightarrow \quad mc\left(\dfrac{98-86}{120}\right) = K\left(\dfrac{98+86}{2} - 22\right)$

$\Rightarrow \quad \dfrac{mc}{10} = 70K$ ... (i)

In second case, $T_1 = 75°\text{C}, T_2 = 69°\text{C}$

$\therefore \quad mc\dfrac{75-69}{t} = K\left(\dfrac{75+69}{2} - 22\right)$

$\Rightarrow \quad \dfrac{6mc}{t} = 50K$ ... (ii)

Dividing Eq. (i) by Eq. (ii), we get

$\dfrac{mc}{10} \times \dfrac{t}{6mc} = \dfrac{70K}{50K} \Rightarrow \dfrac{t}{60} = \dfrac{7}{5}$

$\Rightarrow \quad t = 84\,\text{s} = \dfrac{84}{60}\,\text{min} = 1\cdot 4\,\text{min}$

5. Given

Initially, at

$$t = 0, \Delta T = 60°\text{C},$$

$$T_w = 80°\text{C}$$

$\because \quad \Delta T = T_w - T_s$

By Newton's law of cooling,

$$\frac{\Delta T}{t} = k\left[\frac{T_i + T_f}{2} - T_s\right]$$

Case I

$\dfrac{20}{6} = K\left[\left(\dfrac{60+40}{2} + 20\right) - 20\right]$ ...(i)

Case II

$\dfrac{20}{t_2 - 6} = K\left[\left(\dfrac{40+20}{2} + 20\right) - 20\right]$ ...(ii)

From Eq. (i) and (ii), $\dfrac{t_2 - 6}{6} = \dfrac{5}{3}$

$\Rightarrow \quad t_2 = 16\,\text{min}$

6. As per Newton's law of cooling, for small temperature difference, the rate of heat lost from a substance is directly proportional to temperature difference between the substance and surrounding. Thus, when small temperature difference between a liquid and its surrounding is doubled, the rate of loss of heat of the liquid becomes twice. Hence, statement A is correct and statement D is incorrect.

For statement B,

$$T_1 = 10°\text{C} = (273 + 10)\text{K} = 283\,\text{K}$$

$$T_2 = 20°\text{C} = (273 + 20)\text{K} = 293\,\text{K}$$

According to Stefan's Boltzmann law,

$$E \propto T^4$$

$\Rightarrow \quad \dfrac{E_1}{E_2} = \left(\dfrac{T_1}{T_2}\right)^4 = \left(\dfrac{283}{293}\right)^4 = \dfrac{1}{1.15}$

Hence, statement B is correct.

In statement C, $T_2 = 100\,\text{K}, T_1 = 400\,\text{K}$

We know that, efficiency of carnot's engine,

$$\eta = 1 - \frac{T_2}{T_1} = 1 - \frac{100}{400} = 1 - \frac{1}{4} = \frac{3}{4}$$

$\Rightarrow \quad \eta = \dfrac{3}{4} \times 100\% = 75\%$

Therefore, statement C is also correct.

7. When, $t = 5$ min, $T_1 = 75°$ C, $T_2 = 65°$ C, then

By using Newton's law of cooling,

$$\frac{T_1 - T_2}{t} = k\left[\left(\frac{T_1 + T_2}{2}\right) - T_s\right] \quad ...(i)$$

$$\Rightarrow \quad \frac{75-65}{5} = k\left[\frac{140}{2} - 25\right]$$

$$\Rightarrow \quad \frac{10}{5} = k(70-25) \quad \Rightarrow \quad k = \frac{2}{45}$$

If T_3 be the temperature of body in next 5 min, then

By using Eq. (i) again

$$\frac{65 - T_3}{5} = \frac{2}{45}\left[\frac{65 + T_3}{2} - 25\right]$$

$$\Rightarrow \quad 9(65 - T_3) = 2\left[\frac{65 + T_3 - 50}{2}\right]$$

$$\Rightarrow \quad 585 - 9T_3 = 15 + T_3$$

$$\Rightarrow \quad 570 = 10T_3$$

$$\Rightarrow \quad T_3 = 57° \text{ C}$$

8. As per question, a body takes 4 min to cool from 61°C to 59°C. Temperature of surroundings is 30°C.

$\because$ We know that, $\frac{\Delta T}{\Delta t} = K(T_t - T_s)$

$$\Rightarrow \quad \frac{61° - 59°}{4} = K\left(\frac{61° + 59°}{2} - 30°\right) \quad ...(i)$$

and
$$\frac{51° - 49°}{t} = K\left(\frac{51° + 49°}{2} - 30°\right) \quad ...(ii)$$

On dividing Eqs. (i) and (ii), we get

$$\frac{\dfrac{61° - 59°}{4}}{\dfrac{51° - 49°}{t}} = \frac{K\left(\dfrac{61° + 59° - 60°}{2}\right)}{K\left(\dfrac{51° + 49° - 60°}{2}\right)}$$

On solving, we will get $t = 6$ min

9. $\frac{\theta_i - \theta_f}{\Delta t} = k(\theta_m - \theta_s)$

Where, $\theta_i = 50°$ C,

$\theta_f = 40°$ C,

Mean temperature,

$$\theta_m = \frac{(50+40)}{2} = \frac{90}{2} = 45° \text{ C},$$

temperature of surroundings $\theta_s = 20°$ C,

Δt = time interval = 300 s

and k = proportionality constant.

So, $$\frac{50-40}{300} = k(45-20) \quad ...(i)$$

Now, after next 5 min (= 300 s), if object's temperature is T, then

$$\frac{40 - T}{300} = k\left(\frac{40+T}{2} - 20\right) \quad ...(ii)$$

Dividing Eq. (i) by Eq. (ii), we have

$$\frac{50-40}{40-T} = \frac{45-20}{\left(\dfrac{40+T}{2} - 20\right)}$$

$$\Rightarrow \quad 10\left(\frac{T}{2}\right) = 25(40 - T)$$

$$\Rightarrow \quad T = \frac{100}{3} = 33° \text{ C}$$

Hence, correct option is (d).

10. We know, $m = V \cdot \rho$

where, V = volume and ρ = density.

So, we have

$$\frac{dQ}{dt} = \frac{h}{ms}(T - T_0) = \frac{h(T - T_0)}{V \cdot \rho s}$$

Since, h, $(T - T_0)$ and V are constant for both beaker.

$$\therefore \quad \frac{dQ}{dt} \propto \frac{1}{\rho s}$$

We have given that

$\rho_A = 8 \times 10^2$ kgm^{-3},

$\rho_B = 10^3$ kgm^{-3},

$s_A = 2000$ J kg^{-1} K^{-1}

and $s_B = 4000$ J kg^{-1} K^{-1},

$\rho_A s_A = 16 \times 10^5$

and $\rho_B s_B = 4 \times 10^6$

So, $\rho_A < \rho_B$, $s_A < s_B$

and $\rho_A s_A < \rho_B s_B$

$$\Rightarrow \quad \frac{1}{\rho_A s_A} > \frac{1}{\rho_B s_B} \quad \Rightarrow \quad \frac{dQ_A}{dt} > \frac{dQ_B}{dt}$$

So, for container B, rate of cooling is smaller than the container A.

Hence, graph of B lies above the graph of A and it is not a straight line (slope of A is greater than B).

JEE Advanced

1. $\lambda T = b$

$$\lambda = \frac{b}{T} \quad \Rightarrow \quad E = \frac{hc}{\lambda} = \frac{hcT}{b}$$

$$E = \left(\frac{hc}{eb}\right) \times T \text{ eV}$$

Substituting the values, we get

$E = (0.428 \times 10^{-3} \times T)$ eV

(P) $T = 2000$ K $\Rightarrow$ $E = 0.856$ eV

(Q) $T = 3000$ K $\Rightarrow$ $E = 1.284$ eV

(R) $T = 5000$ K $\Rightarrow$ $E = 2.14$ eV

(S) $T = 10000$ K $\Rightarrow$ $E = 4.28$ eV

2. $T_s = 0$ K

$T_i = 200$ K, $e = 1$

$$-Ms\frac{dT}{dt} = \frac{dQ}{dt} = \sigma e A T^4$$

$$\Rightarrow \quad -\frac{dT}{dt}=\frac{\sigma AT^4}{Ms}$$

$$\frac{\sigma A}{Ms}\int_{t_i}^{t_f} dt=-\int_{T_i}^{T_f}\frac{dT}{T^4}$$

$$\frac{\sigma A}{Ms}(t_f-t_i)=\frac{1}{3}\left(\frac{1}{T_f^3}-\frac{1}{T_i^3}\right)$$

$$\frac{\frac{\sigma A}{Ms}(t_1-0)=\frac{1}{3}\left(\frac{1}{(100)^3}-\frac{1}{(200)^3}\right)}{\frac{\sigma A}{Ms}(t_2-0)=\frac{1}{3}\left(\frac{1}{(50)^3}-\frac{1}{(200)^3}\right)}$$

$$\frac{t_1}{t_2}=\frac{\dfrac{(200)^3-(100)^3}{(100)^3(200)^3}}{\dfrac{(200)^3-(50)^3}{(50)^3(200)^3}}$$

$$\therefore \quad \frac{t_2}{t_1}=\frac{9}{1}$$

3. $\frac{dQ}{dt}=e\sigma A(T^4-T_0^4)$

For small temperature change,

$$\frac{dQ}{dt}=e\sigma AT^3\Delta T \quad \text{... (i)}$$

$$\frac{mCdT}{dt}=e\sigma AT^3\Delta T$$

$$\frac{dT}{dt}=\frac{e\sigma AT^3}{mC}\Delta T$$

$\frac{e\sigma AT^3}{mC}\rightarrow$ constant for Newton law of cooling

$$\frac{e\sigma AT^3}{mC}=0.001$$

$$e\sigma AT^3=mC\times 0.001$$

$$=1\times 4200\times 0.001$$

$$e\sigma AT^3=4.2 \quad \text{... (ii)}$$

$$\frac{dQ}{dt}=700\times 0.05=35 \text{ W} \quad \text{... (iii)}$$

Putting the value of Eqs. (ii) and (iii) in Eq. (i), we get

$$35=4.2\,\Delta T$$

$$\Rightarrow \quad \frac{35}{4.2}=\Delta T \Rightarrow \Delta T=8.33$$

4. Assumption $e=1$ [black body radiation]

$$P=\sigma A(T^4-T_0^4)$$

(c) $P_{rad}=\sigma AT^4=\sigma\cdot 1\cdot(T_0+10)^4$

$$=\sigma\cdot T_0^4\left(1+\frac{10}{T_0}\right)^4 \quad [T_0=300\text{K given}]$$

$$=\sigma\cdot(300)^4\cdot\left(1+\frac{40}{300}\right)\approx 460\times\frac{17}{15}\approx 520 \text{ J}$$

$$P_{net}=520-460\approx 60 \text{ W}$$

$\Rightarrow$ Energy radiated in 1 s = 60 J

(b) $P=\sigma A(T^4-T_0^4)$

$dP=\sigma A(0-4T_0^3\cdot dT)$ and $dT=-\Delta T$

$\Rightarrow dP=4\sigma AT_0^3\Delta T$

(d) If surface area decreases, then energy radiation also decreases.

5. $\log_2\frac{P_1}{P_0}=1$

Therefore, $\frac{P_1}{P_0}=2$

According to Stefan's law, $P\propto T$

$$\Rightarrow \quad \frac{P_2}{P_1}=\left(\frac{T_2}{T_1}\right)^4=\left(\frac{2767+273}{487+273}\right)^4=4^4$$

$$\Rightarrow \quad \frac{P_2}{P_1}=\frac{P_2}{2P_0}=4^4$$

$$\log_2\frac{P_2}{P_0}=\log_2[2\times 4^4]$$

$$=\log_2 2+\log_2 4^4=1+\log_2 2^8=9$$

6. Power, $P=(\sigma T^4A)=\sigma T^4(4\pi R^2)$

or, $P\propto T^4R^2$ ...(i)

According to Wien's law,

$$\lambda\propto\frac{1}{T}$$

(λ is the wavelength at which peak occurs)

$\therefore$ Eq. (i) will become,

$$P\propto\frac{R^2}{\lambda^4} \quad \text{or} \quad \lambda\propto\left[\frac{R^2}{P}\right]^{1/4}$$

$$\Rightarrow \quad \frac{\lambda_A}{\lambda_B}=\left[\frac{R_A}{R_B}\right]^{1/2}\left[\frac{P_B}{P_A}\right]^{1/4}$$

$$=[400]^{1/2}\left[\frac{1}{10^4}\right]^{1/4}=2$$

CHAPTER~05

KINETIC THEORY OF GASES

LEVEL 01 Starter Level

5.1 Kinetic Theory of Gases

1 State whether the followings assumptions of kinetic theory of gas are true or false.

(a) The molecules of a gas are identical, perfectly elastic and hard spheres.

(b) Volume of molecules is negligible as compared with the volume of the gas.

(c) Molecules do not have any preferred direction of motion, motion is completely random.

(d) Molecules of gas never travel in straight line.

(e) The time of the collision between any two molecules is very small.

(f) The collision between molecules and the wall of the container is inelastic.

(g) The motion of molecules is not governed by Newton's laws of motion.

(h) The effect of gravity on the motion of molecules is negligible.

2 Find the average momentum of molecules of hydrogen gas in a container at temperature 300 K.

5.2 Root Mean Square Speed

1 The speeds of three molecules are $3v$, $4v$ and $5v$ respectively. Find their rms speed.

2 You are given the following group of particles, n_i represents the number of molecules with speed v_i

n_i	2	4	8	6	3
v_i (ms^{-1})	1.0	2.0	3.0	4.0	5.0

Calculate : (a) average speed (b) rms speed (c) most probable speed.

3 Calculate rms velocity of oxygen molecules at 27°C.

4 At room temperature (27°C), the rms speed of the molecules of a certain diatomic gas is found to be 1930 m/s. Can you guess name of the gas? Find the temperature at which the rms speed is double of the speed in part one ($R = 25/3$ J/mol-K).

5 At a pressure of 24×10^5 dyne / cm^2, the volume of O_2 is 10 L and mass is 20 g. What will be its rms velocity?

6 The molecules of a given mass of gas have rms speed 200 ms^{-1} at 27°C and 10^5 Nm^{-2} pressure. When the absolue temperature is doubled and the pressure is halved, then find rms speed of the molecules of the same gas.

7 At what temperature is the root mean square velocity of gaseous hydrogen molecules is equal to that of oxygen molecules at 47°C ?

8 Two vessels having equal volume contain molecular hydrogen at one atmosphere, and helium at two atmospheres respectively. What is the ratio of rms speeds of hydrogen molecule to that of helium molecule, if both the samples are at the same temperature?

5.3 Pressure on the Walls of Container

1 A flask contains 10^{-3} m^3 gas. At a temperature, the number of molecules of oxygen are 3.0×10^{22}. The mass of an oxygen molecule is 5.3×10^{-26} kg and at that temperature the rms velocity of molecules is 400 m/s. What is the pressure of the gas in the flask?

2 The root mean square speed of hydrogen molecules of an ideal hydrogen gas kept in a gas chamber at 0°C is 3180 m/s. What is the pressure of the hydrogen gas?

(Density of hydrogen gas = 8.99×10^{-2} kg / m^3, 1 atmosphere = 1.01×10^5 N / m^2).

3 A cubical container having side as l is filled with a gas having N molecules in the container. Mass of each molecule is m. If we assume that at every instant half of the molecules are moving towards the positive X-axis and half of the molecules are moving towards the negative X-axis. Two walls of the container are perpendicular to the X-axis. Find the pressure experienced by each wall. Assume that all the molecules are moving with speed v_0.

4 A cubical box of side 1 m contains helium gas (atomic weight = 4 g) at a pressure of 100 N/m^2. During an observation time of 1 s, an atom travelling with the root mean square speed parallel to one of the edges of the cube, was found to make 500 hits with a particular wall, without any collision with other atoms. Take, $R = 25/3$ J/mol-K and $k = 1.38 \times 10^{-23}$ J/K.

(a) Evaluate the temperature of the gas.

(b) Evaluate the average kinetic energy per atom.

(c) Evaluate the total mass of helium gas in the box.

5.4 Maxwell's Distribution of Speed

1 Find the temperature at which average speed of oxygen molecule be sufficient, so as to escape from the earth. (Escape speed from the earth is 11.0 km/s, $R = 25/3$ J-mol^{-1}K^{-1}).

2 Find the average of magnitude of linear momentum of a helium molecule in a sample of helium gas at 0°C. Mass of a helium molecule $= 6.64 \times 10^{-27}$ kg and $k = 1.38 \times 10^{-23}$ J/K.

3 The mean speed of the molecules of a hydrogen sample equals the mean speed of the molecules of helium sample. Calculate the ratio of the temperature of the hydrogen sample to the temperature of the helium sample.

4 Determine the gas temperature at which,

(a) the root mean square velocity of hydrogen molecules exceeds their most probable velocity by $\Delta v = 400$ m/s.

(b) the velocity of distribution function $F(v)$ for the oxygen molecules will have the maximum value at the velocity $v = 420$ m/s.

5.5 Mean Free Path

1 If the mean free path of atoms is doubled, then what will be the new pressure of gas if the original pressure is p?

2 The mean free path of nitrogen molecules at a pressure of 1.0 atm and temperature 0°C is 0.8×10^{-7} m. If the number of density of molecules is 2.7×10^{25} per m^3, then what is the molecular diameter?

3 Calculate the ratio of the mean free paths of the molecules of two gases having molecular diameters 10 Å and 2 Å. The gases may be considered under identical conditions of temperature, pressure and volume.

5.6 Degree of Freedom

1 Fill the table.

Type of Gas	Number of degree of freedom		
	Translational	Rotational	Total
Monoatomic gas			
Diatomic gas			
Linear polyatomic gas			
Nonlinear polyatomic gas			

2 Calculate the total number of degrees of freedom possessed by the molecules in one cm^3 of H_2 gas at NTP.

5.7 Kinetic Energy

1 Calculate the kinetic theory of a gram molecule of argon at 127°C.

2 A vessel is filled with O_2 at 27°C. Calculate

(a) the average kinetic energy of translation of an oxygen molecule

(b) the average kinetic energy of rotation of an oxygen molecule

(c) the total kinetic energy of an oxygen molecule

3 The average translational kinetic energy of nitrogen gas molecules is 0.02 eV (1 eV $= 1.6 \times 10^{-19}$ J). Calculate the temperature of the gas. Boltzmann constant $k = 1.38 \times 10^{-23}$ J/K.

4 The average kinetic energy of a gas molecule at 27°C is 6.21×10^{-31} J. What will be its average kinetic energy at 227°C?

5 A cylinder of capacity 20 L is filled with H_2 gas. The total average kinetic energy of translatory motion of its molecules is 1.5×10^5 J. What is the pressure of hydrogen in the cylinder?

6 The temperature of a gas consisting of rigid diatomic molecules is $T = 300$ K. Calculate the angular root mean square velocity of a rotating molecule if its moment of inertia is $I = 2.0 \times 10^{-40}$ kg m^2.

5.8 Internal Energy

1 A balloon has 5.0 mole of helium at 7°C. Calculate the total internal energy of the system.

2 2.8 g of N_2 is kept in a closed container initially at 30.0°C. The container is now heated. Neglecting the expansion of the container, calculate the temperature at which the internal energy is increased by 25 J. $[R = 25/3 \text{ J-mol}^{-1}\text{K}^{-1}]$

3 A light container having a diatomic gas enclosed within a moving with velocity v. Mass of the gas is M and number of moles is n.
(a) What is the kinetic energy of gas w.r.t. centre of mass of the system?
(b) What is the kinetic energy of gas w.r.t. ground?

4 16 g of oxygen at 67°C is mixed with 2 g of helium at 27°C. Find the temperature of the mixture.

5 If 2 moles of He are mixed with 3 moles of O_2, find γ for the mixture.

5.9 Ideal Gas Equation

1 Find the number of molecules contained in a vessel of volume 7 L at 0°C at 1.3×10^5 Pa.

2 Find density of methane gas at 27°C and 5 atm pressure. $[R = 25/3 \text{ J-mol}^{-1}\text{K}^{-1}]$

3 By increasing temperature of gas by 5°C, its pressure increases by 0.5% from its initial value at constant volume, then what is initial temperature of gas?

4 During an experiment, an ideal gas is found to obey an additional law Vp^2 = constant. The gas is initially at temperature T and volume V. What will be the temperature of the gas when it expands to a volume $2V$?

5 Equal masses of air are sealed in two vessels, one of the volume V_0 and the other of volume $2V_0$. If the first vessel is maintained at a temperature 300 K and the other at 600 K, find the ratio of the pressures in the two vessels.

6 A cylinder contains gas at 2×10^5 Pa and 47°C. The cylinder is steadily heated. Neglecting any change in its volume, find the temperature at which the cylinder will break if the walls of cylinder can bear a maximum pressure of 8×10^5 Pa.

7 A closed container of volume 0.02 m^3 contains a mixture of neon and argon gases at a temperature of 27°C and pressure of $1 \times 10^5 \text{ Nm}^2$. The total mass of the mixture is 28 g. If the gram molecular weight of neon and argon are 20 and 40 respectively, find the masses of the individual gases in the container, assuming them to be ideal. Given, $R = 8.314$ J/mol/K.

8 When 2 g of a gas A are introduced into an evacuated flask kept at 25°C, the pressure is found to be 1 atm. If 3 g of another gas B added to the same flask, the pressure becomes 1.5 atm. What is the ratio of the molecular weights of gas A and gas B?

9 The capacity of a vessel is 6 L. It contains 16 g oxygen, 14 g nitrogen and 11 g CO_2 mixture at 27°C. If $R = 8.31$ J/mol-K, then what will be the pressure in the vessel?

10 Oxygen is contained in a vessel of volume 0.05 m^3 at a temperature of 47°C and pressure $2 \times 10^5 \text{ N/m}^2$. When some of the gas is used, the pressure in the vessel falls to $0.8 \times 10^5 \text{ N/m}^2$ and temperature remains at 47°C. Find the mass of oxygen used. $(R = 25/3 \text{ J mol}^{-1}\text{K}^{-1})$

11 At a pressure of 2 atm air (treated as an ideal gas) is pumped into the tubes of a cycle rickshaw. The volume of each tube at given pressure is 0.002 m^3. One of the tubes gets punctured and the volume of the tube reduces to 0.0005 m^3. Find the number of moles of air that have leaked out. Assume that the temperature remains constant at 300 K. $(R = 25/3 \text{ J mol}^{-1}\text{K}^{-1})$

12 An open vessel contains air at 27°C. If the vessel is heated, one third of the air escapes from the vessel. What is the temperature to which the vessel is heated?

13 In given figure, A uniform cylindrical tube closed at one end, contains a pallet of mercury 5 cm long. When the tube is kept vertically with the closed end downward, the length of the air column trapped is 30 cm.

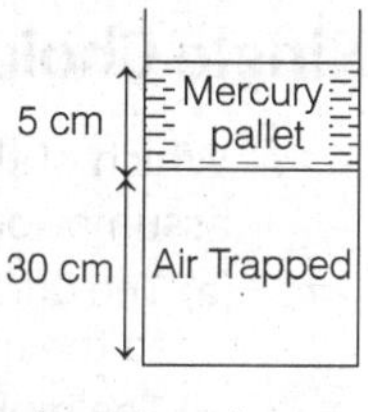

Now the tube is inverted, so that the closed end goes up. Find the new length of the air column trapped. Atmospheric pressure = 75 cm of mercury.

(Assume temperature remains constant in this process)

14 Two identical containers joined by a small pipe initially contain the same gas at pressure p_0 and absolute temperature T_0. One container is now maintained at the same temperature while the other is heated to $2T_0$. What will be the common pressure of the gases?

15 Two non-conducting containers contain monoatomic gas. They are connected as shown in figure. Pressure, volume and temperature in the two containers are $2p_0, 2V_0, T_0$ and $p_0, V_0, 2T_0$ respectively. Initially stopcock is closed, if the stopcock is opened find the final pressure and temperature.

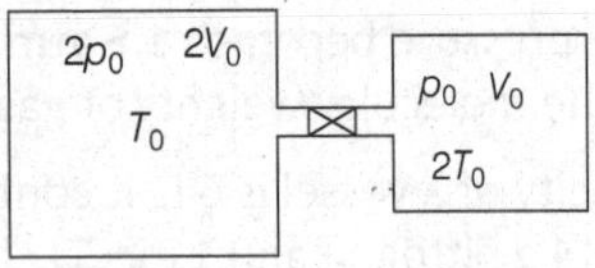

5.10 Graphs of Different Processes

1 Explain whether (a) $T_2 > T_1$ (b) $p_2 > p_1$ (c) $V_2 > V_1$ or otherwise in figure. *a*, *b* and *c* which represent isothermal, isobaric and isochoric process respectively.

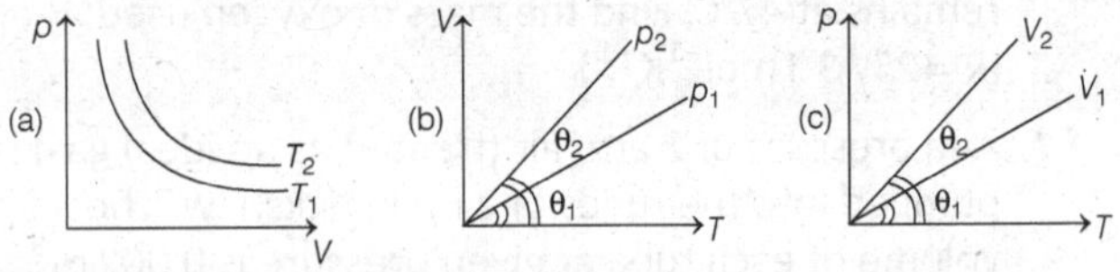

2 Examine the following plots and predict whether in
(a) $p_1 < p_2$ and $T_1 > T_2$, in
(b) $T_1 = T_2 < T_3$, in
(c) $V_1 > V_2$, in
(d) $p_1 > p_2$ or otherwise.

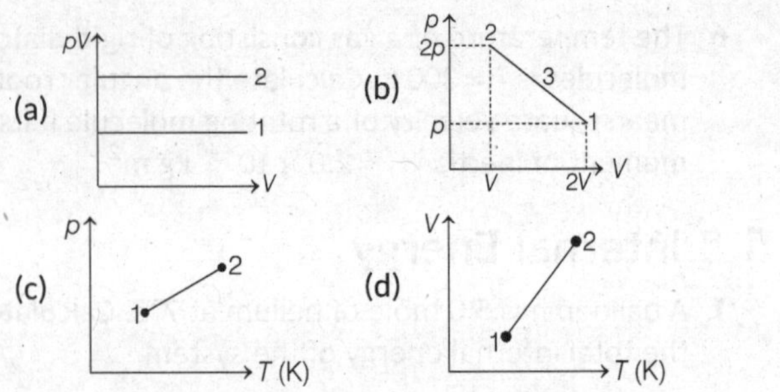

3 In the given *p*-*V* diagram if the temperature of point *A* is T_0, find the temperature at points *B* and *C*. Also, draw *p*-*T* and *V*-*T* diagrams of given process.

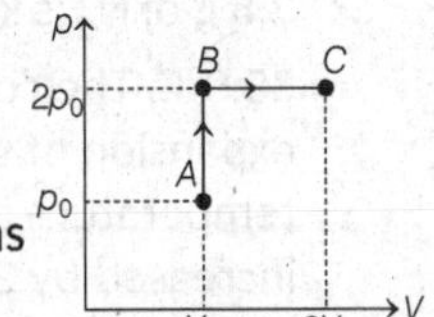

4 An ideal gas undergoes a cycle process *ABCA* as shown in figure. Plot the same process on *p*-*V* and *p*-*T* diagrams.

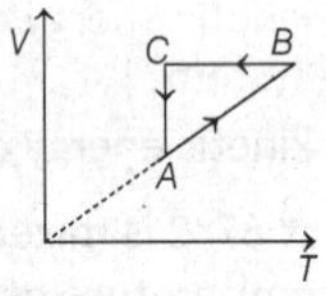

5 An ideal gas is under taken the cyclic process *ABCDA* as shown in the diagram. Draw the corresponding *T*-*V* curve and *p*-*T* curve.

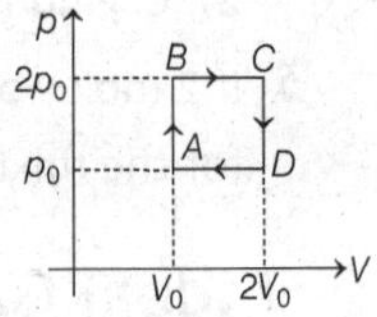

6 The figure shows, the *p*-*V* diagram of a thermodynamic cycle. Process *BC* and *DA* are isothermal. Draw the corresponding *p*-*T* and *V*-*T* diagrams of this cycle.

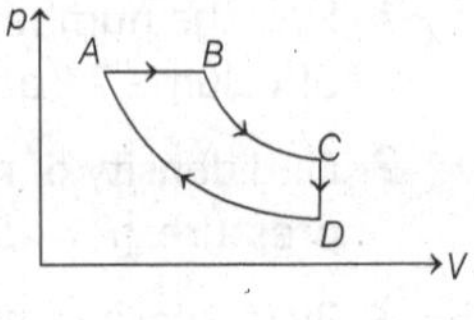

LEVEL 02 JEE Main Level

Single Choice Correct Questions

1 Which of the following statements is/are not an assumption of the kinetic theory for an ideal gas?
(a) The duration of a collision is negligible as compared to the time between successive collisions.
(b) The molecules have negligible attraction for each other.
(c) The molecules have negligible momentum change on collision with the container walls.
(d) There is no total kinetic energy change of the molecules on colliding with each other or with the walls of the container.

2 A gas behaves more closely like an ideal gas at
(a) low pressure and low temperature
(b) low pressure and high temperature
(c) high pressure and low temperature
(d) at all pressure and temperature

3 The average velocity of molecules of a gas of molecular weight *M* at temperature *T* is
(a) 0 (b) $\sqrt{\frac{3RT}{M}}$
(c) $\sqrt{\frac{8RT}{\pi M}}$ (d) $\sqrt{\frac{2RT}{M}}$

4 1 mole of an ideal gas is contained in a cubical volume V, $ABCDEFGH$ at 300 K (Figure). One face of the cube ($EFGH$) is made up of a material which totally absorbs any gas molecule incident on it. At any given time,

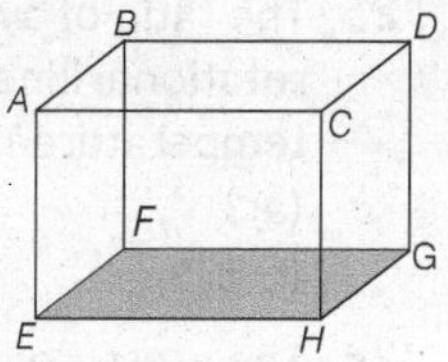

(a) the pressure on $EFGH$ would be zero
(b) the pressure on $EFGH$ would be half that on $ABCD$
(c) the pressure of $EFGH$ would be double the pressure on $ABCD$
(d) the pressure on all the faces will the equal

5 Three particles have speeds of $2u$, $10u$ and $11u$. Which of the following statements is correct?
(a) The rms speed exceeds the mean speed by about u.
(b) the mean speed exceeds the rms speed by about u.
(c) The rms speed equals the mean speed.
(d) The rms speed exceeds the mean speed by more than $2u$.

6 The temperature at which the rms velocity of oxygen molecules equal that of nitrogen molecules at 100°C is nearly
(a) 426.3 K (b) 456.3 K
(c) 436.3 K (d) 446.3 K

7 A temperature T, the root mean square velocity of oxygen molecules is v. If the temperature is doubled, gas dissociates and converts into atomic oxygen. Now the root mean square velocity will be
(a) $v/2$ (b) v
(c) $2v$ (d) $v\sqrt{2}$

8 The root mean square speed of the molecules of a gas enclosed in a vessel is v. If the pressure is doubled while the temperature remains the same, the root mean square speed will be
(a) $v/2$ (b) v
(c) $2v$ (d) $4v$

9 If the rms velocity of oxygen molecule at certain temperature is 0.5 km/s, the rms velocity for hydrogen molecule at the same temperature will be
(a) 2 km/s (b) 4 km/s
(c) 9 km/s (d) 16 km/s

10 The rms speed of the molecules of a gas in a vessel is 400 m/s. If half of the gas leaks out, at constant temperature, the speed of the remaining molecules will be
(a) 800 m/s (b) $400\sqrt{2}$ m/s
(c) 400 m/s (d) 200 m/s

11 The temperature of a gas is doubled (i) on absolute scale (ii) on centigrade scale. The increase in root mean square velocity of gas will be
(a) more in case (i)
(b) more in case (ii)
(c) same in both case
(d) Information not sufficient

12 Three closed vessels A, B, and C are at the same temperature T and contain gases which obey the Maxwell distribution of speed. Vessel A contains only O_2, B only N_2 and C a mixture of equal quantities of O_2 and N_2. If the average speed of O_2 molecules in vessel A is v_1, that of the N_2 molecules in vessel B is v_2, the average speed of the O_2 molecules in vessel C will be
(a) $\frac{v_1 + v_2}{2}$ (b) v_1
(c) $(v_1 v_2)^{1/2}$ (d) $\frac{v_1}{2}$

13 Suppose a container is evacuated to leave just one molecule of a gas in it. Let v_{mp} and v_{av} represent the most probable speed and the average speed of the gas, then
(a) $v_{mp} > v_{av}$ (b) $v_{mp} < v_{av}$
(c) $v_{mp} = v_{av}$ (d) None of these

14 One mole of an ideal gas at STP is heated in an insulated closed container until the average speed of its molecules is doubled. Its pressure would therefore increase by factor.
(a) 1.5 (b) $\sqrt{2}$ (c) 2 (d) 4

15 An ideal gas is held in a container of volume V at pressure p. The average speed of a gas molecule under these conditions is v. If now the volume and pressure are changed to $2V$ and $2p$, the average speed of a molecule will be
(a) $v/2$ (b) v
(c) $2v$ (d) $4v$

16 Gas at pressure p_0 is contained in a vessel. If the masses of all the molecules are halved and their speed doubled, the resulting pressure p will be equal to
(a) $4p_0$ (b) $2p_0$ (c) p_0 (d) $p_0/2$

17 Calculate the value of mean free path for oxygen molecules at temperature 27°C and pressure 1.01×10^5 Pa. Assume the molecular diameter 0.3 nm and the gas is ideal.
(a) 102 nm (b) 32 nm
(c) 58 nm (d) 86 nm

18 The average translational kinetic energy per molecule of an ideal gas at 0°C ($k = 1.38 \times 10^{-23}$ J/K) is

(a) 5.65×10^{-21} J (b) 9.5×10^{-23} J
(c) 6.5×10^{-21} J (d) 11.3×10^{-22} J

19 If the kinetic energy of one gram molecule of a gas at 27°C is E, what will it be at 627°C?

(a) $2E$ (b) $3E$
(c) $(627/27)E$ (d) $(27/627)E$

20 The pressure p of an ideal gas and its translational kinetic energy per unit volume E are related as

(a) $p = \frac{1}{2}E$ (b) $p = E$
(c) $p = \frac{3}{5}E$ (d) $p = \frac{2}{3}E$

21 The average translational energy and the rms speed of molecules in a sample of oxygen gas at 300 K are 6.21×10^{-21} J and 484 m/s respectively. The corresponding values at 600 K are nearly (assuming ideal gas behaviour)

(a) 12.42×10^{-21} J, 968 m/s
(b) 8.78×10^{-21} J, 684 m/s
(c) 6.21×10^{-21} J, 968 m/s
(d) 12.42×10^{-21} J, 684 m/s

22 The average translational kinetic energy of O_2 (molar mass 32) molecules at a particular temperature is 0.048 eV. The translational kinetic energy of N_2 (molar mass 28) molecules in eV at the same temperature is

(a) 0.0015 (b) 0.003
(c) 0.048 (d) 0.768

23 A box contains N molecules of a perfect gas at temperature T_1 and pressure p_1. The number of molecules in the box is doubled keeping the total kinetic energy of the gas same as before. If the new pressure and temperature are p_2 are T_2 respectively, then

(a) $p_2 = p_1, T_2 = T_1$ (b) $p_2 = p_1, T_2 = T_1/2$
(c) $p_2 = 2p_1, T_2 = T_1$ (d) $p_2 = 2p_1, T_2 = T_1/2$

24 A vessel contains a mixture of one mole of oxygen and two moles of nitrogen at 300 K. The ratio of the average rotational kinetic energy per O_2 molecule to that per N_2 molecule is

(a) 1 : 1
(b) 1 : 2
(c) 2 : 1
(d) depend on the moment of inertia of two molecules

25 The ratio of average translational kinetic energy to rotational kinetic energy of a diatomic molecule at temperature T is

(a) 3 (b) 7/5
(c) 5/3 (d) 3/2

26 The pressure, volume and adiabatic exponent of an ideal gas are p, V and γ respectively. Then, the internal energy of the gas is

(a) pV (b) $(3/2)pV$
(c) $pV/(\gamma - 1)$ (d) γpV

27 If the internal energy of n_1 moles of He at temperature $10T$ is equal to the internal energy of n_2 moles of hydrogen at temperature $6T$. The ratio of $\frac{n_1}{n_2}$ is

(a) $\frac{3}{5}$ (b) 2 (c) 1 (d) $\frac{5}{3}$

28 A gas mixture consists of 2 moles of oxygen and 4 moles of argon at temperature T. Neglecting all vibrational modes, the total internal energy of the system is

(a) $4RT$ (b) $15RT$
(c) $9RT$ (d) $11RT$

29 If 2 moles of an ideal monoatomic gas at temperature T_0 is mixed with 4 moles of another ideal monoatomic gas at temperature $2T_0$, then the temperature of the mixture is

(a) $\frac{5}{3}T_0$ (b) $\frac{3}{2}T_0$ (c) $\frac{4}{3}T_0$ (d) $\frac{5}{4}T_0$

30 A diatomic gas of molecules weight 30 g/mol is filled in a container at 27°C. It is moving at a velocity 100 m/s. If it is suddenly stopped, the rise in temperature of gas is

(a) $\frac{60}{R}$ (b) $\frac{600}{R}$
(c) $\frac{6 \times 10^4}{R}$ (d) $\frac{6 \times 10^5}{R}$

31 Two moles of a monoatomic gas are mixed with 1 mole of a diatomic gas. The γ for the mixture is

(a) 5/3 (b) 7/5
(c) 4/3 (d) 17/11

32 The quantity $\frac{pV}{kT}$ represents

(a) mass of the gas
(b) kinetic energy of the gas
(c) number of molecules in the gas
(d) number of moles of the gas

33 A vessel contains 1 mole of O_2 gas (molar mass 32) at a temperature T. The pressure of the gas is p. An identical vessel contaiing one mole of He gas (molar mass 4) at a temperature $2T$ has a pressure of
(a) $p/8$ (b) p (c) $2p$ (d) $8p$

34 A rigid tank contains 35 kg of nitrogen at 6 atm. Sufficient quantity of oxygen is supplied to increase the pressure to 9 atm, while the temperature remains constant. Amount of oxygen supplied to the tank is
(a) 5 kg (b) 10 kg (c) 20 kg (d) 40 kg

35 A closed vessel contain 8 g of oxygen and 7 g of nitrogen. The total pressure is 10 atm at a given temperature. If now oxygen is absorbed by introducing a column absorbent, the pressure of the remaining gas will be
(a) 2 atm (b) 4 atm (c) 5 atm (d) 10 atm

36 A vessel of volume $0.02\ m^3$ contains a mixture of hydrogen and helium at 20°C and 2 atmospheric pressure. The mass of mixture is 5 g. Find the ratio of mass of hydrogen to that of helium in the mixture.
(a) 1 : 2 (b) 1 : 3 (c) 2 : 3 (d) 3 : 2

37 A vessel with open mouth contains air at 60°C. When the vessel is heated upto temperature T, one fourth of the air goes out. The value of T is
(a) 80°C (b) 171°C (c) 333°C (d) 444°C

38 Hydrogen gas is filled in a vessel at 20°C at a certain pressure. Some gas is allowed to escape from the vessel and the temperature of the vessel is then raised to 40°C to obtain the same pressure. Then, the fraction of the gas allowed to escape is
(a) 0.068 (b) 0.500 (c) 0.193 (d) 0.936

39 The gas in vessel is subjected to a pressure of 20 atmosphere at a temperature 27°C. The pressure of the gas in a vessel after one half of the gas is released from the vessel and the temperature of the remainder is raised by 50°C is
(a) 8.5 atm (b) 10.8 atm
(c) 11.7 atm (d) 17 atm

40 Figure shows two flasks connected to each other. The volume of the flask 1 is twice that of flask 2. The system is filled with an ideal gas at temperature 100 K and 200 K respectively. If the mass of the gas in 1 be m, then what is the mass of the gas in flask 2?

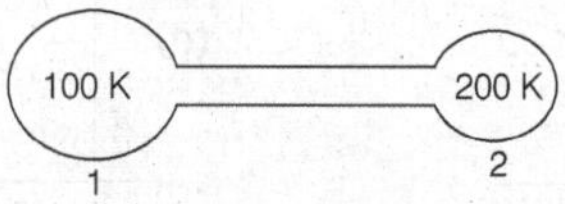

(a) m (b) $m/2$ (c) $m/4$ (d) $m/8$

41 12 g of gas occupy a volume of $4 \times 10^{-3}\ m^3$ at a temperature of 7°C. After the gas is heated at constant pressure, its density becomes 6×10^{-4} g/cc. What is the temperature to which the gas was heated?
(a) 1000 K (b) 1400 K
(c) 1200 K (d) 800 K

42 If a mixture of 28 g of nitrogen, 4 g of hydrogen and 8 g of helium is contained in a vessel at temperature 400 K and pressure 8.3×10^5 Pa, the density of the mixture will be
(a) 3 kg/m^3
(b) 0.2 kg/m^3
(c) 2 g/L
(d) 1.5 g/L

43 Two spherical vessel of equal volume, are connected by a narrow tube. The apparatus contains an ideal gas at 1 atm and 300 K. Now if one vessel is immersed in a bath of constant temperature 600 K and the other in a bath of constant temperature 300 K, then what will be the common pressure?

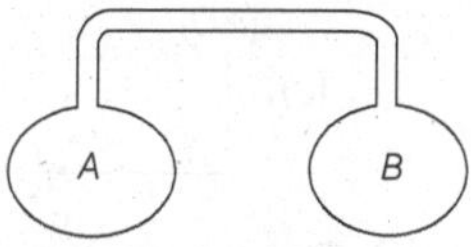

(a) 4/3 atm (b) 5/3 atm
(c) 6/5 atm (d) 8/5 atm

44 A closed gas cylinder is divided into two parts by a piston held tight. The pressure and volume of gas in two parts respectively are (p, $5V$) and ($10p$, V). If now the piston is left free and the system undergoes isothermal process, then the volume of the gas in two parts respectively are
(a) $2V$, $4V$ (b) $3V$, $3V$
(c) $5V$, V (d) $4V$, $2V$

45 A cylinder containing an ideal gas is in vertical position and has a piston of mass that is able to move up or down without friction (Figure). If the temperature is increased

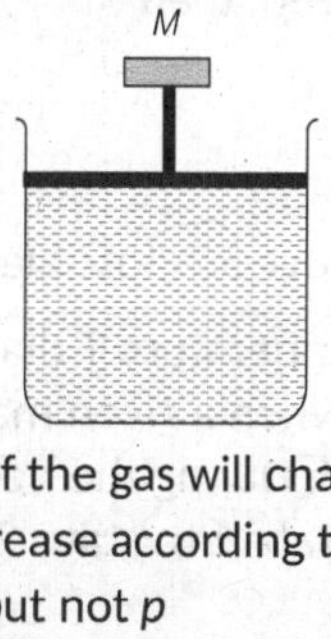

(a) Both p and V of the gas will change
(b) Only p will increase according to Charle's law
(c) V will change but not p
(d) p will change but not V

46 An ideal gas undergoes an adiabatic process obeying the relation $pV^{4/3}$ = constant. If its initial temperature is 300 K and then its pressure is increased upto four times its initial value, then the final temperature is (in Kelvin)
(a) $300\sqrt{2}$ (b) $300\sqrt[3]{2}$ (c) 600 (d) 1200

47 When the temperature of a gas in a vessel is increased by 1°C then its pressure is increased by 0.5%. The initial temperature is
(a) 100 K (b) 200 K (c) 273 K (d) 300 K

48 Which one of the following graphs most correctly illustrates the variation of the product (pressure × volume) for an ideal gas with thermodynamic temperature?

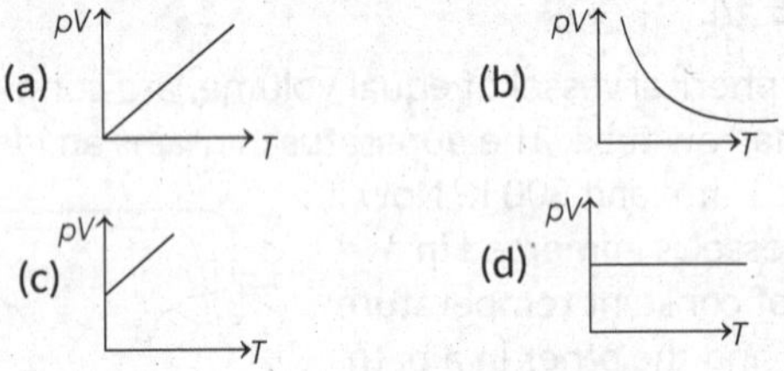

49 The expansion of an ideal gas of mass m at a constant pressure p is given by the straight line B. Then, the expansion of the same ideal gas of mass $2m$ at a pressure $2p$ is given by the straight line

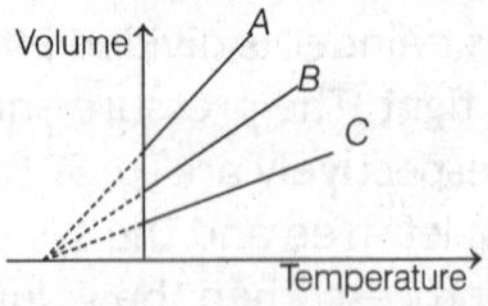

(a) C (b) A
(c) B (d) None of these

50 Two different isotherms representing the relationship between pressure p and volume V at the same temperature of the same ideal gas are shown for masses m_1 and m_2 of the gas respectively in the figure given, then

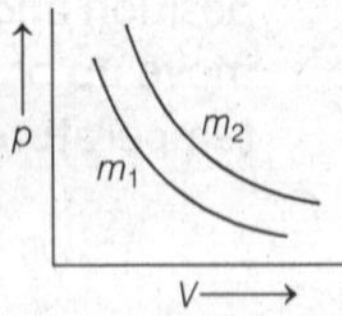

(a) $m_1 > m_2$
(b) $m_1 = m_2$
(c) $m_1 < m_2$
(d) All of the above are possible

51 A volume V-temperature T diagram was obtained when a given mass of gas was heated. During the heating process from state 1 to state 2, the pressure

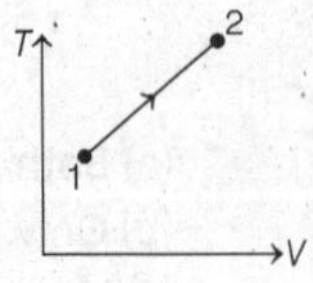

(a) remained constant (b) decreased
(c) increased (d) changed erratically

52 The process AB is shown in the diagram. As the gas is taken from A to B, its temperature

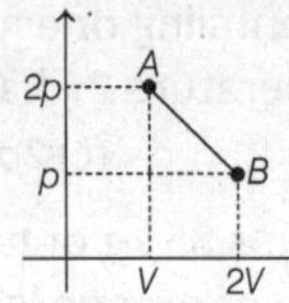

(a) initially increases then decreases
(b) initially decreases then increases
(c) remains constant
(d) variation depends on type of gas

53 Pressure *versus* temperature graph of an ideal gas is as shown in figure. Density of the gas at point A is ρ_0. Density at B will be

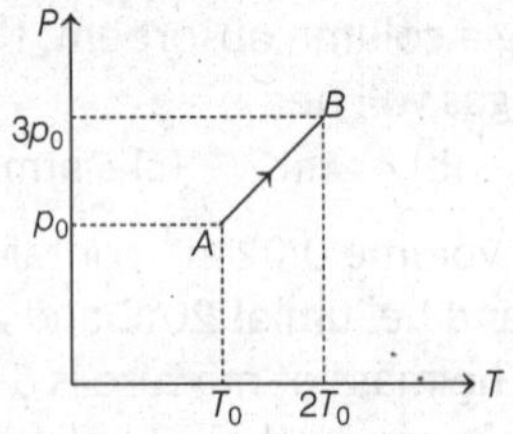

(a) $\frac{3}{4}\rho_0$ (b) $\frac{3}{2}\rho_0$
(c) $\frac{4}{3}\rho_0$ (d) $2\rho_0$

54 Figure shows graphs of pressure *versus* density for an ideal gas at two temperatures T_1 and T_2.

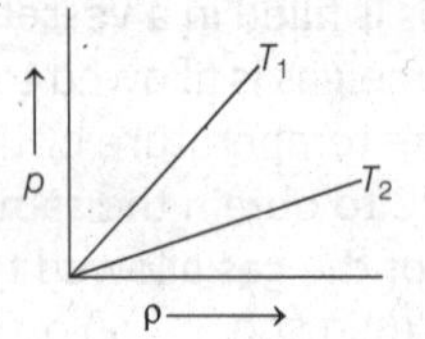

(a) $T_1 > T_2$ (b) $T_1 = T_2$
(c) $T_1 < T_2$ (d) None of these

55 Which of the following graphs correctly represents of variation of $\beta = -\frac{1}{V}\frac{dV}{dp}$ with p for an ideal gas at constant temperature?

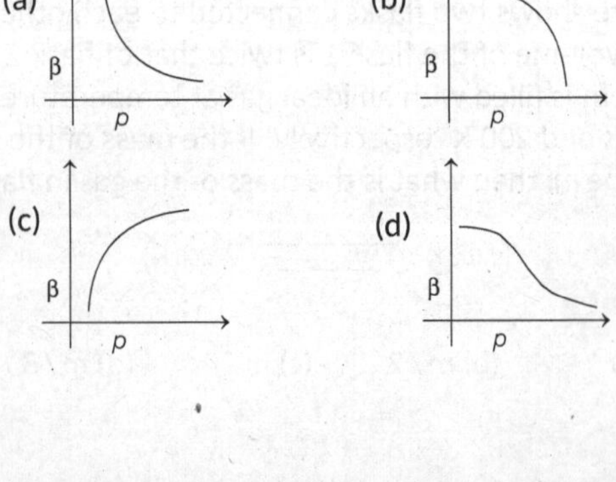

56 Figure shows *V-T* graph of a cyclic process. Which of the following *p-V* graph represents the same process?

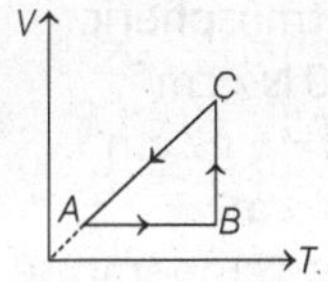

(a) 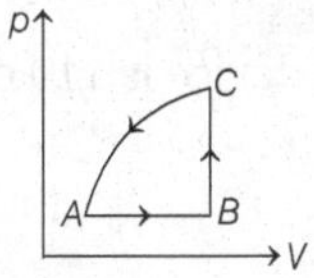

(b) 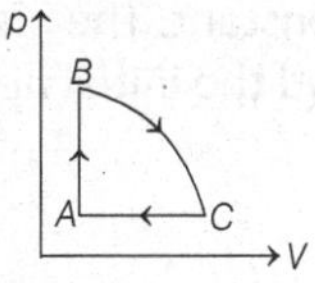

(c) 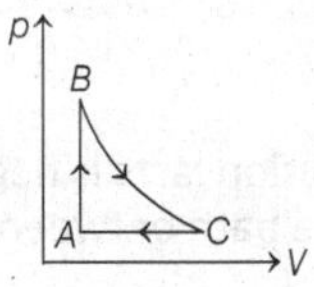

(d) 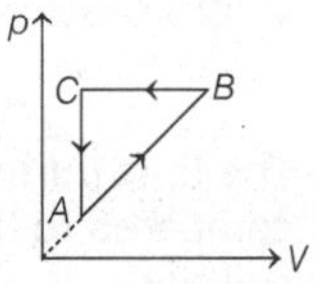

57 A cyclic process is shown on the *V-T* diagram. The same process on a *p-T* diagram is shown by

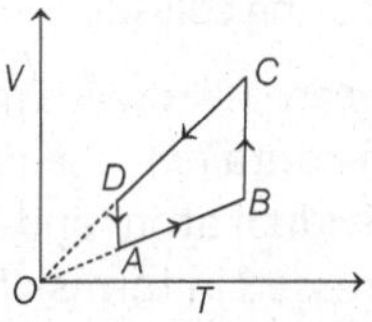

(a) 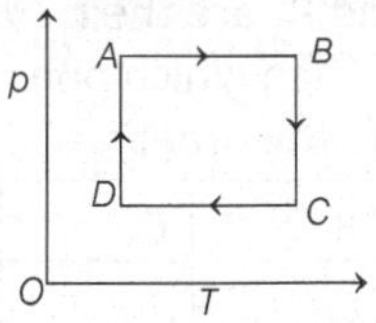

(b) 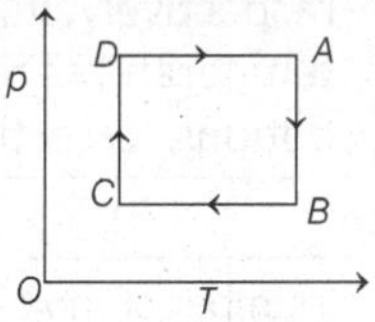

(c) 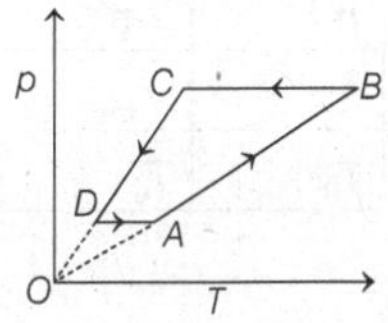

(d) 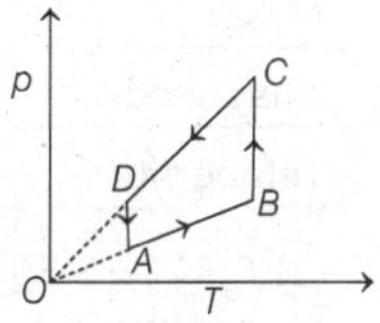

58 One mole of an ideal gas undergoes a process

$$p = p_0\left[1+\left(\frac{2V_0}{V}\right)^2\right]^{-1}$$, where p_0, V_0 are constants. Change in temperature of the gas when volume is changed from $V = V_0$ to $V = 2V_0$ is

(a) $\frac{4}{5}\frac{p_0V_0}{nR}$

(b) $\frac{3}{4}\frac{p_0V_0}{nR}$

(c) $\frac{2}{3}\frac{p_0V_0}{nR}$

(d) $\frac{7}{9}\frac{p_0V_0}{nR}$

Numerical Value Questions

1 A vessel of volume $V = 5$ L contains 1.4 g nitrogen and 0.4 g of He at 1500 K. If 30% of the nitrogen molecules are dissociated into atoms, then the gas pressure becomes $(N/8) \times 10^5$ N/m^2. Find *N* (Assume temperature to be constant). [$R = 25/3$ J/mol K]

2 5 g of helium having rms speed of molecules 1000 m/s and 24 g of oxygen having rms speed of 1000 m/s are introduced in a thermally isolated vessel. Find the rms speed (in m/s) of oxygen when thermal equilibrium is attained.

3 1 kg of diatomic gas is at a pressure of 8×10^4 N/m^2. The density of gas is 4 kg/m^3. What is the energy (in kJ) of the gas due to its thermal motion?

4 In a glass tube filled with a gas and closed by a mercury column of length 8 cm, if you hold the tube such that its open end is up, the length of the gas column is 4 cm, but if you hold the tube with its open end down, the length of the gas column is 5 cm. What is the atmospheric pressure (in cm) of mercury column?

5 *V-T* curve for 2 moles of a gas is straight line as shown in the graph here. If the pressure of gas at *A* is $\beta \times 10^4$ N/m^2, then find the value of β. [$R = 25/3$ J/mol K]

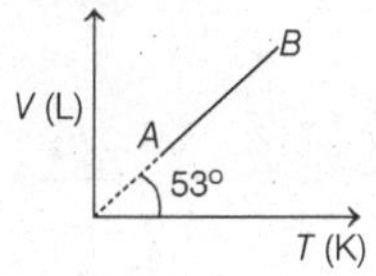

6 At a temperature *T* K, the pressure of 4.0 g argon in a bulb is *p*. The bulb is put in a bath having temperature higher by 50 K, than the first one. 0.8 g of argon gas had to be removed to maintain the original pressure. What is the value of *T*?

7 An empty pressure cooker of volume 10 L contains air at atmospheric pressure 10^5 Pa and temperature of 27°C. It contains a whistle which has area of 0.1 cm^2 and weight of 100 g. What should be the temperature (in °C) of air inside, so that the whistle is just lifted up?

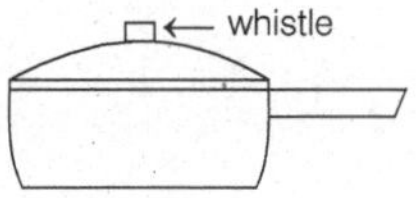

8 A vertical hollow cylinder of height 80 cm is fitted with a freely moving piston of negligible mass and thickness. The lower half portion of the cylinder contains an ideal gas at 31.5°C and the upper half is filled with mercury. To what temperature (in °C) the gas has to be heated, so that half of the mercury comes out of the cylinder? (Neglect thermal expansion of Hg. Atmospheric pressure is 76 cm of Hg).

9 An ideal gas is enclosed in a container as shown in figure. The spring constant is 100 N/m, the area of the piston is 1 cm^2 and the length of the gas column is 100 cm. The compression of the spring is 10 cm. There is no friction between the walls and the piston. The whole system is heated to make the temperature 2.4 times the original temperature. Find the distance moved by the piston (in cm).
Take, atmospheric pressure $= 10^5$ Pa.

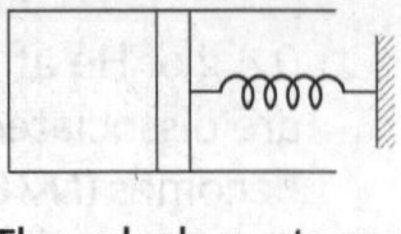

10 How far can one move (in cm) the piston of cross-section A_1, in the device shown in figure, so that 40% of the air enclosed remains? (The atmospheric pressure $p_0 = 10\ N/cm^2$, density of liquid $= 5\ g/cm^3$, $l = 20$ cm, $A_1 = 4\ cm^2$, $A_2 = 1\ cm^2$). The temperature is constant. The piston is massless and the initial height of gas in device is 110 cm.

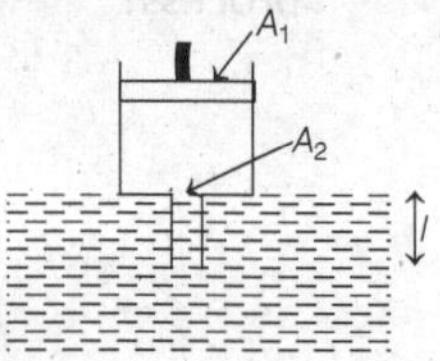

LEVEL 03 JEE Advanced Level

Single Choice Correct Questions

1 Consider a gas with mean density ρ and rms velocity *c*, when it is contained in a vessel. Now the vessel is fitted as shown in figure on a trolley, and the trolley is moving with a constant velocity *v*, then the pressure exerted by the gas on the vessel will be

(a) $\frac{1}{3}\rho c^2$
(b) $\frac{1}{3}\rho (c+v)^2$
(c) $\frac{1}{3}\rho (c-v)^2$
(d) $\frac{1}{3}\rho (c^2 - v^2)$

2 In the figure shown, *n* molecules of a gas of mass *nm* move only along *X*-axis (i.e., either towards +ve *X*-axis or –ve *X*-axis) inside a cube of edge 1 m. Half molecules have speed *v* and other half have 2*v*. The pressure on a wall perpendicular to *X*-axis is

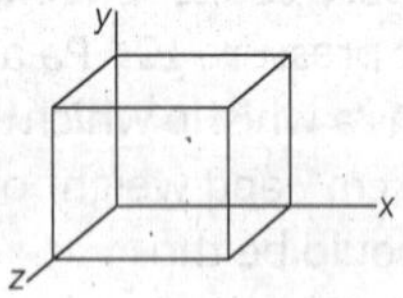

(a) $2.5nmv^2$
(b) $\frac{nmv^2}{5}$
(c) $\frac{3}{2}nmv^2$
(d) None of these

3 Select the incorrect statement about ideal gas.
(a) Molecules of a gas are in incessant random motion colliding against one another and with the walls of the container.
(b) The gas is not isotropic and the constant (1/3) in equation $p = (1/3)\rho v_{rms}^2$ is result of this property.
(c) The time during which a collision lasts is negligible compared to the time of free path between collisions.
(d) There is no force of interaction between molecules among themselves or between molecules and the wall except during collision.

4 Four containers are filled with monoatomic ideal gases. For each container, the number of moles, the mass of an individual atom and the rms speed of the atoms are expressed in terms of *n*, *m* and v_{rms} respectively. If T_A, T_B, T_C and T_D are their temperatures respectively, then which one of the options correctly represents the order?

	A	B	C	D
Number of moles	n	$3n$	$2n$	n
Mass	$4m$	m	$3m$	$2m$
rms speed	v_{rms}	$2v_{rms}$	v_{rms}	$2v_{rms}$
Temperature	T_A	T_B	T_C	T_D

(a) $T_B = T_C > T_A > T_D$
(b) $T_D > T_A > T_C > T_B$
(c) $T_D > T_A = T_B > T_C$
(d) $T_B > T_C > T_A > T_D$

5 The following graph shows two isotherms for a fixed mass of an ideal gas. The ratio of rms speed of the molecules at temperatures T_1 and T_2 is

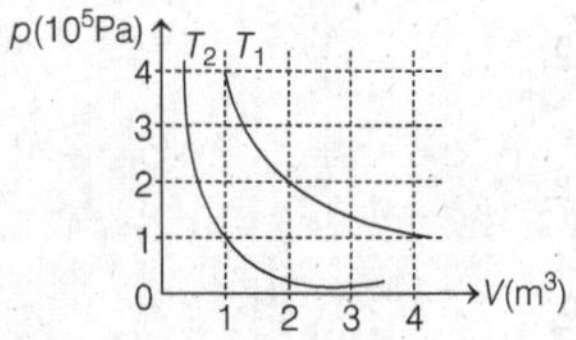

(a) $2\sqrt{2}$
(b) $\sqrt{2}$
(c) 2
(d) 4

6 A gas contains only rigid diatomic molecules at temperature T. If I is the moment of inertia of the molecule, then mean square angular velocity of the molecule is

(a) $\sqrt{kT/I}$ (b) $\sqrt{3kT/I}$
(c) $\sqrt{5kT/I}$ (d) $\sqrt{2kT/I}$

7 The root mean square velocity of all molecules in a mixture containing CO_2 and N_2 in the mole ratio 1 : 7 is found to be x times the root mean square velocity of CO_2 molecules at the same temperature. The value of x is

(a) $\sqrt{\frac{4}{5}}$ (b) $\sqrt{\frac{3}{2}}$
(c) $\sqrt{\frac{2}{3}}$ (d) None of these

8 At temperature T, N molecules of gas A each having mass m and at the same temperature $2N$ molecules of gas B each having mass $2m$ are filled in a container. The mean square velocity of molecules of gas B is v^2 and mean square of x component of velocity of molecules of gas A is w^2. The ratio of w^2/v^2 is

(a) 1 (b) 2 (c) 1/3 (d) 2/3

9 A vessel is partitioned in two equal halves by a fixed diathermic separator. Two different ideal gases are filled in left (L) and right (R) halves. The rms speed of the molecules in L part is equal to the mean speed of molecules in the R part. Then, the ratio of the mass of a molecule in L part to that of a molecule in R part is

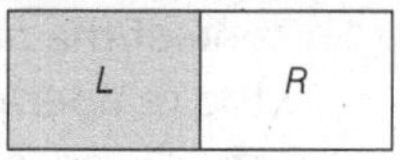

(a) $\sqrt{\frac{3}{2}}$ (b) $\sqrt{\frac{\pi}{4}}$ (c) $\sqrt{\frac{2}{3}}$ (d) $\frac{3\pi}{8}$

10 For a gas sample with N_0 number of molecules, function $N(v)$ is given by : $N(v) = \frac{dN}{dv} = \left(\frac{3N_0}{v_0^3}\right)v^2$ for $0 < v < v_0$ and $N(v) = 0$, for $v > v_0$ where dN is number of molecules in speed range v to $v + dv$. The rms speed of the molecules is

(a) $\sqrt{\frac{2}{5}}\,v_0$ (b) $\sqrt{\frac{3}{5}}\,v_0$ (c) $\sqrt{2}\,v_0$ (d) $\sqrt{3}\,v_0$

11 Assume a sample of a gas in a vessel. The speeds of molecules are between 2 m/s to 5 m/s. The number of molecules for speed v (m/s) is given by $n = 7v - v^2 - 10$. The most probable speed in the sample is

(a) 3.5 m/s (b) 5 m/s
(c) 10 m/s (d) 4 m/s

12 Let v denote the root mean square speed of the molecules in an ideal diatomic gas at absolute temperature T. The mass of a molecule is m. Neglecting vibrational energy terms, which is false?

(a) A molecule can have a speed greater than $\sqrt{2}\,v$
(b) v is proportional to $\sqrt{T}$
(c) The average rotational kinetic energy of a molecule is $\frac{mv^2}{4}$
(d) The average kinetic energy of a molecule is $\frac{5mv^2}{6}$

13 One mole of a diatomic gas undergoes a process $p = \frac{p_0}{1+\left(\frac{V}{V_0}\right)^2}$, where p_0 and V_0 are constants. The translational kinetic energy of the gas, when $V = V_0$ is given by

(a) $\frac{5p_0V_0}{4}$ (b) $\frac{3p_0V_0}{4}$
(c) $\frac{3p_0V_0}{2}$ (d) $\frac{5p_0V_0}{2}$

14 One mole of an ideal gas undergoes a process in which $T = T_0 + aV^3$, where T_0 and a are positive constants and V is volume. The volume for which pressure will be minimum is

(a) $\left(\frac{T_0}{2a}\right)^{1/3}$ (b) $\left(\frac{T_0}{3a}\right)^{1/3}$ (c) $\left(\frac{a}{2T_0}\right)^{2/3}$ (d) $\left(\frac{a}{3T_0}\right)^{2/3}$

15 In the above question, minimum pressure attainable is

(a) $\frac{3}{4}(a^{5/3}R^{2/3}T_0^{2/3})\,2^{1/3}$
(b) $\frac{3}{2}(a^{2/3}RT_0^{2/3})\,3^{1/2}$
(c) $\frac{3}{2}(a^{1/2}R^{2/3}T_0^{3/4})\,4^{1/3}$
(d) $\frac{3}{2}(a^{1/3}RT_0^{2/3})\,2^{1/3}$

16 A cylindrical tube of cross-sectional area A has two air tight frictionless pistons at its two ends. The pistons are tied with a straight piece of metallic wire. The tube contains a gas at atmospheric pressure p_0 and temperature T_0. If temperature of the gas is doubled, then the tension in the wire is

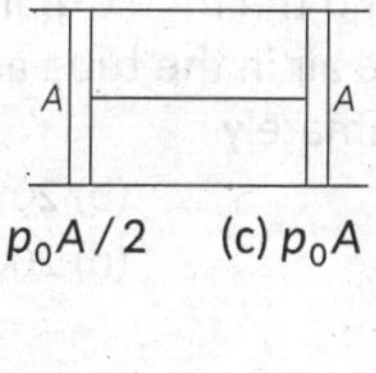

(a) $4p_0A$ (b) $p_0A/2$ (c) p_0A (d) $2p_0A$

17 A ring shaped tube contains two ideal gases with equal masses and molar masses $M_1 = 32$ and $M_2 = 28$. The gaseous are separated by one fixed partition P and another movable stopper S which can move freely without friction inside the ring. The angle α is

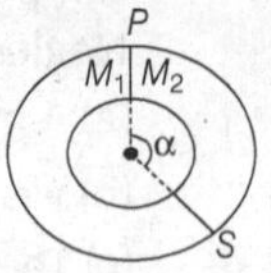

(a) 182° (b) 170°
(c) 192° (d) 180°

18 Two identical containers A and B with frictionless pistons contain the same ideal gas at the same temperature and the same volume V. The mass of the gas in A is m_A and that in B is m_B. The gas in each cylinder is now allowed to expand isothermally to the same final volume $2V$. The change in the pressure in A and B are found to be Δp and $1.5\Delta p$ respectively. Then,

(a) $4m_A = 9m_B$ (b) $2m_A = 3m_B$
(c) $3m_A = 2m_B$ (d) $9m_A = 4m_B$

19 An open and wide glass tube is immersed vertically in mercury in such a way that length 0.05 m extends above mercury level. The open end of the tube is closed and the tube is raised further by 0.43 m. The length of air column above mercury level in the tube will be (Take, $p_{atm} = 76$ cm of mercury)

(a) 0.215 m (b) 0.2 m (c) 0.1 m (d) 0.4 m

20 28 g of N_2 gas is contained in a flask at a pressure of 10 atm and at a temperature of 57°C. It is found that due to leakage in the flask, the pressure is reduced to half and the temperature reduces to 27°C. The quantity of N_2 gas that leaked out is

(a) 11/20 g (b) 20/11 g
(c) 5/63 g (d) 63/5 g

21 Two identical glass bulbs are interconnected by a thin glass tube. A gas is filled in these bulbs at NTP. If one bulb is placed in ice and another bulb is placed in hot bath, then the pressure of the gas become 1.5 times. The temperature of hot bath will be

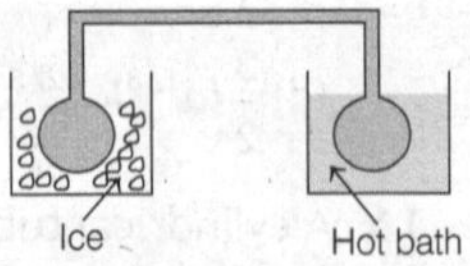

(a) 100°C (b) 182°C (c) 256°C (d) 546°C

22 Air is pumped into an automobile tube upto a pressure of 200 kPa in the morning when the air temperature is 22°C. During the day, temperature rises to 42°C and the tube expands by 2%. The pressure of the air in the tube at this temperature, will be approximately

(a) 212 kPa (b) 209 kPa
(c) 206 kPa (d) 200 kPa

23 An ideal monoatomic gas is confined in a cylinder by a spring-loaded piston of cross-section $8 \times 10^{-3}\ m^2$. Initially the gas is at 300 K and occupies a volume of $2.4 \times 10^{-3}\ m^3$ and the spring is in a relaxed state. The gas is heated by a small heater coil H. The force constant of the spring is 8000 N/m, and the atmospheric pressure is 1.0×10^5 Pa. The cylinder and piston are thermally insulated. The piston and the spring are massless and there is no friction between the piston and cylinder. There is no heat loss through heater coil wire leads and thermal capacity of the heater coil is negligible. With all the above assumptions, if the gas is heated by the heater until the piston moves out slowly by 0.1 m, then the final temperature is

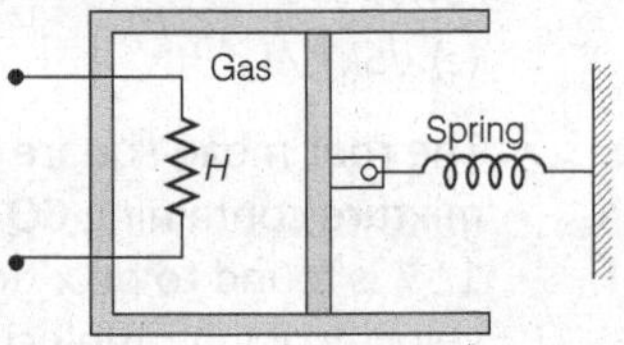

(a) 400 K (b) 800 K
(c) 1200 K (d) 300 K

24 A cylinder made of perfectly non conducting material closed at both ends is divided into two equal parts by a heat proof piston. Both parts of the cylinder contain the same masses of a gas at a temperature $T_0 = 27°C$ and pressure $p_0 = 1$ atm. Now if the gas in one of the parts is slowly heated to $T = 57°C$ while the temperature of other part is maintained at T_0, the distance moved by the piston from the middle of the cylinder will be (length of the cylinder = 84 cm)

(a) 3 cm (b) 5 cm
(c) 2 cm (d) 1 cm

25 An ideal gas of molar mass M is contained in a vertical tube of height H, closed at both ends. The tube is accelerating vertically upwards with acceleration g. Then, the ratio of pressure at the bottom and the mid-point of the tube will be

(a) $e^{\frac{2MgH}{RT}}$ (b) $e^{-\frac{2MgH}{RT}}$ (c) $e^{\frac{MgH}{RT}}$ (d) $\frac{MgH}{RT}$

26 Two pistons having low thermal conductivity divide an adiabatic container in three equal parts as shown. An ideal gas is present in the three parts A, B and C having initial pressures as shown and same temperatures. Now the pistons are released. Then, the final equilibrium length of part A after long time will be

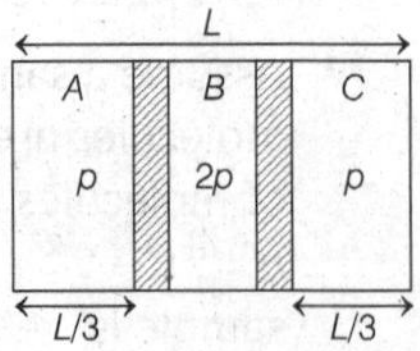

(a) $L/8$ (b) $L/4$
(c) $L/6$ (d) $L/5$

27 Two cylinders fitted with pistons and placed as shown, connected with string through a small tube of negligible volume, are filled with a gas at pressure p_0 and temperature T_0. The radius of smaller cylinder is half of the other. If the temperature is increased to $2T_0$, find the pressure, if the piston of bigger cylinder moves towards left by 1 m.

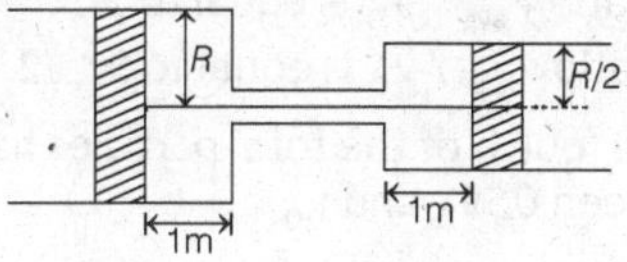

(a) $\frac{4}{5}p_0$ (b) $\frac{3}{5}p_0$ (c) $\frac{2}{5}p_0$ (d) $\frac{5}{4}p_0$

28 A vessel of volume V_0 contains an ideal gas at a pressure p_0. Gas is continuously pumped out of this vessel at a constant rate $\frac{dV}{dt} = r$, keeping the temperature constant. The pressure of the gas taken out equals the pressure inside the vessel. Find the pressure of the gas inside the vessel as a function of time

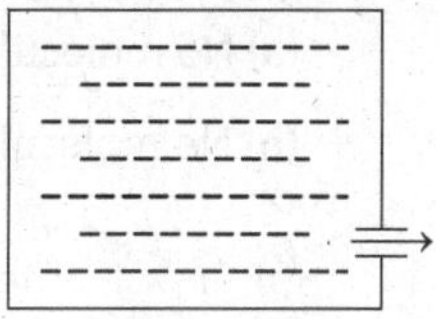

(a) $2p_0e^{-rt/V_0}$ (b) $3p_0e^{-rt/V_0}$
(c) $-p_0e^{-rt/V_0}$ (d) p_0e^{-rt/V_0}

29 An experiment is carried on a fixed amount of gas at different temperatures and at high pressure such that it deviates from the ideal gas behaviour. The variation of $\frac{pV}{RT}$ with p is shown in the diagram. The correct variation will correspond to

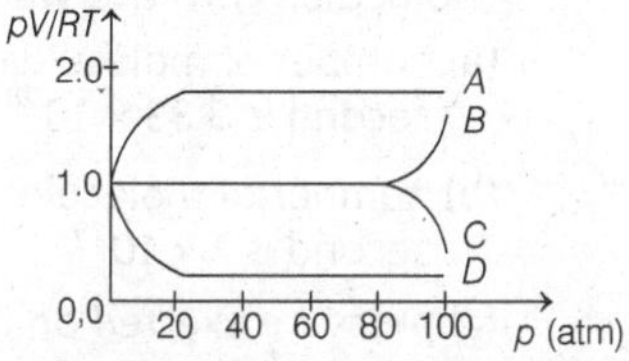

(a) curve A (b) curve B
(c) curve C (d) curve D

30 An ideal gas follows a process pT = constant. The correct graph between pressure and volume is

(a) 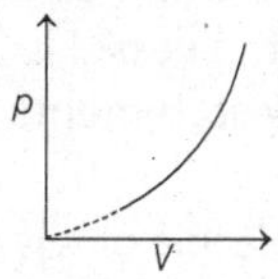

(b) 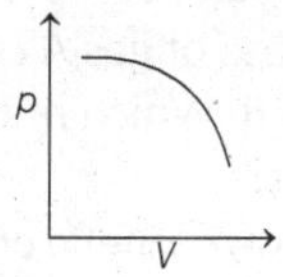

(b) 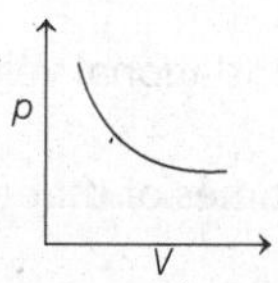

(d) 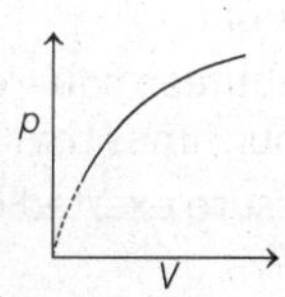

31 *pV versus T* graph of equal masses of H_2, He and CO_2 is shown in figure. Choose the correct alternative

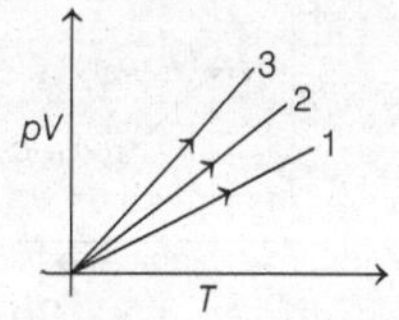

(a) 3 corresponds to H_2, 2 to He and 1 to CO_2
(b) 1 corresponds to He, 2 to H_2 and 3 to CO_2
(c) 1 corresponds to He, 3 to H_2 and 2 to CO_2
(d) 1 corresponds to CO_2, 2 to H_2 and 3 to He

32 Pressure *versus* temperature graphs of an ideal gas are as shown in figure. Choose the wrong statement.

(i) 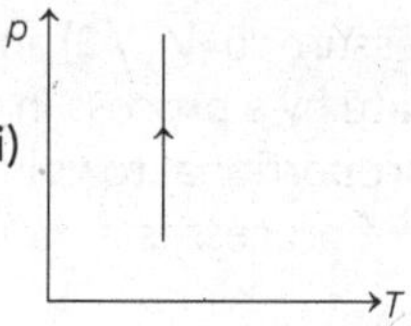

(ii) 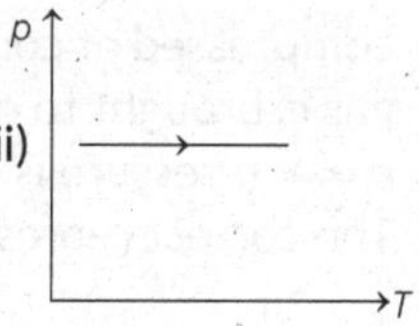

(iii) 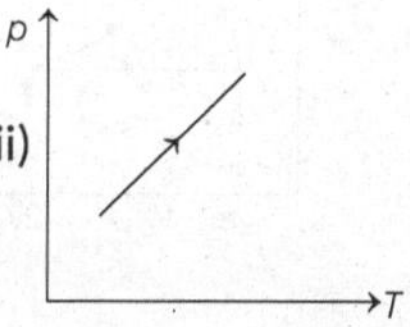

(a) Density of gas is increasing in graph (i)
(b) Density of gas decreasing in graph (ii)
(c) Density of gas is constant in graph (iii)
(d) None of the above

33 Variation of internal energy with density of 1 mole of monoatomic gas is depicted in figure. Corresponding variation of pressure with volume can be depicted as (assume the curve is rectangular hyperbola)

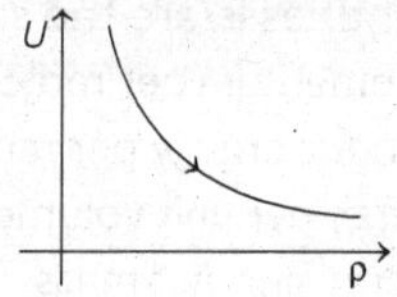

(a) 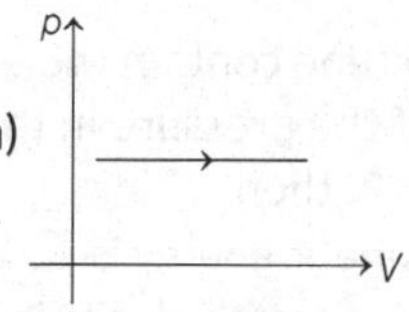

(b) 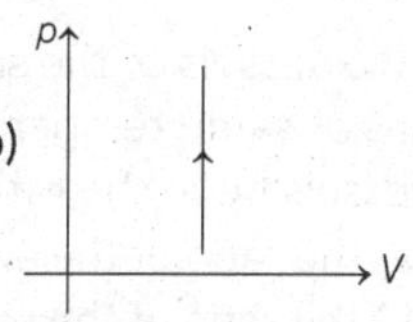

(c) 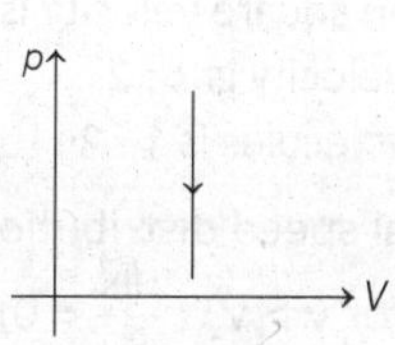

(d) 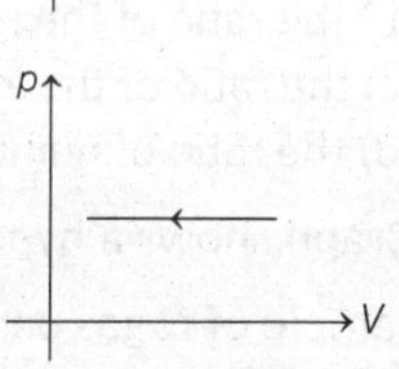

34 One mole of a gas expands obeying the relation as shown in the p-V diagram. The maximum temperature in this process is equal to

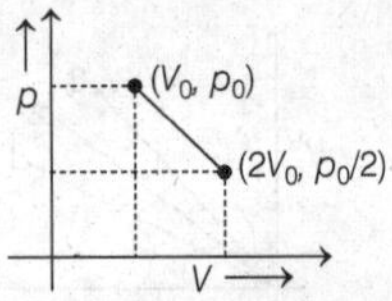

(a) $\frac{p_0V_0}{R}$ (b) $\frac{3p_0V_0}{R}$

(c) $\frac{9p_0V_0}{8R}$ (d) None of these

35 One mole of an ideal gas at pressure p_0, temperature T_0 and volume V_0 is expanded isothermally to twice its volume and then compressed at constant pressure to $(V_0/2)$ and the gas is brought to original state by a process in which $p \propto V$ (Pressure is directly proportional to volume). The correct representation of process is

(a)
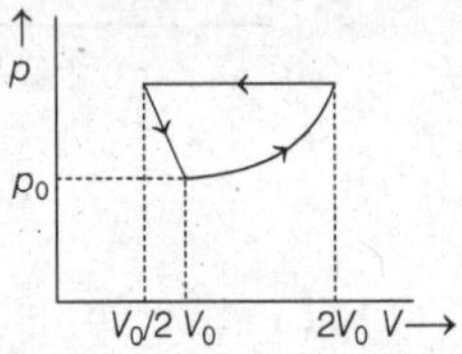

(b)
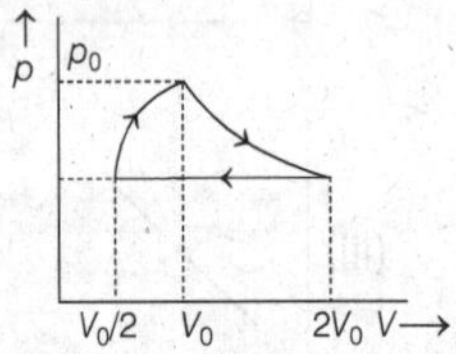

(c)
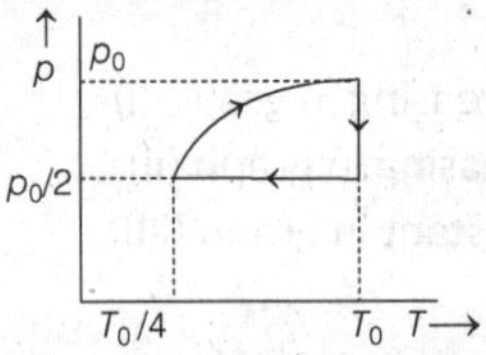

(d)
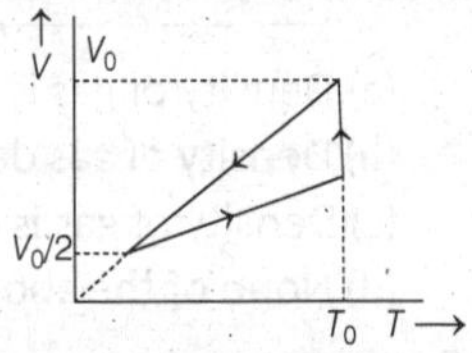

Multiple Choice(s) Correct Questions

1 In case of hydrogen and oxygen at NTP, which of the following quantities is/are the same?

(a) Average momentum per molecule

(b) Average kinetic energy per molecule

(c) Kinetic energy per unit volume

(d) Kinetic energy per unit mass

2 Two vessels of the same volume contain the same gas at same temperature. If the pressure in the vessels be in the ratio of 1 : 2, then

(a) the ratio of the average kinetic energy is 1 : 2

(b) the ratio of the root mean square velocity is 1 : 1

(c) the ratio of the average velocity is 1 : 2

(d) the ratio of number of molecules is 1 : 2

3 Graph shows a hypothetical speed distribution for a sample of N gas particles (for $v > v_0$; $\frac{dN}{dv} = 0$)

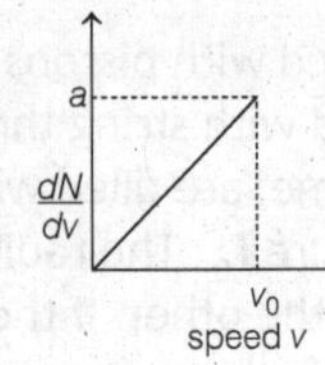

(a) The value of av_0 is $2N$.

(b) The ratio v_{avg}/v_0 is equal to 2/3.

(c) The ratio v_{rms}/v_0 is equal to $1/\sqrt{2}$.

(d) Three fourth of the total particles has a speed between $0.5v_0$ and v_0

4 Let $\bar{v}$, v_{rms} and v_p respectively denote the mean speed, the root mean square speed, and the most probable speed of the molecules in an ideal monoatomic gas at absolute temperature T. The mass of a molecule is m.

(a) No molecule can have speed greater than V_{rms}

(b) No molecule can have speed less than $\frac{V_p}{\sqrt{2}}$

(c) $v_p < \bar{v} < v_{rms}$

(d) The average kinetic energy of a molecule is $\frac{3}{4}mv_p^2$

5 A container holds 10^{26} molecules/m^3, each of mass 3×10^{-27} kg. Assume that 1/6 of the molecules move with velocity 2000 m/s directly towards one wall of the container while the remaining 5/6 of the molecules move either away from the wall or in perpendicular direction, and all collisions of the molecules with the wall are elastic

(a) number of molecules hitting 1 m^2 of the wall every second is 3.33×10^{28}.

(b) number of molecules hitting 1 m^2 of the wall every second is 2×10^{29}.

(c) pressure exerted on the wall by molecules is 24×10^5 Pa.

(d) pressure exerted on the wall by molecules is 4×10^5 Pa.

6 A closed vessel contains a mixture of two diatomic gases A and B. Molar mass of A is 16 times that of B and mass of gas A contained in the vessel is 2 times that of B. Which of the following statements are correct?

(a) Average kinetic energy per molecule of A is equal to that of B.

(b) Root mean square value of translational velocity of B is four times that of A.

(c) Pressure exerted by B is eight times of that exerted by A.

(d) Number of molecules of B, in the cylinder, is eight times that of A.

7 From the following statements, concerning ideal gas at any given temperature T, select the correct one(s).

(a) The coefficient of volume expansion at constant pressure is same for all ideal gases.

(b) The average translational kinetic energy per molecule of oxygen gas is $3kT$ (k being Boltzmann constant).

(c) In a gaseous mixture, the average translational kinetic energy of the molecules of each component is same.

(d) The mean free path of molecules increases with the decrease in pressure.

8 During an experiment, an ideal gas is found to obey a condition $p^2/\rho = \text{constant}$ [ρ = density of the gas]. The gas is initially at temperature T, pressure p and density ρ. The gas expands such that density changes to $\rho/2$.

(a) The temperature of the gas changes to $\sqrt{2}\,p$.

(b) The temperature of the gas changes to $\sqrt{2}\,T$.

(c) The graph of the above process on the p-T diagram is parabola.

(d) The graph of the above process on the p-T diagram is hyperbola.

9 A partition divides a container having insulated walls into two compartments I and II. The same gas fills the two compartments whose initial parameters are given. The partition is a conducting wall which can move freely without friction.

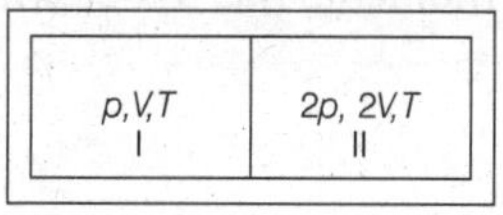

Which of the following statements is/are correct, with reference to the final equilibrium position?

(a) The pressure in the two compartments are equal.

(b) Volume of compartment I is $3V/5$

(c) Volume of compartment II is $12V/5$

(d) Final pressure in compartment I is $5p/3$

10 According to Maxwell's distribution of molecular speeds, for the below graph drawn for two different samples of gases A and B at temperature T_1 and T_2 respectively, while of the following statements is/are incorrect?

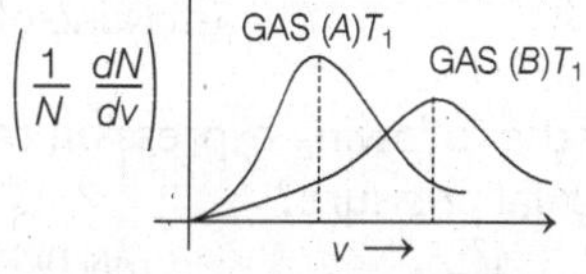

(a) If $T_1 = T_2$, then molecular mass of gas $B(M_B)$ is greater than molecular mass of gas $A(M_A)$.

(b) If molecular mass of gas $A(M_A)$ is equal to molecular mass of gas $B(M_B)$, then $T_1 > T_2$.

(c) If $T_1 < T_2$, then molecular mass of gas $B(M_B)$ is necessarily less than molecular mass of gas $A(M_A)$.

(d) If gas A is O_2 and gas B is N_2, then considering them to be ideal gases, T_1 is necessarily less than T_2.

11 A sample of ideal gas of constant mass is taken through the cyclic process shown in the figure. Plot this cyclic process on the (p, T) and (V, T) diagrams instead of the (p, V).

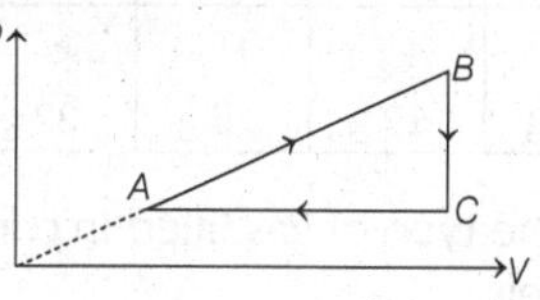

(a)
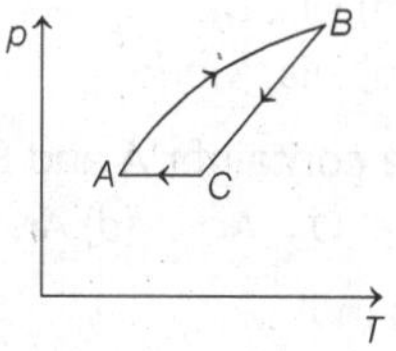

(b)
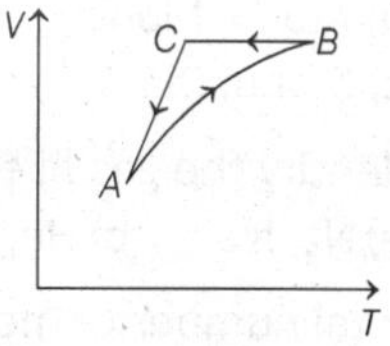

(c)
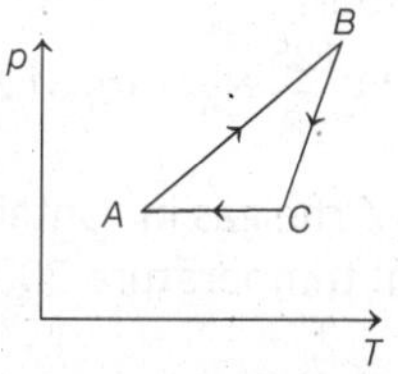

(d)
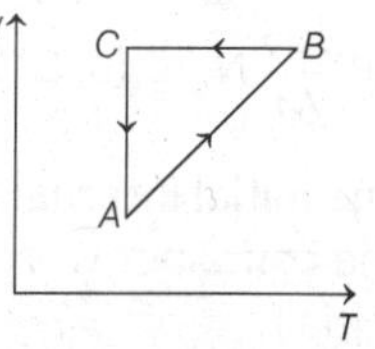

12 An ideal gas undergoes a process in which the number of collisions of the molecules per unit area of the wall in unit time is a constant. Then, for this process

(a) $pV = \text{constant}$ (b) $pV^{\gamma} = \text{constant}$

(c) $pV^{-1} = \text{constant}$ (d) $p^{-1}V = \text{constant}$

Comprehension Based Questions

Comprehension 1

Two closed identical conducting containers are found in the laboratory of an old scientist. For the verification of the gas some experiments are performed on the two boxes and the results are noted.

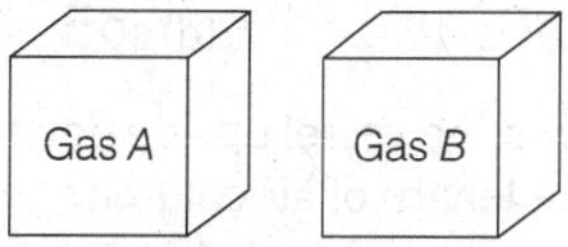

Experiment 1

When the two containers are weighed $W_A = 225$ g, $W_B = 160$ g and mass of evacuated container $W_C = 100$ g.

Experiment 2

When the two containers are given same amount of heat, same temperature rise is recorded. The pressure changes found are $\Delta p_A = 2.5$ atm, $\Delta p_B = 1.5$ atm.

Required data for unknown gas

Mono (molar mass)	He 4g	Ne 20 g	Ar 40 g	Kr 84 g	Xe 131 g	Rd 222 g
Dia (molar mass)	H_2 2 g	F_2 19 g	N_2 28 g	O_2 32 g	Cl_2 71 g	

1 Identify the type of gas filled in container A and B respectively.

(a) Mono, Mono (b) Dia, Dia
(c) Mono, Dia (d) Dia, Mono

2 Identify the gas filled in the container A and B.

(a) N_2, Ne (b) He, H_2 (c) O_2, Ar (d) Ar, O_2

3 Total number of molecules in A
(Here, N_A = Avogadro number)

(a) $\frac{125}{64}N_A$ (b) $3.125N_A$ (c) $\frac{125}{28}N_A$ (d) $31.25N_A$

4 The initial internal energy of the gas in container A, if the container were at room temperature 300 K initially

(a) 1406.25 cal (b) 1000 cal
(c) 2812.5 cal (d) None of these

Comprehension 2

Ram is in a fix. His mother has handed him an airtight container with a frictionless piston in it. The piston is such that, no air can leave the container or enter it. "Having studied so much of Physics, you should be able to get this out!" Commands the mom. Ram estimates that piston area is 10 cm^2 and the piston weighs 100 g. The atmospheric pressure is 1.01×10^5 Pa. He knows air is inside, nothing else. The temperature is 27°C. The height of air column is 10 cm. Take, $R = 25/3$ J/mol K.

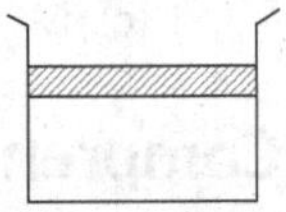

5 How many molecules of air are inside the vessel?

(a) 2.5×10^{21} (b) 5.0×10^{21}
(c) 7.5×10^{21} (d) 10^{22}

6 If Ram turns the vessel upside down isothermally, what is the length of air column?

(a) 9.8 cm (b) 10.2 cm (c) 10.4 cm (d) 10.6 cm

7 How much heat should be supplied to the vessel in this upside down situation, so that the volume doubles and the lid comes out?

(a) 35.7 J (b) 38.2 J (c) 27.3 J (d) 48.1 J

Comprehension 3

Consider the cylinder and piston arrangement as shown in the diagram. Initially the piston is fixed such that the volume of both the compartment is V. Initially the valve is closed.

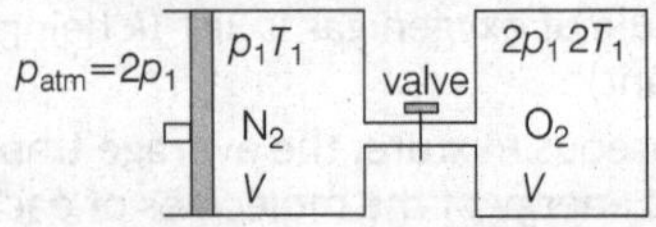

8 The ratio of initial number of moles $\frac{N_{left}}{N_{right}} =$

(a) 2 (b) 1/2 (c) 2/3 (d) 1

9 Now the valve is open and simultaneously piston is moved right side, so that the volume of left part becomes equal to $V/2$. At this moment the piston remains in equilibrium. Find out the final temperature of gas mixture.

(a) $\frac{3T_1}{2}$ (b) $\frac{2T_1}{3}$ (c) T_1 (d) $\frac{T_2}{2}$

Comprehension 4

Consider a cylindrical vessel of radius R and length L. If one molecule is present in it then the motion of that one molecule can be described by radial and axial velocities as shown. Now consider N molecules to be present. Each molecule has a mass m.

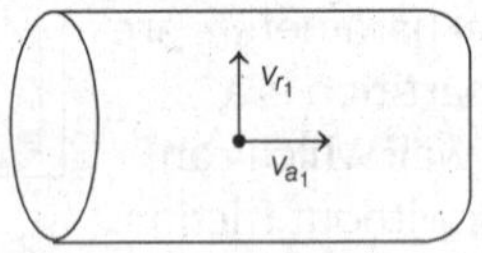

10 Which of the following is correct expression of rms speed of radial speed of the gas sample?

(a) $\sqrt{\frac{kT}{m}}$ (b) $\sqrt{\frac{2kT}{m}}$
(c) $\sqrt{\frac{kT}{2m}}$ (d) None of these

11 Which of the following is correct expression for rms speed of axial speed of the gas sample?

(a) $\sqrt{\frac{kT}{m}}$ (b) $\sqrt{\frac{2kT}{m}}$
(c) $\sqrt{\frac{kT}{2m}}$ (d) None of these

12 Which of the following expression can be used to give the axial pressure?

(a) $\frac{mN(v_{rms\ a})^2}{2\pi R^2 L}$ (b) $\frac{mN(v_{rms\ a})^2}{\pi R^2 L}$
(c) $\frac{mN(v_{rms\ a})^2}{4\pi R^2 L}$ (d) None of these

Match the Columns Questions

1 Hydrogen gas is kept in a conducting container fitted with a piston. Many processes can be carried out on the gas. Match the possible outcome of each of the processes on the gas in the container.

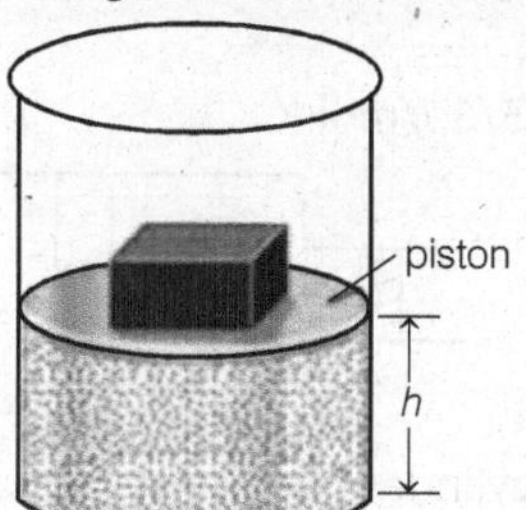

	Column I		Column II
(A)	Some gas is slowly removed from the container keeping piston free	(P)	The pressure of the gas increases
(B)	The gas is heated keeping the piston fixed	(Q)	The volume of the gas increases
(C)	The container is heated keeping the piston free	(R)	The pressure of the gas decreases
(D)	The container is taken to a place where acceleration due to gravity is half of that on the earth but the temperature and pressure of the surroundings is the same. Piston is free.	(S)	The volume of the gas decreases
		(T)	The temperature of the gas is the same as before

2 In each situation of Column I, a process $A \to B \to C$ is given for an ideal gas. Match each situation of Column I with correct result in Column II.

	Column I		Column II
(A)	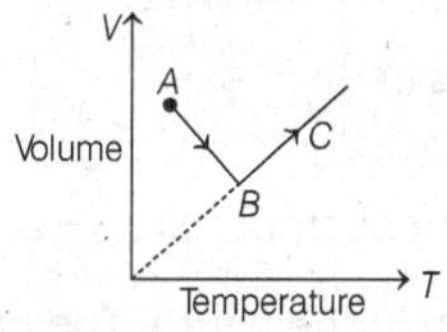	(P)	Temperature increases continuously
(B)	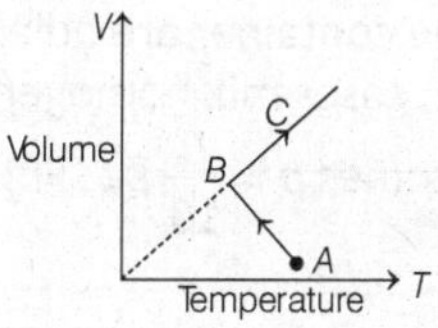	(Q)	Pressure first increases and then remains constant
(C)	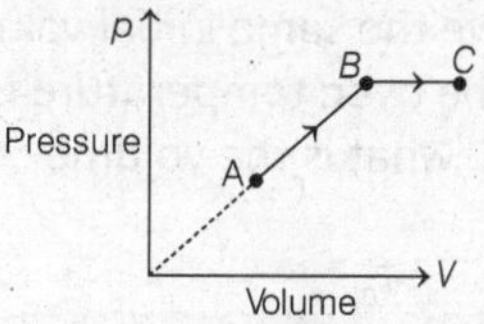	(R)	Temperature first decreases and then increases
(D)	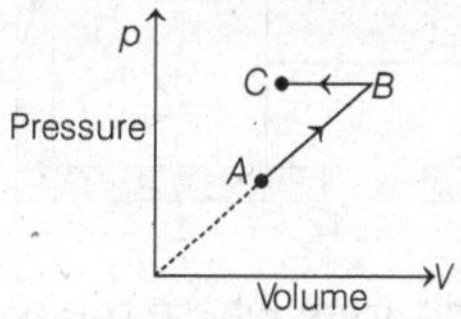	(S)	Pressure first decreases and then remains constant
		(T)	Volume first decreases and then increases

3 For an ideal monoatomic gas, match the following graphs for constant mass in different processes (ρ = Density of gas).

(A) 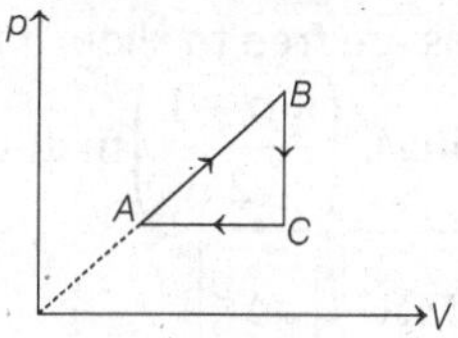

(P) 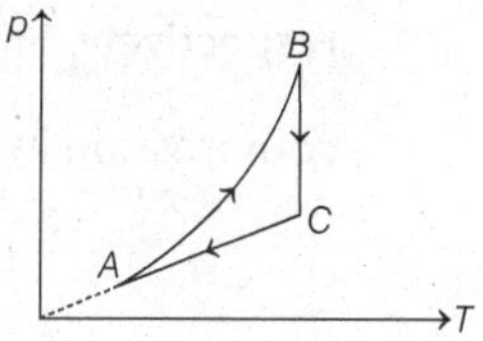

(B) 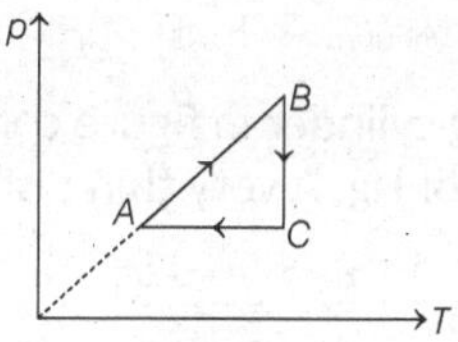

(Q) 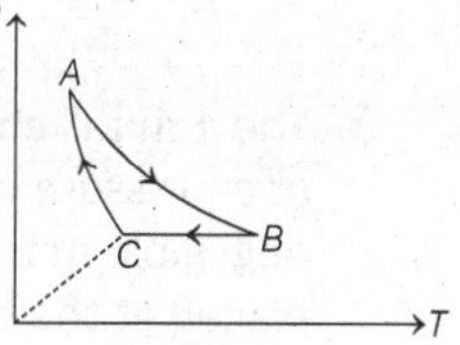

(C) 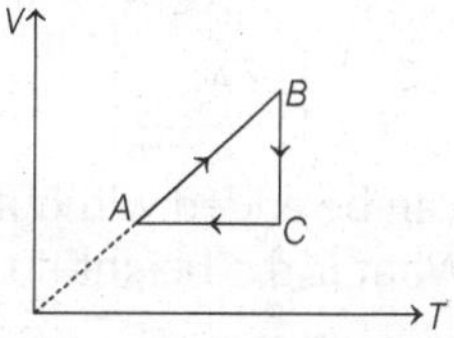

(R) 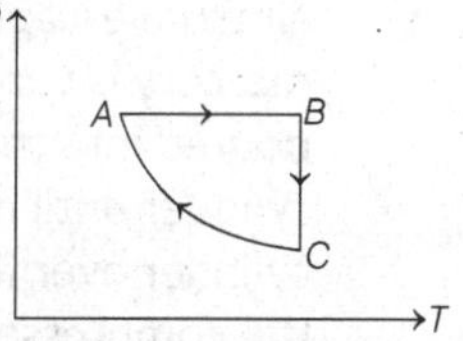

(D) 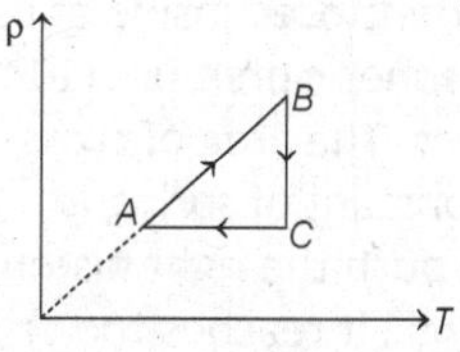

(S) 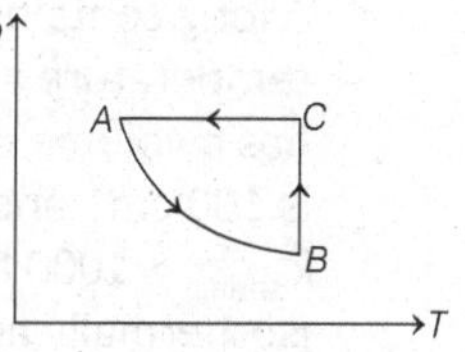

Numerical Value Questions

1 The two conducting cylinder-piston systems shown below are linked. Cylinder 1 is filled with a certain molar quantity of a monoatomic ideal gas, and cylinder 2 is filled with an equal molar quantity of a diatomic ideal gas. The entire apparatus is situated inside an oven whose temperature is $T_a = 27°C$. The cylinder volumes have the same initial value $V_0 = 100$ cc. When the oven temperature is slowly raised to $T_b = 127°C$, what is the volume change ΔV (in cc) of cylinder 1?

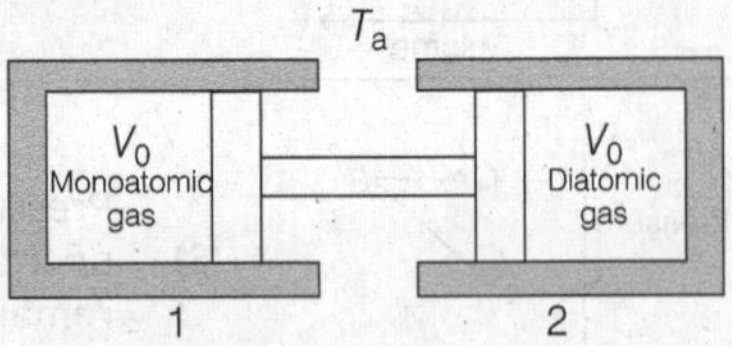

2 Consider the shown diagram where the two chambers separated by piston-spring arrangement contain equal amounts of certain ideal gas. There is vacuum between the tight fitting pistons. Initially when the temperatures of the gas in both the chambers are kept at 300 K, the compression in the spring is 1 m. The temperature of the left and the right chambers are now raised to 400 K and 500 K respectively. The pistons are free to slide. If the final compression in the spring is $\left(\frac{\sqrt{n}-1}{2}\right)$ m, then find n.

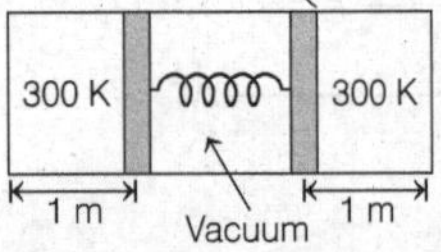

3 The 1 m tall conducting cylinder in figure contains air at a pressure of 76 cm of Hg. A very thin piston of negligible mass is placed at the top of the cylinder to prevent any air from escaping, then mercury is very slowly poured into the cylinder until no more can be added without the cylinder over flowing. What is the height (in cm) of the compressed air?

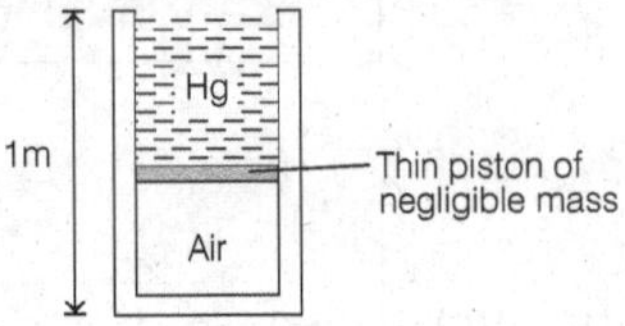

4 A long container has air enclosed inside at room temperature and atmospheric pressure (10^5 Pa). It has a volume of 20000 cc. The area of cross- section is 100 cm^2 and force constant of spring is $k_{spring} = 1000$ N/m. We push the right piston isothermally and slowly till it reaches the original position of the left piston which is movable. What is the final length of air column in cm? Assume that spring is initially relaxed.

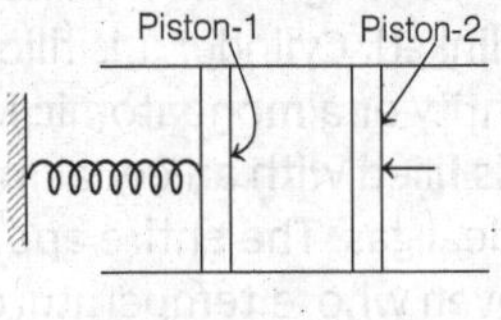

5 A horizontal cylinder has two sections of cross-sections areas 100 cm^2 and 200 cm^2 respectively in which two pistons can move freely. The pistons are joined by a string. 1 mole of gas is trapped between the pistons. If this gas is heated by $\Delta T = 30$ K, find the distance (in cm) moved by the piston.

Use : $R = 25/3$ J/mol-K

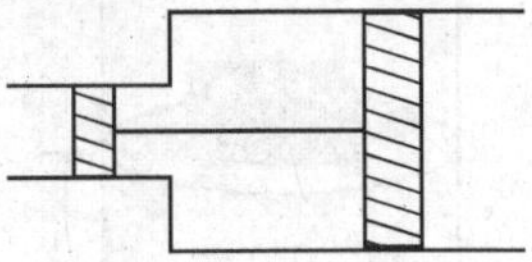

6 A vertical cylinder of cross-sectional area 0.1 m^2 closed at both ends is fitted with a frictionless piston of mass M dividing the cylinder into two parts. Each part contains one mole of an ideal gas in equilibrium at 300 K. The volume of the upper part is 0.1 m^3 and that of the lower part is 0.05 m^3. What force (in N) must be applied to the piston, so that the volumes of the two parts remain unchanged when the temperature is increased to 500 K? Given, $R = 8.3$ J/mol-K.

7 A vessel of volume 30 L is separated into three equal parts by stationary semipermeable membrane. The left, middle and right parts are filled with 30 g of hydrogen, 160 g of oxygen and 70 g of nitrogen respectively. The left partition lets through only hydrogen while the right partition lets through hydrogen and nitrogen. If the temperature in all is 300 K, the ratio of pressure in the three compartments is 4 : x : 5. Find x.

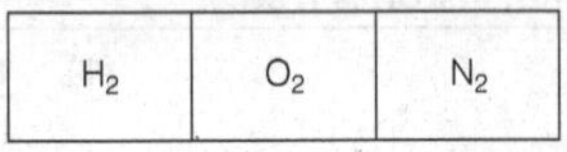

8 Consider the adjacent figure, a piston divides a cylindrical container into two parts. The left part contains 1 mole of helium gas and the right part contains two moles of oxygen gas. The initial temperatures and pressures of the gases in the left chamber are

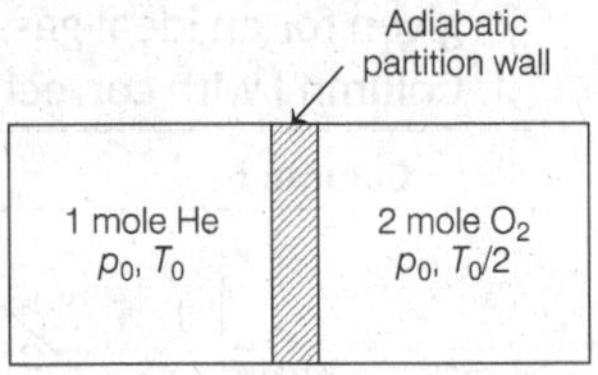

T_0 and p_0 and the right chamber are $\frac{T_0}{2}$ and p_0 respectively, as shown in the figure. The piston as well as the walls of the container are adiabatic. After removal of the piston, gases mix homogeneously and the final pressure becomes $p = \frac{n}{13} p_0$. Find the value of n.

9 A gas is confined in the cylinder under a light piston which is connected to the bottom of the cylinder with a weightless spring as shown in figure, under pressure $p = 0.1$ MPa and temperature $T = 27°C$. The inital pressure of the gas is equal to the external atmospheric pressure. To what temperature (in °C) should we heat the gas to increase its volume to $n = 1.2$ times? If the gas under the piston is fully pumped out, the piston will reach the bottom of the vessel compressing the spring compeltely without touching the bottom.

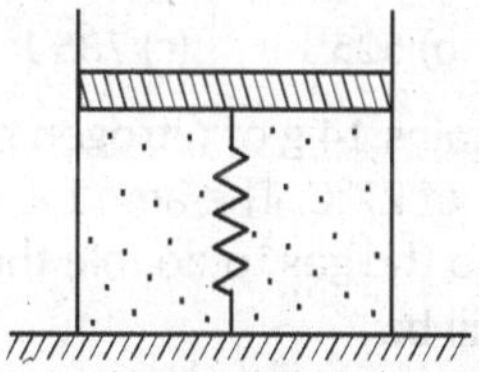

10 The speed distribution of molecules in a sample of a gas is shown in the figure. The graph between $\frac{dN}{du}$ and u is a parabola and total number of molecules in the sample is N_0. Calculate the total translational kinetic energy (in J) of molecules if mass of the sample is 10 g.

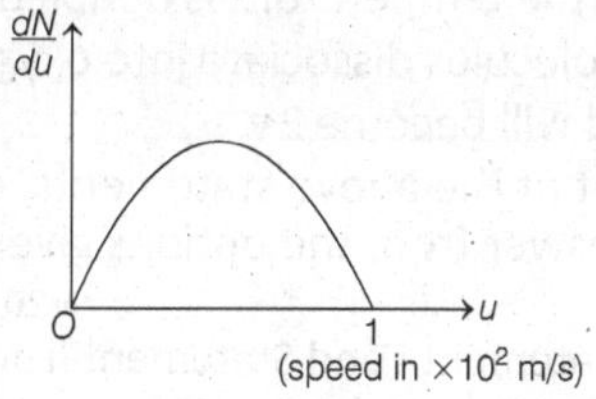

Previous Year's Questions

JEE Main

1 The average kinetic energy of a monoatomic molecule is 0.414 eV at temperature. (Use $k_B = 1.38 \times 10^{-23}$ J/mol-K) **[2024, 27 Jan Shift-I]**
(a) 1600 K (b) 3000 K (c) 1500 K (d) 3200 K

2 The total kinetic energy of 1 mole of oxygen at 27°C is [Use universal gas constant $(R) = 8.31$ J/mole K] **[2024, 27 Jan Shift-II]**
(a) 6845.5 J (b) 6232.5 J
(c) 5670.5 J (d) 5942.0 J

3 Two vessels A and B are of the same size and are at same temperature. A contains 1 g of hydrogen and B contains 1 g of oxygen. p_A and p_B are the pressures of the gases in A and B respectively, then $\frac{p_A}{p_B}$ is **[2024, 29 Jan Shift-I]**
(a) 4 (b) 8 (c) 32 (d) 16

4 The temperature of a gas having 2.0×10^{25} molecules per cubic metre at 1.38 atm (Given, $k = 1.38 \times 10^{-23}$ JK^{-1}) is **[2024, 29 Jan Shift-II]**
(a) 300 K (b) 200 K
(c) 500 K (d) 100 K

5 N moles of a polyatomic gas $(f = 6)$ must be mixed with two moles of a monoatomic gas, so that the mixture behaves as a diatomic gas. The value of N is **[2024, 29 Jan Shift-II]**
(a) 6 (b) 2
(c) 3 (d) 4

6 A flask contains Hydrogen and Argon in the ratio 2 : 1 by mass. The temperature of the mixture is 30°C. The ratio of average kinetic energy per molecule of the two gases ($K_{argon}/K_{hydrogen}$) is (Given, Atomic Weight of Ar = 39.9) **[2023, 15 April Shift-I]**
(a) 2 (b) 39.9
(c) $\frac{39.9}{2}$ (d) 1

7 The number of air molecules per cm^3 increased from 3×10^{19} to 12×10^{19}. The ratio of collision frequency of air molecules before and after the increase in number respectively is **[2023, 6 April Shift-I]**
(a) 0.75 (b) 0.50
(c) 1.25 (d) 0.25

8 The temperature of an ideal gas is increased from 200 K to 800 K. If r.m.s. speed of gas at 200 K is v_0. Then, r.m.s. speed of the gas at 800 K will be **[2023, 6 April Shift-II]**
(a) $v_0/4$ (b) v_0 (c) $4v_0$ (d) $2v_0$

9 The temperature at which the kinetic energy of oxygen molecules becomes double than its value at 27°C is **[2023, 8 April Shift-II]**
(a) 927°C (b) 327°C
(c) 627°C (d) 1227°C

10 Given below are two statements.

Statement I The temperature of a gas is −73°C. When the gas is heated to 527°C, the root mean square speed of the molecules is doubled.

Statement II The product of pressure and volume of an ideal gas will be equal to translational kinetic energy of the molecules. **[2023, 24 Jan Shift-I]**

In the light of the above statements, choose the correct answer from the options given below.
(a) Statement I is false but Statement II is true.
(b) Both Statement I and Statement II are true.
(c) Statement I is true but Statement II is false.
(d) Both Statement I and Statement II are false.

11 For three low density gases A, B, C, pressure *versus* temperature graphs are plotted while keeping them at constant volume, as shown in the figure.

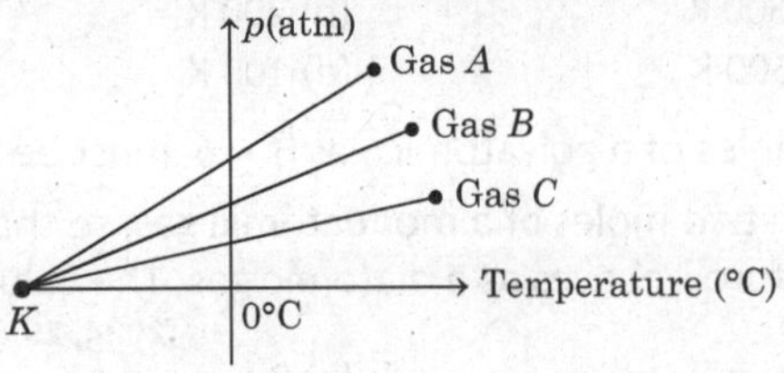

The temperature corresponding to the point K is **[2023, 1 Fbe Shift-II]**

(a) $-40°C$ (b) $-100°C$ (c) $-273°C$ (d) $-373°C$

12 The correct relation between $\gamma = \frac{C_p}{C_V}$ and temperature T is **[2023, 31 Jan Shift-I]**

(a) $\gamma \propto T$ (b) $\gamma \propto \frac{1}{T}$ (c) $\gamma \propto T^0$ (d) $\gamma \propto \frac{1}{\sqrt{T}}$

13 The mean free path of molecules of a certain gas at STP is $1500d$, where d is the diameter of the gas molecules. While maintaining the standard pressure, the mean free path of the molecules at 373K is approximately **[2023, 13 April Shift-II]**

(a) $2049d$ (b) $1500d$ (c) $750d$ (d) $1098d$

14 Three vessels of equal volume contain gases at the same temperature and pressure. The first vessel contains neon (monoatomic), the second contains chlorine (diatomic) and third contains uranium hexafloride (polyatomic). Arrange these on the basis of their root mean square speed (v_{rms}) and choose the correct answer from the options given below **[2023, 11 April Shift-I]**

(a) v_{rms} (mono) $= v_{rms}$ (dia) $= v_{rms}$ (poly)
(b) v_{rms} (mono) $< v_{rms}$ (dia) $< v_{rms}$ (poly)
(c) v_{rms} (dia) $< v_{rms}$ (poly) $< v_{rms}$ (mono)
(d) v_{rms} (mono) $> v_{rms}$ (dia) $= v_{rms}$ (poly)

15 Match List I with List II

List I	List II
A. 3 Translational degrees of freedom	I. Monoatomic gases
B. 3 Translational, 2 rotational degrees of freedoms	II. Polyatomic gases
C. 3 Translational, 2 rotational and 1 vibrational degrees of freedom	III. Rigid diatomic gases
D. 3 Translational, 2 rotational and more than one vibrational degrees of freedom	IV. Nonrigid diatomic gases

Choose the correct answer from the options given below : **[2023, 10 April Shift-I]**

(a) (A)-(IV), (B)-(III), (C)-(II), (D)-(I)
(b) (A)-(I), (B)-(III), (C)-(IV), (D)-(II)
(c) (A)-(IV). (B)-(II), (C)-(I), (D)-(III)
(d) (A)-(I), (B)-(IV), (C)-(III), (D)-(II)

16 Heat energy of 735 J is given to a diatomic gas allowing the gas to expand at constant pressure. Each gas molecule rotates around an internal axis but do not oscillate. The increase in the internal energy of the gas will be **[2023, 31 Jan Shift-II]**

(a) 572 J (b) 525 J (c) 735 J (d) 441 J

17 A vessel contains 14 g of nitrogen gas at a temperature of 27°C. The amount of heat to be transferred to the gas to double the rms speed of its molecules will be
(Take, $R = 8.32$ J mol^{-1}K^{-1}) **[2022, 28 July Shift-II]**

(a) 2229 J (b) 5616 J (c) 9360 J (d) 13,104 J

18 Given below are two statements.

Statement I The average momentum of a molecule in a sample of an ideal gas depends on temperature.

Statement II The rms speed of oxygen molecules in a gas is v. If the temperature is doubled and the oxygen molecules dissociate into oxygen atoms, the rms speed will become $2v$.

In the light of the above statements, choose the correct answer from the options given below. **[2022, 28 July Shift-I]**

(a) Both Statement I and Statement II are true.
(b) Both Statement I and Statement II are false.
(c) Statement I is true but Statement II is false.
(d) Statement I is false but Statement II is true.

19 A vessel contains 16 g of hydrogen and 128 g of oxygen at standard temperature and pressure. The volume of the vessel in cm^{33} is **[2022, 29 June Shift-II]**

(a) 72×10^5 (b) 32×10^5 (c) 27×10^4 (d) 54×10^4

20 A cylinder of fixed capacity of 44.8 L contains helium gas at standard temperature and pressure. The amount of heat needed to raise the temperature of gas in the cylinder by 20.0°C will be (Given, gas constant, $R = 8.3$ JK^{-1}-mol^{-1}) **[2022, 29 June Shift-I]**

(a) 249 J (b) 415 J (c) 498 J (d) 830 J

21 What will be the effect on the root mean square velocity of oxygen molecules, if the temperature is doubled and oxygen molecule dissociates into atomic oxygen? **[2022, 28 June Shift-II]**

(a) The velocity of atomic oxygen remains same.
(b) The velocity of atomic oxygen doubles.

(c) The velocity of atomic oxygen becomes half.
(d) The velocity of atomic oxygen becomes four times.

22 A mixture of hydrogen and oxygen has volume $2000\ cm^3$, temperature 300 K, pressure 100 kPa and mass 0.76 g. The ratio of number of moles of hydrogen to number of moles of oxygen in the mixture will be **[2022, 27 June Shift-I]**

(a) $\frac{1}{3}$ (b) $\frac{3}{1}$ (c) $\frac{1}{16}$ (d) $\frac{16}{1}$

23 The relation between root mean square speed v_{rms} and most probable speed v_p for the molar mass M of oxygen gas molecule at the temperature of 300 K will be **[2022, 25 June Shift-I]**

(a) $v_{rms} = \sqrt{\frac{2}{3}} v_p$ (b) $v_{rms} = \sqrt{\frac{3}{2}} v_p$

(c) $v_{rms} = v_p$ (d) $v_{rms} = \sqrt{\frac{1}{3}} v_p$

24 For a perfect gas, two pressures p_1 and p_2 are shown in figure, The graph shows **[2022, 27 June Shift-II]**

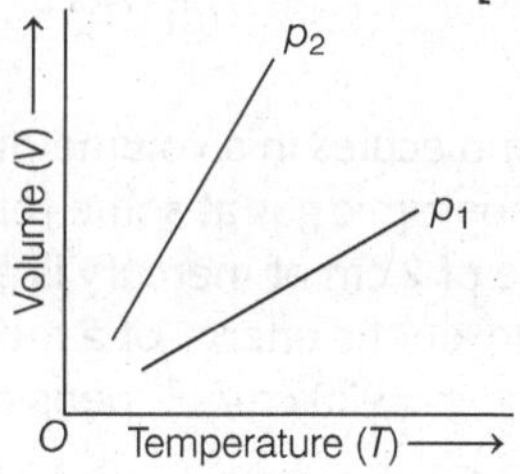

(a) $p_1 > p_2$ (b) $p_1 < p_2$ (c) $p_1 = p_2$
(d) insufficient data to draw any conclusion

25 Which statements are correct about degrees of freedom?

A. A molecule with n degrees of freedom has n^2 different ways of storing energy.
B. Each degree of freedom is associated with $\frac{1}{2}RT$ average energy per mole.
C. A monoatomic gas molecule has 1 rotational degree of freedom whereas diatomic molecule has 2 rotational degrees of freedom.
D. CH_4 has a total of 6 degrees of freedom.

Choose the correct answer from the option given below. **[2022, 27 July Shift-II]**

(a) B and C only (b) B and D only
(c) A and B only (d) C and D only

26 A gas has n degrees of freedom. The ratio of specific heat of gas at constant volume to the specific heat of gas at constant pressure will be **[2022, 26 July Shift-II]**

(a) $\frac{n}{n+2}$ (b) $\frac{n+2}{n}$ (c) $\frac{n}{2n+2}$ (d) $\frac{n}{n-2}$

27 According to kinetic theory of gases,

A. The motion of the gas molecules freezes at 0°C.
B. The mean free path of gas molecules decreases if the density of molecules is increased.
C. The mean free path of gas molecules increases if temperature is increased keeping pressure constant.
D. Average kinetic energy per molecule per degree of freedom is $\frac{3}{2}k_BT$ (for monoatomic gases).

Choose the most appropriate answer from the options given below. **[2022, 27 June Shift-II]**

(a) A and C only (b) B and C only
(c) A and B only (d) C and D only

28 The total internal energy of two mole monoatomic ideal gas at temperature, $T = 300$ K will be .... J.
(Given, $R = 8.31$ J/mol · K) **[2022, 28 June Shift-I]**

29 A mixture of hydrogen and oxygen has volume $500\ cm^3$, temperature 300 K, pressure 400 kPa and mass 0.76 g. The ratio of masses of oxygen to hydrogen will be **[2021, 31 Aug Shift-II]**

(a) 3 : 8 (b) 3 : 16
(c) 16 : 3 (d) 8 : 3

30 If the rms speed of oxygen molecules at 0°C is 160 m/s, find the rms speed of hydrogen molecules at 0°C. **[2021, 27 Aug Shift-II]**

(a) 640 m/s (b) 40 m/s
(c) 80 m/s (d) 332 m/s

31 An ideal gas is expanding such that pT^3 = constant. The coefficient of volume expansion of the gas is **[2021, 27 Aug Shift-I]**

(a) $1/T$ (b) $2/T$
(c) $4/T$ (d) $3/T$

32 A balloon carries a total load of 185 kg at normal pressure and temperature of 27°C. What load will the balloon carry on rising to a height at which the barometric pressure is 45 cm of Hg and the temperature is −7°C?
[Assuming, the volume constant.] **[2021, 27 Aug Shift-I]**

(a) 181.46 kg (b) 214.15 kg
(c) 219.07 kg (d) 123.54 kg

33 A cylindrical container of volume $4.0 \times 10^{-3}\ m^3$ contains one mole of hydrogen and two moles of carbon dioxide. Assume the temperature of the mixture is 400 K. The pressure of the mixture of gases is [Take, gas constant $= 8.3\ J\ mol^{-1}K^{-1}$] **[2021, 26 Aug Shift-II]**

(a) 249×10^1 Pa (b) 24.9×10^3 Pa
(c) 24.9×10^5 Pa (d) 24.9 Pa

34 Which of the following graphs represent the behaviour of an ideal gas ? (Symbols have their usual meanings.) **[2021, 20 July Shift-II]**

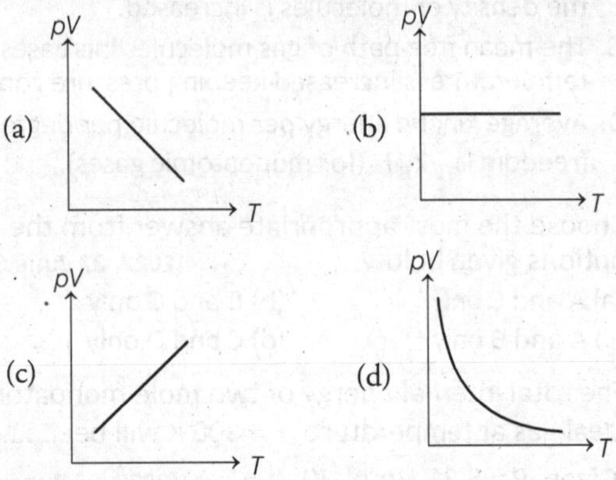

35 Consider a sample of oxygen behaving like an ideal gas. At 300 K, the ratio of root mean square (rms) velocity to the average velocity of gas molecule would be (Molecular weight of oxygen is 32 g/mol; $R = 8.3\ \text{JK}^{-1}\ \text{mol}^{-1}$) **[2021, 18 March Shift-II]**

(a) $\sqrt{\frac{3}{3}}$ (b) $\sqrt{\frac{8}{3}}$

(c) $\sqrt{\frac{3\pi}{8}}$ (d) $\sqrt{\frac{8\pi}{3}}$

36 What will be the average value of energy along one degree of freedom for an ideal gas in thermal equilibrium at a temperature T? (k_B is Boltzmann constant) **[2021, 18 March Shift-I]**

(a) $\frac{1}{2}k_BT$ (b) $\frac{2}{3}k_BT$ (c) $\frac{3}{2}k_BT$ (d) k_BT

37 If one mole of the polyatomic gas is having two vibrational modes and β is the ratio of molar specific heats for polyatomic gas $\left(\beta = \frac{C_p}{C_V}\right)$, then the value of β is **[2021, 17 March Shift-II]**

(a) 1.02 (b) 1.2 (c) 1.25 (d) 1.35

38 Two ideal polyatomic gases at temperatures T_1 and T_2 are mixed so that there is no loss of energy. If f_1 and f_2, m_1 and m_2, n_1 and n_2 be the degrees of freedom, masses, number of molecules of the first and second gas respectively, the temperature of mixture of these two gases is **[2021, 17 March Shift-I]**

(a) $\frac{n_1T_1 + n_2T_2}{n_1 + n_2}$ (b) $\frac{n_1f_1T_1 + n_2f_2T_2}{n_1f_1 + n_2f_2}$

(c) $\frac{n_1f_1T_1 + n_2f_2T_2}{f_1 + f_2}$ (d) $\frac{n_1f_1T_1 + n_2f_2T_2}{n_1 + n_2}$

39 The temperature of 3.00 mol of an ideal diatomic gas is increased by 40.0 °C without changing the pressure of the gas. The molecules in the gas rotate but do not oscillate. If the ratio of change in internal energy of the gas to the amount of workdone by the gas is $x/10$, then the value of x (round off to the nearest integer) is .... (Given, $R = 8.31\ \text{J mol}^{-1}\ \text{K}^{-1}$) **[2021, 1 Sep Shift-II]**

40 An engine takes in 5 moles of air at 20° C and 1 atm and compresses it adiabatically to 1/10th of the original volume. Assuming air to be a diatomic ideal gas made up of rigid molecules, the change in its internal energy during this process comes out to be XkJ. The value of X to the nearest integer is .... **[2020, 2 Sep Shift-I]**

41 In a dilute gas at pressure p and temperature T, the mean time between successive collisions of a molecule varies with T as **[2020, 6 Sep Shift-I]**

(a) T (b) $\frac{1}{\sqrt{T}}$

(c) $\frac{1}{T}$ (d) $\sqrt{T}$

42 Number of molecules in a volume of 4 cm^3 of a perfect monoatomic gas at some temperature T and at a pressure of 2 cm of mercury is close to (Given, mean kinetic energy of a molecule at T is 4×10^{-14} erg, $g = 980\ \text{cm/s}^2$, density of mercury $= 13.6\ \text{g/cm}^3$) **[2020, 5 Sep Shift-I]**

(a) 5.8×10^{16} (b) 4.0×10^{16}

(c) 4.0×10^{18} (d) 5.8×10^{18}

43 An ideal gas in a closed container is slowly heated. As its temperature increases, which of the following statements are true? **[2020, 2 Sep Shift-II]**

A. The mean free path of the molecules decreases.

B. The mean collision time between the molecules decreases.

C. The mean free path remains unchanged.

D. The mean collision time remains unchanged.

(a) B and C (b) A and B

(c) C and D (d) A and D

44 Consider a mixture of n moles of helium gas and $2n$ moles of oxygen gas (molecules taken to be rigid) as an ideal gas. Its C_p/C_V value will be **[2020, 8 Jan Shift-II]**

(a) 40/27

(b) 23/15

(c) 19/13

(d) 67/45

45 The change in the magnitude of the volume of an ideal gas when a small additional pressure Δp is applied at a constant temperature, is the same as the change when the temperature is reduced by a small quantity ΔT at constant pressure. The initial temperature and pressure of the gas are 300 K and 2 atm, respectively. If $|\Delta T| = C|\Delta p|$, then value of C (in K/atm) is .... **[2020, 4 Sep Shift-II]**

46 A gas mixture consists of 3 moles of oxygen and 5 moles of argon at temperature T. Assuming the gases to be ideal and the oxygen bond to be rigid, the total internal energy (in units of RT) of the mixture is **[2020, 2 Sep Shift-I]**

(a) 15 (b) 13 (c) 11 (d) 20

47 Match the C_p/C_V ratio for ideal gases with different type of molecules: **[2020, 4 Sep Shift-I]**

Molecule type		C_p/C_V
(A) Monatomic molecules	I.	7/5
(B) Diatomic rigid molecules	II.	9/7
(C) Diatomic non-rigid molecules	III.	4/3
(D) Triatomic rigid molecules	IV.	5/3

	A	B	C	D
(a)	IV	I	II	III
(b)	III	IV	II	I
(c)	II	III	I	IV
(d)	IV	II	I	III

JEE Advanced

1. An ideal gas is in thermodynamic equilibrium. The number of degrees of freedom of a molecule of the gas is n. The internal energy of one mole of the gas is U_n and the speed of sound in the gas is v_n. At a fixed temperature and pressure, which of the following is the correct option? **(2023 Adv.)**

(a) $v_3 < v_6$ and $U_3 > U_6$

(b) $v_5 > v_3$ and $U_3 > U_5$

(c) $v_5 > v_7$ and $U_5 < U_7$

(d) $v_6 < v_7$ and $U_6 < U_7$

Question Stem

A soft plastic bottle, filled with water of density 1 g/cc, carries an inverted glass test-tube with some air (ideal gas) trapped as shown in the figure. The test-tube has a mass of 5 g and it is made of a thick glass of density 2.5 g/cc. Initially the bottle is sealed at atmospheric pressure $p_0 = 10^5$ Pa, so that the volume of the trapped air is $v_0 = 3.3$ cc. When, the bottle is squeezed from outside at constant temperature, the pressure inside rises and the volume of the trapped air reduces. It is found that the test tube begins to sink at pressure $p_0 + \Delta p$ without changing its orientation. At this pressure, the volume of the trapped air is $v_0 - \Delta v$.

Let $\Delta v = X$ cc and $\Delta p = Y \times 10^3$ Pa.

2. The value of X is ________. **(2021 Adv.)**

3. The value of Y is ________. **(2021 Adv.)**

4. A thermally isolated cylindrical closed vessel of height 8 m is kept vertically. It is divided into two equal parts by a diathermic (perfect thermal conductor) frictionless partition of mass 8.3 kg. Thus the partition is held initially at a distance of 4 m from the top, as shown in the schematic figure below. Each of the two parts of the vessel contains 0.1 mole of an ideal gas at temperature 300 K. The partition is now released and moves without any gas leaking from one part of the vessel to the other. When equilibrium is reached, the distance of the partition from the top (in m) will be ________ (take the acceleration due to gravity = 10 ms^{-2} and the universal gas constant = 9.3 J mol^{-1} K^{-1}). **(2020 Adv.)**

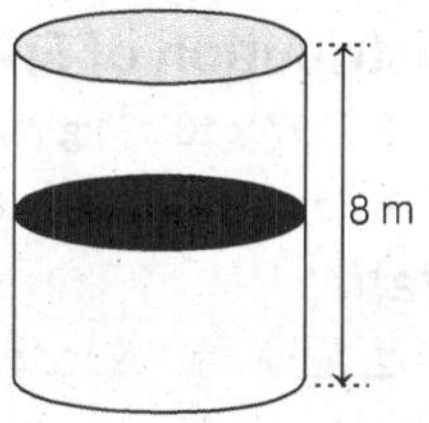

5. A container of fixed volume has a mixture of one mole of hydrogen and one mole of helium in equilibrium at temperature T. Assuming the gases are ideal, the correct statements is/are **(2015 Adv.)**

(a) The average energy per mole of the gas mixture is $2RT$

(b) The ratio of speed of sound in the gas mixture to that in helium gas is $\sqrt{\frac{6}{5}}$

(c) The ratio of the rms speed of helium atoms to that of hydrogen molecules is 1/2

(d) The ratio of the rms speed of helium atoms to that of hydrogen molecules is $\frac{1}{\sqrt{2}}$

6. Two non-reactive monoatomic ideal gases have their atomic masses in the ratio 2 : 3. The ratio of their partial pressures, when enclosed in a vessel kept at a constant temperature, is 4 : 3. The ratio of their densities is **(2013 Adv.)**

(a) 1 : 4 (b) 1 : 2
(c) 6 : 9 (d) 8 : 9

7. A mixture of 2 moles of helium gas (atomic mass = 4 amu) and 1 mole of argon gas (atomic mass = 40 amu) is kept at 300 K in a container. The ratio of the rms speeds $\left(\frac{v_{rms}\text{ (helium)}}{v_{rms}\text{ (argon)}}\right)$ is **(2012 Adv.)**

(a) 0.32 (b) 0.45
(c) 2.24 (d) 3.16

Answer Key

Level 1

5.1 Kinetic Theory of Gases

1. (a) True (b) True (c) True (d) False (e) True (f) False (g) False (h) True
2. 0

5.2 Root Mean Square Speed

1. $\sqrt{\frac{50}{3}}\,v$ 2. (a) 3.17 ms^{-1} (b) 3.36 ms^{-1} (c) 3.0 ms^{-1}
3. 483.6 ms^{-1} 4. H_2, 927°C 5. 600 m/s
6. $200\sqrt{2}\text{ ms}^{-1}$ 7. −253°C 8. $\sqrt{2}$

5.3 Pressure on the Walls of Container

1. $8.48\times10^4\text{ N/m}^2$ 2. 3.0 atm 3. $\frac{mv_0^2N}{2l^3}$
4. (a) 160 K (b) 3.312×10^{-21} J (c) 3.0×10^{-4} kg

5.4 Maxwell's Distribution of Speed

1. 1.82×10^5 K 2. 7.97×10^{-24} kg-m/s
3. 1 : 2 4. (a) 381 K (b) 340 K

5.5 Mean Free Path

1. $p/2$ 2. 3.2 Å 3. 4 : 1

5.6 Degree of Freedom

1.

Type of Gas	Number of degree of freedom		
	Translational	Rotational	Total
Monoatomic gas	3	0	3
Diatomic gas	3	2	5
Linear polyatomic gas	3	2	5
Nonlinear polyatomic gas	3	3	6

2. 1.344×10^{20}

5.7 Kinetic Energy

1. 4986 J
2. (a) 6.21×10^{-21} J (b) 4.14×10^{-21} J (c) 10.35×10^{-21} J
3. 154.6 K 4. 10.35×10^{-21} J
5. $5\times10^6\text{ N/m}^2$ 6. 4.5×10^9 rad/s

5.8 Internal Energy

1. 1.74×10^4 J 2. 42°C
3. (a) $K=\frac{5}{2}nRT$ (b) $K=\frac{1}{2}Mv^2+\frac{5}{2}nRT$
4. 52°C 5. 31/21

5.9 Ideal Gas Equation

1. 2.4×10^{23} 2. 3.2 kg/m^3 3. 1000 K
4. $\sqrt{2}\,T$ 5. 1 : 1 6. 1007°C
7. $m_{Ne}=4\,g, m_{Ar}=24\,g$
8. 1 : 3 9. $5.2\times10^5\text{ N/m}^2$
10. 72 g 11. 0.14 12. 177°C
13. 240/7 cm 14. $\frac{4}{3}p_0$ 15. $\frac{5p_0}{3}, \frac{10T_0}{9}$

5.10 Graphs of Different Processes

1. (a) yes (b) no (c) no
2. (a) $p_1 < p_2, T_1 < T_2$, (b) $T_1 = T_2 < T_3$, (c) $V_2 > V_1$, (d) $p_1 > p_2$
3. $T_B = 2T_0, T_C = 4T_0$

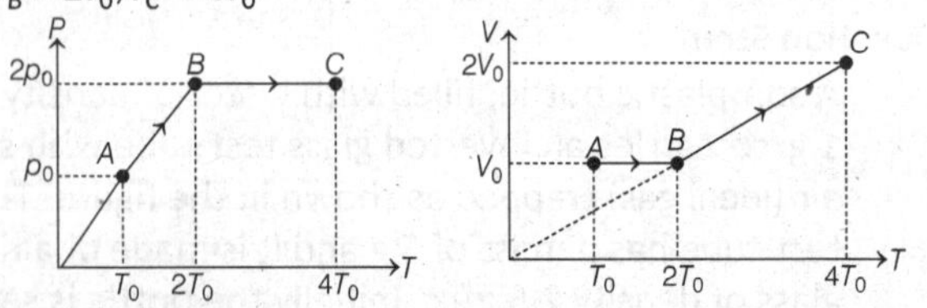

4.

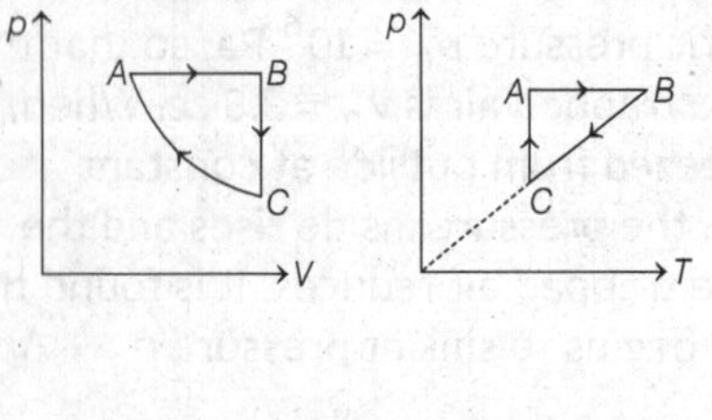

5.

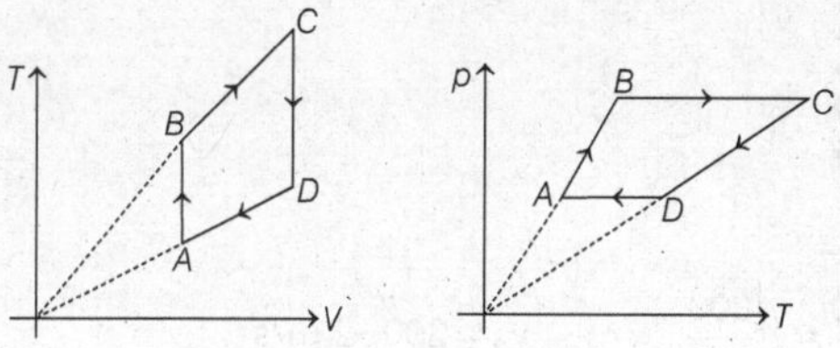

6.

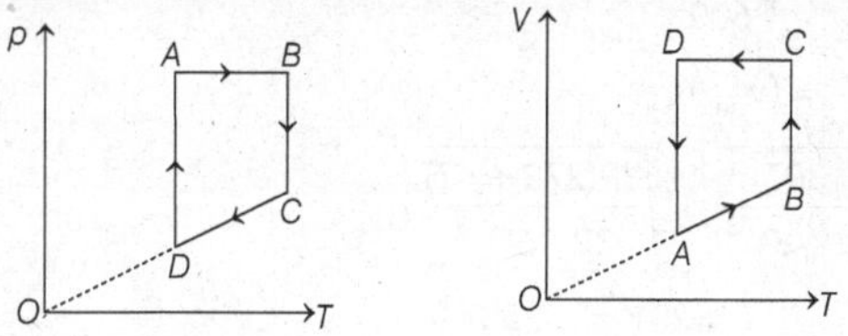

Level 2

Single Choice Correct Questions

1. (c)	2. (b)	3. (a)	4. (b)	5. (a)
6. (a)	7. (c)	8. (b)	9. (a)	10. (c)
11. (a)	12. (b)	13. (c)	14. (d)	15. (c)
16. (b)	17. (a)	18. (a)	19. (b)	20. (d)
21. (d)	22. (c)	23. (b)	24. (a)	25. (d)
26. (c)	27. (c)	28. (d)	29. (a)	30. (a)
31. (d)	32. (c)	33. (c)	34. (c)	35. (c)
36. (a)	37. (b)	38. (a)	39. (c)	40. (c)
41. (b)	42. (c)	43. (a)	44. (a)	45. (c)
46. (a)	47. (b)	48. (a)	49. (c)	50. (c)
51. (b)	52. (a)	53. (b)	54. (a)	55. (a)
56. (c)	57. (a)	58. (a)		

Numerical Value Questions

1 (33)	2 (750)	3 (50)	4 (72)	5 (1.25)
6 (200)	7 (327)	8 (105)	9 (20)	10 (75)

Level 3

Single Choice Correct Questions

1. (a)	2. (a)	3. (b)	4. (c)	5. (c)
6. (d)	7. (b)	8. (d)	9. (d)	10. (b)
11. (a)	12. (c)	13. (b)	14. (a)	15. (d)
16. (c)	17. (c)	18. (c)	19. (c)	20. (d)
21. (d)	22. (b)	23. (b)	24. (c)	25. (c)
26. (b)	27. (d)	28. (d)	29. (b)	30. (c)
31. (a)	32. (c)	33. (d)	34. (c)	35. (c)

Multiple Choice(s) Correct Questions

1. (abc)	2. (abd)	3. (abcd)	4. (cd)
5.(ad)	6. (abcd)	7. (acd)	8. (bd)
9.(abcd)	10. (abcd)	11. (ab)	12. (cd)

Comprehension Based Questions

1. (c)	2. (d)	3. (b)	4. (c)	5. (a)
6. (b)	7. (a)	8. (d)	9. (a)	10. (b)
11. (a)	12. (b)			

Match the Columns Questions

1. A→ S, T B→ P, C → Q, D→ Q, R, T
2. A→ P, Q, T, B→ R, S, C→ P, Q, D→ Q
3. A→ Q, B→ R, C→ S, D→ P

Numerical Value Questions

1 (0)	2 (13)	3 (76)	4 (100)	5 (25)
6 (1660)	7 (9)	8 (3)	9 (159)	10 (15)

Previous Year's Questions

JEE Main

1 (d)	2 (b)	3 (d)	4 (c)	5 (d)
6 (d)	7 (d)	8 (d)	9 (b)	10 (c)
11 (c)	12 (c)	13 (a)	14 (d)	15 (b)
16 (b)	17 (c)	18 (d)	19 (c)	20 (c)
21 (b)	22 (b)	23 (b)	24 (a)	25 (b)
26 (a)	27 (b)	28 (7479)	29 (c)	30 (a)
31 (c)	32 (d)	33 (c)	34 (c)	35 (c)
36 (a)	37 (b)	38 (b)	39 (25)	40 (4)
41 (b)	42 (c)	43 (a)	44 (c)	45 (150)
46 (a)	47 (a)			

JEE Advanced

1. (c)	2. (0.3)	3. (10)	4. (*)	5.(a,b,d)
6. (d)	7. (d)			

SOLUTIONS

Level 1

5.1 Kinetic Theory of Gases

1. (a) True (b) True
   (c) True (d) False
   (e) True (f) False
   (g) False (h) True
2. Average momentum = mass × average velocity
   Since, average velocity of gas molecules is zero, average momentum will be zero.

5.2 Root Mean Square Speed

1. $v_{rms} = \sqrt{\frac{(3v)^2 + (4v)^2 + (5v)^2}{3}} = \sqrt{\frac{50}{3}}\, v$
2. (a) $v_{avg.} = \frac{\Sigma n_i v_i}{\Sigma n_i} = \frac{2(1) + 4(2) + 8(3) + 6(4) + 3(5)}{2 + 4 + 8 + 6 + 3} = 3.17 \text{ m/s}$

   (b) $v_{rms} = \sqrt{\frac{\Sigma n_i v_i^2}{\Sigma n_i}} = \sqrt{\frac{2(1)^2 + 4(2)^2 + 8(3)^2 + 6(4)^2 + 3(5)^2}{2 + 4 + 8 + 6 + 3}}$

   $= 3.36 \text{ m/s}$

   (c) Most probable speed is the speed possessed by the maximum number of molecules. Here 8 molecules have speed of 3.0 m/s. So, $v_{mp} = 3.0$ m/s.
3. $v_{rms} = \sqrt{\frac{3RT}{M}} = \sqrt{\frac{3 \times 8.314 \times 300}{32 \times 10^{-3}}} = 483.6 \text{ m/s}$
4. $v_{rms} = \sqrt{\frac{3RT}{M}}$

   $\Rightarrow 1930 = \sqrt{\frac{3 \times (25/3) \times 300}{M}}$

   $\Rightarrow M = 2 \times 10^{-3} \text{ kg} = 2 \text{ g}$

   So, gas will be H_2.

   $v'_{rms} = 2v_{rms}$

   $\Rightarrow \sqrt{\frac{3RT'}{M}} = 2\sqrt{\frac{3R(300)}{M}}$

   $\Rightarrow T' = 1200 \text{ K} = 927° \text{C}$
5. $\rho = \frac{m}{V} = \frac{20}{10 \times 10^3} = 2 \times 10^{-3} \text{ g/cm}^3$

   $v_{rms} = \sqrt{\frac{3p}{\rho}} = \sqrt{\frac{3 \times 24 \times 10^5}{2 \times 10^{-3}}} = 6 \times 10^4 \text{ cm/s} = 600 \text{ m/s}$
6. $v = \sqrt{\frac{3RT}{M}} \Rightarrow v \propto \sqrt{T}$

   $\therefore \frac{v_1}{v_2} = \sqrt{\frac{T_1}{T_2}}$

   $\Rightarrow \frac{200}{v_2} = \sqrt{\frac{300}{600}} \Rightarrow v_2 = 200\sqrt{2} \text{ m/s}$
7. $(v_{rms})_{H_2} = (v_{rms})_{O_2}$

   $\Rightarrow \sqrt{\frac{3RT}{2 \times 10^{-3}}} = \sqrt{\frac{3R(273 + 47)}{32 \times 10^{-3}}}$

   $\Rightarrow T = 20 \text{ K} = -253° \text{C}$
8. $v_{rms} = \sqrt{\frac{3RT}{M}}$

   $\Rightarrow \frac{(v_{rms})_{H_2}}{(v_{rms})_{He}} = \sqrt{\frac{M_{He}}{M_{H_2}}} = \sqrt{\frac{4}{2}} = \sqrt{2}$

5.3 Pressure on the Walls of Container

1. $p = \frac{1}{3}\frac{mN}{V} v_{rms}^2 = \frac{1}{3} \times \frac{5.3 \times 10^{-26} \times 3.0 \times 10^{22}}{10^{-3}} \times (400)^2$

   $= 8.48 \times 10^4 \text{ N/m}^2$
2. $p = \frac{1}{3}\rho v_{rms}^2 = \frac{1}{3} \times 8.99 \times 10^{-2} \times (3180)^2$

   $= 3.03 \times 10^5 \text{ N/m}^2 = 3.0 \text{ atm}$
3. Force on one wall due to $\frac{N}{2}$ molecules

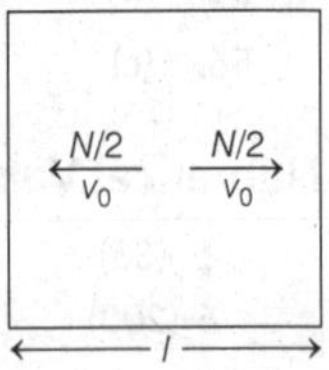

   $F = \frac{\Delta p}{\Delta t} = \left(\frac{2mv_0}{\left(\frac{2l}{v_0}\right)}\right) \times \frac{N}{2} = \frac{mv_0^2 N}{2l}$

   Pressure $= \frac{F}{A} = \frac{mv_0^2 N}{2l(l^2)} = \frac{mv_0^2 N}{2l^3}$
4. Number of hits per second $= \frac{v_{rms}}{2l}$

   $\Rightarrow 500 = \frac{v_{rms}}{2(1)} \Rightarrow v_{rms} = 1000 \text{ m/s}$

   (a) $v_{rms} = \sqrt{\frac{3RT}{M}}$

   $\Rightarrow 100 = \sqrt{\frac{3 \times (25/3) \times T}{4 \times 10^{-3}}} \Rightarrow T = 160 \text{ K}$

   (b) $K = \frac{3}{2}kT = \frac{3}{2} \times 1.38 \times 10^{-23} \times 160 = 3.312 \times 10^{-21} \text{ J}$

   (c) $p = \frac{1}{3}\left(\frac{m}{V}\right) v_{rms}^2$

   $\Rightarrow 100 = \frac{1}{3} \times \frac{m}{(1)^3} \times (1000)^2$

   $\Rightarrow m = 3 \times 10^{-4} \text{ kg}$

5.4 Maxwell's Distribution of Speed

1. $v_{avg} = \sqrt{\dfrac{8RT}{\pi M}}$

$\Rightarrow 11 \times 10^3 = \sqrt{\dfrac{8 \times (25/3) \times T}{3.14 \times 32 \times 10^{-3}}}$

$\Rightarrow \quad T = 1.82 \times 10^5$ K

2. $p_{avg} = mv_{avg} = m\sqrt{\dfrac{8kT}{\pi m}} = \sqrt{\dfrac{8kTm}{\pi}}$

$\therefore p_{avg} = \sqrt{\dfrac{8 \times 1.38 \times 10^{-23} \times 273 \times 6.64 \times 10^{-27}}{\pi}}$

$= 7.98 \times 10^{-24}$ kg-m/s

3. $v_{mean} = \sqrt{\dfrac{8RT}{\pi M}}$

$\Rightarrow \dfrac{(v_{mean})_{H_2}}{(v_{mean})_{He}} = \sqrt{\dfrac{T_{H_2}}{T_{He}}} \times \sqrt{\dfrac{M_{He}}{M_{H_2}}}$

$\Rightarrow \quad 1 = \sqrt{\dfrac{T_{H_2}}{T_{He}}} \times \sqrt{\dfrac{4}{2}} \quad \Rightarrow \quad \dfrac{T_{H_2}}{T_{He}} = \dfrac{1}{2}$

4. (a) $v_{rms} - v_{mp} = \Delta v$

$\Rightarrow \sqrt{\dfrac{3RT}{M}} - \sqrt{\dfrac{2RT}{M}} = \Delta v$

$\Rightarrow \quad T = \dfrac{M}{R}\dfrac{(\Delta v)^2}{(\sqrt{3}-\sqrt{2})^2}$

$= \dfrac{2 \times 10^{-3}}{8.314} \times \left(\dfrac{400}{\sqrt{3}-\sqrt{2}}\right)^2 = 381$ K

(b) $v_{mp} = \sqrt{\dfrac{2RT}{M}} = 420$

$\Rightarrow \sqrt{\dfrac{2 \times 8.314 \times T}{32 \times 10^{-3}}} = 420$

$\Rightarrow \quad T = 340$ K

5.5 Mean Free Path

1. $\lambda \propto \dfrac{1}{p}$

So, if λ is doubled, p will get halved.

$\therefore \quad p' = \dfrac{p}{2}$

2. $\lambda = \dfrac{1}{\sqrt{2}\,\pi n d^2}$

$\Rightarrow 0.8 \times 10^{-7} = \dfrac{1}{\sqrt{2} \times 3.14 \times 2.7 \times 10^{25} \times d^2}$

$\Rightarrow \quad d = 3.2 \times 10^{-10}$ m $= 3.2$ Å

3. $\lambda \propto \dfrac{1}{d^2}$

$\Rightarrow \quad \dfrac{\lambda_1}{\lambda_2} = \left(\dfrac{d_2}{d_1}\right)^2 = \left(\dfrac{2}{1}\right)^2 = 4:1$

5.6 Degree of Freedom

2. Number of molecules in 1 cm^3 of H_2

$= \dfrac{6.023 \times 10^{23}}{22400} \times 1 = 2.688 \times 10^{19}$

Number of degree of fredom of H_2 molecule $= 3 + 2 = 5$

Total number of degrees of freedom $= 2.688 \times 10^{19} \times 5$

$= 1.344 \times 10^{20}$

5.7 Kinetic Energy

1. $K = \dfrac{3}{2}RT = \dfrac{3}{2} \times 8.31 \times 400 = 4986$ J

2. (a) $K_T = 3\left(\dfrac{1}{2}kT\right) = \dfrac{3}{2} \times 1.38 \times 10^{-23} \times 300 = 6.21 \times 10^{-21}$ J

(b) $K_R = 2\left(\dfrac{1}{2}kT\right) = 1.38 \times 10^{-23} \times 300 = 4.14 \times 10^{-21}$ J.

(c) $K_{Total} = 5\left(\dfrac{1}{2}kT\right) = \dfrac{5}{2} \times 1.38 \times 10^{-23} \times 300$

$= 10.35 \times 10^{-21}$ J

3. $K_T = \dfrac{3}{2}kT$

$\Rightarrow 0.02 \times 1.6 \times 10^{-19} = \dfrac{3}{2} \times 1.38 \times 10^{-23} \times T$

$\Rightarrow \quad T = 154.6$ K

4. $K \propto T$

$\Rightarrow \quad \dfrac{K_1}{K_2} = \dfrac{T_1}{T_2}$

$\Rightarrow \dfrac{6.21 \times 10^{-21}}{K_2} = \dfrac{300}{500}$

$\Rightarrow \quad K_2 = 10.35 \times 10^{-21}$ J

5. $K_T = n \times 3 \times \left(\dfrac{1}{2}RT\right) = \dfrac{3}{2}pV$

$\Rightarrow 1.5 \times 10^5 = \dfrac{3}{2} \times p \times (20 \times 10^{-3})$

$\Rightarrow \quad p = 5 \times 10^6$ N/m^2

6. $K_R = 2\left(\dfrac{1}{2}kT\right) = 2\left(\dfrac{1}{2}I\omega^2\right)$

$\Rightarrow \omega = \sqrt{\dfrac{kT}{I}} = \sqrt{\dfrac{1.38 \times 10^{-23} \times 300}{2 \times 10^{-40}}} = 4.5 \times 10^9$ rad/s

5.8 Internal Energy

1. $U = nf\left(\dfrac{1}{2}RT\right)$

$= 5 \times 3 \times \dfrac{1}{2} \times 8.314 \times 280 = 1.74 \times 10^4$ J

2. $\Delta U = n\left(\dfrac{fR}{2}\right)\Delta T$

$$\Rightarrow 25 = \frac{2.8}{28}\left(\frac{5\times(25/3)}{2}\right)(T-30) \quad \Rightarrow T = 42°\text{C}$$

3. Kinetic energy of gas w.r.t. centre of mass of the system is the kinetic energy of molecules due to their random motion. This will be the internal energy of the gas.

(a) $K = nf\left(\frac{1}{2}RT\right) = n(5)\left(\frac{1}{2}RT\right) = \frac{5}{2}nRT$

(b) Kinetic energy of gas w.r.t. ground
= Kinetic energy of centre of mass w.r.t. ground
+ Kinetic energy of gas w.r.t. centre of mass

$$= \frac{1}{2}Mv^2 + \frac{5}{2}nRT$$

4. $U_1 + U_2 = U'_1 + U'_2$

$$\Rightarrow \left(\frac{16}{32}\right)\left(\frac{5R}{2}\right)340 + \left(\frac{2}{4}\right)\left(\frac{3R}{2}\right)300 = \left(\frac{16}{32}\right)\left(\frac{5R}{2}\right)T + \left(\frac{2}{4}\right)\left(\frac{3R}{2}\right)T$$

$$\Rightarrow \quad T = 325\text{ K} = 52°\text{C}$$

5. $$(C_V)_{mix} = \frac{n_1C_{V_1} + n_2C_{V_2}}{n_1 + n_2} = \frac{2\left(\frac{3R}{2}\right) + 3\left(\frac{5R}{2}\right)}{2+3} = \frac{21}{10}R$$

$$(C_V)_{mix} = \frac{R}{\gamma_{mix} - 1} = \frac{21}{10}R$$

$$\Rightarrow \gamma_{mix} = \frac{31}{21}$$

5.9 Ideal Gas Equation

1. $N = \frac{pV}{kT} = \frac{1.3\times10^5 \times 7\times10^{-3}}{1.38\times10^{-23}\times273} = 2.4\times10^{23}$

2. $\rho = \frac{pM}{RT} = \frac{5\times10^5\times16\times10^{-3}}{(25/3)\times300} = 3.2\text{ kg/m}^3$

3. At constant volume, $p \propto T$

$$\therefore \frac{\Delta p}{p}\times100 = \frac{\Delta T}{T}\times100$$

$$\Rightarrow \quad 0.5 = \frac{5}{T}\times100 \quad \Rightarrow T = 1000\text{ K}$$

4. $Vp^2 = $ constant

$$\Rightarrow V\left(\frac{nRT}{V}\right)^2 = \text{constant}$$

$$\Rightarrow \quad V \propto T^2$$

$$\therefore \quad \frac{V_1}{V_2} = \left(\frac{T_1}{T_2}\right)^2 \quad \Rightarrow \frac{V}{2V} = \left(\frac{T}{T_2}\right)^2$$

$$\Rightarrow \quad T_2 = \sqrt{2}T$$

5. $p = \frac{nRT}{V}$

$$\Rightarrow \frac{p_1}{p_2} = \left(\frac{T_1}{T_2}\right)\left(\frac{V_2}{V_1}\right) = \left(\frac{300}{600}\right)\left(\frac{2V_0}{V_0}\right) = 1:1$$

6. At constant volume,

$$\frac{p_1}{T_1} = \frac{p_2}{T_2}$$

$$\Rightarrow \frac{2\times10^5}{320} = \frac{8\times10^5}{T_2}$$

$$\Rightarrow \quad T_2 = 1280\text{ K} = 1007°\text{C}$$

7. Let mass of neon $= m$

$\therefore$ Mass of argon $= 28 - m$

$$pV = nRT$$

$$\Rightarrow 1\times10^5\times0.02 = \left(\frac{m}{20} + \frac{28-m}{40}\right)\times\frac{25}{3}\times300$$

$$\Rightarrow \quad m = 4\text{ g}$$

$\therefore$ Mass of neon = 4 g and mass of argon = 24 g

8. $pV = nRT$

$$\Rightarrow 1\times V = \left(\frac{2}{M_A}\right)RT \quad \text{...(i)}$$

When 3 g of another gas are added,

$$pV = nRT$$

$$\Rightarrow 1.5\times V = \left(\frac{2}{M_A} + \frac{3}{M_B}\right)RT \quad \text{...(ii)}$$

Solving Eqs. (i) and (ii), we get

$$\frac{M_A}{M_B} = 1:3$$

9. $$pV = nRT$$

$$\Rightarrow p\times6\times10^{-3} = \left(\frac{16}{32} + \frac{14}{28} + \frac{11}{44}\right)\times8.31\times300$$

$$\Rightarrow \quad p = 5.2\times10^5\text{ N/m}^2$$

10. $$pV = nRT$$

$$\Rightarrow \quad 2\times10^5\times0.05 = \left(\frac{m_1}{32}\right)\times\left(\frac{25}{3}\right)\times320$$

$$\Rightarrow \quad m_1 = 120\text{ g}$$

$$pV = nRT$$

$$\Rightarrow 0.8\times10^5\times0.05 = \left(\frac{m_2}{32}\right)\left(\frac{25}{3}\right)320$$

$$\Rightarrow \quad m_2 = 48\text{ g}$$

Mass of O_2 used $= 120 - 48 = 72$ g

11. $n = \frac{pV}{RT}$

$$\Rightarrow n_1 = \frac{2\times10^5\times0.002}{(25/3)\times300} = 0.16$$

After tube gets punctured,

$$n = \frac{pV}{RT}$$

$$\Rightarrow n_2 = \frac{1\times10^5\times0.0005}{(25/3)\times300} = 0.02$$

Moles leaked out $= n_1 - n_2 = 0.14$

12. For open vessel, $nT = \text{constant}$

$\Rightarrow \quad n \propto \frac{1}{T}$

$\therefore \quad \frac{n_1}{n_2} = \frac{T_2}{T_1} \Rightarrow \frac{n}{(2n/3)} = \frac{T_2}{300}$

$\Rightarrow \quad T_2 = 450\,\text{K} = 177°\,\text{C}$

13. $p_1 = 75 + 5 = 80$ cm of Hg, $V_1 = A$ (30 cm)

$p_2 = 75 - 5 = 70$ cm of Hg, $V_2 = A(h)$

Since temperature remains constant,

$p_1V_1 = p_2V_2$

$\Rightarrow 80 \times A(30) = 70 \times A(h)$

$\Rightarrow \quad h = \frac{240}{7}$ cm

14. $n_1 + n_2 = n'_1 + n'_2$

$\Rightarrow \frac{p_0V_0}{RT_0} + \frac{p_0V_0}{RT_0} = \frac{pV_0}{RT_0} + \frac{pV_0}{R(2T_0)}$

$\Rightarrow \quad p = \frac{4}{3}p_0$

15. Let final pressure and temperature be p and T, respectively.

Applying internal energy conservation,

$U_1 + U_2 = U'_1 + U'_2$

$$\Rightarrow \left[\frac{(2p_0)(2V_0)}{RT_0}\right]C_VT_0 + \left[\frac{p_0V_0}{R(2T_0)}\right]C_V(2T_0) = \left[\frac{p(2V_0)}{RT}\right]C_VT + \left(\frac{pV_0}{RT}\right)C_VT$$

$\Rightarrow p = \frac{5p_0}{3}$

Applying conservation of moles,

$n_1 + n_2 = n'_1 + n'_2$

$$\Rightarrow \frac{(2p_0)(2V_0)}{RT_0} + \frac{p_0V_0}{R(2T_0)} = \frac{(5p_0/3)(2V_0)}{RT} + \frac{(5p_0/3)V_0}{RT}$$

$\Rightarrow \quad T = \frac{10T_0}{9}$

5.10 Graphs of Different Processes

1. (a)

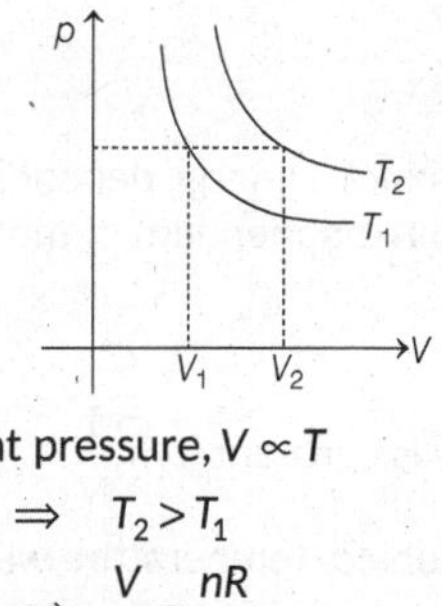

At constant pressure, $V \propto T$

$\because V_2 > V_1 \Rightarrow T_2 > T_1$

(b) $pV = nRT \Rightarrow \frac{V}{T} = \frac{nR}{p}$

$\Rightarrow \text{Slope} \propto \frac{1}{\text{Pressure}}$

$\because (\text{Slope})_2 > (\text{Slope})_1 \Rightarrow p_2 < p_1$

(c) $pV = nRT \Rightarrow \frac{p}{T} = \frac{nR}{V} \Rightarrow \text{Slope} \propto \frac{1}{\text{Volume}}$

$(\text{Slope})_2 > (\text{Slope})_1 \Rightarrow V_2 < V_1$

2. (a) $(pV)_2 > (pV)_1$

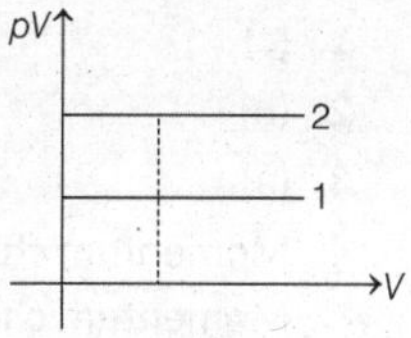

$\Rightarrow nRT_2 > nRT_1 \Rightarrow T_1 < T_2$

At constant volume,

$p_2V > p_1V \Rightarrow p_1 < p_2$

(b) $T_1 = \frac{p(2V)}{nR}, T_2 = \frac{(2p)V}{nR}$

$\therefore T_1 = T_2$

So, 1 and 2 will lie on an isotherm.

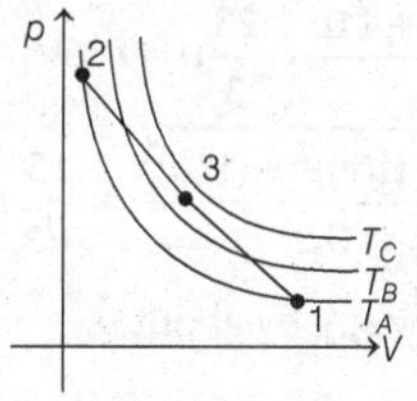

$T_C > T_B > T_A$

So, as we go from 1 to 2, temperature first increases and then decreases.

$\therefore T_1 = T_2 < T_3$

(c) $\text{Slope} = \frac{p}{T} = \frac{nR}{V}$

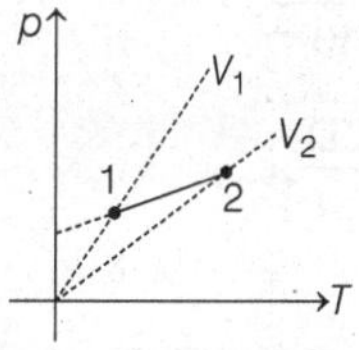

$\therefore \text{Slope} \propto \frac{1}{\text{Volume}}$

$\because (\text{Slope})_1 > (\text{Slope})_2 \Rightarrow V_2 > V_1$

(d) $\text{Slope} = \frac{V}{T} = \frac{nR}{p}$

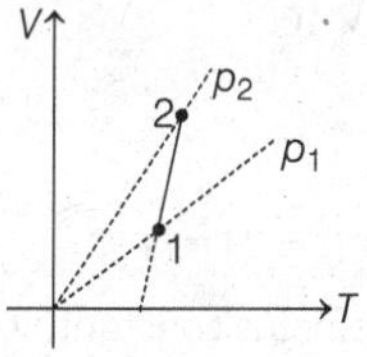

$\therefore \text{Slope} \propto \frac{1}{\text{Pressure}}$

$\because (\text{Slope})_2 > (\text{Slope})_1 \Rightarrow p_1 > p_2$

3. $A \rightarrow B$ is isochoric process.

$\therefore \quad \frac{p_A}{T_A} = \frac{p_B}{T_B} \Rightarrow \frac{p_0}{T_0} = \frac{2p_0}{T_B}$

$\Rightarrow T_B = 2T_0$

$B \rightarrow C$ is isobaric process.

$\therefore \quad \frac{V_B}{T_B} = \frac{V_C}{T_C} \Rightarrow \frac{V_0}{2T_0} = \frac{2V_0}{T_C} \Rightarrow T_C = 4T_0$

Level 2

Single Choice Correct Questions

1. (c)
2. (b)
3. (a)
4. Momentum change when molecule gets absorbed $= mv$
   Momentum change when molecule rebounds with the speed $= mv - (-mv) = 2mv$
   So, pressure on *EFGH* would be half that on *ABCD*.

5. $v_{mean} = \dfrac{2u + 10u + 11u}{3} = \dfrac{23}{3}u = 766u$

$$v_{rms} = \sqrt{\frac{(2u)^2 + (10u)^2 + (11u)^2}{3}} = \frac{15}{\sqrt{3}}u = 8.66u$$

So, v_{rms} exceeds v_{mean} by about u.

6. $(v_{rms})_{O_2} = (v_{rms})_{N_2}$

$$\Rightarrow \sqrt{\frac{3RT}{32 \times 10^{-3}}} = \sqrt{\frac{3R(273 + 100)}{28 \times 10^{-3}}}$$

$$\Rightarrow \quad T = 426.3 \text{ K}$$

7. For O_2, $v = \sqrt{\dfrac{3RT}{32 \times 10^{-3}}}$

   For O, $v' = \sqrt{\dfrac{3R(2T)}{16 \times 10^{-3}}}$

   $\therefore \quad v' = 2v$

8. v_{rms} depends only on temperature. As temperature remains same, v_{rms} will be same.

9. For O_2, $v_{rms} = \sqrt{\dfrac{3RT}{32 \times 10^{-3}}} = 0.5$ km/s

   For H_2, $v'_{rms} = \sqrt{\dfrac{3RT}{2 \times 10^{-3}}}$

   $\therefore \quad \dfrac{v'_{rms}}{v_{rms}} = 4$

   $\Rightarrow \quad v'_{rms} = 4v_{rms} = 2$ km/s

10. As temperature remains constant, v_{rms} will be same.

11. Let T = Temperature on Celsius scale
    K = Temperature on absolute scale
    $T = K - 273 \quad \Rightarrow \quad 2T = 2K - 273$
    So, final temperature in case (i) $= 2K$
    and final temperature in case (ii) $= 2K - 273$
    As $v_{rms} \propto \sqrt{K}$, the increase in v_{rms} will be more in case (i).

12. Average speed of gas molecules depends only on the temperature and molecular weight. Since, vessel *A* and *C* are at the same temperature, average speed of O_2 molecules will be same in both the vessels.

13. For one molecule, $v_{mp} = v_{avg}$

14. $v_{avg} = \sqrt{\dfrac{8RT}{\pi M}} = \sqrt{\dfrac{8p}{\pi \rho}}$

    $\therefore p \propto (v_{avg})^2$

    So, it average speed is doubled, pressure would become 4 times.

15. $T = \dfrac{pV}{nR}$,

    $T' = \dfrac{(2p)(2V)}{nR} = 4T$

    $v_{avg} \propto \sqrt{T}$

    So, if temperature becomes 4 times, average speed will get doubled.

16. $p_0 = \dfrac{1}{3}\left(\dfrac{mN}{V}\right)v_{rms}^2$

    $p = \dfrac{1}{3}\left(\dfrac{(m/2)N}{V}\right)(2v_{rms})^2 = 2p_0$

17. $\lambda = \dfrac{kT}{\sqrt{2}\,\pi d^2 p} = \dfrac{1.38 \times 10^{-23} \times 300}{\sqrt{2} \times 3.14 \times (0.3 \times 10^{-9})^2 (1.01 \times 10^5)}$

    $= 102$ nm

18. $K_T = \dfrac{3}{2}kT = \dfrac{3}{2} \times 1.38 \times 10^{-23} \times 273 = 5.65 \times 10^{-21}$ J

19. $K \propto T$

    $\therefore \dfrac{K_1}{K_2} = \dfrac{T_1}{T_2} \quad \Rightarrow \quad \dfrac{E}{K_2} = \dfrac{300}{900} \quad \Rightarrow \quad K_2 = 3E$

20. $K_T = n(3)\left(\dfrac{1}{2}RT\right) = \dfrac{3}{2}pV$

    $\therefore \dfrac{K_T}{V} = \dfrac{3}{2}p \quad \Rightarrow \quad E = \dfrac{3}{2}p \quad \Rightarrow \quad p = \dfrac{2}{3}E$

21. $K_T \propto T$ and $v_{rms} \propto \sqrt{T}$

    So, when temperature is doubled, kinetic energy will be doubled and rms speed will become $\sqrt{2}$ times.

    $\therefore \quad K = 2(6.21 \times 10^{-21}) = 12.42 \times 10^{-21}$ J

    and $v_{rms} = \sqrt{2}\,(484) = 684$ m/s

22. $K_T = \dfrac{3}{2}kT$

    So, translational kinetic energy depends only on temperature and is independent of molar mass.

23. $K_T = \dfrac{3}{2}NkT$

    As kinetic energy is constant, $T \propto \dfrac{1}{N}$

    So, when N is doubled, temperature will get halved.

    $\therefore \quad T_2 = \dfrac{T_1}{2}$

    $pV = \left(\dfrac{N}{N_A}\right)RT$

As NT = constant, pressure will not change.

$\therefore \quad p_2 = p_1$

24. Both O_2 and N_2 have 2 rotational degrees of freedom. So, for each of them, rotational kinetic energy will be $2\left(\frac{1}{2}kT\right) = kT$.

25. A diatomic molecule has 3 translational and 2 rotational degree of freedom.

$$\therefore \quad \frac{K_T}{K_R} = \frac{3\left(\frac{1}{2}kT\right)}{2\left(\frac{1}{2}kT\right)} = \frac{3}{2}$$

26. $U = nC_VT = n\left(\frac{R}{\gamma-1}\right)T = \frac{pV}{\gamma-1}$

27.
$$U_{He} = U_{H_2}$$
$$\Rightarrow n_1\left(\frac{3R}{2}\right)(10T) = n_2\left(\frac{5R}{2}\right)(6T)$$
$$\Rightarrow \quad \frac{n_1}{n_2} = 1$$

28. $U = U_1 + U_2 = 2\left(\frac{5R}{2}\right)T + 4\left(\frac{3R}{2}\right)T = 11RT$

29.
$$U_1 + U_2 = U'_1 + U'_2$$
$$\Rightarrow 2\left(\frac{3R}{2}\right)T_0 + 4\left(\frac{3R}{2}\right)(2T_0) = 2\left(\frac{3R}{2}\right)T + 4\left(\frac{3R}{2}\right)T$$
$$\Rightarrow \quad T = \frac{5}{3}T_0$$

30. Loss in kinetic energy will be the gain in internal energy

$$\therefore \quad \frac{1}{2}mv^2 = nC_V\Delta T$$
$$\Rightarrow \frac{1}{2}(n \times 30 \times 10^{-3})(100)^2 = n\left(\frac{5R}{2}\right)\Delta T$$
$$\Rightarrow \quad \Delta T = \frac{60}{R}$$

31. $(C_V)_{\text{mix}} = \frac{n_1C_{V_1} + n_2C_{V_2}}{n_1 + n_2} = \frac{2\left(\frac{3R}{2}\right) + 1\left(\frac{5R}{2}\right)}{2+1} = \frac{11R}{6}$

$(C_V)_{\text{mix}} = \frac{R}{\gamma_{\text{mix}} - 1} = \frac{11R}{6} \quad \Rightarrow \quad \gamma_{\text{mix}} = \frac{17}{11}$

32. $pV = nRT$

$\Rightarrow pV = \left(\frac{N}{N_A}\right)RT \quad \Rightarrow \quad pV = N\left(\frac{R}{N_A}\right)T$

$\Rightarrow pV = NkT$

$\Rightarrow \; N = \frac{pV}{kT}$ = Number of molecules

33. For first vessel, $pV = nRT$

$$\Rightarrow \quad pV = 1 \times R \times T$$

For second vessel, $PV = nRT$

$$\Rightarrow \quad p'V = 1 \times R \times 2T$$
$$\therefore \quad p' = 2P$$

34.
$$pV = nRT$$
$$\Rightarrow \quad 6 \times V = \left(\frac{35 \times 10^3}{28}\right)RT$$

When oxygen is added,

$$pV = nRT$$
$$\Rightarrow \quad 9 \times V = \left(\frac{35 \times 10^3}{28} + \frac{m \times 10^3}{32}\right)RT$$

Solving we get, $m = 20$ kg

35. For mixture, $pV = nRT$

$$\Rightarrow \quad 10 \times V = \left(\frac{8}{32} + \frac{7}{28}\right)RT \quad \text{...(i)}$$

When oxygen is absorbed, $pV = nRT$

$$\Rightarrow \quad p \times V = \left(\frac{7}{28}\right)RT \quad \text{...(ii)}$$

Solving Eqs. (i) and (ii), we get $p = 5$ atm

36. Let mass of hydrogen $= m$

and mass of helium $= 5 - m$

$$pV = nRT$$
$$\Rightarrow (2 \text{ atm})(0.02 \times 10^3 \text{ L}) = \left(\frac{m}{2} + \frac{5-m}{4}\right)(0.082)(293)$$
$$\Rightarrow \quad m = 1.66 \text{ g}$$
$$\therefore \quad \frac{m_{H_2}}{m_{He}} = \frac{m}{5-m} = 1:2$$

37. For open vessel, nT = constant

$$\therefore \quad n_1T_1 = n_2T_2$$
$$\Rightarrow n \times (273 + 60) = \left(n - \frac{n}{4}\right)T$$
$$\Rightarrow \quad T = 444\text{ K} = 171°\text{C}$$

38. As $V \propto T$

$$\Rightarrow \quad \frac{V_2}{V_1} = \frac{T_2}{T_1} = \frac{313}{293}$$

Fraction of gas comes out $= \frac{V_2 - V_1}{V_1} = \frac{V_2}{V_1} - 1$

$$= \frac{313}{293} - 1 = \frac{20}{293} = 0.068$$

39.
$$pV = nRT$$
$$\Rightarrow \quad 20 \times V = nR \times 300 \quad \text{...(i)}$$

When half of the gas is released and temperature raised by 50°C,

$$pV = nRT$$
$$\Rightarrow p \times V = \left(n - \frac{n}{2}\right)R \times 350 \quad \text{...(ii)}$$

Solving Eqs. (i) and (ii), we get $p = 11.7$ atm

40. $pV = nRT$

$\Rightarrow \quad pV = \left(\frac{m}{M}\right)RT \quad \Rightarrow \quad m \propto \frac{V}{T}$

$\therefore \quad \frac{m_1}{m_2} = \left(\frac{V_1}{V_2}\right)\left(\frac{T_2}{T_1}\right)$

$\Rightarrow \quad \frac{m}{m_2} = \left(\frac{2V}{V}\right)\left(\frac{200}{100}\right) \quad \Rightarrow \quad m_2 = \frac{m}{4}$

41. $\rho = \frac{m}{V} = \frac{12}{4 \times 10^{-3} \times 10^6} = 3 \times 10^{-3}$ g/cc

$\rho = \frac{pM}{RT} \quad \Rightarrow \quad \frac{\rho_1}{\rho_2} = \frac{T_2}{T_1}$

$\Rightarrow \frac{3 \times 10^{-3}}{6 \times 10^{-4}} = \frac{T_2}{280} \quad \Rightarrow \quad T_2 = 1400$ K

42. $pV = nRT$

$8.3 \times 10^5 \times V = \left(\frac{28}{28} + \frac{4}{2} + \frac{8}{4}\right) \times 8.3 \times 400$

$\Rightarrow \quad V = 0.02\,\text{m}^3 = 20$ L

$\rho = \frac{m}{V} = \frac{28+4+8}{20} = 2$ g/L

43. $n_1 + n_2 = n'_1 + n'_2$

$\Rightarrow \frac{p_0V_0}{R(300)} + \frac{p_0V_0}{R(300)} = \frac{pV_0}{R(600)} + \frac{pV_0}{R(300)}$

$\Rightarrow \quad p = \frac{4p_0}{3} = \frac{4}{3}$ atm

44.

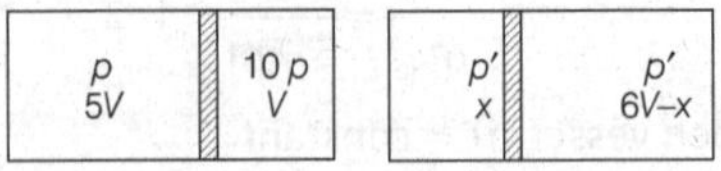

For left part, $p_1V_1 = p_2V_2$

$\Rightarrow \quad p(5V) = p'x \quad$ ...(i)

For right part, $p_1V_1 = p_2V_2$

$\Rightarrow \quad (10p)V = p'(6V - x) \quad$ ...(ii)

$\therefore \quad \frac{6V - x}{x} = 2 \quad \Rightarrow \quad x = 2V$

So, volume of the two parts will be $2V$ and $4V$.

45. Pressure of gas inside cylinder $= p_0 + \frac{Mg}{A} =$ constant

As temperature is increased, V will increase but p will remain unchanged.

46. $pV^{4/3} =$ constant

$\Rightarrow p\left(\frac{nRT}{p}\right)^{4/3} = \text{constant} \quad \Rightarrow \quad T \propto p^{1/4}$

$\therefore \quad \frac{T_2}{T_1} = \left(\frac{p_2}{p_1}\right)^{1/4}$

$\Rightarrow \quad \frac{T_2}{300} = \left(\frac{4p_1}{p_1}\right)^{1/4}$

$\Rightarrow \quad T_2 = 300\sqrt{2}$ K

47. At constant volume, $p \propto T$

$\therefore \quad \frac{\Delta p}{p} \times 100 = \frac{\Delta T}{T} \times 100$

$\Rightarrow \quad 0.5 = \frac{1}{T} \times 100 \quad \Rightarrow \quad T = 200$ K

48. $pV = nRT \quad \Rightarrow \quad y = mx$

So, graph will be straight line passing through origin.

49. Slope $= \frac{V}{T} = \frac{nR}{p} = \frac{mR}{Mp}$

$\therefore$ Slope $\propto \frac{m}{p}$

So, if both m and p are doubled, slope will remain same.

As the slope doesn't change, the straight line will be B.

50.

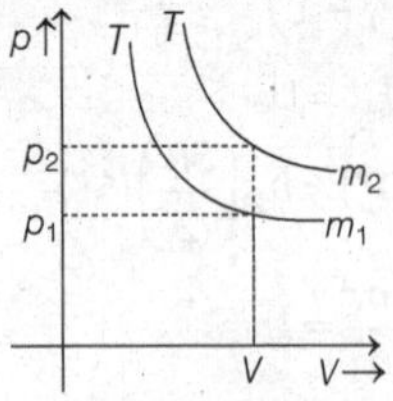

$pV = \left(\frac{m}{M}\right)RT \quad \Rightarrow \quad m = \frac{pVM}{RT}$

At constant volume, $m \propto p$

$\because p_2 > p_1 \quad \Rightarrow \quad m_2 > m_1$

51. Slope $= \frac{T}{V} = \frac{p}{nR}$

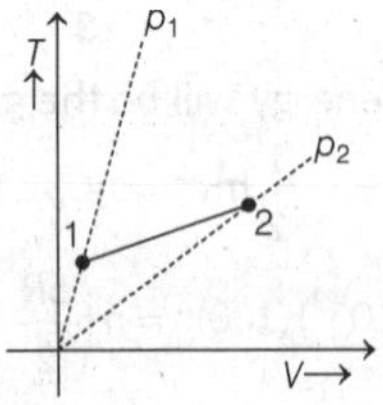

$\therefore$ Slope $\propto$ Pressure

$\because \quad (\text{Slope})_1 > (\text{Slope})_2 \quad \Rightarrow \quad p_2 < p_1$

So, during the heating process from state 1 to state 2, the pressure decreased.

52. $T_A = \frac{(2p)V}{nR}, \quad T_B = \frac{p(2V)}{nR}$

$\therefore T_A = T_B$, so A and B will lie on an isotherm.

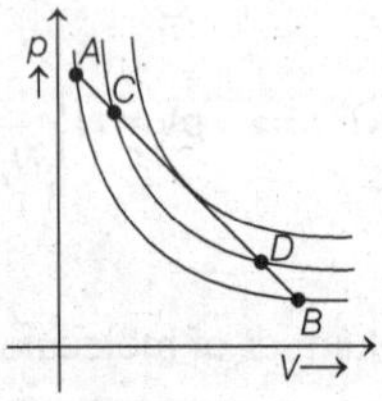

C and D lie on another isotherm of higher temperature

$\therefore \quad T_C = T_D > T_A$ or T_B

So, as the gas is taken from A to B, its temperature initially increases then decreases.

53. $\rho = \frac{pM}{RT}$

At A, $\rho_0 = \frac{p_0 M}{RT_0}$

At B, $\rho = \frac{(3p_0)M}{R(2T_0)} = \frac{3}{2}\rho_0$

54. $\text{Slope} = \frac{p}{\rho} = \frac{RT}{M}$

$\Rightarrow$ Slope $\propto$ Temperature

$\because$ $(\text{Slope})_1 > (\text{Slope})_2 \Rightarrow T_1 > T_2$

55. $pV = nRT \Rightarrow pdV + Vdp = 0$

$\Rightarrow \frac{dV}{dp} = -\frac{V}{p}$

$\beta = -\frac{dV/dp}{V} = -\left(-\frac{V}{p}\right)\frac{1}{V} = \frac{1}{p}$

$\Rightarrow \beta \propto \frac{1}{p}$

So, β *versus* p graph will be rectangular hyperbola.

56. $A \to B$: Isochoric heating
$B \to C$: Isothermal expansion
$C \to A$: Isobaric cooling

57. $A \to B$: Isobaric heating
$B \to C$: Isothermal expansion
$C \to D$: Isobaric cooling
$D \to A$: Isothermal compression

58. When $V = V_0$,

$$p_1 = p_0\left[1 + \left(\frac{2V_0}{V_0}\right)^2\right]^{-1} = \frac{p_0}{5}$$

When $V = 2V_0$,

$$p_2 = p_0\left[1 + \left(\frac{2V_0}{2V_0}\right)^2\right]^{-1} = \frac{p_0}{2}$$

$$T_2 - T_1 = \frac{p_2V_2 - p_1V_1}{nR} = \frac{\left(\frac{p_0}{2}\right)2V_0 - \left(\frac{p_0}{5}\right)V_0}{nR} = \frac{4}{5}\frac{p_0V_0}{nR}$$

Numerical Value Questions

1. $n = \frac{1.4}{28} \times \frac{30}{100} \times 2 + \frac{1.4}{28} \times \frac{70}{100} + \frac{0.4}{4} = 0.165$

$pV = nRT$

$\Rightarrow p = \frac{nRT}{V} = \frac{0.165 \times (25/3) \times 1500}{5 \times 10^{-3}} = 4.125 \times 10^5 \text{ Pa}$

$\therefore \frac{N}{8} = 4.125 \Rightarrow N = 33$

2. For He, $v_{rms} = \sqrt{\frac{3RT_1}{4 \times 10^{-3}}} = 1000$

$\Rightarrow 3RT_1 = 4000$

For O_2, $v_{rms} = \sqrt{\frac{3RT_2}{32 \times 10^{-3}}} = 1000$

$\Rightarrow 3RT_2 = 32000$

Applying internal energy conservation for mixing,

$U_1 + U_2 = U'_1 + U'_2$

$\Rightarrow \left(\frac{5}{4}\right)\left(\frac{3R}{2}\right)T_1 + \left(\frac{24}{32}\right)\left(\frac{5R}{2}\right)T_2 = \left(\frac{5}{4}\right)\left(\frac{3R}{2}\right)T + \left(\frac{24}{32}\right)\left(\frac{5R}{2}\right)T$

$\Rightarrow T = \frac{T_1 + T_2}{2}$

For O_2, $v_{rms} = \sqrt{\frac{3RT}{M}} = \sqrt{\frac{3R(T_1+T_2)}{32 \times 10^{-3} \times 2}}$

$= \sqrt{\frac{4000 + 32000}{32 \times 10^{-3} \times 2}}$

$= 750$ m/s

3. $V = \frac{m}{\rho} = \frac{1}{4} = 0.25 \text{ m}^3$

$E = \frac{5}{2}pV = \frac{5}{2} \times 8 \times 10^4 \times 0.25 = 50 \text{ kJ}$

4. Let atmosphere pressure be h cm of mercury.

$p_1V_1 = p_2V_2$

$\Rightarrow (h+8) \times A(4) = (h-8) \times A(5)$

$\Rightarrow h = 72$

5. At constant pressure,

Slope of line $= \frac{nR}{p} = \tan 53°$

$\Rightarrow \frac{2 \times (25/3) \times 10^3 \text{ Pa-L/mol-K}}{p} = \frac{4}{3}$

$\Rightarrow p = 1.25 \times 10^4 \text{ N/m}^2$

$\therefore \beta = 1.25$

6. $pV = nRT$

$\Rightarrow pV = \left(\frac{4}{36}\right)RT$ ...(i)

After removing argon and raising temperature

$pV = nRT$

$\Rightarrow pV = \left(\frac{4 - 0.8}{36}\right)R(T + 50)$ ...(ii)

Solving Eqs. (i) and (ii), we get $T = 200$ K

7. $p_2 = p_0 + \frac{mg}{A}$

$= 10^5 + \frac{100 \times 10^{-3} \times 10}{0.1 \times 10^{-4}} = 2 \times 10^5 \text{ Pa}$

At constant volume,

$\frac{p_1}{T_1} = \frac{p_2}{T_2} \Rightarrow \frac{10^5}{300} = \frac{2 \times 10^5}{T_2}$

$\Rightarrow T_2 = 600 \text{ K} = 327° \text{C}$

8. $p_1 = 76 + 40 = 116$ cm of Hg

When half of the mercury comes out of the cylinder,

$$p_2 = 76 + 20 = 96 \text{ cm of Hg}$$

$$\frac{p_1V_1}{T_1} = \frac{p_2V_2}{T_2}$$

$$\Rightarrow \frac{116 \times A(40)}{304.5} = \frac{96 \times A(60)}{T_2}$$

$$\Rightarrow T_2 = 378\,\text{K} = 105°\text{C}$$

9. $p_1 = p_0 + \frac{Kx}{A} = 10^5 + \frac{100 \times 10 \times 10^{-2}}{1 \times 10^{-4}} = 2 \times 10^5$ Pa

Let final compression be x' cm

$$p_2 = p_0 + \frac{Kx'}{A} = 10^5 + \frac{100 \times x' \times 10^{-2}}{1 \times 10^{-4}} = 10^4(10 + x')$$

$$\frac{p_1V_1}{T_1} = \frac{p_2V_2}{T_2}$$

$$\Rightarrow \frac{2 \times 10^5 \times (100A)}{T_1} = \frac{10^4(10 + x') \times (90 + x')A}{2.4T_1}$$

$$\Rightarrow (10 + x')(90 + x') = 4800$$

$$\Rightarrow x' = 30$$

$\therefore$ Distance moved by piston $= x' - x$

$$= 30 - 10 = 20 \text{ cm}$$

10. $p_1 = p_0 + \rho gh$

$$= 10^5 + 5 \times 10^3 \times 10 \times 20 \times 10^{-2} = 1.1 \times 10^5 \text{ Pa}$$

$$V_1 = A_1(h_0 - h) + A_2l$$

$$= 4 \times 10^{-4}(1.1 - h) + 1 \times 10^{-4} \times 20 \times 10^{-2}$$

$$= (4.6 - 4h) \times 10^{-4}$$

$$\frac{p_0V_0}{n_0} = \frac{p_1V_1}{n_1}$$

$$\Rightarrow \frac{10^5 \times (4 \times 10^{-4} \times 1.1)}{n_0} = \frac{1.1 \times 10^5 \times (4.6 - 4h) \times 10^{-4}}{0.4n_0}$$

$$\Rightarrow h = 0.75 \text{ m} = 75 \text{ cm}$$

Level 3

Single Choice Correct Questions

1. The motion of the vessel doesn't affect the relative motion of the gas molecules w.r.t. the walls of the vessel. Hence, pressure exerted by the gas on the vessel will remain same.

2. $F = \left(\frac{2mv}{(2l/v)}\right) \times \frac{n}{2} + \left[\frac{2m(2v)}{(2l/2v)}\right] \times \frac{n}{2} = 2.5\frac{nmv^2}{l}$

$$p = \frac{F}{A} = 2.5\frac{nmv^2}{l^3} = 2.5nmv^2$$

3. (b)

4. $v_{rms} = \sqrt{\frac{3kT}{m}} \Rightarrow T \propto mv_{rms}^2$

$\therefore T_D > T_A = T_B > T_C$

5. $T = \frac{pV}{nR} \Rightarrow \frac{T_1}{T_2} = \frac{p_1V_1}{p_2V_2} = \frac{4 \times 1}{1 \times 1} = 4$

$$v_{rms} = \sqrt{\frac{3kT}{m}}$$

$$\Rightarrow \frac{(v_{rms})_1}{(v_{rms})_2} = \sqrt{\frac{T_1}{T_2}} = 2$$

6. $\frac{1}{2}I\omega^2 = 2 \times \left(\frac{1}{2}kT\right) \Rightarrow \omega = \sqrt{\frac{2kT}{I}}$

8. For gas A, $< v_x^2 > = \frac{1}{3} < v_{rms}^2 >$

$$\Rightarrow w^2 = \frac{1}{3}\left(\frac{3kT}{m}\right) = \frac{kT}{m}$$

For gas B, $< v_{rms}^2 > = \frac{3kT}{(2m)}$

$$\Rightarrow v^2 = \frac{3kT}{2m}$$

$$\therefore \frac{w^2}{v^2} = \frac{2}{3}$$

9. $(v_{rms})_L = (v_{mean})_R$

$$\Rightarrow \sqrt{\frac{3kT}{m_L}} = \sqrt{\frac{8kT}{\pi m_R}} \Rightarrow \frac{m_L}{m_R} = \frac{3\pi}{8}$$

7. For mixture of gases,

$$v_{rms}^2 = \frac{N_1\bar{v}_1^2 + N_2\bar{v}_2^2}{N_1 + N_2}$$

$$= \frac{N_1\left(\frac{3RT}{M_1}\right) + N_2\left(\frac{3RT}{M_2}\right)}{N_1 + N_2} = \frac{3RT}{\left(\frac{N_1 + N_2}{\frac{N_1}{M_1} + \frac{N_2}{M_2}}\right)}$$

$$\therefore v_{rms} = \sqrt{\frac{3RT}{\left(\frac{1 + 7}{\frac{1}{44} + \frac{7}{28}}\right)}} = \sqrt{\frac{3RT}{(88/3)}}$$

$$(v_{rms})_{mixture} = x(v_{rms})_{CO_2}$$

$$\Rightarrow \sqrt{\frac{3RT}{(88/3)}} = x\sqrt{\frac{3RT}{44}} \Rightarrow x = \sqrt{\frac{3}{2}}$$

10. $v_{rms}^2 = \frac{\int v^2 dN}{\int dN} = \frac{\int_0^{v_0} v^2\left(\frac{3N_0}{v_0^3}\right)v^2 dv}{\int_0^{N_0} dN}$

$$= \frac{3}{v_0^3}\left[\frac{v^5}{5}\right]_0^{v_0} = \frac{3v_0^2}{5}$$

$$\therefore v_{rms} = \sqrt{\frac{3}{5}}v_0$$

11. For most probable speed,

$$\frac{dn}{dv}=0 \Rightarrow 7-2v_{mp}=0 \Rightarrow v_{mp}=3.5\text{ m/s}$$

12. $\frac{1}{2}mv^2=3\left(\frac{1}{2}kT\right) \Rightarrow v\propto\sqrt{T}$

Average Rotational KE $=2\left(\frac{1}{2}kT\right)=\frac{1}{3}mv^2$

Average KE $=5\left(\frac{1}{2}kT\right)=\frac{5}{6}mv^2$

13. When $V=V_0$,

$$p=\frac{p_0}{1+\left(\frac{V_0}{V_0}\right)^2}=\frac{p_0}{2}$$

Translational KE $=\frac{3}{2}pV=\frac{3}{2}\left(\frac{p_0}{2}\right)V_0=\frac{3}{4}p_0V_0$

14. $T=T_0+aV^3$

$$\Rightarrow \frac{pV}{nR}=T_0+aV^3 \Rightarrow p=R\left(\frac{T_0}{V}+aV^2\right)$$

For minimum pressure,

$$\frac{dp}{dV}=R\left(-\frac{T_0}{V^2}+2aV\right)=0$$

$$\Rightarrow V=\left(\frac{T_0}{2a}\right)^{1/3}$$

15. $p_{min}=R\left[T_0\left(\frac{2a}{T_0}\right)^{1/3}+a\left(\frac{T_0}{2a}\right)^{2/3}\right]=\frac{3}{2}(a^{1/3}RT_0^{2/3})2^{1/3}$

16. At constant volume,

$$\frac{p_1}{T_1}=\frac{p_2}{T_2} \Rightarrow \frac{p_0}{T_0}=\frac{p_2}{2T_0}$$

$$\Rightarrow p_2=2p_0$$

For equilibrium,

$$p_0A+T=2p_0A \Rightarrow T=p_0A$$

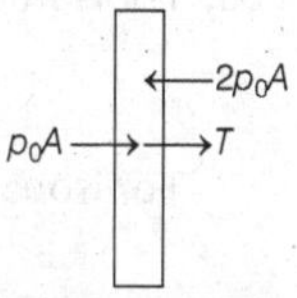

FBD of Piston

17.

$$p_1=p_2$$

$$\Rightarrow \frac{n_1RT}{V_1}=\frac{n_2RT}{V_2}$$

$$\Rightarrow \frac{\left(\frac{m}{32}\right)}{A[r(360-\alpha)]}=\frac{\left(\frac{m}{28}\right)}{A(r\alpha)} \Rightarrow \alpha=192^\circ$$

18. For gas A,

$$\Delta p=(p_A)_i-(p_A)_f=\frac{n_ART}{V}-\frac{n_ART}{2V}=\frac{n_ART}{2V}$$

For gas B,

$$1.5\Delta p=(p_B)_i-(p_B)_f=\frac{n_BRT}{V}-\frac{n_BRT}{2V}=\frac{n_BRT}{2V}$$

$$\therefore \frac{n_A}{n_B}=\frac{2}{3}$$

$$\frac{m_A}{m_B}=\frac{n_A}{n_B}=\frac{2}{3} \Rightarrow 3m_A=2m_B$$

19. Let length of air column finally be x.

For air column,

$$p_1V_1=p_2V_2$$

$$\Rightarrow 76\times A(5)=[76-(48-x)]\times Ax$$

$$\Rightarrow (28+x)x=380$$

$$\Rightarrow x=10\text{ cm}=0.1\text{ m}$$

20.

$$pV=nRT$$

$$\Rightarrow 10\times V=\left(\frac{28}{28}\right)R(330) \quad \text{...(i)}$$

When m g of N_2 leaked out,

$$pV=nRT$$

$$\Rightarrow 5\times V=\left(\frac{28-m}{28}\right)R(300) \quad \text{...(ii)}$$

Solving Eqs. (i) and (ii), we get

$$m=\frac{63}{5}\text{ g}$$

21.

$$n_1+n_2=n'_1+n'_2$$

$$\Rightarrow \frac{1\times V}{R(273)}+\frac{1\times V}{R(273)}=\frac{1.5\times V}{R(273)}+\frac{1.5\times V}{RT}$$

$$\Rightarrow T=819\text{ K}=546^\circ\text{C}$$

22.

$$\frac{p_1V_1}{T_1}=\frac{p_2V_2}{T_2}$$

$$\Rightarrow \frac{200\times V}{295}=\frac{p_2\times 1.02V}{315}$$

$$\Rightarrow p_2=209\text{ kPa}$$

23. $p_1=p_0=1.0\times10^5$ Pa,

$V_1=2.4\times10^{-3}\text{ m}^3, T_1=300\text{ K}$

$$p_2=p_0+\frac{Kx}{A}=10^5+\frac{8000(0.1)}{8\times10^{-3}}=2\times10^5\text{Pa}$$

$$V_2=V_1+Ax=2.4\times10^{-3}+8\times10^{-3}\times0.1=3.2\times10^{-3}\text{ m}^3$$

$$\frac{p_1V_1}{T_1}=\frac{p_2V_2}{T_2}$$

$$\Rightarrow \frac{10^5\times2.4\times10^{-3}}{300}=\frac{2\times10^5\times3.2\times10^{-3}}{T_2}$$

$$\Rightarrow T_2=800\text{ K}$$

24.

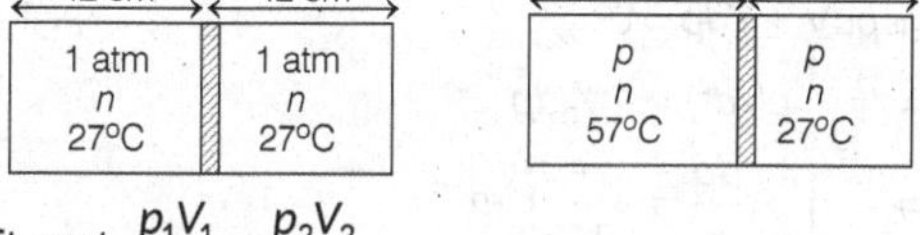

For left part, $\frac{p_1V_1}{T_1}=\frac{p_2V_2}{T_2}$

$$\Rightarrow \frac{1\times A(42)}{300}=\frac{p\times A(42+x)}{330} \quad \text{...(i)}$$

For right part, $\frac{p_1V_1}{T_1}=\frac{p_2V_2}{T_2}$

$$\Rightarrow \frac{1\times A(42)}{300}=\frac{p\times A(42-x)}{300} \quad \text{...(ii)}$$

Solving Eqs. (i) and (ii), we get

$$x = 2\text{ cm}$$

25. Pressure gradient will develop due to the upward acceleration.

$$\frac{dp}{dh} = \rho g_{\text{eff}} = \left(\frac{pM}{RT}\right)(2g)$$

$$\Rightarrow \int_{p_M}^{p_B} \frac{dp}{p} = \frac{2Mg}{RT}\int_0^{H/2} dh$$

$$\Rightarrow \ln\left(\frac{p_B}{p_M}\right) = \frac{2Mg}{RT}\left(\frac{H}{2}\right)$$

$$\Rightarrow \frac{p_B}{p_M} = e^{\frac{MgH}{RT}}$$

26. Total number of moles $= n_A + n_B + n_C$

$$\Rightarrow n = \frac{pA(L/3)}{RT} + \frac{2pA(L/3)}{RT} + \frac{pA(L/3)}{RT}$$

$$\Rightarrow n = \frac{4pAL}{3RT}$$

$$\therefore \frac{n_A}{n} = \frac{1}{4}$$

Since, the temperature and pressure in all the parts will be equal at equilibrium,

$$V \propto n \Rightarrow L \propto n$$

$$\Rightarrow L_A \propto \frac{L}{4}$$

27. $V_1 = \pi R^2(1) + \pi\left(\frac{R}{2}\right)^2(1) = \frac{5}{4}\pi R^2$

$$V_2 = \pi R^2(2) + 0 = 2\pi R^2$$

$$\frac{p_1V_1}{T_1} = \frac{p_2V_2}{T_2}$$

$$\Rightarrow \frac{p_0\left(\frac{5}{4}\pi R^2\right)}{T_0} = \frac{p(2\pi R^2)}{2T_0}$$

$$\Rightarrow p = \frac{5}{4}p_0$$

28. $\frac{dV}{dt} = r \Rightarrow dV = rdt$

$$pV = nRT$$

$$\Rightarrow pdV + Vdp = 0 \qquad [\because T = \text{constant}]$$

$$\Rightarrow p(rdt) = -V_0 dp$$

$$\Rightarrow \int_{p_0}^{p} \frac{dp}{p} = -\frac{r}{V_0}\int_0^t dt$$

$$\Rightarrow \ln\left(\frac{p}{p_0}\right) = -\frac{rt}{V_0}$$

$$\Rightarrow p = p_0 e^{-\frac{rt}{V_0}}$$

29. At lower pressure, we can assume that given gas behaves as an ideal gas. So, $\frac{pV}{RT}$ = constant.

But when pressure increases, the decrease in volume will not take place in same proportion. So, $\frac{pV}{RT}$ increases.

30. $pT = \text{constant} \Rightarrow p\left(\frac{pV}{nR}\right) = \text{constant}$

$$\Rightarrow p \propto \frac{1}{\sqrt{V}}$$

31. Slope $= \frac{pV}{T} = nR = \frac{mR}{M}$

$\therefore$ Slope $\propto \frac{1}{M}$

32. $\rho = \frac{pM}{RT}$

In graph (iii), density would have been constant if the straight line had passed through origin.

33. $U\rho = \text{constant}$

$$\Rightarrow nC_VT\left(\frac{pM}{RT}\right) = \text{constant}$$

$$\Rightarrow p = \text{constant}$$

As density increases, volume decreases.

34. Temperature will be maximum at the mid-point of line *AB*.

$$\therefore \quad p = \frac{p_0 + \frac{p_0}{2}}{2} = \frac{3p_0}{4}$$

and $$V = \frac{2V_0 + V_0}{2} = \frac{3V_0}{2}$$

$$T_{\text{max}} = \frac{pV}{nR} = \frac{(3p_0/4)(3V_0/2)}{1(R)} = \frac{9p_0V_0}{8R}$$

35. For isothermal process,

$$V_f = 2V_0 \Rightarrow p_f = \frac{p_0}{2}$$

For isobaric process,

$$V_f = \frac{V_0}{2} \Rightarrow T_f = \frac{T_0}{4}$$

For $p \propto V$ process,

p-V graph must be straight line.

$T \propto V^2 \Rightarrow$ *V-T* must be parabolic.

$p^2 \propto T \Rightarrow$ *p-T* must be parabolic.

Multiple choice (s) Correct Questions

1. (a) $p_{\text{avg}} = mv_{\text{avg}} = 0$ [$\because$ Average velocity is zero]

(b) $K_{\text{avg}} = f\left(\frac{1}{2}kT\right)$

Since, $f = 5$ for both of them, K_{avg} will be same.

(c) $K = \frac{5}{2}pV$

Kinetic energy per unit volume $= \frac{5}{2}p$

(d) Kinetic energy per unit mass will be different as they have different molecular masses.

2. (a) $K = \frac{3}{2} pV$

$\Rightarrow \frac{K_1}{K_2} = \left(\frac{p_1}{p_2}\right)\left(\frac{V_1}{V_2}\right) = \left(\frac{1}{2}\right)\left(\frac{1}{1}\right) = 1:2$

(b) $v_{rms} \propto \sqrt{T}$

$\Rightarrow \frac{(v_{rms})_1}{(v_{rms})_2} = \sqrt{\frac{T_1}{T_2}} = 1:1$

(c) Average velocity is zero for gas molecules.

(d) $N = \frac{pV}{RT}$

$\Rightarrow \frac{N_1}{N_2} = \frac{p_1}{p_2} = 1:2$

3. $y = mx \quad \Rightarrow \quad \frac{dN}{dv} = \left(\frac{a}{v_0}\right) v$

$\Rightarrow dN = \left(\frac{a}{v_0}\right) v dv$

(a) Number of molecules = Area under the curve

$\Rightarrow \quad N = \frac{1}{2} v_0 \times a$

$\Rightarrow \quad av_0 = 2N$

(b) $v_{avg} = \frac{\int v\, dN}{\int dN} = \frac{\int_0^{v_0} v \left(\frac{a}{v_0}\right) v dv}{\int_0^N dN} = \frac{2}{3} v_0$

$\therefore \quad \frac{v_{avg}}{v_0} = \frac{2}{3}$

(c) $v_{rms}^2 = \frac{\int v^2 dN}{\int dN} = \frac{\int_0^N v^2 \left(\frac{a}{v_0}\right) v dv}{\int_0^N dN} = \frac{v_0^2}{2}$

$\therefore \frac{v_{rms}}{v_0} = \frac{1}{\sqrt{2}}$

(d) Area under the curve from $v = 0.5 v_0$ to $v = v_0$

$= \frac{1}{2} v_0 a - \frac{1}{2}\left(\frac{v_0}{2}\right)\left(\frac{a}{2}\right) = \frac{3}{8} v_0 a$

$\text{Fraction} = \frac{A}{A_0} = \frac{\frac{3}{8} v_0 a}{\frac{1}{2} v_0 a} = \frac{3}{4}$

4. Molecules have speeds ranging from 0 to ∞.

$v_{rms} = \sqrt{\frac{3RT}{M}}, v_{mp} = \sqrt{\frac{2RT}{M}}, \bar{v} = \sqrt{\frac{8RT}{\pi M}}$

$\therefore \; v_{mp} < \bar{v} < v_{rms}$

$K_{avg} = \frac{3}{2} kT$ and $v_{mp} = \sqrt{\frac{2kT}{m}}$

$\therefore \; K_{avg} = \frac{3}{2}\left(\frac{mv_{mp}^2}{2}\right) = \frac{3}{4} mv_{mp}^2$

5. Number of molecules hitting 1 m^2 of the wall per second

$= \frac{1}{6} nv_{rms} = \frac{1}{6} \times 10^{26} \times 2000 = 3.33 \times 10^{28}$

Pressure exerted on the wall by molecules

$= \left(\frac{1}{6} nv_{rms}\right)(2mv_{rms}) = \frac{1}{3} mnv_{rms}^2$

$= \frac{1}{3} \times 3 \times 10^{-27} \times 10^{26} \times (2000)^2 = 4 \times 10^5 \text{ Pa}$

6. (a) K_{avg} per molecule $= \frac{5}{2} kT$

Since, both the gases are contained in the same vessel, temperature of both the gases is same. Hence, average kinetic energy per molecule is also same.

(b) $v_{rms} = \sqrt{\frac{3RT}{M}}$

$\Rightarrow \frac{(v_{rms})_A}{(v_{rms})_B} = \sqrt{\frac{M_B}{M_A}} = \sqrt{\frac{1}{16}} = \frac{1}{4}$

(c) $pV = \left(\frac{m}{M}\right) RT$

$\Rightarrow \quad \frac{p_A}{p_B} = \left(\frac{m_A}{m_B}\right)\left(\frac{M_B}{M_A}\right) = \left(\frac{2}{1}\right)\left(\frac{1}{16}\right) = \frac{1}{8}$

(d) $N = \frac{pV}{KT}$

$\Rightarrow \quad \frac{N_A}{N_B} = \frac{p_A}{p_B} = \frac{1}{8}$

7. (a) $\gamma = \frac{1}{V}\frac{dV}{dT} = \frac{1}{V}\left(\frac{nR}{p}\right) = \frac{1}{T}$

So, coefficient of volume expansion at constant pressure is same for all ideal gases.

(b) $K_{avg} = \frac{3}{2} kT$

(c) The average translational kinetic energy of the molecules is independent of their nature, so each component of the gaseous mixture will have the same value of average translational kinetic energy.

(d) $\lambda \propto \frac{1}{p}$

8. (a) $\frac{p_1^2}{\rho_1} = \frac{p_2^2}{\rho_2}$

$\Rightarrow \frac{p^2}{\rho} = \frac{p_2^2}{\rho/2} \quad \Rightarrow \quad p_2 = \frac{p}{\sqrt{2}}$

(b) $\frac{p^2}{\rho} = \text{constant}$

$\Rightarrow \quad \frac{p^2}{\left(\frac{pM}{RT}\right)} = \text{constant}$

$\Rightarrow \quad pT = \text{constant}$

$\therefore \quad p_1T_1 = p_2T_2$

$\Rightarrow \quad pT = \left(\frac{p}{\sqrt{2}}\right)T_2$

$\Rightarrow \quad T_2 = \sqrt{2}\,T$

(d) $pT =$ constant

So, graph of p *versus* T will be rectangular hyperbola.

9. $n_1 = \frac{pV}{RT}$,

$n_2 = \frac{(2p)(2V)}{RT} = \frac{4pV}{RT}$

Since, final pressure and temperature will be same for both the compartments, $V \propto n$

$\therefore \quad V_1 = \left(\frac{n_1}{n_1 + n_2}\right)(2V + V) = \frac{3V}{5}$

and $\quad V_2 = \left(\frac{n_2}{n_1 + n_2}\right)(3V) = \frac{12V}{5}$

For compartment I, $p_1V_1 = p_2V_2$

$\Rightarrow \quad pV = p'\left(\frac{3V}{5}\right)$

$\Rightarrow \quad p' = \frac{5p}{3}$

10. (a) From graph, $(v_{mp})_B > (v_{mp})_A$

$\Rightarrow \quad \sqrt{\frac{2RT_2}{M_B}} > \sqrt{\frac{2RT_1}{M_A}}$

$\Rightarrow \quad \frac{T_2}{M_B} > \frac{T_1}{M_A}$

If $T_1 = T_2 \quad \Rightarrow \quad M_B < M_A$

(b) If $M_A = M_B \quad \Rightarrow \quad T_2 > T_1$

(c) $M_A > \left(\frac{T_1}{T_2}\right)M_B$

(d) $\frac{T_2}{28} > \frac{T_1}{32} \quad \Rightarrow \quad T_1 < \frac{8}{7}T_2$

So, T_1 is not necessarily less than T_2.

11. $A \rightarrow B : p \propto V$ or $T \propto V^2$ or $T \propto p^2$

So, V-T and p-T graph will be parabola.

$B \rightarrow C$: Isochoric cooling

$C \rightarrow A$: Isobaric cooling

12. $nv_{rms} =$ constant

$\Rightarrow \quad \frac{N}{V}\sqrt{\frac{3kT}{m}} =$ constant

$\Rightarrow \quad T \propto V^2$

$\Rightarrow \quad \frac{pV}{nR} \propto V^2 \quad \Rightarrow \quad p \propto V$

$\Rightarrow \quad pV^{-1} =$ constant or $p^{-1}V =$ constant

Comprehension Based Questions

1. $pV = nRT$

$\Rightarrow \quad \Delta p_A V = n_A R\Delta T$ and $\Delta p_B V = n_B R\Delta T$

$\therefore \quad \frac{n_A}{n_B} = \frac{\Delta p_A}{\Delta p_B} = \frac{2.5}{1.5} = \frac{5}{3}$

At constant volume,

$$Q = n_A C_{V_A}\Delta T = n_B C_{V_B}\Delta T$$

$\Rightarrow \quad \frac{C_{V_B}}{C_{V_A}} = \frac{n_A}{n_B} = \frac{5}{3} = \frac{5R/2}{3R/2}$

So, gas A is monoatomic and gas B is diatomic.

2. $m_A = 225 - 100 = 125$ g

$m_B = 160 - 100 = 60$ g

$n_A = \frac{m_A}{M_A}$ and $n_B = \frac{m_B}{M_B}$

$\therefore \quad \frac{n_A}{n_B} = \left(\frac{m_A}{m_B}\right)\left(\frac{M_B}{M_A}\right)$

$\Rightarrow \quad \frac{5}{3} = \left(\frac{125}{60}\right)\frac{M_B}{M_A}$

$\Rightarrow \quad \frac{M_A}{M_B} = \frac{5}{4} = \frac{40}{32}$

So, A will be argon and B will be oxygen.

3. Number of molecules in $A = \left(\frac{m_A}{M_A}\right)N_A$

$= \left(\frac{125}{40}\right)N_A = 3.125N_A$

4. $R = 2$ cal/mol-K

$U_A = n_A C_{V_A} T_A = \left(\frac{125}{40}\right)\left(\frac{3R}{2}\right)300 = 2812.5$ cal

5. $p = p_0 + \frac{mg}{A} = 1.01 \times 10^5 + \frac{100 \times 10^{-3} \times 10}{10 \times 10^{-4}} = 1.02 \times 10^5$ Pa

$n = \frac{pV}{RT} = \frac{1.02 \times 10^5 \times (10 \times 10^{-4} \times 10 \times 10^{-2})}{\frac{25}{3} \times 300} = 4.08 \times 10^{-3}$

$N = 6 \times 10^{23} \times 4.08 \times 10^{-3} = 2.5 \times 10^{21}$

6. $p_1 = p_0 + \frac{mg}{A} = 1.02 \times 10^5$ Pa

$p_2 = p_0 - \frac{mg}{A} = 1 \times 10^5$ Pa

$$p_1V_1 = p_2V_2$$

$\Rightarrow (1.02 \times 10^5)A(10) = (1 \times 10^5)Ah_2$

$\Rightarrow \quad h_2 = 10.2$ cm

7. $Q = nC_p\Delta T = (4.08 \times 10^{-3})\left(\frac{7R}{2}\right)(600 - 300) = 35.7$ J

8. $n = \frac{pV}{RT}$

$\therefore \quad N_{\text{left}} = \frac{p_1 V}{RT_1}$ and $N_{\text{right}} = \frac{(2p_1)V}{R(2T_1)}$

$\Rightarrow \quad \frac{N_{\text{left}}}{N_{\text{right}}} = 1$

9. As the piston is in equilibrium, pressure in both the compartments will become equal to p_{atm} i.e., $2p_1$.

$$n_1 + n_2 = n'_1 + n'_2$$

$$\Rightarrow \frac{p_1 V}{RT_1} + \frac{(2p_1)V}{R(2T_1)} = \frac{(2p_1)(V/2)}{RT} + \frac{(2p_1)V}{RT}$$

$$\Rightarrow \quad T = \frac{3T_1}{2}$$

10. There are 2 degree of freedom for radial motion and 1 degree of freedom for axial motion.

$\therefore$ For radial speed, $= \frac{1}{2}mv_r^2 = 2\left(\frac{1}{2}kT\right)$

$$\Rightarrow \quad v_r = \sqrt{\frac{2kT}{m}}$$

11. For axial speed, $\frac{1}{2}mv_a^2 = 1\left(\frac{1}{2}kT\right)$

$$\Rightarrow \quad v_a = \sqrt{\frac{kT}{m}}$$

12. $F = \frac{N(2mv_{\text{rms}\,a})}{\left(\frac{2L}{v_{\text{rms}\,a}}\right)} = \frac{mNv_{\text{rms}\,a}^2}{L}$

$$p = \frac{F}{A} = \frac{mNv_{\text{rms}\,a}^2}{\pi R^2 L}$$

Match the Columns Questions

1. A → S, T, B → P, C → Q, D → Q, R, T
2. A → P, Q, T, B → R, S, C → P, Q, D → Q
3. $\rho = \frac{pM}{RT}$

(A) For AB, $p \propto V \Rightarrow T \propto V^2 \Rightarrow T \propto \rho^{-2}$

For BC, V = constant $\Rightarrow \rho$ = constant

For CA, p = constant $\Rightarrow \rho T$ = constant

(B) For AB, $p \propto T \Rightarrow \rho$ = constant

For BC, T = constant $\Rightarrow p \propto \rho$

For CA, p = constant $\Rightarrow \rho T$ = constant

(C) For AB, p = constant $\Rightarrow \rho T$ = constant

For BC, T = constant $\Rightarrow p \propto \rho$

For CA, V = constant $\Rightarrow \rho$ = constant

(D) For AB, $\rho \propto T \Rightarrow p \propto T^2$

For BC, T = constant $\Rightarrow p \propto \rho$

For CA, ρ = constant $\Rightarrow p \propto T$

Numerical Values Questions

1. $p_0 V_0 = nRT_a$

$(p_0 + \Delta p)(V_0 + \Delta V) = nRT_b$

$(p_0 + \Delta p)(V_0 - \Delta V) = nRT_b$

$\therefore \quad \Delta V = 0$

Pressure depends on number of moles and is independent of nature of gas.

2. Let the distances moved by left and right pistons be x_1 and x_2 respectively.

L = Final compression $= 1 + x_1 + x_2$

$p_i = \frac{K(1)}{A}, \quad p_f = \frac{KL}{A}$

For left chamber, $\frac{p_1 V_1}{T_1} = \frac{p_2 V_2}{T_2}$

$$\Rightarrow \frac{\left(\frac{K(1)}{A}\right)A(1)}{300} = \frac{\left(\frac{KL}{A}\right)A(1+x_1)}{400}$$

$$\Rightarrow \quad x_1 = \frac{4}{3L} - 1$$

For right chamber, $\frac{p_1 V_1}{T_1} = \frac{p_2 V_2}{T_2}$

$$\Rightarrow \frac{\left(\frac{K(1)}{A}\right)A(1)}{300} = \frac{\left(\frac{KL}{A}\right)A(1+x_2)}{500}$$

$$\Rightarrow \quad x_2 = \frac{5}{3L} - 1$$

$$L = 1 + x_1 + x_2$$

$$\Rightarrow \quad L = 1 + \frac{4}{3L} - 1 + \frac{5}{3L} - 1$$

$$\Rightarrow \quad L^2 + L - 3 = 0$$

$$\Rightarrow \quad L = \frac{\sqrt{13} - 1}{2}$$

3. $p_1 V_1 = p_2 V_2$

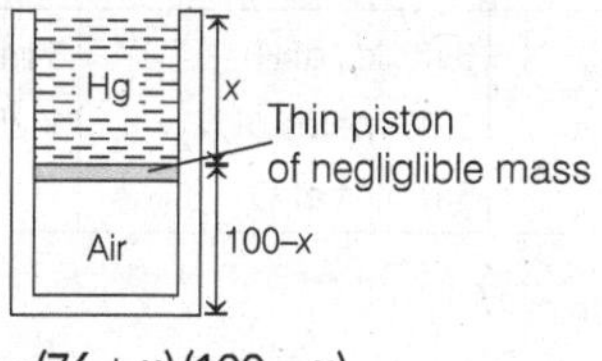

$\Rightarrow 76 \times 100 = (76 + x)(100 - x)$

$\Rightarrow \quad x = 24$ cm

$\therefore$ Air column length = 76 cm

4. Let the compression in the spring be x.

$$p_1 = 10^5 \text{ Pa}, V_2 = 20000 \text{ cm}^3 = 0.02 \text{ m}^3$$

$$p_2 = p_0 + \frac{kx}{A} = 10^5 + \frac{1000\,x}{100 \times 10^{-4}} = 10^5(1 + x)$$

$$p_1 V_1 = p_2 V_2$$

$$\Rightarrow 10^5 \times 0.02 = 10^5(1 + x) \times (100 \times 10^{-4} x)$$

$\Rightarrow \quad x^2 + x - 2 = 0$

$\Rightarrow \quad x = 1\,\text{m} = 100\,\text{cm}$

5. At constant pressure,

$$\Delta V = \frac{nR\Delta T}{p} = \frac{1 \times (25/3) \times 30}{10^5} = 25 \times 10^{-4}\,\text{m}^3 = 2500\,\text{cm}^3$$

Let the distance moved by pistons be x.

$\therefore \quad \Delta V = (A_1 - A_2)x$

$\Rightarrow \quad 2500 = (200 - 100)x \Rightarrow x = 25\,\text{cm}$

6. Let initially p_1 and p_2 be the pressure in upper and lower part of the cylinder.

For equilibrium of piston,

$$p_1A + mg = p_2A \Rightarrow mg = (p_2 - p_1)A$$

On heating, let the pressure in the two sections change to p'_1 and p'_2 and F is the force applied. So,

$p'_1A + mg + F = p'_2A$

$\Rightarrow \quad F = (p'_2 - p'_1)A - mg$

$\Rightarrow \quad F = (p'_2 - p'_1)A - (p_2 - p_1)A$

$\Rightarrow \quad F = (p'_2 - p'_1 - p_2 + p_1)A$

$$= R\left(\frac{T_2}{V_2} - \frac{T_2}{V_1} - \frac{T_1}{V_2} + \frac{T_1}{V_1}\right)(0.1)$$

$$= R\left(\frac{500}{0.05} - \frac{500}{0.1} - \frac{300}{0.05} + \frac{300}{0.1}\right)(0.1)$$

$$= 200R = 200 \times 8.3 = 1660\,\text{N}$$

7. $n_{H_2} = \frac{30}{2} = 15, \quad n_{O_2} = \frac{160}{32} = 5, \quad n_{N_2} = \frac{70}{28} = 2.5$

As hydrogen diffuses through all the partitions, it uniformly spreads in all the three parts of the vessel.

Nitrogen can diffuse only through the right partition, it uniformly spreads in the middle and right parts of the vessel.

Oxygen does not diffuse through the partitions.

A	B	C
5 moles of H_2	5 moles of H_2 1.25 moles of N_2 5 moles of O_2	5 moles of H_2 1.25 moles of N_2

$p \propto n$

$\Rightarrow p_A : p_B : p_C = n_A : n_B : n_C$

$= 5 : (5 + 1.25 + 5) : (5 + 1.25) = 4 : 9 : 5$

$\therefore \quad x = 9$

8. Applying internal energy conservation,

$$U_1 + U_2 = U'_1 + U'_2$$

$$\Rightarrow 1 \times \frac{3R}{2} \times T_0 + 2 \times \frac{5R}{2} \times \frac{T_0}{2} = 1 \times \frac{3R}{2} \times T + 2 \times \frac{5R}{2} \times T$$

$\Rightarrow \quad T = \frac{8T_0}{13}$

$$\text{Total volume of vessel} = V_1 + V_2 = \frac{1RT_0}{p_0} + \frac{2R\left(\frac{T_0}{2}\right)}{p_0} = \frac{2RT_0}{p_0}$$

$$pV = nRT$$

$\Rightarrow \quad p\left(\frac{2RT_0}{p_0}\right) = (1+2)R\left(\frac{8T_0}{13}\right)$

$\Rightarrow \quad p = \frac{12p_0}{13}$

$\therefore \quad n = 12$

9. $kl_0 = p_0A$

$V = A(l_0 + x) = 1.2V_0$

$p = p_0 + \frac{kx}{A} = p_0 + \frac{k(0.2l_0)}{A} = 1.2p_0$

$\frac{p_0V_0}{T_0} = \frac{p_1V_1}{T_1}$

$\Rightarrow \quad \frac{p_0V_0}{300} = \frac{(1.2p_0)(1.2V_0)}{T_1}$

$\Rightarrow \quad T_1 = 300 \times 1.44 = 432\,\text{K} = 159°\,\text{C}$

10. Let the equation of parabola be

$$\frac{dN}{du} = a(u - u^2)$$

$\therefore \quad N_0 = \int_0^1 \left(\frac{dN}{du}\right) du = a\left[\frac{u^2}{2} - \frac{u^3}{3}\right]_0^1$

$\Rightarrow \quad a = 6N_0$

$$\int u^2 dN = \int u^2 \left(\frac{dN}{du}\right) du = 6N_0 \int_0^1 u^2(u - u^2)\,du$$

$$= 6N_0\left[\frac{1}{4} - \frac{1}{5}\right] = \frac{3N_0}{10}$$

$$v_{rms} = \sqrt{\frac{\int u^2 dN}{\int dN}}$$

$$= \sqrt{\frac{\frac{3N_0}{10}}{N_0}} = \sqrt{\frac{3}{10}}\ \text{unit}$$

$$= \sqrt{\frac{3}{10}} \times 100\,\text{m/s}$$

$$K_T = \frac{1}{2}mv_{rms}^2$$

$$= \frac{1}{2} \times (10 \times 10^{-3}) \times 3000 = 15\,\text{J}$$

Previous Year's Questions

JEE Main

1. Average KE = 0.414 eV, for monoatomic $f = 3$

$$\frac{f}{2}kT = \frac{3}{2}kT = 0.414 \times 1.6 \times 10^{-19} \text{ J}$$

$$T = 3200 \text{ K}$$

2. Given, $T = 27°\text{C} = 300 \text{ K}$

$$R = 8.31 \text{ J/molK}$$

The total kinetic energy of 1 mole of oxygen,

$$\text{KE} = \frac{1}{2}fRT = \frac{1}{2} \times 5 \times 8.31 \times 300 = 6232.5 \text{ J}$$

3. Ideal Gas equation,

$$p_A V_A = n_A R T_A \quad \ldots\text{(i)}$$

$$p_B V_B = n_B R T_B \quad \ldots\text{(ii)}$$

$$\frac{p_A V_A}{p_B V_B} = \frac{n_A R T_A}{n_B R T_B}$$

As, $V_A = V_B, T_A = T_B$

$$\frac{p_A V_B}{p_B V_B} = \frac{n_A R T_A}{n_B R T_A}$$

$$\frac{p_A V_B}{p_B V_B} = \frac{n_A T_A}{n_B T_A} \Rightarrow \frac{p_A}{p_B} = \frac{n_A}{n_B}$$

$$\frac{p_A}{p_B} = \frac{1/2}{1/32} = \frac{1}{2} \times \frac{32}{1}$$

$$\frac{p_A}{p_B} = \frac{16}{1}$$

4. Given,

$n = 2 \times 10^{25}$ molecules per cubic metre

$$p = 1.38 \text{ atm} = 1.38 \times 10^5 \text{ N/m}^2$$

$$K = 1.38 \times 10^{-23} \text{ J K}^{-1}$$

we know that

$$pV = nKT$$

$$\Rightarrow \quad T = \frac{pV}{nK} = \frac{1.38 \times 10^5 \times 1}{2 \times 10^{25} \times 1.38 \times 10^{-23}} = 500 \text{ K}$$

5. Given,

$\because \quad f = 6, \mu_1 = N, \mu_2 = 2$

For diatomic gas	For monoatomic gas
$\gamma_1 = 1 + \frac{2}{f} = 1 + \frac{2}{6}$ $= 1 + 0.33 = 1.33$	$\gamma_2 = 1 + \frac{2}{3} = 1.67$

$$\therefore \quad \gamma_{mix} = \frac{\frac{\mu_1\gamma_1}{\gamma_1 - 1} + \frac{\mu_2\gamma_2}{\gamma_2 - 1}}{\frac{\mu_1}{\gamma_1 - 1} + \frac{\mu_2}{\gamma_2 - 1}}$$

$$\because \quad 1.4 = \frac{\frac{N \times 1.33}{1.33 - 1} + \frac{2 \times 1.67}{1.67 - 1}}{\frac{N}{1.33 - 1} + \frac{2}{1.67 - 1}}$$

$$\Rightarrow \quad 1.4 = \frac{N \times 4 + 5}{3N + 3}$$

$$\Rightarrow \quad 4.2N + 4.2 = 4N + 5$$

$$\Rightarrow \quad 0.2N = 0.8$$

$$N = 4$$

6. The average kinetic energy per molecule of any gas (hydrogen argon, O_2, N_2 etc) is always equal to $\frac{3}{2}k_B T$. It depends only on temperature and is independent of the nature of the gas. Since, hydrogen and argon both have the same temperature as 30° in the flask hence, the ratio of average kinetic energy (per molecule) of the two gases will 1 : 1.

7. Collision frequency is given by

$$z = n\pi d^2 v_{\text{avg}}$$

where, n is number of molecules per unit volume

$$\frac{z_1}{z_2} = \frac{n_1}{n_2} = \frac{3}{12} = \frac{1}{4} = 0.25$$

8. Using $v_{\text{rms}} = \sqrt{\frac{3RT}{m}}$

$$v_0 = \sqrt{\frac{3R \times 200}{m}} \quad \ldots\text{(i)}$$

$$v' = \sqrt{\frac{3R \times 800}{m}} \quad \ldots\text{(ii)}$$

On dividing (ii) by (i), we get

$$\frac{v'}{v_0} = \sqrt{\frac{800}{200}} = \sqrt{4} = 2$$

$$v' = 2v_0$$

9. Kinetic energy 'K' of a gas molecule at absolute temperature T is

$$K = \frac{3}{2}k_B T$$

Where, K_B = Boltzmann constant

T = Absolute temperature

So; $\quad \frac{K_2}{K_1} = \frac{T_2}{T_1}$ or $T_2 = \frac{K_2}{K_1} \times T_1$

Here $\quad T_1 = 27°\text{C} = 273 + 27 = 300 \text{ K}$

And $\quad K_2 = 2K$,

$$\Rightarrow \quad T_2 = 2 \times T_1 = 2 \times 300 = 600 \text{ K}$$

$$= (600 - 273)°\text{C} = 327°\text{C}$$

10. **Statement I** As, $v_{\text{rms}} = \sqrt{\frac{3KT}{m}}$

So, at $T = -73°\text{C} = 273 + (-73) = 200 \text{ K}$, we get

$$(v_{\text{rms}})_1 = \sqrt{\frac{3K(200)}{m}} = 10\sqrt{\frac{6K}{m}}$$

and at $T = 527°\text{C} = (527 + 273) \text{ K} = 800 \text{ K}$, we get

$$(v_{\text{rms}})_2 = \sqrt{\frac{3K(800)}{m}} = 20\sqrt{\frac{6K}{m}}$$

So, Statement I is correct, as $(v_{rms})_2 = 2(v_{rms})_1$

Statement II

Translational kinetic energy $= \frac{3}{2} nRT$

As, $pV = nRT$, so, translational KE $= \frac{3}{2} pV$

So, Statement II is false.

11. From ideal gas equation, $pV = \mu RT$

If volume is constant, $p \propto T$

From the given graph, it is clear that all the gases lines of graphs meet at same value or point. On the horizontal axis (temperature axis) pressure is zero but temperature is negative and it will be equal to 0K or $-273°$ C.

12. Molar specific heat capacity C_p and C_V both do not depend on temperature.

γ is ratio of C_p and C_V which is also independent of temperature.

$$\gamma \propto T^{\circ}$$

13. The mean free path λ

$$\lambda = \frac{RT}{\sqrt{2}\pi d^2 N_A P}$$

$$\lambda \propto T$$

$$\frac{1500d}{\lambda} = \frac{273}{373}$$

$$\Rightarrow \quad \lambda = \frac{1500d \times 373}{273}$$

$$\lambda = 2049d$$

14. Given,

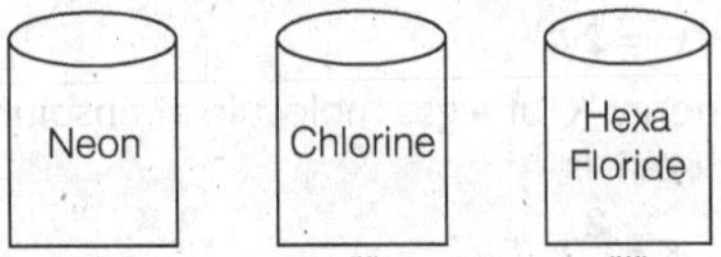

(I) (II) (III)

$$v_{rms} = \sqrt{\frac{\gamma RT}{m}} \quad \text{...(i)}$$

$$\gamma = 1 + \frac{2}{f}$$

$$\gamma_{\text{Monoatomic}} > \gamma_{\text{diatomic}} > \gamma_{\text{polyatomic}}$$

$$v_{rms}' \propto \sqrt{\gamma}$$

$$v_{\text{mono}} > v_{\text{diatomic}} > v_{\text{poly}}$$

15. A-I, B-III, C-IV, D-II

A monoatomic gas molecule has 3-translatory degree of freedom.

A rigid diatomic molecule has 3-translation and 2-rotational degree of freedom.

A non rigid diatomic gas molecule has 3-translation, 2-rotational and 1-vibrational degree of freedom.

A polyatomic gas molecule has 3-translational, 2-rotational and more than one vibrational degree of freedom.

16. Heat given at constant pressure, $Q_p = \mu C_p \Delta T = 735$ J.

Gas molecule does not oscillate, hence vibrational degree of freedom is not considered.

So, Change in internal energy,

$$\Delta U = \mu C_V \Delta T$$

$$\because \quad \frac{C_p}{C_V} = \gamma \quad \text{or} \quad C_V = \frac{C_p}{\gamma}$$

$$\text{or} \quad \Delta U = \mu\left(\frac{C_p}{\gamma}\right)\Delta T = \frac{\mu C_p \Delta T}{\gamma}$$

For diatomic gas, $\gamma = \frac{7}{5}$ thus,

$$\Delta U = \frac{735}{7/5} = 525 \text{ J}$$

17. Given, mass of N_2 gas, $m = 14$ g Initial temperature,

$$T_1 = 27°\text{C} = 27 + 273 = 300 \text{ K}$$

$$R = 8.32 \text{ J mol}^{-1} \text{ K}^{-1}$$

The rms speed of a gas is given by

$$v_{rms} = \sqrt{\frac{3KT}{m}} \Rightarrow v_{rms} \propto \sqrt{T}$$

$$\frac{(v_{rms})_2}{(v_{rms})_1} = \sqrt{\frac{T_2}{T_1}}$$

Given, $(v_{rms})_2 = 2(v_{rms})_1 = 2v_{rms}$

$$\Rightarrow \quad \frac{2v_{rms}}{v_{rms}} = \sqrt{\frac{T_2}{300}} \Rightarrow T_2 = (2)^2 \times 300 = 1200 \text{ K}$$

As, heat transferred,

$$H = \frac{f}{2} nR(T_2 - T_1)$$

For diatomic gas, $f = 5$

Also, $n = \frac{\text{mass } (m)}{\text{molar mass } (M)} = \frac{14}{28} = 0.5$

$$\therefore \quad H = \frac{5}{2} \times 0.5 \times 8.32 \times 900 = 9360 \text{ J}$$

18. Average momentum of a molecule in a sample of an ideal gas is always zero and it does not depend on temperature. Hence, statement I is false.

We know that, $v_{rms} = \sqrt{\frac{3RT}{M}}$

When temperature of gas is doubled to $2T$ and oxygen atoms are used, then atomic mass becomes $M/2$.

$$\therefore \quad v'_{rms} = \sqrt{\frac{3R(2T)}{M/2}}$$

$$= 2\sqrt{\frac{3RT}{M}} = 2v_{rms} = 2v \quad [(\because v_{rms} = v \text{ (given)}]$$

Hence, statement II is correct.

19. Number of moles of hydrogen present,

$$n_1 = \frac{m_1}{M_1} = \frac{16}{2} = 8 \text{ moles}$$

Number of moles of oxygen present,

$$n_2 = \frac{m_2}{M_2} = \frac{128}{32} = 4 \text{ moles}$$

Temperature of vessel $= 27°C = 300$ K

Pressure of vessel $=$ 1atm $= 1.01 \times 10^5$ Pa

Now using, $pV = nRT$, $(\because n = n_1 + n_2)$

we have,

$$V = \frac{(n_1 + n_2)RT}{p} = \frac{12 \times \frac{25}{3} \times 300}{1.01 \times 10^5}$$

$$= 29 \times 10^4 \text{cm}^3 \approx 27 \times 10^4 \text{cm}^3$$

20. Number of moles,

$$n = \frac{\text{Gas Volume}}{\text{Molar Volume}} = \frac{44.8}{22.4} = 2$$

Now, amount of heat required,

$$\Delta Q = nC_V \Delta T = 2 \times \frac{3}{2} R \times \Delta T$$

(He is monoatomic, $\therefore C_V = \frac{3}{2}R$)

So, $\Delta Q = 2 \times \frac{3}{2} \times 8.3 \times 20 = 498$ J

21. RMS speed of a gas molecule,

$$v_{\text{rms}} = \sqrt{\frac{3RT}{M_0}}$$

When temperature is doubled, $T' = 2T$ and when molecule is dissociated,

$$M' = \frac{M_0}{2}$$

Hence, $v'_{\text{rms}} = \sqrt{\frac{3R(2T)}{\left(\frac{M_0}{2}\right)}} = 2\sqrt{\frac{3RT}{M_0}} = 2v_{\text{rms}}$

22. Let n_H and n_O be number of moles of hydrogen and oxygen.

Given, volume $= 2000 \text{ cm}^3 = 2000 \times 10^{-6} \text{m}^3$

By Ideal gas equation, $pV = nRT$

$$100 \times 10^3 \times 2000 \times 10^{-6} = n \times 8.3 \times 300$$

$$n = 0.08$$

$$n_H + n_O = 0.08 \quad \text{...(i)}$$

Both hydrogen and oxygen are diatomic molecules. Therefore,

$$2n_H + 32n_O = 0.76 \quad \text{...(ii)}$$

Solving Eqs. (i) and (ii), we get

$$n_H = 0.06$$

$\Rightarrow$ $n_O = 0.02$

$\therefore$ $\frac{n_H}{n_O} = \frac{3}{1}$

23. We know that, most probable speed (v_p) of gas,

$$v_p = \sqrt{\frac{2RT}{M}} \quad \text{...(i)}$$

$\therefore$ Root mean square speed,

$$v_{\text{rms}} = \sqrt{\frac{3RT}{M}} = \sqrt{\frac{3}{2}}\sqrt{\frac{2RT}{M}} = \sqrt{\frac{3}{2}} \cdot v_p \quad \text{[From Eq. (i)]}$$

24. According to ideal gas equation,

$$pV = nRT \Rightarrow V = \frac{nR}{p}T$$

$\Rightarrow$ $V = mT$, where m = slope of $V - T_{\text{curve}} = \frac{nR}{p}$

Now, as $m_2 > m_1$.

Therefore,

$$\frac{nR}{p_2} > \frac{nR}{p_1} \Rightarrow p_2 < p_1$$

25. Statement A is incorrect because a molecule with n degrees of freedom have n different ways of storing energy.

- Statement B is correct as each degree of freedom is associated with 1/2 RT average energy per mole.
- Statement C is incorrect because a monoatomic gas molecule has no rotational degree of freedom and diatomic gas molecule has 2 rotational degrees of freedom.
- Statement D is correct as CH_4 molecule has 3 translational and 3 rotational, i.e. total 6 degrees of freedom.

26. According to law of equipartition of energy, average kinetic energy of each molecule $= \frac{n}{2}k_BT$

where, n = degree of freedom,

k_B = Boltzmann constant and

T = temperature.

$\therefore$ Internal energy of one mole of the gas,

$$U = \frac{n}{2}k_BT \times N_A = \frac{n}{2}RT$$

$$\therefore \quad C_V = \frac{dU}{dT} = \frac{d}{dt}\frac{n}{2}RT = \frac{nR}{2}$$

and $C_p = C_V + R = \frac{nR}{2} + R = R\left(\frac{n}{2} + 1\right)$

$$\therefore \quad \frac{C_V}{C_p} = \frac{\frac{nR}{2}}{R\left(\frac{n}{2} + 1\right)} = \frac{n}{n+2}$$

27. According to kinetic theory of gases,

A. The motion of gas molecules freezes at 0 K.

B. The mean free path of gas molecules decreases on increasing the number density of gas molecules as

$$\mu = \text{mean free path} = \frac{1}{\sqrt{2}\,\pi n d^2}$$

$$\Rightarrow \mu \propto \frac{1}{n}$$

The mean free path increases with the increase of volume.

C. If pressure is constant and temperature is increased, then volume should increase, hence mean free path increases.

D. Average KE per molecule per degree of freedom is $\frac{1}{2}$ K_BT.

Hence, statements (B) and (C) are correct.

28. For a monoatomic gas, degree of freedom, $f = 3$

So, specific heat at constant volume

$$C_V = \frac{f}{2}R \Rightarrow C_V = \frac{3}{2}R$$

Hence, internal energy of 2 moles at 300 K is

$$U = n \cdot C_V T = 2 \times \frac{3}{2} \times 8.31 \times 300 = 7479 \text{ J}$$

29. Given,

Volume, $V = 500 \text{ cm}^3 = 5 \times 10^2 \times 10^{-6} \text{ m}^3$

$= 5 \times 10^{-4} \text{ m}^3$

Pressure, $p = 400 \text{ kPa} = 4 \times 10^5 \text{ Pa}$

Temperature, $T = 300 \text{ K}$

Total mass, $m = 0.76 \text{ g}$

We know that,

Molar mass of hydrogen, $M_1 = 2 \text{ g}$

Molar mass of oxygen, $M_2 = 32 \text{ g}$

Let n_1 and n_2 be the number of moles of hydrogen and oxygen, respectively.

Total number of moles of mixture,

$$n = n_1 + n_2$$

By using ideal gas equation,

$$pV = nRT$$

$$4 \times 10^5 \times 5 \times 10^{-4} = n \times 8.314 \times 300$$

$$n = 0.08 \text{ mol}$$

Then, $n_1 + n_2 = 0.08$ ...(i)

Let mass of hydrogen in mixture $= m_1$

and mass of oxygen in oxygen $= m_2$

$$n_1M_1 + n_2M_2 = m \quad \left[\because n = \frac{m}{M} \Rightarrow m = nM\right]$$

$$2n_1 + 32n_2 = 0.76$$

$$n_1 + 16n_2 = 0.38 \quad \text{...(ii)}$$

On solving Eqs. (i) and (ii), we get

$$n_1 = 0.06 \text{ and } n_2 = 0.02$$

∴ Ratio of masses,

$$\frac{m_2}{m_1} = \frac{n_2M_2}{n_1M_1} = \frac{0.02 \times 32}{0.06 \times 2} = \frac{16}{3}$$

i.e. $m_2 : m_1 = 16 : 3$

30. Given, rms speed of oxygen $(v_{rms})_{O_2} = 160$ m/s

Let rms speed of hydrogen $= (v_{rms})_{H_2}$

Since, $v_{rms} = \sqrt{\frac{3RT}{M}}$

$$\therefore \frac{(v_{rms})_{O_2}}{(v_{rms})_{H_2}} = \sqrt{\frac{M_{H_2}}{M_{O_2}}}$$

$$\Rightarrow \frac{160}{(v_{rms})_{H_2}} = \sqrt{\frac{1}{16}} \Rightarrow \frac{160}{(v_{rms})_{H_2}} = \frac{1}{4}$$

$$\Rightarrow (v_{rms})_{H_2} = 160 \times 4 = 640 \text{ ms}^{-1}$$

31. Given, $pT^3 =$ constant ...(i)

From ideal gas equation, we have

$$pV = nRT \Rightarrow p = \frac{nRT}{V}$$

From Eq. (i), we get

$$\therefore \left(\frac{nRT}{V}\right)T^3 = \text{constant} \Rightarrow nRT^4V^{-1} = \text{constant}$$

Differentiating above expression, we get

$$nR\left[4T^3V^{-1}dT - \frac{T^4}{V^2}dV\right] = 0$$

$$\Rightarrow 4dT = \frac{T}{V}dV \quad \text{...(ii)}$$

We know that, $dV = \gamma V dT$

$$\Rightarrow \gamma = \frac{dV}{VdT} \quad \text{...(iii)}$$

From Eq. (ii), $\frac{4}{T} = \frac{dV}{VdT}$ ...(iv)

On comparing Eqs. (iii) and (iv), we get

$$\gamma = \frac{4}{T}$$

32. Given, initial load,

$$M_1 = 185 \text{ kg}$$

Initial pressure, $p_1 = 76$ cm of Hg

Initial temperature,

$$T_1 = 27\text{ °C} = (273 + 27)\text{K} = 300 \text{ K}$$

Final pressure at height,

$$p_2 = 45 \text{ cm of Hg}$$

Final temperature, $T_2 = -7\text{°C} = [273 + (-7)]\text{K} = 266 \text{ K}$

Volume of balloon is constant,

$$V_1 = V_2 = V$$

We know that for air,

$$p = \rho RT$$

Now, for initial condition,

$$p_1 = \rho_1 RT_1 \quad \text{...(i)}$$

Similarly, for final condition,

$$p_2 = \rho_2 RT_2 \quad \text{...(ii)}$$

Dividing Eq. (i) by Eq. (ii), we get

$$\frac{p_1}{p_2} = \frac{\rho_1 T_1}{\rho_2 T_2}$$

$$\frac{76}{45} = \frac{\rho_1}{\rho_2}\left(\frac{300}{266}\right)$$

$$\Rightarrow \frac{\rho_1}{\rho_2} = \frac{76 \times 266}{45 \times 300}$$

We know that density of balloon,

$$\rho = \frac{M}{V}$$

As, volume is constant $\rho \propto M$

$$\therefore \quad \frac{\rho_1}{\rho_2} = \frac{M_1}{M_2} = \frac{76 \times 266}{45 \times 300}$$

$$\Rightarrow \quad \frac{M_1}{M_2} = \frac{20216}{13500}$$

Substituting the value of M_1 in above expression, we get

$$M_2 = 185 \times \frac{13500}{20216} = 123.54 \text{ kg}$$

33. Given, volume of container,

$$V = 4.0 \times 10^{-3} \text{ m}^3$$

Gas constant, $R = 8.3 \text{ J mol}^{-1} \text{ K}^{-1}$

Number of moles of hydrogen, $n_1 = 1$

Number of moles of carbon dioxide,

$$n_2 = 2$$

Temperature of mixture, $T = 400$ K

Using Dalton's law,

$$p = p_1 + p_2 = \frac{n_1 RT}{V} + \frac{n_2 RT}{V}$$

$$= \frac{RT}{V}(n_1 + n_2) = \frac{RT}{V}(1+2) = \frac{3RT}{V}$$

$$= \frac{3 \times 8.3 \times 400}{4.0 \times 10^{-3}} = 24.9 \times 10^5 \text{ Pa}$$

34. According to ideal gas equation,

$$pV = nRT \quad \text{...(i)}$$

and T = absolute temperature of gas.

Eq. (i) can be written as $pV = cT$

where, c is any constant.

$$\Rightarrow \quad pV \propto T$$

So, graph in option (c) is correct.

35. We know that,

$$v_{\text{rms}} = \sqrt{\frac{3RT}{M}}$$

The expression of the average velocity of the gas molecules,

$$v_{\text{av}} = \sqrt{\frac{8RT}{\pi M}} \Rightarrow \frac{v_{\text{rms}}}{v_{\text{av}}} = \frac{\sqrt{\frac{3RT}{M}}}{\sqrt{\frac{8RT}{\pi M}}} = \sqrt{\frac{3\pi}{8}}$$

36. We know that, the average value of energy of an ideal gas in thermal equilibrium temperature T,

$$E = \frac{f}{2} k_B T$$

Given, degree of freedom, $f = 1$

Energy per degree of freedom, $E = \frac{1}{2} k_B T$

37. For polyatomic gas molecule has 3 rotational degrees of freedom, 3 translational degrees of freedom, and 2 vibrational modes.

So, number of vibrational degrees of freedom = 2(2) = 4

$\therefore$ Total number of degrees of freedom,

$$f = 3 + 3 + 4 = 10$$

Here, ratio of molar specific heats is given as

$$\beta = \frac{C_p}{C_V}$$

In terms of degrees of freedom,

$$\beta = 1 + \frac{2}{f}$$

Substituting the value of f in above equation, we get

$$\beta = 1 + \frac{2}{10} \Rightarrow \beta = 1.2$$

38. Let the final temperature of this mixture be T.

As per question there is no loss of energy, it means

$$\Delta U = 0 \quad \text{...(i)}$$

As, we know,

$$\Delta U = \frac{f_1 n_1 R\Delta T}{2} + \frac{f_2 n_2 R\Delta T}{2} \quad \text{...(ii)}$$

From Eqs. (i) and (ii), we get

$$\frac{f_1 n_1 R\Delta T}{2} + \frac{f_2 n_2 R\Delta T}{2} = 0$$

$$\Rightarrow \quad f_1 n_1 R\Delta T + f_2 n_2 R\Delta T = 0$$

$$\Rightarrow f_1 n_1 R(T_1 - T) + f_2 n_2 R(T_2 - T) = 0$$

$$T = \frac{f_1 n_1 T_1 + f_2 n_2 T_2}{f_1 n_1 + f_2 n_2}$$

39. Given, the number of diatomic moles, $n = 3$ mol

The increase in temperature of the diatomic mole,

$$\Delta T = 40^\circ \text{C}$$

Now, the degree of freedom,

f = linear + rotational + no oscillation

$$f = 3 + 2 + 0 \Rightarrow f = 5$$

Change in internal energy,

$$\Delta U = nC_V \Delta T \quad \text{...(i)}$$

where, $C_V = \frac{f}{2} R = \frac{5}{2} R$

Substituting the value in Eq. (i), we get

$$\Delta U = \frac{5R}{2} n\Delta T$$

Now, work done by the gas for isobaric process,

$$W = p\Delta V = nR\Delta T$$

The ratio of the change in internal energy to the work done by the gas,

$$\frac{\Delta U}{W} = \frac{\frac{5}{2} nR\Delta T}{nR\Delta T} \Rightarrow \frac{\Delta U}{W} = \frac{5}{2}$$

Multiply and divide the above equation with 5, we get

$$\frac{\Delta U}{W} = \frac{5 \times 5}{2 \times 5} = \frac{25}{10}$$

Comparing with given equation, $\frac{\Delta U}{W}=\frac{x}{10}$

The value of the $x=25$.

40. Given, air is diatomic gas

$\therefore$ Degrees of freedom, $f=5$

So, ratio of specific heats of gas, $\gamma=1+\frac{2}{f}=\frac{7}{5}$

Also, given that $V_i=V$ and $V_f=\frac{V}{10}$

$$T_i=20^\circ\text{C}=273+20=293\text{ K}$$

As for adibatic change,

$$TV^{\gamma-1}=\text{constant} \Rightarrow T_iV_i^{\gamma-1}=T_fV_f^{\gamma-1}$$

$$\Rightarrow 293\cdot V^{\frac{7}{5}-1}=T_f\cdot\left(\frac{V}{10}\right)^{\frac{7}{5}-1} \Rightarrow T_f=293\times10^{2/5}\text{K}$$

Change in internal energy is

$$\Delta U=\frac{n\cdot f\cdot R(T_f-T_i)}{2}=\frac{5\times5\times\frac{25}{3}(293\times10^{2/5}-293)}{2}$$

$$=4.195\times10^3\text{ J}=46144\text{ J}\approx46\text{ kJ}$$

41. The expression of mean time, $\tau=\frac{\lambda}{V_{avg}}$

As, mean free path of gas molecule, $\lambda=\frac{1}{\sqrt{2}\pi d^2 n_V}$

(where, n_V = number of molecules volume)

$$\Rightarrow \lambda\propto(T)^0$$

Also, average speed, $v_{avg}=\sqrt{\frac{8RT}{\pi M}}$

$$\Rightarrow v_{avg}\propto\sqrt{T}$$

$$\therefore \tau\propto\frac{1}{\sqrt{T}}$$

42. According to gas equation,

$$pV=NKT \Rightarrow N=\frac{pV}{KT}$$

For monoatomic gas,

Energy, $U=\frac{3}{2}KT \Rightarrow KT=\frac{2}{3}U$

Now, $N=\frac{3pV}{2U}$

So, $N=\frac{3g\rho hV}{2U}$ $\quad(\because$ Pressure, $p=\rho gh)$

$$\therefore N=\frac{3\times980\times13.6\times2\times4}{2\times4\times10^{-14}}=3.99\times10^{18}\approx4\times10^{18}$$

43. Mean free path,

$$\lambda=\frac{V}{\sqrt{2}\pi d^2N}=\frac{kT}{\sqrt{2}\pi d^2 p}$$

But from gas equation, $\frac{p}{T}=\frac{nR}{V}$

For a constant n and V;

$p/T=$ constant.

So, mean free path does not depend on p/T or p and T. So, in given condition (closed container), mean free path remains constant or unchanged.

$\therefore$ Statement A is incorrect, but C is correct. Also, mean time between two collisions is

$$\tau=\frac{\text{mean free path}}{V_{avg}}=\frac{\lambda}{V_{avg}}$$

As, $V_{avg}\propto\sqrt{T}$

$\Rightarrow$ Average time, $\tau\propto\frac{1}{\sqrt{T}}$

As, the temperature is increasing, so mean collision time (τ) decreases.

$\therefore$ Statement B is correct.

44. For a mixture of two gases,

$$\gamma_{\text{mixture}}=\frac{C_{p\text{mixture}}}{C_{V\text{mixture}}}=\frac{n_1C_{p_1}+n_2C_{p_2}}{n_1C_{V_1}+n_2C_{V_2}} \quad \text{....(i)}$$

Here, gas 1 is helium which is monoatomic, so $n_1=n$,

$$C_{p_1}=\frac{5}{2}R, C_{V_1}=\frac{3}{2}R$$

and gas 2 is oxygen which is diatomic, so $n_2=2n$,

$$C_{p_2}=\frac{7}{2}R, C_{V_2}=\frac{5}{2}R$$

Hence, from Eq. (i), we get

$$\gamma_{\text{mix}}=\frac{n\times\frac{5R}{2}+2n\times\frac{7R}{2}}{n\times\frac{3R}{2}+2n\times\frac{5R}{2}}=\frac{19}{13}$$

45. From ideal gas equation, $pV=nRT$

At constant temperature, for small changes in p and V,

$$\Delta(pV)=\Delta(nRT)$$

$$\Rightarrow p\Delta V+V\Delta p=0 \Rightarrow V\Delta p=-p\Delta V$$

$$\Rightarrow \Delta p=-\frac{p\Delta V}{V} \Rightarrow |\Delta p|=\left|-\frac{p\Delta V}{V}\right|$$

$$\Rightarrow |\Delta p|=\frac{p\Delta V}{V} \quad \text{...(i)}$$

Again, from ideal gas equation,

$$pV=nRT$$

At constant pressure, for small changes in V and T.

$$\Delta(pV)=\Delta(nRT)$$

$$\Rightarrow p\Delta V=nR\Delta T$$

$$\Rightarrow \Delta T=\frac{p\Delta V}{nR} \Rightarrow |\Delta T|=\left|\frac{p\Delta V}{nR}\right|$$

$$\Rightarrow |\Delta T|=\frac{p\Delta V}{nR} \quad \text{...(ii)}$$

If ΔV is same in both the cases (as given), then dividing eq. (ii) by eq. (i), we get

$$\frac{|\Delta T|}{|\Delta p|}=\frac{\left(\frac{p\Delta V}{nR}\right)}{\left(\frac{p\Delta V}{V}\right)} \Rightarrow \frac{|\Delta T|}{|\Delta p|}=\frac{V}{nR}$$

$$\Rightarrow \quad |\Delta T| = \frac{V}{nR}|\Delta p| \quad \Rightarrow \quad |\Delta T| = \frac{T}{p}|\Delta p|$$

$$\left(\because pV = nRT \Rightarrow \frac{V}{nR} = \frac{T}{p}\right)$$

$$\Rightarrow \quad |\Delta T| = \frac{300}{2}|\Delta p| \quad (\text{as } T = 300 \text{ K and } p = 2 \text{ atm})$$

$$\Rightarrow \quad |\Delta T| = 150|\Delta p|$$

Given that, $|\Delta T| = C|\Delta p|$

On comparing both equations, we get

$$C = 150$$

46. Internal energy of a gas mixture

= Sum of internal energies of its' components.

Also, internal energy of a gas is given by

$$U = \frac{f}{2}(nRT)$$

Here, gases are oxygen (diatomic, $f = 5$) and argon (monoatomic, $f = 3$).

So, total internal energy of the mixture is

$$U = \left(\frac{f}{2}nRT\right)_{O_2} + \left(\frac{f}{2}nRT\right)_{Ar}$$

$$= \frac{5}{2}\times 3\times RT + \frac{3}{2}\times 5\times RT = 15RT$$

47. $\because \gamma = \frac{C_p}{C_V} = 1 + \frac{2}{f}$

where, f = degree of freedom.

Now, (A) for monatomic gas, $f = 3$

so, $\gamma = 1 + \frac{2}{3} = \frac{5}{3}$

(B) for diatomic rigid gas, $f = 5$

so, $\gamma = 1 + \frac{2}{5} = \frac{7}{5}$

(C) for diatomic non-rigid gas, $f = 7$

so, $\gamma = 1 + \frac{2}{7} = \frac{9}{7}$

(D) for triatomic rigid gas, $f = 6$

so, $\gamma = 1 + \frac{2}{6} = \frac{8}{6} = \frac{4}{3}$

Therefore, A-IV, B-I, C-II, D-III.

JEE Advanced

1. Given, internal energy $U = \frac{nfRT}{2}$

For one mole gas, $n = 1$

$$\therefore \quad U = \frac{fRT}{2} \quad \text{...(i)}$$

where, f is degree of freedom

$$\therefore \quad v_n = \sqrt{\frac{\gamma RT}{M}}$$

$$v_n = \sqrt{\frac{\left(1 + \frac{2}{f}\right)RT}{M}} \quad \text{...(ii)} \quad \left(\because \gamma = 1 + \frac{2}{f}\right)$$

From Eqs. (i) and (ii), it is clear that when f increases, then U increases but v_n decreases.

Hence, option (c) is correct.

2. & **3.**

When the tube just sinks / floats, then average density = density of water

$$\frac{\text{Mass}}{\text{total volume}} = 1 \text{ gm/cc}$$

$$\Rightarrow \quad \frac{5\text{gm}}{\text{total volume}} = 1 \text{ gm/cc}$$

$\Rightarrow$ Total volume = 5 cc

$\Rightarrow$ Volume of tube + final volume of air in the tube = 5 cc

$$\Rightarrow \quad \frac{5\text{gm}}{2.5 \text{ gm / cc}} + V_f = 5$$

$$\Rightarrow \quad V_f = 5 - 2 = 3 \text{ cc} \quad \Rightarrow \Delta V = 0.3 \text{ cc}$$

For isothermal process,

$$p_iV_i = p_fV_f \quad \Rightarrow \quad p_f = 10^5 \times \frac{3.3}{3}$$

$$p_f = 1.1\times 10^5 - 10^5$$

$$p_f - p_i = 1.1\times 10^5 - 10^5$$

$$= 0.1\times 10^5 = 10\times 10^3 \text{Pa} \Rightarrow Y = 10$$

4. Question was wrong. According to official website of IIT-JEE, marks were given to all students in this question.

5. (a) Total internal energy $U = \frac{f_1}{2}nRT + \frac{f_2}{2}nRT$

$$(U_{\text{ave}})_{\text{per mole}} = \frac{U}{2n} = \frac{1}{4}[5RT + 3RT] = 2RT$$

(b) $$\gamma_{\text{mix}} = \frac{n_1C_{p_1} + n_2C_{p_2}}{n_1C_{V_1} + n_2C_{V_2}} = \frac{(1)\frac{7R}{2} + (1)\frac{5R}{2}}{(1)\frac{5R}{2} + (1)\frac{3R}{2}} = \frac{3}{2}$$

$$M_{\text{mix}} = \frac{n_1M_1 + n_2M_2}{n_1 + n_2} = \frac{M_1 + M_2}{2} = \frac{2+4}{2} = 3$$

Speed of sound $v = \sqrt{\frac{\gamma RT}{M}} \Rightarrow v \propto \sqrt{\frac{\gamma}{M}}$

$$\frac{V_{\text{mix}}}{V_{\text{He}}} = \sqrt{\frac{\gamma_{\text{mix}}}{\gamma_{\text{He}}}\times\frac{M_{\text{He}}}{M_{\text{mix}}}} = \sqrt{\frac{3/2}{5/3}\times\frac{4}{3}} = \sqrt{\frac{6}{5}}$$

(d) $$V_{\text{rms}} = \sqrt{\frac{3RT}{M}}$$

$$\Rightarrow V_{\text{rms}} \propto \frac{1}{\sqrt{M}}, \quad \frac{V_{\text{He}}}{V_{\text{H}}} = \sqrt{\frac{M_{\text{H}}}{M_{\text{He}}}} = \sqrt{\frac{2}{4}} = \frac{1}{\sqrt{2}}$$

6. $\rho = pM / RT \quad \therefore \quad \rho \propto pM$

or $$\frac{\rho_1}{\rho_2} = \left(\frac{p_1}{p_2}\right)\left(\frac{M_1}{M_2}\right) = \left(\frac{2}{3}\right)\left(\frac{4}{3}\right) = \frac{8}{9}$$

7. $$V_{\text{rms}} = \sqrt{\frac{3RT}{M}} \quad \text{or} \quad V_{\text{rms}} \propto \frac{1}{\sqrt{M}}$$

$$\therefore \quad \frac{(V_{\text{rms}})_{\text{He}}}{(V_{\text{rms}})_{\text{Ar}}} = \sqrt{\frac{M_{\text{Ar}}}{M_{\text{He}}}} = \sqrt{\frac{40}{4}} = \sqrt{10} \approx 3.16$$

CHAPTER~06

THERMODYNAMICS

LEVEL 01 Starter Level

6.1 Work Done by Gas

1 During the expansion process, the volume of the gas changes from $4\,m^3$ to $6\,m^3$ while the pressure changes according to $p = 30V + 100$, where pressure is in Pa and volume is in m^3. Find the work done by gas.

2 The pressure in a 2 moles of monoatomic gas increases linearly from 4×10^5 Pa to 8×10^5 Pa when its volume increases from $0.2\,m^3$ to $0.5\,m^3$. Calculate the

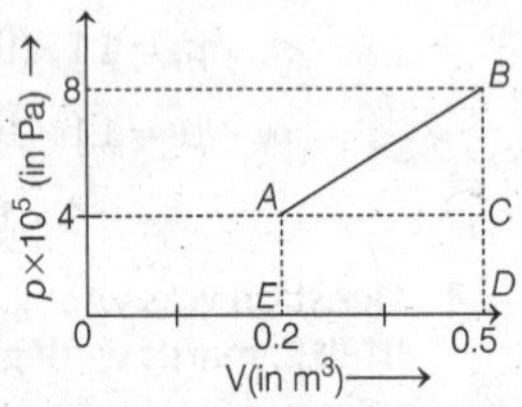

(a) work done by the gas

(b) increase in the internal energy

3 *p-V* diagram of an ideal gas is as shown in figure. What is the work done by the gas in the process *ABCD*?

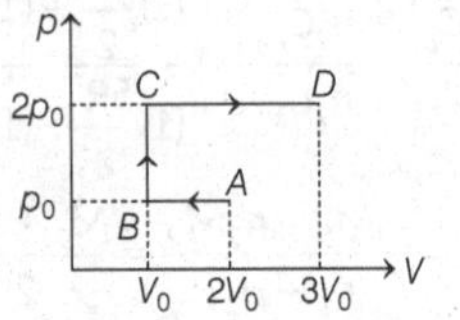

4 In the *p-V* diagram shown in figure, *ABC* is a semicircle. Find the work done in the process *ABC*.

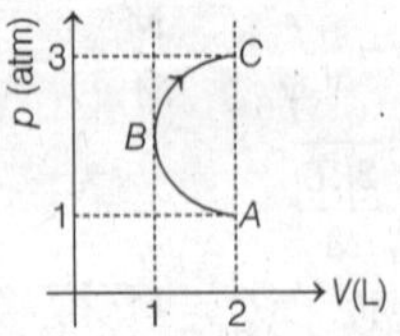

5 Find work done by the gas in the following cyclic processes.

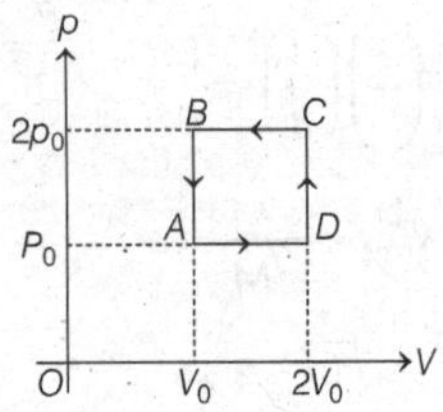

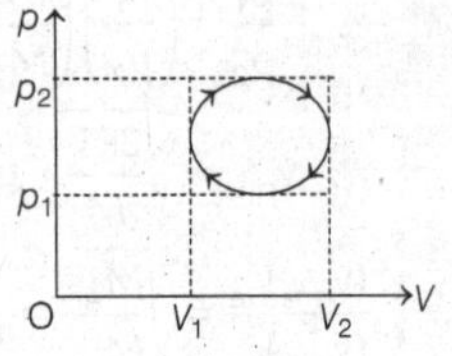

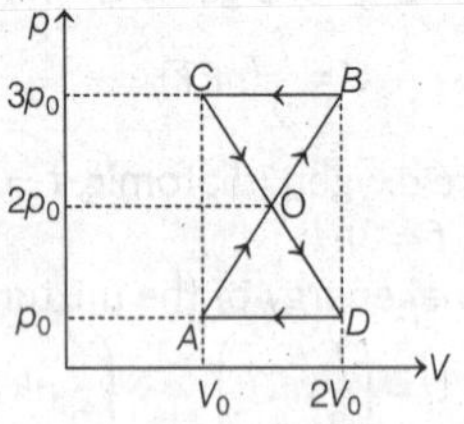

6.2 First Law of Thermodynamics

1 In a thermodynamic process, pressure of a fixed mass of a gas is changed in such a manner that the gas releases 20 J of heat and 8 J of work is done on the gas. If initial internal energy of the gas was 30 J, what will be the final internal energy?

2 A gas undergoes a change of state during which 100 J of heat is supplied to it and it does 20 J of work. The system is brought back to its original state through a process during which 20 J of heat is released by the gas. What is the work done by the gas in the second process?

3 When a system is taken from state *a* to state *b* along the path *acb*, it is found that a quantity of heat $Q = 200$ J is absorbed by the system and a work $W = 80$ J is done by it. Along the path *adb*, $Q = 144$ J.

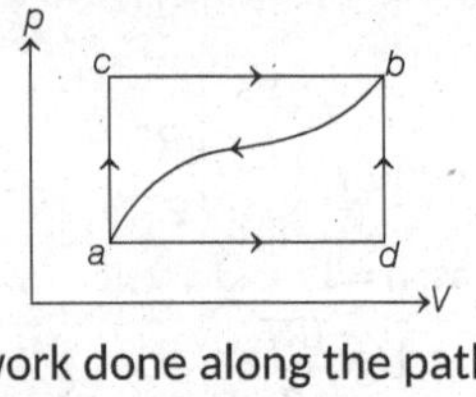

(a) Find the work done along the path *adb*.

(b) If the work done on the system along the curved path *ba* is 52 J, then what is the heat absorbed along this path?

(c) If $U_a = 40$ J, what is the value of U_b?

(d) If $U_d = 88$ J, what is the heat absorbed for the path *db*?

6.3 Molar Heat Capacity of Gas

1 If γ be the ratio of specific heats (C_p and C_V) for a perfect gas, find the number of degrees of freedom of a molecule of the gas.

2 Internal energy of two moles of an ideal gas at a temperature of 127°C is 1200*R*. Then, find the molar specific heat of the gas at constant pressure?

3 Ideal monoatomic gas is taken through a process $dQ = 2dU$. where dQ is heat supplied and dU is change in internal energy. Find the molar heat capacity (in terms of *R*) for the process.

4 Find the molar heat capacity in a process of a diatomic gas, if it does a work of $Q/4$ when a heat of *Q* is supplied to it.

5 Calculate the value of mechanical equivalent of heat from the following data. Specific heat capacity of air at constant volume and at constant pressure are 4.93 cal/mol-K and 6.90 cal/mol-K, respectively. Gas constant $R = 8.3$ J/mol-K.

6 Calculate the difference between two specific heats of 1 g of helium gas at NTP. Molecular weight of helium = 4 g and 1 J = 4.186 J cal^{-1}.

6.4 Isochoric, Isobaric and Isothermal Processes

1 Find the change in internal energy of 2 moles of an ideal diatomic gas when its temperature is increased by 75 K,

(a) keeping the volume constant,
(b) keeping the pressure constant
[Given, $R = 25/3$ J/mol-K]

2 How much heat must be supplied to a mixture of 10 g hydrogen and 40 g of He to increase the temperature by 50°C, if they are kept in a closed vessel?

3 A gas under constant pressure of 4.5×10^5 Pa when subjected to 800 kJ of heat, changes the volume from 0.5 m^3 to 2.0 m^3. Find the change in internal energy of the gas.

4 A diatomic gas is heated at constant pressure. If 105 J of heat is given to the gas, find

(a) the change in internal energy of the gas
(b) the work done by the gas

5 A quantity of heat *Q* is supplied to a monoatomic ideal gas which expands at constant pressure. What is the fraction of heat which increases the internal energy of the gas?

6 The average degree of freedom per molecule for a gas is 6. The gas performs 25 J of work when it expands at constant pressure. Find the heat absorbed by the gas.

7 70 cal of heat is required to raise the temperature of 2 moles of an ideal gas at constant pressure from 30°C to 35°C. Find the amount of heat required to raise the temperature of the same gas through the same range (30°C to 35°C) at constant volume.

8 In given figure, gas is slowly heated for sometime. During the process, the increase in internal energy of the gas is 10 J and the piston is found to move out by 25 cm, then find the amount of heat supplied. The area of cross-section of cylinder = 40 cm^2 and atmospheric pressure = 100 kPa.

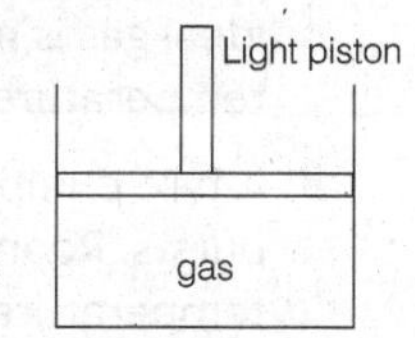

9 2 moles of a diatomic gas at 300 K are enclosed in a cylinder as shown in figure. Piston is light. Find out the heat given (in terms of *R*) if the gas is slowly heated to 400 K in the following cases.

(a) If piston is free to move
(b) If piston does not move

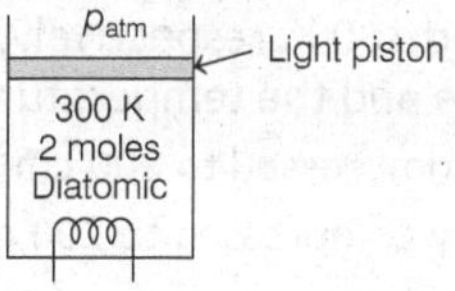

10 When 5 moles of an ideal gas is compressed isothermally, its volume decreases from 5 L to 1 L. If the gas is at 27°C, find the work done on the gas $\left(\log_{10}\left(\frac{1}{5}\right) = -0.6990\right)$.

11 *p*-*V* curve of a diatomic gas is shown in the figure. Find the total heat given to the gas in the process *AB* and *BC*. (ln 2 = 0.7)

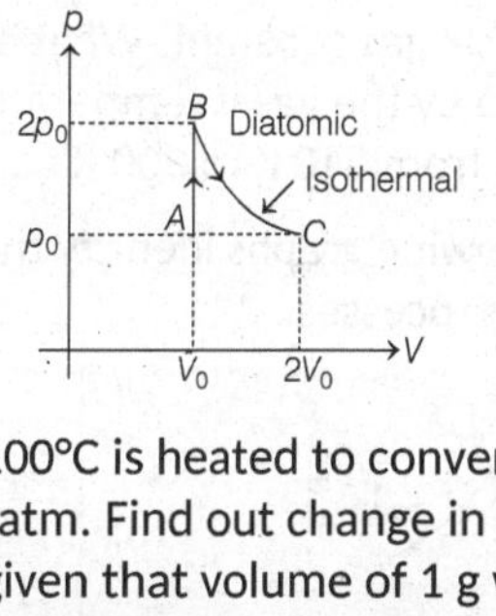

12 1 g water at 100°C is heated to convert into steam at 100°C at 1 atm. Find out change in internal energy of water. Its given that volume of 1 g water at 100°C = 1 cc, volume of 1 g steam at 100°C = 1671 cc. Latent heat of vaporisation = 540 cal/g. (Mechanical equivalent of heat 1 J = 4.18 J/cal.)

6.5 Adiabatic Process and Free Expansion

1 An ideal monoatomic gas is enclosed in a non-conducting cylinder having a piston which can move freely. Suddenly gas is compressed to 1/8 of its initial volume. Find the final pressure and temperature, if initial pressure and temperature are p_0 and T_0 respectively.

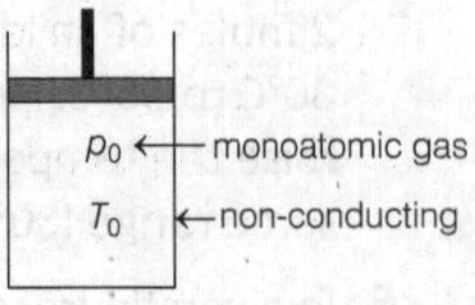

2 During an adiabatic process, if the pressure of an ideal gas is proportional to the cube of its temperature, find γ.

3 A tyre pumped to a pressure of 6 atm suddenly bursts. Room temperature is 27°C. Calculate the temperature of escaping air. ($\gamma = 1.4$ and $6^{-2/7} = 0.6$)

4 In an adiabatic process, the pressure is increased by (2/3%). If $\gamma = 3/2$, then find the decrease in volume

5 In figure the walls of the container and the piston are weakly conducting. The initial pressure, volume and temperature of the gas are 200 kPa, 800 cm^3 and 100 K, respectively. Find the pressure and the temperature of the gas, if it is

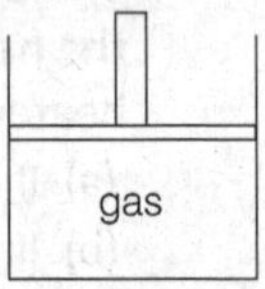

(a) slowly compressed to 200 cm^3

(b) suddenly compressed to 200 cm^3 ($\gamma = 1.5$)

6 At 27°C, 2 moles of an ideal monoatomic gas occupy a volume V. The gas expands adiabatically to a volume $2V$. Calculate : (a) the final temperature of the gas, (b) change in its internal energy and (c) the work done by the gas during the process. (Given, $R = 25/3$ J/mol-K and $2^{-2/3} = 0.63$)

7 Temperature of 1 mole of an ideal gas is increased from 300 K to 310 K under isochoric process. Heat supplied to the gas in this process is $Q = 25R$, where R = universal gas constant. What amount of work has to be done by the gas if temperature of the gas decreases from 310 K to 300 K adiabatically?

8 In the following graphs identify the isothermal and adiabatic processes.

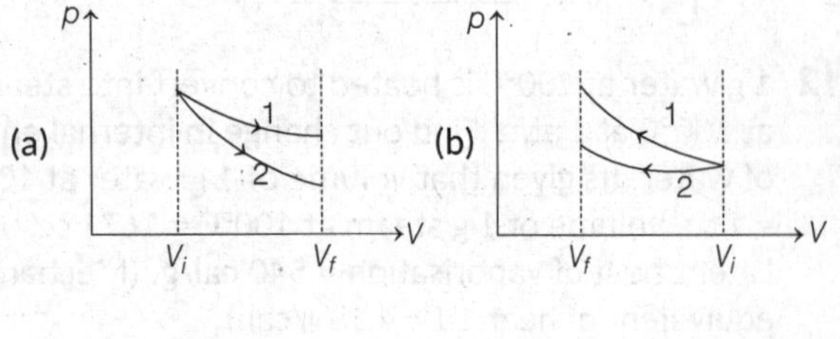

9 Three samples of the same gas A, B and C ($\gamma = 3/2$) have initially equal volume. Now, the volume of each sample is doubled. The process is adiabatic for A, isobaric for B and isothermal for C. If the final pressures are equal for all three samples, find the ratio of their initial pressures.

10 A non-conducting cylinder having volume $2V_0$ is partitioned by a fixed non-conducting wall in two equal parts. Partition is attached with a valve. Right side of the partition is a vacuum and left part is filled with a gas having pressure and temperature p_0 and T_0, respectively. If valve is opened find the final pressure and temperature of the two parts.

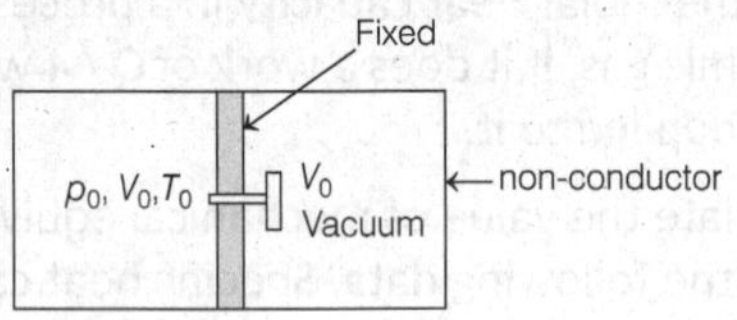

6.6 Polytropic Process

1 Find the molar heat capacity (in terms of R) of a monoatomic ideal gas undergoing the process : $pV^{1/2}$ = constant.

2 An ideal gas ($C_p/C_V = \gamma$) taken through a process in which the pressure and the volume vary as $p = kV^a$, where k = constant. Find the value of a for which the molar specific heat capacity in the process is zero.

3 Find the molar heat capacity of an ideal diatomic gas, during a process obeying : $p\sqrt{T}$ = constant.

4 2 moles of a monoatomic gas are heated up such that the pressure of a gas is directly proportional to its volume. If temperature of the gas rises from 20°C to 50°C, then find

(a) work done by the gas

(b) heat supplied to the gas
[$R = 25/3$ J/mol-K]

6.7 Cyclic Process

1 An ideal gas is taken through a cyclic thermodynamic process through four steps. The amounts of heat involved in these steps are $Q_1 = 5960$ J, $Q_2 = -5585$ J, $Q_3 = -2980$ J and $Q_4 = 3645$ J, respectively. The corresponding works involved are $W_1 = 2200$ J, $W_2 = -825$ J, $W_3 = -1100$ J and W_4, respectively.

(a) Find the value of W_4.

(b) What is the efficiency of the cycle?

2 T-V curve of cyclic process is shown below, number of moles of the gas are n. Find the total work done during the cycle.

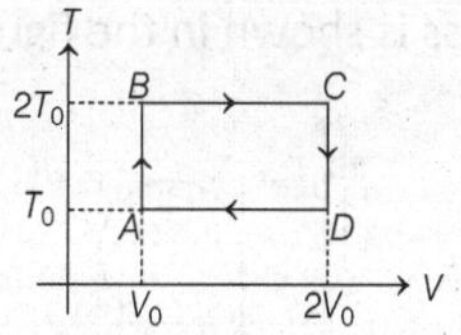

3 p-T curve of a cyclic process is shown. Find out the work done by the gas in the given process, if number of moles of the gas are n.

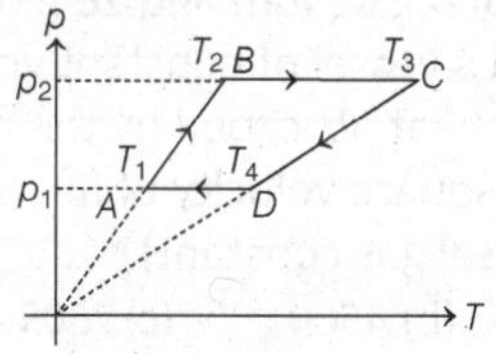

4 One mole of certain diatomic gas is under taken the cyclic process shown in the diagram. Find the efficiency of the cyclic process.

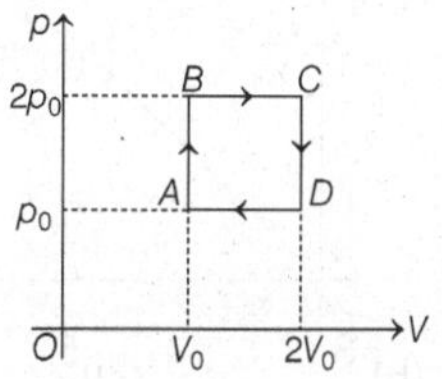

5 An ideal gas initially has pressure p_0, volume V_0 and temperature T_0. It is isothermally expanded to four times of its original volume, then it is compressed at constant pressure to attain its original volume V_0. Finally, the gas is heated at constant volume to get the original temperature T_0.

(a) Draw V-T curve

(b) Calculate the total work done by the gas in the process. (Given, ln 2 = 0.693)

6 In figure, a sample of an ideal gas is taken through the cyclic process *abca*. 800 J of work is done by the gas during process *ab*. If gas absorbs no heat in process *ab*, rejects 100 J of heat during *bc* and absorbs 500 J of heat during process *ca*. Then,

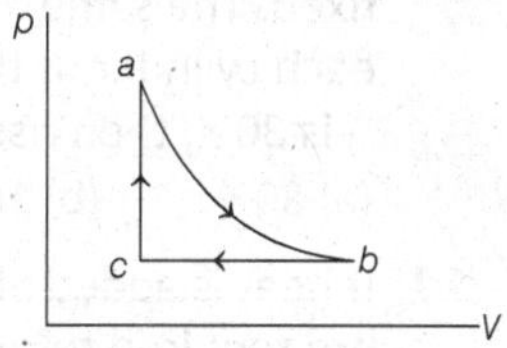

(a) find the internal energy of the gas at *b* and *c*, if it is 1000 J at *a*.

(b) also calculate the work done by the gas during the part *bc*.

7 n moles of a diatomic gas has undergone a cyclic process $ABCA$ as shown in figure. Temperature at A is T_0. Find

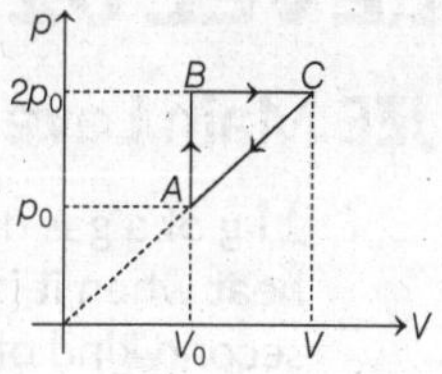

(a) volume at C

(b) maximum temperature

(c) total heat given to gas

(d) how much heat is rejected?

(e) out the efficiency

8 Consider the cyclic process $ABCA$, shown in the figure, performed on a sample of 2.0 moles of an ideal gas. A total of 1200 J of heat is withdrawn from the sample in the process. Find the work done by the gas during the part BC.

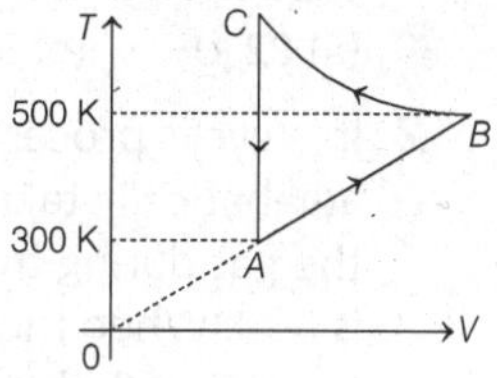

6.8 Heat Engine and Heat Pump

1 A Carnot engine has an efficiency of 40%, when the sink temperature is 27°C. What is the source temperature?

2 A Carnot engine takes 10^3 kcal of heat from a reservoir at 627°C and exhausts it to a sink at 27°C. What will be the (a) efficiency of the engine and (b) work performed by the engine?

3 The efficiency of Carnot's engine is 50%. The temperature of its sink is 7°C. To increase its efficiency to 70%, what should be the increase in temperature of the source?

4 A Carnot engine work as refrigerator in between 0°C and 27°C.

(a) What is the work efficiency coefficient?

(b) How much energy is needed to freeze 10 kg ice at 0°C?

5 A Carnot engine works as a refrigerator in between 250 K and 300 K. If it acquires 750 cal from heat source at low temperature, then what is the heat generated at higher temperature?

6 A refrigerator, whose coefficient of performance β is 5, extracts heat from the cooling compartment at the rate of 250 J per cycle.

(a) How much work per cycle is required to operate the refrigerator?

(b) How much heat per cycle is discharged to the room which acts as the high temperature reservoir?

LEVEL 02 JEE Main Level

JEE Main Level

1 1 kg of a gas does 20 kJ of work are receives 16 kJ of heat when it is expanded between two states. A second kind of expansion can be found between the same initial and final states which requires a heat input of 9 kJ. The work done by the gas in the second expansion is

(a) 32 kJ (b) 5 kJ (c) −4 kJ (d) 13 kJ

2 In a cyclic process shown in the figure, an ideal gas is adiabatically taken from B and A, the work done on the gas during the process $B \rightarrow A$ is 30 J. When the gas is taken from $A \rightarrow B$, the heat absorbed by the gas is 20 J. The change in internal energy of the gas in the process $A \rightarrow B$ is

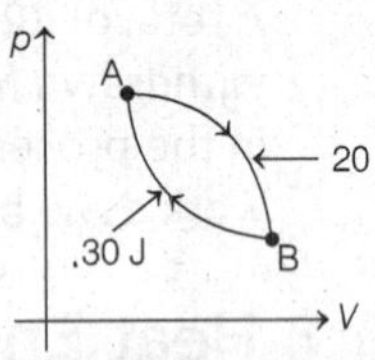

(a) 20 J (b) −30 J (c) 50 J (d) −10 J

3 In figure p-V curve of an ideal gas is given. During the process, the cumulative work done by the gas

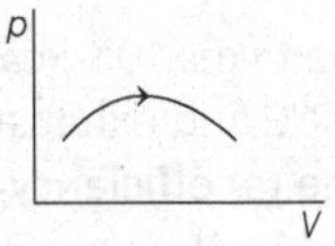

(a) continuously increases
(b) continuously decreases
(c) first increases then decreases
(d) first decreases then increases

4 A process $1 \rightarrow 2$ using monoatomic gas is shown on the p-V diagram on the right. $p_1 = 2p_2 = 10^6\ \text{N/m}^2$, $V_2 = 4V_1 = 0.4\ \text{m}^3$. The heat absorbed by the gas in this process will be

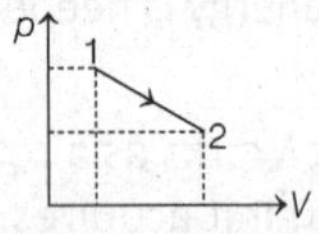

(a) 350 kJ (b) 375 kJ
(c) 425 kJ (d) None of these

5 Find work done by the gas in the process ABC

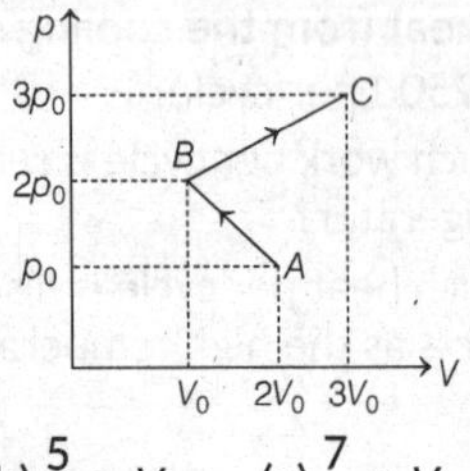

(a) $\frac{3}{2}p_0V_0$ (b) $\frac{5}{2}p_0V_0$ (c) $\frac{7}{2}p_0V_0$ (d) $4p_0V_0$

6 Heat energy absorbed by a system in going through a cyclic process is shown in the figure [V in litres and p in kPa] is

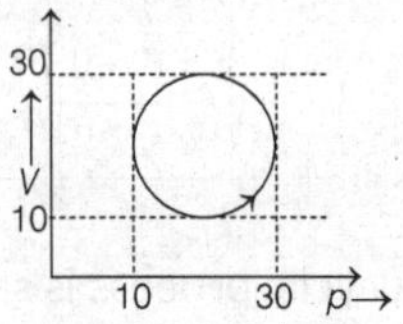

(a) $10^7\ \pi$J (b) $10^4\ \pi$J (c) $10^2\ \pi$J (d) $10^{-7}\ \pi$J

7 A mixture of 4 g helium and 28 g of nitrogen is enclosed in a vessel of constant volume at 300 K. The quantity of heat absorbed by the mixture to increase root mean square velocity of its molecules by 50% is (R is universal gas constant)

(a) $1500R$ (b) $450R$ (c) $750R$ (d) $3000R$

8 Volume *versus* temperature graph of two moles of helium gas is as shown in figure. The ratio of heat absorbed and the work done by the gas in process 1-2 is

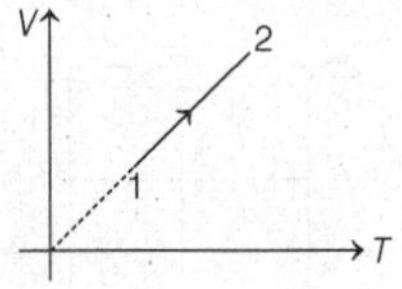

(a) 1 (b) $\frac{3}{2}$ (c) $\frac{5}{3}$ (d) $\frac{5}{2}$

9 10 moles of a diatomic perfect gas are allowed to expand at constant pressure. The initial volume and temperature are V_0 and T_0, respectively. If $7/2\ RT_0$ is transferred to the gas as heat, then the final volume and temperature are

(a) $1.1V_0, 1.1T_0$ (b) $0.9V_0, 0.9T_0$
(c) $1.1V_0, 10T_0/11$ (d) $0.9V_0, 10T_0/9$

10 Two cylinders A and B fitted with pistons contain equal amounts of an ideal diatomic gas at 300 K. The piston of A is free to move, while that of B is held fixed. The same amount of heat is given to the gas in each cylinder. If the rise in temperature of the gas in A is 30 K, then rise in temperature of the gas in B is

(a) 30 K (b) 18 K (c) 50 K (d) 42 K

11 If heat is added at constant volume, 6300 J of heat are required to raise the temperature of an ideal gas by 150 K. If instead, heat is added at constant pressure, 8800 J are required fo the same temperature change. When the temperature of the gas changes by 300 K, the internal energy of the gas changes by

(a) 5000 J (b) 12600 J (c) 17600 J (d) 22600 J

12 One mole of an ideal gas at temperature T was cooled isochorically till the gas pressure fell from p to $\frac{p}{n}$. Then, by an isobaric process, the gas was restored to the initial temperature. The net amount of heat absorbed by the gas in the process is

(a) nRT (b) $\frac{RT}{n}$

(c) $RT(n-1)$ (d) $RT(1-n^{-1})$

13 2 moles of monoatomic gas is expanded from (p_0, V_0) to $(p_0, 2V_0)$ under isobaric condition. Let ΔQ_1, be the heat given to the gas, ΔW_1 the work done by the gas and ΔU_1 the change in internal energy. Now, the monoatomic gas is replaced by a diatomic gas. Other conditions remaining the same. The corresponding values in the case are $\Delta Q_2, \Delta W_2, \Delta U_2$ respectively, then

(a) $\Delta Q_1 - \Delta Q_2 = \Delta U_1 - \Delta U_2$
(b) $\Delta U_2 + \Delta W_2 > \Delta U_1 + \Delta W_1$
(c) $\Delta U_2 > \Delta U_1$
(d) All of the above

14 A diatomic ideal gas is heated at constant volume until its pressure is doubled. It is again heated at constant pressure until its volume is doubled. The molar heat capacity for the whole process is

(a) $23R/5$
(b) $19R/5$
(c) $19R/6$
(d) $13R/4$

15 Ideal gas is taken through process shown in figure.

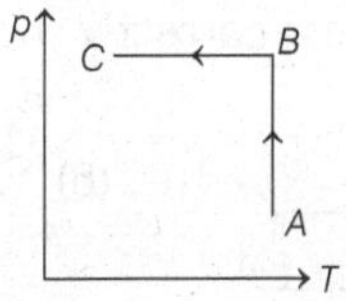

(a) In process AB, work done by system is positive.
(b) In process AB, heat is rejected out of the system.
(c) In process AB, internal energy increases.
(d) In process AB thermal energy decreases and in process BC internal energy increases.

16 The value of the ratio C_p/C_V for hydrogen is 1.67 at 30 K but decreases to 1.4 at 300 K as more degrees of freedom become active. During the rise in temperature,

(a) C_p remains constant but C_V increases
(b) C_p decreases but C_V increases
(c) Both C_p and C_V decrease by the same amount
(d) Both C_p and C_V increase by the same amount

17 An ideal gas undergoes a process such that $p \propto \frac{1}{T}$. The molar heat capacity of this process is 33.24 J/mol-K. (Take, $R = 8.31$ J/mol-K)

(a) The work done by the gas in $nR\Delta T$.
(b) Degree of freedom of the gas is 4.
(c) Degree of freedom of the gas is 3.
(d) γ for the gas is 1.5.

18 The heat capacity at constant volume of a sample of an ideal monoatomic gas is 35 J/K. Following are given three statements. State in order from (i) to (iii) whether they are true (T) or false (F).
Taking, $R = 25/3$ J/mol-K

(i) Number of moles of the gas are 1.5
(ii) Internal energy of the gas at 0°C is 35×273 J
(iii) Molar heat capacity at constant pressure is 125/6 J/mol-K

(a) T T T (b) TFT (c) FTT (d) TFF

19 One mole of an ideal gas is kept enclosed under a light piston (area $= 10^{-2}$ m^2) connected by a compressed spring (spring constant 100 N/m). The volume of gas is 0.83 m^3 and its temperature is 100 K. The gas is heated, so that it compresses the spring further by 0.1 m. The work done the gas in the process is
(Take, $R = 8.3$ J/mol-K and suppose there is no atmosphere)

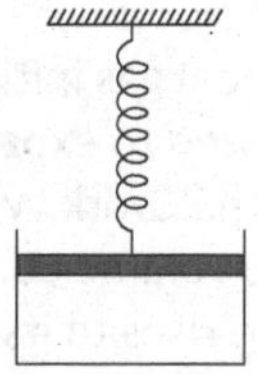

(a) 3 J (b) 6 J (c) 9 J (d) 1.5 J

20 In an adiabatic expansion of air ($\gamma = 7/5$), the volume increases by 5%. Then, the percentage change in pressure is approximately.

(a) +7% (b)+3% (c) −5% (d) −7%

21 A gas iscompressed adiabatically at 27°C, so that its volume becomes 1/9 th of the initial volume. Its final temperature will be ($\gamma = 1.5$)

(a) 27 K (b) 273 K
(c) 300 K (d) 900 K

22 An insulated 0.2 m^3 tank contain helium at 1200 kPa and 47°C. A value is now opened, allowing some helium to escape. The valve is closed when one-half of the initial mass has escaped. The temperature of the gas is ($\sqrt[3]{4} = 1.6$)

(a) −20°C (b) 20°C (c) 73°C (d) −73°C

23 A gaseous mixture of 4 g of oxygen and 2 g of helium expands adiabatically and reversibly from 20 L to 30 L. The initial temperature is 117°C. What is the final temperature?

(a) $390 \times \left(\frac{2}{3}\right)^{\frac{10}{17}}$ K (b) $390 \times \left(\frac{2}{3}\right)^{\frac{27}{17}}$ K

(c) $390 \times \left(\frac{2}{3}\right)$ K (d) $390 \times \left(\frac{3}{2}\right)^{\frac{10}{17}}$ K

24 The relation between U, p and V for a gas in an adiabatic process is given by relation $U = a + bpV$. Find the value of adiabatic exponent γ of this gas

(a) $\frac{b+1}{b}$ (b) $\frac{b+1}{a}$ (c) $\frac{a+1}{b}$ (d) $\frac{a}{a+b}$

25 One of the straight lines in the figure depicts the dependence of the work done $|W|$ on the temperature variations T for an isobaric process. The two of following are the adiabatic curves for argon and nitrogen. This isobaric process which depicts both the gases is

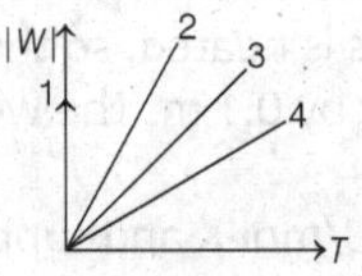

(a) 1 (b) 2 (c) 3 (d) 4

26 A sample of an ideal gas initially having internal energy U_1 is allowed to expand adiabatically performing external work W. Heat Q is then supplied to it, keeping the volume constant at its new value, until the pressure rises to its original value. The internal energy is then U_2. The increase in internal energy, $U_2 - U_1$ is equal to

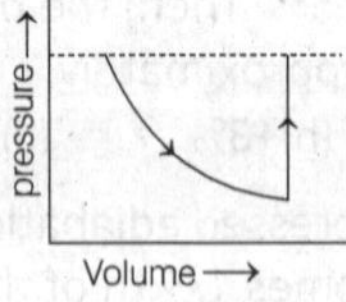

(a) $Q + W$ (b) W (c) $W - Q$ (d) $Q - W$

27 In figure, A and B are two adiabatic curves for two different gases. Then, A and B correspond to

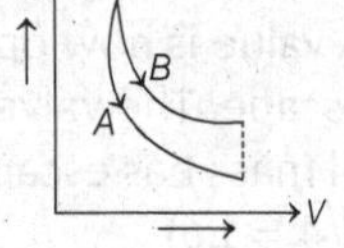

(a) Ar and He respectively

(b) He and H_2 respectively

(c) O_2 and H_2 respectively

(d) H_2 and He respectively

28 Two samples 1 and 2 are initially kept in the same state. The sample 1 is expanded through an isothermal process where as sample 2 through an adiabatic process upto the same final volume. The final temperature in process 1 and 2 are T_1 and T_2 respectively, then

(a) $T_1 > T_2$

(b) $T_1 = T_2$

(c) $T_1 < T_2$

(d) The relation between T_1 and T_2 cannot be deduced

29 Let, p_1 and p_2 be the final pressure of the samples 1 and 2, respectively in the previous question, then

(a) $p_1 < p_2$

(b) $p_1 = p_2$

(c) $p_1 > p_2$

(d) The relation between p_1 and p_2 cannot be deduced

30 Let ΔW_1 and ΔW_2 be the work done by the systems 1 and 2, respectively in the previous question, then

(a) $\Delta W_1 > \Delta W_2$

(b) $\Delta W_1 = \Delta W_2$

(c) $\Delta W_1 < \Delta W_2$

(d) The relation between W_1 and W_2 cannot be deduced

31 A certain mass of an ideal gas is at pressure p_1 and volume V_1. It is compressed isothermally and then allowed to expand adiabatically until its pressure returns to p_1. The gas is then allowed to expand to its original value. Which of the following p-V graphs are these process correctly shown?

(a)
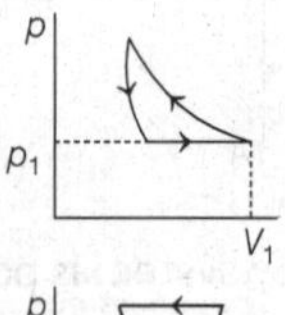

(b)
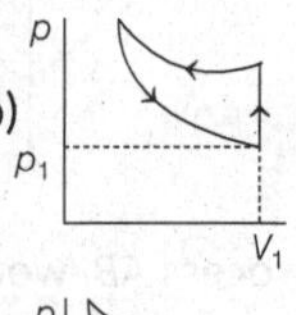

(c)
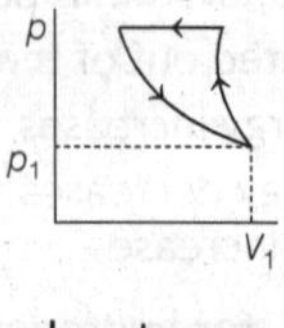

(d)
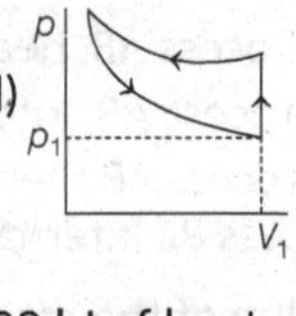

32 A closed system receives 200 kJ of heat at constant volume. It then rejects 100 kJ of heat while it has 50 kJ of work done on it at constant pressure. If an adiabatic process can be found which will restore the system to its initial state, the work done by the system during the process is

(a) 100 kJ (b) 50 kJ

(c) 150 kJ (d) 200 kJ

33 Suppose, 0.5 mole of an ideal gas undergoes an isothermal expansion as energy is added to it as heat Q. Graph shows the final volume V_f *versus* Q. The temperature of gas is (Use $\ln 3 \approx 10$ and $R = 25/3$ J/mol-K)

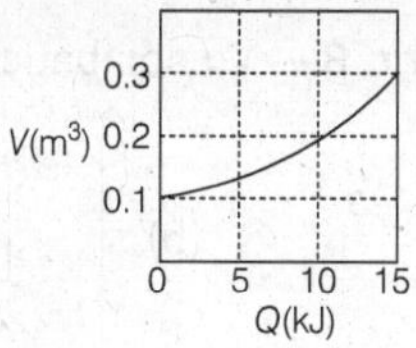

(a) 360 K (b) 260 K (c) 390 K (d) 490 K

34 A closed container is fully insulated from outside. One half of it is filled with an ideal gas X separated by a plate P from the other half Y which contains a vacuum as shown in figure. When P is removed, X moves into Y. Which of the following statements is correct?

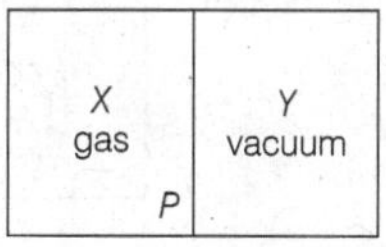

(a) No work is done by X
(b) X decreases in temperature
(c) X increases in internal energy
(d) X doubles in pressure

35 Which of the following graphs correctly shows the change in internal energy of an ideal gas with pressure for the isobaric, isochoric and isothermal processes?

(a)
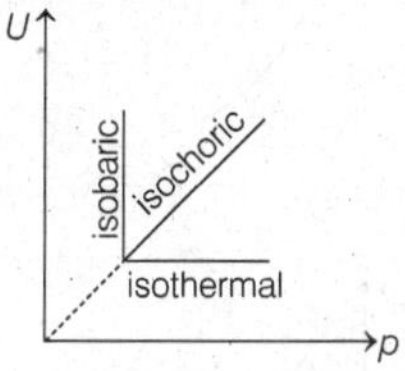

(b)
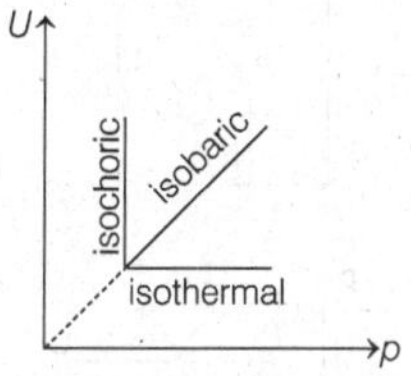

(c)
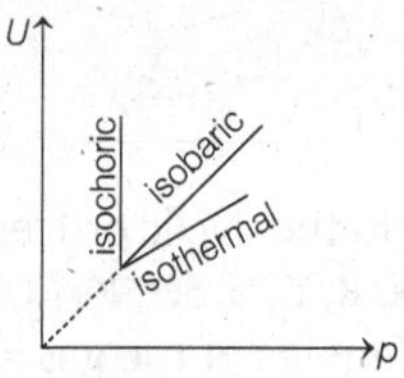

(d)
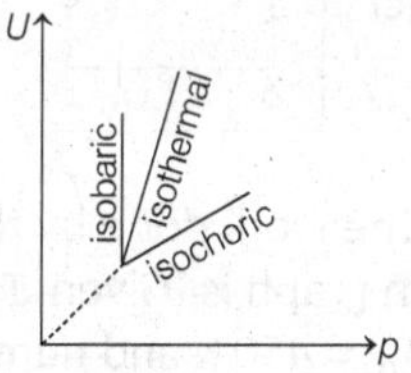

36 Two isochoric cooling process AB and CD are shown in p-V diagram for the same sample of gas. In which case heat exchange will be more?

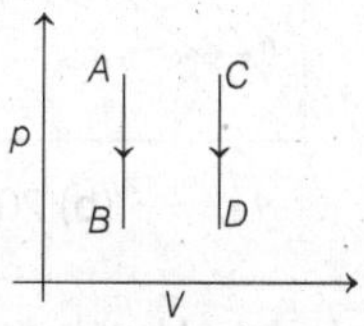

(a) AB (b) Same in both cases
(c) CD (d) Can't say

37 2 moles of a diatomic gas undergoes the process $pT^2/V =$ constant. Then, the molar heat capacity of the gas during the process will be equal to

(a) $5R/2$ (b) $9R/2$ (c) $3R$ (d) $4R$

38 pV-diagram of a monoatomic ideal gas is a straight line passing through origin. The molar heat capacity in the process is

(a) $4R$ (b) $2R$ (c) $3R$ (d) $4/3\,R$

39 A polytropic process for an ideal gas is represented by equation $pV^n =$ constant. If γ is ratio of specific heats $\left(\frac{C_p}{C_V}\right)$, then value of n for which molar heat capacity of the process is negative, is given as

(a) $\gamma > n$ (b) $\gamma > n > 1$
(c) $n > \gamma$ (d) none, as it is not possible

40 If molar heat capacity of the given process (as shown in figure) is C, then

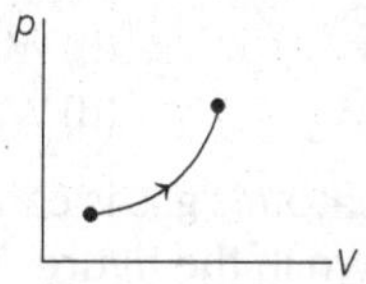

(a) $C < C_V$ (b) $C = 0$
(c) $C > C_V$ (d) $C = C_V$

41 Find the amount of work required to be done to increase the temperature of one mole of an ideal gas by 30°C, if it is expanding under the condition $p \propto V^{2/3}$

(a) 150 J (b) 100 J
(c) 50 J (d) 200 J

42 One mole of a diatomic gas is compressed to one fourth its original volume V_0 according to the law : $VT^2 =$ constant. The initial pressure is p_0. Then, which of the following is not true?

(a) $\Delta Q = p_0V_0/2$ (b) $\Delta p = 7p_0$
(c) $\Delta U = 2.5p_0V_0$ (d) $W = -p_0V_0$

43 If one mole of an ideal monoatomic gas ($\gamma = 5/3$) is mixed with one mole of ideal diatomic gas ($\gamma = 7/5$), the value of γ for the mixture will be

(a) 1.4 (b) 1.5 (c) 1.53 (d) 3.07

44 One mole of an ideal monoatomic gas is taken from point A to C along the path ABC. The initial temperature at A is T_0. For the process $A \to B \to C$,

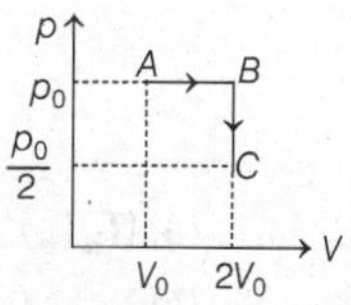

(a) heat absorbed $= RT_0/2$
(b) heat liberated $= 2RT_0$
(c) change in internal energy = 0
(d) work done = 0

45 A student records ΔQ, ΔU and ΔW for a thermodynamic cycle $A \rightarrow B \rightarrow C \rightarrow A$. Certain entries are missing. Find correct entry in following options.

	AB	BC	CA
ΔW	40 J		30 J
ΔU		50 J	
ΔQ	150 J	10 J	

(a) $\Delta W_{BC} = -70$ J (b) $\Delta Q_{CA} = 130$ J
(c) $\Delta U_{AB} = 190$ J (d) $\Delta U_{CA} = -160$ J

46 A given mass of a gas expands from a state A to the state B by three paths 1, 2 and 3 as shown in T-V indicator diagram. If W_1, W_2 and W_3, respectively be the work done by the gas along the three paths, then

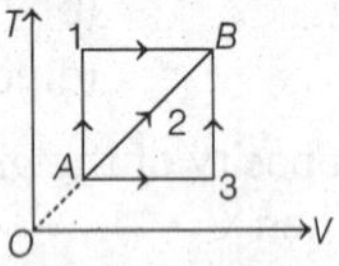

(a) $W_1 > W_2 > W_3$ (b) $W_1 > W_2 < W_3$
(c) $W_1 = W_2 = W_3$ (d) $W_1 < W_2, W_1 > W_3$

47 An ideal monoatomic gas is carried around the cycle $ABCDA$ as shown in the figure. The efficiency of the gas cycle is

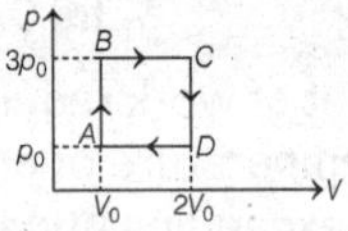

(a) 4/21 (b) 2/21 (c) 4/31 (d) 2/31

48 A sample of nitrogen gas was taken through the cyclic process shown in the figure. What is the ratio of energy released by the gas in the isochoric process to work done by the gas in the isobaric process?

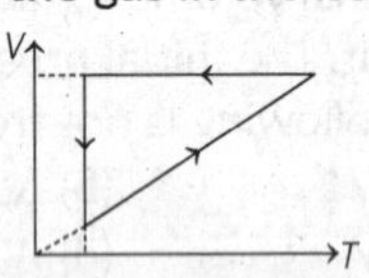

(a) 1.5 (b) 2.5 (c) 0.4 (d) 0.66

49 Figure illustrates a cycle conducted with n moles of an ideal gas. In the states a and b the gas temperature are T_a and T_b, respectively. Temperature of the gas in the state c is

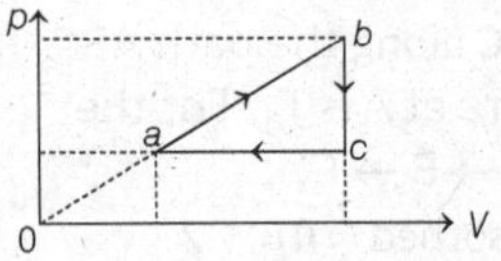

(a) $(T_a T_b)^{1/2}$ (b) $T_a + T_b$
(c) $T_a - T_b$ (d) $(T_a + T_b)/2$

50 For a given thermodynamic process, the p-V diagram is as shown below. Which of the following is the V-T diagram for the process?

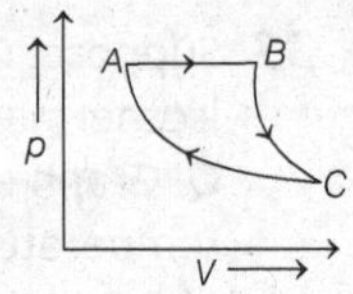

$A \rightarrow B$: isobaric, $B \rightarrow C$: adiabatic, $C \rightarrow A$: isothermal

(a) 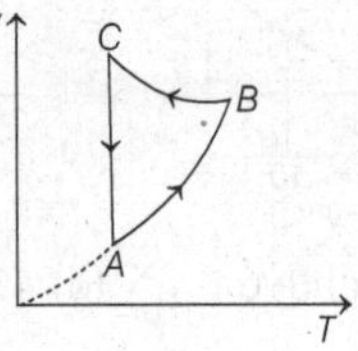
(b) 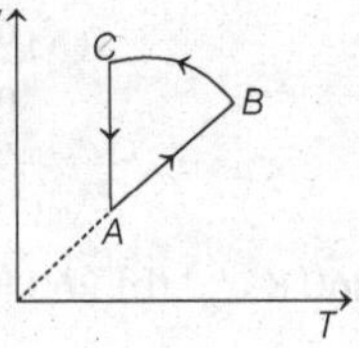
(c) 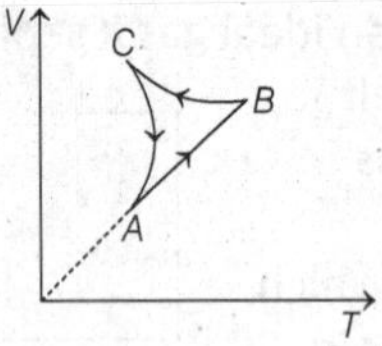
(d) 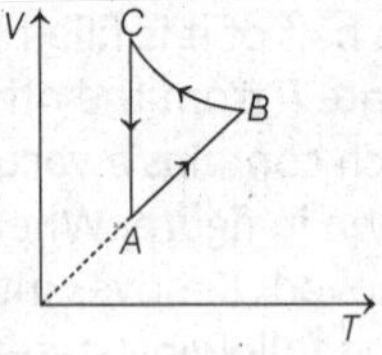

51 Pressure *versus* temperature graph of an ideal gas is as shown in figure. Corresponding density ρ *versus* volume V graph will be

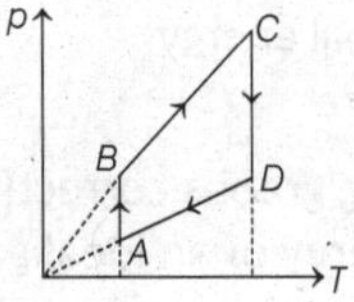

(a) 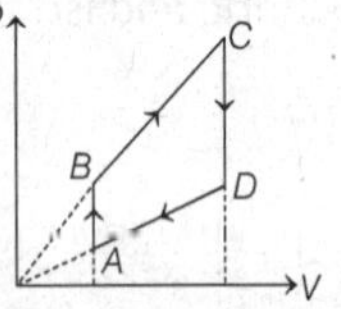
(b) 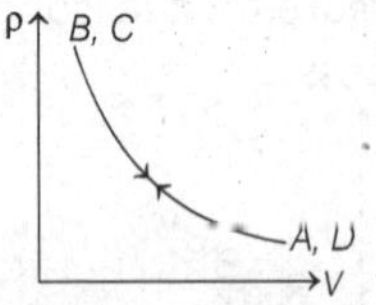
(c) 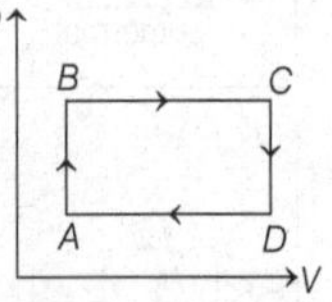
(d) 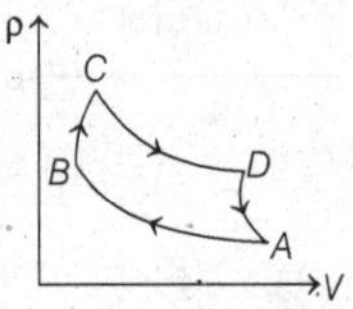

52 The work done by the gas in the cyclic process shown in graph is (Given, $T_A = 300$ K, $T_B = 500$ K, $T_C = 600$ K, $T_D = 450$ K and number of moles of the gas = 4)

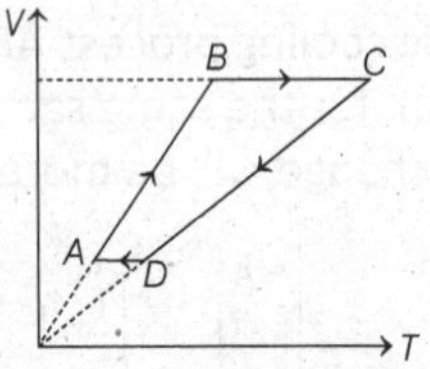

(a) 400 cal (b) 200 cal
(c) 100 cal
(d) cannot be calculated because volumes at different states is unknown

53 On a *T-p* diagram, two moles of ideal gas perform process *AB* and *CD*. If the work done by the gas in the process *AB* is two times the work done in the process *CD*, then what is the value of T_1 / T_2?

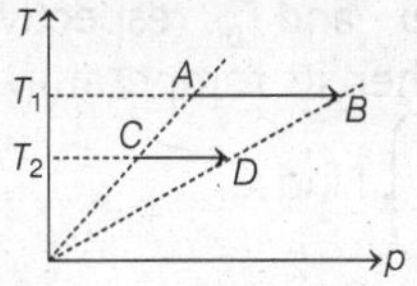

(a) 1/2 (b) 1 (c) 2 (d) 4

54 An ideal gas is taken through a cycle $A \to B \to C \to A$ as shown in figure. If the heat supplied in the cycle is 5 J, then work done by the gas in the process $C \to A$ is

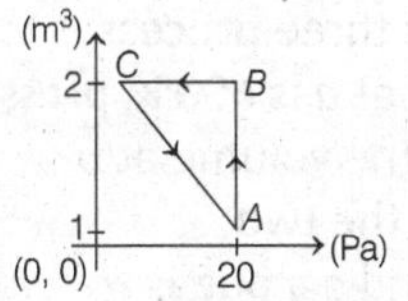

(a) –5 J (b) –10 J (c) –15 J (d) –20 J

55 In the *p-V* diagram shown, the gas does 5 J of work in isothermal process *ab* and 4 J in adiabatic process *bc*. What will be the change in internal energy of the gas in straight path *c* to *a*?

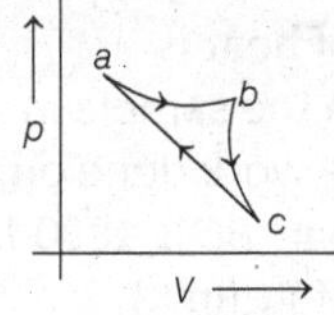

(a) 9 J
(b) 1 J
(c) 4 J
(d) 5 J

56 In the pressure *versus* volume graph shown, in the process of going from *a* to *b* 60 J of heat is added, and in the process of going from *b* to *d* 20 J of heat is added. In the process of going from *a* to *c* to *d*, what is the total heat added?

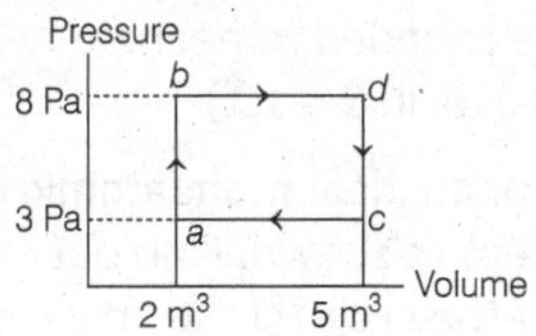

(a) 80 J
(b) 65 J
(c) 60 J
(d) 56 J

57 100 mole of an ideal monoatomic gas undergoes the following thermodynamic process as shown in the figure.

$A \to B$: isothermal expansion,
$B \to C$: adiabatic expansion
$C \to D$: isobaric compression
$D \to A$: isochoric process

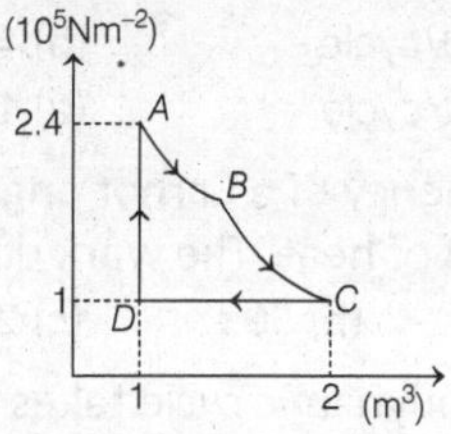

The heat transfere along the process *AB* is 9×10^4 J. The net work done by the gas during the cycle is (Take, $R = 8\ JK^{-1}mol^{-1}$)

(a) -0.5×10^4 J
(b) $+0.5 \times 10^4$ J
(c) -5×10^4 J
(d) $+5 \times 10^4$ J

58 A constant amount of an ideal gas undergoes the cyclic process *ABCA* as shown in the *p-V* diagram. The path *BC* is isothermal. The work done by the gas during one complete cycle, beginning and ending at *A*, is most nearly

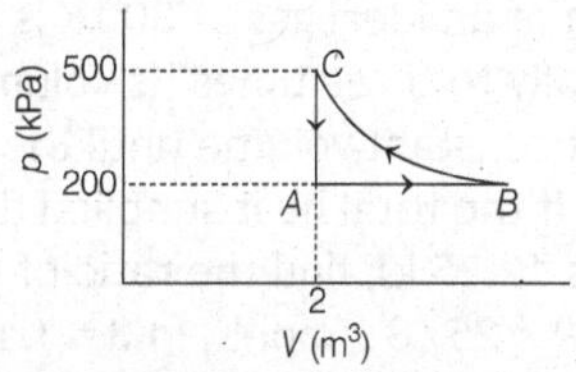

(a) –300 kJ (b) 300 kJ (c) 0 (d) 600 kJ

59 A monoatomic ideal gas is used as the working substance for the Carnot cycle shown in the figure. Processes *AB* and *CD* are isothermal, while processes *BC* and *DA* are adiabatic. During process *AB*, 400 J of work is done by the gas on the surroundings. How much heat is expelled by the gas during process *CD*?

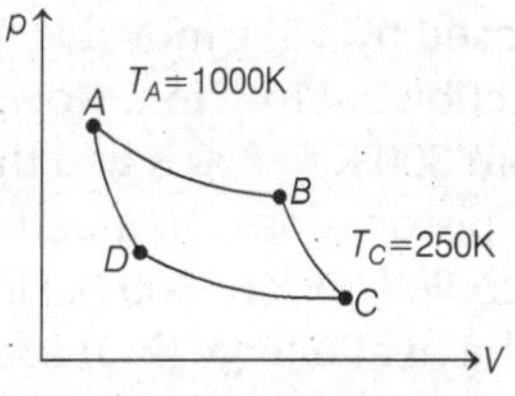

(a) 1600 J
(b) 400 J
(c) 200 J
(d) 100 J

60 An ideal gas heat engine operated in a Carnot's cycle between 227°C and 127°C. It absorbs 6×10^4 J at high temperature. The amount of heat converted into work is

(a) 4.8×10^4 J
(b) 3.5×10^4 J
(c) 1.6×10^4 J
(d) 1.2×10^4 J

61 A Carnot engine working between 300 K and 600 K has work output of 800 J/cycle. What is amount of

heat energy supplied to the engine from source per cycle?
(a) 1800 J/cycle (b) 1000 J/cycle
(c) 2000 J/cycle (d) 1600 J/cycle

62 The efficiency of a Carnot engine is 0.6. It rejects total 20 J of heat. The work done by the engine is
(a) 40 J (b) 50 J (c) 20 J (d) 30 J

63 A thermodynamic cycle takes in heat energy at a high temperature and rejects energy at a lower temperature. If the amount of energy rejected at the low temperature is 3 times the amount of work done by the cycle, the efficiency of the cycle is
(a) 0.25 (b) 0.33 (c) 0.67 (d) 0.9

64 The coefficient of performance of a carnot refrigerator working between 30°C and 0°C is
(a) 10 (b) 1 (c) 9 (d) 0

Numerical Value Questions

1 One mole of an ideal gas at 300 K is expanded isothermally to three times its volume and then heated at constant volume until the initial pressure is attained. If the total heat supplied during the entire process is 17.75 kJ, find the ratio of specific heats of the gas. [$R = 25/3$ J/mol-K, ln 3 = 1.1]

2 A sample of helium is kept in a cylinder of cross-section $A = 8.5\ \text{cm}^2$. The cylinder is closed by a light frictionless piston. The gas is slowly heated in a process during which a total of 42.5 J heat is given to the gas. Find the displacement (in cm) of the piston. [Take, $R = 25/3$ SI unit, atmospheric pressure = 100 kPa]

3 A vertical hollow cylinder contains an ideal gas. The gas is enclosed by a 5 kg movable piston with an area of cross-section $5 \times 10^{-3}\ \text{m}^2$. Now, the gas is slowly heated from 300 K to 350 K and the piston rises by 0.1 m. The piston is now clamped at this position and the gas is cooled back to 300 K. Find the difference between the heat energy (in J) added during heating process and energy lost during the cooling process. [1 atm pressure $= 10^5\ \text{Nm}^{-2}$]

4 p-V graph for an ideal gas undergoing polytropic process $pV^m =$ constant is shown here. Find the value of m.

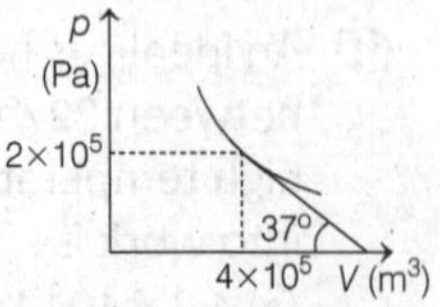

5 One mole of a diatomic gas is taken through the process $p/T^n = C$, where n and C are constant. If the heat capacity of gas is $C = -R/2$, then the value of n is

6 The equation of state for a gas is given by $pV = nRT + \alpha V$, where n is the number of moles and α is a positive constant. The initial pressure and temperature of 1 mole of the gas contained in a cylinder are p_0 and T_0, respectively. The work done by the gas when its temperature doubles isobarically is $\frac{x}{7}\left(\frac{p_0 T_0 R}{p_0 - \alpha}\right)$. Find x.

7 An insulator container contains 4 moles of an ideal diatomic gas at temperature T. Heat Q is supplied to this gas, due to which 2 moles of the gas are dissociated into atoms but temperature of the gas remains constant. If $Q = nRT$, then find n.

8 Figure shows three processes for an ideal gas. The temperature at a is 600 K, pressure 16 atm and volume 1 L. The volume at b is 4 L. Out of the two process ab and ac, one is adiabatic and the other is isothermal. The ratio of specific heats of the gas is 1.5. Find the volume (in L) at c.

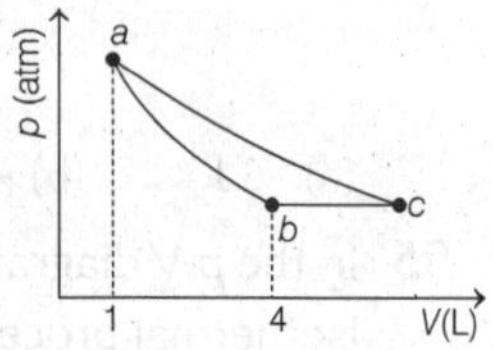

9 Consider the cyclic process $ABCA$ shown in figure, performed on a sample of 1 mole of an ideal gas. A total of 1000 J of heat is withdrawn from the sample in the process. The work done on the gas during part BC is 1830 J. Find the value of T_B (in K). ($R = 8.3$ J/K-mol)

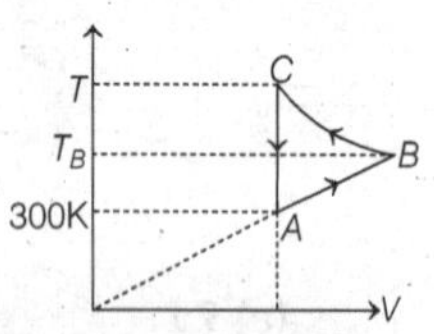

10 A diatomic ideal gas is taken through the cyclic process shown in the figure. In state 1 the pressure of the gas is 100 kPa and its temperature is 350 K. In state 2 the pressure is 300 kPa. What is the efficiency of the cycle in percentage rounded to nearest integer? [Take, ln 3 = 1.1]

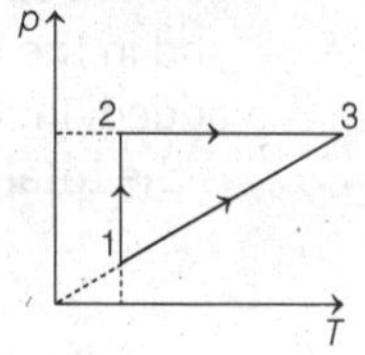

11 One mole of an ideal monoatomic gas undergoes the cyclic process as shown. Find out efficiency (in percent) of the cycle. [Take, ln 2 = 0.7]

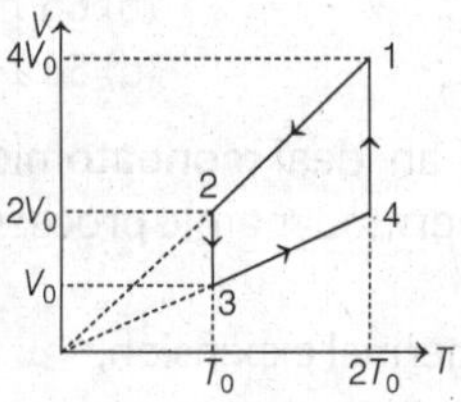

LEVEL 03 JEE Advanced Level

Single Choice Correct Questions

1 Find work done by the gas in the process shown in figure

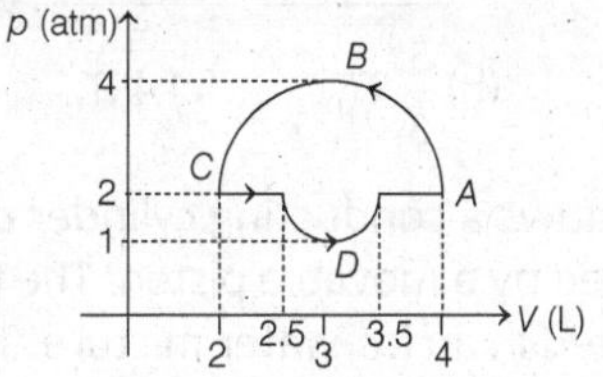

(a) $\frac{5}{2}\pi$ atm-L (b) $\frac{5}{2}$ atm-L

(c) $-\frac{3}{2}\pi$ atm-L (d) $-\frac{5}{4}\pi$ atm-L

2 Figure shows a cyclic process *ABCDBEA* performed on an ideal cycle. If $p_A = 2$ atm, $p_B = 5$ atm and $p_C = 6$ atm, $V_E - V_A = 20$ L, find the work done by the gas in the complete process. (1 atm pressure $= 1 \times 10^5$ Pa)

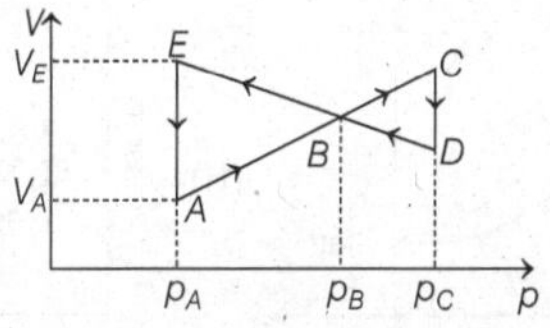

(a) 4.67 kJ (b) 3.67 kJ

(c) 2.67 kJ (d) 1.67 kJ

3 If for hydrogen $C_p - C_V = m$ and for nitrogen $C_p - C_V = n$, where C_p and C_V refer to specific heats per unit mass respectively at constant pressure and constant volume, the relation between *m* and *n* is (molecular weight of hydrogen = 2 and molecular weight of nitrogen = 28)

(a) $n = 14m$ (b) $n = 7m$

(c) $m = 7n$ (d) $m = 14n$

4 The molar heat capacity at constant pressure of nitrogen gas at STP is nearly 3.5*R*. Now, when the temperature is increased, it gradually increases and approaches 4.5*R*. The most appropriate reason for this behaviour is that at high temperatures

(a) nitrogen does not behave as an ideal gas

(b) nitrogen molecules dissociate in atoms

(c) the molecules collide more frequently

(d) molecular vibration gradually become effective

5 The value of $C_p - C_V$ is 1.09*R* for a gas sample in state *A* and is 1.00*R* in state *B*. Let, T_A, T_B denote the temperature and p_A and p_B denote the pressure of the states *A* and *B*, respectively. Then,

(a) $p_A < p_B$ and $T_A > T_B$

(b) $p_A > p_B$ and $T_A > T_B$

(c) $p_A = p_B$ and $T_A < T_B$

(d) $p_A > p_B$ and $T_A < T_B$

6 Sixty percent of given sample of oxygen gas when raised to a high temperature dissociates into atoms. Ratio of its initial heat capacity (at constant volume) to the final heat capacity (at constant volume) will be

(a) $\frac{8}{7}$ (b) $\frac{25}{26}$ (c) $\frac{10}{7}$ (d) $\frac{25}{27}$

7 In the process *ABC* for an ideal monoatomic gas, the temperature at states *A* and *C* are equal. The heat released in the process *BC* is *Q*. The work done in the process *A* to *B* is equal to

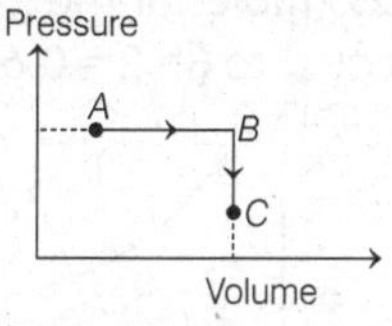

(a) *Q* (b) $Q/2$ (c) $2Q/3$ (d) $3Q/2$

8 An ideal gas undergoes the process $1 \rightarrow 2$ as shown in the figure, the heat supplied and work done in the process is ΔQ and ΔW, respectively. The ratio $\Delta Q : \Delta W$ is

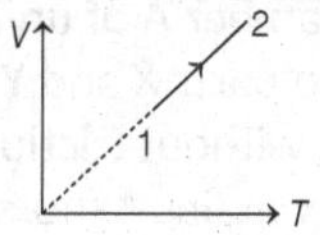

(a) $\gamma : \gamma - 1$ (b) γ (c) $\gamma - 1$ (d) $\gamma - 1 : \gamma$

9 Figure shows an isochore, an isotherm, an adiabatic and two isobars of two gases on a work done *versus* heat supplied curve. The initial states of both gases are the same and the scales for the two axes are same. Which of the following statements is incorrect?

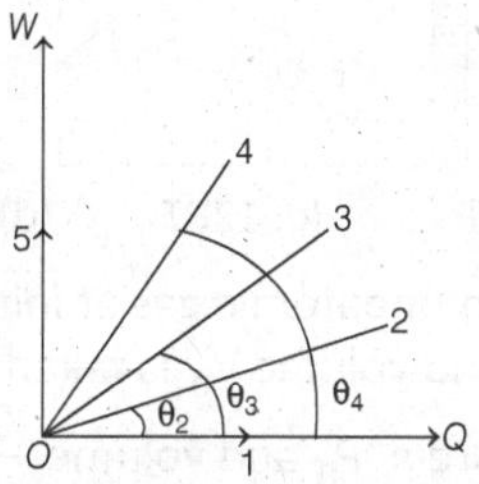

$\tan\theta_2 = 2/7$

$\tan\theta_3 = 2/5$

$\tan\theta_4 = 1$

(a) Straight line 1 corresponds to an isochoric process.

(b) Straight line 2 corresponds to an isobaric process for diatomic gas.

(c) Straight line 4 corresponds to an isothermal process.

(d) Straight line 5 corresponds to an isothermal process.

10 Two moles of helium gas are taken along the path *ABCD* (as shown in figure). The work done by the gas is

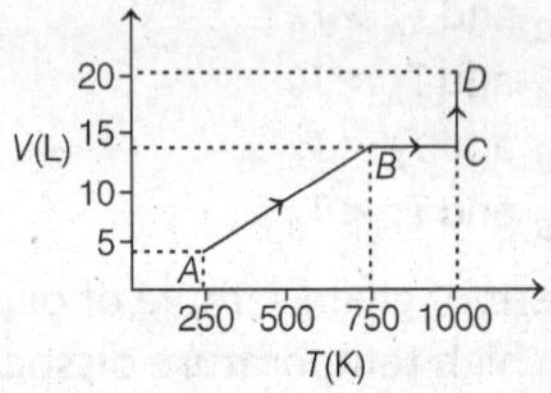

(a) $2000R\left(\frac{1}{2}+\ln\frac{4}{3}\right)$ (b) $500R(3+\ln 4)$

(c) $500R\left(2+\ln\frac{16}{9}\right)$ (d) $1000R\left(1+\ln\frac{16}{9}\right)$

11 Curve in the figure shows an adiabatic compression of an ideal gas from $15\,m^3$ to $12\,m^3$, followed by an isothermal compression to a final volume of $3.0\,m^3$. There are 2.0 moles of the gas. Total heat supplied to the gas is equal to ($\ln 2 = 0.693$)

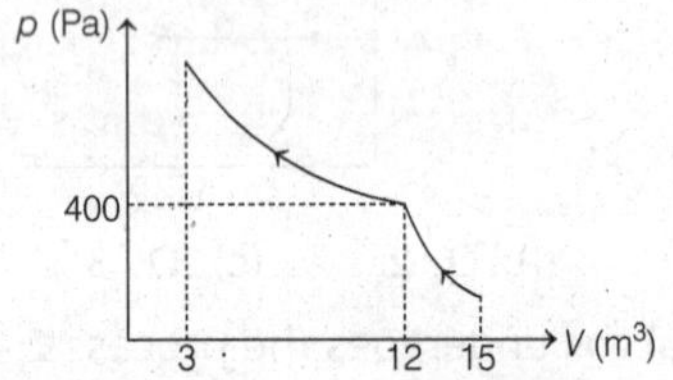

(a) 4521 J (b) – 4521 J
(c) – 6653 J (d) – 8476 J

12 A cylindrical chamber *A* of uniform cross-section is divided into two parts *X* and *Y* by a movable piston *P* which can slide without friction inside the chamber. Initially part *X* contains 1 mole of a monoatomic gas and *Y* contains 2 moles of a diatomic gas, and the volumes of *X* and *Y* are in the ratio 1 : 2 with both parts *X* and *Y* being at the same temperature. Assuming the gases to be ideal, the work *W* that will be done in moving the piston slowly to the position where the ratio of the volumes of *X* and *Y* is 2 : 1 will be

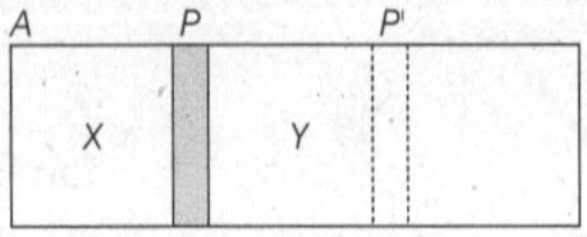

(a) $-5.8T$ (b) $8.3T$ (c) $12.3T$ (d) zero

13 One mole of ideal monoatomic gas at initial state *a* with pressure p_0 and volume V_0 is taken to a final state *d* with pressure e^3P_0 and volume $\frac{V_0}{e}$ through the path $a \to b \to c \to d$ (figure). $a \to b$ and $c \to d$ are adiabatic paths, where $b \to c$ is isothermal with temperature T_0. Find the work done by the gas in the process $b \to c$. (Given, $\ln(e) = 1$)

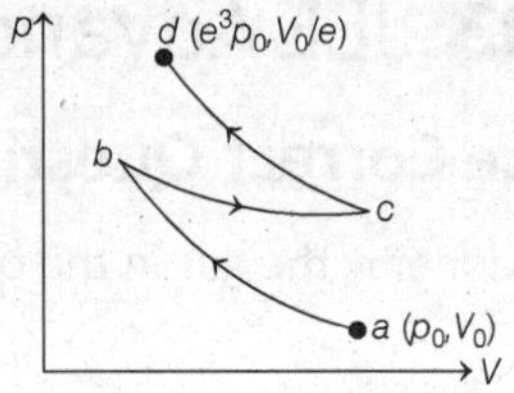

(a) $2RT_0$ (b) $\frac{5}{3}RT_0$ (c) $4RT_0$ (d) $\frac{3}{2}RT_0$

14 Figure shows a conducting cylinder containing gas and closed by a movable piston. The cylinder is submerged in an ice-water mixture. The piston is quickly pushed down from position (1) to position (2). The piston is held at position (2) until the gas is again at 0°C and then is slowly raised back to position (1). *p-V* diagram for the above process will be

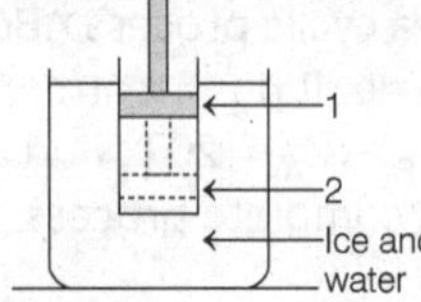

(a)

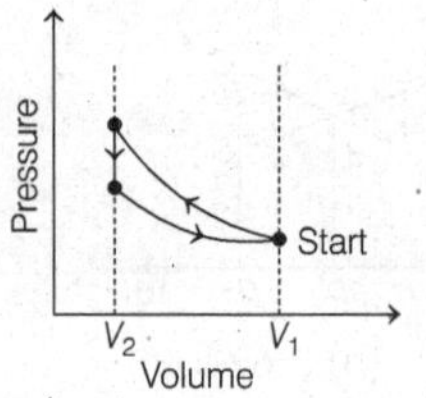

(b)

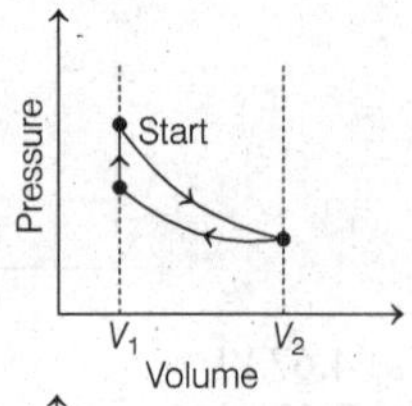

(c)

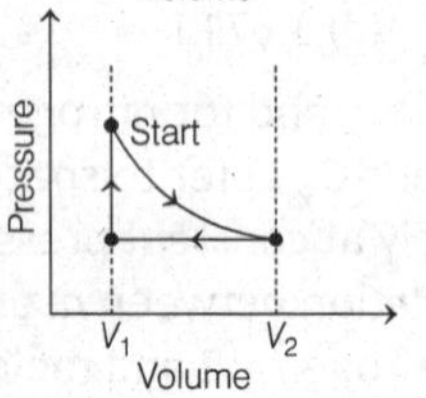

(d)

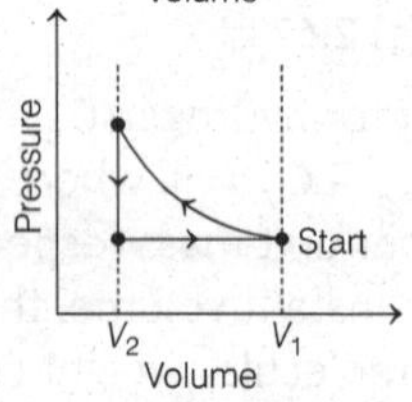

15 One mole of an ideal gas is taken along the process in which pV^x = constant. The graph shown represents the variation of molar heat capacity of such a gas with respect to *x*. The value of *c'* and *x'*, respectively, are given by

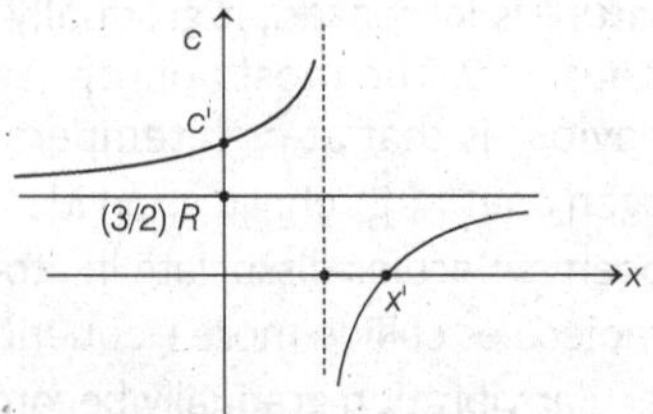

(a) $\frac{5R}{2}, \frac{5}{2}$ (b) $\frac{5R}{2}, \frac{5}{3}$

(c) $\frac{7R}{2}, \frac{7}{2}$ (d) $\frac{5R}{2}, \frac{7}{5}$

16 An amount Q of heat is added to a monoatomic ideal gas in a process in which the gas performs a work $Q/2$ on its surrounding. Find equation of the process.
(a) $pV^{1/3} = \text{constant}$
(b) $pV^{-1/4} = \text{constant}$
(c) $pV^{1/4} = \text{constant}$
(d) $pV^{-1/3} = \text{constant}$

17 In a certain gas, the ratio of the speed of sound and root mean square speed is $\sqrt{\frac{5}{9}}$. The molar heat capacity of the gas in a process given by $pT = \text{constant}$ is
(a) $R/2$ (b) $3R/2$ (c) $5R/2$ (d) $7R/2$

18 In an H_2 gas process, $pV^2 = \text{constant}$. The ratio of work done by gas to change in its internal energy is
(a) 2/3 (b) 0.4
(c) – 0.4 (d) 1.5

19 One mole of an ideal gas undergoes a process whose molar heat capacity is $4R$ and in which work done by gas for small change in temperature is given by the relation $dW = 2RdT$, then the ratio $\frac{C_p}{C_V}$ is
(a) 7/5 (b) 5/3 (c) 3/2 (d) 2

20 Figure demonstrates a polytropic process (*i.e.*, pV^n = constant) for an ideal gas. The work done by the gas in process AB is

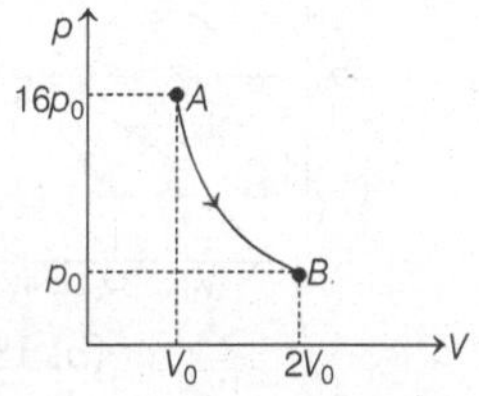

(a) $\frac{15}{2}p_0V_0$ (b) $\frac{14}{3}p_0V_0$
(c) $8p_0V_0$ (d) Insufficient information

21 The molar heat capacity C for an ideal gas going through a process is given by $C = \frac{a}{T}$, where a is a constant. If $\gamma = \frac{C_p}{C_V}$, then the work done by one mole of gas during heating from T_0 to ηT_0 will be
(a) $a\ln\eta$ (b) $\frac{1}{a\ln\eta}$
(c) $a\ln\eta - \left(\frac{\eta-1}{\gamma-1}\right)RT_0$ (d) $a\ln\eta - (\gamma-1)RT_0$

22 For two thermodynamic processes temperature and volume diagram are given. In first process, it is a straight line having initial and final coordinates as (V_0, T_0) and $(2V_0, 2T_0)$, where as in second process it is a rectangular hyperbola having initial and final coordinates (V_0, T_0) and $(2V_0, T_0/2)$. Then, ratio of work done $(W_1 : W_2)$ in the two processes must be

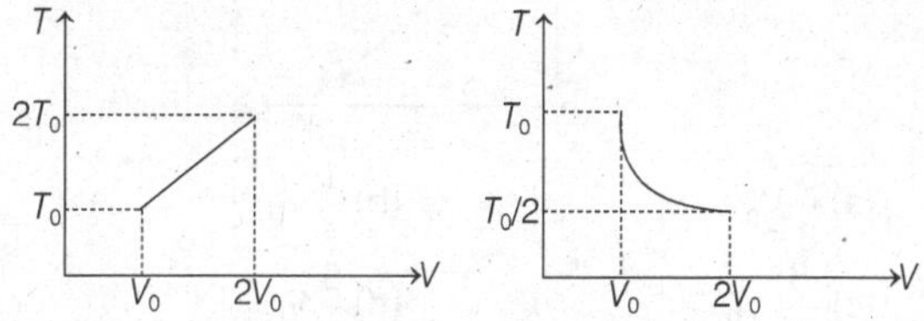

(a) 1 : 2 (b) 2 : 1
(c) 1 : 1 (d) None of these

23 A reversible adiabatic path on a p-V diagram for an ideal gas passes through state A, where $p = 0.7 \times 10^5\ \text{N/m}^{-2}$ and $V = 0.0049\ \text{m}^3$. The ratio of specific heat of the gas is 1.4. The slope of path at A is
(a) $2.0 \times 10^7\ \text{Nm}^{-5}$ (b) $1.0 \times 10^7\ \text{Nm}^{-5}$
(c) $-2.0 \times 10^7\ \text{Nm}^{-5}$ (d) $-1.0 \times 10^7\ \text{Nm}^{-5}$

24 A gas is undergoing an adiabatic process. At a certain state, the value of volume and temperature $= (V_0, T_0)$ and the magnitude of the slope of V-T curve is α. The value of C_V is
(a) $\left(1 + \frac{\alpha T_0}{V_0}\right)R$ (b) $\frac{\alpha R V_0}{T_0}$
(c) $\left(1 - \frac{\alpha T_0}{V_0}\right)R$ (d) $\frac{\alpha R T_0}{V_0}$

25 A gas undergoes an adiabatic process and an isothermal process. The two processes are plotted on a p-V diagram. The resulting curves intersect at a point A. Tangents are drawn to the two curves at A. These make angles of 135° and 121° with the positive V-axis. If $\cos 59° = \frac{3}{\sqrt{34}}$, the gas is likely to be

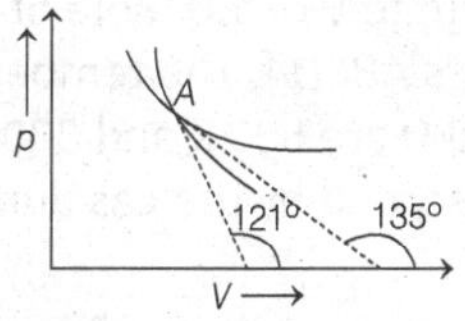

(a) monoatomic
(b) diatomic
(c) triatomic
(d) a mixture of monoatomic and diatomic gases

26 One mole of an ideal monoatomic gas undergoes a linear process from A to B, in p-V diagram. The volume of the gas when the process turns from an endothermic to an exothermic one is

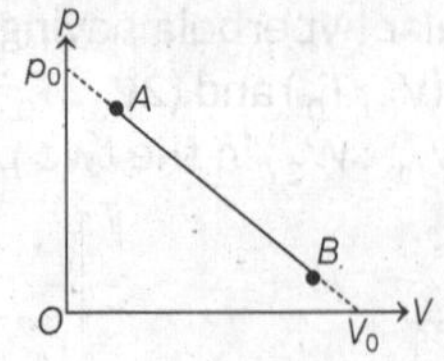

(a) $\frac{5}{8}V_0$ (b) $\frac{1}{2}V_0$
(c) $\frac{8}{15}V_0$ (d) $\frac{3}{5}V_0$

27 Monoatomic, diatomic and non-linear triatomic gases whose initial volume and pressure are the same are compressed till their final pressure is doubled. Then, if the process is

(a) isothermal their final volumes will be different
(b) adiabatic their final volumes will be same
(c) adiabatic then triatomic gas will have maximum final volume
(d) adiabatic then monoatomic gas will have maximum final volume

28 Figure shows a cyclic process $ABCA$ for an ideal diatomic gas. The ratio of the heat energy absorbed in the process $A \to B$ to the work done on the gas in the process $B \to C$ is

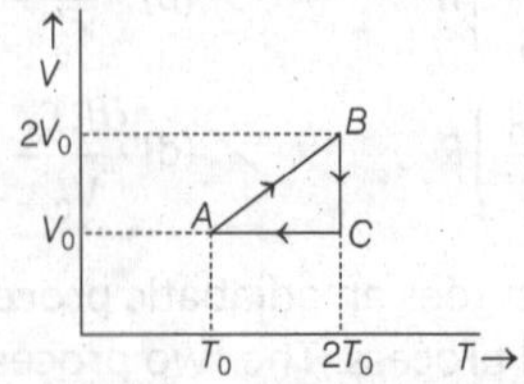

(a) $\frac{7}{4\ln 2}$ (b) $\frac{7}{2\ln 2}$
(c) $\frac{5\ln 2}{4}$ (d) $\frac{5\ln 2}{2}$

29 The figure shows the variation in internal energy U with the volume V of 1.0 mole of an ideal gas in a cyclic process $ABCDA$. The temperatures of the gas at points B and D are 500 K and 300 K, respectively. The net heat absorbed by the gas during the cyclic process is

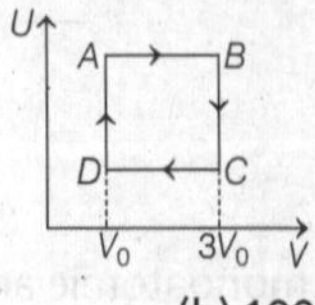

(a) zero (b) $100R \ln 3$
(c) $200R \ln 3$ (d) Data are insufficient

30 Three processes form a thermodynamic cycle as shown on p-V diagram for an ideal gas. Process $1 \to 2$ takes place at constant temperature 300 K. Process $2 \to 3$ takes place at constant volume. During this process 40 J of heat leaves the system. Process $3 \to 1$ is adiabatic and temperature T_3 is 275 K. Work done by the gas during the process $3 \to 1$ is

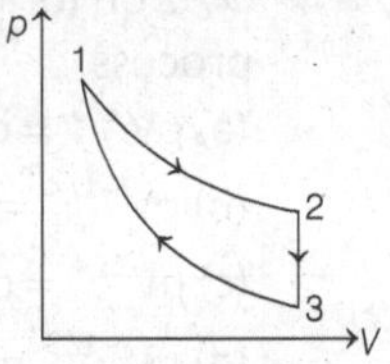

(a) −40 J (b) −20 J (c) +40 J (d) +20 J

31 Consider the thermodynamics cycle shown on PV diagram. The process $A \to B$ is isobaric, $B \to C$ is isochoric and $C \to A$ is a straight line process. The following internal energy and heat are given $\Delta U_{A \to B} = +400$ kJ and $Q_{B \to C} = -500$ kJ. The heat flow in the process $Q_{C \to A}$ is

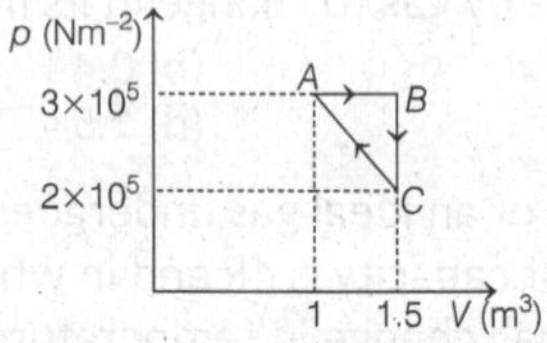

(a) −20 kJ (b) +25 kJ
(c) −25 kJ (d) Data are insufficient

32 A certain quantity of ideal gas mixture takes up 300 J of heat in process AB and its internal energy increases by 1200 J in process AC. Its adiabatic constant γ is

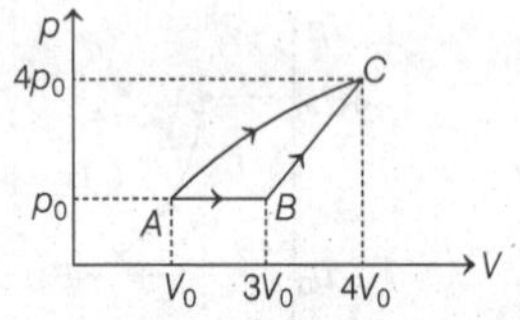

(a) 6/5 (b) 15/8
(c) 7/5 (d) 5/3

33 The density (ρ) *versus* pressure (p) graph of an ideal gas (monoatomic) undergoing a cyclic process is shown in the figure. The gas taken has molecular weight M and 1 mole gas is taken. The heat rejected by gas in process 3 to 1 in cycle is

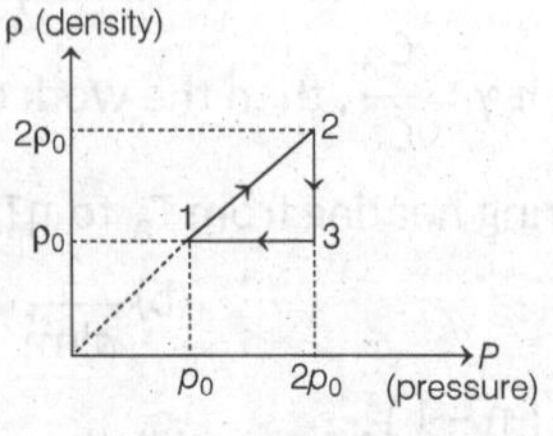

(a) $\frac{3p_0M}{\rho_0}$ (b) $\frac{3p_0M}{2\rho_0}$ (c) $\frac{5p_0M}{2\rho_0}$ (d) $\frac{5p_0M}{3\rho_0}$

34 One mole of an ideal gas is carried through a thermodynamics cycle as shown in the figure. The cycle consists of an isochoric, an isothermal and an adiabatic processes. Find the adiabatic exponent of the gas.

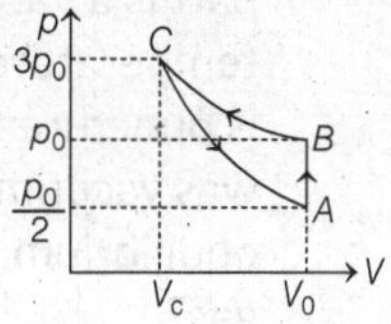

(a) $\frac{\ln 5}{\ln 3}$ (b) $\frac{\ln 6}{\ln 3}$

(c) $\frac{\ln 6}{\ln 2}$ (d) $\frac{\ln 5}{\ln 2}$

35 Calculate the efficiency of a heat engine in a gas (whose ratio of specific heat = γ), while it is being taken through a cycle as shown in the indicator diagram. *AB* and *CD* are adiabatic processes.

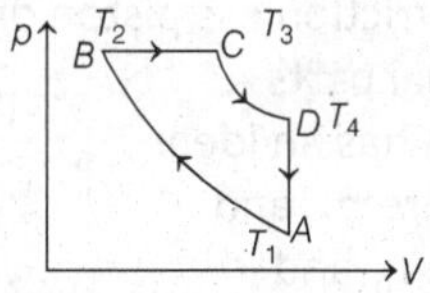

(a) $1-\gamma\left(\frac{T_4-T_1}{T_3-T_2}\right)$ (b) $1-\gamma\left(\frac{T_3-T_2}{T_4-T_1}\right)$

(c) $1-\frac{1}{\gamma}\left(\frac{T_3-T_2}{T_4-T_1}\right)$ (d) $1-\frac{1}{\gamma}\left(\frac{T_4-T_1}{T_3-T_2}\right)$

36 Helium is used as working substance in an engine working on the cycle as shown in the figure. Processes *AB*, *BC*, *CD* and *DA* are isobaric, adiabatic, isochoric and isothermal, respectively. The ratio of maximum to minimum volume of helium during the cycle is $8\sqrt{2}$ and that of maximum to minimum absolute temperature is 4. Calculate efficiency of the cycle.

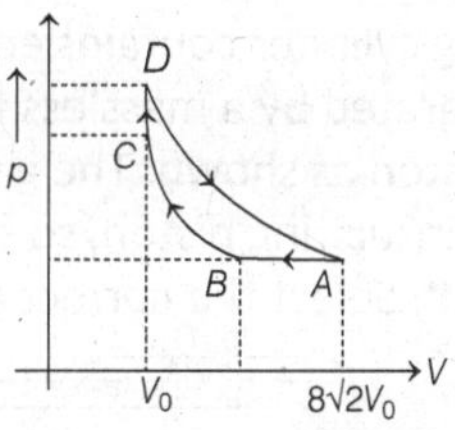

(a) $\frac{28\ln 2-9}{28\ln 2+6}$ (b) $\frac{28\ln 2-6}{28\ln 2+9}$

(c) $\frac{14\ln 2-9}{14\ln 2+6}$ (d) $\frac{14\ln 2-6}{14\ln 2+9}$

37 A Carnot engine works between the temperature of 1092 K to 273 K is used as heat pump. It consumes 1260 W of electrical energy and heat is extracted from the sink containing water at 0°C. Find the rate of freezing of water.

(a) 1.25 g/s (b) 2 g/s
(c) 3 g/s (d) 5 g/s

38 Two Carnot heat engines are put in series such that heat rejected by one engine is used in the second engine as heat input. If efficiency of first engine is 30% and overall combination has efficiency of 65%, then the efficiency of second engine is

(a) 20% (b) 35% (c) 40% (d) 50%

Multiple Choice(s) Correct Questions

1 Figure shows an indicator diagram. During path $1\rightarrow 2\rightarrow 3$, 100 cal are given to the system and 40 cal work is done. During path $1\rightarrow 4\rightarrow 3$, the work done is 10 cal.

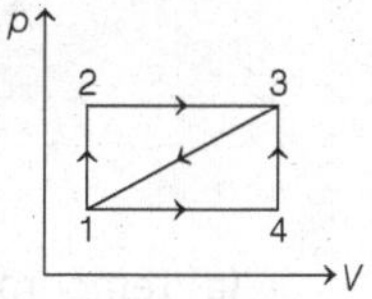

(a) Heat given to the system during path $1\rightarrow 4\rightarrow 3$ is 70 cal.
(b) If the system is brought from 3 to 1 along straight line path $3\rightarrow 1$, work done is 25 cal.
(c) Along straight line path $3\rightarrow 1$, the heat ejected by the system is 85 cal.
(d) The internal energy of the system in state 3 is 140 cal above that in state 1.

2 An ideal gas of one mole is kept in a rigid container of negligible heat capacity. If 25 J of heat is supplied the gas temperature raises by 2°C. Then, the gas may be

(a) helium (b) argon
(c) oxygen (d) carbon dioxide

3 An ideal gas expands in such a way that pV^2 = constant throughout the process.

(a) The graph of the process on *T*-*V* diagram is a parabola
(b) The graph of the process on *T*-*V* diagram is a straight line
(c) Such an expansion is possible only with heating
(d) Such an expansion is possible only with cooling

4 An ideal gas has molar heat capacity at constant pressure $C_p = 5R/2$. The gas is kept in a cylindrical vessel fitted with a piston which is free to move. Mass of the frictionless piston is 9 kg. Initial volume of the gas is 0.0027 m^3 and cross-section area of the piston is 0.09 m^2. The initial temperature of the gas is 300 K. Atmospheric pressure $p_0 = 1.05\times10^5\ N/m^2$. An amount of 2.5×10^4 J of heat energy is supplied to the gas such that piston moves without acceleration, then

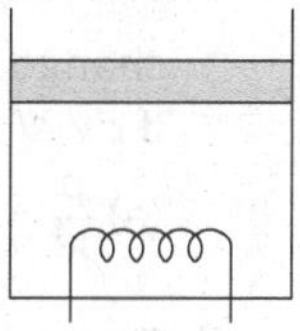

(a) initial pressure of the gas is $1.06\times10^5\ N/m^2$
(b) final temperature of the gas is 1000 K
(c) final pressure of the gas is $1.06\times10^5\ N/m^2$
(d) work done by gas is 10^4 J

5 The graph in the figure shows three different curves relating the pressure and volume of a fixed mass of a perfect gas at three different temperatures. Curve 2 is for 0°C (density of Hg = 13.6×10^3 kg/m^3)

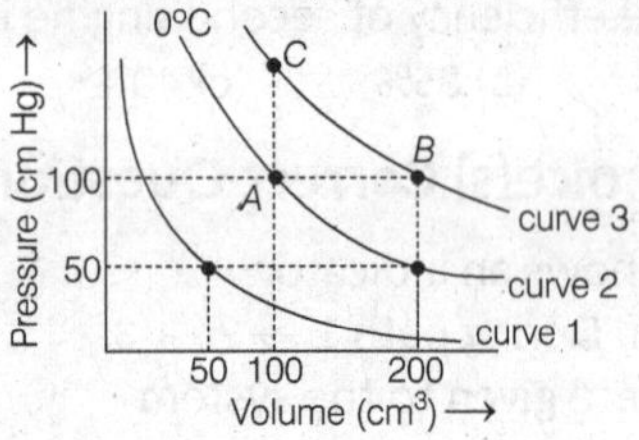

(a) temperature of curve-1 approx. 68 K
(b) temperature of curve-3 is 546 K
(c) pressure at point C is 200 cm of Hg
(d) the work done by the gas from the state A to state B cannot be calculated with the information given in graph

6 For an ideal gas
(a) the change in internal energy in a constant pressure process from temperature T_1 to T_2 is equal to $nC_V(T_2 - T_1)$, where C_V is the molar specific heat at constant volume and n the number of moles of the gas
(b) the change in internal energy of the gas and the work done by the gas are equal in magnitude in an adiabatic process
(c) the internal energy does not change in an isothermal process
(d) no heat is added or removed in an adiabatic process

7 On the p-T graph of an ideal gas
(a) adiabatic process will be a straight line
(b) isochoric process will be a straight line passing through the origin
(c) adiabatic curve will have a positive slope
(d) the slope of adiabatic curve will decrease with increase in T

8 The pressure and density of a diatomic gas $(\gamma = 7/5)$ change adiabatically from (p, d) to (p', d'). If $d/d' = 32$
(a) $\frac{p}{p'} = \frac{1}{128}$ (b) $\frac{V'}{V} = \frac{1}{128}$ (c) $\frac{p}{p'} = 128$ (d) $\frac{V'}{V} = 32$

9 Two moles of O_2 $(\gamma = 7/5)$ at temperature T_0 and 3 moles of CO_2 $(\gamma = 4/3)$ at temperature $2T_0$ are allowed to mix together in a rigid closed adiabatic vessel. The resulting mixture finally comes in thermal equilibrium. Then,
(a) final temperature of the mixture is $23T_0/14$
(b) final temperature of the mixture is $31T_0/19$
(c) adiabatic exponent of the mixture formed is 14/5
(d) adiabatic exponent of the mixture formed is 19/14

10 A thermally insulating container has a membrane separating the container into two equal parts. In one part is a vacuum. In the other part is an ideal gas of temperature T and internal energy U. The membrane is punctured and the gas rushes into region which was vacuum. After the system has returned to equilibrium, which of the following is not true for the gas?
(a) The temperature of the gas decreases
(b) Work done by the gas on the surroundings is positive
(c) There is no heat exchanged by the gas with the surroundings
(d) The internal energy of the gas is unchanged

11 A thermally insulated chamber of volume $2V_0$ is divided by a frictionless piston of area S and mass m into two equal parts A and B. Part A has an ideal gas at pressure p_0 and temperature T_0 and in part B is vacuum. A massless spring of force constant k is connected with the piston and the wall of the container as shown. Initially the spring is underformed. The gas in chamber A is allowed to expand. Let in equilibrium the spring is compressed by x_0. Then,

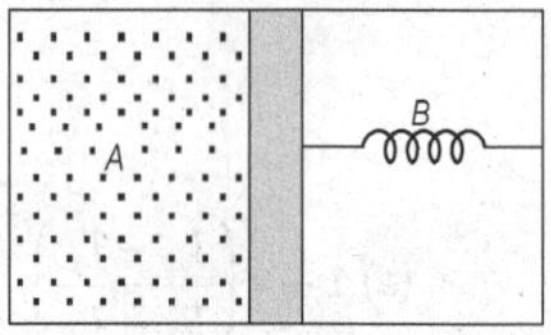

(a) pressure of the gas at equilibrium is $\frac{kx_0}{2S}$
(b) work done by the gas is $\frac{1}{2}kx_0^2$
(c) increase in internal energy of the gas is $\frac{1}{2}kx_0^2$
(d) temperature of the gas is decreased

12 An insulating cylinder contains equal volumes of He and O_2 separated by a massless freely moving adiabatic piston as shown. The gas is compressed by moving the insualting piston, so that volume of He becomes half. Select the correct alternative(s).

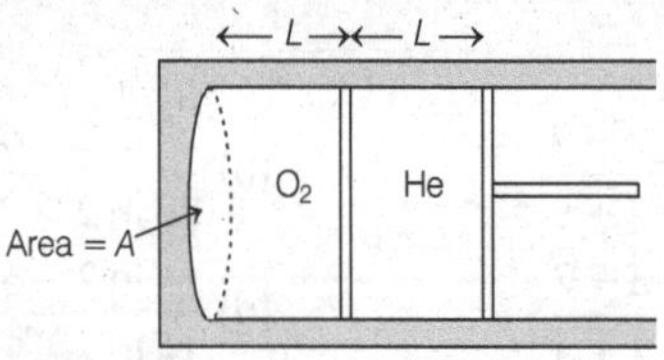

(a) Pressure in He chamber will be equal to pressure in O_2 chamber
(b) Pressure in He chamber will be less than pressure in O_2 chamber
(c) Volume of He chamber will be equal to volume of O_2 chamber
(d) Volume of O_2 chamber will be $\frac{(LA)}{(2)^{25/21}}$

13 A vertical cylinder with heat-conducting walls is closed at the bottom and is fitted with a smooth light piston. It contains one mole of an ideal gas. The temperature of the gas is always equal to the surrounding's temperature, T_0. The piston is moved up slowly to increase the volume of the gas to η times. Which of the following are correct?

(a) Work done by the gas is $RT_0 \ln \eta$

(b) Work done against the atmosphere is $RT_0(\eta - 1)$

(c) There is no change in the internal energy of the gas

(d) The final pressure of the gas is $\frac{1}{(\eta - 1)}$ times its initial pressure

14 Which of the following statements is/are true about specific heats of an ideal gas?

(a) Specific heat of an ideal gas is zero when it undergoes an adiabatic process

(b) Specific heat of an ideal gas is infinite when it undergoes an isothermal process

(c) The difference between specific heats at constant pressure and constant volume is the same for all ideal gases

(d) The ratio of specific heats at constant pressure and constant volume is the same for all ideal gases

15 We make helium gas of 2 g to go through the thermal cycle shown in the figure. The lowest temperature of the gas in the cycle is −17°C, the highest is 127°C and the temperature is equal at points A and B. [R = Universal gas constant]

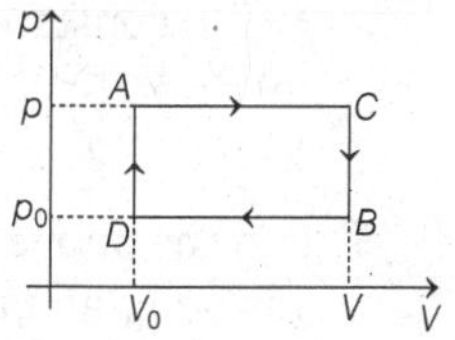

(a) The temperature of A and B is 320 K

(b) The temperature at A and B is 328 K

(c) Net work done by the gas during a cycle is $32R$

(d) Net work done by the gas during a cycle is $8R$

16 Use the following p-T graph to choose the correct option(s)

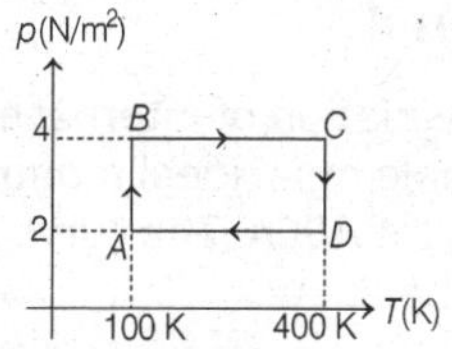

(a) the heat is supplied to the gas during the cycle *ABCDA*

(b) during the process *AB*, work is done on the gas

(c) the area under the graph gives us the work done by the gas during the cycle

(d) the volume of the sample at A is same as the volume of the sample at C

17 A system of ideal gas is taken around cyclic process as shown. The graph of pressure *versus* density is given

(a) maximum temperature during cycle occurs at C

(b) maximum temperature during cycle occurs at B

(c) net heat during the cycle is absobed by the system

(d) net heat during the cycle is rejected by the system

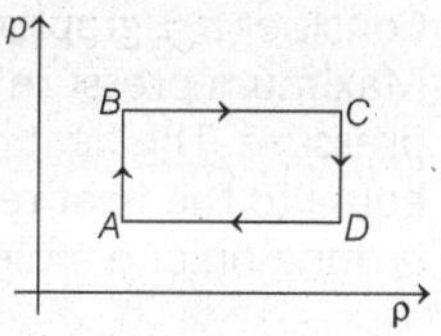

18 One mole of monoatomic gas is taken through cyclic process shown below.

$T_A = 300$ K. Process AB is defined as pT = constant.

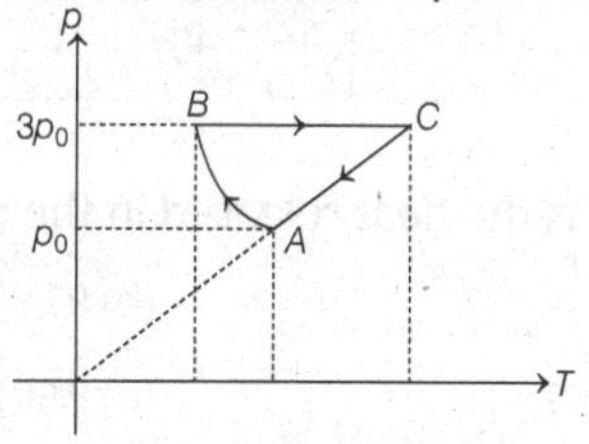

(a) Work done in process AB is $-400R$

(b) Change in internal energy in process CA is $900R$

(c) Heat transferred in the process BC is $2000R$

(d) Change in internal energy in process CA is $-900R$

19 In the given cyclic process from c to b, 40 J heat is exchanged. From b to a, 130 J heat is exchanged, and work done is 80 J.

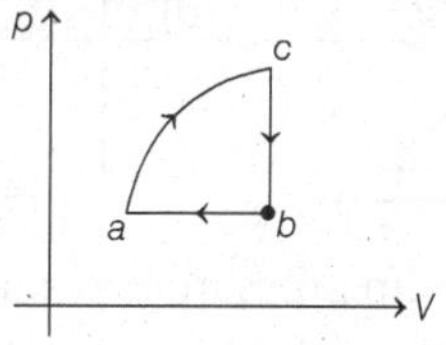

From a to c, 400 J heat is exchanged, then

(a) work done in process a to c is 310 J

(b) net work done in cycle is 230 J

(c) net change in internal energy in cycle is 130 J

(d) efficiency of cycle is 57.5%

20 An ideal gas undergoes a cyclic process *ABCA* as shown in p-V diagram. The gas expands isothermally along *AB* and adiabatically along *BC* and the respective work done are 600 J and 250 J. If during the compression, the gas gives up 50 J of heat to the surrounding, then

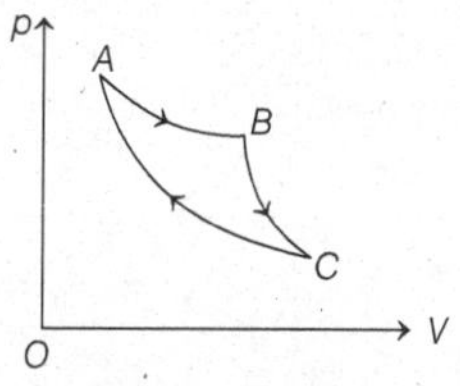

(a) the net change in internal energy is zero during cycle

(b) the amount of work done on the gas along *CA* is 300 J

(c) the net work done is 600 J

(d) the change in the internal energy along *CA* is 250 J

Comprehension Based Questions

Comprehension-1

Consider *p*-*T* graph of cyclic process shown in the figure. Maximum pressure during the cycle is twice the minimum pressure. The heat received by the gas in the process 1-2 is equal to the heat received in the process 3-4. The process is done on one mole of monoatomic gas.

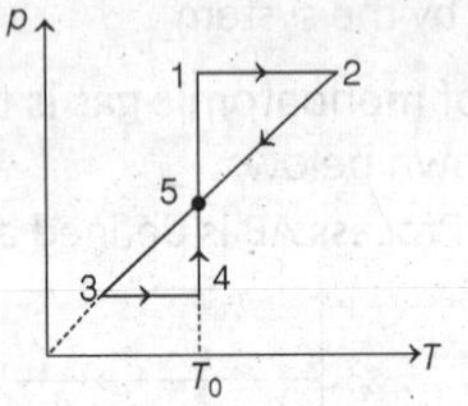

1 What is the heat released in the process 2-3?

(a) $\frac{5RT_0}{3}$ (b) RT_0

(c) $1.5RT_0$ (d) $2.5RT_0$

2 Correct *pV* diagram for the process is

(a)

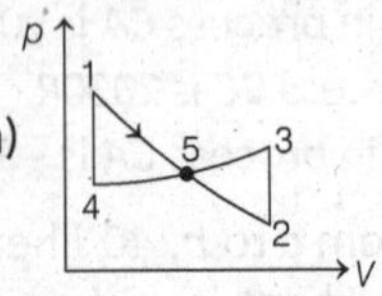

(b)

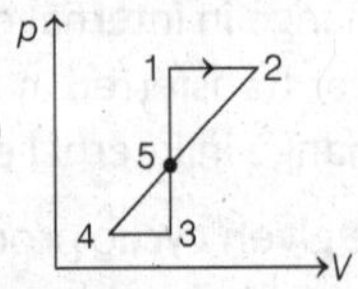

(c)

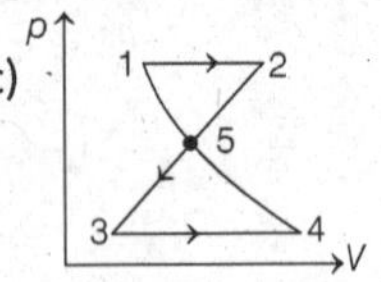

(d)

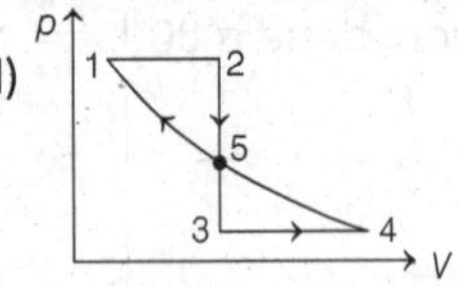

3 If the maximum pressure is *p*, then what is the pressure at the point 5?

(a) $2p/3$ (b) $4p/5$

(c) $3p/4$ (d) None of these

Comprehension-2

A sample of ideal gas is taken through the cyclic process shown in the figure. The temperature of the gas at state *A* is $T_A = 200$ K. At states *B* and *C*, the temperature of the gas is the same.

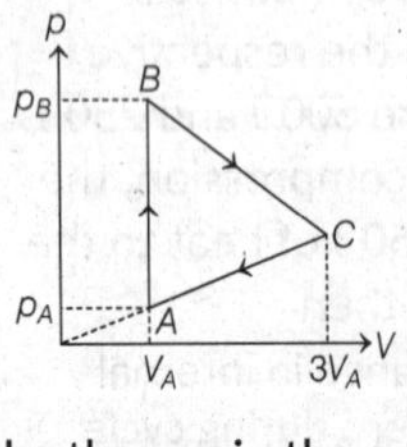

4 Net work done by the gas in the process is

(a) $2p_AV_A$ (b) $4p_AV_A$

(c) $6p_AV_A$ (d) $8p_AV_A$

5 Which of the following graphs best represents the cyclic process in *T*-*V* diagram?

(a)

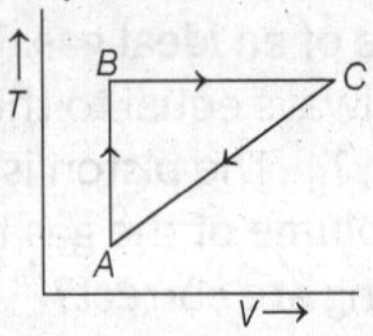

(b)

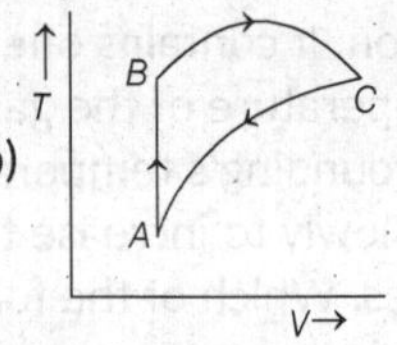

(c)

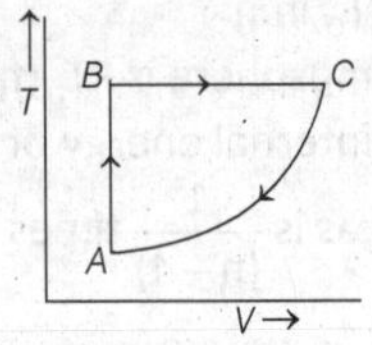

(d)

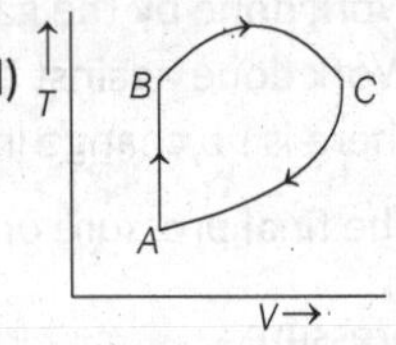

6 What is the greatest temperature of the gas during the cyclic process?

(a) 600 K (b) 1200 K

(c) 2400 K (d) None of these

Comprehension-3

One mole of an ideal diatomic gas is expanded, so that the amount of heat transferred to the gas is equal to the decrease in its internal energy.

7 The molar specific heat of the gas in this process is given by *C* whose value is

(a) $-5R/2$ (b) $-3R/2$ (c) $2R$ (d) $5R/2$

8 The process can be represented by the equation $TV^n =$ constant, where the value of *n* is

(a) $n = 7/5$ (b) $n = 1/5$

(c) $n = 3/2$ (d) $n = 3/5$

9 If in the above process, the initial temperature of the gas be T_0 and the final volume be 32 times the initial volume, the work done by the gas during the process will be

(a) RT_0 (b) $\frac{5RT_0}{2}$

(c) $2RT_0$ (d) $\frac{RT_0}{2}$

Comprehension-4

Figure shows the variation of internal energy *U* with density ρ of one mole of an ideal monoatomic gas for a thermodynamic cycle *ABCA*. The curve *AB* on graph is a rectangular hyperbola.

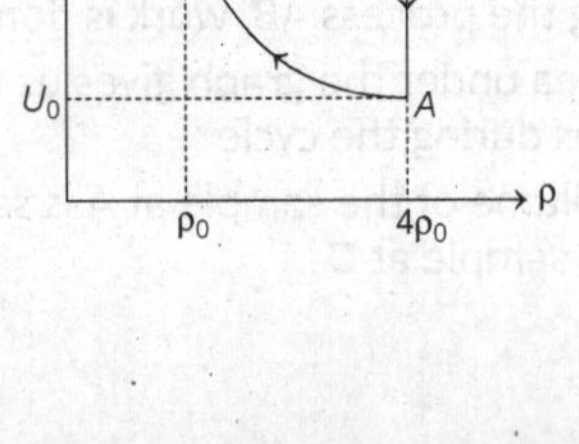

10 The work done by the gas in process A to B is

(a) U_0 (b) $2U_0$
(c) $3U_0$ (d) $4U_0$

11 The work done by the gas in process B to C is

(a) $-\frac{8U_0}{3}\ln 2$ (b) $-\frac{16U_0}{3}\ln 2$
(c) $\frac{8U_0}{3}\ln 2$ (d) $-\frac{16U_0}{3}\ln 2$

12 The molar heat capacity of gas for process CA is

(a) $\frac{3}{2}R$ (b) $\frac{5}{2}R$
(c) $3R$ (d) $\frac{R}{2}$

Comprehension-5

One mole of a diatomic ideal gas ($\gamma = 1.4$) is taken through a cyclic process starting from point A. The process $A \rightarrow B$ is an adiabatic compression. $B \rightarrow C$ is isobaric expansion, $C \rightarrow D$ an adiabatic expansion and $D \rightarrow A$ is isochoric process. The volume ratio are $\frac{V_A}{V_B} = 16$ and $\frac{V_C}{V_B} = 2$ and the temperature at A is $T_A = 27°C$.

($2^{1.6} = 3.03, 2^{1.2} = 2.3$)

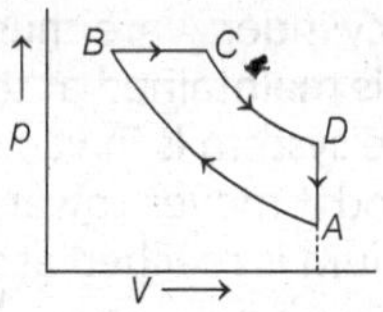

13 Calculate the temperature of the gas at point B

(a) 333°C (b) 636°C (c) 939°C (d) 1242°C

14 Calculate the temperature of the gas at point D

(a) 417.4°C (b) 517.4°C
(c) 617.4°C (d) 717°C

15 Find the efficiency of the cycle.

(a) 38.6% (b) 51.8%
(c) 61.4% (d) 71.5%

Comprehension-6

One mole of an ideal monoatomic gas undergoes a cyclic process as shown in figure. Temperature at point 1 = 300 K and process 2-3 is isothermal.

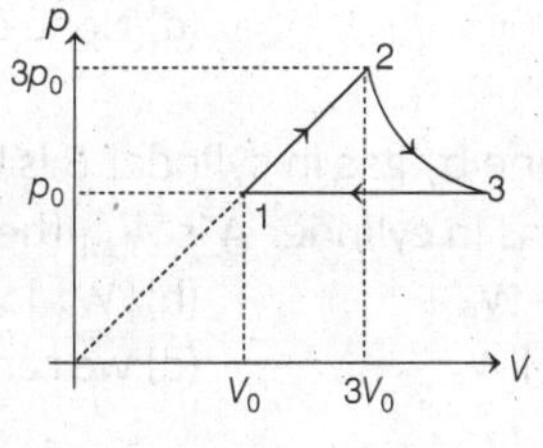

16 Net work done by gas in complete cycle is

(a) $(9\ln 3 + 12)\,p_0V_0$ (b) $(9\ln 3 + 4)\,p_0V_0$
(c) $(9\ln 3 - 4)\,p_0V_0$ (d) $(9\ln 3 - 8)\,p_0V_0$

17 Heat capacity of process $1 \rightarrow 2$ is

(a) $\frac{R}{2}$ (b) $\frac{3R}{2}$ (c) $\frac{5R}{2}$ (d) $2R$

18 The efficiency of cycle is

(a) $\left(\frac{9\ln 3 + 4}{9\ln 3 + 12}\right)$ (b) $\left(\frac{9\ln 3 - 4}{9\ln 3 + 12}\right)$
(c) $\left(\frac{9\ln 3 - 4}{9\ln 3 + 16}\right)$ (d) $\left(\frac{9\ln 3 + 12}{9\ln 3 + 16}\right)$

Comprehension-7

A monoatomic ideal gas of two moles is taken through a cyclic process starting from A as shown in the figure. The volume ratios are $\frac{V_B}{V_A} = 2$ and $\frac{V_D}{V_A} = 4$. If the temperature T_A at A is 27°C, calculate

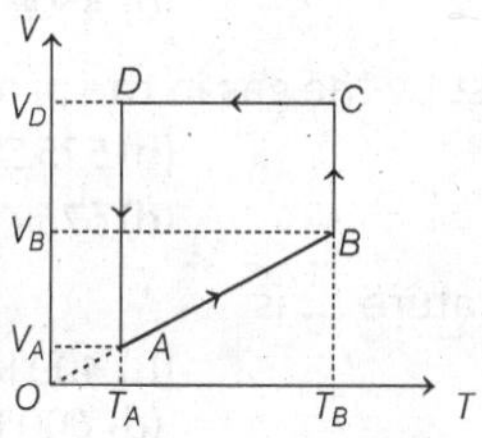

19 the temperature of the gas at point B

(a) 500 K (b) 700 K (c) 600 K (d) 300 K

20 heat absorbed or released by the gas in process $A \rightarrow B$

(a) $1500R$, absorbed (b) $1200R\ln 2$, absorbed
(c) $900R$, released (d) $1200R\ln 2$, released

21 heat absorbed or released by the gas in process $B \rightarrow C$

(a) $1500R$, absorbed (b) $1200R\ln 2$, absorbed
(c) $900R$, released (d) $1200R\ln 2$, released

22 heat absorbed or released by the gas in process $C \rightarrow D$

(a) $1500R$, absorbed (b) $1200R\ln 2$, absorbed
(c) $900R$, released (d) $1200R\ln 2$, released

23 heat absorbed or released by the gas in process $D \rightarrow A$

(a) $1500R$, absorbed (b) $1200R\ln 2$, absorbed
(c) $900R$, released (d) $1200R\ln 2$, released

24 the total work done by the gas during the complete cycle

(a) $500R$ (b) $600R$ (c) $700R$ (d) $300R$

Comprehension-8

One mole of a monoatomic ideal gas is taken through the cycle shown in the figure.

$A \to B$: adiabatic expansion

$B \to C$: cooling at constant volume

$C \to D$: adiabatic compression

$D \to A$: heating at constant volume

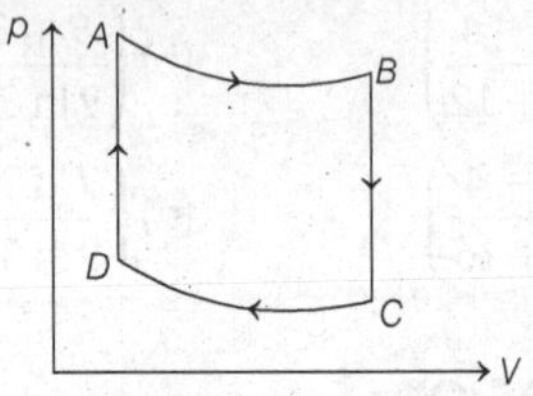

The pressure and temperature at A, B, etc are denoted by p_A, T_A, p_B, T_B etc, respectively. Given that $T_A = 1000$ K, $p_B = (2/3)\, p_A$ and $p_C = (1/3)\, p_A$. [Given $(2/3)^{2/5} = 0.85$]

25 The work done by the gas in the process $A \to B$ is

(a) 150*R* (b) 225*R*
(c) 300*R* (d) 450*R*

26 The heat lost by the gas in the process $B \to C$ is

(a) 450*R* (b) 525.5*R*
(c) 637.5*R* (d) 675*R*

27 The temperature T_D is

(a) 300 K (b) 400 K
(c) 500 K (d) 600 K

Comprehension-9

A massless piston, which can move without friction, closes a sample of Helium in a vertical, thermally insulated cylinder, which is closed at its bottom, and the cross-section of which is $A = 2\,\text{dm}^2$. Above the piston there is a fixed stand to which an unstretched spring of spring constant 2000 N/m is attached, whose bottom end is at a distance of 2 dm from the piston when the volume of the gas is $V_0 = 8\,\text{dm}^3$. The external pressure is $p_0 = 10^5$ Pa, $g = 10\,\text{m/s}^2$. The gas confined in the cylinder is heated with an electric heating element. (1 dm $= 10^{-1}$ m)

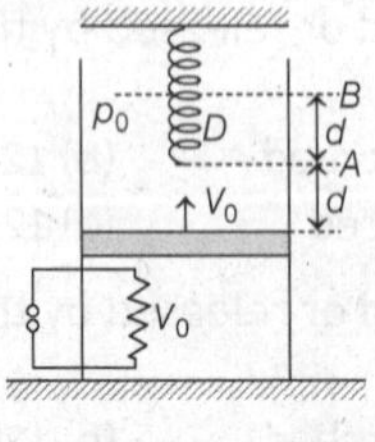

28 How much heat is supplied by the element till it reaches the spring?

(a) Zero (b) 600 J
(c) 8000 J (d) 1000 J

29 How will process look like on a *p*-*V* diagram?

(a)
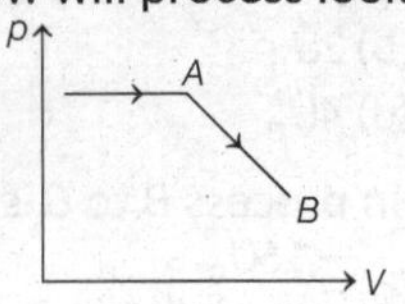

(b)
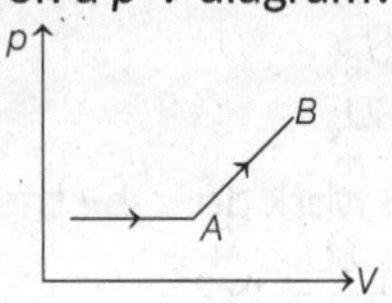

(c)
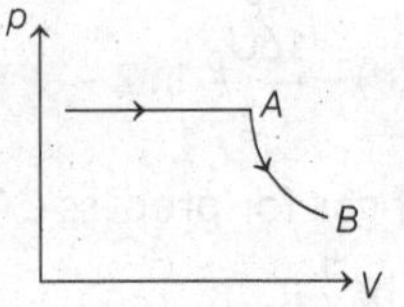

(d)
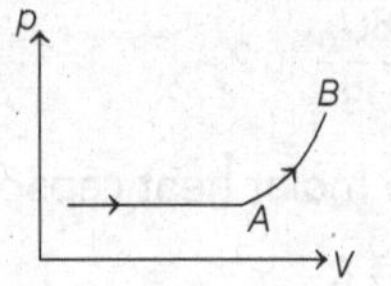

30 What is the ratio of work done by gas in moving the piston from initial position to A, and from there to B?

(a) $\frac{10}{11}$ (b) $\frac{11}{10}$ (c) $\frac{5}{3}$ (d) $\frac{3}{5}$

Comprehension-10

Two cylinders A and B are having piston connected by massless rod (as shown in figure). The cross-sectional area of two cylinders are same and equal to *S*. The cylinder A contains *m* gm of an ideal gas at pressure p_0 and temperature T_0. The cylinder B contains identical gas at same temperature T_0 but has different mass. The piston is held at the state in the position, so that volume of gas in cylinder A and cylinder B are same and is equal to V_0. The walls and piston of cylinder A are thermally insulated, whereas cylinder B is maintained at temperature T_0 reservoir. The whole system is in vacuum. Now, the piston is slowly released and it moves towards left and mechanical equilibrium is reached at the state when the volume of gas in cylinder A becomes $\frac{V_0}{2}$. Then, (Here γ for gas = 1.5)

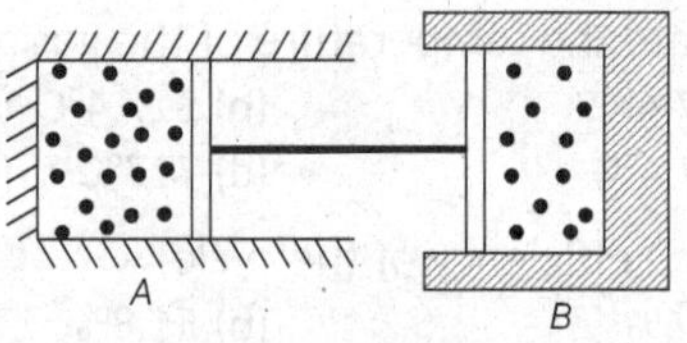

31 The mass of gas in cylinder B is

(a) $2\sqrt{2}$ m (b) $3\sqrt{2}$ m
(c) $\sqrt{2}$ m (d) None of these

32 The change in internal energy of gas in cylinder A is

(a) $(\sqrt{2} - 1)\, p_0 V_0$ (b) $2(\sqrt{2} - 1)\, p_0 V_0$
(c) $\frac{p_0 V_0}{(\sqrt{2} - 1)}$ (d) None of these

33 If work done by gas in cylinder B is W_B and work done by gas in cylinder A is W_A, then

(a) $W_A = -W_B$ (b) $|W_A| > |W_B|$
(c) $|W_A| < |W_B|$ (d) we can't say anything

34 What will be the compressive force in connecting rod at equilibrium?

(a) $p_0 S$ (b) $\sqrt{2} p_0 S$

(c) $2^{3/2} p_0 S$ (d) None of these

Comprehension-11

Two rectangular boxes shown in figure has a partition which can slide without friction along the length of the box. Initially each of the two chambers of the box has one mole of a monoatomic ideal gas ($\gamma = 5/3$) at a pressure p_0, volume V_0 and temperature T_0. The chamber on the left is slowly heated by an electric heater. The walls of the box and the partitions are thermally insulated. Heat loss through the lead wires of the heater is negligible. The gas in the left chamber expands, pushing the partition until the final pressure in both chambers becomes $243 p_0 / 32$.

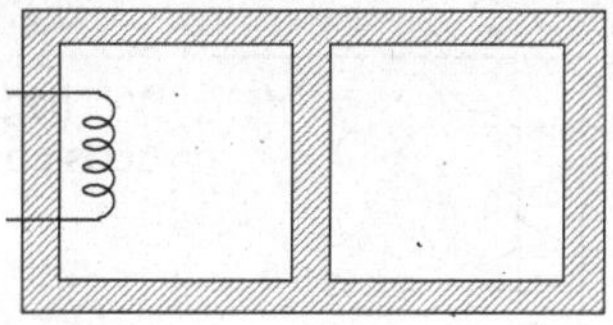

35 The final temperature of the gas in the right chamber will be

(a) $\frac{3}{2} T_0$ (b) $\frac{9}{4} T_0$ (c) $\frac{27}{8} T_0$ (d) $\frac{207}{16} T_0$

36 The final temperature of the gas in the left chamber will be

(a) $\frac{3}{2} T_0$ (b) $\frac{9}{4} T_0$ (c) $\frac{27}{8} T_0$ (d) $\frac{207}{16} T_0$

37 The work done by the gas in the right chamber will be

(a) $-\frac{5}{8} p_0 V_0$ (b) $-\frac{15}{8} p_0 V_0$

(c) $-\frac{15}{4} p_0 V_0$ (d) $-\frac{5}{4} p_0 V_0$

38 Heat supplied by the heater will be

(a) $\frac{211}{32} p_0 V_0$ (b) $\frac{15}{8} p_0 V_0$

(c) $\frac{15}{4} p_0 V_0$ (d) $\frac{633}{32} p_0 V_0$

Match the Columns Questions

1 Match the following for the given process

Column I		Column II	
(A)	Process $J \to K$	(P)	$W > 0$
(B)	Process $K \to L$	(Q)	$W < 0$
(C)	Process $L \to M$	(R)	$Q > 0$
(D)	Process $M \to J$	(S)	$Q < 0$

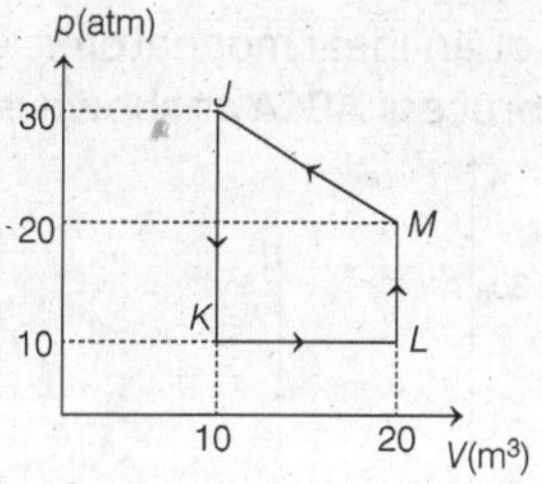

2 Consider the U (Internal energy) *versus* p (Pressure) graph shown. Find out the work by one mole of monoatomic ideal gas in each step.
(Take, ln 2 = 0.3010)

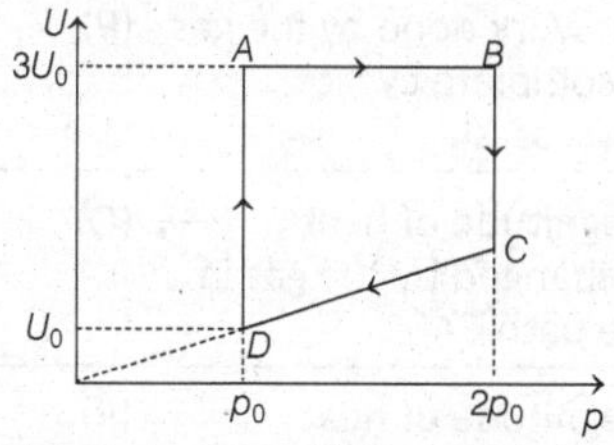

Column I		Column II	
(A)	W_{AB}	(P)	$1.33 U_0$
(B)	W_{BC}	(Q)	0
(C)	W_{CD}	(R)	$-0.602 U_0$
(D)	W_{DA}	(S)	$-0.67 U_0$

3 For an ideal gas, a process on p-V diagram is a circle. An adiabatic from A passes through C. An isotherm from A passes through B. We take a part of the circular cyclic process. Comment on the sign of the quantity of Column I.

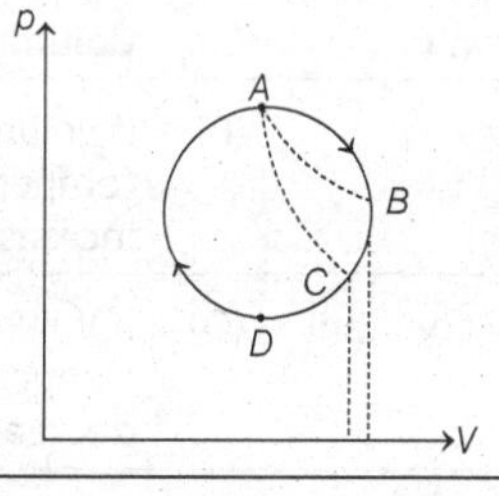

Column I		Column II	
(A)	Heat given to the gas in going from A to C along circle	(P)	Positive
(B)	Heat given to the gas in going from B to C along circle	(Q)	Negative
(C)	Heat given to the gas in going from C to D along circle	(R)	Zero
		(S)	Can't be said

4 One mole of an ideal monoatomic gas is taken round the cyclic process *ABCA* as shown in figure. Then,

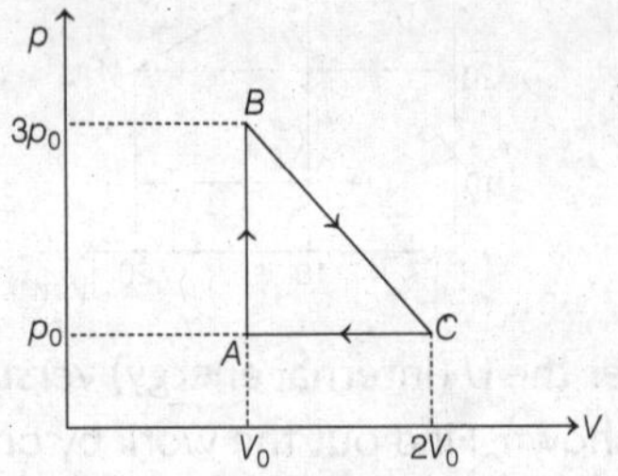

	Column I		Column II
(A)	the work done by the gas in complete cyclic process is	(P)	$\frac{p_0V_0}{2}$
(B)	magnitude of heat exchanged by the gas in the path *CA*	(Q)	$\frac{3p_0V_0}{8}$
(C)	magnitude of heat exchanged by the gas in the path *BC*	(R)	p_0V_0
(D)	the maximum temperature attained by the gas during the cycle (considering universal gas constant $R = 25/3$ unit)	(S)	$\frac{5}{2}p_0V_0$

5 An ideal monoatomic gas undergoes different types of processes which are described in Column I. Match the corresponding effects in Column II. The letters have usual meaning.

	Column I		Column II
(A)	$p = 2V^2$	(P)	If volume increases, then temperature will also increase
(B)	$pV^2 =$ constant	(Q)	If volume increases, then temperature will decrease
(C)	$C = C_V + 2R$	(R)	For expansion, heat will have to be supplied to the gas
(D)	$C = C_V - 2R$	(S)	If temperature increases, then work done by gas is positive

6 A sample of gas goes from state *A* to state *B* in four different manners, as shown by the graphs. Let, *W* be the work done by the gas and ΔU be change in internal energy along the path *AB*. Correctly match the graph with the statements provided.

	Column I		Column II
(A)	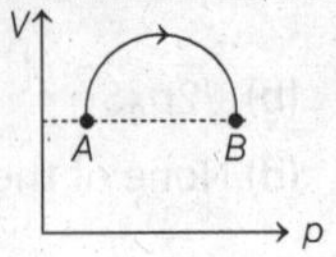	(P)	Both *W* and ΔU are positive
(B)	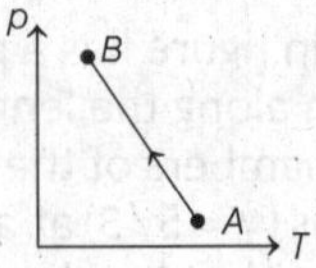	(Q)	Both *W* and ΔU are negative
(C)	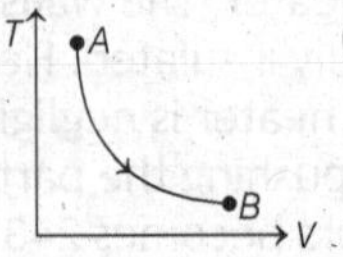	(R)	*W* is positive whereas ΔU is negative
(D)	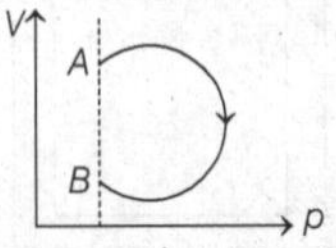	(S)	*W* is negative whereas ΔU is positive

7 Match the Column I with Column II. Following graphs are plotted for an ideal gas of fixed mass filled in a cylinder.

	Column I		Column II
(A)	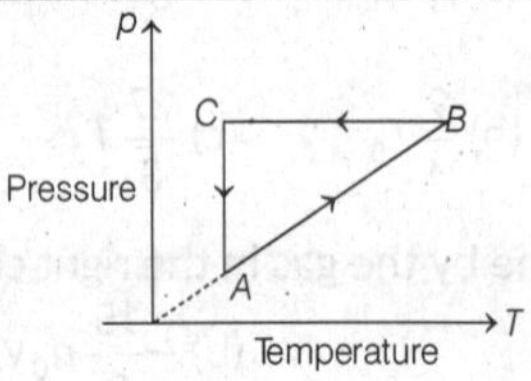	(P)	Work done by the gas is positive
(B)	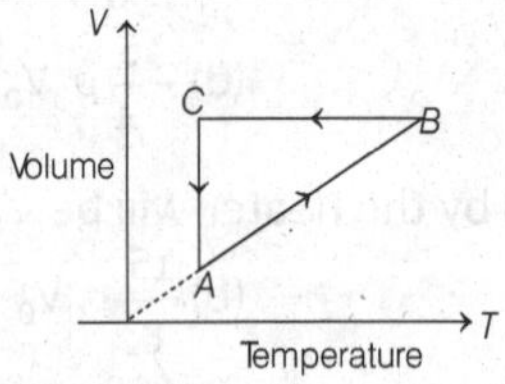	(Q)	Work done by the gas is negative
(C)	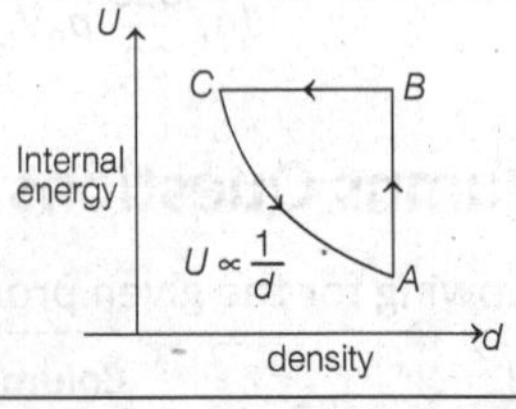	(R)	Heat is supplied to the gas
		(S)	Change in internal energy in process *ABCA* is zero

Numerical Value Questions

1 A container closed by a freely moving piston contains a mixture of hydrogen and helium gases of total mass 12 g. A heat of 150 kJ is transferred to the gas at constant pressure and in this process gas performs 50 kJ work. Find mass of hydrogen (in g) in the mixture.

2 One mole helium in a vessel gets the heat from outside and starts expanding to make its volume 2 times the original volume. The heat capacity of the gas in this process is constant and is $R/2$. What is the final temperature of gas (in K)? Initial temperature is 200 K and initial pressure is 40 kPa.

3 There are two vessels. Each of them contains one mole of a monoatomic ideal gas. Initial volume of the gas in each vessel is 8.3×10^{-3} m^3 at 27°C. Equal amount of heat is supplied to each vessel. In one of the vessel, the volume of the gas is doubled without change in its internal energy, where as the volume of the gas is held constant in the second vessel. The vessels are now connected to allow free mixing of the gas. Find the final temperature of the combined gas in Kelvin. (ln2 =0.693)

4 One mole of an ideal monoatomic gas is taken from state A to state B through the process $p = \frac{3}{2}T^{1/2}$. It is found that its temperature increases by 100 K in this process. Now, it is taken from state B to C through a process for which internal energy is related to volume as $U = \frac{1}{2}V^{1/2}$. Find the total work performed by the gas (in Joule), if it is given that volume at B is 100 m^3 and at C it is 1600 m^3. [Use, $R = 8.3$ J/mol-K]

5 One mole of an ideal monoatomic gas is contained in a piston cylinder arrangement as shown in the figure. The gas is initially at a pressure of 1 atm and temperature 27°C. The piston has cross-sectional area 0.005 m^2 and is connected to an undeformed spring of force constant 10^4 Nm^{-2}. How much heat (in J) must be added to the gas to increase the pressure to 3 atm? [$R = 25/3$ J/mol-K]

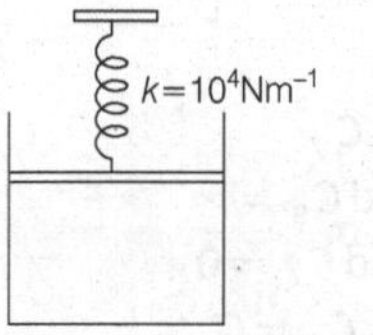

6 In the figure shown, the combined weight of the pistons + connecting rod is 1000 N. The larger piston area is 0.02 m^2 while the smaller pistons area is 0.01 m^2. The region between the two pistons contains 2 moles of a diatomic gas. The pistons as well as the cylinder walls are thermally insulating. The atmospheric pressure is 10^5 Pa. A small electrical heater slowly heats the gas, so that the pistons shift up by 10 cm. Find the amount of heat supplied (in J) by the heater.

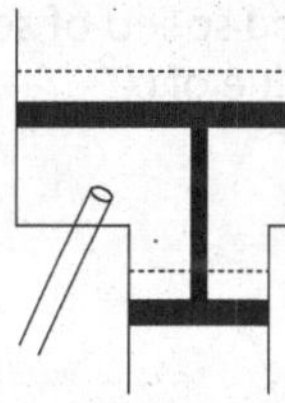

7 0.01 moles of an ideal diatomic gas is enclosed in an adiabatic cylinder of cross-sectional area $A = 10^{-4}$ m^2. In the arrangement shown, a block of mass $M = 0.8$ kg is placed on a horizontal support, and piston of mass $m = 1$ kg is suspended from a spring of stiffness constant $k = 16$ N/m. Initially the spring is relaxed and the volume of the gas is $V = 1.4 \times 10^{-4}$ m^3. When the gas in the cylinder is heated up, the piston starts moving up and the spring gets compressed, so that the block M is just lifted up. Determine the heat supplied (in Joule). (Take, atmospheric pressure, $p_0 = 10^5$ Nm^{-2}, $g = 10$ m/s^2).

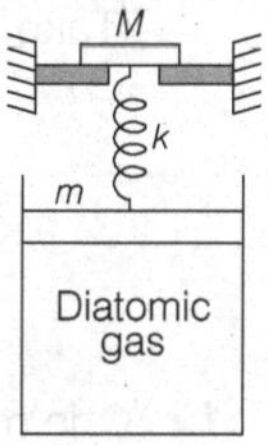

8 A vertical cylinder piston system has cross-section S. It contains 1 mole of an ideal monoatomic gas under a piston of mass M. At a certain instant a heater is switched on which transmits heat q per unit time to the cylinder. Assume that piston is in equilibrium at all times during the process. The velocity v of the piston given the condition that pressure under the piston is constant and the system is thermally insulated is $\frac{xq}{5(p_0S + Mg)}$. Here, the value of x is

9 A cylindrical vessel is divided in two parts by a fixed partition which is perfectly heat conducting. The wall and piston are thermally insulated from surroundings. The left side contains 0.5 moles of gas with $C_V = 2R$ at temperature of 300 K. The right side contains 4 moles of mixture of gas with $C_V = 1.75R$ at same temperature of 300 K. The piston compresses slowly the right side from volume of V_0 to $\frac{V_0}{4}$. Find the total change in internal energy of gases.

If $\Delta U = n \times 10^4$ J, fill n in OMR sheet.

(Take, $R = 25/3$ SI. unit)

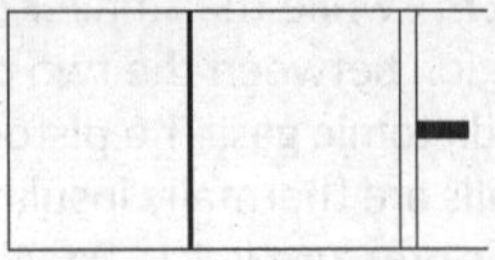

10 Figure shows a parabolic graph between T and $\frac{1}{V}$ for a mixture of a gas undergoing an adiabatic process. If the ratio of v_{rms} and speed of sound in the mixture is α, then find the value of α^2.

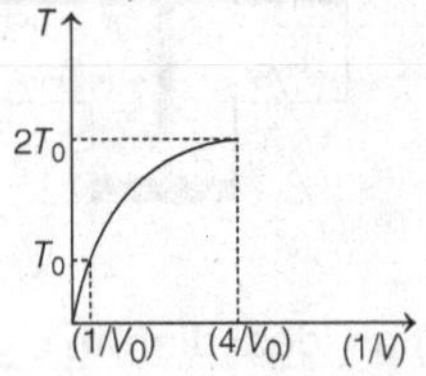

11 Between two isotherms we have a cycle as shown. Find the work done (in J) by the gas during the cycle. (Take, $T_1 = 127°C$, $T_2 = 16°C$, $n = 1$ mol]

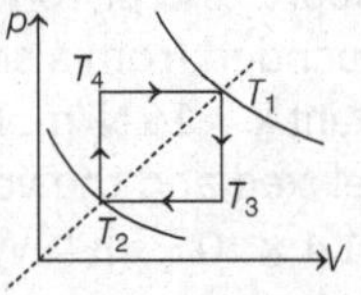

12 One mole of ideal monoatomic gas is taken along a cyclic process as shown in the figure. Process $1 \to 2$ shown is 1/4 th part of a circle, process $2 \to 3$ is isochoric while $3 \to 1$ is isobaric. find the percentage efficiency of the cycle. $\left(\text{Take, } \pi = \frac{22}{7}\right)$

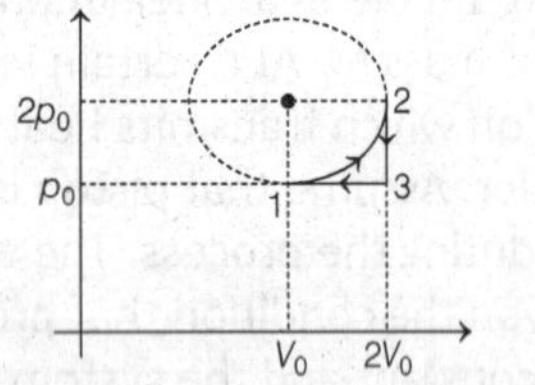

13 A fixed mass of a gas is taken through a process $A \to B \to C \to A$. Here, $A \to B$ is isobaric. $B \to C$ is adiabatic and $C \to A$ is isothermal. If the efficiency of the process is $\frac{X - 2\ln 2}{X}$. Find the value of X.

(Take, $\gamma = 1.5$)

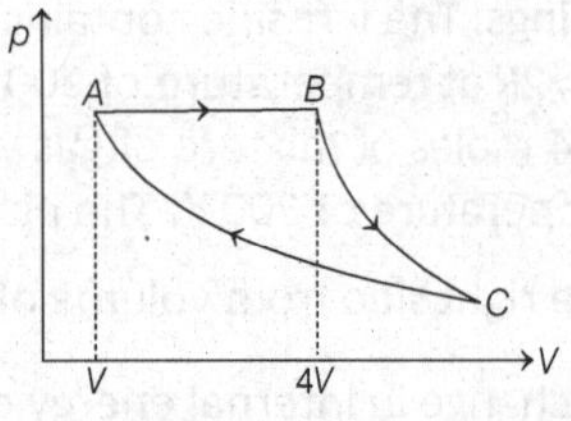

Previous Year's Questions

JEE Main

1 0.08 kg air is heated at constant volume through 5°C. The specific heat of air at constant volume is 0.17 kcal/kg°C and J = 4.18 J/cal. The change in its internal energy is approximately. **[2024, 27 Jan Shift-I]**

(a) 318 J (b) 142 J
(c) 298 J (d) 284 J

2 During an adiabatic process, the pressure of a gas is found to be proportional to the cube of its absolute temperature. The ratio of $\frac{C_p}{C_V}$ for the gas is **[2024, 27 Jan Shift-II]**

(a) $\frac{9}{7}$ (b) $\frac{3}{2}$
(c) $\frac{7}{5}$ (d) $\frac{5}{3}$

3 A thermodynamic system is taken from an original state A to an intermediate state B by a linear process as shown in the figure. It's volume is then reduced to the original value from B to C by an isobaric process. The total work done by the gas from A to B and B to C would be **[2024, 29 Jan Shift-I]**

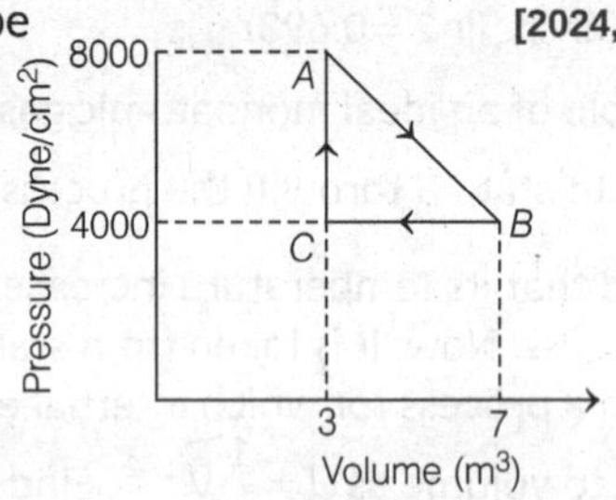

(a) 600 J (b) 2200 J
(c) 33800 J (d) 1200 J

4 Two thermodynamical processes are shown in the figure. The molar heat capacity for process A and B are C_A and C_B. The molar heat capacity at constant pressure and constant volume are represented by C_p and C_V, respectively. Choose the correct statement. **[2024, 30 Jan Shift-I]**

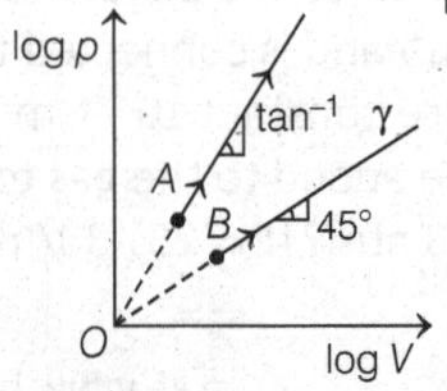

(a) $C_A > C_P > C_V$
(b) $C_A = 0$ and $C_B = \infty$
(c) $C_B = \infty$ and $C_A = 0$
(d) $C_P > C_V > C_A = C_B$

5 Choose the correct statement for processes A and B shown in figure **[2024, 30 Jan Shift-II]**

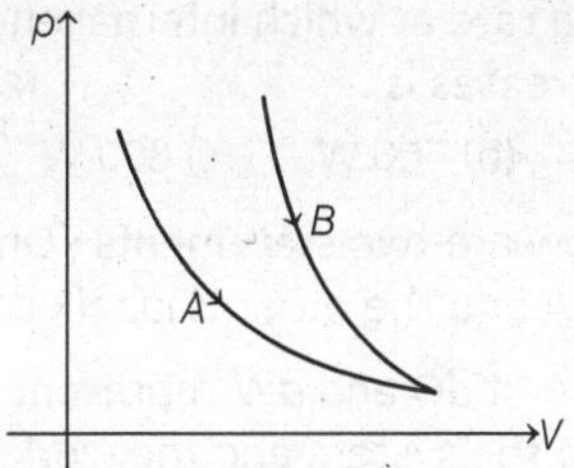

(a) $\frac{p^{\gamma-1}}{T^{\gamma}} = k$ for process B and $T = k$ for process A

(b) $pV = k$ for process B and A

(c) $\frac{T^{\gamma}}{p^{\gamma-1}} = k$ for process A and $pV = k$ for process B

(d) $pV^{\gamma} = k$ for process B and $pV = k$ for process A

6 Given below are two statements : one is labelled as Assertion (A) and other is labelled as Reason (R)

Assertion (A) Efficiency of a reversible heat engine will be highest at – 273°C temperature of cold reservoir.

Reason (R) The efficiency of Carnot's engine depends not only on temperature of cold reservoir but it depends on the temperature of hot reservoir too and is given as $\eta = \left(1 - \frac{T_2}{T_1}\right)$.

In the light of the above statements, choose the correct answer from the options given below : **[30 Jan 2023 Shift-II]**

(a) Both A and R are true but R is not the correct explanation of A
(b) A is true but R is false
(c) A is false but R is true
(d) Both A and R are true and R is the correct explanation of A

7 A carnot engine operating between two reservoirs has efficiency 1/3. When the temperature of cold reservoir raised by x, its efficiency decreases to 1/6. The value of x, if the temperature of hot reservoir is 99°C, will be **[2023, 1 Feb Shift-II]**

(a) 62 K
(b) 16.5 K
(c) 33 K
(d) 66 K

8 Given below are two statements

Statement I If heat is added to a system, its temperature must increase.

Statement II If positive work is done by a system in a thermodynamic process, its volume must increase.

In the light of the above statements, choose the correct answer from the options given below **[2023, 8 April Shift-I]**

(a) Statement I is true but Statement II is false
(b) Statement I is false but Statement II is true
(c) Both Statement I and Statement II are false
(d) Both Statement I and Statement II are true

9 Consider two containers A and B containing monoatomic gases at the same Pressure (p), Volume (V) and Temperature (T). The gas in A is compressed isothermally to $\frac{1}{8}$ of its original volume while the gas in B is compressed adiabatically to 1/8 of its original volume. The ratio of final pressure of gas in B to that of gas in A is **[2023, 11 April Shift-II]**

(a) $\frac{1}{8}$ (b) 4
(c) $8^{3/2}$ (d) 8

10 The thermodynamic process, in which internal energy of the system remains constant is **[2023, 10 April Shift-I]**

(a) isobaric
(b) isochoric
(c) adiabatic
(d) isothermal

11 Under isothermal condition, the pressure of a gas is given by $p = aV^{-3}$, where a is a constant and V is the volume of the gas. The bulk modulus at constant temperature is equal to **[2023, 13 April Shift-I]**

(a) $3p$ (b) $\frac{p}{2}$
(c) $2p$ (d) p

12 A thermodynamic system is taken through cyclic process. The total work done in the process is **[2023, 13 April Shift-I]**

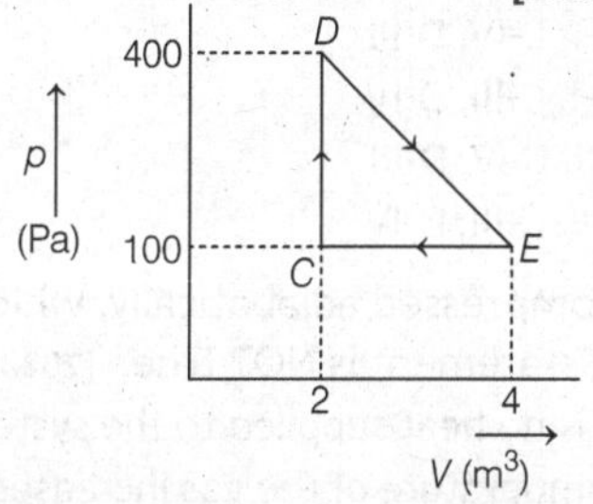

(a) 200 J (b) Zero
(c) 300 J (d) 100 J

13 In an isothermal change, the change in pressure and volume of a gas can be represented for three different temperature $T_3 > T_2 > T_1$ as [2023, 24 Jan Shift-II]

(a)
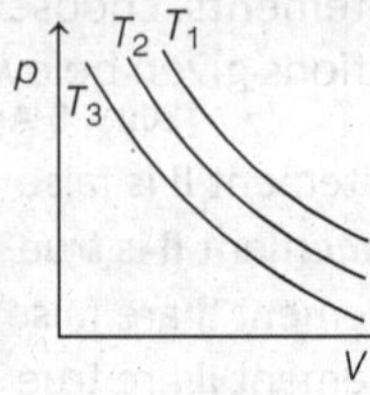

(b)
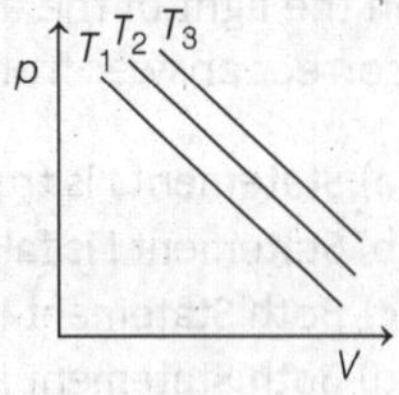

(c)
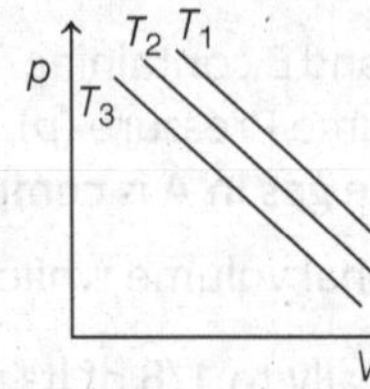

(d)
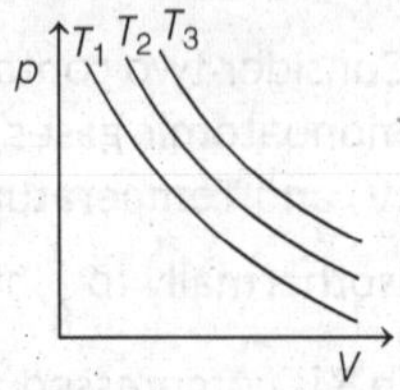

14 1 g of a liquid is converted to vapour at 3×10^5 Pa pressure. If 10% of the heat supplied is used for increasing the volume by 1600 cm^3 during this phase change, then the increase in internal energy is the process will be [2023, 24 Jan Shift-I]

(a) 4.32×10^8 J (b) 432000 J
(c) 4320 J (d) 4800 J

15 Match List I with List II

List I		List II	
A.	Isothermal process	I.	Work done by the gas decreases internal energy
B.	Adiabatic process	II.	No change in internal energy
C.	Isochoric process	III.	The heat absorbed goes partly to increase internal energy and partly to do work
D.	Isobaric process	IV.	No work is done on or by the gas

Choose the correct answer from the options given below. [2023, 25 Jan Shift-II]

(a) A-II, B-I, C-IV, D-III
(b) A-II, B-I, C-III, D-IV
(c) A-I, B-II, C-IV, D-III
(d) A-I, B-II, C-III, D-IV

16 A gas is compressed adiabatically, which one of the following statement is NOT true, [2023, 10 April Shift-II]

(a) There is no heat supplied to the system
(b) The temperature of the gas increases.
(c) There is no change in the internal energy
(d) The change in the internal energy is equal to the work done on the gas.

17 A source supplies heat to a system at the rate of 1000 W. If the system performs work at a rate of 200 W. The rate at which internal energy of the system increases is [2023, 6 April Shift-I]

(a) 600 W (b) 500 W (c) 800 W (d) 1200 W

18 Given below are two statements : One is labelled as **Assertion A** and the other is labelled as **Reason R.**

Assertion A If dQ and dW represent the heat supplied to the system and the work done on the system respectively. Then according to the first law of thermodynamics $dQ = dU - dW$.

Reason R First law of thermodynamics is based on the law of conservation of energy.

In the light of the above statements, choose the correct answer from the options given below [2023, 29 Jan Shift-I]

(a) Both A and R are correct and R is the correct explanation of A
(b) Both A and R are correct but R is not the correct explanation of A
(c) A is not correct but R is correct
(d) A is correct but R is not correct

19 A sample of an ideal gas is taken through the cyclic process $ABCA$ as shown in figure. It absorbs, 40 J of heat during the part AB, no heat during BC and rejects 60 J of heat during CA. A work 50 J is done on the gas during the part BC. The internal energy of the gas at A is 1560 J.

The work done by the gas during the part CA is [2022, 28 June Shift-II]

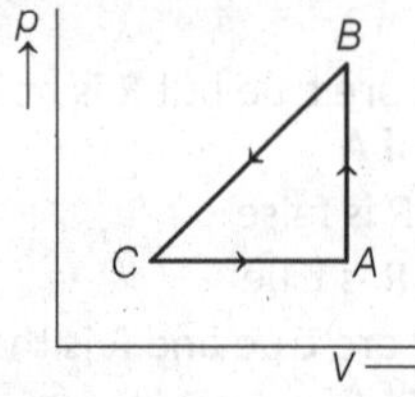

(a) 20 J (b) 30 J (c) – 30 J (d) – 60 J

20 A diatomic gas ($\gamma = 1.4$) does 400 J of work when it is expanded isobarically. The heat given to the gas in the process is ______ J. [2022, 27 June Shift-II]

21 The pressure p_1 and density d_1 of diatomic gas $\left(\gamma = \frac{7}{5}\right)$ changes suddenly to p_2 ($> p_1$) and d_2 respectively during an adiabatic process. The temperature of the gas increases and becomes times of its initial temperature. $\left(\text{given } \frac{d_2}{d_1} = 32\right)$

[2022, 29 July Shift-I]

22 Read the following statements

A. When small temperature difference between a liquid and its surrounding is doubled, the rate of loss of heat of the liquid becomes twice.

B. Two bodies P and Q having equal surface areas are maintained at temperature 10°C and 20°C. The thermal radiation emitted in a given time by p and Q are in the ratio 1 : 1.15.

C A Carnot engine working between 100 K and 400 K has an efficiency of 75%.

D. When small temperature difference between a liquid and its surrounding is quadrupled, the rate of loss of heat of the liquid becomes twice.

Choose the correct answer from the options given below **[2022, 27 July Shift-I]**

(a) A, B, C only (b) A, B only
(c) A, C only (d) B, C, D only

23 A steam engine intakes 50 g of steam at 100°C per minute and cools it down to 20°C. If latent heat of vaporization of steam is 540 cal g^{-1}, then the heat rejected by the steam engine per minute is .... $\times 10^3$ cal. (Given : specific heat capacity of water : 1 cal $g^{-1}°C^{-1}$) **[2022, 25 June Shift-I]**

24 300 cal. of heat is given to a heat engine and it rejects 225 cal. of heat. If source temperature is 227°C, then the temperature of sink will be ....°C. **[2022, 29 June Shift-I]**

25 In a carnot engine, the temperature of reservoir is 527°C and that of sink is 200 K. If the work done by the engine when it transfers heat from reservoir to sink is 12000 kJ, the quantity of heat absorbed by the engine from reservoir is ...... $\times 10^6$ J. **[2022, 27 June Shift-I]**

26 An electric appliance supplies 6000 J/min heat to the system. If the system delivers a power of 90W. How long it would take to increase the internal energy by 2.5×10^3 J? **[2021, 26 Aug Shift-I]**

(a) 2.5×10^2 s (b) 4.1×10^1 s
(c) 2.4×10^3 s (d) 2.5×10^1 s

27 In thermodynamics, heat and work are **[2021, 16 March Shift-I]**

(a) path functions
(b) intensive thermodynamic state variables
(c) extensive thermodynamic state variables
(d) point functions

28 One mole of rigid diatomic gas performs a work of $Q/5$ when heat Q is supplied to it. The molar heat capacity of the gas during this transformation is $\frac{xR}{8}$, The value of x is ....
[R = universal gas constant] **[2021, 26 Feb Shift-II]**

29 The p-V diagram of a diatomic ideal gas system going under cyclic process as shown in figure. The work done during an adiabatic process CD is (use, $\gamma = 1.4$) **[2021, 18 March Shift-I]**

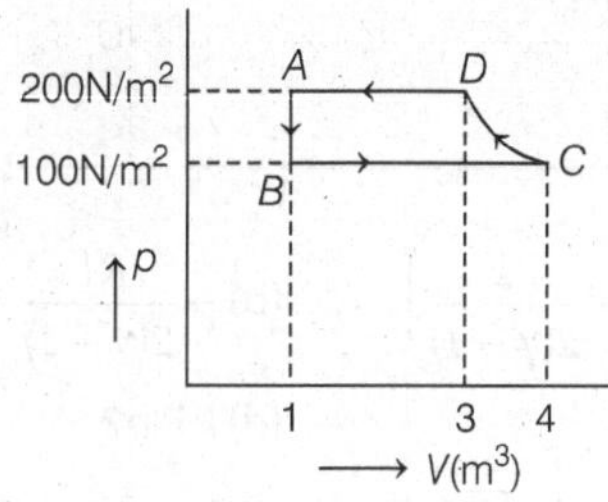

(a) –500 J (b) – 400 J (c) 400 J (d) 200 J

30 Which one is the correct option for the two different thermodynamic processes ? **[2021, 17 March Shift-II]**

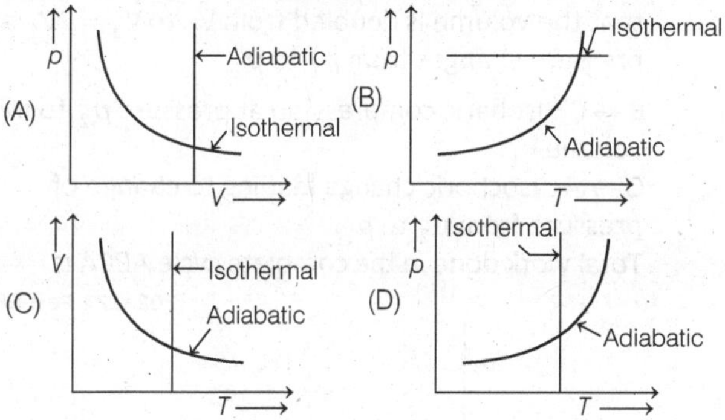

(a) C and A (b) C and D (c) Only A (d) B and C

31 Thermodynamic process is shown below on a p-V diagram for one mole of an ideal gas. If $V_2 = 2V_1$, then the ratio of temperature $\frac{T_2}{T_1}$ is **[2021, 25 Feb Shift-II]**

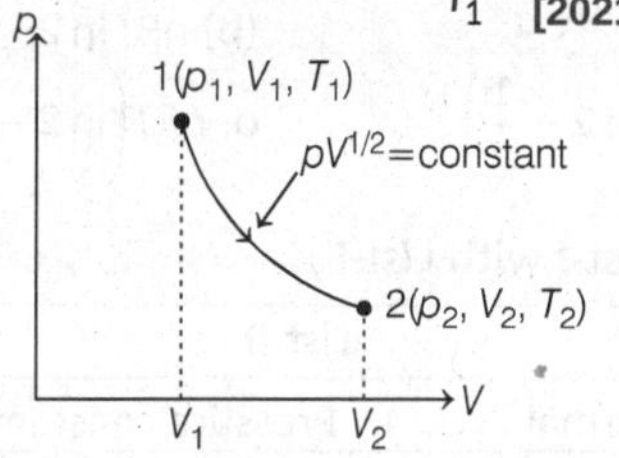

(a) $1/\sqrt{2}$ (b) $\sqrt{2}$ (c) 1/2 (d) 2

32 If one mole of an ideal gas at (p_1, V_1) is allowed to expand reversibly and isothermally (A to B), its pressure is reduced to one-half of the original pressure (see figure). This is followed by a constant volume cooling till its pressure is reduced to one-fourth of the initial value ($B \rightarrow C$). Then, it is restored to its initial state by a reversible adiabatic compression (*C* to *A*). The net work done by the gas is equal to **[2021, 24 Feb Shift-II]**

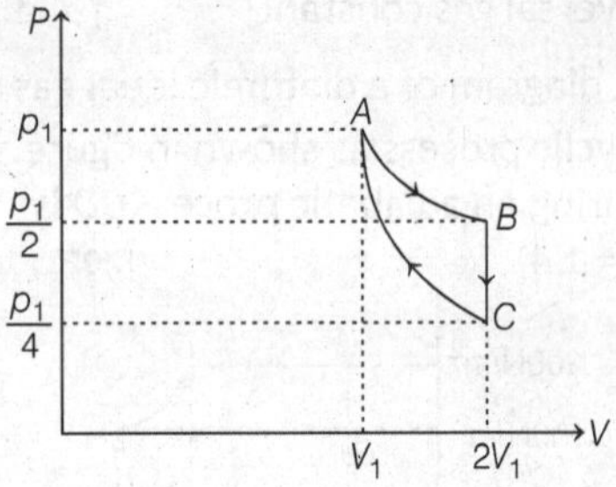

(a) $RT\left(\ln 2-\frac{1}{2(\gamma-1)}\right)$ (b) $-\frac{RT}{2(\gamma-1)}$

(c) 0 (d) $RT\ln 2$

33 *n* mole of a perfect gas undergoes a cyclic process *ABCA* (see figure) consisting of the following processes.

$A \rightarrow B$: Isothermal expansion at temperature *T*, so that the volume is doubled from V_1 to $V_2 = 2V_1$ and pressure changes from p_1 to p_2.

$B \rightarrow C$: Isobaric compression at pressure p_2 to initial volume V_1.

$C \rightarrow A$: Isochoric change leading to change of pressure from p_2 to p_1.

Total work done in the complete cycle *ABCA* is **[2021, 24 Feb Shift-I]**

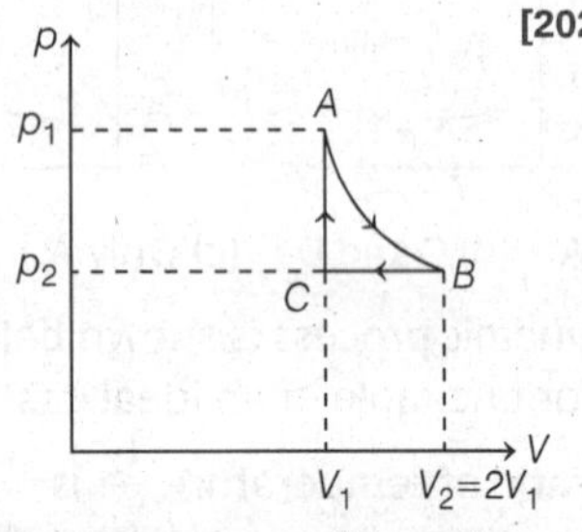

(a) 0 (b) $nRT\ln 2$

(c) $nRT\left(\ln 2+\frac{1}{2}\right)$ d. $nRT\left(\ln 2-\frac{1}{2}\right)$

34 Match List-I with List-II.

List-I	List-II
A. Isothermal	1. Pressure constant
B. Isochoric	2. Temperature constant
C. Adiabatic	3. Volume constant
D. Isobaric	4. Heat content is constant

Choose the correct answer from the options given below. **[2021, 24 Feb Shift-I]**

	A	B	C	D		A	B	C	D
(a)	1	3	2	4	(b)	3	2	1	4
(c)	2	4	3	1	(d)	2	3	4	1

35 A sample of gas with $\gamma = 1.5$ is taken through an adiabatic process in which the volume is compressed from 1200 cm^3 to 300 cm^3. If the initial pressure is 200 kPa. The absolute value of the work done by the gas in the process is .... J. **[2021, 31 Aug Shift-II]**

36 In the reported figure, heat energy absorbed by a system in going through a cyclic process is ...... πJ. **[2021, 20 July Shift-I]**

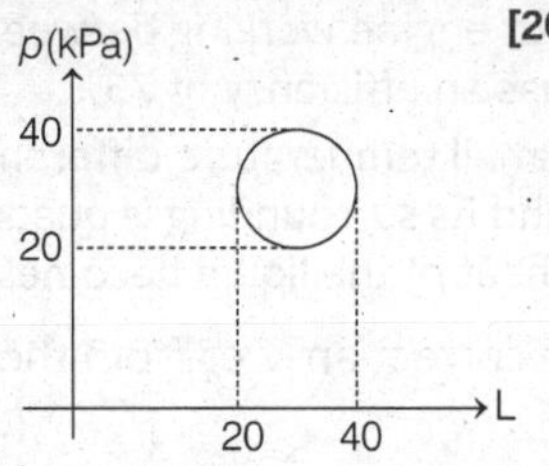

37 In a certain thermodynamical process, the pressure of a gas depends on its volume as kV^3. The work done when the temperature changes from 100°C to 300°C will be .... *nR*, where *n* denotes number of moles of a gas. **[2021, 25 Feb Shift-I]**

38 A heat engine operates between a cold reservoir at temperature $T_2 = 400$ K and a hot reservoir at temperature T_1. It takes 300 J of heat from the hot reservoir and delivers 240 J of heat to the cold reservoir in a cycle. The minimum temperature of the hot reservoir has to be .... K. **[2021, 27 Aug Shift-II]**

39 Starting at temperature 300 K, one mole of an ideal diatomic gas ($\gamma = 1.4$) is first compressed adiabatically from volume V_1 to $V_2 = \frac{V_1}{16}$. It is then allowed to expand isobarically to volume $2V_2$. If all the processes are the quasi-static, then the final temperature of the gas (in °K) is (to the nearest integer) .... **[2020, 9 Jan Shift-II]**

40 Two ideal Carnot engines operate in cascade (all heat given up by one engine is used by the other engine to produce work) between temperatures T_1 and T_2. The temperature of the hot reservoir of the first engine is T_1 and the temperature of the cold reservoir of the second engine is T_2. *T* is temperature of the sink of first engine which is also the source for the second engine. How is *T* related to T_1 and T_2, if both the engines perform equal amount of work? **[2020, 7 Jan Shift-II]**

(a) $T = 0$ (b) $T = \frac{2T_1T_2}{T_1+T_2}$

(c) $T = \sqrt{T_1 T_2}$ (d) $T = \frac{T_1+T_2}{2}$

41 If minimum possible work is done by a refrigerator in converting 100 g of water at 0°C to ice, how much heat (in cal) is released to the surroundings at temperature 27°C to the nearest integer ...... ? (Take, latent heat of ice = 80 cal/g) **[2020, 3 Sep Shift-II]**

JEE Advanced

1. One mole of an ideal gas expands adiabatically from an initial state (T_A, V_0) to final state $(T_f, 5V_0)$. Another mole of the same gas expands isothermally from a different initial state (T_B, V_0) to the same final state $(T_f, 5V_0)$. The ratio of the specific heats at constant pressure and constant volume of this ideal gas is γ. What is the ratio T_A / T_B? **(2023 Adv.)**

(a) $5^{\gamma-1}$ (b) $5^{1-\gamma}$ (c) 5^{γ} (d) $5^{1+\gamma}$

2. A closed container contains a homogeneous mixture of two moles of an ideal monoatomic gas $(\gamma = 5/3)$ and one mole of an ideal diatomic gas $(\gamma = 7/5)$. Here, γ is the ratio of the specific heats at constant pressure and constant volume of an ideal gas. The gas mixture does a work of 66 Joule when heated at constant pressure. The change in its internal energy is .... joule. **(2023 Adv.)**

3. One mole of an ideal gas undergoes two different cyclic processes I and II, as shown in the *p-V* diagrams below. In cycle I, processes *a*, *b*, *c* and *d* are isobaric, isothermal, isobaric and isochoric, respectively. In cycle II, processes *a′*, *b′*, *c′* and *d′* are isothermal, isochoric, isobaric and isochoric, respectively. The total work done during cycle I is W_I and that during cycle II is W_{II}. The ratio W_I / W_{II} is .... . **(2023 Adv.)**

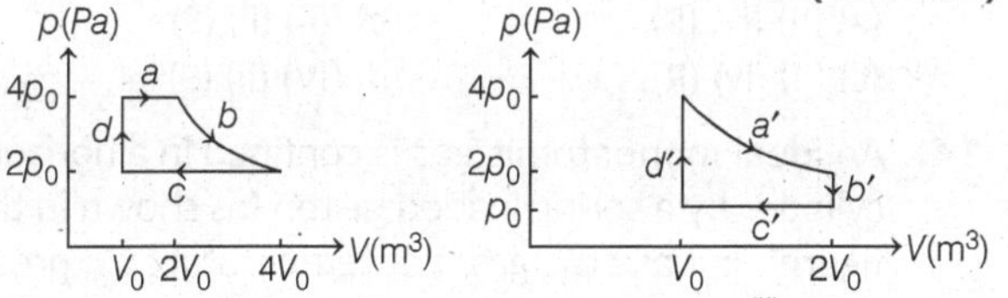

(I) (II)

4. An ideal gas of density $\rho = 0.2$ kg m^{-3} enters a chimney of height *h* at the rate of $\alpha = 0.8$ kg s^{-1} from its lower end, and escapes through the upper end as shown in the figure. The cross-sectional area of the lower end is $A_1 = 0.1$ m^2 and the upper end is $A_2 = 0.4$ m^2. The pressure and the temperature of the gas at the lower end are 600 Pa and 300 K, respectively, while its temperature at the upper end is 150 K. The chimney is heat insulated, so that the gas undergoes adiabatic expansion. Take, $g = 10$ ms^{-2} and the ratio of specific heats of the gas $\gamma = 2$. Ignore atmospheric pressure. **(2022 Adv.)**

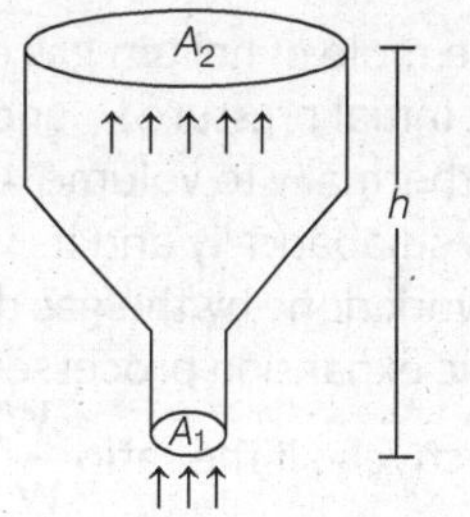

Which of the following statement(s) is(are) correct?

(a) The pressure of the gas at the upper end of the chimney is 300 Pa.

(b) The velocity of the gas at the lower end of the chimney is 40 ms^{-1} and at the upper end is 20ms^{-1}.

(c) The height of the chimney is 590 m.

(d) The density of the gas at the upper end is 0.05 kg m^{-3}.

5. In the given *p-V* diagram, a monoatomic gas $\left(\gamma = \frac{5}{3}\right)$ is first compressed adiabatically from state *A* to state *B*. Then, it expands isothermally from state *B* to state *C*. [Given, $\left(\frac{1}{3}\right)^{0.6} \simeq 0.5$, $\ln 2 \simeq 0.7$]. **(2022 Adv.)**

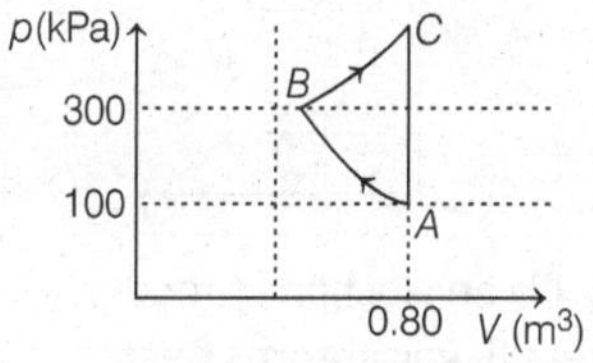

Which of the following statement(s) is(are) correct?

(a) The magnitude of the total work done in the process $A \to B \to C$ is 144 kJ.

(b) The magnitude of the work done in the process $B \to C$ is 84 kJ.

(c) The magnitude of the work done in the process $A \to B$ is 60 kJ.

(d) The magnitude of the work done in the process $C \to A$ is zero.

6. An ideal gas undergoes a four step cycle as shown in the *p-V* diagram below. During this cycle, heat is absorbed by the gas in **(2021 Adv.)**

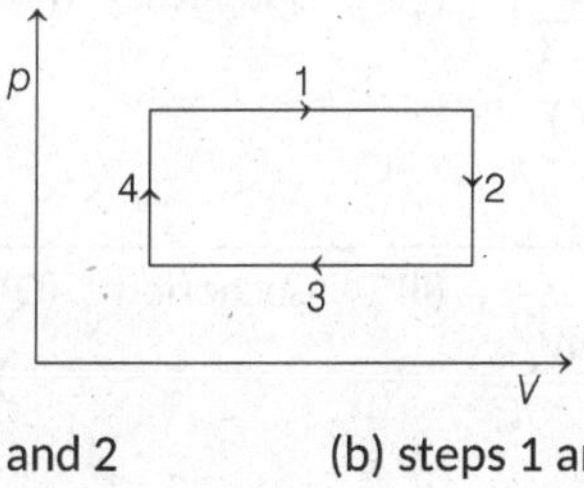

(a) steps 1 and 2 (b) steps 1 and 3
(c) steps 1 and 4 (d) steps 2 and 4

7. Consider one mole of helium gas enclosed in a container at initial pressure P_1 and volume V_1. It expands isothermally to volume $4V_1$. After this, the gas expands adiabatically and its volume becomes $32\ V_1$. The work done by the gas during isothermal and adiabatic expansion processes are W_{iso} and W_{adia}, respectively. If the ratio $\frac{W_{iso}}{W_{adia}} = f \ln 2$, then f is________. **(2020 Adv.)**

8. A spherical bubble inside water has radius R. Take the pressure inside the bubble and the water pressure to be p_0. The bubble now gets compressed radially in an adiabatic manner so that its radius becomes $(R - a)$. For $a << R$ the magnitude of the work done in the process is given by $(4\pi p_0 R a^2)X$, where X is a constant and $\gamma = C_p/C_V = 41/30$. The value of X is________. **(2020 Adv.)**

9. One mole of a monoatomic ideal gas undergoes a cyclic process as shown in the figure (where, V is the volume and T is the temperature). Which of the statements below is (are) true ? **(2018 Adv.)**

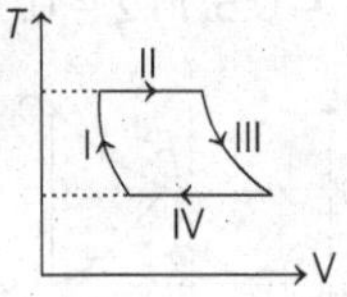

(a) Process I is an isochoric process
(b) In process II, gas absorbs heat
(c) In process IV, gas releases heat
(d) Processes I and III are not isobaric

10. One mole of a monoatomic ideal gas undergoes an adiabatic expansion in which its volume becomes eight times its initial value. If the initial temperature of the gas is 100 K and the universal gas constant $R = 8.0\ \text{J mol}^{-1}\ \text{K}^{-1}$, the decrease in its internal energy in joule, is .... **(2018 Adv.)**

Directions (Q.Nos. 11-13) Matching the information given in the three columns of the following table.

	Column 1		Column 2		Column 3
(I)	$W_{1\to 2} = \frac{1}{\gamma - 1}(p_2V_2 - p_1V_1)$	(i)	Isothermal	(P)	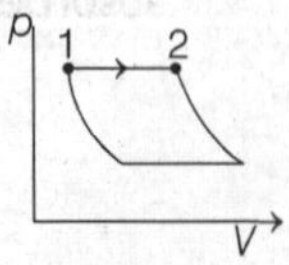
(II)	$W_{1\to 2} = -pV_2 + pV_1$	(ii)	Isochoric	(Q)	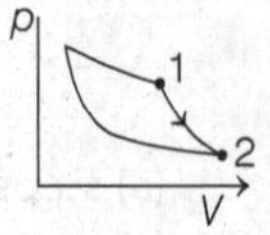
(III)	$W_{1\to 2} = 0$	(iii)	Isobaric	(R)	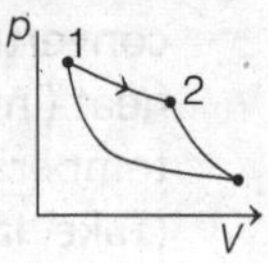
(IV)	$W_{1\to 2} = -nRT \ln\left(\frac{V_2}{V_1}\right)$	(iv)	Adiabatic	(S)	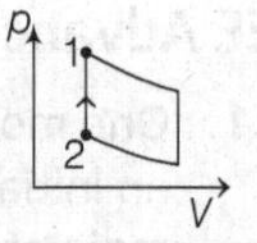

An ideal gas is undergoing a cyclic thermodynamic process in different ways as shown in the corresponding *p*-*V* diagrams in column 3 of the table. Consider only the path from state 1 to state 2. W denotes the corresponding work done on the system. The equations and plots in the table have standards notations and used in thermodynamic processes. Here γ is the ratio of heat capacities at constant pressure and constant volume. The number of moles in the gas is n.

11. Which one of the following options correctly represents a thermodynamic process that is used as a correction in the determination of the speed of sound in an ideal gas?
(a) (IV) (ii) (R) (b) (I) (ii) (Q) **(2017 Adv.)**
(c) (I), (iv) (Q) (d) (III) (iv) (R)

12. Which of the following options is the only correct representation of a process in which $\Delta U = \Delta Q - p\Delta V$?
(a) (II) (iii) (S) (b) (II) (iii) (P) **(2017 Adv.)**
(c) (III) (iii) (P) (d) (II) (iv) (R)

13. Which one of the following options is the correct combination? **(2017 Adv.)**
(a) (II) (iv) (P) (b) (III) (ii) (S)
(c) (II) (iv) (R) (d) (IV) (ii) (S)

14. An ideal monoatomic gas is confined in a horizontal cylinder by a spring loaded piston (as shown in the figure). Initially the gas is at temperature T_1, pressure p_1 and volume V_1 and the spring is in its relaxed state. The gas is then heated very slowly to temperature T_2, pressure p_2 and volume V_2. During this process the piston moves out by a distance x. **(2015 Adv.)**

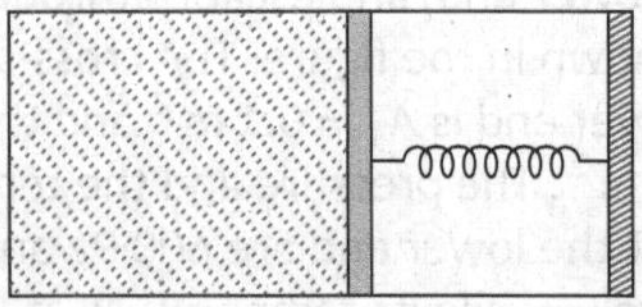

Ignoring the friction between the piston and the cylinder, the correct statements is/are

(a) If $V_2 = 2V_1$ and $T_2 = 3T_1$,
then the energy stored in the spring is $\frac{1}{4}p_1V_1$

(b) If $V_2 = 2V_1$ and $T_2 = 3T_1$,
then the change in internal energy is $3p_1V_1$

(c) If $V_2 = 3V_1$ and $T_2 = 4T_1$,
then the work done by the gas is $\frac{7}{3}p_1V_1$

(d) If $V_2 = 3V_1$ and $T_2 = 4T_1$,
then the heat supplied to the gas is $\frac{17}{6}p_1V_1$

Passage Based Questions

In the figure a container is shown to have a movable (without friction) piston on top. The container and the piston are all made of perfectly insulating material allowing no heat transfer between outside and inside the container. The container is divided into two compartments by a rigid partition made of a thermally conducting material that allows slow transfer of heat.

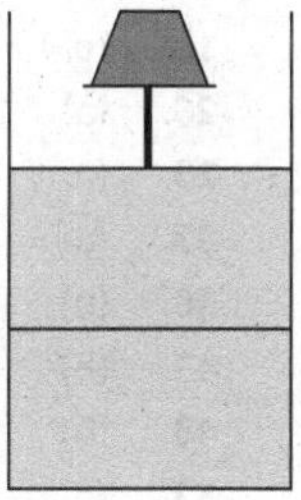

The lower compartment of the container is filled with 2 moles of an ideal monoatomic gas at 700 K and the upper compartment is filled with 2 moles of an ideal diatomic gas at 400 K. The heat capacities per mole of an ideal monoatomic gas are $C_V = \frac{3}{2}R, C_p = \frac{5}{2}R$, and those for an ideal diatomic gas are $C_V = \frac{5}{2}R, C_p = \frac{7}{2}R$.

15. Consider the partition to be rigidly fixed so that it does not move. When equilibrium is achieved, the final temperature of the gases will be **(2014 Adv.)**

(a) 550 K (b) 525 K
(c) 513 K (d) 490 K

16. Now consider the partition to be free to move without friction so that the pressure of gases in both compartments is the same. Then total work done by the gases till the time they achieve equilibrium will be **(2014 Adv.)**

(a) 250R (b) 200R
(c) 100R (d) −100R

17. A thermodynamic system is taken from an initial state i with internal energy $U_i = 100$ J to the final state f along two different paths iaf and ibf, as schematically shown in the figure. The work done by the system along the paths af, ib and bf are $W_{af} = 200$ J, $W_{ib} = 50$ J and $W_{bf} = 100$ J respectively. The heat supplied to the system along the path iaf, ib and bf are Q_{iaf}, Q_{ib} and Q_{bf} respectively. If the internal energy of the system in the state b is $U_b = 200$ J and $Q_{iaf} = 500$ J, the ratio Q_{bf}/Q_{ib} is **(2014 Adv.)**

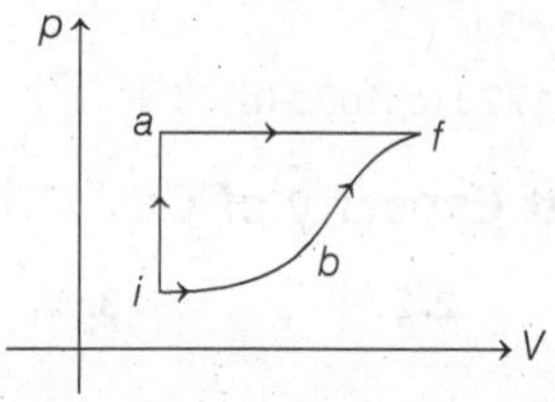

18. One mole of a monatomic ideal gas is taken along two cyclic processes $E \to F \to G \to E$ and $E \to F \to H \to E$ as shown in the p-V diagram. **(2013 Adv.)**

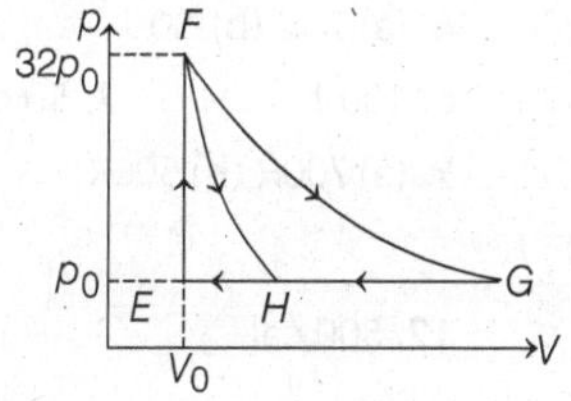

The processes involved are purely isochoric, isobaric, isothermal or adiabatic.

Match the paths in List I with the magnitudes of the work done in List II and select the correct answer using the codes given below the lists.

	List I		List II
P.	$G \to E$	1.	$160\, p_0V_0 \ln 2$
Q.	$G \to H$	2.	$36\, p_0V_0$
R.	$F \to H$	3.	$24\, p_0V_0$
S.	$F \to G$	4.	$31\, p_0V_0$

Codes

	P	Q	R	S
(a)	4	3	2	1
(b)	4	3	1	2
(c)	3	1	2	4
(d)	1	3	2	4

19. 5.6 L of helium gas at STP is adiabatically compressed to 0.7 L. Taking the initial temperature to be T_1, the work done in the process is **(2011 Adv.)**

(a) $\frac{9}{8}RT_1$ (b) $\frac{3}{2}RT_1$ (c) $\frac{15}{8}RT_1$ (d) $\frac{9}{2}RT_1$

Answer Key

Level 1

6.1 Work Done by Gas

1. 500 J 2. (a) 1.8×10^5 J, (b) 4.8×10^5 J 3. $3p_0V_0$

4. $\frac{\pi}{2}$ atm-L 5. (a) $-p_0V_0$ (b) $\frac{\pi}{4}(p_2 - p_1)(V_2 - V_1)$ (c) 0

6.2 First Law of Thermodynamics

1. 18 J 2. 60 J

3. (a) 24 J (b) – 172 J (c) 160 J (d) 72 J

6.3 Molar Heat Capacity of Gas

1. $\frac{2}{\gamma - 1}$ 2. $2.5R$ 3. $3R$ 4. $10R/3$

5. 4.2 J/cal 6. 0.5 cal $g^{-1}K^{-1}$

6.4 Isochoric, Isobaric and Isothermal Processes

1. (a) 3125 J (b) 3125 J 2. 2750 cal

3. 125 kJ 4. (a) 75 J (b) 30 J

5. 3/5 6. 100 J 7. 50 cal

8. 110 J 9. (a) $700R$ (b) $500R$

10. -2.007×10^4 J

11. $3.9p_0V_0$ 12. 500 cal

6.5 Adiabatic Process and Free Expansion

1. $32p_0, 4T_0$ 2. 3/2 3. – 93°C

4. 4/9% 5. (a) 800 kPa, 100 K (b) 1600 kPa, 200 K

6. (a) – 84°C, (b) – 2775 J, (c) 2775 J 7. $25R$

8. (a) 1-isothermal, 2-adiabatic (b) 1-adiabatic, 2-isothermal

9. $p_A : p_B : p_B = (2)^{3/2} : 1 : 2 = 2\sqrt{2} : 1 : 2$

10. $T_{final} = T_0, p_{final} = p_0/2$

6.6 Polytropic Process

1. $3.5R$ 2. $-\gamma$ 3. $4R$

4. (a) 250 J (b) 1000 J

6.7 Cyclic Process

1. (a) 765 J (b) 208/1921

2. $nRT_0 \ln 2$ 3. $nR(T_1 + T_3 - T_4 - T_2)$ 4. 2/19

5. (a)

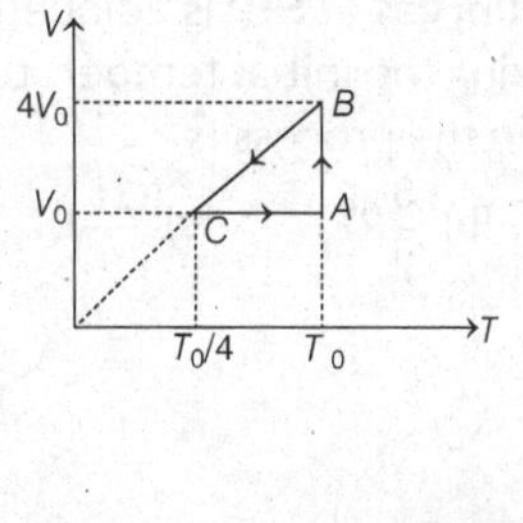

(b) $0.636\,p_0V_0$

6. (a) $U_b = 200$ J, $U_c = 500$ J (b) $W_{bc} = -400$ J

7. (a) $V_c = 2V_0$, (b) $T_{max} = 4T_0$, (c) $\frac{1}{2}p_0V_0$, (d) $9p_0V_0$ (e) $\frac{100}{19}$%

8. – 4526 J

6.8 Heat Engine and Heat Pump

1. 227°C 2. (a) 66.7% (b) 2.8×10^6 J

3. 373.3 K 4. (a) 10.13 (b) 879 kcal

5. $Q_1 = 900$ cal 6. (a) 50 J (b) 300 J

Level 2

Single Choice Correct Questions

1. (d)	2. (b)	3. (a)	4. (b)	5. (c)
6. (c)	7. (a)	8. (d)	9. (a)	10. (d)
11. (b)	12. (d)	13. (d)	14. (c)	15. (b)
16. (d)	17. (a)	18. (c)	19. (d)	20. (d)
21. (d)	22. (d)	23. (a)	24. (a)	25. (d)
26. (d)	27. (b)	28. (a)	29. (c)	30. (a)
31. (a)	32. (c)	33. (a)	34. (a)	35. (a)
36. (c)	37. (d)	38. (b)	39. (b)	40. (c)
41. (a)	42. (d)	43. (b)	44. (c)	45. (d)
46. (a)	47. (a)	48. (b)	49. (a)	50. (d)
51. (b)	52. (a)	53. (c)	54. (c)	55. (c)
56. (b)	57. (d)	58. (a)	59. (d)	60. (d)
61. (d)	62. (d)	63. (a)	64. (c)	

Numerical Value Questions

1. 1.33	2. 20	3. 55	4. 1.5	5. 4
6. 7	7. 1	8. 8	9. 400	10. 13
11. 17.95				

Level 3

Single Choice Correct Questions

1. (d)	2. (c)	3. (d)	4. (d)	5. (d)
6. (c)	7. (c)	8. (a)	9. (d)	10. (a)
11. (c)	12. (a)	13. (a)	14. (a)	15. (b)
16. (a)	17. (d)	18. (c)	19. (c)	20. (b)
21. (c)	22. (b)	23. (c)	24. (d)	25. (a)
26. (a)	27. (d)	28. (a)	29. (c)	30. (a)
31. (c)	32. (b)	33. (b)	34. (b)	35. (d)
36. (a)	37. (a)	38. (d)		

Multiple Choice(s) Correct Questions

1. (ac)	2. (ab)	3. (d)	4. (acd)	5. (abcd)
6. (abcd)	7. (bc)	8. (cd)	9. (ad)	10. (ab)

11. (bd)	**12.** (ad)	**13.** (abc)	**14.** (abc)	**15.** (ad)
16. (ab)	**17.** (bd)	**18.** (acd)	**19.** (abd)	**20.** (abd)

Comprehension Based Questions

1. (b)	**2.** (d)	**3.** (c)	**4.** (d)	**5.** (d)
6. (c)	**7.** (a)	**8.** (b)	**9.** (b)	**10.** (b)
11. (d)	**12.** (a)	**13.** (b)	**14.** (b)	**15.** (c)
16. (c)	**17.** (d)	**18.** (c)	**19.** (c)	**20.** (a)
21. (b)	**22.** (c)	**23.** (d)	**24.** (b)	**25.** (b)
26. (c)	**27.** (c)	**28.** (d)	**29.** (b)	**30.** (a)
31. (b)	**32.** (b)	**33.** (c)	**34.** (c)	**35.** (b)
36. (d)	**37.** (b)	**38.** (d)		

Match the Column Questions

1. A→ S, B→ P, R, C→ R, D→ Q, S
2. A→ R, B→ S, C→ Q, D→ P
3. A→ P, B→ Q, C→ Q
4. A→ R, B→ S, C→ P, D→ Q
5. A→ P, R, S, B→ Q, C→ P, R, S, D→ Q, R
6. A→ S, B→ Q, C→ R, D→ Q
7. A→ Q, S, B→ P, R, S, C→ P, R, S

Numerical Value Questions

1. 4	**2.** 100	**3.** 369.3	**4.** 435	**5.** 7825
6. 700	**7.** 75	**8.** 2	**9.** 2	**10.** 2
11. 75	**12.** 3.75	**13.** 3		

Previous Year's Questions

JEE Main

1. (d)	**2.** (b)	**3.** (*)	**4.** (*)	**5.** (d)
6. (d)	**7.** (a)	**8.** (b)	**9.** (b)	**10.** (d)
11. (a)	**12.** (c)	**13.** (d)	**14.** (c)	**15.** (a)
16. (c)	**17.** (c)	**18.** (a)	**19.** (b)	**20.** (1400)
21. (4)	**22.** (a)	**23.** (31)	**24.** (102)	**25.** (16)
26. (a)	**27.** (a)	**28.** (25)	**29.** (a)	**30.** (b)
31. (b)	**32.** (a)	**33.** (d)	**34.** (d)	**35.** (480)
36. (100)	**37.** (50)	**38.** (500)	**39.** (1819)	**40.** (d)
41. (8791)				

JEE Advanced

1. (a)	**2.** (121)	**3.** (2)	**4.** (b)	**5.** (b,c,d)
6. (c)	**7.** (1.78)	**8.** (2.05)	**9.** (b,c,d)	**10.** (900)
11. (c)	**12.** (b)	**13.** (b)	**14.** (a,b,c)	**15.** (d)
16. (d)	**17.** (2)	**18.** (a)	**19.** (a)	

SOLUTIONS

Level-1

6.1 Work done by Gas

1. $W = \int p\,dV = \int_4^6 (30V + 100)\,dV$

$= [15V^2 + 100V]_4^6 = 500$ J

2. (a) W = Area under p-V curve

$= \frac{1}{2}(4\times10^5 + 8\times10^5)(0.3) = 1.8\times10^5$ J

(b) $\Delta U = nC_V\Delta T$

$= n\left(\frac{3R}{2}\right)(T_2 - T_1) = \frac{3}{2}(p_2V_2 - p_1V_1)$

$= \frac{3}{2}(8\times10^5\times0.5 - 4\times10^5\times0.2)$

$= 4.8\times10^5$ J

3. $W = W_{AB} + W_{BC} + W_{CD}$

$= -p_0(2V_0 - V_0) + 0 + 2p_0(3V_0 - V_0) = 3p_0V_0$

4. W = Area of semi-circle

$= \frac{\pi(1)^2}{2}$ atm-L

5. (a) W = Area of rectangle

$= -(2p_0 - p_0)(2V_0 - V_0) = -p_0V_0$

Work done is negative as the cycle is anti-clockwise.

(b) W = Area of ellipse $= \pi ab$

$= \pi\left(\frac{V_2 - V_1}{2}\right)\left(\frac{p_2 - p_1}{2}\right)$

$= \frac{\pi}{4}(p_2 - p_1)(V_2 - V_1)$

(c) W = +Area of ΔODA – Area of $\Delta OBC = 0$

6.2 First Law of Thermodynamics

1. $Q = \Delta U + W$

$\Rightarrow \quad -20 = (U_2 - 30) + (-8)$

$\Rightarrow \quad U_2 = 18$ J

2. For $A \to B$,

$Q = \Delta U_{AB} + W$

$\Rightarrow \quad 100 = \Delta U_{AB} + 20$

$\Rightarrow \quad \Delta U_{AB} = 80$ J

$\Delta U_{BA} = -\Delta U_{AB} = -80$ J

For $B \to A$,

$Q = \Delta U_{BA} + W$

$\Rightarrow \quad -20 = -80 + W$

$\Rightarrow \quad W = 60$ J

3. (a) Along path acb, $Q = \Delta U_{ab} + W$

$\Rightarrow \quad 200 = \Delta U_{ab} + 80$

$\Rightarrow \quad \Delta U_{ab} = 120$ J

Along path adb, $Q = \Delta U_{ab} + W$

$\Rightarrow \quad 144 = 120 + W$

$\Rightarrow \quad W = 24$ J

(b) Along path ba, $Q = \Delta U_{ba} + W$

$= -120 + (-52) = -172$ J

(c) $\Delta U_{ab} = U_b - U_a$

$\Rightarrow \quad 120 = U_b - 40 \quad \Rightarrow \quad U_b = 160$ J

(d) $U_{db} = U_b - U_d$

$= 160 - 88 = 72$ J

Along path db, $Q = \Delta U_{db} + W$

$\Rightarrow \quad Q = 72 + 0 = 72$ J

6.3 Molar Heat Capacity of Gas

1. $C_V = \frac{fR}{2}, \quad C_p = C_V + R = \frac{fR}{2} + R$

$\gamma = \frac{C_p}{C_V}$

$\Rightarrow \quad \gamma = \frac{\frac{fR}{2} + R}{\frac{fR}{2}} \quad \Rightarrow \quad f = \frac{2}{\gamma - 1}$

2. $U = nC_VT$

$\Rightarrow \quad 1200R = 2C_V(400) \quad \Rightarrow \quad C_V = 1.5R$

$C_p = C_V + R = 1.5R + R = 2.5R$

3. $dQ = 2dU$

$\Rightarrow \quad nCdT = 2nC_VdT$

$\Rightarrow \quad C = 2C_V = 2\left(\frac{3R}{2}\right) = 3R$

4. $Q = \Delta U + W$

$\Rightarrow \quad Q = \Delta U + \frac{Q}{4}$

$\Rightarrow \quad \Delta U = \frac{3Q}{4} \quad \Rightarrow \quad nC_V\Delta T = \frac{3}{4}nC\Delta T$

$\Rightarrow \quad C = \frac{4}{3}C_V = \frac{4}{3}\left(\frac{5R}{2}\right) = \frac{10R}{3}$

5. $C_p - C_V = R$

$\Rightarrow \quad 6.90\text{ J} - 4.93\text{ J} = 8.3$

$J = \frac{8.3}{1.97} = 4.2$ J/cal

6. For 1 mole of gas, $C_p - C_V = R$

$$n = \frac{m}{M} = \frac{1}{4}$$

For 1 g of helium,

$$C_p - C_V = \frac{8.314}{4 \times 4.186} \text{ cal g}^{-1}\text{K}^{-1} = 0.5 \text{ cal g}^{-1}\text{K}^{-1}$$

6.4 Isochoric, Isobaric and Isothermal Processes

1. (a) $\Delta U = nC_V\Delta T$

$$= 2\left(\frac{5R}{2}\right)75 = 375R = 375 \times \frac{25}{3} = 3125 \text{ J}$$

(b) ΔU is independent of the nature of process.

So, $\Delta U = 3125$ J

2. At constant volume, $Q = nC_V\Delta T$

$$\therefore \quad Q = n_1C_{V_1}\Delta T + n_2C_{V_2}\Delta T$$

$$= \left(\frac{10}{2}\right)\left(\frac{5R}{2}\right)50 + \left(\frac{40}{4}\right)\left(\frac{3R}{2}\right)50$$

$$= 1375R = 1375 \times 2 = 2750 \text{ cal}$$

3. $W = p\Delta V = 4.5 \times 10^5(2 - 0.5) = 675$ kJ

$$Q = \Delta U + W$$

$$\Rightarrow \quad 800 = \Delta U + 675$$

$$\Rightarrow \quad \Delta U = 125 \text{ kJ}$$

4.

$$Q = nC_p\Delta T$$

$$\Rightarrow \quad 105 = n\left(\frac{7R}{2}\right)\Delta T$$

$$\Rightarrow \quad nR\Delta T = 30 \text{ J}$$

(a) $\Delta U = nC_V\Delta T$

$$= n\left(\frac{5R}{2}\right)\Delta T = \frac{5}{2} \times 30 = 75 \text{ J}$$

(b) $W = nR\Delta T = 30$ J

5. $\Delta U = nC_V\Delta T$, $Q = nC_p\Delta T$

$$\therefore \quad \frac{\Delta U}{Q} = \frac{nC_V\Delta T}{nC_p\Delta T} = \frac{1}{\gamma} = \frac{1}{5/3} = \frac{3}{5}$$

6. At constant pressure,

$$W = nR\Delta T = 25 \text{ J}$$

$$C_V = \frac{fR}{2} = \frac{6R}{2} = 3R,$$

$$C_p = C_V + R = 4R$$

$$Q = nC_p\Delta T = n(4R)\Delta T = 4 \times 25 = 100 \text{ J}$$

7. At constant pressure, $Q_1 = nC_p\Delta T$

At constant volume, $Q_2 = nC_V\Delta T$

$$\therefore \quad Q_1 - Q_2 = n(C_p - C_V)\Delta T$$

$$\Rightarrow \quad 70 - Q_2 = 2R(35 - 30)$$

$$\Rightarrow \quad 70 - Q_2 = 2 \times 2 \times 5 \qquad [\because R = 2 \text{ cal/mol-K}]$$

$$\Rightarrow \quad Q_2 = 50 \text{ cal}$$

8. $W = p\Delta V = 100 \times 10^3 \times (40 \times 10^{-4} \times 25 \times 10^{-2}) = 100$ J

$$Q = \Delta U + W = 10 + 100 = 110 \text{ J}$$

9. (a) $Q = nC_p\Delta T = 2\left(\frac{7R}{2}\right)(400 - 300) = 700R$

(b) $Q = nC_V\Delta T = 2\left(\frac{5R}{2}\right)(400 - 300) = 500R$

10. $W = nRT\ln\left(\frac{V_2}{V_1}\right) = 5 \times 8.314 \times 300 \ln\left(\frac{1}{5}\right)$

$$= 5 \times 8.314 \times 300 \times 2.303 \times (-0.6990)$$

$$= -2.007 \times 10^4 \text{ J}$$

11. *AB* is isochoric process and *BC* is isothermal process.

$$Q_{AB} = nC_V\Delta T$$

$$= n\left(\frac{5R}{2}\right)(T_B - T_A) = \frac{5}{2}(p_BV_B - p_AV_A)$$

$$= \frac{5}{2}(2p_0V_0 - p_0V_0) = \frac{5}{2}p_0V_0$$

$$Q_{BC} = nRT_B\ln\left(\frac{V_C}{V_B}\right) = p_BV_B\ln\left(\frac{V_C}{V_B}\right)$$

$$= 2p_0V_0\ln\left(\frac{2V_0}{V_0}\right) = 2p_0V_0\ln 2$$

$$Q_{ABC} = Q_{AB} + Q_{BC} = \left(\frac{5}{2} + 2\ln 2\right)p_0V_0 = 3.9p_0V_0$$

12. $W = p\Delta V$

$$= 10^5 \text{ Pa} \times (1671 - 1) \times 10^{-6} \text{ m}^3$$

$$= 167 \text{ J} = \frac{167}{4.18} \text{ cal} = 40 \text{ cal}$$

$$\Delta U = Q - \Delta W = 540 - 40 = 500 \text{ cal}$$

6.5 Adiabatic Process and Free Expansion

1.

$$p_1V_1^\gamma = p_2V_2^\gamma$$

$$\Rightarrow \quad p_0V_0^{5/3} = p_2\left(\frac{V_0}{8}\right)^{5/3}$$

$$\Rightarrow \quad p_2 = 32p_0$$

$$T_1V_1^{\gamma-1} = T_2V_2^{\gamma-1}$$

$$\Rightarrow \quad T_0V_0^{\frac{5}{3}-1} = T_2\left(\frac{V_0}{8}\right)^{\frac{5}{3}-1}$$

$$\Rightarrow \quad T_2 = 4T_0$$

2. $p \propto T^3 \Rightarrow Tp^{-1/3} = \text{constant}$

Comparing it with $Tp^{\frac{1-\gamma}{\gamma}} = \text{constant}$, we get

$$\frac{1-\gamma}{\gamma} = -\frac{1}{3} \quad \Rightarrow \quad \gamma = \frac{3}{2}$$

3. $T_1 = 300\text{ K}, p_1 = 6 \text{ atm}, p_2 = 1 \text{ atm}, T_2 = ?$

$$T_1p_1^{\frac{1-\gamma}{\gamma}} = T_2p_2^{\frac{1-\gamma}{\gamma}}$$

$\Rightarrow \quad 300(6)^{\frac{1-1.4}{1.4}} = T_2(1)^{\frac{1-1.4}{1.4}}$

$\Rightarrow \quad T_2 = 300 \times 6^{-2/7}$

$= 300 \times 0.6 = 180\,K = -93°\,C$

4. $pV^{\gamma} = \text{constant}$

$\Rightarrow \quad \frac{\Delta p}{p} \times 100 + \gamma\left(\frac{\Delta V}{V} \times 100\right) = 0$

$\Rightarrow \quad \frac{\Delta V}{V} \times 100 = -\frac{1}{\gamma}\left(\frac{\Delta p}{p} \times 100\right) = -\frac{1}{3/2} \times \frac{2}{3} = -\frac{4}{9}\%$

So, volume decreases by $\frac{4}{9}\%$.

5. (a) For isothermal process,

$p_1V_1 = p_2V_2$

$\Rightarrow 200 \times 800 = p_2 \times 200$

$\Rightarrow \quad p_2 = 800\text{ kPa}$

$T_2 = T_1 = 100\,K$

(b) For adiabatic process,

$p_1V_1^{\gamma} = p_2V_2^{\gamma}$

$\Rightarrow \quad 200 \times (800)^{1.5} = p_2(200)^{1.5}$

$\Rightarrow \quad p_2 = 200(4)^{3/2} = 1600\text{ kPa}$

$T_1V_1^{\gamma-1} = T_2V_2^{\gamma-1}$

$\Rightarrow 100 \times (800)^{1.5-1} = T_2 \times (200)^{1.5-1}$

$\Rightarrow \quad T_2 = 100(4)^{0.5} = 200\,K$

6. (a) $\quad T_1V_1^{\gamma-1} = T_2V_2^{\gamma-1}$

$\Rightarrow \quad 300V^{\frac{5}{3}-1} = T_2(2V)^{\frac{5}{3}-1}$

$\Rightarrow \quad T_2 = 300 \times 2^{-2/3}$

$= 300 \times 0.63 = 189\,K = -84°\,C$

(b) $\Delta U = nC_V\Delta T = 2\left(\frac{3R}{2}\right)(-84 - 27) = -2775\text{ J}$

(c) $W = -\Delta U = 2775\text{ J}$

7. For isochoric process,

$Q = nC_V\Delta T$

$\Rightarrow \quad 25R = nC_V(310 - 300)$

$\Rightarrow \quad nC_V(10) = 25R$

For adiabatic process,

$W = -\Delta U = -nC_V\Delta T$

$= -nC_V(300 - 310) = 25R$

8. For isothermal process,

$\text{Slope} = \frac{dp}{dV} = -\frac{p}{V}$

For adiabatic process,

$\text{Slope} = \frac{dp}{dV} = -\gamma\left(\frac{p}{V}\right)$

Since $\gamma > 1$, magnitude of slope of p-V curve will be greater for adiabatic process.

(a) Graph 2 is steeper than graph 1. So, graph 2 will be of adiabatic process and graph 1 will be of isothermal process.

(b) Graph 1 is steeper than graph 2. So, 1-adiabatic, 2-isothermal.

9. For isobaric process,

$p_B = p_f$

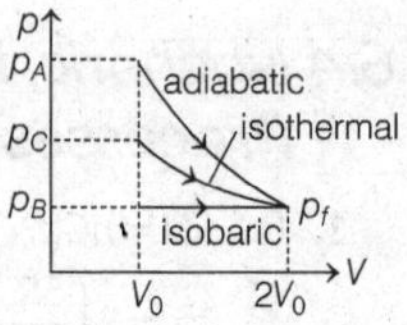

For isothermal process,

$p_1V_1 = p_2V_2$

$\Rightarrow \quad p_CV_0 = p_f(2V_0)$

$\Rightarrow \quad p_C = 2p_f$

For adiabatic process,

$p_1V_1^{\gamma} = p_2V_2^{\gamma}$

$\Rightarrow \quad p_A(V_0)^{3/2} = p_f(2V_0)^{3/2}$

$\Rightarrow \quad p_A = 2\sqrt{2}\,p_f$

$\therefore \quad p_A : p_B : p_C = 2\sqrt{2} : 1 : 2$

10. Since the gas expands freely, $W = 0$

Since no heat is given to gas, $Q = 0$

$Q = \Delta U + W$

$0 = \Delta U + 0 \quad \Rightarrow \quad \Delta U = 0$

$\therefore \quad T_{\text{final}} = T_0$

Since the process is isothermal,

$p_0V_0 = p_{\text{final}} \times 2V_0 \quad \Rightarrow \quad p_{\text{final}} = \frac{p_0}{2}$

6.6 Polytropic Process

1. $C = C_V + \frac{R}{1-m} = \frac{3R}{2} + \frac{R}{1-\frac{1}{2}} = 3.5R$

2. $p = KV^a \quad \Rightarrow \quad pV^{-a} = K$

So, $\quad m = -a$

$C = C_V + \frac{R}{1-m}$

$\Rightarrow \quad 0 = \frac{R}{\gamma - 1} + \frac{R}{1-(-a)}$

$\Rightarrow \quad a = -\gamma$

3. $p\sqrt{T} = \text{constant}$

$\Rightarrow \quad p\left(\frac{pV}{nR}\right)^{1/2} = \text{constant}$

$\Rightarrow \quad pV^{1/3} = \text{constant}$

$\therefore \quad m = \frac{1}{3}$

$C = C_V + \frac{R}{1-m} = \frac{5R}{2} + \frac{R}{1-\frac{1}{3}} = 4R$

4. $p \propto V \quad \Rightarrow \quad pV^{-1} = \text{constant}$

$\therefore \quad m = -1$

$$C = C_V + \frac{R}{1-m} = \frac{3R}{2} + \frac{R}{1-(-1)} = 2R$$

(a) $W = \frac{nR\Delta T}{1-m} = \frac{2R(50-20)}{1-(-1)} = 30R = 30 \times \frac{25}{3} = 250 \text{ J}$

(b) $Q = nC\Delta T = 2(2R)(50-20) = 120R = 120 \times \frac{25}{3} = 1000 \text{ J}$

6.7 Cyclic Process

1. (a) For the cyclic process,

$$Q = Q_1 + Q_2 + Q_3 + Q_4$$
$$= 5960 - 5585 - 2980 + 3645$$
$$= 1040 \text{ J}$$
$$Q = \Delta U + W$$

$\Rightarrow \quad 1040 = 0 + (W_1 + W_2 + W_3 + W_4)$

$\Rightarrow \quad 1040 = 0 + (2200 - 825 - 1100 + W_4)$

$\Rightarrow \quad W_4 = 765 \text{ J}$

(b) $\eta = \frac{\text{Work done}}{\text{Heat input}} = \frac{1040}{5960 + 3645} = \frac{208}{1921}$

2. $W_{AB} = 0,$

$$W_{BC} = nR(2T_0)\ln\left(\frac{2V_0}{V_0}\right) = 2nRT_0 \ln 2$$

$W_{CD} = 0,$

$$W_{DA} = nRT_0 \ln\left(\frac{V_0}{2V_0}\right) = -nRT_0 \ln 2$$

$$W = W_{AB} + W_{BC} + W_{CD} + W_{DA}$$
$$= 0 + 2nRT_0 \ln 2 + 0 - nRT_0 \ln 2 = nRT_0 \ln 2$$

3. $A \rightarrow B$: Isochoric process

$B \rightarrow C$: Isobaric process

$C \rightarrow D$: Isochoric process

$D \rightarrow A$: Isobaric process

$$W_{AB} = W_{CD} = 0$$
$$W_{BC} = nR(T_C - T_B) = nR(T_3 - T_2)$$
$$W_{DA} = nR(T_A - T_D) = nR(T_1 - T_4)$$
$$W = W_{AB} + W_{BC} + W_{CD} + W_{DA}$$
$$= nR(T_1 + T_3 - T_2 - T_4)$$

4. $Q_{AB} = nC_V(T_B - T_A)$

$$= n\left(\frac{5R}{2}\right)(T_B - T_A) = \frac{5}{2}(p_B V_B - p_A V_A)$$

$$= \frac{5}{2}(2p_0V_0 - p_0V_0) = 2.5\,p_0V_0$$

$Q_{BC} = nC_P(T_C - T_B)$

$$= n\left(\frac{7R}{2}\right)(T_C - T_B) = \frac{7}{2}(p_C V_C - p_B V_B)$$

$$= \frac{7}{2}[(2p_0)(2V_0) - (2p_0)V_0] = 7p_0V_0$$

$Q_{CD} = nC_V(T_D - T_C) = -5p_0V_0$

$Q_{DA} = nC_P(T_A - T_D) = -3.5p_0V_0$

Q_1 = Heat input

$$= 2.5p_0V_0 + 7p_0V_0 = 9.5p_0V_0$$

Q_2 = Heat rejected

$$= 5p_0V_0 + 3.5p_0V_0 = 8.5p_0V_0$$

$$\eta = 1 - \frac{Q_2}{Q_1} = 1 - \frac{8.5p_0V_0}{9.5p_0V_0} = \frac{2}{19}$$

5. (a)

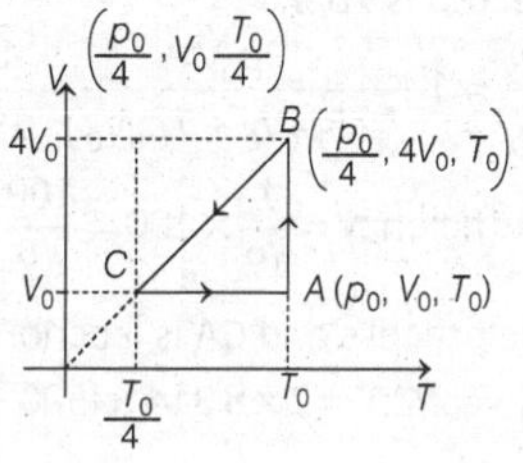

(b) $W_{AB} = nRT_0 \ln\left(\frac{4V_0}{V_0}\right) = 2nRT_0 \ln 2 = 2p_0V_0 \ln 2$

$$W_{BC} = nR\left(\frac{T_0}{4} - T_0\right) = -\frac{3}{4}nRT_0 = -\frac{3p_0V_0}{4}$$

$$W_{CA} = 0$$

$$W = W_{AB} + W_{BC} + W_{CA} = p_0V_0\left(2\ln 2 - \frac{3}{4}\right)$$

$$= p_0V_0[2(0.693) - 0.75] = 0.636p_0V_0$$

6. (a) $W_{ab} = 800 \text{ J}, Q_{ab} = 0,$

$Q_{bc} = -100 \text{ J}, Q_{ca} = 500 \text{ J}$

$Q_{ab} = \Delta U_{ab} + W_{ab}$

$\Rightarrow \quad 0 = (U_b - 1000) + 800$

$\Rightarrow \quad U_b = 200 \text{ J}$

$Q_{ca} = \Delta U_{ca} + W_{ca}$

$\Rightarrow \quad 500 = (U_c - 1000) + 0$

$\Rightarrow \quad U_c = 500 \text{ J}$

(b) $Q_{bc} = \Delta U_{bc} + W_{bc}$

$\Rightarrow -100 = (500 - 200) + W_{bc}$

$\Rightarrow \quad W_{bc} = -400 \text{ J}$

7. (a) $\tan\theta = \frac{p_0}{V_0} = \frac{2p_0}{V_C}$

$\Rightarrow \quad V_C = 2V_0$

(b) $T_{max} = T_C = \frac{p_C V_C}{nR} = \frac{(2p_0)(2V_0)}{nR} = 4T_0$

(c) For cyclic process $ABCA$,

$$Q = \Delta U + W = 0 + \frac{1}{2}(2V_0 - V_0)(2p_0 - p_0) = \frac{p_0V_0}{2}$$

(d) $Q_{AB} = nC_V(T_B - T_A) = n\left(\frac{5R}{2}\right)(T_B - T_A)$

$$= \frac{5}{2}(p_B V_B - p_A V_A) = 2.5p_0V_0$$

$$Q_{BC} = nC_P(T_C - T_B) = \frac{7}{2}(p_C V_C - p_B V_B) = 7p_0V_0$$

For cyclic process *ABCA*,

$$Q = \Delta U + W$$

$\Rightarrow$ $Q_{AB} + Q_{BC} + Q_{CA} = 0 + \text{Area of } \Delta ABC$

$\Rightarrow$ $2.5p_0V_0 + 7p_0V_0 + Q_{CA} = \frac{1}{2}p_0V_0$

$\Rightarrow$ $Q_{CA} = -9p_0V_0$

So, heat rejected is $9p_0V_0$.

(e) $\eta = 1 - \frac{Q_2}{Q_1} = 1 - \frac{9p_0V_0}{2.5p_0V_0 + 7p_0V_0} = \frac{1}{19}$

Percentage efficiency $= \frac{1}{19} \times 100 = \frac{100}{19}\%$

8. *AB* is isobaric process and *CA* is isochoric process.

$W_{AB} = nR\Delta T = 2 \times 8.314 \times (500 - 300) = 3326\text{ J}$

$W_{CA} = 0$

For cyclic process *ABCA*,

$Q = \Delta U + W$

$\Rightarrow$ $-1200 = 0 + (3326 + W_{BC} + 0)$

$\Rightarrow$ $W_{BC} = -4526\text{ J}$

6.8 Heat Engine and Heat Pump

1. $\eta = 1 - \frac{T_2}{T_1}$

$\Rightarrow$ $\frac{40}{100} = 1 - \frac{300}{T_1}$

$\Rightarrow$ $T_1 = 500\text{ K} = 227°\text{C}$

2. (a) $\eta = 1 - \frac{T_2}{T_1} = 1 - \frac{300}{900} = \frac{2}{3}$

Percentage efficiency $= \frac{2}{3} \times 100 = 66.7\%$

(b) $\eta = \frac{W}{Q_1}$

$\Rightarrow$ $\frac{2}{3} = \frac{W}{10^3 \times 10^3 \times 4.2}$

$\Rightarrow$ $W = 2.8 \times 10^6\text{ J}$

3. $\eta = 1 - \frac{T_2}{T_1}$

$\Rightarrow$ $\frac{50}{100} = 1 - \frac{280}{T_1} \Rightarrow T_1 = 560\text{ K}$

$\eta' = 1 - \frac{T_2}{T'_1}$

$\Rightarrow$ $\frac{70}{100} = 1 - \frac{280}{T'_1}$

$\Rightarrow$ $T'_1 = 933.3\text{ K}$

$\Delta T = T'_1 - T_1 = 933.3 - 560 = 373.3\text{ K}$

4. (a) $\beta = \frac{T_2}{T_1 - T_2} = \frac{273}{300 - 273} = 10.1$

(b) Heat extracted $= Q_2 = mL_f = 10 \times 80 = 800\text{ kcal}$

$\beta = \frac{Q_2}{W} \Rightarrow 10.1 = \frac{800}{W}$

$\Rightarrow$ $W = 79\text{ kcal}$

Energy needed, $Q_1 = Q_2 + W = 800 + 79 = 879\text{ kcal}$

5. $\frac{Q_1}{Q_2} = \frac{T_1}{T_2} \Rightarrow \frac{Q_1}{750} = \frac{300}{250}$

$\Rightarrow$ $Q_1 = 900\text{ cal}$

6. (a) $\beta = \frac{Q_2}{W} \Rightarrow 5 = \frac{250}{W}$

$\Rightarrow$ $W = 50\text{ J}$

(b) $Q_1 = Q_2 + W = 250 + 50 = 300\text{ J}$

Level-2

Single Choice Correct Questions

1. $Q = \Delta U + W$

$\Rightarrow$ $16 = \Delta U + 20 \Rightarrow \Delta U = -4\text{ kJ}$

$Q = \Delta U + W$

$\Rightarrow$ $9 = -4 + W \Rightarrow W = 13\text{ kJ}$

2. $B \to A$: Adiabatic process $\Rightarrow Q_{BA} = 0$

$Q_{BA} = \Delta U_{BA} + W_{BA}$

$\Rightarrow$ $0 = \Delta U_{BA} + (-30)$

$\Rightarrow$ $\Delta U_{BA} = 30\text{ J}$

$\Delta U_{AB} = -\Delta U_{BA} = -30\text{ J}$

3. W = Area under *p-V* curve

As gas expands, area continuously increases. So, work done by the gas continuously increases.

4. $\Delta U_{12} = nC_V(T_2 - T_1) = n\left(\frac{3R}{2}\right)(T_2 - T_1)$

$= \frac{3}{2}(p_2V_2 - p_1V_1) = 150\text{ kJ}$

W_{12} = Area under *p-V* curve

$= \frac{1}{2}\left(10^6 + \frac{1}{2} \times 10^6\right) \times 0.3 = 225\text{ kJ}$

$Q_{12} = \Delta U_{12} + W_{12} = 150 + 225 = 375\text{ kJ}$

5. $W_{AB} = -$ Area under line *AB*

$= -\frac{1}{2}(2p_0 + p_0)(2V_0 - V_0) = -\frac{3}{2}p_0V_0$

W_{BC} = Area under line *BC*

$= \frac{1}{2}(2p_0 + 3p_0)(3V_0 - V_0) = 5p_0V_0$

$W_{ABC} = W_{AB} + W_{BC} = -\frac{3}{2}p_0V_0 + 5p_0V_0 = \frac{7}{2}p_0V_0$

6. For cyclic process, $Q = \Delta U + W$

$= 0 + \text{Area of cycle}$

$= \text{Area of cycle}$

$$= \pi\left(\frac{30-10}{2}\right)\times 10^3\,\text{Pa}\times\left(\frac{30-10}{2}\right)\times 10^{-3}\,\text{m}^3$$

$$= 10^2\pi\,\text{J}$$

7. $v_{rms} \propto \sqrt{T}$

$$\Rightarrow \quad \frac{v'_{rms}}{v_{rms}} = \sqrt{\frac{T'}{T}} \quad \Rightarrow \quad \frac{1.5\,v_{rms}}{v_{rms}} = \sqrt{\frac{T'}{T}}$$

$$\Rightarrow \quad T' = 2.25T = 675\,\text{K}$$

At constant volume,

$$Q = n_1 C_{V_1}\Delta T + n_2 C_{V_2}\Delta T$$

$$= \left(\frac{4}{4}\right)\left(\frac{3R}{2}\right)(675-300) + \left(\frac{28}{28}\right)\left(\frac{5R}{2}\right)(675-300)$$

$$= 1500R$$

8. For isobaric process,

$$\frac{Q}{W} = \frac{nC_p\Delta T}{nR\Delta T} = \frac{5R/2}{R} = \frac{5}{2}$$

9. At constant pressure, $Q = nC_p\Delta T$

$$\Rightarrow \quad \frac{7}{2}RT_0 = 10\left(\frac{7R}{2}\right)(T_2 - T_0)$$

$$\Rightarrow \quad T_2 = 1.1T_0$$

$$V \propto T \quad \Rightarrow \quad \frac{V_1}{T_1} = \frac{V_2}{T_2}$$

$$\Rightarrow \quad \frac{V_0}{T_0} = \frac{V_2}{1.1T_0} \quad \Rightarrow \quad V_2 = 1.1V_0$$

10. For A, $Q_1 = nC_p\Delta T = n\left(\frac{7R}{2}\right)(30)$

For B, $Q_2 = nC_V\Delta T = n\left(\frac{5R}{2}\right)\Delta T$

$$Q_1 = Q_2$$

$$\Rightarrow \quad n\left(\frac{7R}{2}\right)(30) = n\left(\frac{5R}{2}\right)\Delta T \quad \Rightarrow \quad \Delta T = 42\,\text{K}$$

11. At constant volume, $Q = nC_V\Delta T$

$$\Rightarrow \quad 6300 = nC_V(150)$$

When the temperature changes by 300 K,

$$\Delta U = nC_V\Delta T = nC_V(300)$$

$$= 2\times 6300 = 12600\,\text{J}$$

12. For $A \to B, T \propto p$

So, temperature will also decrease by a factor of n.

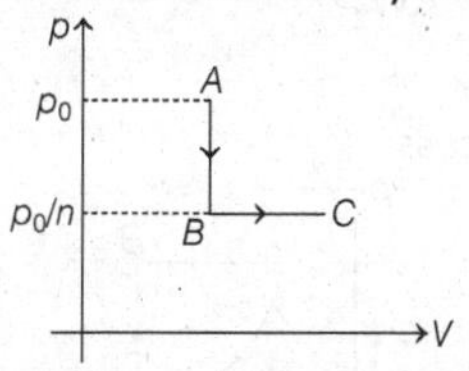

$$\therefore \quad T_A = T, T_B = \frac{T}{n}, T_C = T$$

$$Q = Q_{AB} + Q_{BC} = nC_V\Delta T + nC_p\Delta T$$

$$= (1)C_V\left(\frac{T}{n} - T\right) + (1)C_p\left(T - \frac{T}{n}\right)$$

$$= (C_p - C_V)T(1 - n^{-1}) = RT(1 - n^{-1})$$

13. $\Delta W_1 = \Delta W_2 = nR(T_2 - T_1) = p_0(2V_0) - p_0V_0 = p_0V_0$

$$\Delta Q_1 = nC_p\Delta T = n\left(\frac{5R}{2}\right)(T_2 - T_1) = \frac{5}{2}p_0V_0$$

$$\Delta Q_2 = nC_p\Delta T = n\left(\frac{7R}{2}\right)(T_2 - T_1) = \frac{7}{2}p_0V_0$$

$$\Delta U_1 = nC_V\Delta T = n\left(\frac{3R}{2}\right)(T_2 - T_1) = \frac{3}{2}p_0V_0$$

$$\Delta U_2 = nC_V\Delta T = n\left(\frac{5R}{2}\right)(T_2 - T_1) = \frac{5}{2}p_0V_0$$

14. $Q_{AB} = nC_V\Delta T = n\left(\frac{5R}{2}\right)(2T_0 - T_0) = \frac{5}{2}nRT_0$

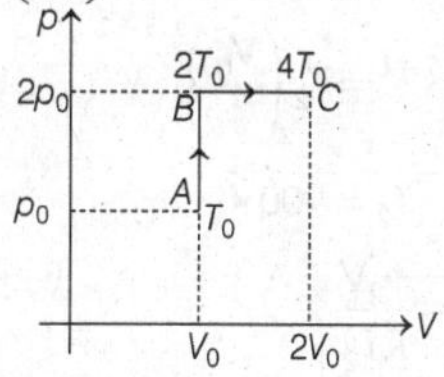

$$Q_{BC} = nC_p\Delta T = n\left(\frac{7R}{2}\right)(4T_0 - 2T_0) = 7nRT_0$$

For process ABC, $C = \dfrac{\Delta Q}{n\Delta T} = \dfrac{\frac{5}{2}nRT_0 + 7nRT_0}{n(4T_0 - T_0)} = \dfrac{19R}{6}$

15. AB is isothermal compression,

$$\therefore \quad \Delta U_{AB} = 0, \; W_{AB} < 0, \; Q_{AB} < 0$$

BC is isobaric cooling. So, temperature decreases.

$$\therefore \quad \Delta U_{BC} < 0$$

16. $C_p - C_V = R$

So, both C_p and C_V increase by the same amount.

17. $\rho \propto \dfrac{1}{T} \quad \Rightarrow \quad \dfrac{pM}{RT} \propto \dfrac{1}{T}$

$$\Rightarrow \quad p = \text{constant}$$

So, the process is isobaric.

$$\therefore \quad W = nR\Delta T$$

$$C = C_p = 33.24 = 4R$$

$$\therefore \quad C_V = C_p - R = 3R$$

$$C_V = \frac{fR}{2} \quad \Rightarrow \quad 3R = \frac{fR}{2} \quad \Rightarrow \quad f = 6$$

$$\gamma = \frac{C_p}{C_V} = \frac{4R}{3R} = 1.33$$

18. $C = nC_V$

$$\Rightarrow \quad 35 = n\left(\frac{3}{2}\times\frac{25}{3}\right) \quad \Rightarrow \quad n = 2.8$$

$$U = nC_VT = 35\times 273\,\text{J}$$

$$C_p = \frac{5R}{2} = \frac{5}{2}\times\frac{25}{3} = \frac{125}{6}\,\text{J/mol-K}$$

19. $pA = Kx_1 \quad \Rightarrow \quad \left(\frac{nRT}{V}\right)A = Kx_1$

$$\Rightarrow \quad \left(\frac{1 \times 8.3 \times 100}{0.83}\right)10^{-2} = 100x$$

$$\Rightarrow \quad x_1 = 0.1\,\text{m}$$

Final compression,

$$x_2 = 0.1 + 0.1 = 0.2\,\text{m}$$

$$W_{gas} = \Delta U_{spring}$$

$$= \frac{1}{2} \times 100 \times (0.2)^2 - \frac{1}{2} \times 100 \times (0.1)^2$$

$$= 1.5\,\text{J}$$

20. $\frac{\Delta p}{p} \times 100 = -\gamma\left(\frac{\Delta V}{V} \times 100\right) = -\frac{7}{5}(5\%) = -7\%$

21. $T_1V_1^{\gamma-1} = T_2V_2^{\gamma-1}$

$$\Rightarrow \quad 300V_0^{1.5-1} = T_2\left(\frac{V_0}{9}\right)^{1.5-1}$$

$$\Rightarrow \quad T_2 = 900\,\text{K}$$

22. $n = \frac{p_1V}{RT_1}$ and $\frac{n}{2} = \frac{p_2V}{RT_2}$

$$\therefore \quad \frac{p_2}{p_1} = \frac{1}{2}\left(\frac{T_2}{T_1}\right)$$

As the tank is insulated, the process is adiabatic.

$$T_2 = T_1\left(\frac{p_2}{p_1}\right)^{\frac{\gamma-1}{\gamma}}$$

$$\Rightarrow \quad \frac{T_2}{T_1} = \left(\frac{1}{2}\frac{T_2}{T_1}\right)^{\frac{(5/3)-1}{(5/3)}}$$

$$\Rightarrow \quad T_2 = \frac{T_1}{2^{2/3}} = \frac{320}{1.6} = 200\,\text{K} = -73°\text{C}$$

23. For mixture of gas,

$$C_{V_{mix}} = \frac{n_1C_{V_1} + n_2C_{V_2}}{n_1 + n_2} = \frac{\left(\frac{4}{32}\right)\left(\frac{5R}{2}\right) + \left(\frac{2}{4}\right)\left(\frac{3R}{2}\right)}{\frac{4}{32} + \frac{2}{4}} = \frac{17}{10}R$$

Also, $C_V = \frac{R}{\gamma - 1} \quad \Rightarrow \quad \frac{17R}{10} = \frac{R}{\gamma_{mix} - 1}$

$$\Rightarrow \quad \gamma_{mix} = \frac{27}{17}$$

$$T_1V_1^{\gamma-1} = T_2V_2^{\gamma-1}$$

$$\Rightarrow \quad 390(20)^{\frac{27}{17}-1} = T_2(30)^{\frac{27}{17}-1}$$

$$\Rightarrow \quad T_2 = 390\left(\frac{2}{3}\right)^{10/17}$$

24. $U = a + bpV = a + bnRT$

$$\Rightarrow \quad dU = nRbdT$$

Comparing it with $dU = nC_VdT$, we get

$$C_V = bR$$

Also, $C_V = \frac{R}{\gamma - 1}$

$$\Rightarrow \quad bR = \frac{1}{\gamma - 1} \quad \Rightarrow \quad \gamma = \frac{b+1}{b}$$

25. For isobaric process, $W = nR\Delta T$

For adiabatic process, $W = -nC_V\Delta T$

$$\Rightarrow \quad |W| = \frac{nR\Delta T}{\gamma - 1}$$

$$\gamma_{argon} = 1.67 \text{ and } \gamma_{N_2} = 1.4$$

So, slope of $|W|$ *versus* T graph will be least for isobaric process. So, line 4 corresponds to isobaric process.

26. $1 \rightarrow 3$: Adiabatic process,

$3 \rightarrow 2$: Isochoric process

For adiabatic process,

$$Q = \Delta U + W$$

$$\Rightarrow \quad 0 = (U_3 - U_1) + W$$

$$\Rightarrow \quad -W = U_3 - U_1 \quad \text{...(i)}$$

For isochoric process,

$$Q = \Delta U + W$$

$$\Rightarrow \quad Q = (U_2 - U_3) + 0 \quad \text{...(ii)}$$

Adding Eqs. (i) and (ii), we get

$$Q - W = U_2 - U_1$$

27. $\frac{dp}{dV} = -\gamma\left(\frac{p}{V}\right)$

Since, $\gamma_{He} > \gamma_{H_2}$, magnitude of slope of p-V graph will be greater for He. Therefore, A corresponds to He and B corresponds to H_2.

28. From graph, $p_1 > p_2$

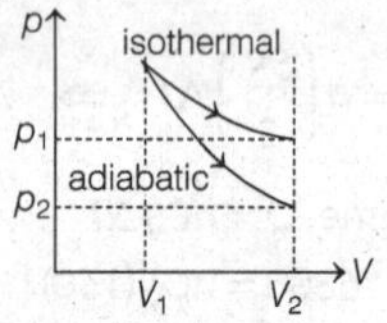

$$\Rightarrow \quad \frac{nRT_1}{V_2} > \frac{nRT_2}{V_2} \quad \Rightarrow \quad T_1 > T_2$$

29. $p_1 > p_2$

30. ΔW = Area under p-V graph

So, $\quad \Delta W_1 > \Delta W_2$

31. (a)

32. For cyclic process,

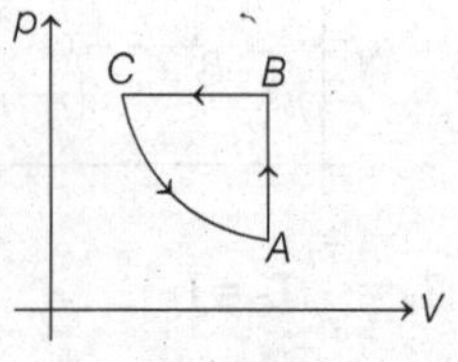

$$Q = \Delta U + W$$

$\Rightarrow \; Q_{AB} + Q_{BC} + Q_{CA} = 0 + (W_{AB} + W_{BC} + W_{CA})$

$\Rightarrow \; (200 - 100 + 0) = 0 + (0 - 50 + W_{CA})$

$\Rightarrow \; W_{CA} = 150 \text{ kJ}$

33. $Q = nRT \ln\left(\frac{V_f}{V_i}\right)$

From graph, $V_i = 0.1 \text{ m}^3$, $V_f = 0.3 \text{ m}^3$ and $Q = 15 \text{ kJ}$

$\therefore \; 15 \times 10^3 = 0.5\left(\frac{25}{3}\right) T \ln\left(\frac{0.3}{0.1}\right)$

$\Rightarrow \; T = 360 \text{ K}$

34. As the gas expands freely, no work is done.

$Q = \Delta U + W \; \Rightarrow \; 0 = \Delta U + 0$

$\Rightarrow \; \Delta U = 0$

So, internal energy and temperature remain constant.

$p_0 V_0 = pV$

$\Rightarrow \; p_0 V_0 = p(2V_0) \; \Rightarrow \; p = \frac{p_0}{2}$

35. $U = nC_V T$

So, U *versus* p will be same as T *versus* p graph.

36. For isochoric process, $Q = nC_V \Delta T = n\left(\frac{fR}{2}\right)\Delta T = \left(\frac{f}{2}\right)(\Delta p) V$

As Δp is same for both the processes, Q will be more for the process taking place at higher volume.

$\therefore \; Q_{CD} > Q_{AB}$

37. $\frac{pT^2}{V} = \text{constant}$

$\Rightarrow \; \frac{p}{V}\left(\frac{pV}{nR}\right)^2 = \text{constant}$

$\Rightarrow \; pV^{1/3} = \text{constant}$

$\therefore \; m = \frac{1}{3}$

$C = C_V + \frac{R}{1-m} = \frac{5R}{2} + \frac{R}{1 - \frac{1}{3}} = 4R$

38. $p \propto V \; \Rightarrow \; pV^{-1} = \text{constant}$

$\therefore \; m = -1$

$C = C_V + \frac{R}{1-m} = \frac{3R}{2} + \frac{R}{1-(-1)} = 2R$

39. $C = C_V + \frac{R}{1-n}$

$\Rightarrow \; C = \frac{R}{\gamma - 1} + \frac{R}{1-n} < 0$

$\Rightarrow \; \frac{(\gamma - n)R}{(\gamma - 1)(1-n)} < 0$

As, $\gamma > 1, \; \gamma > n > 1$

40. $C = \frac{Q}{n\Delta T} = \frac{\Delta U + W}{n\Delta T} = \frac{nC_V \Delta T + W}{n\Delta T} = C_V + \frac{W}{n\Delta T}$

As gas is expanding, $W > 0$

$\therefore \; C > C_V$

41. $p \propto V^{2/3} \; \Rightarrow \; pV^{-2/3} = \text{constant}$

So, $m = -\frac{2}{3}$

Work done for polytropic process,

$W = \frac{nR\Delta T}{1-m} = \frac{1 \times (25/3) \times 30}{1 - \left(-\frac{2}{3}\right)} = 150 \text{ J}$

42. $VT^2 = \text{constant}$

$\Rightarrow \; V\left(\frac{pV}{nR}\right)^2 = \text{constant}$

$\Rightarrow \; pV^{3/2} = \text{constant}$

$p_0 V_0^{3/2} = pV^{3/2}$

$\Rightarrow \; p_0 V_0^{3/2} = p\left(\frac{V_0}{4}\right)^{3/2}$

$\Rightarrow \; p = 8p_0$

$\therefore \; \Delta p = p - p_0 = 8p_0 - p_0 = 7p_0$

$\Delta U = nC_V \Delta T$

$= n\left(\frac{5R}{2}\right)(T - T_0) = \frac{5}{2}(pV - p_0 V_0)$

$= \frac{5}{2}\left[(8p_0)\left(\frac{V_0}{4}\right) - p_0 V_0\right] = 2.5 p_0 V_0$

$W = \frac{nR(T - T_0)}{1-m} = \frac{p_0 V_0}{1 - \frac{3}{2}} = -2p_0 V_0$

$Q = \Delta U + W = 2.5p_0 V_0 - 2p_0 V_0 = \frac{p_0 V_0}{2}$

43. $C_{V_{mix}} = \frac{n_1 C_{V_1} + n_2 C_{V_2}}{n_1 + n_2} = \frac{1\left(\frac{3R}{2}\right) + 1\left(\frac{5R}{2}\right)}{1+1} = 2R$

Also, $C_V = \frac{R}{\gamma - 1}$

$\Rightarrow \; 2R = \frac{R}{\gamma_{mix} - 1} \; \Rightarrow \; \gamma_{mix} = 1.5$

44. $T_A = \frac{p_0 V_0}{nR} = T_0,$

$T_B = \frac{p_0 (2V_0)}{nR} = 2T_0,$

$T_C = \frac{(p_0/2)(2V_0)}{nR} = T_0$

$Q = Q_{AB} + Q_{BC} = (1)\left(\frac{5R}{2}\right)(2T_0 - T_0) + (1)\left(\frac{3R}{2}\right)(T_0 - 2T_0) = RT_0$

$W = W_{AB} + W_{BC} = p_0(2V_0 - V_0) + 0 = p_0 V_0$

$\Delta U = nC_V (T_C - T_A) = 0$

45. $\Delta Q_{AB} = \Delta U_{AB} + \Delta W_{AB}$

$\Rightarrow \quad 150 = \Delta U_{AB} + 40 \Rightarrow \Delta U_{AB} = 110$ J

$\Delta Q_{BC} = \Delta U_{BC} + \Delta W_{BC}$

$\Rightarrow \quad 10 = 50 + \Delta W_{BC} \Rightarrow \Delta W_{BC} = -40$ J

For cyclic process,

$\Delta U = \Delta U_{AB} + \Delta U_{BC} + \Delta U_{CA} = 0$

$\Rightarrow \quad 110 + 50 + \Delta U_{CA} = 0$

$\Rightarrow \quad \Delta U = -160$ J

46. On *p-V* graph :

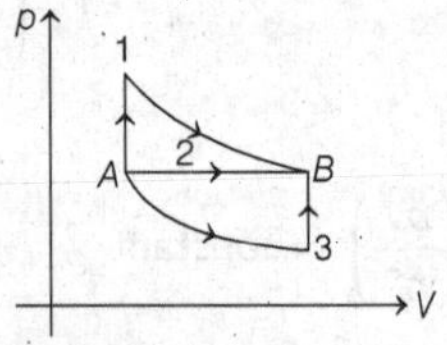

W = Area under *p-V* graph

$\therefore \quad W_1 > W_2 > W_3$

47. $T_A = \dfrac{p_0V_0}{nR} = T_0,$

$T_B = \dfrac{(3p_0)V_0}{nR} = 3T_0,$

$T_C = \dfrac{(3p_0)(2V_0)}{nR} = 6T_0,$

$T_D = \dfrac{p_0(2V_0)}{nR} = 2T_0$

$Q_{AB} = nC_V\Delta T = n\left(\dfrac{3R}{2}\right)(3T_0 - T_0) = 3nRT_0$

$Q_{BC} = nC_p\Delta T = n\left(\dfrac{5R}{2}\right)(6T_0 - 3T_0) = 7.5nRT_0$

$Q_{CD} = nC_V\Delta T = n\left(\dfrac{3R}{2}\right)(2T_0 - 6T_0) = -6nRT_0$

$Q_{DA} = nC_p\Delta T = n\left(\dfrac{5R}{2}\right)(T_0 - 2T_0) = -2.5nRT_0$

Heat input $= Q_1 = 3nRT_0 + 7.5nRT_0 = 10.5nRT_0$

Heat rejected $= Q_2 = 6nRT_0 + 2.5nRT_0 = 8.5nRT_0$

$$\eta = 1 - \frac{Q_2}{Q_1} = 1 - \frac{8.5nRT_0}{10.5nRT_0} = \frac{4}{21}$$

48.

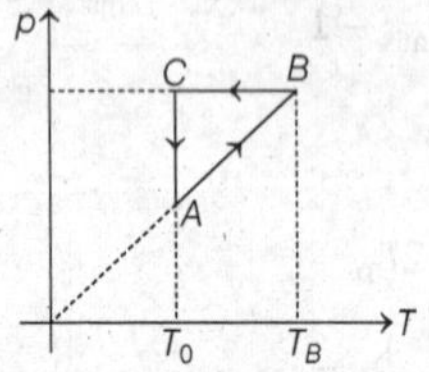

$Q_{BC} = nC_V\Delta T = n\left(\dfrac{5R}{2}\right)(T_0 - T_B)$

$W_{AB} = nR\Delta T = nR(T_B - T_0)$

$\therefore \quad \dfrac{|Q_{BC}|}{W_{AB}} = 2.5$

49. $T_a = \dfrac{p_0V_0}{nR}$

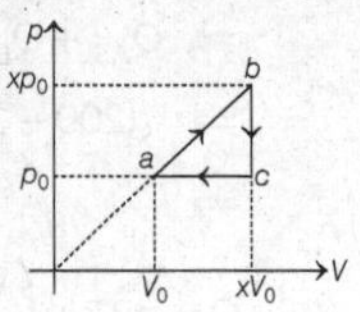

$T_b = \dfrac{(xp_0)(xV_0)}{nR} = x^2\dfrac{p_0V_0}{nR}$

$T_c = \dfrac{p_0(xV_0)}{nR} = x\dfrac{p_0V_0}{nR}$

$\therefore \quad T_c = (T_aT_b)^{1/2}$

50. (d)

51. $\rho = \dfrac{m}{V} \quad \Rightarrow \quad \rho \propto \dfrac{1}{V}$

So, ρ *versus* V graph will be rectangular hyperbola.

52. $W = W_{AB} + W_{BC} + W_{CD} + W_{DA}$

$= nR(T_B - T_A) + 0 + nR(T_D - T_C) + 0$

$= 4(2)(500 - 300) + 0 + 4(2)(450 - 600) + 0$

$= 400$ cal

53. $V_A = V_C$ and $V_B = V_D$

$W_{AB} = nRT_1 \ln\left(\dfrac{V_B}{V_A}\right)$

$W_{CD} = nRT_2 \ln\left(\dfrac{V_D}{V_C}\right) = nRT_2 \ln\left(\dfrac{V_B}{V_A}\right)$

$W_{AB} = 2W_{CD}$

$\Rightarrow \quad nRT_1 \ln\left(\dfrac{V_B}{V_A}\right) = 2nRT_2 \ln\left(\dfrac{V_B}{V_A}\right)$

$\Rightarrow \quad \dfrac{T_1}{T_2} = 2$

54. $W_{AB} = p\Delta V = 20(2 - 1) = 20$ J

$W_{BC} = 0$

For the cyclic process, $Q = \Delta U + W$

$\Rightarrow \quad 5 = 0 + (20 + 0 + W_{CA})$

$\Rightarrow \quad W_{CA} = -15$ J

55. $\Delta U_{ab} = 0 \quad \Rightarrow \quad U_b - U_a = 0$

$Q_{bc} = \Delta U_{bc} + W_{bc}$

$\Rightarrow 0 = (U_c - U_b) + 4$

$\Rightarrow \quad U_c - U_b = -4$

$\therefore \quad U_c - U_a = -4 \quad \Rightarrow \quad U_a - U_c = 4$

$\Rightarrow \quad \Delta U_{ca} = 4$ J

56. For process $a \to b \to d$,

$Q = \Delta U_{ad} + W$

$\Rightarrow \quad 60 + 20 = \Delta U_{ad} + [0 + 8(5 - 2)]$

$\Rightarrow \quad \Delta U_{ad} = 56$ J

For process $a \to c \to d$

$Q = \Delta U_{ad} + W$

$= \Delta U_{ad} + (W_{ac} + W_{cd})$

$= 56 + [3(5 - 2) + 0]$

$= 65$ J

57. $T_A = \dfrac{p_A V_A}{nR} = \dfrac{2.4 \times 10^5 \times 1}{100 \times 8} = 300\,\text{K}$

$T_B = T_A = 300\,\text{K}$

$T_C = \dfrac{p_C V_C}{nR} = \dfrac{1 \times 10^5 \times 2}{100 \times 8} = 250\,\text{K}$

$W_{AB} = Q_{AB} = 9 \times 10^4\,\text{J}$

$W_{BC} = -nC_V \Delta T = -100\left[\dfrac{3(8)}{2}\right](250 - 300) = 6 \times 10^4\,\text{J}$

$W_{CD} = p\Delta V = -1 \times 10^5 \times (2-1) = -10 \times 10^4\,\text{J}$

$W_{DA} = 0$

$\therefore\ W = W_{AB} + W_{BC} + W_{CD} + W_{DA}$

$= 9 \times 10^4 + 6 \times 10^4 - 10 \times 10^4 + 0 = 5 \times 10^4\,\text{J}$

58. $p_B V_B = p_C V_C \Rightarrow 200 \times V_B = 500 \times 2 \Rightarrow V_B = 5\,\text{m}^3$

$W_{AB} = p\Delta V = 200 \times 10^3 \times (5-2) = 600\,\text{kJ}$

$W_{BC} = nRT_B \ln\left(\dfrac{V_C}{V_B}\right) = p_B V_B \ln\left(\dfrac{V_C}{V_B}\right)$

$= 200 \times 10^3 \times 5 \ln\left(\dfrac{2}{5}\right) = -900\,\text{kJ}$

$W_{CA} = 0$

$\therefore\ W = W_{AB} + W_{BC} + W_{CA} = -300\,\text{kJ}$

59. $\dfrac{Q_{AB}}{Q_{CD}} = \dfrac{T_{AB}}{T_{CD}} \Rightarrow \dfrac{400}{Q_{CD}} = \dfrac{1000}{250}$

$\Rightarrow\ Q_{CD} = 100\,\text{J}$

60. $\eta = 1 - \dfrac{T_2}{4} = 1 - \dfrac{400}{500} = \dfrac{1}{5}$

$\eta = \dfrac{W}{Q_1} \Rightarrow \dfrac{1}{5} = \dfrac{W}{6 \times 10^4}$

$\Rightarrow\ W = 1.2 \times 10^4\,\text{J}$

61. $\eta = 1 - \dfrac{T_2}{T_1} = 1 - \dfrac{300}{600} = \dfrac{1}{2}$

$\eta = \dfrac{W}{Q_1} \Rightarrow \dfrac{1}{2} = \dfrac{800}{Q_1}$

$\Rightarrow\ Q_1 = 1600\,\text{J/cycle}$

62. $\eta = 1 - \dfrac{Q_2}{Q_1} \Rightarrow 0.6 = 1 - \dfrac{20}{Q_1}$

$\Rightarrow\ Q_1 = 50\,\text{J}$

$W = Q_1 - Q_2 = 50 - 20 = 30\,\text{J}$

63. $Q_2 = 3W$

$\therefore\ Q_1 = Q_2 + W = 4W$

$\eta = 1 - \dfrac{Q_2}{Q_1} = 1 - \dfrac{3}{4} = 0.25$

64. $\beta = \dfrac{T_2}{T_1 - T_2} = \dfrac{273}{303 - 273} = 9.1$

Numerical Value Questions

1.

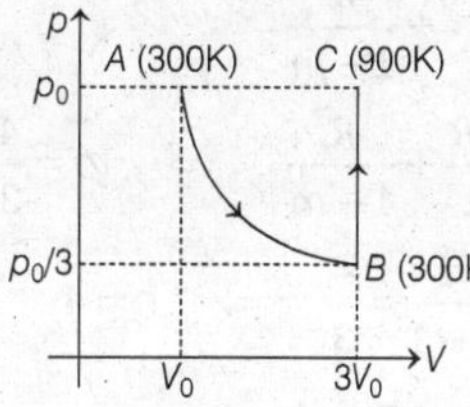

$Q_{AB} = nRT \ln\left(\dfrac{V_B}{V_A}\right) = 1 \times \dfrac{25}{3} \times 300 \ln 3 = 2750\,\text{J}$

$Q_{BC} = nC_V \Delta T = 1 \times \left(\dfrac{R}{\gamma - 1}\right)(900 - 300) = \dfrac{5000}{\gamma - 1}\,\text{J}$

$Q = Q_{AB} + Q_{BC}$

$\Rightarrow\ 17.75 \times 10^3 = 2750 + \dfrac{5000}{\gamma - 1}$

$\Rightarrow\ \gamma = \dfrac{4}{3} = 1.33$

2. As the piston is free to move, the process will be isobaric.

$Q = nC_p \Delta T$

$\Rightarrow\ 42.5 = n\left(\dfrac{5}{2}R\right)\Delta T$

$\Rightarrow\ nR\Delta T = 17$

$W = p\Delta V = nR\Delta T$

$\Rightarrow\ pA\Delta x = nR\Delta T$

$\Rightarrow\ 10^5 \times 8.5 \times 10^{-4} \times \Delta x = 17$

$\Rightarrow\ \Delta x = 0.2\,\text{m} = 20\,\text{cm}$

3. $p = p_0 + \dfrac{mg}{A} = 10^5 + \dfrac{5 \times 10}{5 \times 10^{-3}} = 1.1 \times 10^5\,\text{Pa}$

When the piston is free to move,

$W = p\Delta V = pA\Delta x = 1.1 \times 10^5 \times 5 \times 10^{-3} \times 0.1 = 55\,\text{J}$

$Q_1 = \Delta U + W = nC_V(350 - 300) + 55$

When the piston is clamped,

Energy lost $= Q_2 = nC_V(350 - 300)$

$\therefore\ Q_1 - Q_2 = 55\,\text{J}$

4. $pV^m = \text{constant}$

$\Rightarrow\ \dfrac{dp}{dV} = -m\left(\dfrac{p}{V}\right)$

$\Rightarrow\ \tan(180° - 37°) = -m\left(\dfrac{2 \times 10^5}{4 \times 10^5}\right)$

$\Rightarrow\ -\dfrac{3}{4} = -m\left(\dfrac{1}{2}\right) \Rightarrow m = 1.5$

5. $\dfrac{p}{T^n} = \text{constant}$

$\Rightarrow\ p\left(\dfrac{pV}{nR}\right)^{-n} = \text{constant}$

$\Rightarrow \quad pV^{\frac{n}{n-1}} = \text{constant}$

$$C = C_V + \frac{R}{1-m}$$

$\Rightarrow \quad -\frac{R}{2} = \frac{5R}{2} + \frac{R}{1-m} \quad \Rightarrow \quad m = \frac{4}{3}$

$\therefore \quad m = \frac{n}{n-1} = \frac{4}{3} \quad \Rightarrow \quad n = 4$

6. $pV = nRT + \alpha V$

$\Rightarrow \quad p\Delta V = nR\Delta T + \alpha \Delta V$

$\Rightarrow \quad \Delta V = \frac{nR\Delta T}{p - \alpha}$

$\therefore \quad W = p\Delta V = \frac{pnR\Delta T}{p-\alpha} = \frac{p_0 RT_0}{p_0 - \alpha} \quad [\because \Delta T = 2T_0 - T_0 = T_0]$

So, $\quad x = 7$

7. $U_1 = 4\left(\frac{5R}{2}\right)T = 10RT$

When 2 moles of diatomic gas dissociate, they will form 4 moles of monoatomic gas.

$\therefore \quad U_2 = 2\left(\frac{5R}{2}\right)T + 4\left(\frac{3R}{2}\right)T = 11RT$

$Q = \Delta U + W$

$\Rightarrow \quad Q = (11RT - 10RT) + 0 = RT$

8. *ab* is adiabatic process and *ac* is isothermal process.

For *ab*, $\quad p_a V_a^{\gamma} = p_b V_b^{\gamma}$

$\Rightarrow \quad 16(1)^{1.5} = p_b(4)^{1.5}$

$\Rightarrow \quad p_b = 2\,\text{atm}$

For *bc*, $\quad p_b = p_c = 2\,\text{atm}$

For *ac*, $\quad p_a V_a = p_c V_c$

$\Rightarrow \quad 16(1) = 2(V_c)$

$\Rightarrow \quad V_c = 8\,\text{L}$

9. $W_{BC} = -1830\,\text{J}$, $W_{CA} = 0$

For the cyclic process, $Q = \Delta U + W$

$\Rightarrow \quad -1000 = 0 + (W_{AB} - 1830 + 0)$

$\Rightarrow \quad W_{AB} = 830\,\text{J}$

$W_{AB} = nR\Delta T$

$\Rightarrow \quad 830 = 1 \times 8.3 \times (T_B - 300)$

$\Rightarrow \quad T_B = 400\,\text{K}$

10. For process $3 \rightarrow 1$,

$\frac{p_3}{T_3} = \frac{p_1}{T_1} \quad \Rightarrow \quad \frac{300}{T_3} = \frac{100}{350}$

$\Rightarrow \quad T_3 = 1050\,\text{K}$

$$Q_{12} = nRT\ln\left(\frac{p_1}{p_2}\right) = nR(350)\ln\left(\frac{100}{300}\right) = -385nR$$

$$Q_{23} = nC_p\Delta T = n\left(\frac{7R}{2}\right)(1050 - 350) = 2450nR$$

$$Q_{31} = nC_V\Delta T = n\left(\frac{5R}{2}\right)(350 - 1050) = -1750nR$$

$$\eta = 1 - \frac{Q_{out}}{Q_{in}} = 1 - \frac{385nR + 1750nR}{2450nR} = 0.1285$$

Percentage efficiency $= 0.1285 \times 100 = 12.85\% \simeq 13\%$

11. $Q_{12} = nC_p\Delta T = 1 \times \frac{5R}{2} \times (T_0 - 2T_0) = -2.5RT_0$

$$Q_{23} = nRT\ln\left(\frac{V_3}{V_2}\right) = 1 \times R \times T_0 \ln\left(\frac{V_0}{2V_0}\right) = -0.7RT_0$$

$$Q_{34} = nC_p\Delta T = 1 \times \frac{5R}{2} \times (2T_0 - T_0) = 2.5RT_0$$

$$Q_{41} = nRT\ln\left(\frac{V_1}{V_4}\right) = 1 \times R \times (2T_0)\ln\left(\frac{4V_0}{2V_0}\right) = 1.4RT_0$$

$$\eta = 1 - \frac{Q_{out}}{Q_{in}} = 1 - \frac{2.5RT_0 + 0.7RT_0}{2.5RT_0 + 1.4RT_0} = 0.1795$$

Percentage efficiency = 17.95%

Level-3

Single Choice Correct Questions

1. Area of half ellipse $= \frac{\pi}{2}ab$

$\therefore$ Area of cycle

$$= \frac{\pi}{2}\left(\frac{4-2}{2}\right)(4-2) + \frac{\pi}{2}\left(\frac{3.5-2.5}{2}\right)(2-1) = \frac{5\pi}{4}$$

Since, the cycle is anti-clockwise, work done by the gas will be negative.

So, $\quad W = -\frac{5\pi}{4}$ atm-L

2. From similar triangles,

$$\frac{V_C - V_D}{p_C - p_B} = \frac{V_E - V_A}{p_B - p_A}$$

$\Rightarrow \quad \frac{V_C - V_D}{6-5} = \frac{20}{5-2} \quad \Rightarrow \quad V_C - V_D = \frac{20}{3}\,\text{L}$

Area of $\Delta ABE = \frac{1}{2}(V_E - V_A)(p_B - p_A)$

$= \frac{1}{2} \times 20 \times 3 = 30$ atm-L

Area of $\Delta BCD = \frac{1}{2}(V_C - V_D)(p_C - p_B)$

$= \frac{1}{2} \times \frac{20}{3} \times 1 = \frac{10}{3}$ atm-L

Work done by gas $= 30 - \frac{10}{3} = \frac{80}{3}$ atm-L

$= \frac{80}{3} \times 1 \times 10^5 \times 10^{-3}\,\text{J} = 2.67\,\text{kJ}$

3. $C_p - C_V = R$ for 1 mole of gas

For 1 mole of hydrogen,

$$2C_p - 2C_V = 2m = R$$

For 1 mole of nitrogen,

$$28C_p - 28C_V = 28n = R$$

$\therefore \quad 2m = 28n \quad \Rightarrow \quad m = 14n$

4. (d)

5. For an ideal gas, $C_p - C_V = R$

For non-ideal gas, $C_p - C_V \neq R$

So, in state A, gas behaves non-ideally.

A gas behaves ideally at low pressure and high temperature.

So, $p_A > p_B$ and $T_A < T_B$

6. Initial heat capacity $= \frac{5R}{2}$

Let there be n moles of O_2. $0.6n$ moles of O_2 dissociate to $1.2n$ moles of O. So, the mixture consists of $0.4n$ moles of O_2 and $1.2n$ moles of O.

$$C_{V_{\text{mix}}} = \frac{n_1 C_{V_1} + n_2 C_{V_2}}{n_1 + n_2} = \frac{1.2n\left(\frac{3R}{2}\right) + 0.4n\left(\frac{5R}{2}\right)}{1.2n + 0.4n} = \frac{7R}{4}$$

$$\therefore \quad \frac{(C_V)_{\text{initial}}}{(C_V)_{\text{final}}} = \frac{5R/2}{7R/4} = \frac{10}{7}$$

7. For process BC,

$$Q = nC_V (T_B - T_C) = n\left(\frac{3R}{2}\right)(T_B - T_C)$$

$$\Rightarrow \quad nR(T_B - T_C) = \frac{2Q}{3}$$

For process AB, $W = nR(T_B - T_A) = nR(T_B - T_C) \quad [\because T_A = T_C]$

$$= \frac{2Q}{3}$$

8. $1 \to 2$ is isobaric process.

$$\therefore \quad \frac{\Delta Q}{\Delta W} = \frac{nC_p \Delta T}{nR\Delta T} = \frac{n\left(\frac{\gamma R}{\gamma - 1}\right)\Delta T}{nR\Delta T} = \frac{\gamma}{\gamma - 1}$$

9. For isochoric process, $W = 0$

$$\Rightarrow \quad \frac{W}{Q} = 0$$

For isobaric process,

$$\frac{W}{Q} = \frac{nR\Delta T}{nC_p \Delta T} = \frac{R}{C_p}$$

For diatomic gas, $\frac{W}{Q} = \frac{R}{(7R/2)} = \frac{2}{7} = \tan\theta_2$

For isothermal process, $\Delta U = 0$

$$\Rightarrow \quad \frac{W}{Q} = 1 = \tan\theta_4$$

10. AB is isobaric, BC is isochoric and CD is isothermal process.

$$W = W_{AB} + W_{BC} + W_{CD}$$

$$= nR\Delta T + 0 + nRT \ln\left(\frac{V_D}{V_C}\right)$$

$$= 2R(750 - 250) + 0 + 2R(1000)\ln\left(\frac{20}{15}\right)$$

$$= 2000R\left[\frac{1}{2} + \ln\left(\frac{4}{3}\right)\right]$$

11. For adiabatic process, $Q_1 = 0$

For isothermal process,

$$Q_2 = nRT \ln\left(\frac{V_2}{V_1}\right) = pV \ln\left(\frac{V_2}{V_1}\right) = 400 \times 12 \ln\left(\frac{3}{12}\right)$$

$$= -9600 \ln 2 = -6653 \text{ J}$$

$$\therefore \quad Q = Q_1 + Q_2 = -6653 \text{ J}$$

12. Since, the piston is moved slowly, we assume isothermal condition for both the gases as thermal equilibrium is maintained throughout.

Let the total volume of chamber be V. Then, volume of gas in X increases from $\frac{V}{3}$ to $\frac{2V}{3}$. So, the work done is given by

$$W_X = nRT \ln\left(\frac{V_2}{V_1}\right) = (1) RT \ln\left(\frac{2V/3}{V/3}\right) = RT \ln 2$$

The volume of gas in Y decreases from $2V/3$ to $V/3$.

$$W_Y = nRT \ln\left(\frac{V_2}{V_1}\right) = (2) RT \ln\left(\frac{V/3}{2V/3}\right) = -2RT \ln 2$$

$$W = W_X + W_Y = -RT \ln 2 = -8.3T\,(0.693) = -5.8T$$

13. For $a \to b$, $p_a V_a^\gamma = p_b V_b^\gamma$

$$\Rightarrow \quad p_0 V_0^{5/3} = p_b V_b^{5/3} \quad \text{...(i)}$$

For $c \to d$, $p_c V_c^\gamma = p_d V_d^\gamma$

$$\Rightarrow \quad p_c V_c^{5/3} = (e^3 p_0)\left(\frac{V_0}{e}\right)^{5/3} \quad \text{...(ii)}$$

From Eqs. (i) and (ii), we get

$$\frac{p_b}{p_c} = \frac{1}{e^{4/3}}\left(\frac{V_c}{V_b}\right)^{5/3} \quad \text{...(iii)}$$

For $b \to c$, $p_b V_b = p_c V_c$

$$\Rightarrow \quad \frac{p_b}{p_c} = \frac{V_c}{V_b} \quad \text{...(iv)}$$

From Eqs. (iii) and (iv), we get

$$\frac{V_c}{V_b} = \frac{1}{e^{4/3}}\left(\frac{V_c}{V_b}\right)^{5/3} \quad \Rightarrow \quad \frac{V_c}{V_b} = e^2$$

$$W_{bc} = nRT \ln\left(\frac{V_c}{V_b}\right) = (1) RT_0 \ln(e^2) = 2RT_0$$

14. (a)

15. For polytropic process, $pV^x =$ constant

$$C = C_V + \frac{R}{1 - x}$$

For $x \to \infty$, $C = \frac{3R}{2}$

$$\Rightarrow \quad \frac{3R}{2} = C_V + 0 \quad \Rightarrow \quad C_V = \frac{3R}{2}$$

$$\therefore \quad C = \frac{3R}{2} + \frac{R}{1-x}$$

For $x = 0, C' = \frac{3R}{2} + \frac{R}{1-0} = \frac{5R}{2}$

For $x = x', C = \frac{3R}{2} + \frac{R}{1-x'} = 0 \quad \Rightarrow \quad x' = \frac{5}{3}$

16. $Q = \Delta U + W \quad \Rightarrow \quad Q = \Delta U + \frac{Q}{2}$

$$\Rightarrow \quad \Delta U = \frac{Q}{2}$$

$$\therefore \quad Q = 2\Delta U$$

$$\Rightarrow nC\Delta T = 2nC_V\Delta T$$

$$\Rightarrow \quad C = 2C_V = 3R$$

$$C = C_V + \frac{R}{1-m}$$

$$\Rightarrow \quad 3R = \frac{3R}{2} + \frac{R}{1-m} \quad \Rightarrow \quad m = \frac{1}{3}$$

So, the equation of polytropic process,

$$pV^{1/3} = \text{constant}$$

17. $v = \sqrt{\frac{\gamma RT}{M}}, \quad v_{rms} = \sqrt{\frac{3RT}{M}}$

$$\frac{v}{v_{rms}} = \sqrt{\frac{\gamma}{3}} = \sqrt{\frac{5}{9}} \quad \Rightarrow \quad \gamma = \frac{5}{3}$$

$pT = \text{constant}$

$$\Rightarrow p\left(\frac{pV}{nR}\right) = \text{constant}$$

$$\Rightarrow \quad pV^{1/2} = \text{constant}$$

$$C = C_V + \frac{R}{1-m} = \frac{R}{\gamma-1} + \frac{R}{1-m}$$

$$= \frac{R}{\frac{5}{3}-1} + \frac{R}{1-\frac{1}{2}} = \frac{7R}{2}$$

18. $pV^2 = \text{constant} \quad \Rightarrow \quad m = 2$

$$W = \frac{nR\Delta T}{1-m} = \frac{nR\Delta T}{1-2} = -nR\Delta T$$

$$\Delta U = nC_V\Delta T = n\left(\frac{5R}{2}\right)\Delta T = \frac{5}{2}nR\Delta T$$

$$\therefore \quad \frac{W}{\Delta U} = -\frac{2}{5} = -0.4$$

19. $dW = 2RdT$

$$\Rightarrow \quad \frac{(1)RdT}{1-m} = 2RdT \quad \Rightarrow \quad m = \frac{1}{2}$$

$$C = \frac{R}{\gamma-1} + \frac{R}{1-m}$$

$$\Rightarrow \quad 4R = \frac{R}{\gamma-1} + \frac{R}{1-\frac{1}{2}} \quad \Rightarrow \quad \gamma = \frac{3}{2}$$

20. $p_A V_A^n = p_B V_B^n$

$$\Rightarrow (16p_0)(V_0)^n = p_0(2V_0)^n \quad \Rightarrow \quad n = 4$$

$$W = \frac{nR\Delta T}{1-m} = \frac{p_B V_B - p_A V_A}{1-m}$$

$$= \frac{p_0(2V_0) - (16p_0)V_0}{1-4} = \frac{14}{3}p_0V_0$$

21. $Q = \int nCdT = \int_{T_0}^{\eta T_0} (1)\frac{a}{T}\,dT = a\ln\eta$

$$\Delta U = nC_V\Delta T = (1)\frac{R}{\gamma-1}(\eta T_0 - T_0) = \left(\frac{\eta-1}{\gamma-1}\right)RT_0$$

$$\therefore \quad W = Q - \Delta U = a\ln\eta - \left(\frac{\eta-1}{\gamma-1}\right)RT_0$$

22. First process is isobaric.

$$\therefore \quad W = nR\Delta T$$

$$\Rightarrow \quad W_1 = nR(2T_0 - T_0) = nRT_0$$

Second process is polytropic.

Equation of hyperbola, $TV = \text{constant}$

$$\Rightarrow \quad \left(\frac{pV}{nR}\right)V = \text{constant}$$

$$\Rightarrow \quad pV^2 = \text{constant}$$

$$\therefore \quad m = 2$$

$$W_2 = \frac{nR\Delta T}{1-m} = \frac{nR\left(\frac{T_0}{2} - T_0\right)}{1-2} = \frac{nRT_0}{2}$$

$$\therefore \quad \frac{W_1}{W_2} = 2:1$$

23. Slope $= \frac{dp}{dV} = -\gamma\left(\frac{p}{V}\right) = -1.4\left(\frac{0.7\times10^5}{0.0049}\right) = -2.0\times10^7\ \text{Nm}^{-5}$

24. $TV^{\gamma-1} = \text{constant}$

$$\Rightarrow \frac{dV}{dT} = -\frac{1}{\gamma-1}\left(\frac{V}{T}\right)$$

Magnitude of slope $= \left(\frac{1}{\gamma-1}\right)\left(\frac{V_0}{T_0}\right) = \alpha$

$$\Rightarrow \quad \frac{1}{\gamma-1} = \frac{\alpha T_0}{V_0}$$

$$\therefore \quad C_V = \frac{R}{\gamma-1} = \frac{\alpha R T_0}{V_0}$$

25. Slope of isothermal curve $= -\frac{p}{V} = \tan 135°$

Slope of adiabatic curve $= -\gamma\left(\frac{p}{V}\right) = \tan 121°$

$$\therefore \quad \gamma = \frac{\tan 121°}{\tan 135°} = \frac{\tan(180° - 59°)}{\tan(180° - 45°)} = \tan 59°$$

We know, $\cos 59° = \frac{3}{\sqrt{34}}$

$\Rightarrow \quad \tan 59° = \frac{5}{3}$

So $\quad \gamma = \frac{5}{3}$

Therefore, the gas is monoatomic.

26. The process turns from an endothermic to an exothermic one when $dQ = 0$. So, at that point, line AB should be tangent to an adiabatic curve.

Equation of line AB,

$$p = \left(-\frac{p_0}{V_0}\right)V + p_0$$

Slope of adiabatic curve = Slope of line AB

$$\Rightarrow \quad -\gamma\left(\frac{p}{V}\right) = -\left(\frac{p_0}{V_0}\right)$$

$$\Rightarrow \quad \frac{5}{3}\frac{1}{V}\left[\left(-\frac{p_0}{V_0}\right)V + p_0\right] = \frac{p_0}{V_0} \quad \Rightarrow \quad V = \frac{5V_0}{8}$$

27. $\frac{dp}{dV} = -\gamma\left(\frac{p}{V}\right)$

As $\gamma_{mono} > \gamma_{dia} > \gamma_{tri}$, p-V graph for monoatomic gas will be steepest.

From graph,

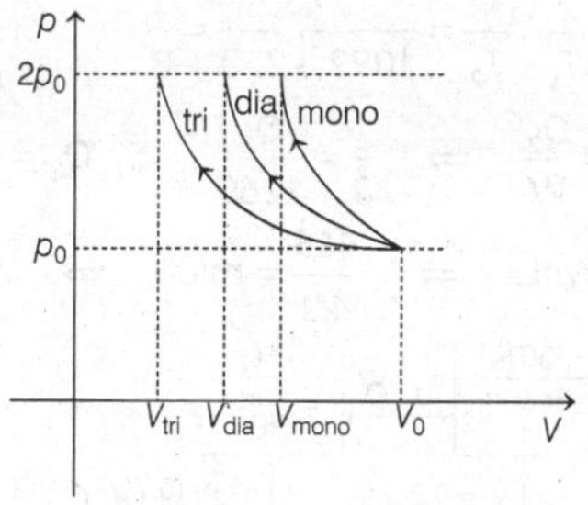

$$V_{mono} > V_{dia} > V_{tri}$$

28. AB is isobaric process.

$\therefore \quad Q_{AB} = nc_p\Delta T = n\left(\frac{7R}{2}\right)(2T_0 - T_0) = \frac{7}{2}nRT_0$

BC is isothermal process

$\therefore$ Work done on the gas $= W_{BC} = -nRT\ln\left(\frac{V_C}{V_B}\right)$

$$= -nR(2T_0)\ln\left(\frac{V_0}{2V_0}\right)$$

$$= 2nRT_0\ln 2$$

$$\therefore \quad \frac{Q_{AB}}{W_{BC}} = \frac{7}{4\ln 2}$$

29. AB and CD are isothermal processes while BC and DA are isochoric processes.

For cyclic process, $\quad Q = \Delta U + W$

$\Rightarrow \quad Q = 0 + W = W$

$$W = W_{AB} + W_{BC} + W_{CD} + W_{DA}$$

$$= (1)R(500)\ln\left(\frac{3V_0}{V_0}\right) + 0 + (1)R(300)\ln\left(\frac{V_0}{3V_0}\right) + 0$$

$$= 500R\ln 3 - 300R\ln 3 = 200R\ln 3$$

$\therefore Q = W = 200R\ln 3$

30. $1 \to 2$ is isothermal process.

So, $\quad \Delta U_{12} = 0 \quad \Rightarrow \quad U_2 - U_1 = 0$

$\Rightarrow \quad U_2 = U_1$

$2 \to 3$ is isochoric process.

$\therefore \quad Q_{23} = \Delta U_{23} \quad \Rightarrow \quad -40 = U_3 - U_2$

$\Rightarrow \quad -40 = U_3 - U_1 \quad \Rightarrow \quad \Delta U_{31} = 40\text{ J}$

$3 \to 1$ is adiabatic process.

$\therefore \quad W_{31} = -\Delta U_{31} = -40\text{ J}$

31. $B \to C$ is isochoric process.

$\therefore \quad Q_{BC} = \Delta U_{BC} + W_{BC}$

$\Rightarrow \quad -500 = \Delta U_{BC} + 0$

$\Rightarrow \quad \Delta U_{BC} = -500\text{ kJ}$

For cyclic process,

$$\Delta U = \Delta U_{AB} + \Delta U_{BC} + \Delta U_{CA} = 0$$

$\Rightarrow \quad 400 - 500 + \Delta U_{CA} = 0$

$\Rightarrow \quad \Delta U_{CA} = 100\text{ kJ}$

$W_{CA} = -$ Area under line CA

$$= -\frac{1}{2}(3\times 10^5 + 2\times 10^5)(1.5 - 1) = -125\text{ kJ}$$

$$Q_{CA} = \Delta U_{CA} + W_{CA}$$

$$= 100 - 125 = -25\text{ kJ}$$

32. AB is isobaric process.

$$Q_{AB} = nC_p\Delta T$$

$\Rightarrow \quad 300 = nC_p(T_B - T_A)$

$\Rightarrow \quad 300 = nC_p\left(\frac{p_0(3V_0)}{nR} - \frac{p_0V_0}{nR}\right)$

$\Rightarrow \quad C_p(p_0V_0) = 150R \quad$ ...(i)

For process AC,

$$\Delta U_{AC} = nC_V(T_C - T_A)$$

$\Rightarrow \quad 1200 = nC_V\left(\frac{(4p_0)(4V_0)}{nR} - \frac{p_0V_0}{nR}\right)$

$\Rightarrow \quad C_V(p_0V_0) = 80R \quad$ ...(ii)

Dividing Eq. (i) by (ii), we get

$$\frac{C_p}{C_V} = \frac{15}{8} \quad \Rightarrow \quad \gamma = \frac{15}{8}$$

33. For process $3 \to 1$, ρ = constant

$\Rightarrow \quad V$ = constant

Let $T_1 = T_0$

$$\frac{p_1}{T_1} = \frac{p_3}{T_3} \quad \Rightarrow \quad \frac{p_0}{T_0} = \frac{2p_0}{T_3}$$

$\Rightarrow \quad T_3 = 2T_0$

Heat rejected in process $3 \to 1$,

$$Q = nC_V(T_3 - T_1) = n\left(\frac{3R}{2}\right)(2T_0 - T_0)$$

$$= \frac{3}{2}nRT_0 = \frac{3}{2}p_0V_0 = \frac{3}{2}\left(\frac{p_0M}{\rho_0}\right)$$

34. BC is isothermal process.

$$p_BV_B = p_CV_C$$

$$\Rightarrow \quad p_0V_0 = (3p_0)V_C$$

$$\Rightarrow \quad \frac{V_C}{V_0} = \frac{1}{3}$$

CA is adiabatic process.

$$p_CV_C^\gamma = p_AV_A^\gamma$$

$$\Rightarrow \quad (3p_0)V_C^\gamma = \left(\frac{p_0}{2}\right)V_0^\gamma$$

$$\Rightarrow \quad \left(\frac{V_C}{V_0}\right)^\gamma = \frac{1}{6} \quad \Rightarrow \quad \left(\frac{1}{3}\right)^\gamma = \frac{1}{6}$$

$$\Rightarrow \quad 3^\gamma = 6 \quad \Rightarrow \quad \gamma \ln 3 = \ln 6$$

$$\Rightarrow \quad \gamma = \frac{\ln 6}{\ln 3}$$

35. $Q_{AB} = Q_{CD} = 0$

$Q_{BC} = nC_p\Delta T = nC_p(T_3 - T_2)$

$Q_{DA} = nC_V\Delta T = nC_V(T_1 - T_4)$

Since, $\quad T_4 > T_1, Q_{DA} < 0$

Heat input $= nC_p(T_3 - T_2)$

Heat output $= nC_V(T_4 - T_1)$

$$\eta = 1 - \frac{Q_{out}}{Q_{in}} = 1 - \frac{nC_V(T_4 - T_1)}{nC_p(T_3 - T_2)}$$

$$= 1 - \frac{1}{\gamma}\left(\frac{T_4 - T_1}{T_3 - T_2}\right)$$

36. AB is isobaric compression $\Rightarrow T_B < T_A$

BC is adiabatic compression $\Rightarrow T_C > T_B$

CD is isochoric heating $\Rightarrow T_D > T_C$

DA is isothermal expansion $\Rightarrow T_D = T_A$

$\therefore \quad T_A = T_D > T_C > T_B$

Let $\quad T_B = T_0 \quad \Rightarrow \quad T_A = T_D = 4T_0$

$$p_A = p_B = p_0$$

For process AB, $\dfrac{V_A}{T_A} = \dfrac{V_B}{T_B}$

$$\Rightarrow \quad \frac{8\sqrt{2}\,V_0}{4T_0} = \frac{V_B}{T_0} \quad \Rightarrow \quad V_B = 2\sqrt{2}\,V_0$$

For process BC,

$$p_BV_B^\gamma = p_CV_C^\gamma$$

$$\Rightarrow \quad p_0(2\sqrt{2}\,V_0)^{5/3} = p_C(V_0)^{5/3}$$

$$\Rightarrow \quad p_C = 4\sqrt{2}\,p_0$$

For process DA,

$$p_AV_A = p_DV_D$$

$$\Rightarrow \quad p_0(8\sqrt{2}\,V_0) = p_DV_0$$

$$\Rightarrow \quad p_D = 8\sqrt{2}\,p_0$$

For process CD, $\dfrac{p_C}{T_C} = \dfrac{p_D}{T_D}$

$$\Rightarrow \quad \frac{4\sqrt{2}\,p_0}{T_C} = \frac{8\sqrt{2}\,p_0}{4T_0}$$

$$\Rightarrow \quad T_C = 2T_0$$

$$Q_{AB} = nC_p\Delta T = n\left(\frac{5R}{2}\right)(T_0 - 4T_0) = -\frac{15}{2}nRT_0$$

$$Q_{BC} = 0$$

$$Q_{CD} = nC_V\Delta T = n\left(\frac{3R}{2}\right)(4T_0 - 2T_0) = 3nRT_0$$

$$Q_{DA} = nRT\ln\left(\frac{V_A}{V_D}\right) = nR(4T_0)\ln\left(\frac{8\sqrt{2}\,V_0}{V_0}\right) = 14nRT_0\ln 2$$

$$\eta = 1 - \frac{Q_{out}}{Q_{in}} = 1 - \frac{\frac{15}{2}nRT_0}{14nRT_0\ln 2 + 3nRT_0}$$

$$= 1 - \frac{15}{2(14\ln 2 + 3)} = \frac{28\ln 2 - 9}{28\ln 2 + 6}$$

37.

$$\beta = \frac{T_2}{T_1 - T_2} = \frac{273}{1092 - 273} = \frac{1}{3}$$

$$\beta = \frac{Q_2}{W} \quad \Rightarrow \quad \frac{1}{3} = \frac{Q_2}{1260} \quad \Rightarrow \quad Q_2 = 415\text{ J}$$

$$Q = mL_f \quad \Rightarrow \quad \frac{415}{4.2} = m(80) \quad \Rightarrow \quad m = 1.25\text{ g/s}$$

38.

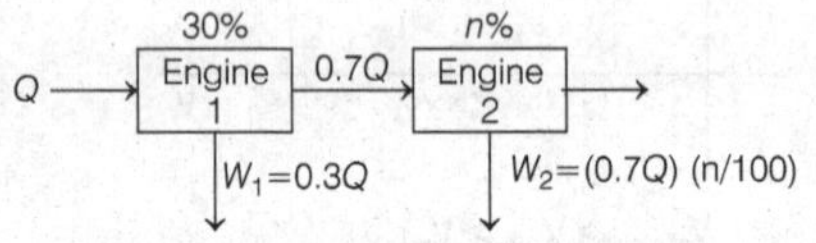

$$\text{Overall efficiency} = \frac{W_1 + W_2}{Q} = \frac{65}{100}$$

$$\Rightarrow \quad \frac{0.3Q + (0.7Q)\left(\frac{n}{100}\right)}{Q} = \frac{65}{100}$$

$$\Rightarrow \quad n = 50\%$$

Multiple Choice(s) Correct Questions

1. For path $1 \to 2 \to 3$, $Q = \Delta U_{13} + W$

$$\Rightarrow \quad 100 = \Delta U_{13} + 40$$

$$\Rightarrow \quad \Delta U_{13} = 60\text{ cal}$$

For path $1 \to 4 \to 3$, $Q = \Delta U_{13} + W$

$$\Rightarrow \quad Q = 60 + 10 = 70\text{ cal}$$

Considering areas, work done in path $1 \to 3$ is mean of that for paths $1 \to 2 \to 3$ and $1 \to 4 \to 3$

$$W_{3\to 1} = \frac{W_{1\to 2\to 3} + W_{1\to 4\to 3}}{2} = \frac{40+10}{2} = 25 \text{ cal}$$

$\therefore W_{3\to 1} = -25$ cal

For path $3 \to 1$, $Q = \Delta U_{31} + W = -60 - 25 = -85$ cal

2. At constant volume, $Q = nC_V \Delta T$

$$\Rightarrow \quad 25 = (1)\left(\frac{fR}{2}\right)2$$

$$\Rightarrow \quad 25 = f\left(\frac{25}{3}\right) \Rightarrow f = 3$$

So, the gas has to be monoatomic.

3. $pV^2 = \text{constant}$

$$\Rightarrow \quad \left(\frac{nRT}{V}\right)V^2 = \text{constant}$$

$$\Rightarrow \quad TV = \text{constant}$$

So, T-V diagram will be rectangular hyperbola.

Since, $T \propto \frac{1}{V}$, as volume increases, temperature decreases.

So, such an expansion is possible only with cooling.

4. As piston moves without acceleration, pressure of gas will remain constant.

$$p_i = p_f = p_0 + \frac{mg}{A} = 1.05 \times 10^5 + \frac{9\times 10}{0.09}$$

$$= 1.06 \times 10^5 \text{ N/m}^2$$

$$n = \frac{pV}{RT} = \frac{1.06\times 10^5 \times 0.0027}{(25/3)\times 300} = 0.11448$$

$$Q = nC_p \Delta T$$

$$\Rightarrow 2.5 \times 10^4 = 0.11448 \times \frac{5}{2}\left(\frac{25}{3}\right)(T_f - 300)$$

$$\Rightarrow \quad T_f = 1348.2 \text{ K}$$

$$W = nR\Delta T = \frac{2Q}{5} = \frac{2}{5} \times 2.5 \times 10^4 = 10^4 \text{ J}$$

5. $$\frac{p_1V_1}{T_1} = \frac{p_2V_2}{T_2}$$

$$\Rightarrow \quad \frac{50\times 50}{T_1} = \frac{100\times 100}{273}$$

$$\Rightarrow \quad T_1 = 68.25 \text{ K}$$

$$\frac{p_2V_2}{T_2} = \frac{p_3V_3}{T_3}$$

$$\Rightarrow \quad \frac{100\times 100}{273} = \frac{100\times 200}{T_3}$$

$$\Rightarrow \quad T_3 = 546 \text{ K}$$

For curve 3, $p_C V_C = p_B V_B$

$$\Rightarrow \quad p_C \times 100 = 100 \times 200$$

$$\Rightarrow \quad p_C = 200 \text{ cm of Hg}$$

Work done cannot be calculated unless path is known between states A and B.

6. (a, b, c, d)

7. For adiabatic process,

$$pT^{\frac{\gamma}{1-\gamma}} = \text{constant} \quad \Rightarrow \quad p \propto T^{\frac{\gamma}{\gamma-1}}$$

Slope, $$\frac{dp}{dT} \propto \left(\frac{\gamma}{\gamma-1}\right)T^{\frac{1}{\gamma-1}}$$

So, slope is positive.

As, $\frac{1}{\gamma-1} > 1$, slope increases with increase in temperature.

8. $pV^\gamma = \text{constant}$

$$\Rightarrow \quad p\left(\frac{m}{d}\right)^\gamma = \text{constant} \quad \Rightarrow \quad p \propto d^\gamma$$

$$\therefore \quad \frac{p}{p'} = \left(\frac{d}{d'}\right)^\gamma = (32)^{7/5} = 128$$

$$V \propto \frac{1}{d} \quad \Rightarrow \quad \frac{V'}{V} = \frac{d}{d'} = 32$$

9. From internal energy conservation,

$$U_1 + U_2 = U'_1 + U'_2$$

$$\Rightarrow \quad 2\left(\frac{5R}{2}\right)T_0 + 3(3R)\,2T_0 = 2\left(\frac{5R}{2}\right)T + 3(3R)T$$

$$\Rightarrow \quad T = \frac{23}{14}T_0$$

$$C_{V_{\text{mix}}} = \frac{n_1C_{V_1} + n_2C_{V_2}}{n_1+n_2} = \frac{2\left(\frac{5R}{2}\right) + 3(3R)}{2+3} = \frac{14}{5}R$$

$$C_V = \frac{R}{\gamma - 1} \quad \Rightarrow \quad \frac{14R}{5} = \frac{R}{\gamma_{\text{mix}} - 1}$$

$$\Rightarrow \gamma_{\text{mix}} = \frac{19}{14}$$

10. As the gas expands freely, $W = 0$

$$Q = \Delta U + W \quad \Rightarrow \quad 0 = \Delta U + 0 \quad \Rightarrow \quad \Delta U = 0$$

So, internal energy of the gas is unchanged and temperature remains unchanged.

11. For equilibrium of piston, $kx_0 = PS$

$$\Rightarrow \quad P = \frac{kx_0}{S}$$

Work done by gas = Elastic potential energy of spring

$$= \frac{1}{2}kx_0^2$$

Since the chamber is thermally insulated, $Q = 0$

So, the work is done by the gas at the expense of its internal energy. Therefore, internal energy of the gas is decreased by $\frac{1}{2}kx_0^2$.

12. For He, $$p_1V_1^\gamma = p_2V_2^\gamma$$

$$\Rightarrow \quad p_{\text{He}}(AL)^{5/3} = p'_{\text{He}}\left(\frac{AL}{2}\right)^{5/3}$$

$\Rightarrow \quad p'_{He} = (2)^{5/3}\, p_{He}$

For O_2, $\quad p_1V_1^{\gamma} = p_2V_2^{\gamma}$

$\Rightarrow \quad p_{O_2}(AL)^{7/5} = p'_{O_2}(AL')^{7/5}$

$\Rightarrow \quad p'_{O_2} = p_{O_2}\left(\frac{L}{L'}\right)^{7/5}$

For equilibrium of moving piston,

$$p_{O_2} = p_{He} \text{ and } p'_{O_2} = p'_{He}$$

$$\frac{p'_{O_2}}{p_{O_2}} = \frac{p'_{He}}{p_{He}}$$

$\Rightarrow \quad \left(\frac{L}{L'}\right)^{7/5} = (2)^{5/3} \Rightarrow L' = \frac{L}{(2)^{25/21}}$

$\therefore$ Volume of O_2 chamber $= \frac{LA}{(2)^{25/21}}$

13. For isothermal process,

$$W_{gas} = nRT\ln\left(\frac{V_2}{V_1}\right) = (1)RT_0\ln(\eta) = RT_0\ln\eta$$

Work done against the atmosphere,

$$W = p_0\Delta V = p_0(\eta V_0 - V_0)$$
$$= p_0V_0(\eta - 1) = RT_0(\eta - 1)$$
$$\Delta U = 0$$
$$p_0V_0 = p_1V_1$$

$\Rightarrow \quad p_0V_0 = p_1(\eta V_0) \Rightarrow p_1 = \frac{p_0}{\eta}$

14. $C = \frac{dQ}{ndT}$

For adiabatic process,

$$dQ = 0 \Rightarrow C = 0$$

For isothermal process,

$$dT = 0 \Rightarrow C = \infty$$

For all ideal gases, $C_p - C_V = R$

$\frac{C_p}{C_V} = \gamma$ and γ depends on the type of gas.

15. For process DA,

$$\frac{p_D}{T_D} = \frac{p_A}{T_A} \Rightarrow \frac{p_D}{p_A} = \frac{T_D}{T_A}$$

For process CB,

$$\frac{p_C}{T_C} = \frac{p_B}{T_B} \Rightarrow \frac{p_C}{p_B} = \frac{T_C}{T_B}$$

$\because \quad p_A = p_C$ and $p_D = p_B$

$\Rightarrow \quad \frac{T_D}{T_A} = \frac{T_B}{T_C}$

$\Rightarrow \quad T_A = \sqrt{T_CT_D} \quad [\because T_A = T_B]$

$\Rightarrow \quad T_A = \sqrt{256 \times 400} = 320\,\text{K}$

$$W = W_{DA} + W_{AC} + W_{CB} + W_{BD}$$
$$= 0 + \left(\frac{2}{4}\right)R(T_C - T_A) + 0 + \left(\frac{2}{4}\right)R(T_D - T_B)$$
$$= 8R$$

16. $Q = Q_{AB} + Q_{BC} + Q_{CD} + Q_{DA}$

$$= nR(100)\ln\left(\frac{2}{4}\right) + nC_p(400 - 100)$$
$$+ nR(400)\ln\left(\frac{4}{2}\right) + nC_p(100 - 400)$$
$$= nR(100)\ln 2$$

Since, $Q > 0$, the heat is supplied.

$$W_{AB} = nR(100)\ln\left(\frac{2}{4}\right) = -nR(100)\ln 2 < 0$$

Since, $W_{AB} < 0$, work is done on the gas.

Line joining A and C doesn't pass through origin. So, $V_A \neq V_C$.

17. $\rho = \frac{m}{V} \Rightarrow \rho \propto \frac{1}{V}$

For process AB, ρ = constant

$\Rightarrow \quad V$ = constant

So, AB is isochoric heating. Therefore, $p \propto T$

$$p_B > p_A \Rightarrow T_B > T_A$$

For process BC, p = constant

Density increases $\Rightarrow$ Volume decreases

So, BC is isobaric compression.

$\because \quad V_C < V_B \Rightarrow T_C < T_B$

For process CD, ρ = constant

$\Rightarrow \quad V$ = constant

So, CD is isochoric cooling.

For process DA, p = constant

Density decreases $\Rightarrow$ Volume increases

So, DA is isobaric expansion.

p-V graph of the cyclic process will be anti-clockwise.

So, $\quad W < 0 \Rightarrow Q < 0$

Therefore, net heat during the cycle is rejected by the system.

18. For process AB, pT = constant

$\Rightarrow \quad p_AT_A = p_BT_B$

$\Rightarrow \quad p_0(300) = (3p_0)T_B \Rightarrow T_B = 100\,\text{K}$

$$pT = \text{constant}$$

$\Rightarrow \quad p\left(\frac{pV}{nR}\right) = \text{constant}$

$\Rightarrow \quad pV^{1/2} = \text{constant}$

So, AB is polytropic process.

$$W_{AB} = \frac{nR\Delta T}{1 - m} = \frac{(1)R(100 - 300)}{1 - \frac{1}{2}} = -400R$$

$$\Delta U_{CA} = nC_V\Delta T = (1)\left(\frac{3R}{2}\right)(300 - 900) = -900R$$

$$Q_{BC} = nC_p\Delta T = (1)\left(\frac{5R}{2}\right)(900 - 100) = 2000R$$

For process CA, $\frac{p_A}{T_A} = \frac{p_C}{T_C}$

$\Rightarrow \quad \frac{p_0}{300} = \frac{3p_0}{T_C} \Rightarrow T_C = 900\,\text{K}$

19. $Q_{cb} = \Delta U_{cb} + W_{cb}$

$\Rightarrow \quad -40 = \Delta U_{cb} + 0$

$\Rightarrow \quad \Delta U_{cb} = -40\,\text{J}$

$Q_{ba} = \Delta U_{ba} + W_{ba}$

$\Rightarrow \quad -130 = \Delta U_{ba} - 80$

$\Rightarrow \quad \Delta U_{ba} = -50\,\text{J}$

For the cyclic process,

$\Delta U_{ba} + \Delta U_{ac} + \Delta U_{cb} = 0$

$\Rightarrow \quad -50 + \Delta U_{ac} - 40 = 0$

$\Rightarrow \quad \Delta U_{ac} = 90\,\text{J}$

$Q_{ac} = \Delta U_{ac} + W_{ac}$

$\Rightarrow \quad 400 = 90 + W_{ac}$

$\Rightarrow \quad W_{ac} = 310\,\text{J}$

$W = W_{ba} + W_{ac} + W_{cb} = -80 + 310 + 0 = 230\,\text{J}$

$\eta = 1 - \frac{Q_{\text{out}}}{Q_{\text{in}}} = 1 - \frac{40+130}{400} = \frac{23}{40}$

Percentage efficiency of cycle $= \frac{23}{40} \times 100 = 57.5\%$

20. $Q_{AB} = \Delta U_{AB} + W_{AB} = 0 + 600 = 600\,\text{J}$

$Q_{BC} = \Delta U_{BC} + W_{BC}$

$\Rightarrow \quad 0 = \Delta U_{BC} + 250$

$\Rightarrow \quad \Delta U_{BC} = -250\,\text{J}$

For the cycle,

$\Delta U_{AB} + \Delta U_{BC} + \Delta U_{CA} = 0$

$\Rightarrow \quad 0 - 250 + \Delta U_{CA} = 0$

$\Rightarrow \quad \Delta U_{CA} = 250\,\text{J}$

$Q_{CA} = \Delta U_{CA} + W_{CA}$

$\Rightarrow \quad -50 = 250 + W_{CA}$

$\Rightarrow \quad W_{CA} = -300\,\text{J}$

$W = W_{AB} + W_{BC} + W_{CA}$

$= 600 + 250 - 300 = 550\,\text{J}$

Comprehension Based Questions

1. Process $2 \to 3$ is isochoric.

$\therefore \quad \frac{p_2}{T_2} = \frac{p_3}{T_3}$

$\Rightarrow \quad \frac{2p_0}{T_2} = \frac{p_0}{T_3} \Rightarrow T_2 = 2T_3$

$Q_{12} = Q_{34}$

$\Rightarrow \quad nC_p(T_2 - T_0) = nC_p(T_0 - T_3)$

$\Rightarrow \quad T_2 + T_3 = 2T_0$

$\Rightarrow \quad 2T_3 + T_3 = 2T_0$

$\Rightarrow \quad T_3 = \frac{2T_0}{3}$

Heat released in the process $2 \to 3$,

$$Q = nC_V(T_2 - T_3) = (1)\left(\frac{3R}{2}\right)\left(\frac{4T_0}{3} - \frac{2T_0}{3}\right) = RT_0$$

2. $1 \to 2$: Isobaric heating

$2 \to 3$: Isochoric cooling

$3 \to 4$: Isobaric heating

$4 \to 1$: Isothermal compression

3. From similar triangles,

$\frac{T_2 - T_1}{T_4 - T_3} = \frac{p_1 - p_5}{p_5 - p_4}$

$\Rightarrow \quad 1 = \frac{p - p_5}{p_5 - \frac{p}{2}} \Rightarrow p_5 = \frac{3p}{4}$

4. For process CA, $\frac{p_C}{V_C} = \frac{p_A}{V_A}$

$\Rightarrow \quad \frac{p_C}{3V_A} = \frac{p_A}{V_A} \Rightarrow p_C = 3p_A$

$T_B = T_C \Rightarrow \frac{p_B V_B}{nR} = \frac{p_C V_C}{nR}$

$\Rightarrow \quad p_B V_A = (3p_A)(3V_A) \Rightarrow p_B = 9p_A$

Work done in the cyclic process = Area of cycle

$\Rightarrow \quad W = \frac{1}{2}(p_B - p_A)(3V_A - V_A) = 8p_A V_A$

5. AB : Isochoric heating

$BC : y = mx + C$

$\Rightarrow \quad p = mV + C$

$\Rightarrow \quad \frac{nRT}{V} = mV + C$

$\Rightarrow \quad T = \left(\frac{m}{nR}\right)V^2 + \left(\frac{C}{nR}\right)V$

So, T-V graph will be parabola opening down as $m < 0$.

$CA : p \propto V$

$\Rightarrow \quad \frac{nRT}{V} \propto V \Rightarrow T \propto V^2$

So, T-V graph will be parabola.

6. Greatest temperature will occur at the mid-point of line BC.

$$T_{\max} = \frac{pV}{nR} = \frac{\left(\frac{p_B + p_C}{2}\right)\left(\frac{V_B + V_C}{2}\right)}{nR}$$

$$= \frac{\left(\frac{9p_A + 3p_A}{2}\right)\left(\frac{V_A + 3V_A}{2}\right)}{nR}$$

$$= \frac{12p_A V_A}{nR} = 12T_A = 2400\,\text{K}$$

7. $dQ = -dU \Rightarrow nCdT = -nC_V dT$

$\Rightarrow \quad C = -C_V = -\frac{5R}{2}$

8. $C = C_V + \frac{R}{1-m}$

$\Rightarrow \quad -\frac{5R}{2} = \frac{5R}{2} + \frac{R}{1-m} \quad \Rightarrow \quad m = \frac{6}{5}$

So, the equation of polytropic process will be

$pV^{6/5} = \text{constant}$

$\Rightarrow \quad \left(\frac{nRT}{V}\right)V^{6/5} = \text{constant}$

$\Rightarrow \quad TV^{1/5} = \text{constant}$

9. $T_1V_1^{1/5} = T_2V_2^{1/5}$

$\Rightarrow T_0V_0^{1/5} = T_2(32V_0)^{1/5} \quad \Rightarrow \quad T_2 = \frac{T_0}{2}$

$$W = \frac{nR\Delta T}{1-m} = \frac{nR\left(\frac{T_0}{2} - T_0\right)}{1 - \frac{6}{5}} = \frac{5RT_0}{2}$$

10. For process AB,

Equation of rectangular hyperbola,

$U\rho = \text{constant}$

$\Rightarrow \quad (nC_VT)\left(\frac{PM}{RT}\right) = \text{constant}$

$\Rightarrow \quad p = \text{constant}$

So, AB is isobaric process.

$$W_{AB} = nR\Delta T = nR(T_B - T_A)$$
$$= \frac{2}{3}\left[n\left(\frac{3R}{2}\right)(T_B - T_A)\right]$$
$$= \frac{2}{3}(U_B - U_A) = \frac{2}{3}(4U_0 - U_0) = 2U_0$$

11. For process BC, $U = \text{constant}$

$\Rightarrow \quad T = \text{constant}$

So, BC is isothermal process.

$$W_{BC} = nRT\ln\left(\frac{V_C}{V_B}\right) = \frac{2}{3}\left[n\left(\frac{3R}{2}\right)T\right]\ln\left(\frac{\rho_B}{\rho_C}\right)$$
$$= \frac{2}{3}(4U_0)\ln\left(\frac{1}{4}\right) = -\frac{16U_0}{3}\ln 2$$

12. For process CA, $\rho = \text{constant}$

$\Rightarrow \quad V = \text{constant}$

So, CA is isochoric process.

$C = C_V = \frac{3R}{2}$

13. For process AB, $T_AV_A^{\gamma-1} = T_BV_B^{\gamma-1}$

$$\Rightarrow \quad T_B = T_A\left(\frac{V_A}{V_B}\right)^{\gamma-1} = 300(16)^{2/5}$$
$$= 300 \times 3.03 = 909\,\text{K} = 636°\,\text{C}$$

14. For process BC, $\frac{V_C}{V_B} = \frac{T_C}{T_B}$

$$\Rightarrow \quad T_C = T_B\left(\frac{V_C}{V_B}\right) = 2T_B = 1818\,\text{K}$$

$\frac{V_A}{V_B} = 16, \quad \frac{V_C}{V_B} = 2$

$\Rightarrow \quad \frac{V_A}{V_C} = 8 \quad \Rightarrow \quad \frac{V_D}{V_C} = 8$

For process CD, $T_CV_C^{\gamma-1} = T_DV_D^{\gamma-1}$

$$\Rightarrow \quad T_D = T_C\left(\frac{V_C}{V_D}\right)^{\gamma-1} = 1818(2)^{-6/5}$$
$$= 790.4\,\text{K} = 517.4°\,\text{C}$$

15. $Q_{AB} = 0,$

$Q_{BC} = nC_p(T_C - T_B) = nC_p(1818 - 909) = nC_p(909)$

$Q_{CD} = 0$

$Q_{DA} = nC_V(T_A - T_D) = nC_V(300 - 790.4) = -nC_V(490.4)$

$$\eta = 1 - \frac{Q_{out}}{Q_{in}} = 1 - \frac{nC_V(490.4)}{nC_p(909)} = 1 - \frac{490.4}{1.4(909)} = 0.614$$

Percentage efficiency $= 0.614 \times 100 = 61.4\%$

16. For the isothermal process,

$p_2V_2 = p_3V_3$

$\Rightarrow (3p_0)(3V_0) = (p_0)V_3 \Rightarrow V_3 = 9V_0$

$W_{12} = \text{Area under line } 1 \rightarrow 2$

$= \frac{1}{2}(p_0 + 3p_0)(3V_0 - V_0) = 4p_0V_0$

$$W_{23} = nRT_2\ln\left(\frac{p_2}{p_3}\right)$$
$$= (3p_0)(3V_0)\ln\left(\frac{3p_0}{p_0}\right) = 9\ln 3(p_0V_0)$$

$W_{31} = \text{Area under line } 3 \rightarrow 1$

$= p_0(9V_0 - V_0) = -8p_0V_0$

$W = W_{12} + W_{23} + W_{31} = (9\ln 3 - 4)\,p_0V_0$

17. Equation of line $1 \rightarrow 2$,

$y = mx \quad \Rightarrow \quad p = \left(\frac{p_0}{V_0}\right)V$

$\Rightarrow \quad pV^{-1} = \text{constant}$

$$C = C_V + \frac{R}{1-m} = \frac{3R}{2} + \frac{R}{1-(-1)} = 2R$$

18. $T_1 = \frac{p_0V_0}{nR} = 300\text{K},$

$T_2 = T_3 = \frac{(3p_0)(3V_0)}{nR} = 2700\,\text{K}$

$Q_{12} = nC(T_2 - T_1) = (1)(2R)(2700 - 300) = 4800R$

$$Q_{23} = nRT_2\ln\left(\frac{p_1}{p_2}\right) = (1)R(2700)\ln\left(\frac{3p_0}{p_0}\right) = (2700\ln 2)R$$

$$Q_{31} = nC_p(T_1 - T_3) = (1)\left(\frac{5R}{2}\right)(300 - 2700) = -6000R$$

$$\eta = 1 - \frac{Q_{out}}{Q_{in}} = 1 - \frac{6000R}{(2700\ln 2)R + 4800R} = \frac{9\ln 3 - 4}{9\ln 3 + 16}$$

19. *AB* is isobaric process.

$$\therefore \quad \frac{V_A}{T_A} = \frac{V_B}{T_B}$$

$$\Rightarrow \quad T_B = T_A\left(\frac{V_B}{V_A}\right) = 300 \times 2 = 600\,\text{K}$$

20. $Q_{AB} = nC_p(T_B - T_A) = (2)\left(\frac{5R}{2}\right)(600 - 300) = 1500R$

Since, $Q_{AB} > 0 \quad \Rightarrow$ Heat is absorbed

21. *BC* is isothermal process.

$$Q_{BC} = nRT_B \ln\left(\frac{V_C}{V_B}\right) = (2)R(600)\ln\left(\frac{4V_A}{2V_A}\right) = 1200R\ln 2$$

Heat is absorbed.

22. *CD* is isochoric process.

$$Q_{CD} = nC_V(T_D - T_C) = (2)\left(\frac{3R}{2}\right)(300 - 600) = -900R$$

Heat is released.

23. $Q_{DA} = nRT_A \ln\left(\frac{V_A}{V_D}\right) = (2)R(300)\ln\left(\frac{1}{4}\right) = -1200R\ln 2$

Heat is released.

24. For the cyclic process,

$$Q = Q_{AB} + Q_{BC} + Q_{CD} + Q_{DA} = 600R$$

$$Q = \Delta U + W \quad \Rightarrow \quad 600R = 0 + W$$

$$\Rightarrow W = 600R$$

25. For process $A \to B$,

$$T_A p_A^{\frac{1-\gamma}{\gamma}} = T_B p_B^{\frac{1-\gamma}{\gamma}}$$

$$\Rightarrow \quad T_B = T_A\left(\frac{p_A}{p_B}\right)^{\frac{1-\gamma}{\gamma}} = 1000\left(\frac{3}{2}\right)^{\frac{1-(5/3)}{5/3}}$$

$$= 1000 \times 0.85 = 850\,\text{K}$$

$$W_{AB} = -\Delta U_{AB} = -nC_V\Delta T$$

$$= -(1)\left(\frac{3R}{2}\right)(850 - 1000) = 225R$$

26. For process $B \to C$,

$$\frac{p_B}{T_B} = \frac{p_C}{T_C}$$

$$\Rightarrow \quad T_C = \left(\frac{p_C}{p_B}\right)T_B = \left(\frac{p_A/3}{2p_A/3}\right)(850) = 425\,\text{K}$$

$$Q_{BC} = nC_V\Delta T = (1)\left(\frac{3R}{2}\right)(425 - 850) = 637.5R$$

27. For $A \to B$, $p_A V_A^{\gamma} = p_B V_B^{\gamma}$

$$\Rightarrow \quad \frac{V_B}{V_A} = \left(\frac{p_A}{p_B}\right)^{1/\gamma} = \left(\frac{3}{2}\right)^{3/5}$$

For $C \to D$, $T_C V_C^{\gamma-1} = T_D V_D^{\gamma-1}$

$$\Rightarrow \quad T_D = T_C\left(\frac{V_C}{V_D}\right)^{\gamma-1} = T_C\left(\frac{V_B}{V_A}\right)^{\gamma-1}$$

$$= 425\left(\frac{3}{2}\right)^{\frac{3}{5}\times\frac{2}{3}} = \frac{425}{0.85} = 500\,\text{K}$$

28. $W_{\text{gas}} = p_0\Delta V = p_0 A\Delta x = 10^5 \times (2\times10^{-2}) \times (2\times10^{-1}) = 400\,\text{J}$

$$Q = nC_p\Delta T = n\left(\frac{5R}{2}\right)\Delta T = \frac{5}{2}(p_0\Delta V) = \frac{5}{2}\times 400 = 100\,\text{J}$$

29. From initial position to *A*,

$$p = p_0 = \text{constant}$$

From *A* to *B*, $p = p_0 + \frac{Kx}{A}$

30. From initial position to *A*, $W_1 = 400$ J

From *A* to *B*, $W_2 = p_0\Delta V + \frac{1}{2}Kx^2$

$$= 400 + \frac{1}{2}\times 2000 \times (2\times10^{-1})^2 = 440\,\text{J}$$

$$\therefore \quad \frac{W_1}{W_2} = \frac{400}{440} = \frac{10}{11}$$

31. For cylinder *A*,

$$p_0 V_0^{\gamma} = p_f V_f^{\gamma}$$

$$\Rightarrow \quad p_0 V_0^{1.5} = p_f\left(\frac{V_0}{2}\right)^{1.5} \quad \Rightarrow \quad p_f = 2\sqrt{2}\,p_0$$

Finally in equilibrium, $p_A = p_B = 2\sqrt{2}\,p_0$

For *A*, $\quad p_0V_0 = \left(\frac{m}{M}\right)RT_0$ ...(i)

For *B*, $(2\sqrt{2}\,P_0)\left(\frac{3V_0}{2}\right) = \left(\frac{m_B}{M}\right)RT_0$ ...(ii)

Dividing Eq. (i) by (ii), we get

$$m_B = 3\sqrt{2}\,m$$

32. $\Delta U = nC_V\Delta T = \frac{nR\Delta T}{\gamma - 1} = \frac{p_fV_f - p_0V_0}{\gamma - 1}$

$$= \frac{(2\sqrt{2}\,p_0)\left(\frac{V_0}{2}\right) - p_0V_0}{1.5 - 1} = 2(\sqrt{2} - 1)\,p_0V_0$$

33. $W_A = -\Delta U = -2(\sqrt{2} - 1)\,p_0V_0 = -0.828p_0V_0$

$$W_B = nRT_0\ln\left(\frac{V_f}{V_i}\right) = (2\sqrt{2}\,p_0)\left(\frac{3V_0}{2}\right)\ln\left(\frac{3V_0/2}{V_0}\right)$$

$$= \left[3\sqrt{2}\ln\left(\frac{3}{2}\right)\right]p_0V_0 = 1.719p_0V_0$$

$$\therefore \quad |W_B| > |W_A|$$

34. For equilibrium of piston,

$$F_{\text{compressive}} = p_f S = 2\sqrt{2}\,p_0 S$$

35. For the right chamber,

$$T_0 p_0^{\frac{1-\gamma}{\gamma}} = T p^{\frac{1-\gamma}{\gamma}}$$

$$\Rightarrow \quad T = T_0\left(\frac{p_0}{p}\right)^{\frac{1-\gamma}{\gamma}} = T_0\left(\frac{32}{243}\right)^{\frac{(1-(5/3))}{5/3}} = \frac{9T_0}{4}$$

36. For the right chamber,

$$\frac{p_0V_0}{T_0} = \frac{pV}{T}$$

$$\Rightarrow \quad \frac{p_0V_0}{T_0} = \frac{\left(\frac{243}{32}\right)p_0V}{\left(\frac{9T_0}{4}\right)} \quad \Rightarrow \quad V = \frac{8}{27}V_0$$

For the left chamber,

$$\frac{p_0V_0}{T_0} = \frac{pV}{T}$$

$$\Rightarrow \quad \frac{p_0V_0}{T_0} = \frac{\left(\frac{243}{32}p_0\right)\left(2V_0 - \frac{8V_0}{27}\right)}{T} \quad \Rightarrow \quad T = \frac{207}{16}T_0$$

37. $W = -nC_V\Delta T = -n\left(\frac{3R}{2}\right)(T_2 - T_1) = -\frac{3}{2}(pV - p_0V_0)$

$$= -\frac{3}{2}\left[\left(\frac{243}{32}p_0\right)\left(\frac{8V_0}{27}\right) - p_0V_0\right] = -\frac{15}{8}p_0V_0$$

38. $\Delta U_1 = nC_V\Delta T = n\left(\frac{3R}{2}\right)(T_2 - T_1) = \frac{3}{2}(pV - p_0V_0)$

$$= \frac{3}{2}\left[\left(\frac{243}{32}p_0\right)\left(\frac{46}{27}\right)V_0 - p_0V_0\right] = \frac{573}{32}p_0V_0$$

$$Q = \Delta U_1 + \Delta U_2 = \frac{573}{32}p_0V_0 + \frac{15}{8}p_0V_0 = \frac{633}{32}p_0V_0$$

Match the Columns Questions

1. (A) $J \to K$ is isochoric cooling. So, $\Delta T < 0$

$\therefore Q = nC_V\Delta T < 0, \quad W = 0$

(B) $K \to L$ is isobaric heating. So, $\Delta T > 0$

$\therefore Q = nC_p\Delta T > 0, \quad W = nR\Delta T > 0$

(C) $L \to M$ is isochoric heating. So, $\Delta T > 0$

$\therefore Q = nC_V\Delta T > 0, \quad W = 0$

(D) $M \to J$,

$$T_M = \frac{(20)(20)}{nR}, \quad T_J = \frac{(30)(10)}{nR}$$

$\therefore \quad T_M > T_J \Rightarrow \Delta T < 0$

$\Delta U = nC_V\Delta T < 0$

$W < 0$ as gas undergoes compression.

$\therefore \quad Q = \Delta U + W < 0$

2. (A) AB is isothermal process.

$$W_{AB} = nRT_A \ln\left(\frac{p_A}{p_B}\right)$$

$$= \frac{2}{3}\left[n\left(\frac{3R}{2}\right)T_A\right]\ln\left(\frac{p_0}{2p_0}\right) = \frac{2}{3}(3U_0)\ln\left(\frac{1}{2}\right)$$

$$= -2\ln 2\, U_0 = -0.602U_0$$

(B) BC is isobaric process.

For CD, $\frac{U_0}{p_0} = \frac{U_C}{2p_0} \quad \Rightarrow \quad U_C = 2U_0$

$$W_{BC} = nR\Delta T = nR(T_C - T_B)$$

$$= \frac{2}{3}\left[n\left(\frac{3R}{2}\right)(T_C - T_B)\right] = \frac{2}{3}(U_C - U_B) = -0.67U_0$$

(C) For CD, $\frac{U}{p} = \text{constant}$

$$\Rightarrow \quad \frac{nC_VT}{p} = \text{constant} \quad \Rightarrow V = \text{constant}$$

So, CD is isochoric process. Therefore, $W_{CD} = 0$.

(D) DA is isobaric process.

$$W = nR\Delta T = \frac{2}{3}\left[n\left(\frac{3R}{2}\right)\Delta T\right]$$

$$= \frac{2}{3}\Delta U = \frac{2}{3}(3U_0 - U_0) = 1.33U_0$$

3. (A) In going from $A \to C$,

$$\Delta U = (Q_{AC})_{adi} - (W_{AC})_{adi}$$

$$= (Q_{AC})_{circle} - (W_{AC})_{circle}$$

$$\Rightarrow \quad 0 - (W_{AC})_{adi} = (Q_{AC})_{circle} - (W_{AC})_{circle}$$

$$\Rightarrow \quad (Q_{AC})_{circle} = (W_{AC})_{circle} - (W_{AC})_{adi}$$

$$= (W_{AC})_{circle} + (W_{CA})_{adi} = W_{cycle}$$

Since, the cycle is clockwise, $W_{cycle} > 0$

$\therefore \quad (Q_{AC})_{circle} > 0$

(B) In going from $B \to C$, both pressure and volume decrease. So, $T_C < T_B$

$\therefore \quad \Delta U_{BC} < 0$

$W_{BC} < 0$ [$\because$ Gas undergoing compression]

$\therefore \quad Q = \Delta U_{BC} + W_{BC} < 0$

(C) For $C \to D$, $\Delta U_{CD} < 0$ and $W_{CD} < 0$

$\therefore \quad Q = \Delta U_{CD} + W_{CD} < 0$

4. (A) W_{cycle} = Area of cycle

$$= \frac{1}{2}(2V_0 - V_0)(3p_0 - p_0) = p_0V_0$$

(B) CA is isobaric process.

$$Q_{CA} = nC_p\Delta T = n\left(\frac{5R}{2}\right)\Delta T = \frac{5}{2}p\Delta V$$

$$= \frac{5}{2}p_0(V_0 - 2V_0) = -\frac{5}{2}p_0V_0$$

(C) $\Delta U_{BC} = n\left(\frac{3R}{2}\right)\Delta T = \frac{3}{2}(p_CV_C - p_BV_B)$

$$= \frac{3}{2}(p_0(2V_0) - (3p_0)V_0) = -\frac{3}{2}p_0V_0$$

W_{BC} = Area under line BC

$$= \frac{1}{2}(3p_0 - p_0)(2V_0 - V_0) = p_0V_0$$

$$Q_{BC} = \Delta U_{BC} + W_{BC}$$

$$= -\frac{3}{2}p_0V_0 + p_0V_0 = -\frac{p_0V_0}{2}$$

(D) Equation of line BC,

$$p - p_0 = -\left(\frac{3p_0 - p_0}{2V_0 - V_0}\right)(V - 2V_0)$$

$$\Rightarrow \quad p = -\left(\frac{2p_0}{V_0}\right)V + 5p_0$$

Substituting $p = \frac{nRT}{V}$, we get

$$\frac{RT}{V} = -\left(\frac{2p_0}{V_0}\right)V + 5p_0$$

$$T = \frac{1}{R}\left[-\left(\frac{2p_0}{V_0}\right)V^2 + (5p_0)V\right]$$

For T to be maximum, $\frac{dT}{dV} = 0$

$$\Rightarrow \quad \frac{dT}{dV} = \frac{1}{R}\left[-\left(\frac{2p_0}{V_0}\right)(2V) + 5p_0\right] = 0 \quad \Rightarrow \quad V = \frac{5V_0}{4}$$

At $\quad V = \frac{5V_0}{4}$,

$$T_{max} = \frac{1}{R}\left[-\left(\frac{2p_0}{V_0}\right)\left(\frac{5V_0}{4}\right)^2 + 5p_0\left(\frac{5V_0}{4}\right)\right]$$

$$= \frac{25p_0V_0}{8R} = \frac{25p_0V_0}{8(25/3)} = \frac{3p_0V_0}{8}$$

5. (A) $p = 2V^2 \quad \Rightarrow \quad \frac{nRT}{V} = 2V^2 \quad \Rightarrow \quad T \propto V^3$

Hence as volume increases, temperature will also increase. As gas is expanding on increasing temperature, $W > 0$ and $\Delta U > 0$.

$\therefore \quad Q = \Delta U + W > 0$

(B) $\quad pV^2 = \text{constant}$

$$\Rightarrow \quad \left(\frac{nRT}{V}\right)V^2 = \text{constant} \quad \Rightarrow \quad TV = \text{constant}$$

So, if volume increases, temperature will decrease.

$$C = C_V + \frac{R}{1-m} = \frac{3R}{2} + \frac{R}{1-2} = \frac{R}{2}$$

$$Q = nC\Delta T$$

For expansion, $Q < 0$ $\quad [\because C > 0 \text{ and } \Delta T < 0]$

If temperature increases, volume decreases. So, $W < 0$

(C) $\quad C = C_V + 2R$

$$\Rightarrow \quad C_V + \frac{R}{1-m} = C_V + 2R$$

$$\Rightarrow \quad m = \frac{1}{2}$$

$$\therefore \quad pV^{1/2} = \text{constant}$$

$$\Rightarrow \quad \left(\frac{nRT}{V}\right)V^{1/2} = \text{constant} \quad \Rightarrow \quad T \propto \sqrt{V}$$

So, as volume increases, temperature will increase.

$Q = nC\Delta T > 0$ $\quad [\because C > 0, \Delta T > 0]$

As gas is expanding on increasing temperature, $W > 0$

(D) $\quad C = C_V - 2R$

$$\Rightarrow \quad C_V + \frac{R}{1-m} = C_V - 2R \quad \Rightarrow \quad m = \frac{3}{2}$$

$$\therefore \quad pV^{3/2} = \text{constant} \quad \Rightarrow \quad TV^{1/2} = \text{constant}$$

So, if volume increases, temperature will decrease.

$Q = nC\Delta T > 0$ $\quad [\because C < 0, \Delta T < 0]$

As volume decreases on increasing temperature, $W < 0$.

6. (A)

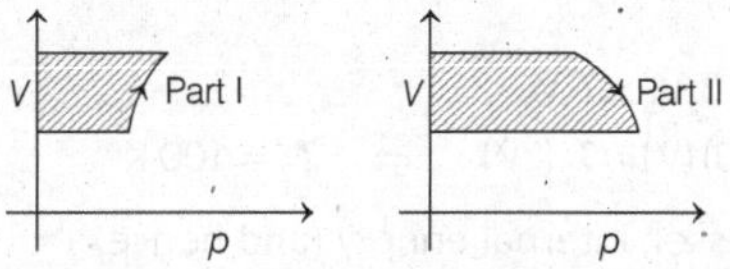

In part I, as volume is increasing, W is positive.
In part II, as volume is decreasing, W is negative.
As negative work in part II is greater than positive work in part I, net work done during the process is negative.

As $\quad V_A = V_B, p_B > p_B$

$\Rightarrow \quad T_B > T_A \quad \Rightarrow \quad \Delta U > 0$

(B) $\quad V = \frac{nRT}{p}$

So, as T decreases and p increases $\Rightarrow V$ will decrease

$\therefore \quad W < 0$ and $\Delta U < 0$

(C) Volume increases while temperature decreases.

$\therefore \quad W > 0$ and $\Delta U < 0$

(D) As volume decreases $\Rightarrow W < 0$

$$p_A = p_B, V_A > V_B$$

$\Rightarrow \quad T_A > T_B \quad \Rightarrow \quad \Delta U < 0$

7. $\Delta U_{cycle} = 0$

If p-V graph is clockwise, work done by the gas is positive. If p-V graph is anti-clockwise, work done by the gas is negative.

$$Q_{cycle} = W_{cycle}$$

Numerical Value Questions

1. Let mass of $H_2 = m$

$$Q = \Delta U + W \quad \Rightarrow \quad 150 = \Delta U + 50$$

$$\Rightarrow \quad \Delta U = 100 \text{ kJ}$$

$$\Delta U = nC_V\Delta T = 100 \text{ kJ}$$

$$W = nR\Delta T = 50 \text{ kJ}$$

$$\therefore \quad \frac{\Delta U}{W} = \frac{C_V}{R} = \frac{100}{50} \quad \Rightarrow \quad C_V = 2R$$

For mixture,

$$C_{V_{mix}} = \frac{n_1C_{V_1} + n_2C_{V_2}}{n_1 + n_2}$$

$$\Rightarrow \quad 2R = \frac{\left(\frac{m}{2}\right)\left(\frac{5R}{2}\right) + \left(\frac{12-m}{4}\right)\left(\frac{3R}{2}\right)}{\frac{m}{2} + \frac{12-m}{4}}$$

$$\Rightarrow \quad m = 4 \text{ g}$$

2. $C = C_V + \dfrac{R}{1-m}$

$$\Rightarrow \quad \frac{R}{2} = \frac{3R}{2} + \frac{R}{1-m} \quad \Rightarrow \quad m = 2$$

So, the equation of polytropic process,
$pV^2 = \text{constant}$

$$\Rightarrow \quad \left(\frac{nRT}{V}\right)V^2 = \text{constant} \quad \Rightarrow \quad TV = \text{constant}$$

$$\therefore \quad T_1V_1 = T_2V_2$$

$$\Rightarrow \quad (200)(V) = T_2(2V) \quad \Rightarrow \quad T_2 = 100\text{ K}$$

3. For the first vessel, internal energy (and hence, temperature) remains constant.

$$Q_1 = nRT\ln\left(\frac{V_2}{V_1}\right) = (1)R(300)\ln 2 = 207.9R$$

For the second vessel, volume is kept constant.

$$Q_2 = nC_V\Delta T = (1)\left(\frac{3R}{2}\right)(T_2 - 300)$$

According to given problem,

$$Q_1 = Q_2 \quad \Rightarrow \quad 207.9R = \left(\frac{3R}{2}\right)(T_2 - 300)$$

$$\Rightarrow \quad T_2 = 438.6\text{ K}$$

Now when the free mixing is allowed,

$$U_1 + U_2 = U'_1 + U'_2$$

$$\Rightarrow n_1C_VT_1 + n_2C_VT_2 = n_1C_VT + n_2C_VT$$

$$\Rightarrow \quad T = \frac{T_1 + T_2}{2} = \frac{300 + 438.6}{2} = 369.3\text{ K}$$

4. For process $A \to B$,

$$p = \frac{3}{2}T^{1/2} \quad \Rightarrow \quad p = \frac{3}{2}\left(\frac{PV}{nR}\right)^{1/2}$$

$$\Rightarrow \quad pV^{-1} = \text{constant}$$

$$W_1 = \frac{nR\Delta T}{1-m} = \frac{(1)(8.3)(100)}{1-(-1)} = 415\text{ J}$$

For process $B \to C$,

$$U = \frac{1}{2}V^{1/2}$$

$$\Rightarrow \quad (1)\left(\frac{3R}{2}\right)T = \frac{1}{2}\sqrt{V} \quad \Rightarrow \quad T = \frac{\sqrt{V}}{3R}$$

$\therefore$ When $V_B = 100\text{ cm}^3$, $T_B = \dfrac{\sqrt{100}}{3R} = \dfrac{10}{3R}$

$$V_B = 1600, T_B = \frac{\sqrt{1600}}{3R} = \frac{40}{3R}$$

$$T \propto \sqrt{V} \Rightarrow pV^{1/2} = \text{constant}$$

$$W_2 = \frac{nR\Delta T}{1-m} = \frac{(1)(R)\left(\frac{40}{3R} - \frac{10}{3R}\right)}{1 - \frac{1}{2}} = 20\text{ J}$$

$$W = W_1 + W_2 = 415 + 20 = 435\text{ J}$$

5. For equilibrium of piston finally,

$$\Delta pA = kx$$

$$\Rightarrow \quad (3-1)\times 10^5 \times 0.005 = 10^4 x$$

$$\Rightarrow \quad x = 0.1\text{ m}$$

For gas, $\quad V_1 = \dfrac{nRT_1}{p_1} = \dfrac{1\times(25/3)\times 300}{1\times 10^5} = 2.5\times 10^{-2}\text{ m}^3$

$$V_2 = V_1 + Ax = 2.55\times 10^{-3}\text{ m}^3$$

$$\frac{p_1V_1}{T_1} = \frac{p_2V_2}{T_2}$$

$$\Rightarrow \quad \frac{1\times 10^5 \times 2.5\times 10^{-2}}{300} = \frac{3\times 10^5 \times 2.55\times 10^{-2}}{T_2}$$

$$\Rightarrow \quad T_2 = 918\text{ K}$$

$$\Delta U = nC_V\Delta T = 1\left(\frac{3R}{2}\right)(918 - 300) = 7725\text{ J}$$

$$W = p_0\Delta V + \frac{1}{2}kx^2$$

$$= 1\times 10^5 \times (0.005\times 0.1) + \frac{1}{2}\times 10^4 \times (0.1)^2 = 100\text{ J}$$

$$\therefore \quad Q = \Delta U + W = 7725 + 100 = 7825\text{ J}$$

6. For equilibrium of combined system,

$$p(A_1 - A_2) = mg + p_0(A_1 - A_2)$$

$$\Rightarrow \quad p = p_0 + \frac{mg}{A_1 - A_2}$$

$$= 10^5 + \frac{1000}{0.02 - 0.01} = 2\times 10^5\text{ Pa}$$

As pistons are free to move, pressure of gas remains constant.

$$Q = nC_p\Delta T = n\left(\frac{7R}{2}\right)\Delta T = \frac{7}{2}p\Delta V$$

$$= \frac{7}{2}\times 2\times 10^5 \times [(0.02 - 0.01)\times 0.1]$$

$$= 700\text{ J}$$

7. For just lifting the block,

$$kx = mg \quad \Rightarrow \quad 16x = 0.8\times 10$$

$$\Rightarrow \quad x = 0.5\text{ m}$$

$$p_1 = p_0 + \frac{mg}{A} = 10^5 + \frac{1\times 10}{10^{-4}} = 2\times 10^5\text{ Pa}$$

$$p_2 = p_1 + \frac{Kx}{A} = 2\times 10^5 + \frac{16\times 0.5}{10^{-4}} = 2.8\times 10^5\text{ Pa}$$

$$V_1 = 1.4\times 10^{-4}\text{ m}^3$$

$$V_2 = V_1 + Ax = 1.4\times 10^{-4} + 10^{-4}\times 0.5 = 1.9\times 10^{-4}\text{ m}^3$$

$$\Delta U = nC_V\Delta T = n\left(\frac{5R}{2}\right)\Delta T = \frac{5}{2}(p_2V_2 - p_1V_1) = 63\text{ J}$$

$$W_{gas} = (p_0A)x + mgx + \frac{1}{2}Kx^2 = 12\text{ J}$$

$$Q = \Delta U + W_{gas} = 63 + 12 = 75\text{ J}$$

8. $Q = nC_p\Delta T = n\left(\frac{5R}{2}\right)\Delta T = \frac{5}{2}p\Delta V = \frac{5}{2}p(S\Delta x)$

$$\frac{dQ}{dt} = \frac{5}{2}pS\frac{\Delta x}{\Delta t}$$

$$\Rightarrow \quad q = \frac{5}{2}\left(p_0 + \frac{Mg}{S}\right)Sv$$

$$\Rightarrow \quad v = \frac{2q}{5(p_0S + Mg)}$$

$\therefore \quad x = 2$

9. $$dQ = dU + dW$$

$$\Rightarrow \quad 0 = (n_1C_{V_1}dT + n_2C_{V_2}dT) + pdV$$

$$\Rightarrow \quad 0 = \frac{1}{2}(2R)\,dT + 4\left(\frac{7R}{4}\right)dT + \left(\frac{4RT}{V}\right)dV = 0$$

$$\Rightarrow \quad 2\int_{300}^{T_f}\frac{dT}{T} + \int_{V_0}^{V_0/4}\frac{dV}{V} = 0$$

$$\Rightarrow \quad 2\ln\left(\frac{T_f}{300}\right) + \ln\left(\frac{V_0/4}{V_0}\right) = 0$$

$$\Rightarrow \quad T_f = 600\text{ K}$$

$$\Delta U = n_1C_{V_1}\Delta T + n_2C_{V_2}\Delta T$$

$$= \frac{1}{2}(2R)(600-300) + 4\times\frac{7R}{4}(600-300)$$

$$= 2400R = 2400\times\frac{25}{3} = 2\times10^4\text{ J}$$

$\therefore \quad n = 2$

10. Equation of parabola,

$$x = ay^2 \quad \Rightarrow \quad \left(\frac{1}{V}\right) = aT^2$$

$\Rightarrow \quad TV^{1/2} = \text{constant}$

Comparing it with $TV^{\gamma-1} = \text{constant}$, we get

$$\gamma - 1 = \frac{1}{2} \quad \Rightarrow \gamma = \frac{3}{2}$$

$$\frac{v_{rms}}{v_{sound}} = \frac{\sqrt{\frac{3RT}{M}}}{\sqrt{\frac{\gamma RT}{M}}} = \sqrt{\frac{3}{\gamma}} = \sqrt{2}$$

$\therefore \quad \alpha^2 = 2$

11. $$T_1 = \frac{p_1V_1}{R}, T_2 = \frac{p_2V_2}{R},$$

$$T_3 = \frac{p_1V_2}{R}, T_4 = \frac{p_2V_1}{R}$$

$$\tan\theta = \frac{p_1}{V_1} = \frac{p_2}{V_2}$$

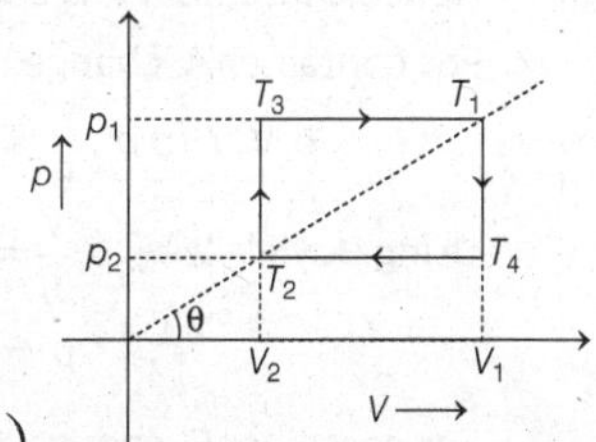

$$\Rightarrow \quad p_1V_2 = p_2V_1$$

$\therefore \quad T_3 = T_4$

$$T_3T_4 = \left(\frac{p_1V_2}{R}\right)\left(\frac{p_2V_1}{R}\right)$$

$$\Rightarrow \quad T_3^2 = \left(\frac{p_1V_1}{R}\right)\left(\frac{p_2V_2}{R}\right) \Rightarrow T_3^2 = T_1T_2$$

$$\Rightarrow \quad T_3 = \sqrt{T_1T_2} = \sqrt{400\times289} = 340\text{ K}$$

$$W = \text{Area of cycle} = (p_1 - p_2)(V_1 - V_2)$$

$$= p_1V_1 + p_2V_2 - p_1V_2 - p_2V_1$$

$$= R(T_1 + T_2 - T_3 - T_4)$$

$$= \frac{25}{3}(400 + 289 - 340 - 340) = 75\text{ J}$$

12. $Q_{12} = \Delta U_{12} + W_{12} = n\left(\frac{3R}{2}\right)(T_2 - T_1) + \left(2p_0V_0 - \frac{\pi\pi_0V_0}{4}\right)$

$$= \frac{3}{2}[(2p_0)(2V_0) - p_0V_0] + \left(2p_0V_0 - \frac{\pi p_0V_0}{4}\right)$$

$$= \left(\frac{13}{2} - \frac{\pi}{4}\right)p_0V_0 = \frac{40}{7}p_0V_0$$

$$Q_{23} = nC_V\Delta T = n\left(\frac{3R}{2}\right)(T_3 - T_2)$$

$$= \frac{3}{2}[p_0(2V_0) - (2p_0)(2V_0)] = -3p_0V_0$$

$$Q_{31} = nC_p\Delta T = n\left(\frac{5R}{2}\right)(T_1 - T_3)$$

$$= \frac{5}{2}(p_0V_0 - p_0(2V_0)) = -\frac{5}{2}p_0V_0$$

$$\eta = 1 - \frac{Q_{out}}{Q_{in}} = 1 - \frac{3p_0V_0 + \frac{5}{2}p_0V_0}{\frac{40}{7}p_0V_0} = \frac{3}{80}$$

$$\text{Percentage efficiency} = \frac{3}{80}\times100 = 3.75\%$$

13. $$p_A = p_B \qquad \text{...(i)}$$

For process BC,

$$p_BV_B^\gamma = p_CV_C^\gamma \qquad \text{...(ii)}$$

For process CA,

$$p_AV_A = p_CV_C \qquad \text{...(iii)}$$

Solving Eqs. (i), (ii) and (iii), we get

$$V_C = \left(\frac{V_B^\gamma}{V_A}\right)^{\frac{1}{\gamma-1}} = \left(\frac{(4V)^{3/2}}{V}\right)^{\left(\frac{1}{(3/2)-1}\right)} = 64\,V$$

$$Q_{AB} = nC_p\Delta T = n(3R)(T_B - T_A) = 9p_AV$$

$$Q_{BC} = 0$$

$$Q_{CA} = nRT_A\ln\left(\frac{V_A}{V_C}\right)$$

$$= p_AV\ln\left(\frac{V}{64V}\right) = (-6\ln2)\,p_AV$$

$$\eta = 1 - \frac{Q_{out}}{Q_{in}} = 1 - \frac{(6\ln2)\,p_AV}{9p_AV} = \frac{3 - 2\ln2}{3}$$

$\therefore \quad X = 3$

Previous Year's Questions

JEE Main

1. $m = 0.08\,\text{kg}$

$S_V = 0.17$ kcal/kg-°C

$\Delta T = 5°\text{C}$

Change in internal energy is,

$\Delta U = mS_V\Delta T$

$\Delta U = 0.08 \times 0.17 \times 10^3 \times 5$

$\Delta U = 68\,\text{cal} \Rightarrow 68 \times 4.184\,\text{J}$

$\Delta U = 284.24\,\text{J} \simeq 248\,\text{J}$

2. For an adiabatic process

$$pT^{\frac{\gamma}{1-\gamma}} = \text{constant} \quad ...(i)$$

Given, $p \propto T^3$

$\therefore \quad pT^{-3} = \text{constant} \quad ...(ii)$

From Eqs. (i) and (ii), we get

$$\frac{\gamma}{1-\gamma} = -3 \Rightarrow \gamma = \frac{3}{2}$$

$$\therefore \quad \frac{C_p}{C_V} = \frac{3}{2}$$

3.

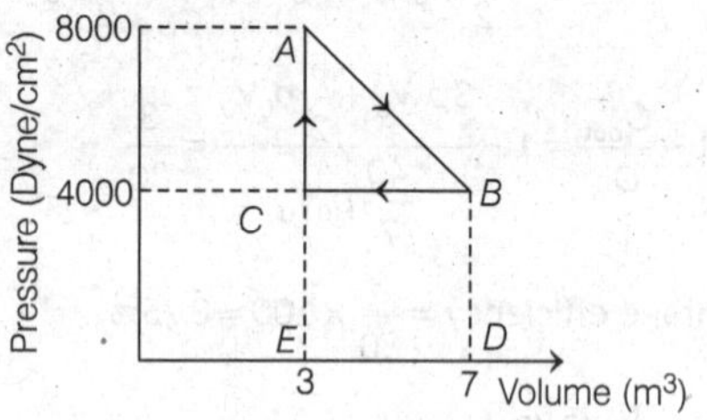

W_{AB} = Area of trapezium $ABDECA$

$$= \frac{1}{2} \times (8000 + 4000) \times 10^{-1} \times 4 = 2400\,\text{J}$$

W_{BC} = Area of rectangle $CBDEC$

$$= 4000 \times 10^{-1} \times 4 = 1600\,\text{J}$$

$\therefore$ Total work done,

$$W = W_{AB} - W_{BC} = 2400 - 1600 = 800\,\text{J}$$

4. For thermodynamic process A,

$\log p = \gamma \log V$

$p = V^\gamma, (\gamma > 1)$

$pV^{\gamma - 1} = \text{constant}$

$$C_A = C_V + \frac{R}{1+\gamma} \quad ...(i)$$

Now for process B,

$pV^{-1} = \text{constant}$

$$C_B = C_V + \frac{R}{1+1}$$

$$C_B = C_V + \frac{R}{2} \quad ...(ii)$$

$$C_p = C_V + R \quad ...(iii)$$

From Eqs. (i), (ii) and (iii)

$$C_p > C_B > C_A > C_V$$

5. Process B is adiabatic (higher slope) and process A is isothermal (Lower slope).

So, $pV^\gamma = k$ for process B

and $pV = k$ for process A.

6. Efficiency of heat engine is given by

$$\eta = 1 - \frac{T_2}{T_1}$$

Where, T_2 = temperature of sink.
or temperature of cold reservoir
T_1 = temperature of source.

For highest value of η, temperature of cold reservoir should be minimum.

But minimum possible temperature is 0K

i.e., $T_2 = 0\,\text{K} = (0 - 273)°\text{C} = -273°\text{C}$

Thus, efficiency of a reversible heat engine will be highest at $-273°\text{C}$ temperature of cold reservoir.

7. The efficiency of a carnot engine is given as,

$$\eta = 1 - \frac{T_2}{T_1}$$

where, T_2 = absolute temperature of sink
T_1 = absolute temperature of reservoir.

In case (i), $\frac{1}{3} = 1 - \frac{T}{273 + 99}$

$$\frac{T}{372} = \frac{2}{3} \text{ or } T = 248\,\text{K}$$

In case (ii), $\frac{1}{6} = 1 - \frac{T + x}{273 + 99}$

$$\Rightarrow \quad \frac{T + x}{372} = \frac{5}{6} \Rightarrow \frac{248 + x}{372} = \frac{5}{6}$$

$\Rightarrow \quad 248 + x = 5 \times 62 = 310$

$\Rightarrow \quad x = 62\,\text{K}$

8. When heat is added to a system isothermally its temperature remains constant. So, statement I is incorrect.

Expansion work of a gas is given by;

$$W = p(V_f - V_i)$$

As $V_f > V_i$ so; work done is positive

Hence, statement II is correct.

9. For container A, change is isothermal.

$$p, V, T \text{ to } p', \frac{V}{8}, T$$

Using Boyle's law; $p'\frac{V}{8} = pV$

or $\quad p' = 8p \quad ...(i)$

For container B, change is adiabatic $\left(\gamma = \frac{5}{3}\right)$.

$$p, V, T \text{ to } p'', \frac{V}{8}, T'$$

Using $p \cdot V^{\gamma} = p''\left(\frac{V}{8}\right)^{\gamma}$

We have;

So, $p'' = p \cdot (8)^{\gamma} = p(8)^{\frac{5}{3}}$ ...(ii)

Ratio of final pressures of B and A samples is;

$$\frac{p''}{p'} = \frac{p \cdot 8^{\frac{5}{3}}}{p \cdot 8} = 8^{\frac{5}{3}-1} = 8^{\frac{2}{3}} = 2^2 = 4$$

10. $dU = nC_V \Delta T$

$\Delta T =$ Constant $\rightarrow$ Isothermal Process

11. Since, $p = aV^{-3}$

$$\frac{dp}{dV} = -3aV^{-4}$$

$$-V\frac{dp}{dV} = (-3aV^{-4})(-V)$$

$$-V\frac{dp}{dV} = +3aV^{-3}$$

$$-V\frac{dp}{dV} = 3p$$

Bulk modulus $= -V\frac{dp}{dV} = 3p$

12. Work done in the cyclic process,

$W =$ area of closed curve

$= \text{Area of } \Delta DCE = \frac{1}{2} \times CE \times CD$

$= \frac{1}{2} \times (4-2) \times (400-100) = 300 \text{ J}$

13. For an isothermal change,

$pV =$ constant or $p \propto \frac{1}{V}$.

Also pV value will be more at higher temperature.

∴ Correct isotherms will be,

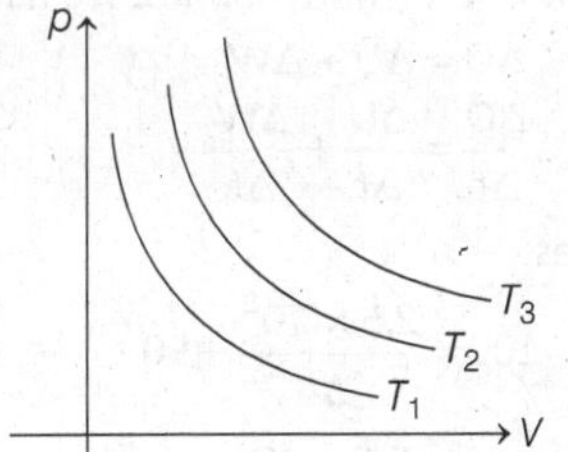

14. Total energy used in doing work $= p\Delta V$

$= 3 \times 10^5 \times 1600 \times 10^{-6} = 480 \text{ J}$

If only 10% energy = 480 J, is used in doing work.

Then, total energy = 4800 J

Therefore, the rest 90% of the remaining energy is used in increasing internal energy.

So, increase in internal energy = 90% of 4800 J

$$= \frac{90}{100} \times 4800 \text{ J} = 4320 \text{ J}$$

15. A $\rightarrow$ II, For an isothermal process, the temperature remains constant. So, the change in internal energy is zero.

B $\rightarrow$ I, In adiabatic process, no heat transfer takes place. Hence, by first law of thermodynamics, work done by the gas is equal to decrease in internal energy.

C $\rightarrow$ IV, In isochoric process, change in volume is zero.

i.e., $\Delta V = 0$

Hence, work done,

$$W = p \cdot \Delta V = p \times 0 = 0$$

Thus, in isochoric process, no work is done on or by the gas.

D $\rightarrow$ III, In isobaric process, when heat is supplied, a part of it goes in the expansion of gas an remaining part is used to increase the temperature of the gas which is turn increase in the internal energy.

16. Since, the given process is adiabatic, hence $\Delta Q = 0$ from first law of thermodynamics, we get

$$\Delta Q = \Delta U + \Delta W \Rightarrow \Delta U = -\Delta W$$

The process is adiabatic compression, therefore volume decreases. Hence,

$$\Delta W = -\text{ve} \Rightarrow \Delta U = +\text{ve}$$

Thus, internal energy of the system increases positively with change in temperature as gas is compressed adiabatically.

Hence, option (c) is not true.

17. From the first law of thermodynamics,

$$dQ = dU + dW$$

Also, we can write this as,

$$\frac{dQ}{dt} = \frac{dU}{dt} + \frac{dW}{dt}$$

$$1000 W = \frac{dU}{dt} + 200 W$$

$$\frac{dU}{dt} = 800 W$$

18. When a system is given heat dQ and the work done on system is dW

Then, $dQ + dW = dU$

or $dQ = dU - dW$

Both, statements are correct and R explains A.

19. For the given cyclic process :

AB is isochoric process, hence work done is zero.

$\Rightarrow \Delta Q_{AB} = \Delta U_{AB} + \Delta W_{AB}$

$\Rightarrow \Delta Q_{AB} = \Delta U_{AB}$

$\Rightarrow \Delta U_{AB} = \Delta Q_{AB} = 40 \text{ J}$ (given)

BC is adiabatic process and

$\Delta Q_{BC} = 0$ (given)

$\Rightarrow \Delta U_{BC} + \Delta W_{BC} = 0$

$\Rightarrow \Delta U_{BC} = -\Delta W_{BC} = -(-50)$

$\Rightarrow \Delta U_{BC} = 50 \text{ J}$ (given, $\Delta W_{BC} = -50$ J)

Now, as process is cyclic,

$\Delta U_{ABCA} = 0$

$\Rightarrow \Delta U_{AB} + \Delta U_{BC} + \Delta U_{CA} = 0$

$\Rightarrow \quad \Delta U_{CA} = -(\Delta U_{AB} + \Delta U_{BC}) = -(40+50) = -90$ J

Now, for process CA,

$$\Delta U_{CA} + \Delta W_{CA} = \Delta Q_{CA}$$

$\Rightarrow \quad -90 + \Delta W_{CA} = -60$

Given, $\quad \Delta Q_{CA} = -60$

So, $\quad \Delta W_{CA} = 90 - 60 = 30$ J

20. Given, for diatomic gas, $\gamma = 1.4$

$W = 400$ J (isobaric expansion)

To find the heat given to the gas.

Work done, $W = nR\Delta T = 400$ J ... (i)

Heat given to gas,

$$\Delta Q = nC_p \Delta T$$

$$\Rightarrow \quad \Delta Q = \frac{n \times 7R}{2} \times \Delta T$$

Using Eq. (i), $\Delta Q = \frac{7}{2} \times 400 = 1400$ J

21. Since we know, for an adiabatic process, $pV^{\gamma} = K$

$p_1V_1^{\gamma} = p_2V_2^{\gamma}$; m is constant

$$p_1\left(\frac{m}{d_1}\right)^{\gamma} = p_2\left(\frac{m}{d_2}\right)^{\gamma}; \frac{p_1}{p_2} = \left(\frac{d_1}{d_2}\right)^{\gamma}$$

$$\frac{p_1}{p_2} = \left(\frac{1}{32}\right)^{7/5}; \frac{p_1}{p_2} = \frac{1}{128}$$

As $\quad pV = nRT$

$$\frac{p_1V_1}{p_2V_2} = \frac{T_1}{T_2}; \frac{1}{128} \times \frac{d_2}{d_1} = \frac{T_1}{T_2};$$

$$\frac{1}{128} \times 32 = \frac{T_1}{T_2}; T_2 = 4T_1$$

22. (A) According to Newton's law of cooling, the rate of loss of heat of a body is directly proportional to the temperature difference between the body and it's surroundings.

i.e., $\frac{d\theta}{dt} \propto \Delta T$

(B) We know $p_{radiation} \propto T^4$

$T_P = 10°C = 283$ K; $T_Q = 20°C = 293$ K;

$$\frac{p_P}{p_Q} = \frac{(283)^4}{(293)^4} = \frac{1}{1.15}$$

(C) Here, $T_1 = 400$ K; $T_2 = 100$ K

$$\eta = \left(1 - \frac{T_2}{T_1}\right) \times 100\% = \left(1 - \frac{100}{400}\right) \times 100\% = 75\%$$

Hence, statement (A), (B) and (C) are correct and statement (D) is incorrect.

23. Given, mass of steam,

$m = 50$ g at $T = 100$ °C Time,

$t = 1$ min, $C_{water} = 1$ cal/g°C,

$T = 20$ °C, $L_V = 540$ cal/g

Heat rejected per minute is

$$\Delta Q = mL + mC\Delta T$$

$\Delta Q = 50 \times 540 + 50 \times 1 \times (100 - 20)$;

$\Delta Q = 540 \times 50 + 50 \times 80$;

$\Delta Q = 31000$ cal, $\Delta Q = 31 \times 10^3$ cal

24. Here, $T_1 = 227°C = 500$ K,

$T_2 = ?, Q_1 = 300$ cal

and $Q_2 = 225$ cal

Work done,

$$W = Q_1 - Q_2$$

$\therefore \quad W = 300 - 225 = 75$ Cal

Thus, we have $\frac{W}{Q} = 1 - \frac{T_2}{T_1}$

or $\frac{75}{300} = 1 - \frac{T_2}{500}$ or $\frac{1}{4} = 1 - \frac{T_2}{500}$

or $T_2 = \frac{3}{4} \times 500 = 375$ K or $T_2 = 102°$ C

25. Given, temperature of reservoir

$(T_H) = 527 + 273 = 800$ K

Temperature of sink $(T_C) = 200$ K

Efficiency of Carnot engine is given by

$$\eta = 1 - \frac{T_C}{T_H} = \frac{W}{Q}$$

$$\Rightarrow \quad \frac{W}{Q} = 1 - \frac{200}{800} = \frac{3}{4}$$

$$\Rightarrow \quad Q = \frac{4}{3} \times W = \frac{4}{3} \times 12000 \text{ kJ} = 16000 \text{ kJ} = 16 \times 10^6 \text{ J}$$

26. Given, heat supplied to the system,

$$\frac{\Delta Q}{\Delta t} = 6000 \text{ J/min} = \frac{6000}{60} \text{ J/s} = 100 \text{ J/s}$$

Power delivered, $P = \frac{\Delta W}{\Delta t} = 90$ W

Increase in internal energy, $\Delta U = 2.5 \times 10^3$ J

From first law of thermodynamics, we have

$$\Delta Q = \Delta U + \Delta W$$

or $\quad \frac{\Delta Q}{\Delta t} = \frac{\Delta U}{\Delta t} + \frac{\Delta W}{\Delta t}$ ...(i)

Putting values

$$100 = \frac{2.5 \times 10^3}{\Delta t} + 90$$

$$\Rightarrow \quad 10 = \frac{2.5 \times 10^3}{\Delta t}$$

$$\Rightarrow \quad \Delta t = \frac{2.5 \times 10^3}{10} \Rightarrow \Delta t = 2.5 \times 10^2 \text{ s}$$

27. In thermodynamic process ΔQ and ΔW depend on the path followed by the system between two states. Thus, they are path functions.

28. Given, number of mole, $n = 1$

Heat supplied $= Q$

Work done $= Q/5$

By using first law of thermodynamics,

$$\Delta Q = \Delta U + \Delta W$$

$\Rightarrow$ $Q = \Delta U + Q/5$

$\Rightarrow$ $\Delta U = 4Q/5 = nC_V \Delta T$ ...(i)

$\because$ $f = 5$

$\therefore$ $Q = \frac{5}{4}\frac{f}{2}R\Delta T$ [from Eq. (i)]

$\Rightarrow$ $\frac{Q}{\Delta T} = C = \frac{5}{4} \times \frac{5}{2} R = \frac{25}{8} R$

Hence, $x = 25$

29. Given,

The final pressure of the adiabatic process, $p_f = 200\ \text{N/m}^3$

The initial pressure of the adiabatic process, $p_i = 100\ \text{N/m}^3$

$$V_i = 4\ \text{m}^3$$
$$V_f = 3\ \text{m}^3$$

We know that, for an adiabatic process

$$W = \frac{p_f V_f - p_i V_i}{1-\gamma}$$

$\Rightarrow$ $W = \frac{200\,(3) - (100)\,(4)}{1 - 1.4}$

$\Rightarrow$ $W = -500\ \text{J}$

Negative sign represents the work done on the system.

30. In graph (A) vertical line is isochoric process, so the graph (A) is incorrect.

In graph (B) horizontal line is isobaric process, so the graph (B) is incorrect.

In graph (C) and (D) vertical line is isothermal process and the curve line is adiabatic process. So, the correct representation of thermodynamic process graph is (C) and (D).

So, the correct option is (b)

31. Here, p_1 and p_2, T_1 and T_2, V_1 and V_2 are initial and final pressures, temperatures and volumes, respectively.

Given, $V_2 = 2V_1$

$pV^{1/2} = \text{constant}$

From graph, $\gamma = \text{adiabatic constant} = 1/2$

$\Rightarrow$ $p_1 V_1^{1/2} = p_2 V_2^{1/2}$

$\Rightarrow$ $\frac{p_1}{p_2} = \left(\frac{2V_1}{V_1}\right)^{1/2} = 2^{1/2}$

Also, $p^{1-\gamma}T^{\gamma} = \text{constant}$ (for adiabatic process)

$\Rightarrow$ $p_1^{1-\gamma}T_1^{\gamma} = p_2^{1-\gamma}T_2^{\gamma}$

$\Rightarrow$ $\left(\frac{p_1}{p_2}\right)^{1-\gamma} = \left(\frac{T_2}{T_1}\right)^{\gamma}$ $\Rightarrow$ $\left(\frac{p_1}{p_2}\right)^{\frac{1-\gamma}{\gamma}} = \frac{T_2}{T_1}$

$\therefore$ $T_2/T_1 = (2^{1/2})^{\frac{1-0.5}{0.5}} = \sqrt{2}$

32. Let p_i, p_f, V_i and V_f be the initial and final pressure and volume.

Given, AB is isothermal $(\Delta T = 0)$,

BC is isochoric $(\Delta V = 0)$

and CA is adiabatic $(\Delta Q = 0)$

Since, isothermal work

$(W_{AB}) = p_1 V_1 \ln \frac{V_f}{V_i}$

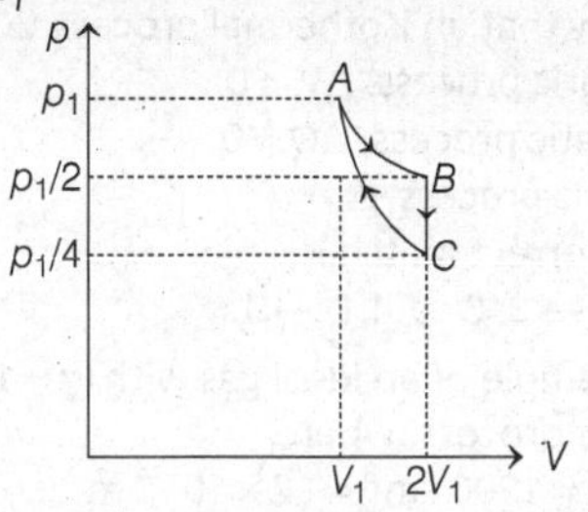

where, V_i and V_f are volume at A and B, respectively.

$\therefore$ $W_{AB} = p_1 V_1 \ln \frac{2V_1}{V_1} = p_1 V_1 \ln 2$

$\therefore$ $\Delta V = 0$

$\therefore$ $W_{BC} = 0$

Since, W_{CA} is an adiabatic work done, i.e.

$$W_{CA} = \frac{1}{1-\gamma}(p_f V_f - p_i V_i)$$

$\Rightarrow$ $W_{CA} = \frac{1}{1-\gamma}\left(p_1 V_1 - \frac{p_1}{4} \times 2V_1\right) = \frac{1}{1-\gamma}\frac{p_1 V_1}{2}$

$\therefore$ Net work done,

$$W_{\text{net}} = W_{AB} + W_{BC} + W_{CA}$$
$$= p_1 V_1 \ln 2 + 0 + \frac{1}{1-\gamma}\frac{p_1 V_1}{2}$$
$$= p_1 V_1 [\ln 2 + 1/2(1-\gamma)]$$

From ideal gas law,

$$pV = nRT$$

$\therefore$ $W_{\text{net}} = RT[\ln 2 - 1/2(\gamma - 1)]$ $(\because n = 1)$

33. As, AB is isothermal process, so work done in isothermal process is given by

$$W_{AB} = nRT \ln\left(\frac{V_2}{V_1}\right)$$
$$W_{AB} = nRT \ln\left(\frac{2V_1}{V_1}\right) = nRT \ln 2$$

As, BC is isobaric process, so work done in isobaric process is given by

$$W_{BC} = p\Delta V = p_2(V_1 - V_2)$$
$$= p_2\left(\frac{V_2}{2} - V_2\right) = -\frac{p_2 V_2}{2}$$
$$= \frac{-nRT}{2} \quad \left[\begin{matrix}\because pV = nRT \\ \therefore p_2 V_2 = nRT\end{matrix}\right]$$

As, CA is isochoric process, so work done in isochoric process is given by, $W_{CA} = 0$ $[\because \Delta V = 0]$

Total work done in the cycle $ABCA$,

$$W_{ABCA} = W_{AB} + W_{BC} + W_{CA}$$

$$= nRT\ln 2 + \left(\frac{-nRT}{2}\right) + 0$$

$$= nRT\left(\ln 2 - \frac{1}{2}\right)$$

34. We know that, in isothermal process, $\Delta T = 0$
In isochoric process, $\Delta V = 0$
In adiabatic process, $\Delta Q = 0$
In isobaric process, $\Delta p = 0$
So, the correct match is,
$A \to 2, B \to 3, C \to 4, D \to 1.$

35. Given, sample of an ideal gas with ($\gamma = 1.5$) is taken through adiabatic process, where

$V_1 = 1200\ \text{cm}^3 = 12 \times 10^{-4}\ \text{m}^3$
$V_2 = 300\ \text{cm}^3 = 3 \times 10^{-4}\ \text{m}$
$p_1 = 200\ \text{kPa} = 2 \times 10^5\ \text{Pa} = p_2$

Using equation of adiabatic process,

$$p_1V_1^\gamma = p_2V_2^\gamma,\ p_2 = p_1\left(\frac{V_1}{V_2}\right)^\gamma$$

$$= 2 \times 10^5\left(\frac{12 \times 10^{-4}}{3 \times 10^{-4}}\right)^{1.5} = 16 \times 10^5\ \text{Pa}$$

Work done in adiabatic process,

$$W = \frac{p_1V_1 - p_2V_2}{\gamma - 1}$$

Substituting the values, we get

$$W = \frac{(2 \times 10^5 \times 12 \times 10^{-4} - 16 \times 10^5 \times 3 \times 10^{-4})}{1.5 - 1} = -480\ \text{J}$$

Hence, work done in adiabatic compression is 480 J.

36. Consider the given diagram,

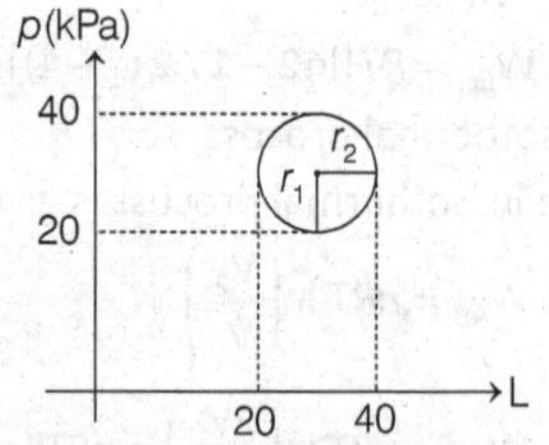

Here, $r_1 = 10 \times 10^3$ m and $r_2 = 10 \times 10^{-3}$m

We know that for a complete cyclic process, change in internal energy,

$$(\Delta U) = 0 \quad \text{...(i)}$$

According to 1st law of thermodynamics,

$$\Delta Q = \Delta U + W \quad \text{...(ii)}$$

From Eqs. (i) and (ii), we get

$\Rightarrow \quad \Delta Q = 0 + W$

$\Rightarrow \quad \Delta Q = W \quad \text{...(iii)}$

$\because \quad W = \text{Area} = \pi r_1 r_2$

$= \pi \times (10 \times 10^3) \times (10 \times 10^{-3})$

$W = 100\pi\ \text{J} \quad \text{...(iv)}$

From Eqs. (iii) and (iv), we get

$$\Delta Q = 100\,\pi\ \text{J}$$

37. Given, pressure, $(p) \propto kV^3$

$$T_1 = 100°\text{C}, T_2 = 300°\text{C}$$

$\Rightarrow \quad \Delta T = T_2 - T_1 = 300 - 100 = 200°\text{C}$

By using ideal gas equation,

$$pV = nRT$$

$\Rightarrow \quad kV^3 \cdot V = nRT \Rightarrow kV^4 = nRT$

On differentiating both sides w.r.t temperature, we get

$$4kV^3\frac{dV}{dT} = nR$$

$\Rightarrow \quad 4kV^3dV = nRdT$

$\Rightarrow \quad kV^3dV = nRdT/4$

$\Rightarrow \quad pdV = nRdT/4$

As, work done $(W) = pdV = nRdT/4$

$$= \frac{nR}{4}\Delta T = \frac{nR}{4} \times 200 = 50\,nR$$

38. Given, temperature of hot reservoir $= T_1$
Temperature of cold reservoir, $T_2 = 400\ \text{K}$
Heat of hot reservoir, $Q_1 = 300$ J
Heat of cold reservoir, $Q_2 = 240$ J
Since, efficiency

$$(\eta) = 1 - \frac{T_2}{T_1} = \frac{Q_1 - Q_2}{Q_1}$$

$$1 - \frac{T_2}{T_1} = 1 - \frac{Q_2}{Q_1}$$

$\Rightarrow 1 - \frac{400}{T_1} = 1 - \frac{240}{300} \Rightarrow \frac{400}{T_1} = \frac{4}{5}$

$\Rightarrow \quad T_1 = 500\ \text{K}$

39. Initially gas is compressed adiabatically.
Initial temperature, $T_1 = 300$ K
Number of moles = 1, $\gamma = 1.4$
Initial volume $= V_1$
Final volume $= \frac{V_1}{16}$

Process equation is,

$$T_1V_1^{\gamma-1} = T_2V_2^{\gamma-1}$$

$\Rightarrow 300V_1^{1.4-1} = T_2\left(\frac{V_1}{16}\right)^{1.4-1}$

$\Rightarrow \quad T_2 = 300 \times 2^{\frac{8}{5}} \quad \text{...(i)}$

In next process, gas is expanded isobarically. Initial volume,

$$V_2 = \frac{V_1}{16}$$

Final volume, $V_3 = 2\left(\frac{V_1}{16}\right) = \frac{V_1}{8}$

Now, for isobaric expansion,

$$\frac{V_2}{T_2} = \frac{V_3}{T_3}$$

$$\Rightarrow \quad \frac{V_2}{300 \times 2^{\frac{8}{5}}} = \frac{2V_2}{T_3}$$

$$\Rightarrow \quad T_3 = 2 \times 300 \times 2^{\frac{8}{5}} = 300 \times 2^{\frac{13}{5}} = 1818.85$$

or $\quad T_3 = 1819\ \text{K}$

40. Carnot engines given are operating in cascade configuration as shown in the figure.

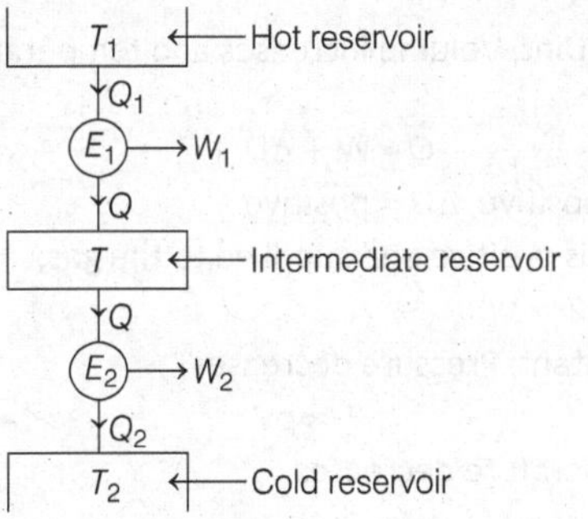

Work done by engine 1,

$$W_1 = Q_1 - Q = k(T_1 - T)$$

Work done by engine 2,

$$W_2 = Q - Q_2 = k(T - T_2)$$

So, $\dfrac{W_1}{W_2} = \dfrac{T_1 - T}{T - T_2}$

As, $\dfrac{W_1}{W_2} = 1$ (given)

$$\Rightarrow T - T_2 = T_1 - T$$

$$\Rightarrow \quad T = \frac{T_1 + T_2}{2}$$

41. To convert 100 g water at 0°C to ice at 0°C, heat absorbed by refrigerator,

$Q_1 = mL = 100 \times 80 = 8000$ cal

W = work done or energy supplied to refrigerator

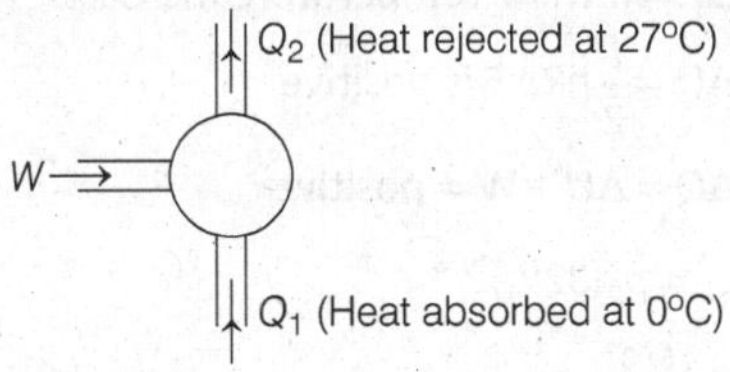

From figure, we have

$$W + Q_1 = Q_2 \quad \Rightarrow \quad W = Q_2 - Q_1$$

Now, coefficient of performance of refrigerator is

$$\beta = \frac{Q_1}{W} = \frac{Q_1}{Q_2 - Q_1} = \frac{T_1}{T_2 - T_1}$$

Here, $T_1 = 0°\ \text{C} = 273\ \text{K}$

$T_2 = 27°\ \text{C} = 300\ \text{K}$

So, $\dfrac{Q_1}{Q_2 - Q_1} = \dfrac{273}{300 - 273}$

$$\Rightarrow \quad 27Q_1 = (Q_2 - Q_1)273$$

$$\Rightarrow \quad 300\,Q_1 = Q_2 \times 273$$

$$\Rightarrow \quad Q_2 = 300 \times \frac{8000}{273} = \frac{2400000}{273}$$

$$= 8791.2\ \text{cal} \approx 8791\ \text{cal}$$

JEE Advanced

1.

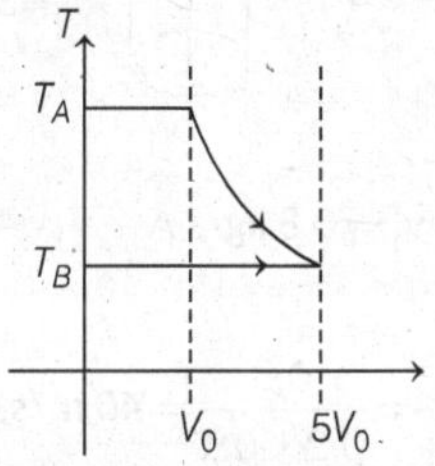

$$T_A V_0^{\gamma - 1} = T_B (5V_0)^{\gamma - 1}$$

$$\Rightarrow \quad T_A = 5^{\gamma - 1} T_B \quad \Rightarrow \quad T_A / T_B = 5^{\gamma - 1}$$

2. We know that for isobaric process, work done,

$$W = (n_1 + n_2)R\Delta T$$

$$\Rightarrow \quad 66 = (2 + 1)R\Delta T \quad \Rightarrow \quad 66 = 3R\Delta T$$

$$\Rightarrow \quad R\Delta T = 22 \quad \text{...(i)}$$

Change in internal energy,

$$\Delta U = \frac{f_1}{2} n_1 R\Delta T + \frac{f_2}{2} n_2 R\Delta T = \frac{R\Delta T}{2}[f_1 n_1 + f_2 n_2]$$

$$= \frac{22}{2}[f_1 n_1 + f_2 n_2] \quad \text{[from Eq. (i)]}$$

$$\Rightarrow \Delta U = 11[f_1 n_1 + f_2 n_2] \quad \text{...(ii)}$$

Now, $f_1 = \dfrac{2}{\gamma_1 - 1} = \dfrac{2}{\left(\dfrac{5}{3} - 1\right)} = 3$

and $f_2 = \dfrac{2}{\gamma_2 - 1} = \dfrac{2}{\left(\dfrac{7}{5} - 1\right)} = 5$

Now, puting the values of $n_1, n_2\ f_1$ and f_2 in Eq. (ii), we get

$$\Delta U = 11(3 \times 2 + 5 \times 1) = 121\ \text{J}$$

3. $W_I = W_a + W_b + W_c + W_d$

$$= 4p_0(2V_0 - V_0) + (4p_0)(2V_0)\ln\frac{4V_0}{2V_0} + 2p_0(V_0 - 4V_0) + 0$$

$$= 8p_0V_0\ln 2 - 2p_0V_0$$

$$W_{II} = W'_a + W'_b + W'_c + W'_d$$

$$= 4p_0V_0\ln\left(\frac{2V_0}{V_0}\right) + 0 + p_0(V_0 - 2V_0) + 0$$

$$= 4p_0V_0\ln 2 - p_0V_0$$

$$\frac{W_I}{W_{II}} = \frac{2}{1} = 2$$

4.

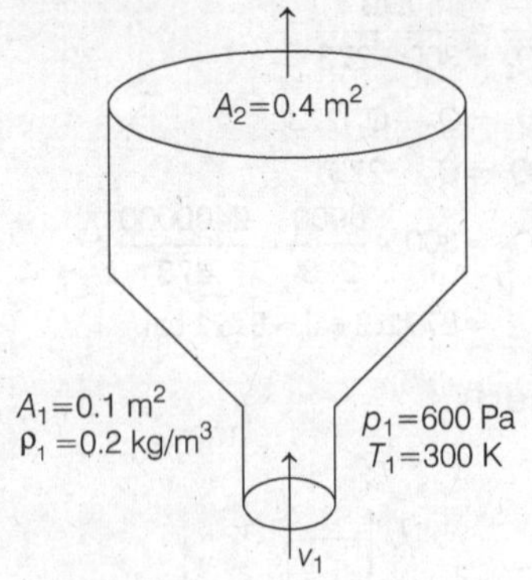

$$\frac{dm}{dt}=\rho_1 A_1 v_1 = 0.8\ \text{kg/s A}$$

$$\Rightarrow \quad v_1=\frac{\frac{dm}{dt}}{\rho_1 A_1}=\frac{0.8}{0.2\times 0.1}=40\ \text{m/s},$$

$$g=10\ \text{m/s}^2,\ \gamma=2$$

Gas undergoes adiabatic expansion,

$$p^{1-\gamma}T^{\gamma}=\text{constant}$$

$$\frac{p_2}{p_1}=\left(\frac{T_1}{T_2}\right)^{\frac{\gamma}{1-\gamma}}$$

$$\Rightarrow \quad p_2=\left(\frac{300}{150}\right)^{\frac{2}{-1}}\times 600 \ \Rightarrow\ p_2=\frac{600}{4}=150\ \text{Pa}$$

Now, $\rho=\frac{pM}{RT}\ \Rightarrow\ \rho\propto\frac{p}{T}$

$$\because\ \frac{\rho_1}{\rho_2}=\left(\frac{p_1}{p_2}\right)\left(\frac{T_1}{T_2}\right)=\left(\frac{150}{600}\right)\left(\frac{300}{150}\right)=\frac{1}{2}$$

$$\Rightarrow \quad \rho_2=\frac{\rho_1}{2}=0.1\ \text{kg/m}^3$$

Now, $\rho_2A_2v_2=0.8\ \Rightarrow\ v_2=\frac{0.8}{0.1\times 0.4}=20$ m/s

5. For adiabatic process ($A\to B$),

$$p_AV_A^{\gamma}=p_BV_B^{\gamma}$$

$$10^5\times(0.8)^{5/3}=3\times 10^5\,(V_B)^{5/3}$$

$$\Rightarrow \quad V_B=0.8\times\left(\frac{1}{3}\right)^{0.6}=0.4$$

Work done in process $A\to B$,

$$W_{AB}=\frac{p_AV_A-p_BV_B}{\gamma-1}$$

$$\Rightarrow \quad W_{AB}=\frac{10^5\times 0.8-3\times 10^5\times 0.4}{\frac{5}{3}-1}$$

$$\Rightarrow \quad W_{AB}=-60\ \text{kJ}\ \Rightarrow\ |W_{AB}|=60\ \text{kJ}$$

Work done in process $B\to C$ (isothermal process),

$$W_{BC}=nRT\ln\frac{V_C}{V_B}=p_BV_B\ln\frac{V_C}{V_B}$$

$$\Rightarrow \quad W_{BC}=3\times 10^5\times 0.4\ln\frac{0.8}{0.4}$$

$$\Rightarrow \quad W_{BC}=84\ \text{kJ}$$

Work done in process $C\to A$,

$$W_{CA}=p\Delta V=0 \qquad (\because \Delta V=0)$$

So, total work done in the process $A\to B\to C$,

$$W_{ABC}=W_{AB}+W_{BC}+W_{CA}=-60+84+0$$

$$\Rightarrow \quad W_{ABC}=24\ \text{kJ}$$

So, correct options are (b, c, d).

6. **Process 1**

$p=$ constant, Volume increases and temperature also increases

$$Q=W+\Delta U$$

$\therefore\ W=$ positive, $\Delta U=$ positive

$\Rightarrow$ Heat is positive and supplied to the gas.

Process 2

$V=$ constant, Pressure decreases

$$T\propto pV \qquad [\text{as } V=\text{constant}]$$

$\Rightarrow$ Temperature decreases

$$W=0$$

ΔT is negative and $\Delta U=\frac{f}{2}nR\Delta T$

$\therefore\ \Delta U$ is also negative, $Q=\Delta U+W$

$\therefore$ Heat is negative and rejected by gas.

Process 3

$p=$ constant, Volume decreases

$\Rightarrow$ Temperature also decreases

$W=p\Delta V=$ negative

$\Delta U=\frac{f}{2}nR\Delta T=$ negative

$Q=W+\Delta U=$ negative

$\therefore$ Heat is negative and rejected by gas.

Process 4

$V=$ constant, Pressure increases

$$W=0 \qquad (\text{as } V=\text{constant})$$

$pV=nRT\Rightarrow$ Temperature increase

$$\Rightarrow \quad \Delta U=\frac{f}{2}nR\Delta T \text{ is positive}$$

$$\Delta Q=\Delta U+W=\text{positive}$$

7. $\frac{p_1}{4}(4V_1)^{5/3}=p_2(32V_1)^{5/3}$

$$p_2=\frac{p_1}{4}\left(\frac{1}{8}\right)^{5/3}=\frac{p_1}{128}$$

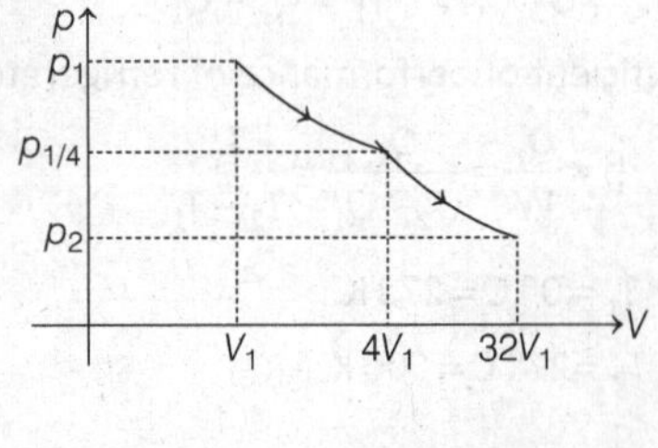

$$W_{adi} = \frac{p_1V_1 - p_2V_2}{\gamma - 1} = \frac{p_1V_1 - \frac{p_1}{128}(32\,V_1)}{\frac{5}{3} - 1}$$

$$= \frac{p_1V_1(3/4)}{2/3} = \frac{9}{8}p_1V_1$$

$$W_{iso} = p_1V_1 \ln\left(\frac{4V_1}{V_1}\right) = 2p_1V_1 \ln 2$$

$$\therefore \quad \frac{W_{iso}}{W_{adi}} = \frac{16}{9}\ln 2$$

$$\Rightarrow \quad f = \frac{16}{9} = 1.7778 \approx 1.78$$

8. $W = (\Delta p)_{avg} \times 4\pi R^2 a$

$$\approx \left| \frac{dp}{2} \cdot 4\pi R^2 a \right|$$

[for small change $(\Delta p)_{avg} < p >$ arithmetic mean]

For adiabatic process, $\frac{dp}{dV} = -\gamma\left(\frac{p}{V}\right)$

$$\therefore \quad dp = -\gamma \frac{p}{V} dV = -\frac{\gamma p_0}{V} 4\pi R^2 a$$

$$= \frac{\gamma p_0}{2V} \times 4\pi R^2 a \times 4\pi R^2 a$$

$$= \frac{\gamma p_0}{2 \times 4\pi R^3} 4\pi R^2 a \times 4\pi R^2 a = (4\pi R p \times a^2)\frac{3\gamma}{2}$$

$$\therefore \quad x \approx 2.05$$

9. Process-II is isothermal expansion,

$\Delta U = 0, W > 0$

$\Delta Q = W > 0$

Process-IV is isothermal compression,

$\Delta U = 0, W < 0$

$\Delta Q = W < 0$

Process-I and III are not isobaric because in isobaric process $T \propto V$ hence, T-V graph should be a straight line passing through origin.

Options b, c and d are true.

10. Given, $n = 1, \gamma = 5/3$

T-V equation in adiabatic process is

$$TV^{\gamma - 1} = \text{constant}$$

$$\therefore \quad T_1V_1^{\gamma - 1} = T_2V_2^{\gamma - 1}$$

$$\Rightarrow \quad T_2 = T_1\left(\frac{V_1}{V_2}\right)^{\gamma - 1} = 100 \times \left(\frac{1}{8}\right)^{\frac{2}{3}}$$

$$\Rightarrow \quad T_2 = 25\,\text{K}$$

$$C_V = \frac{3}{2}R \text{ for monoatomic gas}$$

$$\therefore \quad \Delta U = nC_V\Delta T = n \times \left(\frac{3R}{2}\right)(T_2 - T_1)$$

$$= 1 \times \frac{3}{2} \times 8 \times (25 - 100) = -900\,\text{J}$$

$\therefore$ Decrease in internal energy = 900 J

11. $v_{sound} = \sqrt{\frac{\gamma RT}{M}}$. As the sound wave propagates, the air in a chamber undergoes compression and rarefaction very fastly, hence undergo a adiabatic process. So, curves are steeper than isothermal.

$$\left(\frac{dp}{dV}\right)_{Adi} = -\gamma\left(\frac{p}{V}\right) \quad \text{...(i)}$$

$$\left(\frac{dp}{dV}\right)_{Iso} = -\left(\frac{p}{V}\right) \quad \text{...(ii)}$$

Graph 'Q' satisfies Eq. (i)

12. $\Delta U = \Delta Q - p\Delta V$

$\Delta U + p\Delta V = \Delta Q$

As $\Delta U \neq 0, W \neq 0, \Delta Q \neq 0$. The process represents, isobaric process

$$W_{gas} = -p(\Delta V) = -p(V_2 - V_1) = -pV_2 + pV_1$$

Graph 'P' satisfies isobaric process.

13. Work done in isochoric process is zero.

$W_{12} = 0$ as $\Delta V = 0$

Graph 'S' represents isochoric process.

14. **NOTE** This question can be solved if right hand side chamber is assumed to be open, so that its pressure remains constant.

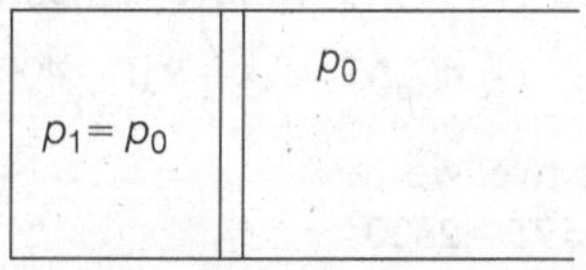

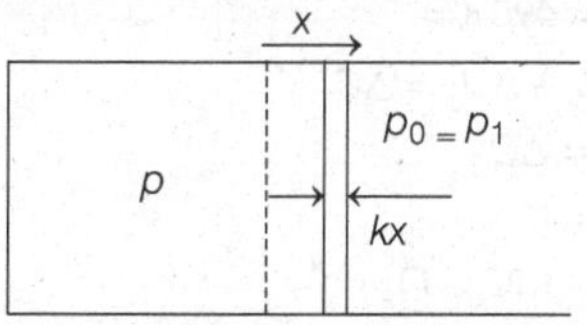

(a) $pV = nRT \Rightarrow p \propto \frac{T}{V}$

Temperature is made three times and volume is doubled

$$\Rightarrow \quad p_2 = \frac{3}{2}p_1$$

Further $x = \frac{\Delta V}{A} = \frac{V_2 - V_1}{A} = \frac{2V_1 - V_1}{A} = \frac{V_1}{A}$

$$p_2 = \frac{3p_1}{2} = p_1 + \frac{kx}{A} \Rightarrow kx = \frac{p_1A}{2}$$

Energy of spring

$$\frac{1}{2}kx^2 = \frac{p_1A}{4}x = \frac{p_1V_1}{4}$$

(b) $\Delta U = nc_v\Delta T = n\left(\frac{3}{2}R\right)\Delta T = \frac{3}{2}(p_2V_2 - p_1V_1)$

$$= \frac{3}{2}\left[\left(\frac{3}{2}p_1\right)(2V_1) - p_1V_1\right] = 3\,p_1V_1$$

(c) $p_2 = \frac{4p_1}{3}$

$$\Rightarrow \quad p_2 = \frac{4}{3}p_1 = p_1 + \frac{kx}{A}$$

$$\Rightarrow \quad kx = \frac{p_1 A}{3} \quad \Rightarrow x = \frac{\Delta V}{A} = \frac{2V_1}{A}$$

$$W_{gas} = (p_0\,\Delta V + W_{spring}) = (p_1 A x + \frac{1}{2}kx \cdot x)$$

$$= + \left(p_1 A \cdot \frac{2V_1}{A} + \frac{1}{2} \cdot \frac{p_1 A}{3} \cdot \frac{2V_1}{A} \right)$$

$$= 2p_1V_1 + \frac{p_1V_1}{3} = \frac{7p_1V_1}{3}$$

(d) $\Delta Q = W + \Delta U$

$$= \frac{7p_1V_1}{3} + \frac{3}{2}(p_2V_2 - p_1V_1)$$

$$= \frac{7p_1V_1}{3} + \frac{3}{2}\left(\frac{4}{3}p_1 \cdot 3V_1 - p_1V_1\right)$$

$$= \frac{7p_1V_1}{3} + \frac{9}{2}p_1\,V_1 = \frac{41p_1V_1}{6}$$

15. Let final equilibrium temperature of gases is T.

Heat rejected by gas by lower compartment

$$= nC_V\Delta T = 2 \times \frac{3}{2}R\,(700 - T)$$

Heat received by the gas in above compartment

$$= nC_p\Delta T = 2 \times \frac{7}{2}R\,(T - 400)$$

Equating the two, we get

$2100 - 3T = 7T - 2800$

$\Rightarrow \quad T = 490\,\text{K}$

16. $\Delta W_1 + \Delta U_1 = \Delta Q_1$ ...(i)

$\Delta W_2 + \Delta U_2 = \Delta Q_2$ ...(ii)

$\Delta Q_1 + \Delta Q_2 = 0$

$\therefore \ (nC_p\Delta T)_1 + (nC_p\Delta T)_2 = 0$

But $\quad n_1 = n_2 = 2$

$$\therefore \quad \frac{5}{2}R\,(T - 700) + \frac{7}{2}R\,(T - 400) = 0$$

Solving, we get $T = 525\,\text{K}$

Now, from Eqs. (i) and (ii), we get

$$\Delta W_1 + \Delta W_2 = -\Delta U_1 - \Delta U_2$$

as $\quad \Delta Q_1 + \Delta Q_2 = 0$

$$\therefore \quad \Delta W_1 + \Delta W_2 = -[(nC_V\Delta T)_1 + (nC_V\Delta T)_2]$$

$$= -\left[2 \times \frac{3}{2}R \times (525 - 700) + 2 \times \frac{5}{2}R \times (525 - 400)\right]$$

$$= -100R$$

17. $W_{ibf} = W_{ib} + W_{bf} = 50\,\text{J} + 100\,\text{J} = 150\,\text{J}$

$W_{iaf} = W_{ia} + W_{af} = 0 + 200\,\text{J} = 200\,\text{J}$

$Q_{iaf} = 500\,\text{J}$

So $\quad \Delta U_{iaf} = Q_{iaf} - W_{iaf} = 500\,\text{J} - 200\,\text{J} = 300\,\text{J} = U_f - U_i$

So, $\quad U_f = U_{iaf} + U_i = 300\,\text{J} + 100\,\text{J} = 400\,\text{J}$

$\Delta U_{ib} = U_b - U_i = 200\,\text{J} - 100\,\text{J} = 100\,\text{J}$

$Q_{ib} = \Delta U_{ib} + W_{ib} = 100\,\text{J} + 50\,\text{J} = 150\,\text{J}$

$Q_{ibf} = \Delta U_{ibf} + W_{ibf} = \Delta U_{iaf} + W_{ibf}$

$= 300\,\text{J} + 150\,\text{J} = 450\,\text{J}$

So, the required ratio

$$\frac{Q_{bf}}{Q_{ib}} = \frac{Q_{ibf} - Q_{ib}}{Q_{ib}} = \frac{450 - 150}{150} = 2$$

18.

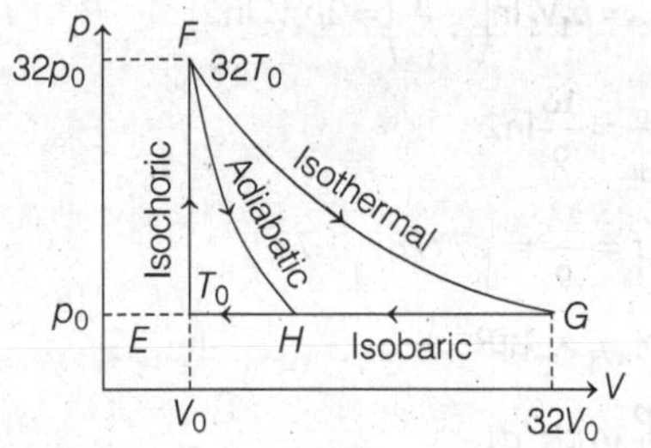

In $F - G$ process:

$T = \text{constant}$

$$V \propto \frac{1}{p} \quad \Rightarrow \quad p_G = \frac{p_F}{32}$$

$$\therefore \quad V_G = 32\,V_F = 32V_0$$

In $F \to G$ work done in isothermal process is

$$nRT\ln\left(\frac{V_f}{V_i}\right) = 32\,p_0V_0\ln\left(\frac{32\,V_0}{V_0}\right)$$

$$= 32\,p_0V_0\ln 2^5 = 160p_0\,V_0\ln 2$$

In $G \to E$, $\Delta W = p_0\Delta V = p_0(31\,V_0) = 31\,p_0V_0$

In $G \to H$ work done is less than $31\,p_0V_0$ i.e. $24\,p_0V_0$

In $F \to H$ work done is $36\,p_0V_0$

19. At STP, 22.4 L of any gas is 1 mole.

$$\therefore \quad 5.6\,\text{L} = \frac{5.6}{22.4} = \frac{1}{4}\text{ moles} = n$$

In adiabatic process, $TV^{\gamma-1} = \text{constant}$

$$\therefore \quad T_2V_2^{\gamma-1} = T_1V_1^{\gamma-1} \text{ or } T_2 = T_1\left(\frac{V_1}{V_2}\right)^{\gamma-1}$$

$$\gamma = \frac{C_p}{C_V} = \frac{5}{3} \text{ for monoatomic He gas.}$$

$$\therefore \quad T_2 = T_1\left(\frac{5.6}{0.7}\right)^{\frac{5}{3}-1} = 4T_1$$

Further in adiabatic process, $Q = 0$

$\therefore \quad W + \Delta U = 0$

or $\quad W = -\Delta U = -nC_V\Delta T$

$$= -n\left(\frac{R}{\gamma - 1}\right)(T_2 - T_1)$$

$$= -\frac{1}{4}\left(\frac{R}{\frac{5}{3} - 1}\right)(4T_1 - T_1) = -\frac{9}{8}RT_1$$

CHAPTER~07

SIMPLE HARMONIC MOTION

LEVEL 01 Starter Level

7.1 Equation of SHM

1. For a particle performing SHM, equation of motion is given as $\frac{d^2x}{dt^2} + 4x = 0$. Find the time period.

2. The equation of particle executing simple harmonic motion is $x = (5\text{m}) \sin\left[(\pi \text{ s}^{-1}) t + \frac{\pi}{3}\right]$. Write down the
   (a) amplitude (b) phase constant
   (c) time period (d) maximum speed
   (e) maximum acceleration
   (f) velocity and the acceleration at $t = 1$ s.

3. The figure shows the displacement-time graph of a particle executing SHM. If the time period of oscillation is 2s, then the equation of motion is given by $x =$ ....

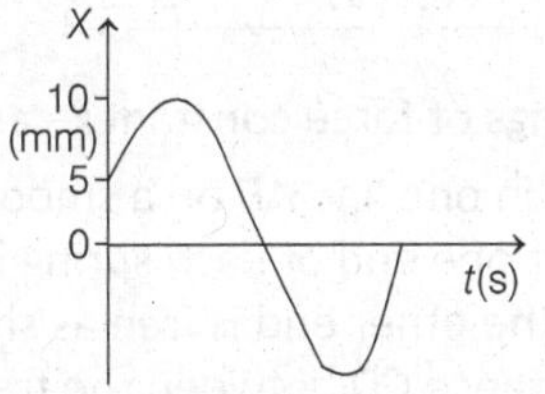

4. A particle executing simple harmonic motion has time period 1 s and amplitude 10 cm. Find
   (a) the speed when the displacement is 6 cm from the mean position,
   (b) the acceleration when the displacement is 3 cm from the mean position.

5. A particle executing SHM has maximum velocity and maximum acceleration of 100 cm/s and 157 cm/s^2, respectively. Find the time period.

6. A particle is vibrating in SHM. If its velocities are v_1 and v_2 when the displacements from the mean position are y_1 and y_2 respectively, then find its time period.

7. A particle of mass 0.50 kg executes a simple harmonic motion under a force $F = -(50 \text{ N/m})\, x$. If it crosses the centre of oscillation with a speed of 10 m/s, find the amplitude of the motion.

8. A particle of mass 2 kg is moving on a straight line under the action of force $F = (8 - 2x)$ N. It is released at rest from $x = 6$ m.
   (a) Find the equilibrium position of the particle.
   (b) Write the equation of motion of the particle.

9. The acceleration-displacement (a-x) graph of a particle executing simple harmonic motion is shown in the figure. Find the frequency of oscillation.

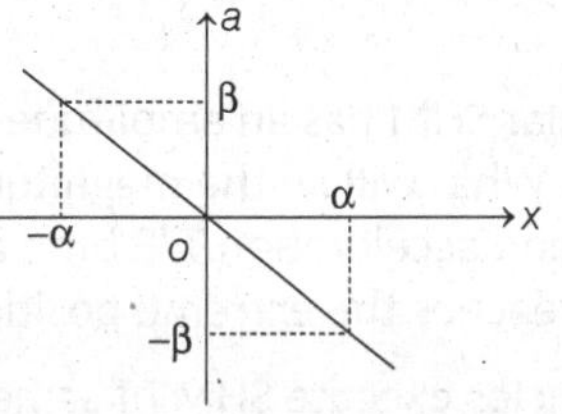

10. The figure shows graph between velocity v and displacement x from mean position of a particle performing simple harmonic motion
    (a) What is the time period of motion of particle?
    (b) What is the maximum acceleration of particle?
    (c) What is the velocity of particle when it is at a distance 1.5 m from mean position?

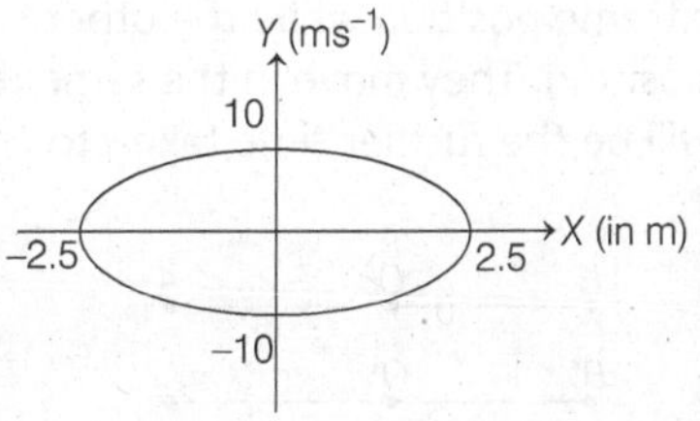

7.2 Phasor Diagrams

1. The equation of motion of a particle which started at $t = 0$ is given by $x = 5\sin\left[\left(\frac{\pi}{12}\right)t + \frac{\pi}{3}\right]$, where, x is in centimetre and t in second. When does the particle
   (a) first come to rest?
   (b) first have maximum speed?

2. A particle executing simple harmonic motion has an amplitude A and time period T. Find the time required by it to travel diectly from
   (a) $x = 0$ to $x = \frac{A}{2}$ (b) $x = 0$ to $x = \frac{A}{\sqrt{2}}$
   (c) $x = A$ to $x = \frac{A}{2}$ (d) $x = -\frac{A}{\sqrt{2}}$ to $x = \frac{\sqrt{3}A}{2}$

3. A particle executes simple harmonic motion with an amplitude of 10 cm and time period 6 s. At $t = 0$ it is at position $x = 5$ cm from mean positon and going towards negative x-direction. Write the equation for the displacement x at time t.

4. A body undergoing SHM about the origin has its equation is giiven by $x = 0.2\cos 5\pi t$. Find its average speed from $t = 0$ to $t = 0.7$ s.

5. The period of a particle is 8 s. At $t = 0$ it is at the mean position. What will be the ratio of distance covered by the particle in first second and second second?

6. A particular SHM has an amplitude of A and time period T. What will be the magnitude of its velocity and acceleration T/8 time after the particle reaches the extreme position?

7. Two particles execute SHM of same amplitude and frequency on parallel lines. They cross each another when moving in opposite directions each time their displacement is half their amplitude. Find phase difference between them.

8. Two particles undergo SHM along parallel lines with the same time period (T) and equal amplitudes. At a particular instant, one particle is at its extreme position while the other is at its mean position. They move in the same direction. What will be the further time taken to cross each other?

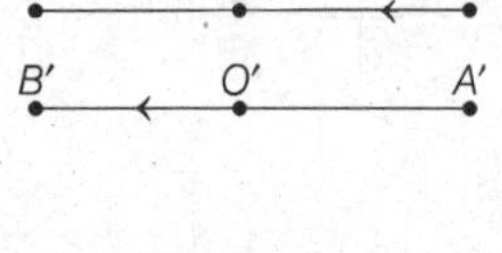

7.3 Energy in SHM

1. In case of simple harmonic motion, at what displacement from the mean position, the kinetic and potential energies are equal?

2. A particle performing SHM with amplitude 10 cm. At what distance from mean position, the kinetic energy of the particle is three-fourth of its total energy?

3. A particle of mass 1 kg is executing SHM with an amplitude of 1 m and time period π s. Calculate kinetic energy of the particle at the moment when the displacement is 0.8 m.

4. A particle of mass 10 g executes a linear SHM of amplitude 5 cm with a period of 2 s. Find the PE and KE, $\frac{1}{6}$ s after crossing the mean position. (Use $\pi^2 = 10$)

5. The potential energy of a harmonic oscillation of mass 2 kg at its mean position is 5 J. If its energy is 9 J and its amplitude is 0.01 m, find its time period.

6. A linear harmonic oscillator of force constant 2×10^6 Nm^{-1} and amplitude 0.01 m has a total mechanical energy of 160 J. Then, find maximum and minimum values of potential energy and kinetic energy.

7.4 Spring Block System

1. A block of mass 100 g attached to a spring of stiffness 100 N/m is lying on a frictionless floor as shown. The block is moved to compress the spring by 10 cm and released. If the collision with the wall is elastic, find the time period of motion.

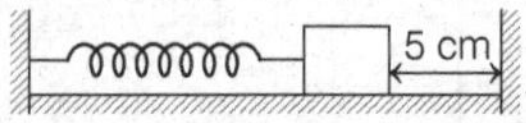

2. Two light springs of force constant k_1 and k_2 and a block of mass m are in one line AB on a smooth horizontal table such that one end of each spring is fixed to rigid supports and the other end is free as shown in the figure. The distance CD between the free ends of the spring is 60 cm. if the block moves along AB with a velocity 120 cm/s in between the springs, calculate the period of oscillation of the block. ($k_1 = 1.8$ N/m, $k_2 = 3.2$ N/m, $m = 200$ g)

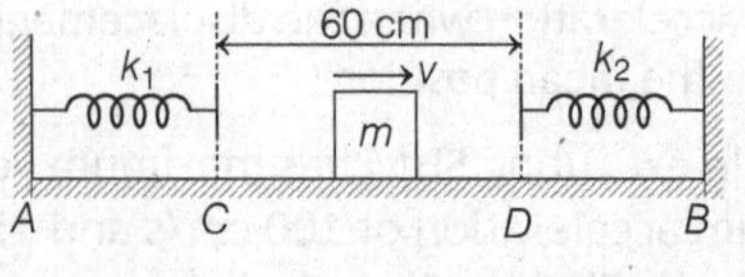

3. A particle of mass m connected with a spring of force constant k is executing simple harmonic motion with amplitude A. When it is at $+A/2$ from equilibrium

position moving towards the right, it receives an impulse which doubles its velocity without changing direction. Find

(a) the new amplitude after the impulse.

(b) time taken by the block to reach the right extreme position.

4. Block P of mass m is performing SHM of amplitude A. Another block Q of mass m is gently placed on P when it passes through mean position and Q sticks to P.

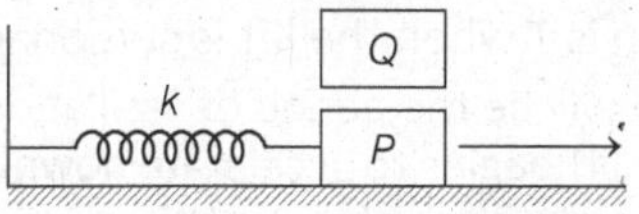

(a) Find the time period and amplitude of new SHM.

(b) Repeat the above problem assuming Q is placed on P at a distance $A/2$ from mean position.

5. The friction coefficient between the two blocks shown in figure is μ and the horizontal plane is smooth.

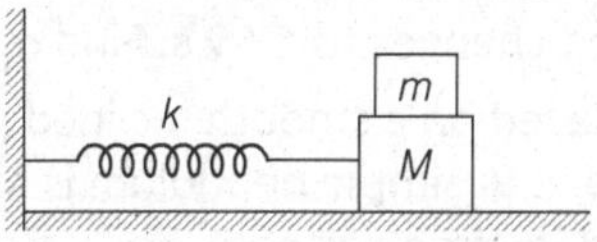

(a) Find the magnitude of the frictional force between the blocks when the displacement from the mean position is x. Assume that both the blocks oscillate together.

(b) What can be the maximum amplitude if the upper block does not slip relative to the lower block?

6. A spring mass system is shown in figure. Spring is initially unstretched. A man starts puling the block with constant force F. Find

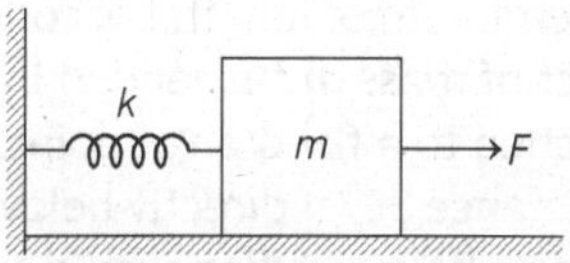

(a) the amplitude and the time period of motion of the block.

(b) the KE of the block at mean position.

(c) the energy stored in the spring when the block passes through the mean position.

7. Find time period of oscillations of the block in the following systems.

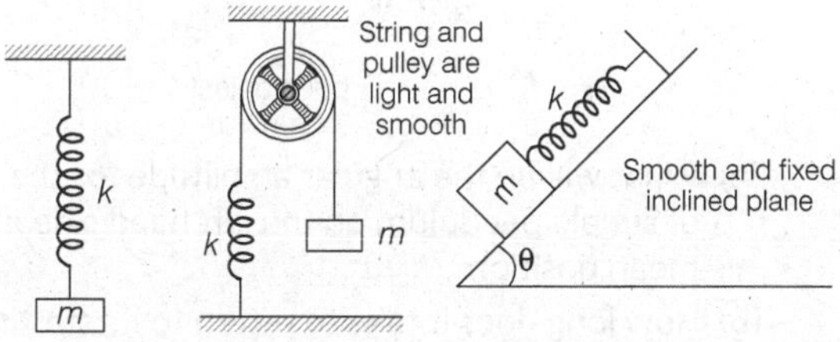

(a) (b) (c)

8. A block of mass 1 kg hanging from a vertical spring executes SHM of amplitude 0.2 m and time period $\pi / 10$ s. Find the maximum force exerted by the spring on the block.

9. A block of mass m is suspended from the ceiling of a stationary elevator through a spring of spring constant k and suddenly, the cable breaks and the elevator starts falling freely. Show that, block now executes a simple harmonic motion of amplitude mg/k in the elevator.

10. The system is in equilibrium and at rest. Now mass m_1 is removed from m_2. Find the amplitude of resultant motion. Spring constant is k.

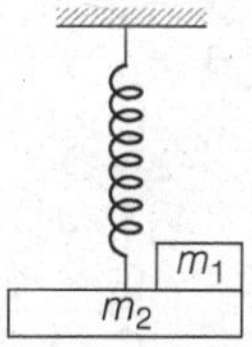

7.5 Two Blocks Spring System

1. The system shown in the figure can move on a smooth surface. The spring is initially compressed by 6 cm and then released. Find

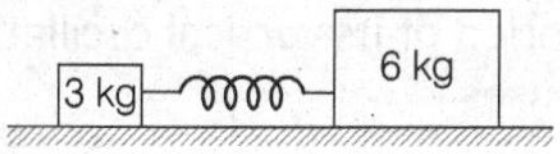

(a) time period.

(b) amplitude of 3 kg block.

(c) maximum momentum of 6 kg block.

2. All the surfaces shown in figure are frictionless. The mass of the car is M, that of the block is m and the spring has spring constant k. Initially, the car and the block are at rest and the spring is stretched through a length x_0, when the system is released. Find the time period of the oscillations of the system.

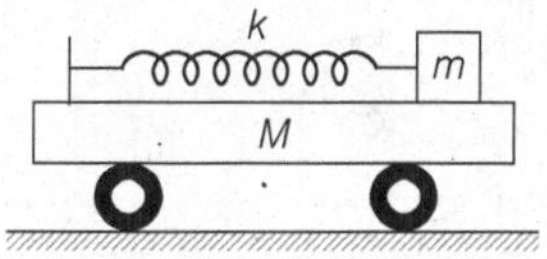

7.6 Combination of Springs

1. Find the time period of oscillations of the following spring mass systems as shown in figure.

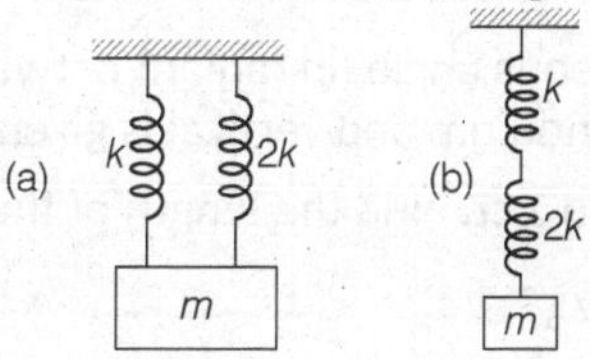

2. A spring of stiffness constant k and natural length l is cut into two parts of length $3l/4$ and $l/4$ respectively, and an arrangement is made as shown in the figure. If the mass is m sightly displaced, find the time period of oscillation.

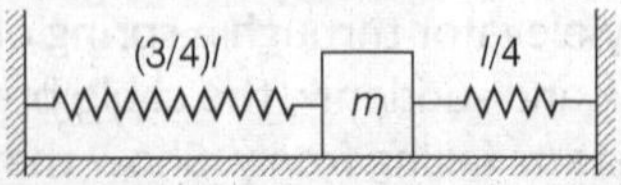

3. A particle of mass m is attached to three identical springs A, B and C each of force constant k as shown in figure. If the particle of mass m is pushed slightly against the spring A and released, then find the time period of its oscillations.

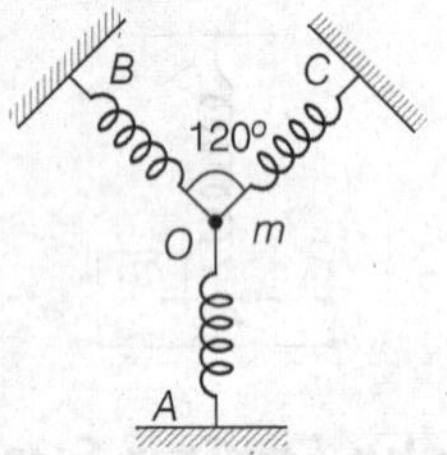

4. Figure shows a system consisting of a massless pulley, a spring of force constant k and a block of mass m. If the block is slightly displaced vertically down from its equilibrium position and released, find the time period of its vertical oscillation in the following cases.

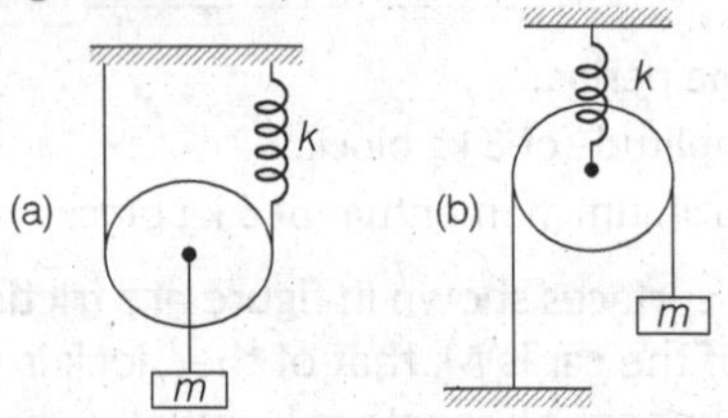

5. Find the time period of oscillation of the block of mass m in the following cases. All pulleys are light and smooth.

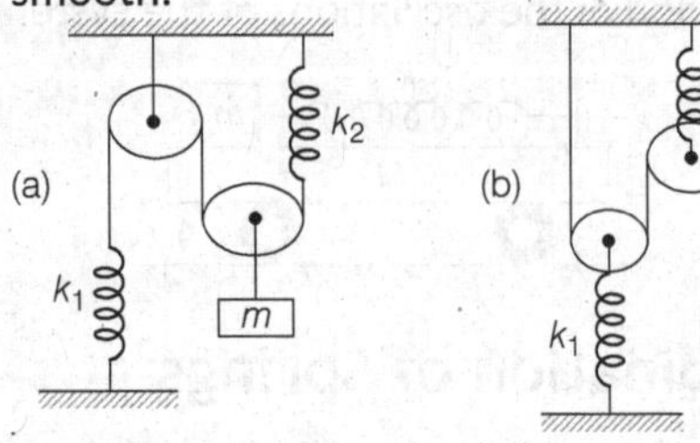

7.7 Simple Pendulum

1. Instantaneous angle (in radian) between string of a simple pendulum and vertical is given by $\theta = \dfrac{\pi}{180} \sin 2\pi t$. Find the length of the pendulum, if $g = \pi^2 \text{ m/s}^2$.

2. A simple pendulum of length 40 cm oscillates with an angular amplitude of 0.04 rad. Find

(a) the time period,

(b) the linear amplitude of the bob,

(c) the speed of the bob when the string makes 0.02 rad with the vertical and

(d) the angular acceleration when the bob is in momentary rest. Take, $g = 10 \text{ m/s}^2$.

3. A pendulum is suspended in a lift and its period of oscillation is T when the lift is stationary.

(a) What will be the period of oscillation of pendulum, if the lift begins to accelerate downwards with an acceleration equal to $3g/4$?

(b) What must be the acceleration of the lift for the period of oscillation of the pendulum to be $T/2$?

4. A simple pendulum suspended through the ceiling of a car at rest oscillates with time period 2s. If car suddenly starts moving with acceleration a_0, then time period changes to 1.99 s. Find a_0.

5. A box is placed on a smooth inclined plane and it is free to move. A simple pendulum is attached in the block. Find its time period.

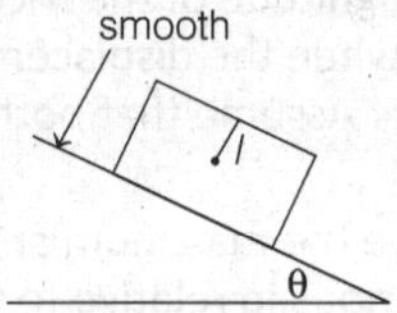

6. A simple pendulum of length l and having bob of density σ is doing angular SHM inside liquid of density ρ. Find the time period of oscillations.

7. A simple pendulum of length L is constructed from a point object of mass m suspended by a massless string attached to a fixed pivot point. A small peg is placed a distance $3L/4$ directly below the fixed pivot point, so that the pendulum would swing as shown in the figure below. The mass is displaced 2° from the vertical and released.

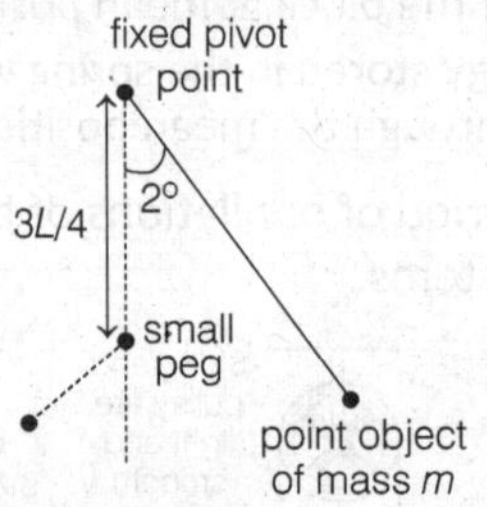

(a) What will be the angular amplitude for the motion of simple pendulum on the left hand side of the mean position?

(b) How long does it take to return to its starting position?

8. Two simple pendula of length 36 cm and 64 cm are initially at opposite extremes of their swings. After how much time will they be in phase? (Take, $g = \pi^2$)

7.8 Compound Pendulum

1. Find the time period of small oscillations in the vertical plane in each of the following cases of compound pendulum.

(a) A rod of mass m and length l suspended through one of its ends.

(b) A ring of mass m and radius r suspended through a point on its periphery.

(c) A uniform square plate of edge a suspended through a corner.

(d) A uniform disc of mass m and radius r suspended through a point $r/2$ away from the centre.

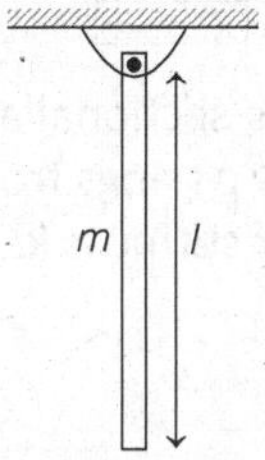

(a)

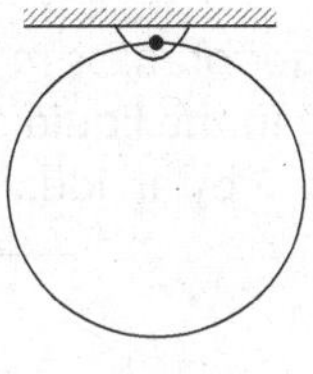

(b)

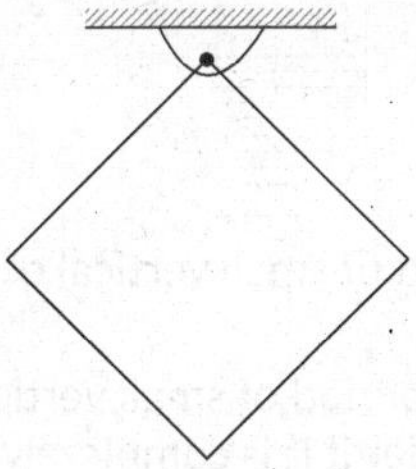

(c)

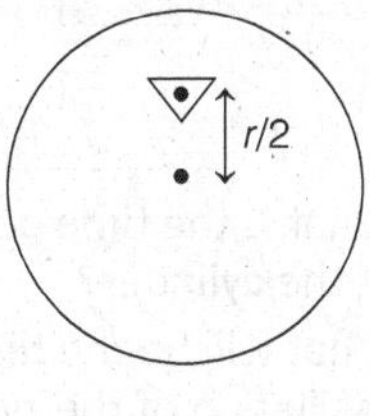

(d)

2. A uniform rod of length L is pivoted at a distance x from its centre, so that it is free to rotate about a horizontal axis as shown in figure. Find the value of x, so that time period of oscillations is minimum and also find the minimum possible time period.

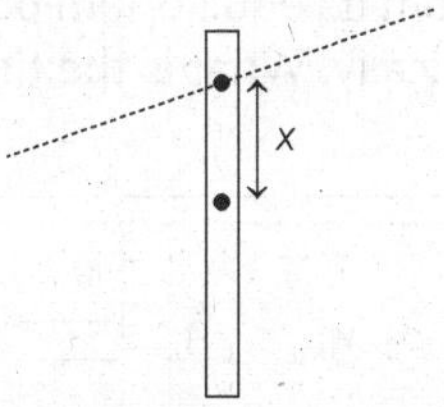

3. A half ring of mass m, radius R is hanged at its one end in vertical plane and is free to oscillate in its plane. Find frequency for small oscillations about mean position of the half ring.

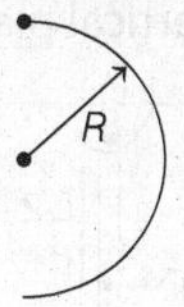

4. Two identical rods each of mass m and length L, are rigidly joined and then suspended in a vertical plane so as to oscillate freely about an axis normal to the plane of paper passing through S (point of suspension). Find the time period of such small oscillations.

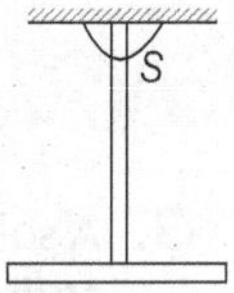

7.9 Torsional Pendulum

1. A uniform disc of radius 5.0 cm and mass 200 g is fixed at its centre to a metal wire, the other end of which is fixed to a ceiling. The hanging disc is rotated about the wire through an angle and is released. If the disc makes torsional oscillations with time period 0.20 s, find the torsional constant of the wire.

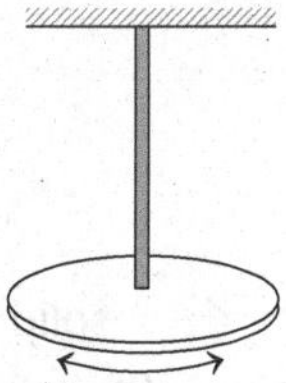

2. A 25 kg uniform solid sphere with a 20 cm radius is suspended by a vertical wire such that the point of suspension is vertically above the centre of the sphere. A torque of 0.10 N-m is required to rotate the sphere through an angle of 1.0 rad and then maintain the orientation. If the sphere is then released, what will be its time period of the oscillation?

7.10 Angular SHM

1. The uniform stick of mass m, length L is pivoted at the centre. In the equilibrium position shown in the figure, the identical light springs have their natural length. If the stick is turned through a small angle θ, it executes SHM. What is the frequency of the motion?

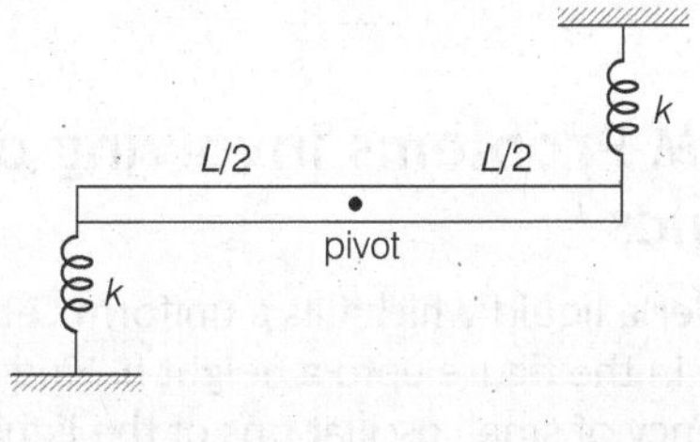

2. Find the frequency of small oscillations of a thin uniform vertical rod of mass *m* and length *l* hinged at one end in the vertical plane as shown in figure.

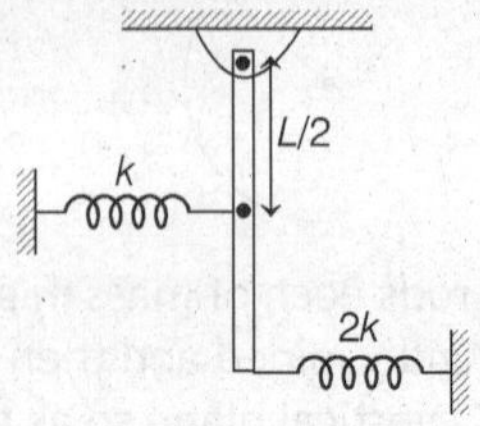

3. A solid sphere of mass *m* attached to a massless spring of force constant *k* is placed on a horizontal surface in such a way that the sphere can roll without slipping. If the system is released from the stretched position of the spring, then what is the time period of oscillations?

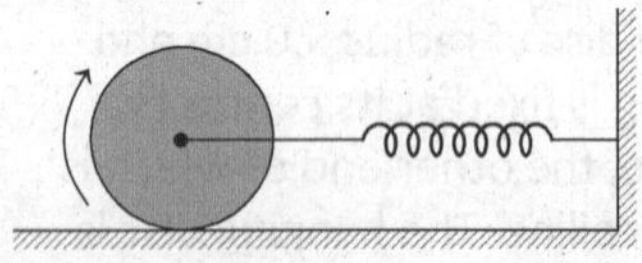

4. A solid uniform cylinder of mass *m* performs small oscillations due to the action of two springs, each having stiffness *k*. Find the period of these oscillations in absence of any sliding (springs have their natural length initially).

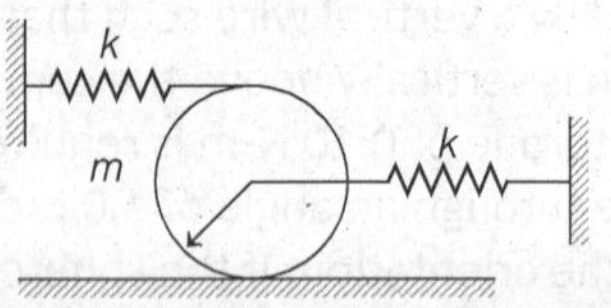

5. Find the time period of the system. The radius of the pulley is *R*, its moment of inertia relative to the rotation axis is *I*, the mass of the body is *m* and the spring constant is *k*.

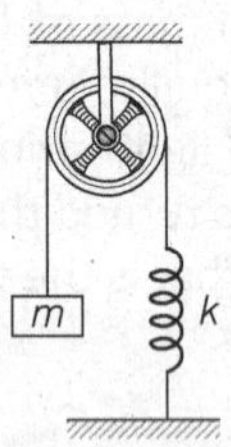

7.11 SHM Problems involving other Topics

1. Consider a liquid which fills a uniform U-tube, as shown in the figure upto a height *h*. Find the frequency of small oscillations of the liquid in the U-tube.

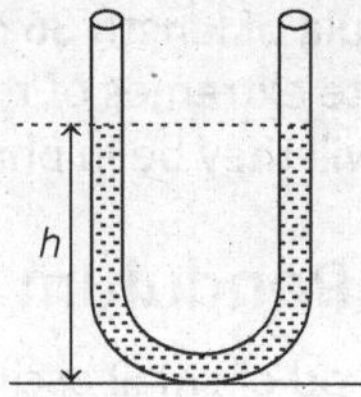

2. Consider a solid cylinder of density σ, cross-sectional area *A* and height *h* floating in a liquid of density ρ, as shown in the adjacent figure (ρ > σ). It is depressed slightly and allowed to oscillate vertically. Find the time period of small oscillations.

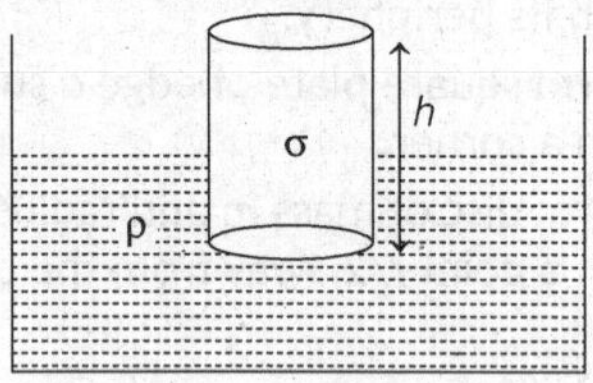

3. A cylinder of mass *m* and cross-sectional area *A* floating in the liquid of density ρ hangs from a rigid support *P* by an ideal spring of stiffness *k*.

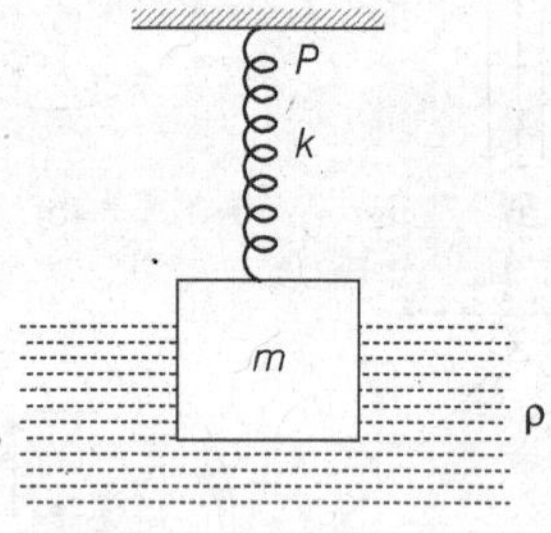

(a) What is the time period of small vertical oscillation of the cylinder?

(b) What will be the time period of small vertical oscillation of the cylinder if it is completely immersed in the liquid?

4. A cylindrical piston of mass *M* and area of cross-section *A* slides smoothly inside a long cylinder closed at one end, enclosing a certain mass of a gas at pressure p_0 and volume V_0. The cylinder is kept with its axis horizontal. If the piston is slightly compressed isothermally from its equilibrium position, it oscillates simple harmonically. What is the time period of oscillation?

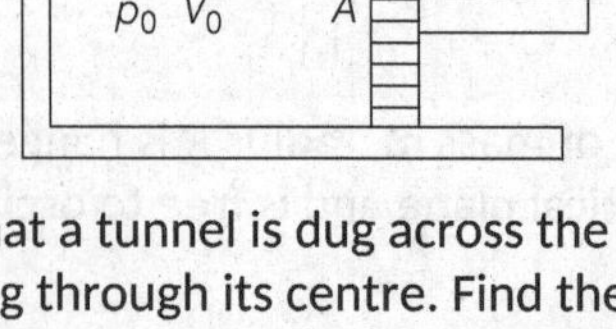

5. Assume that a tunnel is dug across the earth (radius = *R*) passing through its centre. Find the time a particle takes to cover the length of the tunnel if

(a) it is projected into the tunnel with a speed of $\sqrt{gR}$,

(b) it is released from a height R above the tunnel.

6. Assume that a tunnel is dug along a chord of the earth, at a perpendicular distance $R/2$ from the earth's centre where R is the radius of the earth. The wall of the tunnel is frictionless. A particle of mass m is placed in the tunnel at a distance x from the centre of the tunnel. Show that the motion of the particle in the tunnel is simple harmonic and find the time period.

7.12 Superposition of SHMs

1. A particle is subjected to two SHM's simultaneously $x_1 = A_1 \sin \omega t$ and $x_2 = A_2 \sin(\omega t + \phi)$ where, $A_1 = 3.0$ cm $A_2 = 4.0$ cm. Find the resultant amplitude, if the phase difference ϕ has values

(a) 0° (b) 60°

(c) 90°

2. $x_1 = 3 \sin \omega t$; $x_2 = 4 \cos \omega t$

Find

(a) amplitude of resultant SHM.

(b) equation of the resultant SHM.

3. If two SHMs are represented by

$y_1 = 10 \sin\left(4\pi t + \frac{\pi}{2}\right)$ and

$y_2 = 5(\sin 2\pi t + \sqrt{3} \cos 2\pi t)$, find the ratio of their amplitudes.

4. $A \cos(\omega t) + \frac{A}{2} \cos\left(\omega t + \frac{\pi}{2}\right) + \frac{A}{4} \cos(\omega t + \pi) + \frac{A}{8} \cos\left(\omega t + \frac{3\pi}{2}\right) = A' \cos(\omega t + \delta)$

Find resulting amplitude A' and the phase of the vibrations δ.

5. A particle is subjected to three SHM's in same direction simultaneously each having equal amplitude a and equal time period. The phase of the second motion is 30° ahead of the first and the phase of the third motion is 30° ahead of the second. Find the amplitude of the resultant motion.

6. A particle simultaneously participates in two mutually perpendicular oscillations $x = \sin 2\pi t$ and $y = 2 \cos 2\pi t$. Write the equation of trajectory of the particle.

LEVEL 02 JEE Main Level

1. The equation of motion of a particle of mass 1 g is $\frac{d^2x}{dt^2} + \pi^2 x = 0$ where, x is displacement (in m) from mean position. The frequency of oscillation is (in Hz)

(a) $\frac{1}{2}$ (b) 2

(c) $5\sqrt{10}$ (d) $\frac{1}{5\sqrt{10}}$

2. Part of a simple harmonic motion is graphed in the figure, where y is the displacement from the mean position. The correct equation describing this SHM is

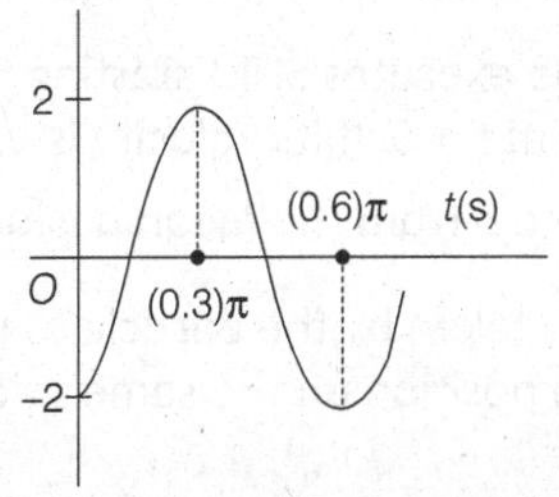

(a) $y = 4 \cos(0.6t)$ (b) $y = 2 \sin\left(\frac{10}{3}t - \frac{\pi}{2}\right)$

(c) $y = 4 \sin\left(\frac{10}{3}t + \frac{\pi}{2}\right)$ (d) $y = 2 \cos\left(\frac{10}{3}t + \frac{\pi}{2}\right)$

3. An object of mass 0.8 kg is attached to one end of a spring and the system is set into simple harmonic motion. The displacement x of the object as a function of time is shown in the figure. The magnitude of the object's acceleration at $t = 1.0$ is

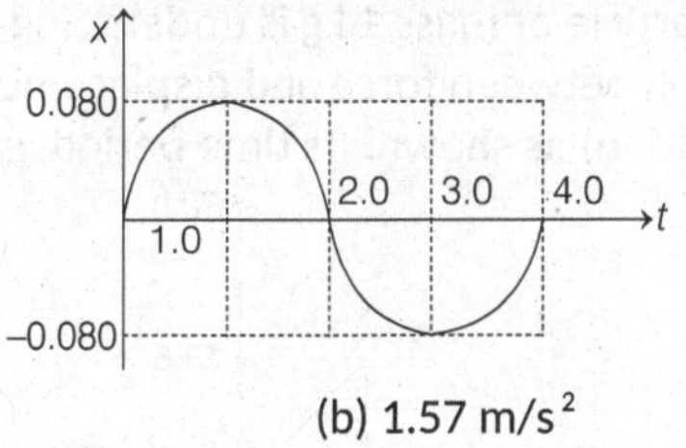

(a) zero (b) 1.57 m/s^2

(c) 0.197 m/s^2 (d) 0.157 m/s^2

4. A particle performing SHM is found at its equilibrium at $t = 1$ s and it is found to have a speed of 0.25 m/s at $t = 2$ s. If the period of oscillation is 6 s, calculate amplitude of oscillation

(a) $\frac{3}{2\pi}$ m (b) $\frac{3}{4\pi}$ m (c) $\frac{6}{\pi}$ m (d) $\frac{3}{8\pi}$ m

5. A particle is executing SHM. Maximum magnitudes of its velocity and acceleration are 10 cm/s and 50 cm/s^2 respectively. Find the distance of the particle from mean position where its speed is 8 cm/s.

(a) 1 cm (b) 1.2 cm
(c) 1.5 cm (d) 1.8 cm

6. The velocities of a particle executing SHM are 30 cm/s and 16 cm/s when its displacements are 8 cm and 15 cm from the equilibrium position. Then, its amplitude of oscillation in cm is

(a) 25 (b) 21 (c) 17 (d) 13

7. The period of oscillation in seconds of the particle in the previous problem is

(a) $\frac{\pi}{2}$ (b) $\frac{3\pi}{4}$ (c) π (d) $\frac{3\pi}{2}$

8. A particle executes SHM on a straight line. At two positions, its velocities are u and v while accelerations are a and b, respectively $[b > a > 0]$. The distance between these two positions will be

(a) $\frac{u^2+v^2}{a+b}$ (b) $\frac{u^2-v^2}{a+b}$
(c) $\frac{u^2-v^2}{b-a}$ (d) $\frac{u^2+v^2}{b-a}$

9. A particle executes SHM on a straight line path. The amplitude of oscillation is 2 cm. When the displacement of the particle from the mean position is 1 cm, the numerical value of magnitude of acceleration is equal to the numerical value of magnitude of velocity. The frequency of SHM (in second^{-1}) is

(a) $2\pi\sqrt{3}$ (b) $2\pi/\sqrt{3}$
(c) $\sqrt{3}/(2\pi)$ (d) $1/(2\pi\sqrt{3})$

10. A particle of mass 1 kg is undergoing SHM, for which graph between force and displacement (from mean position) as shown. Its time period, in seconds, is

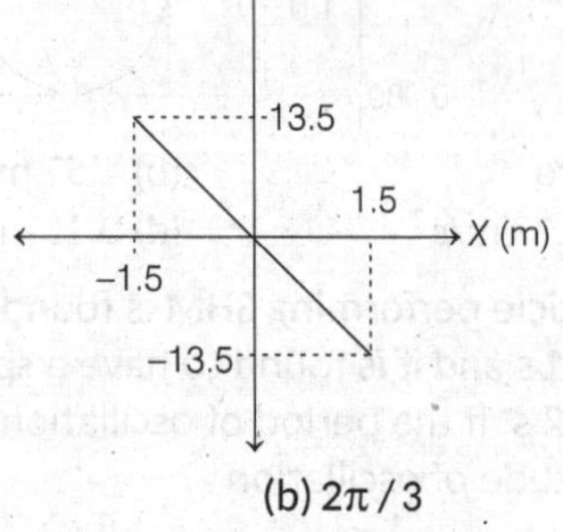

(a) $\pi/3$ (b) $2\pi/3$
(c) $\pi/6$ (d) $3/\pi$

11. Speed v of a particle moving along a straight line, when it is at a distance x from a fixed point on the line is given by $v^2 = 108 - 9x^2$ (all quantities in SI. unit). Then,

(a) the motion is uniformly accelerated along the straight line
(b) the magnitude of the acceleration at a distance 3 cm from the fixed point is 0.27 m/s^2
(c) the motion is simple harmonic about $x = \sqrt{12}$ m
(d) the maximum displacement from the fixed point is 4 cm.

12. A particle is performing simple harmonic motion.

(i) Its velocity-displacement graph is parabolic in nature.
(ii) Its velocity-time graph is sinusoidal in nature.
(iii) Its velocity-acceleration graph is elliptical in nature.

Which of the above statements are correct?

(a) (i), (ii) and (iii) (b) (ii) and (iii)
(c) (i) and (ii) (d) (i) and (iii)

13. A particle moves on X-axis according to relation $x = 2\cos(50\pi t + \pi/5)$. The motion is started at $t = 0$. When does the particle come to rest 9th time?

(a) 176×10^{-3} s (b) 196×10^{-3} s
(c) 256×10^{-3} s (d) None of these

14. A particle is performing SHM according to the equation $x = (3\text{ cm})\sin\left(\frac{2\pi}{18}t + \frac{\pi}{6}\right)$, where t is in second. The distance travelled by the particle in 39s is

(a) 24 cm (b) 1.5 cm
(c) 25.5 cm (d) none of these

15. A small mass executes linear SHM about O with amplitude a and period T. Its displacement from O at time $T/8$ after passing through O is

(a) $\frac{a}{8}$ (b) $\frac{a}{2\sqrt{2}}$
(c) $\frac{a}{2}$ (d) $\frac{a}{\sqrt{2}}$

16. A particle executes SHM starting from its mean position at $t = 0$. If its velocity is $\sqrt{3}b\omega$, when it is at a distance b from the mean position, when $\omega = \frac{2\pi}{T}$.

The time taken by the particle to move from b to the extreme position on the same side is

(a) $\frac{5\pi}{6\omega}$ (b) $\frac{\pi}{3\omega}$
(c) $\frac{\pi}{2\omega}$ (d) $\frac{\pi}{4\omega}$

17. A particle executes SHM along a straight line with mean position $x = 0$, period 20 s and amplitude 5 cm. The shortest time taken by the particle to go from $x = 4$ to $x = -3$ cm is
(a) 4 s (b) 7 s (c) 5 s (d) 6 s

18. A particle performs SHM on the X-axis with amplitude A and time period T. The time taken by the particle to travel a distance $A/5$ starting from rest is
(a) $\frac{T}{2\pi}$ (b) $\frac{T}{2\pi}\cos^{-1}\left(\frac{4}{5}\right)$
(c) $\frac{T}{2\pi}\cos^{-1}\left(\frac{1}{5}\right)$ (d) $\frac{T}{2\pi}\sin^{-1}\left(\frac{1}{5}\right)$

19. A particle performing SHM crosses points P and Q with the same velocity. Having taken 2 s in passing from P to Q, it returns to Q after another 2 s. The periodic time is
(a) 2 s (b) 4 s (c) 6 s (d) 8 s

20. A particle performs SHM in a straight line. In the first second, starting from rest, it travels a distance a and in the next second, it travels a distance b in the same direction. The amplitude of the SHM is
(a) $a - b$ (b) $\frac{2a-b}{3}$
(c) $\frac{2a^2}{3a-b}$ (d) None of these

21. A particle performs SHM with a period T and amplitude a. The mean velocity of the particle over the time interval during which it travels a distance $a/2$ from the extreme position is
(a) $2a/T$ (b) $3a/T$
(c) $a/2T$ (d) None of these

22. A particle executes SHM with amplitude of oscillation A and time period T. Find the magnitude of average acceleration for the period of time in which it moves from mean position by a distance $A/2$.
(a) $\frac{3\pi A}{T^2}$ (b) $\frac{12\pi A}{T^2}$
(c) $\frac{12\pi A(2-\sqrt{3})}{T^2}$ (d) None of these

23. A particle performs SHM on X-axis from $x = -2$ to $x = 6$ cm with time period of 0.5 s. It was located at $x = 4$ cm and moving in positive x at $t = 0$.
(a) the equation of SHM of the particle is $x = 2 + 4\sin(4\pi t + 30°)$.
(b) the equation of SHM of the particle is $x = -2 + 2\cos 4\pi t$.
(c) the velocity of the particle at $x = 4$ cm is 3 cm/s.
(d) the acceleration at $x = 4$ cm is $32\pi^2$ cm/s^2

24. Two particles are in SHM with same angular frequency and amplitudes A and $2A$ respectively along same straight line with same mean position. They cross each other at position $A/2$ distance from mean position in opposite direction. The phase difference between them is
(a) $\frac{5\pi}{6} - \sin^{-1}\left(\frac{1}{4}\right)$ (b) $\frac{\pi}{6} - \sin^{-1}\left(\frac{1}{4}\right)$
(c) $\frac{5\pi}{6} - \cos^{-1}\left(\frac{1}{4}\right)$ (d) $\frac{\pi}{6} - \cos^{-1}\left(\frac{1}{4}\right)$

25. Two particles are in SHM in a straight line about same equilibrium position. Amplitude A and time period T of both the particles are equal. At time $t = 0$, one particle is at displacement $y_1 = +A$ and the other at $y_2 = -A/2$, and they are approaching towards each other. After what time they cross each other?
(a) $T/3$ (b) $T/4$ (c) $5T/6$ (d) $T/6$

26. Two particles execute SHM of same amplitude of 20 cm with same period along the same line about the same equilibrium position. The maximum distance between the two is 20 cm. Their phase difference in radians is
(a) $\frac{2\pi}{3}$ (b) $\frac{\pi}{2}$ (c) $\frac{\pi}{3}$ (d) $\frac{\pi}{4}$

27. The total energy of a vibrating particle in SHM is E. If its amplitude and time period are doubled, its total energy will be
(a) $16E$ (b) $8E$ (c) $4E$ (d) E

28. Starting from the mean position, a body oscillates simple harmonically with a period of 2 s. After what time will its kinetic energy be 25% of the total energy?
(a) $\frac{1}{6}$ s (b) $\frac{1}{4}$ s
(c) $\frac{1}{3}$ s (d) $\frac{1}{12}$ s

29. A heavy particle of mass 8 kg is executing SHM on the X-axis with time period 6.28 s. If its maximum and minimum potential energy during motion is 80 J and 16 J respectively, then find out amplitude of the motion of particle
(a) 16 m (b) 32 m
(c) 8 m (d) 4 m

30. When a particle oscillates simple harmonically, its kinetic energy varies periodically. If frequency of the oscillation of particle is n, then the frequency of oscillations of KE is
(a) n (b) $2n$ (c) $3n$ (d) $4n$

31. The time period of a particle in simple harmonic motion is equal to the smallest time between the particle acquiring a particular velocity v. The value of v is

(a) v_{max} (b) 0
(c) between 0 and v_{max} (d) between 0 and $-v_{max}$

32. A particle is executing SHM according to $y = a \cos \omega t$. Then, which of the graphs represents variations of potential energy?

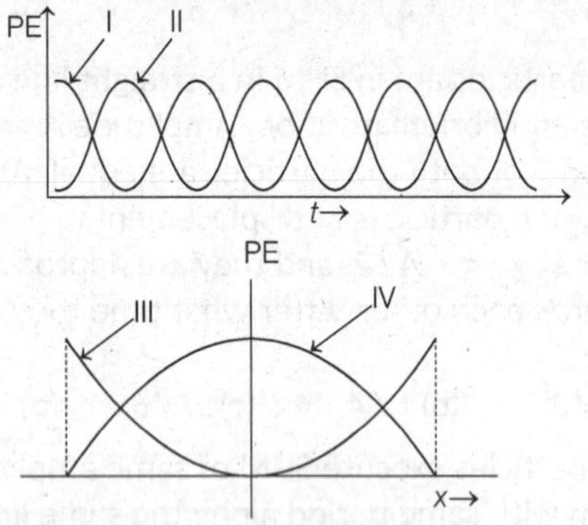

(a) (I) and (III) (b) (II) and (IV)
(c) (I) and (IV) (d) (II) and (III)

33. Acceleration a and time period T of a body in SHM is given by a curve shown below. Then, corresponding graph between kinetic energy KE and time t is correctly represented by

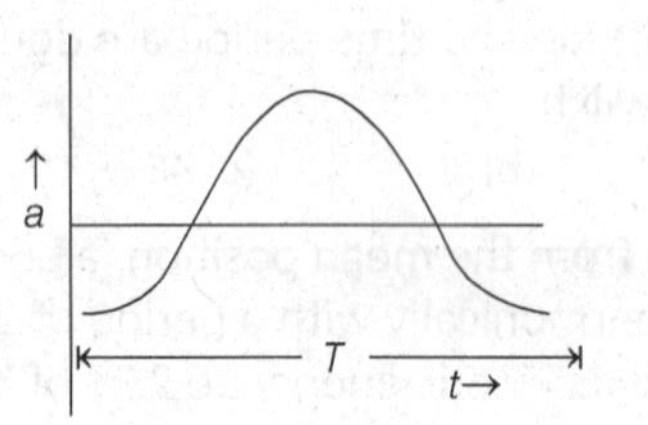

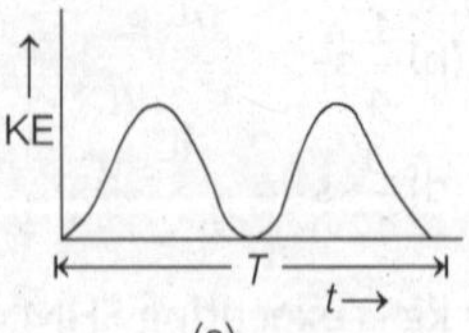

(a)

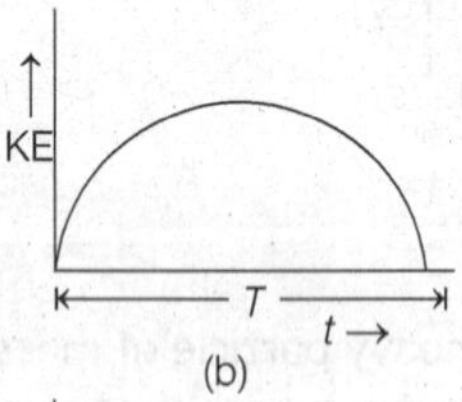

(b)

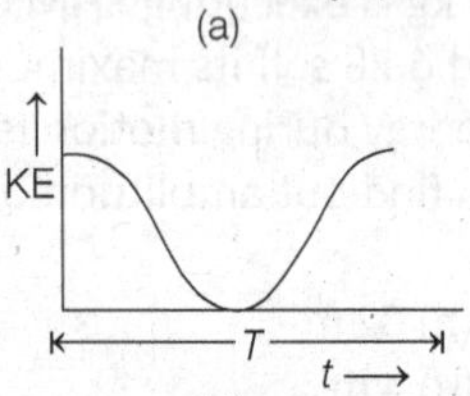

(c)

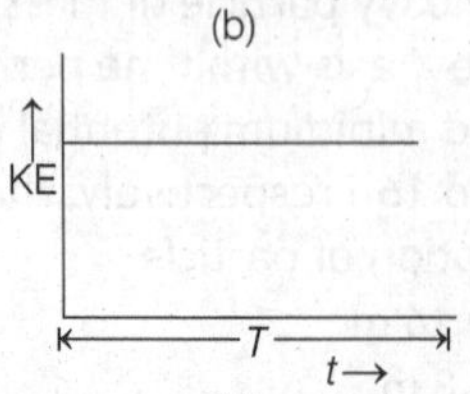

(d)

34. A particle performs SHM of amplitude A with angular frequency ω along a straight line. When it is at a distance $\frac{\sqrt{3}}{2} A$ from mean position, its kinetic energy gets increased by an amount $\frac{1}{2} m\omega^2 A^2$ due to an impulsive force. Then, its new amplitude becomes

(a) $\frac{\sqrt{5}}{2} A$ (b) $\frac{\sqrt{3}}{2} A$
(c) $\sqrt{2} A$ (d) $\sqrt{5} A$

35. A particle of mass m moves in a one-dimensional potential energy $U(x) = -ax^2 + bx^4$, where 'a' and 'b' are positive constants. The angular frequency of small oscillations about the minima of the potential energy is equal to

(a) $\pi \sqrt{\frac{a}{2b}}$ (b) $2\sqrt{\frac{a}{m}}$ (c) $\sqrt{\frac{2a}{m}}$ (d) $\sqrt{\frac{a}{2m}}$

36. A man of mass 60 kg standing on a platform executing SHM in the vertical plane. The displacement from the mean position varies as $y = 0.5 \sin (2\pi ft)$. The minimum value of f for which the man will feel weightlessness at the highest point is (y is in metres)

(a) $\frac{g}{4\pi}$ (b) $4\pi g$
(c) $\frac{\sqrt{2g}}{2\pi}$ (d) $2\pi \sqrt{2g}$

37. A plank with a small block on top of it is under going vertical SHM. Its time period is 2. The minimum amplitude at which the block will separate from plank is

(a) $\frac{10}{\pi^2}$ (b) $\frac{\pi^2}{10}$ (c) $\frac{20}{\pi^2}$ (d) $\frac{\pi}{10}$

38. In the figure, the block of mass m attached to the spring of stiffness k is in contact with the completely elastic wall and the compression in the spring is 'e'. The spring is compressed further by 'e' by displacing the block towards left and is then released. If the collision between the block and the wall is completely elastic, then the time period of oscillations of the block will be

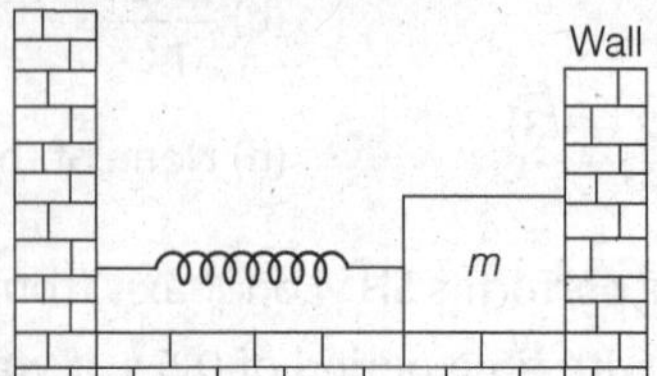

(a) $\frac{2\pi}{3}\sqrt{\frac{m}{k}}$ (b) $2\pi\sqrt{\frac{m}{k}}$
(c) $\frac{\pi}{3}\sqrt{\frac{m}{k}}$ (d) $\frac{\pi}{6}\sqrt{\frac{m}{k}}$

39. The angular frequency of a spring block system is ω_0. This system is suspended from the ceiling of an elevator moving downwards with a constant speed v_0. The block is at rest relative to the elevator. Lift is suddenly stopped. Assuming the downwards as a positive direction, choose the wrong statement

(a) The amplitude of the block is $\frac{v_0}{\omega_0}$.

(b) The initial phase of the block is π.

(c) The equation of motion for the block is $\frac{v_0}{\omega_0}\sin\omega_0 t$.

(d) The maximum speed of the block is v_0.

40. A block of mass 1 kg hangs without vibrating at the end of a spring with a force constant 1 N/cm attached to the ceiling of an elevator. The elevator is rising with an upward acceleration of $g/4$. The acceleration of the elevator suddenly ceases. What is the amplitude of the resulting oscillations?

(a) 2.5 cm (b) 5 cm (c) 10 cm (d) 12.5 cm

41. Two blocks P and Q of masses 0.3 kg and 0.4 kg respectively are stuck to each other by some weak glue as shown in the figure. They hang together at the end of a spring with a spring constant $k = 2\ \text{N cm}^{-1}$. The block Q suddenly falls free due to failure of glue. Find the amplitude of oscillations of P now.

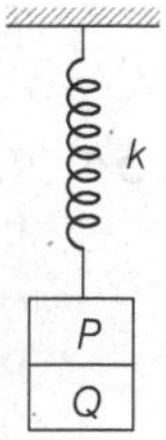

(a) 1.5 cm (b) 2.0 cm (c) 3.5 cm (d) 7.0 cm

42. A block of mass M_1 resting on a frictionless horizontal surface connected to a spring of spring constant k that is anchored to a wall. A block of mass $M_2 = \alpha M_1$ is placed on the top of the first block. The two bodies move as a unit with SHM. What is the maximum amplitude of oscillation so that the two bodies move as a unit? The coefficient of friction between two bodies is μ.

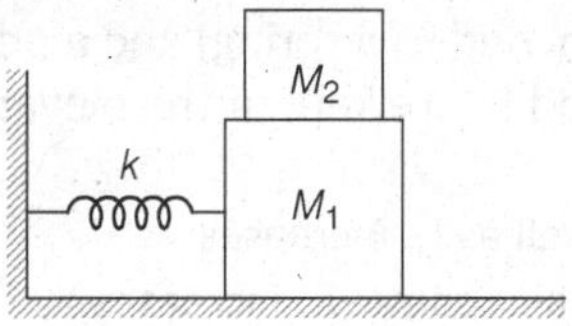

(a) $\frac{(1+\alpha)g\,\mu M_1}{k}$ (b) $\frac{(1+\alpha)\,g\mu M_2}{k}$

(c) $\frac{\alpha M_1 g\mu}{k}$ (d) $\frac{\alpha M_2 g\mu}{k}$

43. A horizontal spring-block system of mass 2 kg executes SHM. When the block is passing through its equilibrium position, an object of mass 1 kg is put on it and the two move together. The new amplitude of vibration is (A being ts initial amplitude)

(a) $\frac{2}{3}A$ (b) $\sqrt{\frac{2}{3}}A$

(c) $\sqrt{2}A$ (d) $\frac{A}{\sqrt{2}}$

44. A block of mass 1 kg kept over a smooth surface is given velocity 2 m/s towards a spring of spring constant 1 N/m at a distance of 10 m. Find after what time, block will be passing through P again

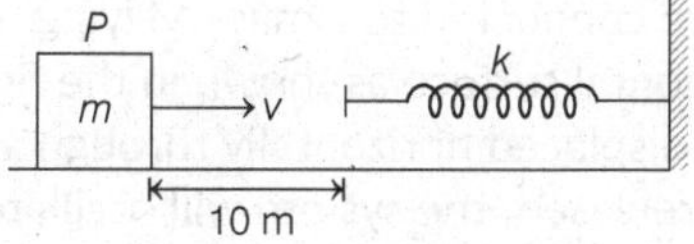

(a) $(10-\pi)$ s (b) 10 s

(c) $(10+2\pi)$ s (d) $(10+\pi)$ s

45. A mass of 0.98 kg suspended using a spring of constant $k = 300\ \text{Nm}^{-1}$ is hit by a bullet of 20 g moving with a velocity 3.0 m/s vertically. The bullet gets embedded and oscillates with the mass. Neglecting gravity, the amplitude of oscillation will be

(a) 0.15 cm (b) 0.35 cm

(c) 1.2 cm (d) None of these

46. Find the ratio of time periods of two identical springs, if they are first joined in series and then in parallel and a mass m is suspended from them

(a) 4 (b) 2

(c) 1 (d) 3

47. The springs in figure A and B are identical but length in A is three times each of that in B. The ratio of time period T_A/T_B is

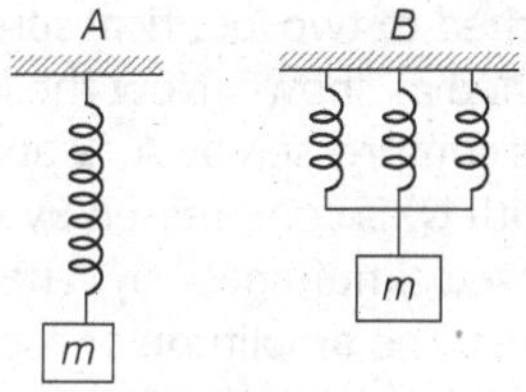

(a) $\sqrt{3}$ (b) 1/3

(c) 3 (d) $1/\sqrt{3}$

48. Some springs are combined in series and parallel arrangement as shown in the figure and a mass m is suspended from them. The ratio of their frequencies will be

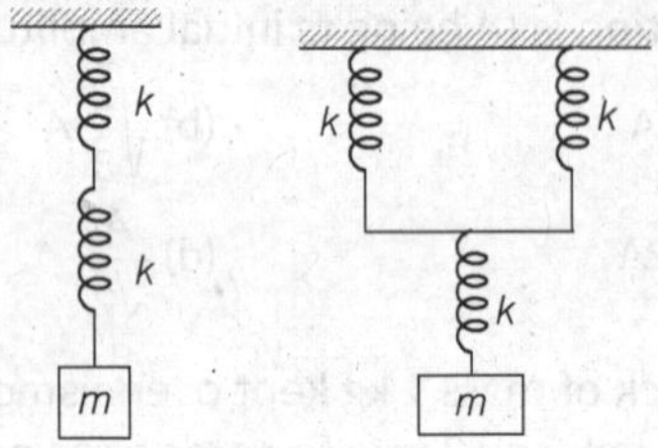

(a) 1 : 1 (b) 2 : 1 (c) $\sqrt{3} : 2$ (d) 4 : 1

49. Four massless springs of force constant $2k$, $2k$, k and $2k$ are connected to a mass M lying on a smooth horizontal surface as shown in the figure. If the mass M is displaced horizontally through a small distance and released, the system will oscillate with a frequency

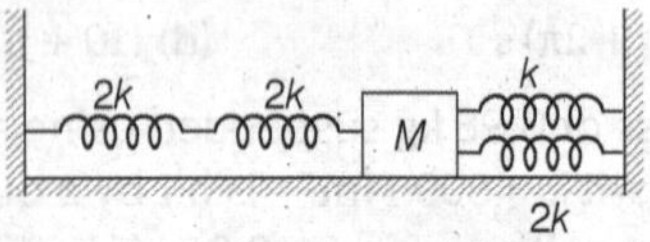

(a) $\frac{1}{2\pi}\sqrt{\frac{7k}{M}}$ (b) $\frac{1}{2\pi}\sqrt{\frac{4k}{M}}$

(c) $\frac{1}{2\pi}\sqrt{\frac{k}{3M}}$ (d) $\frac{1}{2\pi}\sqrt{\frac{k}{4M}}$

50. Two identical springs are fixed at one end and masses 1 kg and 4 kg are suspended at their other ends. They are both stretched down from their mean position and let go simultaneously. If they are in the same phase after every 4 s, then the spring constant k is

(a) π Nm^{-1} (b) π^2 Nm^{-1}

(c) 2π Nm^{-1} (d) given data is insufficient

51. Two identical blocks P and Q have mass m each. They are attached to two identical springs initially unstretched as shown. Now the left spring (along with P) is compressed by $A/2$ and the right spring (along with Q) is compressed by A. Both the blocks are released simultaneously. They collide and stick to each other. The amplitude of oscillation of combined mass is

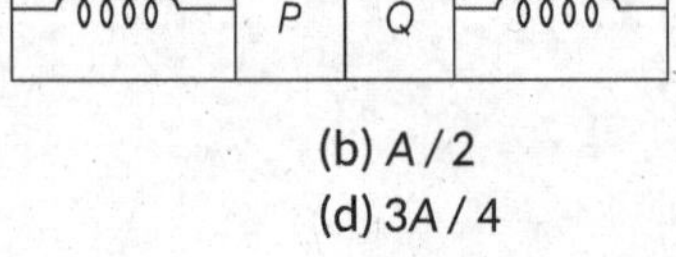

(a) $A/4$ (b) $A/2$

(c) $2A/3$ (d) $3A/4$

52. Suppose that a block of mass m is attached to a fixed spring on one side and rests (i.e., is not attached to) against an identical spring on the other side. It is now allowed to oscillate. The frequency of small oscillations is

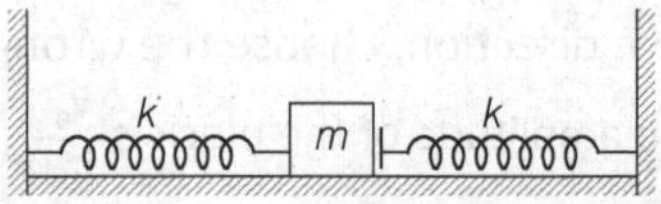

(a) $\frac{1}{\pi}\sqrt{\frac{k}{m}}$ (b) $\frac{1}{\pi}(2-\sqrt{2})\sqrt{\frac{k}{m}}$

(c) $\frac{(4-2\sqrt{2})}{\pi}\sqrt{\frac{k}{m}}$ (d) $\frac{(2+\sqrt{2})}{\pi}\sqrt{\frac{k}{m}}$

53. A system is shown in the figure. The time period for small oscillations of the two blocks will be

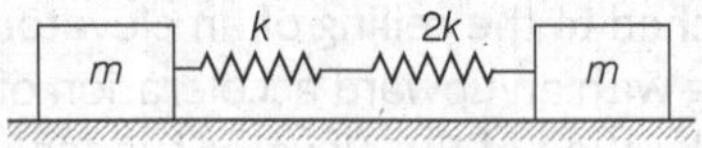

(a) $2\pi\sqrt{\frac{3m}{k}}$ (b) $2\pi\sqrt{\frac{3m}{2k}}$

(c) $2\pi\sqrt{\frac{3m}{4k}}$ (d) $2\pi\sqrt{\frac{3m}{8k}}$

54. The displacement x of a particle at a time t is given by $x = 5\sin 2t$, where x is in metre and t is in second. A simple pendulum has the same period as the particle when the length of the pendulum is

(a) 10.0 m (b) 5.0 m

(c) 2.5 m (d) 2.0 m

55. A simple pendulum has time period 2 s. The point of suspension is now moved upward according to relation $y = (6t - 3.75t^2)$ m, where t is in second and y is the vertical displacement in upward direction. The new time period of simple pendulum will be ($g = 10$ ms^{-2})

(a) 2 s (b) 1 s

(c) 4 s (d) None of these

56. In an elevator, a spring clock of time period T_s (mass attached to a spring) and a pendulum clock of time period T_p are kept. If the elevator accelerates upwards

(a) T_s as well as T_p increases.

(b) T_s remains same, T_p increases.

(c) T_s remains same, T_p decreases.

(d) T_s as well as T_p decreases.

57. A heavy brass sphere is hung from a spiral spring and it executes vertical vibrations with time period T. The ball is now immersed in non-viscous liquid with a density one-tenth that of brass. When set into vertical vibrations with the sphere remaining inside the liquid all the time, the time period will be

(a) $\left[\frac{9}{10}\right]T$ (b) $T\sqrt{\left(\frac{10}{9}\right)}$ (c) T (d) $T\sqrt{\left(\frac{9}{10}\right)}$

58. Two pendulums of lengths 121 cm and 100 cm start vibrating. At some instant, the two are in the mean position in the same phase. After how many vibrations of the shorter pendulum, the two will be in phase in the mean position?

(a) 10 (b) 11 (c) 20 (d) 21

59. If the length of a simple pendulum is equal to the radius of the earth, its time period will be

(a) $2\pi\sqrt{\frac{R}{g}}$ (b) $2\pi\sqrt{\frac{R}{2g}}$ (c) $2\pi\sqrt{\frac{2R}{g}}$ (d) ∞

60. A man is swinging on a swing made of 2 ropes of equal length L and in direction perpendicular to the plane of paper. The time period of the small oscillations about the mean position is

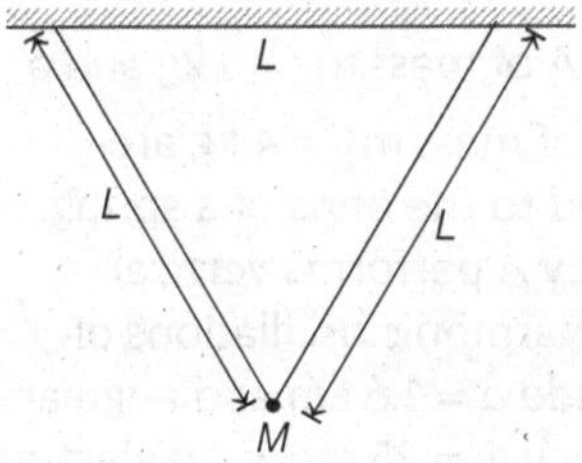

(a) $2\pi\sqrt{\frac{L}{2g}}$ (b) $2\pi\sqrt{\frac{\sqrt{3}L}{2g}}$

(c) $2\pi\sqrt{\frac{L}{2\sqrt{3}g}}$ (d) $\pi\sqrt{\frac{L}{g}}$

61. A ring of diameter 2 m oscillates as a compound pendulum about a horizontal axis passing through a point at its rim. It oscillates such that its centre move in a plane which is perpendicular to the plane of the ring. The equivalent length of the simple pendulum is

(a) 2 m (b) 4 m

(c) 1.5 m (d) 3 m

62. A metre stick swinging in vertical plane about a fixed horizontal axis passing through its one end undergoes small oscillations of frequency f_0 as shown in figure. If the bottom half of the stick were cut off, then its new frequency of small oscillations would become

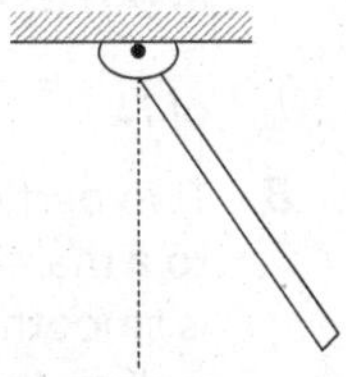

(a) f_0 (b) $\sqrt{2}f_0$

(c) $2f_0$ (d) $2\sqrt{2}f_0$

63. A system of two identical rods (L-shaped) of mass m and length l are resting on a peg P as shown in the figure. If the system is displaced in its plane by a small angle θ, find the period of oscillations

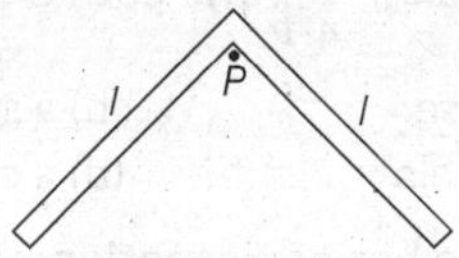

(a) $2\pi\sqrt{\frac{\sqrt{2}l}{3g}}$ (b) $2\pi\sqrt{\frac{2\sqrt{2}l}{3g}}$ (c) $2\pi\sqrt{\frac{2l}{3g}}$ (d) $3\pi\sqrt{\frac{l}{3g}}$

64. A circular disc has a tiny hole in it at a distance z from its centre. Its mass is M and radius R $(R > z)$. A horizontal shaft is passed through the hole and held fixed so that the disc can freely swing in the vertical plane. For small disturbance, the disc performs SHM whose time period is minimum for $z =$

(a) $R/2$ (b) $R/3$

(c) $R/\sqrt{2}$ (d) $R/\sqrt{3}$

65. A thin spherical shell full of water is attached to the end of a rope and allowed to swing back and forth as a pendulum from a fixed support. It has a hole in its bottom that allows water to leak out. How does the period of motion change with the loss of water?

(a) The period does not change.

(b) The period continuously decreases.

(c) The period continuously increases.

(d) The period increases to some maximum and then decreases again.

66. A rod of mass m, length l is held horizontal using a vertical string through its centre. If it is turned a little, the frequency of oscillation will be proportional to [C = Torsional constant of the string]

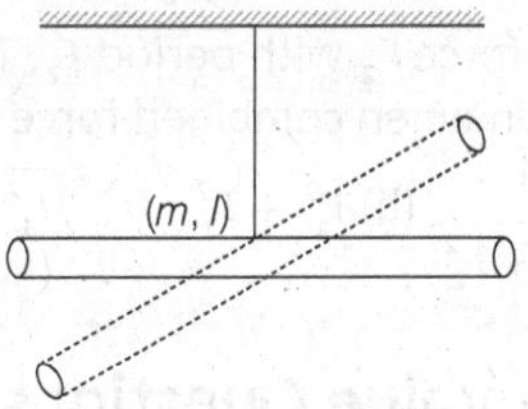

(a) $\sqrt{\frac{3C}{ml^2}}$ (b) $\sqrt{\frac{12C}{m}}$ (c) $\sqrt{\frac{ml^2}{12C}}$ (d) $\sqrt{\frac{m}{12C}}$

67. Equations $y_1 = 2A\cos^2\omega t$ and $y_2 = A(\sin\omega t + \sqrt{3}\cos\omega t)$ represent the motion of two particles.

(a) Only one of these is SHM.

(b) Ratio of maximum speeds is 2 : 1.

(c) Ratio of maximum speeds is 1 : 1.

(d) Ratio of maximum accelerations is 1 : 4.

68. A particle is subjected to two mutually perpendicular simple harmonic motions such that its x and y coordinates are given by $x = 2 \sin \omega t$, $y = 2 \sin\left(\omega t + \frac{\pi}{4}\right)$. The path of the particle will be

(a) an ellipse (b) a straight line
(c) a parabola (d) a circle

69. Two simple harmonic motions $y_1 = A \sin \omega t$ and $y_2 = A \cos \omega t$ are superimposed on a particle of mass m. The total mechanical energy of the particle is

(a) $\frac{1}{2} m\omega^2 A^2$ (b) $m\omega^2 A^2$
(c) $\frac{1}{4} m\omega^2 A^2$ (d) zero

70. A point mass is subjected to two simultaneous sinusoidal displacements in x-direction, $x_1(t) = A \sin \omega t$ and $x_2(t) = A \sin\left(\omega t + \frac{2\pi}{3}\right)$. Adding a third sinusoidal displacement $x_3(t) = B \sin(\omega t + \phi)$ brings the mass to a complete rest. The values of B and ϕ are

(a) $\sqrt{2}A, \frac{3\pi}{4}$ (b) $A, \frac{4\pi}{3}$ (c) $\sqrt{3}A, \frac{5\pi}{6}$ (d) $A, \frac{\pi}{3}$

71. The function $\sin^2(\pi t)$ represents (t is in s)

(a) a periodic, but not simple harmonic motion with a period 2 s.
(b) a periodic, but not simple harmonic motion with a period 1 s.
(c) a simple harmonic motion with a period 2 s.
(d) a simple harmonic motion with a period 1 s.

72. A force F_1 makes a body oscillate with period T_1 and another force F_2 with period T_2. The time period of oscillation when combined force acts

(a) $\frac{T_1 T_2}{\sqrt{T_1^2 + T_2^2}}$ (b) $T_1^2 + T_2^2$ (c) $\sqrt{T_1^2 + T_2^2}$ (d) $\frac{2T_1 T_2}{\sqrt{T_1^2 + T_2^2}}$

Numerical Value Questions

1. A particle executing SHM on a straight line. A and B are two points at which its velocity is zero. It passes through a certain point P ($AP < PB$) at successive intervals of 0.5 and 1.5 s with a speed of $3\sqrt{2}$ m/s. Determine the maximum speed (in m/s).

2. Two particles P and Q describe simple harmonic motions of same period, same amplitude, along the same line about the same equilibrium position O. When P and Q are on opposite sides of O at the same distance from O, they have the same speed of 1.2 m/s in the same direction. When their displacements are the same, they have the same speed of 1.6 m/s in opposite directions. Find the maximum velocity (in m/s) of either particle.

3. A point object of mass 0.1 kg is executing SHM of amplitude 0.1 m. When the particle passes through the mean position, its kinetic energy is 8×10^{-3} J. If equation of motion of the particle is $y = A \sin(bt)$, then find the value of $10 Ab$ in SI units.

4. A particle of mass 2 kg is executing SHM about origin along X-axis and its potential energy at extreme is 10 J. Velocity at mean position is $2\sqrt{2}$ m/s. Find potential energy at $x = A/2$ (where, A is amplitude).

5. A body is executing SHM under the action of force whose maximum magnitude is $10\sqrt{2}$ N. Find the magnitude of force (in N) acting on the particle at the time when its energy is half kinetic and half potential.

6. A body A of mass $m_1 = 1$ kg and a body B of mass $m_2 = 4$ kg are attached to the ends of a spring. The body A performs vertical simple harmonic oscillations of amplitude $a = 1.6$ cm and angular frequency $\omega = 25$ rad/s. Neglecting the mass of the spring, determine the ratio of maximum and minimum values of force, the system exerts on the surface on which it rests. [Take, $g = 10 \text{ m/s}^2$]

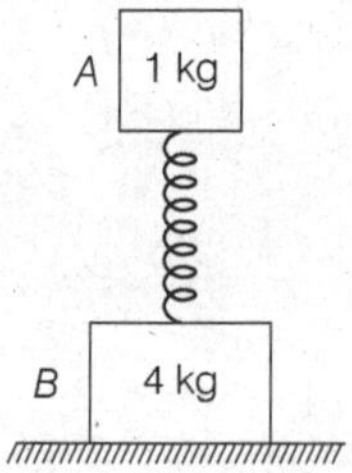

7. Two identical springs are attached to a small block P. The outer ends of the springs are fixed at A and B such that AB is vertical. When P is in equilibrium, the extension of top spring is 20 cm and extension of bottom spring is 10 cm. If the period of small vertical oscillations of P about its equilibrium position is $\frac{\pi}{N\sqrt{2}}$ s, fill the value of N.

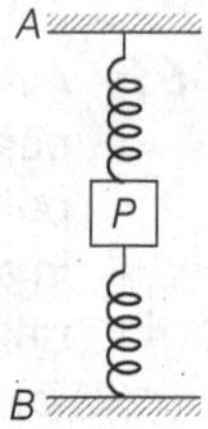

8. Two particles of mass m each are fixed to a massless rod of length $2l$. The rod is smoothly hinged at one end to a ceiling. It performs oscillation of small angle in vertical plane. If the length of the equivalent simple pendulum is $\left(\frac{xl}{3}\right)$, then find the value of x.

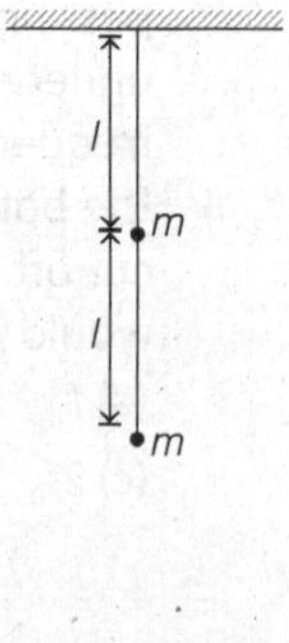

9. Two springs of spring constant $\frac{mg}{l}$ each are attached to the end of a uniform rod of mass m and length $l = 1.25$ m which is hinged in vertical plane as shown in figure. As the rod is rotated slightly about the hinge, it undergoes SHM with angular frequency ω. Find ω (in rad/s).

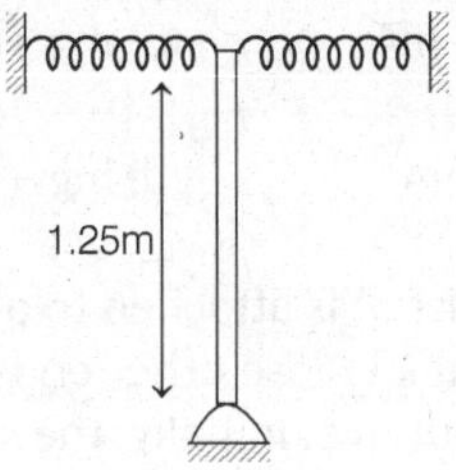

10. A cart consists of a body of mass m and two wheels each of mass m and radius R. The cart is attached to a spring of constant k. The other end of the spring is fixed to a wall as shown in figure. If time period of oscillation is $\beta \times 2\pi\sqrt{\frac{m}{k}}$, then find the value of β.

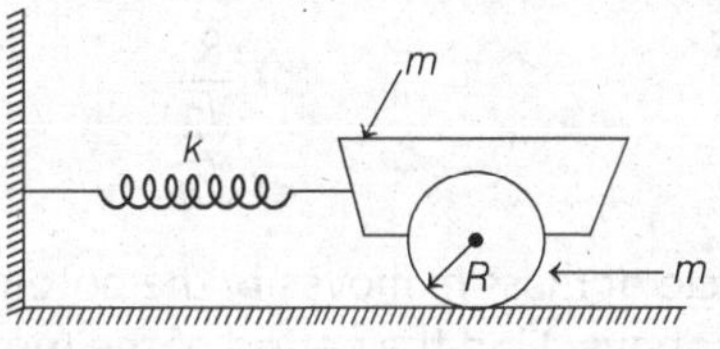

LEVEL 03 JEE Advanced Level

1. Two particles P and Q are executing SHM across same straight line whose equations are given as $y_P = A\sin(\omega t + \phi_1)$ and $y_Q = A\cos(\omega t + \phi_2)$. An observer, at $t = 0$, observes the particle P at a distance $A/\sqrt{2}$ moving to the right from mean position O while Q at $\frac{\sqrt{3}}{2}A$ moving to the left from mean position O as shown. Then, $(\phi_2 - \phi_1)$ is equal to

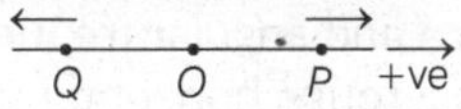

(a) $\pi/12$ (b) $7\pi/12$
(c) $5\pi/12$ (d) None of these

2. The following figure shows the displacement *versus* time graph for two particles A and B executing simple harmonic motions. The ratio of their maximum velocities is

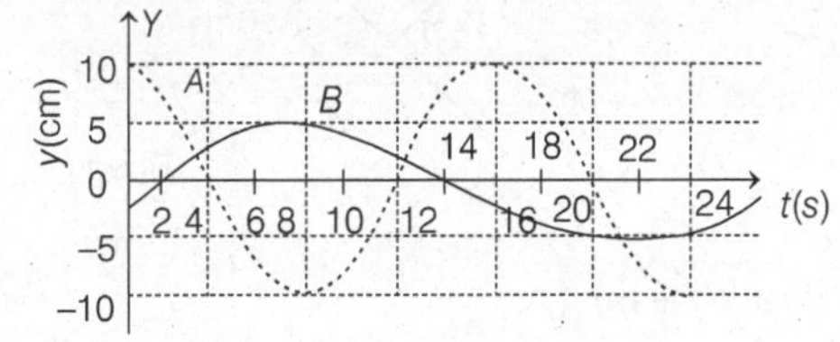

(a) 3 : 1 (b) 1 : 3
(c) 1 : 9 (d) 9 : 1

3. Two particles A and B perform SHM along the same straight line with the same amplitude a, same frequency f and same equilibrium position O. The greatest distance between them is found to be $3a/2$. At some instant of time, they have the same displacement from mean position. What is this displacement?

(a) $\frac{a}{2}$ (b) $\frac{\sqrt{7}}{4}a$ (c) $\frac{\sqrt{3}}{2}a$ (d) $\frac{3a}{4}$

4. The period of a particle executing linear SHM is T. There is a point P, at a distance x from the mean position O. When the particle passes P towards O, it has speed v, then find the time in which it returns to P again.

(a) $\frac{T}{\pi}\left[\pi - \tan^{-1}\left(\frac{vT}{2\pi x}\right)\right]$ (b) $\frac{T}{\pi}\tan^{-1}\left(\frac{vT}{2\pi x}\right)$

(c) $T\sin^{-1}\left(\frac{vT}{x}\right)$ (d) $\frac{T}{2\pi}\cot^{-1}\left(\frac{vT}{2\pi x}\right)$

5. A particle of mass m is executing oscillations about the origin on the X-axis. Its potential energy is $U(x) = k|x|^3$, where k is a positive constant. If the amplitude of oscillation is a, then its time period T is

(a) proportional to $1/\sqrt{a}$ (b) independent of a
(c) proportional to $\sqrt{a}$ (d) proportional to $a^{3/2}$

6. Potential energy of a particle of mass 0.1 kg moving along X-axis is given as $U = 5x(x-4)$ J, here x is in metres, then which of the following is correct?

(i) Particle is acted upon by a constant force.
(ii) Speed of particle is maximum at $x = 2$ m.
(iii) Particle executes SHM.
(iv) Period is $\pi/5$ s

(a) i, ii, iii (b) ii, iii, iv
(c) i, ii, iv (d) i, ii, iii and iv

7. A body performs simple harmonic oscillations along the straight line *ABCDE* with *C* as the midpoint of *AE*. Its kinetic energies at *B* and *D* are each one-fourth of its maximum value. If $AE = 2R$, the distance between *B* and *D* is

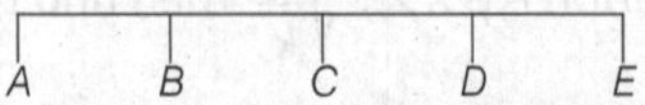

(a) $\frac{\sqrt{3}R}{2}$ (b) $\frac{R}{\sqrt{2}}$

(c) $\sqrt{3}R$ (d) $\sqrt{2}R$

8. A particle of mass *m* moves in the potential energy *U* shown above. Find the period of the motion when the particle has total energy *E*.

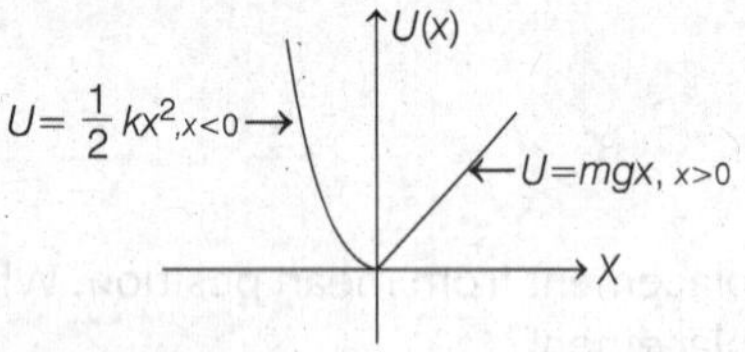

(a) $2\pi\sqrt{\frac{m}{k}} + 4\sqrt{\frac{2E}{mg^2}}$ (b) $2\pi\sqrt{\frac{m}{k}}$

(c) $\pi\sqrt{\frac{m}{k}} + 2\sqrt{\frac{2E}{mg^2}}$ (d) $2\sqrt{\frac{2E}{mg^2}}$

9. Vertical displacement of a plank with a body of mass *m* on it is varying according to law $y = \sin \omega t + \sqrt{3}\cos \omega t$. The minimum value of ω for which the mass just breaks off the plank and the moment it occurs first after $t = 0$ are given by (*y* is positive vertically upwards)

(a) $\sqrt{\frac{g}{2}}, \frac{\sqrt{2}}{6}\frac{\pi}{\sqrt{g}}$ (b) $\frac{g}{\sqrt{2}}, \frac{2}{3}\sqrt{\frac{\pi}{g}}$

(c) $\sqrt{\frac{g}{2}}, \frac{\pi}{3}\sqrt{\frac{2}{g}}$ (d) $\sqrt{2g}, \sqrt{\frac{2\pi}{3g}}$

10. A block of mass *m* is placed on an ideal spring and is in equilibrium. The block is not attached to the spring. The spring is compressed by x_0 in equilibrium. If the spring is further compressed by $2x_0$ and released, find the time period of oscillations.

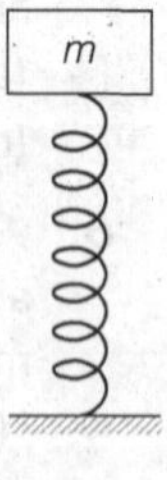

(a) $2\sqrt{\frac{x_0}{g}}(\pi + 1)$ (b) $2\pi\sqrt{\frac{x_0}{g}}$

(c) $2\sqrt{\frac{x_0}{g}}\left(\frac{2\pi}{3} + \sqrt{3}\right)$ (d) $2\pi\sqrt{\frac{m}{k}} + \sqrt{\frac{x_0}{g}}$

11. A block of mass *m* is suspended from a spring and executes vertical SHM of time period *T* as shown in figure. The amplitude of the SHM is *A* and spring is never in compressed state during the oscillation. The magnitude of minimum force exerted by spring on the block is

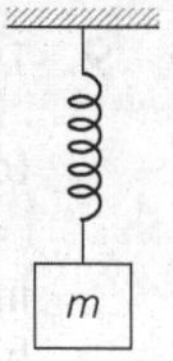

(a) $mg - \frac{4\pi^2}{T^2}mA$ (b) $mg + \frac{4\pi^2}{T^2}mA$

(c) $mg - \frac{\pi^2}{T^2}mA$ (d) $mg + \frac{\pi^2}{T^2}mA$

12. A block of mass *m* is attached to a spring of force constant *k* whose other end is fixed to a horizontal surface. Initially, the spring is in its natural length and the block is released from rest. If average force acting on the surface by the spring till the instant when the block has zero acceleration for the first time is *F*, then find *F*.

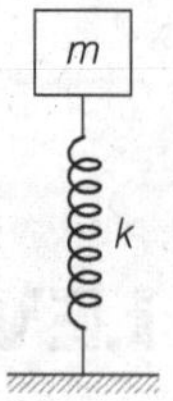

(a) $\frac{mg}{\pi}$ (b) $\frac{2mg}{\pi}$

(c) $\frac{3mg}{\pi}$ (d) $\frac{4mg}{\pi}$

13. A block of mass *m* attached to a fixed position *O* on a smooth inclined wedge of mass *M* oscillates with amplitude *A* and angular frequency ω. The wedge is located on a rough horizontal surface. If the angle of the wedge is 60°, then the force of friction acting on the wedge is given by (coefficient of static friction $= \mu$)

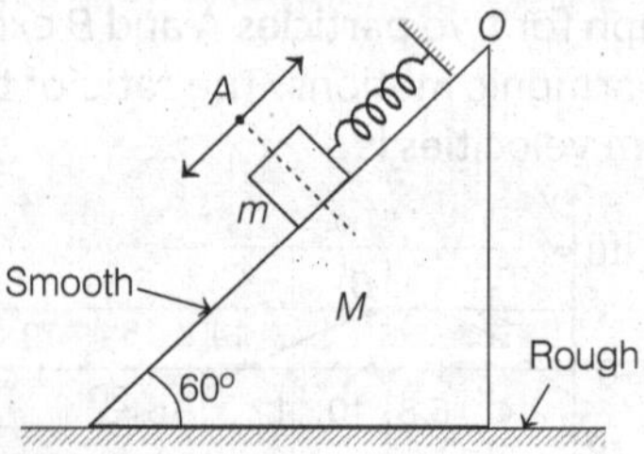

(a) $\mu(M + m)g$

(b) $\frac{1}{2}m\omega^2 A \sin \omega t$

(c) $\mu\left[(M + m)g + \frac{\sqrt{3}}{2}m\omega^2 A \sin \omega t\right]$

(d) $\mu(M + m)\omega^2 A \sin \omega t$

14. The coefficient of friction between blocks of mass m and $2m$ is $\mu = 2\tan\theta$. There is no friction between block of mass $2m$ and inclined plane. The maximum amplitude of two block system for which there is no relative motion between the blocks is

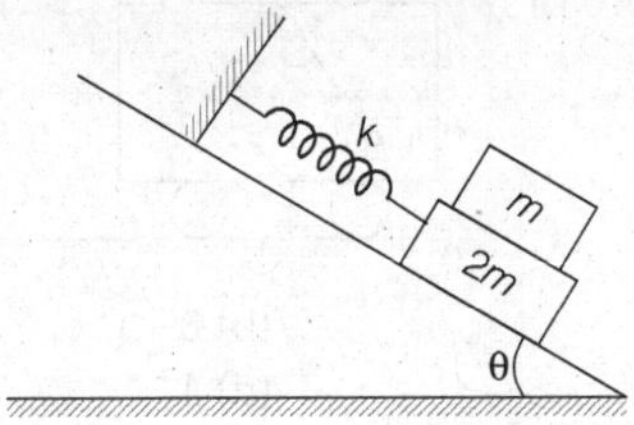

(a) $g\sin\theta\sqrt{\dfrac{k}{m}}$ (b) $\dfrac{mg\sin\theta}{k}$

(c) $\dfrac{3mg\sin\theta}{k}$ (d) $\dfrac{2mg\sin\theta}{k}$

15. A spring block system is fixed in a train, suddenly train starts moving with constant acceleration a_0. Taking origin at initial position of block, what is equation of motion for block in reference frame of train. Force constant of spring is k. Neglect friction between block and train.

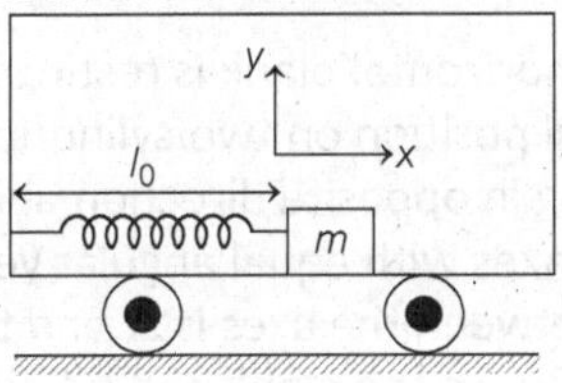

(a) $-\dfrac{ma_0}{k} + \dfrac{ma_0}{k}\cos\left(\sqrt{\dfrac{k}{m}}\right)t$

(b) $\dfrac{ma_0}{k} - \dfrac{ma_0}{k}\cos\left(\sqrt{\dfrac{k}{m}}\right)t$

(c) $-\dfrac{ma_0}{k} - \dfrac{ma_0}{k}\cos\left(\sqrt{\dfrac{k}{m}}\right)t$

(d) $\dfrac{ma_0}{k} + \dfrac{ma_0}{k}\cos\left(\sqrt{\dfrac{k}{m}}\right)t$

16. A block of mass m is connected to two springs of spring constants $2k$ and $3k$ respectively, as shown in the diagram, with both the springs being vertical and fixed at their other ends. Both springs are initially unstretched and the mass m is given an initial velocity u in the downward direction. The block oscillates. The amplitude of oscillation of the block is given by

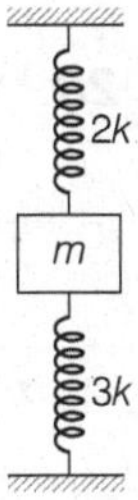

(a) $\sqrt{\dfrac{mu^2}{5k} + \dfrac{mg}{5k}}$ (b) $\dfrac{mg}{5k}$

(c) $\sqrt{\dfrac{mu^2}{5k} + \left(\dfrac{mg}{5k}\right)^2}$ (d) $\left|\sqrt{\dfrac{mu^2}{5k}} - \dfrac{mg}{5k}\right|$

17. A block of mass m is supported by string spring combination as shown in the diagram. The string is sufficiently long. The system is at rest in equilibrium. The block is pulled by a distance x from equilibrium position and released. It performs oscillatory motion and let $x = x_0$, is maximum possible value for which string is not becoming slacked in subsequent motion. If $x = 2x_0$, then time for which string becomes slacked in one complete oscillation is

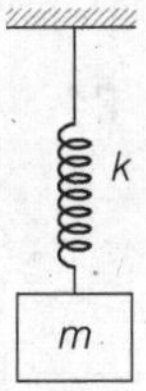

(a) $\sqrt{\dfrac{3m}{k}}$ (b) $\sqrt{\dfrac{6m}{k}}$ (c) $3\sqrt{\dfrac{m}{k}}$ (d) $\sqrt{\dfrac{12m}{k}}$

18. The system shown lies on a horizontal smooth surface. The mass m is given a small displacement along the X-axis. The time period will be

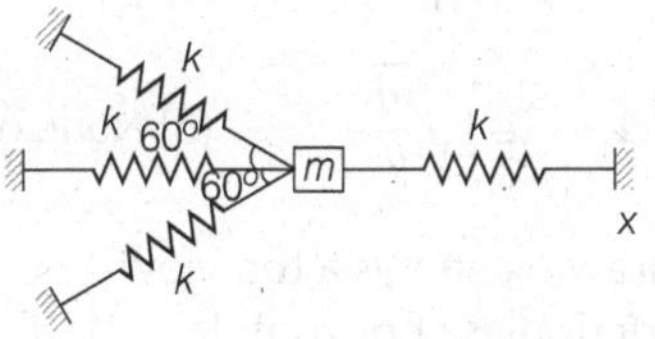

(a) $2\pi\sqrt{\dfrac{2m}{5k}}$ (b) $2\pi\sqrt{\dfrac{5m}{2k}}$

(c) $2\pi\sqrt{\dfrac{3m}{2k}}$ (d) None of these

19. The mass M shown in the figure oscillates in simple harmonic motion with amplitude A. The amplitude of the point P is

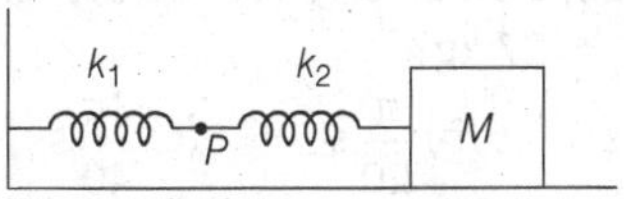

(a) $\dfrac{k_1A}{k_2}$ (b) $\dfrac{k_2A}{k_1}$ (c) $\dfrac{k_1A}{k_1+k_2}$ (d) $\dfrac{k_2A}{k_1+k_2}$

20. In the figure shown, a block of mass m is rigidly attached to two identical springs of stiffness k each with other ends of the springs connected to the fixed walls. When the block is in equilibrium, length of each spring is b, which is greater than the natural length l of the spring. The time period of the oscillation of the block if it is displaced by small distance x perpendicular to the length of the spring and released (motion of the block is unaffected from gravity) is

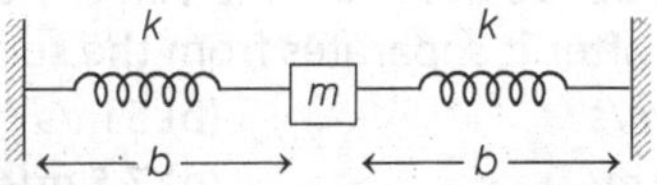

(a) $2\pi\sqrt{\dfrac{mb}{k(b-l)}}$ (b) $2\pi\sqrt{\dfrac{mb}{2k(b-l)}}$

(c) $\sqrt{\dfrac{m(b-l)}{kb}}$ (d) $2\pi\sqrt{\dfrac{m(b-l)}{2kb}}$

21. A smooth wedge of mass m and angle of inclination 60° rests unattached between two springs of spring constant k and $4k$, on a smooth horizontal plane, both springs in the unextended position. The time period of small oscillations of the wedge (assuming that the springs are constrained to get compressed along their length) equals

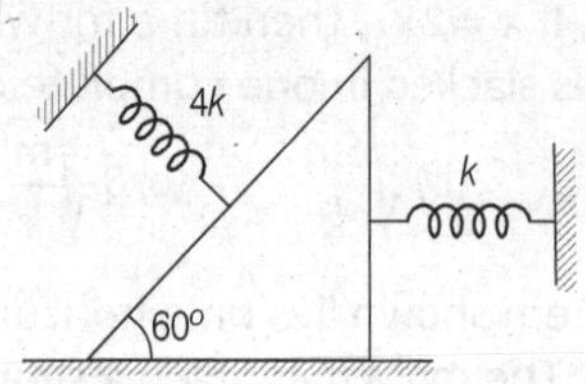

(a) $\pi\left(1+\frac{1}{2}\right)\sqrt{\frac{m}{k}}$ (b) $\pi\left(1+\frac{1}{\sqrt{3}}\right)\sqrt{\frac{m}{k}}$

(c) $\pi\left(1+\frac{2}{\sqrt{3}}\right)\sqrt{\frac{m}{k}}$ (d) None of these

22. The drawing shows a top view of a frictionless horizontal surface, where there are two identical springs with particles of mass m_1 and m_2 attached to them. Each spring has a spring constant of 1200 N/m. The particles are pulled to the right and then released from the positions shown in the drawing. How much time passes before the particles are again side by side for the first time if $m_1 = 3.0$ kg and $m_2 = 27$ kg?

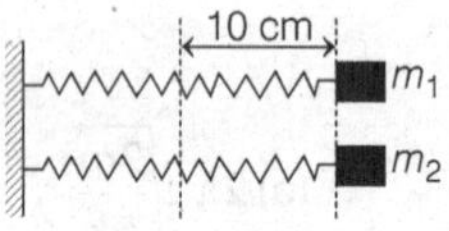

Natural length

(a) $\frac{\pi}{40}$ s (b) $\frac{\pi}{20}$ s (c) $\frac{3\pi}{40}$ s (d) $\frac{\pi}{10}$ s

23. A 2 kg block moving with 10 m/s strikes a spring of constant π^2 N/m attached to 2 kg block at rest kept on a smooth floor. The time for which rear moving block remains in contact with spring will be

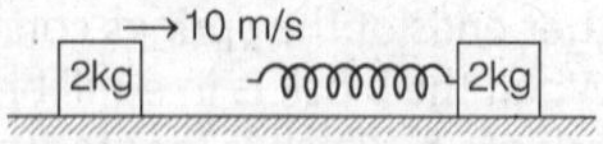

(a) $\sqrt{2}$ s (b) $\frac{1}{\sqrt{2}}$ s

(c) 1 s (d) $\frac{1}{2}$ s

24. In the above question, the velocity of the rear 2 kg block after it separates from the spring will be

(a) 0 m/s (b) 5 m/s

(c) 10 m/s (d) 7.5 m/s

25. A bob B of mass 1 kg is suspended from the ceiling of a toy train as shown in the figure. The train oscillates simple harmonically in hozional direction with angular frequency $\omega = 5$ rad/s and amplitude $a = 0.1$ m. What is the ratio of maximum and minimum tensions in the string AB during the motion? ($g = 10$ m/s^2 and $\tan 37° = \frac{3}{4}$)

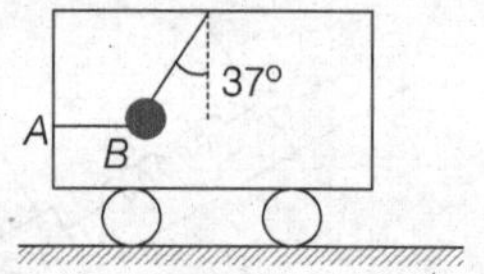

(a) 2 (b) 3

(c) 4 (d) 1

26. A bar of mass m is suspended horizontally on two vertical springs of spring constant k and $3k$. The bar bounces up and down while remaining horizontal. Find the time period of oscillation of the bar (Neglect mass of springs and friction everywhere).

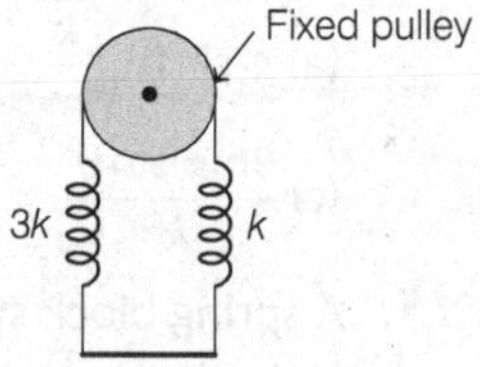

(a) $2\pi\sqrt{\frac{m}{k}}$ (b) $2\pi\sqrt{\frac{m}{3k}}$ (c) $\pi\sqrt{\frac{2m}{3k}}$ (d) $\pi\sqrt{\frac{3m}{4k}}$

27. A uniform horizontal plank is resting symmetrically in a horizontal position on two cylindrical drums, which are spinning in opposite direction about their horizontal axes with equal angular velocity. The distance between the axes is $2L$ and the coefficient of friction between the plank and cylinder is μ. If the plank is displaced slightly from the equilibrium position along its length and released, calculate the time period of motion.

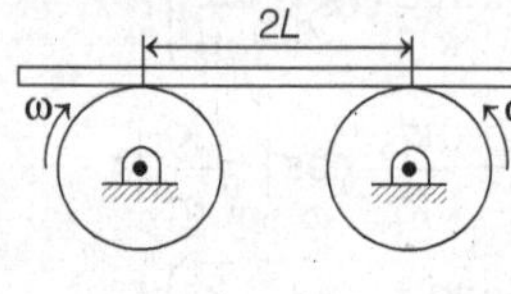

(a) $2\pi\sqrt{\frac{2L}{\mu g}}$ (b) $2\pi\sqrt{\frac{L}{\mu g}}$ (c) $2\pi\sqrt{\frac{L}{2\mu g}}$ (d) $4\pi\sqrt{\frac{L}{\mu g}}$

28. What is the period of small oscillations of the block of mass m if the springs are ideal and pulleys are massless?

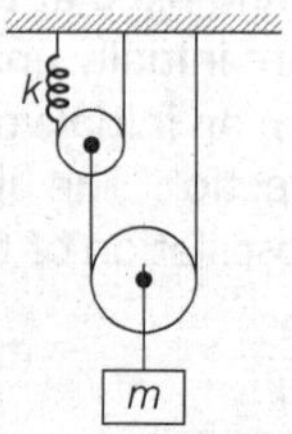

(a) $\frac{\pi}{2}\sqrt{\frac{m}{k}}$ (b) $\frac{\pi}{2}\sqrt{\frac{m}{2k}}$ (c) $\frac{\pi}{2}\sqrt{\frac{2m}{k}}$ (d) $\pi\sqrt{\frac{m}{2k}}$

29. A non-viscous liquid of density ρ is filled in a tube with A as the area of cross-section, as shown in the figure. If the liquid is slightly depressed in one of the arms, the liquid column oscillates with a frequency

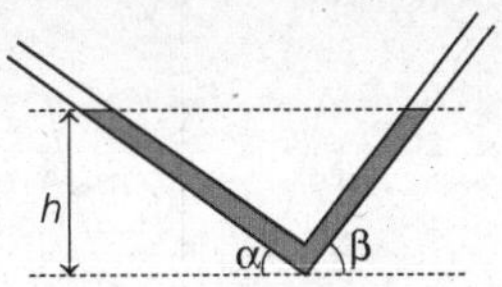

(a) $\frac{1}{2\pi}\sqrt{\frac{g}{h}}$ (b) $\frac{1}{2\pi}\sqrt{\frac{g(\sin\alpha+\sin\beta)}{h}}$

(c) $\frac{1}{2\pi}\sqrt{\frac{g\sin\alpha\sin\beta}{h}}$ (d) $\frac{1}{2\pi}\sqrt{\frac{g\sin(\beta-\alpha)}{h}}$

30. The angular frequency of oscillation of the liquid in the vertical circular tube is

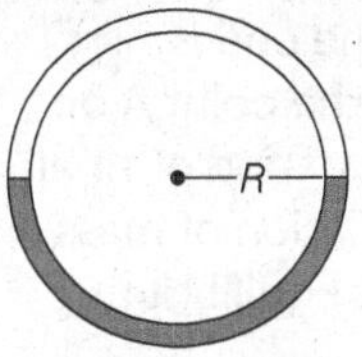

(a) $\sqrt{\frac{g}{R}}$ (b) $\sqrt{\frac{2g}{R}}$

(c) $\sqrt{\frac{\pi g}{R}}$ (d) $\sqrt{\frac{2g}{\pi R}}$

31. A vertical pole of height h, density ρ, area of cross-section A, floats in two immiscible liquids of densities ρ_1 and ρ_2. In equilibrium position the bottom end is at the interface of the liquids. When the cylinder is displaced vertically, the time period of oscillation is ....

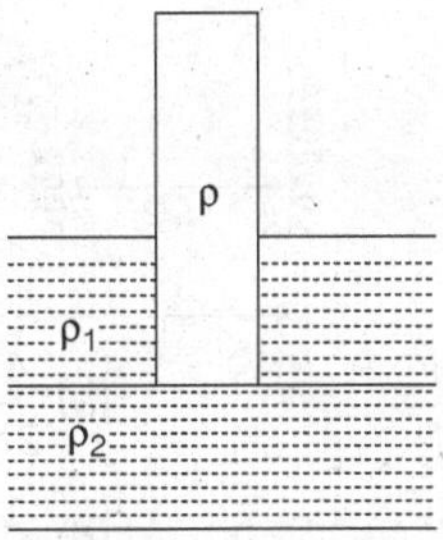

(a) $\pi\sqrt{\frac{\rho h}{(\rho_1+\rho_2)g}}$ (b) $\pi\sqrt{\frac{\rho h}{g}}\left(\frac{1}{\sqrt{\rho_1}}+\frac{1}{\sqrt{\rho_2}}\right)$

(c) $\pi\sqrt{\frac{(\rho_1+\rho_2)h}{\rho g}}$ (d) $\pi\sqrt{\frac{h}{\rho g}}(\sqrt{\rho_1}+\sqrt{\rho_2})$

32. An air chamber of volume V has a neck area of cross-section a into which a ball of mass m can move up and down without friction. If the ball is pressed down a little and released, then find the time period of oscillation of ball. Here, air is ideal and its temperature remains constant. Bulk modulus of air is B.

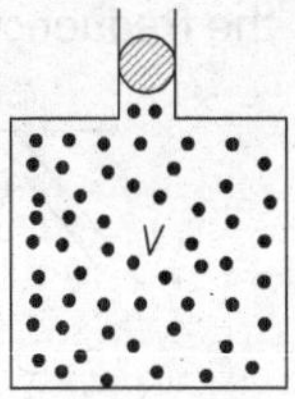

(a) $T=2\pi\sqrt{\frac{2Vm}{Ba^2}}$ (b) $T=2\pi\sqrt{\frac{Vm}{Ba^2}}$

(c) $T=2\pi\sqrt{\frac{Vm}{2Ba^2}}$ (d) None of these

33. A ball is suspended by a thread of length L at the point O on the wall PQ which is inclined to the vertical through an angle α. The thread with the ball is now displaced through a small angle β ($\beta > \alpha$) away from the vertical and released from rest. Assuming the collision of the ball against the wall to be perfectly elastic, the time period of oscillation of the pendulum will be

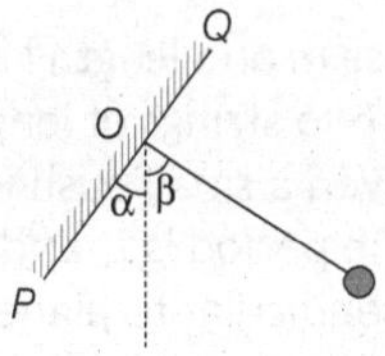

(a) $2\pi\sqrt{\frac{L}{g}}$ (b) $\sqrt{\frac{L}{g}}\left[\pi+\sin^{-1}\left(\frac{\alpha}{\beta}\right)\right]$

(c) $2\sqrt{\frac{L}{g}}\left[\frac{\pi}{2}+\sin^{-1}\left(\frac{\alpha}{\beta}\right)\right]$ (d) $2\sqrt{\frac{L}{g}}\left[\frac{\pi}{2}+\cos^{-1}\left(\frac{\alpha}{\beta}\right)\right]$

34. A long, straight, and massless rod pivots about one end in a vertical plane. In configuration I, shown, two small identical masses are attached to the free end, in configuration II, one mass is moved to the centre of the rod. What is the ratio of the frequency of small oscillations of configuration II to that of configuration I?

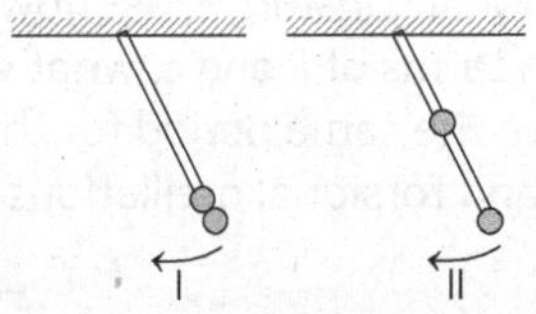

(a) $(6/5)^{1/2}$ (b) $(3/2)^{1/2}$

(c) 6/5 (d) 5/3

35. A *L*-shaped bar of mass *M* is pivoted at one of its end so that it can freely rotate in a vertical plane as shown. If it is slightly displaced from its equilibrium position, then the frequency of oscillation is ...

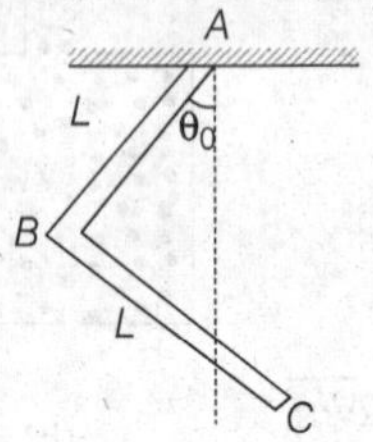

(a) $\frac{1}{2\pi}\sqrt{\frac{3g}{\sqrt{10}L}}$ (b) $\frac{1}{2\pi}\sqrt{\frac{g}{L}\left(\frac{\sqrt{10}}{4}\right)}$

(c) $\frac{1}{2\pi}\sqrt{\frac{g}{L}(\sqrt{2})}$ (d) $\frac{1}{2\pi}\sqrt{\frac{g}{\sqrt{2}L}}$

36. A thin uniform plate shaped as an equilateral triangle with a height *h* performs small oscillations about the horizontal axis coinciding with one of its sides. The time period of oscillation is

(a) $2\pi\sqrt{\frac{h}{g}}$ (b) $\pi\sqrt{\frac{h}{g}}$ (c) $\pi\sqrt{\frac{2h}{g}}$ (d) $2\pi\sqrt{\frac{2h}{g}}$

37. A rod of mass *m* and length *l* is suspended from ceiling with two strings of length *l* as shown. When the rod is given a small push in the plane of page and released time period is T_1 and when the rod is given a push perpendicular to plane, time period of oscillation is T_2. The ratio $\frac{T_1^2}{T_2^2}$ is

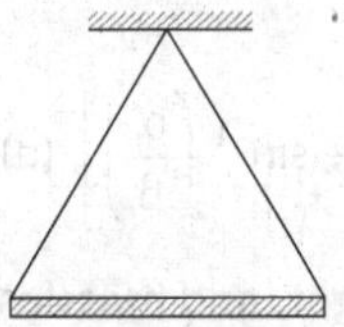

(a) 1 (b) $\frac{10}{9}$

(c) $\frac{9}{10}$ (d) $\frac{\sqrt{3}}{2}$

38. A solid disk of radius *R* is suspended from a spring of linear spring constant *k* and torsional constant *c*, as shown in figure. In terms of *k* and *c*, what value of *R* will give the same period for the vertical and torsional oscillations of this system?

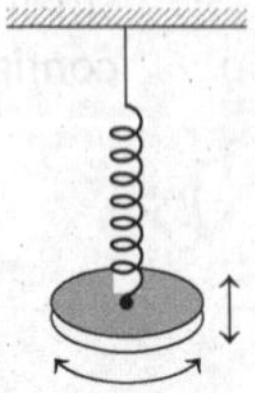

(a) $\sqrt{\frac{2c}{k}}$ (b) $\sqrt{\frac{c}{2k}}$ (c) $2\sqrt{\frac{c}{k}}$ (d) $\frac{1}{2}\sqrt{\frac{c}{k}}$

39. A particle of mass *m* is allowed to oscillate near the minimum of a vertical parabolic path having the equation $x^2 = 4ay$. The angular frequency of small oscillation is given by

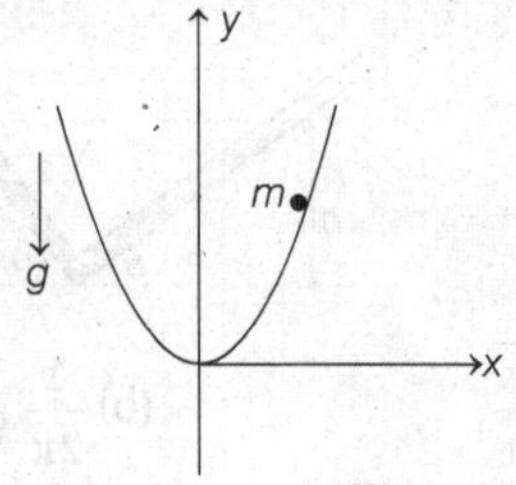

(a) $\sqrt{gh}$ (b) $\sqrt{2gh}$ (c) $\sqrt{\frac{g}{2a}}$ (d) $\sqrt{\frac{g}{a}}$

40. A massless rod is pivoted at point *O*. A string carrying a mass *m* at one end is attached to the point *A* on the rod. The period of small vertical oscillation of mass *m* around its equilibrium position is

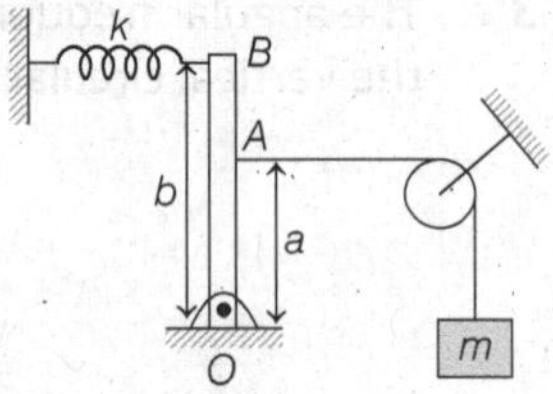

(a) $T = 2\pi\frac{a}{b}\sqrt{\frac{m}{k}}$ (b) $T = \pi\frac{a}{b}\sqrt{\frac{m}{k}}$

(c) $T = 2\pi\frac{b}{a}\sqrt{\frac{m}{k}}$ (d) $T = \pi\frac{b}{a}\sqrt{\frac{m}{k}}$

41. A long uniform rod of length *L*, mass *M* is free to rotate in a horizontal plane about a vertical axis through its end. Two springs of constant *k* each are connected as shown. On equilibrium, the rod was horizontal. The frequency will be

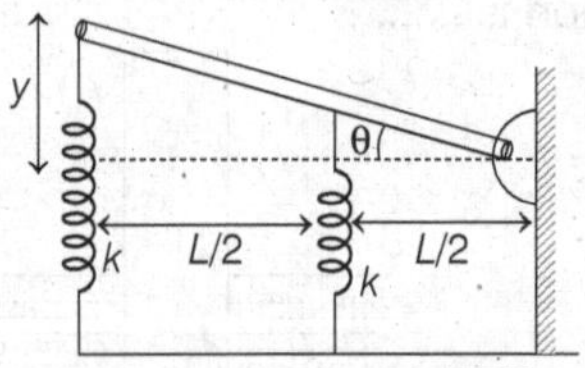

(a) $\frac{1}{2\pi}\sqrt{\frac{15k}{M}}$ (b) $\frac{1}{2\pi}\sqrt{\frac{5k}{4M}}$

(c) $\frac{1}{2\pi}\sqrt{\frac{3k}{4M}}$ (d) $\frac{1}{2\pi}\sqrt{\frac{15k}{4M}}$

42. A spherical ball of mass *m* and radius *r* rolls without slipping on a rough concave surface of large radius *R*. It makes small oscillations about the lowest point. Find the time period.

(a) $2\pi\sqrt{\frac{7(R-r)}{5g}}$ (b) $2\pi\sqrt{\frac{5(R-r)}{7g}}$

(c) $2\pi\sqrt{\frac{2(R-r)}{5g}}$ (d) $2\pi\sqrt{\frac{5(R-r)}{2g}}$

43. A uniform plank of mass m, free to move in the horizontal direction only, is placed at the top of a solid cylinder of mass $2m$ and radius R. The plank is attached to a fixed wall by means of a light spring of spring constant k. There is no slipping between the cylinder and the plank and between the cylinder and the ground. Find the time period of small oscillations of the system.

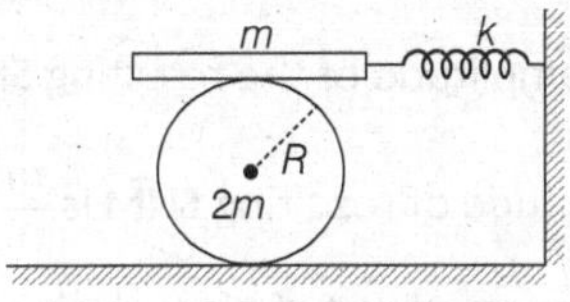

(a) $2\pi\sqrt{\frac{17m}{5k}}$ (b) $2\pi\sqrt{\frac{27m}{10k}}$

(c) $2\pi\sqrt{\frac{7m}{4k}}$ (d) $2\pi\sqrt{\frac{19m}{5k}}$

44. A thin walled tube of mass m and radius R has a rod of mass m and very small cross-section soldered on its inner surface. The side-view of the arrangement is as shown. The entire arrangement is placed on a rough horizontal surface. The system is given a small angular displacement from its equilibrium position, as a result, the system performs oscillations. The time period of resulting oscillations, if the tube rolls without slipping is

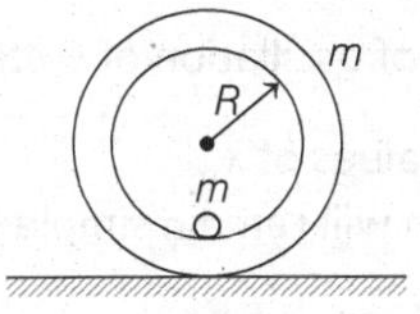

(a) $2\pi\sqrt{\frac{4R}{g}}$ (b) $2\pi\sqrt{\frac{2R}{g}}$

(c) $2\pi\sqrt{\frac{R}{g}}$ (d) None of these

Multiple Choice(s) Correct Questions

1. The displacement of a particle of mass 100 g from its mean position is given by $y = 0.05 \sin 4\pi (5t + 0.4)$, y in metres and t in seconds.

(a) The time period of motion is 0.1 s.
(b) The maximum acceleration of the particle is $10\pi^2$ m/s^2.
(c) The total energy of SHM of the particle is $0.05\pi^2$ J.
(d) The force acting on the particle is zero, when displacement is 0.05 m.

2. The displacement-time graph of a particle executing SHM is shown. Which of the following statements is/are true?

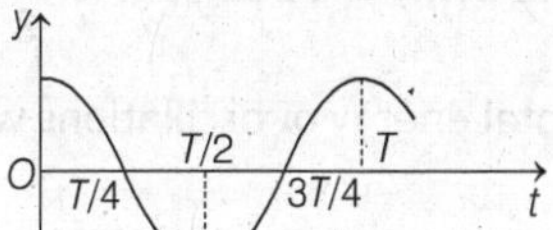

(a) The velocity is maximum at $t = T/2$.
(b) The acceleration is maximum at $t = T$.
(c) The force is zero at $t = 3T/4$.
(d) The potential energy equals the oscillation energy at $t = T/2$.

3. A particle of mass 1 kg, executing simple harmonic motion of period 20 s, crosses the mean position at $t = 0$ with velocity π cm/s.

(a) The maximum acceleration of the particle is 10 cm/s^2.
(b) When it is 4 cm from the mean position, its velocity is $6\pi/10$ cm/s.
(c) The kinetic energy of the particle when its displacement is 5 cm from the mean position is $\frac{3\pi^2}{8\times 10^4}$ J.
(d) Its velocity at displacement 6 cm from the mean position is $8\pi/10$ cm/s.

4. The figure shows a graph between velocity and displacement (from mean position) of a particle performing SHM,

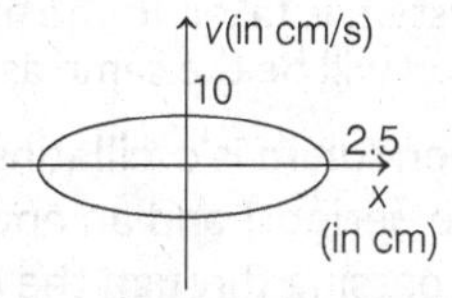

(a) the time period of the particle is 1.57 s.
(b) the maximum acceleration will be 40 cm/s^2.
(c) the velocity of particle is $2\sqrt{21}$ cm/s, when it is at a distance 1 cm from the mean position.
(d) None of these

5. Consider a spring that exerts the following restoring force

$$F = -kx \text{ for } x > 0, \quad F = -4kx \text{ for } x < 0$$

A mass m on a frictionless surface is attached to the spring displaced to $x = A$ by stretching the spring and released.

(a) The period of motion will be $T = \frac{3\pi}{2}\sqrt{\frac{m}{k}}$.
(b) The most negative value the mass m can reach will be $x = -\frac{A}{2}$.

(c) The time taken to move from $x = A$ to $x = -\frac{A}{\sqrt{2}}$, straight away will be equal to $\frac{5\pi}{8}\sqrt{\frac{m}{k}}$.

(d) The total energy of oscillations will be $\frac{5}{2}kA^2$.

6. Figure shows the potential energy diagram and the total energy line of a particle oscillating on a spring.

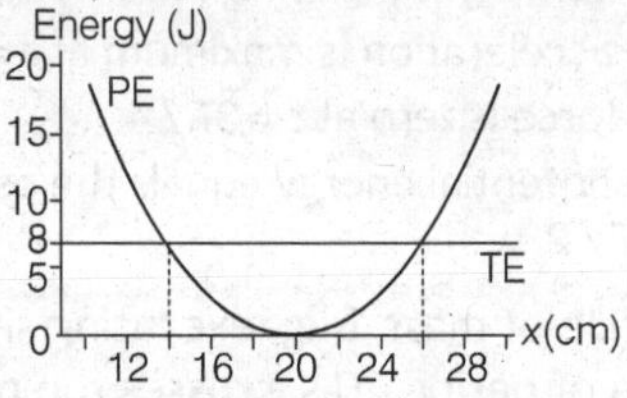

(a) The amplitude of oscillation of particle is 6 cm.
(b) The spring constant is 4.44 kN/m.
(c) The mass of particle is 1 kg.
(d) The maximum kinetic energy of particle is at $x = 20$ cm.

7. A mass of 0.2 kg is attached to the lower end of a massless spring of force constant 200 N/m, the upper end of which is fixed to a rigid support. Which of the following statements is/are true?
(a) In equilibrium, the spring will be stretched by 1 cm.
(b) If the mass is raised till the spring is unstretched state and then released, it will go down by 2 cm before moving upwards.
(c) The frequency of oscillation will be nearly 5 Hz.
(d) If the system is taken to the moon, the frequency of oscillation will be the same as on the earth.

8. A simple pendulum is oscillating in a stationary lift with a time period T and an angular amplitude θ_0. When it is passing through the mean position, the lift started accelerating upwards.

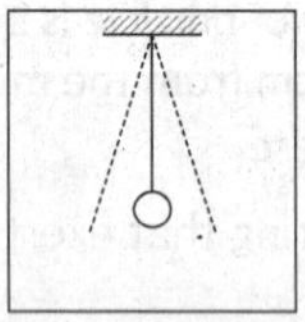

(a) The time period of its oscillation will increase.
(b) Its angular amplitude would increase.
(c) The time period of its oscillation would decrease.
(d) Its angular amplitude would decrease.

9. A spring mass system is hanging from the ceiling of an elevator in equilibrium. The elevator suddenly starts accelerating upwards with acceleration a, consider all the options in the reference frame of elevator.

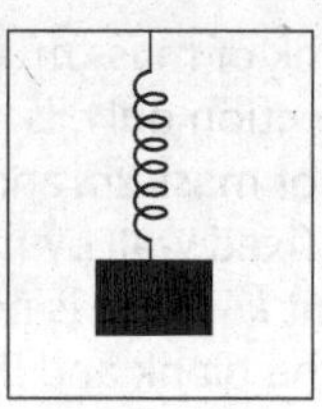

(a) The frequency of oscillation is $\frac{1}{2\pi}\sqrt{\frac{k}{m}}$.
(b) The amplitude of the resulting SHM is $\frac{ma}{k}$.
(c) Amplitude of resulting SHM is $\frac{m(g+a)}{k}$.
(d) Maximum speed of block during oscillation is $\left(\sqrt{\frac{m}{k}}\right)a$.

10. A bob of mass $2m$ hangs by a string attached to the block of mass m of a spring block system. The whole arrangement is in a state of equilibrium. The bob of mass $2m$ is pulled down slowly by a distance x_0 and released.

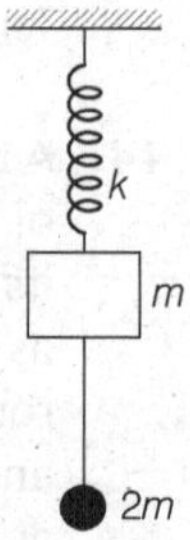

(a) For $x_0 = \frac{3mg}{k}$, maximum tension in string is $4mg$.
(b) For $x_0 > \frac{3mg}{k}$, minimum tension in string is mg.
(c) Frequency of oscillation of system is $\frac{1}{2\pi}\sqrt{\frac{k}{3m}}$, for all non-zero values of x_0.
(d) The motion will remain simple harmonic for $x_0 \le \frac{3mg}{k}$.

11. Two blocks of masses 3 kg and 6 kg rest on a horizontal smooth surface. The 3 kg block is attached to a spring with a force constant $k = 900\ \text{Nm}^{-1}$ which is compressed 2 m from beyond the equilibrium position. The 6 kg mass is at rest 1 m from the mean position. 3 kg mass strikes the 6 kg mass and the two stick together.

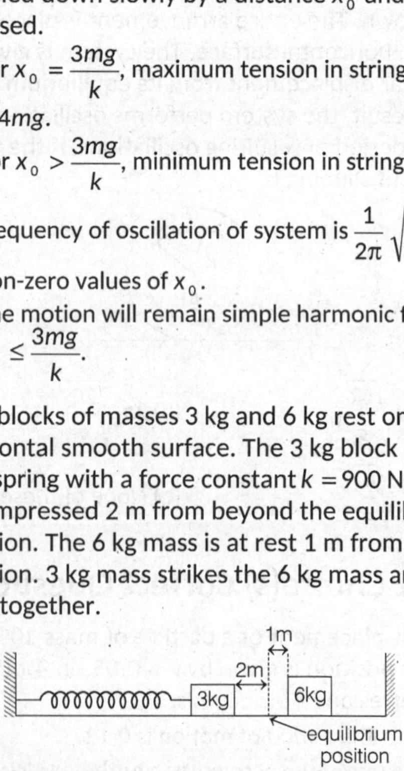

(a) Velocity of the combined masses immediately after the collision is $10\ \text{ms}^{-1}$.
(b) Velocity of the combined masses immediately after the collision is $5\ \text{ms}^{-1}$.
(c) Amplitude of the resulting oscillation is $\sqrt{2}$ m.
(d) Amplitude of the resulting oscillation is $\sqrt{5/2}$ m.

12. Initially, spring is compressed by x_0 and blocks are in contact when system is released, then blocks start moving and after some time, contact between blocks breaks, then

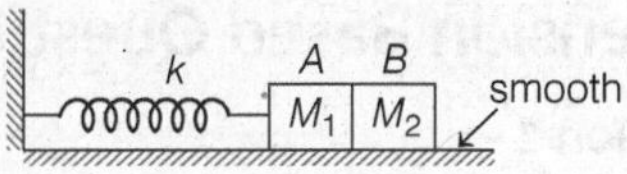

(a) blocks will separated at natural length of spring.

(b) after separation, block A performs SHM of amplitude $x_0\sqrt{\dfrac{m_1}{m_1+m_2}}$.

(c) after separation, maximum velocity of block A is $x_0\sqrt{\dfrac{k}{m_1+m_2}}$.

(d) after separation, block A will perform SHM of amplitude x_0.

13. When displaced and released, the 2 kg mass in the figure oscillates on the frictionless horizontal surface with time period $\pi/6$ s. A small mass m is placed on the 2 kg block and the coefficient of static friction between the small mass and the 2 kg block is 0.1. (Assume the period is unaffected by adding the small mass).

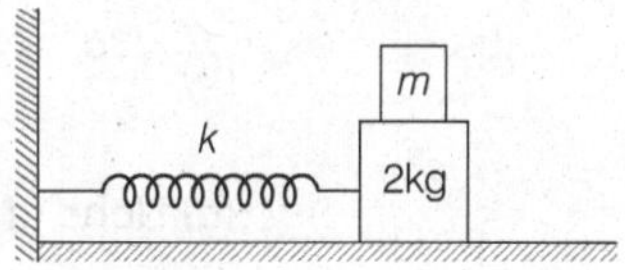

(a) The maximum amplitude of oscillation before the small mass slips is $\dfrac{1}{144}$ m.

(b) The maximum amplitude of oscillation before the small mass slips is $\dfrac{1}{72}$ m.

(c) maximum velocity of blocks assuming no slipping is $\dfrac{1}{12}$ m/s.

(d) maximum velocity of blocks assuming no slipping is $\dfrac{1}{24}$ m/s.

14. A uniform rod of mass m and length l is pivoted at top and it can perform angular SHM in vertical plane according to equation $\theta=\theta_0\sin\omega t$. At time $t=\dfrac{2\pi}{\omega}$, a point mass m (at rest) sticks to lowest end of rod.

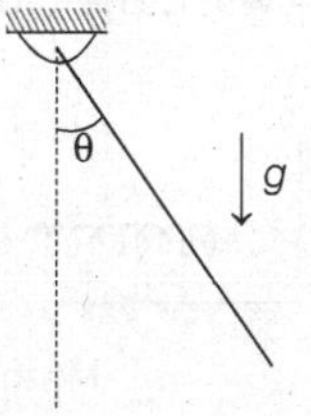

(a) New time period of rod will be $\dfrac{2}{\sqrt{3}}$ times of the time period before collision.

(b) New angular amplitude is $\dfrac{\theta_0}{\sqrt{12}}$.

(c) New angular amplitude is $\dfrac{\theta_0}{4}$.

(d) There will always be loss of kinetic energy of rod, irrespective of time at which mass sticks to rod.

15. A block of mass $M=3m$ is connected to a spring of mass m and oscillates in simple harmonic motion on a horizontal, frictionless track (figure). The force constant of the spring is k and the equilibrium length is l. Assume all portions of the spring oscillate in phase and the velocity of a segment dx is proportional to the distance x from the fixed end, that is, $v_x=(x/l)\,v$. Also, notice that the mass of a segment of the spring is $dm=(m/l)\,dx$.

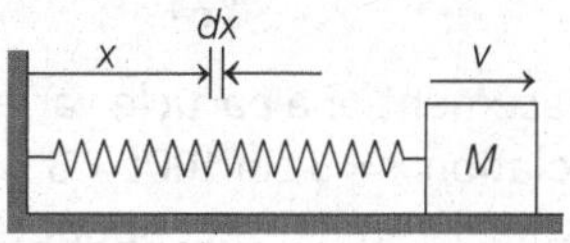

(a) The kinetic energy of the system when the block has a speed v is $\dfrac{5}{3}mv^2$.

(b) The kinetic energy of the system when the block has a speed v is $\dfrac{4}{3}mv^2$.

(c) The period of oscillation is $2\pi\sqrt{\dfrac{10m}{3k}}$.

(d) The period of oscillation is $2\pi\sqrt{\dfrac{8m}{3k}}$.

16. A particle of mass m is moving in a potential well for which the potential energy is given by $U(x)=U_0(1-\cos ax)$, where U_0 and a are constants. Then, for small oscillations,

(a) the time period of small oscillation is $T=2\pi\sqrt{\dfrac{m}{aU_0}}$.

(b) the speed of particle is maximum at $x=0$.

(c) the amplitude of oscillation is $\dfrac{\pi}{2a}$.

(d) the time period of small oscillation is $2\pi\sqrt{\dfrac{m}{a^2U_0}}$.

17. Consider a hollow cylinder of radius R rolling without slipping on an inclined plane. The mass of the cylinder is M and its moment of inertia is $I=MR^2$. The axis of the cylinder is connected to a fixed wall at the top of the inclined plane by a light spring of constant k as shown in the figure. In equilibrium, the cylinder is at some distance x_0 from the top.

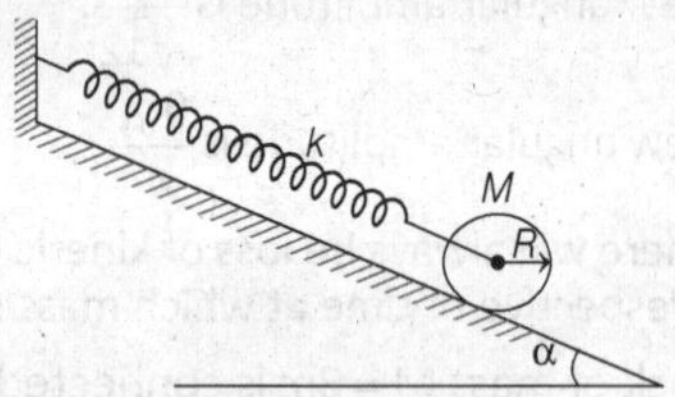

(a) For hollow cylinder, angular frequency of small oscillations is $\sqrt{\frac{k}{2M}}$.
(b) Friction force on cylinder varies simple harmonically.
(c) In case of pure rolling of cylinder, friction force at equilibrium position during oscillation is zero.
(d) Instead of rolling without slipping, the cylinder were moving on smooth surface, then angular frequency of small oscillations is $\sqrt{\frac{k}{M}}$.

18. The displacement of a particle varies according to the the relation $x = 3\sin 100t + 8\cos^2 50t$. Which of the following is/are correct about this motion?
(a) The motion of the particle is not SHM.
(b) The amplitude of the SHM of the particle is 5 units.
(c) The amplitude of the resultant SHM is $\sqrt{73}$ units.
(d) The maximum displacement of the particle from the origin is 9 units.

19. A 20 g particle is subjected to two simple harmonic motions $x_1 = 2\sin 10t$, $x_2 = 4\sin\left(10t + \frac{\pi}{3}\right)$, where x_1 and x_2 are in m and t is in s.
(a) The displacement of the particle at $t = 0$ will be $2\sqrt{3}$ m.
(b) Maximum speed of the particle will be $20\sqrt{7}$ m/s.
(c) Magnitude of maximum acceleration of the particle will be $200\sqrt{7}\ \text{m/s}^2$.
(d) Energy of the resultant motion will be 28 J.

20. The position vector of a particle that is moving in three dimensions is given by
$\mathbf{r} = (1 + 2\cos 2\omega t)\,\hat{\mathbf{i}} + (3\sin^2 \omega t)\,\hat{\mathbf{j}} + (3)\,\hat{\mathbf{k}}$
in the ground frame. All units are in SI. Choose the correct statement(s).
(a) The particle executes SHM in the ground frame about the mean position $\left(1, \frac{3}{2}, 3\right)$.
(b) The particle executes SHM in a frame moving along the Z-axis with a velocity of 3 m/s.
(c) The amplitude of the SHM of the particle is $\frac{5}{2}$ m.
(d) The direction of the SHM of the particle is given by the vector $\left(\frac{4}{5}\hat{\mathbf{i}} - \frac{3}{5}\hat{\mathbf{j}}\right)$.

Comprehension Based Questions

Comprehension 1

The block of mass m is attached to 2 springs as shown. In the equilibrium position, the springs are at their natural length. The mass oscillates along the line of springs with amplitude d. At $t = 0$, mass is at $+d/2$ from equilibrium and moving to right. The right spring is removed at that instant without changing velocity of block.

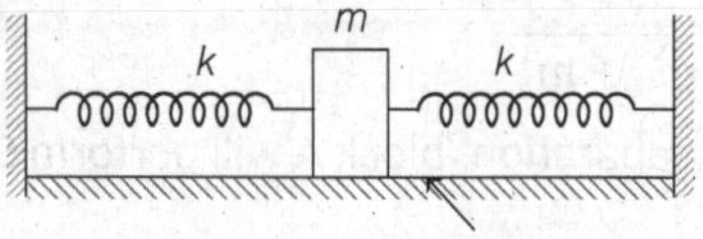

1. Find the new time period of oscillation, if original time period was T_0.
(a) $2T_0$ (b) $\frac{T_0}{2}$ (c) $\frac{T_0}{\sqrt{2}}$ (d) $\sqrt{2}T_0$

2. The new amplitude of mass is
(a) d (b) $\frac{\sqrt{3}d}{2}$
(d) $\frac{\sqrt{7}d}{2}$ (d) None of these

3. The velocity of the mass when it passes through equilibrium position is
(a) $\frac{\sqrt{19}\pi d}{T_0}$ (b) $\frac{\sqrt{2}\pi d}{T_0}$
(c) $\frac{\sqrt{14}\pi d}{T_0}$ (d) None of these

Comprehension 2

A horizontal spring block system executes SHM ($x = A\sin(\omega t + \phi)$) with amplitude $A = 10$ cm, initial phase $\phi = 0$ and angular frequency ω. The mass of block is $M = 25$ kg and there is no friction between the block and the horizontal surface. The spring constant is 2500 N/m. At $t = t_1$ s [for which $\omega t_1 = \phi_1 = 30°$], a mass $m = 75$ kg is gently put on the block. [Assume that collision between the block and the mass is perfectly inelastic and mass m remains stationary w.r.t. the block M always].

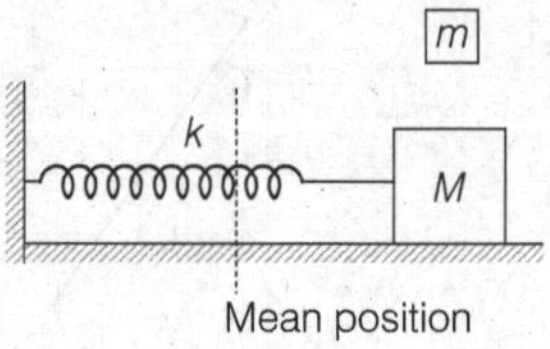

Read above passage carefully and answer the following questions.

4. The new angular frequency of the system will be
(a) 5 rad/s (b) 10 rad/s
(c) 15 rad/s (d) 20 rad/s

5. The total energy of system after collision at any moment of time is
(a) $\frac{175}{32}$ J (b) $\frac{88}{15}$ J
(c) $\frac{96}{25}$ J (d) None of these

6. The new amplitude of the system will be
(a) $\frac{\sqrt{7}}{40}$ m (b) $\frac{\sqrt{3}}{40}$ m
(c) $\frac{\sqrt{5}}{40}$ m (d) None of these

Comprehension 3

A cylinder of mass M contains water of mass m. The spring has a constant k and the cylinder executes pure rolling.

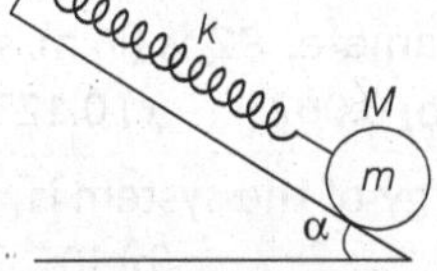

7. What is the angular frequency of the small oscillations of the system?
(a) $\sqrt{\frac{k}{M+m}}$
(b) $\sqrt{\frac{k}{2M+m}}$
(c) $\sqrt{\frac{2k}{(4M+3m)}}$
(d) $\sqrt{\frac{2k}{(2M+3m)}}$

8. What will be the angular frequency when the water in the cylinder freezes?
(a) $\sqrt{\frac{k}{M+m}}$ (b) $\sqrt{\frac{k}{2M+m}}$
(c) $\sqrt{\frac{2k}{(4M+3m)}}$ (d) $\sqrt{\frac{2k}{(2M+3m)}}$

Comprehension 4

A man having mass 50 kg is standing on a platform of mass 10 kg which oscillates up and down (doing SHM) of frequency 0.5 s^{-1} and amplitude 0.4 m. Platform has a weighing machine fitted in it (which is massless) on which person is standing. (Take $\pi^2 = 10$ and $g = 10\ m/s^2$). Assume that at $t = 0$ (platform + man) is at their highest point of oscillation.

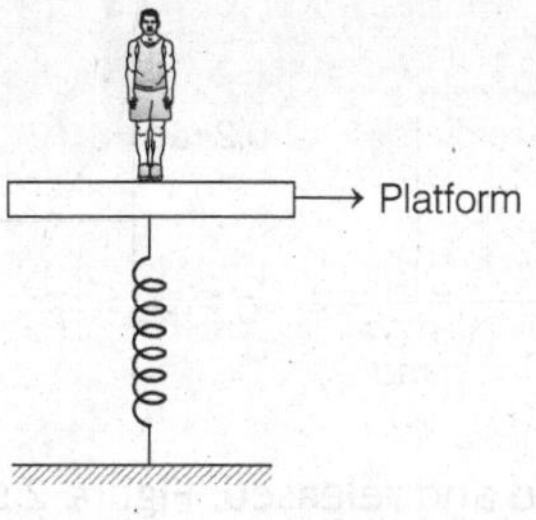

9. Maximum reading of weighing machine is
(a) 60 kg (b) 70 kg (c) 84 kg (d) 50 kg

10. Find compression in spring when weighing machine reads 55 kg
(a) 1 m (b) 1.1 m (c) 1.4 m (d) 0.1 m

11. Find minimum time after which speed of person is 0.2π m/s
(a) $\frac{1}{6}$ s (b) $\frac{1}{3}$ s (c) 1 s (d) $\frac{1}{4}$ s

Comprehension 5

A long plank P is placed on a horizontal frictionless surface and connected to two springs of spring constant k and $2k$ respectively. A cylinder of mass m is placed on the plank. The plank is displaced towards right (positive direction) and released at $t = 0$, it oscillates with amplitude A. The cylinder does not slip on the plank during the oscillation.

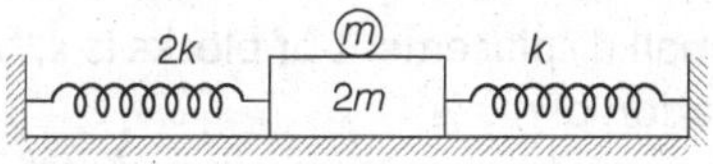

12. The maximum friction force acting on the cylinder during the oscillation is
(a) $3kA$ (b) $\frac{2kA}{3}$
(c) $\frac{3kA}{7}$ (d) $\frac{2kA}{7}$

13. The friction force acting on the cylinder as a function of time is shown as (Take the right side as positive)

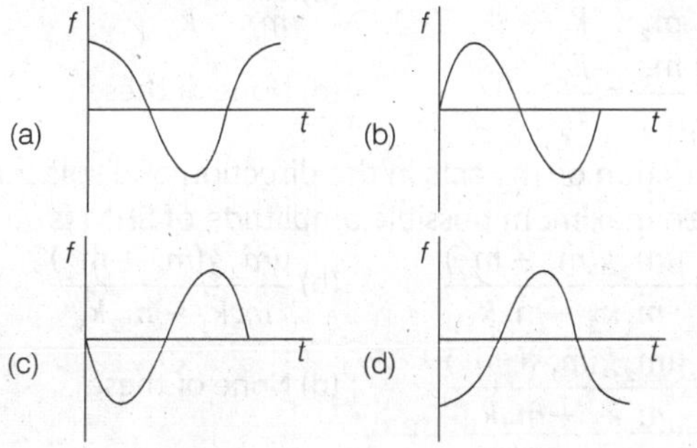

Comprehension 6

A torsional pendulum is made by attaching a disc to a wire. Figure 1 gives the magnitude of torque needed to rotate the disc about its centne *versus* rotational angle θ.

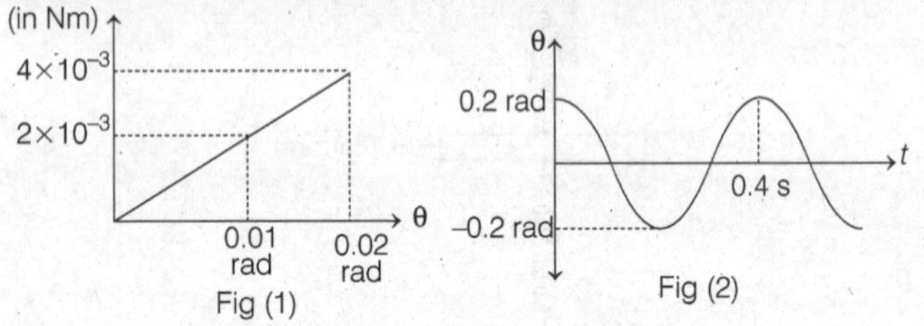

Fig (1) Fig (2)

The disc is rotated and released. Figure 2 shows the angular position (θ) with time (*t*). Take, $\pi^2 = 10$.

14. What is the moment of inertia of the disc?
(a) 4×10^{-5} kgm^2 (b) 8×10^{-4} kgm^2
(c) 8×10^{-5} k gm^2 (d) 8×10^{-6} kgm^2

15. What is the maximum angular speed of the disc?
(a) π rad/s (b) 5π rad/s (c) 2π rad/s (d) 3π rad/s

Comprehension 7

In the shown arrangement, both springs are relaxed. The coefficient of friction between m_2 and m_1 is μ. There is no friction between m_1 and surface. If the blocks are displaced slightly, they perform SHM together.

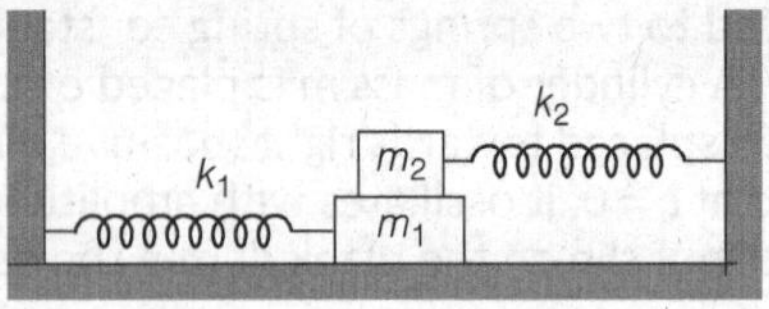

16. If the small displacement of blocks is *x*, then acceleration of m_2 is
(a) $\frac{k_2 x}{m_2}$ (b) $\frac{(k_1+k_2)x}{m_2}$
(c) $\left(\frac{k_1+k_2}{m_1+m_2}\right)x$ (d) None of these

17. The condition in which frictional force on m_2 acts in the direction of its displacement from mean position is
(a) $\frac{m_1}{m_2} > \frac{k_1}{k_2}$ (b) $\frac{m_2}{m_1} > \frac{k_1}{k_2}$
(c) $\frac{m_1}{m_2} = \frac{k_1}{k_2}$ (d) None of these

18. If friction on m_2 acts in the direction of displacement, then maximum possible amplitude of SHM is
(a) $\frac{\mu m_2 g(m_1+m_2)}{m_1k_2 - m_2k_1}$ (b) $\frac{\mu m_2 g(m_1+m_2)}{m_1k_1 - m_2k_2}$
(c) $\frac{\mu m_2 g(m_1+m_2)}{m_1k_2 + m_2k_1}$ (d) None of these

Comprehension 8

Two identical balls *A* and *B*, each of mass 0.1 kg, are attached to two identical massless springs. The spring-mass system is constrained to move inside a rigid smooth pipe bent in the form of a circle as shown in figure. The pipe is fixed in a horizontal plane. The centres of the balls can move in a circle of radius 0.06 m. Each spring has a natural length of 0.06π m and spring constant 0.1 N/m. Initially, both the balls are displaced by an angle θ = π/6 rad with respect to the diameter *PQ* of the circle as shown in fig. and released from rest.

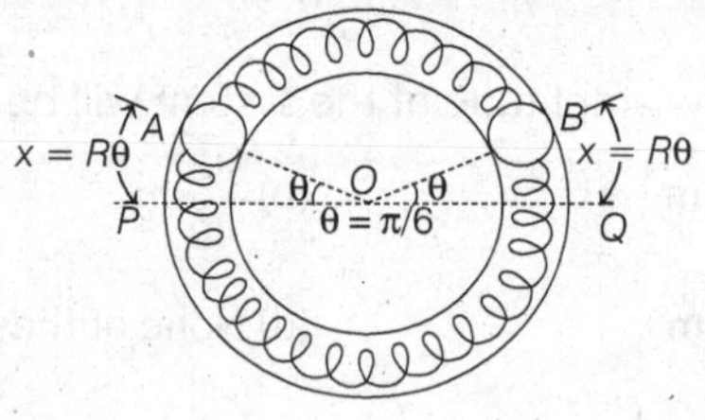

19. The frequency of oscillation of ball *B* is
(a) $\frac{1}{\pi}$ Hz (b) $\frac{1}{2\pi}$ Hz (c) $\frac{6}{\pi}$ Hz (d) $\frac{2}{\pi}$ Hz

20. The speed of ball *A* when *A* and *B* are at the two ends of the diameter *PQ* is (in m/s)
(a) 0.0314 (b) 0.0628 (c) 0.1256 (d) zero

21. The total energy of the system is
(a) 3.9×10^{-4} J (b) 10^{-4} J
(c) 6×10^{-4} J (d) 2×10^{-4} J

Comprehension 9

A small block of mass *m* is fixed at upper end of a massive vertical spring of spring constant $k = 4mg/L$ and natural length 10*L*. The lower end of spring is free and is at a height *L* from fixed horizontal floor as shown. The spring is initially unstretched and the spring-block system is released from rest in the shown position.

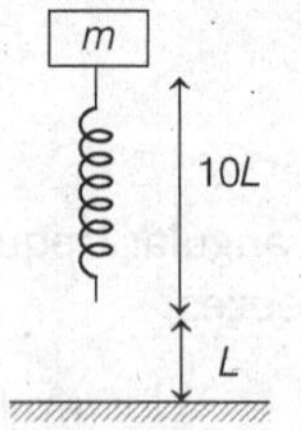

22. At the instant, the speed of block is maximum, the magnitude of force exerted by the spring on the block is
(a) $\frac{mg}{2}$ (b) *mg*
(c) zero (d) None of these

23. As the block is coming down, the maximum speed attained by the block is

(a) $\sqrt{gL}$ (b) $\sqrt{3gL}$ (c) $\frac{3}{2}\sqrt{gL}$ (d) $\sqrt{\frac{3}{2}gL}$

24. Till the block reaches its lowest position for the first time, the time duration for which the spring remains compressed is

(a) $\pi\sqrt{\frac{L}{2g}}+\sqrt{\frac{L}{4g}}\sin^{-1}\frac{1}{3}$ (b) $\frac{\pi}{4}\sqrt{\frac{L}{g}}+\sqrt{\frac{L}{4g}}\sin^{-1}\frac{1}{3}$

(c) $\pi\sqrt{\frac{L}{2g}}+\sqrt{\frac{L}{4g}}\sin^{-1}\frac{2}{3}$ (d) $\frac{\pi}{2}\sqrt{\frac{L}{2g}}+\sqrt{\frac{L}{4g}}\sin^{-1}\frac{2}{3}$

Match the Columns Questions

1. A simple harmonic oscillator consists of a block attached to a spring with $k = 100$ N/m. The block slides on a frictionless horizontal surface with equilibrium point $x = 0$. A graph of block's velocity as a function of time is shown. Correctly match the two columns ($\pi^2 = 10$)

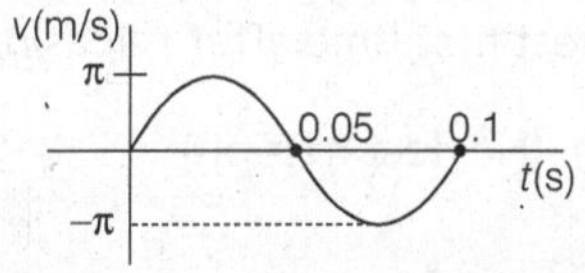

	Column I		Column II
(A)	The block's mass in kg	(P)	0.025
(B)	The block's displacement at $t = 0$ in m	(Q)	200
(C)	The block's acceleration at $t = 0.1$ s in m/s^2	(R)	−0.05
(D)	The block's maximum kinetic energy in J	(S)	0.125

2. Two particles A and B start SHM at $t = 0$. Their positions as a function of time are given by $x_A = A\sin\omega t$, $x_B = A\sin(\omega t + \pi/3)$.

	Column I		Column II
(A)	Minimum time when x is same	(P)	$\frac{5\pi}{6\omega}$
(B)	Minimum time when velocity is same	(Q)	$\frac{\pi}{3\omega}$
(C)	Minimum time after which $v_A < 0$ and $v_B < 0$	(R)	$\frac{\pi}{\omega}$
(D)	Minimum time after which $x_A < 0$ and $x_B < 0$	(S)	$\frac{\pi}{2\omega}$

3. A body executing SHM has an amplitude (A). Match the following.

	Column I		Column II
(A)	Velocity becomes half of maximum at $x =$	(P)	$\frac{-\sqrt{3}}{2}A$
(B)	$\frac{PE}{KE} = 3$, at $x =$	(Q)	$\frac{\sqrt{3}}{2}A$
(C)	$\frac{KE}{TE} = 1$, at $x =$	(R)	$\pm\frac{A}{4}$
(D)	Acceleration one-fourth of maximum at $x =$	(S)	Zero

4. A block of mass $m = 2$ kg is connected with spring ($k = 3200$ N/m) and placed on a frictionless horizontal surface as shown in figure. Initially, it is compressed by a distance 10 cm. It is then released at $t = 0$.

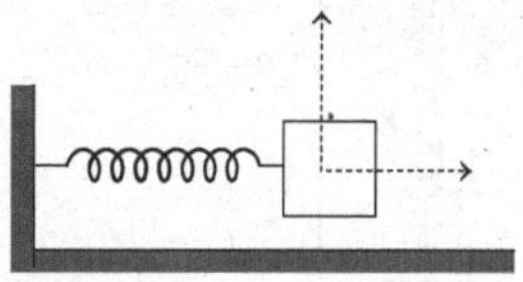

	Column I		Column II
(A)	Time for the mass to move by first 5 cm distance	(P)	$\frac{\pi}{160}$ s
(B)	Time for the mass to move by next 5 cm distance	(Q)	$\frac{\pi}{240}$ s
(C)	Time at which kinetic energy and potential energy becomes equal for the first time	(R)	$\frac{\pi}{120}$ s
(D)	Time at which kinetic energy become one-fourth of its maximum value	(S)	$\frac{\pi}{40}$ s

5. Column I describes various spring block arrangements. Column II gives values of different parameters of SHM and symbols have their usual meaning.

	Column I		Column II
(A)	Block is attached to spring of spring constant k kept at its natural length. A force of $2mg$ is applied to the block towards left. 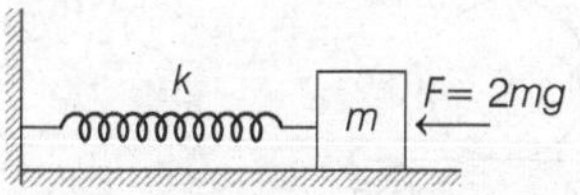	(P)	$\omega=\sqrt{\frac{k}{m}}$

(B) Block is attached to a vertical spring of spring constant k and the system is in equilibrium. A force of $2mg$ is applied on the block in vertically downward direction.

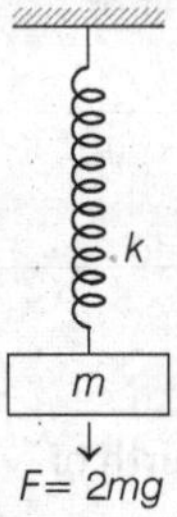

(Q) $A = \frac{2mg}{k}$

(C) Block is attached to a vertical spring of spring constant k and the system is in equilibrium. The lift is accelerated upward with acceleration $2g$.

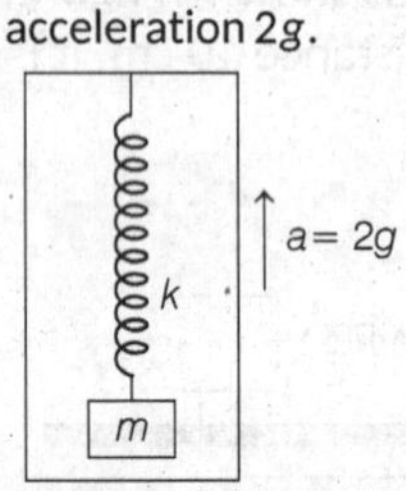

(R) Maximum energy stored in spring is $\frac{2m^2g^2}{k}$

(D) Block is attached to spring of spring constant k which is at its natural length and the surface of cart is smooth. Now the cart is accelerated with an acceleration $2g$ towards right.

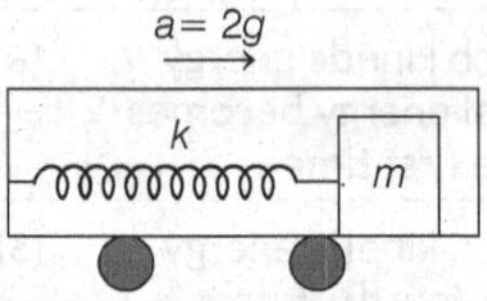

(S) Separation between relaxed length and equilibrium position is $\frac{2mg}{k}$.

(T) Minimum energy in spring is zero.

6. In Column I, the systems are performing SHM and in Column II, the time period of SHM is shown, then match Column I with Column II.

Column I	Column II
(A) 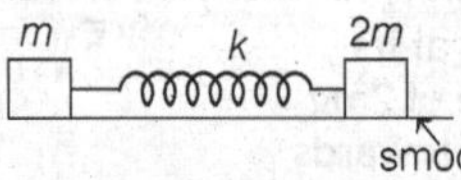	(P) $\left[2\pi\sqrt{\frac{11m}{10k}}\right]$
(B) 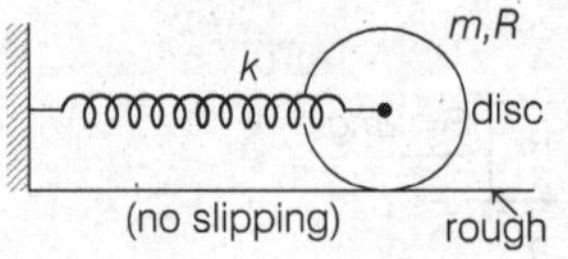	(Q) $2\pi\sqrt{\frac{m}{4k}}$
(C) 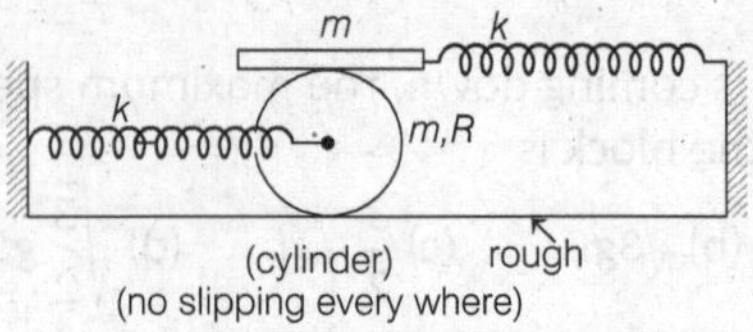	(R) $2\pi\sqrt{\frac{3m}{2k}}$
(D) 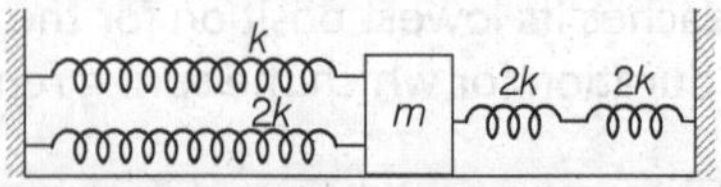	(S) $2\pi\sqrt{\frac{2m}{3k}}$

Numerical Value Questions

1. Two bodies with a mass of 1 kg each hang on a spring with a force constant of 250 N/m attached to each other using a thread with a length of 10 cm, as shown in the figure. We burn the thread. What is the distance (in cm) between the two bodies when the top body first arrives at its highest position? ($\pi^2 = 10$)

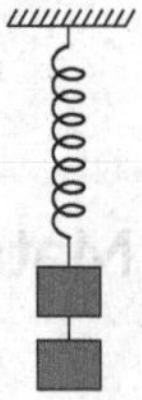

2. In the figure shown, the spring is relaxed. The spring is compressed by $2A$ and released. Mass m collides with the wall and loses two-third of its kinetic energy and returns. If the time after which the mass m comes to rest first time after releasing is $\frac{n\pi}{12}\sqrt{\frac{m}{k}}$, then find n. (Neglect friction)

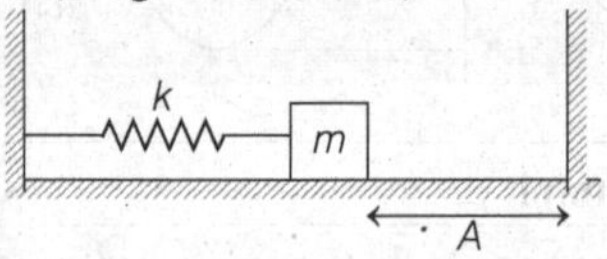

3. On a corner on a smooth horizontal surface, we kept two masses m_1 and m_2 attached to a spring as shown. The spring has a spring constant of 150 N/m. Now m_2 is suddenly given a velocity to the left. It is seen that spring first comes to natural length at $\frac{\pi}{5\sqrt{2}}$ s. It next comes to natural length after $\frac{\pi}{10\sqrt{2}}$ s. What is mass m_1 (in kg)?

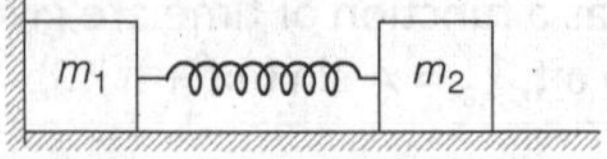

4. A small block of mass $m = 0.5$ kg is attached to two springs each of force constant $k = 10$ N/m as shown in figure. The block is executing SHM with amplitude $A = 50$ cm. When the block is at equilibrium position, one of the spring breaks without changing momentum of block. What is new amplitude (in cm) of oscillation?

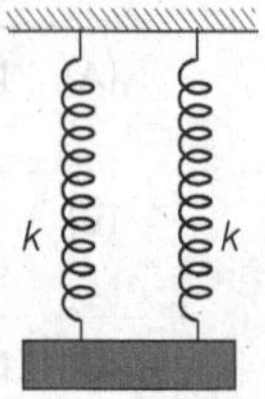

5. A sphere of mass M and radius R is on a smooth fixed inclined plane in equilibrium as shown in the figure. If now the sphere is displaced through a small distance along the plane, what will be the angular frequency (in rad/s) of the resulting SHM? (Given, $k = 4M/3$)

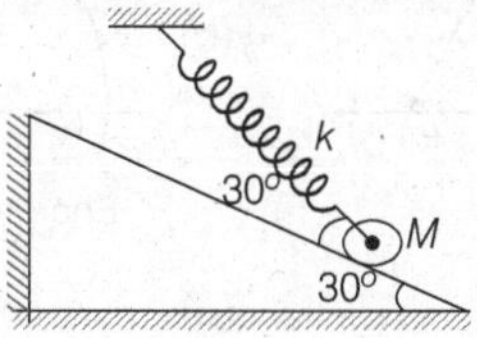

6. Figure shows a small block of mass m attached to a spring of force constant k and an identical spring hangs from ceiling. Initially, lower spring is in compressed state with compression equal to $3mg/k$ from natural length of spring. When block is released, it strikes upper spring and sticks to it. What is the amplitude of oscillation (in cm) after sticking?

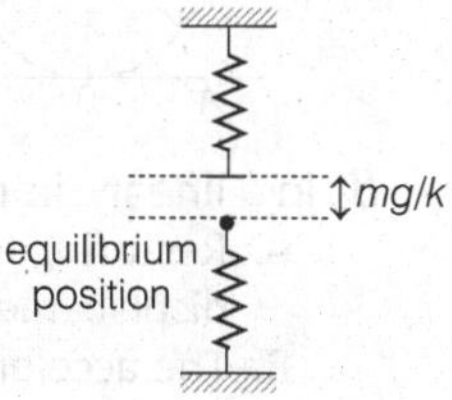

Given, $mg = 10$ N, $k = 100\sqrt{7}$ N/m.

7. In the arrangement shown in figure pulleys are light, springs are ideal and $k_1 = 25\pi^2$ N/m, $k_2 = 2k_1$, $k_3 = 3k_1$ and $k_4 = 4k_1$ are the force constants of the springs. Calculate the period (in sec) of small vertical oscillations of block of mass $m = 3$ kg.

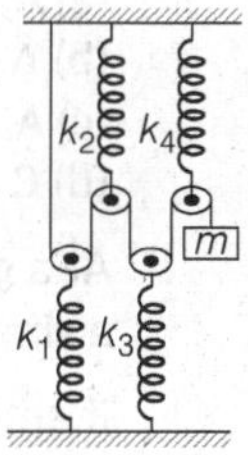

8. In the figure shown, a plate of mass 60 g is at rest and in equilibrium. A particle of mass $m = 30$ g is released from height $4.5\ mg/k$ from the plate. The particle sticks to the plate. Neglecting the duration of collision, find the time from the collision of the particle and plate to the moment when the spring has maximum compression. Spring has force constant 1 N/m. Calculate the value of time in the form π/n and find the value of n.

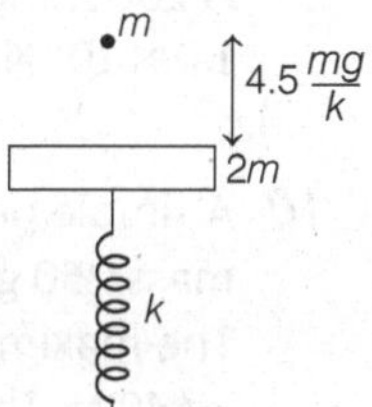

9. A cylindrical block of height 1 m is in equilibrium in a beaker as shown. Cross-sectional area of cylindrical block is one-fourth of cross-sectional area of beaker. Density of cylindrical block is one-third of liquid. Determine the time period of small oscillation (in seconds). (Given, $g = \pi^2$ m/s^2)

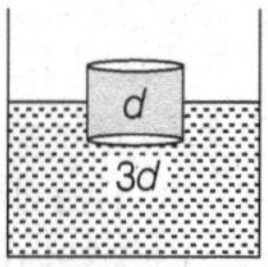

10. Two uniform ropes having linear mass densities m and $4m$ are joined to form a closed loop. The loop is hanging over a fixed frictionless small pulley with the lighter rope above as shown in the figure (in the figure equilibrium position is shown). Now, if point A (joint) is slightly displaced in downward direction and released, it is found that the loop performs SHM with the period of oscillation equal to N. Find the value of N. (Take $l = \dfrac{150}{4\pi^2}$, $g = 10$ ms^{-2})

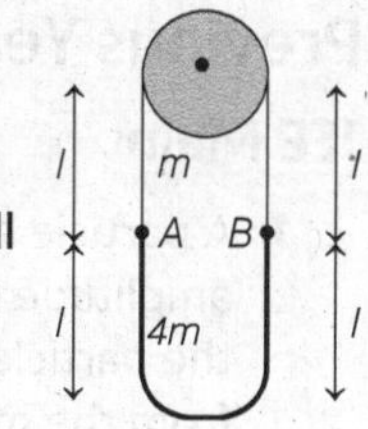

11. A uniform disc of mass m and radius $R = \dfrac{80}{23\pi^2}$ m is pivoted smoothly at P. If a uniform ring of mass m and radius R is welded at the lowest point of the disc, find the period (in seconds) of SHM of the system (disc + ring).

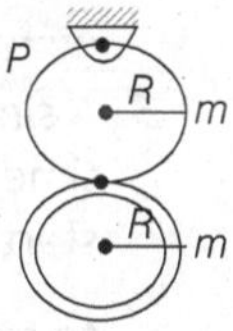

12. A rod of mass m and length l hinged at one end is connected by two springs of spring constants k_1 and k_2, so that it is horizontal at equilibrium. What is the angular frequency of the system? (in rad/s)

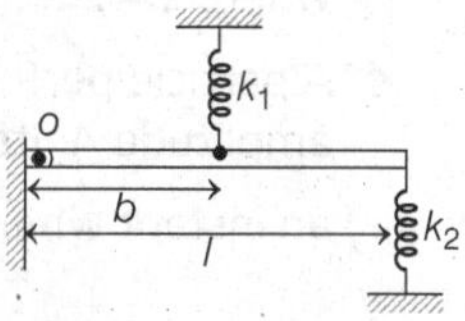

(Take, $l = 1$ m, $b = 0.25$ m, $k_1 = 16$ N/m, $k_2 = 63$ N/m, $m = 3$ kg)

13. A pulley in the form of a circular disc of mass m and radius r has the groove cut all along its perimeter. A string whose one end is attached to the ceiling passes over this disc pulley and its other end is attached to a spring of spring constant k. The other end of the spring is attached to ceiling as shown in the figure. If the time period of vertical oscillations of the centre of mass assuming that the string does not slip over the pulley is $\pi\sqrt{\dfrac{3m}{nk}}$, then find the value of n.

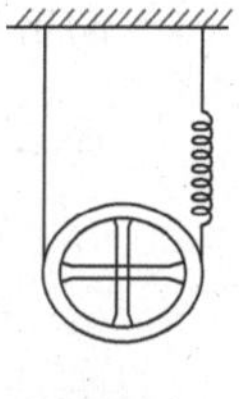

14. A solid cylinder is kept over a rough plank which is oscillating along X-axis according to equation $x = A\cos(10)t$, where x is in m and t is in s. If coefficient of friction between cylinder and plank is 0.3, then find maximum amplitude of plank (in cm) possible, so that cylinder never slips on plank.

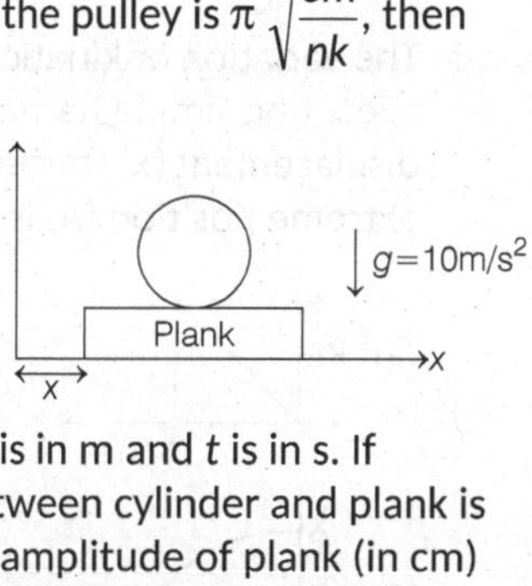

Previous Year's Questions

JEE Main

1 A particle executes simple harmonic motion with an amplitude of 4 cm. At the mean position, velocity of the particle is 10 cm/s. The distance of the particle from the mean position, when its speed becomes 5 cm/s is $\sqrt{\alpha}$ cm, where $\alpha =$ .... **[2024, 27 Jan Shift-I]**

2 When the displacement of a simple harmonic oscillator is one third of its amplitude, the ratio of total energy to the kinetic energy is $\frac{x}{8}$, where $x =$ .... **[2024, 29 Jan Shift-I]**

3 A simple harmonic oscillator has an amplitude A and time period 6π second. Assuming the oscillation starts from its mean position, the time required by it to travel from $x = A$ to $x = \frac{\sqrt{3}}{2}A$ will be $\frac{\pi}{x}$ s, where $x =$ .... **[2024, 29 Jan Shift-II]**

4 A particle performs simple harmonic motion with amplitude A. Its speed is increased to three times at an instant when its displacement is $\frac{2A}{3}$. The new amplitude of motion is $\frac{nA}{3}$. The value of n is .... **[2024, 31 Jan Shift-I]**

5 The time period of simple harmonic motion of mass M in the given figure is $\pi\sqrt{\frac{\alpha M}{5k}}$, where the value of α is .... **[2024, 31 Jan Shift-II]**

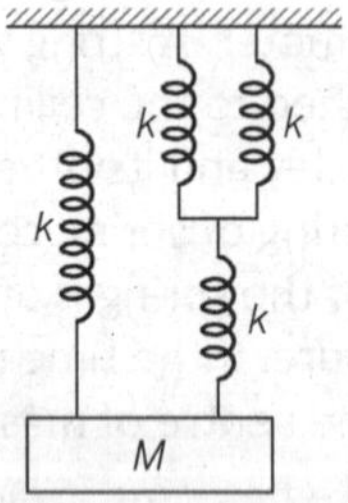

6 The variation of kinetic energy (KE) of a particle executing simple harmonic motion with the displacement (x) starting from mean position to extreme position (A) is given by **[2023, 11 April Shift-I]**

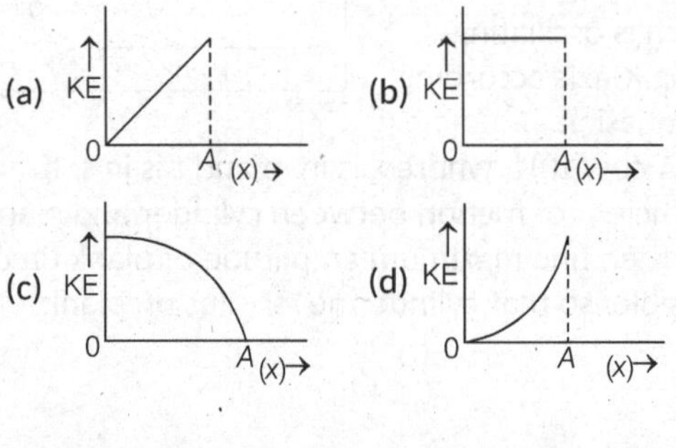

7 Which graph represents the difference between total energy and potential energy of a particle executing SHM versus it's distance from mean position? **[2023, 13 April Shift-I]**

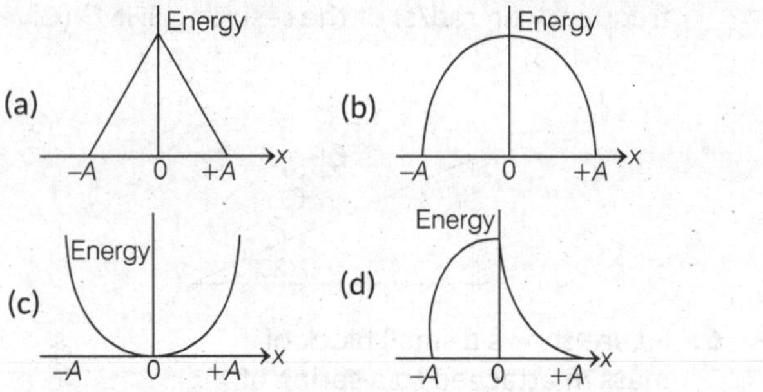

8 In a linear Simple Harmonic Motion (SHM)

A. Restoring force is directly proportional to the displacement.
B. The acceleration and displacement are opposite in direction.
C. The velocity is maximum at mean position.
D. The acceleration is minimum at extreme points.

Choose the correct answer from the options given below. **[2023, 15 April Shift-I]**

(a) A, B and C only
(b) A, B and D only
(c) A, C and D only
(d) C and D only

9 At a given point of time the value of displacement of a simple harmonic oscillator given as $y = \cos(30°)$. If amplitude is 40 cm and kinetic energy at that time is 200 J, the value of force constant is $1.0 \times 10^{x}\ \text{Nm}^{-1}$. The value of x is .... **[2023, 13 April Shift-I]**

10 A simple pendulum with length 100 cm and bob of mass 250 g is executing S.H.M. of amplitude 10 cm. The maximum tension in the string is found to be $x/40$ N. The value of x is .... **[2023, 6 April Shift-II]**

11 The general displacement of a simple harmonic oscillator is $x = A \sin \omega t$. Let T be its time period. The slope of its potential energy (U)-time (t) curve will be maximum when $t = T/\beta$. The value of β is .... **[2023, 30 Jan Shift-I]**

12 The amplitude of a particle executing SHM is 3 cm. The displacement at which its kinetic energy will be 25% more than the potential energy is .... cm. **[2023, 1 Feb Shift-I]**

13 Choose the correct length (L) *versus* square of time period (T^2) graph for a simple pendulum executing simple harmonic motion. **[2023, 1 Feb Shift-II]**

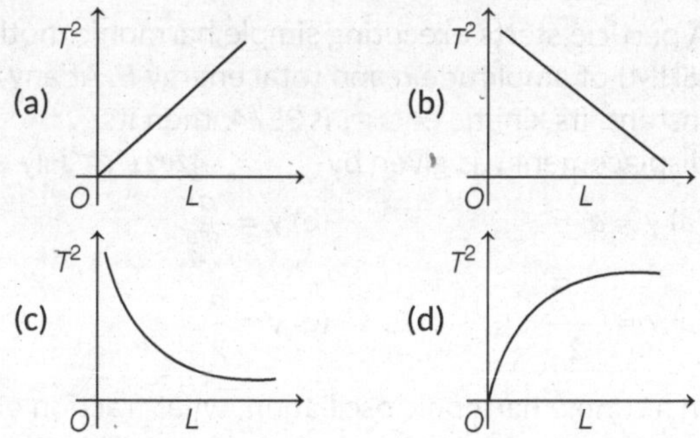

14 Assume that the earth is a solid sphere of uniform density and a tunnel is dug along its diameter throughout the earth. It is found that when a particle is released in this tunnel. It executes a simple harmonic motion. The mass of the particle is 100 g. The time period of the motion of the particle will be (approximately)
(Take, $g = 10\ ms^{-2}$, radius of earth = 6400 km) **[2023, 25 Jan Shift-I]**

(a) 24 hours
(b) 1 hour 40 minutes
(c) 1 hour 24 minutes
(d) 12 hours

15 T is the time period of simple pendulum on the earth's surface. Its time period becomes xT when taken to a height R (equal to earth's radius) above the earth's surface. Then, the value of x will be **[2023, 25 Jan Shift-I]**

(a) 2 (b) $\frac{1}{2}$
(c) 4 (d) $\frac{1}{4}$

16 Given below are two statements: One is labelled as Assertion A and the other is labelled as Reason R.

Assertion (A) A pendulum clock when taken to Mount Everest becomes fast.

Reason (R) The value of g (acceleration due to gravity) is less at Mount Everest than its value on the surface of earth.

In the light of the above statements, choose the most appropriate answer from the options given below. **[2023, 24 Jan Shift-II]**

(a) Both A and R are correct and R is the correct explanation of A.
(b) Both A and R are correct but R is not the correct explanation of A.
(c) A is not correct but R is correct.
(d) A is correct but R is not correct.

17 For a simple harmonic motion in a mass spring system shown, the surface is frictionless. When the mass of the block is 1 kg, the angular frequency is ω_1. When the mass block is 2 kg the angular frequency is ω_2. The ratio ω_2/ω_1 is **[2023, 30 Jan Shift-II]**

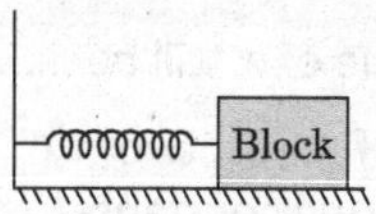

(a) $\frac{1}{\sqrt{2}}$ (b) $\frac{1}{2}$
(c) 2 (d) $\sqrt{2}$

18 The equation of a particle executing simple harmonic motion is given by $x = \sin\pi\left(t + \frac{1}{3}\right)$ m. At $t = 1$ s the speed of particle will be (Given: $\pi = 3.14$) **[2022, 27 June Shift-II]**

(a) $0\ cm\ s^{-1}$ (b) $157\ cm\ s^{-1}$
(c) $272\ cm\ s^{-1}$ (d) $314\ cm\ s^{-1}$

19 A particle executes simple harmonic motion. Its amplitude is 8 cm and time period is 6s. The time it will take to travel from its position of maximum displacement to the point corresponding to half of its amplitude, is ...... s. **[2022, 27 June Shift-II]**

20 Two waves executing simple harmonic motions travelling in the same direction with same amplitude and frequency are superimposed. The resultant amplitude is equal to the $\sqrt{3}$ times of amplitude of individual motions.

The phase difference between the two motions is ...... (degree). **[2022, 25 July Shift-II]**

21 The time period of oscillation of a simple pendulum of length L suspended from the roof of a vehicle, which moves without friction down an inclined plane of inclination α, is given by **[2022, 29 July Shift-I]**

(a) $2\pi\sqrt{L/(g\cos\alpha)}$
(b) $2\pi\sqrt{L/(g\sin\alpha)}$
(c) $2\pi\sqrt{L/g}$
(d) $2\pi\sqrt{L/(g\tan\alpha)}$

22 Two massless springs with spring constants 2 k and 9 k, carry 50 g and 100 g masses at their free ends. These two masses oscillate vertically such that their maximum velocities are equal. Then, the ratio of their respective amplitudes will be **[2022, 24 June Shift-II]**

(a) 1 : 2 (b) 3 : 2
(c) 3 : 1 (d) 2 : 3

23 A mass 0.9 kg, attached a horizontal spring, executes SHM with an amplitude A_1. When this mass passes through its mean position, then a smaller mass of 124 g is placed over it and both masses move together with amplitude A_2. If the ratio $\frac{A_1}{A_2}$ is $\frac{\alpha}{\alpha - 1}$, then the value of α will be ....**[2022, 27 July Shift-I]**

24 As per given figures, two springs of spring constants k and $2k$ are connected to mass m. If the period of oscillation in Fig. (a) is 3 s, then the period of oscillation in Fig. (b) will be $\sqrt{x}$ s. The value of x is .... **[2022, 26 July Shift-II]**

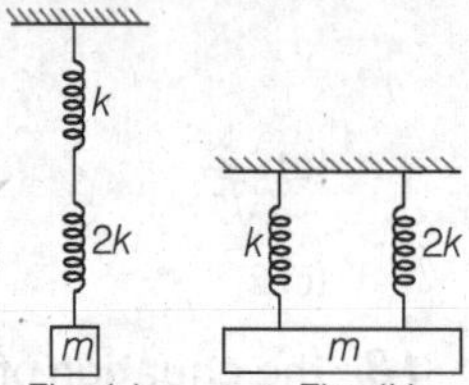

Fig. (a) Fig. (b)

25 For a body executing SHM

A. potential energy is always equal to its kinetic energy.

B. average potential and kinetic energy over any given time interval are always equal.

C. sum of the kinetic and potential energy at any point of time is constant.

D. average kinetic energy in one time period is equal to average potential energy in one time period.

Choose the most appropriate option from the options given below. **[2021, 31 Aug Shift-II]**

(a) (C) and (D)
(b) Only (C)
(c) (B) and (C)
(d) Only (B)

26 The variation of displacement with time of a particle executing free simple harmonic motion is shown in the figure.

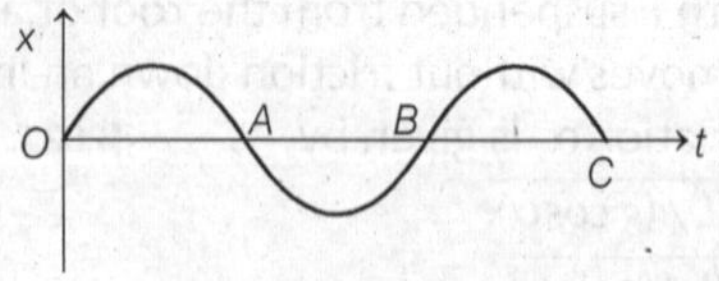

The potential energy $U(x)$ *versus* time (t) plot of the particle is correctly shown in figure **[2021, 27 Aug Shift-I]**

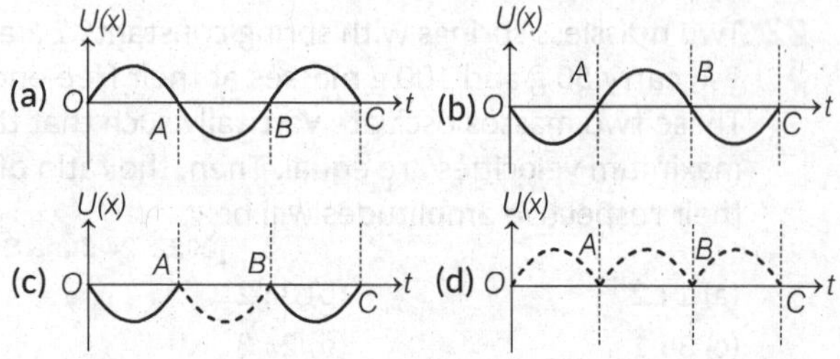

27 A particle starts executing simple harmonic motion (SHM) of amplitude a and total energy E. At any instant, its kinetic energy is $3E/4$, then its displacement y is given by **[2021, 27 July Shift-I]**

(a) $y = a$ (b) $y = \frac{a}{\sqrt{2}}$

(c) $y = \frac{a\sqrt{3}}{2}$ (d) $y = \frac{a}{2}$

28 In a simple harmonic oscillation, what fraction of total mechanical energy is in the form of kinetic energy, when the particle is midway between mean and extreme position. **[2021, 25 July Shift-II]**

(a) $\frac{1}{2}$ (b) $\frac{3}{4}$

(c) $\frac{1}{3}$ (d) $\frac{1}{4}$

29 A particle is making simple harmonic motion along the X-axis. If at a distances x_1 and x_2 from the mean position, the velocities of the particle are v_1 and v_2 respectively, then the time period of its oscillation is given as **[2021, 20 July Shift-II]**

(a) $T = 2\pi\sqrt{\frac{x_2^2 + x_1^2}{v_1^2 - v_2^2}}$ (b) $T = 2\pi\sqrt{\frac{x_2^2 + x_1^2}{v_1^2 + v_2^2}}$

(c) $T = 2\pi\sqrt{\frac{x_2^2 - x_1^2}{v_1^2 + v_2^2}}$ (d) $T = 2\pi\sqrt{\frac{x_2^2 - x_1^2}{v_1^2 - v_2^2}}$

30 When a particle executes SHM, the nature of graphical representation of velocity as a function of displacement is **[2021, 24 Feb Shift-II]**

(a) circular (b) elliptical
(c) parabolic (d) straight line

31 A mass of 5 kg is connected to a spring. The potential energy curve of the simple harmonic motion executed by the system is shown in the figure. A simple pendulum of length 4 m has the same period of oscillation as the spring system. What is the value of acceleration due to gravity on the planet where these experiments are performed? **[2021, 1 Sep Shift-II]**

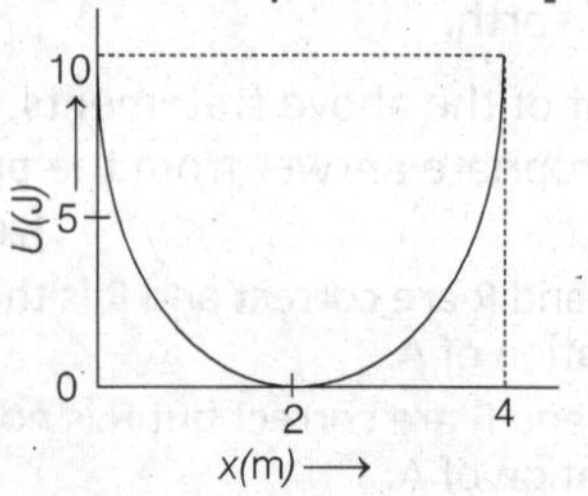

(a) $10\ m/s^2$ (b) $5\ m/s^2$
(c) $4\ m/s^2$ (d) $9.8\ m/s^2$

32 A bob of mass m suspended by a thread of length l undergoes simple harmonic oscillations with time period T. If the bob is immersed in a liquid that has density 1/4 times that of the bob and the length of the thread is increased by 1/3rd of the original length, then the time period of the simple harmonic oscillations will be **[2021, 31 Aug Shift-II]**

(a) T (b) $\frac{3}{2}T$ (c) $\frac{3}{4}T$ (d) $\frac{4}{3}T$

33 T_0 is the time period of a simple pendulum at a place. If the length of the pendulum is reduced to 1/16 times of its initial value, then the modified time period is **[2021, 22 July Shift-II]**

(a) T_0 (b) $8\pi T_0$ (c) $4T_0$ (d) $1/4\,T_0$

34 A particle of mass 1 kg is hanging from a spring of force constant 100 Nm^{-1}. The mass is pulled slightly downward and released, so that it executes free simple harmonic motion with time period T. The time when the kinetic energy and potential energy of the system will become equal, is T/x. The value of x is. **[2021, 31 Aug Shift-I]**

35 In the reported figure, two bodies A and B of masses 200 g and 800 g are attached with the system of springs. Springs are kept in a stretched position with some extension when the system is released.
The horizontal surface is assumed to be frictionless. The angular frequency will be .... rad/s when $k = 20$ N/m. **[2021, 25 July Shift-I]**

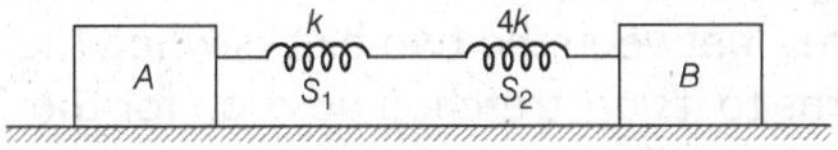

36 Consider two identical springs each of spring constant k and negligible mass compared to the mass M as shown. Fig.1 shows one of them and Fig.2 shows their series combination. The ratios of time period of oscillation of the two SHM is $T_b/T_a = \sqrt{x}$, where value of x is .... **[2021, 17 March Shift-I]**
(Round off to the nearest integer)

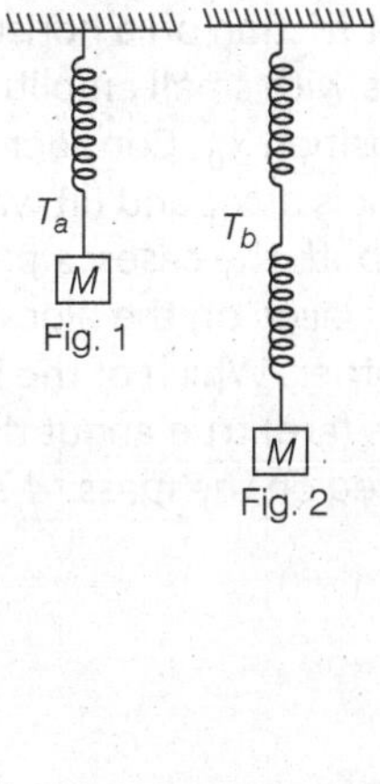

Fig. 1 Fig. 2

37 Time period of a simple pendulum is T. The time taken to complete 5/8 oscillations starting from mean position is $\alpha/\beta\,T$. The value of α is .... **[2021, 26 Feb Shift-II]**

38 Amplitude of a mass-spring system which is executing simple harmonic motion decreases with time. If mass = 500 g. Decay constant = 20 g/s then how much time is required for the amplitude of the system to drop to half of its initial value?
($\ln 2 = 0.693$) **[2021, 6 March Shift-II]**

(a) 17.32 s (b) 15.01 s (c) 34.65 s (d) 0.034 s

39 The displacement-time graph of a particle executing SHM is given in figure (sketch is schematic and not to scale) **[2020, 2 Sep Shift-II]**

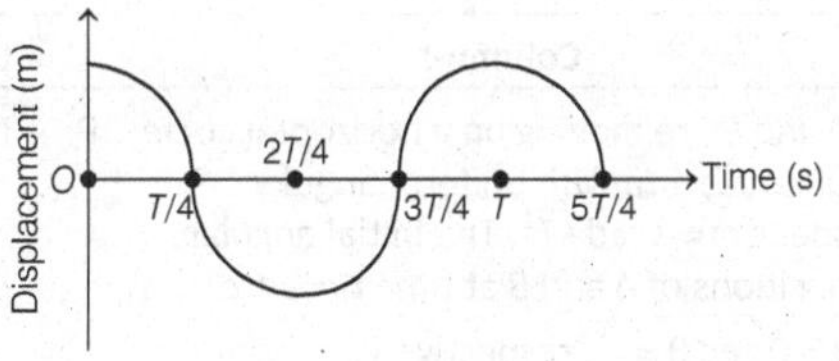

Which of the following statement(s) is/are true for this motion?

A. The force is zero at $t = \frac{3T}{4}$.
B. The acceleration is maximum at $t = T$.
C. The speed is maximum at $t = \frac{T}{4}$.
D. The potential energy is equal to kinetic energy of the oscillation at $t = \frac{T}{2}$.

(a) A, B and D (b) B, C and D
(c) A, B and C (d) A and D

JEE Advanced

1. Two point-like objects of masses 20 g and 30 g are fixed at the two ends of a rigid massless rod of length 10 cm. This sytem is suspended vertically from a rigid ceiling using a thin wire attached to its centre of mass, as shown in the figure. The resulting torsional pendulum undergoes small oscillations. The torsional constant of the wire is 1.2×10^{-8} N-m rad^{-1}. The angular frequency of the oscillations in $n \times 10^{-1}$ rad s^{-1}. The value of n is .... **(2023 Adv.)**

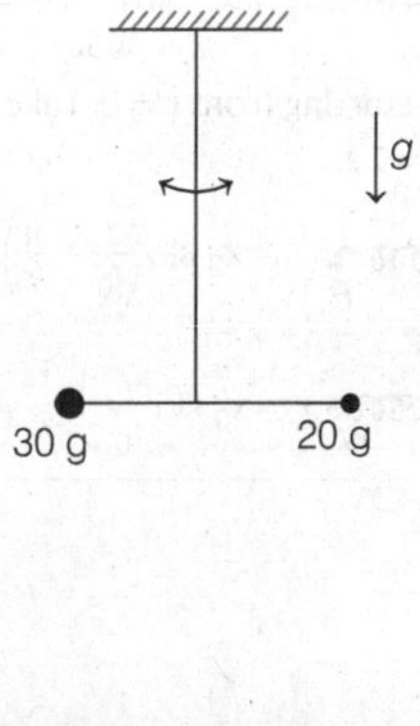

2. On a frictionless horizontal plane, a bob of mass $m = 0.1$ kg is attached to a spring with natural length $l_0 = 0.1$ m. The spring constant is $k_1 = 0.009$ N m^{-1} when the length of the spring $l > l_0$ and is $k_2 = 0.016$ N m^{-1} when $l < l_0$. Initially, the bob is released from $l = 0.15$ m. Assume that Hooke's law remains valid throughout the motion. If the time period of the full oscillation is $T = (n\pi)$ s, then the integer closest to n is .... **(2022 Adv.)**

3. Column-I describes four systems, each with two particles A and B in relative motion as shown in figures. Column-II gives possible magnitudes of their relative velocities (in ms^{-1}) at time $t = \frac{\pi}{3}$ s. **(2022 Adv.)**

	Column-I	Column-II
I.	A and B are moving on a horizontal circle of radius 1 m with uniform angular speed $\omega = 1$ rad s^{-1}. The initial angular positions of A and B at time $t = 0$ are $\theta = 0$ and $\theta = \frac{\pi}{2}$, respectively. 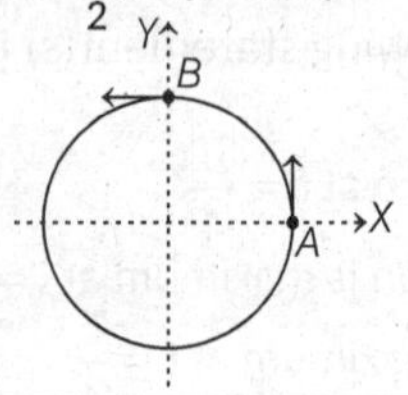	P. $\frac{\sqrt{3}+1}{2}$
II.	Projectiles A and B are fired (in the same vertical plane) at $t = 0$ and $t = 0.1$ s respectively, with the same speed $v = \frac{5\pi}{\sqrt{2}}$ ms^{-1} and at 45° from the horizontal plane. The initial separation between A and B is large enough, so that they do not collide. ($g = 10$ ms^{-2}) 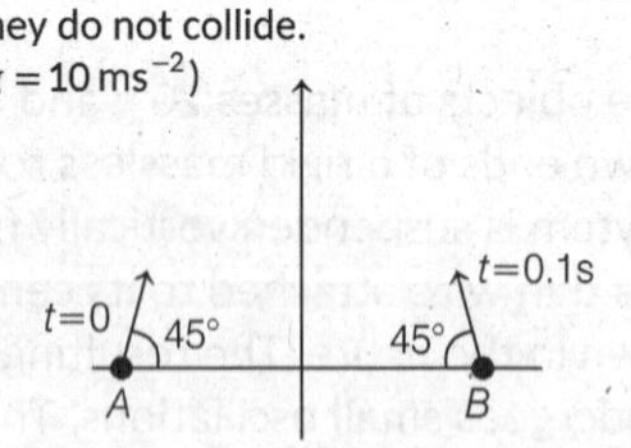	Q. $\frac{(\sqrt{3}-1)}{\sqrt{2}}$
III.	Two harmonic oscillators A and B moving in the x-direction according to $x_A = x_0 \sin\frac{t}{t_0}$ and $x_B = x_0 \sin\left(\frac{t}{t_0} + \frac{\pi}{2}\right)$ respectively, starting from $t = 0$. Take $x_0 = 1$ m, $t_0 = 1$ s. 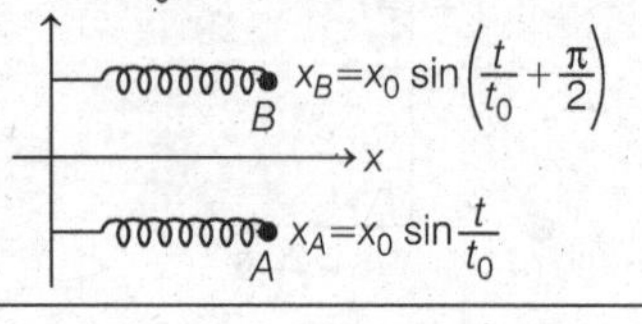	R. $\sqrt{10}$
IV.	Particle A is rotating in a horizontal circular path of radius 1 m on the XY-plane, with constant angular speed $\omega = 1$ rad s^{-1}. Particle B is moving up at a constant speed 3 ms^{-1} in the vertical direction as shown in the figure. (Ignore gravity.) 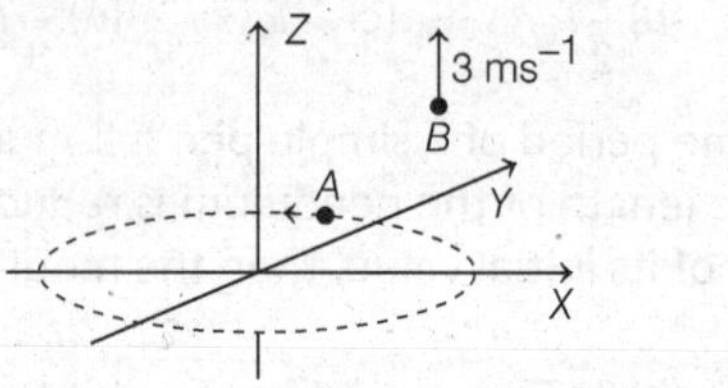	S. $\sqrt{2}$
		T. $\sqrt{25\pi^2 + 1}$

Which one of the following options is correct?

	I	II	III	IV
(a)	R	T	P	S
(b)	S	P	Q	R
(c)	S	T	P	R
(d)	T	P	R	S

4. A spring block system is resting on a frictionless floor as shown in the figure. The spring constant is 2.0 Nm^{-1} and the mass of the block is 2.0 kg. Ignore the mass of the spring. Initially, the spring is in an unstretched condition. Another block of mass 1.0 kg moving with a speed of 2.0 ms^{-1} collides elastically with the first block. The collision is such that the 2.0 kg block does not hit the wall. The distance, in metres, between the two blocks when the spring returns to its unstretched position for the first time after the collision is .... **(2018 Adv.)**

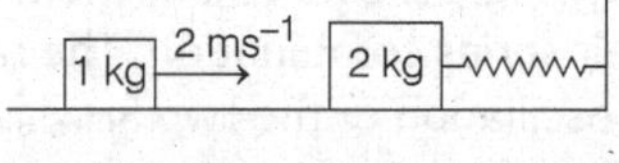

5. A block with mass M is connected by a massless spring with stiffness constant k to a rigid wall and moves without friction on a horizontal surface. The block oscillates with small amplitude A about an equilibrium position x_0. Consider two cases : (i) when the block is at x_0 and (ii) when the block is at $x = x_0 + A$. In both the cases, a particle with mass m ($< M$) is softly placed on the block after which they stick to each other. Which of the following statement(s) is (are) true about the motion after the mass m is placed on the mass M ? **(2016 Adv.)**

(a) The amplitude of oscillation in the first case changes by a factor of $\sqrt{\frac{M}{m+M}}$, whereas in the second case it remains unchanged

(b) The final time period of oscillation in both the cases is same

(c) The total energy decreases in both the cases

(d) The instantaneous speed at x_0 of the combined masses decreases in both the cases

6. Two independent harmonic oscillators of equal masses are oscillating about the origin with angular frequencies ω_1 and ω_2 and have total energies E_1 and E_2, respectively. The variations of their momenta p with positions x are shown in the figures. If $\frac{a}{b} = n^2$ and $\frac{a}{R} = n$, then the correct equations is/are **(2015 Adv.)**

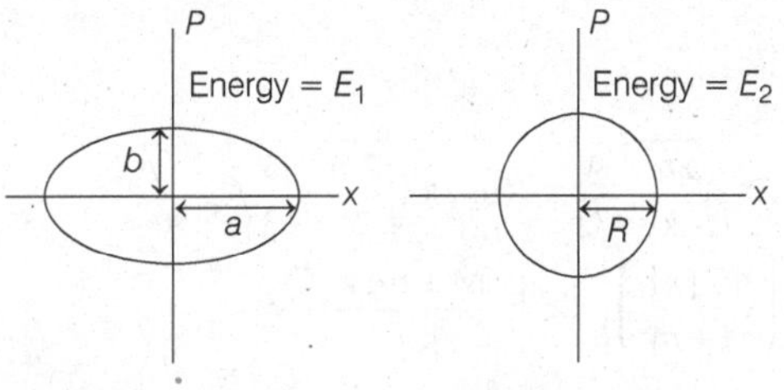

(a) $E_1\omega_1 = E_2\omega_2$ (b) $\frac{\omega_2}{\omega_1} = n^2$

(c) $\omega_1\omega_2 = n^2$ (d) $\frac{E_1}{\omega_1} = \frac{E_2}{\omega_2}$

7. A particle of mass m is attached to one end of a massless spring of force constant k, lying on a frictionless horizontal plane. The other end of the spring is fixed. The particle starts moving horizontally from its equilibrium position at time $t = 0$ with an initial velocity u_0. When the speed of the particle is $0.5\,u_0$, it collides elastically with a rigid wall. After this collision **(2013 Adv.)**

(a) the speed of the particle when it returns to its equilibrium position is u_0

(b) the time at which the particle passes through the equilibrium position for the first time is $t = \pi\sqrt{\frac{m}{k}}$

(c) the time at which the maximum compression of the spring occurs is $t = \frac{4\pi}{3}\sqrt{\frac{m}{k}}$

(d) the time at which the particle passes through the equilibrium position for the second time is $t = \frac{5\pi}{3}\sqrt{\frac{m}{k}}$

8. A small block is connected to one end of a massless spring of unstretched length 4.9 m. The other end of the spring (see the figure) is fixed. The system lies on a horizontal frictionless surface. The block is stretched by 0.2 m and released from rest at $t = 0$. It then executes simple harmonic motion with angular frequency $\omega = \frac{\pi}{3}$ rad/s. Simultaneously at $t = 0$, a small pebble is projected with speed v from point P at an angle of 45° as shown in the figure.

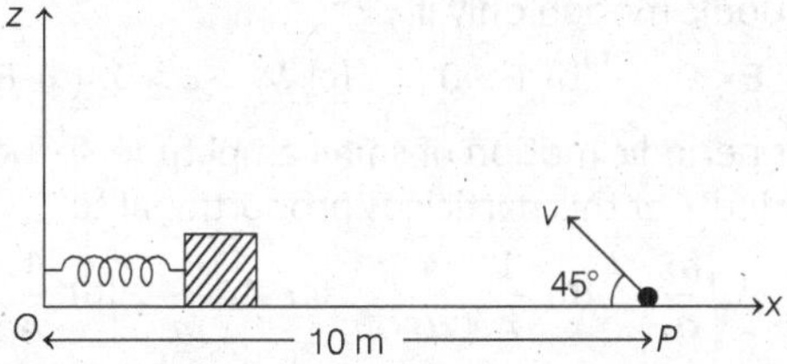

Point P is at a horizontal distance of 10 m from O. If the pebble hits the block at $t = 1$ s, the value of v is (Take, $g = 10\ \text{m/s}^2$) **(2012 Adv.)**

(a) $\sqrt{50}$ m/s (b) $\sqrt{51}$ m/s (c) $\sqrt{52}$ m/s (d) $\sqrt{53}$ m/s

9. A metal rod of length L and mass m is pivoted at one end. A thin disc of mass M and radius $R\,(<L)$ is attached at its centre to the free end of the rod. Consider two ways the disc is attached. **case A**—the disc is not free to rotate about its centre and **case B**—the disc is free to rotate about its centre. The rod-disc system performs SHM in vertical plane after being released from the same displaced position. Which of the following statement(s) is/are true? **(2011)**

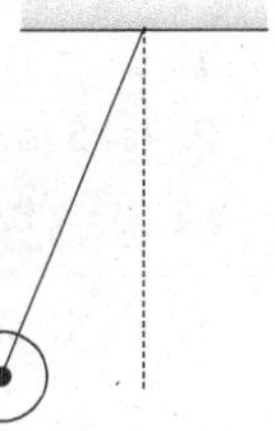

(a) Restoring torque in case A = Restoring torque in case B

(b) Restoring torque in case A < Restoring torque in case B

(c) Angular frequency for case A > Angular frequency for case B

(d) Angular frequency for case A < Angular frequency for case B

Passage Based Questions

When a particle of mass m moves on the X-axis in a potential of the form $V(x) = kx^2$, it performs simple harmonic motion. The corresponding time period is proportional to $\sqrt{m/k}$, as can be seen easily using dimensional analysis. However, the motion of a particle can be periodic even when its potential energy increases on both sides of $x = 0$ in a way different from kx^2 and its total energy is such that the particle does not escape to infinity. Consider a particle of mass m moving on the

X-axis. Its potential energy is $V(x) = \alpha x^4 (\alpha > 0)$ for $|x|$ near the origin and becomes a constant equal to V_0 for $|x| \geq X_0$ (see figure).

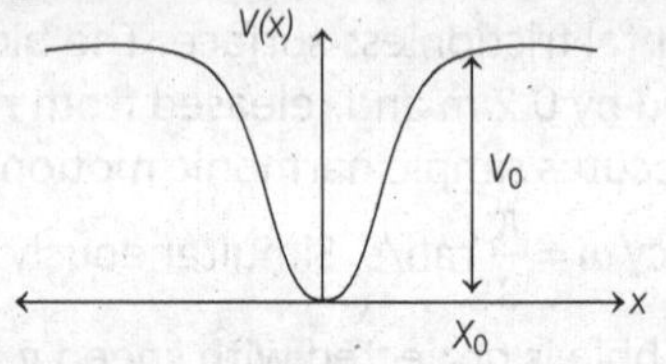

10. If the total energy of the particle is E, it will perform periodic motion only if **(2010)**

(a) $E < 0$ (b) $E > 0$ (c) $V_0 > E > 0$ (d) $E > V_0$

11. For periodic motion of small amplitude A, the time period T of this particle is proportional to **(2010)**

(a) $A\sqrt{\frac{m}{\alpha}}$ (b) $\frac{1}{A}\sqrt{\frac{m}{\alpha}}$ (c) $A\sqrt{\frac{\alpha}{m}}$ (d) $\frac{1}{A}\sqrt{\frac{\alpha}{m}}$

12. The acceleration of this particle for $|x| > X_0$ is **(2010)**

(a) proportional to V_0

(b) proportional to $\frac{V_0}{mX_0}$

(c) proportional to $\sqrt{\frac{V_0}{mX_0}}$

(d) zero

13. A 0.1 kg mass is suspended from a wire of negligible mass. The length of the wire is 1 m and its cross-sectional area is 4.9×10^{-7} m^2. If the mass is pulled a little in the vertically downward direction and released, it performs simple harmonic motion of angular frequency 140 rad s^{-1}. If the Young's modulus of the material of the wire is $n \times 10^9$ Nm^{-2}, the value of n is. **(2010)**

Answer Key

Level 1

7.1 Equation of SHM

1. π

2. (a) 5 m (b) $\pi/3$ (c) 2 s (d) 5π m/s (e) 50 m/s (f) $-\frac{5\pi}{2}$ m/s, $-\frac{5\sqrt{3}\pi^2}{2}$ m/s^2

3. $x = 10\sin(\pi t + \pi/6)$ **4.** (a) 50.2 cm/s (b) -120 cm/s^2

5. 4s **6.** $T = 2\pi\sqrt{\frac{y_2^2 - y_1^2}{v_1^2 - v_2^2}}$ **7.** 1 m

8. (a) $x = 4$ (b) $x = 4 + 2\cos t$ **9.** $\frac{1}{2\pi}\sqrt{\frac{\beta}{\alpha}}$

10. (a) $\frac{\pi}{2}$ s (b) 40 ms^{-2} (c) 8 ms^{-1}

7.2 Phasor Diagrams

1. (a) 2 s (b) 8 s

2. (a) $T/12$ (b) $T/8$ (c) $T/6$ (d) $7T/24$

3. $x = (10 \text{ cm})\sin\left[\frac{\pi}{3}t + \frac{5\pi}{6}\right]$

4. 2 m/s **5.** $\frac{1}{\sqrt{2}-1}$ **6.** $\frac{\sqrt{2}\pi A}{T}, \frac{2\sqrt{2}\pi^2 A}{T^2}$ **7.** $\frac{2\pi}{3}$ **8.** $\frac{3T}{8}$

7.3 Energy in SHM

1. $\pm\frac{A}{\sqrt{2}}$ **2.** ± 5 cm **3.** 0.72 J **4.** 3.125×10^{-5} J, 9.375×10^{-5} J

5. $\pi/100$ s **6.** $K_{min} = 0, U_{max} = 160$ J, $K_{max} = 100$ J, $U_{min} = 60$ J

7.4 Spring Block System

1. 0.133 s **2.** 2.83 s **3.** (a) $\frac{\sqrt{13}}{2}A$ (b) $\sqrt{\frac{m}{k}}\cos^{-1}\left(\frac{1}{\sqrt{13}}\right)$

4. (a) $2\pi\sqrt{\frac{2m}{k}}, \frac{A}{\sqrt{2}}$ (b) $2\pi\sqrt{\frac{2m}{k}}, \sqrt{\frac{5}{8}}A$

5. (a) $\left(\frac{mk|x|}{M+m}\right)$ (b) $\frac{\mu(M+m)g}{k}$

6. (a) $\frac{F}{k}, 2\pi\sqrt{\frac{m}{k}}$ (b) $\frac{F^2}{2k}$ (c) $\frac{F^2}{2k}$ **8.** 90 N **10.** $\frac{m_1 g}{k}$

7.5 Two Blocks Spring System

1. (a) $\frac{\pi}{10}$ sec, (b) 4 cm (c) 2.40 kg m/s **2.** $2\pi\sqrt{\frac{mM}{k(M+m)}}$

7.6 Combination of Springs

1. (a) $2\pi\sqrt{\frac{m}{3k}}$ (b) $2\pi\sqrt{\frac{3m}{2k}}$ **2.** $\frac{\pi}{2}\sqrt{\frac{3m}{k}}$ **3.** $2\pi\sqrt{\frac{2m}{3k}}$

4. (a) $\pi\sqrt{\frac{m}{k}}$ (b) $4\pi\sqrt{\frac{m}{k}}$

5. (a) $2\pi\sqrt{\frac{m(k_1+k_2)}{4k_1k_2}}$ (b) $4\pi\sqrt{\frac{m(k_1+k_2)}{k_1k_2}}$

7.7 Simple Pendulum

1. 0.25 m **2.** (a) 1.26 s (b) 1.6 cm (c) 6.8 cm/s (d) 1 rad/s^2

3. (a) $2T$ (b) $3g$ (upwards) **4.** $a = \frac{\sqrt{2}g}{10}$ **5.** $T = 2\pi\sqrt{\frac{l}{g\cos\theta}}$

6. $2\pi.\sqrt{\frac{l}{g\left(1-\frac{\rho}{\sigma}\right)}}$ **7.** (a) 4° (b) $\frac{3\pi}{2}\sqrt{\frac{L}{g}}$ **8.** 2.4 s

7.8 Compound Pendulum

1. (a) $2\pi\sqrt{\frac{2l}{3g}}$ (b) $2\pi\sqrt{\frac{2r}{g}}$ (c) $2\pi\sqrt{\frac{2\sqrt{2}a}{3g}}$ (d) $2\pi\sqrt{\frac{3r}{2g}}$

2. $\frac{L}{2\sqrt{3}}, 2\pi\sqrt{\frac{L}{\sqrt{3}g}}$ 3. $\frac{1}{2\pi}\sqrt{\frac{g}{2r}}\sqrt{1+\frac{4}{\pi^2}}$ 4. $2\pi\sqrt{\frac{17L}{18g}}$

7.9 Torsional Pendulum

1. $0.25\ \text{kg-m}^2/\text{s}^2$ 2. 4π s

7.10 Angular SHM

1. $\frac{1}{2\pi}\sqrt{\frac{6k}{m}}$ 2. $\frac{1}{2\pi}\sqrt{\frac{27k}{4m}+\frac{3g}{2l}}$ 3. $2\pi\sqrt{\frac{7m}{5k}}$

4. $2\pi\sqrt{\frac{3m}{10k}}$ 5. $2\pi\sqrt{\frac{1}{k}\left(m+\frac{I}{R^2}\right)}$

7.11 SHM Problems involving other Topics

1. $\frac{1}{2\pi}\sqrt{\frac{g}{h}}$ 2. $2\pi\sqrt{\frac{\sigma h}{\rho g}}$ 3. (a) $2\pi\sqrt{\frac{m}{k+A\rho g}}$ (b) $2\pi\sqrt{\frac{m}{k}}$

4. $2\pi\sqrt{\frac{MV_0}{P_0A^2}}$ 5. (a) $\frac{\pi}{2}\sqrt{\frac{R}{g}}$ (b) $\frac{\pi}{2}\sqrt{\frac{R}{g}}$ 6. $2\pi\sqrt{\frac{R}{g}}$

7.12 Superposition of SHMs

1. (a) 7 cm (b) 6.1 cm (c) 5 cm 2. 5, $x = 5\sin(\omega t + 53°)$

3. 1 : 1 4. $\frac{3\sqrt{5}A}{8}, \tan^{-1}\left(\frac{1}{2}\right)$ 5. $(\sqrt{3}+1)a$ 6. $x^2+\frac{y^2}{4}=1$

Level 2

Single Choice Correct Questions

1. (a)	2. (b)	3. (c)	4. (a)	5. (b)
6. (c)	7. (c)	8. (b)	9. (c)	10. (b)
11. (b)	12. (b)	13. (a)	14. (c)	15. (d)
16. (b)	17. (c)	18. (b)	19. (d)	20. (c)
21. (b)	22. (c)	23. (a)	24. (a)	25. (d)
26. (c)	27. (d)	28. (c)	29. (d)	30. (b)
31. (a)	32. (a)	33. (a)	34. (c)	35. (b)
36. (c)	37. (a)	38. (a)	39. (b)	40. (a)
41. (b)	42. (a)	43. (b)	44. (d)	45. (b)
46. (b)	47. (c)	48. (c)	49. (b)	50. (b)
51. (a)	52. (b)	53. (c)	54. (c)	55. (c)
56. (c)	57. (b)	58. (b)	59. (b)	60. (b)
61. (c)	62. (b)	63. (b)	64. (c)	65. (d)
66. (c)	67. (c)	68. (a)	69. (b)	70. (b)
71. (d)	72. (a)			

Numerical Value Questions

1. (6)	2. (2)	3. (4)	4. (4)	5. (10)
6. (1.5)	7. (5)	8. (5)	9. (6)	10. (2)

Level 3

Single Choice Correct Questions

1. (b)	2. (a)	3. (b)	4. (b)	5. (a)
6. (b)	7. (c)	8. (c)	9. (a)	10. (c)
11. (a)	12. (b)	13. (b)	14. (c)	15. (a)
16. (c)	17. (d)	18. (a)	19. (d)	20. (b)
21. (b)	22. (c)	23. (c)	24. (a)	25. (a)
26. (b)	27. (b)	28. (a)	29. (c)	30. (d)
31. (b)	32. (b)	33. (c)	34. (a)	35. (a)
36. (c)	37. (b)	38. (a)	39. (c)	40. (a)
41. (d)	42 (a)	43. (c)	44. (a)	

Multiple Choice(s) Correct Questions

1. (ac)	2. (bcd)	3. (cd)	4. (abc)
5. (abc)	6. (abd)	7. (abcd)	8. (cd)
9. (abd)	10. (ad)	11. (ac)	12. (abc)
13. (ac)	14. (ab)	15. (ac)	16. (bcd)
17. (abcd)	18. (bd)	19. (abcd)	20. (ac)

Comprehension Based questions

1. (d)	2. (c)	3. (d)	4. (a)	5. (a)
6. (a)	7. (b)	8. (c)	9. (b)	10. (b)
11. (a)	12. (c)	13. (d)	14. (b)	15. (a)
16. (c)	17. (a)	18. (a)	19. (a)	20. (b)
21. (a)	22. (b)	23. (c)	24. (b)	

Match the Columns Questions

1. A → P, B → R, C → Q, D → S
2. A → Q, B → P, C → S, D → R
3. A → PQ, B → PQ, C → S, D → R
4. A → R, B → Q, C → P, D → Q
5. A → PQST, B → PQ, C → PQ, D → PQST
6. A → S, B → R, C → P, D → Q

Numerical Value Questions

1. 38	2. 17	3. 1	4. 75	5. 1
6. 5	7. 2	8. 5	9. 1	10. 5
11. 2	12. 8	13. 2	14. 9	

Previous Year's Questions

JEE Main

1. (3)	2. (9)	3. (2)	4. (7)	5. (12)
6. (c)	7. (b)	8. (a)	9. (4)	10. (99)
11. (8)	12. (2)	13. (a)	14. (c)	15. (a)
16. (c)	17. (a)	18. (b)	19. (1)	20. (60)
21. (a)	22. (b)	23. (1.9)	24. (2)	25. (a)
26. (d)	27. (d)	28. (b)	29. (d)	30. (b)
31. (c)	32. (d)	33. (d)	34. (8)	35. (10)
36. (2)	37. (7)	38. (c)	39. (c)	

JEE Advanced

1. (10)	2. (6)	3. (c)	4. (2.09)	5. (a)
6. (a,b,d)	7. (a,d)	8. (a)	9. (a,d)	10. (c)
11. (b)	12. (d)	13. (4)		

SOLUTIONS

Level 01

7.1 Equation of SHM

1. Comparing with $\frac{d^2x}{dt^2} + \omega^2 x = 0$, we get

$$\omega^2 = 4 \Rightarrow \omega = 2 \text{ rad/s}$$

$$T = \frac{2\pi}{\omega} = \frac{2\pi}{2} = \pi \text{ s}$$

2. $x = A\sin(\omega t + \phi) = (5\text{m})\sin\left(\pi t + \frac{\pi}{3}\right)$

(a) $A = 5\text{m}$

(b) $\phi = \frac{\pi}{3}$

(c) $\omega = \pi$ rad/s

$$\therefore \quad T = \frac{2\pi}{\omega} = 2\text{s}$$

(d) $v_{max} = \omega A = \pi(5) = 5\pi$ m/s

(e) $a_{max} = \omega^2 A = \pi^2(5) = 50$ m/s

(f) $v = 5\pi\cos\left(\pi t + \frac{\pi}{3}\right)$

$$a = -5\pi^2 \sin\left(\pi t + \frac{\pi}{3}\right)$$

At $t = 1$ s,

$$v = 5\pi\cos\left(\pi + \frac{\pi}{3}\right) = -\frac{5\pi}{2} \text{ m/s}$$

$$a = -5\pi^2\sin\left(\pi + \frac{\pi}{3}\right) = -\frac{5\sqrt{3}\,\pi^2}{2} \text{ m/s}^2$$

3. $\omega = \frac{2\pi}{T} = \frac{2\pi}{2} = \pi$ rad/s

$$x = A\sin(\omega t + \phi)$$

At $t = 0, x = 5$ mm

$$5 = 10\sin[\pi(0) + \phi]$$

$$\Rightarrow \quad \sin\phi = \frac{1}{2} \Rightarrow \phi = \frac{\pi}{6}$$

$$\therefore \quad x = 10\sin\left(\pi t + \frac{\pi}{6}\right)$$

4. $\omega = \frac{2\pi}{T} = \frac{2\pi}{1} = 2\pi$ rad/s

(a) $v = \omega\sqrt{A^2 - x^2} = 2\pi\sqrt{(10)^2 - (6)^2} = 50.3$ cm/s

(b) $a = -\omega^2 x = (-2\pi)^2 3 = -120$ cm / s^2

5. $v_{max} = \omega A = 100$ cm/s

$a_{max} = \omega^2 A = 157$ cm/s^2

$$\therefore \quad \frac{\omega^2 A}{\omega A} = \frac{157}{100} \Rightarrow \omega = 1.57 \text{ rad/s}$$

$$T = \frac{2\pi}{\omega} = \frac{2\pi}{1.57} = 4\text{ s}$$

6. $v = \omega\sqrt{A^2 - x^2}$

$$\therefore \quad v_1 = \omega\sqrt{A^2 - y_1^2} \quad \text{...(i)}$$

$$v_2 = \omega\sqrt{A^2 - y_2^2} \quad \text{...(ii)}$$

Squaring and subtracting the equations, we get

$$v_1^2 - v_2^2 = \omega^2(y_2^2 - y_1^2)$$

$$\Rightarrow \quad \omega = \sqrt{\frac{v_1^2 - v_2^2}{y_2^2 - y_1^2}}$$

$$T = \frac{2\pi}{\omega} = 2\pi\sqrt{\frac{y_2^2 - y_1^2}{v_1^2 - v_2^2}}$$

7. $\omega = \sqrt{\frac{k}{m}} = \sqrt{\frac{50}{0.5}} = 10$ rad/s

$$v_{max} = \omega A \Rightarrow 10 = 10(A)$$

$$\Rightarrow \quad A = 1\text{m}$$

8. (a) $F = 8 - 2x = 0 \Rightarrow x = 4$

(b) $F = -2(x - 4) = -2x$

$$\omega = \sqrt{\frac{k}{m}} = \sqrt{\frac{2}{2}} = 1 \text{ rad/s}$$

The particle is released from rest from $x = 6$.

So, the particle is at the right extreme initially.

$$A = 6 - 4 = 2$$

$$X = A\sin(\omega t + \phi)$$

$$\Rightarrow \quad x - 4 = 2\sin\left[(1)t + \frac{\pi}{2}\right] \Rightarrow x = 4 + 2\cos t$$

9. $a = -\omega^2 x \Rightarrow -\beta = -\omega^2\alpha$

$$\Rightarrow \quad \omega = \sqrt{\frac{\beta}{\alpha}}$$

$$f = \frac{\omega}{2\pi} = \frac{1}{2\pi}\sqrt{\frac{\beta}{\alpha}}$$

10. (a) $A = 2.5$ m

$$v_{max} = 10 \text{ m/s} \Rightarrow A\omega = 10$$

$$\Rightarrow \quad (2.5)\omega = 10$$

$$\Rightarrow \quad \omega = 4 \text{ rad/s}$$

$$T = \frac{2\pi}{\omega} = \frac{2\pi}{4} = \frac{\pi}{2}\text{ s}$$

(b) $a_{max} = \omega^2 A = (4)^2(2.5) = 40$ m/s^2

(c) $v = \omega\sqrt{A^2 - x^2} = 4\sqrt{(2.5)^2 - (1.5)^2} = 8$ ms^{-1}

7.2 Phasor Diagrams

1. (a) The particle will first come to rest at the right extreme,

$$\therefore \quad \left(\frac{\pi}{12}\right)t + \frac{\pi}{3} = \frac{\pi}{2} \Rightarrow t = 2\text{ s}$$

(b) The particle will first have maximum speed at the mean position.

$\therefore \quad \left(\frac{\pi}{12}\right)t + \frac{\pi}{3} = \pi \quad \Rightarrow \quad t = 8\text{ s}$

2. (a) $\sin\theta = \frac{A/2}{2} = \frac{1}{2}$

$\Rightarrow \quad \theta = \frac{\pi}{6}$

$\theta = \omega t$

$\Rightarrow \quad \frac{\pi}{6} = \left(\frac{2\pi}{T}\right)t$

$\Rightarrow \quad t = \frac{T}{12}$

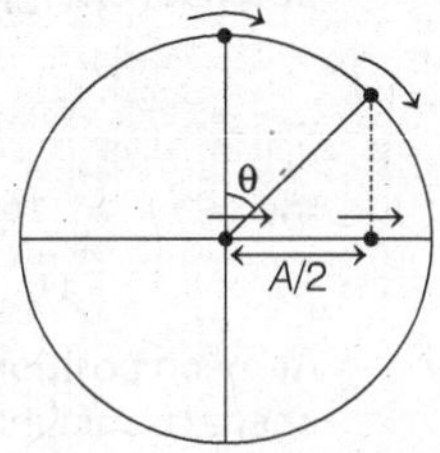

(b) $\sin\theta = \frac{A/\sqrt{2}}{A} = \frac{1}{\sqrt{2}}$

$\Rightarrow \quad \theta = \frac{\pi}{4}$

$\theta = \omega t \Rightarrow \frac{\pi}{4} = \left(\frac{2\pi}{T}\right)t$

$\Rightarrow \quad t = \frac{T}{8}$

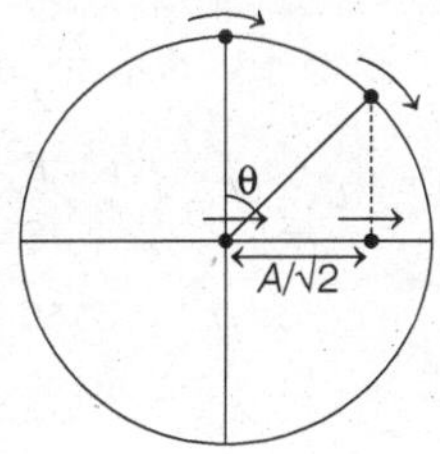

(c) $\cos\theta = \frac{A/2}{A} \quad \Rightarrow \quad \theta = \frac{\pi}{3}$

$\theta = \omega t$

$\Rightarrow \frac{\pi}{3} = \left(\frac{2\pi}{T}\right)t$

$\Rightarrow t = \frac{T}{6}$

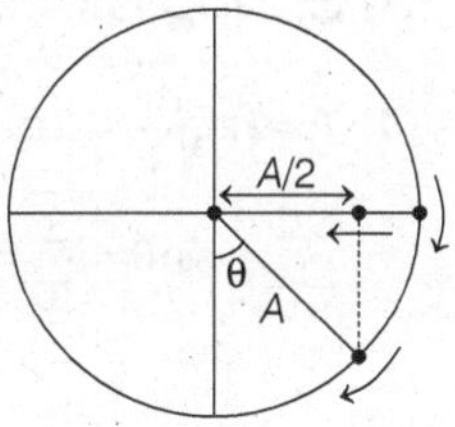

(d) $\sin\alpha = \frac{A/\sqrt{2}}{A} = \frac{1}{\sqrt{2}}$

$\Rightarrow \quad \alpha = \frac{\pi}{4}$

$\sin\beta = \frac{\sqrt{3}A/2}{A} = \frac{\sqrt{3}}{2}$

$\Rightarrow \quad \beta = \frac{\pi}{3}$

$\theta = \omega t$

$\Rightarrow \quad \frac{\pi}{4} + \frac{\pi}{3} = \left(\frac{2\pi}{T}\right)t$

$\Rightarrow \quad t = \frac{7T}{24}$

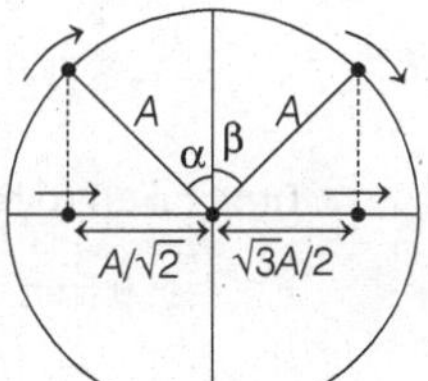

3. $\cos\theta = \frac{5}{10} \quad \Rightarrow \theta = \frac{\pi}{3}$

$\phi = \frac{\pi}{2} + \frac{\pi}{3} = \frac{5\pi}{6}$

$\omega = \frac{2\pi}{T} = \frac{2\pi}{6} = \frac{\pi}{3}$

$x = A\sin(\omega t + \phi)$

$\Rightarrow \quad x = (10\text{ cm})\sin\left(\frac{\pi}{3}t + \frac{5\pi}{6}\right)$

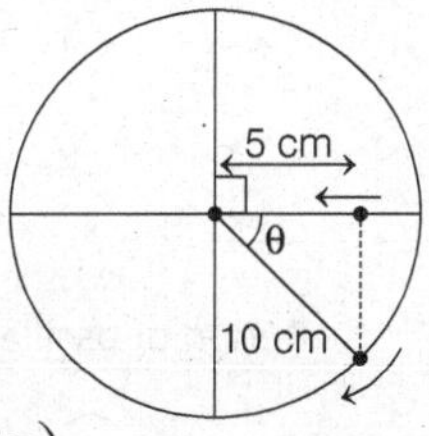

4. $T = \frac{2\pi}{\omega} = \frac{2\pi}{5\pi} = 0.4\text{s}$

$t_0 = \frac{T}{4} = 0.1\text{ s}$

Distance travelled in $T/4$ time $= A = 0.2$ m

At $t = 0$, the particle is at the right extreme. So, in every 0.1 s, it will travel 0.2 m.

Distance travelled in 0.7 s $= 7 \times 0.2 = 1.4$ m

Average speed $= \frac{\text{Total distance}}{\text{Total time}} = \frac{1.4}{0.7} = 2$ m/s

5. $\omega = \frac{2\pi}{T} = \frac{2\pi}{8} = \frac{\pi}{4}$

$\theta = \omega t$

In one second interval,

$$\theta = \left(\frac{\pi}{4}\right)1 = \frac{\pi}{4}$$

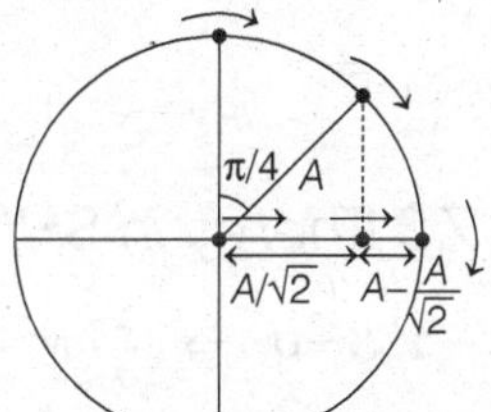

Distance covered in first second,

$$d_1 = \frac{A}{\sqrt{2}}$$

Distance covered in next one second,

$$d_2 = A - \frac{A}{\sqrt{2}}$$

$$\therefore \quad \frac{d_1}{d_2} = \frac{A/\sqrt{2}}{A - \frac{A}{\sqrt{2}}} = \frac{1}{\sqrt{2} - 1}$$

6. If the particle starts from the right extreme position, then

$x = A\cos\omega t$

$$v = \frac{dx}{dt} = -A\omega\sin\omega t$$

$$a = \frac{dv}{dt} = -A\omega^2\cos\omega t$$

At $t = \frac{T}{8}$,

$$v = -A\left(\frac{2\pi}{T}\right)\sin\left[\frac{2\pi}{T}\left(\frac{T}{8}\right)\right] = -\frac{\sqrt{2}\pi A}{T}$$

$$a = -A\left(\frac{2\pi}{T}\right)^2\cos\left[\frac{2\pi}{T}\left(\frac{T}{8}\right)\right] = -\frac{2\sqrt{2}\pi^2 A}{T^2}$$

7. $\cos\theta = \frac{A/2}{A} = \frac{1}{2}$

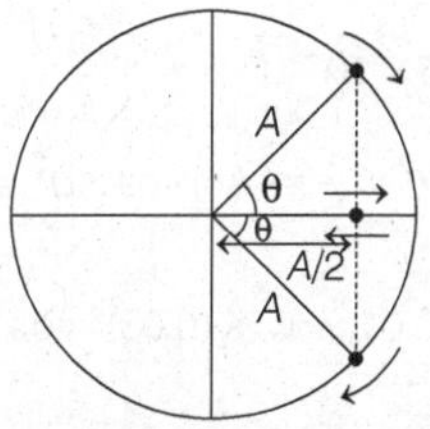

$\Rightarrow \quad \theta = \frac{\pi}{3}$

Phase difference $= 2\theta = \frac{2\pi}{3}$

8. For the particle starting from A,

$$x_1 = A\sin\left(\omega t + \frac{\pi}{2}\right) = A\cos\omega t$$

For the particle starting from O′ and moving left,

$$x_2 = A\sin(\omega t + \pi) = -A\sin\omega t$$

The particle will cross when

$$x_1 = x_2$$

$$\Rightarrow \quad A\cos\omega t = -A\sin\omega t$$

$$\Rightarrow \quad \tan\omega t = -1 \Rightarrow \omega t = \frac{3\pi}{4}$$

$$\Rightarrow \quad \left(\frac{2\pi}{T}\right)t = \frac{3\pi}{4} \Rightarrow t = \frac{3T}{8}$$

7.3 Energy in SHM

1. $K = U \Rightarrow \frac{1}{2}mv^2 = \frac{1}{2}kx^2$

$$\Rightarrow \quad \frac{1}{2}m\left(\omega\sqrt{A^2 - x^2}\right)^2 = \frac{1}{2}(m\omega^2)x^2$$

$$\Rightarrow \quad x = \pm\frac{A}{\sqrt{2}}$$

2. $K = \frac{3}{4}E$

$$\Rightarrow \quad \frac{1}{2}m\left(\omega\sqrt{A^2 - x^2}\right)^2 = \frac{3}{4}\left(\frac{1}{2}m\omega^2A^2\right)$$

$$\Rightarrow \quad x = \pm\frac{A}{2} = \pm 5\text{ cm}$$

3. $\omega = \frac{2\pi}{T} = \frac{2\pi}{\pi} = 2\text{ rad/s}$

$$K = \frac{1}{2}mv^2 = \frac{1}{2}m\left(\omega\sqrt{A^2 - x^2}\right)^2 = \frac{1}{2}m\omega^2(A^2 - x^2)$$

$$\therefore \quad K = \frac{1}{2}\times 1\times 2^2[1^2 - (0.8)^2] = 0.72\text{ J}$$

4. $\omega = \frac{2\pi}{T} = \frac{2\pi}{2} = \pi$

$$U = \frac{1}{2}kx^2 = \frac{1}{2}m\omega^2(A\sin\omega t)^2 = \frac{1}{2}m\omega^2A^2\sin^2\omega t$$

$$\therefore \quad U = \frac{1}{2}\times 0.01\times\pi^2\times(0.05)^2\sin^2\left[\pi\left(\frac{1}{6}\right)\right]$$

$$= 3.125\times 10^{-5}\text{ J}$$

$$K = \frac{1}{2}mv^2 = \frac{1}{2}m(A\omega\cos\omega t)^2 = \frac{1}{2}m\omega^2A^2\cos^2\omega t$$

$$\therefore \quad K = \frac{1}{2}\times 0.01\times\pi^2\times(0.05)^2\cos^2\left[\pi\left(\frac{1}{6}\right)\right] = 9.375\times 10^{-5}\text{ J}$$

5. At mean position,

$$K_{max} = E - U = 9 - 5 = 4\text{ J}$$

$$K_{max} = \frac{1}{2}m\omega^2A^2 = 4$$

$$\Rightarrow \quad \frac{1}{2}\times 2\times\omega^2(0.01)^2 = 4$$

$$\Rightarrow \quad \omega = 200\text{ rad/s}$$

$$T = \frac{2\pi}{\omega} = \frac{2\pi}{200} = \frac{\pi}{100}\text{ s}$$

6. At extreme position, kinetic energy is minimum and potential energy is maximum.

$$E = K + U$$

$$\Rightarrow \quad E = K_{min} + U_{max}$$

$$\Rightarrow \quad 160 = 0 + U_{max}$$

$$\Rightarrow \quad U_{max} = 160\text{ J}$$

At mean position, kinetic energy is maximum and potential energy is minimum.

$$K_{max} = \frac{1}{2}m\omega^2A^2 = \frac{1}{2}kA^2 = \frac{1}{2}\times 2\times 10^6(0.01)^2 = 100\text{ J}$$

$$E = K + U$$

$$\Rightarrow \quad E = K_{max} + U_{min}$$

$$\Rightarrow \quad 160 = 100 + U_{min}$$

$$\Rightarrow \quad U_{min} = 60\text{ J}$$

7.4 Spring Block System

1. $T = 2\pi\sqrt{\frac{m}{k}} = 2\pi\sqrt{\frac{0.1}{100}} = 0.2\text{ s}$

$$\sin\theta = \frac{5}{10} = \frac{1}{2} \Rightarrow \theta = \frac{\pi}{6}$$

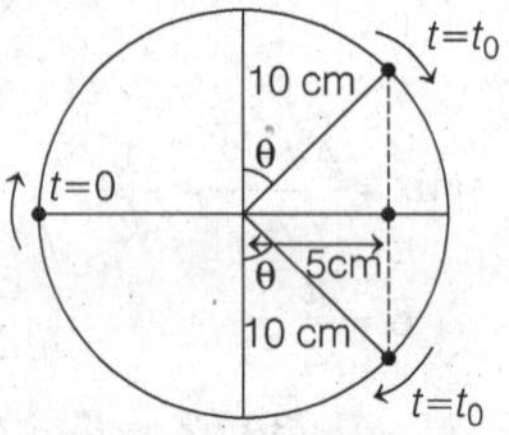

Time taken to reach wall,

$$\theta = \omega t \Rightarrow \frac{\pi}{2} + \frac{\pi}{6} = \left(\frac{2\pi}{0.2}\right)t_0 \Rightarrow t_0 = \frac{1}{15}\text{ s}$$

$$\text{Time period of motion} = 2t_0 = \frac{2}{15}\text{ s} = 0.133\text{ s}$$

2. Time for which the block remains in contact with a spring $= \frac{T}{2}$

$$T_1 = 2\pi\sqrt{\frac{m}{k_1}} = 2\pi\sqrt{\frac{0.2}{1.8}} = \frac{2\pi}{3}$$

$$T_2 = 2\pi\sqrt{\frac{m}{k_2}} = 2\pi\sqrt{\frac{0.2}{3.2}} = \frac{\pi}{2}$$

$$\text{Period of oscillation} = \frac{2(CD)}{v} + \frac{T_1}{2} + \frac{T_2}{2}$$

$$= \frac{2(60)}{120} + \frac{1}{2}\left(\frac{2\pi}{3}\right) + \frac{1}{2}\left(\frac{\pi}{2}\right) = 2.83\text{ s}$$

3. (a) $v = \omega\sqrt{A^2 - x^2} = \omega\sqrt{A^2 - \left(\frac{A}{2}\right)^2} = \frac{\sqrt{3}\omega A}{2}$

After receiving impulse, speed gets doubled.

$$\therefore \quad v = \omega\sqrt{A'^2 - x^2}$$

$$\Rightarrow \quad 2\left(\frac{\sqrt{3}\omega A}{2}\right) = \omega\sqrt{A'^2 - \left(\frac{A}{2}\right)^2}$$

$$\Rightarrow \quad A' = \frac{\sqrt{13}A}{2}$$

(b) $\cos\theta = \frac{A/2}{A'} = \frac{1}{\sqrt{13}}$

$$\theta = \omega t$$

$$\Rightarrow \cos^{-1}\left(\frac{1}{\sqrt{13}}\right) = \left(\sqrt{\frac{k}{m}}\right)t$$

$$\Rightarrow \quad t = \sqrt{\frac{m}{k}}\cos^{-1}\left(\frac{1}{\sqrt{13}}\right)$$

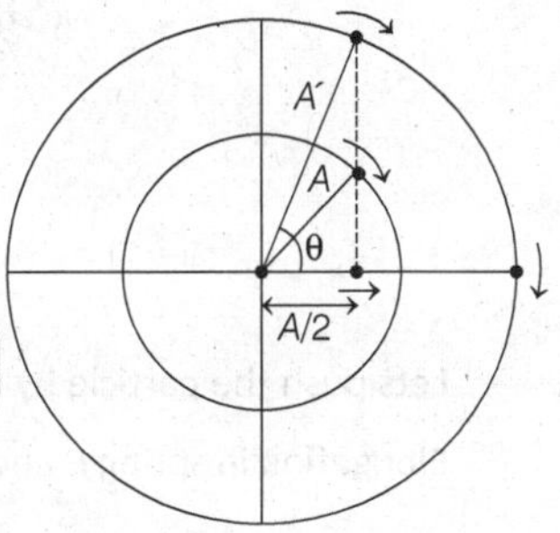

4. (a) $T = 2\pi\sqrt{\frac{m'}{k}} = 2\pi\sqrt{\frac{2m}{k}}$

Applying linear momentum conservation,

$$m(\omega A) + 0 = 2m(\omega' A')$$

$$\Rightarrow \quad m\left(\sqrt{\frac{k}{m}}A\right) = 2m\left(\sqrt{\frac{k}{2m}}\right)A'$$

$$\Rightarrow \quad A' = \frac{A}{\sqrt{2}}$$

(b) $T = 2\pi\sqrt{\frac{m'}{k}} = 2\pi\sqrt{\frac{2m}{k}}$

Applying linear momentum conservation,

$$m(\omega\sqrt{A^2 - x^2}) + 0 = 2m(\omega'\sqrt{A'^2 - x^2})$$

$$\Rightarrow m\left(\sqrt{\frac{k}{m}}\sqrt{A^2 - \left(\frac{A}{2}\right)^2}\right) = 2m\left(\sqrt{\frac{k}{2m}}\sqrt{A'^2 - \left(\frac{A}{2}\right)^2}\right)$$

$$\Rightarrow \quad A' = \sqrt{\frac{5}{8}}A$$

5. (a) Common acceleration of blocks $= \omega^2|x|$

$$= \left(\frac{k}{M+m}\right)|x|$$

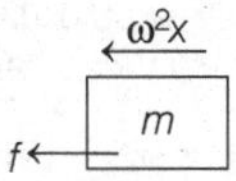

For the upper block,

$$\Sigma F = ma$$

$$\Rightarrow \quad f = m\omega^2|x| = \frac{mk|x|}{M+m}$$

(b) $f_{max} = m\omega^2 A$

$$f_{max} \le f_L$$

$$\Rightarrow \quad m\omega^2 A \le \mu mg$$

$$\Rightarrow \quad A_{max} = \frac{\mu g}{\omega^2} = \frac{\mu(M+m)g}{k}$$

6. (a) Initially the block is at the left extreme position.

At the mean position, $\Sigma F = 0$

$$\Rightarrow \quad F - kx = 0$$

$$\Rightarrow \quad x = \frac{F}{k}$$

So, amplitude will be $\frac{F}{k}$.

Due to applied constant force, only mean position will be shifted. Time period is not affected.

So, $\quad T = 2\pi\sqrt{\frac{m}{k}}$

(b) Applying work-energy theorem between the left extreme position and mean position,

$$W_F + W_{spring} = \Delta K$$

$$\Rightarrow \quad F\left(\frac{F}{k}\right) + \frac{1}{2}k\left(0^2 - \left(\frac{F}{k}\right)^2\right) = K_{mean} - 0$$

$$\Rightarrow \quad K_{mean} = \frac{F^2}{2k}$$

(c) $U = \frac{1}{2}kx^2 = \frac{1}{2}k\left(\frac{F}{k}\right)^2 = \frac{F^2}{2k}$

7. Time period in each case will be $2\pi\sqrt{\frac{m}{k}}$. Gravity doesn't affect the time period of the spring block system. It only changes the equilibrium position.

8. At the lower extreme position,

$$F_S - mg = m(\omega^2 A)$$

$$\Rightarrow \quad F_S = mg + m\omega^2 A$$

$$= 1(10) + 1\left(\frac{2\pi}{\pi/10}\right)^2(0.2) = 90\,\text{N}$$

9. When the elevator is stationary, the spring is stretched by $\frac{mg}{k}$. In freely falling elevator, pseudo force (mg) will balance the weight (mg). Thus, the block is subjected to a net force kx by the spring when it is at a diistance x from the position of unstretched spring. Hence its motion in the elevator is simple harmonic with its mean position corresponding to the unstretched spring. Initially the block is at the lower extreme position. Thus, the amplitude of the resulting SHM is mg/k.

10. For equilibrium of system,

$$kx_0 = (m_1 + m_2)g$$

$$\Rightarrow \quad x_0 = \frac{(m_1 + m_2)g}{k}$$

When m_1 is removed, m_2 will move up. So, initially m_2 is at the lower extreme position.

For new equilibrium position,

$$kx_2 = m_2 g$$

$$\Rightarrow \quad x_2 = \frac{m_2 g}{k}$$

Distance between lower extreme position and new mean position $= x_0 - x_2 = \dfrac{m_1 g}{k}$

Thus, the amplitude of resultant SHM will be $m_1 g / k$.

7.5 Two Blocks Spring System

1. (a) $\mu = \dfrac{m_1 m_2}{m_1 + m_2} = \dfrac{3(6)}{3+6} = 2\text{ kg}$

$$T = 2\pi\sqrt{\frac{m}{K}} = 2\pi\sqrt{\frac{2}{800}} = \frac{\pi}{10}\text{ s}$$

(b) $m_1 A_1 = m_2 A_2$

$\Rightarrow \quad 3A_1 = 6A_2 \quad \Rightarrow \quad A_1 = 2A_2$

$A_1 + A_2 = 6\text{ cm}$

$\Rightarrow \quad A_1 + \dfrac{A_1}{2} = 6 \quad \Rightarrow \quad A_1 = 4\text{ cm}$

(c) Let velocities of 3 kg and 6 kg block be v_1 and v_2, respectively when the spring acquires natural length.

Loss in potential energy = Gain in kinetic energy

$\Rightarrow \quad \dfrac{1}{2} \times 800 \times (0.06)^2 = \dfrac{1}{2} \times 3 \times v_1^2 + \dfrac{1}{2} \times 6 \times v_2^2$

$\Rightarrow \quad v_1^2 + 2v_2^2 = 0.96 \quad$ ...(i)

Applying linear momentum conservation,

$0 + 0 = 3v_1 + 6(-v_2)$

$\Rightarrow \quad v_1 = 2v_2 \quad$ ...(ii)

Solving Eqs. (i) and (ii), we get

$v_2 = 0.4\text{ m/s}$

$\therefore \quad p_{2\max} = 6 \times 0.4 = 2.4\text{ kg ms}^{-1}$

2. $\mu = \dfrac{Mm}{M+m}$

$$T = 2\pi\sqrt{\frac{\mu}{k}} = 2\pi\sqrt{\frac{Mm}{k(M+m)}}$$

7.6 Combination of Springs

1. (a) For springs in parallel,

$k_{\text{eff}} = k_1 + k_2 = k + 2k = 3k$

$$T = 2\pi\sqrt{\frac{m}{k_{\text{eff}}}} = 2\pi\sqrt{\frac{m}{3k}}$$

(b) For springs in series,

$$\frac{1}{k_{\text{eff}}} = \frac{1}{k_1} + \frac{1}{k_2}$$

$\Rightarrow \quad \dfrac{1}{k_{\text{eff}}} = \dfrac{1}{k} + \dfrac{1}{2k} \quad \Rightarrow \quad k_{\text{eff}} = \dfrac{2k}{3}$

$$T = 2\pi\sqrt{\frac{m}{k_{\text{eff}}}} = 2\pi\sqrt{\frac{3m}{2k}}$$

2. $kl = k_1 l_1 = k_2 l_2$

$\Rightarrow \quad kl = k_1\left(\dfrac{3l}{4}\right) = k_2\left(\dfrac{l}{4}\right)$

$\Rightarrow \quad k_1 = \dfrac{4k}{3}, k_2 = 4k$

$k_{\text{eff}} = k_1 + k_2 = \dfrac{4k}{3} + 4k = \dfrac{16k}{3}$

$$T = 2\pi\sqrt{\frac{m}{k_{\text{eff}}}} = 2\pi\sqrt{\frac{3m}{16k}} = \frac{\pi}{2}\sqrt{\frac{3m}{k}}$$

3. (a)

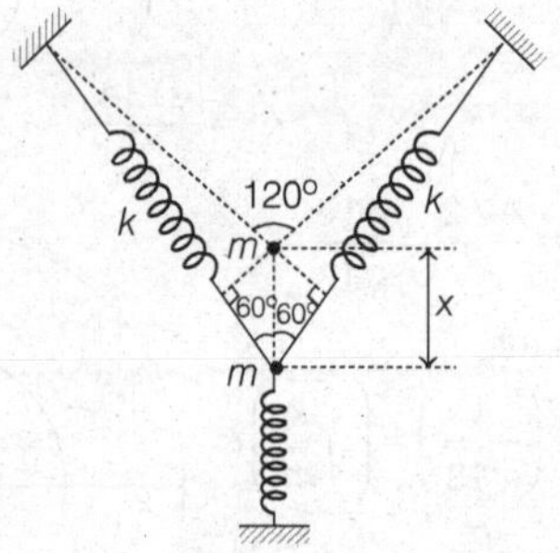

Lets push the particle by a distance x against the spring A.

Elongation in spring B and spring $C = x\cos 60° = \dfrac{x}{2}$

Net restoring force

$$= kx + k\left(\frac{x}{2}\right)\cos 60° + k\left(\frac{x}{2}\right)\cos 60°$$

$\Rightarrow \quad F = -\left(\dfrac{3k}{2}\right)x$

$\therefore \quad T = 2\pi\sqrt{\dfrac{m}{k_{eq}}} = 2\pi\sqrt{\dfrac{2m}{3k}}$

4. (a) Lets displace the block vertically down by a distance x and increase in elongation of spring be x_1.

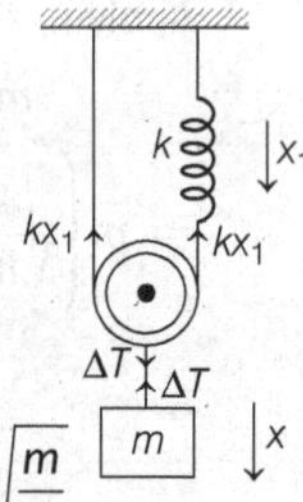

By constraint, $x_1 = 2x$

For equilibrium of pulley,

$\Delta T = 2kx_1$

$\Rightarrow \quad \Delta T = 2k(2x)$

$\Rightarrow \quad \Delta T = 4kx$

$\therefore \quad K_{\text{eff}} = 4k$

$$T = 2\pi\sqrt{\frac{m}{K_{\text{eff}}}} = 2\pi\sqrt{\frac{m}{4k}} = \pi\sqrt{\frac{m}{k}}$$

(b) Lets displace the block vertically down by distance x and increase in elongation of spring be x_1.

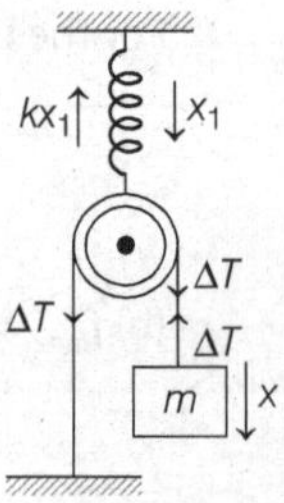

By constraint, $x_1 = \dfrac{x}{2}$

For equilibrium of pulley,

$2\Delta T = kx_1$

$\Rightarrow \quad 2\Delta T = k\left(\dfrac{x}{2}\right)$

$\Rightarrow \quad \Delta T = \left(\dfrac{k}{4}\right)(x)$

$\therefore \quad k_{\text{eff}} = \dfrac{k}{4}$

$$T=2\pi\sqrt{\frac{m}{k_{eff}}}=2\pi\sqrt{\frac{m}{k/4}}=4\pi\sqrt{\frac{m}{k}}$$

5. (a) Lets displace the block by a distance x from its equilibrium position and due to this further elongations in spring 1 and spring 2 be x_1 and x_2, respectively.

$$\frac{F}{2}=k_1x_1=k_2x_2$$

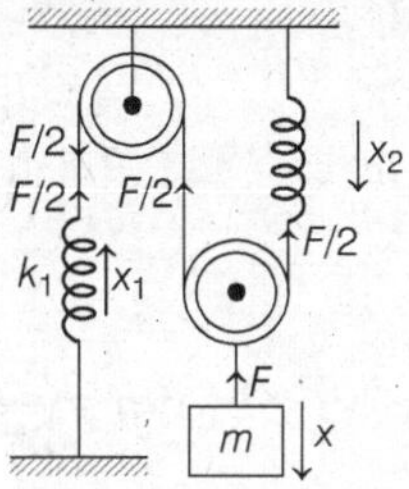

Using constraint relation,

$$x_1+x_2=2x$$

$$\Rightarrow \quad \frac{F}{2k_1}+\frac{F}{2k_2}=2x$$

$$\Rightarrow \quad F=\left(\frac{4k_1k_2}{k_1+k_2}\right)x$$

$$\therefore \quad k_{eff}=\frac{4k_1k_2}{k_1+k_2}$$

$$T=2\pi\sqrt{\frac{m}{k_{eff}}}=2\pi\sqrt{\frac{m(k_1+k_2)}{4k_1k_2}}$$

$$=\pi\sqrt{\frac{m(k_1+k_2)}{k_1k_2}}$$

(b) $2F=k_1x_1=k_2x_2$

$$x=2x_1+2x_2$$

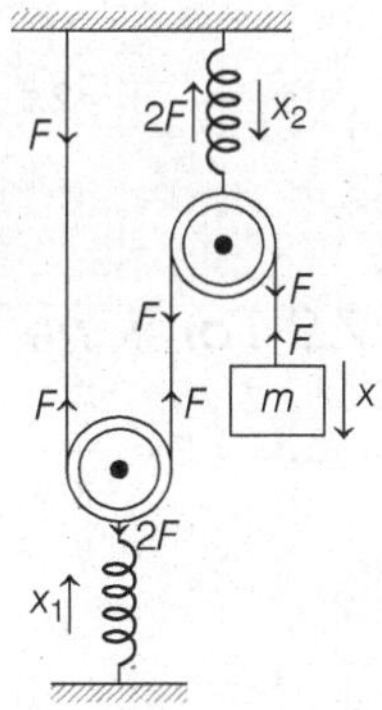

$$\Rightarrow \quad x=2\left(\frac{2F}{k_1}\right)+2\left(\frac{2F}{k_2}\right)$$

$$\Rightarrow \quad F=\frac{k_1k_2}{4(k_1+k_2)}x$$

$$\therefore \quad k_{eff}=\frac{k_1k_2}{4(k_1+k_2)}$$

$$T=2\pi\sqrt{\frac{m}{k_{eff}}}$$

$$=2\pi\sqrt{\frac{4(k_1+k_2)m}{k_1k_2}}$$

$$=4\pi\sqrt{\frac{m(k_1+k_2)}{k_1k_2}}$$

7.7 Simple Pendulum

1. $\theta=\theta_0\sin\omega t$

Comparing, we get $\omega=2\pi$

$$\therefore \quad T=\frac{2\pi}{\omega}=1\text{ s}$$

$$T=2\pi\sqrt{\frac{l}{g}}$$

$$\Rightarrow \quad 1=2\pi\sqrt{\frac{l}{\pi^2}} \quad \Rightarrow \quad l=0.25\text{ m}$$

2. (a) $T=2\pi\sqrt{\frac{l}{g}}=2\pi\sqrt{\frac{0.4}{10}}=1.26\text{ s}$

(b) $A=l\theta_0=40\times0.04=1.6\text{ cm}$

(c) $\Omega=\omega\sqrt{\theta_0^2-\theta^2}=5\sqrt{(0.04)^2-(0.02)^2}=0.17\text{ rad/s}$

$$v=\Omega l=0.17\times40=6.8\text{ cm/s}$$

(d) $|\alpha|=\omega^2\theta_0=(5)^2(0.04)=1\text{ rad/s}^2$

3. (a) $g_{eff}=g-\frac{3g}{4}=\frac{g}{4}$

$$T=2\pi\sqrt{\frac{l}{g}}$$

$$T'=2\pi\sqrt{\frac{l}{g_{eff}}}=2\pi\sqrt{\frac{l}{(g/4)}}=2T$$

(b) $T'=\frac{T}{2}$

$$\Rightarrow \quad 2\pi\sqrt{\frac{l}{g_{eff}}}=\frac{1}{2}\left(2\pi\sqrt{\frac{l}{g}}\right)$$

$$\Rightarrow \quad g_{eff}=4g$$

$$g_{eff}=g+a$$

$$\Rightarrow \quad 4g=g+a$$

$$\Rightarrow \quad a=3g\text{ (upwards)}$$

4. $T=2\pi\sqrt{\frac{l}{g}},$

$$T'=2\pi\sqrt{\frac{l}{g_{eff}}}=2\pi\sqrt{\frac{l}{\sqrt{g^2+a_0^2}}}$$

$$\therefore \quad \frac{T}{T'}=\sqrt{\frac{\sqrt{g^2+a_0^2}}{g}}$$

$$\Rightarrow \quad \left(\frac{2}{1.99}\right)^4=\frac{g^2+a_0^2}{g^2} \quad \Rightarrow \quad a_0^2=\left(\left(\frac{2}{1.99}\right)^4-1\right)g^2$$

$$\Rightarrow \quad a_0^2=\left(\left(\frac{2}{2-0.01}\right)^4-1\right)g^2$$

$$\Rightarrow \quad a_0^2=\left(\left(\frac{1}{1-0.005}\right)^4-1\right)g^2$$

$$\Rightarrow \quad a_0=((1-0.005)^{-4}-1)^{1/2}g$$

$$\Rightarrow \quad a_0=(1+4(0.005)-1)^{1/2}g$$

$$\Rightarrow \quad a_0=\frac{\sqrt{2}g}{10}$$

5. $T=2\pi\sqrt{\frac{l}{g_{eff}}}=2\pi\sqrt{\frac{l}{g\cos\theta}}$

6. $mg_{eff}=mg-B$

$$\Rightarrow \quad \sigma Vg_{eff}=\sigma Vg-\rho Vg$$

$$\Rightarrow \quad g_{eff}=g\left(1-\frac{\rho}{\sigma}\right)$$

$$T=2\pi\sqrt{\frac{l}{g_{eff}}}=2\pi\sqrt{\frac{l}{g\left(1-\frac{\rho}{\sigma}\right)}}$$

7. (a) $v_1 = v_2$

$$\Rightarrow \quad \Omega_1 r_1 = \Omega_2 r_2$$

$$\Rightarrow \quad \theta_1\omega_1 r_1 = \theta_2\omega_2 r_2$$

$$\Rightarrow \quad 2^\circ\left(\sqrt{\frac{g}{L}}\right)L = \theta_2\left(\sqrt{\frac{g}{L-\frac{3L}{4}}}\right)\left(L-\frac{3L}{4}\right)$$

$$\Rightarrow \quad \theta_2 = 4^\circ$$

(b) $t = \frac{T_1}{2} + \frac{T_2}{2} = \pi\sqrt{\frac{L}{g}} + \pi\sqrt{\frac{L/4}{g}} = \frac{3\pi}{2}\sqrt{\frac{L}{g}}$

8. $\omega_1 = \sqrt{\frac{g}{l_1}} = \sqrt{\frac{\pi^2}{0.36}} = \frac{5\pi}{3}$ rad/s

$$\omega_2 = \sqrt{\frac{g}{l_2}} = \sqrt{\frac{\pi^2}{0.64}} = \frac{5\pi}{4} \text{ rad/s}$$

$$\Delta\phi = (\omega_1 - \omega_2)t$$

$$\Rightarrow \quad \pi = \left(\frac{5\pi}{3} - \frac{5\pi}{4}\right)t \quad \Rightarrow \quad t = 2.4 \text{ s}$$

7.8 Compound Pendulum

1. (a) $T = 2\pi\sqrt{\frac{I}{mgd}} = 2\pi\sqrt{\frac{ml^2/3}{mg\left(\frac{l}{2}\right)}} = 2\pi\sqrt{\frac{2l}{3g}}$

(b) $T = 2\pi\sqrt{\frac{I}{mgd}} = 2\pi\sqrt{\frac{2mr^2}{mgr}} = 2\pi\sqrt{\frac{2r}{g}}$

(c) $T = 2\pi\sqrt{\frac{I}{mgd}} = 2\pi\sqrt{\frac{2ma^2/3}{mg\left(\frac{a}{\sqrt{2}}\right)}} = 2\pi\sqrt{\frac{2\sqrt{2}a}{3g}}$

(d) $T = 2\pi\sqrt{\frac{I}{mgd}} = 2\pi\sqrt{\frac{\frac{mr^2}{2} + m\left(\frac{r}{2}\right)^2}{mg\left(\frac{r}{2}\right)}} = 2\pi\sqrt{\frac{3r}{2g}}$

2. $I = \frac{mL^2}{12} + mx^2$

$$T = 2\pi\sqrt{\frac{I}{mgd}} = 2\pi\sqrt{\frac{\frac{mL^2}{12} + mx^2}{mgx}} = 2\pi\sqrt{\frac{1}{g}\left(\frac{L^2}{12x} + x\right)}$$

Let $\quad y = \frac{L^2}{12x} + x$

For T to be minimum, y should be minimum.

So, $\quad \frac{dy}{dx} = -\frac{L^2}{12x^2} + 1 = 0 \quad \Rightarrow \quad x = \frac{L}{2\sqrt{3}}$

$$T_{min} = 2\pi\sqrt{\frac{1}{g}\left(\frac{L^2}{12\left(\frac{L}{2\sqrt{3}}\right)} + \frac{L}{2\sqrt{3}}\right)} = 2\pi\sqrt{\frac{L}{\sqrt{3}g}}$$

3.

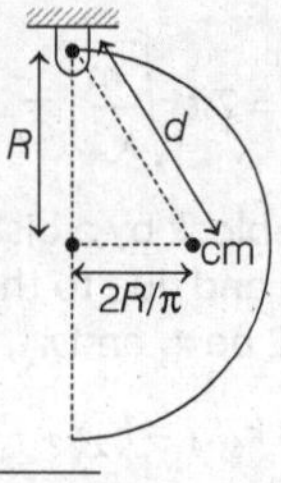

$$d = \sqrt{\left(\frac{2R}{\pi}\right)^2 + R^2},\ I = 2mR^2$$

$$f = \frac{1}{2\pi}\sqrt{\frac{mgd}{I}} = \frac{1}{2\pi}\sqrt{\frac{mg\sqrt{\left(\frac{2R}{\pi}\right)^2 + R^2}}{2mR^2}}$$

$$= \frac{1}{2\pi}\sqrt{\frac{g}{2R}\sqrt{1 + \frac{4}{\pi^2}}}$$

4. $I = I_1 + I_2 = \frac{mL^2}{3} + \left(\frac{mL^2}{12} + mL^2\right) = \frac{17}{12}mL^2$

$$d = \frac{m_1 r_1 + m_2 r_2}{m_1 + m_2} = \frac{m\left(\frac{L}{2}\right) + mL}{m + m} = \frac{3L}{4}$$

$$T = 2\pi\sqrt{\frac{I}{mgd}} = 2\pi\sqrt{\frac{\frac{17}{12}mL^2}{2mg\left(\frac{3L}{4}\right)}} = 2\pi\sqrt{\frac{17L}{18g}}$$

7.9 Torsional Pendulum

1. $T = 2\pi\sqrt{\frac{I}{k}}$

$$\Rightarrow \quad 0.2 = 2\pi\sqrt{\frac{(0.2)(0.05)^2}{2k}}$$

$$\Rightarrow \quad k = 0.25 \text{ kgm}^2\text{s}^{-2}$$

2. $\tau = k\theta \quad \Rightarrow \quad 0.1 = k(1)$

$$\Rightarrow \quad k = 0.1 \text{ N-m/rad}$$

$$I = \frac{2}{5}mR^2 = \frac{2}{5} \times 25 \times (0.2)^2 = 0.4 \text{ kg - m}^2$$

$$T = 2\pi\sqrt{\frac{I}{k}} = 2\pi\sqrt{\frac{0.4}{0.1}} = 4\pi \text{ s}$$

7.10 Angular SHM

1. $\tau = -\left(k\left(\frac{L}{2}\theta\right)\frac{L}{2} + k\left(\frac{L}{2}\theta\right)\frac{L}{2}\right)$

$$\Rightarrow \quad \left(\frac{mL^2}{12}\right)\alpha = -\frac{kL^2}{2}\theta \quad \Rightarrow \quad \alpha = -\frac{6k}{m}\theta$$

$$\therefore \quad \omega = \sqrt{\frac{6k}{m}},$$

$$f = \frac{\omega}{2\pi} = \frac{1}{2\pi}\sqrt{\frac{6k}{m}}$$

2. Lets displace the rod by an angle θ from the equilibrium position.

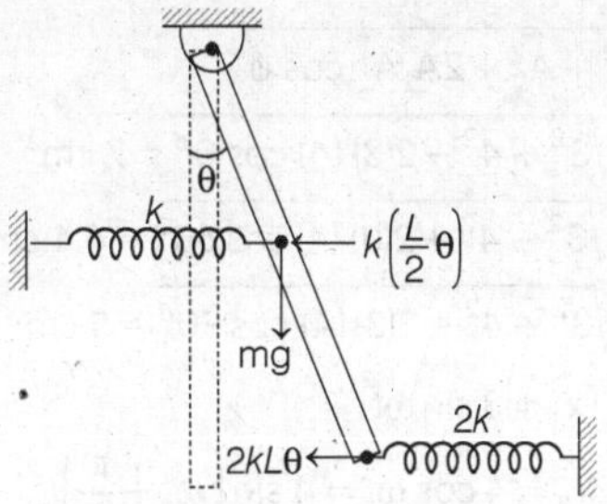

$$\tau = -\left((2kL\theta)L + \left(k\frac{L}{2}\theta\right) + mg\sin\theta\left(\frac{L}{2}\right)\right)$$

$$\Rightarrow \quad \left(\frac{mL^2}{3}\right)\alpha = -\left(\frac{9}{4}kL^2 + \frac{mgL}{2}\right)\theta$$

$$\Rightarrow \quad \alpha = -\left(\frac{27k}{4m} + \frac{3g}{2L}\right)\theta$$

$$\therefore \quad \omega = \sqrt{\frac{27k}{4m} + \frac{3g}{2l}}$$

$$f = \frac{1}{2\pi}\sqrt{\frac{27k}{4m} + \frac{3g}{2l}}$$

3. Lets displace the centre of the sphere by a distance x.

$$E = \frac{1}{2}kx^2 + \left(\frac{1}{2}mv^2 + \frac{1}{2}\left(\frac{2}{5}mR^2\right)\left(\frac{v}{R}\right)^2\right)$$

$$E = \frac{1}{2}kx^2 + \frac{7}{10}mv^2$$

$$\therefore \quad k_{eff} = k, \quad m_{eff} = \frac{7m}{5}$$

$$T = 2\pi\sqrt{\frac{m_{eff}}{k_{eff}}} = 2\pi\sqrt{\frac{7m}{5k}}$$

4. Lets displace the centre of the cylinder by a distance x.

$$E = \left(\frac{1}{2}kx^2 + \frac{1}{2}k(2x)^2\right) + \left(\frac{1}{2}mv^2 + \frac{1}{2}\left(\frac{mR^2}{2}\right)\left(\frac{v}{R}\right)^2\right)$$

$$\Rightarrow \quad E = \frac{1}{2}(5k)x^2 + \frac{1}{2}\left(\frac{3m}{2}\right)v^2$$

$$\therefore \quad k_{eff} = 5k, \quad m_{eff} = \frac{3m}{2}$$

$$T = 2\pi\sqrt{\frac{m_{eff}}{k_{eff}}} = 2\pi\sqrt{\frac{3m}{10k}}$$

5. Lets displace the block down by a distance x.

$$E = \frac{1}{2}kx^2 + \left(\frac{1}{2}mv^2 + \frac{1}{2}I\left(\frac{v}{R}\right)^2\right)$$

$$E = \frac{1}{2}kx^2 + \frac{1}{2}\left(m + \frac{I}{R^2}\right)v^2$$

$$\therefore \quad k_{eff} = x, \quad m_{eff} = m + \frac{I}{R^2}$$

$$T = 2\pi\sqrt{\frac{m_{eff}}{k_{eff}}} = 2\pi\sqrt{\frac{1}{k}\left(m + \frac{I}{R^2}\right)}$$

7.11 SHM Problems involving other Topics

1. Lets depress liquid in one of the limbs by distance x.

Restoring force = Weight of the liquid column of height 2x

$$\Rightarrow \quad F = -\rho A(2x)g$$

$$\Rightarrow \quad \rho A(2h)a = -\rho A(2x)g \quad \Rightarrow \quad a = -\frac{g}{h}x$$

$$\therefore \quad \omega = \sqrt{\frac{g}{h}}, \quad f = \frac{1}{2\pi}\sqrt{\frac{g}{h}}$$

2. Lets displace the cylinder down by a distance x from its equilibrium position.

Restoring force = Additional buoyant force

$$\Rightarrow \quad F = -\rho Axg$$

$$\Rightarrow \quad (\sigma Ah)a = -\rho Axg$$

$$\Rightarrow \quad a = -\left(\frac{\rho g}{\sigma h}\right)x$$

$$\therefore \quad \omega = \sqrt{\frac{\rho g}{\sigma h}}, \quad T = 2\pi\sqrt{\frac{\sigma h}{\rho g}}$$

3. (a) Lets displace the block down by a distance x from its equilibrium position.

Restoring force = $\Delta F_S + \Delta F_B$

$$\Rightarrow \quad F = -(kx + \rho Axg)$$

$$\Rightarrow \quad a = -\left(\frac{k + \rho Ag}{m}\right)x$$

$$\therefore \quad T = 2\pi\sqrt{\frac{m}{k + \rho Ag}}$$

(b) If the cylinder is completely immersed in the liquid, buoyant force will be constant and restoring force will be provided only by the spring.

$$\therefore \quad T = 2\pi\sqrt{\frac{m}{k}}$$

4. Lets displace the piston by a distance x towards left from its equilibrium position.

For the gas, $\quad p_0V_0 = pV$

$$\Rightarrow \quad p_0V_0 = p(V_0 - Ax)$$

$$\Rightarrow \quad p = p_0\left(\frac{V_0}{V_0 - Ax}\right)$$

$$\Rightarrow \quad p = p_0\left(1 - \frac{Ax}{V_0}\right)^{-1}$$

$$\Rightarrow \quad p = p_0\left(1 + \frac{Ax}{V_0}\right)$$

For the piston,

Restoring force = $pA - p_0A$

$$\Rightarrow \quad F = -(p - p_0)A$$

$$\Rightarrow \quad a = -\left(\frac{A^2p_0}{mV_0}\right)x$$

$$\therefore \quad T = 2\pi\sqrt{\frac{mV_0}{A^2p_0}}$$

5. (a) When the particle is at a distance x from the centre,

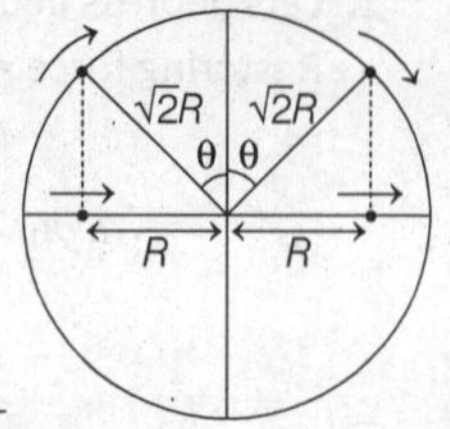

$$F = -m\left(\frac{GM}{R^3}x\right)$$

$$\Rightarrow \quad a = -\left(\frac{GM}{R^3}\right)x$$

$$\therefore \quad \omega = \sqrt{\frac{GM}{R^3}},$$

$$T = 2\pi\sqrt{\frac{R^3}{GM}} = 2\pi\sqrt{\frac{R}{g}}$$

$$v = \omega\sqrt{A^2 - x^2}$$

$$\Rightarrow \quad \sqrt{gR} = \sqrt{\frac{g}{R}}\sqrt{A^2 - R^2}$$

$$\Rightarrow \quad A = \sqrt{2}R$$

$$\sin\theta = \frac{R}{\sqrt{2}R} = \frac{1}{\sqrt{2}} \Rightarrow \theta = \frac{\pi}{4}$$

For the time taken to cross the tunnel,

$$\theta = \omega t$$

$$\Rightarrow \quad \frac{\pi}{4} + \frac{\pi}{4} = \left(\sqrt{\frac{g}{R}}\right)t$$

$$\Rightarrow \quad t = \frac{\pi}{2}\sqrt{\frac{R}{g}}$$

(b) $K_1 + U_1 = K_2 + U_2$

$$\Rightarrow \quad 0 - \frac{mgR}{1 + \frac{R}{R}} = \frac{1}{2}mv^2 - mgR$$

$$\Rightarrow \quad v = \sqrt{gR}$$

So, the particle will enter the tunnel with speed $\sqrt{gR}$.

Hence, time taken to cross the tunnel will be $\frac{\pi}{2}\sqrt{\frac{R}{g}}$.

6. $F = \left(\frac{GM}{R^3}r\right)m$

Restoring force on the particle along the tunnel $= F\cos\theta$

$$\Rightarrow \quad ma = -\frac{GMm}{R^3}r\cos\theta$$

$$\Rightarrow \quad a = -\frac{GM}{R^3}x \qquad [\because r\cos\theta = x]$$

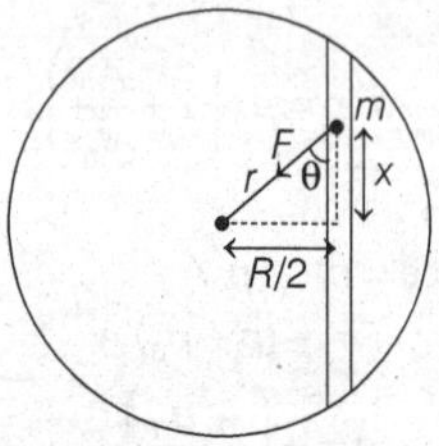

So, the particle will perform SHM

$$T = 2\pi\sqrt{\frac{R^3}{GM}} = 2\pi\sqrt{\frac{R}{g}}$$

7.12 Superposition of SHMs

1. $A = \sqrt{A_1^2 + A_2^2 + 2A_1A_2\cos\phi}$

(a) $A = \sqrt{3^2 + 4^2 + 2(3)(4)\cos 0°} = 7$ cm

(b) $A = \sqrt{3^2 + 4^2 + 2(3)(4)\cos 60°} = 6.1$ cm

(c) $A = \sqrt{3^2 + 4^2 + 2(3)(4)\cos 90°} = 5$ cm

2.

$$x_1 = 3\sin\omega t,$$

$$x_2 = 4\cos\omega t = 4\sin\left(\omega t + \frac{\pi}{2}\right)$$

$$\phi = \left(\omega t + \frac{\pi}{2}\right) - \omega t = \frac{\pi}{2}$$

(a) $A = \sqrt{3^2 + 4^2 + 2(3)(4)\cos\left(\frac{\pi}{2}\right)} = 5$

(b) $\tan\psi = \frac{A_2\sin\phi}{A_1 + A_2\cos\phi}$

$$\Rightarrow \quad \tan\psi = \frac{4\sin\left(\frac{\pi}{2}\right)}{3 + 4\cos\frac{\pi}{2}} = \frac{4}{3}$$

$$\Rightarrow \quad \psi = 53°$$

$$\therefore \quad x = 5\sin(\omega t + 53°)$$

3. $A_1 = 10$

$$A_2 = \sqrt{5^2 + (5\sqrt{3})^2} = 10$$

$$\therefore \quad \frac{A_1}{A_2} = 1:1$$

4.

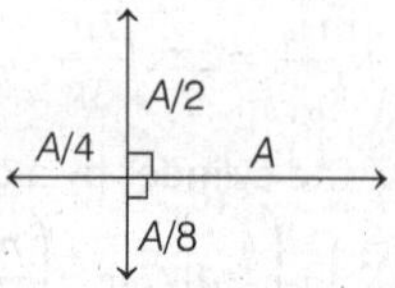

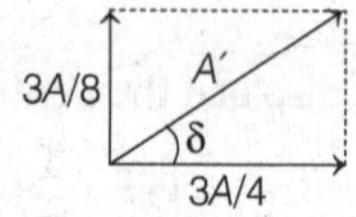

$$A' = \sqrt{\left(\frac{3A}{4}\right)^2 + \left(\frac{3A}{8}\right)^2} = \frac{3\sqrt{5}A}{8}$$

$$\tan\delta = \frac{3A/8}{3A/4}$$

$$\Rightarrow \quad \delta = \tan^{-1}\left(\frac{1}{2}\right)$$

5. Resultant amplitude

$$= a + a\cos 30° + a\cos 30°$$

$$= (\sqrt{3} + 1)\,a$$

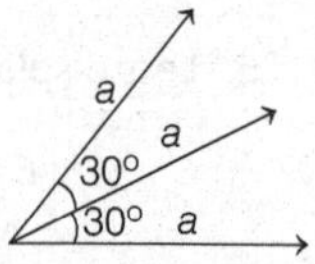

6. $\sin^2(2\pi t) + \cos^2(2\pi t) = 1$

$$\Rightarrow \quad x^2 + \left(\frac{y}{2}\right)^2 = 1$$

$$\Rightarrow \quad x^2 + \frac{y^2}{4} = 1$$

Level 02

Single Choice Correct Questions

1. Comparing the given equation with $\frac{d^2x}{dt^2} + \omega^2 x = 0$,

we get $\omega^2 = \pi^2 \Rightarrow \omega = \pi$

$$\therefore \quad f = \frac{\omega}{2\pi} = \frac{1}{2}$$

2. $A = 2, \; \frac{T}{2} = 0.3\pi$

$$\Rightarrow \quad T = 0.6\pi$$

$$\omega = \frac{2\pi}{T} = \frac{10}{3}, \quad \phi = -\frac{\pi}{2}$$

$$y = A\sin(\omega t + \phi) = 2\sin\left(\frac{10}{3}t - \frac{\pi}{2}\right)$$

3. $\omega = \frac{2\pi}{T} = \frac{2\pi}{4} = \frac{\pi}{2}$ rad/s

At $t = 1$ s,

$$a_{max} = \omega^2 A = \left(\frac{\pi}{2}\right)^2 (0.080) = 0.197\,\text{m/s}^2$$

4. $\omega = \frac{2\pi}{T} = \frac{2\pi}{6} = \frac{\pi}{3}$

$$v = A\omega\cos(\omega t + \phi) = A\frac{\pi}{3}\cos\left(\frac{\pi}{3}(t-1)\right)$$

At $t = 2$ s,

$$0.25 = A\frac{\pi}{3}\cos\left(\frac{\pi}{3}(2-1)\right) \Rightarrow A = \frac{3}{2\pi}\,\text{m}$$

5.

$$v_{max} = \omega A = 10\,\text{cm/s},$$

$$a_{max} = \omega^2 A = 50\,\text{cm/s}^2$$

$$\frac{\omega^2 A}{\omega A} = \frac{50}{10} \Rightarrow \omega = 5\,\text{rad/s}$$

$$\frac{(\omega A)^2}{\omega^2 A} = \frac{(10)^2}{50} \Rightarrow A = 2\,\text{cm}$$

$$v = \omega\sqrt{A^2 - x^2}$$

$$\Rightarrow \quad 8 = 5\sqrt{2^2 - x^2} \Rightarrow x = 1.2\,\text{cm}$$

6.

$$v = \omega\sqrt{A^2 - x^2}$$

$$30 = \omega\sqrt{A^2 - 8^2} \quad \text{...(i)}$$

$$16 = \omega\sqrt{A^2 - 15^2} \quad \text{...(ii)}$$

Dividing Eqs. (i) and (ii), we get

$$\frac{30}{16} = \sqrt{\frac{A^2 - 64}{A^2 - 225}} \Rightarrow A = 17\,\text{cm}$$

7. Substituting $A = 17$ cm, we get

$$30 = \omega\sqrt{17^2 - 8^2}$$

$$\Rightarrow \quad \omega = 2\,\text{rad/s}$$

$$\therefore \quad T = \frac{2\pi}{\omega} = \pi\,\text{s}$$

8. Let, the two positions be at distances x_1 and x_2 from the mean position,

$$u^2 = \omega^2(A^2 - x_1^2) \quad \text{...(i)}$$

$$v^2 = \omega^2(A^2 - x_2^2) \quad \text{...(ii)}$$

$$a = \omega^2 x_1 \quad \text{...(iii)}$$

$$b = \omega^2 x_2 \quad \text{...(iv)}$$

Subtracting Eq. (ii) from Eq. (i), we get

$$u^2 - v^2 = \omega^2(x_2^2 - x_1^2) \quad \text{...(v)}$$

Adding, Eqs. (iii) and (iv), we get

$$a + b = \omega^2(x_1 + x_2) \quad \text{...(vi)}$$

Dividing Eq. (v) by Eq. (vi),

$$x_2 - x_1 = \frac{u^2 - v^2}{a + b}$$

9. $|a| = v$

$$\Rightarrow \quad \omega^2 x = \omega\sqrt{A^2 - x^2} \Rightarrow \omega^2(1) = \omega\sqrt{2^2 - 1^2}$$

$$\Rightarrow \quad \omega = \sqrt{3}\,\text{rad/s}$$

$$f = \frac{\omega}{2\pi} = \frac{\sqrt{3}}{2\pi}\,\text{s}^{-1}$$

10. $F = -kx$

$$\Rightarrow \quad -13.5 = -k(1.5) \Rightarrow k = 9$$

$$T = 2\pi\sqrt{\frac{m}{k}} = 2\pi\sqrt{\frac{1}{9}} = \frac{2\pi}{3}\,\text{s}$$

11. $v^2 = 9(12 - x^2) = \omega^2(A^2 - x^2)$

$$\therefore \quad \omega^2 = 9$$

$$|a| = \omega^2 x = 9(0.03) = 0.27\,\text{m/s}^2$$

12. (b)

13. The particle will first come to rest at the right extreme position.

$$\therefore \quad 50\pi t_1 + \frac{\pi}{5} = \pi$$

$$\Rightarrow \quad t_1 = 16 \times 10^{-3}\,\text{s}$$

Now, the particle will come to rest after every $\frac{T}{2}$ interval

$$T = \frac{2\pi}{\omega} = \frac{2\pi}{50\pi} = 40 \times 10^{-3}\,\text{s}$$

Time when the particle comes to rest for the 9th time,

$$t_9 = t_1 + 8\left(\frac{T}{2}\right) = 176 \times 10^{-3}\,\text{s}$$

14. $\theta = \omega t = \left(\frac{2\pi}{18}\right)39 = \frac{13\pi}{3}$

$$\frac{13\pi}{3} = 2(2\pi) + \frac{\pi}{3}$$

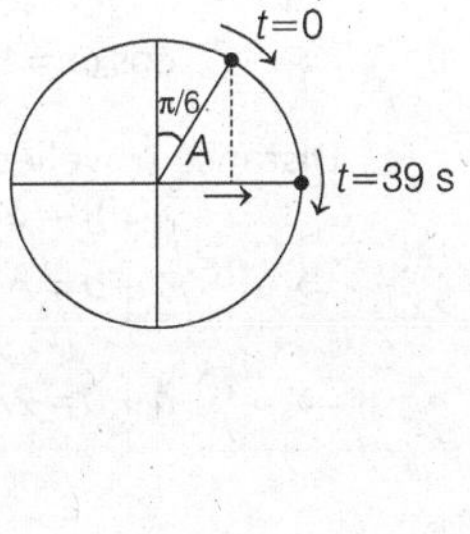

In one complete oscillation, particle travels distance equal to 4A.

Total distance travelled

$$= 2(4A) + A\cos\left(\frac{\pi}{3}\right)$$

$$= 24 + 1.5 = 25.5\,\text{cm}$$

15. $x = a\sin\left(\frac{2\pi}{T}t\right)$

At $t = \frac{T}{8}$, $x = a\sin\left(\frac{2\pi}{T}\left(\frac{T}{8}\right)\right) = \frac{a}{\sqrt{2}}$

16. $v = \omega\sqrt{A^2 - x^2}$

$\Rightarrow \quad \sqrt{3}b\omega = \omega\sqrt{A^2 - b^2}$

$\Rightarrow \quad A = 2b$

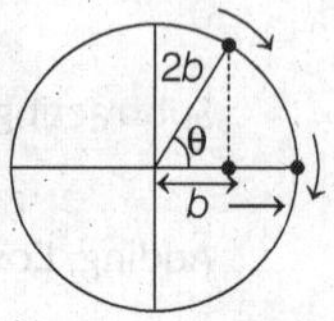

$\cos\theta = \frac{b}{2b} = \frac{1}{2} \quad \Rightarrow \quad \theta = \frac{\pi}{3}$

$\theta = \omega t \quad \Rightarrow \quad \frac{\pi}{3} = \omega t$

$\Rightarrow \quad t = \frac{\pi}{3\omega}$

17. $\sin\alpha = \frac{4}{5} \quad \Rightarrow \quad \alpha = 53°$

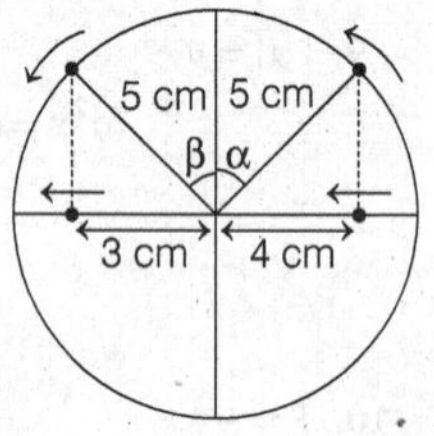

$\sin\beta = \frac{3}{5} \quad \Rightarrow \quad \beta = 37°$

$\theta = \alpha + \beta = 90° = \frac{\pi}{2}$ rad

$\theta = \omega t \quad \Rightarrow \quad \frac{\pi}{2} = \left(\frac{2\pi}{20}\right)t$

$\Rightarrow \quad t = 5$ s

18. $\cos\theta = \frac{4A/5}{A} = \frac{4}{5}$

$\Rightarrow \quad \theta = \cos^{-1}\left(\frac{4}{5}\right)$

$\theta = \omega t$

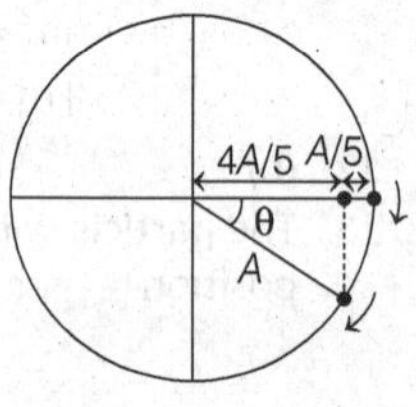

$\Rightarrow \quad \cos^{-1}\left(\frac{4}{5}\right) = \left(\frac{2\pi}{T}\right)t$

$\Rightarrow \quad t = \frac{T}{2\pi}\cos^{-1}\left(\frac{4}{5}\right)$

19. $t_{OQ} = \frac{t_{PQ}}{2} = 1$ s

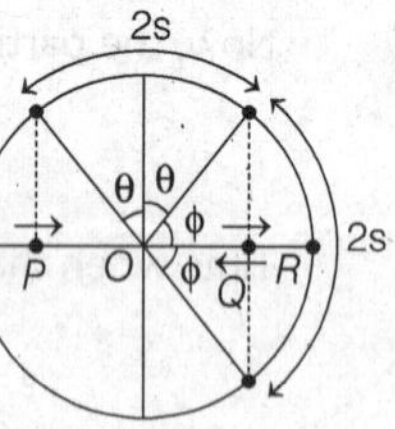

$t_{QR} = \frac{2}{2} = 1$ s

$t_{OR} = t_{OQ} + t_{QR} = 1 + 1 = 2$ s

$T = 4t_{OR} = 4(2) = 8$ s

20. Since, the particle starts from rest,

$x = A\cos\omega t$

Distance travelled in the first second,

$a = A - A\cos\omega \quad (1)$

$\Rightarrow \quad \cos\omega = 1 - \frac{a}{A}$

Distance travelled in two seconds,

$a + b = A - A\cos\omega \quad (2)$

$\Rightarrow \quad a + b = A - A(2\cos^2\omega - 1)$

$\Rightarrow \quad a + b = 2A\left(1 - \left(1 - \frac{a}{A}\right)^2\right)$

$\Rightarrow \quad a + b = 2A\left(1 + 1 - \frac{a}{A}\right)\left(1 - 1 + \frac{a}{A}\right)$

$\Rightarrow \quad a + b = 2a\left(2 - \frac{a}{A}\right) \Rightarrow A = \frac{2a^2}{3a - b}$

21. $\cos\theta = \frac{a/2}{a} = \frac{1}{2} \quad \Rightarrow \quad \theta = \frac{\pi}{3}$

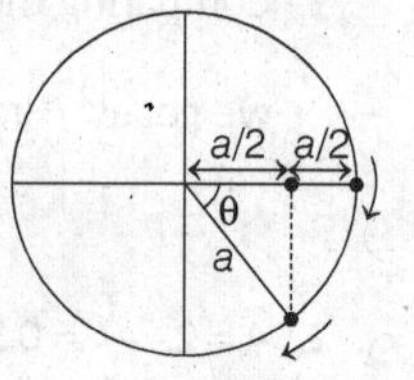

$\theta = \omega t \quad \Rightarrow \quad \frac{\pi}{3} = \left(\frac{2\pi}{T}\right)t$

$\Rightarrow \quad t = \frac{T}{6}$

$v_{avg} = \frac{a/2}{t} = \frac{a/2}{T/6} = \frac{3a}{T}$

22. At mean position, $v_1 = \omega A$

At $x = \frac{A}{2}$, $v_2 = \omega\sqrt{A^2 - \left(\frac{A}{2}\right)^2} = \frac{\sqrt{3}A\omega}{2}$

$x = A\sin\left(\frac{2\pi t}{T}\right)$

$\Rightarrow \quad \frac{A}{2} = A\sin\left(\frac{2\pi t}{T}\right) \quad \Rightarrow \quad t = \frac{T}{12}$

$a_{avg} = \left|\frac{v_2 - v_1}{t}\right| = \frac{12\pi A(2 - \sqrt{3})}{T^2}$

23.

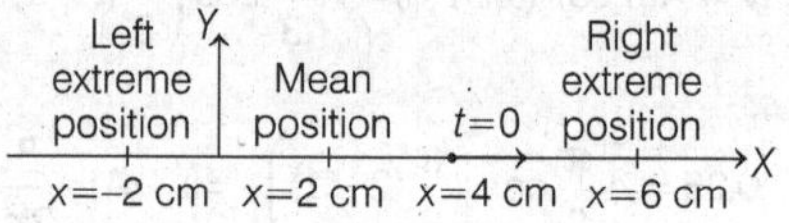

Mean position will be at $x_0 = 2$ cm

Amplitude = 4 cm

$x - x_0 = A\sin(\omega t + \phi)$

$\Rightarrow \quad x - 2 = 4\sin(\omega t + \phi)$

At $t = 0$, $x = 4$ cm,

$4 - 2 = 4\sin\phi$

$\Rightarrow \quad \sin\phi = \frac{1}{2} \quad \Rightarrow \quad \phi = 30°$

$\therefore \quad x = 2 + 4\sin(4\pi t + 30°)$

24. $\cos\theta = \frac{A/2}{A} = \frac{1}{2} \quad \Rightarrow \quad \theta = \frac{\pi}{3}$

$\cos\phi = \frac{A/2}{2A} = \frac{1}{4}$

$\Rightarrow \quad \phi = \cos^{-1}\left(\frac{1}{4}\right)$

Phase difference $= \theta + \phi$

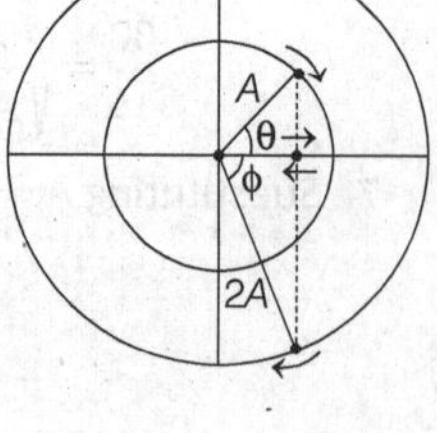

$= \frac{\pi}{3} + \cos^{-1}\left(\frac{1}{4}\right)$

$= \frac{\pi}{3} + \frac{\pi}{2} - \sin^{-1}\left(\frac{1}{4}\right)$

$= \frac{5\pi}{6} - \sin^{-1}\left(\frac{1}{4}\right)$

25. $\sin\theta = \dfrac{A/2}{A} = \dfrac{1}{2}$

$\Rightarrow \quad \theta = \dfrac{\pi}{6}$

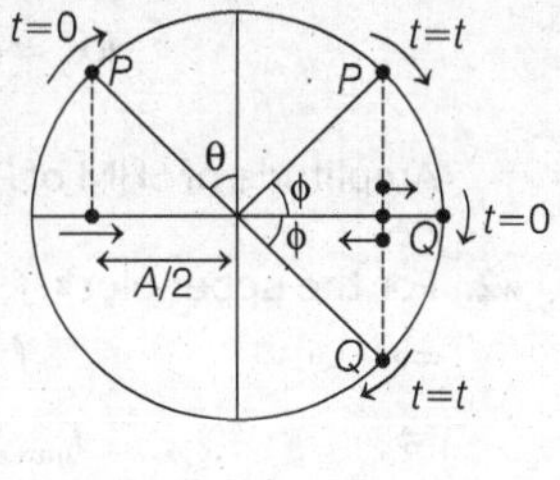

Phase difference $= \dfrac{\pi}{2} + \dfrac{\pi}{6} = \dfrac{2\pi}{3}$

When they cross each other,

$$2\phi = \frac{2\pi}{3} \Rightarrow \phi = \frac{\pi}{3}$$

For Q, $\theta = \omega t$

$$\Rightarrow \quad \frac{\pi}{3} = \left(\frac{2\pi}{T}\right)t \Rightarrow t = \frac{T}{6}$$

26. Separation is maximum when their relative velocity is zero i.e. they have same velocity.

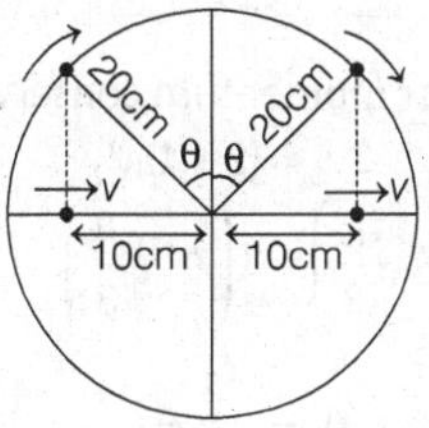

$$\sin\theta = \frac{10}{20} = \frac{1}{2} \Rightarrow \theta = \frac{\pi}{6}$$

Phase difference $= 2\theta = \dfrac{\pi}{3}$

27. $E = \dfrac{1}{2}m\omega^2A^2 = \dfrac{1}{2}m\left(\dfrac{2\pi}{T}\right)^2 A^2$

$$\Rightarrow \quad E \propto \left(\frac{A}{T}\right)^2$$

If amplitude and time period are doubled, total energy will remain same.

28. $K = \dfrac{1}{2}mv^2,$

$$\frac{K'}{K} = \left(\frac{v'}{v}\right)^2 \Rightarrow \frac{\frac{25K}{100}}{K} = \left(\frac{v'}{v}\right)^2$$

$$\Rightarrow \quad v' = \frac{v}{2} \Rightarrow A\omega\cos\omega t = \frac{A\omega}{2}$$

$$\Rightarrow \quad \cos\omega t = \frac{1}{2} \Rightarrow \omega t = \frac{\pi}{3}$$

$$\Rightarrow \quad \left(\frac{2\pi}{2}\right)t = \frac{\pi}{3} \Rightarrow t = \frac{1}{3}\text{ s}$$

29. $K_{max} + U_{min} = K_{min} + U_{max}$

$$\Rightarrow \quad K_{max} + 16 = 0 + 80$$

$$\Rightarrow \quad K_{max} = 64\text{ J}$$

$$K_{max} = \frac{1}{2}m\omega^2A^2$$

$$\Rightarrow \quad 64 = \frac{1}{2} \times 8 \times \left(\frac{2\pi}{6.28}\right)^2 A^2 \Rightarrow A = 4\text{ m}$$

30. $K = \dfrac{1}{2}mv^2 = \dfrac{1}{2}m(A\omega\cos\omega t)^2 = \dfrac{1}{2}m\omega^2A^2\left(\dfrac{1+\cos 2\omega t}{2}\right)$

So, frequency of oscillations of kinetic energy will be double that of the frequency of oscillations of the particle.

31. Velocity is a vector, means it has magnitude as well as direction. The maximum velocity at the mean position is acquired by the particle after a single time period. Other velocities occur twice between the two extreme positions.

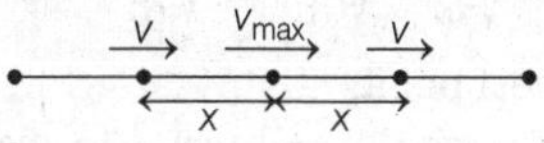

32. $U = \dfrac{1}{2}ky^2 = \dfrac{1}{2}k(a\cos\omega t)^2$

At $t = 0$, U is maximum

$$U = \frac{1}{2}kx^2$$

At $x = 0$, U is minimum

33. $a = -\omega^2A\cos\omega t$

$$\Rightarrow \quad v = -\omega A\sin\omega t$$

$$K = \frac{1}{2}mv^2 = \frac{1}{2}m\omega^2A^2\sin^2\omega t$$

34. $K = \dfrac{1}{2}m\omega^2(A^2 - x^2)$

At $x = \dfrac{\sqrt{3}}{2}A,$

$$K = \frac{1}{2}m\omega^2\left[A^2 - \left(\frac{\sqrt{3}A}{2}\right)^2\right] = \frac{1}{8}m\omega^2A^2$$

New kinetic energy $= \dfrac{1}{8}m\omega^2A^2 + \dfrac{1}{2}m\omega^2A^2$

$$= \frac{5}{8}m\omega^2A^2$$

$$\therefore \quad K' = \frac{1}{2}m\omega^2(A'^2 - x^2)$$

$$\Rightarrow \quad \frac{5}{8}m\omega^2A^2 = \frac{1}{2}m\omega^2\left[A'^2 - \left(\frac{\sqrt{3}A}{2}\right)^2\right]$$

$$\Rightarrow \quad A' = \sqrt{2}A$$

35. $F = -\dfrac{dU}{dx} = 2ax - 4bx^3$

At mean position,

$$F = 2ax_0 - 4bx_0^3 = 0$$

$$\Rightarrow \quad 2x_0(a - 2bx_0^2) = 0$$

$$\Rightarrow \quad x_0 = 0 \text{ and } x_0 = \pm\sqrt{\frac{a}{2b}}$$

Lets displace the particle by a distance y from the mean position.

$$F = 2a(x_0 + y) - 4b(x_0 + y)^3$$

$$\Rightarrow \quad F = 2a(x_0 + y) - 4bx_0^3\left(1 + \frac{y}{x_0}\right)^3$$

$$\Rightarrow \quad F = 2a(x_0 + y) - 4bx_0^3\left(1 + \frac{3y}{x_0}\right)$$

$$\Rightarrow \quad F = (2ax_0 - 4bx_0^3) + (2a - 12bx_0^2)\,y$$

$$\Rightarrow \quad F = 0 + \left(2a - 12b\left(\frac{a}{2b}\right)\right)y$$

$$\Rightarrow \quad F = -4ay$$

$$\omega = \sqrt{\frac{k}{m}} = \sqrt{\frac{4a}{m}} = 2\sqrt{\frac{a}{m}}$$

36. At the highest point,

$$mg - N = ma_{max} \Rightarrow mg - 0 = m\omega^2 A$$

$$\Rightarrow \quad g = (2\pi f)^2\,(0.5) \Rightarrow f = \frac{\sqrt{2g}}{2\pi}$$

37. $\omega = \frac{2\pi}{T} = \frac{2\pi}{2} = \pi$ rad/s

$$mg - N = ma$$

$$\Rightarrow \quad mg - 0 = m\omega^2 A$$

$$\Rightarrow \quad A = \frac{g}{\omega^2} = \frac{10}{\pi^2}$$

38. $\cos\theta = \frac{e}{2e} = \frac{1}{2}$

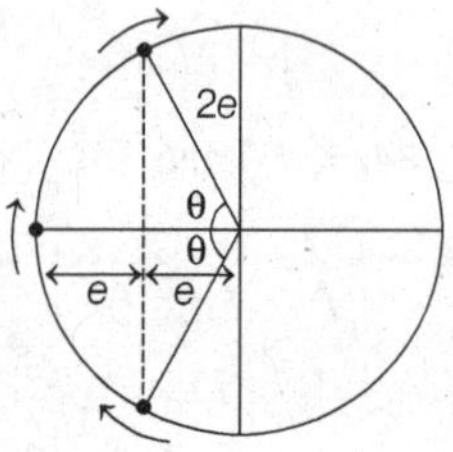

$$\Rightarrow \quad \theta = \frac{\pi}{3}$$

$$\theta = \omega t$$

$$\Rightarrow \quad 2\left(\frac{\pi}{3}\right) = \left(\sqrt{\frac{k}{m}}\right)t$$

$$\Rightarrow \quad t = \frac{2\pi}{3}\sqrt{\frac{m}{k}}$$

39. The block is in mean position initially. So,

$$v_{max} = A\omega \Rightarrow v_0 = A\omega_0 \Rightarrow A = \frac{v_0}{\omega_0}$$

$$x = A\sin\omega t \Rightarrow x = \frac{v_0}{\omega_0}\sin\omega_0 t$$

40. For the block,

$$kx_0 - mg = m\left(\frac{g}{4}\right)$$

$$\Rightarrow \quad x_0 = \frac{5mg}{4k} = \frac{5(1)(10)}{4(1)} = 12.5 \text{ cm}$$

After acceleration of elevator ceases, we have to find new mean position as initial position will be the extreme position.

$$kx_1 = mg \Rightarrow (1)\,x_1 = (1)\,(10)$$

$$\Rightarrow \quad x_1 = 10 \text{ cm}$$

Amplitude $= x_0 - x_1 = 12.5 - 10 = 2.5$ cm

41. When P and Q hang together, let elongation in the spring be x_0 in mean position.

$$kx_0 = (m_1 + m_2)\,g$$

$$\Rightarrow \quad x_0 = \frac{(m_1 + m_2)\,g}{k}$$

When Q falls, P will move up. Initial position is now lower extreme position of P.

For new mean position,

$$kx_1 = m_1 g \Rightarrow x_1 = \frac{m_1 g}{k}$$

Amplitude of SHM of $P = x_0 - x_1 = \frac{m_2 g}{k} = \frac{0.4 \times 10}{2} = 2$ cm

42. For the upper block, $f = M_2 a$

$$\Rightarrow \quad f = M_2\omega^2 x$$

$$\Rightarrow \quad f_{max} = M_2\omega^2 A$$

$$f_{max} \le f_L$$

$$\Rightarrow \quad M_2\left(\frac{k}{M_1 + M_2}\right)A \le \mu M_2 g$$

$$\Rightarrow \quad A_{max} = \frac{\mu g M_1(1+\alpha)}{k}$$

43. Applying linear momentum conservation,

$$2v_1 = (2+1)\,v_2$$

$$\Rightarrow \quad 2\left(A\sqrt{\frac{k}{2}}\right) = 3\left(A'\sqrt{\frac{k}{3}}\right) \qquad \left[\because v = A\omega = A\sqrt{\frac{k}{m}}\right]$$

$$\Rightarrow \quad A' = \sqrt{\frac{2}{3}}A$$

44. $T = 2\pi\sqrt{\frac{m}{k}} = 2\pi\sqrt{\frac{1}{1}} = 2\pi$

The block will be in contact with the spring for time interval of $\frac{T}{2}$.

So, $$t = \frac{2(10)}{v} + \frac{T}{2} = \frac{20}{2} + \frac{2\pi}{2} = (10 + \pi)\text{ s}$$

45. Applying linear momentum conservation,

$$(0.02)\,3 + 0.98(0) = (0.02 + 0.98)\,v$$

$$\Rightarrow \quad v = 0.06 \text{ m/s}$$

At mean position, $v_{max} = A\omega$

$$\Rightarrow \quad 0.06 = A\left(\sqrt{\frac{300}{1}}\right) \Rightarrow A = 0.35 \text{ cm}$$

46. $T = 2\pi\sqrt{\frac{m}{k}}$

$$\Rightarrow \quad \frac{T_S}{T_P} = \sqrt{\frac{k_P}{k_S}} = \sqrt{\frac{2k}{k/2}} = 2$$

47. $k_1 l_1 = k_2 l_2$

$$\Rightarrow \quad k_1(3l_2) = k_2 l_2$$

$$\Rightarrow \quad k_2 = 3k_1$$

Let $k_A = k$,

$$k_B = k_2 + k_2 + k_2 = 3k_2 = 9k$$

$$T = 2\pi\sqrt{\frac{m}{k}}$$

$$\Rightarrow \quad \frac{T_A}{T_B} = \sqrt{\frac{k_B}{k_A}} = \sqrt{\frac{9k}{k}} = 3$$

48. $k_1 = \frac{k(k)}{k+k} = \frac{k}{2}$,

$$k_2 = \frac{(2k)\,k}{2k+k} = \frac{2k}{3}$$

$$f = \frac{1}{2\pi}\sqrt{\frac{k}{m}}$$

$$\Rightarrow \quad \frac{f_1}{f_2} = \sqrt{\frac{k_1}{k_2}} = \sqrt{\frac{k/2}{2k/3}} = \frac{\sqrt{3}}{2}$$

49. The two springs to the left of the block are in series. The rest all are in parallel.

$$k_1 = \frac{(2k)(2k)}{2k+2k} = k$$

$$k_{eff} = k_1 + k_2 + k_3 = k + k + 2k = 4k$$

$$f = \frac{1}{2\pi}\sqrt{\frac{k_{eff}}{M}} = \frac{1}{2\pi}\sqrt{\frac{4k}{M}}$$

50. $\omega_1 = \sqrt{\frac{k}{m_1}} = \sqrt{k}$, $\quad \omega_2 = \sqrt{\frac{k}{m_2}} = \frac{\sqrt{k}}{2}$

$$\omega_{rel} = \omega_1 - \omega_2 = \frac{\sqrt{k}}{2} \quad \Rightarrow \quad \omega_{rel} = \frac{2\pi}{T}$$

$$\Rightarrow \quad \frac{\sqrt{k}}{2} = \frac{2\pi}{4} \quad \Rightarrow k = \pi^2$$

51. Velocity at mean position, $v = A\omega$

$$v_P = \frac{A}{2}\sqrt{\frac{k}{m}}, \quad v_Q = A\sqrt{\frac{k}{m}}$$

Applying linear momentum conservation,

$$mv_P + m(-v_Q) = 2m(-v_{P+Q})$$

$$\Rightarrow \quad m\left(\frac{A}{2}\sqrt{\frac{k}{m}}\right) + m\left(-A\sqrt{\frac{k}{m}}\right) = 2m\left(-A'\sqrt{\frac{2k}{2m}}\right)$$

$$\Rightarrow \quad A' = \frac{A}{4}$$

52. $T = \frac{T_1}{2} + \frac{T_2}{2} = \pi\sqrt{\frac{m}{k}} + \pi\sqrt{\frac{m}{2k}}$

$$f = \frac{1}{T} = \frac{1}{\pi}(2-\sqrt{2})\sqrt{\frac{k}{m}}$$

53. $k_{eff} = \frac{(2k)\,k}{2k+k} = \frac{2k}{3}$, $\quad \mu = \frac{m(m)}{m+m} = \frac{m}{2}$

$$T = 2\pi\sqrt{\frac{\mu}{k_{eff}}} = 2\pi\sqrt{\frac{3m}{4k}}$$

54. $x = A\sin\omega t = 5\sin 2t$

$$T = \frac{2\pi}{\omega} = \frac{2\pi}{2} = \pi$$

For simple pendulum, $T = 2\pi\sqrt{\frac{l}{g}}$

$$\Rightarrow \quad \pi = 2\pi\sqrt{\frac{l}{10}} \quad \Rightarrow l = 2.5\text{ m}$$

55. $a = \frac{d^2y}{dt^2} = -7.5\text{ m/s}^2$

$$g_{eff} = g + a = 10 - 7.5 = 2.5\text{ m/s}^2$$

$$T = 2\pi\sqrt{\frac{l}{g}}, \quad T' = 2\pi\sqrt{\frac{l}{g_{eff}}}$$

$$\therefore \quad \frac{T'}{T} = \sqrt{\frac{g}{g_{eff}}}$$

$$\Rightarrow \quad \frac{T'}{2} = \sqrt{\frac{10}{2.5}} \quad \Rightarrow \quad T' = 4\text{ s}$$

56. $T_S = 2\pi\sqrt{\frac{m}{k}}, T_P = 2\pi\sqrt{\frac{l}{g_{eff}}}$

T_S is independent of acceleration of the elevator.

57. $$mg_{eff} = mg - B$$

$$\Rightarrow \quad \sigma V g_{eff} = \sigma V g - \left(\frac{\sigma}{10}\right)Vg$$

$$\Rightarrow \quad g_{eff} = \frac{9g}{10}$$

$$T = 2\pi\sqrt{\frac{l}{g}}, \; T' = 2\pi\sqrt{\frac{l}{g_{eff}}} = 2\pi\sqrt{\frac{10l}{9g}}$$

$$\therefore \quad \frac{T'}{T} = \sqrt{\frac{10}{9}} \quad \Rightarrow \quad T' = \left(\sqrt{\frac{10}{9}}\right)T$$

58. $\omega_1 = \sqrt{\frac{g}{l_1}} = \frac{\sqrt{g}}{1.1}$, $\quad \omega_2 = \sqrt{\frac{g}{l_2}} = \sqrt{g}$

$$\omega_{rel} = \omega_2 - \omega_1 = \frac{\sqrt{g}}{11}$$

$$t = \frac{2\pi}{\omega_{rel}} = \frac{22\pi}{\sqrt{g}}$$

Number of oscillations of the shorter pendulum $= \frac{t}{T_2}$

$$= \frac{22\pi/\sqrt{g}}{2\pi/\sqrt{g}} = 11$$

59. $T = 2\pi\sqrt{\frac{1}{g\left(\frac{1}{l}+\frac{1}{R}\right)}} = 2\pi\sqrt{\frac{1}{g\left(\frac{1}{R}+\frac{1}{R}\right)}} = 2\pi\sqrt{\frac{R}{2g}}$

60. $T = 2\pi\sqrt{\frac{l_{eff}}{g}} = 2\pi\sqrt{\frac{l\sin 60°}{g}} = 2\pi\sqrt{\frac{\sqrt{3}L}{2g}}$

61. $I = I_{cm} + md^2 = \frac{mR^2}{2} + mR^2 = 1.5mR^2$

$$T_1 = T_2$$

$$\Rightarrow \quad 2\pi\sqrt{\frac{I}{mgd}} = 2\pi\sqrt{\frac{l}{g}}$$

$$\Rightarrow \quad l = \frac{I}{md} = \frac{1.5mR^2}{mR} = 1.5R = 1.5\text{ m}$$

62. $f = \frac{1}{2\pi}\sqrt{\frac{mgd}{I}} = \frac{1}{2\pi}\sqrt{\frac{mg(L/2)}{(mL^2/3)}} = \frac{1}{2\pi}\sqrt{\frac{3g}{2L}}$

$$\therefore \quad f \propto \frac{1}{\sqrt{L}}$$

$$\Rightarrow \quad \frac{f_1}{f_2}=\sqrt{\frac{L_2}{L_1}} \quad \Rightarrow \quad \frac{f_0}{f_2}=\sqrt{\frac{L/2}{L}}$$

$$\Rightarrow \quad f_2=\sqrt{2}f_0$$

63. $I=\frac{ml^2}{3}+\frac{ml^2}{3}=\frac{2}{3}ml^2$

$$T=2\pi\sqrt{\frac{I}{mgd}}=2\pi\sqrt{\frac{(2ml^2/3)}{(2m)\,g\left(\frac{l}{2}\cos 45^\circ\right)}}$$

$$=2\pi\sqrt{\frac{2\sqrt{2}l}{3g}}$$

64. $T=2\pi\sqrt{\frac{I}{mgd}}=2\pi\sqrt{\frac{\frac{mR^2}{2}+mz^2}{mgz}}=2\pi\sqrt{\frac{1}{g}\left(\frac{R^2}{2z}+z\right)}$

Let $y=\frac{R^2}{2z}+z$

To minimise T, z has to be minimised.

$$\frac{dy}{dz}=-\frac{R^2}{2z^2}+1=0 \quad \Rightarrow \quad z=\frac{R}{\sqrt{2}}$$

65. The length of the pendulum is the distance between the point of suspension and the centre of gravity of the sphere. The centre of gravity (CG) of a sphere is at its centre when it is empty and completely filled with water.

The CG falls below the centre of the sphere as the water flows out until the sphere is half full after which the CG begins to rise. Hence, the effective length of the pendulum (and hence time period) will increase at first and decrease until the sphere is empty when it becomes equal to the time period when the sphere was full of water.

66. $f=\frac{1}{2\pi}\sqrt{\frac{I}{C}}=\frac{1}{2\pi}\sqrt{\frac{ml^2}{12C}} \quad \Rightarrow \quad f\propto\sqrt{\frac{ml^2}{12C}}$

67. $y_1=2A\cos^2\omega t=A(1+\cos 2\omega t)$

$\therefore \quad A_1=A$ and $\omega_1=2\omega$

$$y_2=A(\sin\omega t+\sqrt{3}\cos\omega t)=2A\sin(\omega t+\phi)$$

$\therefore \quad A_2=2A, \omega_2=\omega$

$$v_{max\,1}=A_1\omega_1, v_{max\,2}=A_2\omega_2$$

$\therefore \quad \frac{v_{max\,1}}{v_{max\,2}}=\frac{A_1\omega_1}{A_2\omega_2}=1,$

$$\frac{a_{max\,1}}{a_{max\,2}}=\frac{\omega_1^2A_1}{\omega_2^2A_2}=2$$

68. $\sin\omega t=\frac{x}{2},$

$$\cos\omega t=\sqrt{1-\sin^2\omega t}=\sqrt{1-\frac{x^2}{4}}$$

$$y=2\sin\left(\omega t+\frac{\pi}{4}\right)$$

$$\Rightarrow \quad y=\sqrt{2}\,(\sin\omega t+\cos\omega t)$$

$$\Rightarrow \quad y=\sqrt{2}\left(\frac{x}{2}+\sqrt{1-\frac{x^2}{4}}\right)$$

$$\Rightarrow \quad \sqrt{2}y-x=\sqrt{4-x^2}$$

$$\Rightarrow \quad 2y^2+x^2-2\sqrt{2}\,xy=4-x^2$$

$$\Rightarrow \quad x^2+y^2-\sqrt{2}xy-2=0$$

This is an equation of ellipse.

69. $y=y_1+y_2=A(\sin\omega t+\cos\omega t)=\sqrt{2}A\sin\left(\omega t+\frac{\pi}{4}\right)$

$$E=\frac{1}{2}m\omega^2A^2=\frac{1}{2}m\omega^2(\sqrt{2}A)^2=m\omega^2A^2$$

70. For superposition of x_1 and x_2,

$$A'=\sqrt{A^2+A^2+2(A)(A)\cos\left(\frac{2\pi}{3}\right)}=A$$

$$\psi=\tan^{-1}\left[\frac{A\sin\left(\frac{2\pi}{3}\right)}{A+A\cos\left(\frac{2\pi}{3}\right)}\right]=\tan^{-1}(\sqrt{3})=\frac{\pi}{3}$$

$$(x_1+x_2)+x_3=0$$

$$\Rightarrow \quad A\sin\left(\omega t+\frac{\pi}{3}\right)+B\sin(\omega t+\phi)=0$$

$$\Rightarrow \quad B\sin(\omega t+\phi)=-A\sin\left(\omega t+\frac{\pi}{3}\right)$$

$$\Rightarrow \quad B\sin(\omega t+\phi)=A\sin\left(\omega t+\frac{\pi}{3}+\pi\right)$$

$$\Rightarrow \quad B\sin(\omega t+\phi)=A\sin\left(\omega t+\frac{4\pi}{3}\right)$$

$$\therefore \quad B=A, \phi=\frac{4\pi}{3}$$

71. $y=\sin^2\pi t=\frac{1}{2}(1-\cos 2\pi t)$

$$T=\frac{2\pi}{\omega}=\frac{2\pi}{2\pi}=1\text{ s}$$

So, it is SHM with a period of 1 s.

72. $F=F_1+F_2$

$$\Rightarrow \quad m\omega^2x=m\omega_1^2x+m\omega_2^2x$$

$$\Rightarrow \quad \omega^2=\omega_1^2+\omega_2^2$$

$$\Rightarrow \quad \left(\frac{2\pi}{T}\right)^2=\left(\frac{2\pi}{T_1}\right)^2+\left(\frac{2\pi}{T_2}\right)^2$$

$$\Rightarrow \quad T=\frac{T_1T_2}{\sqrt{T_1^2+T_2^2}}$$

Numerical Value Questions

1.

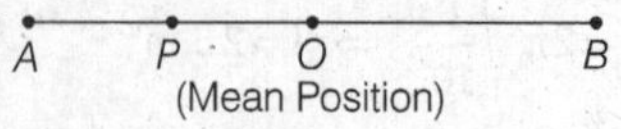

Time to go from P to A and back to $P=0.5$ s

Time to go from P to B and back to $P = 1.5$ s

$\therefore \quad T = 0.5 + 1.5 = 2$ s

$$\omega = \frac{2\pi}{T} = \pi \text{ rad/s}$$

Time to go from A to $P = \frac{0.5}{2} = 0.25$ s

Lets say the particle starts from A.

$\therefore \quad v = v_{max} \sin \omega t$

At P, $\quad 3\sqrt{2} = v_{max} \sin(\pi(0.25))$

$$\Rightarrow \quad 3\sqrt{2} = v_{max}\left(\frac{1}{\sqrt{2}}\right) \quad \Rightarrow \quad v_{max} = 6 \text{ m/s}$$

2.

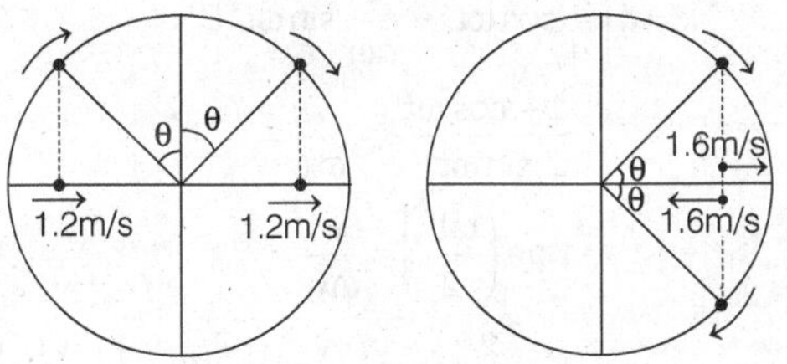

$$A\omega \cos\theta = 1.2 \quad \text{...(i)}$$

$$A\omega \cos(90° - \theta) = 1.6$$

$$\Rightarrow \quad A\omega \sin\theta = 1.6 \quad \text{...(ii)}$$

Squaring and adding Eqs. (i) and (ii), we get

$$A\omega = \sqrt{(1.2)^2 + (1.6)^2} \quad \Rightarrow \quad v_{max} = 2 \text{ m/s}$$

3. $K = \frac{1}{2} m\omega^2 A^2$

$$\Rightarrow \quad 8 \times 10^{-3} = \frac{1}{2} \times 0.1 \times \omega^2 \times (0.1)^2$$

$$\Rightarrow \quad \omega = 4 \text{ rad/s}$$

$$A = 0.1, \quad b = \omega = 4$$

$$10Ab = 10(0.1)(4) = 4$$

4. At extreme position,

$$E = K_{min} + U_{max} = 0 + 10 = 10 \text{ J}$$

At mean position,

$$K_{max} = \frac{1}{2} \times 2 \times (\sqrt{8})^2 = 8 \text{ J}$$

$$E = K_{max} + U_{min}$$

$$\Rightarrow \quad 10 = 8 + U_{min} \quad \Rightarrow \quad U_{min} = 2 \text{ J}$$

At $x = \frac{A}{2}$, $v = \omega\sqrt{A^2 - \left(\frac{A}{2}\right)^2} = \frac{\sqrt{3}}{2} A\omega = \frac{\sqrt{3}}{2} \times \sqrt{8} = \sqrt{6}$ m/s

$$K = \frac{1}{2} mv^2 = \frac{1}{2} \times 2 \times (\sqrt{6})^2 = 6 \text{ J}$$

$$E = K + U$$

$$\Rightarrow \quad 10 = 6 + U_0 \quad \Rightarrow \quad U_0 = 4 \text{ J}$$

5. $F = m\omega^2 x$,

$$F_{max} = m\omega^2 A = 10\sqrt{2} \text{ N}$$

$$K = U$$

$$\Rightarrow \quad \frac{1}{2} m\left[\omega\sqrt{A^2 - x^2}\right]^2 = \frac{1}{2} m\omega^2 x^2$$

$$\Rightarrow \quad x = \pm\frac{A}{\sqrt{2}}$$

$$F = m\omega^2\left(\frac{A}{\sqrt{2}}\right) = \frac{10\sqrt{2}}{\sqrt{2}} = 10 \text{ N}$$

6. For block A,

$$a_{max} = \omega^2 A = (25)^2 (1.6 \times 10^{-2}) = 10 \text{ m/s}^2$$

When A is at the lower extreme position,

For A, $kx - mg = ma$

$$\Rightarrow \quad kx - 1(10) = 1(10)$$

$$\Rightarrow \quad kx = 20 \text{ N}$$

For B, $\quad \Sigma F = 0$

$$\Rightarrow \quad N_{max} = mg + kx = 40 + 20 = 60 \text{ N}$$

When A is at the upper extreme position,

For A, $\quad mg - kx = ma$

$$\Rightarrow \quad 1(10) - kx = 1(10)$$

$$\Rightarrow \quad kx = 0$$

For B, $\quad N_{min} = mg - kx = 40 - 0 = 40 \text{ N}$

$$\therefore \quad \frac{N_{max}}{N_{min}} = \frac{60}{40} = 1.5$$

7. For equilibrium of block P,

$$\Sigma F = 0 \quad \Rightarrow \quad kx_1 = mg + kx_2$$

$$\Rightarrow \quad k(0.2) = mg + k(0.1) \quad \Rightarrow \quad \frac{m}{k} = 0.01$$

$$T = 2\pi\sqrt{\frac{m}{k_{eff}}} = 2\pi\sqrt{\frac{m}{2k}} = 2\pi\sqrt{\frac{0.01}{2}} = \frac{\pi}{5\sqrt{2}} \text{ s}$$

$$\therefore \quad N = 5$$

8. $I = ml^2 + m(2l)^2 = 5ml^2$, $d = \frac{3l}{2}$

$$T_1 = T_2$$

$$\Rightarrow \quad 2\pi\sqrt{\frac{I}{mgd}} = 2\pi\sqrt{\frac{l'}{g}}$$

$$\Rightarrow \quad \frac{5ml^2}{2mg\left(\frac{3l}{2}\right)} = \frac{l'}{g} \quad \Rightarrow \quad l' = \frac{5l}{3}$$

$$\therefore \quad x = 5$$

9. Lets displace the rod by an angle θ from its equilibrium position

$$\tau = -\left[k(l\theta)l + K(l\theta)l - (mg \sin\theta)\frac{l}{2}\right]$$

$$\Rightarrow \quad \left(\frac{ml^2}{3}\right)\alpha = -\left(2kl^2 - \frac{mgl}{2}\right)\theta$$

$$\Rightarrow \quad \alpha = -\left(\frac{6k}{m} - \frac{3g}{2l}\right)\theta$$

$$\therefore \quad \omega = \sqrt{\frac{6k}{m} - \frac{3g}{2l}} = \sqrt{\frac{9g}{2l}} = \sqrt{\frac{9(10)}{2(1.25)}} = 6 \text{ rad/s}$$

10. Lets displace the cart by a distance x from its mean position,

$$E=\frac{1}{2}kx^2+\frac{1}{2}mv^2+2\left[\frac{1}{2}mv^2+\frac{1}{2}\left(\frac{mR^2}{2}\right)\left(\frac{v}{R}\right)^2\right]$$

$$\Rightarrow \quad E=\frac{1}{2}kx^2+\frac{1}{2}(4m)v^2$$

$$T=2\pi\sqrt{\frac{m_{\text{eff}}}{k_{\text{eff}}}}=2\pi\sqrt{\frac{4m}{k}}=2\times 2\pi\sqrt{\frac{m}{k}}$$

$$\therefore \quad \beta=2$$

Level 3

Single Choice Correct Questions

1. $\sin\phi_1=\frac{A/\sqrt{2}}{A}=\frac{1}{\sqrt{2}}$

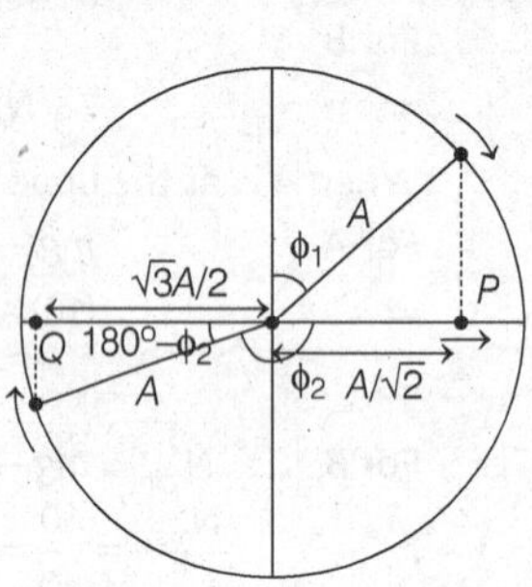

$$\Rightarrow \quad \phi_1=\frac{\pi}{4}$$

$$\cos(\pi-\phi_2)=\frac{\sqrt{3}A/2}{A}=\frac{\sqrt{3}}{2}$$

$$\Rightarrow \quad \pi-\phi_2=\frac{\pi}{6}$$

$$\Rightarrow \quad \phi_2=\frac{5\pi}{6}$$

$$\therefore \quad \phi_2-\phi_1=\frac{5\pi}{6}-\frac{\pi}{4}=\frac{7\pi}{12}$$

2. $T_A=16$ s, $\quad \omega_A=\frac{2\pi}{T_A}=\frac{\pi}{8}$ rad/s

$$T_B=24\text{ s},\ \omega_B=\frac{2\pi}{T_B}=\frac{\pi}{12}\text{ rad/s}$$

$$\frac{(v_{\max})_A}{(v_{\max})_B}=\frac{\omega_A A_A}{\omega_B A_B}=\frac{(\pi/8)(10)}{(\pi/12)(5)}=3$$

3. Separation will be maximum when their relative velocity is zero i.e., they have the same velocity.

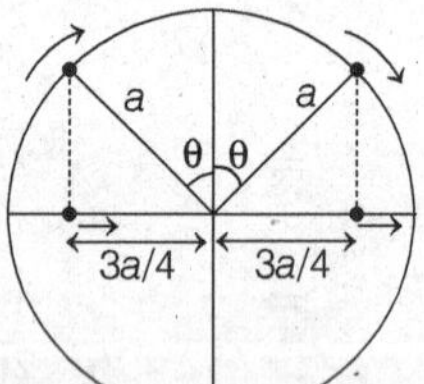

$$\sin\theta=\frac{3a/4}{a}=\frac{3}{4}$$

$$\cos\theta=\sqrt{1-\sin^2\theta}$$

$$=\sqrt{1-\left(\frac{3}{4}\right)^2}=\frac{\sqrt{7}}{4}$$

When they have the same displacement from mean position,

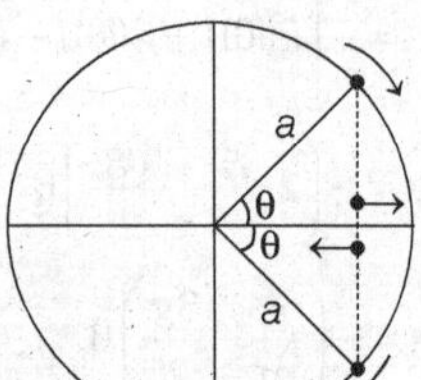

$$x=a\cos\theta=a\left(\frac{\sqrt{7}}{4}\right)$$

4. Let the particle is at P at an instant t starting from mean position and it returns to P again after interval t'.

Then, $\quad x=a\sin\omega t \quad$ ...(i)

Also, $\quad x=a\sin\omega(t+t') \quad$ ...(ii)

From Eq. (i),

$$v=\frac{dx}{dt}=a\omega\cos\omega t$$

$$\Rightarrow \quad \cos\omega t=\frac{v}{a\omega} \quad \text{...(iii)}$$

From Eq. (ii),

$$x=a[\sin\omega t\cos\omega t'+\cos\omega t\sin\omega t']$$

$$\Rightarrow \quad x=a\left[\frac{x}{a}\cos\omega t'+\frac{v}{a\omega}\sin\omega t'\right]$$

$$\Rightarrow \quad \frac{1-\cos\omega t'}{\sin\omega t'}=\frac{v}{\omega x}$$

$$\Rightarrow \quad \tan\left(\frac{\omega t'}{2}\right)=\frac{v}{\omega x}$$

$$\Rightarrow \quad t'=\frac{2}{\omega}\tan^{-1}\left(\frac{v}{\omega x}\right)=\frac{T}{\pi}\tan^{-1}\left(\frac{vT}{2\pi x}\right)$$

5. $U=k|x|^3$, $\quad U_{\max}=ka^3$

$$E=\frac{1}{2}m\omega^2a^2=ka^3$$

$$\Rightarrow \quad \omega=\sqrt{\frac{2ka}{m}}$$

$$T=\frac{2\pi}{\omega}=2\pi\sqrt{\frac{m}{2ka}}$$

$$\therefore \quad T\propto\frac{1}{\sqrt{a}}$$

6. $F=-\frac{dU}{dx}=-10(x-2)$

So, the particle executes SHM.

$$F=-10(x-2)=0 \Rightarrow x=2\text{ m}$$

So, mean position is at $x=2$ m and hence speed will be maximum.

$$T=2\pi\sqrt{\frac{m}{k}}=2\pi\sqrt{\frac{0.1}{10}}=\frac{\pi}{5}\text{ s}$$

7. $\quad K=\frac{1}{4}E$

$$\Rightarrow \quad \frac{1}{2}m\omega^2(A^2-x^2)=\frac{1}{4}\left(\frac{1}{2}m\omega^2A^2\right)$$

$$\Rightarrow \quad x=\frac{\sqrt{3}A}{2}$$

Distance between B and $D=2x=\sqrt{3}A=\sqrt{3}R$

8. For $x<0$, $U=\frac{1}{2}kx^2$

$$\Rightarrow \quad F=-\frac{dU}{dx}=-kx$$

So, the motion is SHM $\quad t_1=\pi\sqrt{\frac{m}{k}}$

For $x > 0$, $U = mgx$

$\Rightarrow$ $F = -\dfrac{dU}{dx} = -mg$

So, the motion is under constant gravity.

At $x = 0, E = K + U$

$\Rightarrow$ $E = K + 0 \Rightarrow K = E$

$\therefore$ $\dfrac{1}{2}mu^2 = E$

$\Rightarrow$ $u = \sqrt{\dfrac{2E}{m}}$

$$t_2 = \frac{2u}{g} = 2\sqrt{\frac{2E}{mg^2}}$$

Time period $= t_1 + t_2 = \pi\sqrt{\dfrac{m}{k}} + 2\sqrt{\dfrac{2E}{mg^2}}$

9. $y = \sin\omega t + \sqrt{3}\cos\omega t = 2\sin\left(\omega t + \dfrac{\pi}{3}\right)$

For the body at the upper extreme position,

$$mg - N = m\omega^2 A$$

$\Rightarrow$ $mg - 0 = m\omega^2 A$ [$\because N = 0$ for losing contact]

$\Rightarrow$ $\omega = \sqrt{\dfrac{g}{A}} = \sqrt{\dfrac{g}{2}}$

$$\omega t + \frac{\pi}{3} = \frac{\pi}{2}$$

$\Rightarrow$ $\left(\sqrt{\dfrac{g}{2}}\right)t = \dfrac{\pi}{6}$

$\Rightarrow$ $t = \dfrac{\sqrt{2}}{6}\dfrac{\pi}{\sqrt{g}}$

10. The block will lose contact when the spring first acquires the natural length.

$$\sin\theta = \frac{x_0}{2x_0} = \frac{1}{2} \Rightarrow \theta = \frac{\pi}{6}$$

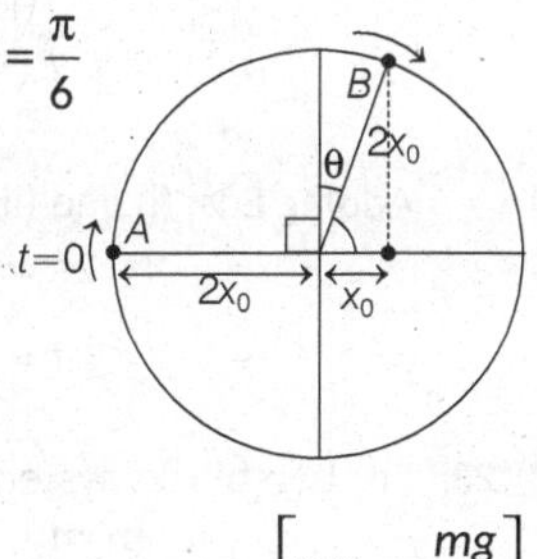

$$\omega t_{AB} = \theta$$

$\Rightarrow$ $\left(\sqrt{\dfrac{k}{m}}\right)t_{AB} = \dfrac{\pi}{2} + \dfrac{\pi}{6}$

$\Rightarrow$ $t_{AB} = \dfrac{2\pi}{3}\sqrt{\dfrac{m}{k}}$

$\Rightarrow$ $t_{AB} = \dfrac{2\pi}{3}\sqrt{\dfrac{x_0}{g}}$ $\left[\because x_0 = \dfrac{mg}{k}\right]$

At B, $v = \omega\sqrt{A^2 - x^2} = \sqrt{\dfrac{k}{m}}\sqrt{(2x_0)^2 - x_0^2} = \sqrt{3gx_0}$

For the motion under gravity,

$$t' = \frac{2v}{g} = 2\sqrt{3}\sqrt{\frac{x_0}{g}}$$

Time period $= T = 2t_{AB} + t'$

$$= 2\sqrt{\frac{x_0}{g}}\left(\frac{2\pi}{3} + \sqrt{3}\right)$$

11. At the upper extreme position,

$$mg - (F_S)_{min} = m\omega^2 A$$

$\Rightarrow$ $(F_S)_{min} = mg - m\left(\dfrac{2\pi}{T}\right)^2 A$

$$= mg - \frac{4\pi^2}{T^2}mA$$

12. $F_{avg} = \dfrac{mv_{max} - 0}{(T/4)} = \dfrac{mA\omega}{(\pi/2\omega)} = \dfrac{2m}{\pi}\left(\dfrac{mg}{k}\right)\left(\dfrac{k}{m}\right) = \dfrac{2mg}{\pi}$

13. The small block oscillates along the inclined plane with an amplitude A. As a result, the centre of mass of the system undergoes SHM along the horizontal direction.

$$x_{cm} = \frac{m(A\sin\omega t\cos 60°)}{M + m} = \frac{1}{2}\left(\frac{m}{M + m}\right)A\sin\omega t$$

$a_{cm} = -\omega^2 x_{cm}$ along the horizontal

f = Net horizontal force

$$= (M + m)\,a_{cm} = \frac{1}{2}m\omega^2 A\sin\omega t$$

14. The maximum tendency of slipping is at the extreme point, as acceleration is maximum at the extreme position.

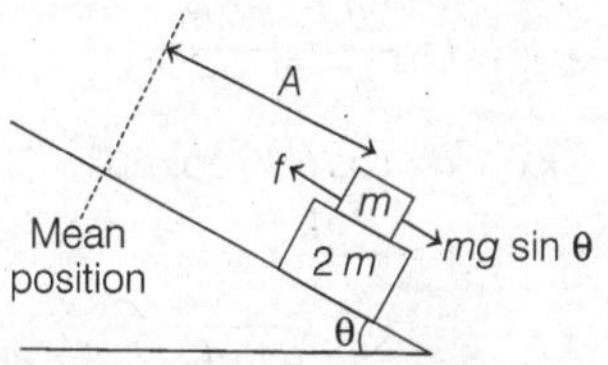

For the upper block,

$$\Sigma F = ma$$

$\Rightarrow$ $f - mg\sin\theta = m\omega^2 A$

$\Rightarrow$ $f = mg\sin\theta + m\omega^2 A$

We know that $f \le f_L$

$\Rightarrow$ $mg\sin\theta + m\omega^2 A \le \mu\,(mg\cos\theta)$

$\Rightarrow$ $mg\sin\theta + m\omega^2 A \le (2\tan\theta)(mg\cos\theta)$

$\Rightarrow$ $A_{max} = \dfrac{g\sin\theta}{\omega^2} = \dfrac{g\sin\theta}{(k/3m)} = \dfrac{3mg\sin\theta}{k}$

15. The block starts from rest. So, initially it is at the right extreme position.

At the mean position, $\Sigma F = 0$

$\Rightarrow$ $kx_0 = ma_0$

$\Rightarrow$ $x_0 = \dfrac{ma_0}{k}$

$\therefore$ Amplitude of SHM $= A = \dfrac{ma_0}{k}$

Displacement from mean position $= \dfrac{ma_0}{k}\cos\omega t$

$\therefore$ $x = -\dfrac{ma_0}{k}(1 - \cos\omega t)$

$$= -\frac{ma_0}{k} + \frac{ma_0}{k}\cos\left(\sqrt{\frac{k}{m}}\right)t$$

16. $k_{eq} = k_1 + k_2 = 2k + 3k = 5k$

At mean position, $k_{eq} x_0 = mg$

$$\Rightarrow \quad x_0 = \frac{mg}{5k}$$

$$v = \omega \sqrt{A^2 - x^2}$$

$$\Rightarrow \quad u = \sqrt{\frac{5k}{m}} \sqrt{A^2 - \left(\frac{mg}{5k}\right)^2}$$

$$\Rightarrow \quad A = \sqrt{\frac{mu^2}{5k} + \left(\frac{mg}{5k}\right)^2}$$

17. The string gets slacked when the spring starts getting compressed. Therefore, $x_0 = \dfrac{mg}{k}$

When $x = 2x_0$,

Speed of the block at $x = x_0$,

$$u = \omega \sqrt{A^2 - x^2} = \sqrt{\frac{k}{m}} \sqrt{(2x_0)^2 - x_0^2} = \sqrt{\frac{3m}{k}}\, g$$

When the string gets slacked, the block will move under the influence of only gravity.

$$t = \frac{2u}{g} = \sqrt{\frac{12m}{k}}$$

18. $F = -(kx + kx + k(x \cos 60°) \cos 60° \times 2)$

$$\Rightarrow \quad F = -\frac{5k}{2} x$$

$$\therefore \quad T = 2\pi \sqrt{\frac{m}{(5K/2)}} = 2\pi \sqrt{\frac{2m}{5k}}$$

19. Let the maximum elongations in the springs be x_1 and x_2, respectively.

$$x_1 + x_2 = A \quad \text{...(i)}$$

$$k_1 x_1 = k_2 x_2 \quad \text{...(ii)}$$

From Eqs. (i) and (ii), we get

$$x_1 = \frac{k_2 A}{k_1 + k_2}$$

$\therefore$ Amplitude of point $P = x_1 = \dfrac{k_2 A}{k_1 + k_2}$

20.

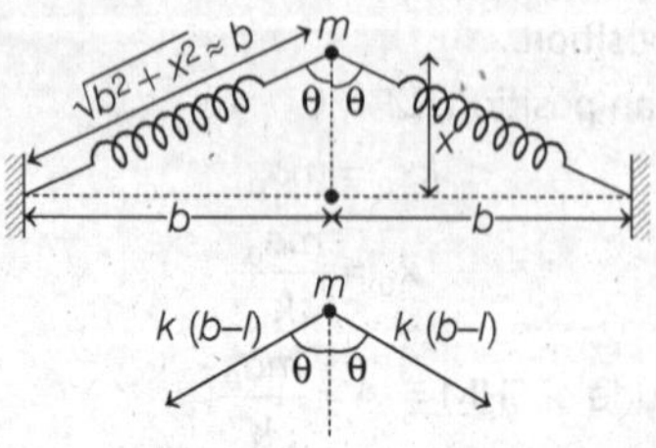

$$F = -2k(b - l) \cos \theta$$

$$\Rightarrow \quad F = -2k(b - l)\left(\frac{x}{b}\right)$$

$$\Rightarrow \quad F = -\left(\frac{2k(b - l)}{b}\right) x$$

$$\therefore \quad T = 2\pi \sqrt{\frac{mb}{2k(b - l)}}$$

21. When the wedge is displaced by a distance x towards left,

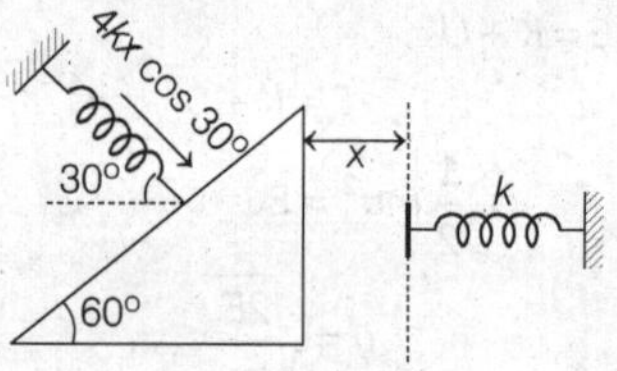

$$F = -(4kx \cos 30°) \cos 30°$$

$$\Rightarrow \quad F = -(\sqrt{3}k)\, x$$

$$t_1 = \frac{T_1}{2} = \pi \sqrt{\frac{m}{\sqrt{3}k}}$$

When the wedge is displaced by a distance x towards right,

$$F = -kx$$

$$t_2 = \frac{T_2}{2} = \pi \sqrt{\frac{m}{k}}$$

$$T = t_1 + t_2 = \pi \sqrt{\frac{m}{k}} \left[1 + \frac{1}{\sqrt{3}}\right]$$

22. $\omega_1 = \sqrt{\dfrac{k}{m_1}} = 20 \text{ rad/s}$

$$\omega_2 = \sqrt{\frac{k}{m_2}} = \frac{20}{3} \text{ rad/s}$$

$$\pi + \theta = \omega_1 t \quad \text{...(i)}$$

$$\pi - \theta = \omega_2 t \quad \text{...(ii)}$$

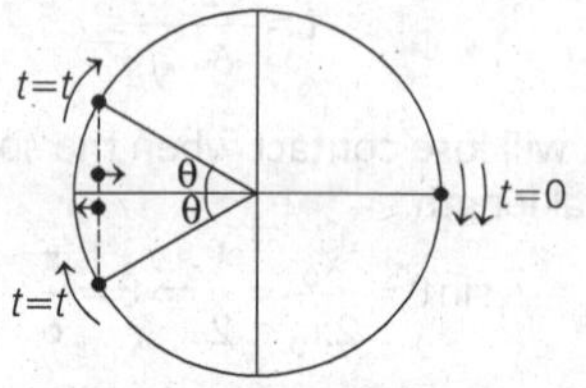

Adding Eqs. (i) and (ii), we get

$$2\pi = (\omega_1 + \omega_2)\, t$$

$$\Rightarrow \quad t = \frac{2\pi}{\omega_1 + \omega_2} = \frac{3\pi}{40} \text{ s}$$

23. For two blocks system,

$$\mu = \frac{m_1 m_2}{m_1 + m_2} = \frac{(2)(2)}{2 + 2} = 1 \text{ kg}$$

$$\therefore \quad T = 2\pi \sqrt{\frac{\mu}{k}} = 2\pi \sqrt{\frac{1}{\pi^2}} = 2 \text{ s}$$

The rear block will be in contact with the spring as long as the spring is compressed.

$$\therefore \quad t = \frac{T}{2} = 1 \text{ s}$$

24. Let the velocities of the two blocks be v_1 and v_2 when the rear block separates from the spring.

From linear momentum conservation,

$$2 \times 10 + 2 \times 0 = 2v_1 + 2v_2$$

$$\Rightarrow \quad v_1 + v_2 = 10 \quad \text{...(i)}$$

From energy conservation,

$$K_1 + U_1 = K_2 + U_2$$

$$\Rightarrow \quad \left(\frac{1}{2} \times 2 \times 10^2 + 0\right) + 0 = \left(\frac{1}{2} \times 2v_1^2 + \frac{1}{2} \times 2v_2^2\right) + 0$$

$$\Rightarrow \quad v_1^2 + v_2^2 = 100 \quad \text{...(ii)}$$

Solving Eqs. (i) and (ii), we get

$$v_1 = 0 \text{ and } v_2 = 10 \text{ m/s}$$

25. $\Sigma F_y = 0$

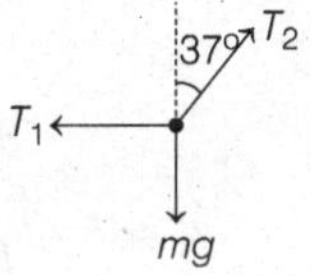

$$\Rightarrow \quad T_2 \cos 37° = mg$$

$$\Rightarrow \quad T_2 = \frac{5mg}{4}$$

$$\Sigma F_x = ma_x$$

$$\Rightarrow \quad (T_1)_{max} - T_2 \sin 37° = m\omega^2 A$$

$$\Rightarrow \quad (T_1)_{max} = m\omega^2 A + T_2 \sin 37°$$

$$= (1)(5)^2(0.1) + \frac{5(1)(10)}{4}\left(\frac{3}{5}\right) = 10 \text{ N}$$

$$T_2 \sin 37° - (T_1)_{min} = m\omega^2 A$$

$$\Rightarrow \quad (T_1)_{min} = T_2 \sin 37° - m\omega^2 A = 5 \text{ N}$$

$$\therefore \quad \frac{(T_1)_{max}}{(T_1)_{min}} = 2$$

26. x = Distance moved by the rod

x_1 = Extension in the left spring

x_2 = Extension in the right spring

$$T = 3kx_1 = kx_2$$

$$\Rightarrow \quad x_2 = 3x_1$$

Constraint relation, $x_1 + x_2 = 2x$

$$\Rightarrow \quad x_1 + 3x_1 = 2x$$

$$\Rightarrow \quad x_1 = \frac{x}{2} \text{ and } x_2 = \frac{3x}{2}$$

$$F = -(3kx_1 + kx_2)$$

$$\Rightarrow \quad F = -\left[3k\left(\frac{x}{2}\right) + k\left(\frac{3x}{2}\right)\right]$$

$$\Rightarrow \quad F = -3kx$$

$$\therefore \quad T = 2\pi\sqrt{\frac{m}{3k}}$$

27. Let displace the plank by a distance x.

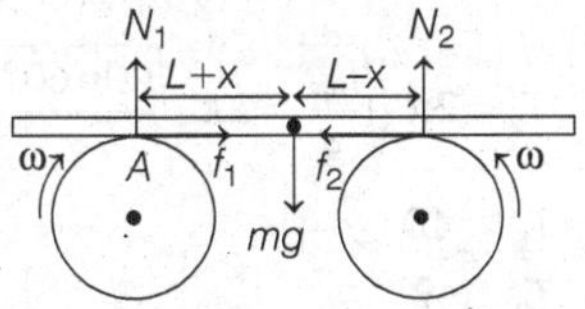

$$\Sigma F_y = 0$$

$$\Rightarrow \quad N_1 + N_2 = mg \quad \text{...(i)}$$

$$\Sigma \tau = 0$$

$$\Rightarrow \quad N_1(L + x) = N_2(L - x) \quad \text{...(ii)}$$

From Eqs. (i) and (ii), we get

$$N_1 = \left(\frac{L - x}{2L}\right) mg$$

and

$$N_2 = \left(\frac{L + x}{2L}\right) mg$$

Restoring force on plank $= f_2 - f_1$

$$\Rightarrow \quad F = -\mu(N_2 - N_1)$$

$$\Rightarrow \quad F = -\left(\frac{\mu mg}{L}\right)x$$

$$\therefore \quad T = 2\pi\sqrt{\frac{m}{(\mu mg / L)}} = 2\pi\sqrt{\frac{L}{\mu g}}$$

28. Lets displace the block by a distance x from its mean position.

Constraint relation,

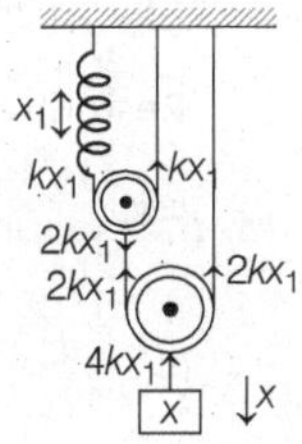

$$x_1 = 4x$$

Restoring force $= 4kx_1$

$$\Rightarrow \quad F = -4k(4x)$$

$$\Rightarrow \quad F = -16kx$$

$$\therefore \quad T = 2\pi\sqrt{\frac{m}{16k}} = \frac{\pi}{2}\sqrt{\frac{m}{k}}$$

29.

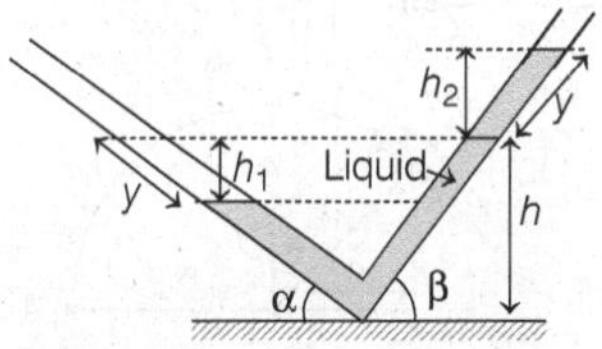

$$m = \rho A\left(\frac{h}{\sin\alpha} + \frac{h}{\sin\beta}\right) = \frac{\rho Ah(\sin\alpha + \sin\beta)}{\sin\alpha \sin\beta}$$

Initially the level of liquid in the two limbs will be at the same height. If the liquid is depressed by y in one limb, it will rise by y along the length of the tube in the other limb. The force that is responsible for restoring the liquid levels in the two arms of the tube is,

$$F = -\Delta pA = -(h_1 + h_2)\rho gA$$

$$\Rightarrow \quad F = -(y \sin\alpha + y \sin\beta)\rho gA$$

$$\Rightarrow \quad F = -[\rho gA(\sin\alpha + \sin\beta)]y$$

$$\therefore \quad f = \frac{1}{2\pi}\sqrt{\frac{k}{m}} = \frac{1}{2\pi}\sqrt{\frac{g \sin\alpha \sin\beta}{h}}$$

30. Lets depress the liquid on one side as shown in figure.

$$F = -\Delta pA$$

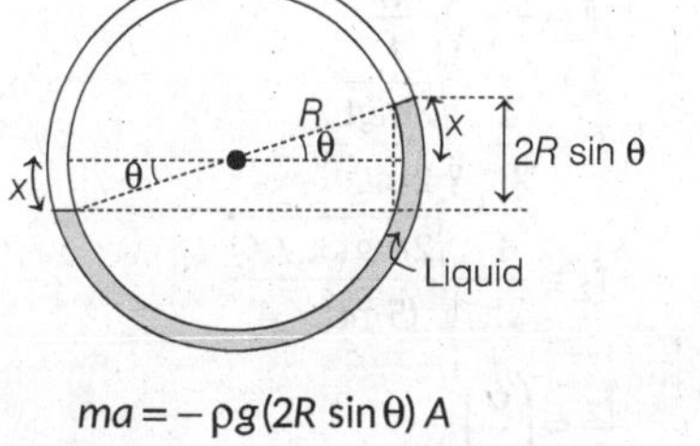

$$\Rightarrow \quad ma = -\rho g(2R \sin\theta) A$$

$$\Rightarrow \quad [\rho A(\pi R)]\, a = -\rho g(2R\theta)\, A$$

$$\Rightarrow \quad a = -\left(\frac{2g}{\pi R}\right)x \qquad [\because R\theta = x]$$

$$\therefore \quad \omega = \sqrt{\frac{2g}{\pi R}}$$

31. Here interface acts as the mean position of SHM.

$$\therefore \quad T = \frac{T_1}{2} + \frac{T_2}{2} = \pi\sqrt{\frac{\rho h}{\rho_1 g}} + \pi\sqrt{\frac{\rho h}{\rho_2 g}}$$

32. Let displace the ball down by distance y.

$$B = \frac{\Delta p}{\Delta V / V} \quad \Rightarrow \quad B = \frac{\Delta p}{ay / V}$$

$$\Rightarrow \quad \Delta p = \left(\frac{Ba}{V}\right)y$$

Restoring force $= -(\Delta p)\, a$

$$\Rightarrow \quad F = -\left(\frac{Ba^2}{V}\right)y$$

$$\therefore \quad T = 2\pi\sqrt{\frac{mV}{Ba^2}}$$

33. $\sin\theta = \dfrac{\alpha}{\beta} \quad \Rightarrow \quad \theta = \sin^{-1}\left(\dfrac{\alpha}{\beta}\right)$

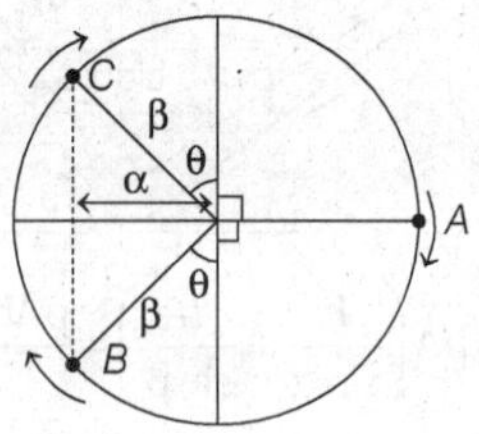

$$\theta = \omega t$$

$$\Rightarrow \quad \frac{\pi}{2} + \sin^{-1}\left(\frac{\alpha}{\beta}\right) = \left(\sqrt{\frac{g}{L}}\right)t_{AB}$$

$$\Rightarrow \quad t_{AB} = \sqrt{\frac{L}{g}}\left[\frac{\pi}{2} + \sin^{-1}\left(\frac{\alpha}{\beta}\right)\right]$$

$$T = t_{AB} + t_{CA} = 2t_{AB} = 2\sqrt{\frac{L}{g}}\left[\frac{\pi}{2} + \sin^{-1}\left(\frac{\alpha}{\beta}\right)\right]$$

34. $I_1 = 2mL^2, \quad d_1 = L$

$$I_2 = mL^2 + m\left(\frac{L}{2}\right)^2 = \frac{5}{4}mL^2, \quad d_2 = \frac{3L}{4}$$

$$f = \frac{1}{2\pi}\sqrt{\frac{mgd}{I}}$$

$$f_1 = \frac{1}{2\pi}\sqrt{\frac{2mgL}{2mL^2}},$$

$$f_2 = \frac{1}{2\pi}\sqrt{\frac{2mg(3L/4)}{(5mL^2/4)}}$$

$$\therefore \quad \frac{f_2}{f_1} = \left(\frac{6}{5}\right)^{1/2}$$

35.

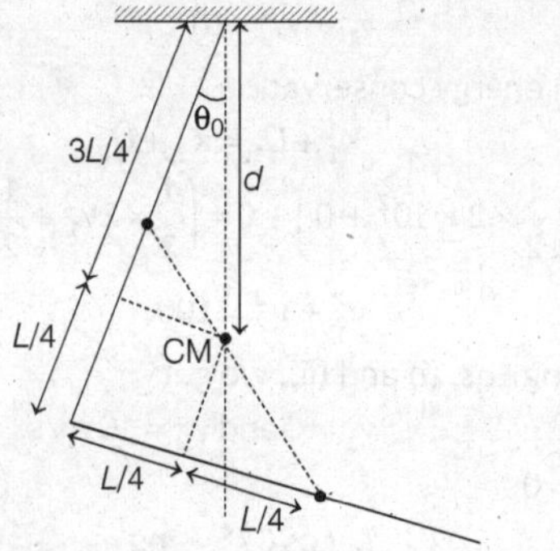

$$d = \sqrt{\left(\frac{3L}{4}\right)^2 + \left(\frac{L}{4}\right)^2} = \frac{L}{4}\sqrt{10}$$

$$I = I_1 + I_2$$

$$= \left(\frac{M}{2}\right)\frac{L^2}{3} + \left[\left(\frac{M}{2}\right)\frac{L^2}{12} + \frac{M}{2}\left(L^2 + \left(\frac{L}{2}\right)^2\right)\right] = \frac{5}{6}mL^2$$

$$f = \frac{1}{2\pi}\sqrt{\frac{mgd}{I}} = \frac{1}{2\pi}\sqrt{\frac{Mg\left(\frac{L}{4}\sqrt{10}\right)}{\left(\frac{5}{6}mL^2\right)}} = \frac{1}{2\pi}\sqrt{\frac{3g}{\sqrt{10}L}}$$

36.

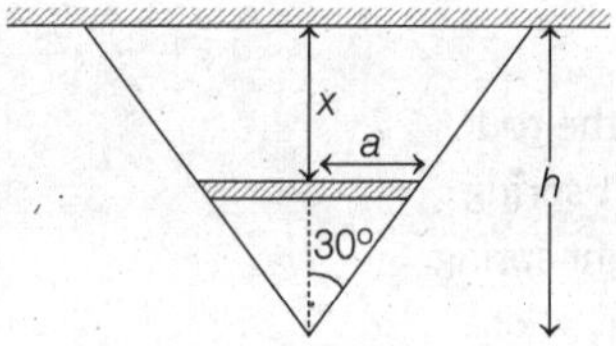

$$\tan 30° = \frac{a}{h-x} \quad \Rightarrow \quad a = \frac{h-x}{\sqrt{3}}$$

$$I = \int dmx^2 = \int_0^h \sigma\,(2a)\, dx\, x^2$$

$$= \frac{2\sigma}{\sqrt{3}}\int_0^h (hx^2 - x^3)\, dx = \frac{\sigma h^4}{6\sqrt{3}} = \frac{mh^2}{6}$$

$$T = 2\pi\sqrt{\frac{I}{mgd}} = 2\pi\sqrt{\frac{(mh^2/6)}{mg(h/3)}} = 2\pi\sqrt{\frac{h}{2g}} = \pi\sqrt{\frac{2h}{g}}$$

37. $T_1 = 2\pi\sqrt{\dfrac{I}{mgd}} = 2\pi\sqrt{\dfrac{\dfrac{ml^2}{12} + m\left(\dfrac{\sqrt{3}l}{2}\right)^2}{mg\left(\dfrac{\sqrt{3}l}{2}\right)}} = 2\pi\sqrt{\dfrac{5l}{3\sqrt{3}g}}$

$$T_2 = 2\pi\sqrt{\frac{l_{\text{eff}}}{g}} = 2\pi\sqrt{\frac{l\sin 60°}{g}} = 2\pi\sqrt{\frac{\sqrt{3}l}{2g}}$$

$$\therefore \quad \frac{T_1^2}{T_2^2} = \frac{10}{9}$$

38. For vertical oscillations,

$$T_1 = 2\pi\sqrt{\frac{m}{k}}$$

For torsional oscillations,

$$T_2 = 2\pi\sqrt{\frac{I}{C}} = 2\pi\sqrt{\frac{mR^2}{2C}}$$

$$T_1 = T_2$$

$$\Rightarrow \quad 2\pi\sqrt{\frac{m}{k}} = 2\pi\sqrt{\frac{mR^2}{2C}}$$

$$\Rightarrow \quad R = \sqrt{\frac{2C}{k}}$$

39. $x^2 = 4ay \quad \Rightarrow \quad y = \dfrac{x^2}{4a}$

$$\tan\theta = \frac{dy}{dx} = \frac{x}{2a}$$

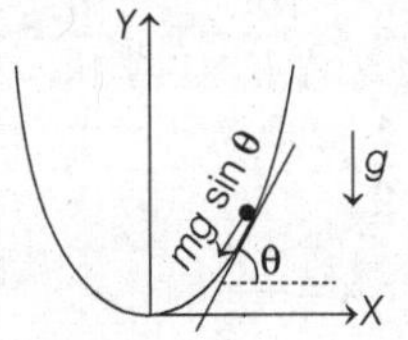

Restoring force $= mg\sin\theta$

$$\Rightarrow \quad F = -mg\theta \qquad [\because \sin\theta \approx \theta \text{ for small } \theta]$$

$$\Rightarrow \quad ma = -mg\left(\frac{x}{2a}\right) \qquad [\because \tan\theta \approx \theta = \frac{x}{2a}]$$

$$\Rightarrow \quad a = -\left(\frac{g}{2a}\right)x$$

$$\therefore \quad \omega = \sqrt{\frac{g}{2a}}$$

40.

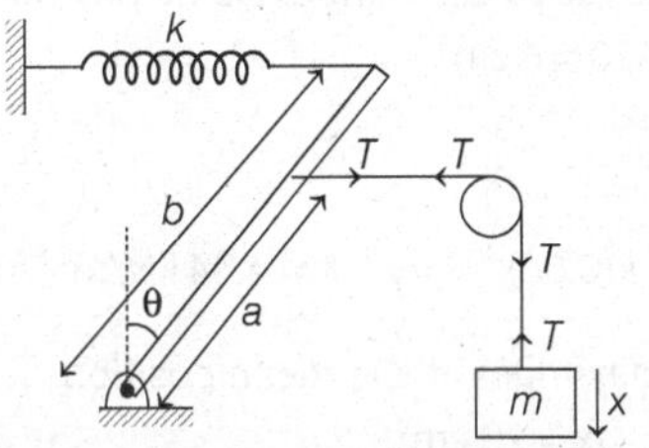

Lets displace the rod by an angle θ from its mean position.

For massless rod, $\Sigma\tau = 0$

$$\Rightarrow \quad k(b\theta)b = Ta$$

$$\Rightarrow \quad T = \left(\frac{kb^2}{a}\right)\theta$$

For the block,

Restoring force $= T$

$$\Rightarrow \quad F = -\left(\frac{kb^2}{a}\right)\theta$$

$$\Rightarrow \quad ma = -\left(\frac{kb^2}{a}\right)\left(\frac{x}{a}\right)$$

$$\Rightarrow \quad a = -\left(\frac{kb^2}{ma^2}\right)x$$

$$\therefore \quad T = 2\pi\frac{a}{b}\sqrt{\frac{m}{k}}$$

41. When the rod is displaced by an angle θ,

$$\tau = -\left[k(L\theta)L + k\left(\frac{L}{2}\theta\right)\frac{L}{2}\right]$$

$$\Rightarrow \quad \frac{ML^2}{3}\alpha = -\frac{5kL^2}{4}\theta$$

$$\Rightarrow \quad \alpha = -\left(\frac{15k}{4M}\right)\theta$$

$$\therefore \quad f = \frac{1}{2\pi}\sqrt{\frac{15k}{4M}}$$

42. Lets displace the centre of sphere by a distance x from the mean position.

$$v_{cm} = \omega'(R-r)$$

$$v_{cm} = \frac{d\theta}{dt}(R-r)$$

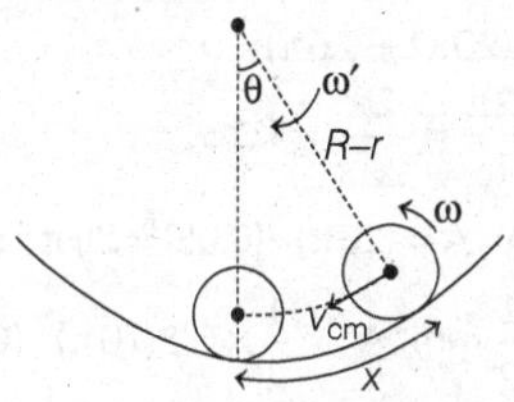

$$E = mg(R-r)(1-\cos\theta) + \left(\frac{1}{2}mv_{cm}^2 + \frac{1}{2}I_{cm}\omega^2\right)$$

$$\Rightarrow \quad E = mg(R-r)(1-\cos\theta) + \left[\frac{1}{2}mv_{cm}^2 + \frac{1}{2}\left(\frac{2mr^2}{5}\right)\left(\frac{v_{cm}}{r}\right)^2\right]$$

$$\Rightarrow \quad E = mg(R-r)(1-\cos\theta) + \frac{7}{10}mv_{cm}^2$$

Differentiating both sides w.r.t. t

$$0 = mg(R-r)\sin\theta\frac{d\theta}{dt} + \frac{7}{10}m(2v_{cm})\frac{dv_{cm}}{dt}$$

$$\Rightarrow \quad 0 = mgv_{cm}\theta + \frac{7}{5}mv_{cm}a_{cm}$$

$$\Rightarrow \quad 0 = g\left(\frac{x}{R-r}\right) + \frac{7}{5}a_{cm}$$

$$\Rightarrow \quad a_{cm} = -\left(\frac{5g}{7(R-r)}\right)x$$

$$\therefore \quad T = 2\pi\sqrt{\frac{7(R-r)}{5g}}$$

43. Lets displace the centre of the cylinder by a distance x.

$$E = \frac{1}{2}k(2x)^2 + \left[\frac{1}{2}m(2v)^2 + \left(\frac{1}{2}(2m)v^2 + \frac{1}{2}\left(\frac{2mR^2}{2}\right)\left(\frac{v}{R}\right)^2\right)\right]$$

$$E = \frac{1}{2}(4k)x^2 + \frac{1}{2}(7m)v^2$$

$$T = 2\pi\sqrt{\frac{m_{eff}}{K_{eff}}} = 2\pi\sqrt{\frac{7m}{4k}}$$

44. Rolling can be considered as pure rotation about the point of contact. We can consider this system as a compound pendulum oscillating about P.

$$T = 2\pi\sqrt{\frac{I_P}{mgd}}$$

$$I_P = mR^2 + mR^2 = 2mR^2$$

The centre of mass of the tube and the rod will be at a height $\frac{R}{2}$ from P.

Hence, $d = \frac{R}{2}$

$$T = 2\pi\sqrt{\frac{2mR^2}{mg\,(R/2)}} = 2\pi\sqrt{\frac{4R}{g}}$$

Multiple Choice(s) Correct Questions

1. $y = 0.05\sin(20\pi t + 1.6\pi)$

$$T = \frac{2\pi}{\omega} = \frac{2\pi}{20\pi} = 0.1\text{ s}$$

$$a_{max} = \omega^2 A = (20\pi)^2(0.05) = 20\pi^2\text{ m/s}^2$$

$$E = \frac{1}{2}m\omega^2 A^2 = \frac{1}{2}\times 0.1\,(20\pi)^2(0.05)^2 = 0.05\pi^2\text{ J}$$

$$F = -m\omega^2 y = 0$$

$\Rightarrow$ $y = 0$

2. $y = A\cos\omega t \quad \Rightarrow \quad v = -A\omega\sin\omega t$

$\Rightarrow$ $a = -A\omega^2\cos\omega t$

At $t = \frac{T}{2}, v = -A\omega\sin\left(\frac{2\pi}{T}\times\frac{T}{2}\right) = 0$

At $t = T, a = -A\omega^2\cos\left(\frac{2\pi}{T}\times T\right) = -A\omega^2$

At $t = \frac{3T}{4}, a = -A\omega^2\cos\left(\frac{2\pi}{T}\times\frac{3T}{4}\right) = 0$

$\therefore$ $F = ma = 0$

At $t = \frac{T}{2}, K = \frac{1}{2}mv^2 = 0$

$\therefore$ $E = U$

3. $\omega = \frac{2\pi}{T} = \frac{2\pi}{20} = \frac{\pi}{10}$ rad/s

$$v_{max} = A\omega = \pi$$

$\Rightarrow$ $A\left(\frac{\pi}{10}\right) = \pi$

$\Rightarrow$ $A = 10$ cm

$$a_{max} = \omega^2 A = \left(\frac{\pi}{10}\right)^2 10 = \frac{\pi^2}{10}\text{ cm/s}^2$$

At $x = 4$ cm, $v = \omega\sqrt{A^2 - x^2} = \frac{\pi}{10}\sqrt{10^2 - 4^2} = \sqrt{84}\,\frac{\pi}{10}$ cm/s

At $x = 6$ cm, $v = \omega\sqrt{A^2 - x^2} = \frac{\pi}{10}\sqrt{10^2 - 6^2} = \frac{8\pi}{10}$ cm/s

At $x = 5$ cm, $K = \frac{1}{2}m\omega^2(A^2 - x^2)$

$$= \frac{1}{2}\times 1\times\left(\frac{\pi}{10}\right)^2(10^2 - 5^2)\times 10^{-4} = \frac{3\pi^2}{8\times 10^4}\text{ J}$$

4. $v_{max} = A\omega \quad \Rightarrow \quad 10 = 2.5\omega$

$\Rightarrow$ $\omega = 4$ rad/s

$$T = \frac{2\pi}{\omega} = \frac{2\pi}{4} = 1.57\text{ s}$$

$$a_{max} = \omega^2 A = (4)^2(2.5) = 40\text{ cm/s}^2$$

$$v = \omega\sqrt{A^2 - x^2} = 4\sqrt{(2.5)^2 - 1^2} = 2\sqrt{21}\text{ cm/s}$$

5. (a) $T = \frac{T_1}{2} + \frac{T_2}{2} = \pi\sqrt{\frac{m}{k}} + \pi\sqrt{\frac{m}{4k}} = \frac{3}{2}\pi\sqrt{\frac{m}{k}}$

(b) $\frac{1}{2}(4k)x^2 = \frac{1}{2}kA^2$

$\Rightarrow$ $x = -\frac{A}{2}$

(c) $t = \frac{T_1}{4} + \frac{T_2}{8} = \frac{5\pi}{8}\sqrt{\frac{m}{k}}$

(d) $E = \frac{1}{2}kA^2$

6. (a) PE is minimum at $x = 20$ cm. So, the mean position is at $x = 20$ cm.

At $x = 26$ cm, $E = K + U$

$\Rightarrow$ $8 = K + 8 \quad \Rightarrow \quad K = 0$

So, $x = 26$ cm corresponds to the right extreme position

$$A = 26 - 20 = 6\text{ cm}$$

(b) $(PE)_{max} = \frac{1}{2}kA^2$

$\Rightarrow$ $8 = \frac{1}{2}k(0.06)^2 \quad \Rightarrow \quad k = 4.44$ kN/m

(d) Kinetic energy is maximum at the mean position i.e. $x = 20$ cm

7. (a) In equilibrium, $kx_0 = mg$

$\Rightarrow$ $x_0 = \frac{mg}{k} = \frac{0.2\times 10}{200} = 1$ cm

(b) Distance between the exteme positions $= 2A = 2$ cm

(c) $f = \frac{1}{2\pi}\sqrt{\frac{k}{m}}$

$$f = \frac{1}{2\pi}\sqrt{\frac{200}{0.2}} \simeq 5\text{ Hz}$$

(d) f is independent of the effect of gravity.

8. $T = 2\pi\sqrt{\frac{l}{g_{eff}}} = 2\pi\sqrt{\frac{l}{g + a}}$

So, time period would decrease.

At the mean position,

Angular speed $= \theta_0\omega_0 = \theta\omega$

$$\Rightarrow \quad \theta_0\sqrt{\frac{g}{l}} = \theta\sqrt{\frac{g+a}{l}}$$

$$\Rightarrow \quad \theta = \theta_0\sqrt{\frac{g}{g+a}}$$

So, the angular amplitude would decrease.

9. (a) Constant pseudo force doesn't affect the frequency of oscillation.

(b) For new mean position,

$$kx = mg + ma$$

$$\Rightarrow \quad x = \frac{m(g+a)}{k}$$

For old mean position (or new extreme position)

$$kx_0 = mg \Rightarrow x_0 = \frac{mg}{k}$$

$$A = \text{Amplitude} = x - x_0 = \frac{ma}{k}$$

(d) $v_{max} = A\omega = \frac{ma}{k}\sqrt{\frac{k}{m}} = a\sqrt{\frac{m}{k}}$

10. (a) For the bob, $\Sigma F = ma$

$$\Rightarrow \quad T_{max} - 2mg = (2m)(\omega^2 x_0)$$

$$\Rightarrow \quad T_{max} - 2mg = (2m)\left(\frac{k}{3m}\right)\left(\frac{3mg}{k}\right)$$

$$\Rightarrow \quad T_{max} = 4mg$$

(b) For $x_0 > \frac{3mg}{k}$, when the spring will get compressed, string will get slacked. Hence, $T_{min} = 0$

(d) The motion will remain simple harmonic motion

$$x_0 \le \frac{3mg}{k}$$

11. (a) Just before collision for 3 kg block,

$$v = \omega\sqrt{A^2 - x^2}$$

$$= \sqrt{\frac{900}{3}}\sqrt{2^2 - 1^2} = 30 \text{ m/s}$$

Applying linear momentum conservation for collision,

$$3 \times 30 + 6 \times 0 = (3+6)\,v$$

$$\Rightarrow \quad v = 10 \text{ m/s}$$

(c) For the combined masses,

$$v = \omega\sqrt{A^2 - x^2}$$

$$\Rightarrow \quad 10 = \sqrt{\frac{900}{9}}\sqrt{A^2 - 1^2}$$

$$\Rightarrow \quad A = \sqrt{2} \text{ m}$$

12. (a) Block will be separated at natural length of spring.

(b) $v_{max} = x_0\omega_0 = x\omega$

$$\Rightarrow \quad x_0\sqrt{\frac{k}{m_1+m_2}} = x\sqrt{\frac{k}{m_1}}$$

$$\Rightarrow \quad x = x_0\sqrt{\frac{m_1}{m_1+m_2}}$$

(c) $v_{max} = x_0\omega_0 = x_0\sqrt{\frac{k}{m_1+m_2}}$

13. $T = 2\pi\sqrt{\frac{m}{k}}$

$$\Rightarrow \quad \frac{\pi}{6} = 2\pi\sqrt{\frac{2}{k}} \quad \Rightarrow \quad k = 288 \text{ N/m}$$

For smaller mass, $f = m\omega^2 x$

$$\Rightarrow \quad f_{max} = m\omega^2 A$$

$$f_{max} = f_L \quad \Rightarrow \quad m\omega^2 A = \mu mg$$

$$\Rightarrow \quad A = \frac{\mu g}{\omega^2} = \frac{1}{144} \text{ m}$$

$$v_{max} = A\omega = \frac{1}{144}(12) = \frac{1}{12} \text{ m/s}$$

14. (a) $T = 2\pi\sqrt{\frac{I}{mgd}} = 2\pi\sqrt{\frac{ml^2/3}{mg(l/2)}} = 2\pi\sqrt{\frac{2l}{3g}}$

$$T' = 2\pi\sqrt{\frac{I'}{m'gd'}} = 2\pi\sqrt{\frac{\frac{ml^2}{3} + ml^2}{2mg\left(\frac{3l}{4}\right)}} = 2\pi\sqrt{\frac{8l}{9g}}$$

$$\therefore \quad T' = \frac{2}{\sqrt{3}}T$$

(b) Applying angular momentum conservation,

$$\left(\frac{ml^2}{3}\right)(\theta_0\omega) = \left(\frac{ml^2}{3} + ml^2\right)(\theta\omega')$$

$$\Rightarrow \left(\frac{ml^2}{3}\right)\left(\theta_0 \times \frac{2\pi}{T}\right) = \left(\frac{4}{3}ml^2\right)\left(\theta \times \frac{2\pi}{T'}\right)$$

$$\Rightarrow \quad \theta = \frac{1}{4}\left(\frac{T'}{T}\right)\theta_0 = \frac{1}{4}\left(\frac{2}{\sqrt{3}}\right)\theta_0 = \frac{\theta_0}{\sqrt{12}}$$

15. (a) Kinetic energy of the spring,

$$K_S = \int \frac{1}{2}dm v_x^2 = \frac{1}{2}\int_0^l \left(\frac{m}{l}dx\right)\left(\frac{x}{l}\right)^2 v^2 = \frac{1}{6}mv^2$$

$$K = K_S + K_{block} = \frac{1}{6}mv^2 + \frac{1}{2}(3m)\,v^2 = \frac{5}{3}mv^2$$

(c) $E = \frac{5}{3}mv^2 + \frac{1}{2}kx^2$

$$\frac{dE}{dt} = \frac{5}{3}m\,2v\frac{dv}{dt} + \frac{1}{2}k(2x)\frac{dx}{dt} = 0$$

$$\Rightarrow \quad \frac{dv}{dt} = -\left(\frac{3k}{10m}\right)x$$

$$\therefore \quad T = 2\pi\sqrt{\frac{10m}{3k}}$$

16. $F = -\frac{dU}{dx} = -aU_0 \sin ax$

For small oscillations, $\sin ax \approx ax$

$$\therefore \quad F = -a^2U_0 x$$

$$T = 2\pi\sqrt{\frac{m}{a^2U_0}}$$

Speed is maximum at the mean position i.e. at $x = 0$.
Force is maximum at extreme position.

$\therefore \quad ax_{max} = \frac{\pi}{2} \Rightarrow x_{max} = \frac{\pi}{2a}$

17. (a) $E = \frac{1}{2}kx^2 + \left[\frac{1}{2}Mv^2 + \frac{1}{2}(MR^2)\left(\frac{v}{R}\right)^2\right]$

$$E = \frac{1}{2}kx^2 + \frac{1}{2}(2M)v^2$$

$\therefore \quad \omega = \sqrt{\frac{k_{eq}}{M_{eq}}} = \sqrt{\frac{k}{2M}}$

(b) $\tau = I\alpha \Rightarrow fR = (MR^2)\alpha$

$\Rightarrow \quad f = M(R\alpha)$

$\Rightarrow \quad f = Ma_{cm}$

$\Rightarrow \quad f = -M\omega^2 x$

So, friction varies simple harmonically.

(c) At $x = 0, f = 0$

(d) $E = \frac{1}{2}kx^2 + \frac{1}{2}Mv^2$

$\therefore \quad \omega = \sqrt{\frac{k}{M}}$

18. $x = 3\sin 100t + 4(2\cos^2 50t)$

$\Rightarrow \quad x = 3\sin 100t + 4(1 + \cos 100t)$

$\Rightarrow \quad x - 4 = 3\sin 100t + 4\cos 100t$

$\Rightarrow \quad X = 3\sin 100t + 4\cos 100t$

$= 5\sin(100t + 53^\circ)$

So, the motion of the particle is SHM.

Amplitude $= \sqrt{3^2 + 4^2} = 5$ units

$x_{max} - 4 = 5 \Rightarrow x_{max} = 9$ units

19. (a) $x = x_1 + x_2 = 2\sin 10t + 4\sin\left(10t + \frac{\pi}{3}\right)$

At $t = 0$,

$$x = 0 + 4\sin\left(\frac{\pi}{3}\right) = 2\sqrt{3}\ \text{m}$$

(b) $A = \sqrt{2^2 + 4^2 + 2(2)(4)\cos\left(\frac{\pi}{3}\right)} = 2\sqrt{7}$ m

$$v_{max} = A\omega = (2\sqrt{7})(10) = 20\sqrt{7}\ \text{m/s}$$

(c) $a_{max} = A\omega^2 = (2\sqrt{7})(10)^2 = 200\sqrt{7}\ \text{m/s}^2$

(d) $E = \frac{1}{2}m\omega^2A^2 = \frac{1}{2}\times 0.02(10)^2(2\sqrt{7})^2 = 28$ J

20. $\mathbf{r} = (1 + 2\cos 2\omega t)\,\hat{\mathbf{i}} + \frac{3}{2}(2\sin^2\omega t)\,\hat{\mathbf{j}} + 3\hat{\mathbf{k}}$

$\Rightarrow \mathbf{r} = (1 + 2\cos 2\omega t)\,\hat{\mathbf{i}} + \frac{3}{2}(1 - \cos 2\omega t)\,\hat{\mathbf{j}} + 3\hat{\mathbf{k}}$

$\Rightarrow \mathbf{r} - \left(\hat{\mathbf{i}} + \frac{3}{2}\hat{\mathbf{j}} + 3\hat{\mathbf{k}}\right) = \left(2\hat{\mathbf{i}} - \frac{3}{2}\hat{\mathbf{j}}\right)\cos 2\omega t$

$\Rightarrow \quad \Delta\mathbf{r} = \left(2\hat{\mathbf{i}} - \frac{3}{2}\hat{\mathbf{j}}\right)\cos 2\omega t$

(a) For mean position, $\Delta\mathbf{r} = 0$

$\Rightarrow \quad \mathbf{r}_0 - \left(\hat{\mathbf{i}} + \frac{3}{2}\hat{\mathbf{j}} + 3\hat{\mathbf{k}}\right) = 0$

$\Rightarrow \quad \mathbf{r}_0 = \hat{\mathbf{i}} + \frac{3}{2}\hat{\mathbf{j}} + 3\hat{\mathbf{k}}$

(c) Amplitude $= \sqrt{2^2 + \left(\frac{3}{2}\right)^2} = \frac{5}{2}$ m

Comprehension Based Questions

1. $T_0 = 2\pi\sqrt{\frac{m}{k_{eff}}} = 2\pi\sqrt{\frac{m}{2k}}$

$$T = 2\pi\sqrt{\frac{m}{k}}$$

$\therefore \quad T = \sqrt{2}T_0$

2. At $x = \frac{d}{2}$,

$$v = \omega_0\sqrt{A_0^2 - x^2} = \omega\sqrt{A^2 - x^2}$$

$\Rightarrow \quad \left(\frac{2\pi}{T_0}\right)\sqrt{d^2 - \left(\frac{d}{2}\right)^2} = \left(\frac{2\pi}{T}\right)\sqrt{A^2 - \left(\frac{d}{2}\right)^2}$

$\Rightarrow \quad A^2 - \frac{d^2}{4} = \left(\frac{T}{T_0}\right)^2\left(\frac{3d^2}{4}\right)$

$\Rightarrow \quad A^2 - \frac{d^2}{4} = (\sqrt{2})^2\left(\frac{3d^2}{4}\right)$

$\Rightarrow \quad A = \frac{\sqrt{7}d}{2}$

3. $v_{max} = A\omega = \left(\frac{\sqrt{7}d}{2}\right)\left(\frac{2\pi}{\sqrt{2}T_0}\right) = \frac{\sqrt{14}\,\pi d}{2T_0}$

4. $\omega' = \sqrt{\frac{k}{M+m}} = \sqrt{\frac{2500}{100}} = 5$ rad/s

5. At $t = t_1$, $x = A\sin\omega t_1 = 10\sin 30^\circ = 5$ cm

$$v = A\omega\cos\omega t_1 = 10\left(\sqrt{\frac{2500}{25}}\right)\cos 30^\circ = 50\sqrt{3}\ \text{cm/s}$$

Applying linear momentum conservation for collision,

$$25 \times 50\sqrt{3} = (25 + 75)v'$$

$\Rightarrow \quad v' = 12.5\sqrt{3}$ cm/s

$$E = K + U$$

$$= \frac{1}{2}(100)\left(\frac{12.5\sqrt{3}}{100}\right)^2 + \frac{1}{2}(2500)(5\times 10^{-2})^2$$

$$= \frac{175}{32}\ \text{J}$$

6. $v' = \omega' \sqrt{A'^2 - x^2}$

$$\Rightarrow \quad 12.5\sqrt{3} = \sqrt{\frac{2500}{100}}\sqrt{A'^2 - 5^2}$$

$$\Rightarrow \quad A' = \frac{5\sqrt{7}}{2}\text{ cm} = \frac{\sqrt{7}}{40}\text{ m}$$

7. $E = \frac{1}{2}kx^2 + \left(\frac{1}{2}mv^2 + \frac{1}{2}I\omega^2\right)$

$$\Rightarrow \quad E = \frac{1}{2}kx^2 + \left[\frac{1}{2}(M+m)v^2 + \frac{1}{2}(MR^2)\left(\frac{v}{R}\right)^2\right]$$

$$\Rightarrow \quad E = \frac{1}{2}kx^2 + \frac{1}{2}(2M+m)v^2$$

$$\omega = \sqrt{\frac{k_{eff}}{m_{eff}}} = \sqrt{\frac{k}{2M+m}}$$

8. When water freezes,

$$E = \frac{1}{2}kx^2 + \left[\frac{1}{2}(M+m)v^2 + \frac{1}{2}(MR^2)\left(\frac{v}{R}\right)^2 + \frac{1}{2}\left(\frac{mR^2}{2}\right)\left(\frac{v}{R}\right)^2\right]$$

$$E = \frac{1}{2}kx^2 + \frac{1}{2}\left(2M + \frac{3m}{2}\right)v^2$$

$$\omega = \sqrt{\frac{k_{eff}}{m_{eff}}} = \sqrt{\frac{2k}{4M+3m}}$$

9. At the lower extreme position,

$$N_{max} - mg = m\omega^2 A$$

$$\Rightarrow \quad N_{max} - 50(10) = 50[2\pi(0.5)]^2(0.4)$$

$$\Rightarrow \quad N_{max} = 700\text{ N}$$

Maximum reading of weighing machine $= \frac{N_{max}}{g} = 70$ kg

10. $N - mg = m\omega^2 x$

$$\Rightarrow \quad 55\times 10 - 50\times 10 = 50\pi^2 x$$

$$\Rightarrow \quad x = 0.1\text{ m}$$

$$x_0 = \frac{(M+m)g}{k} = \frac{(50+10)(10)}{60\pi^2} = 1\text{ m}$$

Compression in the spring $= x_0 + x = 1.1$ m

11. $x = A\cos\omega t$

$$\Rightarrow \quad v = -A\omega\sin\omega t$$

$$\Rightarrow \quad -0.2\pi = -0.4\pi\sin\pi t$$

$$\Rightarrow \quad \pi t = \frac{\pi}{6} \Rightarrow t = \frac{1}{6}\text{ s}$$

12. At the extreme position

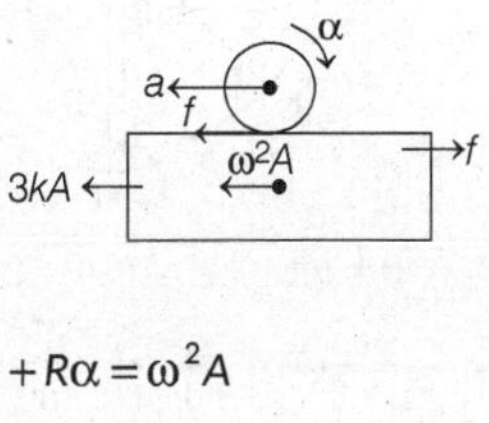

For no slipping,

$$a + R\alpha = \omega^2 A \qquad \text{...(i)}$$

For plank,

$$3kA - f = 2m\omega^2 A \qquad \text{...(ii)}$$

For cylinder, $\quad f = ma \qquad$ ...(iii)

$$\tau = I\alpha \Rightarrow fR = \left(\frac{mR^2}{2}\right)\alpha$$

$$\Rightarrow \quad f = \frac{mR\alpha}{2} \qquad \text{...(iv)}$$

Substituting values in Eq. (i),

$$\frac{f}{m} + \frac{2f}{m} = \frac{3kA - f}{2m}$$

$$\Rightarrow \quad f = \frac{3kA}{7}$$

13. $f = -\frac{3k}{7}x = -\frac{3k}{7}A\cos\omega t$

14. $\tau = k\theta \quad \Rightarrow \quad k = \frac{\tau}{\theta} = \frac{2\times 10^{-3}}{0.01} = 0.2$ N-m/rad

$$T = 0.4\text{ s}$$

$$T = 2\pi\sqrt{\frac{I}{k}}$$

$$\Rightarrow \quad I = \frac{kT^2}{4\pi^2} = \frac{0.2(0.4)^2}{4(10)} = 8\times 10^{-4}\text{ kg - m}^2$$

15. $(\Omega)_{max} = \theta_0\omega = 0.2\left(\frac{2\pi}{0.4}\right) = \pi$ rad/s

16. $a = \omega^2 x = \left(\frac{k_1 + k_2}{m_1 + m_2}\right)x$

17.

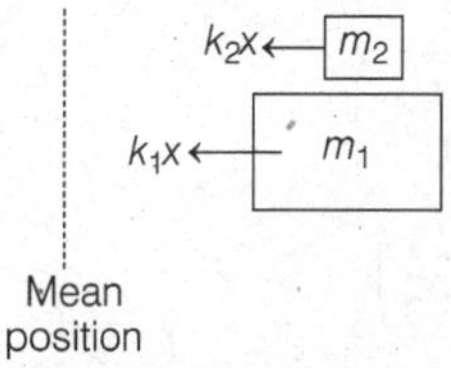

In absence of friction,

$$a_1 = \frac{k_1 x}{m_1}, \quad a_2 = \frac{k_2 x}{m_2}$$

For friction on m_2 to act in the direction of its displacement from the mean position,

$$a_2 > a_1 \quad \Rightarrow \quad \frac{k_2 x}{m_2} > \frac{k_1 x}{m_1}$$

$$\Rightarrow \quad \frac{m_1}{m_2} > \frac{k_1}{k_2}$$

18. For m_2,

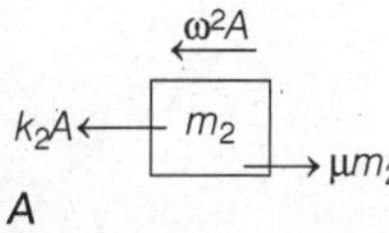

$$k_2 A - \mu m_2 g = m_2\omega^2 A$$

$$\Rightarrow \quad k_2 A - \mu m_2 g = m_2\left(\frac{k_1 + k_2}{m_1 + m_2}\right)A$$

$$\Rightarrow \quad A = \frac{\mu m_2 g(m_1 + m_2)}{m_1 k_2 - m_2 k_1}$$

19. $\mu = \dfrac{m_1 m_2}{m_1 + m_2} = 0.05$ kg

$$k_{eq} = k_1 + k_2 = 0.2 \text{ N/m}$$

$$f = \frac{1}{2\pi}\sqrt{\frac{k_{eq}}{\mu}} = \frac{1}{2\pi}\sqrt{\frac{0.2}{0.05}} = \frac{1}{\pi} \text{ Hz}$$

20. $v_{max} = A\omega = (R\theta)\,\omega = (0.06)\dfrac{\pi}{6} \times 2 = 0.0628$ m/s

21. $E = 2 \times \dfrac{1}{2} m v_{max}^2 = 3.9 \times 10^{-4}$ J

22. The speed of the block is maximum at equilibrium position,

$$\therefore \quad kx - mg = 0 \quad \Rightarrow \quad kx = mg$$

23. Compression in the spring when the speed is maximum,

$$x = \frac{mg}{k} = \frac{L}{4}$$

$$v = \omega\sqrt{A^2 - x^2}$$

$$\Rightarrow \quad \sqrt{2gL} = \sqrt{\frac{k}{m}}\sqrt{A^2 - \left(\frac{L}{4}\right)^2}$$

$$\Rightarrow \quad \sqrt{2gL} = \sqrt{\frac{4g}{L}}\sqrt{A^2 - \left(\frac{L}{4}\right)^2}$$

$$\Rightarrow \quad A = \frac{3L}{4}$$

$$v_{max} = A\omega = \frac{3L}{4}\sqrt{\frac{4g}{L}} = \frac{3}{2}\sqrt{gL}$$

24. t_0 = time taken from start of compression till the block reaches mean position

$$x = A \sin \omega t_0$$

$$\Rightarrow \quad \frac{L}{4} = \frac{3L}{4}\sin\left(2\sqrt{\frac{g}{L}}\,t_0\right)$$

$$\Rightarrow \quad t_0 = \sqrt{\frac{L}{4g}}\sin^{-1}\left(\frac{1}{3}\right)$$

Time taken by the block to go from the mean position to bottom most position,

$$t = \frac{T}{4} = \frac{\pi}{4}\sqrt{\frac{L}{g}}$$

$$\text{Required time} = t_0 + t = \frac{\pi}{4}\sqrt{\frac{L}{g}} + \sqrt{\frac{L}{4g}}\sin^{-1}\left(\frac{1}{3}\right)$$

Match the Columns Questions

1. (A) $\omega = \dfrac{2\pi}{T} = \dfrac{2\pi}{0.1} = 20\pi$ rad/s

$$\omega = \sqrt{\frac{k}{m}}$$

$$\Rightarrow \quad 20\pi = \sqrt{\frac{100}{m}} \quad \Rightarrow \quad m = 0.025 \text{ kg}$$

(B) $v_{max} = A\omega \quad \Rightarrow \quad \pi = A(20\pi) \quad \Rightarrow \quad A = 0.05$ m

$$v = A\omega \sin \omega t \quad \Rightarrow \quad x = -A\cos\omega t$$

At $t = 0$, $x = -0.05$ m

(C) $a = \dfrac{dv}{dt} = A\omega^2 \cos \omega t$

At $t = 0.1$ s,

$$a = 0.05(20\pi)^2 \cos[20\pi(0.1)] = 200 \text{ m/s}^2$$

(D) $K_{max} = \dfrac{1}{2} m v_{max}^2 = \dfrac{1}{2} \times 0.025 \times \pi^2 = 0.125$ J

2. (A)

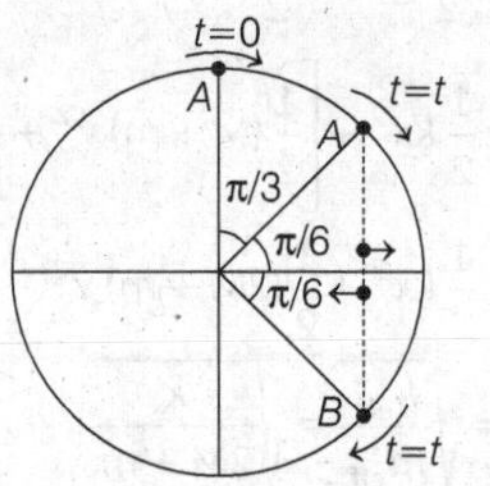

For A, $\theta = \omega t \quad \Rightarrow \quad \dfrac{\pi}{3} = \omega t \quad \Rightarrow \quad t = \dfrac{\pi}{3\omega}$

(B)

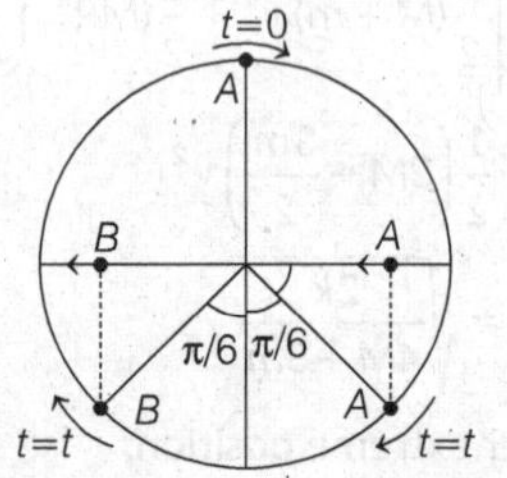

For A, $\theta = \omega t$

$$\Rightarrow \quad \frac{5\pi}{6} = \omega t \quad \Rightarrow \quad t = \frac{5\pi}{6\omega}$$

(C)

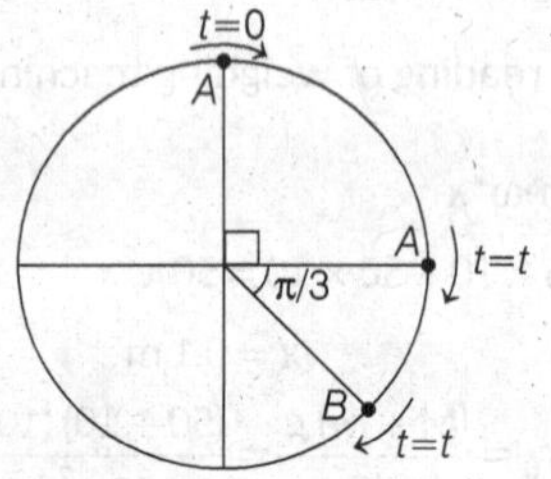

For A, $\theta = \omega t$

$$\Rightarrow \quad \frac{\pi}{2} = \omega t \quad \Rightarrow \quad t = \frac{\pi}{2\omega}$$

(D)

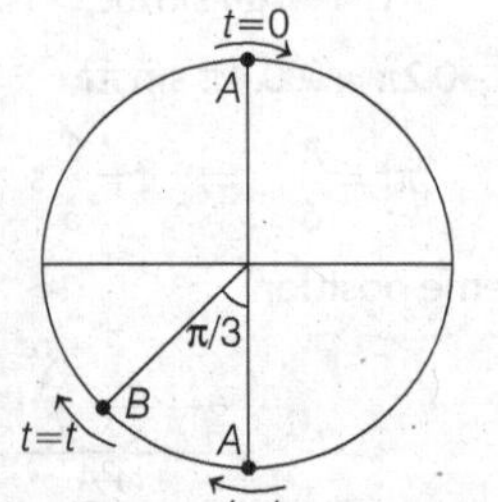

For A, $\theta = \omega t$

$$\Rightarrow \quad \pi = \omega t \quad \Rightarrow \quad t = \frac{\pi}{\omega}$$

3. (A) $v=\omega\sqrt{A^2-x^2} \Rightarrow \frac{A\omega}{2}=\omega\sqrt{A^2-x^2} \Rightarrow x=\pm\frac{\sqrt{3}A}{2}$

(B) $\frac{PE}{KE}=\frac{\frac{1}{2}m\omega^2x^2}{\frac{1}{2}m\omega^2(A^2-x^2)}=3 \Rightarrow x=\pm\frac{\sqrt{3}A}{2}$

(C) $\frac{KE}{TE}=\frac{\frac{1}{2}m\omega^2(A^2-x^2)}{\frac{1}{2}m\omega^2A^2}=1 \Rightarrow x=0$

(D) $a=-\omega^2x \Rightarrow \pm\frac{1}{4}(\omega^2A)=-\omega^2x \Rightarrow x=\pm\frac{A}{4}$

4. (A) $\omega=\sqrt{\frac{k}{m}}=\sqrt{\frac{3200}{2}}=40$ rad/s,

$$T=\frac{2\pi}{\omega}=\frac{\pi}{20}\text{ s}$$

$$x=A\sin\left(\omega t+\frac{3\pi}{2}\right)=-10\cos 40t$$

$$x=-5=-10\cos 40t$$

$$\Rightarrow 40t=\frac{\pi}{3} \Rightarrow t=\frac{\pi}{120}\text{ s}$$

(B) $t=\frac{T}{4}-\frac{\pi}{120}=\frac{\pi}{80}-\frac{\pi}{120}=\frac{\pi}{240}$ s

(C) $K=U \Rightarrow \frac{1}{2}m\omega^2(A^2-x^2)=\frac{1}{2}m\omega^2x^2 \Rightarrow x=\pm\frac{A}{\sqrt{2}}$

$$x=-\frac{10}{\sqrt{2}}=-10\cos 40t$$

$$\Rightarrow 40t=\frac{\pi}{4} \Rightarrow t=\frac{\pi}{160}\text{ s}$$

(D) $K=\frac{1}{4}K_{max} \Rightarrow \frac{1}{2}m\omega^2(A^2-x^2)=\frac{1}{4}\left(\frac{1}{2}m\omega^2A^2\right)$

$$\Rightarrow x=\pm\frac{\sqrt{3}A}{2}$$

$$x=-\frac{\sqrt{3}}{2}(10)=-10\cos 40t$$

$$\Rightarrow 40t=\frac{\pi}{6} \Rightarrow t=\frac{\pi}{240}\text{ s}$$

5. (A) PQST (B) PQ (C) PQ (D) PQST

6. (A) $\mu=\frac{m_1m_2}{m_1+m_2}=\frac{(2m)m}{2m+m}=\frac{2m}{3}$

$$T=2\pi\sqrt{\frac{\mu}{k}}=2\pi\sqrt{\frac{2m}{3k}}$$

(B) $E=\frac{1}{2}kx^2+\left[\frac{1}{2}mv^2+\frac{1}{2}\left(\frac{mR^2}{2}\right)\left(\frac{v}{R}\right)^2\right]$

$$E=\frac{1}{2}kx^2+\frac{1}{2}\left(\frac{3m}{2}\right)v^2$$

$$T=2\pi\sqrt{\frac{m_{eff}}{k_{eff}}}=2\pi\sqrt{\frac{3m}{2k}}$$

(C) Lets displace the centre of the cylinder by a distance x.

$$E=\left[\frac{1}{2}kx^2+\frac{1}{2}k(2x)^2\right]$$

$$+\left[\frac{1}{2}m(2v)^2+\frac{1}{2}mv^2+\frac{1}{2}\left(\frac{mR^2}{2}\right)\left(\frac{v}{R}\right)^2\right]$$

$$E=\frac{1}{2}(5k)x^2+\frac{1}{2}\left(\frac{11m}{2}\right)v^2$$

$$T=2\pi\sqrt{\frac{11m/2}{5k}}=2\pi\sqrt{\frac{11m}{10k}}$$

(D) $k_{eq}=k+2k+\left(\frac{1}{2k}+\frac{1}{2k}\right)^{-1}=4k$

$$T=2\pi\sqrt{\frac{m}{4k}}$$

Numerical Value Questions

1. Initial elongation in the spring,

$$x_0=\frac{2mg}{k}=8\text{ cm}$$

Elongation in new mean position,

$$x_1=\frac{mg}{k}=4\text{ cm}$$

$\therefore$ Amplitude $=x_0-x_1=4$ cm

Time taken to go from lower extreme position to the upper extreme position

$$t=\frac{T}{2}=\pi\sqrt{\frac{1}{250}}$$

Distance fallen by the lower body $=\frac{1}{2}gt^2$

$$=\frac{1}{2}\times 10\times\pi^2\times\frac{1}{250}=0.2\text{ m}=20\text{ cm}$$

Separation $=20+10+2(4)=38$ cm

2. Time taken to reach the wall,

$$\theta=\omega t$$

$$\Rightarrow \frac{\pi}{2}+\sin^{-1}\left(\frac{A}{2A}\right)=\sqrt{\frac{k}{m}}t_0$$

$$\Rightarrow t_0=\frac{2\pi}{3}\sqrt{\frac{m}{k}}$$

Speed just before hitting the wall,

$$v=\omega\sqrt{A^2-x^2}=\omega\sqrt{(2A)^2-A^2}=\sqrt{3}\,\omega A$$

As the block loses two third of its kinetic energy, KE remaining will be one third. Hence, speed will reduce by a factor of $\sqrt{3}$.

$$v=\omega\sqrt{A^2-x^2}$$

$$\Rightarrow \frac{\sqrt{3}\,\omega A}{\sqrt{3}}=\omega\sqrt{A'^2-A^2}$$

$$\Rightarrow A'=\sqrt{2}A$$

Time taken to reach left extreme position from wall,

$$\theta = \omega t$$

$$\Rightarrow \quad \frac{\pi}{2} + \sin^{-1}\left(\frac{A}{\sqrt{2}A}\right) = \sqrt{\frac{k}{m}}\, t_1$$

$$\Rightarrow \quad t_1 = \frac{3\pi}{4}\sqrt{\frac{m}{k}}$$

$$\text{Total time} = t_0 + t_1 = \frac{17\pi}{12}\sqrt{\frac{m}{k}}$$

3. As long as the spring is compressed, m_1 will not lose contact with the wall. Only m_2 is oscillating. Spring will first come to natural length in time $\frac{T}{2}$.

$$\therefore \quad \frac{T}{2} = \frac{\pi}{5\sqrt{2}}$$

$$\Rightarrow \quad \pi\sqrt{\frac{m_2}{150}} = \frac{\pi}{5\sqrt{2}}$$

$$\Rightarrow \quad m_2 = 3\,\text{kg}$$

When the spring starts getting elongated, m_1 will break contact from the wall. So, it will be two block system now.

$$\therefore \quad \frac{T'}{2} = \frac{\pi}{10\sqrt{2}}$$

$$\Rightarrow \quad \pi\sqrt{\frac{\mu}{150}} = \frac{\pi}{10\sqrt{2}}$$

$$\Rightarrow \quad \mu = \frac{3}{4}\,\text{kg}$$

$$\mu = \frac{m_1 m_2}{m_1 + m_2} \quad \Rightarrow \quad \frac{3}{4} = \frac{m_1(3)}{m_1 + 3}$$

$$\Rightarrow \quad m_1 = 1\,\text{kg}$$

4. $v_{max} = A\omega = (0.5)\sqrt{\frac{2(10)}{0.5}} = \sqrt{10}$ m/s

Elongation in old mean position $= \frac{mg}{2k} = 25$ cm

Elongation in new mean position $= \frac{mg}{k} = 50$ cm

$$x = 50 - 25 = 25\,\text{cm}$$

$$v = \omega\sqrt{A^2 - x^2}$$

$$\Rightarrow \quad \sqrt{10} = \sqrt{\frac{10}{0.5}}\sqrt{A^2 - (0.25)^2}$$

$$\Rightarrow \quad A = \frac{3}{4}\,\text{m} = 75\,\text{cm}$$

5. Let the sphere be displaced by a distance x along the plane from its equilibrium position.

Restoring force, $F = -(kx\cos 30°)\cos 30°$

$$\Rightarrow \quad F = -\left(\frac{3k}{4}\right)x$$

$$\therefore \quad \omega = \sqrt{\frac{3k}{4M}} = 1\,\text{rad/s}$$

6. Initial amplitude $= \frac{3mg}{k} - \frac{mg}{k} = \frac{2mg}{k}$

Speed just before sticking,

$$v = \omega\sqrt{A^2 - x^2}$$

$$= \sqrt{\frac{k}{m}}\sqrt{\left(\frac{2mg}{k}\right)^2 - \left(\frac{mg}{k}\right)^2}$$

$$= \sqrt{3}g\sqrt{\frac{m}{k}}$$

Mean position after sticking, $x_0 = \frac{mg}{2k}$

$$v = \omega\sqrt{A^2 - x^2}$$

$$\Rightarrow \sqrt{3}g\sqrt{\frac{m}{k}} = \sqrt{\frac{2k}{m}}\sqrt{A^2 - \left(\frac{mg}{2k}\right)^2}$$

$$\Rightarrow \quad A = \sqrt{7}\frac{mg}{2k} = 0.05\,\text{m} = 5\,\text{cm}$$

7.

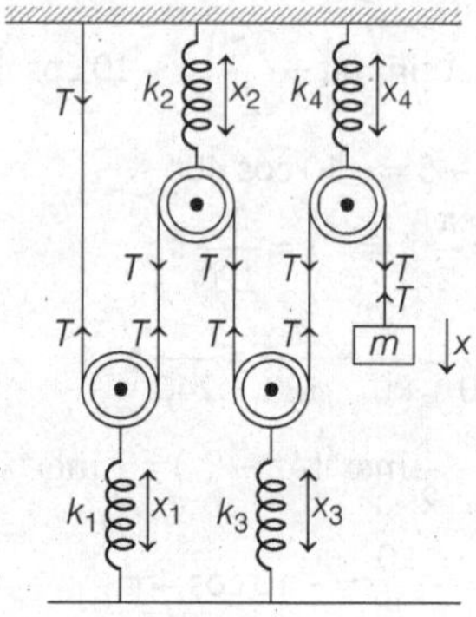

$$2T = k_1x_1 = k_2x_2 = k_3x_3 = k_4x_4$$

$$x = 2x_1 + 2x_2 + 2x_3 + 2x_4$$

$$\Rightarrow \quad x = 2\left(\frac{2T}{k_1} + \frac{2T}{k_2} + \frac{2T}{k_3} + \frac{2T}{k_4}\right)$$

$$\Rightarrow \quad T = \left(\frac{1}{4\left(\frac{1}{k_1} + \frac{1}{k_2} + \frac{1}{k_3} + \frac{1}{k_4}\right)}\right)x$$

$$\therefore \quad \frac{1}{k_{eq}} = 4\left(\frac{1}{k_1} + \frac{1}{k_2} + \frac{1}{k_3} + \frac{1}{k_4}\right)$$

$$\Rightarrow \quad k_{eq} = \frac{3k_1}{25} = 3\pi^2\,\text{N/m}$$

$$T = 2\pi\sqrt{\frac{m}{k_{eq}}} = 2\pi\sqrt{\frac{3}{3\pi^2}} = 2\,\text{s}$$

8. Velocity of the particle just before collision,

$$u = \sqrt{2gh} = \sqrt{2g\left(\frac{4.5mg}{k}\right)} = 3g\sqrt{\frac{m}{k}}$$

Applying momentum conservation for the collision,

$$mu = (2m + m)\,v$$

$$\Rightarrow \qquad v = \frac{u}{3} = g\sqrt{\frac{m}{k}}$$

Initial compression in the spring $= \dfrac{2mg}{k}$

Compression in new mean position $= \dfrac{3mg}{k}$

$$x = \frac{3mg}{k} - \frac{2mg}{k} = \frac{mg}{k}$$

$$v = \omega\sqrt{A^2 - x^2}$$

$$\Rightarrow \qquad g\sqrt{\frac{m}{k}} = \sqrt{\frac{k}{3m}}\sqrt{A^2 - \left(\frac{mg}{k}\right)^2}$$

$$\Rightarrow \qquad A = \frac{2mg}{k}$$

$$\theta = \omega t$$

$$\Rightarrow \qquad \sin^{-1}\left(\frac{mg/k}{2mg/k}\right) + \frac{\pi}{2} = \left(\sqrt{\frac{1}{0.09}}\right)t$$

$$\Rightarrow \qquad t = \frac{\pi}{5}\text{ s}$$

$$\therefore \qquad n = 5$$

9. Lets displace the block down by a distance x from the equilibrium position.

y = Rise in the level of liquid in the beaker

$$Ax = (4A - A)\,y \quad \Rightarrow \quad y = \frac{x}{3}$$

Restoring force = Additional buoyant force

$$\Rightarrow \qquad F = -\rho A\left(x + \frac{x}{3}\right)g$$

$$\Rightarrow \qquad F = -\left(\frac{4\rho A g}{3}\right)x$$

Mass of block $= \sigma A(1) = \dfrac{\rho A}{3}$

$$T = 2\pi\sqrt{\frac{m}{k}} = 2\pi\sqrt{\frac{\rho A/3}{4\rho A g/3}} = 1\text{ s}$$

10. Let the linear mass densities of the two ropes be λ and 4λ.

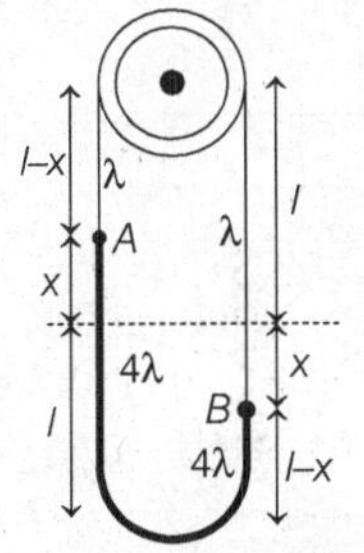

Restoring force = Difference in weight of two sides

$$\Rightarrow \qquad F = [-4\lambda\,(l + x) + \lambda\,(l - x) - \lambda\,(l + x) - 4\lambda\,(l - x)]\,g$$

$$\Rightarrow \qquad F = -(6\lambda g)\,x$$

$$\Rightarrow \qquad [4\lambda\,(2l) + \lambda\,(2l)]\,a = -6\lambda g x$$

$$\Rightarrow \qquad a = -\frac{3g}{5l}x$$

$$\therefore \qquad T = 2\pi\sqrt{\frac{5l}{3g}} = 5\text{ s}$$

11. $I = I_1 + I_2 = \dfrac{3}{2}mR^2 + [mR^2 + m(3R)^2] = \dfrac{23}{2}mR^2$

$d = 2R$

$$T = 2\pi\sqrt{\frac{I}{mgd}} = 2\pi\sqrt{\frac{23mR^2/2}{2mg(2R)}}$$

$$= 2\pi\sqrt{\frac{23R}{8g}} = 2\text{ s}$$

12. Lets rotate the rod by angle θ from the mean position.

$$\tau = -[k_1(b\theta)\,b + k_2(l\theta)\,l]$$

$$\Rightarrow \qquad \frac{ml^2}{3}\alpha = -(k_1b^2 + k_2l^2)\theta$$

$$\Rightarrow \qquad \alpha = -\frac{3(k_1b^2 + k_2l^2)}{ml^2}\theta$$

$$\therefore \qquad \omega = \sqrt{\frac{3(k_1b^2 + k_2l^2)}{ml^2}} = 8\text{ rad/s}$$

13. Lets displace the centre of the pulley down by a distance x.

$$E = \frac{1}{2}k(2x)^2 + \left[\frac{1}{2}mv^2 + \frac{1}{2}\left(\frac{mR^2}{2}\right)\left(\frac{v}{R}\right)^2\right]$$

$$E = \frac{1}{2}(4k)\,x^2 + \frac{1}{2}\left(\frac{3m}{2}\right)v^2$$

$$T = 2\pi\sqrt{\frac{3m/2}{4k}}$$

$$= 2\pi\sqrt{\frac{3m}{8k}} = \pi\sqrt{\frac{3m}{2k}}$$

$$\therefore \qquad n = 2$$

14. For cylinder,

$$\Sigma F = ma \;\Rightarrow\; f = ma \;\Rightarrow\; a = \frac{f}{m}$$

$$\Sigma\tau = I\alpha \;\Rightarrow\; fR = \left(\frac{mR^2}{2}\right)\alpha$$

$$\Rightarrow \qquad R\alpha = \frac{2f}{m}$$

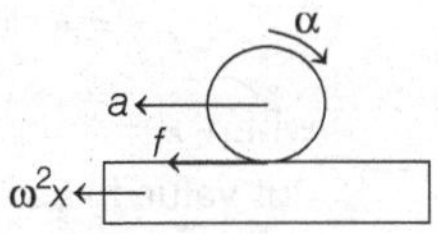

For no slipping, $a + R\alpha = \omega^2 x$

$$\Rightarrow \qquad \frac{f}{m} + \frac{2f}{m} = \omega^2 x$$

$$\Rightarrow \qquad f = \frac{m\omega^2 x}{3}$$

$$f \le f_L \;\Rightarrow\; \frac{m\omega^2 x}{3} \le \mu mg$$

$$\Rightarrow \qquad \frac{m\omega^2 A}{3} = \mu mg$$

$$\Rightarrow \qquad A = \frac{3\mu g}{\omega^2} = \frac{3(0.3)(10)}{10^2} = 9\text{ cm}$$

Previous year's Questions

JEE Main

1. At mean position speed is maximum,

$$v_{max} = A\omega = 10 \text{ cm}$$

and using $v = \omega\sqrt{A^2 - x^2} = 5$ cm

$$5 \text{ cm/s} = \omega\sqrt{A^2 - x^2} \quad \text{...(i)}$$

$$\frac{10 \text{ cm / s}}{5 \text{ cm / s}} = \frac{A\omega}{\omega\sqrt{A^2 - x^2}} \quad \text{...(ii)}$$

$$2 = \frac{A}{\sqrt{A^2 - x^2}} \Rightarrow 4 = \frac{A^2}{A^2 - x^2}$$

$$4A^2 - 4x^2 = A^2 \Rightarrow 3A^2 = 4x^2$$

$$\frac{3}{4}A^2 = x^2 \Rightarrow x = \frac{\sqrt{3}}{2}A$$

$$A = 4 \text{ cm} \Rightarrow x = \frac{\sqrt{3}}{2} \times 4$$

$$x = 2\sqrt{3} \text{ cm} \Rightarrow \alpha = 3$$

2. Total kinetic energy, $E = \frac{1}{2}KA^2$

$$U = \frac{1}{2}K\left(\frac{A}{3}\right)^2 = \frac{1}{2}\frac{KA^2}{9} = \frac{E}{9}$$

$$KE = E - \frac{E}{9} = \frac{8E}{9}$$

$$\frac{\text{Total KE}}{\text{KE}} = \frac{E}{8E/9} = \frac{9}{8}$$

$$\Rightarrow \quad x = 9$$

3. In simple harmonic motion

$$x = A\sin\omega t$$

$$x = A\sin\frac{2\pi}{T}t \quad \left(\because \omega = \frac{2\pi}{T}\right)$$

when, $T = 6\pi$ s

then, $x = A\sin\left(\frac{2\pi}{6\pi}\cdot t\right)$

$$x = A\sin\frac{t}{3} \quad \text{...(i)}$$

when, $x = A$, then $t = t_1$

Put value in Eq. (i),

$$A = A\sin\frac{t_1}{3}$$

$$1 = \sin\frac{t_1}{3}$$

$$\sin\frac{\pi}{2} = \sin\frac{t_1}{3}$$

$$t_1 = \frac{3\pi}{2}$$

when, $x = \frac{\sqrt{3}}{2}A$, then $t = t_2$

Put value in Eq. (i),

$$\frac{\sqrt{3}}{2}A = A\sin\frac{t_2}{3}$$

$$\sin\frac{\pi}{3} = \sin\frac{t_2}{3} \Rightarrow t_2 = \pi$$

Time required, $\Delta t = t_1 - t_2 = \frac{3\pi}{2} - \pi = \frac{\pi}{2} = \frac{\pi}{x}$ s (given)

$$\therefore \quad x = 2$$

4.

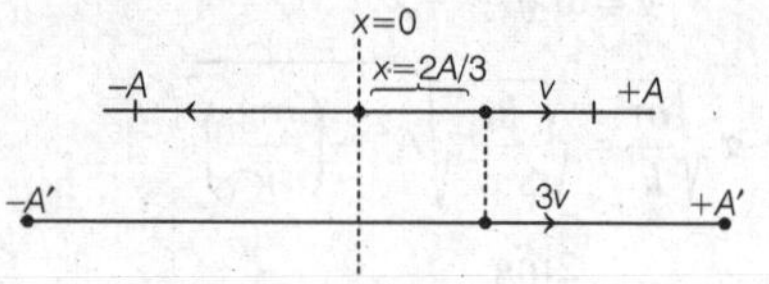

Velocity at $x = \frac{2A}{3}$ is,

$$v = \omega\sqrt{A^2 - x^2} = \omega\sqrt{A^2 - \left(\frac{2A}{3}\right)^2} = \omega A\left(\sqrt{\frac{5}{9}}\right)$$

At $x = \frac{2A}{3}$, an impulse causes velocity to become three times.

$$\therefore \quad v' = 3\omega A\frac{\sqrt{5}}{3} = \sqrt{5}\,\omega A$$

As now, $v' = \omega\sqrt{(A')^2 - x^2}$

$$\Rightarrow \quad \sqrt{5}\,\omega A = \omega\sqrt{(A')^2 - \left(\frac{2A}{3}\right)^2}$$

$$\Rightarrow \quad 5A^2 = (A')^2 - \frac{4A^2}{9}$$

$$\Rightarrow \quad A'^2 = \left(5 + \frac{4}{9}\right)A^2 = \frac{49}{9}A^2$$

or $A' = \frac{7}{3}A = \frac{nA}{3}$ (given)

$$\therefore \quad n = 7$$

5.

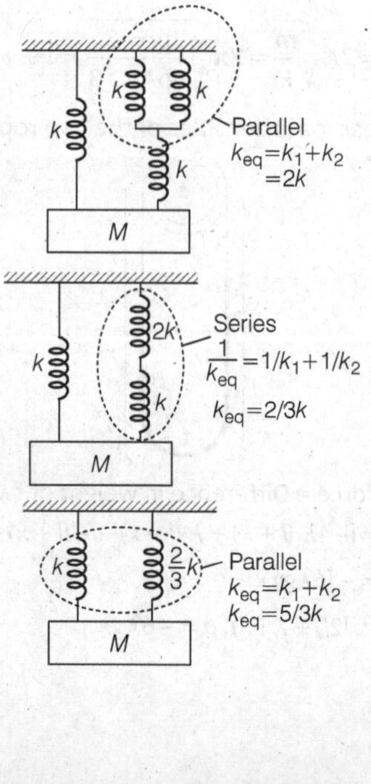

Time period, $T = 2\pi\sqrt{\frac{m}{k_{eq}}} = 2\pi\sqrt{\frac{3m}{5k}}$

$= \pi\sqrt{\frac{12m}{5k}} = \pi\sqrt{\frac{\alpha m}{5k}}$ (given)

$\therefore \quad \alpha = 12$

6. Given,

$$KE = \frac{1}{2}k(A^2 - x^2)$$

Graph between KE and x will be parabola.

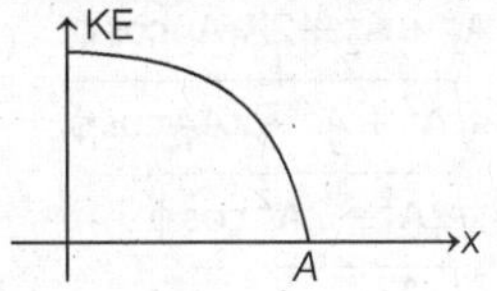

7. We know that in SHM,

TE = KE + PE, KE = TE − PE

But, $KE = \frac{1}{2}mv^2$ ...(i)

$KE = \frac{1}{2}m\omega^2(A^2 - x^2)$ $[\because v = \omega\sqrt{A^2 - x^2}]$

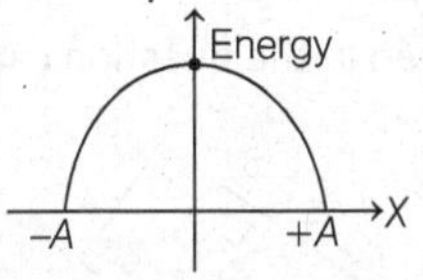

8. In simple harmonic motion, restoring force, $F = -Kx$ where, K is force constant.

$\therefore \quad F \propto x$

Acceleration, $a = -\omega^2 x$

Here, negative sign indicates that acceleration acts in opposite to the displacement.

At extreme position, $x = A$

$\therefore \quad a_{max} = -\omega^2 A$

Hence, acceleration is maximum at extreme points

Velocity, $v = \omega\sqrt{A^2 - x^2}$

At mean position, $x = 0$.

$\therefore \quad v_{max} = \omega A$

Thus, from above discussion, we found that statement (A), (B) and (C) are correct.

9. Given, $y = A\cos 30° = \frac{A\sqrt{3}}{2} = \frac{40\sqrt{3}}{2}$ cm $[\because A = 40 \text{ cm}]$

$= 0.2\sqrt{3}$ m

Since, Kinetic energy,

$$E_K = \frac{1}{2}m\omega^2(A^2 - y^2) = \frac{1}{2}k(A^2 - y^2)$$

$\Rightarrow \quad k = \frac{2E_K}{A^2 - y^2} = \frac{2 \times 200}{(0.4)^2 - (0.2\sqrt{3})^2}$

$= \frac{400}{0.16 - 0.12} = 1 \times 10^4$ N/m

$= 1 \times 10^x$ N/m (given)

$\therefore \quad x = 4$

10. For pendulum

$$T_{max} = mg + \frac{mv^2}{L} \quad \text{...(i)}$$

Given $m = \frac{1}{4}$ kg, $L = 1$ m, $g = 9.8$ m/s^2

$A = \frac{1}{10}$ m

For SHM, $KE_{max} = \frac{1}{2}mv^2 = \frac{1}{2}m\omega^2 A^2$

$\therefore \quad mv^2 = m\omega^2 A^2$

Using $\omega = \sqrt{\frac{g}{L}}$

$$mv^2 = m\left(\sqrt{\frac{g}{l}}\right)^2 A^2 = \frac{mgA^2}{L} \quad \text{...(ii)}$$

Using Eqs. (ii) in (i)

$$T_{max} = 2mg + \frac{mgA^2}{L^2} = mg\left[1 + \frac{1}{10^2}\right] = \frac{1}{4} \times 9.8 \times \frac{101}{100}$$

$T_{max} = \frac{98.98}{40} \Rightarrow x \cong 99$

11. $U = \frac{1}{2}M\omega^2 A^2 \sin^2\omega t$

So, $\frac{dU}{dt} = \frac{M\omega^3 A^2}{2}\sin 2\omega t$

It's value will be maximum, when

$\sin 2\omega t = 1$

$\Rightarrow \quad 2\omega t = \frac{\pi}{2}$

$\Rightarrow \quad 2 \times \frac{2\pi}{T} \times t = \frac{\pi}{2} \Rightarrow t = \frac{T}{8}$

So, $\beta = 8$

12. In SHM kinetic energy,

$$KE = \frac{1}{2}K(A^2 - x^2)$$

Potential energy, $U = \frac{1}{2}Kx^2$

Given that, amplitude,

$A = 3$ cm

$KE = U + 25\%$ of $U = U + 0.25U$

$\Rightarrow \quad KE = 1.25U$

$\Rightarrow \frac{1}{2}K(A^2 - x^2) = 1.25 \times \frac{1}{2}Kx^2$

$\Rightarrow \quad A^2 - x^2 = 1.25x^2 \quad \Rightarrow 2.25x^2 = A^2$

$x^2 = \frac{A^2}{2.25}$ or $x = \frac{A}{1.5}$

$\Rightarrow \quad x = \frac{3}{1.5} = 2$ cm

13. As we know, time period of simple pendulum is

$$T = 2\pi\sqrt{\frac{L}{g}} \quad \text{or} \quad T^2 = \frac{4\pi^2 L}{g} \quad \text{or } T^2 \propto L$$

14. Given, $m = 100\text{ g} = 0.1\text{ kg}$

$R_e = 6400\text{ km} = 6.4\times 10^6\text{ m}$

According to given situation, time period of oscillation of solid sphere,

$$T = 2\pi\sqrt{\frac{R_e}{g}} = 2\times 3.14 = \sqrt{\frac{6.4\times 10^6}{10}}$$

$$= 5028.6\text{ s} = 83.8\text{ min}$$

$$\simeq 84\text{min} \simeq 1\text{ h }24\text{ min}$$

15. Time period of simple pendulum on the earth's surface,

$$T = 2\pi\sqrt{\frac{l}{g}} \quad \text{...(i)}$$

Where, l is length of pendulum.

At height $h = R$, gravitational acceleration g_h is given as

$$g_h = \frac{g}{\left(1+\frac{h}{R}\right)^2} = \frac{g}{\left(1+\frac{R}{R}\right)^2} = \frac{g}{4}$$

∴ New time period of simple pendulum at height h.

$$T' = 2\pi\sqrt{\frac{l}{g_h}} = 2\pi\sqrt{\frac{l}{g/4}} = 2\times 2\pi\sqrt{\frac{l}{g}}$$

$$= 2T \quad \text{[From Eq. (i)]}$$

$$= xT \quad \text{[Given]}$$

$$\therefore \quad x = 2$$

16. For a pendulum, $T = 2\pi\sqrt{\frac{l}{g}}$; at mount Everest g reduces, so time period increases. Hence a pendulum clock will go slow (Assertion is false). As g decreases with height hence, its value at mount Everest is less than it's value on surface. (Reason is true).

17. We know that $\omega = \sqrt{\frac{k}{m}}$

For same spring, k remains constant.

$$\therefore \quad \frac{\omega_1}{\omega_2} = \sqrt{\frac{m_2}{m_1}}$$

Here, $m_1 = 1\text{ kg}, m_2 = 2\text{ kg}$

$$\therefore \quad \frac{\omega_1}{\omega_2} = \sqrt{\frac{2}{1}}$$

$$\frac{\omega_1}{\omega_2} = \sqrt{2} \Rightarrow \frac{\omega_2}{\omega_1} = \frac{1}{\sqrt{2}}$$

18. At $t = 1$ s, displacement of the particle,

$$x = \sin\pi\left(1+\frac{1}{3}\right) = \sin\frac{4\pi}{3} = -\sin\left(\frac{\pi}{3}\right) = -\frac{\sqrt{3}}{2}\text{ m}$$

So, $v = \omega\sqrt{A^2 - x^2} = \pi\sqrt{1-\frac{3}{4}} = \frac{\pi}{2}\text{ m/s}$

$$= 1.57\text{ ms}^{-1} = 157\text{ cm s}^{-1}$$

19. Here, $A = 8\text{ cm}, T = 6\text{ s}$

we know that $x = A\sin\omega t$, when

$x = A/2$

$$\frac{A}{2} = A\cos\omega t \Rightarrow \cos\omega t = \frac{1}{2}$$

So, $\omega t = \frac{\pi}{3} \Rightarrow \frac{2\pi}{T}\times t = \frac{\pi}{3}$

$$t = \frac{T}{6} = \frac{6}{6} = 1\text{ s}$$

20. Given, amplitude of two SHM,

$$A_1 = A_2 = A$$

Amplitude of resultant wave,

$$A' = \sqrt{3}A$$

If ϕ be the phase difference between the two motion, then

$$A' = \sqrt{A_1^2 + A_2^2 + 2A_1A_2\cos\phi}$$

$$\Rightarrow \quad \sqrt{3}A = \sqrt{A^2 + A^2 + 2AA\cos\phi}$$

$$\Rightarrow \quad \sqrt{3}A = \sqrt{2A^2 + 2A^2\cos\phi}$$

$$\Rightarrow \quad \sqrt{3}A = \sqrt{A^2(2+2\cos\phi)}$$

On squaring both sides, we get

$$3A^2 = A^2(2+2\cos\phi)$$

$$\Rightarrow \quad 3 = 2 + 2\cos\phi$$

$$\Rightarrow \quad \cos\phi = 1/2 \Rightarrow \cos\phi = \cos 60^\circ$$

$$\Rightarrow \quad \phi = 60^\circ$$

21. The situation given in the question can be depicted as shown below

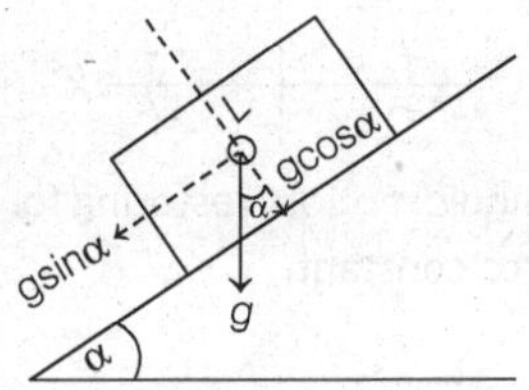

$$\therefore g_{\text{effective}} = g\cos\alpha$$

$$\therefore \quad T = 2\pi\sqrt{\frac{L}{g_{\text{effective}}}} = 2\pi\sqrt{\frac{L}{g\cos\alpha}}$$

22. According to given situation,

$$(v_{max})_1 = (v_{max})_2$$

$$\Rightarrow \quad \omega_1A_1 = \omega_2A_2 \quad [\because v_{max} = \omega A]$$

$$\Rightarrow \quad \frac{A_1}{A_2} = \frac{\omega_2}{\omega_1} = \frac{\sqrt{\frac{k_2}{m_2}}}{\sqrt{\frac{k_1}{m_1}}} \quad \left[\because \omega = \sqrt{\frac{k}{m}}\right]$$

$$= \sqrt{\frac{k_2}{k_1}}\sqrt{\frac{m_1}{m_2}} = \sqrt{\frac{9k}{2k}}\sqrt{\frac{0.05}{0.1}} = \frac{3}{2}$$

$$\therefore \quad A_1 : A_2 = 3:2$$

23. Given, mass of the first body attached to spring, $M_1 = 0.9$ kg

Mass of small body attached to first body of mass M, $m = 124\text{ g} = 0.124\text{ kg}$

At mean position, $F_{net} = 0$

Therefore, by conservation of linear momentum,

$$Mv_1 = (M+m)v_2$$

$$\Rightarrow \quad M\omega_1A_1 = (M+m)\omega_2A_2$$

$$\Rightarrow \quad \frac{M}{M+m} = \frac{\omega_2 A_2}{\omega_1 A_1} \quad ...(i)$$

$$\Rightarrow \text{But, } \omega_1 = \sqrt{\frac{k}{M}} \text{ and } \omega_2 = \sqrt{\frac{k}{M+m}}$$

$$\therefore \quad \frac{\omega_2}{\omega_1} = \frac{\sqrt{\frac{k}{(M+m)}}}{\sqrt{\frac{k}{M}}} = \sqrt{\frac{M}{M+m}}$$

$$\Rightarrow \quad \frac{\omega_2}{\omega_1} = \sqrt{\frac{M}{M+m}} \quad ...(ii)$$

From Eqs. (i) and (ii), we get

$$\frac{M}{M+m} = \sqrt{\frac{M}{M+m}} \cdot \frac{A_2}{A_1}$$

$$\Rightarrow \quad \frac{A_1}{A_2} = \sqrt{\frac{M+m}{M}}$$

$$\Rightarrow \quad \frac{\alpha}{\alpha - 1} = \sqrt{\frac{0.9 + 0.124}{0.9}} \quad \left[\because \frac{A_1}{A_2} = \frac{\alpha}{\alpha - 1} \text{ (given)}\right]$$

$$\Rightarrow \quad \frac{\alpha}{1-\alpha} = 1.07 \quad \Rightarrow \quad \alpha = 1.07 - 1.07\alpha$$

$$\Rightarrow \quad \alpha + 1.07\alpha = 1.07$$

$$\Rightarrow \quad \alpha = \frac{1.07}{2.07} = 1.9$$

$$\alpha = 1.9$$

24. Case - I

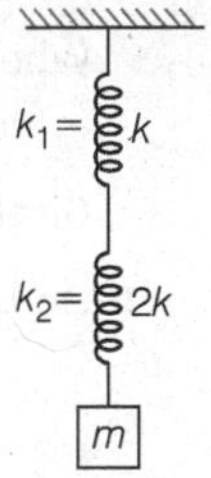

For series connection of spring equivalent force, constant k' is given as

$$\frac{1}{k'} = \frac{1}{k_1} + \frac{1}{k_2} = \frac{1}{k} + \frac{1}{2k}$$

$$\Rightarrow \quad \frac{1}{k'} = \frac{3}{2k} \Rightarrow k' = \frac{2k}{3}$$

Period of oscillation,

$$T' = 2\pi\sqrt{m/k'}$$

$$\Rightarrow \quad 3 = 2\pi\sqrt{\frac{m}{\frac{2k}{3}}} \quad [\because T' = 3\text{ s}]$$

$$\Rightarrow \quad 3 = 2\pi\sqrt{\frac{3}{2}}\sqrt{\frac{m}{k}}$$

$$\Rightarrow \quad \sqrt{\frac{m}{k}} = \left(\sqrt{\frac{3}{2}}\right)\frac{1}{\pi} \quad ...(i)$$

Case -2 For parallel combination,

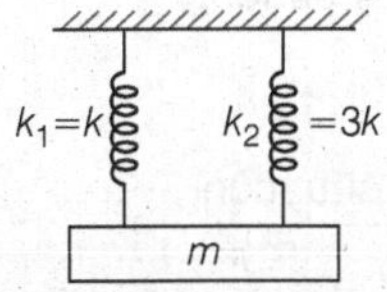

Equivalent force constant,

$$k'' = k_1 + k_2 = k + 2k = 3k$$

$\therefore$ Period of oscillation,

$$T'' = 2\pi\sqrt{\frac{m}{k''}} = 2\pi\sqrt{\frac{m}{3k}} = \frac{2\pi}{\sqrt{3}}\sqrt{\frac{m}{k}}$$

$$\Rightarrow \quad T'' = \frac{2\pi}{\sqrt{3}}\left(\sqrt{\frac{3}{2}}\right)\frac{1}{\pi} \quad \text{[From Eq. (i)]}$$

$$= \sqrt{2}\text{ s} = \sqrt{x}\text{ s} \quad \text{[Given]}$$

$$x = 2$$

25. In SHM,

$$KE_{av} = PE_{av} = \frac{1}{4}m\omega^2 a^2$$

$\therefore$ Total mechanical energy at any time

$= $ Sum of kinetic and potential energy $= \frac{1}{2}m\omega^2 a^2$

$= $ constant.

Where, m = mass of body executing SHM,

ω = angular frequency

and a = amplitude of SHM.

26. We know that $PE = \frac{1}{2}kx^2$

$$PE = \frac{1}{2}kx_0^2 \sin^2 \omega t \quad [\because x = x_0 \sin\omega t]$$

$$PE = C\sin^2 \omega t \quad \left(\therefore C = \frac{1}{2}kx_0^2\right)$$

Simplify the value of $\sin^2\omega t$, we get

$$PE = C\left[\frac{1 - \cos 2\omega t}{2}\right]$$

The value of function $\cos 2\omega t$ will always lies between -1 and 1.

Thus, the value of potential energy will be greater than or equal to zero.

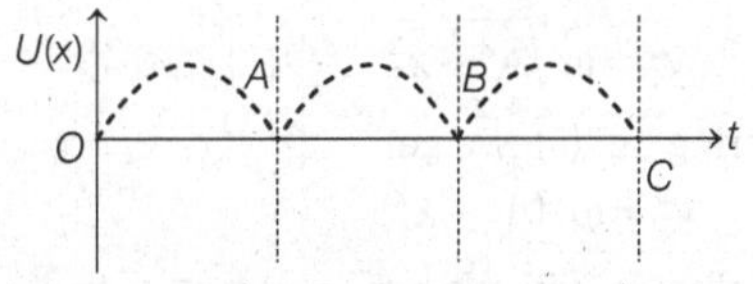

$$0 \leq PE$$

This condition is only satisfied by graph (d).

27. In first scenario, a particle is executing SHM of amplitude a and energy E.

$$\therefore \quad \text{Energy, } E = \frac{1}{2}Ka^2 \quad ....(i)$$

In second scenario,

$$\frac{3E}{4} = \frac{1}{2}K(a^2 - y^2) \quad ...(ii)$$

Where, y is the displacement.

On dividing Eqs. (i) and (ii), we get

$$\frac{E}{\frac{3E}{4}} = \frac{\frac{1}{2}Ka^2}{\frac{1}{2}K(a^2 - y^2)}$$

$$\Rightarrow \frac{4}{3}=\frac{a^2}{a^2-y^2}$$

$$\Rightarrow 4a^2-4y^2=3a^2 \Rightarrow -4y^2=-a^2$$

$$\Rightarrow y^2=\frac{a^2}{4} \Rightarrow y=\frac{a}{2}$$

28. Given, wave displacement, $x=\frac{A}{2}$

As we know that,

$$ME = KE + PE$$

In SHM, $KE=\frac{1}{2}m\omega^2(A^2-x^2)=\frac{1}{2}m\omega^2\left(A^2-\frac{A^2}{4}\right)$

$$=\frac{3}{8}m\omega^2A^2 \quad \text{...(i)}$$

$$\therefore \quad PE=\frac{1}{2}m\omega^2\frac{A^2}{4}=\frac{1}{8}m\omega^2A^2$$

Now, $ME = KE + PE=\frac{3}{8}m\omega^2A^2+\frac{1}{8}m\omega^2A^2$

$$=\frac{4m\omega^2A^2}{8}=\frac{m\omega^2A^2}{2} \quad \text{...(ii)}$$

On dividing Eq. (i) by Eq. (ii), we get

$$\frac{KE}{ME}=\frac{\frac{3}{8}m\omega^2A^2}{\frac{1}{2}m\omega^2A^2}=\frac{3}{4}$$

29. Velocity of particle performing simple harmonic motion,

$$v=\pm\omega\sqrt{(A^2-x^2)} \quad \text{...(i)}$$

According to given situation,

$$v_1=\omega\sqrt{A^2-x_1^2} \quad \text{...(ii)}$$

and $$v_2=\omega\sqrt{A^2-x_2^2} \quad \text{...(iii)}$$

On squaring Eq. (ii), we get

$$v_1^2=\omega^2(A^2-x_1^2) \quad \text{...(iv)}$$

On squaring Eq. (iii), we get

$$v_2^2=\omega^2(A^2-x_2^2) \quad \text{...(v)}$$

On subtracting Eq. (iv) from Eq. (v), we get

$$v_1^2-v_2^2=\omega^2(x_2^2-x_1^2)$$

$$\Rightarrow v_1^2-v_2^2=\left(\frac{2\pi}{T}\right)^2(x_2^2-x_1^2)$$

$$\Rightarrow T=2\pi\sqrt{\frac{(x_2^2-x_1^2)}{(v_1^2-v_2^2)}}$$

30. Since, the particle is executing SHM.

$$y=A\sin\omega t \Rightarrow y/A=\sin\omega t$$

and wave velocity equation will be

$$v_y=\frac{dy}{dt}=A\omega\cos\omega t$$

$$\Rightarrow v_y/A\omega=\cos\omega t$$

Now, $\sin^2\omega t+\cos^2\omega t=1$

$$\therefore \quad (y/A)^2+(v_y/A\omega)^2=1$$

This equation is similar to the equation of ellipse.

31. From the potential energy curve,

$$U_{max}=\frac{1}{2}kA^2 \Rightarrow 10=\frac{1}{2}k(2)^2$$

$$\Rightarrow \quad k=5\text{ N/m}$$

The length of the simple pendulum, $L=4$ m

Time period of spring, $T=2\pi\sqrt{\frac{k}{m}}$

Time period of simple pendulum, $T=2\pi\sqrt{\frac{l}{g}}$

The time period of simple pendulum is same as the time period of the spring oscillation.

$$\Rightarrow \quad 2\pi\sqrt{\frac{l}{g}}=2\pi\sqrt{\frac{k}{m}}$$

On substituting the values in the above equations, we get

$$2\pi\sqrt{\frac{4}{g}}=2\pi\sqrt{\frac{5}{5}} \Rightarrow g=4\text{ m/s}^2$$

32. Given that a bob of mass m suspended by a thread of length l undergoes SHM with time period,

$$T_1=T=2\pi\sqrt{\frac{l}{g}} \quad \text{...(i)}$$

In liquid, effective gravity, $g_{eff}=g\left(\frac{\sigma-\rho}{\sigma}\right)$

Where, ρ = density of liquid

and σ = density of body (bob).

Given, $\rho=\frac{\sigma}{4} \Rightarrow \sigma=4\rho$

On substituting this value, we get

$$g_{eff}=g\left(\frac{4\rho-\rho}{4\rho}\right)=\frac{3g}{4}$$

Now, the new time period of pendulum in liquid is

$$T'=2\pi\sqrt{\frac{l'}{g_{eff}}} \quad \text{...(ii)}$$

Here, $l'=l+\frac{1}{3}=\frac{4\ell}{3}$

On substituting the values in Eq. (ii), we get

$$T'=2\pi\sqrt{\frac{4l}{3}\times\frac{4}{3g}}=\left(2\pi\sqrt{\frac{l}{g}}\right)\frac{4}{3}$$

$$\Rightarrow \quad T'=\frac{4T}{3} \quad \text{[From Eq. (i)]}$$

33. According to first situation.

$$T_0=2\pi\sqrt{\frac{l}{g}} \quad \text{...(i)}$$

According to final situation,

$$T'=2\pi\sqrt{\frac{l}{16\times g}}=\frac{2\pi}{4}\sqrt{\frac{l}{g}}=\frac{T_0}{4} \quad \text{[From Eq. (i)]}$$

34. Given, mass of particle, $m=1$ kg

Spring constant, $k = 100\,\text{Nm}^{-1}$

Let time period is T.

Kinetic energy (KE) = Potential energy (PE) = E

KE in SHM = PE in SHM

$$\Rightarrow \quad \frac{1}{2}m\omega^2(A^2 - x^2) = \frac{1}{2}kx^2$$

$$\Rightarrow \quad m\omega^2(A^2 - x^2) = kx^2 \quad \text{... (i)}$$

Since, force, $F = m\omega^2 x = kx$

$$\Rightarrow \quad k = m\omega^2$$

On substituting the value in Eq. (i), we get

$$\Rightarrow m\omega^2(A^2 - x^2) = m\omega^2 x^2$$

$$\Rightarrow \quad A^2 - x^2 = x^2 \Rightarrow A^2 = 2x^2$$

$$\Rightarrow \quad x = A/\sqrt{2}$$

Since, wave displacement,

$$x = A\sin\omega t$$

$$\Rightarrow \quad \frac{A}{\sqrt{2}} = A\sin\omega t \Rightarrow$$

$$\sin(\pi/4) = \sin\omega t$$

$$\Rightarrow \quad \omega t = \frac{\pi}{4} \Rightarrow \frac{2\pi}{T}\cdot t = \frac{\pi}{4}$$

$$\Rightarrow \quad t = \frac{T}{8} = \frac{4}{x} \quad \text{[Given]}$$

$$\therefore \quad x = 8$$

35. Given, spring constants of springs k_1 and k_2 are k and $4k$.

Where, $k = 20\,\text{N/m}$

$$m_A = 200\,\text{g} = 200 \times 10^{-3}\,\text{kg}$$

$$m_B = 800\,\text{g} = 800 \times 10^{-3}\,\text{kg}$$

As we know that

$$T = 2\pi\sqrt{\frac{m_{eq}}{k_{eq}}} \quad \text{...(i)}$$

Where, equivalent or reduced mass,

$$m_{eq} = \frac{m_A m_B}{m_A + m_B}$$

$$\Rightarrow \quad m_{eq} = \frac{(200 \times 10^{-3})(800 \times 10^{-3})}{200 \times 10^{-3} + 800 \times 10^{-3}} = 16 \times 10^{-2}\,\text{kg}$$

and equivalent spring constant,

$$k_{eq} = \frac{k_1 k_2}{k_1 + k_2} = \frac{k \times 4k}{k + 4k} = \frac{4k}{5} = \frac{4}{5} \times 20 = 16\,\text{N/m}$$

On putting these values in Eq. (i), we get

$$T = 2\pi\sqrt{\frac{16 \times 10^{-2}}{16}} = 2\pi \times 10^{-1} = \frac{2\pi}{10}$$

As, $\quad \omega = \frac{2\pi}{T} = \frac{2\pi}{2\pi} \times 10 = 10\,\text{rads}^{-1}$

36. Time period of Fig. 1 can be given as

$$T_a = 2\pi\sqrt{\frac{M}{k}}$$

Time period can be given as

$$T_b = 2\pi\sqrt{\frac{M}{k_{eq}}} = 2\pi\sqrt{\frac{M}{k/2}} \quad \left(\because k_{eq} = \frac{k \times k}{k + k}\right)$$

Now, $\quad \frac{T_b}{T_a} = \frac{2\pi\sqrt{\frac{M}{k/2}}}{2\pi\sqrt{\frac{M}{k}}}$

$$\Rightarrow \quad \frac{T_b}{T_a} = \sqrt{2} = \sqrt{x} \quad \text{[Given] ...(i)}$$

$$\therefore \quad x = 2$$

37. Given, angular displacement to complete $\frac{5}{8}\left(= \frac{1}{2} + \frac{1}{8}\right)$ rev

$$= \left(\pi + \frac{\pi}{6}\right)\text{rad} = \left(\frac{7\pi}{6}\right)\text{rad}$$

Since, $\quad \omega = \frac{2\pi}{T} = \frac{\theta}{t}$

$$\Rightarrow \quad \theta = \frac{2\pi}{T}\cdot t \Rightarrow \frac{7\pi}{6} = \frac{2\pi}{T}t \Rightarrow t = \frac{7T}{12} = \frac{\alpha}{\beta}T$$

Hence, $\alpha = 7$

38. Given mass,

$$m = 500, \quad g = 0.5\,\text{kg}$$

Decay constant = 20 g / s

when spring-mass system performs damping motion, then its amplitude is given as,

$$A = A_0 e^{-bt/2m} \Rightarrow \frac{A}{A_0} = e^{-bt/2m}$$

according to question,

$$\frac{A_{0/2}}{A_0} = \frac{1}{2} = e^{-bt/2m}$$

$$\frac{-bt}{2m} = \ln\left(\frac{1}{2}\right)$$

$$\Rightarrow \quad \frac{bt}{2m} = \ln 2 = 0.693$$

or $\quad t = \frac{2m \times 0.693}{b} = \frac{2 \times 0.5 \times 0.693}{20 \times 10^{-3}} = 34.65\,\text{s}$

39. The displacement-time graph is as shown below,

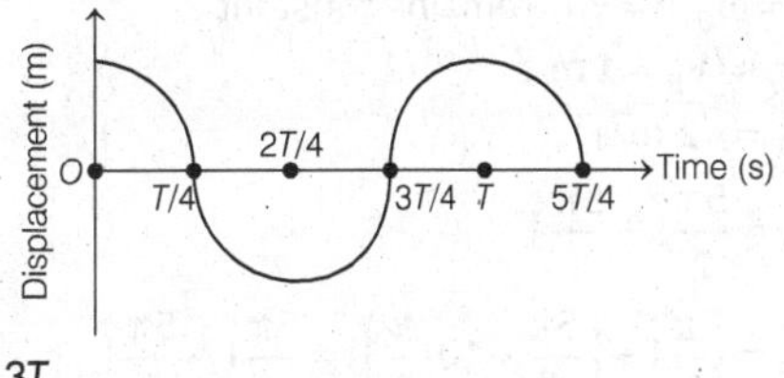

At $t = \frac{3T}{4}$, particle is at mean position.

At mean position of SHM, acceleration of particle is zero. i.e. force is zero.

Statement (A) is correct.

At $t = T$, particle is at extreme position. As direction is changing, so its acceleration is maximum. Statement (B) is correct.

At $t = \frac{T}{4}$, particle is at mean position, so whole of energy is kinetic. i.e. its speed is maximum. Statement (C) is correct.

Since, PE = KE at $t = \frac{T}{8}$, so Statement (D) is incorrect.

Hence, option (c) is correct.

JEE Advanced

1. $$T = \frac{2\pi}{\omega} = 2\pi\sqrt{\frac{I}{C}}$$

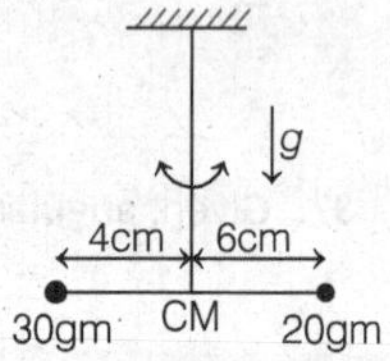

$$\Rightarrow \quad \omega = \sqrt{\frac{C}{I}} \quad \text{...(i)}$$

C = Torsional constant

where, I = moment of inertia

$$I = (30)(4)^2 + (20)(6)^2$$
$$= 1200\ \text{gm - cm}^2 = 1.2 \times 10^{-4}\ \text{kg - m}^2$$

From Eq. (i),

$$\omega = \sqrt{\frac{1.2\times10^{-4}}{1.2\times10^{-4}}} \Rightarrow \omega = \sqrt{10^{-4}} = (10^{-2})$$

$$\therefore\ n \times 10^{-3} = 10^{-2} \Rightarrow n = 10$$

2. $$l > l_0 \to k = k_1$$
$$l < l_0 \to k = k_2$$

Half of the oscillation will be completed with k_1 and the other half with k_2.

Time period of oscillation,

$$T = \frac{T_1}{2} + \frac{T_2}{2} \Rightarrow T = \pi\sqrt{\frac{m}{k_1}} + \pi\sqrt{\frac{m}{k_2}}$$

$$T = \pi\sqrt{\frac{0.1}{0.009}} + \pi\sqrt{\frac{0.1}{0.016}}$$

$$T = \frac{\pi}{0.3} + \frac{\pi}{0.4} \Rightarrow T = \frac{0.7}{0.12}\pi$$

$$\Rightarrow \quad T = 5.83\pi \Rightarrow T \approx 6\pi$$

So, $\quad n = 6$

3. (I) $v_{BA}^2 = v_A^2 + v_B^2 - 2v_{AB}\cos\theta$

As $\omega_A = \omega_B, \theta = 90°$ remains constant

Also, $v_A = v_B = 1$ m/s

So, $v_{BA} = \sqrt{2}$ m/s

(II) $\mathbf{u}_A = \frac{5\pi}{2}\hat{i} + \frac{5\pi}{2}\hat{j}$

$$\mathbf{v}_A = \frac{5\pi}{2}\hat{i} + \left(\frac{5\pi}{2} - 10\cdot\frac{\pi}{3}\right)\hat{j} = \frac{5\pi}{2}\hat{i} - \frac{5\pi}{6}\hat{j}$$

$$\mathbf{u}_B = -\frac{5\pi}{2}\hat{i} + \frac{5\pi}{2}\hat{j}$$

$$\mathbf{u}_B = -\frac{5\pi}{2}\hat{i} - \left(\frac{5\pi}{6} + 1\right)\hat{j}$$

$$\mathbf{v}_{B,A} = -5\pi\hat{i} - \hat{j}$$

$$v_{BA} = \sqrt{25\pi^2 + 1}$$

(III) $x_A = \sin t$

$$v_A = \cos t = \frac{1}{2}\ \text{m/s}$$
$$x_B = \cos$$
$$v_B = -\sin t = -\frac{\sqrt{3}}{2}\ \text{m/s}$$
$$v_{BA} = -\frac{\sqrt{3}}{2} - \frac{1}{2}$$

(IV) $\mathbf{v}_A$ and $\mathbf{v}_B$ are always perpendicular.

So, $|\mathbf{v}_{BA}| = \sqrt{v_A^2 + v_B^2} = \sqrt{10}$ m/s

4. Just Before Collision,

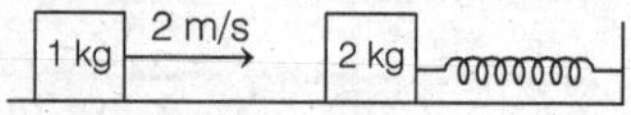

Just After Collision

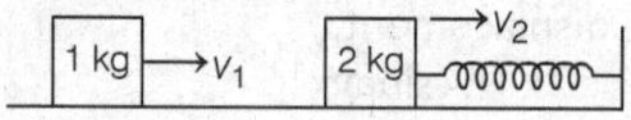

Let velocities of 1 kg and 2 kg blocks just after collision be v_1 and v_2 respectively.

From momentum conservation principle,

$$1 \times 2 = 1v_1 + 2v_2 \quad \text{...(i)}$$

Collision is elastic. Hence $e = 1$ or relative velocity of separation = relation velocity of approach.

$$v_2 - v_1 = 2 \quad \text{...(ii)}$$

From Eqs. (i) and (ii),

$$v_2 = \frac{4}{3}\ \text{m/s},\ v_1 = \frac{-2}{3}\ \text{m/s}$$

2 kg block will perform SHM after collision,

$$t = \frac{T}{2} = \pi\sqrt{\frac{m}{k}} = 3.14\ \text{s}$$

$$\text{Distance} = |v_1|t = \frac{2}{3} \times 3.14 = 2.093 = 2.09\ \text{m}$$

5. Case-1

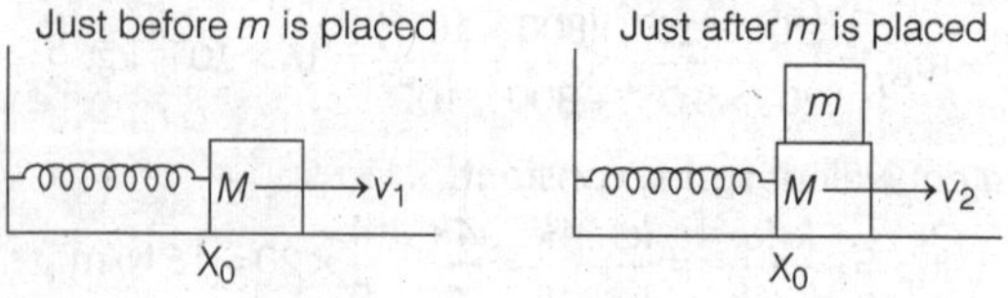

Case-2

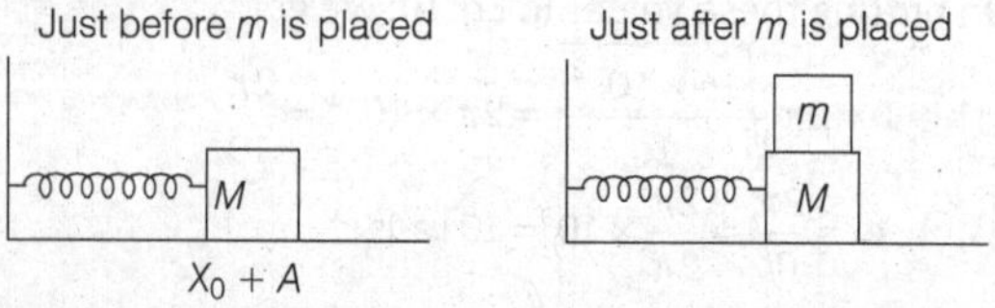

In case-1,

$$Mv_1 = (M+m)v_2 \Rightarrow v_2 = \left(\frac{M}{M+m}\right)v_1$$

Here, $\quad v_2 = \omega_2 A_2$

$$v_1 = \omega_1 A_1 \text{ and } \omega = \sqrt{\frac{k}{m}}$$

$$\sqrt{\frac{k}{M+m}}\, A_2 = \left(\frac{M}{M+m}\right)\sqrt{\frac{k}{M}}\, A_1$$

$$A_2 = \sqrt{\frac{k}{M+m}}\, A_1$$

In case-2 $A_2 = A_1$

Further, $T = 2\pi\sqrt{\frac{M+m}{k}}$ in both cases.

Total energy decreases in first case whereas remain same in 2nd case. Instantaneous speed at x_0 decreases in both cases.

6. Ist Particle

$$P = 0 \text{ at } x = a$$

$\Rightarrow$ 'a' is the amplitude of oscillation 'A_1'.

At $x = 0, P = b$ (at mean position)

$$\Rightarrow \quad mv_{max} = b \Rightarrow v_{max} = \frac{b}{m}$$

$$E_1 = \frac{1}{2}mv_{max}^2 = \frac{m}{2}\left[\frac{b}{m}\right]^2 = \frac{b^2}{2m}$$

$$A_1\omega_1 = v_{max} = \frac{b}{m}$$

$$\Rightarrow \quad \omega_1 = \frac{b}{ma} = \frac{1}{mn^2} \quad (A_1 = a, \frac{a}{b} = n^2)$$

IInd Particle

$$P = 0 \text{ at } x = R$$

$$\Rightarrow \quad A_2 = R$$

At $x = 0, P = R$

$$\Rightarrow \quad v_{max} = \frac{R}{m}$$

$$E_2 = \frac{1}{2}mv_{max}^2 = \frac{m}{2}\left[\frac{R}{m}\right]^2 = \frac{R^2}{2m}$$

$$A_2\omega_2 = \frac{R}{m}$$

$$\Rightarrow \quad \omega_2 = \frac{R}{mR} = \frac{1}{m}$$

(b) $\frac{\omega_2}{\omega_1} = \frac{1/m}{1/mn^2} = n^2$

(c) $\omega_1\omega_2 = \frac{1}{mn^2} \times \frac{1}{m} = \frac{1}{m^2n^2}$

(d) $\frac{E_1}{\omega_1} = \frac{b^2/2m}{1/mn^2} = \frac{b^2n^2}{2} = \frac{a^2}{2n^2} = \frac{R^2}{2}$

$$\frac{E_2}{\omega_2} = \frac{R^2/2m}{1/m} = \frac{R^2}{2} \quad \Rightarrow \quad \frac{E_1}{\omega_1} = \frac{E_2}{\omega_2}$$

7. At equilibrium ($t = 0$) particle has maximum velocity u_0. Therefore velocity at time t can be written as

$$u = u_0 \cos\omega t$$

writing, $u = 0.5u_0 = u_0\cos\omega t$

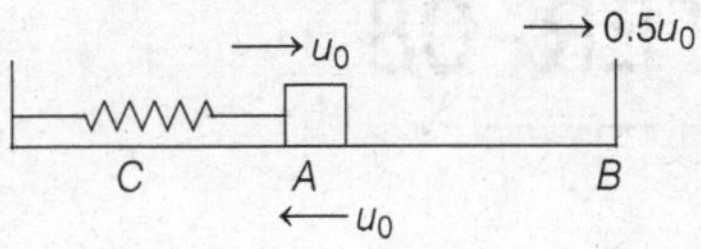

$$\therefore \quad \omega t = \frac{\pi}{3}$$

$$\therefore \quad \frac{2\pi}{T}t = \frac{\pi}{3}$$

$$\therefore \quad t = \frac{T}{6}$$

(b) $t = t_{AB} + t_{BA} = \frac{T}{6} + \frac{T}{6} = \frac{T}{3} = \frac{2\pi}{3}\sqrt{\frac{m}{k}}$

(c) $t = t_{AB} + t_{BA} + t_{AC} = \frac{T}{6} + \frac{T}{6} + \frac{T}{4} = \frac{7}{12}T = \frac{7\pi}{6}\sqrt{\frac{m}{k}}$

(d) $t = t_{AB} + t_{BA} + t_{AC} + t_{CA} = \frac{t}{6} + \frac{T}{6} + \frac{T}{4} + \frac{T}{4} = \frac{5}{6}T = \frac{5\pi}{3}\sqrt{\frac{m}{k}}$

8. t = time of flight of projectile $= \frac{2v\sin\theta}{g}$ $(\theta = 45°)$

$$\therefore \quad v = \frac{gt}{2\sin\theta} = \frac{10\times 1}{2\times 1/\sqrt{2}} = \sqrt{50}\text{ m/s}$$

9. $\tau_A = \tau_B = \left(mg\frac{L}{2}\sin\theta + MgL\sin\theta\right)$

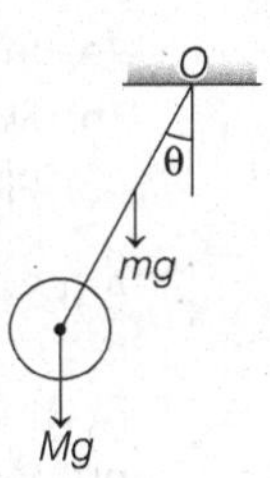

= Restoring torque about point O.

In case A, the moment of inertia is more as compared to B, so $\omega_A < \omega_B$.

10. If $E > V_0$, particle will escape. But simultaneously for oscillations, $E > 0$.

Hence, the correct answer is $V_0 > E > 0$

or the correct option is (c).

11. $[\alpha] = \left[\frac{PE}{x^4}\right] = \left[\frac{ML^2T^{-2}}{L^4}\right] = [ML^{-2}T^{-2}]$

$$\therefore \quad \left[\frac{m}{\alpha}\right] = [L^2T^2]$$

$$\Rightarrow \quad \left[\frac{1}{A}\sqrt{\frac{m}{\alpha}}\right] = [T]`1$$

As dimensions of amplitude A is [L].

Hence, the correct option is (b).

12. For $|x| > X_0$, potential energy is constant. Hence, kinetic energy, speed or velocity will also remain constant.

$\therefore$ Acceleration will be zero.

Hence, the correct option is (d).

13. $\omega = \sqrt{\frac{K}{m}} = \sqrt{\frac{YA}{lm}} = \sqrt{\frac{(n\times 10^9)(4.9\times 10^{-7})}{1\times 0.1}}$

Putting, $\omega = 140$ rad s^{-1} in above equation we get, $n = 4$

$\therefore$ Answer is 4.

CHAPTER~08

TRAVELLING WAVES

LEVEL 01 Starter Level

8.1 Wave Function

1 A wave pulse moving along the X-axis is represented, by the wave function $y(x, t) = \frac{2}{(x-3t)^2 + 1}$ where x and y are measured in cm and t is in seconds.

(a) In which direction is the wave moving?

(b) Find speed of the wave

(c) Plot the waveform at $t = 0, t = 2$ s.

2 A travelling wave pulse is given by $y = \frac{10}{5 + (x + 2t)^2}$.

In which direction and with what velocity is the pulse propagating? What is the amplitude of pulse?

3 At $t = 0$, a transverse wave pulse on a wire is described by the function $y = \frac{6}{x^3 + 3}$ where x and y are in m. Write the function $y(x, t)$ that describes this wave, if it is travelling in the positive X-direction with a speed of 4 m/s.

4 A wave pulse is travelling on a string at 2 m/s, Displacement y of the particle at $x = 0$ at any time t is given by $y = \frac{2}{t^2 + 1}$. Find expression of the function $y = (x, t)$ i.e., displacement of a particle at position x and time t.

5 A wave is propagating on a long stretched string along its length taken as the positive X-axis. The wave, equation is given as $y_0 e^{-\left(\frac{t}{T} - \frac{x}{\lambda}\right)^2}$ where $y_0 = 4$ mm, $T = 1.0$ s and $\lambda = 4$ cm.

(a) Find the velocity of the wave.

(b) Find the function $f(t)$ giving the displacement of the particle at $x = 0$.

(c) Find the function $g(x)$ giving the shape of the string at $t = 0$.

8.2 Equation of Travelling Sinusoidal Wave

1 Consider the wave

$y = (10 \text{ mm}) \sin [(5\pi \text{ cm}^{-1})\, x - (60\pi \text{ s}^{-1})\, t + \frac{\pi}{4}]$.

Find the

(a) amplitude (b) wavelength

(c) frequency (d) wave velocity

2 A sinusoidal wave travelling in the negative X-direction has an amplitude of 15 cm, wavelength 40 cm and frequency 8 Hz. The vertical displacement of the medium at $t = 0$ and $x = 0$ is also 15 cm, as shown. Write a general expression for the wave function.

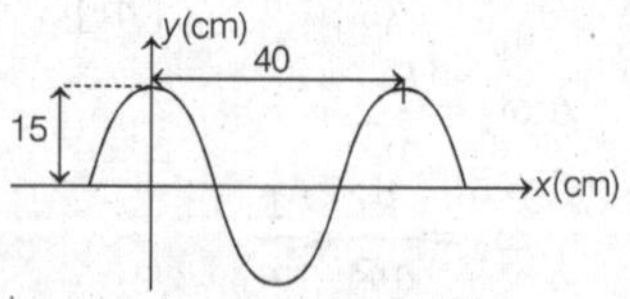

3 The sketch in the figure shows displacement time curve of a sinusoidal wave at $x = 8$ m. Taking velocity of wave $v = 6$ m/s along positive X-axis, write the equation of the wave.

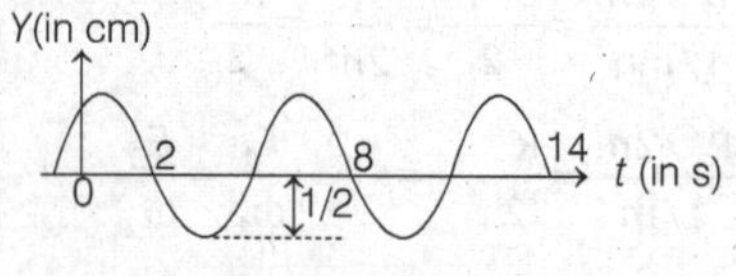

4 Figure shows a snapshot of a sinusoidal travelling wave taken at $t = 0.3$ s. The wavelength is 7.5 cm and the amplitude is 2 cm. If the crest P was at $x = 0$ at $t = 0$, write the equation of travelling wave.

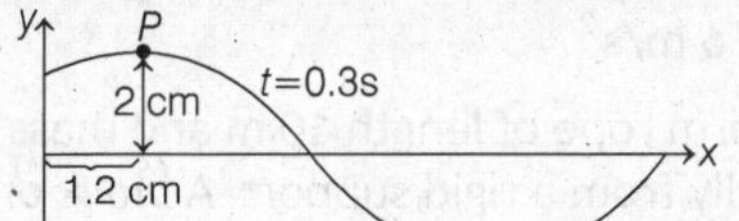

8.3 Phase Difference

1 Equation of a wave travelling along X-axis is given by $y = 4 \sin \frac{\pi}{2}\left(2t + \frac{x}{8}\right)$. Calculate

(a) the phase difference for two positions of the same particle which are occupied at time interval 0.4 s apart and

(b) the phase difference at any given instant of two particles 12 cm apart.

2 What is the phase difference between the paticles 1 and 2 located as shown in figure?

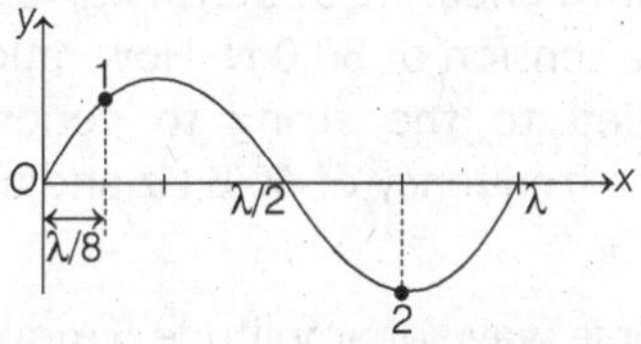

3 Consider a sinusoidal travelling wave shown in figure. The velocity is +40 cm/s. Find

(a) the frequency

(b) the phase difference between points 2.5 cm apart

(c) how long it takes for the phase at a given position to change by 60°?

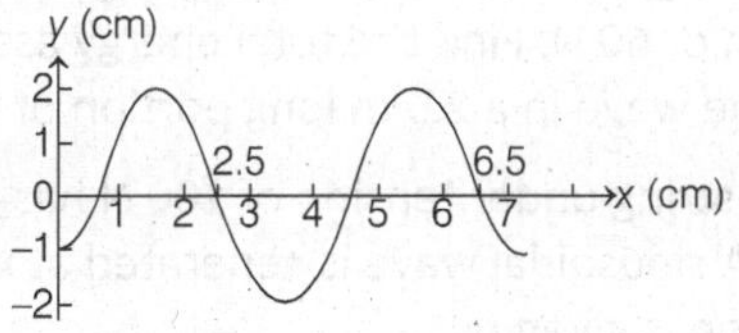

4 A transverse harmonic wave of amplitude 1.0 cm and wavelength 3.0 m is travelling in positive X-direction on a stretched string. At an instant, the particle at $x = 5.0$ m is at $y = +0.5$ cm and is travelling in positive y-direction. Find the coordinate of the nearest particle ($x > 5.0$ m) which is at its positive extreme at this instant.

8.4 Particle Velocity and Acceleration

1 A transverse progressive wave is given by the equation $y = (0.05 \text{ m}) \sin \pi (400t + x)$. Find

(a) velocity of the wave.

(b) maximum particle velocity and acceleration.

(c) velocity and acceleration of particle at $x = \frac{1}{6}$ m at $t = 0.01$ s

2 The transverse wave shown in the figure is travelling in the positive x-direction with speed 20 cm/s. At a particular instant of time, the tangent to the string at point P makes an angle of 60° with the X-axis. Find the velocity of string particle P at this instant.

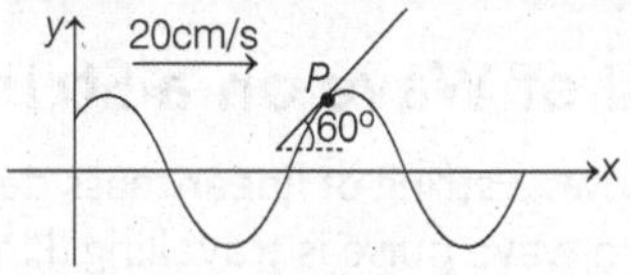

3 A transverse wave is travelling along a string from left to right. The figure represents the shape of the string (snap-shot) at a given instant. At this instant,

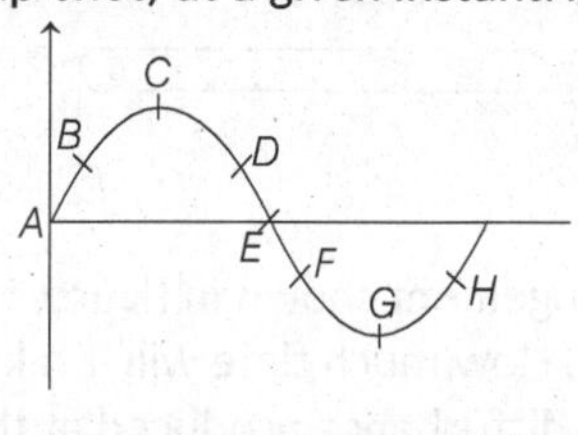

(a) which points have an upward velocity?

(b) which points have downward velocity?

(c) which points have zero velocity?

(d) which points have maximum magnitude of velocity?

4 For a wavelength described by, $y = A \sin(\omega t - kx)$, consider the following points

(a) $x = 0$ (b) $x = \frac{\pi}{4k}$

(c) $x = \frac{\pi}{2k}$ (d) $x = \frac{3\pi}{4k}$

For a particle at each of these points at $t = 0$, describe whether the particle is moving or not and in what direction and describe whether the particle is speeding up, slowing down or instantaneously not accelerating.

5 A sinusoidal wave propagates along a string. In figure (a) and (b), y represents displacement of particle from the mean position. x and t have usual meanings. Find

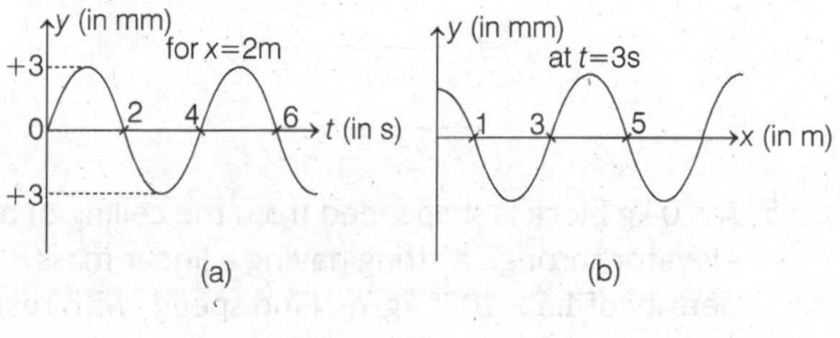

(a) (b)

(a) speed of the wave

(b) maximum velocity and maximum acceleration of the particles

(c) the magnitude of slope of the string at $x = 2$ and $t = 4$ s.

6 If a travelling wave satisfies the relation $\frac{\partial^2 y}{\partial x^2} = \frac{1}{9}\frac{\partial^2 y}{\partial t^2}$, then find the speed of the wave.

8.5 Speed of Wave on a String

1 Figure shows a string of linear mass density 1.0 g/cm on which a wave pulse is travelling. Find the time taken by the pulse in travelling through a distance of 60 cm on the string. Take, $g = 10\ \text{m/s}^2$.

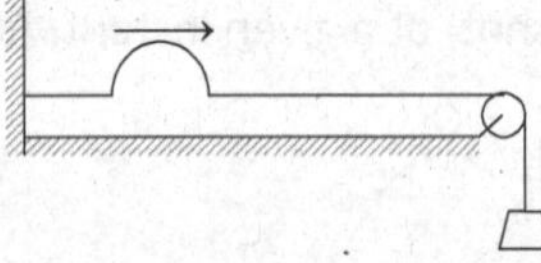

2 In the arrangement shown in figure, the string has mass of 5g. How much time will it take for a transverse disturbance produced at the floor to reach the pulley A? Take, $g = 10\ \text{m/s}^2$.

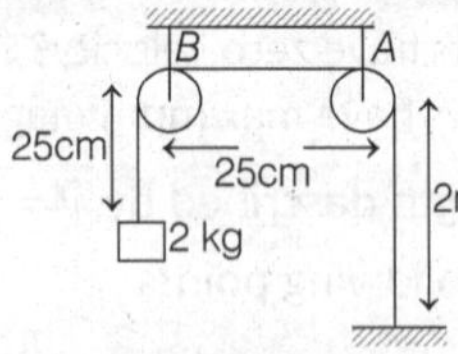

3 Two wires of different densities but same area of cross-section are soldered together at one end and are stretched to a tension T. The velocity of a transverse wave in the first wire is half of that in the second wire. Find the ratio of the density of the first wire to that of the second wire

4 A taut string having tension 100 N and linear mass density 0.25 kg/m is used inside a cart to generate a wave pulse starting at the left end, as shown. What should be the velocity of the cart so that pulse remains stationary w.r.t. ground?

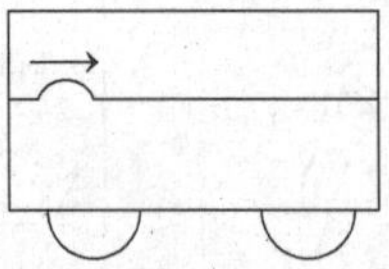

5 A 4.0 kg block is suspended from the ceiling of an elevator through a string having a linear mass density of 1.6×10^{-3} kg/m. Find speed (with respect to the string) with which a wave pulse can proceed on the string if the elevator accelerates up at the rate of 6 m/s^2.

6 A uniform rope of length 10 m and mass 15 kg hangs vertically from a rigid support. A block of mass 5 kg is attached to the free end of the rope. A transverse pulse of wavelength 0.04 m is produced at the lower end of the rope. What is the wavelength of the pulse when it reaches the top of the rope?

7 A uniform rope of mass m and length L hangs from a ceiling.

(a) Find the speed of a transverse wave on the rope at a distance y from the lower end.

(b) If the string is plucked sideways at the lower end, find the time taken by the disturbance to reach the upper end of the rope.

8.6 Power Transmitted along the String

1 A string with linear mass density $\mu = 5.00 \times 10^{-2}$ kg/m is under a tension of 80.0 N. How much power must be supplied to the string to generate sinusoidal waves at a frequency of 60.0 Hz and an amplitude of 6.00 cm?

2 A transverse wave of amplitude 5 mm and frequency 10 Hz is produced on a wire stretched to a tension of 100 N. If the wave speed is 100 m/s, what average power is the source transmitting to the wire? ($\pi^2 = 10$)

3 A 200 Hz wave with amplitude 1 mm travels on a long string of linear mass density 6 g/m kept under a tension of 60 N. Find the total energy associated with the wave in a 2.0 m long portion of the string.

4 A long string under tension of 100 N has one end at $x = 0$. A sinusoidal wave is generated at $x = 0$ whose equation is given by

$$y = (0.01\ \text{cm}) \sin\left[\left(\frac{\pi x}{10}\ \text{m}\right) - 50\pi t\ (\text{s})\right]$$

Find the average power transmitted by the wave.

5 A stretched string is forced to transmit transverse waves by means of an oscillator coupled to one end. The string has a diameter of 4 mm. The amplitude of the oscillation is 10^{-4} m and the frequency is 10 Hz. Tension in the string is 100 N and mass density of wire is 4200 kgm^{-3}. Find the average intensity transmitted through the string.

LEVEL 02 JEE Main Level

Single Choice Correct Questions

1 The transverse displacement $y(x, t)$ of a wave on a string is given by $y(x, t) = e^{-(ax^2 + bt^2 + 2\sqrt{ab}xt)}$. This represents a

(a) wave moving in –ve x-direction with speed $\sqrt{\frac{b}{a}}$

(b) wave moving in +ve x-direction with speed $\sqrt{\frac{b}{a}}$

(c) standing wave of frequency $\sqrt{b}$

(d) standing wave of frequency $\frac{1}{\sqrt{b}}$

2 The displacement of a wave disturbance propagating in the positive X-direction is given by $y = \frac{1}{(1+x^2)}$ at time $t = 0$ and $y = \frac{1}{[1+(x-1)^2]}$ at $t = 2$ s where x and y are in m. The shape of the wave disturbance does not change during the propagation. The velocity of the wave is

(a) 2.5 m/s (b) 0.25 m/s (c) 0.5 m/s (d) 5 m/s

3 In wave, displacement of origin is varying according to $y(0, t) = 2t$ mm $\quad 0 \le t \le 2$

$= (6 - t)$ mm $\quad 2 < t \le 4$

of disturbance propagating in +x-direction with speed 2 cm/s, then displacement of particle at $x = 4$ cm at $t = 5$ s is

(a) 0 (b) 1 mm (c) 3 mm (d) 6 mm

4 Which of the following function correctly represents the travelling wave equation for finite positive values of x and t

(a) $y = x^2 - t^2$

(b) $y = \cos x^2 \sin t$

(c) $y = \log (x^2 - t^2) - \log (x - t)$

(d) $y = e^{2x} \sin t$

5 Two small boats are 10 m apart on a lake. Each pops up and down with a period of 4.0 s due to wave motion on the surface of water. When one boat is at its highest point, the other boat is at its lowest point. Both boats are always within a single cycle of the waves. The speed of the waves is

(a) 2.5 m/s (b) 5.0 m/s (c) 14 m/s (d) 40 m/s

6 A sinusoidal progressive wave is generated in a string. Its equation is given by $y = (2\text{ mm}) \sin (2\pi x - 100\pi t + \pi/3)$. The time when particle at $x = 4$ m first passes through mean position, will be

(a) $\frac{1}{150}$ s (b) $\frac{1}{12}$ s (c) $\frac{1}{300}$ s (d) $\frac{1}{100}$ s

7 The wave motion has the function $y = a_0 \sin (\omega t - kx)$. The graph in the figure shows how the displacement y at a fixed point varies with time t. Which one of the labelled points shows a displacement equal to that at the position $x = \pi/2k$ at time $t = 0$?

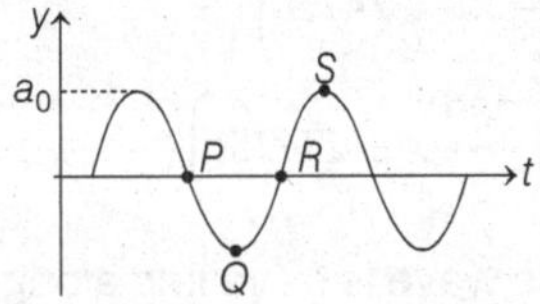

(a) P (b) Q (c) R (d) S

8 A transverse wave of amplitude 0.50 m, wavelength 1 m and frequency 2 Hz is propagating on a string in the negative x-direction. The expression of the wave is

(a) $y(x, t) = 0.5 \sin (2\pi x + 2\pi t)$

(b) $y(x, t) = 0.5 \cos (2\pi x + 4\pi t)$

(c) $y(x, t) = 0.5 \sin (\pi x - 2\pi t)$

(d) $y(x, t) = 0.5 \cos (2\pi x - 2\pi t)$

9 Figure shown the shape of part of a long string in which transverse waves are produced by attaching one end of the string to tuning fork of frequency 250 Hz. What is the velocity of the waves?

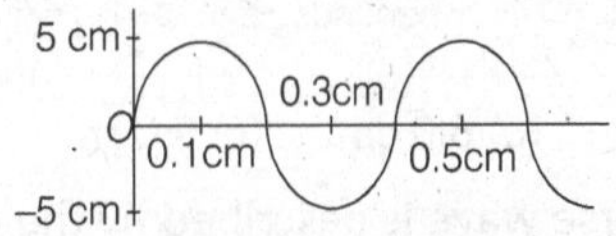

(a) 1.0 ms^{-1} (b) 1.5 ms^{-1}

(c) 2.0 ms^{-1} (d) 2.5 ms^{-1}

10 The equation of a wave travelling along the positive X-axis, as shown in figure at $t = 0$ is given by

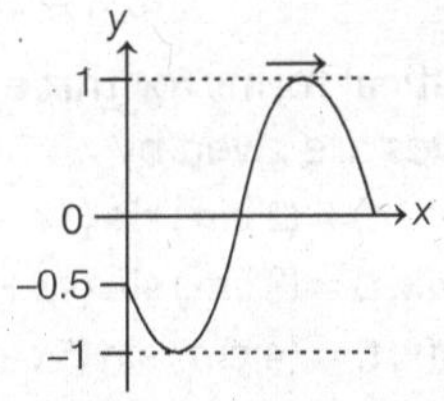

(a) $\sin\left(kx - \omega t + \frac{\pi}{6}\right)$ (b) $\sin\left(kx - \omega t - \frac{\pi}{6}\right)$

(c) $\sin\left(\omega t - kx + \frac{\pi}{6}\right)$ (d) $\sin\left(\omega t - kx - \frac{\pi}{6}\right)$

11 For the wave shown in figure, the equation for the wave, travelling along +X-axis with velocity 350 ms^{-1} when its position at $t = 0$ is as shown

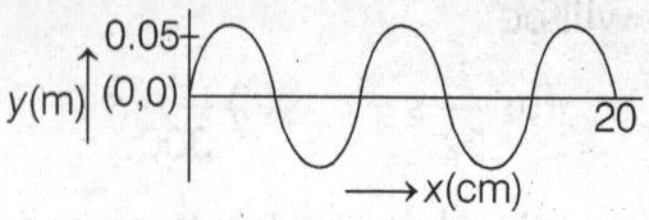

(a) $0.05 \sin\left(\frac{314}{4}x - 27475t\right)$

(b) $0.05 \sin\left(\frac{379}{5}x - 27475t\right)$

(c) $1 \sin\left(\frac{314}{4}x - 27475t\right)$

(d) $0.05 \sin\left(\frac{289}{5}x + 27475t\right)$

12 A transverse wave is travelling along a horizontal string. The first picture shows the shape of the string at an instant of time. This picture is superimposed on a coordinate system to help you make any necessary measurements. The second picture is a graph of the vertical displacement of one point along the string as a function of time. How far does this wave travel along the string in 2s?

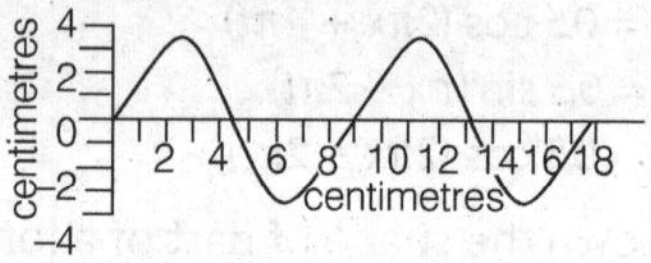

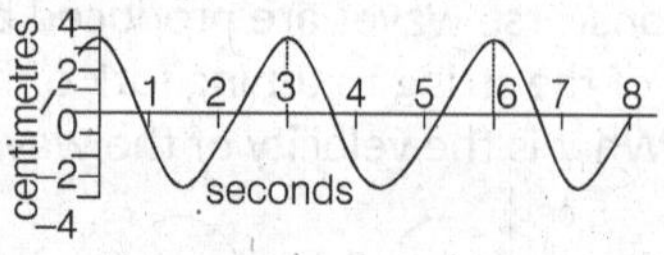

(a) 3.0 cm (b) 6.0 cm (c) 9.0 cm (d) 18 cm

13 A transverse wave is described by the equation $Y = Y_0 \sin 2\pi\left[ft - \frac{x}{\lambda}\right]$. The maximum particle velocity is equal to four times the wave velocity, if

(a) $\lambda = \pi Y_0 / 4$ (b) $\lambda = \pi Y_0 / 2$

(c) $\lambda = \pi Y_0$ (d) $\lambda = 2\pi Y_0$

14 The mathematical forms for three sinusoidal travelling waves are given by

wave 1 : $y(x, t) = (2 \text{ cm}) \sin(3x - 6t)$

wave 2 : $y(x, t) = (3 \text{ cm}) \sin(4x - 12t)$

wave 3 : $y(x, t) = (4 \text{ cm}) \sin(5x - 11t)$

where x is in m and t is in s. Of these waves

(a) wave 1 has the greatest wave speed and the greatest maximum transverse string speed

(b) wave 2 has the greatest wave speed and wave 1 has the greatest maximum transverse string speed

(c) wave 3 has the greatest wave speed and the greatest maximum transverse string speed

(d) wave 2 has the greatest wave speed and wave 3 has the greatest maximum transverse string speed

15 A travelling wave on a string is given by $y = A \sin\left[\alpha x + \beta t + \frac{\pi}{6}\right]$. If $\alpha = 0.56$/cm, $\beta = 12$/s $A = 7.5$ cm, then find the velocity of particle at $x = 1$ cm and $t = 1$ s is

(a) 46.5 cm s^{-1} (b) 77.94 cm s^{-1}

(c) 7.5 cm s^{-1} (d) 75 cm s^{-1}

16 A progressive wave is given by $y = 3 \sin 2\pi\left[\frac{t}{0.04} - \frac{x}{0.01}\right]$ where x, y are in cm and t in s. The frequency of wave and maximum acceleration will be

(a) 100 Hz, 4.7×10^3 m/s^2 (b) 50 Hz, 7.5×10^3 m/s^2

(c) 25 Hz, 4.7×10^4 m/s^2 (d) 25 Hz, 7.5×10^4 m/s^2

17 The equation of a transverse wave is $y = a \sin 2\pi\left[t - \frac{x}{5}\right]$, then the ratio of maximum particle velocity and wave velocity is

(a) $\frac{2\pi a}{\sqrt{5}}$ (b) $\frac{2\pi a}{5}$ (c) $\frac{a}{5}$ (d) $2\pi a\sqrt{5}$

18 The equation of a wave is $y = 4 \sin\left[\frac{\pi}{2}\left(2t + \frac{x}{8}\right)\right]$ where y, x are in cm and time in s. The acceleration of particle located at $x = 8$ cm and $t = 1$ s is

(a) $4\pi^2$ cm/s^2 (b) $-4\pi^2$ cm/s^2

(c) $16\pi^2$ cm/s^2 (d) $-16\pi^2$ cm/s^2

19 At $t = 0$, a transverse wave pulse travelling in the +ve x-direction with a speed of 2 m/s in a wire is described by $y = \frac{6}{x^2}$, given that $x \neq 0$. Transverse velocity of a particle at $x = 2$ m and $t = 2$ s is

(a) 3 m/s (b) –3 m/s

(c) 8 m/s (d) –8 m/s

20 The displacement of a string carrying a travelling sinusoidal wave is given by

$$y(x, t) = y_m \sin(kx - \omega t - \phi)$$

At time $t = 0$ the point at $x = 0$ has velocity v_0 and displacement y_0. The phase constant ϕ is given by $\tan \phi =$

(a) $\frac{v_0}{\omega y_0}$ (b) $\frac{\omega y_0}{v_0}$

(c) $\frac{\omega v_0}{y_0}$ (d) $\omega v_0 y_0$

21 A wave pulse is generated in a string that lies along X-axis. At the points A and B, as shown in figure, if R_A and R_B are ratio of wave speed to the particle speed respectively, then

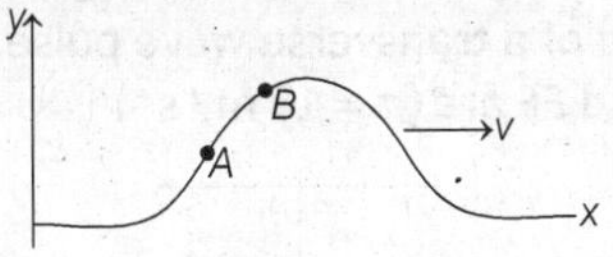

(a) $R_A > R_B$
(b) $R_B > R_A$
(c) $R_A = R_B$
(d) Information is not sufficient to decide

22 The transverse wave shown is travelling from right to left in a medium. The direction of the instantaneous velocity of a particle of the medium at point P is

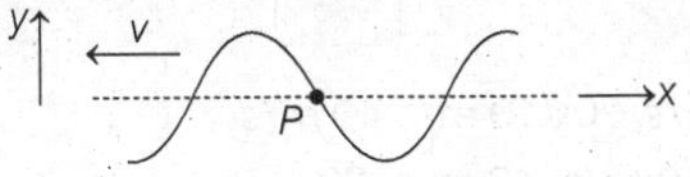

(a) ↑ (b) ↓
(c) ↖ (d) ←

23 Wave pulse on a string shown in figure is moving to the right without changing shape. Consider two particles at positions $x_1 = 1.5$ m and $x_2 = 2.5$ m. Their transverse velocities at the moment shown in figure are along directions

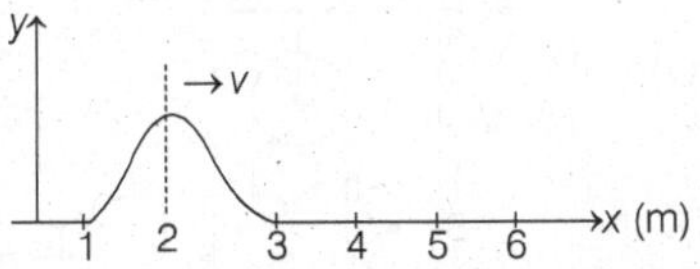

(a) positive Y-axis and positive Y-axis respectively
(b) negative Y-axis and positive Y-axis respectively
(c) positive Y-axis and negative Y-axis respectively
(d) negative Y-axis and negative Y-axis respectively

24 The figure shows a simple harmonic progressive transverse wave, progressing towards the right. The particle having the maximum acceleration directed downwards is represented by

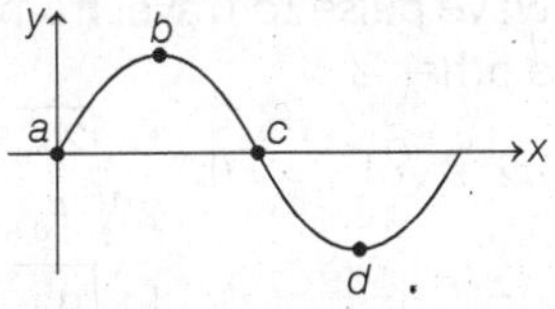

(a) a (b) b
(c) c (d) d

25 A certain transverse sinusoidal wave of wavelength 20 cm is moving in the positive x-direction. The transverse velocity of the particle at $x = 0$ as a function of time is shown. The amplitude of the motion is

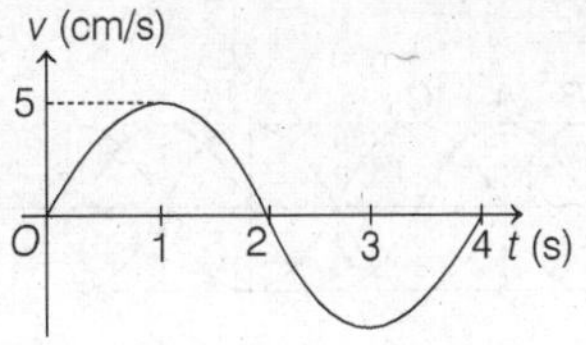

(a) $\frac{5}{\pi}$ cm (b) $\frac{\pi}{2}$ cm
(c) $\frac{10}{\pi}$ cm (d) 2π cm

26 Graph shows three waves that are separately sent along a string that is stretched under a certain tension along X-axis. If ω_1, ω_2 and ω_3 are their angular frequencies respectively, then

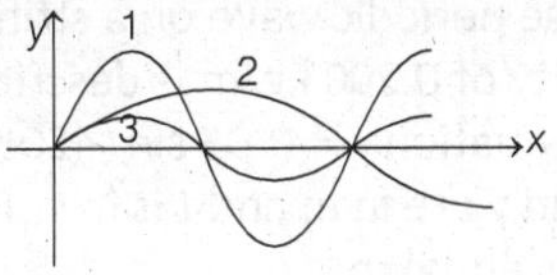

(a) $\omega_1 = \omega_3 > \omega_2$ (b) $\omega_1 > \omega_2 > \omega_3$
(c) $\omega_2 > \omega_1 = \omega_3$ (d) $\omega_1 = \omega_2 = \omega_3$

27 The following figure depicts a wave travelling in a medium. Which pair of particles are in phase?

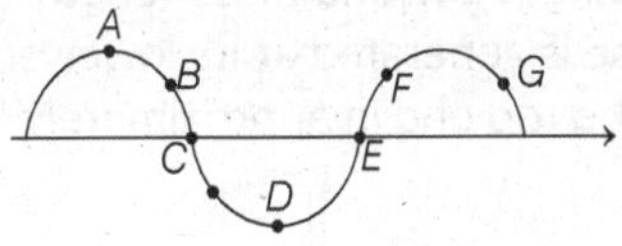

(a) A and D (b) B and F
(c) C and E (d) B and G

28 A small-amplitude progressive wave in a stretched string has a velocity of 10 ms^{-1} and a frequency of 100 Hz. What is the phase difference, in radians, between two points 2.5 cm apart in the string?

(a) $\frac{\pi}{8}$ (b) $\frac{\pi}{4}$ (c) $\frac{3\pi}{8}$ (d) $\frac{\pi}{2}$

29 The equation of a wave is given by (all quantity expressed in MKS units) $y = 5 \sin 10\pi (t - 0.01x)$ along the X-axis. The phase difference between the points separated by a distance of 10 m along X-axis is

(a) $\pi/2$ (b) π (c) 2π (d) $\pi/4$

30 Transverse wave of amplitude 0.1 m is generated at one end ($x = 0$) of a long string by a tuning fork of frequency 500 Hz. At a certain instant of time, the displacement of particle A at $x = 1.0$ m is -0.1 m and of particle B at $x = 2.0$ m is $+0.1$ m. How long can the wave take to travel from A to B?

(a) 1 s (b) 1/10 s (c) 1/100 s (d) 1/1000 s

31 Three progressive waves *A*, *B* and *C* are shown in figure. With respect to wave *A*

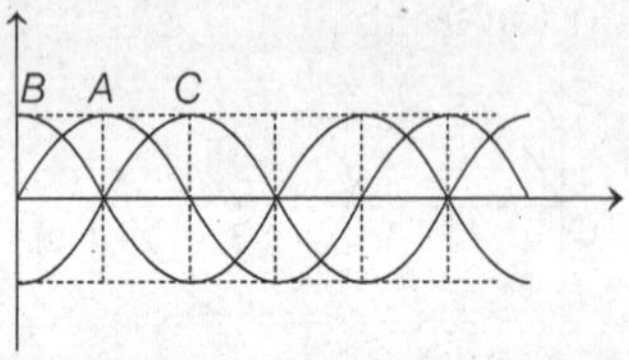

(a) The wave *C* lags behind in phase by $\pi/2$ and *B* leads by $\pi/2$
(b) The wave *C* leads in phase by π and *B* lags behind by π
(c) The wave *C* leads in phase by $\pi/2$ and *B* lags behind by $\pi/2$
(d) The wave *C* lags behind in phase by π and *B* leads by π

32 A transverse periodic wave on a string with a linear mass density of 0.200 kg/m is described by the following equation $y = 0.05 \sin(420t - 21.0x)$ where *x* and *y* are in m and *t* is in s. The tension in the string is equal to

(a) 32 N (b) 42 N
(c) 66N (d) 80 N

33 A block of mass 1 kg is hanging vertically from a string of length 1 m and mass/length = 0.001 kg/m. A small pulse is generated at its lower end. The pulse reaches the top end in approximately

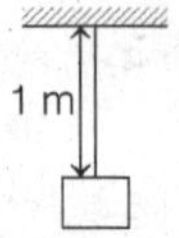

(a) 0.2 s (b) 0.1 s (c) 0.02 s (d) 0.01 s

34 A 4 kg block is suspended from a ceiling of an elevator through a string having a linear mass density of 19.2×10^{-3} kg/m. Find the speed (with respect to the string) with which a wave pulse can proceed on the string, if the elevator accelerates up at the rate of 2.0 m/s^2. ($g = 10\text{ m/s}^2$)

(a) 35 m/s (b) 57 m/s
(c) 45 m/s (d) 50 m/s

35 A heavy ball is suspended from the ceiling of a motor car through a light string. A transverse pulse travels at a speed of 50 cm/s on the string when the car is at rest and 52 cm/s when the car accelerates on a horizontal road. Then acceleration of the car is (Take $g = 10\text{ m/s}^2$)

(a) 2.7 m/s^2 (b) 3.7 m/s^2
(c) 2.4 m/s^2 (d) 4.1 m/s^2

36 Three blocks I, II and III having mass of 1.6 kg, 1.6 kg and 3.2 kg, respectively are connected as shown in the figure. The linear mass density of the wire *AB*, *CD* and *EF* are 10 g/m, 8 g/m and 10 g/m respectively. The speed of a transverse wave pulse produced in *AB*, *CD* and *EF* are ($g = 10\text{ m/s}^2$)

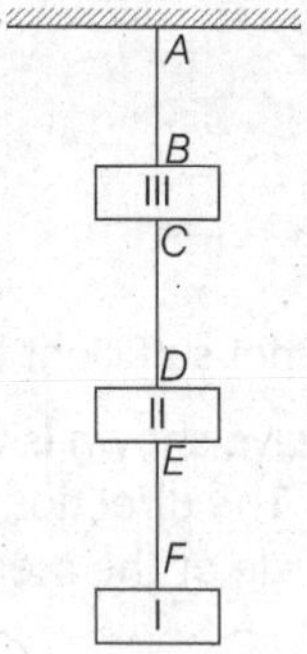

(a) 80 m/s, $20\sqrt{10}$ m/s 40 m/s
(b) $20\sqrt{10}$ m/s, 40 m/s, 80 m/s
(c) $20\sqrt{10}$ m/s in all
(d) 80 m/s in all

37 Both the strings, shown in figure are made of same material and diameter of *CD* is double that of *AB*. The pulleys are light. The speed of a transverse wave in the string *AB* is v_1 and in *CD* it is v_2, then $\frac{v_1}{v_2}$ is

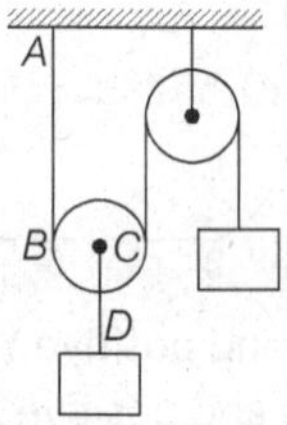

(a) 1 (b) 2 (c) $\sqrt{2}$ (d) $\frac{1}{\sqrt{2}}$

38 A string of length *L* consists of two distinct sections. The left half has linear mass density $\mu = \mu_0/2$, while the right half has linear mass density $\mu' = 3\mu_0$. Tension in the string is F_0. The time required for a transverse wave pulse to travel from one end of the string to the other is

(a) $\frac{L}{4}\sqrt{\frac{\mu_0}{F_0}}(\sqrt{2}+\sqrt{6})$ (b) $\frac{L}{2}\sqrt{\frac{2\mu_0}{F_0}}(1+\sqrt{3})$

(c) $\frac{L}{2}\sqrt{\frac{\mu_0}{2F_0}}(\sqrt{2}+\sqrt{6})$ (d) $\frac{L}{2}\sqrt{\frac{\mu_0}{2F_0}}(1+\sqrt{6})$

39 A uniform rope having some mass hanges vertically from a rigid support. A transverse wave pulse is produced at the lower end. The speed (v) of the wave pulse varies with height (h) from the lower end as

(a) 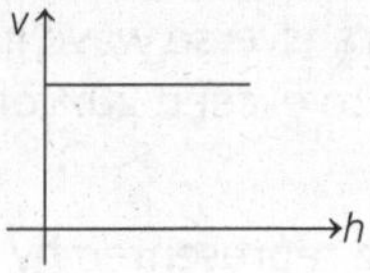

(b) 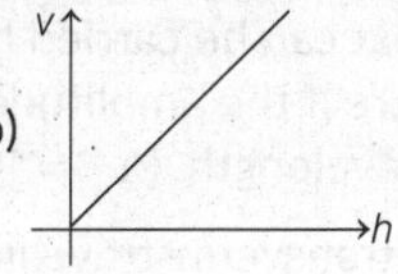

(c) 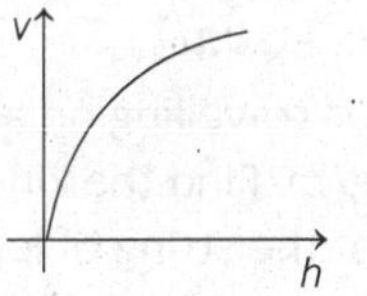

(d) 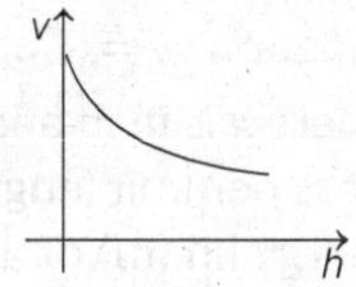

40 A heavy but uniform rope of length L is suspended from a ceiling. A particle is dropped from the ceiling at the instant when the bottom end is given the jerk. Where will the particle meet the pulse?
(a) At a distance $2L/3$ from the bottom
(b) At a distance $L/3$ from the bottom
(c) At a distance $3L/4$ from the bottom
(d) None of the above

41 A wire of variable mass per unit length $\mu = \mu_0 x$, is hanging from the ceiling as shown in figure. The length of wire is l_0. A small transverse disturbance is produced at its lower end. Find the time after which the disturbance will reach to the other end.

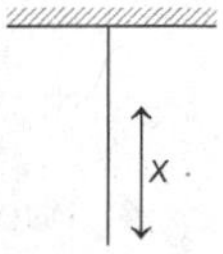

(a) $\sqrt{\frac{l_0}{2g}}$ (b) $\sqrt{\frac{2l_0}{g}}$ (c) $\sqrt{\frac{4l_0}{g}}$ (d) $\sqrt{\frac{8l_0}{g}}$

42 When a 100 Hz oscillator is used to generate a sinusoidal wave on a certain string, the wavelength is 10 cm. When the tension in the string is doubled, the generator produces a wave with a frequency and wavelength of
(a) 200 Hz and 20 cm (b) 141 Hz and 10 cm
(c) 100 Hz and 20 cm (d) 100 Hz and 14 cm

43 Two identical but separate strings, with the same tension, carry sinusoidal waves with the same frequency. Wave A has an amplitude that is twice that of wave B and transmits energy at a rate that is .... that of wave B.
(a) half (b) twice
(c) one-fourth (d) four times

44 Sinusoidal waves 5.00 cm in amplitude are to be transmitted along a string having a linear mass density equal to 4.00×10^{-2} kg/m. If the source can deliver an average power of 90 W and the string is under a tension of 100 N, then the highest frequency at which the source can operate is (Take $\pi^2 = 10$)
(a) 45 Hz (b) 50 Hz (c) 30 Hz (d) 62 Hz

45 The prong of an electrically operated tuning fork is connected to a long string of $\mu = 1$ kg/m and tension 25 N. The maximum velocity of the prong is 1 cm/s, then the average power needed to drive the prong is

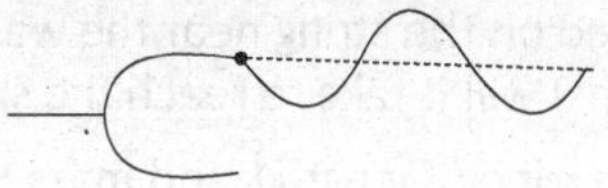

(a) 5×10^{-4} W (b) 2.5×10^{-4} W
(c) 1×10^{-4} W (d) 10^{-3} W

Numerical Value Questions

1 A particle on a stretched string supporting a travelling wave, takes minimum time 5.0 ms to move from its mean position to the mean position. The distance between two consecutive particles, which are at their mean positions, is 2.0 cm. Find the wave speed (in m/s).

2 A progressive wave of frequency 500 Hz is travelling with a velocity of 360 m/s. How far apart (in cm) are two points 60° out of phase?

3 A plane progressive wave is given by $x = (40 \text{ cm}) \cos (50\pi t - 0.02\pi y)$ where y is in cm and t is in s. The particle velocity at $y = 25$ m and at time $t = 0.005$ s will be $10\pi \sqrt{n}$ m/s. What is the value of n?

4 A transverse wave is passing through a string shown in figure. Mass density of the string is 1 kg/m^3 and cross-section area of string is 0.01 m^2. Equation of wave in string is $y = 2 \sin (20t - 10x)$ where t is time in s and x is position in m. If the hanging mass is $n \times 10^{-3}$ kg, then find the value of n.

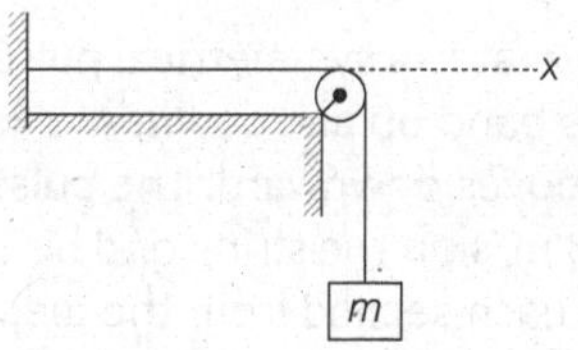

5 Find out the time taken (in ms) by the pulse generated at the right end to reach the left end. The system is released from the rest in the figure shown. Mass per unit length of the string is 12 g/m. Neglect the effect of mass of string in calculation of tension and acceleration. Pulleys are smooth and frictionless. [Take, $g = 10$ m/s^2]

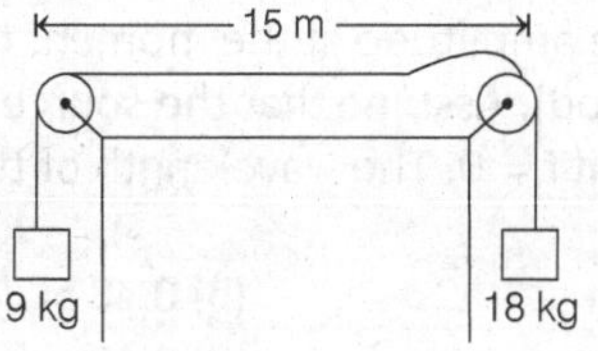

6 A string of length 40 cm and weighing 10 g is attached to a spring at one end and to a fixed wall at the other end. The spring has a spring constant of 160 N/m and is stretched by 1.0 cm. If a wave pulse is produced on the string near the wall, how much time (in ms) will it take to reach the spring?

7 A uniform rope of length L and mass M hangs vertically from a rigid support. A block of mass m $(m = M)$ is attached to the free end of the rope. A transverse pulse of wavelength λ is produced at the lower end of the rope. The wavelength of the pulse, when it reaches the top of the rope, is $a\lambda$. Find the value of a^2.

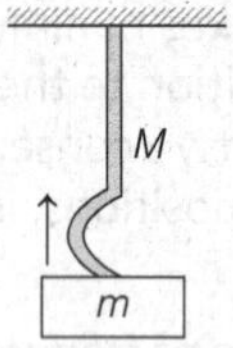

8 A steel wire has a mass of 5 g/m and is under tension 450 N. Find the maximum average power (in kW) that can be carried by the transverse wave in the wire if the amplitude is not to exceed 20% of the wavelength. $(\pi^2 = 10)$

9 A transverse travelling wave represented by a equation : $y = (1\text{ cm}) \sin [2\pi x - 20\pi t]$, where x is in m and t is in s, is travelling on a string of mass per unit length 0.01 kg/m. Find the kinetic energy (in mJ) of a portion of the string of length equal to one wavelength.

10 A transverse wave is passing through a stretched string with a speed of 20 m/s. The tension in the string is 20 N. At a certain point P on the string, it is observed that energy is being transferred at a rate of 40 mW at a given instant. Find the speed (in cm/s) of point P.

LEVEL 03 JEE Advanced Level

Single Choice Correct Questions

1 A wave is propagating along X-axis. The displacement of particles of the medium in z-direction at $t = 0$ is given by : $z = \exp[-(x+2)^2]$, where x is in m. At $t = 1$ s, the same wave disturbance is given by : $z = \exp[-(2-x)^2]$. Then, the wave propagation velocity is

(a) 4 m/s in $+x$-direction (b) 4 m/s in $-x$-direction
(c) 2 m/s in $+x$-direction (d) 2 m/s in $-x$-direction

2 A man generates a symmetrical pulse in a string by moving his hand up and down. At $t = 0$, the point on his hand moves downward. The pulse travels with speed of 3 m/s on the string and his hands passes 6 times in each second from the mean position. Then, at what time the point on the string at a distance 3 m from the hand will reach its upper extreme first time?

(a) 1.25 s (b) 1 s
(c) 13/12 s (d) None of these

3 The displacement from the position of equilibrium of a point 4 cm from a source of sinusoidal oscillations is half the amplitude at the moment $t = T/6$ (T is the time period). Assume that the source was at mean position at $t = 0$. The wavelength of the running wave is

(a) 0.96 m (b) 0.48 m
(c) 0.24 m (d) 0.12 m

4 Two particles of medium disturbed by the wave propagation are at $x_1 = 0$ and $x_2 = 1$ cm. The respective displacement (in cm) of the particles can be given by equations

$y_1 = 2 \sin 3\pi t$, $y_2 = 2 \sin \left(3\pi t - \frac{\pi}{2}\right)$.

Wave velocity can be

(a) 6 cm/s (b) 7 cm/s (c) 8 cm/s (d) 9 cm/s

5 The figure below shows a snap photogaph of a simple harmonic progressive wave, progressing in the negative X-axis, at a given instant. The direction of the velocity of the particle at the stage P on the figure is best represented by the arrow.

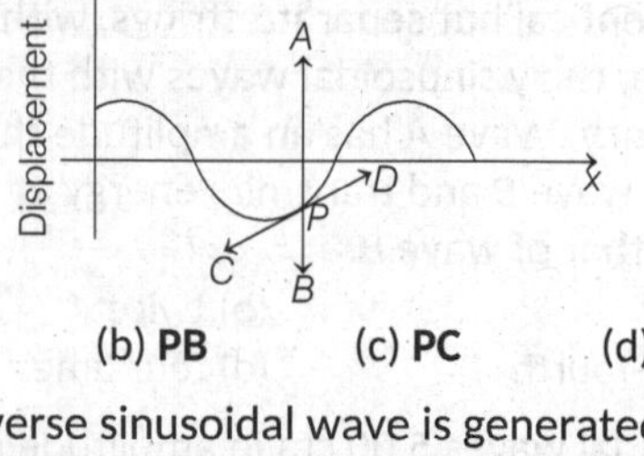

(a) **PA** (b) **PB** (c) **PC** (d) **PD**

6 A transverse sinusoidal wave is generated at one end of a long horizontal string by a bar that moves the end up and down through a distance by 2.0 cm. The motion of bar is continuous and is repeated regularly 125 times per second. If the distance between adjacent wave crests is observed to be 15.6 cm and the wave is moving along positive x-direction, and at $t = 0$ the element of the string at $x = 0$ is at mean position $y = 0$ and is moving downward, the equation of the wave is best described by

(a) $y = (1\text{ cm}) \sin[(40.3\text{ rad/m})\, x - (786\text{ rad/s})\, t]$
(b) $y = (2\text{ cm}) \sin[40.3\text{ rad/m})\, x - (786\text{ rad/s})\, t]$
(c) $y = (1\text{ cm}) \cos[(40.3\text{ rad/m})\, x - (786\text{ rad/s})\, t]$
(d) $y = (2\text{ cm}) \cos[(40.3\text{ rad/m})\, x - (786\text{ rad/s})\, t]$

7 A transverse sinusoidal wave moves along a string in the positive x-direction at a speed of 10 cm/s. The wavelength of the wave is 0.5 m and its amplitude is 10 cm. At a particular time t, the snapshot of the wave is shown in figure. The velocity of point P when its displacement is 5 cm is

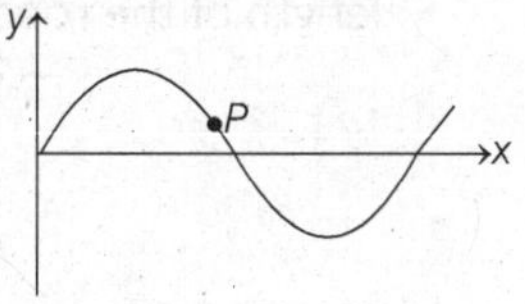

(a) $\frac{\sqrt{3}\pi}{50}\,\hat{j}$ m/s (b) $-\frac{\sqrt{3}\pi}{50}\,\hat{j}$ m/s
(c) $\frac{\sqrt{3}\pi}{50}\,\hat{i}$ m/s (d) $-\frac{\sqrt{3}\pi}{50}\,\hat{i}$ m/s

8 The following figure shows a snapshot of a vibrating string at $t = 0$. The particle P is observed to be moving up with velocity $20\sqrt{3}$ cm/s. The tangent to the string at P makes an angle of 60° with the X-axis. The equation of the wave is

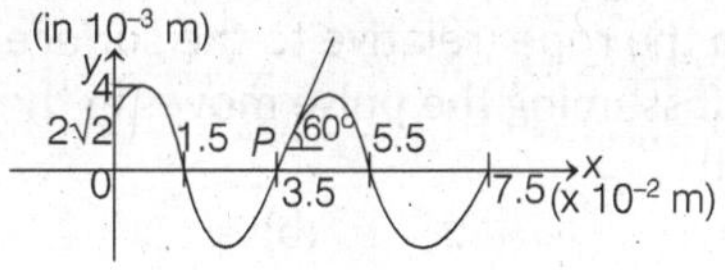

(a) $y = (4 \times 10^{-3}) \sin\left(10\pi t + \frac{\pi}{2}x + \frac{\pi}{4}\right)$

(b) $y = (4 \times 10^{-3}) \sin\left(10\pi t - \frac{\pi}{2}x + \frac{\pi}{4}\right)$

(c) $y = (4 \times 10^{-3}) \sin\left(10\pi t + \frac{\pi}{2}x + \frac{3\pi}{4}\right)$

(d) $y = (4 \times 10^{-3}) \sin\left(10\pi t - \frac{\pi}{2}x + \frac{3\pi}{4}\right)$

9 Figure shows two snapshots of medium particles within a time interval of 1/60 s. Find the possible time periods of the wave

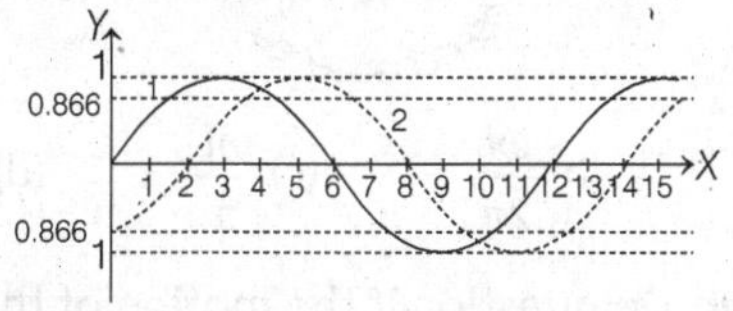

(a) $\frac{1}{10(6n+1)}$ (b) $\frac{1}{10(5n+1)}$
(c) $\frac{1}{10(6n-1)}$ (d) $\frac{1}{20(6n+1)}$

10 Adjoining figure shows the snapshot of two waves A and B at any time t. The equation for A is $y = A \sin(kx - \omega t - \phi)$, and for B it is $y = A \sin(kx - \omega t)$. It is clearly shown in the figure that wave A is ahead of B by a distance ϕ/k. The motion of a single point in time, i.e., y *versus* t for two waves is best represented by

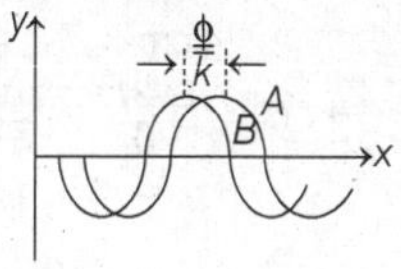

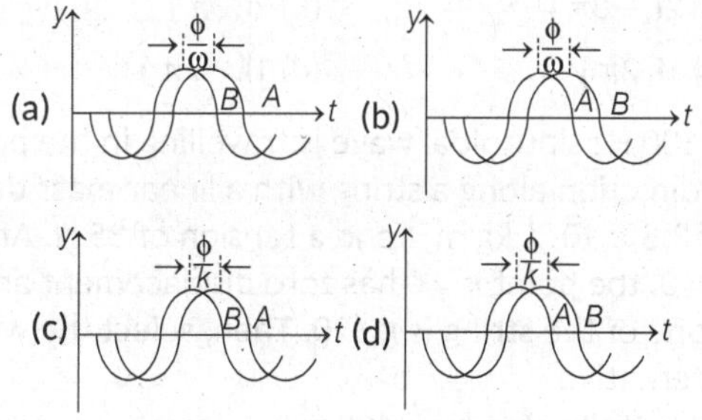

11 A transverse wave on a string travelling along +ve X-axis has been shown in the figure below. The mathematical form of the shown wave is $y = (3.0\text{ cm}) \sin\left[2\pi \times 0.1t - \frac{2\pi}{100}x\right]$ where t is in s and x is in cm.

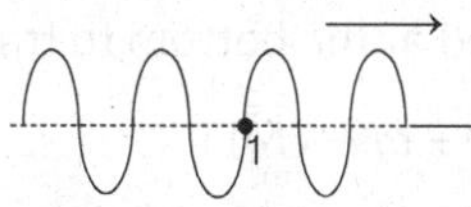

Find the total distance travelled by the particle at (1) in 10 min 15 s, measured from the instant shown in the figure and direction of its motion at the end of this time

(a) 6 cm, in upward direction
(b) 6 cm, in downward direction
(c) 738 cm, in upward direction
(d) 732 cm, in upward direction

12 A harmonic wave is travelling on a stretched string. At any particular instant, the smallest distance between two particles having same displacement, equal to half of amplitude is 8 cm. Find the smallest separation between two particles which have same value of displacement (magnitude only) equal to half of amplitude

(a) 8 cm
(b) 24 cm
(c) 12 cm
(d) 4 cm

13 A transverse sinusoidal wave moves along a string in the positive x-direction. In figure (1) displacement of particle at P as a function of time is given and in figure (II) at a paticular time t-the snapshot of wave is shown. The wave velocity (cm/s) and velocity of particle at P (cm/s) will be

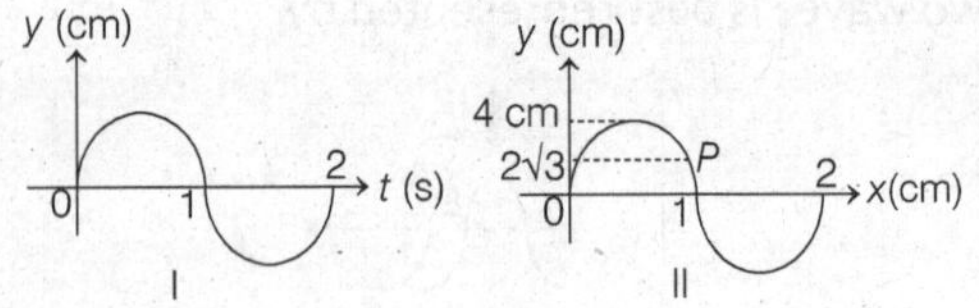

(a) $2\hat{\mathbf{i}}, -3\pi\,\hat{\mathbf{j}}$ (b) $2\hat{\mathbf{i}}, 3\pi\,\hat{\mathbf{j}}$
(c) $1\hat{\mathbf{i}}, 2\pi\,\hat{\mathbf{j}}$ (d) $1\hat{\mathbf{i}}, -2\pi\,\hat{\mathbf{j}}$

14 A 100 Hz sinusoidal wave is travelling in the positive X-direction along a string with a linear mass density of 3.5×10^{-3} kg m^{-1} and a tension of 35 N. At time $t = 0$, the point $x = 0$ has zero displacement and the slope of the string is $\pi / 20$. Then, select the wrong alternative
(a) velocity of wave is 100 m/s
(b) angular frequency is 200π rad/s
(c) amplitude of wave is 0.025 m
(d) propagation constant is $4\pi\ m^{-1}$

15 A rope of mass m and length L is suspended vertically. If a mass M is suspended from the free end of the rope, the time taken by a transverse wave pulse generated at the bottom to travel to the top is
(a) $2\sqrt{\frac{L}{mg}}(\sqrt{M+m}-\sqrt{M})$
(b) $\sqrt{\frac{L}{mg}}(\sqrt{M+m}-\sqrt{M})$
(c) $\frac{1}{2}\sqrt{\frac{L}{mg}}(\sqrt{M}-\sqrt{m})$
(d) $\sqrt{\frac{L}{mg}}(\sqrt{M}-\sqrt{m})$

16 In the figure shown, strings AB and BC have masses m and 2m, respectively. Both are of the same length 1. Mass of each string is uniformly distributed on its length. The string is suspended vertically from the ceiling of a room. A small jerk wave pulse is given at the end C. If time taken by it to reach upper end A is $a(b+\sqrt{c}-\sqrt{d})\sqrt{\frac{l}{g}}$, then find the value of $a+b+c+d$

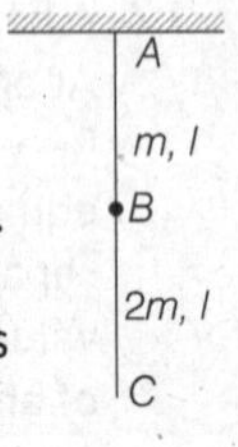

(a) 5 (b) 6 (c) 7 (d) 8

17 A rope hangs from a rigid support. A pulse is set by jiggling the bottom end. We want to design a rope in which velocity v of pulse is independent of z, the distance of the pulse from fixed end of the rope. If the rope is very long the desired function for mass per unit length $\mu(z)$ in terms of μ_0 (mass per unit length of the rope at the top ($z = 0$), g, v and z is

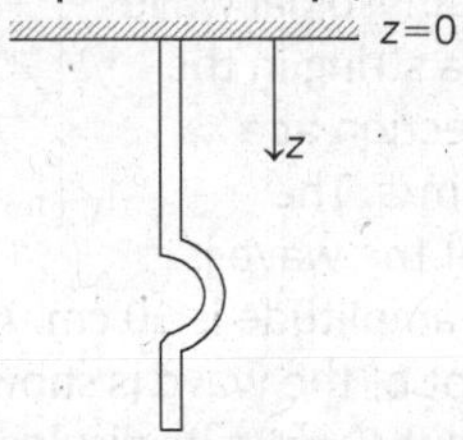

(a) $\mu(z) = \mu_0 e^{-[g/v^2]z}$ (b) $\mu(z) = \mu_0 e^{+[g/v^2]z}$
(c) $\mu(z) = \mu_0 \log_e\left(\frac{g}{v^2}\right)z$ (d) $\mu(z) = \mu_0 e + \left(\frac{v^2}{g}\right)z$

18 A loose coil of flexible rope of length L and mass m rests on a frictionless table. A force S is applied at one end of the rope and more and more rope is pulled from the coil with a constant velocity v. A transverse pulse is produced in the rope while the rope is being pulled from the coil. The velocity of the pulse in the rope (relative to the surface of the table) will be (assuming the pulse moves in the direction of the pull)
(a) zero (b) 2v
(c) $\sqrt{\frac{SL}{m}}$ (d) $\frac{1}{2}\sqrt{\frac{SL}{m}}$

19 A circular loop of rope of length L rotates with uniform angular velocity ω about an axis through its centre on a horizontal smooth platform. Velocity of pulse (with respect to rope) produced due to slight radial displacement is given by

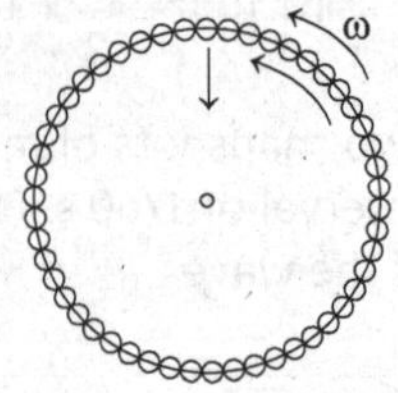

(a) ωL (b) $\frac{\omega L}{2\pi}$ (c) $\frac{\omega L}{\pi}$ (d) $\frac{\omega L}{4\pi^2}$

20 In the above question if the motion of the pulse and rotation of the loop, both are in same direction, then the velocity of the pulse w.r.t. to ground will be
(a) ωL (b) $\frac{\omega L}{2\pi}$ (c) $\frac{\omega L}{\pi}$ (d) $\frac{\omega L}{4\pi^2}$

21 In the above question, if both are in opposite direction, then the velocity of the pulse w.r.t. to ground will be

(a) ωL (b) $\frac{\omega L}{2\pi}$ (c) $\frac{\omega L}{\pi}$ (d) 0

22 A uniform rope of length L and mass m is held at one end and whirled in a horizontal circle with angular velocity ω. Ignore gravity. Find the time period required for a transverse wave to travel from one end of the rope to the other.

(a) $\frac{\pi}{\sqrt{2}\omega}$ (b) $\frac{\sqrt{2}\pi}{\omega}$ (c) $\frac{2\pi}{\omega}$ (d) $\frac{\pi}{2\omega}$

23 A stretched rope having linear mass density 5×10^{-2} kg/m is under a tension of 80 N. The power that has to be supplied to the rope to generate harmonic waves at a frequency of 60 Hz and an amplitude of $\frac{2\sqrt{2}}{15\pi}$ m is

(a) 215 W (b) 251 W
(c) 512 W (d) 521 W

24 The displacement vs time graph for two waves A and B which travel along the same string are shown in the figure. Their intensity ratio I_A/I_B is

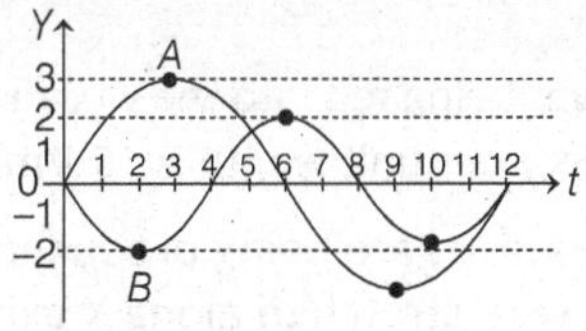

(a) $\frac{9}{4}$ (b) 1 (c) $\frac{81}{16}$ (d) $\frac{3}{2}$

25 The wave function of a triangular wave pulse is defined by the relation below at time $t = 0$ s

$$y = \begin{cases} mx & \text{for } 0 \le x \le \frac{a}{2} \\ -m(x-a) & \text{for } \frac{a}{2} \le x \le a \\ 0 & \text{everywhere else, where } m << 1 \end{cases}$$

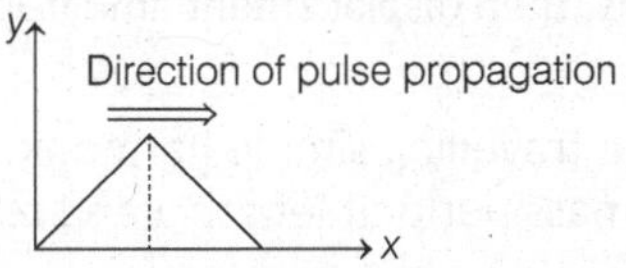

The wave pulse is moving in the +x-direction in a string having tension T and mass per unit length μ. The total energy present with the wave pulse is

(a) $\frac{m^2Ta}{2}$ (b) m^2Ta (c) mTa (d) $\frac{mTa}{2}$

Multiple Choice(s) Correct Questions

1. Which of the following functions could represent a travelling wave?

(a) $A\cos(kx+\omega t)$ (b) $\frac{(x-vt)}{1+(x-vt)^2}$

(c) $(x-vt)^2+1$ (d) $\frac{1}{1+(x-bt^2)}$

2 $y(x,t) = \frac{0.8}{[(4x+5t)^2+5]}$ represents a moving pulse, where x and y are in m and t in s. Then,

(a) pulse is moving in +x-direction
(b) In 2 s it will travel a distance of 2.5 m
(c) its maximum displacement is 0.16 m
(d) it is a symmetric pulse

3 The plane wave represented by an equation of the form $y = f(x - vt)$ implies the propagation along the positive x-axis without change of shape with constant velocity v

(a) $\frac{\partial y}{\partial t} = -v\left(\frac{\partial y}{\partial x}\right)$ (b) $\frac{\partial y}{\partial t} = -v\left(\frac{\partial^2 y}{\partial x^2}\right)$

(c) $\frac{\partial^2 y}{\partial t^2} = -v^2\left(\frac{\partial^2 y}{\partial x^2}\right)$ (d) $\frac{\partial^2 y}{\partial t^2} = v^2\left(\frac{\partial^2 y}{\partial x^2}\right)$

4 A transverse wave travelling on a taut string is represented by $y = 0.01\sin 2\pi(10t - x)$ where y and x are in m and t in s. Then,

(a) the speed of the wave is 10 m/s
(b) closest points on the string which differ in phase by 60° are separated by (1/6) m
(c) Maximum particle velocity in $\pi/4$ m/s
(d) The phase of a certain point on the string changes by 120° in (1/20) s

5 Figure shows a snapshot graph and a history graph for a wave pulse on a stretched string. They describe the same wave from two perspectives.

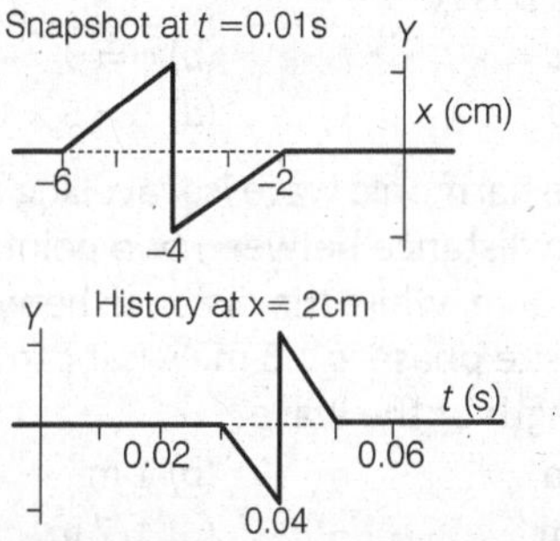

(a) the wave is travelling in positive x-direction
(b) the wave is travelling in negative x-direction
(c) the speed of the wave is 2 m/s
(d) the peak is located at $x = -6$ cm at $t = 0$

6 The figure represents two snaps of a travelling wave on a string of mass per unit length $\mu = 0.25$ kg/m. The first snap is taken at $t = 0$ and the second is taken at $t = 0.05$ s. Choose the correct option(s).

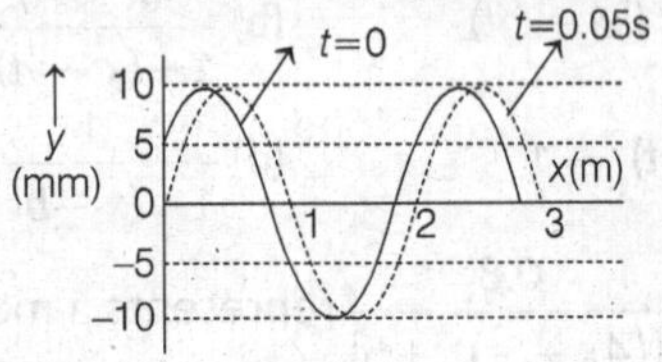

(a) $y = 10 \sin\left(\pi x - \frac{10}{3}\pi t + \frac{\pi}{6}\right)$

(b) $y = 10 \sin\left(\pi x - \frac{10}{3}\pi t + \frac{5\pi}{6}\right)$

(c) Tension in the string is 25/3 N

(d) Tension in the string is 25/9 N

7 Shape of a string transmitting wave along X-axis at some instant is shown. Velocity of point P is $v = 4\pi$ cm/s and angle $\theta = \tan^{-1}(0.004\pi)$.

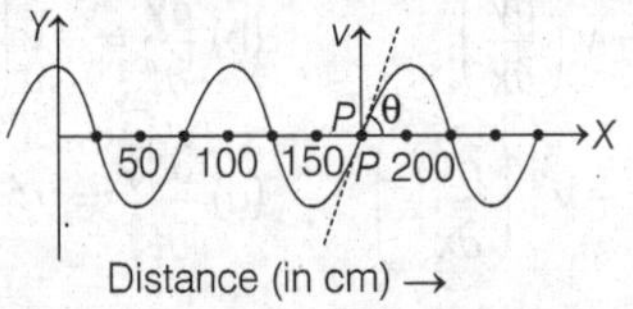

(a) Amplitude of wave is 2 mm

(b) Velociity of wave is 10 m/s

(c) Maximum acceleration of particle is $80\pi^2$ cm/s^2

(d) Wave is travelling in negative x-direction

8 A plane progressive wave of frequency 25 Hz, amplitude 2.5×10^{-5} m and initial phase zero moves along the negative X-direction with a velocity of 300 m/s. A and B are two points 6 m apart on the line of propagation of the wave. At any instant the phase difference between A and B is ϕ. The maximum difference in the displacements of particle at A and B is Δ.

(a) $\phi = \pi$ (b) $\phi = 0$

(c) $\Delta = 0$ (d) $\Delta = 5 \times 10^{-5}$ m

9 A simple harmonic wave is travelling along a straight line. The distance between two points in the same phase is 5 m, while the distance between two points in opposite phase is 1.5 m. What can be the wavelength of the wave?

(a) 0.5 m (b) 1 m

(c) 1/3 m (d) 1/7 m

10 A perfectly elastic uniform string is suspended vertically with its upper end fixed to the ceiling and the lower end loaded with the weight. If a transverse wave is imparted to the lower end of the string, the pulse will

(a) not travel along the length of the string

(b) travel upwards with increasing speed

(c) travel upwards with decreasing speed

(d) travel upwards with constant acceleration

11 One end of a string of length L is tied to the ceiling of a lift accelerating upwards with an acceleration $2g$. The other end of the string is free. The linear mass density of the string varies linearly from 0 to λ from bottom to top.

(a) The velocity of the wave in the string will be 0

(b) The acceleration (relative to string) of the wave on the string will be $3g/4$ everywhere

(c) The time taken by a pulse to reach from bottom to top will be $\sqrt{8L/3g}$

(d) The time taken by a pulse to reach from bottom to top will be $\sqrt{4L/3g}$

12 Waves are moving along + X-direction with amplitude 0.4 m, speed 6 m/s and frequency 17 Hz on a string with mass per unit length $\mu = 0.02$ kg/m. (Use $\pi^2 = 10$)

(a) The energy per unit length is 18.5 J/m.

(b) The power being fed into the vibrating string is 111 W.

(c) The power being fed into the vibrating string is 90 W.

(d) The energy per unit length is 15 J/m.

13 Transverse waves are being produced at the one end ($x = 0$) of a wire stretched along X-axis by a tuning fork oscillating along Y-axis. The frequency of the fork is 400 Hz and linear mass density of wire is 0.05 kg/m. It is observed that at a certain moment of time two consecutive particles at extreme are located at $x = 100$ cm and $x = 200$ cm. Now, choose the correct statement(s)

(a) Tension in the string is 32×10^3 N

(b) Speed of the wave is 800 m/s

(c) Wavelength of the wave is 2 m

(d) If maximum velocity of particle of the wire is 80π m/s, then displacement amplitude of particle is 10 cm

14 Consider a travelling simple harmonic wave on a string of mass per unit length μ and tension T. Kinetic energy per unit length is given by $u_k = \frac{1}{2}\mu\left(\frac{\partial y}{\partial t}\right)^2$ and potential energy per unit length is given by $u_p = \frac{1}{2}T\left(\frac{\partial y}{\partial x}\right)^2$. Mark the correct option.

(a) Power transmitted by wave equals $(u_k + u_p)\sqrt{\dfrac{T}{\mu}}$

(b) u_k and u_p simultaneously attain their maximum and minimum values

(c) Total energy per unit length of a string is constant when a harmonic wave travels on it

(d) A small part of string has maximum potential enegy when it is at its equilibrium position

Comprehension Based Questions

Comprehension-1

Figure shows two snapshots of medium particle supporting a plane progressive wave travelling along positive X-axis, corresponding to instants $t = 0.002$ s and $t = 0.008$ s, respectively shown by curves numbered 1 and 2. Assume that the interval between the two snapshots is less than the time period.

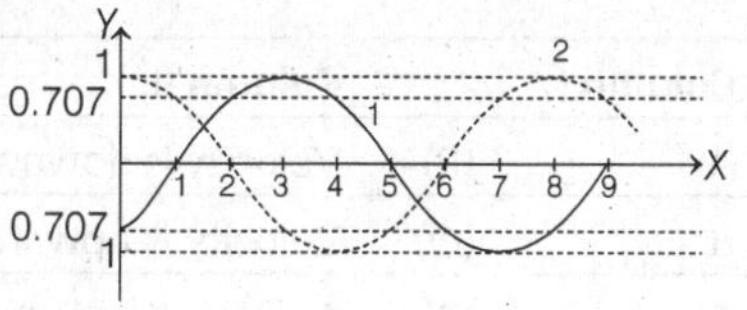

1 Velocity of the wave is

(a) 1700/3 m/s
(b) 1700/5 m/s
(c) 2500/7 m/s
(d) 2500/3 m/s

2 The frequency of the wave is

(a) 52.6 Hz (b) 205.3 Hz
(c) 104.2 Hz (d) 84.5 Hz

Comprehension-2

A simple harmonic plane wave propagates along X-axis in a medium. The displacement of the particles as a function of time is shown in figure, for $x = 0$ (curve 1) and $x = 7$ (curve 2). The two particles are within a span of one wavelength.

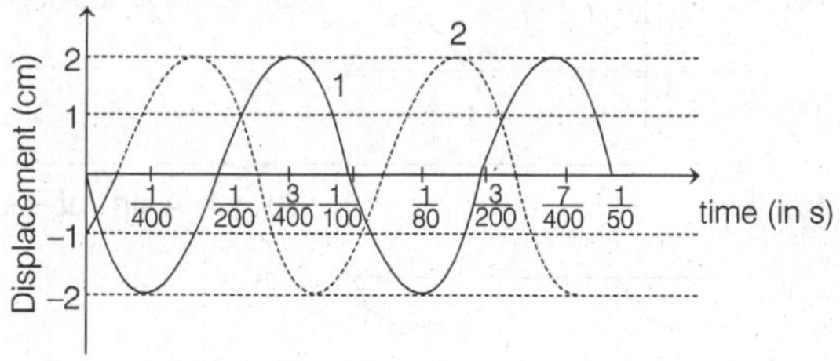

3 The wavelength of the wave is

(a) 6 cm (b) 24 cm
(c) 12 cm (d) 16 cm

4 The speed of the wave is

(a) 12 m/s (b) 24 m/s
(c) 8 m/s (d) 16 m/s

Comprehension-3

A pulse is started at a time $t = 0$ along the +x-direction on a long, taut string. The shape of the pulse at $t = 0$ is given by function y with

$$y = \begin{cases} \dfrac{x}{4} + 1 & \text{for } -4 < x \le 0 \\ -x + 1 & \text{for } 0 < x < 1 \\ 0 & \text{otherwise} \end{cases}$$

here y and x are in cm. The linear mass density of the string is 50 g/m and it is under a tension of 5 N.

5 The shape of the string is drawn at $t = 0$ and the area of the pulse enclosed by the string and the X-axis is measured. It will be equal to

(a) 2 cm^2 (b) 2.5 cm^2
(c) 4 cm^2 (d) 5 cm^2

6 The vertical displacement of the particle of the string at $x = 7$ cm and $t = 0.01$ s will be

(a) 0.75 cm (b) 0.5 cm
(c) 0.25 cm (d) zero

7 The transverse velocity of the particle at $x = 13$ cm and $t = 0.015$ s will be

(a) –250 cm/s (b) –500 cm/s
(c) 500 cm/s (d) –1000 cm/s

Comprehension-4

The figure represents the instantaneous picture of a transverse harmonic wave travelling along the negative X-axis. Choose the correct alternative (s) related to the movement of the nine points shown in the figure.

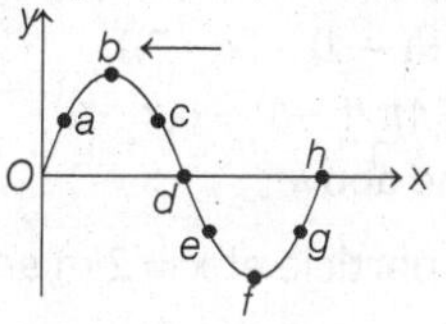

8 The points moving upward is/are

(a) a (b) c
(c) f (d) g

9 The points moving downwards is/are

(a) o (b) b
(c) d (d) h

10 The stationary points is/are

(a) o (b) b
(c) f (d) h

11 The points moving with maximum velocity is/are

(a) b (b) c
(c) d (d) h

Comprehension-5

Sinusoidal waves travel on five identical strings. Use the mathematical forms of the waves given below. In the expressions given below x is in m and y is in mm and t is in s.

(a) $y = (2\text{ mm})\sin(2x - 4t)$
(b) $y = (3\text{ mm})\sin(4x - 10t)$
(c) $y = (2.5\text{ mm})\sin(6x - 12t)$
(d) $y = (1\text{ mm})\sin(8x - 16t)$
(e) $y = (4\text{ mm})\sin(10x - 20t)$

12 Four of the strings have the same tension, but the fifth has a different tension. Identify it.
(a) *a* (b) *b* (c) *d* (d) *e*

13 Two of the strings have the same energy in one wavelength, Identify the pair.
(a) *b* and *c* (b) *a* and *e*
(c) *a* and *d* (d) *b* and *d*

14 Which string has maximum slope at $x = 8$ m and $t = 4$ s?
(a) *a* (b) *c* (c) *d* (d) *e*

Comprehension-6

A sinusoidal wave is propagating in negative *x*-direction in a string stretched along X-axis. A particle of string at $x = 2$ m is found at its mean position and it is moving in positive Y-direction at $t = 1$. The amplitude of the wave, the wavelength and the angular frequency of the wave are 0.1 m, $\frac{\pi}{4}$ m and 4π rad/s, respectively.

15 The equation of the wave is
(a) $y = 0.1\sin(4\pi(t-1) + 8(x-2))$
(b) $y = 0.1\sin((t-1)-(x-2))$
(c) $y = 0.1\sin(4\pi(t-1) - 8(x-2))$
(d) None of the above

16 The speed of particle at $x = 2$ m and $t = 1$ s is
(a) 0.2π m/s (b) 0.6π m/s
(c) 0.4π m/s (d) 0

17 The instantaneous power transfer through $x = 2$ m and $t = 1.125$ s, is
(a) 10 J/s (b) $\frac{4\pi}{3}$ J/s
(c) $\frac{2\pi}{3}$ J/s (d) 0

Match the Columns Questions

1 Following is given the equation of a travelling wave (all in SI units)
$y = (0.02)\sin 2\pi(10t - 5x)$

Match the followings.

Column I		Column II (only magnitude in SI units)	
(A)	Speed of wave	(P)	10
(B)	Frequency of wave	(Q)	0.4π
(C)	Wavelength of wave	(R)	2
(D)	Maximum paticle speed	(S)	0.2

2 A transverse sine wave is travelling in a string towards right as shown. Comment on the velocity and acceleration of points marked *A*, *B* and *C*.

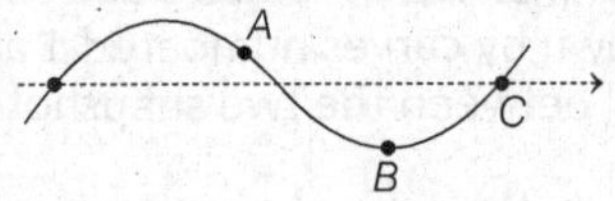

Column I		Column II	
(A)	A	(P)	Velocity is downwards
(B)	B	(Q)	Velocity is upwards
(C)	C	(R)	Acceleration is downwards
		(S)	Acceleration is upwards

3 For four sinusoidal waves, moving on a string along positive *x*-direction, displacement-distance curves (*y*-*x* curves) are shown at time $t = 0$. In the right column, expressions for *y* as function of distance *x* and time *t* for sinusoidal waves are given. All terms in the equations have general meaning. Correctly match *y*-*x* curves with corresponding equations.

Column I		Column II
(A)	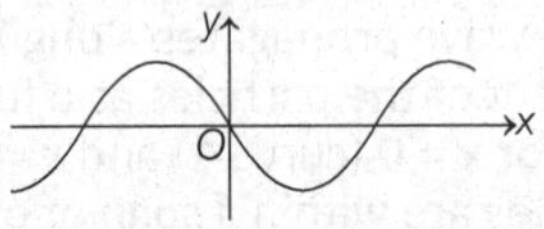	(P) $y = A\cos(\omega t - kx)$
(B)	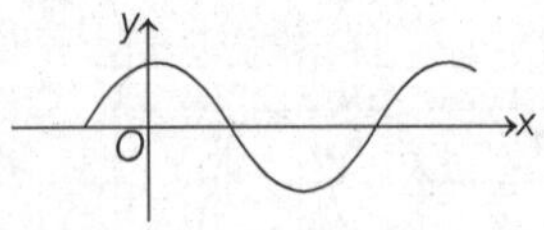	(Q) $y = -A\cos(kx - \omega t)$
(C)	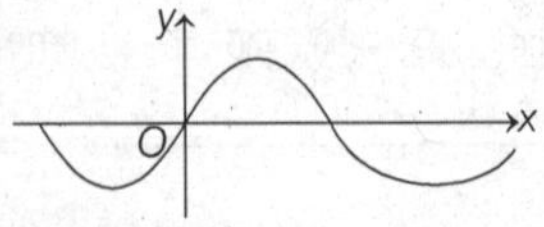	(R) $y = A\sin(\omega t - kx)$
(D)	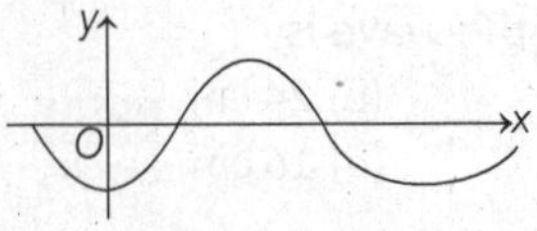	(S) $y = A\sin(kx - \omega t)$
		(T) $y = A\cos(kx - \omega t)$

4 From a single source, two wave trains are sent in two different strings. Strings 2 is 4 times heavier than string 1. The two wave equations are : (area of cross-section and tension of both strings is same)

$y_1 = A \sin(\omega_1 t - k_1 x)$ and $y_2 = 2A \sin(\omega_2 t - k_2 x)$

Suppose, u = energy density, P = power transmitted and I = intensity of the wave.

	Column I		Column II
(a)	u_1 / u_2 is equal to	(p)	1/8
(B)	P_1 / P_2 is equal to	(q)	1/16
(C)	I_1 / I_2 is equal to	(r)	1/4

Numerical Value Questions

1 A travelling wave pulse is given by

$y = \dfrac{0.8}{3x^2 + 12xt + 12t^2 + 4}$, where x and y are in m and t is in s. Find the velocity (in m/s) of the wave.

2 The equation of a transverse wave is given by $\Psi = 10^{-2} \sin \pi [30t - x\sqrt{3} - y]$ where x, y and Ψ are in m, and t in s. If phase difference between two points $A(2\sqrt{3}$ m, 2 m) and $B(3\sqrt{3}$ m, 3 m) be $n\pi$, find the value of n.

3 An ant with mass m is standing peacefully on top of a horizontal, stretched rope. The rope has mass per unit length μ and is under tension F. Without warning, a student starts a sinusoidal transverse wave of wavelength λ propagating along the rope. The motion of the rope is in a vertical plane. What minimum wave amplitude (in mm) will make the ant feel weightless momentarily? Assume that m is so small that the presence of the ant has no effect on the propagation of the wave.

[Given, $\lambda = 0.5$ m, $\mu = 0.1$ kg/m, $F = 3.125$ N, $g = \pi^2$]

4 In the given figure, a string of linear mass density 3×10^{-2} kg/m and length $L = 1$ m, is stretched by a force $F = (3 - kt)$ N, where k is a constant and t is time in s. At the time $t = 0$, a pulse is generated at the end P of the string. Find the value of k (in N/s) if the value of force becomes zero as the pulse reaches point Q.

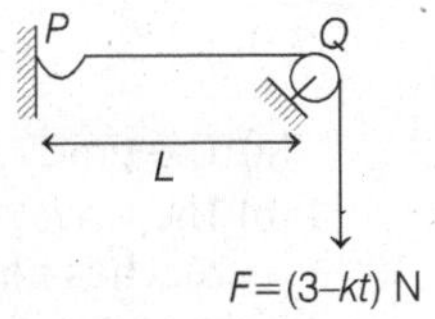

5 Calculate the ratio of the average power (P_1 / P_2) carried by the following two waves. Assume that the strings carrying the waves are identical.

$y_1 = 3.0 \sin(3.2t - 200x)$ cm,

$y_2 = 6.0 \sin(0.4t - 25x)$ cm

6 Sinusoidal progressive wave of amplitude 10 cm is to be sent along a string that has linear mass density of 4×10^{-2} kg/m and a tension of 100 N. The source can deliver a maximum average power of 40 W. What is the maximum frequency (in Hz) at which source can operate? (Take, $\pi^2 = 10$)

7 Find the kinetic energy (in μJ) of pulse travelling in a taut string.

Given, $T = 10$ N and $\mu = 0.1$ kg/m.

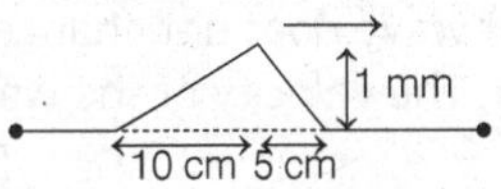

8 The equation (wave function) of a transverse wave travelling on a stretched string is $y = (4 \text{ mm})\, e^{-(2x + 5t)^2}$, where x is in cm and t in s. If tension in the string be 20 N, determine the rate of energy flow along +X-axis through the point $x = 0$ at a time $t = 0$.

Previous Year's Questions

JEE Main

1 A travelling wave is described by the equation $y(x, t) = [0.05 \sin(8x - 4t)]$ m

The velocity of the wave is (all the quantities are in SI unit **[2023, 24 Jan Shift-I]**

(a) 0.5 ms^{-1}
(b) 8 ms^{-1}
(c) 2 ms^{-1}
(d) 4 ms^{-1}

2 A steel wire with mass per unit length $7.0 \times 10^{-3} \text{ kg m}^{-1}$ is under tension of 70 N. The speed of transverse waves in the wire will be **[2023, 1 Feb Shift-I]**

(a) 10 m/s
(b) 200π m/s
(c) 100 m/s
(d) 50 m/s

3 A transverse harmonic wave on a string is given by $y(x, t) = 5 \sin(6t + 0.003x)$ where, x and y are in cm and t in sec. The wave velocity is .... ms^{-1}. **[2023, 10 April Shift-I]**

4 The equation of wave is given by

$$Y = 10^{-2} \sin 2\pi(160t - 0.5x + 4\pi/4)$$

where x and Y are in meter and t in second. The speed of the wave is .... kmh^{-1}. **[2023, 11 April Shift-I]**

5 A longitudinal wave is represented by $y = 10 \sin 2\pi\left(nt - \dfrac{x}{\lambda}\right)$ cm. The maximum particle velocity will be four times the wave velocity, if the determined value of wavelength is equal to **[2022, 29 June Shift-I]**

(a) 2π (b) 5π
(c) π (d) $5\pi/2$

6 The amplitude of wave disturbance propagating in the positive x-direction is given by $= \frac{1}{(1+x)^2}$ at time $t = 0$ and $y = \frac{1}{1+(x-2)^2}$ at $t = 1$ s, where x and y are in metre.

The shape of wave does not change during the propagation. The velocity of the wave will be ...... m/s. **[2021, 20 July Shift-I]**

7 The mass per unit length of a uniform wire is 0.135 g/cm. A transverse wave of the form $y = -0.21 \sin(x + 30t)$ is produced in it, where x is in metre and t is in second. Then, the expected value of tension in the wire is $x \times 10^{-2}$ N. Value of x is .... (Round-off to the nearest integer) **[2021, 26 Feb Shift-I]**

8 For a transverse wave travelling along a straight line, the distance between two peaks (crests) is 5 m, while the distance between one crest and one trough is 1.5 m. The possible wavelengths (in metre) of the waves are **[2020, 4 Sep Shift-I]**

(a) 1, 2, 3,...... (b) $\frac{1}{1}, \frac{1}{3}, \frac{1}{5}$,.....
(c) 1, 3, 5,..... (d) $\frac{1}{2}, \frac{1}{4}, \frac{1}{6}$,.....

9 A progressive wave travelling along the positive x-direction is represented by
$y(x, t) = A \sin(kx - \omega t + \phi)$.
Its snapshot at $t = 0$ is given in the figure. **[2019, 12 April Shift-I]**

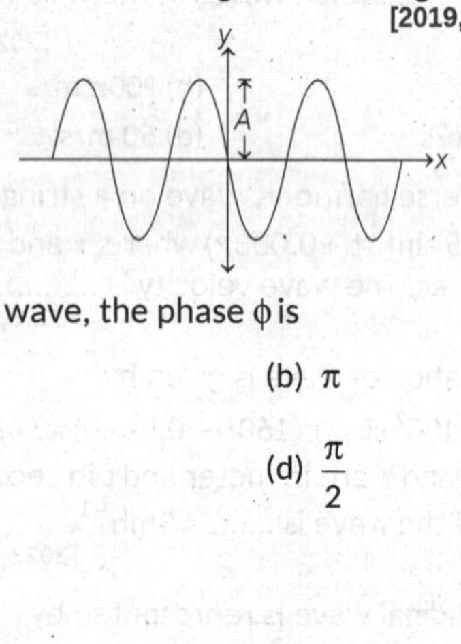

For this wave, the phase ϕ is

(a) $-\frac{\pi}{2}$ (b) π
(c) 0 (d) $\frac{\pi}{2}$

10 A travelling harmonic wave is represented by the equation $y(x, t) = 10^{-3} \sin(50t + 2x)$, where x and y are in metre and t is in second. Which of the following is a correct statement about the wave? **[2019, 12 Jan Shift-I]**

(a) The wave is propagating along the negative X-axis with speed 25 ms^{-1}
(b) The wave is propagating along the positive X-axis with speed 25 ms^{-1}
(c) The wave is propagating along the positive X-axis with speed 100 ms^{-1}.
(d) The wave is propagating along the negative X-axis with speed 100 ms^{-1}

11 A heavy ball of mass M is suspended from the ceiling of a car by a light string of mass $m (m << M)$. When the car is at rest, the speed of transverse waves in the string is 60 ms^{-1}. When the car has acceleration a, the wave speed increases to 60.5 ms^{-1}. The value of a, in terms of gravitational acceleration g is closest to **[2019, 9Jan Shift-I]**

(a) $g/20$ (b) $g/5$ (c) $g/30$ (d) $g/10$

JEE Advanced

1. A block M hangs vertically at the bottom end of a uniform rope of constant mass per unit length. The top end of the rope is attached to a fixed rigid support at O. A transverse wave pulse (Pulse 1) of wavelength λ_0 is produced at point O on the rope. The pulse takes time T_{OA} to reach point A. If the wave pulse of wavelength λ_0 is produced at point A (Pulse 2) without disturbing the position of M it takes time T_{AO} to reach point O. Which of the following options is/are correct? **(2017 Adv.)**

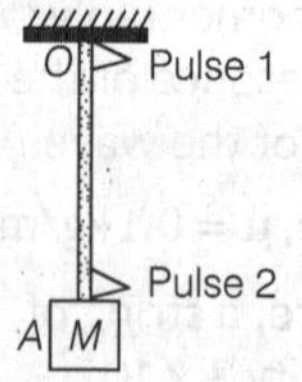

(a) The time $T_{AO} = T_{OA}$
(b) The wavelength of Pulse 1 becomes longer when it reaches point A
(c) The velocity of any pulse along the rope is independent of its frequency and wavelength
(d) The velocities of the two pulses (Pulse 1 and Pulse 2) are the same at the mid-point of rope

Answer Key

Level 1

8.1 Wave Function

1. (a) Positive X-axis (b) 3 cm/s

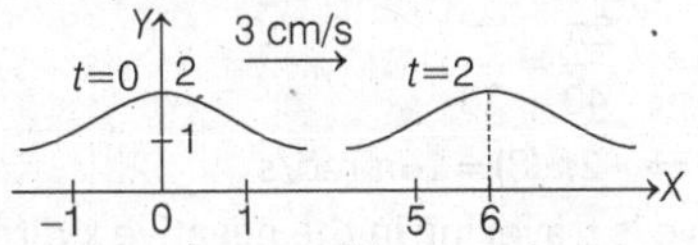

(c)

2. Negative X-axis, $v = 2$ m/s, $y_{max} = 2$ m
3. $\dfrac{6}{(x-4t)^2+3}$ 4. $y = \dfrac{2}{\left(t-\dfrac{x}{2}\right)^2+1}$
5. (a) 4 cm/s (b) $f(t) = y_0 e^{-(t/T)^2}$ (c) $g(x) = y_0 e^{-(x/\lambda)^2}$

8.2 Equation of Travelling Sinusoidal Wave

1. (a) 10 mm (b) 0.4 cm (c) 30 Hz (d) 12 cm/s
2. $y = (15\text{ cm})\sin\left[16t + \left(\dfrac{\pi}{20}\right)x + \dfrac{\pi}{2}\right]$
3. $(0.5\text{ cm})\sin\left(\dfrac{\pi}{3}t - \dfrac{\pi}{18}x + \dfrac{7\pi}{9}\right)$
4. $y(x,t) = (2\text{ cm})\cos\left[\left(\dfrac{16\pi}{15}\right)t - \left(\dfrac{4\pi}{15}\right)x\right]$

8.3 Phase Difference

1. (a) $2\pi/5$ (b) $3\pi/4$ 2. $5\pi/4$
3. (a) 10 Hz (b) $5\pi/4$ (c) 1/60 s 4. 7.5 m

8.4 Particle Velocity and Acceleration

1. (a) 400 m/s (b) 20π m/s, 8×10^4 m/s^2
   (c) $10\sqrt{3}$ m/s, -4×10^4 m/s^2
2. $20\sqrt{3}$ cm/s (downward)
3. (a) D, E, F (b) A, B, H (c) C, G (d) A, E
4. (a) moving upwards, acceleration is zero-S;
   (b) moving upwards, speeding up
   (c) stationary, speeding up,
   (d) moving downwards, slowing down
5. (a) 1 m/s, (b) $\dfrac{3\pi}{2}$ mm/s, $\dfrac{3\pi^2}{4}$ mm/s^2, (c) $\dfrac{3\pi}{2}$
6. 3 m/s

8.5 Speed of Wave on a String

1. 0.03 s 2. 0.02 s 3. 4
4. $\mathbf{v}_{CG} = -20\hat{\mathbf{i}}$ m/s 5. 200 m/s
6. 0.08 m 7. (a) $\sqrt{gy}$ (b) $2\sqrt{L/g}$

8.6 Power Transmitted along the String

1. 512 W 2. 0.05 W 3. 9.6 mJ 4. 25×10^{-6} W 5. 3.6 W/m^2

Level 2

Single Choice Correct Questions

1. (a)	2. (c)	3. (c)	4. (c)	5. (b)
6. (c)	7. (b)	8. (b)	9. (a)	10. (d)
11. (a)	12. (b)	13. (b)	14. (d)	15. (b)
16. (d)	17. (b)	18. (a)	19. (b)	20. (b)
21. (b)	22. (b)	23. (b)	24. (b)	25. (c)
26. (a)	27. (d)	28. (d)	29. (b)	30. (d)
31. (a)	32. (d)	33. (d)	34. (d)	35. (d)
36. (a)	37. (c)	38. (d)	39. (c)	40. (b)
41. (d)	42. (d)	43. (d)	44. (c)	45. (b)

Numerical Value Questions

1. 4	2. 12	3. 2	4. 4	5. 150
6. 50	7. 2	8. 108	9. 1	10. 20

Level 3

Single Choice Correct Questions

1. (a)	2. (a)	3. (b)	4. (a)	5. (a)
6. (a)	7. (a)	8. (a)	9. (a)	10. (b)
11. (c)	12. (d)	13. (c)	14. (d)	15. (a)
16. (d)	17. (a)	18. (b)	19. (b)	20. (c)
21. (d)	22. (a)	23. (c)	24. (b)	25. (b)

Multiple Choice(s) Correct Questions

1. (ab)	2. (bcd)	3. (ad)	4. (ab)	5. (acd)
6. (ad)	7. (abcd)	8. (ad)	9. (bcd)	10. (bd)
11. (bc)	12. (ab)	13. (abcd)	14. (abd)	

Comprehension Bsed Questions

1. (d)	2. (c)	3. (c)	4. (a)	5. (b)
6. (c)	7. (a)	8. (ad)	9. (c)	10. (bc)
11. (cd)	12. (b)	13. (c)	14. (d)	15. (a)
16. (c)	17. (d)			

Match the Columns Questions

1. A → R, B → P, C → S, D → Q 2. A → QR, B → S, C → Q
3. A → R, B → PT, C → S, D → Q 4. A → Q, B → P, C → P

Numerical Value Questions

1. 2	2. 4	3. 2	4. 20
5. 16	6. 10	7. 150	8. 0

Previous Year's Questions

JEE Main

1. (a)	2. (c)	3. (20)	4. (1152)	5. (b)
6. (2)	7. (1215)	8. (b)	9. (b)	10. (a)
11. (b)				

JEE Advanced

1. (a, c)

SOLUTIONS

Level 01

8.1 Wave Function

1. (a) Comparing the given expression with $y = f(x - vt)$, we get

$$v = 3 \text{ cm/s}$$

So, wave is moving in positive x-direction with speed 3 cm/s.

(b) $v = 3$ cm/s

(c) At $t = 0$, $y(x, 0) = \dfrac{2}{x^2 + 1}$

At $t = 2$, $y(x, 2) = \dfrac{2}{(x-6)^2 + 1}$

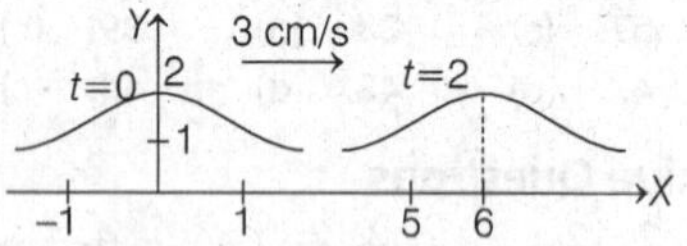

2. Comparing the given wave function with $y = f(x - vt)$, we get $v = -2$ m/s

So, the wave is travelling in negative x-direction with speed 2 m/s.

$$y_{max} = \frac{10}{5+0} = 2 \text{ m}$$

3. $y(x,t) = f(x - vt) = \dfrac{6}{(x-4t)^2 + 3}$

4. Replacing t with $t - \dfrac{x}{v}$, we get

$$y(x,t) = \frac{2}{\left(t - \dfrac{x}{2}\right)^2 + 1}$$

5. (a) $y = y_0 e^{-\left(\frac{t}{T} - \frac{x}{\lambda}\right)^2} = y_0 e^{-\frac{1}{T^2}\left(t - \frac{x}{\lambda/T}\right)^2}$

Comparing with the general equation, $y = f\left(t - \dfrac{x}{v}\right)$, we get

$$v = \frac{\lambda}{T} = \frac{4 \text{ cm}}{1.0 \text{ s}} = 4 \text{ cm/s}$$

(b) Putting $x = 0$ in the given equation,

$$f(t) = y_0 e^{-(t/T)^2}$$

(c) Putting $t = 0$ in the given equation,

$$g(x) = y_0 e^{-(x/\lambda)^2}$$

8.2 Equation of Travelling Sinusoidal Wave

1. Comparing the given equation with $y = A \sin(kx - \omega t)$,

(a) $A = 10$ mm

(b) $k = 5\pi$, $\lambda = \dfrac{2\pi}{k} = \dfrac{2\pi}{5\pi} = 0.4$ cm

(c) $\omega = 60\pi$, $f = \dfrac{\omega}{2\pi} = \dfrac{60\pi}{2\pi} = 30$ Hz

(d) $v = \dfrac{\omega}{k} = \dfrac{60\pi}{5\pi} = 12$ cm/s

2. $k = \dfrac{2\pi}{\lambda} \Rightarrow \dfrac{2\pi}{40} = \dfrac{\pi}{20}$,

$\omega = 2\pi f \Rightarrow 2\pi(8) = 16\pi$ rad/s

Since, wave is travelling in the negative x-direction,

$$y = A \sin(\omega t + kx + \phi)$$

At $t = 0, x = 0, y = 15$

$$15 = 15 \sin(0 + 0 + \phi)$$

$$\Rightarrow \sin\phi = 1 \Rightarrow \phi = \frac{\pi}{2}$$

$$\therefore \quad y = (15 \text{ cm}) \sin\left(16\pi t + \frac{\pi}{20} x + \frac{\pi}{2}\right)$$

3. From figure, $T = 8 - 2 = 6$ s

$$\omega = \frac{2\pi}{T} = \frac{2\pi}{6} = \frac{\pi}{3} \text{ rad/s}$$

$$k = \frac{\omega}{v} = \frac{\pi/3}{6} = \frac{\pi}{18} \text{ rad/m}$$

$$y = A \sin(\omega t - kx + \phi)$$

At $x = 8$ m, $t = 2$ s, $y = 0$

$$\therefore \quad 0 = (0.5 \text{ cm}) \sin\left(\frac{\pi}{3}(2) - \frac{\pi}{18}(8) + \phi\right)$$

$$\Rightarrow \quad \frac{2\pi}{3} - \frac{4\pi}{9} + \phi = \pi$$

$$\Rightarrow \quad \phi = \frac{7\pi}{9}$$

$$\therefore \quad y = (0.5 \text{ cm}) \sin\left(\frac{\pi}{3} t - \frac{\pi}{18} x + \frac{7\pi}{9}\right)$$

4. Displacement of first along X-axis in 0.3 is 1.2 cm.

$$\therefore \quad v = \frac{1.2}{0.3} = 4 \text{ cm/s}$$

$$k = \frac{2\pi}{\lambda} = \frac{2\pi}{7.5} = \frac{4\pi}{15} \text{ rad/cm}$$

$$\omega = kv = \frac{4\pi}{15}(4) = \frac{16\pi}{15} \text{ rad/s}$$

$$y = A \sin(\omega t - kx + \phi)$$

$$\therefore \quad y = (2 \text{ cm}) \sin\left(\frac{16\pi}{15} t - \frac{4\pi}{15} x + \frac{\pi}{2}\right)$$

$$= (2 \text{ cm}) \cos\left(\frac{16\pi}{15} t - \frac{4\pi}{15} x\right)$$

8.3 Phase Difference

1. $y = 4 \sin\left(\pi t + \dfrac{\pi}{16} x\right)$

$\therefore \quad \omega = \pi$ rad/s, $k = \frac{\pi}{16}$ rad/cm

(a) $\Delta\phi = \omega\Delta t = \pi(0.4) = \frac{2\pi}{5}$

(b) $\Delta\phi = k\,\Delta x = \frac{\pi}{16}(12) = \frac{3\pi}{4}$

2. $\Delta x = x_2 - x_1$

$\Rightarrow \quad \frac{3\lambda}{4} - \frac{\lambda}{8} = \frac{5\lambda}{8}$

$\Delta\phi = k\,\Delta x$

$\Rightarrow \quad \frac{2\pi}{\lambda}\left(\frac{5\lambda}{8}\right) = \frac{5\pi}{4}$

3. (a) $\lambda = 6.5 - 2.5 = 4$ cm

$f = \frac{v}{\lambda} = \frac{40}{4} = 10$ Hz

(b) $\Delta\phi = k\,\Delta x$

$\frac{2\pi}{4}(2.5) = \frac{5\pi}{4}$

(c) $\Delta\phi = \omega\Delta t$

$\Rightarrow \quad 60 \times \frac{\pi}{180} = (2\pi(10)\pi)\Delta t$

$\Rightarrow \quad \Delta t = \frac{1}{60}$ s

4.

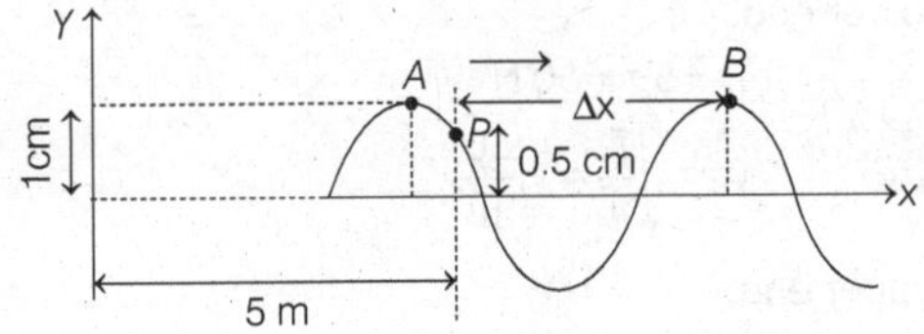

The position of point P is taken at the right side of point A as it is travelling in positive y-direction.

Phase difference between points A and B $= 2\pi$

$y = A\cos\phi$

$\Rightarrow \quad 0.5 = (1)\cos\phi \quad \Rightarrow \quad \phi = \frac{\pi}{3}$

$\therefore$ Phase difference between points P and $B = 2\pi - \frac{\pi}{3} = \frac{5\pi}{3}$

$\Delta\phi = k\Delta x$

$\Rightarrow \quad \frac{5\pi}{3} = \frac{2\pi}{3}\Delta x$

$\Rightarrow \quad \Delta x = 2.5$ m

$\therefore \quad x_B = 5 + 2.5 = 7.5$ m

8.4 Particle Velocity and Acceleration

1. (a) $y = (0.05\text{ m})\sin(400\pi t + \pi x)$

$\therefore \quad \omega = 400\pi$ rad/s, $k = \pi$ rad/m

$v = \frac{\omega}{k} = \frac{400\pi}{\pi} = 400$ m/s

(b) $v_{max} = \omega A = (400\pi)(0.05) = 20\pi$ m/s

$a_{max} = \omega^2 A = (400\pi)^2(0.05) = 8\times10^4$ m/s^2

(c) $v_p = \frac{\partial y}{\partial t} = (0.05)(400\pi)\cos(400\pi t + \pi x)$

$a_p = \frac{\partial^2 y}{\partial t^2} = -(0.05)(400\pi)^2\sin(400\pi t + \pi x)$

At $x = \frac{1}{6}$ m, $t = 0.01$ s

$v_p = 20\pi\cos\left(400\pi(0.01) + \pi\left(\frac{1}{6}\right)\right) = 10\sqrt{3}$ m/s

$a_p = -8\times10^4\sin\left(400\pi(0.01) + \pi\left(\frac{1}{6}\right)\right)$

$= -4\times10^4$ m/s^2

2. $v_p = -v\times\text{slope} = -(20\text{ cm/s})\times\tan 60°$

$= -20\sqrt{3}$ cm/s

$= 20\sqrt{3}$ cm/s, downward

3. $v_p = -v\times\text{slope}$

(a) Slope is negative at points D, E and F. So, $v_p > 0$.

(b) Slope is positive at points A, B and H. So, $v_p < 0$.

(c) Slope is zero at C and G. So $v_p = 0$.

(d) Slope is maximum at A and E. So, maximum magnitude of velocity occurs at points A and E.

4. $y = A\sin(\omega t - kx)$

$v_p = \frac{\partial y}{\partial t} = A\omega\cos(\omega t - kx)$

$a_p = \frac{\partial^2 y}{\partial t^2} = -A\omega^2\sin(\omega t - kx)$

(a) At $t = 0, x = 0$,

$v_p = A\omega > 0$

$\therefore$ Particle is moving upwards

$a_p = 0$

(b) At $t = 0, x = \frac{\pi}{4k}$

$v_p = A\omega\cos\left[-k\left(\frac{\pi}{4k}\right)\right] = \frac{A\omega}{\sqrt{2}}$

$\because v_p > 0$, particle is moving upwards

$a_p = -A\omega^2\sin\left(-k\left(\frac{\pi}{4k}\right)\right) = \frac{\omega^2 A}{\sqrt{2}}$

$\therefore \quad a_p > 0$

Since, v_p and a_p both are in the same direction, the particle will be speeding up.

(c) At $t = 0, x = \frac{\pi}{2k}$

$v_p = \omega A\cos\left(-\frac{\pi}{2}\right) = 0$

$a_p = -\omega^2 A\sin\left(-\frac{\pi}{2}\right) = \omega^2 A > 0$

So, the particle is stationary and speeding up.

(d) At $t = 0, x = \frac{3\pi}{4k}$

$$v_p = \omega A \cos\left(-\frac{3\pi}{4}\right) = -\frac{\omega A}{\sqrt{2}} < 0$$

$$a_p = -\omega^2 A \sin\left(-\frac{3\pi}{4}\right) = \frac{\omega^2 A}{\sqrt{2}} > 0$$

Since, $v_p < 0$, the particle is moving downward.

As v_p and a_p have opposite signs, the particle will be slowing down.

5. (a) In figure (a), $T = 4$ s

In figure (b), $\lambda = 5 - 1 = 4$ m

$$v = \frac{\lambda}{T} = \frac{4}{4} = 1 \text{ m/s}$$

(b) $\omega = \frac{2\pi}{T} = \frac{2\pi}{4} = \frac{\pi}{2}$ rad/s

$$v_{max} = \omega A = \left(\frac{\pi}{2}\right)(3\text{ mm}) = \frac{3\pi}{2} \text{ mm/s}$$

$$a_{max} = \omega^2 A = \left(\frac{\pi}{2}\right)^2 (3\text{ mm}) = \frac{3\pi^2}{4} \text{ mm/s}^2$$

(c) $k = \frac{2\pi}{\lambda} = \frac{2\pi}{4} = \frac{\pi}{2}$

$$y = A\sin[(\omega t - k(x-2))]$$

$$\therefore \quad y = (3\text{ mm})\sin\left(\frac{\pi}{2}t - \frac{\pi}{2}(x-2)\right)$$

$$\text{Slope} = \frac{\partial y}{\partial x} = -\frac{3\pi}{2}\cos\left(\frac{\pi}{2}t - \frac{\pi}{2}(x-2)\right)$$

At $t = 4, x = 2$

$$|\text{Slope}| = \left|-\frac{3\pi}{2}\cos\left(\frac{\pi}{2}(4) - \frac{\pi}{2}(2-2)\right)\right| = \frac{3\pi}{2}$$

6. Comparing the given relation with the general relation $\frac{\partial^2 y}{\partial x^2} = \frac{1}{v^2}\frac{\partial^2 y}{\partial t^2}$, we get

$$v^2 = 9 \Rightarrow v = 3 \text{ m/s}$$

8.5 Speed of Wave on a String

1. $\mu = 1$ gm/cm $= 0.1$ kg/m, $T = mg = 40$ N

$$v = \sqrt{\frac{T}{\mu}} = \sqrt{\frac{40}{0.1}} = 20 \text{ m/s}$$

$$t = \frac{l}{v} = \frac{60 \times 10^{-2}}{20} = 0.03 \text{ s}$$

2. $l = 2 + 0.25 + 0.25 = 2.5$ m

$$\mu = \frac{m}{l} = \frac{5 \times 10^{-3}}{2.5} = 2 \times 10^{-3} \text{ kg/m}$$

$$v = \sqrt{\frac{T}{\mu}} = \sqrt{\frac{20}{2 \times 10^{-3}}} = 100 \text{ m/s}$$

$$t = \frac{L}{v} = \frac{2}{100} = 0.02 \text{ s}$$

3. $\mu = \frac{m}{L} = \frac{\rho(AL)}{L} = \rho A$

$$v = \sqrt{\frac{T}{\mu}} = \sqrt{\frac{T}{\rho A}}$$

$$\therefore \quad v \propto \frac{1}{\sqrt{\rho}}$$

$$\Rightarrow \quad \frac{v_1}{v_2} = \sqrt{\frac{\rho_2}{\rho_1}}$$

$$\Rightarrow \quad \frac{v_2/2}{v_2} = \sqrt{\frac{\rho_2}{\rho_1}}$$

$$\Rightarrow \quad \frac{\rho_1}{\rho_2} = 4$$

4. Velocity of pulse w.r.t. cart $= \sqrt{\frac{T}{\mu}} = \sqrt{\frac{100}{0.25}} = 20$ m/s

$$\therefore \quad \mathbf{v}_{pc} = 20\hat{\mathbf{i}}$$

$$\Rightarrow \quad \mathbf{v}_p - \mathbf{v}_c = 20\hat{\mathbf{i}}$$

$$\Rightarrow \quad 0 - \mathbf{v}_c = 20\hat{\mathbf{i}}$$

$$\Rightarrow \quad \mathbf{v}_c = -20\hat{\mathbf{i}}$$

5. $T = m(g + a) = 4(10 + 6) = 64$ N

$$v = \sqrt{\frac{T}{\mu}} = \sqrt{\frac{64}{1.6 \times 10^{-3}}} = 200 \text{ m/s}$$

6. At the lower end,

$$T_1 = 5g = 50 \text{ N}$$

$$v_1 = \sqrt{\frac{T_1}{\mu}} = \sqrt{\frac{50}{\mu}}$$

At the upper end,

$$T_2 = (5 + 15)\,g = 20g = 200 \text{ N}$$

$$v_2 = \sqrt{\frac{T_2}{\mu}} = \sqrt{\frac{200}{\mu}}$$

Frequency doesn't change

$$f = \frac{v_1}{\lambda_1} = \frac{v_2}{\lambda_2}$$

$$\Rightarrow \quad \frac{\lambda_2}{\lambda_1} = \frac{v_2}{v_1} \quad \Rightarrow \quad \frac{\lambda_2}{0.04} = 2$$

$$\Rightarrow \quad \lambda_2 = 0.08 \text{ m}$$

7. (a) At a distance y from the lower end,

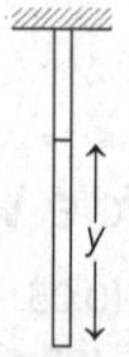

$$T = \left(\frac{m}{L}y\right)g = \mu y g$$

$$v = \sqrt{\frac{T}{\mu}} = \sqrt{gy}$$

(b) $v = \sqrt{gy} \quad \Rightarrow \quad \frac{dy}{dt} = \sqrt{gy}$

$$\Rightarrow \quad \int_0^t dt = \frac{1}{\sqrt{g}}\int_0^L \frac{dy}{\sqrt{y}}$$

$$\Rightarrow \quad t = \frac{1}{\sqrt{g}}[2\sqrt{y}]_0^L = 2\sqrt{\frac{L}{g}}$$

8.6 Power Transmitted along the String

1. $v=\sqrt{\frac{T}{\mu}}=\sqrt{\frac{80}{5\times10^{-2}}}=40$ m/s

$$P_{avg}=\frac{1}{2}\mu v\omega^2A^2=\frac{1}{2}\times5\times10^{-2}\times40\times(2\pi(60))^2(0.06)^2$$
$$=512 \text{ W}$$

2. $\mu=\frac{T}{v^2}=\frac{100}{(100)^2}=0.01$ kg/m

$$P_{avg}=\frac{1}{2}\mu v\omega^2A^2=\frac{1}{2}\times0.01\times100\times[2\pi(10)]^2\times(0.005)^2$$
$$=0.05 \text{ W}$$

3. $v=\sqrt{\frac{T}{\mu}}=\sqrt{\frac{60}{6\times10^{-3}}}=100$ m/s

$$P_{avg}=\frac{1}{2}\mu v\omega^2A^2=\frac{1}{2}\times6\times10^{-3}\times100(2\pi(200))^2(1\times10^{-3})^2$$
$$=0.48 \text{ W}$$
$$t=\frac{l}{v}=\frac{2}{100}=0.02 \text{ s}$$
$$E=P_{avg}\times t=0.48\times0.02=9.6\times10^{-3}\text{ J}=9.6 \text{ mJ}$$

4. Comparing the given equation with the general equation $y=A\sin(kx-\omega t)$, we get.

$$k=\frac{\pi}{10},\ \omega=50\pi$$
$$v=\frac{\omega}{k}=\frac{50\pi}{\pi/10}=500 \text{ m/s}$$
$$\mu=\frac{T}{v^2}=\frac{100}{(500)^2}=4\times10^{-4}\text{ kg/m}$$
$$P_{avg}=\frac{1}{2}\mu v\omega^2A^2=\frac{1}{2}\times4\times10^{-4}\times500(50\pi)^2(0.01\times10^{-2})^2$$
$$=25\times10^{-6}\text{ W}$$

5. $v=\sqrt{\frac{T}{\mu}}=\sqrt{\frac{T}{\rho\pi r^2}}=\sqrt{\frac{100}{4200\times3.14(0.002)^2}}=43.53$ m/s

$$I_{avg}=\frac{1}{2}\rho v\omega^2A^2=\frac{1}{2}\times4200\times43.53[2\pi(10)]^2(10^{-4})^2$$
$$=3.6 \text{ W/m}^2$$

Level 02

Single Choice Correct Questions

1. $y(x,t)=e^{-(\sqrt{ax}+\sqrt{bt})^2}=e^{-b\left(t+\frac{x}{\sqrt{b/a}}\right)^2}$

Comparing it with $y=f\left(t-\frac{x}{v}\right)$, we get

$$v=-\sqrt{\frac{b}{a}}$$

So, it represents a wave moving in negative x-direction with speed $\sqrt{\frac{b}{a}}$.

2. $y=f(x-vt)$

At $t=2$ s,

$$x-vt=x-1$$
$$\Rightarrow\quad x-v(2)=x-1$$
$$\Rightarrow\quad v=0.5 \text{ m/s}$$

3. $y(x,t)=f\left(t-\frac{x}{v}\right)$

$$\Rightarrow\quad y(4,5)=f\left(5-\frac{4}{2}\right)=f(3)$$
$$y(0,3)=6-3=3 \text{ mm}$$

4. Equation of travelling wave,

$$y=f(x\pm vt)$$

5. $\frac{\lambda}{2}=10\ \Rightarrow\ \lambda=20$ m

$$f=\frac{1}{T}=\frac{1}{4}=0.25 \text{ Hz}$$
$$v=\lambda f=20\times0.25=5.0 \text{ m/s}$$

6. $y=(2\text{ mm})\sin\left(2\pi(4)-100\pi t+\frac{\pi}{3}\right)$

$$y=(2\text{ mm})\sin\left(\frac{\pi}{3}-100\pi t\right)$$

At mean position, $y=0$

$$\Rightarrow\quad \frac{\pi}{3}-100\pi t=0$$
$$\Rightarrow\quad t=\frac{1}{300}\text{ s}$$

7. $y=a_0\sin(\omega t-kx)=a_0\sin\left(\omega(0)-k\left(\frac{\pi}{2k}\right)\right)=-a_0$

At point Q, $y=-a_0$

8. $\omega=2\pi f=2\pi(2)=4\pi$

$$k=\frac{2\pi}{\lambda}=\frac{2\pi}{1}=2\pi$$

For a wave travelling in negative x-direction,

$$y(x,t)=f(kx+\omega t)=\cos(2\pi x+4\pi t)$$

9. $\lambda=0.4$ cm

$$v=\lambda f=(0.4\times10^{-2})(250)=1.0 \text{ m/s}$$

10. $y=A\sin(\omega t-kx+\phi)$

$v=A\omega\cos(\omega t-kx+\phi)$

At $t=0, x=0, y=-0.5, v>0$

$$\Rightarrow\quad \phi=-\frac{\pi}{6}$$
$$\therefore\quad y=(1)\sin\left(\omega t-kx-\frac{\pi}{6}\right)$$

11. From figure, $2.5\lambda=20\ \Rightarrow\ \lambda=8$ cm

$$k=\frac{2\pi}{\lambda}=\frac{2\pi}{0.08}=\frac{314}{4}\text{ rad/m}$$
$$\omega=kv=\frac{314}{4}\times350=27475 \text{ rad/s}$$

$$y = A\sin(kx - \omega t) = 0.05\sin\left(\frac{314}{4}x - 27475t\right)$$

12. From first figure, $\lambda = 9$ cm

From second figure, $T = 3$ s

$$v = \frac{\lambda}{T} = \frac{9}{3} = 3 \text{ cm/s}$$

$$s = vt = 3(2) = 6 \text{ cm}$$

13. $(v_p)_{max} = 4v \Rightarrow A\omega = 4\left(\frac{\omega}{k}\right)$

$$\Rightarrow \quad Y_0 = 4\left(\frac{1}{2\pi/\lambda}\right)$$

$$\Rightarrow \quad \lambda = \frac{\pi Y_0}{2}$$

14. $v_{max} = A\omega, \; v = \frac{\omega}{k}$

$$v_{max\,1} = 2(6) = 12 \text{ cm/s},$$

$$v_{max\,2} = 3(12) = 36 \text{ cm/s},$$

$$v_{max\,3} = 4(11) = 44 \text{ cm/s}$$

$$v_1 = \frac{6}{3} = 2 \text{ m/s},$$

$$v_2 = \frac{12}{4} = 3 \text{ m/s},$$

$$v_3 = \frac{11}{5} = 2.2 \text{ m/s}$$

So, wave 2 has greatest wave speed and wave 3 has the greatest maximum transverse string speed.

15. $v_p = \frac{\partial y}{\partial t} = A\beta\cos\left(\alpha x + \beta t + \frac{\pi}{6}\right)$

At $x = 1$ cm, $t = 1$ s,

$$v_p = 7.5(12)\cos\left(0.56(1) + 12(1) + \frac{\pi}{6}\right)$$

$$= 90\cos\left(4\pi + \frac{\pi}{6}\right) = 90 \times \frac{\sqrt{3}}{2}$$

$$= 45\sqrt{3} \text{ cm/s} = 77.94 \text{ cm/s}$$

16. $\omega = 2\pi f \Rightarrow \frac{2\pi}{0.04} = 2\pi f$

$$\Rightarrow \quad f = 25 \text{ Hz}$$

$$a_{max} = \omega^2 A = \left(\frac{2\pi}{0.04}\right)^2 (3) = 7.5 \times 10^4 \text{ m/s}^2$$

17. $v_{max} = A\omega = a(2\pi), \quad v = \frac{\omega}{k} = 5$

$$\therefore \quad \frac{v_{max}}{v} = \frac{2\pi a}{5}$$

18. $a_p = \frac{\partial^2 y}{\partial t^2} = -4\pi^2\sin\left[\frac{\pi}{2}\left(2t + \frac{x}{8}\right)\right]$

At $x = 8$ cm, $t = 1$ s,

$$a_p = -4\pi^2\sin\left[\frac{\pi}{2}\left(2(1) + \frac{8}{8}\right)\right] = 4\pi^2 \text{ cm/s}^2$$

19. $y = f(x - vt) = \frac{6}{(x - 2t)^2}$

$$v_p = \frac{\partial y}{\partial t} = -\frac{12}{(x-2t)^3}(-2) = \frac{24}{(x-2t)^3}$$

At $x = 2, t = 2$,

$$v_p = \frac{24}{[2 - 2(2)]^3} = -3 \text{ m/s}$$

20. $y = y_m\sin(kx - \omega t - \phi)$

At $t = 0, x = 0, y = y_0$,

$$y_0 = y_m\sin(0 - 0 - \phi)$$

$$\Rightarrow \quad y_0 = -y_m\sin\phi \quad \text{...(i)}$$

$$v_p = \frac{\partial y}{\partial t} = -y_m\omega\cos(kx - \omega t - \phi)$$

At $t = 0, x = 0, v = v_0$

$$v_0 = -y_m\omega\cos(0 - 0 - \phi)$$

$$\Rightarrow \quad \frac{v_0}{\omega} = -y_m\cos\phi \quad \text{...(ii)}$$

Dividing Eqs. (i) by (ii), we get

$$\tan\phi = \frac{\omega y_0}{v_0}$$

21. $R = \frac{v}{v_p} = -\frac{1}{\text{slope}}$

$$\Rightarrow \quad R \propto \frac{1}{\text{slope}}$$

$$(\text{slope})_A > (\text{slope})_B$$

$$\Rightarrow \quad R_B > R_A$$

22. $v_p = -v \times \text{slope}$

Since, v and slope both are negative

$$\Rightarrow \quad v_p < 0$$

Therefore, velocity of point P will be directed downwards.

23. $v_p = -v \times \text{slope}$

At $x_1 = 1.5$ m, slope is positive

$$\Rightarrow \quad v_p < 0$$

At $x_2 = 2.5$ m, slope is negative

$$\Rightarrow \quad v_p > 0$$

24. Particle acceleration is maximum at the extreme positions and directed towards the mean position. So, acceleration is maximum at b and d. At b, acceleration is directed downwards.

25. $T = 4$ s, $\omega = \frac{2\pi}{T} = \frac{2\pi}{4} = \frac{\pi}{2}$ rad/s

$$v_{max} = A\omega \Rightarrow 5 = A\left(\frac{\pi}{2}\right)$$

$$\Rightarrow \quad A = \frac{10}{\pi} \text{ cm}$$

26. $v = \sqrt{\frac{T}{\mu}} = \text{constant}$

$$\omega = kv = \frac{2\pi v}{\lambda}$$

$\Rightarrow \quad \omega \propto \frac{1}{\lambda}$

Since, $\quad \lambda_2 > \lambda_1 = \lambda_3$

$\Rightarrow \quad \omega_1 = \omega_3 > \omega_2$

27. Both *B* and *G* are at the same distance from the mean position and are moving up. Hence, *B* and *G* are in phase.

28. $v = \lambda f \quad \Rightarrow \quad 10 = \lambda(100)$

$\Rightarrow \quad \lambda = 0.1 \text{ m}$

$$\Delta\phi = \frac{2\pi}{\lambda}\Delta x = \frac{2\pi}{0.1} \times 2.5 \times 10^{-2} = \frac{\pi}{2}$$

29. $k = 10\pi(0.01) = \frac{\pi}{10}$ rad/m

$$\Delta\phi = k\,\Delta x = \frac{\pi}{10} \times 10 = \pi$$

30. For adjacent crest and trough, $\Delta\phi = \pi$

$$\Delta\phi = \omega\,\Delta t$$

$\Rightarrow \quad \pi = 2\pi(500)\,\Delta t$

$\Rightarrow \quad \Delta t = \frac{1}{1000}$ s

31. $y_A = A\sin(\omega t - kx)$

$$y_B = A\sin\left(\omega t - kx + \frac{\pi}{2}\right)$$

$$y_C = A\sin\left(\omega t - kx - \frac{\pi}{2}\right)$$

32. $v = \frac{\omega}{k} = \frac{420}{21} = 20$ m/s

$$v = \sqrt{\frac{T}{\mu}} \quad \Rightarrow \quad 20 = \sqrt{\frac{T}{0.2}}$$

$\Rightarrow \quad T = 80$ N

33. $v = \sqrt{\frac{T}{\mu}} = \sqrt{\frac{mg}{\mu}} = \sqrt{\frac{1(10)}{0.001}} = 100$ m/s

$$t = \frac{L}{v} = \frac{1}{100} = 0.01 \text{ s}$$

34. $T = m(g + a) = 48$ N

$$v = \sqrt{\frac{T}{\mu}} = \sqrt{\frac{48}{19.2 \times 10^{-3}}} = 50 \text{ m/s}$$

35. When the car is at rest,

$$v_1 = \sqrt{\frac{T_1}{\mu}} = \sqrt{\frac{mg}{\mu}}$$

When the car accelerates horizontally,

$$v_2 = \sqrt{\frac{T_2}{\mu}} = \sqrt{\frac{m\sqrt{g^2 + a^2}}{\mu}}$$

$\therefore \quad \left(\frac{v_2}{v_1}\right)^4 = \frac{g^2 + a^2}{g^2}$

$\Rightarrow \quad a = 10\sqrt{\left(\frac{52}{50}\right)^4 - 1} = 4.1 \text{ m/s}^2$

36. $T_{AB} = (1.6 + 1.6 + 3.2)\,g = 64$ N

$T_{CD} = (1.6 + 1.6)\,g = 32$ N

$T_{EF} = 1.6g = 16$ N

$$v_{AB} = \sqrt{\frac{T_{AB}}{\mu_{AB}}} = \sqrt{\frac{64}{10 \times 10^{-3}}} = 80 \text{ m/s}$$

$$v_{CD} = \sqrt{\frac{T_{CD}}{\mu_{CD}}} = \sqrt{\frac{32}{8 \times 10^{-3}}} = 20\sqrt{10} \text{ m/s}$$

$$v_{EF} = \sqrt{\frac{T_{EF}}{\mu_{EF}}} = \sqrt{\frac{16}{10 \times 10^{-3}}} = 40 \text{ m/s}$$

37. $v = \sqrt{\frac{T}{\mu}} = \sqrt{\frac{T}{\rho\pi r^2}}$

$\therefore \quad \frac{v_1}{v_2} = \left(\frac{r_2}{r_1}\right)\left(\frac{T_1}{T_2}\right)^{1/2} = \left(\frac{2r}{r}\right)\left(\frac{T}{2T}\right)^{1/2} = \sqrt{2}$

38. $v_1 = \sqrt{\frac{T}{\mu}} = \sqrt{\frac{F_0}{(\mu_0/2)}} = \sqrt{\frac{2F_0}{\mu_0}}$

$$v_2 = \sqrt{\frac{T}{\mu'}} = \sqrt{\frac{F_0}{3\mu_0}}$$

$$T = t_1 + t_2 = \frac{L/2}{v_1} + \frac{L/2}{v_2} = \frac{L}{2}\sqrt{\frac{\mu_0}{2F_0}}(1 + \sqrt{6})$$

41. $T = \int_0^x (\mu_0 x)\,dx g = \frac{\mu_0 x^2 g}{2}$

$$v = \sqrt{\frac{T}{\mu}} = \sqrt{\frac{\mu_0 x^2 g}{2(\mu_0 x)}} = \sqrt{\frac{g}{2}}\sqrt{x}$$

$$v = \frac{dx}{dt} = \sqrt{\frac{g}{2}}\sqrt{x}$$

$\Rightarrow \quad \int_0^t dt = \sqrt{\frac{2}{g}}\int_0^{l_0} \frac{dx}{\sqrt{x}}$

$\Rightarrow \quad t = \sqrt{\frac{2}{g}}[2\sqrt{x}]_0^{l_0}$

$\Rightarrow \quad t = \sqrt{\frac{8l_0}{g}}$

39. $T = \mu hg$

$$v = \sqrt{\frac{T}{\mu}} = \sqrt{\frac{\mu hg}{\mu}} = \sqrt{gh}$$

$\therefore \quad v \propto \sqrt{h}$

40. Let the particle meets the pulse at a distance *h* from the bottom.

For the pulse, $\quad v = \sqrt{\frac{T}{\mu}} = \sqrt{\frac{\mu xg}{\mu}} = \sqrt{gx}$

$$v = \sqrt{gx}$$

$\Rightarrow \quad \frac{dx}{dt} = \sqrt{gx}$

$\Rightarrow \quad \int_0^t dt = \frac{1}{\sqrt{g}} \int_0^h \frac{dx}{\sqrt{x}}$

$\Rightarrow \quad t = 2\sqrt{\frac{h}{g}}$

For the particle,

$s = ut + \frac{1}{2}at^2$

$\Rightarrow \quad L - h = 0 + \frac{1}{2}g\left(2\sqrt{\frac{h}{g}}\right)^2$

$\Rightarrow \quad h = \frac{L}{3}$

42. Frequency will remain same.

$\lambda = \frac{v}{f} = \frac{1}{f}\sqrt{\frac{T}{\mu}}$

$\Rightarrow \quad \lambda \propto \sqrt{T}$

As tension is doubled, λ will become $\sqrt{2}$ times.

$\therefore \quad \lambda' = 10\sqrt{2} = 14$ cm

43. $P_{avg} = \frac{1}{2}\mu v\omega^2 A^2$

$\Rightarrow \quad P_{avg} \propto A^2$

44. $v = \sqrt{\frac{T}{\mu}} = \sqrt{\frac{100}{4 \times 10^{-2}}} = 50$ m/s

$P_{avg} = \frac{1}{2}\mu v\omega^2 A^2$

$\Rightarrow \quad 90 = \frac{1}{2} \times 4 \times 10^{-2} \times 50(2\pi f)^2 (0.05)^2$

$\Rightarrow \quad f = 30$ Hz

45. $v = \sqrt{\frac{T}{\mu}} = \sqrt{\frac{25}{1}} = 5$ m/s

$P_{avg} = \frac{1}{2}\mu v(\omega A)^2 = \frac{1}{2}\mu v^2_{max}$

$= \frac{1}{2} \times 1 \times 5 \times (0.01)^2 = 2.5 \times 10^{-4}$ W

Numerical Value Questions

1. $\frac{T}{2} = 5 \times 10^{-3} \Rightarrow T = 0.01$ s

$\frac{\lambda}{2} = 2 \times 10^{-2} \Rightarrow \lambda = 0.04$ m

$v = \frac{\lambda}{T} = \frac{0.04}{0.01} = 4$ m/s

2. $k = \frac{\omega}{v} = \frac{2\pi(500)}{360} = \frac{25\pi}{9}$

$\Delta\phi = k\,\Delta x$

$\Rightarrow \quad 60\left(\frac{\pi}{180}\right) = \frac{25\pi}{9}\Delta x$

$\Rightarrow \quad \Delta x = 12$ cm

3. $v_p = \frac{\partial x}{\partial t} = -(40\text{ cm})(50\pi)\sin(50\pi t - 0.02\pi y)$

At $y = 25$ m and $t = 0.005$ s,

$v_p = -(0.4)(50\pi)\sin[50\pi(0.005) - 0.02\pi(25)]$

$\Rightarrow \quad v_p = 20\pi\left(\frac{1}{\sqrt{2}}\right) = 10\pi\sqrt{2}$ m/s

$\therefore \quad n = 2$

4. $v = \frac{\omega}{k} = \frac{20}{10} = 2$ m/s

$v = \sqrt{\frac{T}{\mu}} = \sqrt{\frac{T}{\rho A}}$

$\Rightarrow \quad 2 = \sqrt{\frac{m(10)}{1 \times 0.01}} \Rightarrow m = 4 \times 10^{-3}$ kg

$\therefore \quad n = 4$

5. $180 - T = 18a$ ...(i)

$T - 90 = 9a$ ...(ii)

Solving Eqs. (i) and (ii), we get $T = 120$ N

$v = \sqrt{\frac{T}{\mu}} = \sqrt{\frac{120}{12 \times 10^{-3}}} = 100$ m/s

$t = \frac{L}{v} = \frac{15}{100} = 0.15$ s $= 150$ ms

6. $T = kx = 160 \times 0.01 = 1.6$ N

$\mu = \frac{m}{L} = \frac{10 \times 10^{-3}}{40 \times 10^{-2}} = 2.5 \times 10^{-2}$ kg/m

$v = \sqrt{\frac{T}{\mu}} = \sqrt{\frac{1.6}{2.5 \times 10^{-2}}} = 8$ m/s

$t = \frac{L}{v} = \frac{0.4}{8} = 0.05$ sec $= 50$ ms

7. At the lower end, $T_1 = mg$,

$v_1 = \sqrt{\frac{T_1}{\mu}} = \sqrt{\frac{mg}{\mu}}$

At the top end, $T_2 = mg + mg = 2mg$

$v_2 = \sqrt{\frac{T_2}{\mu}} = \sqrt{\frac{2mg}{\mu}}$

Frequency remains constant,

$\therefore \quad \lambda = \frac{v}{f} \Rightarrow \frac{\lambda_1}{\lambda_2} = \frac{v_1}{v_2}$

$\Rightarrow \quad \frac{\lambda}{\lambda_2} = \frac{1}{\sqrt{2}} \Rightarrow \lambda_2 = \sqrt{2}\lambda$

$\therefore \quad a = \sqrt{2} \Rightarrow a^2 = 2$

8. $v = \sqrt{\frac{T}{\mu}} = \sqrt{\frac{450}{5 \times 10^{-3}}} = 300$ m/s

$A = \left(\frac{20}{100}\right)\lambda = \frac{\lambda}{5}$

$P_{max} = \frac{1}{2}\mu v(\omega A)^2 = \frac{1}{2}\mu v\left[2\pi f\left(\frac{\lambda}{5}\right)\right]^2 = \frac{2}{25}\pi^2\mu v^3$

$\therefore \quad P_{max} = \frac{2}{25} \times 10 \times 5 \times 10^{-3} \times (300)^3 = 108\text{ kW}$

9. $\frac{dK}{dt} = \frac{1}{2}\frac{dm}{dt}v_p^2 = \frac{1}{2}\mu v\omega^2 A^2 \cos^2(\omega t - kx)$

$\left(\frac{dK}{dt}\right)_{avg} = \frac{1}{4}\mu v\omega^2 A^2$

$= \frac{1}{4} \times 0.01 \times 10 (20\pi)^2 (0.01)^2 = 10^{-2}\text{ W}$

$K = \left(\frac{dK}{dt}\right)_{avg} \times \text{time}$

$= 10^{-2} \times \left(\frac{2\pi}{20\pi}\right) = 10^{-3}\text{ J} = 1\text{ mJ}$

10. Instantaneous power is given by

$P = \frac{FA^2\omega^2}{v}\cos^2(\omega t - kx) = \frac{F}{v}v_p^2$

$\therefore \quad v_p = \sqrt{\frac{Pv}{F}} = \sqrt{\frac{40 \times 10^{-3} \times 20}{20}} = 0.2\text{ m/s} = 20\text{ cm/s}$

Level 03

Single Choice Correct Questions

1. $z = f(x - vt) = e^{-(x - vt + 2)^2}$

At $t = 1$ s, $x - vt + 2 = x - 2$

$\Rightarrow \quad -v(1) + 2 = -2$

$\Rightarrow \quad v = 4\text{ m/s}$

So, the wave is travelling with speed 4 m/s in +x-direction.

2. One upward and successive downward movement of hand will generate a complete wave.

$f = \frac{6}{2} = 3\text{ Hz}$

$T = \frac{1}{f} = \frac{1}{3}\text{ s},$

$\lambda = \frac{v}{f} = \frac{3}{3} = 1\text{ m}$

Time taken by the pulse to reach the point at distance 3 m,

$t_1 = \frac{x}{v} = \frac{3}{3} = 1\text{ s}$

Time taken by the particle at 3m distance to reach its upper extreme position,

$t_2 = \frac{3T}{4}$ [$\because$ particle will initially move downwards]

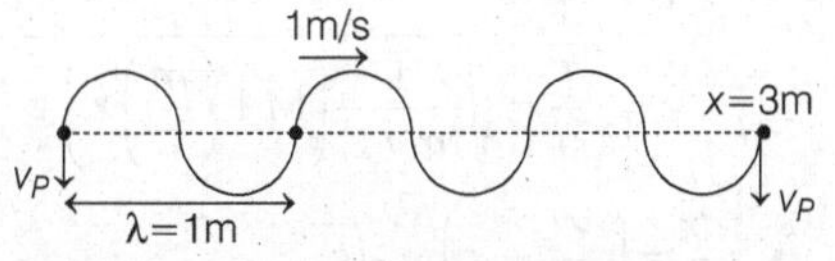

Hence, time taken by the particle to reach its upper extreme for the first time,

$t = t_1 + t_2 = 1 + \frac{3}{4}\left(\frac{1}{3}\right) = \frac{5}{4} = 1.25\text{ s}$

3. $y = A\sin(\omega t - kx)$

$\Rightarrow \quad \frac{A}{2} = A\sin(\omega t - kx)$

$\Rightarrow \quad \sin(\omega t - kx) = \frac{1}{2}$

$\Rightarrow \quad \omega t - kx = \frac{\pi}{6}$

$\Rightarrow \quad \left(\frac{2\pi}{T}\right)\left(\frac{T}{6}\right) - \left(\frac{2\pi}{\lambda}\right)(0.04) = \frac{\pi}{6}$

$\Rightarrow \quad \lambda = 0.48\text{ m}$

4. $y(x,t) = f\left(t - \frac{x}{v}\right) = 2\sin\left[3\pi\left(t - \frac{x}{v}\right)\right]$

At $x_2 = 1$ cm,

$3\pi\left(t - \frac{1}{v}\right) = 3\pi t - \frac{\pi}{2}$

$\Rightarrow \quad v = 6\text{ cm/s}$

5. $v_p = -v \times \text{slope}$

Since, v is negative and slope is positive, $v_p > 0$

Hence, velocity of the particle at the stage P will be along **PA.**

6. $f = 125\text{ Hz}, A = \frac{2}{2} = 1\text{ cm}, \lambda = 15.6\text{ cm}$

$\omega = 2\pi f = 250\pi = 786\text{ rad/s}$

$k = \frac{2\pi}{\lambda} = \frac{2\pi}{0.156} = 40.3\text{ rad/m}$

$y = A\sin(kx - \omega t + \phi)$

$y(0, 0) = A\sin\phi = 0 \quad$ ...(i)

$v_p = \frac{\partial y}{\partial t} = -A\omega\cos(kx - \omega t + \phi)$

At $t = 0, x = 0, v_p < 0$

$v_p = -A\omega\cos\phi < 0 \quad$ ...(ii)

From Eqs. (i) and (ii), we get $\phi = 0°$

$\therefore y = (1\text{ cm})\sin[(40.3\text{ rad/m})\,x - (786\text{ rad/s})\,t]$

7. $f = \frac{v}{\lambda} = \frac{10}{50} = \frac{1}{5}\text{ Hz}$

$\omega = 2\pi f = \frac{2\pi}{5}\text{ rad/s}$

$v_p = \omega\sqrt{A^2 - x^2} = \frac{2\pi}{5}\sqrt{(0.1)^2 - (0.05)^2} = \frac{\sqrt{3}\pi}{50}\text{ m/s}$

$v_p = -v \times \text{slope}$

Since, v is positive and slope is negative, $v_p > 0$

$\therefore \quad \mathbf{v}_p = \left(\frac{\sqrt{3}\pi}{50}\hat{\mathbf{j}}\right)\text{ m/s}$

8. $v_p = -v \times \text{slope}$

$\Rightarrow \quad +20\sqrt{3} = -v \times \tan 60°$

$\Rightarrow \quad v = -20\text{ cm/s}$

So, the wave is travelling in negative x-direction with speed 20 cm/s.

$$\lambda = 7.5 - 3.5 = 4\text{ cm},$$

$$k = \frac{2\pi}{\lambda} = \frac{\pi}{2}\text{ rad/cm}$$

$$\omega = kv = \frac{\pi}{2}(20) = 10\pi\text{ rad/s}$$

$$y = A\sin(\omega t + kx + \phi)$$

At $t = 0$ and $x = 0$,

$$2\sqrt{2} = 4\sin\phi$$

$$\Rightarrow \quad \sin\phi = \frac{1}{\sqrt{2}}$$

$$\Rightarrow \quad \phi = \frac{\pi}{4}\text{ or }\frac{3\pi}{4}$$

$$\text{Slope} = \frac{\partial y}{\partial x} = Ak\cos(\omega t + kx + \phi)$$

At $t = 0, x = 0$,

$$\text{Slope} = Ak\cos\phi > 0$$

Hence $\quad \phi = \dfrac{\pi}{4}$

$$\therefore \quad y = (4\times 10^{-3})\sin\left(10\pi t + \frac{\pi}{2}x + \frac{\pi}{4}\right)$$

9. $\lambda = 12 - 0 = 12$ units

Distance moved by the wave in $\dfrac{1}{60}$ s time,

$$d = 2 + n\lambda = 2 + n(12) = 2(6n+1)$$

$$\text{Velocity of wave, } v = \frac{d}{t} = \frac{2(6n+1)}{(1/60)} = 120(6n+1)$$

$$T = \frac{\lambda}{v} = \frac{12}{120(6n+1)} = \frac{1}{10(6n+1)}$$

10. For wave A,

$$y = A\sin(kx - \omega t - \phi)$$

$$= A\sin\left[kx - \omega\left(t + \frac{\phi}{\omega}\right)\right]$$

For wave B, $y = A\sin(kx - \omega t)$

So, wave A is ahead of wave B by a time difference of $\dfrac{\phi}{\omega}$.

In y *versus* t, 'ahead of' means 'to the left of' while in y versus x, 'ahead of' means 'to the right of' if the wave is travelling in positive x-direction and *vice-versa*.

11. $\Delta\phi = \omega\Delta t = 2\pi \times 0.1 \times 615 = 123\pi$

$$123\pi = 61(2\pi) + 1(\pi)$$

So, the particle completes 61 full cycles and one half cycle.

If one complete cycle, particle travels a distance four times the amplitude.

$\therefore$ distance travelled $= 61 \times (4\times 3) + 1\times(2\times 3) = 738$ cm

$$v_p = -v \times \text{slope}$$

Initially $v_p < 0$ i.e., the particle is moving downward.

Hence, after the last half cycle, it will be moving in upward direction.

12. $y = A\sin(kx - \omega t)$

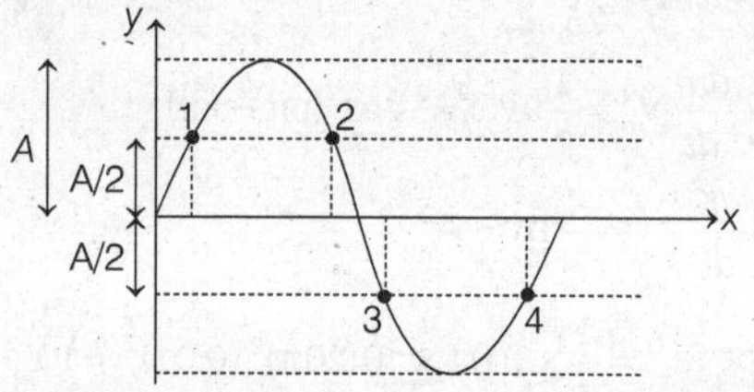

At $t = 0$, $\quad \dfrac{A}{2} = A\sin kx$

$$\Rightarrow \quad kx = \frac{\pi}{6}, \frac{5\pi}{6}, \ldots$$

$$\Rightarrow \quad x = \frac{\lambda}{12}, \frac{5\lambda}{12}, \ldots$$

$$x_2 - x_1 = 8$$

$$\Rightarrow \quad \frac{5\lambda}{12} - \frac{\lambda}{12} = 8$$

$$\Rightarrow \quad \lambda = 24\text{ cm}$$

$$x_3 - x_2 = (x_3 - x_1) - (x_2 - x_1)$$

$$= \frac{\lambda}{2} - \frac{\lambda}{3} = \frac{\lambda}{6} = 4\text{ cm}$$

13. From figure 1, $T = 2$ s

From figure 2, $\lambda = 2$ cm

$$\text{Wave velocity, } v = \frac{\lambda}{T} = \frac{2}{2} = 1\text{ cm/s}$$

$$v_p = \omega\sqrt{A^2 - x^2} = \left(\frac{2\pi}{2}\right)\sqrt{4^2 - (2\sqrt{3})^2} = 2\pi\text{ cm/s}$$

$$v_p = -v \times \text{slope}$$

Since, v is positive and slope is negative, $v_p > 0$

14. $v = \sqrt{\dfrac{T}{\mu}} = \sqrt{\dfrac{35}{3.5\times 10^{-3}}} = 100$ m/s

$$\omega = 2\pi f = 2\pi(100) = 200\pi\text{ rad/s}$$

$$k = \frac{\omega}{v} = \frac{200\pi}{100} = 2\pi\text{ m}^{-1}$$

$$y = A\sin(kx - \omega t)$$

$$\Rightarrow \quad \frac{\partial y}{\partial x} = Ak\cos(kx - \omega t)$$

At $t = 0$ and $x = 0$,

$$\text{Slope} = \frac{\partial y}{\partial x} = A(2\pi)\cos 0^\circ = \frac{\pi}{20}$$

$$\Rightarrow \quad A = 0.025\text{ m}$$

15. $T = \left[M + \left(\dfrac{m}{L}\right)x\right]g$

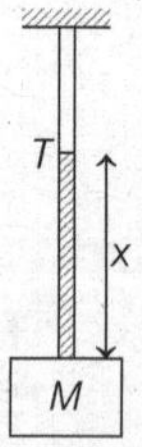

$$v = \sqrt{\frac{T}{\mu}} = \sqrt{\frac{1}{(m/L)}\left(M + \left(\frac{m}{L}\right)x\right)g}$$

$$\frac{dx}{dt} = \left(\frac{ML}{m} + x\right)^{1/2}\sqrt{g}$$

$$\Rightarrow \quad \int_0^L \frac{dx}{\left(\frac{ML}{m} + x\right)^{1/2}} = \sqrt{g}\int_0^t dt$$

$$\Rightarrow \quad \left[2\sqrt{\frac{ML}{m}+x}\right]_0^L = \sqrt{g}\,[t]_0^t$$

$$\Rightarrow \quad t = 2\sqrt{\frac{L}{mg}}\,(\sqrt{M+m}-\sqrt{M})$$

16. For string BC,

At a distance y from end C,

$$T = \mu y g$$

$$v_{BC} = \sqrt{\frac{T}{\mu}} = \sqrt{gy}$$

$$\frac{dy}{dt} = \sqrt{gy}$$

$$\Rightarrow \quad \int_0^l \frac{dy}{\sqrt{y}} = \sqrt{g}\int_0^{t_1} dt \quad \Rightarrow \quad t_1 = 2\sqrt{\frac{l}{g}}$$

For string AB,

At a distance y from end B,

$$T = 2mg + \mu y g$$

$$v_{AB} = \sqrt{\frac{T}{\mu}} = \sqrt{\frac{(2m+\mu y)\,g}{\mu}} = \sqrt{g(y+2l)}$$

$$\frac{dy}{dt} = \sqrt{g(y+2l)}$$

$$\Rightarrow \quad \sqrt{g}\int_0^{t_2} dt = \int_0^l \frac{dy}{\sqrt{y+2l}}$$

$$\Rightarrow \quad t_2 = 2(\sqrt{3}-\sqrt{2})\sqrt{\frac{l}{g}}$$

$$t = t_1 + t_2 = 2(\sqrt{3}-\sqrt{2}+1)\sqrt{\frac{l}{g}}$$

$$\therefore \quad a+b+c+d = 2+1+3+2 = 8$$

17. $\Sigma F_z = 0$

$$\Rightarrow \quad (T+dT) + \mu dz g - T = 0$$

$$\Rightarrow \quad dT = -\mu dz g$$

Also, $\quad T = \mu v^2$

$$\Rightarrow \quad dT = d\mu v^2 + 2v\,dv\,d\mu$$

As v is independent of z, $dv = 0$

$$\therefore \quad dT = d\mu v^2$$

$$\Rightarrow \quad -\mu dz g = d\mu v^2$$

$$\Rightarrow \quad \int_{\mu_0}^{\mu} \frac{d\mu}{\mu} = -\frac{g}{v^2}\int_0^z dz$$

$$\Rightarrow \quad \mu = \mu_0 e^{-(g/v^2)\,z}$$

18. $F_{ext} = \dfrac{dm}{dt} v_{rel}$

$$\Rightarrow \quad S = (\mu v)\,v = \mu v^2$$

Velocity of pulse w.r.t. the rope $= \sqrt{\dfrac{S}{\mu}} = v$

Velocity of pulse w.r.t. ground

$$= v_{pulse,\ rope} + v_{rope} = v + v = 2v$$

19. $2T\sin\left(\dfrac{d\theta}{2}\right) = dm\omega^2 R$

$$\Rightarrow \quad T d\theta = \frac{m}{L}(R d\theta)\,\omega^2 R$$

$$\Rightarrow \quad T = \frac{m\omega^2 R^2}{L} = \frac{m\omega^2 L}{4\pi^2}$$

$$\Rightarrow \quad v = \sqrt{\frac{T}{\mu}} = \sqrt{\frac{1}{(m/L)}\,\frac{m\omega^2 L}{4\pi^2}} = \frac{\omega L}{2\pi}$$

20. $v_{pulse} = v_{pulse,\ rope} + v_{rope} = \dfrac{\omega L}{2\pi} + \omega\left(\dfrac{L}{2\pi}\right) = \dfrac{\omega L}{\pi}$

21. $v_{pulse} = v_{pulse,\ rope} + v_{rope} = -\dfrac{\omega L}{2\pi} + \omega\left(\dfrac{L}{2\pi}\right) = 0$

22. $\Sigma F = ma_{cm}$

$$\Rightarrow \quad T = \left(\frac{m}{L}(L-x)\right)\omega^2\left(x + \frac{L-x}{2}\right)$$

$$\Rightarrow \quad T = \frac{\mu\omega^2(L^2-x^2)}{2}$$

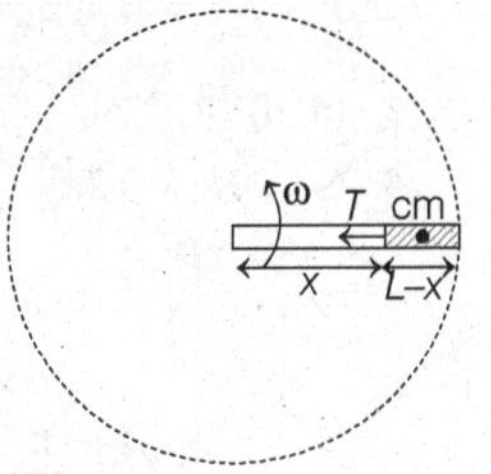

$$v = \sqrt{\frac{T}{\mu}}$$

$$\Rightarrow \quad \frac{dx}{dt} = \frac{\omega}{\sqrt{2}}\sqrt{L^2-x^2}$$

$$\Rightarrow \quad \int_0^t dt = \frac{\sqrt{2}}{\omega}\int_0^L \frac{dx}{\sqrt{L^2-x^2}}$$

$$\Rightarrow \quad t = \frac{\sqrt{2}}{\omega}\left[\sin^{-1}\left(\frac{x}{L}\right)\right]_0^L$$

$$\Rightarrow \quad t = \frac{\sqrt{2}}{\omega}\left(\frac{\pi}{2} - 0\right) = \frac{\pi}{\sqrt{2}\omega}$$

23. $v = \sqrt{\dfrac{T}{\mu}} = \sqrt{\dfrac{80}{5\times 10^{-2}}} = 40$ m/s

$$P = \frac{1}{2}\mu v\omega^2 A^2$$

$$= \frac{1}{2}\times 5\times 10^{-2}\times 40\times(2\pi(60))^2\times\left(\frac{2\sqrt{2}}{15\pi}\right)^2 = 512\ \text{W}$$

24. $\omega_A = \dfrac{2\pi}{T_A} = \dfrac{2\pi}{12} = \dfrac{\pi}{6}$,

$$\omega_B = \frac{2\pi}{T_B} = \frac{2\pi}{8} = \frac{\pi}{4}$$

$$I = \frac{1}{2}\rho v\omega^2 a^2$$

$$\Rightarrow \quad I \propto \omega^2 a^2$$

$$\therefore \quad \frac{I_A}{I_B} = \left(\frac{\omega_A}{\omega_B}\right)^2\left(\frac{a_A}{a_B}\right)^2 = \left(\frac{\pi/6}{\pi/4}\right)^2\left(\frac{3}{2}\right)^2 = 1$$

25. $\quad v_p = -v\times\text{slope} \quad \Rightarrow \quad |v_p| = v\,m$

$$v = \sqrt{\frac{T}{\mu}} \quad \Rightarrow \quad T = \mu v^2$$

$$E = K + U = \int \frac{1}{2}(\mu dx)\, v_p^2 + \int \frac{1}{2}(Tdx)\left(\frac{dy}{dx}\right)^2$$

$$= \frac{\mu (mv)^2}{2}\int dx + \frac{Tm^2}{2}\int dx = m^2 Ta$$

Multiple Choice(s) Correct Questions

1. Function should be in the form of $f(ax \pm bt)$ and it should have finite value for all x and t.

2. $y(x,t) = \dfrac{0.8}{16\left(x + \frac{5}{4}t\right)^2 + 5} = f(x + vt)$

So, the pulse is moving in negative x-direction.

and $v = \frac{5}{4} = 1.25$ m/s

$x = vt = 1.25 \times 2 = 2.5$ m

$y_{max} = \frac{0.8}{5} = 0.16$ m

3. (a, d)

4. $\omega = 20\pi, k = 2\pi$

$$v = \frac{\omega}{k} = \frac{20\pi}{2\pi} = 10 \text{ m/s}$$

$$\Delta\phi = k\,\Delta x$$

$$\Rightarrow \quad 60\left(\frac{\pi}{180}\right) = 2\pi\,\Delta x$$

$$\Rightarrow \quad \Delta x = \frac{1}{6}\text{ m}$$

$$v_{max} = \omega A = (20\pi)(0.01) = \frac{\pi}{5}\text{ m/s}$$

$$\Delta\phi = \omega\,\Delta t$$

$$\Rightarrow \quad \Delta\phi = (20\pi)\left(\frac{1}{20}\right) = \pi \text{ rad} = 180°$$

5. $\lambda = -2 - (-6) = 4$ cm $= 0.04$ m

$T = 0.05 - 0.03 = 0.02$ s

$v = \frac{\lambda}{T} = \frac{0.04}{0.02} = 2$ m/s

At $t = 0.01$ s, the peak is at $x = -4$ cm

At $t = 0.04$ s, the peak is at $x = 2$ cm

So, the wave is travelling in positive x-direction

Distance travelled in 0.01s $= 2 \times 0.01 = 0.02$ m $= 2$ cm

So, at $t = 0$, the peak will be at $x = -4 - 2 = -6$ cm.

6. $y = A\sin(kx - \omega t + \phi)$

At $t = 0, x = 0, y = 5$,

$$5 = 10\sin\phi \Rightarrow \sin\phi = \frac{1}{2}$$

$$\Rightarrow \quad \phi = \frac{\pi}{6}, \frac{5\pi}{6}$$

$$\frac{\partial y}{\partial x} = Ak\cos(kx - \omega t + \phi)$$

At $t = 0, x = 0$,

$$\text{Slope} = \frac{\partial y}{\partial x} = Ak\cos\phi > 0$$

Hence, $\phi = \frac{\pi}{6}$

At $t = 0.05, x = 0, y = 0$

$$0 = 10\sin\left[0 - \omega(0.05) + \frac{\pi}{6}\right]$$

$$\Rightarrow \quad \omega = \frac{10\pi}{3}$$

$$k = \frac{2\pi}{\lambda} = \frac{2\pi}{2} = \pi$$

$$\therefore \quad y = 10\sin\left(\pi x - \frac{10}{3}\pi t + \frac{\pi}{6}\right)$$

$$v = \frac{\omega}{k} = \frac{10\pi/3}{\pi} = \frac{10}{3}\text{ m/s}$$

$$T = \mu v^2 = 0.25\left(\frac{10}{3}\right)^2 = \frac{25}{9}\text{ N}$$

7. $v_p = -v \times \text{slope}$

$$\Rightarrow \quad 4\pi = -v \times 0.004\pi$$

$$\Rightarrow \quad v = -1000\text{ cm/s} = -10\text{ m/s}$$

So, the wave is travelling in negative x-direction with speed 10 m/s.

$$\lambda = 10\text{ cm} = 1\text{ m}$$

$$f = \frac{v}{\lambda} = \frac{10}{1} = 10\text{ Hz}$$

$$\omega = 2\pi f = 2\pi(10) = 20\pi\text{ rad/s}$$

$$v_{max} = A\omega \Rightarrow 4\pi = A(20\pi)$$

$$\Rightarrow \quad A = 0.2\text{ cm} = 2\text{ mm}$$

$$a_{max} = \omega^2 A = (20\pi)^2(0.2) = 80\pi^2\text{cm/s}^2$$

8. $\omega = 2\pi f = 2\pi(25) = 50\pi$ rad/s

$$k = \frac{\omega}{v} = \frac{50\pi}{300} = \frac{\pi}{6}\text{ rad/m}$$

$$\Delta\phi = k\,\Delta x = \frac{\pi}{6}(6) = \pi$$

$$\lambda = \frac{v}{f} = \frac{300}{25} = 12\text{ m}$$

$$\Delta x = \frac{\lambda}{2} \text{ and } \Delta\phi = \pi$$

So, $\Delta = 2A = 2(2.5 \times 10^{-5}) = 5 \times 10^{-5}$ m

9. $n_1\lambda = 5$ ...(i)

$$(2n_2 + 1)\frac{\lambda}{2} = 1.5 \quad \text{...(ii)}$$

$$\therefore \quad \frac{2n_1}{2n_2 + 1} = \frac{5}{1.5}$$

$$\Rightarrow \quad 3n_1 = 10n_2 + 5$$

Possible solutions are $n_2 = 1, n_1 = 5$

$n_2 = 4, n_1 = 15$

$n_2 = 7, n_1 = 25$

$$n_2 = 10, n_1 = 35$$

$$\therefore \quad \lambda = \frac{5}{n_1} = 1\,\text{m}, \frac{1}{3}\,\text{m}, \frac{1}{5}\,\text{m}, \frac{1}{7}\,\text{m}, \ldots$$

10. $v = \sqrt{\frac{T}{\mu}} = \sqrt{\frac{\mu y g}{\mu}} = \sqrt{gy}$

$$a = v\frac{dv}{dy} = \sqrt{gy}\,\sqrt{g}\left(\frac{1}{2\sqrt{y}}\right) = \frac{g}{2}$$

So, the pulse travels upward with increasing speed and constant acceleration.

11. $\mu = \left(\frac{\lambda}{L}\right)y$

$$T = \int_0^y \mu dy g_{\text{eff}} = \int_0^y \left(\frac{\lambda}{L}\right) y dy\,(3g) = \frac{3\lambda g y^2}{2L}$$

$$v = \sqrt{\frac{T}{\mu}} = \sqrt{\frac{3gy}{2}}$$

$$v = \frac{dy}{dt} = \sqrt{\frac{3g}{2}}\sqrt{y}$$

$$\Rightarrow \quad \int dt = \sqrt{\frac{2}{3g}}\int_0^L \frac{dy}{\sqrt{y}} \quad \Rightarrow \quad t = \sqrt{\frac{8L}{3g}}$$

$$a = v\frac{dv}{dy} = \frac{3g}{4}$$

12. $P_{\text{avg}} = \frac{1}{2}\mu v\omega^2 A^2 = \frac{1}{2} \times 0.02 \times 6 \times (2\pi(17))^2\,(0.4)^2 = 111\,\text{W}$

Energy per unit length $= P_{\text{avg}} \times \left(\frac{1}{v}\right) = 111 \times \frac{1}{6} = 18.5\,\text{J/m}$

13. $\frac{\lambda}{2} = 200 - 100$

$$\Rightarrow \quad \lambda = 200\,\text{cm} = 2\,\text{m}$$

$$v = \lambda f = 2(400) = 800\,\text{m/s}$$

$$T = \mu v^2 = 0.05(800)^2 = 32 \times 10^3\,\text{N}$$

$$v_{\max} = A\omega$$

$$\Rightarrow \quad 80\pi = A(2\pi\,(400))$$

$$\Rightarrow \quad A = 0.1\,\text{m} = 10\,\text{cm}$$

14. Power $= \frac{dE}{dt} = \frac{(u_k + u_p)\,dl}{dt} = (u_k + u_p)\sqrt{\frac{T}{\mu}}$

Comprehension Based Questions

1. At $t_1 = 0.002$ s, Crest is at $x_1 = 3$ m

At $t_2 = 0.008$ s, Crest is at $x_2 = 8$ m

$$v = \frac{x_2 - x_1}{t_2 - t_1} = \frac{8-3}{0.008 - 0.002} = \frac{2500}{3}\,\text{m/s}$$

2. $\lambda = 9 - 1 = 8$ m

$$f = \frac{v}{\lambda} = \frac{2500}{3 \times 8} = 104.2\,\text{Hz}$$

3. $y = A\sin(\omega t - kx + \phi)$

$$v_p = \frac{dy}{dt} = A\omega\cos(\omega t - kx + \phi)$$

For curve 1,

At $t = 0, x = 0, y = 0,$

$$\Rightarrow \quad 0 = A\sin\phi \quad \Rightarrow \quad \phi = 0 \text{ or } \pi$$

Here, ϕ will be π because particle velocity is negative.

For curve 2,

At $t = 0, x = 7$ cm, $y = -1,$

$$\Rightarrow \quad -1 = 2\sin[-k(7) + \pi]$$

$$\Rightarrow \quad \sin(-7k + \pi) = -\frac{1}{2}$$

$$\Rightarrow \quad -7k + \pi = 2n\pi + \frac{7\pi}{6} \quad \text{or} \quad 2n\pi + \frac{11\pi}{6}$$

Here, $-7k + \pi = 2n\pi + \frac{11\pi}{6}$ because at $t = 0$, particle velocity is positive.

$$\therefore \quad -7\left(\frac{2\pi}{\lambda}\right) = 2n\pi + \frac{5\pi}{6}$$

$$\Rightarrow \quad \lambda = \frac{-14\pi}{2n\pi + \frac{5\pi}{6}} = \frac{-84}{12n+5}$$

For $n = -1, \lambda = 12$ cm

$n = -2, \lambda = \frac{84}{19}$ cm (not possible as $\lambda > 7$ cm)

$$\therefore \quad \lambda = 12\,\text{cm}$$

4. $T = \frac{1}{100}$ s

$$v = \frac{\lambda}{T} = \frac{0.12}{(1/100)} = 12\,\text{m/s}$$

5.

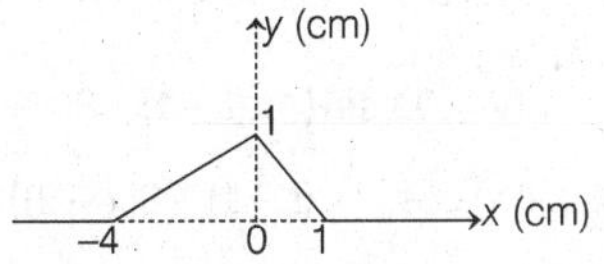

$$\text{Area} = \frac{1}{2} \times \text{base} \times \text{height}$$

$$= \frac{1}{2} \times 5 \times 1 = 2.5\,\text{cm}^2$$

6. $v = \sqrt{\frac{T}{\mu}} = \sqrt{\frac{5}{50 \times 10^{-3}}} = 10\,\text{m/s}$

$x = vt = 10 \times 0.01 = 0.1$ m $= 10$ cm

So, the peak wil be at $x = 10$ cm at 0.01 s.

Hence, $x = 7$ cm will lie left of the peak.

$$y(x,t) = \frac{x - vt}{4} + 1 = \frac{7 - 10}{4} + 1 = 0.25\,\text{cm}$$

7. $x = vt = 10 \times 0.015 = 0.15$ m $= 15$ cm

So, $x = 13$ cm will lie left of the peak

$$v_p = -v \times \frac{dy}{dx} = -10\left(\frac{1}{4}\right) = -2.5\,\text{m/s} = -250\,\text{cm/s}$$

8. $v_p = -v \times \text{slope}$

Here, v is negative. Thats why v_p will be positive when slope is positive and v_p will be negative when slope is negative.

Slope is positive for a and g. So, a and g will be moving upward.

9. For d, slope is negative. So, d will be moving downwards.

10. Slope is zero for b and f. So, b and f are momentarily at rest.

11. Slope is maximum for points d and h. So, points d and h are moving with maximum velocity.

12. $T = \mu v^2 \Rightarrow T \propto v^2$

Speed for (b),
$$v = \frac{\omega}{k} = \frac{10}{4} = 2.5 \text{ m/s}$$
Speed for other four strings,
$$v = \frac{\omega}{k} = 2 \text{ m/s}$$
So, b will be different tension

13. Energy in one wavelength = Power × time
$$\Rightarrow \quad E = \frac{1}{2}\mu v \omega^2 A^2 \times \left(\frac{2\pi}{\omega}\right)$$
$$\Rightarrow \quad E \propto v\omega A^2$$

14. Slope $= \frac{\partial y}{\partial x} = Ak\cos(kx - \omega t)$

15. The equation of wave moving in negative x-direction, assuming origin of position at $x = 2$ and origin of time (i.e., initial time) at $t = 1$s
$$y = 0.1\sin(4\pi t + 8x)$$
Now, shifting the origin of position to left by 2m, to $x = 0$. Also shifting the origin of time backwards by 1 s, that is to $t = 0$ s.
$$y = 0.1\sin(4\pi(t-1) + 8(x-2))$$

16. $v_p = \frac{\partial y}{\partial t} = (0.1)(4\pi)\cos(4\pi(t-1) + 8(x-2))$

At $x = 2$ m and $t = 1$s,
$$v_p = 0.4\pi \text{ m/s}$$

17. At $x = 2$ m, $t = 1.125$ s,
$$v_p = (0.1)\,4\pi\cos(4\pi(1.125-1) + 8(2-2)) = 0$$
Hence, $\quad P = Fv_p = 0$

Match the Columns Questions

1. $y = A\sin(\omega t - kx)$

Comparing we get, $\omega = 20\pi$, $k = 10\pi$
$$v = \frac{\omega}{k} = \frac{20\pi}{10\pi} = 2 \text{ m/s}$$
$$f = \frac{\omega}{2\pi} = \frac{20\pi}{2\pi} = 10 \text{ Hz}$$
$$\omega = \frac{2\pi}{k} = \frac{2\pi}{10\pi} = 0.2 \text{ m}$$
$$v_{max} = A\omega = (0.02)(20\pi) = 0.4\pi \text{ m/s}$$

2. $v_p = -v \times$ slope

Acceleration is directed towards the mean position and at mean position acceleration is zero.

3. Check value of y and $\frac{\partial y}{\partial x}$ (slope) at $x = 0, t = 0$

4. As both waves are sent from the same source, $\omega_1 = \omega_2$
$$v = \sqrt{\frac{T}{\mu}} \Rightarrow v \propto \frac{1}{\sqrt{\mu}}$$
$$\therefore \quad v_1 = 2v_2 \qquad [\because \mu_2 = 4\mu_1]$$
$$A_1 = A \text{ and } A_2 = 2A$$
Power, $\quad P = \frac{1}{2}\mu v\omega^2 A^2$
$$\Rightarrow \quad \frac{P_1}{P_2} = \frac{\mu_1 v_1 A_1^2}{\mu_2 v_2 A_2^2} = \left(\frac{1}{4}\right)\left(\frac{2}{1}\right)\left(\frac{1}{2}\right)^2 = \frac{1}{8}$$
Intensity, $\quad I = \frac{P}{S}$
$$\Rightarrow \quad \frac{I_1}{I_2} = \frac{P_1}{P_2} = \frac{1}{8}$$
Energy density, $u \propto \mu\omega^2 A^2$
$$\Rightarrow \quad \frac{u_1}{u_2} = \left(\frac{\mu_1}{\mu_2}\right)\left(\frac{A_1}{A_2}\right)^2 = \left(\frac{1}{4}\right)\left(\frac{1}{2}\right)^2 = \frac{1}{16}$$

Numerical Value Questions

1. $y = \frac{0.8}{3(x+2t)^2 + 4} = f(x + vt)$
$$\therefore \quad v = -2 \text{ m/s}$$

2. $\phi = \pi[30t - x\sqrt{3} - y]$
$$\phi_A = \pi[30t - (2\sqrt{3})\sqrt{3} - 2] = \pi[30t - 8]$$
$$\phi_B = \pi[30t - (3\sqrt{3})\sqrt{3} - 3] = \pi[30t - 12]$$
$$\phi_A - \phi_B = 4\pi$$
$$\therefore \quad n = 4$$

3. $v = \sqrt{\frac{F}{\mu}}$, $\omega = 2\pi f = \frac{2\pi v}{\lambda} = \frac{2\pi}{\lambda}\sqrt{\frac{F}{\mu}}$
$$a_{max} = \omega^2 A = g$$
$$\Rightarrow \quad \left(\frac{2\pi}{\lambda}\sqrt{\frac{F}{\mu}}\right)^2 A = g$$
$$\Rightarrow \quad A = \frac{\lambda^2\mu g}{4\pi^2 F} = \frac{\lambda^2\mu}{4F} = 2 \times 10^{-3} \text{ m} = 2 \text{ mm}$$

4. At point Q, $F = 3 - kt_0 = 0$
$$\Rightarrow \quad t_0 = \frac{3}{k}$$
Time taken by the pulse to travel from P to $Q = t_0 = \frac{3}{k}$
$$v = \sqrt{\frac{T}{\mu}} = \sqrt{\frac{3-kt}{3 \times 10^{-2}}}$$
$$\Rightarrow \quad \frac{dx}{dt} = \frac{10}{\sqrt{3}}(3 - kt)^{1/2}$$
$$\Rightarrow \quad \int_0^1 dx = \frac{10}{\sqrt{3}}\int_0^{t_0}(3 - kt)^{1/2}dt$$

$$\Rightarrow \quad [x]_0^1 = \frac{10}{\sqrt{3}}\left[\frac{(3-kt)^{3/2}}{-k(3/2)}\right]_0^{t_0}$$

$$\Rightarrow \quad 1-0 = -\frac{20}{3\sqrt{3}k}((3-kt_0)^{3/2} - 3^{3/2})$$

$$\Rightarrow \quad k = 20$$

5. $P = \frac{1}{2}\mu v\omega^2 A^2$

$\Rightarrow P \propto v\omega^2 A^2$

$$\therefore \quad \frac{P_1}{P_2} = \left(\frac{v_1}{v_2}\right)\left(\frac{\omega_1}{\omega_2}\right)^2\left(\frac{A_1}{A_2}\right)^2 = \left(\frac{3.2/200}{0.4/25}\right)\left(\frac{3.2}{0.4}\right)^2\left(\frac{3}{6}\right)^2 = 16$$

6. $v = \sqrt{\frac{T}{\mu}} = \sqrt{\frac{100}{4\times 10^{-2}}} = 50$ m/s

$$P_{avg} = \frac{1}{2}\mu v\omega^2 A^2$$

$$\Rightarrow \quad 40 = \frac{1}{2}\times 4\times 10^{-2}\times 50\times(2\pi f)^2 (0.1)^2$$

$$\Rightarrow \quad f = 10 \text{ Hz}$$

7. $v = \sqrt{\frac{T}{\mu}} = \sqrt{\frac{10}{0.1}} = 10$ m/s

$v_p = -v\times$ slope

To the left of the peak, $v_p = -10\times\left(\frac{0.1}{10}\right) = -0.1$ m/s

To the right of the peak,

$$v_p' = -10\times\left(-\frac{0.1}{5}\right) = 0.2 \text{ m/s}$$

$$K = \int_{-10}^{0}\frac{1}{2}(\mu dx)\,v_p^2 + \int_0^5 \frac{1}{2}(\mu dx)\,v_p'^2$$

$$\Rightarrow \quad K = \frac{1}{2}\times 0.1\times(0.1)^2[x]_{-0.1}^{0} + \frac{1}{2}\times 0.1\times(0.2)^2[x]_0^{0.05}$$

$$\Rightarrow \quad K = 150\times 10^{-6}\text{ J} = 150\,\mu\text{J}$$

8. $v_p = \frac{\partial y}{\partial t} = 4e^{-(2x+5t)^2}\times 2(2x+5t)\times 5$

At $t=0, x=0, v_p = 0$

$\therefore$ Rate of energy flow = 0

Previous Year's Questions

JEE Main

1. Given, wave equation is ,

$$y = 0.05\sin(8x-4t),$$

Comparing it with general equation

$$\Rightarrow \quad y = A\sin(kx-\omega t).$$

we have $\quad k = 8$ and $\omega = 4$

So, wave speed is given by

$$v = \frac{\omega}{k} = \frac{4}{8} = 0.5 \text{ m/s}$$

2. Given that, Mass per unit length,

$$\mu = 7.0\times 10^{-3}\text{kg m}^{-1}$$

Tension in string, $T = 70$ N

Speed of transverse wave,

$$v = \sqrt{\frac{T}{\mu}} = \sqrt{\frac{70}{7.0\times 10^{-3}}}$$

$$v = 100 \text{ m/s}$$

3. Transverse harmonic wave is,

$$y(x,t) = 5\sin(6t + 0.003x)$$

So here, $\omega = 6$ rad/s

and $\quad k = 0.003\text{ cm}^{-1}$

So, wave speed is given by

$$v = \frac{\omega}{k} = \frac{6}{0.003}\text{ cm/s} = 2000 \text{ cm/s} = 20 \text{ m/s}$$

4. Given,

$$Y = 10^{-2}\sin 2\pi(160t - 0.5x + \pi/4)$$

Speed of wave $= \frac{\omega}{k} = \frac{160}{0.5} = 320$ m/s

$$= 320\times\frac{18}{5} = 1152 \text{ km/h}$$

5. Wave equation is given as

$$y = 10\sin\left(2\pi nt - \frac{2\pi}{\lambda}\cdot x\right)$$

Wave speed $= \frac{\omega}{k} = \frac{2\pi n}{(2\pi/\lambda)} = n\lambda$

Maximum speed of oscillating particle $= A\omega = 10(2\pi n)$

Given, maximum particle speed = 4 × wave speed

$$\Rightarrow \quad 10\times 2\pi n = 4\times n\lambda$$

$$\Rightarrow \quad \frac{10\times 2\pi}{4} = \lambda \text{ or } \lambda = 5\pi \text{ units}$$

6. As per question,

at $\quad t = 0, y = \frac{1}{(1+x)^2}$

and at $\quad t = 1$ s, $y = \frac{1}{1+(x-2)^2}$ ...(i)

As we know,

At $\quad t = t$ s, $y = \frac{1}{1+(x-vt)^2}$

So, at $\quad t = 1$ s, $y = \frac{1}{1+(x-v)^2}$ ...(ii)

On comparing Eqs. (i) and (ii), we get

$$v = 2 \text{ ms}^{-1}$$

Hence,the velocity of the wave will be 2 m/s.

7. Given, mass per unit length,

$$\mu = 0.135 \text{ g/cm} = 1.35\times 10^{-2}\text{ kg/m}$$

Transverse wave equation,

$$y = -0.21\sin(x + 30t)$$

From given equation,

$$\omega = 30 \text{ rad/s}, k = 1$$

Speed of wave,

$$v = \frac{\omega}{k} = \frac{30}{1} = 30 \text{ ms}^{-1}$$

Also, $v = \sqrt{\dfrac{T}{\mu}} \Rightarrow T = v^2\mu$

$$T = (30)^2 \times 1.35 \times 10^{-2}$$
$$= 900 \times 0.0135 = 12.15 \text{ N}$$
$$= 1215 \times 10^{-2} \text{ N}$$

Hence, $x = 1215$

8. Distance between any two crests

$$n\lambda = 5 \text{ (} n \text{ is an integer)} \quad \text{...(i)}$$

Distance between any crest and any trough $(2m+1)\dfrac{\lambda}{2} = 1.5$

(m is an integer)

$$\Rightarrow \quad (2m+1)\lambda = 3 \quad \text{...(ii)}$$

Dividing Eq. (i) by Eq. (ii), we get

$$\Rightarrow \quad \frac{n\lambda}{(2m+1)\lambda} = \frac{5}{3}$$
$$3n = 5(2m+1)$$
$$3n = 10m + 5 \quad \text{...(iii)}$$

(I) $m = 1$ and $n = 5$
Now, on putting these values in Eqs. (i) and (ii), we get
$\lambda = 1$

(II) $m = 4$ and $n = 15$
Now, on putting these values in Eqs. (i) and (ii), we get
$\lambda = \dfrac{1}{3}$

(III) $m = 7$ and $n = 25$
Now, on putting these values in Eqs. (i) and (ii), we get
$\lambda = \dfrac{1}{5}$ and so on.

So, possible values of $\lambda = 1, \dfrac{1}{3}, \dfrac{1}{5}, \ldots\ldots$ Hence, correct option is (b).

9. From the given snapshot at $t = 0$,

$$y = 0 \text{ at } x = 0$$

and $y = -$ ve when x increases from zero.
Standard expression of any progressive wave is given by

$$y = A\sin(kx - \omega t + \phi)$$

Here, ϕ is the phase difference, we need to get at $t = 0$,
$y = A\sin(kx + \phi)$
Clearly $\phi = \pi$, so that

$$y = A\sin(kx + \pi)$$
$$y = -A\sin(kx)$$
$$\Rightarrow \quad y = 0 \text{ at } x = 0$$

and $\quad y = -\text{ve at } x > 0$

Which satisfies the given snapshot.

10. Wave equation is given by,

$$y = 10^{-3}\sin(50t + 2x)$$

Speed of wave is obtained by differentiating phase of wave.
Now, phase of wave from given equation is $\phi = 50t + 2x =$ constant
Differentiating 'ϕ' w.r.t. 't',
we get

$$\frac{d}{dx}(50t + 2x) = \frac{d}{dt} \quad \text{(constant)}$$
$$\Rightarrow \quad 50 + 2\left(\frac{dx}{dt}\right) = 0$$
$$\Rightarrow \quad \frac{dx}{dt} = \frac{-50}{2} = -25 \text{ ms}^{-1}$$

So, wave is propagating in negative x–direction with a speed of 25 ms^{-1}.

11. When the car is at rest, the situation can be shown in the figure below.

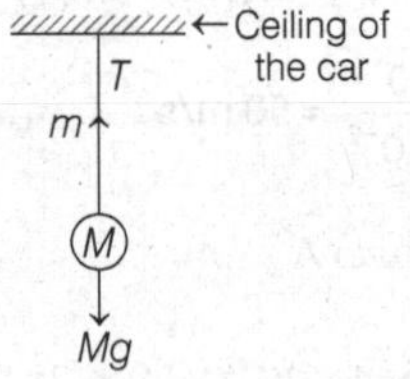

Since, $m << M$, then we can neglect the mass of the string.
So, the initial velocity of the wave in the string can be given as,

$$v = \sqrt{\frac{T}{\mu}} = \sqrt{\frac{Mg}{\frac{M}{l}}} = 60 \text{ m/s} \quad \text{...(i)}$$

Now, when the car has acceleration 'a', then the situation can be shown in the figure given below.

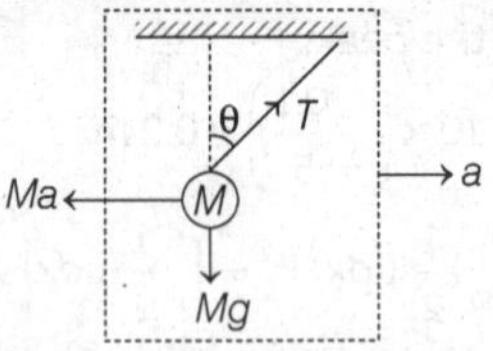

Resolving the components of 'T' along X-and Y-axis, we get

$$T\cos\theta = Mg \quad \text{...(ii)}$$
$$T\sin\theta = Ma \quad \text{...(iii)}$$

Squaring both sides of Eqs. (ii) and (iii) and adding them, we get

$$T^2(\sin^2\theta + \cos^2\theta) = M^2(g^2 + a^2)$$
$$\Rightarrow \quad T = M(g^2 + a^2)^{\frac{1}{2}} \quad \text{...(iv)}$$

Now, the velocity of the wave in the string would be given as

$$v' = \sqrt{\frac{T}{\mu}} = \sqrt{\frac{M(g^2 + a^2)^{\frac{1}{2}}}{\frac{M}{l}}} = 60.5 \text{ m/s} \quad \text{...(v)}$$

Dividing Eq. (i) and Eq. (v), we get

$$\frac{v}{v'} = \frac{\sqrt{\dfrac{Mg}{\frac{M}{l}}}}{\sqrt{\dfrac{M(g^2 + a^2)^{\frac{1}{2}}}{\frac{M}{l}}}} = \sqrt{\frac{g}{(g^2 + a^2)^{\frac{1}{2}}}}$$

$$= \frac{60}{60.5} \text{ or } \frac{60.5}{60} = \sqrt{\frac{(g^2+a^2)^{\frac{1}{2}}}{g}}$$

Squaring both the sides, we get

$$\frac{(60.5)^2}{(60)^2} = \frac{(g^2+a^2)^{\frac{1}{2}}}{g}$$

or $$\left(1+\frac{0.5}{60}\right)^2 = \sqrt{1+\left(\frac{a}{g}\right)^2}$$

Using binomial expansion,

$$(1+x)^n = 1+\frac{nx}{1!}+\ldots$$

On both sides, we get

$$1+2\times\frac{0.5}{60} = 1+\frac{1}{2}\cdot\frac{a^2}{g^2}$$

$$\Rightarrow \quad 1+\frac{1}{60} = 1+\frac{1}{2}\cdot\frac{a^2}{g^2} \text{ or } \frac{a}{g} = \frac{1}{\sqrt{30}}$$

or $$a = \frac{g}{\sqrt{30}} = \frac{g}{5.4} \simeq \frac{g}{5}$$

JEE Advanced

1. $v = \sqrt{\frac{T}{\mu}}$, so speed at any position will be same for both pulses, therefore time taken by both pulses will be same.

$$\lambda f = v$$

$$\Rightarrow \quad \lambda = \frac{v}{f} \Rightarrow \lambda \propto v \propto T$$

When pulse 1 reaches at A tension and hence speed decreases therefore λ decreases.

CHAPTER~09

Standing Waves

LEVEL 01 Starter Level

9.1 Superposition of Waves

1. Two waves passing through a region are represented by
$y_1 = 5\sqrt{2}$ mm sin $[(2\pi \text{ cm}^{-1})x - (50\pi \text{ s}^{-1})t]$
and $y_2 = 10$ mm sin $[(\pi \text{ cm}^{-1})x - (100\pi \text{ s}^{-1})t]$
Find the displacement of the particle at $x = 1$ cm at time $t = 5.0$ ms.

2. Figure shows a rectangular pulse and triangular pulse approaching each other. The speed of each pulse is 0.5 cm/s. Sketch the resultant pulse at $t = 2$ s.

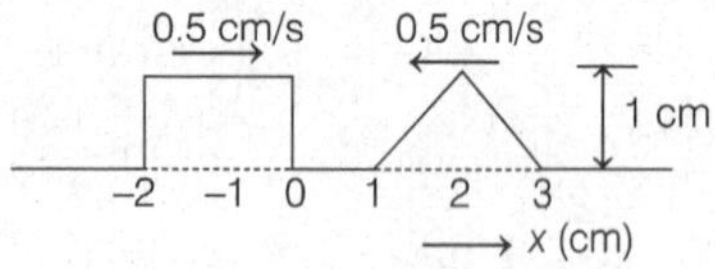

3. Two waves are described by
$y_1 = (3 \text{ cm}) \sin [\pi (5x - 200t)]$
and $y_2 = (4 \text{ cm}) \sin [\pi (5x - 200t) + \pi/3]$
where, x is in m and t is in s. When these two waves are combined, a travelling wave is produced. What is the
(a) amplitude,
(b) wave speed, and
(c) wavelength of that travelling wave?

4. Find the resultant wave equation due to superposition of two waves $y_1 = 5 \sin (\omega t - kx)$ and $y_2 = -5 \cos (\omega t - kx - 150°)$.

5. Two waves each having a frequency of 100 Hz and a wavelength of 2 cm are travelling in the same direction on a string. What is the phase difference between the waves
(a) if the second wave was produced 10 ms later than the first one at the same place?
(b) if the two waves were produced at a distance 1 cm behind the second one?
(c) if each of the waves has an amplitude of 2.0 mm, what would be the amplitudes of the resultant waves in part (a) and (b)?

9.2 Reflected and Transmitted Waves

1. Two strings A and B with $\mu = 2$ kg/m and $\mu = 8$ kg/m respectively are joined in series and kept on a horizontal table with both the ends fixed. The tension in the string is 200 N. If a pulse of amplitude 6 mm travels in A towards the junction, then find the amplitude of reflected and transmitted pulse.

2. A plane wave given by equation
$y = 0.04 \sin (0.6\pi x - 100\pi t)$, where x and y are in m and t in s is incident normally on a boundary between two media beyond which wave speed becomes tripled. Find the equation of the reflected and transmitted waves. Take $x = 0$ as the boundary between two media.

3. The harmonic wave
$y_i = (2.0 \times 10^{-3}) \cos \pi (2.0x - 60t)$ travels along a string towards a boundary at $x = 0$ with a second string. The wave speed on the second string is 20 m/s. Find the percentage of energy transmitted.

4. The figures show a triangular pulse on a rope at $t = 0$. It is moving with speed 2 cm/s. Draw the pulse at $t = 2$ s for the following two cases.

(a)

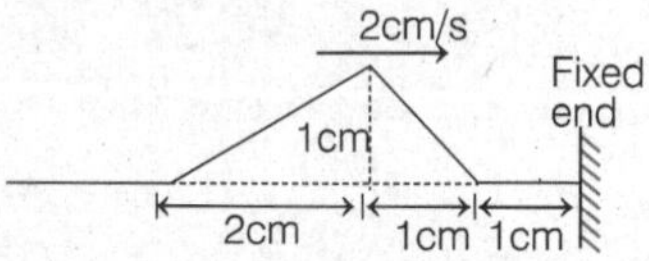

(b)

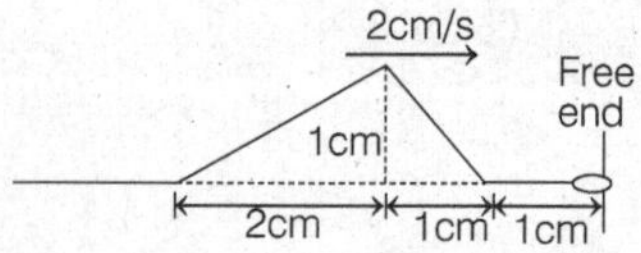

9.3 Standing Waves

1. Two waves travelling in opposite directions produce a standing wave. The individual wave functions are
$y_1 = (4 \text{ cm}) \sin(3\pi x - 2\pi t)$,
$y_2 = (4 \text{ cm}) \sin(3\pi x + 2\pi t)$, where x is in m and t is in s.
(a) Find the maximum displacement of a particle of the medium at $x = 1/12$ m.
(b) Find the position of the nodes and anti-nodes.
(c) What is the amplitude of the SHM of a particle located at an anti-node?

2. The vibration of a string of length 60 cm is represented by the equation,
$y = 3\cos\left(\frac{\pi x}{20}\right)\cos(72\pi t)$, where x and y are in cm ant t in s.
(a) Write down the component waves whose superposition gives the above wave.
(b) Where are the nodes and anti-nodes located along the string?
(c) What is the velocity of the particle of the string at the position $x = 5$ cm and $t = 0.25$ s?

3. The equation of wave in a string fixed at both ends is $y = 4\sin(\pi x)\cos(\pi t)$. Find
(a) the distance between adjacent nodes.
(b) the phase difference between oscillations of two particles located at $x = 0.8$ m and $x = 1.2$ m.
(c) Write down the component waves.

9.4 Vibrations of a String Fixed at both Ends

1. A 10.0 m long wire of mass 100 g is fixed at both ends and is stretched under a tension of 25 N. Find the frequency of
(a) fundamental mode (b) 2nd overtone
(c) 5th harmonic

2. A string 1 m long is drawn by a 300Hz vibrator attached to its end. The string vibrates in 3 segments. What is the speed of transverse waves in the string?

3. The length of the wire shown in figure between the pulleys is 1.5 m and its mass is 15 g. Find the frequency of vibration with which the wire vibrates in four loops leaving the middle point of the wire between the pulleys at rest. ($g = 10 \text{ m/s}^2$)

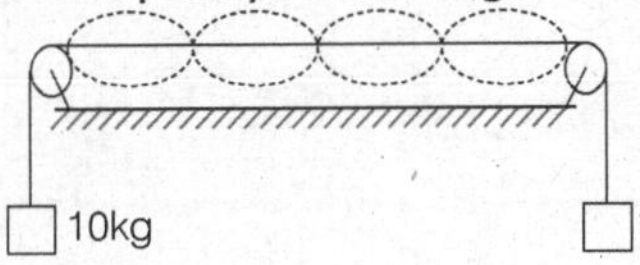

4. A rope under a tension of 200 N and fixed at both ends, oscillates in a second harmonic standing wave pattern. The displacement of the rope is given by
$y = (0.10 \text{ m}) \sin\left(\frac{\pi x}{2}\right)\sin 12\pi t$
where, $x = 0$ at one end of the rope, x is in m and t is in s. What is
(a) the length of the rope,
(b) the speed of the progressive waves on the rope, and
(c) the mass of the rope?
(d) If the rope oscillates in a third-harmonic standing wave pattern, what will be the period of oscillation?

5. A 60.0 cm guitar string under a tension of 50.0 N has a mass per unit length of 0.100 g/cm. What is the highest resonance frequency of the string that can be heard by a person able to hear frequencies upto 20,000 Hz?

6. A string with linear mass density 4×10^{3} kg/m is under a tension of 360 N and is fixed at both ends. One of its resonance frequencies is 375 Hz. The next higher frequency is 450 Hz.
(a) What is the fundamental frequency of string?
(b) Which harmonics are the ones given?
(c) What is the length of string?

7. A string fixed at both ends has consecutive standing wave modes for which the distances between adjacent nodes are 18 cm and 16 cm respectively.
(a) What is the length of the string?
(b) If the tension is 10 N and the linear mass density is 4 g/m, what is the fundamental frequency?

8. A uniform horizontal rod of length 40 cm and mass 1.2 kg is supported by two identical wires as shown in figure. Where should a mass of 4.8 kg be placed on the rod so that the same tuning fork may excite the wire on left into its fundamental vibrations and that on right into its first overtone? Take $g = 10 \text{ m/s}^2$.

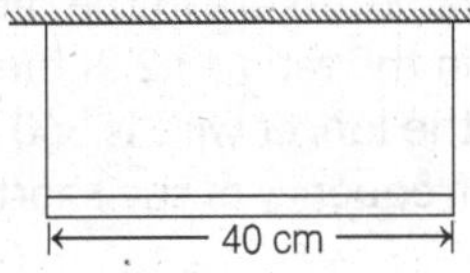

9.5 Vibrations of a String Fixed at one End

1. A 1 m long rope having a mass of 40 g is fixed at one end and is tied to a light string at the other end. The tension in the string is 400 N. Find the frequencies of the fundamental and the first two overtones.

2. Three successive resonance frequencies for a certain string are 90 Hz, 150 Hz and 210 Hz.
(a) What is the fundamental frequency?
(b) Which harmonics are these resonance frequencies?
(c) Which overtone are these frequencies?
(d) If the speed of transverse waves on this string is 96 m/s, find the length of the string.

9.6 Resonance in an Oscillating String

1. In the arrangement shown in figure, a mass can be hung from a string (with linear mass density of $\mu = 2$ g/m) that passes over a light pulley. The string is connected to a vibrator (of constant frequency f), and the length of the string between point P and the pulley is $L = 2.0$ m. When the mass m is either 16.0 kg or 25.0 kg, standing waves are observed, however, no standing waves are observed with any mass between these values. ($g = 9.8\ \text{m/s}^2$)

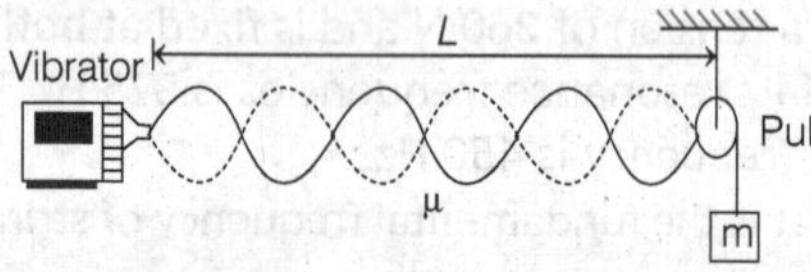

(a) What is the frequency of the vibrator?
(b) What is the largest mass for which standing waves could be observed?

2. A string passing over a smooth pulley carries a stone at one end, while its other end is attached to a fixed end. A vibrating tuning fork is brought in contact with the stretched string and the string vibrates forming 8 loops. When the stone is completely immersed in water, 10 loops are formed. What is the specific gravity of the stone?

9.7 Sonometer

1. Two wires are fixed on a sonometer. Their tensions are in the ratio 8 : 1, their lengths are in the ratio 36 : 35, the diameters are in the ratio 4 : 1 and densities are in the ratio 1 : 2. If the fundamental frequency of the longer wire is 360 Hz, then find the fundamental frequency of the shorter wire.

2. An addition of 24 kgf to the tension of sonometer wire of fixed length increases its fundamental frequency 3 fold. What is the original tension in the string?

3. A sonometer wire has a length of 114 cm between two fixed ends. Where should two bridges be placed to divide the wire into three segments whose fundamental frequencies are in the ratio 1 : 3 : 4?

4. A sonometer wire fixed at one end has a solid mass M hanging from its other end to produce tension in it. It is found that 70 cm length of the wire produces a certain fundamental frequency when plucked. When the same mass M is hanging in water, completely submerged in it, it is found that the length of the wire has to be changed by 5 cm in order to produce the same fundamental frequency. Calculate the density of the material of mass M.

9.8 Vibrations of a Composite String

1. A light string of length $5L$ is tied at one end to a fixed support and to a heavy string of length L at the other end as shown in figure. Mass per unit length of the strings are μ and 9μ and the tension is T. Find the minimum possible value of frequency such that point A is (a) a node (b) an anti-node.

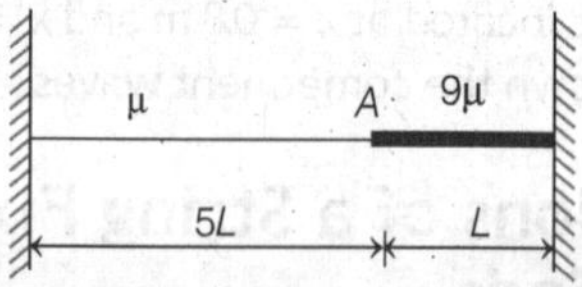

2. Figure shows an aluminium wire of length 60 cm joined to a steel wire of length 80 cm and stretched between two fixed supports. The tension produced is 40 N. The cross-sectional area of the steel wire is $1.0\ \text{mm}^2$ and that of the aluminium wire is $3.0\ \text{mm}^2$. What could be the minimum frequency of a tuning fork which can produce standing waves in the system with the joint as a node? The density of aluminium is $2.6\ \text{g/cm}^3$ and that of steel is $7.8\ \text{g/cm}^3$.

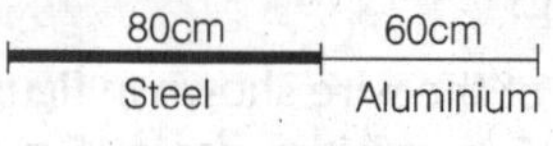

LEVEL 02 \ JEE Main Level

Single Choice Correct Questions

1. Two waves are represented by $y_1 = a_1 \cos(\omega t - kx)$ and $y_2 = a_2 \sin\left(\omega t - kx + \frac{\pi}{3}\right)$. Then, the phase difference between them is

   (a) $\frac{\pi}{3}$ (b) $\frac{\pi}{2}$

   (c) $\frac{5\pi}{6}$ (d) $\frac{\pi}{6}$

2. Find the resultant of two waves progressing along X-axis.

   $y_1 = 3\sin(3t - 6x)$

   $y_2 = -4\cos(3t - 6x)$

   (a) $5\sin(3t - 6x - 37°)$

   (b) $5\sin(3t - 6x + 53°)$

   (c) $5\sin(3t - 6x - 53°)$

   (d) None of the above

3. Three waves of equal frequency having amplitudes 10 mm, 4 mm and 7 mm arrive at a given point with a successive phase difference of $\pi/2$. The amplitude of the resulting wave is

   (a) 7 mm (b) 6 mm

   (c) 5 mm (d) 4 mm

4. Five waveforms moving with equal speeds on the X-axis

   $y_1 = 8\sin(\omega t + kx)$,

   $y_2 = 6\sin\left(\omega t + \frac{\pi}{2} + kx\right)$,

   $y_3 = 4\sin(\omega t + \pi + kx)$,

   $y_4 = 2\sin\left(\omega t + \frac{3\pi}{2} + kx\right)$,

   $y_5 = 4\sqrt{2}\sin\left(\omega t - kx + \frac{\pi}{4}\right)$

   are superimposed on each other. The resulting wave is

   (a) $8\sqrt{2}\cos kx \sin\left(\omega t + \frac{\pi}{4}\right)$

   (b) $8\sqrt{2}\sin\left(\omega t - kx + \frac{\pi}{4}\right)$

   (c) $8\sqrt{2}\sin kx \cos\left(\omega t + \frac{\pi}{4}\right)$

   (d) $8\sin(\omega t + kx)$

5. The diagram shows two transverse pulses moving along a string. One pulse is moving to the right and the second is moving to the left. Both pulses reach point x at the same instant. What would be the resulting motion of point x as the two pulses pass each other?

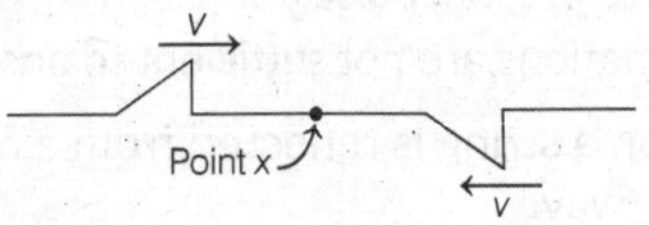

   (a) Up then down.

   (b) Down then up.

   (c) Up, down, up.

   (d) There would be no motion, the pulses cancel one another.

6. Two pulses on a string approach each other at speed of 1 m/s. What is the shape of the string at $t = 6$ s?

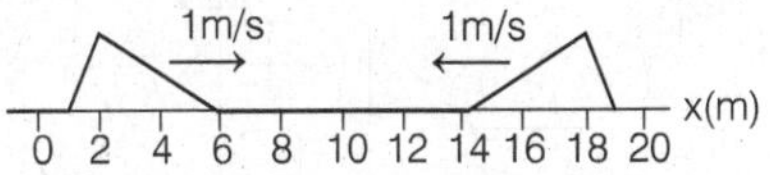

Approaching waves at $t = 0$ s

(a)
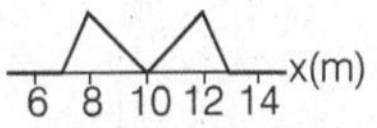

(b)
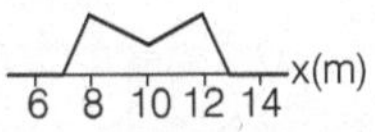

(c)
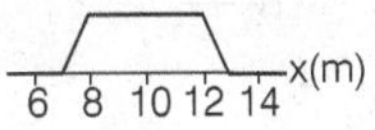

(d)
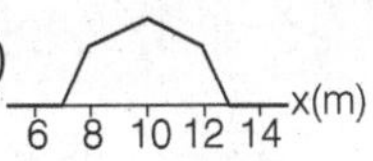

7. Two strings whose linear mass densities are 25 g cm^{-1} and 9 g cm^{-1} are joined together. The ratio of amplitude of reflected and incident wave for the vibration waves is

   (a) $\frac{9}{16}$ (b) $\frac{3}{4}$ (c) $\frac{1}{4}$ (d) $\frac{1}{3}$

8. A composition string is made up by joining two strings of different masses per unit length $\rightarrow \mu$ and 4μ. The composite string is under the same tension. A transverse wave pulse $y = (6\text{ mm})\sin(5t + 40x)$, where t is in s and x in m, is sent along the lighter string towards the joint. The joint is at $x = 0$. The equation of the wave pulse reflected from the joint is

   (a) $(2\text{ mm})\sin(5t - 40x)$ (b) $(4\text{ mm})\sin(40x - 5t)$

   (c) $-(2\text{ mm})\sin(5t - 40x)$ (d) $(2\text{ mm})\sin(5t - 10x)$

9. In the previous question, the percentage of power transmitted to the heavier string through the joint is approximately

   (a) 33% (b) 89%

   (c) 67% (d) 75%

10. A transverse pulse travelling in a rope is reflected at the boundary with another rope. If the reflected pulse is not inverted, then wavelength of transmitted pulse is
(a) longer than original pulse.
(b) shorter than original pulse.
(c) equal to original pulse.
(d) informations are not sufficient to answer.

11. A wave on a string is reflected from a fixed end. The reflected wave
(a) is in phase with the original wave at the end.
(b) is 180° out of phase with the original wave at the end.
(c) has a larger amplitude than the original wave.
(d) has a larger speed than the original wave.

12. A pulse is incident on a free end, then the possible form of reflected pulse is

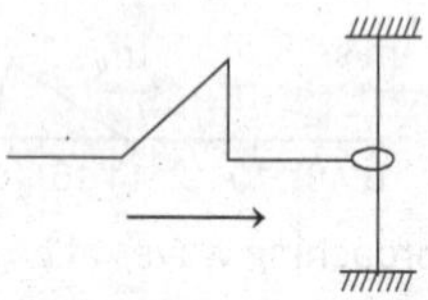

(a) 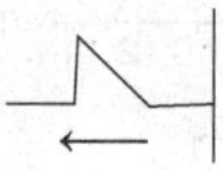 (b) 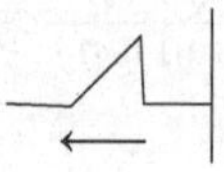

(c) 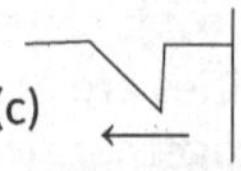 (d) 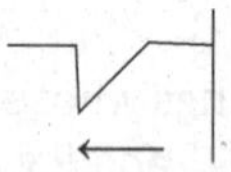

13. Two identical pulses in a stretched string whose centres are initially 8 cm apart are moving towards each other as shown in figure. The speed of each pulse is 2 cm/s. After 2 s, the total energy of the pulse will be

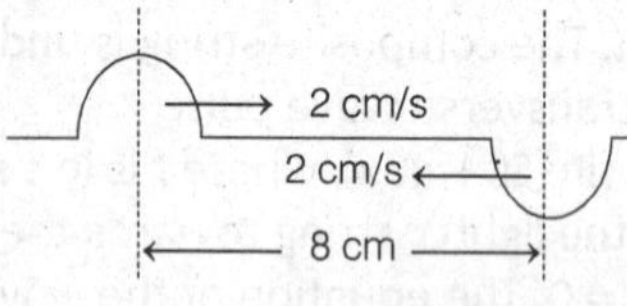

(a) zero
(b) purely kinetic
(c) purely potential
(d) partly kinetic and partly potential

14. Two interfering harmonic waves are described by
$y_1 = 12 \sin \pi [(x/25) - 40t]$
$y_2 = 12 \cos \pi [(x/25) - 40t]$,
where distances are measured in cm and time is in s. Which of the following best describes the resultant wave?
(a) Travelling wave, frequency = 20 Hz.
(b) Travelling wave, wavelength = 25 cm.
(c) Standing wave, 50 cm between adjacent nodes.
(d) Standing wave, frequency = 20 Hz.

15. A wave represented by the equation $y = A \cos (kx - \omega t)$ is superimposed with another wave to form a stationary wave such that the point $x = 0$ is a node. The equation of the other wave is
(a) $-A \sin (kx + \omega t)$ (b) $-A \cos (kx + \omega t)$
(c) $A \sin (kx + \omega t)$ (d) $A \cos (kx + \omega t)$

16. Equations of a stationary wave and a travelling wave are $y_1 = a \sin kx \cos \omega t$ and $y_2 = a \sin (\omega t - kx)$. The phase difference between two points $x_1 = \frac{\pi}{3k}$ and $x_2 = \frac{3\pi}{2k}$ is ϕ_1 for the first wave and ϕ_2 for the second wave. The ratio $\frac{\phi_1}{\phi_2}$ is
(a) 1 (b) 5/6 (c) 3/4 (d) 6/7

17. Two harmonic waves are described by
$y_1 = 3 \sin \pi (x + 0.6t)$ cm, $y_2 = 3 \sin \pi (x - 0.6t)$ cm
The three smallest values of x corresponding to anti-nodes are
(a) $\frac{1}{4}, \frac{1}{3}, \frac{1}{2}$ (b) $\frac{1}{2}, \frac{3}{2}, \frac{5}{2}$
(c) $\frac{1}{3}, \frac{1}{6}, \frac{1}{9}$ (d) $0, \frac{1}{2}, 1$

18. The shape of a string on which standing waves are produced at $t = 0$ is shown here. The suitable equation of standing wave can be

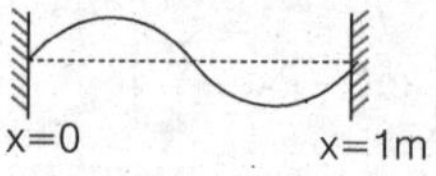

(a) $y = A \sin kx \cos \omega t$ (b) $y = A \sin kx \sin \omega t$
(c) $y = A \cos kx \sin \omega t$ (d) $y = A \cos kx \cos \omega t$

19. The equation of a wave disturbance is given as

$$y = 0.02 \cos \left(\frac{\pi}{2} + 50\pi t\right) \cos (10\pi x),$$

where x and y are in m and t in s. Choose the wrong statement.
(a) Anti-node occurs at $x = 0.3$ m.
(b) The wavelength is 0.2 m.
(c) The speed of the constituent waves is 4 m/s.
(d) Node occurs at $x = 0.15$ m.

20. A wave is represented by the equation
$y = 10 \sin 2\pi (100t - 0.02x) + 10 \sin 2\pi (100t + 0.02x)$.
The maximum amplitude and loop length are respectively
(a) 20 units and 30 units. (b) 20 units and 25 units.
(c) 30 units and 20 units. (d) 25 units and 20 units.

21. A standing wave on a string is given by
$y = (4 \text{ cm}) \cos(\pi x) \sin(50\pi t)$,
where x is in m and t is in s. The velocity of the string section at $x = 1/3$ m and $t = 1/5$ s is
(a) zero (b) π m/s
(c) 840π m/s (d) None of these

22. A string of length L is clamped at each end and vibrates in a standing wave pattern. The wavelengths of the constituent travelling waves cannot be
(a) $3L$ (b) $2L$
(c) $2L/3$ (d) $L/2$

23. A steel wire of mass 4.0 g and length 80 cm is fixed at the two ends. The tension in the wire is 50 N. The frequency of the fourth harmonic of the fundamental will be
(a) 75 Hz (b) 125 Hz
(c) 250 Hz (d) 300 Hz

24. A taut string at both ends vibrates in its nth overtone. The distance between adjacent node and anti-node is found to be d. If the length of the string is L, then
(a) $L = 2d(n+1)$ (b) $L = d(n+1)$
(c) $L = 2dn$ (d) $L = 2d(n-1)$

25. Two uniform stretched strings A and B, made of steel are vibrating under the same tension. If the first overtone of A is equal to the second overtone of B and if the radius of A is twice that of B, the ratio of the lengths of the strings is
(a) 2 : 3 (b) 1 : 2 (c) 1 : 3 (d) 1 : 4

26. A uniform string clamped at both ends is vibrated at constant frequency f. Initially, its vibration forms a standing wave with three anti-nodes. The tension in the string is gradually increased until the next standing wave mode appears. What is the ratio of final and initial tensions in the string? Assume that the string maintains the same dimensions throughout the tightening.
(a) $\frac{4}{3}$ (b) $\frac{9}{16}$
(c) $\frac{16}{9}$ (d) $\frac{9}{4}$

27. A string is firmly attached at both ends. When a frequency of 60 Hz is applied, the string vibrates in the standing wave pattern as shown. Assume the tension in the string and its mass per unit length do not change. Which of the following frequencies could not also produce a standing wave pattern in the string?

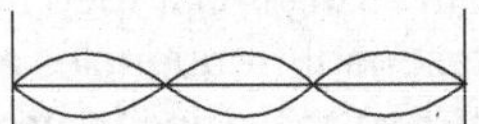

(a) 30 Hz (b) 40 Hz
(c) 80 Hz (d) 100 Hz

28. A wave with a frequency of 30 Hz travels along a string at a speed of 36 m/s and reflects off a free end. How far is the first node from the end of the string?
(a) 0.2 m (b) 0.3 m (c) 0.4 m (d) 0.6 m

29. One end of a 2.4 m string is held fixed and the other end is attached to a weightless ring that can slide along a frictionless rod as shown in figure. The three longest possible wavelength for standing waves in this string are respectively

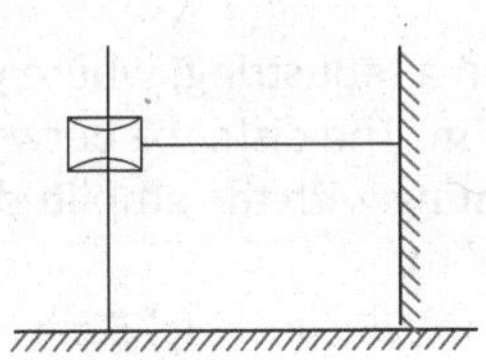

(a) 4.8 m, 1.6 m and 0.96 m.
(b) 9.6 m, 3.2 m and 1.92 m.
(c) 2.4 m, 0.8 m and 0.48 m.
(d) 1.2 m, 0.4 m and 0.24 m.

30. A string of length 1 m and linear mass density 0.01 kgm^{-1} is stretched to a tension of 100 N. When both ends of the string are fixed, the three lowest frequencies for standing wave are f_1, f_2 and f_3. When only one end of the string is fixed, the three lowest frequencies for standing wave are n_1, n_2 and n_3. Then,
(a) $n_3 = 5n_1 = f_3 = 125$ Hz (b) $f_3 = 5f_1 = n_2 = 125$ Hz
(c) $f_3 = n_2 = 3f_1 = 150$ Hz (d) $n_2 = \frac{f_1 + f_2}{2} = 75$ Hz

31. A stretched string of length 1 m fixed at both ends, having a mass of 5×10^{-4} kg is under a tension of 20 N. It is plucked at a point situated at 25 cm from one end. The stretched string would vibrate with a frequency of
(a) 400 Hz (b) 100 Hz
(c) 200 Hz (d) 256 Hz

32. A wire of density 9 g/cm^3 is stretched between two clamps 1.00 m apart while subjected to an extension of 0.049 cm. The lowest frequency of transverse vibrations in the wire is
(Assume Young's modulus, $Y = 9 \times 10^{10}$ N/m^2)
(a) 35 Hz (b) 45 Hz (c) 75 Hz (d) 90 Hz

33. When a certain string is clamped at both ends, the lowest four resonant frequencies are 50, 100, 150 and 200 Hz. When the string is also clamped at its mid-point, the lowest four resonant frequencies are
(a) 50, 100, 150 and 200 Hz
(b) 50, 150, 250 and 300 Hz
(c) 100, 200, 300 and 400 Hz
(d) 25, 50, 75 and 100 Hz

34. A 75 cm string fixed at both ends produces resonant frequencies 384 Hz and 288 Hz without there being any other resonant frequency between these two. Wave speed for the string is
(a) 144 m/s (b) 216 m/s
(c) 108 m/s (d) 72 m/s

35. A standing wave $y = A \sin\left(\frac{20}{3}\pi x\right)\cos(1000\pi t)$ is maintained in a taut string, where y and x are expressed in m. The distance between the successive points oscillating with the amplitude $A/2$ across a node is equal to
(a) 2.5 cm (b) 25 cm (c) 5 cm (d) 10 cm

36. A string of length L is fixed at both ends. It is vibrating in its 3rd overtone with maximum amplitude a. The amplitude at a distance $L/3$ from one end is
(a) a (b) 0 (c) $\frac{\sqrt{3}a}{2}$ (d) $\frac{a}{2}$

37. In a stationary wave
(a) particles at all anti-nodes vibrate in the same phase.
(b) particles at all nodes vibrate in the same phase.
(c) all particles between consecutive nodes vibrate in the same phase.
(d) all particles between consecutive anti-nodes vibrate in the same phase.

38. In a stationary wave that form as a result of reflection of waves from an obstacle, the ratio of the amplitude at an anti-node to the amplitude at node is n. The fraction of energy reflected is
(a) $\left(\frac{n-1}{n}\right)^2$ (b) $\left(\frac{n-1}{n+1}\right)^2$
(c) $\left(\frac{1}{n}\right)^2$ (d) $\left(\frac{n}{n+1}\right)^2$

39. At a certain instant, a stationary transverse wave is found to have maximum kinetic energy. The appearance of string at that instant is
(a) sinusoidal shape with amplitude $A/3$.
(b) sinusoidal shape with amplitude $A/2$.
(c) sinusoidal shape with amplitude A.
(d) straight line.

40. The length of a sonometer wire is 90 cm and the stationary wave setup in the wire is represented by an equation $y = 6 \sin\left(\frac{\pi x}{30}\right)\cos(250t)$, where x, y are in cm and t is in second. The number of loops is
(a) 1 (b) 2
(c) 4 (d) 3

41. The fundamental frequency of a sonometer wire is increased by 5 Hz, if its tension is increased by 21%. Instead, if the length of wire is decreased by 10%, then the fundamental frequency becomes
(a) 45.45 Hz
(b) 50 Hz
(c) 55.55 Hz
(d) None of the above

42. A sonometer consists of two wires of lengths 1.5 m and 1 m made up of different materials whose densities are 5 g/cc, 8 g/cc and their respective radii are in the ratio 4 : 3. The ratio of tensions in those two wires if their fundamental frequencies are equal is
(a) 5 : 3 (b) 5 : 2
(c) 2 : 5 (d) 3 : 5

43. A one metre long sonometer wire is stretched with a force of 4 kg weight. Another wire of same material and diameter is arranged alongside the first and stretched with a force of 16 kg weight. What should be the length of second wire so that its second harmonic is same as fifth harmonic of first?
(a) 40 cm (b) 50 cm
(c) 70 cm (d) 80 cm

44. A sonometer wire is divided in many segments using bridges. If fundamental natural frequencies of the segments are $n_1, n_2, n_3, \ldots$, then the fundamental natural frequency (n) of entire sonometer wire will be (if the divisions were not made)
(a) $n = n_1 + n_2 + n_3 + \ldots$
(b) $n = \sqrt{n_1 \times n_2 \times n_3 \times \ldots}$
(c) $\frac{1}{n} = \frac{1}{n_1} + \frac{1}{n_2} + \frac{1}{n_3} + \ldots$
(d) None of the above

45. A 110 cm long wire is to be divided into 3 segments by placing two bridges on a sonometer so that their fundamental frequency are in the ratio 1 : 2 : 3. The positions of the two bridges should be
(a) 40 and 50 cm from one end.
(b) 60 and 90 cm from one end.
(c) 30 and 50 cm from one end.
(d) 35 and 50 cm from one end.

46. A sonometer wire of length L is plucked at a distance $L/8$ from one end, then it vibrates with a minimum frequency n. If the same wire is plucked at a distance $L/6$ from another end, the minimum frequency with which it vibrates is
(a) $\frac{\sqrt{3}}{2}n$ (b) $\frac{3}{2}n$ (c) $\frac{3n}{4}$ (d) $\frac{4n}{3}$

47. In an experiment, it was found that string vibrates in n loops when a mass M is placed on the pan. The mass that should be placed on the pan to make it vibrate in $2n$ loops with same frequency (neglect the mass of pan) is
(a) $2M$ (b) $M/4$ (c) $4M$ (d) $M/2$

48. A sonometer is set on the floor of a lift. When the lift is at rest, the sonometer wire vibrates with fundamental frequency 256 Hz. When the lift goes up with acceleration $a = 9g/16$, the frequency of vibration of the same wire changes to
(a) 512 Hz (b) 320 Hz
(c) 256 Hz (d) 204 Hz

49. An object of specific gravity ρ is hung from a thin steel wire. The fundamental frequency for transverse standing waves in the wire is 300 Hz. The object is immersed in water so that one half of its volume is submerged. The new fundamental frequency in Hz is
(a) $300\left(\frac{2\rho-1}{2\rho}\right)^{1/2}$ (b) $300\left(\frac{2\rho}{2\rho-1}\right)^{1/2}$
(c) $300\left(\frac{2\rho}{2\rho-1}\right)$ (d) $300\left(\frac{2\rho-1}{2\rho}\right)$

50. One end of two wires of the same metal and of same length (with radius r and $2r$) are joined together. The wire is used as sonometer wire and the junction is placed in between two bridges. The tension T is applied to the wire. If at a junction, a node is formed, then the ratio of number of loops formed in the wires will be
(a) 1 : 2 (b) 2 : 3
(c) 3 : 4 (d) 4 : 5

Numerical Value Questions

1. A string of length 20 cm and linear mass density 0.40 g/cm is fixed at both ends and is kept under a tension of 16 N. A wave pulse is produced at $t = 0$, near an end as shown in figure which travels towards the other end. At what time will the string have the shape shown in the figure again?
(in $\times 10^{-2}$ s)

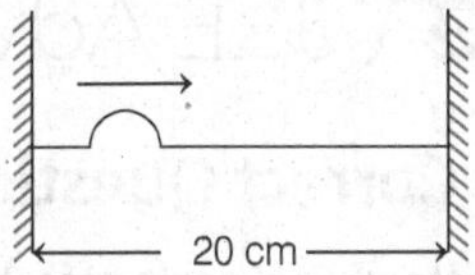

2. A parabolic pulse given by equation, y (in cm) $= 0.3 - 0.1(x - 5t)^2$ $(y \geq 0)$, x in m and t in s, travelling in a uniform string. The pulse passes through a boundary beyond which its velocity becomes 2.5 m/s. What will be the amplitude (in mm) of pulse in this medium after transmission?

3. A steel string of area 10 mm^2 and length 60 cm is fixed at both ends. It vibrates at 600 Hz in the third harmonic. What is the tension in the string (in N)? The density of steel is 8000 kg/m^3.

4. Two identical sinusoidal waves travel in opposite direction in a wire 15 m long and produce a standing wave in the wire. If the speed of the waves is 30 m/s and there are six nodes in the standing wave, find the frequency (in Hz).

5. The equation for the vibration of a string fixed at both ends vibrating in its second overtone is given by $y = (2\text{ cm})\sin[(0.05\pi\text{ cm}^{-1})x]\cos[(500\pi\text{ s}^{-1})t]$. What is the length (in cm) of the string?

6. The length, radius, tension and density of a string A are twice the same parameters of a string B. Find the ratio of fundamental frequency of B to the fundamental frequency of A.

7. A wire having a linear density 0.1 kg/m is kept under a tension of 490 N. It is observed that it resonates at a frequency of 400 Hz and the next higher frequency 450 Hz. Find the length (in cm) of the wire.

8. The fundamental frequency f_0 of a sonometer wire decreases to $f_0/2$, when the weights producing the tension are completely immersed in water. The frequency of the sonometer decreases to $f_0/4$, if it is immersed in certain liquid. Find the specific gravity of the liquid.

9. A guitar string is 90 cm long and has a fundamental frequency of 124 Hz. It is pressed at a distance $10x$ cm from one end to produce a fundamental frequency of 186 Hz. Find the value of x.

10. Two identical wires, one made of iron and the other of aluminium are stretched along side on a sonometer board by equal stretching forces.
[Density of iron = 7.5 gm/cc, density of aluminium = 2.7 g/cc]
Find the frequency of lowest harmonic for which both wires vibrate in unison, given that the length of the wires is 1 m, their diameters 1 mm and tension 75π N.

LEVEL 03 \ JEE Advanced Level

Single Choice Correct Questions

1. A string consists of two parts attached at $x = 0$. The right part of the string ($x > 0$) has mass μ_r per unit length and the left part of the string ($x < 0$) has mass μ_l per unit length. The string tension is T. If a wave of unit amplitude travels along the left part of the string, as shown in the figure, what is the amplitude of the wave that is transmitted to the right part of the string?

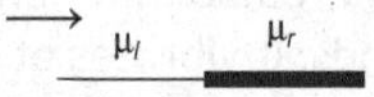

(a) 1
(b) $\dfrac{2}{1+\sqrt{\mu_l/\mu_r}}$
(c) $\dfrac{2\sqrt{\mu_l/\mu_r}}{1+\sqrt{\mu_l/\mu_r}}$
(d) $\dfrac{\sqrt{\mu_l/\mu_r}-1}{\sqrt{\mu_l/\mu_r}+1}$

2. A wave travels on a light string. The equation of the wave is $y = A \sin (kx - \omega t + 30°)$. It is reflected from a heavy string tied to an end of the light string at $x = 0$. If 64% of the incident energy is reflected, the equation of the reflected wave is
(a) $y = 0.8A \sin (kx - \omega t + 30° + 180°)$
(b) $y = 0.8A \sin (kx + \omega t + 30° + 180°)$
(c) $y = 0.8A \sin (kx + \omega t - 30°)$
(d) $y = 0.8A \sin (kx + \omega t + 30°)$

3. A pulse shown here is reflected from the rigid wall A and then from free end B. The shape of the string after these two reflections will be

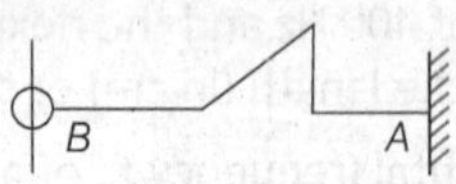

(a)
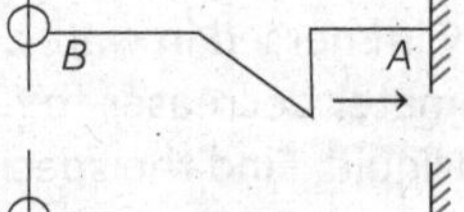

(b)
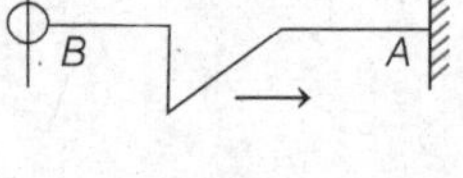

(c)
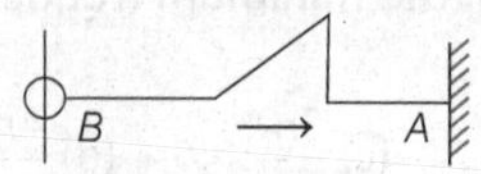

(d)
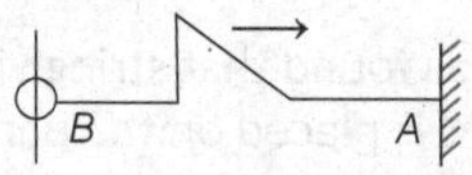

4. A wave pulse on a string has the dimension shown in figure. The wave speed is $v = 1$ cm/s. The point O is a free end. The shape of wave at time $t = 3$ s is

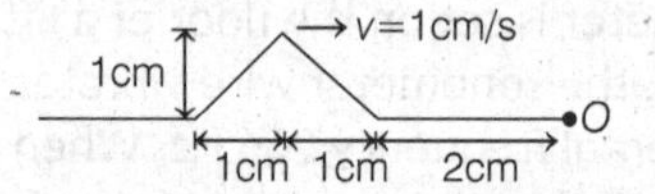

(a)

(b)
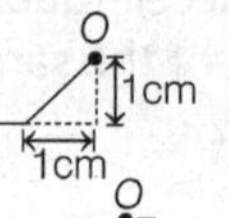

(c)
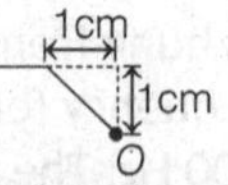

(d)
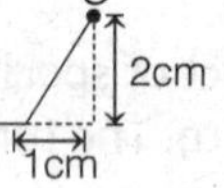

5. A string of length 0.4 m and mass 10^{-2} kg is tightly clamped at its ends. The tension in the string is 1.6 N. Identical wave pulses are produced at one end at equal intervals of time Δt. The minimum value of Δt which allows constructive interference between successive pulses is
(a) 0.05 s
(b) 0.10 s
(c) 0.20 s
(d) 0.40 s

6. Figure shows a stationary wave between two fixed points P and Q. Which point(s) of 1, 2 and 3 are in phase with the point X?

(a) 1, 2 and 3
(b) 1 and 2 only
(c) 2 and 3 only
(d) 3 only

7. A string of length 1.5 m with its two ends clamped is vibrating in fundamental mode. Amplitude at the centre of the string is 4 mm. Distance between the two points having amplitude 2 mm is
(a) 1 m (b) 75 cm
(c) 60 cm (d) 50 cm

8. A string of length $3L$ is fixed at both ends. It resonates with a tuning fork in third harmonic with amplitude at anti-node equal to A_0. At time $t = 0$, a string element at position of anti-node is at half its positive amplitude and moving towards mean position. Displacement of a string element at $L/2$ is given by
(a) $\frac{A_0}{2}\sin\left(\omega t + \frac{11\pi}{6}\right)$ (b) $\frac{\sqrt{3}A_0}{2}\sin\left(\omega t + \frac{5\pi}{6}\right)$
(c) $A_0 \sin\left(\omega t + \frac{5\pi}{6}\right)$ (d) $\frac{A_0}{2}\sin\left(\omega t + \frac{5\pi}{6}\right)$

9. Standing wave produced in a metal rod of length 1 m is represented by the equation,
$y = 10^{-6}\sin\frac{\pi x}{2}\sin 200\pi t$, where x is in m and t is in s. The maximum tensile stress at the mid-point of the rod is (Young's modulus of material of rod $= 10^{12}$ N/m^2).
(a) $\frac{\pi}{2} \times 10^6$ N/m^2 (b) $2\pi \times 10^6$ N/m^2
(c) $\frac{\pi}{2\sqrt{2}} \times 10^6$ N/m^2 (d) $\frac{2\pi}{\sqrt{3}} \times 10^6$ N/m^2

10. A light rod PQ of length L is hung from two identical wires A and B. A block of mass m is hung at point R of the rod as shown in figure. The value of x so that the fundamental mode in wire A is in resonance with first overtone of B is

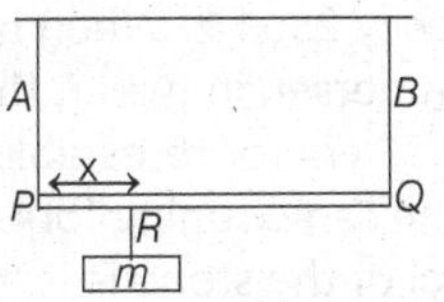

(a) $\frac{4L}{5}$ (b) $\frac{L}{4}$ (c) $\frac{L}{5}$ (d) $\frac{2L}{3}$

11. An aluminium wire of length 60 cm is joined to a steel wire of length 80 cm and stretched between two fixed supports. The tension produced is 40 N. The cross-sectional areas of the steel and aluminium wire are 1.0 mm^2 and 3.0 mm^2, respectively. The densities of steel and aluminium are 7.8 g/cm^3 and 2.6 g/cm^3, respectively. The frequency of first overtone of this composite wire with the joint as a node is nearly

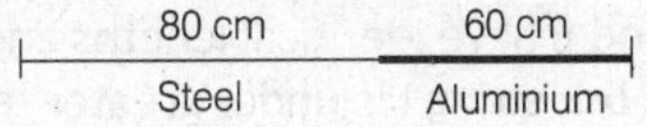

(a) 180 Hz (b) 240 Hz
(c) 360 Hz (d) 480 Hz

12. A metallic wire with tension T and at temperature 30°C vibrates with its fundamental frequency of 1 kHz. The same wire with the same tension but at 10°C temperature vibrates with a fundamental frequency of 1.001 kHz. The coefficient of linear expansion of the wire is
(a) 2×10^{-4} °C^{-1} (b) 1.5×10^{-4} °C^{-1}
(c) 1×10^{-4} °C^{-1} (d) 0.5×10^{-4} °C^{-1}

13. A steel wire of length 1 m and mass 0.1 kg and having a uniform cross-sectional area of 10^{-6} m^2 is rigidly fixed at both ends. The temperature of the wire is lowered by 20°C. If the transverse waves are set up by plucking the string in the middle, the frequency of the fundamental note of vibration is ($Y_{steel} = 2 \times 10^{11}$ N/m^2, $\alpha_{steel} = 1.21 \times 10^{-5}$ /°C)
(a) 44 Hz (b) 88 Hz (c) 22 Hz (d) 11 Hz

14. You have a microwave generator that can produce microwaves at any frequency between 1 GHz and 10 GHz. The microwave radiation enters a 10 cm long cylinder with reflective end caps, as shown in the figure. What frequency of the microwave generator, in GHz, will produce the lowest order standing wave with an antinode (maximum) in the centre of the cavity? Note that with reflectors at both ends, the electromagnetic standing wave acts just like the standing wave on a string that is tied at both ends. (Take, velocity of waves as 3×10^8 m/s)

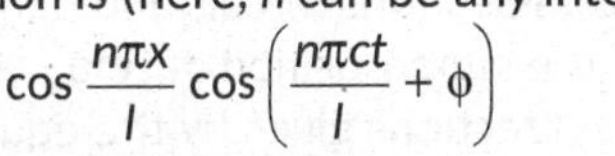

(a) 4.5 (b) 3.0 (c) 1.5 (d) 7.5

15. The two ends of a uniform stretched string are fastened to light rings that can slide freely on two fixed parallel rods at $x = 0$ and $x = l$, one ring being on each rod. The equation of possible normal modes of vibration is (here, n can be any integer)
(a) $y = A\cos\frac{n\pi x}{l}\cos\left(\frac{n\pi ct}{l} + \phi\right)$
(b) $y = A\sin\frac{n\pi x}{l}\sin\left(\frac{n\pi ct}{l} + \phi\right)$
(c) $y = A\sin\frac{n\pi x}{2l}\cos\left(\frac{n\pi ct}{l} + \phi\right)$
(d) $y = A\cos\frac{n\pi x}{2l}\sin\left(\frac{n\pi ct}{l} + \phi\right)$

16. String I and II have identical lengths and linear mass densities but string I is under greater tension than string II. The accompanying figure shows four different situations, A to D, in which standing wave patterns exist on the two strings. In which situation is it possible that strings I and II are oscillating at the same resonant frequency?

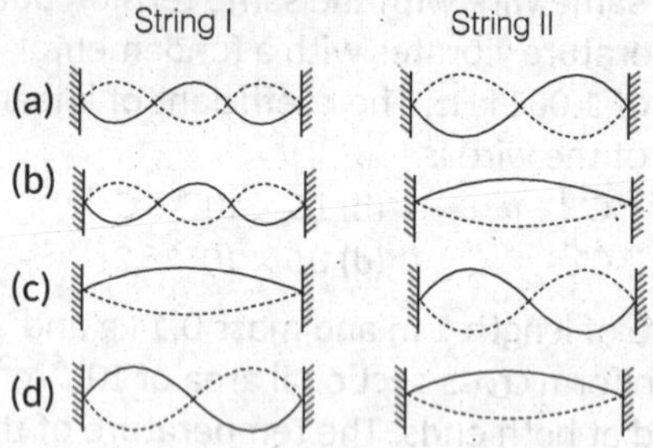

17. The ends of a stretched wire of length L are fixed at $x = 0$ and $x = L$. In one experiment, the displacement of the wire is $y_1 = A \sin\left(\frac{\pi x}{L}\right) \sin \omega t$ and energy is E_1 and in other experiment, its displacement is $y_2 = A \sin\left(\frac{2\pi x}{L}\right) \sin 2\omega t$ and energy is E_2. Then,

(a) $E_2 = E_1$ (b) $E_2 = 2E_1$
(c) $E_2 = 4E_1$ (d) $E_2 = 16E_1$

18. A snapshot of a travelling wave is shown in figure 1 and a snapshot of standing wave is shown in figure 2. (Particles are at their respective extremes. The amplitude, frequency and the speed of both the waves are the same. The string in both the cases is identical). The energy per unit length of system at point A in figure 1 is x_1 and that in fig. 2 is x_2. What is value of $\frac{x_1}{x_2}$?

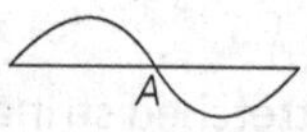

fig. 1

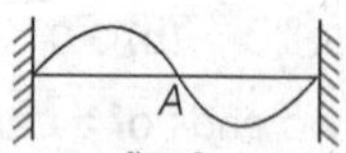

fig. 2

(a) 2 : 1 (b) 1 : 2 (c) 1 : 1 (d) 3 : 1

19. A standing wave is maintained in a homogeneous string of cross-sectional area s and density ρ. It is formed by the superposition of two waves travelling in opposite directions given by the equation $y_1 = a \sin(\omega t - kx)$ and $y_2 = 2a \sin(\omega t + kx)$. The total mechanical energy confined between the sections corresponding to the adjacent anti-node is

(a) $\frac{3\pi s\rho\omega^2 a^2}{2k}$ (b) $\frac{\pi s\rho\omega^2 a^2}{2k}$
(c) $\frac{5\pi s\rho\omega^2 a^2}{2k}$ (d) $\frac{2\pi s\rho\omega^2 a^2}{2k}$

20. **Statement 1** In a standing wave on a string, kinetic energy and potential energy of any small part of string are equal at an instant.

Statement 2 In a standing wave on a string total energy from a node to next anti-node on a string remains constant.

(a) Statement 1 is true, statement 2 is true and statement 2 is correct explanation for statement 1.
(b) Statement 1 is true, statement 2 is true and statement 2 is not the correct explanation for statement 1.
(c) Statement 1 is true, statement 2 is false.
(d) Statement 1 is false, statement 2 is true.

21. The fundamental frequency of a sonometer wire increases by 6 Hz, if its tension is increased by 44%, keeping the length constant. What is the change in the fundamental frequency of the sonometeer wire when the length of the wire is increased by 20%, keeping the original tension in the wire constant.

(a) 2 Hz (b) 4 Hz
(c) 5 Hz (d) 10 Hz

22. A sonometer wire resonates with a given tuning fork forming standing waves with five anti-nodes between the two bridges when a mass of 9 kg is suspended from the wire. When this mass is replaced by mass M, the wire resonates with the same tuning fork forming three anti-nodes for the same positions of the bridges. The value of M is

(a) 25 kg (b) 5 kg
(c) 12.5 kg (d) 1/25 kg

23. A stone is hung in air from a wire which is stretched over a sonometer. The bridges of the sonometer are 40 cm apart when the wire is in unison with a tuning fork of frequency 256 Hz. When the stone is completely immersed in water, the length between the bridges is 22 cm for re-establishing (same mode) unison with the same tuning fork. The specific gravity of the material of the stone is

(a) $\frac{(40)^2}{(40)^2 + (22)^2}$ (b) $\frac{(40)^2}{(40)^2 - (22)^2}$
(c) $256 \times \frac{22}{40}$ (d) $256 \times \frac{40}{22}$

24. A string fixed at both ends, vibrates in a resonant mode with a separation 2.0 cm between the consecutive nodes. For the next higher resonant frequency, this separation is reduced to 1.6 cm. The length of the string is

(a) 4.0 cm (b) 8.0 cm
(c) 12.0 cm (d) 16.0 cm

Multiple Choice(s) Correct Questions

1. The vibrations of a string of length 600 cm fixed at both ends are represented by the equation
$y = 4\sin\left(\frac{\pi x}{15}\right)\cos(96\pi t)$, where x and y are in cm and t in seconds.
(a) The maximum displacement of a point $x = 5$ cm is $2\sqrt{3}$ cm.
(b) The nodes located along the string are at a distance of $15n$, where integer n varies from 0 to 40.
(c) The velocity of the particle at $x = 7.5$ cm at $t = 0.25$ s is 0.
(d) The equations of the component waves whose superposition gives the above wave are
$2\sin 2\pi\left(\frac{x}{30} + 48t\right)$, $2\sin 2\pi\left(\frac{x}{30} - 48t\right)$.

2. Following are equations of four waves
(i) $y_1 = a\sin\omega\left(t - \frac{x}{v}\right)$
(ii) $y_2 = a\cos\omega\left(t + \frac{x}{v}\right)$
(iii) $z_1 = a\sin\omega\left(t - \frac{x}{v}\right)$
(iv) $z_2 = a\cos\omega\left(t + \frac{x}{v}\right)$
Which of the following statements is/are correct?
(a) On superposition of waves (i) and (iii), a travelling wave having amplitude $a\sqrt{2}$ will be formed.
(b) Superposition of waves (ii) and (iii) is not possible
(c) On superposition of (i) and (ii), a stationary wave having amplitude $a\sqrt{2}$ will be formed.
(d) On superposition of (iii) and (iv), a transverse stationary wave will be formed

3. Standing waves can be produced
(a) on a string clamped at both the ends.
(b) on a string clamped at one end and free at the other.
(c) when incident wave gets reflected from a wall.
(d) when two identical waves with a phase difference of π are moving in same direction.

4. A string of length L fixed at the two ends is oscillating such that the point at $3L/8$ is an anti-node. What is the possible number of loops in the string?
(a) 4 (b) 8 (c) 12 (d) 16

5. The equation of a standing wave in a string is given by $y = A\sin\omega t\sin kx$. Distance between two points having amplitude $A/2$ may be
(a) $\frac{5\pi}{6k}$ (b) $\frac{2\pi}{3k}$ (c) $\frac{7\pi}{6k}$ (d) $\frac{5\pi}{3k}$

6. In a stationary wave,
(a) all the particles of the medium vibrate either in phase or in opposite phase.
(b) all the anti-nodes vibrate in opposite phase.
(c) the alternate anti-nodes vibrate in phase.
(d) all the particles between consecutive nodes vibrate in phase.

7. A narrow steel rod of length L is rigidly clamped at its mid-point and transverse standing waves of frequency f are set up in it. The speed of transverse waves in the rod is c. Then,
(a) the free ends of the rod must be anti-nodes.
(b) the fundamental frequency of the rod is c/L.
(c) The second overtone frequency of the rod is $5c/(2L)$.
(d) f can be any integral multiple of the fundamental frequency.

8. The length, tension, diameter and density of a wire B are double than the corresponding quantities for another stretched wire A. Then,
(a) fundamental frequency of B is $\frac{1}{2\sqrt{2}}$ times that of A.
(b) the velocity of wave in B is $\frac{1}{\sqrt{2}}$ times that of velocity in A.
(c) the fundamental frequency of A is equal to the third overtone of B.
(d) the velocity of wave in B is half that of velocity in A.

9. Mark out the correct statement(s) regarding standing waves.
(a) Standing waves appear to be stationary but transfer of energy from one particle to another continues to take place.
(b) A standing wave not only appears to be stationary but net transfer of energy from one particle to the other is also equal to zero.
(c) A standing wave does not appear to be stationary and net transfer of energy from one particle to the other is also non-zero.
(d) A standing wave does not appear to be stationary but net transfer of energy from one particle to the other is zero.

10. A clamped string is oscillating in nth harmonic, then
(a) total energy of oscillations will be proportional to n^2 times that of fundamental frequency.
(b) total energy of oscillations will be proportional to $(n-1)^2$ times that of fundamental frequency.
(c) average kinetic energy of the string over a complete oscillation is half of that of the total energy of the string.
(d) None of the above

11. A standing wave of time period T is set up in a string clamped between two rigid supports. At $t = 0$, anti-node is at its maximum displacement $2A$.
(a) The energy density of a node is equal to energy density of an anti-node for the first time at $t = T/4$.
(b) The energy density of node and anti-node becomes equal after time $T/2$.
(c) The displacement of the particle at anti-node at $t = \frac{T}{8}$ is $\sqrt{2}A$.
(d) The displacement of the particle at node is zero.

Comprehension Based Questions

Comprehension 1

In the figure shown a sinusoidal wave is generated at the end A. The wave travels along positive X-axis and during its motion it encounters another string BC at the junction B at $x = 0$. The density of strings AB and BC are ρ and 9ρ respectively and their radii of cross-sections are $2r$ and r. The wave function, amplitude and wavelength of incident wave are respectively y_i, A_i and λ_i. Similarly, for reflected and transmitted wave, these parameters are y_r, A_r, λ_r and y_t, A_t, λ_t respectively.

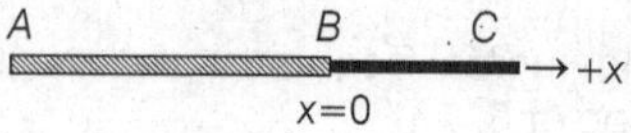

1. Which of the following statement regarding phase difference, $\Delta\phi$ between waves at $x = 0$ is true?
(a) $\Delta\phi = 0$, between y_i and y_r.
(b) $\Delta\phi = 0$, between y_r and y_t.
(c) $\Delta\phi = \pi$, between y_i and y_t.
(d) $\Delta\phi = \pi$, between y_r and y_t.

2. The ratio of wavelengths λ_r to λ_t (i.e., $\lambda_r : \lambda_t$) will be
(a) 1 : 1 (b) 3 : 2
(c) 2 : 3 (d) None of these

3. The ratio of amplitudes A_r to A_t is (i.e., $A_r : A_t$) will be
(a) 1 : 1 (b) 1 : 4
(c) 4 : 1 (d) None of these

Comprehension 2

A string of mass m is fixed at both ends. It is excited to vibrate in its fundamental mode, the equation of the stationary wave being $y = A \sin kx \sin(\omega t + \pi/4)$.

4. The amplitude of oscillation of a point on the string which is at a distance of one-third of the length of the string from one of the fixed ends is
(a) A (b) $\frac{A}{2}$ (c) $\frac{A}{\sqrt{2}}$ (d) $\frac{\sqrt{3}A}{2}$

5. The minimum time after $t = 0$ at which the kinetic energy of the string is maximum is
(a) $\frac{\pi}{\omega}$ (b) $\frac{\pi}{4\omega}$ (c) $\frac{3\pi}{4\omega}$ (d) $\frac{2\pi}{3\omega}$

6. The maximum kinetic energy of the string is
(a) $mA^2\omega^2$ (b) $\frac{1}{2}mA^2\omega^2$
(c) $\frac{1}{4}mA^2\omega^2$ (d) $\frac{1}{8}mA^2\omega^2$

Comprehension 3

A string whose ends are tied to the walls are separated by a distance of 120 cm. Waves produced on such a string travel back and forth between the walls and standing waves are set up. It is found that the points on the string at which displacement amplitude is 3.5 mm are separated by 15 cm.

7. The string is oscillating in
(a) 3rd harmonic (b) 4th harmonic
(c) 2nd harmonic (d) 1st harmonic

8. The maximum displacement amplitude is
(a) 3.5 mm (b) $3.5\sqrt{2}$ mm
(c) $\frac{3.5}{\sqrt{2}}$ mm (d) 7 mm

Comprehension-4

In the arrangement shown in figure, mass can be hung from a string with a linear mass density of 2×10^{-3} kg/m that passes over a light pulley. The string is connected to a vibrator of frequency 700 Hz and the length of the string between the vibrator and the pulley is 1 m.

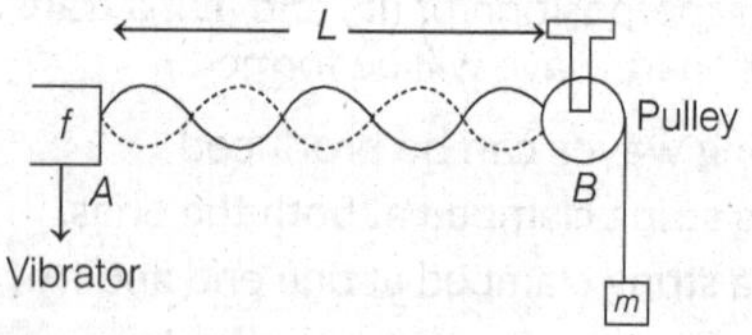

9. If the standing waves are observed, the largest mass to be hung is
(a) 16 kg (b) 25 kg (c) 32 kg (d) 400 kg

10. If the mass suspended is 16 kg, then the number of loops formed in the string is
(a) 1 (b) 3 (c) 5 (d) 8

11. The string is set into vibrations and represented by the equation $y = 6\sin\left(\frac{\pi x}{10}\right)\cos(14 \times 10^3 \pi t)$
where, x and y are in cm, and t in s. The maximum displacement at $x = 5$ m from the vibrator is
(a) 6 cm (b) 3 cm (c) 5 cm (d) 2 cm

Comprehension 5

A wave represented by equation
$y = (2\text{ mm}) \sin[4\pi (s^{-1}) t - 2\pi (m^{-1}) x]$
is superimposed with another wave
$y = (2\text{ mm}) \sin\left[4\pi (s^{-1}) t + 2\pi (m^{-1}) x + \frac{\pi}{3}\right]$
on a tight string.

12. Phase difference between two particles which are located at $x_1 = 1/7$ and $x_2 = 5/12$ is
(a) 0 (b) $\frac{5\pi}{6}$ (c) π (d) $\frac{5\pi}{3}$

13. Which of the following is not a location of anti-node?
(a) $\frac{2}{3}$ (b) $\frac{11}{12}$ (c) $\frac{5}{12}$ (d) $\frac{17}{12}$

14. The location having maximum potential energy is
(a) $\frac{1}{7}$ (b) $\frac{1}{6}$
(c) $\frac{5}{12}$ (d) $\frac{23}{12}$

Match the Columns Questions

1. Column I shows different sets of standing waves in a string of length L whose ends are fixed or free according to respective figure and Column II shows possible equations for them where symbols have usual meaning.

Column I	Column II
(A) 	(P) $y = A \sin\frac{\pi x}{L} \cos\omega t$
(B) 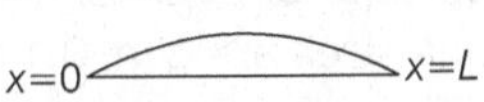	(Q) $y = A \sin\frac{2\pi x}{L} \cos\omega t$
(C) 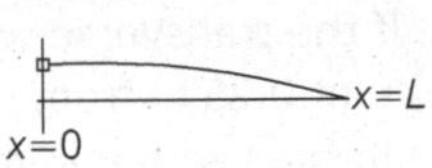	(R) $y = A \cos\frac{\pi x}{2L} \cos\omega t$
(D) 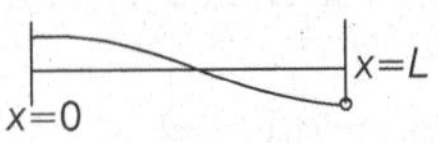	(S) $y = A \cos\frac{\pi x}{L} \cos\omega t$

2. String of length L whose one end is $x = 0$ vibrates according to the relations given in Column I. Select matching entries from Column II including nodes or anti-nodes at the end points of string.

Column I	Column II
(A) $y = A \sin\frac{\pi x}{L} \sin\omega t$	(P) 1 anti-node, 2 nodes
(B) $y = A \cos\frac{\pi x}{L} \sin\omega t$	(Q) 3 nodes, 2 anti-nodes
(C) $y = A \sin\frac{2\pi x}{L} \sin\omega t$	(R) 2 anti-nodes, 1 node
(D) $y = A \cos\frac{2\pi x}{L} \sin\omega t$	(S) 3 anti-nodes, 2 nodes

3. In case of string waves, match the statements in Column I with the statements in Column II.

Column I	Column II
(A) A tight string is fixed at both ends and sustaining standing wave	(P) At the middle, anti-node is formed in odd harmonic
(B) A tight string is fixed at one end and free at the other end	(Q) At the middle, node is formed in even harmonic
(C) A tight string is fixed at both ends and vibrating in four loops	(R) The frequency of vibration is 300% more than its fundamental frequency
(D) A tight string is fixed at one end and free at the other end, vibrating in 2nd overtone	(S) Phase difference between SHMs of any two particles will be either π or zero
	(T) The frequency of vibration is 400% more than fundamental frequency

4. The graph show the standing wave on a string at two successive instants of time t_1 and t_2. A, B, C are points on the string (S_0 is the maximum displacement amplitude of the standing wave). Column II gives observations about net mechanical energy for the time interval between t_1 and t_2.

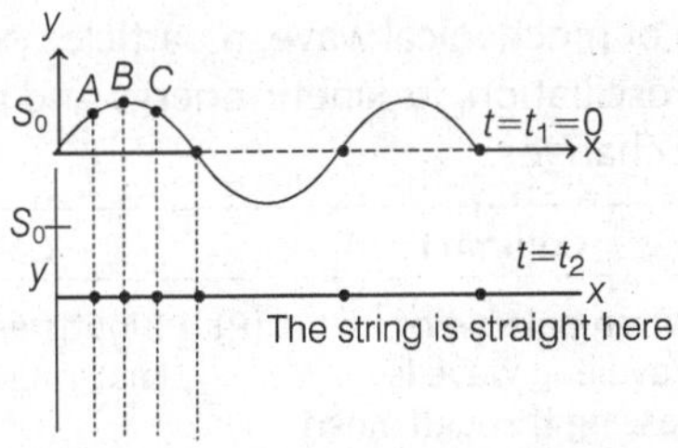

Column I	Column II
(A) A	(P) Kinetic energy at this element is increasing.
(B) B	(Q) Energy is flowing towards right through this point.
(C) C	(R) Energy is flowing left through this point.
	(S) No net energy ever crosses this point.

5. The three graphs shown in Column I are snapshots of three different waves in string. The arrows represent the direction of velocity of particles at that moment. Match with description in Column II.

Column I		Column II
(A) 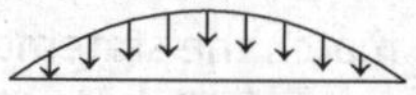	(P)	Right going travelling wave.
(B) 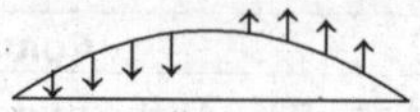	(Q)	Left going travelling wave.
(C) 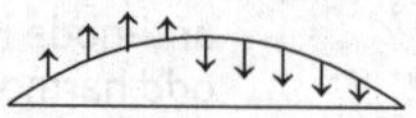	(R)	A standing wave growing in displacement.
	(S)	A standing wave shrinking in displacement.

6. A string of linear mass density 5×10^{-3} kg/m is stretched under a tension of 72 N between two rigid supports 60 cm apart. The string is vibrating in second overtone so that amplitude at one of its anti-node is 0.25 cm (values in column II are in CGS unit)

Column I		Column II
(A) Maximum velocity of a particle at anti-node	(P)	$\frac{150\pi}{\sqrt{2}}$
(B) Maximum velocity of a particle at 5 cm from any node	(Q)	$\frac{90000\pi^2}{\sqrt{2}}$
(C) Maximum acceleration of a particle at anti-node	(R)	150π
(D) Maximum acceleration of particle at 5 cm from any node	(S)	$90000\pi^2$

7. In case of mechanical wave, a particle oscillates and during oscillation, its kinetic energy and potential energy changes.

Column I		Column II
(A) When particle of travelling wave is passing through mean position	(P)	Kinetic energy is maximum
(B) When particle of travelling wave is at extreme position	(Q)	Potential energy is maximum
(C) When particle between node and anti-node in standing wave is passing through mean position	(R)	Kinetic energy is minimum
(D) When particle between node and anti-node in standing wave is at extreme position	(S)	Potential energy is minimum

Numerical Value Questions

1. A 16 kg object hangs in equilibrium from a string with a total length of $L = 16$ m and a linear density of $\mu = 0.01$ kg/m. The string is wrapped around two light small frictionless pulleys that are separated by distance $d = 6$ m. At what frequency (in Hz) must the string between the pulleys vibrate to form the standing wave pattern with three loops on the string.

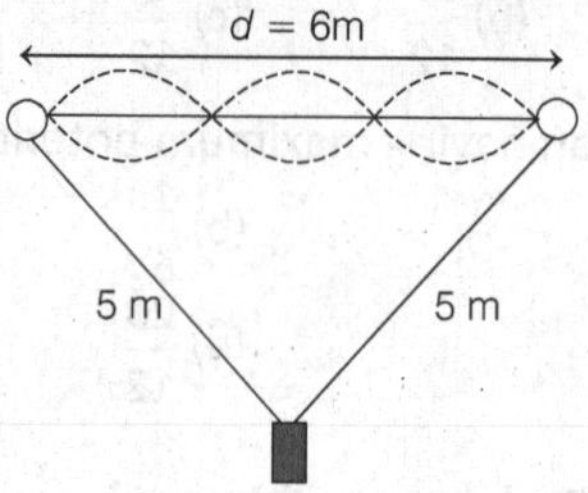

2. A string will break apart, if it is placed under too much tensile stress. One type of steel has density, $\rho_{steel} = 10^4$ kg/m^3 and breaking stress $\sigma = 9 \times 10^8$ N/m^2. We make a guitar string from (4π) gram of this type of steel. It should be able to withstand (900π) N without breaking. What is highest possible fundamental frequency (in Hz) of standing waves on the string, if the entire length of the string vibrates.

3. A steel wire is rigidly fixed at both ends. Its length, mass and cross-sectional area are 1 m, 0.1 kg and 10^{-6} m^2 respectively. Then, the temperature of the wire is lowered by 20°C. If the transverse waves are setup by plucking the wire at 0.25 m from one end and assuming that wire vibrates with minimum number of loops possible for such a case, find the frequency of vibration.

[coefficient of linear expansion of steel $= 1.21 \times 10^{-5}$ /°C and Young's modulus $= 2 \times 10^{11}$ N/m^2]

4. A wooden flexible plank is placed over a pit which is 5 m wide. Student begins to jump up and down at the centre such that she jumps at a frequency of 2 Hz. The plank forms a standing wave pattern with minimum possible loops. Now student moves at

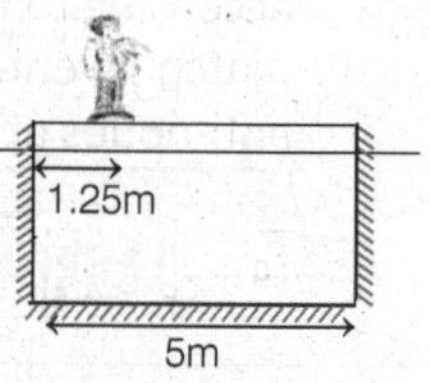

1.25 m from edge of the pit and jumps at this position such that this point has maximum amplitude. What is minimum frequency (in Hz) of her jumping?

5. The string fixed at both ends has standing wave nodes for which distance between adjacent nodes is x_1. The same string has another standing wave nodes for which distance between adjacent nodes is x_2. If l is the length of the string, then $\frac{x_2}{x_1} = \frac{l}{(l + 2x_1)}$. What is the difference in the number of the loops in the two cases?

6. Imagine a very thin uniform wire of length L and total mass 1 g. Fix one end of the wire in the ceiling, hang a large mass of 1 kg from the other end and then pluck the wire $L/4$ from the top. Assume that as the wire vibrates, the large mass is not moving. The lowest frequency heard by us is 100 Hz. What is the length of the wire (in m)? (You may ignore the effect of gravity on the mass of the string).

7. A stretched string is fixed at both ends. When it is vibrating in the fundamental mode, the maximum kinetic energy of the string is E_1 and amplitude at anti-node is A_1. When it is vibrating in the 3rd harmonic, the maximum kinetic energy of the string is E_2 and amplitude at anti-node is A_2. If $E_1 = E_2$, find A_1 / A_2.

8. A heavy string is tied at one end to a movable support and to a light thread at the other end as shown in figure. The thread goes over a fixed pulley and supports a weight to produce a tension. The lowest frequency with which the heavy string resonates is 120 Hz. If the movable support is pushed to the right by 20 cm so that the joint is placed on the pulley, what will be the minimum frequency (in Hz) at which the heavy string can resonate?

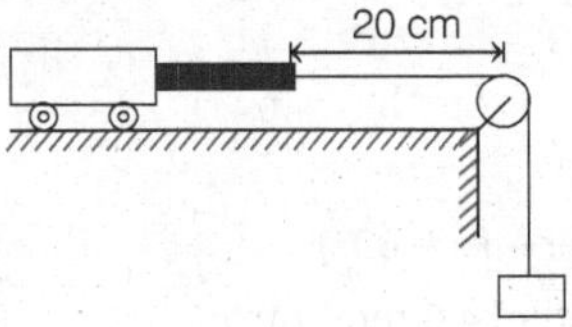

9. Figure shows a string stretched by a block going over a pulley. The string vibrates in its tenth harmonic in resonance with a particular tuning fork. When a beaker containing water is brought under the block so that the block is completely dipped into the beaker, the string vibrates in its eleventh harmonic. If the specific gravity of the material of the block is $\frac{121}{n}$, then find the value of n. (node is formed at the pulley)

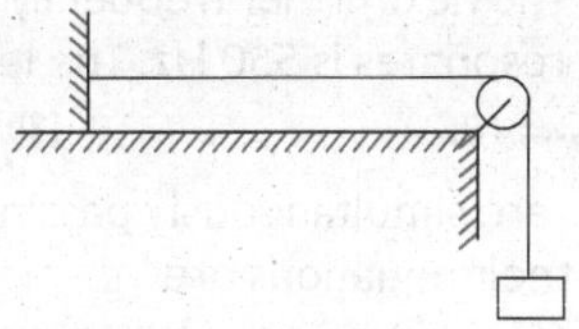

Previous Year's Questions

JEE Main

1 The fundamental frequency of vibration of a string stretched between two rigid support is 50 Hz. The mass of the string is 18 g and its linear mass density is 20 g/m. The speed of the transverse waves produced in the string is .... ms^{-1} **[2023, 15 April Shift-I]**

2 A guitar string of length 90 cm vibrates with a fundamental frequency of 120 Hz. The length of the string producing a fundamental frequency of 180 Hz will be .... cm. **[2023, 8 April, Shift-II]**

3 The displacement equations of two interfering waves are given by $y_1 = 10 \sin\left(\omega t + \frac{\pi}{3}\right)$ cm, $y_2 = 5[\sin \omega t + \sqrt{3} \cos \omega t]$ cm, respectively. The amplitude of the resultant wave is ...... cm. **[2023, 31 Jan, Shift-II]**

4 A wire of length of 30 cm, stretched between rigid supports, has it's nth and $(n+1)$th harmonics at 400 Hz and 450 Hz, respectively. If tension in the string is 2700 N, its linear mass density is .... kg/m. **[2022, 27 July Shift-II]**

5 Two travelling waves of equal amplitudes and equal frequencies move in opposite directions along a string. They interfere to produce a stationary wave whose equation is given by

$$y = \left(10 \cos \pi x \sin \frac{2\pi t}{T}\right) \text{cm.}$$

The amplitude of the particle at $x = \frac{4}{3}$ cm will be .... cm. **[2022, 24 June Shift-II]**

6 The equations of two waves are given by

$$y_1 = 5 \sin 2\pi(x - vt) \text{ cm}$$
$$y_2 = 3 \sin 2\pi(x - vt + 1.5) \text{ cm}$$

These waves are simultaneously passing through a string. The amplitude of the resulting wave is **[2022, 24 June Shift-I]**

(a) 2 cm (b) 4 cm (c) 5.8 cm (d) 8 cm

7 A wire having a linear mass density 9.0×10^{-4} kg/m is stretched between two rigid supports with a tension of 900 N. The wire resonates at a frequency of 500 Hz. The next higher frequency at which the same wire resonates is 550 Hz. The length of the wire is .... m. **[2021, 31 Aug, Shift-I]**

8 Two waves are simultaneously passing through a string and their equations are
$y_1 = A_1 \sin k(x - vt), y_2 = A_2 \sin k(x - vt + x_0)$. Given amplitudes $A_1 = 12$ mm and $A_2 = 5$ mm, $x_0 = 3.5$ cm and wave number $k = 6.28\text{ cm}^{-1}$. The amplitude of resulting wave will be ...... mm. **[2021, 26 Aug Shift-II]**

9 Two travelling waves produce a standing wave represented by equation,
$y = 1.0\text{ mm} \cos(1.57\text{ cm}^{-1})x \sin(78.5\text{ s}^{-1})t$.
The node closest to the origin in the region $x > 0$ will be at $x =$ .... cm. **[2021, 26 Aug Shift-I]**

10 A wire of density 9×10^{-3} kg-cm^{-3} is stretched between two clamps 1 m apart. The resulting strain in the wire is 4.9×10^{-4}. The lowest frequency of the transverse vibrations in the wire is (Young's modulus of wire, $Y = 9 \times 10^{10}\text{ Nm}^{-2}$), (to the nearest integer) .... **[2020, 2 Sep Shift-II]**

11 Two identical strings X and Z made of same material have tensions T_X and T_Z in them. If their fundamental frequencies are 450 Hz and 300 Hz respectively, then the ratio of T_X / T_Z is **[2020, 2 Sep Shift-I]**
(a) 1.25 (b) 2.25 (c) 0.44 (d) 1.5

12 Three harmonic waves having equal frequency ν and same intensity I_0, have phase angles 0, $\pi/4$ and $-\frac{\pi}{4}$, respectively. When they are superimposed, the intensity of the resultant wave is closed to **[2020, 9 Jan Shift-I]**
(a) $0.2I_0$ (b) I_0 (c) $3I_0$ (d) $5.8I_0$

13 A string of length 1 m and mass 5 g is fixed at both ends. The tension in the string is 8.0 N. The string is set into vibration using an external vibrator of frequency 100 Hz. The separation between successive nodes on the string is close to **[2019, 10 Jan Shift-I]**
(a) 16.6 cm (b) 33.3 cm (c) 10.0 cm (d) 20.0 cm

JEE Advanced

1. A string of length 1 m and mass 2×10^{-5} kg is under tension T. When the string vibrates, two successive harmonics are found to occur at frequencies 750 Hz and 1000 Hz. The value of tension T is ...... Newton. **(2023 Adv.)**

2. One end of a taut string of length 3 m along the X-axis is fixed at $x = 0$. The speed of the waves in the string is 100 ms^{-1}. The other end of the string is vibrating in the y-direction so that stationary waves are set up in the string. The possible waveform(s) of these stationary wave is (are) **(2014 Adv.)**
(a) $y(t) = A \sin\frac{\pi x}{6} \cos\frac{50\pi t}{3}$
(b) $y(t) = A \sin\frac{\pi x}{3} \cos\frac{100\pi t}{3}$
(c) $y(t) = A \sin\frac{5\pi x}{6} \cos\frac{250\pi t}{3}$
(d) $y(t) = A \sin\frac{5\pi x}{2} \cos 250\pi t$

3. A horizontal stretched string, fixed at two ends, is vibrating in its fifth harmonic according to the equation,
$y(x, t) = (0.01\text{ m}) [\sin(62.8\text{ m}^{-1})x] \cos[(628\text{ s}^{-1})t]$.
Assuming $\pi = 3.14$, the correct statement(s) is (are) **(2012 Adv.)**
(a) the number of nodes is 5
(b) the length of the string is 0.25 m
(c) the maximum displacement of the mid-point of the string from its equilibrium position is 0.01 m
(d) the fundamental frequency is 100 Hz

Answer Key

Level 1

9.1 Superposition of Waves

1. 5 mm
2. 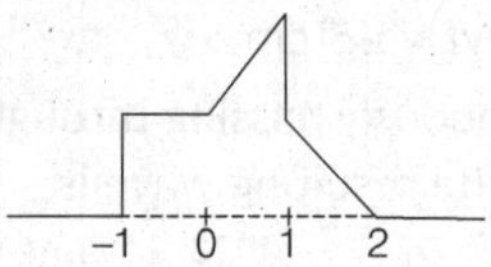

3. (a) 6.1 cm, (b) 40 m/s, (c) 0.40 m
4. $y = 5 \sin(\omega t - kx + 60°)$
5. (a) 2π (b) π (c) 4.0 mm, zero

9.2 Reflected and Transmitted Waves

1. $A_r = -2$ mm, $A_t = 4$ mm
2. $y_r = 0.02 \sin(0.6\pi x + 100\pi t)$,
$y_t = 0.06 \sin(0.2\pi x - 100\pi t)$
3. 96%

4. (a) 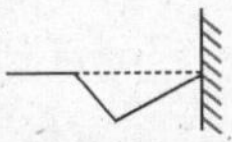 (b) 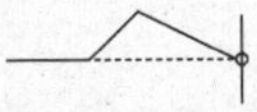

9.3 Standing Waves

1. (a) $4\sqrt{2}$ cm (b) $x_{node} = \left(\frac{n}{3}\right)$ m $(n = 0, 1, 2, 3, ...)$,

$x_{anti\text{-}node} = \left(\frac{n}{6}\right)$ m $(n = 1, 3, 5, \ldots)$, (c) 8 cm

2. (a) $y_1 = 1.5\cos[(\pi/20)x - 72\pi t]$,
$y_2 = 1.5\cos[(\pi/20)x + 72\pi t]$
(b) 10 cm, 30 cm, 50 cm and 0, 20 cm, 40 cm, 60 cm (c) 0
3. (a) 1 m (b) π
(c) $y_1 = 2\sin(\pi x - \pi t)$, $y_2 = 2\sin(\pi x + \pi t)$

9.4 Vibrations of a String Fixed at both Ends

1. (a) 2.5 Hz, (b) 7.5 Hz, (c) 12.5 Hz
2. 200 m/s
3. 400/3 Hz
4. (a) 4 m (b) 24 m/s (c) 25/18 kg (d) 1/9 s
5. 19976 Hz
6. (a) 75 Hz, (b) 5, 6 (c) 2 m
7. (a) 144 cm (b) 17.36 Hz
8. 5 cm from the left end

9.5 Vibrations of a String Fixed at one End

1. 25 Hz, 75 Hz, 125 Hz
2. (a) 30 Hz, (b) 3rd, 5th, 7th harmonic
(c) 1st, 2nd, 3rd (d) 80 cm

9.6 Resonance in an Oscillating String

1. (a) 350 Hz (b) 400 kg 2. 2.78

9.7 Sonometer

1. 350 Hz 2. 3 kgf
3. First bridge at 72 cm and second bridge at 96 cm from one end
4. 7.26×10^3 kg / m^3

9.8 Vibrations of a Composite String

1. (a) $\frac{1}{2L}\sqrt{\frac{T}{\mu}}$ (b) $\frac{1}{4L}\sqrt{\frac{T}{\mu}}$
2. 180 Hz

Level 2

Single Choice Correct Questions

1	(d)	2	(c)	3	(c)	4	(a)	5	(c)
6	(c)	7	(c)	8	(c)	9	(b)	10	(a)
11	(b)	12	(a)	13	(b)	14	(a)	15	(b)
16	(d)	17	(b)	18	(a)	19	(c)	20	(b)
21	(b)	22	(a)	23	(c)	24	(a)	25	(c)
26	(d)	27	(a)	28	(b)	29	(b)	30	(d)
31	(c)	32	(a)	33	(c)	34	(a)	35	(c)
36	(c)	37	(c)	38	(b)	39	(d)	40	(d)
41	(c)	42	(b)	43	(d)	44	(c)	45	(b)
46	(c)	47	(b)	48	(b)	49	(a)	50	(a)

Numerical Value Questions

1	(2)	2	(2)	3	(4608)	4	(5)	5	(60)
6	(4)	7	(70)	8	(1.25)	9	(6)	10	(500)

Level 3

Single Choice Correct Questions

1	(c)	2	(c)	3	(a)	4	(d)	5	(b)
6	(c)	7	(a)	8	(c)	9	(c)	10	(c)
11	(c)	12	(c)	13	(d)	14	(c)	15	(a)
16	(c)	17	(c)	18	(a)	19	(c)	20	(d)
21	(c)	22	(a)	23	(b)	24	(b)		

Multiple Choice(s) Correct Questions

1	(abcd)	2	(ad)	3	(abc)	4	(ac)	5	(bd)
6	(acd)	7	(ac)	8	(cd)	9	(b)	10	(ac)
11	(cd)								

Comprehension Based Questions

1	(d)	2	(b)	3	(b)	4	(d)	5	(c)
6	(c)	7	(b)	8	(b)	9	(d)	10	(c)
11	(a)	12	(c)	13	(a)	14	(b)		

Match the Columns Questions

1 (A)-Q, (B)-P, (C)-R, (D)-S
2 (A)-P, (B)-R, (C)-Q, (D)-S
3 (A) P, Q, S (B) S (C) Q, R, S (D) S, T
4 (A) P, Q (B) P, S (C) P, R
5 (A) S (B) P (C) Q
6 $A \rightarrow R$, $B \rightarrow P$, $C \rightarrow S$, $D \rightarrow Q$
7 $A \rightarrow PQ$, $B \rightarrow RS$, $C \rightarrow PS$, $D \rightarrow QR$

Numerical Value Questions

1	(25)	2	(375)	3	(22)	4	(4)	5	(2)
6	(1)	7	(3)	8	(240)	9	(21)		

Previous Year's Questions

JEE Main

1	(90)	2	(60)	3	(20)	4	(3)	5	(−5)
6	(a)	7	(10)	8	(7)	9	(1)	10	(35)
11	(b)	12	(d)	13	(d)				

JEE Advanced

1	(5)	2	(a,c,d)	3	(b, c)

SOLUTIONS

Level 1

9.1 Superposition of Waves

1. At $x = 1$ cm and $t = 5$ ms,

$$y_1 = 5\sqrt{2}\sin[2\pi(1) - 50\pi \times 5 \times 10^{-3}]$$
$$= 5\sqrt{2}\sin\left(2\pi - \frac{\pi}{4}\right) = -5 \text{ mm}$$
$$y_2 = 10\sin[\pi(1) - 100\pi \times 5 \times 10^{-3}]$$
$$= 10\sin\left(\pi - \frac{\pi}{2}\right) = 10 \text{ mm}$$

According to the principle of superposition,
$y = y_1 + y_2 = -5 + 10 = 5$ mm

2. In 2 s, each pulse will travel a distance of 1 cm.
The two pulses will overlap between 0 and 1 cm as shown in figure. So, A_1 and A_2 can be added as shown in resultant pulse figure.

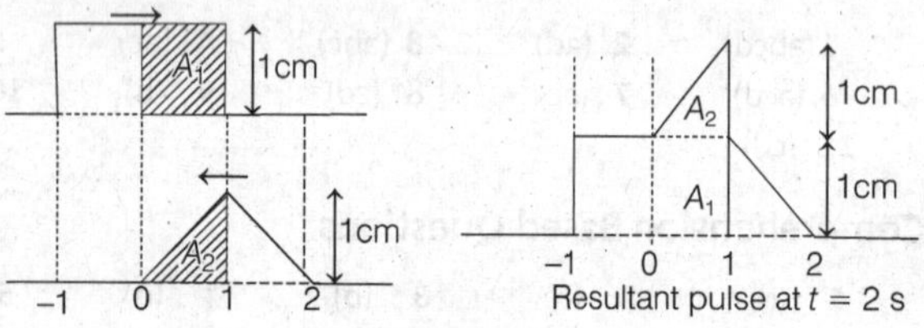

3. (a) $A = \sqrt{A_1^2 + A_2^2 + 2A_1A_2\cos\Delta\phi}$

$$= \sqrt{3^2 + 4^2 + 2(3)(4)\cos\left(\frac{\pi}{3}\right)} = 6.1 \text{ cm}$$

(b) Wavelength and wave speed will be same as those of individual waves.

$$v = \frac{\omega}{k} = \frac{200\pi}{5\pi} = 40 \text{ m/s}$$

(c) $\lambda = \frac{2\pi}{k} = \frac{2\pi}{5\pi} = 0.4$ m

4.
$$y_1 = 5\sin(\omega t - kx)$$
$$y_2 = -5\cos(\omega t - kx - 150°)$$
$$= 5\sin(270° + \omega t - kx - 150°)$$
$$= 5\sin(\omega t - kx + 120°)$$
$$A = \sqrt{A_1^2 + A_2^2 + 2A_1A_2\cos\Delta\phi}$$
$$= \sqrt{5^2 + 5^2 + 2(5)(5)\cos 120°} = 5$$
$$y = y_1 + y_2 = 5\sin(\omega t - kx + 60°)$$

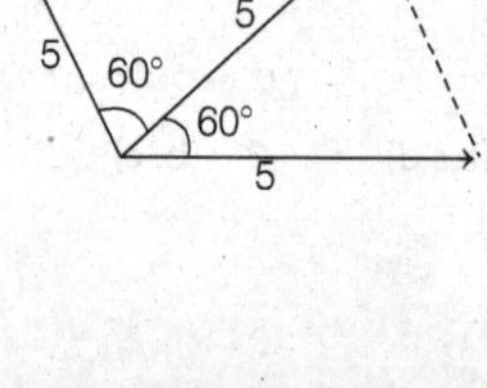

5. (a) $\Delta\phi = \omega\Delta t = 2\pi(100) \times 10 \times 10^{-3} = 2\pi$

(b) $\Delta\phi = k\,\Delta x = \frac{2\pi}{2} \times 1 = \pi$

(c) $A = \sqrt{A_1^2 + A_2^2 + 2A_1A_2\cos\Delta\phi}$

When $\Delta\phi = 2\pi$,
$$A = \sqrt{2^2 + 2^2 + 2(2)(2)\cos 2\pi} = 4 \text{ mm}$$

When $\Delta\phi = \pi$
$$A = \sqrt{2^2 + 2^2 + 2(2)(2)\cos\pi} = 0$$

9.2 Reflected and Transmitted Waves

1. $v_1 = \sqrt{\frac{T}{\mu_1}} = \sqrt{\frac{200}{2}} = 10$ m/s,

$$v_2 = \sqrt{\frac{T}{\mu_2}} = \sqrt{\frac{200}{8}} = 5 \text{ m/s}$$
$$A_r = \left(\frac{v_2 - v_1}{v_2 + v_1}\right)A_i = \left(\frac{5 - 10}{5 + 10}\right)6 = -2 \text{ mm}$$
$$A_t = \left(\frac{2v_2}{v_1 + v_2}\right)A_i = \left(\frac{2(5)}{10 + 5}\right)6 = 4 \text{ mm}$$

2. $v_2 = 3v_1$

$$A_r = \left(\frac{v_2 - v_1}{v_2 + v_1}\right)A_i = 0.02 \text{ m}$$
$$A_t = \left(\frac{2v_2}{v_1 + v_2}\right)A_i = 0.06 \text{ m}$$

As second medium is rarer, reflected pulse will not undergo a phase change of π.

$$v_2 = 3v_1$$
$$\Rightarrow \quad k_2 = \frac{k_1}{3} = \frac{0.6\pi}{3} = 0.2\pi$$
$$\therefore \quad y_r = 0.02\sin(0.6\pi x + 100\pi t)$$
$$y_t = 0.06\sin(0.2\pi x - 100\pi t)$$

3. $v_1 = \frac{\omega}{k} = \frac{60\pi}{2\pi} = 30$ m/s, $v_2 = 20$ m/s

$$\frac{A_r}{A_i} = \frac{v_2 - v_1}{v_2 + v_1} = -\frac{1}{5}$$
$$I \propto A^2$$
$$\Rightarrow \quad \frac{I_r}{I_i} \times 100 = \left(\frac{A_r}{A_i}\right)^2 \times 100 = 4\%$$

$\therefore$ Percentage of energy transmitted $= 100 - 4 = 96\%$

4. Reflection will just get completed at $t = 2$ s

(a) Incident pulse after reflection from a fixed end undergoes a phase change of π. So, the reflected pulse will get inverted.

(b) As reflection takes place from a free end, reflected pulse will not get inverted.

9.3 Standing Waves

1. (a) $y = y_1 + y_2 = (8 \sin 3\pi x) \cos 2\pi t$

$A = 8 \sin 3\pi x$

At $x = \frac{1}{12}$ m,

$$A = 8 \sin\left[3\pi\left(\frac{1}{12}\right)\right] = 4\sqrt{2} \text{ cm}$$

(b) For nodes, $A = 8 \sin(3\pi x) = 0$

$\Rightarrow 3\pi x = n\pi$

$\Rightarrow x = \left(\frac{n}{3}\right)$ m where $n = 0, 1, 2, 3, \ldots$

For antinodes, $A = 8 \sin(3\pi x) = 8$

$\Rightarrow 3\pi x = \frac{n\pi}{2}$

$\Rightarrow x = \left(\frac{n}{6}\right)$ m, where $n = 1, 3, 5, \ldots$

(c) At an antinode, $A = 8$ cm

2. (a) Using, $2 \cos A \cos B = \cos(A - B) + \cos(A + B)$, we get

$$y = 1.5 \cos\left[\left(\frac{\pi}{20}\right)x - 72\pi t\right] + 1.5 \cos\left[\left(\frac{\pi}{20}\right)x + 72\pi t\right]$$

$\therefore \quad y_1 = 1.5 \cos\left[\left(\frac{\pi}{20}\right)x - 72\pi t\right],$

$y_2 = 1.5 \cos\left[\left(\frac{\pi}{20}\right)x + 72\pi t\right]$

(b) $A = 3 \cos\left(\frac{\pi x}{20}\right)$

For nodes, $A = 3 \cos\left(\frac{\pi x}{20}\right) = 0$

$\Rightarrow \frac{\pi x}{20} = (2n - 1)\frac{\pi}{2}$, where $n \in I$

$\Rightarrow x = 10$ cm, 30 cm, 50 cm

For antinode, $A = 3 \cos\left(\frac{\pi x}{20}\right) = 3$

$\Rightarrow \frac{\pi x}{20} = n\pi$, where $n \in I$

$\Rightarrow x = 0$, 20 cm, 40 cm, 60 cm

(c) $v_p = \frac{\partial y}{\partial t} = -3 \cos\left(\frac{\pi x}{20}\right) \sin(72\pi t) \times 72$

At $x = 5$ cm and $t = 0.25$ s,

$$v_p = -216 \cos\left[\frac{\pi}{20}(5)\right] \sin[72\pi(0.25)] = 0$$

3. (a) $k = \frac{2\pi}{\lambda} \Rightarrow \pi = \frac{2\pi}{\lambda} \Rightarrow \lambda = 2$ m

Distance between adjacent nodes $= \frac{\lambda}{2} = 1$ m

(b) $x = 0$ is a node and next node is at $x = 1$ m.

So, the given two points are on two sides of a node.

Hence, their phase difference will be π.

(c) Using, $2 \sin A \cos B = \sin(A - B) + \sin(A + B)$

$4 \sin \pi x \cos \pi t = 2 \sin(\pi x - \pi t) + 2 \sin(\pi x + \pi t)$

$\therefore \quad y_1 = 2 \sin(\pi x - \pi t),$

$y_2 = 2 \sin(\pi x + \pi t)$

9.4 Vibrations of a String Fixed at both Ends

1. (a) $\mu = \frac{0.1 \text{ kg}}{10.0 \text{ m}} = 0.01$ kg/m

$$v = \sqrt{\frac{T}{\mu}} = \sqrt{\frac{25}{0.01}} = 50 \text{ m/s}$$

$$f = \frac{v}{2l} = \frac{50}{2(10)} = 2.5 \text{ Hz}$$

(b) 2nd overtone corresponds to 3rd harmonic

$$f = \frac{nv}{2l} = 3(2.5) = 7.5 \text{ Hz}$$

(c) $f = \frac{nv}{2l} = 5(2.5) = 12.5$ Hz

2. $3\left(\frac{\lambda}{2}\right) = 1 \Rightarrow \lambda = \frac{2}{3}$ m

$v = \lambda f = \frac{2}{3} \times 300 = 200$ m/s

3. $\mu = \frac{15 \times 10^{-3}}{1.5} = 0.01$ kg/m

$$v = \sqrt{\frac{T}{\mu}} = \sqrt{\frac{10(10)}{0.01}} = 100 \text{ m/s}$$

$$f = \frac{nv}{2L} = \frac{4(100)}{2(1.5)} = \frac{400}{3} \text{ Hz}$$

4. (a) $\lambda = \frac{2\pi}{k} = \frac{2\pi}{\pi/2} = 4$ m

$$L = n\left(\frac{\lambda}{2}\right) = 2\left(\frac{4}{2}\right) = 4 \text{ m}$$

(b) $f = \frac{\omega}{2\pi} = \frac{12\pi}{2\pi} = 6$ Hz

$$v = \lambda f = 4 \times 6 = 24 \text{ m/s}$$

(c) $v = \sqrt{\frac{T}{\mu}} \Rightarrow 24 = \sqrt{\frac{200}{\mu}}$

$$\mu = \frac{25}{72} \text{ kg/m}$$

$$m = \mu L = \frac{25}{72} \times 4 = \frac{25}{18} \text{ kg}$$

(d) $f = \frac{nv}{2L} = \frac{3(24)}{2(4)} = 9$ Hz, $T = \frac{1}{f} = \frac{1}{9}$ s

5. $\mu = \frac{0.1 \times 10^{-3}}{1 \times 10^{-2}}$ kg/m $= 0.01$ kg/m

$$v = \sqrt{\frac{T}{\mu}} = \sqrt{\frac{50}{0.01}} = 50\sqrt{2} \text{ m/s}$$

$$f = \frac{nv}{2L} \leq 20000$$

$$\Rightarrow \quad \frac{n(50\sqrt{2})}{2(0.6)} \le 20000$$

$$\Rightarrow \quad n_{max} = [339.4] = 339$$

$$\therefore \quad f_{max} = \frac{339(50\sqrt{2})}{2(0.6)} = 19976 \text{ Hz}$$

6. (a) Let, the fundamental frequency be f.

$$nf = 375 \quad \text{...(i)}$$

$$(n+1)f = 450 \quad \text{...(ii)}$$

Dividing Eq. (ii) by Eq. (i), we get

$$n = 5 \text{ and } f = 75 \text{ Hz}$$

(b) 375 Hz corresponds to 5th harmonic and 450 Hz corresponds to 6th harmonic.

(c) $v = \sqrt{\frac{T}{\mu}} = \sqrt{\frac{360}{4 \times 10^3}} = 300$ m/s

$$f = \frac{v}{2l} \Rightarrow 75 = \frac{300}{2l} \Rightarrow l = 2 \text{ m}$$

7. (a)

$$L = n(18) \quad \text{...(i)}$$

$$L = (n+1)(16) \quad \text{...(ii)}$$

From Eqs. (i) and (ii), we get

$$n = 8, L = 144 \text{ cm}$$

(b) For fundamental frequency, $\lambda = 2L = 288$ cm

$$v = \sqrt{\frac{T}{\mu}} = \sqrt{\frac{10}{4 \times 10^{-3}}} = 50 \text{ m/s}$$

Fundamental frequency, $f = \frac{v}{\lambda} = \frac{50}{2.88} = 17.36$ Hz

8. Let the mass be suspended at a distance x from the left end.

$$f_1 = f_2 \Rightarrow \frac{v_1}{2L} = 2\left(\frac{v_2}{2L}\right)$$

$$\Rightarrow \quad \sqrt{\frac{T_1}{\mu}} = 2\sqrt{\frac{T_2}{\mu}}$$

$$\Rightarrow \quad T_1 = 4T_2 \quad \text{...(i)}$$

$$\Sigma F_y = 0$$

$$\Rightarrow \quad T_1 + T_2 = (4.8 + 1.2)\text{ g}$$

$$\Rightarrow \quad T_1 + T_2 = 60 \quad \text{...(ii)}$$

From Eqs. (i) and (ii), we get

$$T_1 = 48 \text{ N}, T_2 = 12 \text{ N}$$

About the centre of rod, $\Sigma\tau = 0$

$$\Rightarrow \quad T_1\left(\frac{L}{2}\right) - T_2\left(\frac{L}{2}\right) - (4.8\text{ g})\left(\frac{L}{2} - x\right) = 0$$

$$\Rightarrow \quad 48(0.2) - 12(0.2) - 48(0.2 - x) = 0$$

$$\Rightarrow \quad x = 0.05 \text{ m} = 5 \text{ cm}$$

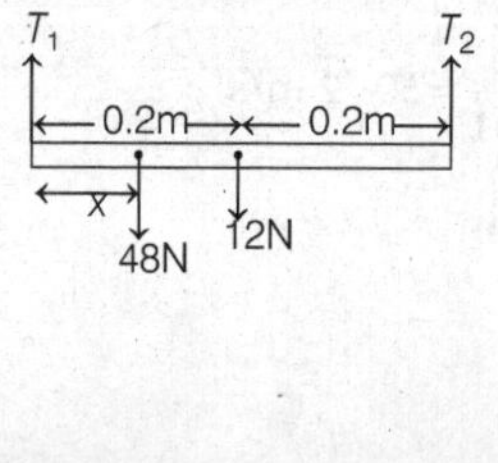

9.5 Vibrations of a String Fixed at One End

1. $v = \sqrt{\frac{T}{\mu}} = \sqrt{\frac{400}{(40 \times 10^{-3}/1)}} = 100$ m/s

Fundamental frequency, $f = \frac{v}{4L} = 25$ Hz

First overtone frequency, $f = \frac{3v}{4L} = 75$ Hz

2nd overtone frequency, $f = \frac{5v}{4L} = 125$ Hz

2. (a) Let the fundamental frequency be f.

$$nf = 90 \quad \text{...(i)}$$

$$(n+2)f = 150 \quad \text{...(ii)}$$

$$(n+4)f = 210 \quad \text{...(iii)}$$

Solving Eqs., we get $n = 3$ and $f = 30$ Hz.

(b) nth, $(n+2)$th, $(n+4)$th harmonics i.e., 3rd, 5th, 7th harmonics.

(c) Ist, 2nd, 3rd

(d) $f = \frac{v}{4L} \Rightarrow 30 = \frac{96}{4L}$

$$\Rightarrow L = 0.8 \text{ m} = 80 \text{ cm}$$

9.6 Resonance in an Oscillating String

1. (a) Let the string oscillates in n loops with 25kg and $(n+1)$ loops with 16 kg.

$$f = \frac{n}{2L}\sqrt{\frac{T_1}{\mu}} = \frac{n+1}{2L}\sqrt{\frac{T_2}{\mu}}$$

$$\Rightarrow \quad \frac{n}{2L}\sqrt{\frac{25g}{\mu}} = \frac{n+1}{2L}\sqrt{\frac{16g}{\mu}}$$

$$\Rightarrow \quad \frac{n+1}{n} = \frac{5}{4} \Rightarrow n = 4$$

$$\therefore \quad f = \frac{n}{2L}\sqrt{\frac{T_1}{\mu}} = \frac{4}{2(2)}\sqrt{\frac{25 \times 9.8}{2 \times 10^{-3}}} = 350 \text{ Hz}$$

(b) For the largest mass, number of loops should be minimum i.e., $n = 1$

$$\Rightarrow \quad 350 = \frac{1}{2(2)}\sqrt{\frac{m(9.8)}{2 \times 10^{-3}}} \Rightarrow m = 400 \text{ kg}$$

2. $f_1 = \frac{n_1 v_1}{2L} = \frac{n_1}{2L}\sqrt{\frac{T_1}{\mu}}$

$$\Rightarrow \quad f_1 = \frac{8}{2L}\sqrt{\frac{\sigma V g}{\mu}} \quad \text{...(i)}$$

When the stone is immersed in water,

$$f_2 = \frac{n_2}{2L}\sqrt{\frac{T_2}{\mu}} = \frac{n_2}{2L}\sqrt{\frac{mg - B}{\mu}}$$

$$\Rightarrow \quad f_2 = \frac{10}{2L}\sqrt{\frac{\sigma V g - (1) V g}{\mu}}$$

$$f_1 = f_2 \Rightarrow 16\sigma = 25\sigma - 25$$

$$\Rightarrow \quad \sigma = \frac{25}{9} = 2.78$$

9.7 Sonometer

1. $f = \frac{v}{2L} = \frac{1}{2L}\sqrt{\frac{4T}{\rho\pi d^2}}$

$\Rightarrow \quad f \propto \frac{1}{Ld}\sqrt{\frac{T}{\rho}}$

$\therefore \quad \frac{f_1}{f_2} = \left(\frac{L_2}{L_1}\right)\left(\frac{d_2}{d_1}\right)\left(\frac{T_1}{T_2}\right)^{1/2}\left(\frac{\rho_2}{\rho_1}\right)^{1/2}$

$\Rightarrow \quad \frac{350}{f_2} = \left(\frac{35}{36}\right)\left(\frac{1}{4}\right)\left(\frac{8}{1}\right)^{1/2}\left(\frac{2}{1}\right)^{1/2}$

$\Rightarrow \quad f_2 = 360 \text{ Hz}$

2. $f = \frac{1}{2L}\sqrt{\frac{T}{\mu}}$ ...(i)

$3f = \frac{1}{2L}\sqrt{\frac{T+24g}{\mu}}$ ...(ii)

From Eqs. (i) and (ii), we get $T = 3$ kgf

3. $f = \frac{v}{2l} \Rightarrow l \propto \frac{1}{f}$

$l_1 : l_2 : l_3 = \frac{1}{f_1} : \frac{1}{f_2} : \frac{1}{f_3} = \frac{1}{1} : \frac{1}{3} : \frac{1}{4} = 12 : 4 : 3$

$l_1 = \left(\frac{12}{12+4+3}\right)114 = 72 \text{ cm}$

$l_2 = \left(\frac{4}{12+4+3}\right)114 = 24 \text{ cm}$

So, the first bridge should be placed 72 cm from one end and the second bridge $(72+24=)$ 96 cm from the same end.

4. Let density of the solid be σ,

$f = \frac{1}{2L}\sqrt{\frac{T}{\mu}}$

$\Rightarrow \quad f = \frac{1}{2(70)}\sqrt{\frac{\sigma V g}{\mu}}$ ...(i)

When mass M hangs in water,

$f = \frac{1}{2(65)}\sqrt{\frac{\sigma V g - 1000 V g}{\mu}}$ ...(ii)

From Eqs. (i) and (ii), we get

$\sigma = 7.26 \times 10^3 \text{ kg/m}^3$

9.8 Vibrations of a Composite String

1. $v_1 = \sqrt{\frac{T}{\mu}}, \quad v_2 = \sqrt{\frac{T}{9\mu}}$

(a) Let the left string oscillates in n_1 loops and the right string in n_2 loops.

$f = \frac{n_1 v_1}{2L_1} = \frac{n_2 v_2}{2L_2}$

$\Rightarrow \quad \frac{n_1}{2(5L)}\sqrt{\frac{T}{\mu}} = \frac{n_2}{2L}\sqrt{\frac{T}{9\mu}} \Rightarrow 3n_1 = 5n_2$

For minimum frequency, $n_1 = 5$ and $n_2 = 3$

$\therefore \quad f_{min} = \frac{5v_1}{2L_1} = \frac{1}{2L}\sqrt{\frac{T}{\mu}}$

(b) Let the left string oscillates in $\left(n_1 + \frac{1}{2}\right)$ loops and the right string in $\left(n_2 + \frac{1}{2}\right)$ loops.

$f = \left(n_1 + \frac{1}{2}\right)\frac{v_1}{2L_1} = \left(n_2 + \frac{1}{2}\right)\frac{v_2}{2L_2}$

$\Rightarrow \quad \frac{2n_1+1}{2n_2+1} = \frac{5}{3}$

For minimum frequency, $n_1 = 2$ and $n_2 = 1$

$\therefore \quad f_{min} = \left(n_1 + \frac{1}{2}\right)\frac{v_1}{2L_1} = \frac{1}{4L}\sqrt{\frac{T}{\mu}}$

2. $\mu_S = \rho_S A_S = 7.8 \times 1 \times 10^{-2} = 7.8 \times 10^{-2}$ g/cm

$\mu_{Al} = \rho_{Al} A_{Al} = 2.6 \times 3 \times 10^{-2} = 7.8 \times 10^{-2}$ g/cm

As $\quad \mu_S = \mu_{Al} \Rightarrow v_S = v_{Al}$

Let, there be n_1 loops on steel wire and n_2 loops on aluminium wire.

$f = \frac{n_1 v_1}{2L_1} = \frac{n_2 v_2}{2L_2}$

$\Rightarrow \quad \frac{n_1}{80} = \frac{n_2}{60} \Rightarrow 3n_1 = 4n_2$

For minimum frequency, $n_1 = 4$ and $n_2 = 3$

$\therefore \quad f_{min} = \frac{4v_1}{2L_1} = \frac{2}{0.8}\sqrt{\frac{40}{7.8 \times 10^{-3}}} = 180 \text{ Hz}$

Level 2

Single Choice Correct Questions

1. $y_1 = a_1 \cos(\omega t - kx) = a_1 \sin\left(\omega t - kx + \frac{\pi}{2}\right)$

$y_2 = a_2 \sin\left(\omega t - kx + \frac{\pi}{3}\right)$

$\Delta\phi = \phi_1 - \phi_2 = \left(\omega t - kx + \frac{\pi}{2}\right) - \left(\omega t - kx + \frac{\pi}{3}\right) = \frac{\pi}{6}$

2. $y_1 = 3\sin(3t - 6x)$

$y_2 = -4\cos(3t - 6x) = 4\sin(3t - 6x + 270°)$

$\tan\theta = \frac{4}{3} \Rightarrow \theta = 53°$

$y = y_1 + y_2 = 5\sin(3t - 6x - 53°)$

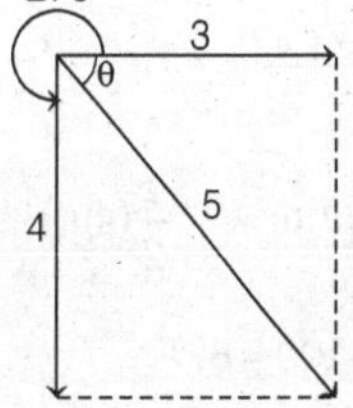

3. $A = \sqrt{(10-7)^2 + 4^2} = 5$ mm

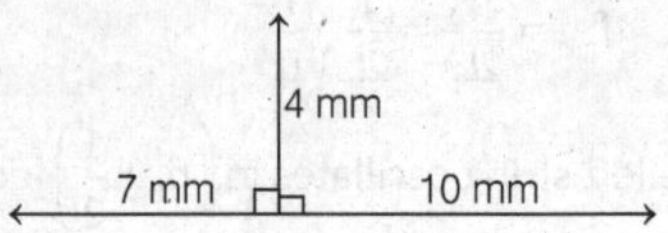

4. $y' = y_1 + y_2 + y_3 + y_4 = 4\sqrt{2} \sin\left(\omega t + kx + \frac{\pi}{4}\right)$

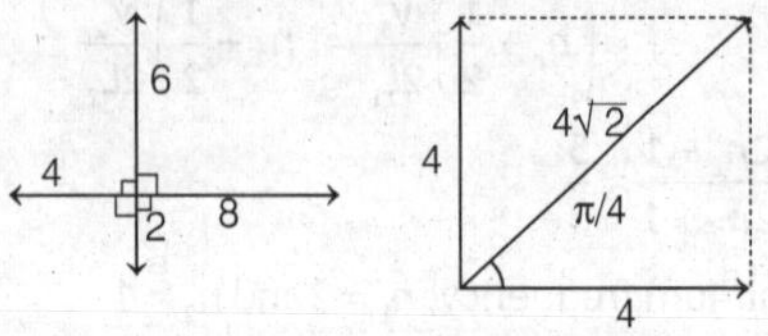

$$y = y' + y_5 = 4\sqrt{2} \sin\left(\omega t + kx + \frac{\pi}{4}\right) + 4\sqrt{2} \sin\left(\omega t - kx + \frac{\pi}{4}\right)$$

$$= 8\sqrt{2} \cos kx \sin\left(\omega t + \frac{\pi}{4}\right)$$

5. Use superposition to see how the amplitudes add. At first, the amplitude jumps up rapidly, then the amplitude moves down as the right most negative pulse continues to propagate. At the very end of their passing, the amplitude will be all the wave down and then, once they pass, the point will jump back to equilibrium.

6. Distance moved by each pulse in 6 s $= 1 \times 6 = 6$ m

The pulses will overlap in the region, $x = 8$ to $x = 12$.

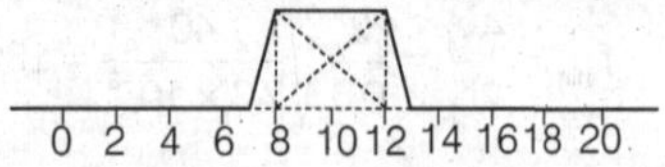

7. $\frac{v_1}{v_2} = \sqrt{\frac{\mu_2}{\mu_1}} = \sqrt{\frac{9}{25}} = \frac{3}{5}$

$$\frac{A_r}{A_i} = \frac{v_2 - v_1}{v_2 + v_1} = \frac{(v_2/v_1) - 1}{(v_2/v_1) + 1} = \frac{(5/3) - 1}{(5/3) + 1} = \frac{1}{4}$$

8.

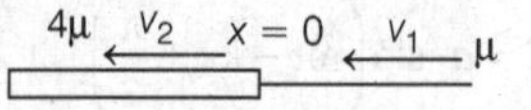

$$\frac{v_2}{v_1} = \sqrt{\frac{\mu_1}{\mu_2}} = \sqrt{\frac{\mu}{4\mu}} = \frac{1}{2}$$

$\Rightarrow \quad v_1 = 2v_2$

$$A_r = \left(\frac{v_2 - v_1}{v_1 + v_2}\right) A_i = \left(\frac{v_2 - 2v_2}{2v_2 + v_2}\right) 6 = -2 \text{ mm}$$

The reflected pulse will travel in positive x-direction

$y_r = (-2 \text{ mm}) \sin(5t - 40x)$

9. $\frac{A_t}{A_i} = \frac{2v_2}{v_1 + v_2} = \frac{2v_2}{2v_2 + v_2} = \frac{2}{3}$

$$P_t = \frac{1}{2}\mu_2 v_2 \omega^2 A_t^2 = \frac{1}{2}(4\mu_1)\left(\frac{v_1}{2}\right)\omega^2\left(\frac{2}{3}A_i\right)^2 = \frac{8}{9}P_i$$

$\therefore \quad \frac{P_t}{P_i} \times 100 = \frac{8}{9} \times 100 = 89\%$

10. As the reflected pulse is not inverted, the second medium is rarer.

$v_2 > v_1 \Rightarrow \lambda_2 > \lambda_1$ [$\because$ Frequency doesn't change]

11. (b)

12. As the reflection happens from a free end, the reflected pulse will not get inverted.

13. After 2 s, both pulses will cancel out each other and string will become flat. So, potential energy will be zero and total energy will be purely kinetic.

14. As both waves are travelling in the same direction, the resultant wave will be travelling wave of same frequency.

$$f = \frac{\omega}{2\pi} = \frac{40\pi}{2\pi} = 20 \text{ Hz}$$

15. $y = y_1 + y_2 = A\cos(kx - \omega t) + y_2$

At $x = 0, y = 0 \quad \Rightarrow \quad y_2 = -A\cos(kx + \omega t)$

16. $x_1 = \frac{\pi}{3k} = \frac{\pi}{3(2\pi/\lambda)} = \frac{\lambda}{6}$,

$x_2 = \frac{3\pi}{2k} = \frac{3\pi}{2(2\pi/\lambda)} = \frac{3\lambda}{4}$

Distance between two adjacent nodes is $\frac{\lambda}{2}$.

$x = 0$ is a node and next node will be at $x = \frac{\lambda}{2}$.

So, the two points are on the opposite sides of a node. So, their phase difference will be π.

$\therefore \quad \phi_1 = \pi$

For a travelling wave, $\Delta\phi = k\,\Delta x$

$\Rightarrow \quad \phi_2 = k\left(\frac{3\pi}{2k} - \frac{\pi}{3k}\right) = \frac{7\pi}{6}$

$\therefore \quad \frac{\phi_1}{\phi_2} = \frac{6}{7}$

17. $y = y_1 + y_2 = 6\sin(\pi x)\cos(0.6\pi t)$

For anti-nodes, $A = 6\sin(\pi x) = 6$

$\Rightarrow \quad \sin(\pi x) = 1$

$\Rightarrow \quad \pi x = (2n-1)\frac{\pi}{2}$, where $n \in I$

$\Rightarrow \quad x = \frac{2n-1}{2} \quad \Rightarrow \quad x = \frac{1}{2}, \frac{3}{2}, \frac{5}{2}$

18. (a)

19. $v = \frac{\omega}{k} = \frac{50\pi}{10\pi} = 5$ m/s

20. Maximum amplitude $= 2A = 2(10) = 20$ units

$$\lambda = \frac{2\pi}{k} = \frac{2\pi}{2\pi(0.02)} = 50 \text{ units}$$

Loop length $= \frac{\lambda}{2} = \frac{50}{2} = 25$ units

21. $v_p = \frac{\partial y}{\partial t} = 4 \times 50\pi \cos(\pi x)\cos(50\pi t)$

At $x = \frac{1}{3}$ m and $t = \frac{1}{5}$ s,

$$v_P = 200\pi \cos\left(\frac{\pi}{3}\right)\cos\left(\frac{50\pi}{5}\right) = 100\pi \text{ cm/s} = \pi \text{ m/s}$$

22. $L = n\left(\frac{\lambda}{2}\right) \Rightarrow \lambda = \frac{2L}{n}$, where $n = 1, 2, 3, 4, \ldots$

23. $\mu = \frac{4\times 10^{-3}}{80\times 10^{-2}} = 5\times 10^{-3}$ kg/m

$$v = \sqrt{\frac{T}{\mu}} = \sqrt{\frac{50}{5\times 10^{-3}}} = 100 \text{ m/s}$$

Frequency of the fourth harmonic,

$$f = 4\left(\frac{v}{2L}\right) = \frac{2\times 100}{0.8} = 250 \text{ Hz}$$

24. nth overtone $\Rightarrow$ $(n+1)$ loops

Distance between adjacent node and anti-node $= d = \frac{\lambda}{4}$

$\therefore$ $\lambda = 4d$

Length of string, $L = (n+1)\frac{\lambda}{2} = 2d(n+1)$

25. $v = \sqrt{\frac{T}{\mu}} = \sqrt{\frac{T}{\rho\pi r^2}} \Rightarrow v \propto \frac{1}{r}$

$\therefore$ $\frac{v_A}{v_B} = \frac{r_B}{r_A} = \frac{1}{2}$

Ist overtone of A = 2nd overtone of B

$\Rightarrow$ $2\left(\frac{v_A}{2L_A}\right) = 3\left(\frac{v_B}{2L_B}\right)$

$\Rightarrow$ $\frac{L_A}{L_B} = \frac{1}{3}$

26. $f = \frac{n}{2L}\sqrt{\frac{T}{\mu}}$ = constant

$\Rightarrow$ $T \propto \frac{1}{n^2}$

$\therefore$ $\frac{T_2}{T_1} = \left(\frac{n_1}{n_2}\right)^2 = \left(\frac{3}{2}\right)^2 = \frac{9}{4}$

As tension increases, n will decrease.

27. $f = \frac{nv}{2L} \Rightarrow 60 = 3\left(\frac{v}{2L}\right) \Rightarrow \frac{v}{2L} = 20$

$f = \frac{nv}{2L} = n(20)$, where $n \in I$

So, 30 Hz is not possible.

28. $\lambda = \frac{v}{f} = \frac{36}{30} = 1.2$ m

Distance of node from the free end $= \frac{\lambda}{4} = 0.3$ m

29. $L = \left(n + \frac{1}{2}\right)\frac{\lambda}{2}$

$\Rightarrow$ $\lambda = \frac{4L}{2n+1} = \frac{9.6}{2n+1}$

If $n = 0, \lambda = 9.6$ m

$n = 1, \lambda = 3.2$ m

$n = 2, \lambda = 1.92$ m

30. $v = \sqrt{\frac{T}{\mu}} = \sqrt{\frac{100}{0.01}} = 100$ m/s

$f_1 = \frac{v}{2L} = 50$ Hz, $f_2 = \frac{v}{L} = 100$ Hz, $f_3 = \frac{3v}{2L} = 150$ Hz

$n_1 = \frac{v}{4L} = 25$ Hz, $n_2 = \frac{3v}{4L} = 75$ Hz, $n_3 = \frac{5v}{4L} = 125$ Hz

$\therefore$ $n_2 = \frac{f_1 + f_2}{2} = 75$ Hz

31. At 25 cm, there will be an anti-node. So, the string will vibrate in 2 loops.

$$v = \sqrt{\frac{T}{\mu}} = \sqrt{\frac{20}{5\times 10^{-4}}} = 200 \text{ m/s}$$

For 2nd harmonic,

$$f = \frac{v}{L} = \frac{200}{1} = 200 \text{ Hz}$$

32. $Y = \frac{\text{Stress}}{\text{Strain}} = \frac{T/A}{\Delta l/l}$

$\Rightarrow$ $T = \frac{AY\,\Delta l}{l}$

$$v = \sqrt{\frac{T}{\mu}} = \sqrt{\frac{AY\,\Delta l}{l(\rho A)}} = \sqrt{\frac{Y\,\Delta l}{l\rho}}$$

$$f = \frac{v}{2l} = \frac{1}{2l}\sqrt{\frac{Y\,\Delta l}{l\rho}} = \frac{1}{2(1)}\sqrt{\frac{9\times 10^{10}\times 4.9\times 10^{-4}}{1\times 9\times 10^3}} = 35 \text{ Hz}$$

33. $f \propto \frac{1}{L}$

As length gets halved, all frequencies will get doubled.

34. $(n+1)\frac{v}{2L} = 384$ ...(i)

$n\frac{v}{2L} = 288$ ...(ii)

From Eqs. (i) and (ii), we get

$$\frac{n+1}{n} = \frac{4}{3} \Rightarrow n = 3$$

From Eq. (ii),

$\therefore$ $\frac{3v}{2(0.75)} = 288 \Rightarrow v = 144$ m/s

35. Amplitude $= A\sin\left(\frac{20}{3}\pi x\right) = \frac{A}{2}$

$\Rightarrow$ $\frac{20\pi x}{3} = \frac{\pi}{6}$

$\Rightarrow$ $x = 0.025$ m $= 2.5$ cm

Distance between successive points oscillating with the amplitude $\frac{A}{2}$

$= 2x = 2\times 2.5 = 5$ cm

36. 3rd overtone $\Rightarrow$ 4 loops

$$L = 4\left(\frac{\lambda}{2}\right) \Rightarrow \lambda = \frac{L}{2}$$

$$k = \frac{2\pi}{\lambda} = \frac{2\pi}{L/2} = \frac{4\pi}{L}$$

$$y = 2A \sin kx \cos \omega t$$

$$\text{Amplitude} = 2A \sin kx = a \sin\left(\frac{4\pi x}{L}\right)$$

At $x = \frac{L}{3}$,

$$\text{Amplitude} = a\left|\sin\left(\frac{4\pi}{L} \times \frac{L}{3}\right)\right| = \frac{\sqrt{3}a}{2}$$

37. (c)

38. $\frac{A_i + A_r}{A_i - A_r} = n \Rightarrow \frac{A_i}{A_r} = \frac{n+1}{n-1}$

$$E \propto A^2 \Rightarrow \frac{E_r}{E_i} = \left(\frac{n-1}{n+1}\right)^2$$

39. Kinetic energy is maximum at mean position.

40. $\lambda = \frac{2\pi}{k} = \frac{2\pi}{\pi/30} = 60 \text{ cm}$

$$L = n\left(\frac{\lambda}{2}\right) \Rightarrow 90 = n\left(\frac{60}{2}\right) \Rightarrow n = 3$$

41. $f = \frac{1}{2L}\sqrt{\frac{T}{\mu}}, \quad f + 5 = \frac{1}{2L}\sqrt{\frac{1.21T}{\mu}}$

$$\therefore \quad \frac{f+5}{f} = 1.1 \Rightarrow f = 50 \text{ Hz}$$

If length is decreased by 10%,

$$f' = \frac{1}{2(0.9L)}\sqrt{\frac{T}{\mu}} = \frac{50}{0.9} = 55.55 \text{ Hz}$$

42. $f = \frac{1}{2L}\sqrt{\frac{T}{\mu}} = \frac{1}{2L}\sqrt{\frac{T}{\rho\pi r^2}}$

$$\Rightarrow \quad T \propto L^2 r^2 \rho$$

$$\therefore \quad \frac{T_1}{T_2} = \left(\frac{L_1}{L_2}\right)^2\left(\frac{r_1}{r_2}\right)^2\left(\frac{\rho_1}{\rho_2}\right) = \left(\frac{1.5}{1}\right)^2\left(\frac{4}{3}\right)^2\left(\frac{5}{8}\right) = \frac{5}{2}$$

43. $f = \frac{1}{2L}\sqrt{\frac{T}{\mu}} = \frac{1}{2L}\sqrt{\frac{T}{\rho\pi r^2}}$

5th harmonic of 1st wire = 2nd harmonic of 2nd wire

$$\Rightarrow \quad 5\left(\frac{1}{2L_1}\sqrt{\frac{4g}{\rho\pi r^2}}\right) = 2\left(\frac{1}{2L_2}\sqrt{\frac{16g}{\rho\pi r^2}}\right)$$

$$\Rightarrow \quad \frac{L_2}{100} = \frac{4}{5} \Rightarrow L_2 = 80 \text{ cm}$$

44. $n_1 = \frac{v}{2l_1}, \quad n_2 = \frac{v}{2l_2}, \quad n_3 = \frac{v}{2l_3}$

For complete wire, $n = \frac{v}{2l}$

$$l = l_1 + l_2 + l_3 + \ldots$$

$$\Rightarrow \quad \frac{v}{2n} = \frac{v}{2n_1} + \frac{v}{2n_2} + \frac{v}{2n_3} + \ldots$$

$$\Rightarrow \quad \frac{1}{n} = \frac{1}{n_1} + \frac{1}{n_2} + \frac{1}{n_3} + \ldots$$

45. $l \propto \frac{1}{f}$

$$\Rightarrow \quad l_1 : l_2 : l_3 = \frac{1}{f_1} : \frac{1}{f_2} : \frac{1}{f_3} = 1 : \frac{1}{2} : \frac{1}{3} = 6:3:2$$

$$l_1 = \left(\frac{6}{6+3+2}\right)110 = 60 \text{ cm}$$

$$l_2 = \left(\frac{3}{6+3+2}\right)110 = 30 \text{ cm}$$

Position of the first bridge $= l_1 = 60$ cm from one end.

Position of the second bridge $= l_1 + l_2 = 90$ cm from one end.

46. The point where the wire is plucked will be an anti-node.

When plucked at $L/8$, length of one loop will be $\frac{L}{4}$.

So, the wire will oscillate in 4 loops.

$$\therefore \quad n = 4\left(\frac{v}{2L}\right) \Rightarrow \frac{v}{2L} = \frac{n}{4}$$

When plucked at $L/6$, length of one loop will be $\frac{L}{3}$.

So, the wire will oscillate in 3 loops.

$$n' = 3\left(\frac{v}{2L}\right) = 3\left(\frac{n}{4}\right) = \frac{3n}{4}$$

47. $f = \frac{n}{2L}\sqrt{\frac{T}{\mu}} = \frac{n}{2L}\sqrt{\frac{Mg}{\mu}}$

$$\Rightarrow \quad M \propto \frac{1}{n^2}$$

$$\therefore \quad \frac{M_1}{M_2} = \left(\frac{n_2}{n_1}\right)^2$$

$$\Rightarrow \quad \frac{M}{M_2} = \left(\frac{2n}{n}\right)^2 \Rightarrow M_2 = \frac{M}{4}$$

48. $f = \frac{1}{2L}\sqrt{\frac{Mg}{\mu}}, \quad f' = \frac{1}{2L}\sqrt{\frac{M(g+a)}{\mu}}$

$$\therefore \quad \frac{f'}{f} = \left(\frac{g+a}{g}\right)^{1/2} \Rightarrow \frac{f'}{256} = \left(1 + \frac{9}{16}\right)^{1/2}$$

$$\Rightarrow \quad f' = 320 \text{ Hz}$$

49. $f = \frac{1}{2L}\sqrt{\frac{Mg}{\mu}}, \quad f' = \frac{1}{2L}\sqrt{\frac{Mg - B}{\mu}}$

$$\therefore \quad \frac{f'}{f} = \left(\frac{Mg - B}{Mg}\right)^{1/2}$$

$$\Rightarrow \quad \frac{f'}{300} = \left(\frac{\rho V g - 1(V/2)g}{\rho V g}\right)^{1/2}$$

$$\Rightarrow \quad f' = 300\left(\frac{2\rho - 1}{2\rho}\right)^{1/2}$$

50. $f = n_1\left(\frac{1}{2L}\sqrt{\frac{T}{\rho\pi r^2}}\right) = n_2\left(\frac{1}{2L}\sqrt{\frac{T}{\rho\pi(2r)^2}}\right) \Rightarrow \frac{n_1}{n_2} = \frac{1}{2}$

Numerical Value Questions

1. In one reflection, pulse gets inverted. So, after two reflections, shape will become same. Hence, the pulse will have to travel a distane of $2\times 20 = 40$ cm.

$$\text{Time taken} = \frac{\text{Distance}}{\text{Speed}} = \frac{40\times 10^{-2}}{\sqrt{\frac{16}{0.04}}} = 2\times 10^{-2}\text{ s}$$

2. $y = f(x - vt)$

$\Rightarrow v_1 = 5$ m/s, $v_2 = 2.5$ m/s

$$A_t = \left(\frac{2v_2}{v_1+v_2}\right)A_i = \frac{2(2.5)}{5+2.5}\times 0.3 = 0.2\text{ cm} = 2\text{ mm}$$

3. $L = n\left(\frac{\lambda}{2}\right)$

$$\Rightarrow \lambda = \frac{2L}{n} = \frac{2(0.6)}{3} = 0.4\text{ m}$$

$$v = \lambda f = 0.4\times 600 = 240\text{ m/s}$$

$$T = \mu v^2 = \rho A v^2 = 8000\times 10\times 10^{-6}\times(240)^2 = 4608\text{ N}$$

4. 6 nodes $\Rightarrow$ 5 loops

$$L = n\left(\frac{\lambda}{2}\right)$$

$$\Rightarrow \lambda = \frac{2L}{n} = \frac{2(15)}{5} = 6\text{ m}$$

$$f = \frac{v}{\lambda} = \frac{30}{6} = 5\text{ Hz}$$

5. $\lambda = \frac{2\pi}{k} = \frac{2\pi}{0.05\pi} = 40$ cm

2nd overtone $\Rightarrow$ 3rd harmonic

$$L = n\left(\frac{\lambda}{2}\right) = 3\left(\frac{40}{2}\right) = 60\text{ cm}$$

6. $f = \frac{1}{2L}\sqrt{\frac{T}{\mu}} = \frac{1}{2L}\sqrt{\frac{T}{\rho\pi r^2}}$

$$\Rightarrow f \propto \frac{1}{Lr}\left(\frac{T}{\rho}\right)^{1/2}$$

$$\therefore \frac{f_B}{f_A} = \left(\frac{L_A}{L_B}\right)\left(\frac{r_A}{r_B}\right)\left(\frac{T_B}{T_A}\right)^{1/2}\left(\frac{\rho_A}{\rho_B}\right)^{1/2}$$

$$= (2)(2)\left(\frac{1}{2}\right)^{1/2}(2)^{1/2} = 4$$

7. $v = \sqrt{\frac{T}{\mu}} = \sqrt{\frac{490}{0.1}} = 70$ m/s

$$n\left(\frac{v}{2L}\right) = 400 \quad \text{...(i)}$$

$$(n+1)\left(\frac{v}{2L}\right) = 450 \quad \text{...(ii)}$$

Subtracting Eq. (i) from Eq. (ii), we get

$$\frac{v}{2L} = 50$$

$$\Rightarrow L = \frac{v}{100} = \frac{70}{100} = 0.7\text{ m} = 70\text{ cm}$$

8. $T = mg = \sigma Vg$

$T_1 = mg - B_1 = \sigma Vg - (1)Vg = (\sigma - 1)Vg$

$T_2 = mg - B_2 = \sigma Vg - \rho Vg = (\sigma - \rho)Vg$

$$f_0 = \frac{1}{2L}\sqrt{\frac{\sigma Vg}{\mu}} \quad \text{...(i)}$$

$$\frac{f_0}{2} = \frac{1}{2L}\sqrt{\frac{(\sigma-1)Vg}{\mu}} \quad \text{...(ii)}$$

From Eqs. (i) and (ii), we get

$$\frac{\sigma}{\sigma-1} = 4 \Rightarrow \sigma = \frac{4}{3}\text{ g/cm}^3$$

When immersed in certain liquid,

$$\frac{f_0}{4} = \frac{1}{2L}\sqrt{\frac{(\sigma-\rho)Vg}{\mu}} \quad \text{...(iii)}$$

From Eqs. (i) and (iii), we get

$$16 = \frac{\sigma}{\sigma-\rho}$$

$$\Rightarrow \rho = \frac{15}{16}\sigma = \frac{15}{16}\times\frac{4}{3} = 1.25$$

9. $f \propto \frac{1}{L} \Rightarrow \frac{f_1}{f_2} = \frac{L_2}{L_1}$

$$\Rightarrow \frac{124}{186} = \frac{L_2}{90} \Rightarrow L_2 = 60\text{ cm}$$

$$\therefore x = 6$$

10. $f = \frac{n_1}{2L}\sqrt{\frac{T}{(7.5)\pi r^2}} = \frac{n_2}{2L}\sqrt{\frac{T}{(2.7)\pi r^2}}$

$$\Rightarrow 3n_1 = 5n_2$$

For lowest harmonic, $n_1 = 5$ and $n_2 = 3$

$$f_{min} = \frac{5}{2(1)}\sqrt{\frac{75\pi}{7.5\times 10^3\times\pi(0.5)^2}} = 500\text{ Hz}$$

Level 3

Single Choice Correct Questions

1. $v \propto \frac{1}{\sqrt{\mu}} \Rightarrow \frac{v_r}{v_i} = \sqrt{\frac{\mu_i}{\mu_r}}$

$$A_t = \left(\frac{2v_2}{v_1+v_2}\right)A_i = \frac{2(v_2/v_1)}{1+(v_2/v_1)} = \frac{2\sqrt{\mu_i/\mu_r}}{1+\sqrt{\mu_i/\mu_r}}$$

2. $E \propto A^2$

$$\Rightarrow \frac{A_r}{A_i} = \sqrt{\frac{E_r}{E_i}} = \sqrt{0.64} = 0.8$$

$$\Rightarrow A_r = 0.8A_i = 0.8A$$

The reflected pulse will undergo a phase change of 180° and travel in negative *x*-direction.

3. At end A, reflected pulse will get inverted. At end B, there will not be any inversion.

4. Distance travelled by each pulse in 3 s $= 1 \times 3 = 3$ cm

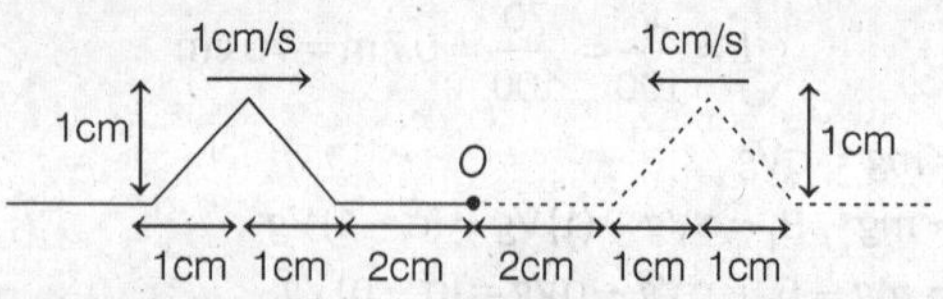

At $t = 3$ s, both pulses will completely overlap each other. So, the resultant amplitude at O will be $1 + 1 = 2$ cm.

5. $v = \sqrt{\dfrac{T}{\mu}} = \sqrt{\dfrac{1.6}{(10^{-2}/0.4)}} = 8$ m/s

For constructive interference between successive pulses

$$\Delta t_{min} = \frac{2L}{v} = \frac{2(0.4)}{8} = 0.1 \text{ s}$$

After two reflections, the wave pulse is in same phase as it was produced since, in each reflection, its phase changes by π and if at this instant, next identical pulse is produced, then constructive interference will be obtained.

6. All particles within a loop oscillate in the same phase. Particles of adjacent loops oscillate with a phase difference of π. So, X and 1 oscillate with a phase difference of π while X, 2 and 3 oscillate in phase.

7. $y = 2A \sin kx \cos \omega t$

In fundamental mode,

$$\frac{\lambda}{2} = L \Rightarrow \lambda = 2L$$

$$k = \frac{2\pi}{\lambda} = \frac{\pi}{L}$$

$$y = 4 \sin\left(\frac{\pi x}{L}\right) \cos \omega t$$

$$\text{Amplitude} = 4 \sin\left(\frac{\pi x}{L}\right) = 2$$

$$\Rightarrow \quad \frac{\pi x}{L} = \frac{\pi}{6} \text{ or } \frac{5\pi}{6}$$

$$\Rightarrow \quad x = \frac{L}{6} \text{ or } \frac{5L}{6}$$

$$\Delta x = x_2 - x_1 = \frac{5L}{6} - \frac{L}{6} = \frac{2L}{3} = \frac{2(1.5)}{3} = 1 \text{ m}$$

8. $l = 3\left(\dfrac{\lambda}{2}\right) \Rightarrow 3L = \dfrac{3\lambda}{2} \Rightarrow \lambda = 2L$

$$k = \frac{2\pi}{\lambda} = \frac{2\pi}{2L} = \frac{\pi}{L}$$

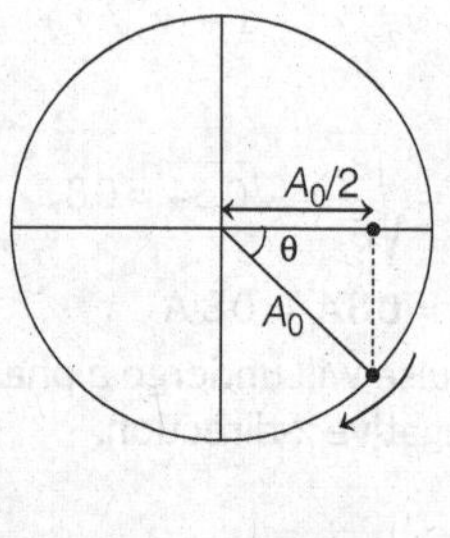

$$\cos\theta = \frac{A_0/2}{A_0} = \frac{1}{2}$$

$$\Rightarrow \quad \theta = \frac{\pi}{3}$$

$$y = A_0 \sin kx \sin(\omega t + \phi)$$

$$y = A_0 \sin\left(\frac{\pi x}{L}\right) \sin\left(\omega t + \frac{\pi}{2} + \frac{\pi}{3}\right)$$

At $x = \dfrac{L}{2}$,

$$y = A_0 \sin\left(\frac{\pi}{L}\left(\frac{L}{2}\right)\right) \sin\left(\omega t + \frac{5\pi}{6}\right)$$

$$= A_0 \sin\left(\omega t + \frac{5\pi}{6}\right)$$

9. Tensile strain $= \dfrac{\partial y}{\partial x} = 10^{-6}\left(\dfrac{\pi}{2}\right) \cos\left(\dfrac{\pi x}{2}\right) \sin(200\pi t)$

Tensile stress $= Y \times$ tensile strain

$$= 10^{12} \times 10^{-6}\left(\frac{\pi}{2}\right) \cos\left(\frac{\pi x}{2}\right) \sin(200\pi t)$$

At $x = \dfrac{1}{2}$ m,

$$\text{Maximum tensile stress} = 10^6\left(\frac{\pi}{2}\right) \cos\left(\frac{\pi}{2}\left(\frac{1}{2}\right)\right)$$

$$= \frac{\pi}{2\sqrt{2}} \times 10^6 \text{ N/m}$$

10. $\Sigma\tau = 0 \Rightarrow T_1 x = T_2(L - x)$

$$\Rightarrow \quad \frac{T_1}{T_2} = \frac{L - x}{x}$$

$$f_A = f_B \Rightarrow \frac{v_A}{2L} = 2\left(\frac{v_B}{2L}\right)$$

$$\Rightarrow \quad \frac{1}{2}\sqrt{\frac{T_1}{\mu}} = \sqrt{\frac{T_2}{\mu}}$$

$$\Rightarrow \quad \frac{T_1}{T_2} = 4$$

$$\therefore \quad \frac{L - x}{x} = 4 \Rightarrow x = \frac{L}{5}$$

11. $\mu_1 = \rho_1 A_1 = 7.8 \times 10^3 \times 1 \times 10^{-6} = 7.8 \times 10^{-3}$ kg/m

$\mu_2 = \rho_2 A_2 = 2.6 \times 10^3 \times 3 \times 10^{-6} = 7.8 \times 10^{-3}$ kg/m

$\because \quad \mu_1 = \mu_2 \Rightarrow v_1 = v_2$

Let, there be n_1 loops on the steel wire and n_2 loops on the aluminium wire.

$$f = n_1\left(\frac{v_1}{2L_1}\right) = n_2\left(\frac{v_2}{2L_2}\right)$$

$$\Rightarrow \quad \frac{n_1}{80} = \frac{n_2}{60}$$

$$\Rightarrow \quad 3n_1 = 4n_2$$

For fundamental mode,

$$n_1 = 4 \text{ and } n_2 = 3$$

For first overtone,

$$n_1 = 8 \text{ and } n_2 = 6$$

$$\therefore \quad f = 8\left(\frac{v_1}{2L_1}\right) = \frac{4}{0.8}\sqrt{\frac{40}{7.8\times10^{-3}}} = 360 \text{ Hz}$$

12. $f = \frac{1}{2L}\sqrt{\frac{T}{\mu}} = \frac{1}{2L}\sqrt{\frac{T}{(m/L)}} \quad \Rightarrow \quad f \propto \frac{1}{\sqrt{L}}$

$$\therefore \quad \frac{\Delta f}{f} = -\frac{1}{2}\frac{\Delta L}{L} \quad \Rightarrow \quad \frac{\Delta f}{f} = -\frac{\alpha\,\Delta T}{2}$$

$$\Rightarrow \quad \frac{1.001-1}{1} = -\frac{\alpha\,(10-30)}{2} \quad \Rightarrow \quad \alpha = 1\times10^{-4}/^\circ\text{C}$$

13. $f = \frac{1}{2L}\sqrt{\frac{T}{\mu}} = \frac{1}{2L}\sqrt{\frac{AY\alpha\Delta T}{\mu}}$

$$\therefore \quad f = \frac{1}{2(1)}\sqrt{\frac{10^{-6}\times2\times10^{11}\times1.21\times10^{-5}\times20}{(0.1/1)}} = 11 \text{ Hz}$$

14. $f = \frac{v}{2L} = \frac{3\times10^8}{2(0.1)} = 1.5\times10^9 \text{ Hz} = 1.5 \text{ GHz}$

15. $x = 0$ and $x = l$, points will be anti-nodes as they are free ends.

16. $f = \frac{n}{2L}\sqrt{\frac{T}{\mu}} = \text{constant}$

$$\Rightarrow \quad n \propto \frac{1}{\sqrt{T}}$$

So, the string with greater tension will oscillate in lesser number of loops.

17. $E_1 = \frac{\mu A^2\omega^2 L}{2}, \quad E_2 = \frac{\mu A^2(2\omega)^2 L}{2}$

$$\therefore \quad E_2 = 4E_1$$

18. In figure 1, energy at A is potential as well as kinetic. In figure 2, energy at A is only potential.

19. Let u_1 and u_2 be the energy densities due to individual waves. So,

$$u_1 = \frac{1}{2}\rho\omega^2 a^2, \quad u_2 = \frac{1}{2}\rho\omega^2(2a)^2 = 2\rho\omega^2 a^2$$

Volume of string in a loop of standing wave,

$$V = S\times L = S\times\frac{\lambda}{2} = \frac{\pi S}{k}$$

Total mechanical energy confined in a loop,

$$E = (u_1+u_2)V = \left(\frac{5}{2}\rho\omega^2 a^2\right)\frac{\pi S}{k} = \frac{5\rho\omega^2 a^2\pi S}{2k}$$

20. (d)

21. $f_0 = \frac{1}{2L}\sqrt{\frac{T}{\mu}}$ ...(i)

$$f_0 + 6 = \frac{1}{2L}\sqrt{\frac{1.44T}{\mu}} \quad \text{...(ii)}$$

Dividing Eq. (ii) by Eq. (i), we get

$$\frac{f_0+6}{f_0} = 1.2 \quad \Rightarrow \quad f_0 = 30 \text{ Hz}$$

When the length is increased by 20%,

$$f = \frac{1}{2(1.2L)}\sqrt{\frac{T}{\mu}} = \frac{30}{1.2} = 25 \text{ Hz}$$

$$\Delta f = f_0 - f = 30 - 25 = 5 \text{ Hz (decrease)}$$

22. $f = \frac{n}{2L}\sqrt{\frac{Mg}{\mu}} \quad \Rightarrow \quad M \propto \frac{1}{n^2}$

$$\therefore \quad \frac{M_1}{M_2} = \left(\frac{n_2}{n_1}\right)^2$$

$$\Rightarrow \quad \frac{9}{M} = \left(\frac{3}{5}\right)^2 \quad \Rightarrow \quad M = 25 \text{ kg}$$

23. $f = \frac{1}{2L}\sqrt{\frac{T}{\mu}}$

$$\Rightarrow \quad 256 = \frac{1}{2(40)}\sqrt{\frac{\sigma Vg}{\mu}} \quad \text{...(i)}$$

When the stone is completely immersed in water,

$$256 = \frac{1}{2(22)}\sqrt{\frac{\sigma Vg - (1)Vg}{\mu}} \quad \text{...(ii)}$$

Dividing Eq. (i) by Eq. (ii), we get

$$\sigma = \frac{(40)^2}{(40)^2 - (22)^2}$$

24. $L = n(2) = (n+1)1.6$

$$\Rightarrow \quad n = 4$$

$$\therefore \quad L = 4(2) = 8 \text{ cm}$$

Multiple Choice(s) Correct Questions

1. (A) $A = 4\sin\left(\frac{\pi x}{15}\right)$

At $x = 5$ cm,

$$A = 4\sin\left(\frac{\pi(5)}{15}\right) = 2\sqrt{3} \text{ cm}$$

(B) For nodes, $A = 4\sin\left(\frac{\pi x}{15}\right) = 0$

$$\Rightarrow \quad \frac{\pi x}{15} = n\pi \quad \Rightarrow \quad x = 15n$$

$$x_{max} = 15n_{max} = 600 \quad \Rightarrow \quad n_{max} = 40$$

$\therefore$ Integer n varies from 0 to 40.

(C) $v_p = \frac{\partial y}{\partial t} = -4\times96\pi\sin\left(\frac{\pi x}{15}\right)\sin(96\pi t)$

At $x = 7.5$ cm, $t = 0.25$ s, $v_p = 0$

(D) $2\sin A\cos B = \sin(A+B) + \sin(A-B)$

Using above result, we can write

$$4\sin\left(\frac{\pi x}{15}\right)\cos(96\pi t)$$

$$= 2\sin\left(\frac{\pi x}{15} + 96\pi t\right) + 2\sin\left(\frac{\pi x}{15} - 96\pi t\right)$$

2. Superposition of two travelling waves moving in the same directions produces also a travelling wave.

Waves (i) and (iii) are moving in x-direction but displacement of particles are along X-axis and Y-axis, respectively. So, the resultant amplitude will be $\sqrt{2}a$.
Superposition of two travelling waves moving in opposite directions produces stationary wave.

$$z_1 + z_2 = a \sin \omega\left(t - \frac{x}{v}\right) + a \sin\left[\omega\left(t - \frac{x}{v}\right) + \frac{\pi}{2}\right]$$

3. (a, b, c)
4. $y = 2A \sin kx \cos \omega t,$

$$n\left(\frac{\lambda}{2}\right) = L \Rightarrow \lambda = \frac{2L}{n}$$

For anti-nodes, $2A \sin kx = 2A$

$$\Rightarrow \frac{2\pi}{\lambda}\left(\frac{3L}{8}\right) = m\frac{\pi}{2}, \text{ where } m \text{ is odd integer}$$

$$\Rightarrow \frac{2\pi}{(2L/n)}\left(\frac{3L}{8}\right) = m\frac{\pi}{2} \Rightarrow 3n = 4m$$

Possible solutions, $n = 4$ and $m = 3$

$n = 12$ and $m = 9$

5. $y = A \sin kx \cos \omega t$

For nodes, $A \sin kx = 0$

$$\Rightarrow x = \frac{\pi}{k}, \frac{2\pi}{k}, \ldots$$

For amplitude $\frac{A}{2}$, $A \sin kx = \frac{A}{2}$

$$\Rightarrow x = \frac{\pi}{6k}, \frac{5\pi}{6k}, \frac{7\pi}{6k}, \frac{11\pi}{6k}$$

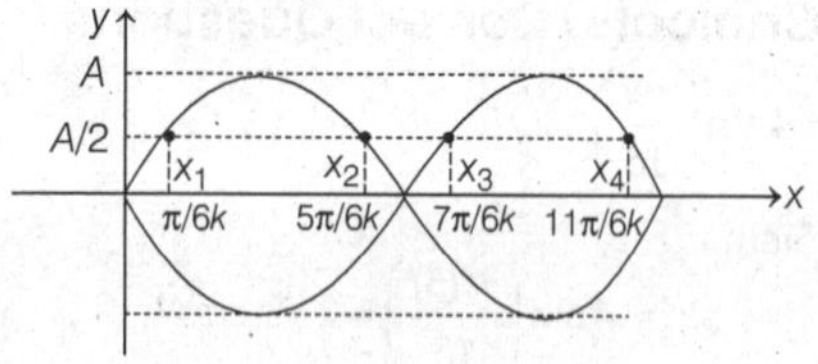

$$x_2 - x_1 = \frac{5\pi}{6k} - \frac{\pi}{6k} = \frac{2\pi}{3k}$$

$$x_3 - x_2 = \frac{7\pi}{6k} - \frac{5\pi}{6k} = \frac{\pi}{3k}$$

$$x_4 - x_1 = \frac{11\pi}{6k} - \frac{\pi}{6k} = \frac{5\pi}{3k}$$

6. (a, c, d)
7. Free ends must be anti-nodes and midpoint will be a node. In fundamental mode, 2 half loops will form.

$$2\left(\frac{\lambda}{4}\right) = L \Rightarrow \lambda = 2L$$

$$\therefore f = \frac{c}{\lambda} = \frac{c}{2L}$$

In first overtone, (2 half loops + 2 full loops) will form.
In second overtone, (2 half loops + 4 full loops) will form.

$$2\left(\frac{\lambda}{4}\right) + 4\left(\frac{\lambda}{2}\right) = L$$

$$\Rightarrow \lambda = \frac{2L}{5}$$

$$\therefore f = \frac{c}{\lambda} = \frac{5c}{2L}$$

8. $v = \sqrt{\frac{T}{\mu}} = \sqrt{\frac{T}{\rho\pi r^2}}$

$$\Rightarrow v \propto \frac{1}{r}\sqrt{\frac{T}{\rho}}$$

$$\therefore \frac{v_A}{v_B} = \left(\frac{r_B}{r_A}\right)\sqrt{\frac{T_A}{T_B}}\sqrt{\frac{\rho_B}{\rho_A}} = (2)\left(\frac{1}{\sqrt{2}}\right)\sqrt{2} = 2$$

$$\Rightarrow v_B = \frac{v_A}{2}$$

$$f = \frac{v}{2L} \Rightarrow f \propto \frac{v}{L}$$

$$\therefore \frac{f_A}{f_B} = \left(\frac{v_A}{v_B}\right)\left(\frac{L_B}{L_A}\right) = (2)(2) = 4$$

Third overtone of $B = 4f_B = f_A$

9. (b)
10. $E = \frac{1}{2}\mu\omega^2 A^2 = \frac{1}{2}\mu(2\pi f)^2 A^2 = 2\pi^2 f^2 \mu A^2$

$$E_n = 2\pi^2 (nf)^2 \mu A^2 = n^2 E$$

$$\langle KE \rangle = \langle PE \rangle = \frac{TE}{2}$$

11. Equation of a particle which is at anti-node,

$$y = 2A \sin\left(\frac{2\pi}{T}t\right)$$

At $t = \frac{T}{8}$, $y = 2A \sin\left[\frac{2\pi}{T}\left(\frac{T}{8}\right)\right] = \sqrt{2}A$

Displacement of particle at node is always zero.

Comprehension Based Questions

1. As reflection takes place from denser medium, reflected pulse will undergo a phase change of π while transmitted wave will be in phase with the incident wave.
2. $\frac{\lambda_r}{\lambda_t} = \frac{v_1}{v_2} = \sqrt{\frac{\mu_2}{\mu_1}}$

$$\mu_1 = \rho\pi(2r)^2 = 4\rho\pi r^2$$

$$\mu_2 = 9\rho\pi r^2$$

$$\therefore \frac{v_1}{v_2} = \sqrt{\frac{9}{4}} = \frac{3}{2}$$

3. $A_r = \left(\frac{v_2 - v_1}{v_1 + v_2}\right)A_i$, $A_t = \left(\frac{2v_2}{v_1 + v_2}\right)A_i$

$$\therefore \frac{A_r}{A_t} = \frac{v_2 - v_1}{2v_2} = \frac{1}{2}\left(1 - \frac{3}{2}\right) = -\frac{1}{4}$$

4. Amplitude $= A \sin kx = A \sin\left(\frac{2\pi}{\lambda} \times \frac{L}{3}\right)$

$$= A \sin\left(\frac{2\pi}{2L} \times \frac{L}{3}\right) = \frac{\sqrt{3}A}{2}$$

5. Kinetic energy is maximum at mean position.

$$\therefore \quad \omega t + \frac{\pi}{4} = \pi \Rightarrow \omega t = \frac{3\pi}{4} \Rightarrow t = \frac{3\pi}{4\omega}$$

6. $K = \int_0^L \frac{1}{2}\left(\frac{m}{L}dx\right)[(A \sin kx)\,\omega]^2 = \frac{1}{4} m\omega^2 A^2$

7.

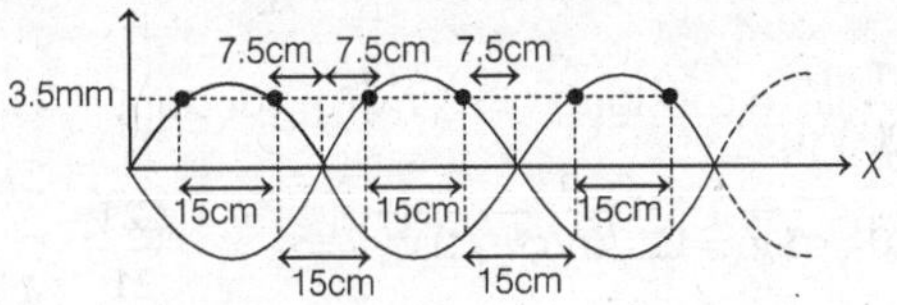

Length of one loop $= 15 + 7.5 + 7.5 = 30$ cm

Number of loops $= \frac{120}{30} = 4$

So, the string is oscillating in 4th harmonic.

8. $\frac{\lambda}{2} = 30 \Rightarrow \lambda = 60$ cm

$y = A \sin kx \cos \omega t$

Amplitude $= A \sin \frac{2\pi}{\lambda} x$

At $x = 7.5$ cm, $\quad A \sin\left(\frac{2\pi}{60}(7.5)\right) = 3.5 \Rightarrow A = 3.5\sqrt{2}$ mm

9. $f = \frac{n}{2L}\sqrt{\frac{mg}{\mu}} \Rightarrow m = \frac{4\mu f^2 L^2}{n^2 g}$

For m to be maximum, $n = 1$

$$\therefore \quad m_{max} = \frac{4 \times 2 \times 10^{-3} \times (700)^2 (1)^2}{(1)^2 (9.8)} = 400 \text{ kg}$$

10. $m \propto \frac{1}{n^2} \Rightarrow \frac{m_1}{m_2} = \left(\frac{n_2}{n_1}\right)^2$

$$\Rightarrow \quad \frac{16}{400} = \left(\frac{1}{n_1}\right)^2 \Rightarrow n_1 = 5$$

11. Maximum displacement $= 6 \sin\left(\frac{\pi}{10}(5)\right) = 6$ cm

12. Equation of resultant wave,

$$y = (4\,\text{mm}) \sin\left[4\pi t + \frac{\pi}{6}\right] \cos\left[2\pi x + \frac{\pi}{6}\right]$$

Position of node, $x = \frac{1}{6}, \frac{4}{6}, \frac{7}{6}, \ldots$

Points $x = \frac{1}{7}$ and $x_2 = \frac{5}{12}$ are on different sides of a node.

So, their phase difference will be π.

13. For anti-nodes, $\cos\left[2\pi x + \frac{\pi}{6}\right] = \pm 1$

$$\Rightarrow \quad 2\pi x + \frac{\pi}{6} = n\pi, \text{ where } n \in I$$

$$\Rightarrow \quad x = \frac{5}{12}, \frac{11}{12}, \frac{17}{12}, \ldots$$

14. (b)

Match the Columns Questions

1. Check values of y at $x = 0$ and $x = L$.

2. $A \to P$, $B \to R$, $C \to Q$, $D \to S$

3. $A \to PQS$, $B \to S$, $C \to QRS$, $D \to ST$

4. As particles are going from extreme position to mean position, kinetic energy will increase.

At $t = t_1$, energy of A, B, C is zero but at $t = t_2$, it is more for B. So, energy flows from A to B and C to B during t_1 and t_2.

5. For travelling wave, $v_P = -v \times$ slope

6. $v = \sqrt{\frac{T}{\mu}} = \sqrt{\frac{72}{5 \times 10^{-3}}} = 120$ m/s

2nd overtone $\Rightarrow$ 3rd harmonic $\Rightarrow n = 3$

$$L = n\left(\frac{\lambda}{2}\right)$$

$$\Rightarrow \quad 60 = 3\left(\frac{\lambda}{2}\right) \Rightarrow \lambda = 40 \text{ cm}$$

$$f = \frac{v}{\lambda} = \frac{120}{0.4} = 300 \text{ Hz}$$

$$\omega = 2\pi f = 600\pi \text{ rad/s}$$

At anti-node, $v_{max} = A\omega = (0.25)(600\pi) = 150\pi$ cm/s

$$a_{max} = A\omega^2 = 90000\pi^2 \text{ cm/s}^2$$

Amplitude $= A \sin\left(\frac{2\pi}{40} x\right)$

At $x = 5$ cm from node,

Amplitude $= 0.25 \sin\left(\frac{2\pi}{40} \times 5\right) = \frac{0.25}{\sqrt{2}}$ cm/s

$$v_{max} = A\omega = \frac{150\pi}{\sqrt{2}} \text{ cm/s}$$

$$a_{max} = A\omega^2 = \frac{90000\pi^2}{\sqrt{2}} \text{ cm/s}^2$$

7. $A \to PQ$, $B \to RS$, $C \to PS$, $D \to QR$

Numerical Value Questions

1. $2T \cos\theta = mg$

$$\Rightarrow \quad 2T\left(\frac{4}{5}\right) = 16 \times 10 \Rightarrow T = 100 \text{ N}$$

$$v = \sqrt{\frac{T}{\mu}} = \sqrt{\frac{100}{0.01}} = 100 \text{ m/s}$$

$$f = \frac{3v}{2L} = \frac{3 \times 100}{2 \times 6} = 25 \text{ Hz}$$

2. $\sigma = \frac{T}{A}$

$$\Rightarrow \quad 9 \times 10^8 = \frac{900\pi}{A}$$

$$\Rightarrow \quad A = \pi \times 10^{-6} \text{ m}^2$$

$$\mu = \rho A = 10^4 \times \pi \times 10^{-6} = \pi \times 10^{-2} \text{ kg/m}$$

$$v = \sqrt{\frac{T}{\mu}} = \sqrt{\frac{900\pi}{\pi \times 10^{-2}}} = 300 \text{ m/s}$$

$$m = \mu L$$

$\Rightarrow \quad 4\pi \times 10^{-3} = (\pi \times 10^{-2})L$

$\Rightarrow \quad L = 0.4$ m

$$f = \frac{v}{2L} = \frac{300}{2(0.4)} = 375 \text{ Hz}$$

3. $v = \sqrt{\frac{T}{\mu}} = \sqrt{\frac{AY\alpha\Delta T}{\mu}} = \sqrt{\frac{10^{-6} \times 2 \times 10^{11} \times 1.21 \times 10^{-5} \times 20}{(0.1/1)}}$

$= 22$ m/s

There will be an anti-node at 0.25 m from one end.

$\therefore$ Distance between node and anti-node $= \frac{\lambda}{4} = 0.25$

$\Rightarrow \quad \lambda = 1$ m

$$f = \frac{v}{\lambda} = \frac{22}{1} = 22 \text{ Hz}$$

4.

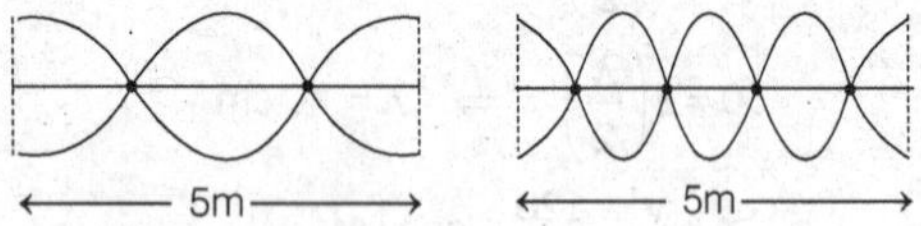

In 1st case, $\frac{\lambda}{4} + \frac{\lambda}{2} + \frac{\lambda}{4} = 5$

$\Rightarrow \quad \lambda = 5$ m

$v = \lambda f = 5(2) = 10$ m/s

In 2nd case, $2\left(\frac{\lambda}{4}\right) + 3\left(\frac{\lambda}{2}\right) = 5$

$\Rightarrow \quad \lambda = 2.5$ m

$\therefore \quad f = \frac{v}{\lambda} = \frac{10}{2.5} = 4$ Hz

5. $n_1 x_1 = l$ and $n_2 x_2 = l$

$\therefore \quad \frac{x_2}{x_1} = \frac{n_1}{n_2}$

Given that, $\frac{x_2}{x_1} = \frac{l}{l + 2x_1}$

$\Rightarrow \quad \frac{n_1}{n_2} = \frac{l}{l + 2\left(\frac{l}{n_1}\right)}$

$\Rightarrow \quad n_2 = n_1 + 2 \Rightarrow n_2 - n_1 = 2$

6. Distance between node and anti-node $= \frac{\lambda}{4} = \frac{L}{4}$

$\therefore \quad \lambda = L$

$$v = \sqrt{\frac{T}{\mu}} = \sqrt{\frac{1 \times 10}{(1 \times 10^{-3}/L)}} = 100\sqrt{L}$$

$v = \lambda f \Rightarrow 100\sqrt{L} = L(100)$

$\Rightarrow \quad L = 1$ m

7. $K = \frac{1}{4} m\omega^2 A^2 = \frac{1}{4} m(2\pi f)^2 A^2 = \pi^2 m f^2 A^2$

$\therefore \quad E_1 = \pi^2 m f^2 A_1^2$ and $E_2 = \pi^2 m (3f)^2 A_2^2$

$E_1 = E_2$

$\Rightarrow \quad \pi^2 m f^2 A_1^2 = 9\pi^2 m f^2 A_2^2$

$\Rightarrow \quad \frac{A_1}{A_2} = 3$

8. For a string fixed at one end, $f = \frac{v}{4L} = 120$ Hz

For a string fixed at both ends, $f = \frac{v}{2L} = 2 \times 120 = 240$ Hz

9. $f = \frac{n}{2L}\sqrt{\frac{T}{\mu}} = \text{constant} \Rightarrow n\sqrt{T} = \text{constant}$

$\therefore \quad 10\sqrt{\sigma V g} = 11\sqrt{\sigma V g - (1) V g} \Rightarrow \sigma = \frac{121}{21}$

$\therefore \quad n = 21$

Previous Year's Questions

JEE Main

1. Given, mass of the string, $m = 18 \text{ g} = 0.018$ kg

Linear mass density, $\mu = 20 \text{ g/m} = 0.02$ kg/m

If l be the length of the string, then

$$\mu = \frac{m}{l} \Rightarrow l = \frac{m}{\mu} = \frac{0.018}{0.02} = 0.9 \text{ m}$$

Speed of transverse wave in the string,

$v = f_0 \lambda = f_0\left(\frac{2l}{n}\right) \qquad \left(\because \lambda = \frac{2l}{n}\right)$

$= f_0 \frac{2l}{1} \qquad$ (for fundamental node, $n = 1$)

$= 50 \times 2 \times 0.9 \qquad (\because f_0 = 50 \text{ Hz})$

$= 90$ m/s

2. Using $f = \frac{v}{2L}$, we get

$120 = \frac{v}{2L_1} \qquad$ ...(i)

and $\quad 180 = \frac{v}{2L'} \qquad$ ...(ii)

Dividing Eq. (ii) from Eq. (i), we get;

$$\frac{L'}{L} = \frac{120}{180} = \frac{2}{3}$$

$\Rightarrow \quad L' = 90 \times \frac{2}{3} = 60$ cm

3. Given, $y_1 = 10\sin\left(\omega t + \frac{\pi}{3}\right)$ cm

$y_2 = 5[\sin\omega t + \sqrt{3}\cos\omega t]$

$y_2 = 5[\sin\omega t + \sqrt{3}\cos\omega t] \times \frac{2}{2}$

$y_2 = 10\left[\sin\omega t \times \frac{1}{2} + \cos\omega t \times \frac{\sqrt{3}}{2}\right]$

$y_2 = 10\left[\sin\omega t \cos\frac{\pi}{3} + \cos\omega t \sin\frac{\pi}{3}\right]$

$y_2 = 10\sin\left(\omega t + \frac{\pi}{3}\right)$ cm

From given equation, $A_1 = 10$ cm, $A_2 = 10$ cm, $\phi = \frac{\pi}{3} - \frac{\pi}{3} = 0$

Amplitude of resultant wave,

$$R = \sqrt{A_1^2 + A_2^2 + 2A_1A_2 \cos\phi}$$

$$= \sqrt{(10)^2 + (10)^2 + 2(10)(10)\cos 0^\circ}$$

$$R = 20 \text{ cm}$$

4. We know, $\frac{nv}{0.6} = f$

where, n = Harmonic number,

v = Speed of waves and

f = Frequency

$\therefore \quad \frac{nv}{0.6} = 400$ and $\frac{(n+1)v}{0.6} = 450$

$\Rightarrow \quad nv = 400 \times 0.6$ and $nv + v = 450 \times 0.6$

$\Rightarrow \quad nv = 240$ and $240 + v = 270$

$\therefore \quad v = 30$

Now, we know that speed of wave in a string $= \sqrt{T/\mu}$

where, T = tension and $\mu = \frac{\text{mass}}{\text{length}}$

$\therefore \quad v = \sqrt{\frac{T}{\mu}} \Rightarrow 30 = \sqrt{\frac{2700}{\mu}}$

$\Rightarrow \quad 900 = \frac{2700}{\mu} \Rightarrow \mu = 3$ kg/m

5. Equation of stationary wave is given as

$$y = \left(10 \cos \pi x \sin \frac{2\pi t}{T}\right) \text{cm}$$

$\therefore$ Amplitude, $A = 10 \cos \pi x$

$\therefore$ Amplitude of particle at $x = \frac{4}{3}$ cm

$$A = 10 \cos \pi \times \frac{4}{3} = 10 \cos \frac{4\pi}{3} = 10 \cos\left(\pi + \frac{\pi}{3}\right)$$

$$= 10\left(-\cos\frac{\pi}{3}\right) = 10\left(-\frac{1}{2}\right) = -5 \text{ cm}$$

6. Equations of the two waves are given as

$$y_1 = 5 \sin 2\pi(x - vt) \text{ cm}$$

$\therefore$ Amplitude, $A_1 = 5$ cm

and $\quad y_2 = 3 \sin 2\pi(x - vt + 1.5)$ cm

$\therefore$ Amplitude, $A_2 = 3$ cm

Phase difference between waves y_1 and y_2 is given as

$$\Delta\phi = 2\pi(1.5) = 3\pi$$

$\therefore$ Amplitude of resultant wave,

$$A = \sqrt{A_1^2 + A_2^2 + 2A_1A_2\cos(\Delta\phi)}$$

$$= \sqrt{A_1^2 + A_2^2 + 2A_1A_2(-1)} \quad [\because \cos 3\pi = \cos\pi = -1]$$

$$= \sqrt{(A_1 - A_2)^2} = A_1 - A_2$$

$$= 5 - 3 = 2 \text{ cm}$$

7. Given that,

Linear mass density,

$$\mu = 9.0 \times 10^{-4} \frac{\text{kg}}{\text{m}}$$

Tension, $T = 900$ N

$\therefore$ Velocity of wire,

$$v = \sqrt{\frac{T}{\mu}} = \sqrt{\frac{900}{9 \times 10^{-4}}} = 10^3 \text{ m/s}$$

$$f_n = \frac{nv}{2l} = 500 \quad \text{... (i)}$$

And $(n+1)v = 550$ ...(ii)

From Eqs. (i) and (ii),

$$f_{n+1} - f_n = \frac{v}{2l} = 50$$

$\therefore \quad l = \frac{10^3}{2 \times 50} = 10$ m

8. Given, $y_1 = A_1 \sin k(x - vt)$

$$y_1 = 12 \sin 6.28(x - vt)$$

$$y_2 = 5 \sin 6.28(x - vt + 3.5)$$

We know,

Phase difference,

$$\Delta\phi = k(\Delta x) = 6.28 \times 3.5 = 7\pi$$

For resultant amplitude,

$$A^2 = A_1^2 + A_2^2 + 2A_1A_2\cos\phi$$

$\Rightarrow \quad A = \sqrt{(12)^2 + (5)^2 + 2(12)(5)\cos(7\pi)}$

$$= \sqrt{144 + 25 - 120} = \sqrt{49} = 7 \text{ mm}$$

9. Given, $y = 1.0$ mm

$\cos(1.57 \text{ cm}^{-1})x \sin(78.5 \text{ s}^{-1})t$

$\therefore \quad A = 1$ mm

$$k = 1.57 \text{ cm}^{-1}$$

$$\omega = 78.5 \text{ s}^{-1}$$

At node, displacement, $y = 0$

$$\cos(1.57 \text{ cm}^{-1} x) = 0$$

$\Rightarrow \quad 1.57 \text{ cm}^{-1} x = \frac{\pi}{2}$

$$x = 1 \text{ cm}$$

10. Density of wire,

$$d = 9 \times 10^{-3} \text{kg/cm}^3 = 9 \times 10^3 \text{ kg/m}^3$$

Strain in the wire,

$$\varepsilon = 4.9 \times 10^{-4}$$

Young's modulus of wire is

$$Y = 9 \times 10^{10} \frac{\text{N}}{\text{m}^2}$$

Lowest frequency of vibration in wire will be

$$f = \frac{1}{2L}\sqrt{\frac{T}{(M/L)}} \quad \text{...(i)}$$

Now, $\frac{T}{M/L} = \frac{T}{V\rho/L} = \frac{T}{\left(\frac{LA \cdot \rho}{L}\right)} = \frac{T}{A\rho}$

But $\frac{T}{A}$ = stress = $Y \times$ strain = $Y \times \varepsilon$

So, from Eq (i), frequency will be

$$f = \frac{1}{2L}\sqrt{\frac{Y \times \varepsilon}{\rho}} = \frac{1}{2 \times 1} \times \sqrt{\frac{9 \times 10^{10} \times 4.9 \times 10^{-4}}{9 \times 10^{3}}} = 35 \text{ Hz}$$

11. Fundamental frequency of oscillation of a taut string is

$$f = \frac{1}{2l}\sqrt{\frac{T}{\mu}}$$

Given, X and Z are identical strings.

$\therefore$ l and μ are same for both X and Z.

$$\Rightarrow \quad f \propto \sqrt{T} \quad \Rightarrow \quad \frac{f_X}{f_Z} = \sqrt{\frac{T_X}{T_Z}}$$

$$\Rightarrow \quad \frac{T_X}{T_Z} = \frac{f_X^2}{f_Z^2} = \left(\frac{450}{300}\right)^2 = \frac{9}{4} = 2.25$$

12. We can represent a wave vectorially with a phasor.

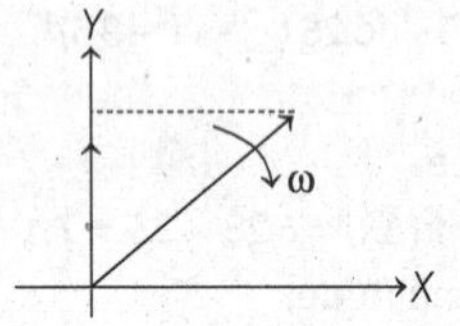

Here, we are given with following phasors.

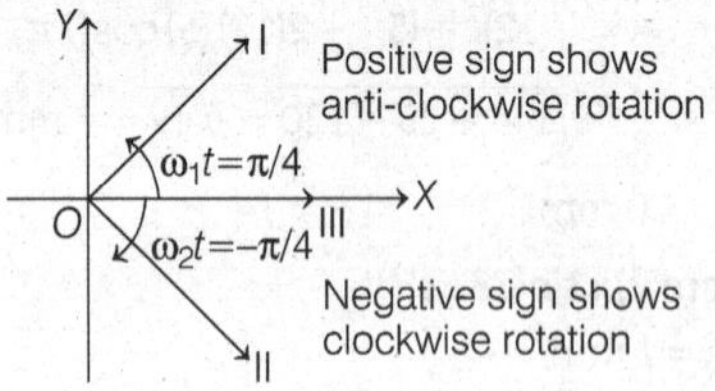

Each phasor is of same amplitude, $A^2 = I_0$

From phasor diagram, amplitude of resultant of phasors I and II,

$$A' = A\cos\frac{\pi}{4} + A\cos\frac{\pi}{4} = 2A \times \frac{1}{\sqrt{2}} = \sqrt{2}\,A$$

Now, this resultant phasor is along the direction of IIIrd phasor.

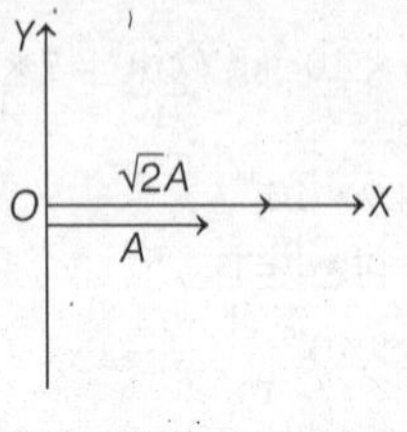

$\therefore$ Resultant amplitude of these two will be

$$A_R = \sqrt{2}A + 1A = (\sqrt{2} + 1)\,A$$

As intensity is proportional to square of amplitude, resultant intensity is given by

$$I_R = A_R^2 = (\sqrt{2} + 1)^2 A^2 = (\sqrt{2} + 1)^2 I_0$$

$$= (2 + 1 + 2\sqrt{2})\,I_0 = (3 + 2\sqrt{2})\,I_0$$

$$= (3 + 2 \times 1.4)\,I_0 = 5.8\,I_0$$

13. Velocity 'v' of the wave on the string $= \sqrt{\frac{T}{\mu}}$

Substituting the given values, we get

$$v = \sqrt{\frac{8}{5} \times 1000} = 40 \text{ ms}^{-1}$$

Wavelength of the wave on the string, $\lambda = \frac{v}{f}$

where, f = frequency of wave.

$$\Rightarrow \quad \lambda = \frac{40}{100}\text{ m} = 40 \text{ cm}$$

$\therefore$ Separation between two successive nodes is,

$$d = \frac{\lambda}{2} = \frac{40}{2} = 20.0 \text{ cm}$$

JEE Advanced

1. $\frac{nv}{2l} = 750$ Hz

$\frac{(n+1)\,v}{2l} = 1000$ Hz

$\therefore \quad \frac{v}{2l} = 1000 - 750 = 250$ Hz

$\Rightarrow \quad v = 2 \times 250 \times 1 \quad \Rightarrow \quad \sqrt{\frac{T}{\mu}} = 500$

$\therefore \quad T = 5$ N

2. There should be a node at $x = 0$ and antinode at $x = 3$ m.

Also, $\quad v = \frac{\omega}{k} = 100$ m / s.

$\therefore \quad y = 0$ at $x = 0$ and $y = \pm A$ at $x = 3$ m.

Only (a), (c) and (d) satisfy the condition.

3.

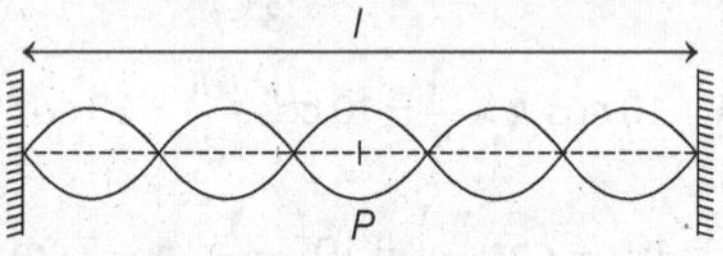

Number of nodes = 6

From the given equation, we can see that

$$k = \frac{2\pi}{\lambda} = 62.8 \text{ m}^{-1}$$

$$\therefore \quad \lambda = \frac{2\pi}{62.8}\text{ m} = 0.1 \text{ m}$$

$$l = \frac{5\lambda}{2} = 0.25 \text{ m}$$

The mid-point of the string is P, an antinode

$\therefore$ maximum displacement = 0.01 m

$$\omega = 2\pi f = 628 \text{ s}^{-1} \quad \Rightarrow \quad f = \frac{628}{2\pi} = 100 \text{ Hz}$$

But this is fifth harmonic frequency.

$\therefore$ Fundamental frequency $f_0 = \frac{f}{5} = 20$ Hz

CHAPTER~10

SOUND WAVES

LEVEL 01 Starter Level

10.1 Displacement Wave, Pressure Wave and Density Wave

1. Find the following for given wave equation. $\Delta p = 0.02 \sin [\pi (3000t - 2x)]$ (all quantities are in SI units.)
   (a) Frequency (b) Wavelength
   (c) Speed of sound wave
   (d) If the equilibrium pressure of air is 10^5 Pa, then find maximum and minimum pressure.
2. A sound wave of wavelength 40 cm travels in air. If the difference between the maximum and minimum pressures at a given point is $2.0 \times 10^{-3}\ N/m^2$, find the amplitude of vibration of the particles of the medium. The bulk modulus of air is $1.4 \times 10^5\ N/m^2$.
3. Corresponding to displacement equation $y = A \sin [kx + \omega t]$ of a longitudinal sound wave, make its pressure and density wave also. Bulk modulus of the medium is B and density is ρ.
4. The figure shows an instantaneous displacement position graph of a sound wave travelling along the positive X-axis. Identify the points of

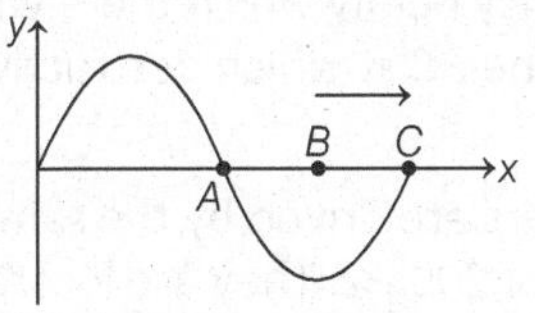

   (a) maximum pressure,
   (b) minimum pressure and
   (c) atmospheric pressure (or normal pressure)

10.2 Speed of Sound

1. Calculate the velocity of sound in air at NTP. The density of air at NTP is 1.29 g/L. Assume air to be diatomic with $\gamma = 1.4$. Also calculate the velocity of sound in air at 27°C.
2. Find the speed of sound in H_2 at temperature T, if the speed of sound in O_2 is 450 m/s at this temperature.
3. (a) Find the speed of sound in a mixture of 1 mol of helium and 2 mol of oxygen at 27°C.
   (b) If now temperature is raised by 1K from 300 K. Find the percentage change in the speed of sound in the gaseous mixture.
4. If the bulk modulus of water is 4000 MPa, what is the speed of sound in water?
5. Find the change in the volume of 1 L kerosene when it is subjected to an extra pressure of $2 \times 10^5\ N/m^2$ from the following data. Density of kerosene is $800\ kg/m^3$ and speed of sound in kerosene is 1330 m/s.

10.3 Intensity of Sound

1. A point source of sound emits 50π W power at 2.5 kHz frequency uniformly and spherically. The density of air is $1.25\ kg/m^3$ and speed of sound in air is 320 m/s. Find
   (a) the intensity at a distance 10 m away from source.
   (b) pressure amplitude at this point.
   (c) displacement amplitude at this point.
2. Find the intensity of sound wave whose frequency is 250 Hz. The displacement amplitude of particles of the medium at this position is 1×10^{-8} m. The density of the medium is 1 kg/m^3, bulk modulus of elasticity of the medium is 400 N/m^2.
3. The pressure amplitude in a sound wave from a radio receiver is $2.0 \times 10^{-3}\ N/m^2$ and the intensity at a point is $10^{-6}\ W/m^2$. If by turning the "Volume" knob the pressure amplitude is increased to $3 \times 10^{-3}\ N/m^2$, evaluate the intensity.
4. Two sound waves one in air and the other in fresh water are equal in intensity.
   (a) Find the ratio of pressure amplitudes of the wave in water to that of the wave in air.

(b) If the pressure amplitudes of the waves are equal, then what will be the ratio of the intensities of the waves? [$v_{sound} = 340$ m/s in air and $\rho_{air} = 1.25\ kg/m^3$, $v_{sound} = 1530$ m/s in water, $\rho_{water} = 1000\ kg/m^3$]

10.4 Decibel Scale

1. A source of sound emits 200π W power which is uniformly distributed over a sphere of radius 10 m. What is the loudness of sound on the surface of the sphere?
2. If the intensity is increased by a factor of 20, by how many decibels is the intensity level increased?
3. A sound source of small size produces a spherical sound wave with a frequency of 3 kHz in air. At a distance $r_1 = 100$ m from the source, the sound loudness level is $L_1 = 60$ dB. Find the sound loudness level at a distance of $r_2 = 200$ m and the distance at which the sound stops being heard.
4. The noise level in a classroom in absence of the teacher is 50 dB when 30 students are present. Assuming that on an average each student outputs same sound energy per second, what will be the noise level if the number of students is increased to 90?
5. If the sound level in a room is increased from 50 dB to 60 dB, by which factor is the pressure amplitude increased?

10.5 Interference of Sound Waves

1. Two point sound sources A and B each of power 25π W and frequency 850 Hz are 1 m apart. The sources are in phase.

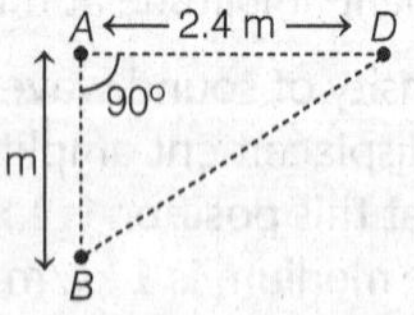

(a) Determine the phase difference between the waves emitting from A and B received by detector D as shown in figure.

(b) Also determine the intensity of the resultant sound wave as recorded by detector D.

Velocity of sound = 340 m/s.

2. Two coherent sources are placed at the corners of a rectangular track of sides 3 m and 4 m. The source S_1 lags S_2 by phase angle π. A detector is moved along path ABC. Then, find

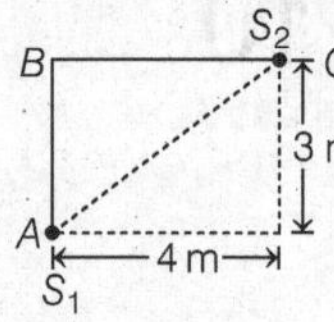

(a) the position of detector, where the phase difference between the sound waves of sources S_1 and S_2 is zero.

(b) Find the ratio of total number of minima detected on line AB to the total number of minima on line BC.

[Velocity of sound = 330 m/s, Frequency of sources S_1 and $S_2 = 165$ Hz]

3. Figure shows a tube having sound source at one end and observer at other end. Source produces frequencies upto 10000 Hz. Speed of sound is 400 m/s. Find the frequencies at which person hears maximum intensity.

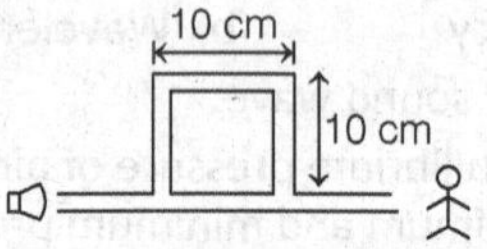

4. Sound of wavelength λ passes through a Quincke's tube, which is adjusted to give a maximum intensity I_0. Find the distance through which the sliding tube should be moved to give an intensity $\frac{I_0}{2}$.

5. Two identical loudspeakers are located at points A and B, 2 m apart. The loudspeakers are driven by the same amplifier (coherent and are in phase). A small detector is moved out from point B along a line perpendicular to the line connecting A and B. Taking speed of sound in air as 332 m/s, find the frequency below which there will be no position along the line BC at which destructive interference occurs.

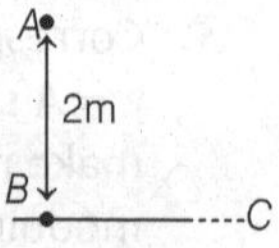

6. Two speakers are driven by the same oscillator with frequency of 200 Hz. They are located 4 m apart on a vertical pole. A man walks straight towards the lower speaker in a direction perpendicular to the pole, as shown in figure.

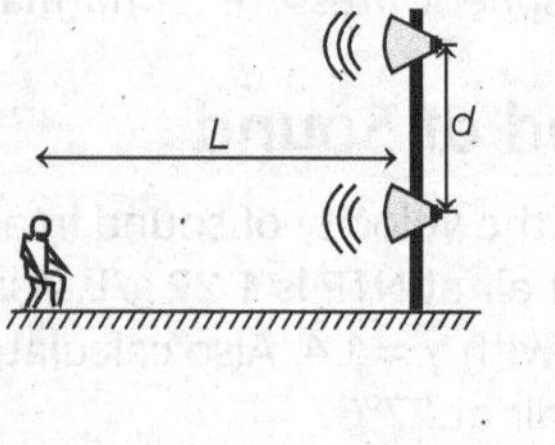

(a) How many times will he hear a minimum in sound intensity, and

(b) How far is he from the pole at these moments? Take the speed of sound to be 330 m/s and ignore any sound reflections coming of the ground.

7. Two sources of sound, S_1 and S_2, emitting waves of equal wavelength 2 cm, are placed with a separation of 3 cm between them. A detector can be moved on a line parallel to S_1S_2 and at a distance of 24 cm from it. Initially, the detector is equidistant from the two sources. Assuming that the waves emitted by the sources are in phase, find the minimum distance through which the detector should be shifted to detect a minimum of sound.

8. Two coherent sources S_1 and S_2 (in phase with each other) are placed at a distance of 2λ as shown, where λ is wavelength of sound. A detector moves on line AB parallel to S_1S_2. Find the θ, where detector detects maximum intensity at finite distance from O.

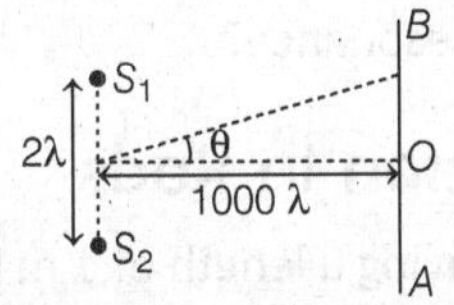

9. A source emitting sound of frequency 180 Hz is placed in front of a wall at a distance of 2 m from it. A detector is also placed in front of the wall at the same distance from it. Find the minimum distance between the source and the detector for which the detector detects a maximum of sound. Speed of sound in air = 360 m/s.

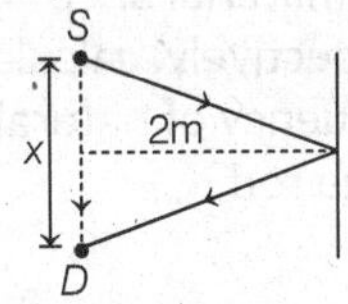

10.6 Equation of Stationary Sound Waves

1. The equation of a longitudinal standing wave due to superposition of the progressive waves produced by two sources of sound is $s = -20 \sin 10\pi x \sin 100\pi t$, where s is the displacement from mean position measured in mm, x is in m and t is in s. The specific gravity of the medium is 10^{-3}. Density of water $= 10^3$ kg/m^3. Find

(a) wavelength, frequency and velocity of the progressive waves.

(b) bulk modulus of the medium and the pressure amplitude.

(c) minimum distance between pressure antinode and a displacement antinode.

2. A metallic rod of length 1 m is rigidly clamped at its end points. Longitudinal stationary waves are setup in the rod in such a way that there are five antinodes of displacement wave observed along the rod. The amplitude of the antinode is 2×10^{-6} m. Write the equation of the stationary waves.

[Young's modulus $= 2 \times 10^{11}$ N/m^2, density $= 8000$ kg/m^3]

10.7 Organ Pipes

1. In an organ pipe the distance between the adjacent nodes is 4 cm. Find the frequency of source if speed of sound in air is 336 m/s.

2. Find the fundamental, first overtone and second overtone frequencies of an organ pipe of length 80 cm if the pipe is

(a) open at both ends.

(b) closed at one end.

The speed of sound in air is 320 m/s.

3. Find the number of possible natural oscillations of air column in a closed pipe, whose frequencies lie below $f_0 = 1250$ Hz. The length of the pipe is $L = 85$ cm. The velocity of sound is $v = 340$ m/s.

4. Two adjacent resonance frequencies of an open organ pipe are 1800 Hz and 2100 Hz. Find the length of the tube. The speed of sound in air is 330 m/s.

5. For a certain organ pipe, three successive resonant frequencies are observed at 425 Hz, 595 Hz and 765 Hz respectively. Taking the speed for sound in air to be 340 m/s,

(a) explain whether the pipe is closed at one end or open at both ends

(b) determine the fundamental frequency and length of the pipe.

6. Two pipes P_1 and P_2 are closed and open respectively. P_1 has a length of 30 cm. Find the length of P_2, if third harmonic of P_1 is same as first overtone of P_2.

7. A cylindrical resonance tube open at both ends has a fundamental frequency f in air. Half of the length of the tube is dipped vertically in water. What will be the fundamental frequency of the air column now?

8. A closed organ pipe of length $L = 100$ cm is cut into two unequal pieces. The fundamental frequency of the new closed organ pipe piece is found to be same as the frequency of first overtone of the open organ pipe piece. Determine the length of the two pieces and the fundamental tone of the open pipe piece. Take, velocity of sound = 320 m/s.
9. A standing wave in second overtone is maintained in a open organ pipe of length L. What will be the distance between consecutive displacement node and pressure node?
10. A closed organ pipe has length L. The air in it is vibrating in 3rd overtone with maximum amplitude a. Find the amplitude at a distance of $L/7$ from closed end of the pipe.
11. A 0.5 m wire of mass 5g in its second overtone is in resonance with organ pipe of 1 m in its fundamental mode. Find the tension in wire if speed of sound in air is 320 m/s.

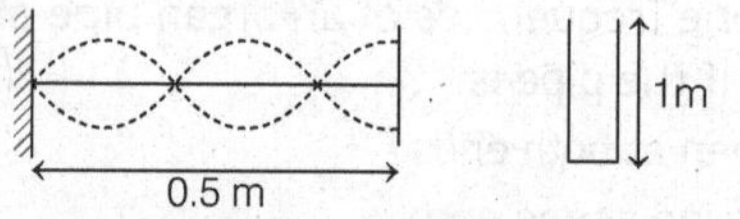

10.8 End Correction

1. A tube of certain diameter and of length 48 cm is open at both ends. Its fundamental frequency of resonance is found to be 320 Hz. The velocity of sound in air is 320 m/s. What is the diameter of the tube?
2. An open pipe 40 cm long and a closed pipe 31 cm long, both having same diameter, are producing their first overtone, and these are in unison. Determine the end correction of these pipes.

10.9 Resonance Tube

1. A tuning fork vibrating at frequency 800 Hz produces resonance in a resonance column tube. The upper end is open and the lower end is closed by the water surface which can be changed. Successive resonances are observed at lengths 9.75 cm, 31.25 cm and 52.75 cm. Calculate the speed of sound in air from these data.
2. A resonance occurs with a tuning fork and an air column of size 12 cm. The next higher resonance occurs with an air column of 38 cm. What is the frequency of the tuning fork? Assume that the speed of sound is 312 m/s.

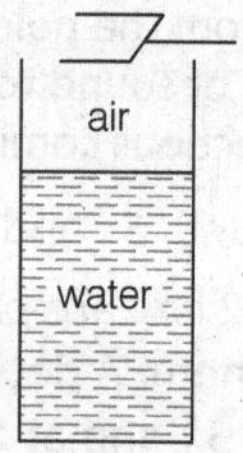

3. A resonance tube is resonated with tuning fork of frequency 256 Hz. If the length of first and second resonating air columns are 32 cm and 100 cm, then what is the end correction?
4. The first resonance length of a resonance tube is 40 cm and the second resonance length is 122 cm. What will be the third resonance length of the tube?
5. A tuning fork of frequency 340 Hz is vibrated just above a cylindrical tube of length 120 cm. Water is slowly poured in the tube. If the speed of sound is 340 ms^{-1}, then what is the minimum height of water required for resonance?

10.10 Vibration in Rods

1. A steel rod having a length of 1 m is fastened at its middle. Assuming Young's modulus to be 2×10^{11} Pa and density to be 8 g/cm^3, find the fundamental frequency of the longitudinal vibration and frequency of first overtone.
2. A metal rod of length $l = 100$ cm is clamped at two points. Distance of each clamp from nearer end is $a = 30$ cm. If density and Young's modulus of elasticity of rod material are $\rho = 9000$ kg m^{-3} and $Y = 144$ GPa respectively, calculate minimum and next higher frequency of natural longitudinal oscillations of the rod.

10.11 Beats

1. What is the speed of sound in a gas, in which two waves of wavelength 1.0 m and 1.02 m produce 6 beats per second?
2. Two tuning fork having frequency 300 Hz and 305 Hz produce beat phenomena. Then,
   (a) how many beats are produced in 5 s?
   (b) determine minimum time interval in which maximum intensity become minimum.
3. Tuning fork A when sounded with a tuning fork B of frequency 480 Hz gives 5 beats per second. When

the prongs of A are loaded with wax, it gives 3 beats per second. Find the frequency of A before and after loading.

4. Tuning fork A having frequency 158 Hz, produces 3 beats/s with another tuning fork B. As we file the arm of B, beats become 7 per second then calculate the frequency of B.

5. Two strings X and Y of a sitar produces a beat of frequency 4 Hz. When the tension of string Y is slightly increased, the beat frequency is found to be 2 Hz. If the frequency of X is 300 Hz, then what is the original frequency of Y?

6. Length of a sonometer wire is either 95 cm or 100 cm. In both the cases a tuning fork produces 4 beats per second, then what will be the frequency of tuning fork?

7. A metal wire is held on two knife edges separated by a distance of 50 cm. The tension in the wire is 100 N. The wire vibrating in its fundamental frequency and a vibrating tuning fork together produces 5 beats per second. The tension in the wire is, then reduced to 81 N. When the two are excited, beats are produced again at the same rate. Calculate the frequency of the fork.

8. Two identical piano wires have a fundamental frequency of 600 vib/sec, when kept under the same tension. What fractional increase in the tension of one wire will lead to the occurrence of six beats per second, when both wires vibrate simultaneously?

9. A string 25 cm long fixed at both ends and having a mass of 2.5 g is under tension. A pipe closed from one end is 40 cm long. When the string is set vibrating in its first overtone and the air in the pipe in its fundamental frequency, 8 beats per second are heard. It is observed that decreasing the tension in the string decreases the beat frequency. If the speed of sound in air is 320 m/s, find tension in the string.

LEVEL 02 JEE Main Level

Single Choice Correct Questions

1. For displacement(s)-x graph shown for a sound wave, select appropriate excess pressure (p)-x graph.

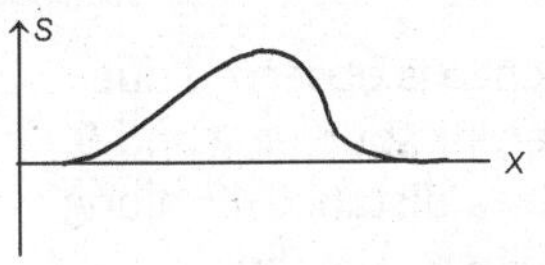

(a) 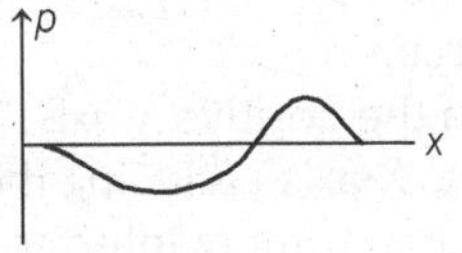

(b) 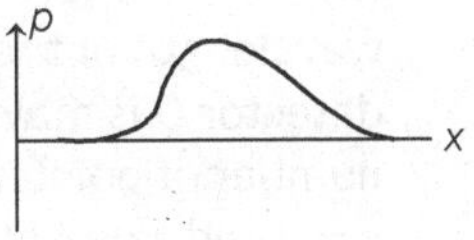

(c) 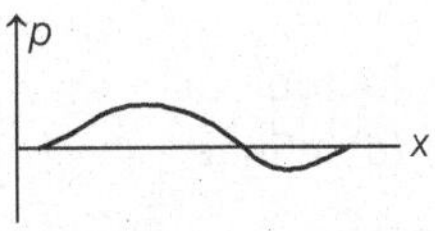

(d) 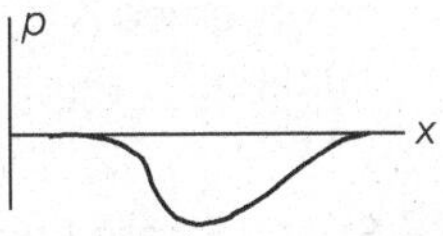

2. The velocity of sound at temperature 27°C is v, then velocity will be $2v$, at

(a) 54°C (b) 327°C
(c) 927°C (d) –123°C

3. The temperature at which the speed of sound will be same in oxygen as the speed in nitrogen at 15°C is

(a) 561°C (b) 56.1°C
(c) 5.61°C (d) 5.061°C

4. The speed of sound in hydrogen at STP is v. The speed of sound in a mixture containing 3 parts of hydrogen and 2 parts of oxygen at STP will be

(a) $\frac{v}{2}$ (b) $\frac{v}{\sqrt{5}}$
(c) $\sqrt{7}v$ (d) $\frac{v}{\sqrt{7}}$

5. The equations of two displacement sound waves propagating in a medium are given by $s_1 = 2\sin(200\pi t)$ and $s_2 = 5\sin(150\pi t)$. The ratio of intensities of sound produced is

(a) 4 : 25 (b) 9 : 100
(c) 8 : 15 (d) 64 : 225

6. A 10 W source of sound of frequency 1000 Hz and sends out waves in air. The displacement amplitude at a distance of 10 m from the source is (speed of sound in air = 340 m/s and density of air = 1.29 kg/m^3)

(a) 0.62 μm (b) 4.2 μm (c) 1.6 μm (d) 0.96 μm

7. The intensity of a plane progressive wave of frequency 1 kHz is 10^{-10} W/m^2. If the density of air is 1.3 kg/m^3 and the speed of sound is equal to 330 m/s, then pressure amplitude of the wave is

(a) 3×10^{-5} N/m^2 (b) 3×10^{-4} N/m^2
(c) 3×10^{-6} N/m^2 (d) 3×10^{-3} N/m^2

8. A 40 dB sound wave strikes an eardrum whose area is 10^{-6} m^2. To receive a total enery of 1 J, time received is ($I_0 = 10^{-12}$ W/m^2)
(a) 10^{-8} s (b) 10^{10} s (c) 10^6 s (d) 10^{14} s

9. The power of sound from the speaker of a radio is 20 MW by tuning the knob of the volume control, the power of the sound is increased to 400 MW. The power increase in decibel as compared to the original power is
(a) 13 dB (b) 10 dB
(c) 20 dB (d) 800 dB

10. A listener *X* hears a sound level of 50 dB when he is at a distance 1 km from the instrument. Another listener *Y* at a distance 10 km from the listener *X* hears a sound level of
(a) 30 dB (b) 20 dB
(c) 10 dB (d) 5 dB

11. A person is talking in a small room and the sound intensity level is 60 dB everywhere within the room. If there are eight people talking simultaneously in the room, what is the sound intensity level?
(a) 60 dB (b) 69 dB
(c) 74 dB (d) 81 dB

12. In a city, sound intensity level increases uniformly by about 1 dB annually. How many years will it take for intensity of sound to become double?
(a) 1 year (b) 2 year
(c) 3 year (d) 4 year

13. The ratio of intensities between two coherent sound sources is 4 : 1. The difference of loudness in dB between maximum and minimum intensities when they interfere in space is
(a) 10 log 2 (b) 20 log 3
(c) 10 log 3 (d) 20 log 2

14. Two waves of sound having intensities *I* and 4*I* interfere to produce interference pattern. The phase difference between the waves is $\pi/2$ at point *A* and π at point *B*. Then, the difference between the resultant intensities at *A* and *B* is
(a) 2*I* (b) 4*I*
(c) 5*I* (d) 7*I*

15. Sources P and Q emit radio waves of wavelength 200 m, with the phase of emission from P ahead of that from source Q by 90°. The distance r_1 from P to detector at A is greater than the corresponding distance r_2 by 50 m. The phase difference between the waves reaching *A* is

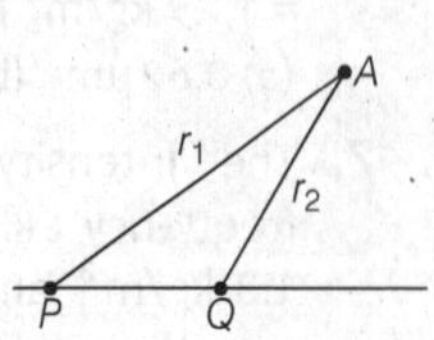

(a) 0 (b) π
(c) $\frac{\pi}{2}$ (d) $\frac{\pi}{4}$

16. Sound signal is sent through a composite tube as shown in the figure. The radius of the semicircular portion of the tube is *r*. Speed of sound in air is *v*. The source of sound is capable of giving varied frequencies in the range of n_1 and n_2 (where $n_2 > n_1$). If *n* is an integer, then frequency for maximum intensity is given by

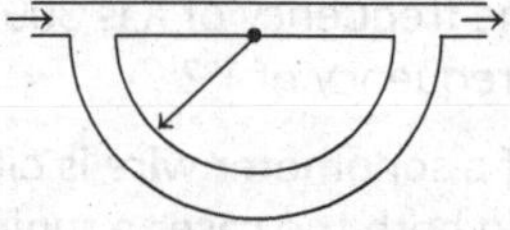

(a) $\frac{nv}{r}$ (b) $\frac{nv}{r(\pi - 2)}$
(c) $\frac{nv}{\pi r}$ (d) $\frac{nv}{(r-2)\pi}$

17. Sound waves from a tuning fork *F* reach a point *P* by two separate routes *FAP* and *FBP*. When *FBP* is greater than *FAP* by 12 cm, there is silence at *P*. If the difference is 24 cm, the sound becomes maximum at *P* but at 36 cm, there is silence again and so on. If velocity of sound in air is 330 ms^{-1}, the least frequency of tuning fork is
(a) 1537 Hz (b) 1735 Hz
(c) 1400 Hz (d) 1375 Hz

18. An interference is observed due to two coherent sources A and B separated by a distance 4λ along the *Y*-axis, where λ is the wavelength of the source. A detector *D* is moved on the positive *X*-axis. The number of points on the *X*-axis excluding the points, $x = 0$ and $x = \infty$ at which maximum interference will be observed is

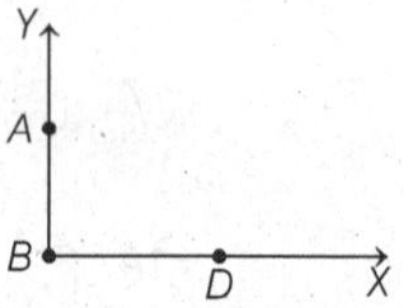

(a) three (b) four
(c) two (d) infinite

19. S_1 and S_2 are two coherent sources of sound. $OA = OB$. $AB = 2.7\lambda$, when λ is the wavelength of sound waves. Number of points of maximum intensity as one moves around the circular path centered at O shown in the figure will be

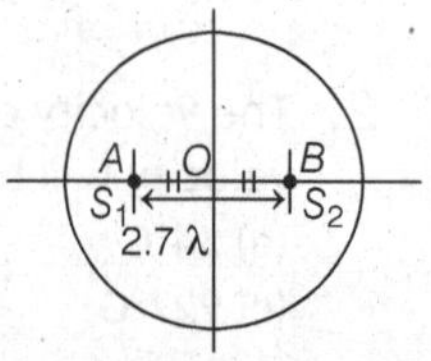

(a) 12 (b) 9
(c) 10 (d) 11

20. Two loudspeakers are emitting sound waves of wavelength λ with an initial phase difference of $\frac{\pi}{2}$. At what minimum distance from O on line AB will one hear a maxima?

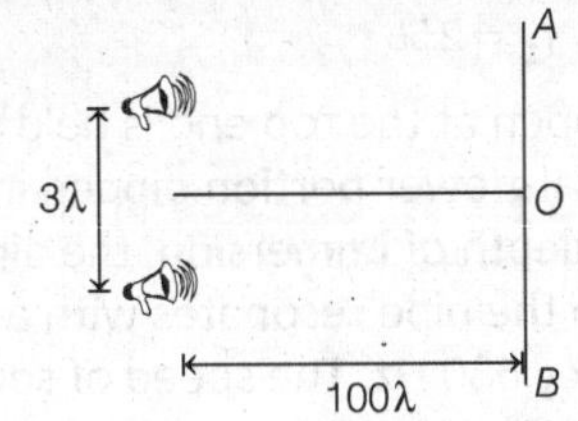

(a) 25λ (b) $\frac{100\lambda}{\sqrt{15}}$
(c) $\frac{25\lambda}{3}$ (d) 50λ

21. In a hall, a person receives direct sound waves from a source 120 m away. He also receives waves from the same source which reach him after being reflected from the 25 m high ceiling at a point half way between them. The two waves interfere constructively for wavelength (in m).
(a) 10, 10/2, 10/3, 10/4, ...
(b) 20, 20/3, 20/5, 20/7, ...
(c) 30, 20, 10, ...
(d) 10, 10/3, 10/5, 10/7,...

22. In Quincke's tube, a detector detects minimum intensity. Now, one of the tubes is displaced by 5 cm. During displacement, detector detects maximum intensity 10 times, then finally a minimum intensity (when displacement is complete). The wavelength of sound is
(a) 10/9 cm (b) 1 cm
(c) 1/2 cm (d) 5/9 cm

23. The three lowest frequencies (in Hz) with which a 20 cm long pipe, closed at one end, can vibrate are (speed of sound = 340 m/s)
(a) 425, 850, 1275 (b) 425, 1275, 2125
(c) 900, 1800, 2700 (d) 900, 2700, 4500

24. An organ pipe closed at one end has fundamental frequency of 1400 Hz. The number of overtones a normal person can hear is
(a) 6 (b) 7 (c) 13 (d) 14

25. The fundamental frequency of a closed organ pipe is same as the first overtone frequency of an open pipe. If the length of open pipe is 50 cm, the length of closed pipe is
(a) 25 cm (b) 12.5 cm
(c) 100 cm (d) 200 cm

26. An organ pipe P_1, closed at one end, is vibrating in its first overtone. Another pipe P_2 open at both ends is vibrating in its third overtone. They are in a resonance with a given tuning fork. The ratio of the length of P_1 to that of P_2 is
(a) 8/3 (b) 3/8 (c) 1/2 (d) 1/3

27. An open pipe is suddenly closed at one end with the result that the frequency of third harmonic of the closed pipe is found to be higher by 100 Hz than the fundamental frequency of the open pipe. The fundamental frequency of the open pipe is
(a) 200 Hz (b) 300 Hz
(c) 240 Hz (d) 480 Hz

28. A pipe open at both ends has a fundamental resonant frequency $= f$. One-third length of the pipe is now immersed in a dense liquid, while the upper end is kept open. The new fundamental frequency of the air column in the pipe will be
(a) $3f$ (b) $\frac{2f}{3}$ (c) $\frac{f}{3}$ (d) $\frac{3f}{4}$

29. An open pipe resonates with frequency 100 Hz and a closed pipe resonates with frequency 50 Hz. If they are joined to form a longer tube, then it will resonate with frequency of (neglect end corrections)
(a) 25 Hz (b) 50 Hz (c) 75 Hz (d) 100 Hz

30. Four open organ pipes of different lengths and different gases at same temperature as shown in figure. Let, f_A, f_B, f_C and f_D be their fundamental frequencies, then [Take $\gamma_{CO_2} = 7/5$]

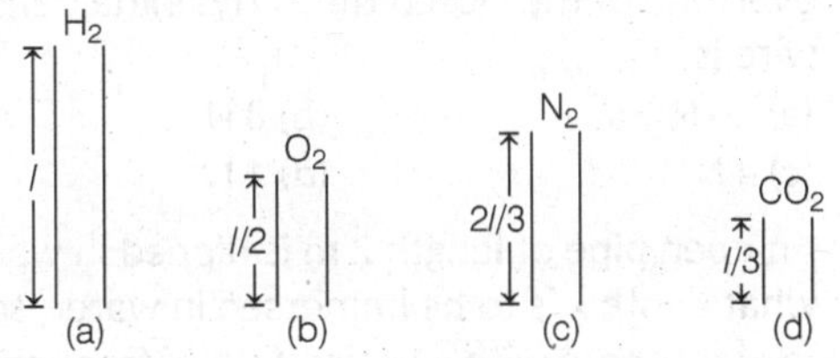

(a) $\frac{f_A}{f_B} = \sqrt{2}$ (b) $\frac{f_B}{f_C} = \sqrt{\frac{72}{28}}$
(c) $\frac{f_C}{f_D} = \sqrt{\frac{11}{28}}$ (d) $\frac{f_D}{f_A} = \sqrt{\frac{76}{11}}$

31. An ideal organ pipe resonates at successive frequencies of 50 Hz, 150 Hz, 250 Hz, etc. (speed of sound = 340 m/s). The pipe is
(a) open at both ends and of length 3.4 m.
(b) open at both ends and of length 6.8 m.
(c) closed at one end, open at the other and of length 1.7 m.
(d) closed at one end, open at the other and of length 3.4 m.

32. A train of sound waves is propagated along a wide pipe and it is reflected from an open end. If the displacement amplitude of the wave is 0.002 cm, the frequency 1000 Hz and the wavelength 40 cm, then the displacement amplitude of vibration at a point at distance 10 cm from open end and inside the pipe will be

(a) 0.004 cm (b) 0.001 cm
(c) 0 (d) 0.002 cm

33. A closed organ pipe is vibrating in its second overtone. The length of the pipe is 10 cm and maximum amplitude of vibration of particles of the air in the pipe is 2 mm. Then, the amplitude of SHM of the particles at 9 cm from the open end is

(a) $\sqrt{3}$ mm (b) $\sqrt{2}$ mm
(c) $\frac{\sqrt{3}}{2}$ mm (d) None of these

34. A closed organ pipe of length 1.2 m vibrates in its first overtone mode. The pressure variation is maximum at

(a) 0.8 m from the open end.
(b) 0.4 m from the open end.
(c) at the open end.
(d) 1.0 m from the open end.

35. The frequency of a stretched uniform wire under tension is in resonance with the fundamental frequency of a closed tube. If the tension in the wire is increased by 8 N, it is in resonance with first overtone of the closed tube. The initial tension in the wire is

(a) 16 N (b) 8 N
(c) 4 N (d) 1 N

36. An open pipe of length 2 m is dipped in water. To what depth x is to be immersed in water, so that it may resonate with a tuning fork of frequency 170 Hz, when vibrating in its first overtone. Speed of sound in air is 340 m/s

(a) 0.5 m (b) 0.75 m
(c) 1 m (d) 1.5 m

37. An open pipe of length 24 cm is in resonance with a frequency 660 Hz in fundamental mode. The radius of pipe is (speed of sound in air = 330 ms^{-1})

(a) 3 cm (b) 0.83 cm
(c) 3.5 cm (d) 2 cm

38. A closed organ pipe of radius r_1 and an open organ pipe of radius r_2 and having same length L resonate, when excited with a given tuning fork. Closed organ pipe resonates in its fundamental mode whereas open organ pipe resonates in its first overtone, then

(a) $r_2 - r_1 = L$
(b) $r_2 - r_1 = L/2$
(c) $r_2 - 2r_1 = 2.5L$
(d) $2r_2 - r_1 = 2.5L$

39. A pipe open at the top end is held vertically with some of its lower portion dipped in water. At a certain depth of immersion, the air column of length 3/8 m in the pipe resonates with a tuning fork of frequency 680 Hz. The speed of sound in air is 340 m/s. The pipe is now raised up by a distance x until it resonates in the next overtone with the same tuning fork. The value of x is

(a) 20 cm (b) 40 cm
(c) 50 cm (d) 25 cm

40. An open pipe resonates with a tuning fork of frequency 500 Hz. It is observed that two successive notes are formed at distance 16 cm and 46 cm from the open end. The speed of sound in air in the pipe is

(a) 230 m/s (b) 300 m/s
(c) 320 m/s (d) 360 m/s

41. A tuning fork with a frequency of $f = 850$ Hz sounds above a cylindrical pipe one metre high. Water is slowly poured into the pipe. At what minimum level of the water in the pipe will the sound of the tuning fork be appreciably intensified?

Take, $v_{\text{sound}} = 340$ m/s and neglect end correction.

(a) 5 cm (b) 10 cm
(c) 20 cm (d) 35 cm

42. A long tube at the top is fixed vertically and water level inside the tube can be moved up or down. A vibrating tuning fork is held above the open end and the water level is pushed down gradually, so as to get first and second resonance at 24.1 cm and 74.1 cm, respectively below the open end. The diameter of the tube is

(a) 5 cm (b) 4 cm
(c) 3 cm (d) 2 cm

43. In a resonance tube experiment, the first two resonances are observed at length 10.5 cm and 29.5 cm. The third resonance is observed at the length .... (cm).

(a) 47.5 (b) 58.5
(c) 48.5 (d) 82.8

44. A glass tube of 1.0 m length is filled with water. The water can be drained out slowly at the bottom of the tube. If a vibrating tuning fork of frequency 500 c/s is brought at the upper end of the tube and the velocity of sound is 330 m/s, then the total number of resonances obtained will be

(a) 4 (b) 3
(c) 2 (d) 1

45. A long cylindrical tube is mounted vertically and contains water. The cylinder has radius 2.5 cm. A tuning fork of frequency 170 Hz is placed at the open end of the tube. Water is draining from the tube at a constant rate of 55 cm^3/s. If the speed of sound is 340 m/s, how much time passes between consecutive resonances as the water drains?

(a) $\frac{125}{7}$ s (b) $\frac{375}{11}$ s
(c) $\frac{250}{7}$ s (d) $\frac{250}{11}$ s

46. If L_1 and L_2 are the lengths of air column for the first and second resonance, when a tuning fork of frequency n is sounded on a resonance tube, then the distance of the displacement antinode from the top end of the resonance tube is

(a) $2(L_2 - L_1)$ (b) $\frac{1}{2}(2L_1 - L_2)$
(c) $\frac{L_2 - 3L_1}{2}$ (d) $\frac{L_2 - L_1}{2}$

47. In a resonance column method, resonance occurs at two successive levels of $l_1 = 30.7$ cm and $l_2 = 63.2$ cm using a tuning fork of $f = 512$ Hz. What is the maximum error in measuring speed of sound using relations $v = f\lambda$ and $\lambda = 2(l_2 - l_1)$?

(a) 256 cm/s (b) 92 cm/s
(c) 128 cm/s (d) 102.4 cm/s

48. A 100 m long rod of density 10.0×10^4 kg/m^3 and having Young's modulus $Y = 10^{11}$ Pa, is clamped at one end. It is hammered at the other free end. The longitudinal pulse goes to right end, gets reflected and again returns to the left end. How much time the pulse takes to go back to initial point?

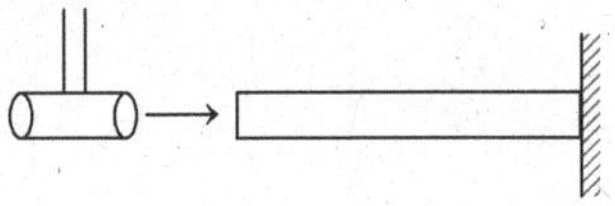

(a) 0.1 s (b) 0.2 s
(c) 0.3 s (d) 2s

49. In a Kundt's tube, the length of the iron rod is 1 m. The stationary waves of frequency 2500 Hz are produced in it. The velocity of sound in iron is

(a) 1250 m/s (b) 2500 m/s
(c) 5000 m/s (d) 10000 m/s

50. Wavelengths of two notes in air are 1 m and $1\frac{1}{164}$ m. Each note produces 1 beat per second with a third note of a fixed frequency. The speed of sound in air is

(a) 330 m/s (b) 340 m/s
(c) 350 m/s (d) 328 m/s

51. Two vibrating tuning forks produce progressive waves given by $y_1 = 4 \sin 500\pi t$ and $y_2 = 2 \sin 506\pi t$. Number of beats produced per minute is

(a) 3 (b) 360
(c) 180 (d) 60

52. When beats are produced by two progressive waves of nearly the same frequency, which one of the following is correct?

(a) The amplitude of vibrations at any point changes simple harmonically with a frequency equal to the difference in frequencies of the two waves.
(b) The particles vibrate simple harmonically, with the frequency equal to the difference in the component frequencies.
(c) The frequency of beats depends on the position, where the observer is.
(d) The frequency of beats changes as the time progresses.

53. The number of beats heard per second, if there are three sources of sound of frequencies $(n-1)$, n and $(n+1)$ of equal intensities sounded together is

(a) 2 (b) 1 (c) 4 (d) 3

54. Two tuning forks of frequency 250 Hz and 256 Hz are sounded together. What shall be the time interval between maximum and minimum sound at a point?

(a) 6 s (b) 3 s
(c) 1/6 s (d) 1/12 s

55. Two tuning forks A and B produce notes of frequencies 256 Hz and 262 Hz respectively. An unknown note sounded with A produces certain beats. When the same note is sounded with B, beat frequency is twice as large. The unknown frequency could be

(a) 268 Hz (b) 260 Hz
(c) 250 Hz (d) 242 Hz

56. Frequency of tuning fork A is 256 Hz. It produces 4 beats per second with tuning fork B. When wax is applied at tuning fork B, then 2 beats per second are heard. Frequency of B is

(a) 250 Hz (b) 260 Hz
(c) 252 Hz
(d) (b) and (c) both may be possible

57. Two parts of a sonometer wire divided by a movable bridge differ in length by 0.2 cm and produce one beat per second, when sounded together. The total length of wire is 1 m, then the frequencies are

(a) 250.5 and 249.5 Hz (b) 230.5 and 229.5 Hz
(c) 220.5 and 219.5 Hz (d) 210.5 and 209.5 Hz

58. Two instruments having stretched strings are being played in unison. When, the tension in one of the instruments is increased by 1%, 3 beats are produced in 2 s. The initial frequency of vibration of each wire is

(a) 600 Hz (b) 300 Hz
(c) 200 Hz (d) 150 Hz

59. On vibrating an air column at 27°C and a tuning fork simultaneosuly, 5 beats per second are produced. The frequency of the fork is less than that of air column. No beats are heard at −3°C. The frequency of the fork is

(a) 70 Hz
(b) 147 Hz
(c) 104 Hz
(d) 90 Hz

60. Match the Column A and B.

Column A		Column B	
(A)	Pitch	(i)	Quality
(B)	Loudness	(ii)	Intensity
(C)	Waveform	(iii)	Frequency

(a) A-(i), B-(iii), C-(ii) (b) A-(i), B-(ii), C-(iii)
(c) A-(iii), B-(ii), C-(i) (d) A-(iii), B-(i), C-(ii)

Numerical Value Questions

1. Two identical sounds A and B reach a point in the same phase. The resultant sound is C. The loudness of C is n dB higher than the loudness of A. Find the value of n.

2. Two point sound sources S_1 and S_2 are both of same power and send out sound waves in the same phase. The wavelength of both the waves is $\frac{48}{5}$ m. The intensity due to S_2 alone at D is 25 W/m^2. The resultant intensity at D is I. Find I (in W/m^2).

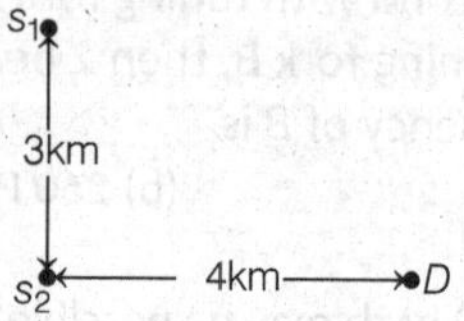

3. A sound source, detector and a cardboard are arranged as shown in figure. The wave is reflected from the cardboard at the line of symmetry of source and detector. Initially the path difference between the reflected wave and the direct wave is one third of the wavelength of sound. Find the minimum distance (in cm) by which the cardboard should be moved upwards, so that both waves are in phase.

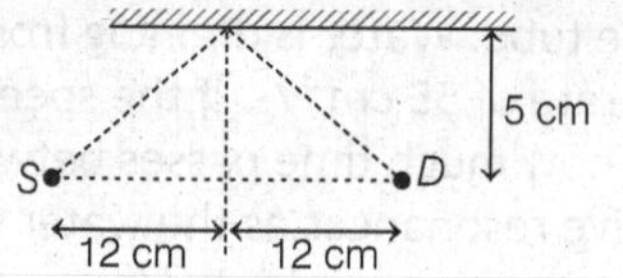

4. nth harmonic of a closed organ pipe is equal to mth harmonic of a open pipe. First overtone frequency of the closed organ pipe is also equal to first overtone frequency of the open organ pipe. Find the value of n, if $m = 6$.

5. A U-tube having uniform cross-section but unequal arm length $l_1 = 100$ cm and $l_2 = 50$ cm has same liquid of density ρ_1 filled in it upto a height $h = 30$ cm as shown in figure. Another liquid of density $\rho_2 = \rho_1 / 2$ is poured in arm A. Both liquids are immiscible. What length of the second liquid (in cm) should be poured in A, so that second overtone of A is in unison with fundamental tone of B? (Neglect end correction)

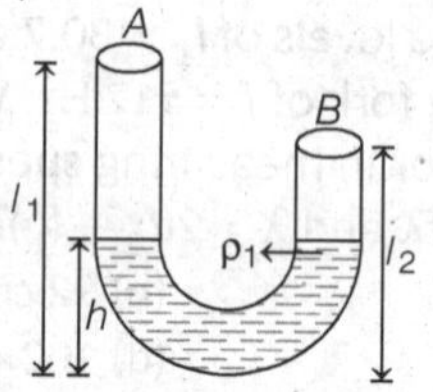

6. A closed organ pipe is vibrating in fundamental mode. There are two points A and B in the organ pipe as shown, at a distance $AB = \frac{L}{n}$. Ratio of maximum pressure variation at point A to point B is $\frac{2}{\sqrt{3}}$. Find value of n.

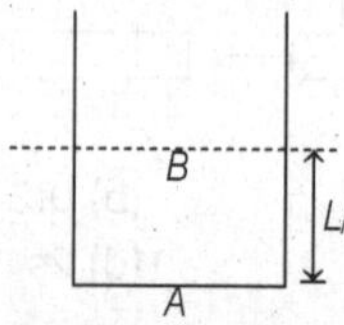

7. In a resonance column apparatus, first resonance is obtained when the water filling beaker (of cylindrical shape) is just empty as shown. The water filling beaker is lowered down and it is seen that second resonance is obtained when beaker is filled upto brim. If the tuning fork has a frequency 420 Hz, what is the velocity (in m/s) of sound in air?

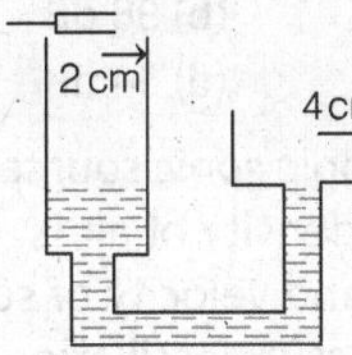

8. A set of 56 tuning forks are arranged in a series of increasing order of their frequencies. If each fork gives 4 beats with preceding one and frequency of the last one is twice that of the first. What is the frequency (in Hz) of the 3rd fork?

9. A closed and an open organ pipe of same length are set into vibrations simultaneously in their fundamental mode to produce 2 beats per second. The length of open organ pipe is now halved and of closed organ pipe is doubled. Now find the number of beats produced per second.

10. A string 25 cm long, having a mass of 0.25 g/cm, is under tension. A pipe closed at one end is 40 cm long. When the string is set vibrating in its first overtone, and the air in the pipe is in its fundamental frequency, 8 beats per second are heard. It is observed that decreasing the tension in the string, decreases the beat frequency. If the speed of sound in air is 320 m/s, find the tension (in N) in the string.

LEVEL 03 JEE Advanced Level

Single Choice Correct Questions

1. A girl stands 130 m away from a high wall. She claps her hands together at steady rate such that 37 claps are made in 30 s, starting at time $t = 0$ and ending at $t = 30$ s. Each clap, except the first, coincides with the echo of the one before. Calculate the speed of sound

(a) 320 m/s (b) 327 m/s (c) 340 m/s (d) 312 m/s

2. A sound wave is travelling in a uniform pipe with gas of adiabatic exponent γ. If u is particle velocity at any point in medium and c is wave velocity, then relative change in pressure dp/p while wave passes through this point is

(a) $\dfrac{u}{\gamma c}$ (b) $\gamma\sqrt{\dfrac{u}{c}}$ (c) $\dfrac{\gamma u}{c}$ (d) $\dfrac{u^2}{\gamma c^2}$

3. How long will it take sound waves to travel the distance l between the points A and B if the air temperature between them varies linearly from T_1 to T_2? The velocity of sound propagation in air is equal to $v = \alpha\sqrt{T}$, where α is constant.

(a) $t = \dfrac{2l}{\alpha[\sqrt{T_2} + \sqrt{T_1}]}$ (b) $t = \dfrac{4l}{\alpha[\sqrt{T_1} + \sqrt{T_2}]}$

(c) $t = \dfrac{4l}{\alpha[\sqrt{T_1}\sqrt{T_2}]}$ (d) $t = \dfrac{2l}{\alpha[\sqrt{T_1 + T_2}]}$

4. A plane progressive sound wave of frequency 160 Hz is moving along vector $3\hat{i} + 4\hat{j}$. Find the phase difference between point $A(1, 0, 2)$ and point $B(3, 1, 4)$ is (Given, velocity of sound = 320 m/s)

(a) $\dfrac{\pi}{3}$ (b) $\dfrac{\pi}{2}$ (c) 2π (d) 3π

5. Figure represents the displacement y *versus* distance x along the direction of propagation of a longitudinal wave. The pressure is maximum at position marked

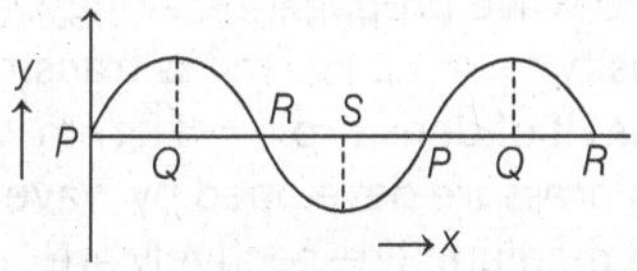

(a) P (b) Q (c) R (d) S

6. Figure shown is a graph, at a certain time t, of the displacement function $S(x, t)$ of three sound waves 1, 2 and 3 as marked on the curves that travel along X-axis through air. If p_1, p_2 and p_3 represent their pressure amplitudes respectively, then correct relation between them is

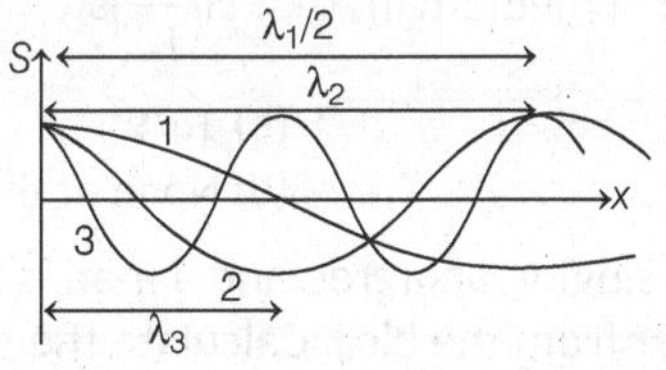

(a) $p_1 > p_2 > p_3$ (b) $p_3 > p_2 > p_1$
(c) $p_1 = p_2 = p_3$ (d) $p_2 > p_3 > p_1$

7. A plane longitudinal wave of angular frequency 10^3 rad/s is travelling along negative x-direction in a homogeneous gaseous medium of density $\rho = 1\,kg/m^3$. Intensity of the wave is $I = 10^{-10}\,W/m^2$ and maximum pressure change is $(\Delta p)_m = 2 \times 10^{-4}\,N/m^2$. Assuming at $x = 0$, initial phase of medium particles to be $\pi/2$, the equation of the wave is

(a) $y = 10^{-9} \sin\left(1000t - 5x + \frac{\pi}{2}\right)$
(b) $y = 10^{-9} \cos(1000t + 5x)$
(c) $y = 10^{-8} \tan(1000t - 50x)$
(d) $y = 10^{-8} \cos(1000t + 50x)$

8. A sound waves is travelling towards right and its s-t graph is as shown for $x = 0$. What will be density *versus* x graph at $T = T/4$?

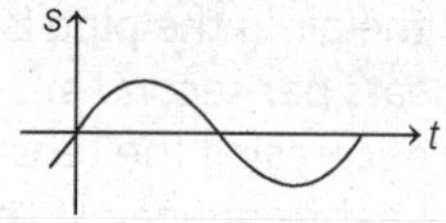

(a)
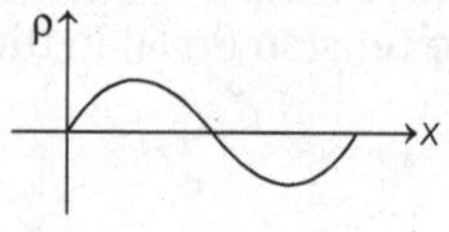

(b)
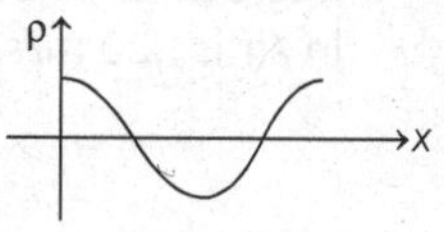

(c)
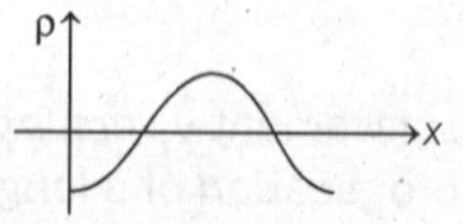

(d)
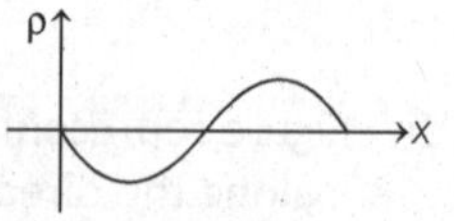

9. A sound wave propagating along X-axis, in medium I of density $\rho_1 = 1.5\ kg/m^3$ is transmitted to a medium II of density $\rho_2 = 3\ kg/m^3$. The equation of excess pressure developed by wave in medium I and that in medium II respectively are

$$p_1 = 4 \times 10^{-2} \cos\omega\left(t - \frac{x}{400}\right) \text{(in SI units)},$$

$$p_2 = 3 \times 10^{-2} \cos\omega\left(t - \frac{x}{1200}\right) \text{(in SI units)}$$

Then, the ratio of intensity of transmitted wave I_1 (wave in medium I) to the intensity of incident wave I_2 (wave in medium II), that is, $\frac{I_1}{I_2}$ is

(a) 4/3
(b) 16/9
(c) 32/3
(d) None of these

10. A bird is singing on a tree and a man is hearing at a distance r from the bird. Calculate the displacement of the man towards the bird, so that the loudness heard by man increases by 20 dB. Assume that the motion of man is along the line joining the bird and the man.

(a) $\frac{9r}{10}$
(b) $\frac{r}{10}$
(c) $\frac{3r}{5}$
(d) $\frac{4r}{5}$

11. 200 students are taking an examination in a room and the sounds of pens scratching on paper, sighs, groans and muttered imprecations has created a more or less continuous sound level of this noise of 60 dB. Assuming each student contributes equally to this noise and nothing else changes or adds to it, what will be sound level in the room be, when only 50 students are left? ($\log 2 = 0.3$)

(a) 40 dB
(b) 38 dB
(c) 48 dB
(d) 54 dB

12. Due to a point isotropic sonic source, loudness at a point is $L = 60$ dB. If density of air is $\rho = (15/11)\ kg/m^3$ and velocity of sound in air is $v = 330$ m/s, the pressure oscillation amplitude at the point of observation is $[I_0 = 10^{-12}\ W/m^2]$

(a) $0.3\ N/m^2$
(b) $0.03\ N/m^2$
(c) $3 \times 10^{-3}\ N/m^2$
(d) $3 \times 10^{-4}\ N/m^2$

13. Spherical sound waves are emitted uniformly in all directions from a point source. The variation in sound level SL as a function of distance r (> 0) from the source can be written as, where a and b are positive constant.

(a) $SL = -b \log r^a$
(b) $SL = a - b \log r$
(c) $SL = a - b(\log r)^2$
(d) $SL = a - \frac{b}{r^2}$

14. S_1 and S_2 are two coherent sound sources separated by distance 100.25λ, where λ is the wavelength of sound waves. S_1 leads S_2 in phase by $\pi/2$. A and B are two points on the line joining S_1 and S_2. The ratio of amplitude of sources S_1 and S_2 is in ratio 1 : 2. The ratio of intensity at A to that at B ($I_A : I_B$) is

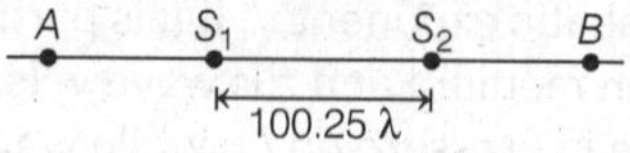

(a) ∞
(b) 1/9
(c) 0
(d) 9

15. When a sound wave is reflected from a wall, the phase difference between the reflected and incident pressure wave is

(a) 0
(b) $\frac{\pi}{4}$
(c) $\frac{\pi}{2}$
(d) π

16. A sound consists of four frequencies → 300 Hz, 600 Hz, 1200 Hz and 2400 Hz. A sound filter is made by passing this sound through a bifurcated pipe as shown. The sound waves have to travel a distance of 50 cm more in the right branch-pipe than in the straight pipe. The speed of sound in air is 300 m/s. Then, which of the following frequencies will be almost completely muffled or "silenced" at the outlet?

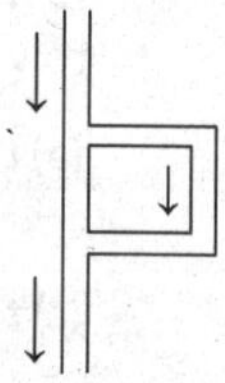

(a) 300 Hz
(b) 600 Hz
(c) 1200 Hz
(d) 2400 Hz

17. Radio waves coming at angle α to vertical are received by a ladder after reflection from a nearby water surface and also directly. What can be height of antenna from water surface so, that it records a maximum intensity (a maxima)? (wavelength = λ)

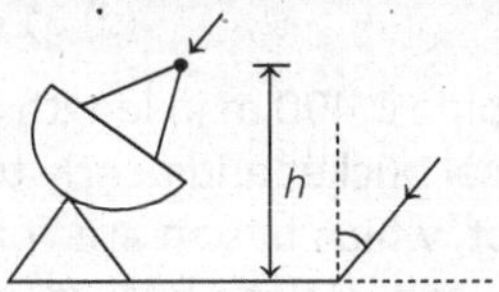

(a) $\frac{h}{2\cos\alpha}$ (b) $\frac{h}{2\sin\alpha}$

(c) $\frac{h}{4\sin\alpha}$ (d) $\frac{h}{4\cos\alpha}$

18. Two speakers connected to the same source of fixed frequency are placed 2 m apart in a box. A sensitive microphone placed at a distance of 4 m from the mid-point along the perpendicular bisector shows maximum response. The box is slowly rotated till the speakers are in line with the microphone. The distance between the mid-point of the speakers and the microphone remains unchanged. Exactly 5 maximum responses are observed in the microphone in doing this, the wavelength of the sound wave is

(a) 0.8 m (b) 0.4 m

(c) 0.2 m (d) 1.6 m

19. A loudspeaker which emits sound of frequency 1000 Hz is placed several metres from a plane reflecting wall *A* in a large chamber containing a gas. A small microphone *M*, detects a series of low and high intensity signals as it moves along the line joining the loudspeaker *B* and the wall. If the microphone detects tenth low intensity signals, while moving through a distance *S* of 2 m, what is the speed of sound in the chamber?

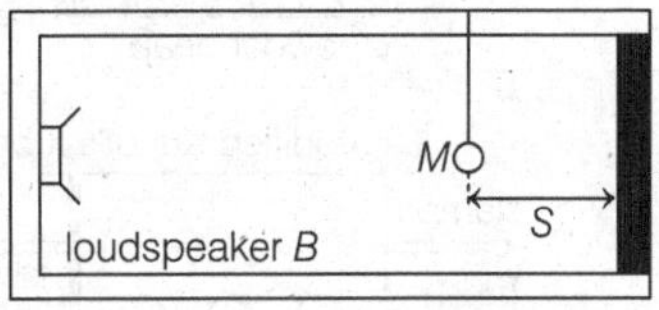

(a) 110 m/s (b) 220 m/s

(c) 330 m/s (d) 421 m/s

20. An open and a closed pipe have same length. The ratio of frequency of their *n*th overtone is

(a) $\frac{n+1}{2n+1}$ (b) $\frac{2(n+1)}{2n+1}$

(c) $\frac{n}{2n+1}$ (d) $\frac{n+1}{2n}$

21. An open pipe resonates to a frequency f_1 and a closed pipe resonates to a frequency f_2. If they are joined together to form a longer tube, then it will resonate to a frequency of (neglect end corrections)

(a) $\frac{f_1 f_2}{2f_2 + f_1}$ (b) $\frac{f_1 f_2}{f_2 + 2f_1}$

(c) $\frac{2f_1 f_2}{f_2 + f_1}$ (d) $\frac{f_1 + 2f_2}{f_1 f_2}$

22. A closed organ pipe of length *L* and an open organ pipe contain gases of densities ρ_1 and ρ_2 respectively. The compressibility of gases are equal in both the pipes. Both the pipes are vibrating in their first overtone with same frequency. The length of open organ pipe is

(a) $\frac{4L}{3}\left(\frac{\rho_1}{\rho_2}\right)^{1/2}$ (b) $\frac{4L}{3}\left(\frac{\rho_2}{\rho_1}\right)^{1/2}$

(c) $\frac{L}{3}$ (d) $\frac{4L}{3}$

23. An open pipe of sufficient length is dipping in water with a speed *v* vertically. If at any instant *l* is length of cube above water then the rate at which fundamental frequency of pipe changes is (*c* is the speed of sound in air)

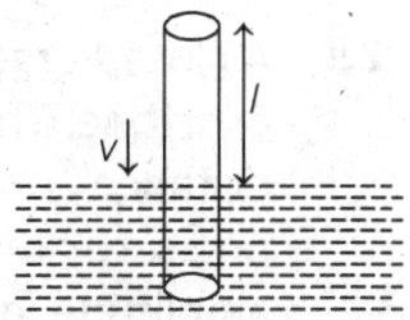

(a) $\frac{cv}{2l^2}$ (b) $\frac{cv}{4l^2}$ (c) $\frac{cv}{2v^2t^2}$ (d) $\frac{cv}{4v^2t^2}$

24. Which of the figures, which show the pressure difference from regular atmospheric pressure for an organ pipe of length *L* closed at one end, corresponds to the 1st overtone for the pipe?

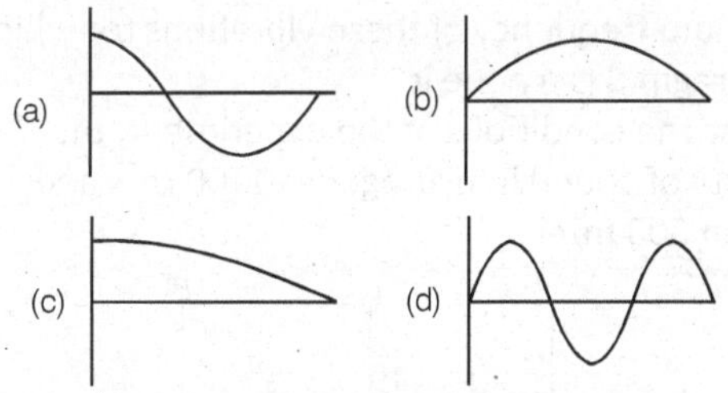

25. A longitudinal sound wave given by $p = 25 \sin \frac{\pi}{2}(x - 660t)$ (where *p* is in N/m^2, *x* is in m and *t* is in s) is sent down a closed organ pipe. If the pipe vibrates in second overtone, then the length of the pipe is

(a) 6 m (b) 8 m

(c) 5 m (d) 10 m

26. In an organ pipe whose one end is at $x = 0$, the pressure is expressed by

$p = p_0 \cos \frac{3\pi x}{2} \sin 300\pi t$, where x is in m and t is in s.

The organ pipe can be

(a) closed at one end, open at another with length = 0.5 m
(b) open at both ends, length = 1 m
(c) closed at both ends, length = 2 m
(d) closed at one end, open at another with length = 2/3 m

27. In a standing wave pattern obtained in a tube filled with iodine, due to vibrations of frequency 800 cycle/s, the distance between eleven consecutive nodes is found to be 1 m, when the temperature of iodine vapours is 352°C. If the temperature is 127°C, the distance between consecutive nodes is

(a) 0.08 m (b) 0.072 m
(c) 1.25 m (d) $\sqrt{\frac{127}{352}} \times 0.1$ m

28. A closed organ pipe of length L is vibrating in its first overtone. There is a point Q inside the pipe at a distance $7L/9$ from the open end. The ratio of pressure amplitude at Q to the maximum pressure amplitude in the pipe is

(a) 1 : 2 (b) 2 : 1
(c) 1 : 1 (d) 2 : 3

29. AB is a cylinder of length 1 m fitted with a thin flexible diaphragm C at middle and two other thin flexible diaphragms A and B at the ends as shown. The portions AC and BC contain hydrogen and oxygen gases respectively. The diaphragms A and B are set into vibrations of the same frequency. The minimum frequency of these vibrations for which diaphragm C is a node is
(Under the conditions of the experiment, the velocity of sound in hydrogen is 1100 m/s and oxygen 300 m/s)

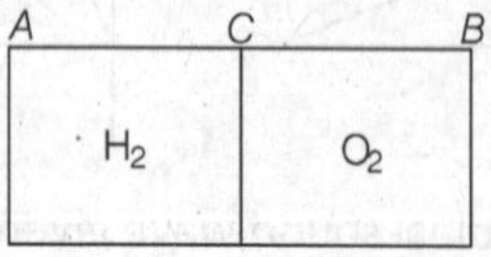

(a) 1100 Hz (b) 3300 Hz
(c) 1650 Hz (d) 1500 Hz

30. A vertical tube is completely filled with water. A small sound source of constant frequency is held a little above the open upper end and water is run out from the lower end. A number of resonance positions are detected. The first of these occurs when the water surface is 7 cm below the top of the tube and another occurs at 39 cm. At which of the following distances should resonance also be detected?

(a) 14 cm (b) 18 cm
(c) 23 cm (d) 31 cm

31. An open pipe 0.400 m in length is placed vertically in a cylindrical bucket and nearly touches the bottom of the bucket, which has an area of 0.100 m^2. Water is slowly poured into the bucket until a sounding tuning fork of frequency 440 Hz, held over the pipe, produces resonance. Find the mass of water in the bucket at this moment. Take, velocity of sound in air as 330 m/s.

(a) 18.75 kg (b) 21.25 kg
(c) 40.00 kg (d) 26.75 kg

32. An open organ pipe containing air resonates in fundamental mode due to a tuning fork. The measured values of length l (in cm) of the pipe and radius r (in cm) of the pipe are $l = 94 \pm 0.1$, $r = 5 \pm 0.05$. The velocity of the sound in air is accurately known. The maximum percentage error in the measurement of the frequency of that tuning fork by this experiment, will be

(a) 0.16 (b) 0.64
(c) 1.2 (d) 1.6

33. In the Kundts tube experiment (shown in figure (i)), the rod is clamped at the end instead of clamping it at the centre as shown in figure (ii). It is known that speed of sound in air is 330 m/s, powder piles up at successive distance of 0.6 m and length of rod used is 1 m, speed of sound in rod is

(i) Standard Kundt's tube

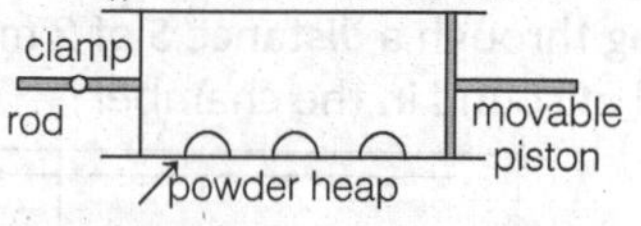

(ii) Modified Kundt's tube

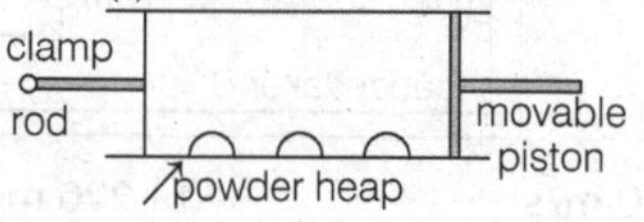

(a) 550 m/s (b) 1100 m/s
(c) 1200 m/s (d) 600 m/s

34. A man standing in front of a mountain at a certain distance beats a drum at regular intervals. The drumming rate is gradually increased and he finds that the echo is not heard distinctly when the rate becomes 40 per minute. He then moves nearer to the mountain by 90 m and finds that the echo is again not heard when the drumming rate becomes 60 per minute. The distance between the mountain and the initial position of the man is

(a) 330 m (b) 300 m
(c) 240 m (d) 270 m

35. Two tuning forks *A* and *B* produce 8 beats per second when sounded together. A gas column 37.5 cm long in a pipe closed at one end and resonate to its fundamental mode with fork *A* whereas a column of length 38.5 cm of the same gas in a similar pipe is required for a similar resonance with fork *B*. The frequencies of two tuning forks are

(a) 308 Hz, 300 Hz (b) 208 Hz, 200 Hz
(c) 300 Hz, 400 Hz (d) 350 Hz, 500 Hz

36. In an experiment three tuning forks are used, one of frequency f_1 and other two of frequency f_2. When f_1 and f_2 are struck together, a beat of frequency 5 Hz is observed. When wax is applied on f_2 and struck along with f_1, beat frequency increases to 6 Hz. When f_1 is filed and struck along with f_2, it produced beats of frequency 7 Hz. What will be the beat frequency (in Hz) when filed f_1 and waxed f_2 are struck together? (Assume $f_1 > f_2$)

(a) 18 (b) 8
(c) 6 (d) 4

37. The fundamental frequency of a sonometer wire of length l is n_0. A bridge is now introduced at a distance of Δl ($<< l$) from the centre of the wire. The lengths of wire on the two sides of the bridge are now vibrated in their fundamental modes. Then, the beat frequency nearly is

(a) $\frac{n_0 \Delta l}{l}$ (b) $\frac{8 n_0 \Delta l}{l}$ (c) $\frac{2 n_0 \Delta l}{l}$ (d) $\frac{n_0 \Delta l}{2lx}$

38. Four tuning forks of frequencies 200, 201, 204 and 206 Hz are sounded together. The beat frequency will be

(a) 6 (b) 12
(c) 15 (d) None of these

Multiple Choice(s) Correct Questions

1. The equation of motion of a longitudinal wave is $s = 0.15 \sin[4\pi t - \pi x]$, where x and s are measured in m at t in s.

(a) The distance between two successive points having phase difference of π is 1 m.
(b) The wave travels along negative X-axis.
(c) The frequency of the wave is 2 Hz.
(d) At $t = 4$ s and at $x = 20$ cm, kinetic energy of the particle is zero.

2. The particle displacement of a travelling longitudinal wave is represented by $s = f(x, t)$. The mid-points of a compression zone and an adjacent rarefaction zone are represented by the letter C and R. Which of the following is true?

(a) $\left|\frac{\partial s}{\partial x}\right|_C = \left|\frac{\partial s}{\partial x}\right|_R$

(b) $\left|\frac{\partial s}{\partial t}\right|_C = \left|\frac{\partial s}{\partial t}\right|_R = 0$

(c) $(\text{Pressure})_C - (\text{Pressure})_R = 2\left|\frac{\partial s}{\partial x}\right|_C \times$ Bulk modulus of air.

(d) Particles of air are stationary mid-way between C and R

3. Two sound waves move in the same direction in the same medium. The pressure amplitude of the waves are equal but the wavelength of the first wave is doubled that of the second. Let the average power transmitted across a cross-section by the two waves be P_1 and P_2 and their displacement amplitudes be s_1 and s_2, then

(a) $\frac{P_1}{P_2} = 1$ (b) $\frac{P_1}{P_2} = 2$
(c) $\frac{s_1}{s_2} = \frac{1}{2}$ (d) $\frac{s_1}{s_2} = \frac{2}{1}$

4. Consider a tuning fork oscillating in air. Assume the wavefronts to be similar to that in a plane wave. Mark the correct statements about that plane sound wave.

(a) Compression pulse is formed at equilibrium position of prong's simple harmonic oscillation with prong moving in the direction of wave propagation.
(b) Rarefaction pulse is formed at extreme position of prong's simple harmonic oscillation.
(c) The maximum density occurs at the centre of compression.
(d) When the prongs are at extreme position of their simple harmonic oscillation, pressure has no variation.

5. Sounds from two identical sources S_1 and S_2 reach a point P. When the sounds reach directly and in the same phase, the intensity at P is I_0. The power of S_1 is now reduced by 64% and the phase difference between S_1 and S_2 is varied continuously. The maximum and minimum intensities recorded at P are now I_{max} and I_{min}

(a) $I_{max} = 0.64 I_0$ (b) $I_{min} = 0.36 I_0$
(c) $\frac{I_{max}}{I_{min}} = 16$ (d) $\frac{I_{max}}{I_{min}} = \frac{1.64}{0.36}$

6. Two monochromatic sources of electromagnetic wave, *P* and *Q* emit waves of wavelength $\lambda = 20$ m and separated by 5 m as shown. *A*, *B* and *C* are three points where interference of these waves is observed. If phase of a wave generated by *P* is ahead of wave generated by *Q* is $\pi/2$, then (given intensity of both waves is *I*)

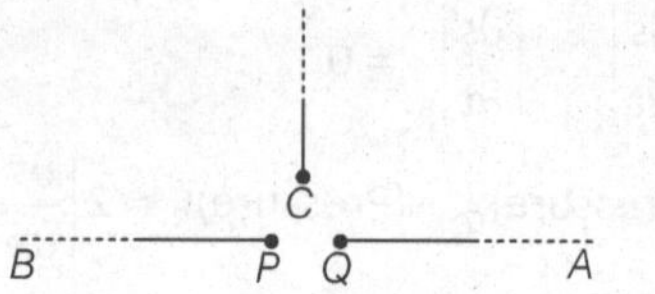

C is symmetrical with respect to *P* and *Q*

(a) phase difference of these waves at *B* is 180°.
(b) intensities at *A*, *B* and *C* are in the ratio 2 : 0 : 1 respectively.
(c) intensities at *A*, *B* and *C* are in the ratio 1 : 2 : 0 respectively.
(d) phase difference at *A* is 0°

7. In a large room, a person receives direct sound from source at 120 m away. He also receives waves from same source after reflection from 25 m high ceiling at a point half ways between them. Find wavelength(s) for which two sound waves interfere constructively

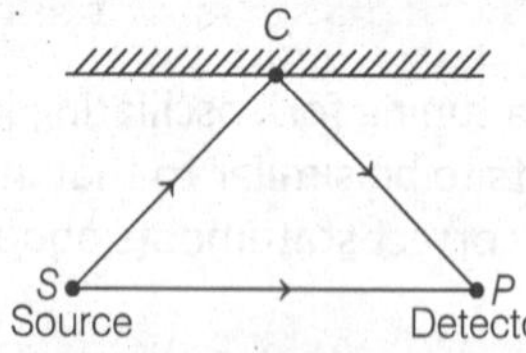

(a) 10 m (b) 5 m (c) 7 m (d) 10/3 m

8. A narrow organ pipe of length 28 cm closed at one end is found to be at resonance when a tuning fork of frequency 850 Hz is sounded near the open end. If velocity of sound in air is 340 m/s, then the

(a) air in the pipe is vibrating in fundamental mode.
(b) air in the pipe is vibrating in first overtone
(c) end correction of the pipe is 1 cm.
(d) end correction of the pipe is 2 cm.

9. Standing sound waves produced in a pipe that is 1.20 m long. For the first overtone, determine the locations along the pipe (measured from the left end) of the displacement nodes (S_N) and the pressure nodes (P_N) if

(a) the pipe is open at both ends, S_N at 0.3 m, 0.9 m.
(b) the pipe is open at both ends, P_N at 0 m, 0.6 m, 1.2 m.
(c) the pipe is closed at the left end and open at the right end, S_N at 0 m, 0.8 m.
(d) the pipe is closed at the left end and open at the right end, P_N at 0.4 m, 1.2 m.

10. The second overtone of an open organ pipe *A* and a closed pipe *B* have the same frequency at a given temperature. It follows that the ratio of the

(a) length of *A* and *B* is 4 : 3.
(b) fundamental frequencies of *A* and *B* is 5 : 6.
(c) length of *B* to that of *A* is 5 : 6.
(d) frequencies of first overtone of *A* and *B* is 10 : 9.

11. If the third harmonic of vibration in an open air pipe equals the fifth harmonic of vibration in a closed pipe, then the possible values of the length of air column in the closed pipe and open pipe, respectively, are (neglect end corrections)

(a) 100 cm, 120 cm (b) 60 cm, 72 cm
(c) 200 cm, 120 cm (d) 180 cm, 150 cm

12. A cylindrical tube, open at one end and closed at the other, is in acoustic unison (resonance) with an external source of sound of single frequency held at the open end of the tube, in its fundamental note. Then,

(a) the displacement wave from the source gets reflected with a phase change of π at the closed end.
(b) the pressure wave from the source gets reflected without a phase change at the closed end.
(c) the wave reflected from the closed end again gets reflected at the open end.
(d) the wave reflected from the closed end does not suffer reflection at the open end.

13. A closed pipe resonates at its fundamental frequency of 300 Hz. Which of the following statement(s) is/are correct?

(a) If the pressure rises, the fundamental frequency increases.
(b) If the temperature rises, the fundamental frequency increases.
(c) The first overtone is of frequency 600 Hz.
(d) If the pipe is filled with a gas of lower density, the fundamental frequency increases.

14. In a resonance tube experiment, a closed organ pipe of length 120 cm is used. Initially, it is completely filled with water. It is vibrated with tuning fork of frequency 340 Hz. To achieve resonance, the water level is lowered, then (given $v_{air} = 340$ m/s, neglect end correction)

(a) minimum length of water column to have the resonance is 45 cm.
(b) the distance between two successive nodes is 50 cm.

(c) the maximum length of water column to create the resonance is 95 cm.

(d) the distance between two successive nodes is 25 cm.

15. Two identical straight wires are stretched so as to produce 6 beats per second when vibrating simultaneously. On changing the tension slightly in one of them, the beat frequency remains unchanged. Denoting by T_1, T_2, the higher and the lower initial tensions in the strings, then it could be said that while making the above changes in tension

(a) T_2 was decreased.

(b) T_2 was increased.

(c) T_1 was increased.

(d) T_1 was decreased.

Comprehension Based Questions

Comprehension-1

The figure represents the instantaneous picture of a longitudinal harmonic wave travelling along the negative X-axis. Identify the correct statement(s) related to the movement of the points shown in the figure.

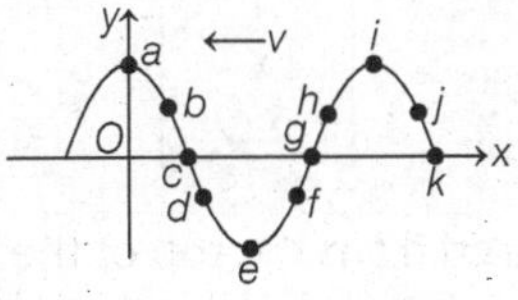

1. The points moving in the direction of wave is/are

(a) b (b) c

(c) f (d) i

2. The points moving opposite to the direction of propagation is/are

(a) a (b) d

(c) f (d) j

3. The stationary points is/are

(a) a (b) e

(c) g (d) k

4. The maximum displaced points is/are

(a) a (b) e

(c) g (d) i

5. The points of maximum compression is/are

(a) c (b) g

(c) e (d) k

6. The points of maximum rarefaction is/are

(a) a (b) e

(c) g (d) i

Comprehension-2

A narrow tube is bent in the form of a circle of radius R, as shown in the figure. Two small holes S and D are made in the tube at the positions right angle to each other. A source placed at S generated a wave of intensity I_0 which is equally divided into two parts : One part travels along the longer path, while the other travels along the shorter path. Both the part waves meet at the point D where a detector is placed.

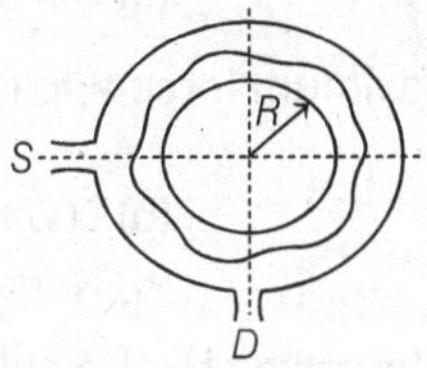

7. If a maxima is formed at the detector then, the magnitude of wavelength λ of the wave produced is given by

(a) πR (b) $\frac{\pi R}{2}$

(c) $\frac{\pi R}{4}$ (d) $\frac{2\pi R}{3}$

8. If the minima is formed at the detector then, the magnitude of wavelength λ of the wave produced is given by

(a) $2\pi R$ (b) $\frac{3\pi R}{2}$ (c) $\frac{2\pi R}{3}$ (d) $\frac{2\pi R}{5}$

9. The maximum intensity produced at D is given by

(a) $4I_0$ (b) $2I_0$ (c) I_0 (d) $3I_0$

10. The maximum value of λ to produce a maxima at D is given by

(a) πR (b) $2\pi R$ (c) $\frac{\pi R}{2}$ (d) $\frac{3\pi R}{2}$

11. The maximum value of λ to produce a minima at D is given by

(a) πR (b) $2\pi R$ (c) $\frac{\pi R}{2}$ (d) $\frac{3\pi R}{2}$

Comprehension-3

A plane pressure pulse, triangular in shape, approaches a rigid wall along normal at a speed of 400 m/s. At time $t = 0$, situation is shown in the figure. The peak pressure is 100 Pa. By the wall pulse gets reflected and pressure near the wall gets doubled. Height of the wall is 2 m and width is also 2 m. A detector on the wall records a minimum excess pressure of 16 Pa .

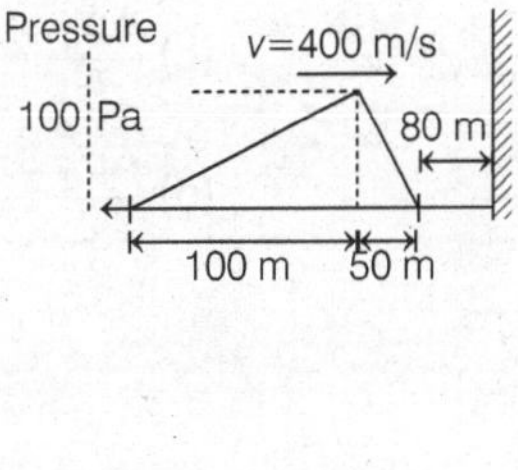

12. When for the first time detector will record the pressure pulse?
(a) 22×10^{-2} s (b) 21×10^{-2} s
(c) 31.5×10^{-2} s (d) None of these

13. For how much time, the detector will record the pulse?
(a) 37.5×10^{-2} s (b) 34.5×10^{-2} s
(c) 31.5×10^{-2} s (d) None of these

14. What is the maximum force applied by the pulse on the wall?
(a) 400 N (b) 800 N
(c) 200 N (d) None of these

15. Total impulse imparted by the pulse on the wall will be
(a) 300 N-s (b) 150 N-s
(c) 750 N-s (d) None of these

Comprehension-4

In a Kundt's tube, a gas is filled and it is found that the heaps of lycopodium powder were formed at a distance of 10 cm from each other. When the gas was replaced with helium gas, the heaps were formed at a distance of $\frac{50}{\sqrt{42}}$ cm. The first gas was diatomic. Assume that the temperature of system remains the same. The velocity of the sound wave in the rod used in Kundt's tube is 10 times that in the first gas. The rod is clamped at the centre.

16. What is the molar mass of the first gas?
(a) 2 g (b) 32 g
(c) 28 g (d) None of these

17. What is the length of the rod, if it is oscillating in the fundamental mode?
(a) 2 m (b) 1 m
(c) 0.5 m (d) None of these

Comprehension-5

The air column in a pipe closed at one end is made to vibrate in its second overtone by a tuning fork of frequency 440 Hz. The speed of the sound in air is 330 m/s. End corrections may be neglected. Let p_0 denote the mean pressure at any point in the pipe and Δp_0 the maximum amplitude of pressure variation then

18. the amplitude of pressure variation at the middle of the column is
(a) $\frac{\Delta p_0}{\sqrt{2}}$ (b) $\frac{\Delta p_0}{\sqrt{3}}$
(c) $\frac{\Delta p_0}{2}$ (d) $\frac{\Delta p_0}{3}$

19. the maximum and minimum pressure at the open end of the pipe are respectively
(a) p_0, p_0 (b) $\frac{p_0}{2}, \frac{p_0}{2}$
(c) $2p_0, 2p_0$ (d) $p_0, \frac{p_0}{2}$

20. the maximum and minimum pressure at the closed end of the pipe are respectively
(a) $p_0 + \Delta p_0, p_0 - \Delta p_0$
(b) $p_0 + \frac{\Delta p_0}{2}, p_0 - \frac{\Delta p_0}{2}$
(c) $p_0 - \Delta p_0, p_0 - 2\Delta p_0$
(d) p_0, p_0

Comprehension-6

In an organ pipe (may be closed or open) of 99 cm length, standing wave is setup, whose equation is given by longitudinal displacement

$$\xi = (0.1\,\text{mm}) \cos \frac{2\pi}{80} (y + 1\,\text{cm}) \cos 2\pi\,(400)\,t$$

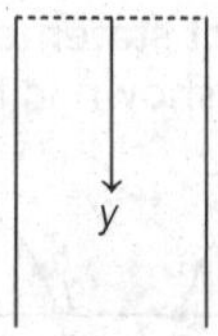

where, y is measured from the top of the tube in centimeters and t in second. Here, 1 cm is the end correction.

21. The upper end and the lower end of the tube are respectively
(a) open-closed (b) closed-open
(c) open-open (d) closed-closed

22. The air column is vibrating in
(a) first overtone
(b) second overtone
(c) third harmonic
(d) fundamental mode

23. Equation of the standing wave in terms of excess pressure is
(Bulk modulus of air, $B = 5 \times 10^5\ \text{N/m}^2$)
(a) $p_{ex} = (125\pi\ \text{N/m}^2) \sin \frac{2\pi}{80} (y + 1\,\text{cm}) \cos 2\pi\,(400t)$
(b) $p_{ex} = (125\pi\ \text{N/m}^2) \cos \frac{2\pi}{80} (y + 1\,\text{cm}) \sin 2\pi\,(400t)$
(c) $p_{ex} = (225\pi\ \text{N/m}^2) \sin \frac{2\pi}{80} (y + 1\,\text{cm}) \cos 2\pi\,(200t)$
(d) $p_{ex} = (225\pi\ \text{N/m}^2) \cos \frac{2\pi}{80} (y + 1\,\text{cm}) \sin 2\pi\,(200t)$

Comprehension-7

A metallic rod of length 1 m has one end free and other end rigidly clamped. Longitudinal stationary waves are set up in the rod in such a way that there are total six antinodes present along the rod. The amplitude of an antinode is 4×10^{-6} m. Young's modulus and density of the rod are 6.4×10^{10} N/m^2 and 4×10^3 kg/m^3 respectively. Consider the free end to be at origin and at $t = 0$, particles at free end are at positive extreme.

24. The equation describing displacements of particles about their mean positions is

(a) $s = 4 \times 10^{-6} \cos\left(\frac{11\pi}{2}x\right)\cos(22\pi \times 10^3 t)$

(b) $s = 4 \times 10^{-6} \cos\left(\frac{11\pi}{2}x\right)\sin(22\pi \times 10^3 t)$

(c) $s = 4 \times 10^{-6} \cos(5\pi x)\cos(20\pi \times 10^3 t)$

(d) $s = 4 \times 10^{-6} \cos(5\pi x)\sin(20\pi \times 10^3 t)$

25. The equation describing stress developed in the rod is

(a) $140.8\pi \times 10^4 \cos\left(\frac{11}{2}\pi x + \pi\right)\cos(22\pi \times 10^3 t)$

(b) $140.8\pi \times 10^4 \sin\left(\frac{11}{2}\pi x + \pi\right)\cos(22\pi \times 10^3 t)$

(c) $128\pi \times 10^4 \cos(5\pi x + \pi)\cos(20\pi \times 10^3 t)$

(d) $128\pi \times 10^4 \sin(5\pi x + \pi)\cos(20\pi \times 10^3 t)$

26. The magnitude of strain at mid-point of the rod at $t = 1$ s is

(a) $11\sqrt{3}\,\pi \times 10^{-6}$ (b) $11\sqrt{2}\,\pi \times 10^{-6}$

(c) $10\sqrt{3}\,\pi \times 10^{-6}$ (d) $10\sqrt{2}\,\pi \times 10^{-6}$

Match the Columns Questions

1. Sound is travelling in a long tube towards right and the graph of excess pressure variation *versus* position (at some instant) is given below. Match velocities in Column I with Column II. *P, Q, R, S, T* are medium particles inside the tube.

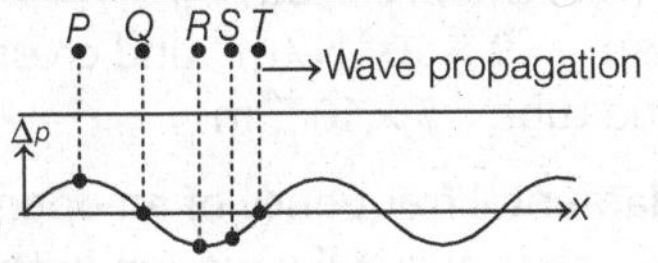

Column I		Column II	
(A)	Velocity is towards right	(P)	P
(B)	Velocity is towards left	(Q)	Q
(C)	Velocity is zero	(R)	R
(D)	Speed is maximum	(S)	S
		(T)	T

2. Match the graph in Column I to quantity described in Column II.

Column I		Column II	
(A)	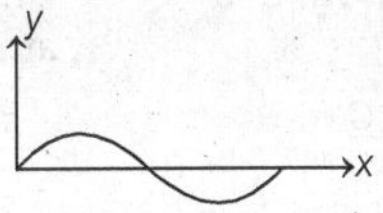	(P)	A sine wave $y = A\sin(kx - \omega t)$ travelling in *x*-direction. The snapshot of wave at $t = \pi/\omega$.
(B)	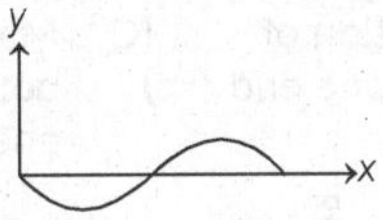	(Q)	A pendulum bob is executing SHM. At $t = 0$, it is at the positive extreme. Its velocity *versus* time graph.
(C)	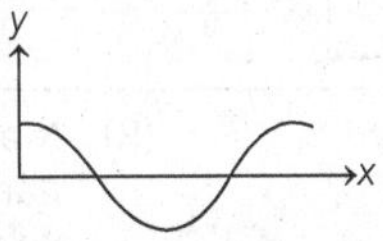	(R)	A string fixed at both ends is oscillating in 2nd harmonic. The particles are at their respective extreme. Slope of string *versus* position graph.
(D)	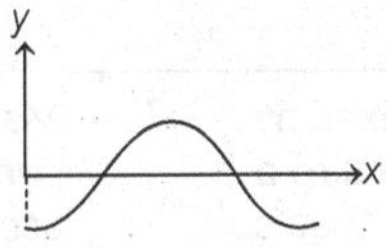	(S)	A pipe open at both ends is oscillating in 1st overtone. The pressure at pressure antinodes is maximum at $t = 0$. Displacement of particles at the end from their mean position *versus* time graph.
		(T)	A block is hanging from a vertical spring. The block is suddenly kicked in vertical direction (at $t = 0$). Acceleration of block *versus* time graph.

3. Column I represents the standing waves in air Columns and string. Column II represents frequency of the note. Match the Column I with Column II. [v = velocity of the sound in the medium]

Column I		Column II	
(A)	Second harmonic for the tube open at both ends	(P)	$\frac{v}{4l}$
(B)	Fundamental frequency for the tube closed at one end	(Q)	$\frac{v}{2l}$
(C)	First overtone for the tube closed at one end	(R)	$\frac{3v}{4l}$
(D)	Fundamental frequency for the string fixed at both ends	(S)	$\frac{v}{l}$
		(T)	$\frac{5v}{4l}$

4.

	Column I		Column II
(A)	Graphical representation of pressure variation in both end open organ pipe. 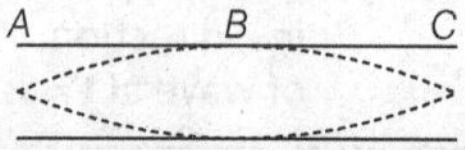	(P)	Maximum kinetic energy at B
(B)	Graphical representation of pressure variation in one end closed organ pipe. 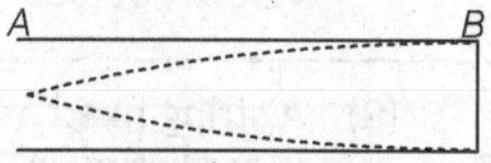	(Q)	Maximum potential energy at B
(C)	Snapshot of string fixed at both ends. 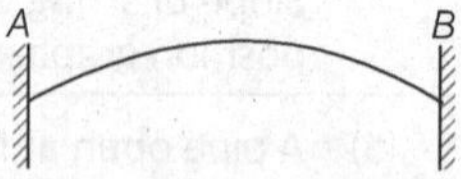	(R)	Maximum particle velocity at B
(D)	Snapshot of a string fixed at one end and connected to a smooth massless ring that is constrained to move vertically. 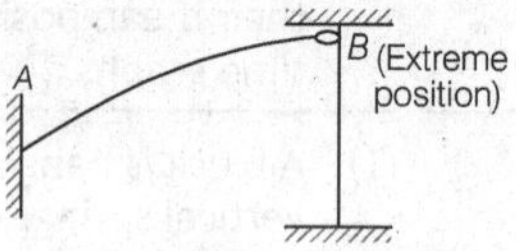	(S)	Maximum particle acceleration at B

5. Match the informations about mechanical waves given in Column I with that given in Column II. Note that any information in Column II may have more than one matching options in Column II.

	Column I (Nature of wave)		Column II (Properties)
(A)	Transverse progressive wave	(P)	Amplitude of all particles same.
(B)	Longitudinal progressive wave	(Q)	Phase of all particles may be same.
(C)	Transverse standing wave	(R)	May occur in gases.
(D)	Longitudinal standing wave	(S)	KE and PE of a small element may be maximum simultaneously.

Numerical Value Questions

1. A person produces sound of 70 dB at 4 m distance away from him. For hearing sound clearly, if threshold sound level is 10 dB, then up to how much distance (in km) from person his sound can be heard clearly?

2. A plane longitudinal wave having angular frequency $\omega = 500$ rad/s is travelling in positive x-direction in a medium of density $\rho = 1\,\text{kg/m}^3$ and bulk modulus $= 4 \times 10^4\,\text{N/m}^2$. The loudness at a point in the medium is observed to be 20 dB. The pressure amplitude of the pressure wave is given by $\alpha \times 10^{-4}\,\text{N/m}^2$. Find the value of α.

3. The three identical loud speakers in figure play a 170 Hz frequency tone in a room where speed of sound is 340 m/s. At point exactly infront of sources S_2, the amplitude of the wave from each speaker is a. What is the ratio of resultant intensity at P and intensity due to single speaker?

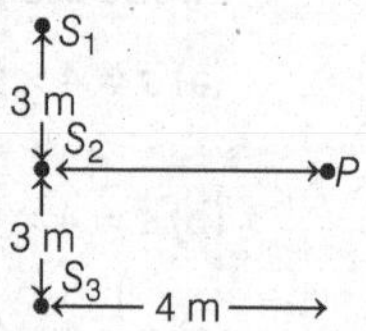

4. As shown in the figure, two loudspeakers are located at point A and B. Both are vibrating in phase at a frequency ν and P_1 and P_2 are their respective power outputs. Point C lies on a line joining the two loudspeakers at a distance of d_1 from A and d_2 from B. With both speakers switched on, what is the power (in W/m^2) at point C? Take velocity of sound = 300 m/s, frequency $\nu = 100$ Hz, $d_1 = 1$ m and $d_2 = 1.5$ m, $P_1 = 8\pi$ W and $P_2 = 18\pi$ W. Also assume that loudspeakers behave like isotropic sources and emit sound uniformly in all directions.

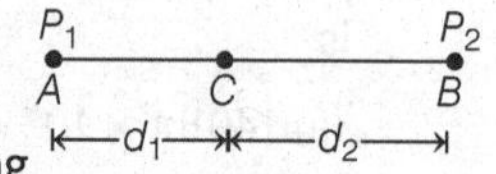

5. Pressure variation due to a sonic wave propagating along positive x-direction is given by the equation $\Delta p(x) = \Delta p_0 \sin[2\pi(vt - x)]$. One end of an open organ pipe is closed by a cap and held at rest with its axis parallel to X-axis and the open end at the origin. What is the minimum value of limiting frictional force (in N) between the cap and the pipe, so that the pipe will remain closed? (Given, $\Delta p_0 = 2 \times 10^3\,\text{N/m}^2$ and cross-sectional area of the tube $= 5 \times 10^{-4}\,\text{m}^2$)

6. The fundamental frequency of an open pipe would be independent of small variation in temperature at a temperature $T_0 = \dfrac{\eta}{14\alpha}$, where α is the coefficient of linear expansion of the material of the tube. Find the value of η.

7. A student is performing a resonance column experiment with pipe of length 2 m and tuning fork of frequency 325 Hz. During the experiment, first resonance is heard at 20 cm from top and then possibly due to some lack of concentration in between, second resonance is skipped and after that next resonance is observed at 108 cm. How many total number of resonances are possible in the pipe?

8. As shown in the figure, water is pumped into a tall vertical cylinder at a volume flow rate R. The radius of the cylinder is r and at the open top of the cylinder, a tuning fork is vibrating with a frequency f. As the water rises, time interval elapsed between successive resonances is given by $t = \dfrac{\pi r^2 v}{\alpha R f}$, where v is speed of sound in air. Find α.

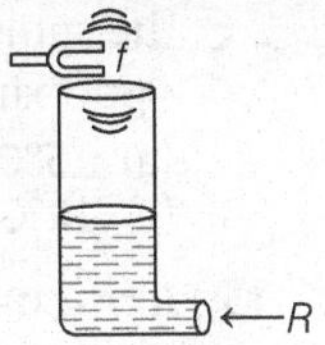

9. Two sound waves of frequencies 100 Hz and 102 Hz and having same amplitude A interfering. A detector which can detect waves of amplitude greater than or equal to A is kept at rest. In a time interval of 12 s, find the total duration (in s) in which detector is active.

10. A piano has two strings for some of its low keys, which are to be perfectly tuned to each other. In a given piano, on a particular key, one of the strings is tuned correctly to 100 Hz. When the two strings are sounded together, three beats per second is heard. The beating is between the fundamental tones. By what percent must a piano tuner change the tension of untuned string to make it match perfectly?

Previous Year's Questions

JEE Main

1 The fundamental frequency of a closed organ pipe is equal to the first overtone frequency of an open organ pipe. If length of the open pipe is 60 cm, then the length of the closed pipe will be **[2024, 31 Jan Shift-I]**

(a) 60 cm (b) 30 cm (c) 45 cm (d) 15 cm

2 A point source is emitting sound waves of intensity 16×10^{-8} Wm^{-2} at the origin. The difference in intensity (magnitude only) at two points located at a distances of 2 m and 4 m from the origin respectively will be .... $\times 10^{-8}$ Wm^{-2}. **[2024, 30 Jan Shift-II]**

3 In a closed organ pipe, the frequency of fundamental note is 30 Hz. A certain amount of water is now poured in the organ pipe, so that the fundamental frequency is increased to 110 Hz. If the organ pipe has a cross-sectional area of 2 cm^2, the amount of water poured to the organ tube is .... g. (Take speed of sound in air is 330 m/s) **[2024, 30 Jan Shift-I]**

4 A closed organ pipe 150 cm long gives 7 beats per second with an open organ pipe of length 350 cm, both vibrating in fundamental mode. The velocity of sound is .... m/s. **[2024, 27 Jan Shift-II]**

5 An organ pipe 40 cm long is open at both ends. The speed of sound in air is 360 ms^{-1}. The frequency of the second harmonic is .... Hz. **[2023, 8 April, Shift-I]**

6 In an experiment to determine the velocity of sound in air at room temperature using a resonance is observed when the air column has a length of 20.0 cm for a tuning fork of frequency 400 Hz is used. The velocity of the sound at room temperature is 336 ms^{-1}. The third resonance is observed when the air column has a length of .... cm. **[2022, 29 June, Shift-II]**

7 A tuning fork of frequency 340 Hz resonates in the fundamental mode with an air column of length 125 cm in a cylindrical tube closed at one end. When water is slowly poured in it, the minimum height of water required for observing resonance once again is ... cm. (Velocity of sound in air is 340 ms^{-1}) **[2022, 28 June, Shift-II]**

8 The velocity of sound in a gas in which two wavelengths 4.08 m and 4.16 m produce 40 beats in 12 s, will be : **[2022, 28 June Shift-I]**

(a) 282.8 ms^{-1} (b) 175.5 ms^{-1}
(c) 353.6 ms^{-1} (d) 707.2 ms^{-1}

9 A set of 20 tuning forks is arranged in a series of increasing frequencies. If each fork gives 4 beats with respect to the preceding fork and the frequency of the last fork is twice the frequency of the first, then the frequency of last fork is ...... Hz. **[2022, 26 June Shift-II]**

10 A tunning fork is vibrating at 250 Hz. The length of the shortest closed organ pipe that will resonate with the tuning fork will be .... cm. (Take, speed of sound in air as 340 ms^{-1}) **[2021, 27 Aug Shift-II]**

11 A closed organ pipe of length L and an open organ pipe contain gases of densities ρ_1 and ρ_2, respectively. The compressibility of gases are equal in both the pipes. Both the pipes are vibrating in their first overtone with same frequency. The length of the open pipe is $\dfrac{x}{3}L\sqrt{\dfrac{\rho_1}{\rho_2}}$ where x is ....

(Round off to the nearest integer) **[2021, 16 March Shift-II]**

12 A tuning fork A of unknown frequency produces 5 beats/s with a fork of known frequency 340 Hz. When fork A is filled, the beat frequency decreases to 2 beats/s. What is the frequency of fork A? **[2021, 26 Feb Shift-II]**

(a) 342 Hz (b) 345 Hz (c) 335 Hz (d) 338 Hz

13 A student is performing the experiment of resonance column. The diameter of the column tube is 6 cm. The frequency of the tuning fork is 504 Hz. Speed of the sound at the given temperature is 336 m/s. The zero of the metre scale coincides with the top end of the resonance column tube. The reading of the water level in the column when the first resonance occurs is **[2021, 25 Feb, Shift-I]**

(a) 13 cm (b) 16.6 cm (c) 14.8 cm (d) 18.4 cm

14 Assume that the displacement of air is proportional to the pressure difference Δp created by a sound wave. Displacement further depends on the speed of sound v, density of air ρ and the frequency f. If $\Delta p \sim 10$ Pa, $v \sim 300$ m/s, $\rho \sim 1$ kg/m^3 and $f \sim 1000$ Hz, then s will be of the order of (Take the multiplicative constant to be 1.) **[2020, 5 Sep Shift-I]**

(a) 10 mm (b) 1 mm

(c) $\frac{1}{10}$ mm (d) $\frac{3}{100}$ mm

15 In a resonance tube experiment, when the tube is filled with water up to a height of 17.0 cm from bottom, it resonates with a given tuning fork. When the water level is raised, the next resonance with the same tuning fork occurs at a height of 24.5 cm. If the velocity of sound in air is 330 m/s, the tuning fork frequency is **[2020, 5 Sep Shift-I]**

(a) 1100 Hz (b) 3300 Hz

(c) 2200 Hz (d) 550 Hz

16 A one metre long (both ends open) organ pipe is kept in a gas that has double the density of air at STP. Assuming the speed of sound in air at STP is 300 m/s, the frequency difference between the fundamental and second harmonic of this pipe is ...... Hz. **[2020, 8 Jan Shift-I]**

17 A tuning fork of frequency 480 Hz is used in an experiment for measuring speed of sound (v) in air by resonance tube method. Resonance is observed to occur at two successive lengths of the air column $l_1 = 30$ cm and $l_2 = 70$ cm. Then, v is equal to **[2019, 12 April Shift-II]**

(a) 332 ms^{-1} (b) 384 ms^{-1}

(c) 338 ms^{-1} (d) 379 ms^{-1}

18 The pressure wave $p = 0.01 \sin [1000t - 3x]$ Nm^{-2}, corresponds to the sound produced by a vibrating blade on a day when atmospheric temperature is 0°C. On some other day when temperature is T, the speed of sound produced by the same blade and at the same frequency is found to be 336 ms^{-1}. Approximate value of T is **[2019, 9 April Shift-I]**

(a) 15°C (b) 11°C

(c) 12°C (d) 4°C

19 A resonance tube is old and has jagged end. It is still used in the laboratory to determine velocity of sound in air. A tuning fork of frequency 512 Hz produces first resonance when the tube is filled with water to a mark 11 cm below a reference mark. near the open end of the tube. The experiment is repeated with another fork of frequency 256 Hz which produces first resonance when water reaches a mark 27 cm below the reference mark. The velocity of sound in air, obtained in the experiment is close to **[2019, 12 Jan Shift-II]**

(a) 328 ms^{-1} (b) 341 ms^{-1}

(c) 322 ms^{-1} (d) 335 ms^{-1}

JEE Advanced

1 A stationary tuning fork is in resonance with an air column in a pipe. If the tuning fork is moved with a speed of 2 ms^{-1} in front of the open end of the pipe and parallel to it, the length of the pipe should be changed for the resonance to occur with the moving tuning fork. If the speed of sound in air is 320 ms^{-1}, the smallest value of the percentage change required in the length of the pipe is ______ **(2020 Adv.)**

2 In an experiment to measure the speed of sound by a resonating air column, a tuning fork of frequency 500 Hz is used. The length of the air column is varied by changing the level of water in the resonance tube. Two successive resonances are heard at air columns of length 50.7 cm and 83.9 cm. Which of the following statements is (are) true? **(2015 Adv.)**

(a) The speed of sound determined from this experiment is 332 m s^{-1}.

(b) The end correction in this experiment is 0.9 cm.

(c) The wavelength of the sound wave is 66.4 cm

(d) The resonance at 50.7 cm corresponds to the fundamental harmonic.

3 Four harmonic waves of equal frequencies and equal intensities I_0 have phase angles 0, $\frac{\pi}{3}$, $\frac{2\pi}{3}$ and π. When they are superposed, the intensity of the resulting wave is nI_0. The value of n is **(2015 Adv.)**

4 A student is performing an experiment using a resonance column and a tuning fork of frequency $244\ s^{-1}$. He is told that the air in the tube has been replaced by another gas (assume that the column remains filled with the gas). If the minimum height at which resonance occurs is (0.350 ± 0.005) m, the gas in the tube is **(2014)**

(Useful information : $\sqrt{167RT} = 640\ J^{1/2}\ \text{mole}^{-1/2}$; $\sqrt{140RT} = 590\ J^{1/2}\ \text{mole}^{-1/2}$. The molar masses M in grams are given in the options. Take the value of $\sqrt{10/M}$ for each gas as given there.)

(a) Neon ($M = 20, \sqrt{10/20} = 7/10$)
(b) Nitrogen ($M = 28, \sqrt{10/28} = 3/5$)
(c) Oxygen ($M = 32, \sqrt{10/32} = 9/16$)
(d) Argon ($M = 36, \sqrt{10/36} = 17/32$)

5 A student is performing the experiment of resonance column. The diameter of the column tube is 4 cm. The frequency of the tuning fork is 512 Hz. The air temperature is 38° C in which the speed of sound is 336 m/s. The zero of the meter scale coincides with the top end of the resonance column tube. When the first resonance occurs, the reading of the water level in the column is **(2012)**

(a) 14.0 cm (b) 15.2 cm
(c) 16.4 cm (d) 17.6 cm

6 A person blows into open-end of a long pipe. As a result, a high-pressure pulse of air travels down the pipe. When this pulse reaches the other end of the pipe, **(2012)**

(a) a high-pressure pulse starts travelling up the pipe, if the other end of the pipe is open.
(b) a low-pressure pulse starts travelling up the pipe, if the other end of the pipe is open.
(c) a low-pressure pulse starts travelling up the pipe, if the other end of the pipe is closed.
(d) a high-pressure pulse starts travelling up the pipe, if the other end of the pipe is closed.

7 **Column I** shows four systems, each of the same length L, for producing standing waves. The lowest possible natural frequency of a system is called its fundamental frequency, whose wavelength is denoted as λ_f. Match each system with statements given in
Column II describing the nature and wavelength of the standing waves. **(2011)**

Column I	Column II
(A) Pipe closed at one end 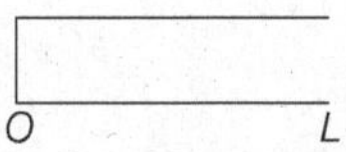	(P) Longitudinal waves
(B) Pipe open at both ends 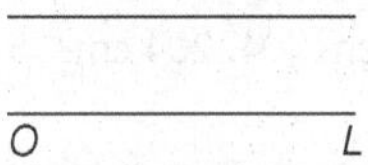	(Q) Transverse waves
(C) Stretched wire clamped at both ends 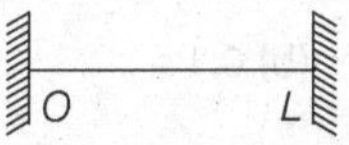	(R) $\lambda_f = L$
(D) Stretched wire clamped at both ends and at mid-point 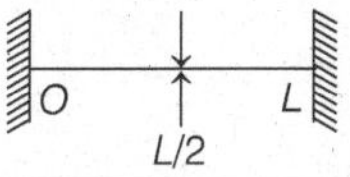	(S) $\lambda_f = 2L$
	(T) $\lambda_f = 4L$

Answer Key

Level 1

10.1 Displacement Wave, Pressure Wave and Density Wave

1. (a) 1500 Hz (b) 1 m (c) 1500 m/s (d) $(1.0 \times 10^5 \pm 0.02)\ N/m^2$
2. 4.54 Å **3.** $\Delta p = -BAk \cos(kx + \omega t)$, $\Delta \rho = -\rho Ak \cos(kx + \omega t)$
4. (a) A (b) C (c) B

10.2 Speed of Sound

1. 331.6 m/s, 347.6 m/s **2.** 1800 m/s
3. (a) 400.9 m/s (b) 0.167% **4.** 2000 ms^{-1} **5.** 0.14 mL

10.3 Intensity of Sound

1. (a) 125 mW/m^2 (b) 10 Pa (c) 1.6 μm **2.** $2.5 \times 10^{-9}\ W/m^2$
3. $2.25 \times 10^{-6}\ W/m^2$ **4.** (a) 60 (b) 1/3600

10.4 Decibel Scale

1. 117 dB **2.** 13 dB **3.** 54 dB, 100 km
4. 54.8 dB **5.** 3.16

10.5 Interference of Sound Waves

1. (a) π (b) $I = (25/312)^2$ **2.** (a) at B (b) 2 : 3
3. 2000 Hz, 4000 Hz, 6000 Hz, 8000 Hz, 10000 Hz

4. $\lambda/8$ 5. 83 Hz
6. (a) 2 (b) 9.28 m, 1.99 m 7. 8.5 cm 8. $\pm 30°$ 9. 3 m

10.6 Equation of Stationary Sound Waves

1. (a) $f = 50$ Hz, $\lambda = 0.2$ m, $v = 10\,\text{ms}^{-1}$ (b) $B = 100\,\text{Nm}^{-2}$, $\Delta p_m = 62.8\,\text{Nm}^{-2}$ (c) $\lambda/4 = 0.05$ m
2. $y(x,t) = (2\times10^{-6}\text{ m})\sin 5\pi x\cos(25000\pi t + \phi)$

10.7 Organ Pipes

1. 4.2 kHz 2. (a) 200 Hz, 400 Hz, 600 Hz (b) 100 Hz, 300 Hz, 500 Hz 3. 6
4. 55 cm 5. (a) closed at one end (b) 85 Hz, 1 m
6. 40 cm 7. f 8. 20 cm, 80 cm, 200 Hz 9. $L/6$
10. a 11. 10.24

10.8 End Correction

1. 3.33 cm 2. 2 cm

10.9 Resonance Tube

1. 344 m/s 2. 600 Hz 3. 2 cm 4. 204 cm 5. 45 cm

10.10 Vibration in Rods

1. 2.5 kHz, 7.5 kHz 2. 10 kHz, 30 kHz

10.11 Beats

1. 306 m/s 2. (a) 25 beats (b) 0.1 s
3. Before loading, $f_A = 485$ Hz.
After loading, $f_A = 483$ Hz or 477 Hz
4. 155 Hz or 161 Hz
5. 296 Hz 6. 156 Hz 7. 95 Hz 8. 2%
9. 27.04 N

Level 2

Single Choice Correct Questions

1. (a)	2. (c)	3. (b)	4. (d)	5. (d)
6. (d)	7. (b)	8. (d)	9. (a)	10. (a)
11. (b)	12. (c)	13. (b)	14. (b)	15. (b)
16. (b)	17. (d)	18. (a)	19. (c)	20. (c)
21. (a)	22. (b)	23. (b)	24. (a)	25. (b)
26. (b)	27. (a)	28. (d)	29. (a)	30. (c)
31. (c)	32. (c)	33. (b)	34. (b)	35. (d)
36. (a)	37. (b)	38. (c)	39. (d)	40. (b)
41. (b)	42. (c)	43. (c)	44. (b)	45. (c)
46. (c)	47. (d)	48. (b)	49. (c)	50. (a)
51. (c)	52. (a)	53. (a)	54. (d)	55. (c)
56. (b)	57. (a)	58. (b)	59. (d)	60. (c)

Numerical Value Questions

1. 6	2. 61	3. 4	4. 9
5. 60	6. 3	7. 336	8. 228
9. 7	10. 67.6		

Level 3

Single Choice Correct Questions

1. (d)	2. (c)	3. (a)	4. (c)	5. (c)
6. (b)	7. (b)	8. (a)	9. (c)	10. (a)
11. (d)	12. (b)	13. (b)	14. (b)	15. (a)
16. (a)	17. (d)	18. (b)	19. (d)	20. (b)
21. (a)	22. (a)	23. (b)	24. (a)	25. (c)
26. (c)	27. (a)	28. (a)	29. (c)	30. (c)
31. (b)	32. (a)	33. (b)	34. (d)	35. (a)
36. (b)	37. (b)	38. (b)		

Multiple Choice(s) Correct Questions

1. (a,c)	2. (a,c,d)	3. (a,d)	4. (a,c,d)
5. (a,c)	6. (a,b,d)	7. (a,b,d)	8. (b,d)
9. (a,b,c,d)	10. (c,d)	11. (a,b)	12. (a,b,c)
13. (b,d)	14. (a,b,c)	15. (b,d)	

Comprehension Based Questions

1. (a,b)	2. (c)	3. (a,b)	4. (a,b,d)
5. (a,d)	6. (c)	7. (a,b,c)	8. (a,c,d)
9. (b)	10. (a)	11. (b)	12. (b)
13. (b)	14. (b)	15. (b)	16. (a)
17. (b)	18. (a)	19. (a)	20. (a)
21. (a)	22. (b)	23. (a)	24. (a)
25. (b)	26. (b)		

Match the Columns Questions

1. (A) P, (B) R, S, (C) Q, T, (D) P, R
2. (A) T, (B) P, Q, T, (C) R, S, (D) R, S
3. (A) S, (B) P, (C) R, (D) Q
4. (A) Q, (B) Q, (C) Q, (D) S
5. (A) P, S, (B) P, R, S, (C) Q, (D) Q, R

Numerical Value Questions

1. (4)	2. (2)	3. (1)	4. (6)	5. (2)
6. (7)	7. (5)	8. (2)	9. (8)	10. (6)

Previous Year's Questions

JEE Main

1. (d)	2. (3)	3. (400)	4. (294)	5. (900)
6. (104)	7. (50)	8. (d)	9. (152)	10. (34)
11. (4)	12. (c)	13. (c)	14. (d)	15. (c)
16. (106.06)	17. (b)	18. (d)	19. (a)	

JEE Advanced

1. (0.625) 2. (abc) 3. (3) 4. (d)
5. (b) 6. (b, d)
7. A→ (P, T); B→ (P, S); C→ (Q, S); D→ (Q, R)

SOLUTIONS

Level 01

10.1 Displacement Wave, Pressure Wave and Density Wave

1. (a) $f = \frac{\omega}{2\pi} = \frac{3000\pi}{2\pi} = 1500$ Hz

(b) $\lambda = \frac{2\pi}{k} = \frac{2\pi}{2\pi} = 1$ m

(c) $v = \frac{\omega}{k} = \frac{3000\pi}{2\pi} = 1500$ m/s

(d) Pressure amplitude $= \Delta p_0 = 0.02\ \text{N/m}^2$

$\therefore\ p = p_0 \pm \Delta p_0 = (1.0 \times 10^5 \pm 0.02)\ \text{N/m}^2$

2. $\Delta p_0 = \frac{p_{max} - p_{min}}{2} = 1.0 \times 10^{-3}\ \text{N/m}^2$

$\Delta p_0 = BAk$

$\Rightarrow\ 1.0 \times 10^{-3} = 1.4 \times 10^5 (A) \times \left(\frac{2\pi}{0.4}\right)$

$\Rightarrow\ A = 4.54$ Å

3. $\Delta p = -B\frac{\partial y}{\partial x} = -BAk\cos(kx + \omega t)$

$\frac{\Delta \rho}{\rho} = -\frac{\Delta V}{V} = -\frac{\Delta y}{\Delta x}$

$\therefore\ \Delta \rho = -\rho\frac{\partial y}{\partial x} = -\rho Ak\cos(kx + \omega t)$

4. $\Delta p = -B\left(\frac{\partial y}{\partial x}\right)$

(a) Maximum pressure occurs at the points of maximum negative slope i.e., at point *A*.

(b) Minimum pressure occurs at the points of maximum positive slope i.e., at point *C*.

(c) Atmospheric pressure occurs at the points of zero slope i.e., at point *B*.

10.2 Speed of Sound

1. $v = \sqrt{\frac{\gamma p}{\rho}} = \sqrt{\frac{1.4 \times 1.013 \times 10^5}{1.29}} = 331.6$ m/s

$v \propto \sqrt{T} \Rightarrow \frac{v_2}{v_1} = \sqrt{\frac{T_2}{T_1}}$

$\Rightarrow\ \frac{v_2}{331.6} = \sqrt{\frac{300}{273}}$

$\Rightarrow\ v_2 = 347.6$ m/s

2. $v = \sqrt{\frac{\gamma RT}{M}}$

$\Rightarrow\ v \propto \frac{1}{\sqrt{M}}$

$\therefore\ \frac{v_1}{v_2} = \sqrt{\frac{M_2}{M_1}}$

$\Rightarrow\ \frac{v_1}{450} = \sqrt{\frac{32}{2}}$

$\Rightarrow\ v_1 = 1800$ m/s

3. (a) $M_{avg} = \frac{n_1M_1 + n_2M_2}{n_1 + n_2} = \frac{1 \times 4 + 2 \times 32}{1 + 2} = \frac{68}{3}$ g

$(C_V)_{mix} = \frac{n_1C_{V_1} + n_2C_{V_2}}{n_1 + n_2} = \frac{1(3R/2) + 2(5R/2)}{1 + 2} = \frac{13R}{6}$

$C_V = \frac{R}{\gamma - 1}$

$\Rightarrow\ \frac{13R}{6} = \frac{R}{\gamma_{mix} - 1}$

$\Rightarrow\ \gamma_{mix} = \frac{19}{13}$

$v = \sqrt{\frac{\gamma RT}{M}} = \sqrt{\frac{(19/13) \times 8.31 \times 300}{(68/3) \times 10^{-3}}}$

$= 400.9$ m/s

(b) $v = \sqrt{\frac{\gamma RT}{M}}$

$\Rightarrow\ \frac{\Delta v}{v} = \frac{1}{2}\frac{\Delta T}{T}$

$\therefore\ \frac{\Delta v}{v} \times 100 = \frac{1}{2}\left(\frac{\Delta T}{T} \times 100\right)$

$= \frac{1}{2}\left(\frac{1}{300} \times 100\right) = 0.167\%$

4. $v = \sqrt{\frac{B}{\rho}} = \sqrt{\frac{4000 \times 10^6}{1000}} = 2000$ m/s

5. $B = \rho v^2 = 800 \times (1330)^2 = 1.415 \times 10^9\ \text{N/m}^2$

$B = \frac{\Delta p}{(\Delta V/V)}$

$\Rightarrow\ 1.415 \times 10^9 = \frac{2 \times 10^5}{(\Delta V/1)}$

$\Rightarrow\ \Delta V = 0.14$ mL

10.3 Intensity of Sound

1. (a) $I = \frac{P}{4\pi r^2} = \frac{50\pi}{4\pi(10)^2} = 125\ \text{mW/m}^2$

(b) $I = \frac{\Delta p_m^2}{2\rho v}$

$\Rightarrow\ 125 \times 10^{-3} = \frac{\Delta p_m^2}{2(1.25)\,320}$

$\Rightarrow\ \Delta p_m = 10$ Pa

(c) $I=\frac{1}{2}\rho v\omega^2A^2$

$$\Rightarrow \quad 125\times10^{-3}=\frac{1}{2}\times1.25\times320(2\pi\times2500)^2A^2$$

$$\Rightarrow \quad A=1.6\,\mu\text{m}$$

2. $v=\sqrt{\frac{B}{\rho}}=\sqrt{\frac{400}{1}}=20$ m/s

$$I=\frac{1}{2}\rho v\omega^2A^2=\frac{1}{2}\times1\times20[2\pi(250)]^2(10^{-8})^2$$

$$=2.5\times10^{-9}\text{ W/m}^2$$

3. $I\propto\Delta p_m^2$

$$\therefore \quad \frac{I_1}{I_2}=\left(\frac{\Delta p_{m_1}}{\Delta p_{m_2}}\right)^2$$

$$\Rightarrow \quad \frac{10^{-6}}{I_2}=\left(\frac{2\times10^{-3}}{3\times10^{-3}}\right)^2$$

$$\Rightarrow \quad I_2=2.25\times10^{-6}\text{ W/m}^2$$

4. (a) $I_a=I_\omega$

$$\Rightarrow \quad \frac{\Delta p_{ma}^2}{2\rho_a v_a}=\frac{\Delta p_{m\omega}^2}{2\rho_\omega v_\omega}$$

$$\Rightarrow \quad \frac{\Delta p_{m\omega}}{\Delta p_{ma}}=\sqrt{\frac{\rho_\omega v_\omega}{\rho_a v_a}}=\sqrt{\frac{1000\times1530}{1.25\times340}}=60$$

(b) $\frac{I_\omega}{I_a}=\frac{\rho_a v_a}{\rho_\omega v_\omega}=\frac{1.25\times340}{1000\times1530}=\frac{1}{3600}$

10.4 Decibel Scale

1. $I=\frac{P}{4\pi r^2}=\frac{200\pi}{4\pi(10)^2}=0.5\text{ W/m}^2$

$$L=10\log_{10}\left(\frac{I}{I_0}\right)=10\log_{10}\left(\frac{0.5}{10^{-12}}\right)=117\text{ dB}$$

2. $\Delta L=10\log_{10}\left(\frac{I_2}{I_1}\right)=10\log_{10}\left(\frac{20I_1}{I_1}\right)=13\text{ dB}$

3. $I=\frac{P}{4\pi r^2}$

$$\Rightarrow \quad \frac{I_2}{I_1}=\left(\frac{r_1}{r_2}\right)^2=\left(\frac{100}{200}\right)^2=\frac{1}{4}$$

$$\Delta L=10\log_{10}\left(\frac{I_2}{I_1}\right)$$

$$\Rightarrow \quad L-60=10\log_{10}\left(\frac{1}{4}\right) \Rightarrow L=54\text{ dB}$$

When sound stops being heard, $L=0$

$$L_2-L_1=10\log_{10}\left(\frac{r_1}{r_2}\right)^2$$

$$\Rightarrow \quad 0-60=10\log_{10}\left(\frac{100}{r_2}\right)^2 \Rightarrow r_2=100\text{ km}$$

4. $\Delta L=10\log_{10}\left(\frac{I_2}{I_1}\right)$

$$\Rightarrow \quad L-50=10\log_{10}\left(\frac{90I}{30I}\right)$$

$$\Rightarrow \quad L=54.8\text{ dB}$$

5. $I=\frac{\Delta p_m^2}{2\rho v} \Rightarrow \frac{I_2}{I_1}=\left(\frac{\Delta p_{m_2}}{\Delta p_{m_1}}\right)^2$

$$\Delta L=10\log_{10}\left(\frac{I_2}{I_1}\right)=10\log_{10}\left(\frac{\Delta p_{m_2}}{\Delta p_{m_1}}\right)^2$$

$$\Rightarrow \quad 60-50=10\log_{10}\left(\frac{\Delta p_{m_2}}{\Delta p_{m_1}}\right)^2$$

$$\Rightarrow \quad \frac{\Delta p_{m_2}}{\Delta p_{m_1}}=\sqrt{10}=3.16$$

10.5 Interference of Sound Waves

1. (a) $\Delta x=BD-AD=\sqrt{(2.4)^2+1^2}-2.4=0.2$ m

$$\Delta\phi=\frac{2\pi}{\lambda}\Delta x=\frac{2\pi}{(340/850)}(0.2)=\pi$$

(b) $I_A=\frac{P}{4\pi r_A^2}=\frac{25\pi}{4\pi(2.4)^2}$, $I_B=\frac{P}{4\pi r_B^2}=\frac{25\pi}{4\pi(2.6)^2}$

$$I=I_A+I_B+2\sqrt{I_A}\sqrt{I_B}\cos\pi=(\sqrt{I_A}-\sqrt{I_B})^2$$

$$=\left[\frac{5}{2(2.4)}-\frac{5}{2(2.6)}\right]^2=\left(\frac{25}{312}\right)^2$$

2. (a) Phase angle for S_1,

$$\phi_1=\omega t-kx_1$$

Phase angle for S_2,

$$\phi_2=\omega t-kx_2+\pi$$

$$\phi_1=\phi_2$$

$$\Rightarrow \quad \omega t-kx_1=\omega t-kx_2+\pi$$

$$\Rightarrow \quad \frac{2\pi}{\lambda}(x_2-x_1)=\pi$$

$$\Rightarrow \quad \frac{2\pi}{(330/165)}(x_2-x_1)=\pi$$

$$\Rightarrow \quad x_2-x_1=1$$

On the path ABC, it is possible at B where $x_2=4$ m and $x_1=3$ m.

(b) At A, phase difference is 4π and at B it is zero.

So, minima in between these will be at π and 3π phase difference. So, total 2 minima.

At C, phase difference is 6π. So, between B and C, there will be minima at $\pi, 3\pi$ and 5π phase difference.

So, total 3 minima.

$\therefore$ Required ratio $=2:3$

3.

$$\Delta x=n\lambda$$

$$\Rightarrow \quad (30-10)\times10^{-2}=n\left(\frac{400}{f}\right)$$

$$\Rightarrow \quad f=2000n$$

For $n=1, f=2000$ Hz

$n=2, f=4000$ Hz

$n=3, f=6000$ Hz

$n=4, f=8000$ Hz

$n=5, f=10000$ Hz

4. Let, intensity of each wave $= I$

$$I_{max} = (\sqrt{I}+\sqrt{I})^2 = I_0$$

$$\Rightarrow \quad I = \frac{I_0}{4}$$

$$I = I_1 + I_2 + 2\sqrt{I_1}\sqrt{I_2}\cos\Delta\phi$$

$$\Rightarrow \quad \frac{I_0}{2} = \frac{I_0}{4} + \frac{I_0}{4} + 2\sqrt{\frac{I_0}{4}}\sqrt{\frac{I_0}{4}}\cos\Delta\phi$$

$$\Rightarrow \quad \Delta\phi = \frac{\pi}{2}$$

$$\Delta\phi = \frac{2\pi}{\lambda}\Delta x$$

$$\Rightarrow \quad \frac{\pi}{2} = \frac{2\pi}{\lambda}\Delta x$$

$$\Rightarrow \quad \Delta x = \frac{\lambda}{4}$$

Let, the distance moved by the sliding tube $= y$

$$\therefore \quad \Delta x = 2y = \frac{\lambda}{4}$$

$$\Rightarrow \quad y = \frac{\lambda}{8}$$

5. At B, $\Delta x_{max} = 2 - 0 = 2$ m

At ∞, $\Delta x_{min} = 2 - 2 = 0$

So, as we go from B to C, path difference decreases.

For no position of destructive interference along the line BC,

$$\Delta x_{max} = \frac{\lambda}{2} = 2$$

$$\Rightarrow \quad \lambda = 4 \text{ m}$$

$$f = \frac{v}{\lambda} = \frac{332}{4} = 83 \text{ Hz}$$

6. (a) $\lambda = \frac{v}{f} = \frac{330}{200} = 1.65$ m,

$$\frac{d}{\lambda} = \frac{4}{1.65} = 2.42$$

At infinity, path difference $= 0$

At pole, path difference $= d = 4$ m

As the man approaches the pole, the path difference changes as $0, \frac{\lambda}{2}, \lambda, \frac{3\lambda}{2}, 2\lambda$.

So, there will be 2 minima corresponding to the path difference $\frac{\lambda}{2}$ and $\frac{3\lambda}{2}$

(b) $\Delta x = \sqrt{L_1^2 + d^2} - L_1 = \frac{\lambda}{2}$ and $\sqrt{L_2^2 + d^2} - L_2 = \frac{3\lambda}{2}$

$\Rightarrow L_1 = 9.28$ m, $L_2 = 1.99$ m

7. $2d = 3$ cm $\Rightarrow d = 1.5$ cm

$\lambda = 2$ cm, $D = 24$ cm

Let, the detection be shifted by a distance y.

$$S_2P - S_1P = \frac{\lambda}{2}$$

$$\Rightarrow \quad \sqrt{D^2 + (y+d)^2} - \sqrt{D^2 + (y-d)^2} = \frac{\lambda}{2}$$

$$\Rightarrow \quad \sqrt{24^2 + (y+1.5)^2} - \sqrt{24^2 + (y-1.5)^2} = 1$$

$$\Rightarrow \quad y = 8.5 \text{ cm}$$

8. $\Delta x = d\sin\theta = n\lambda$

$\Rightarrow 2\lambda \sin\theta = n\lambda$

$$\Rightarrow \quad \sin\theta = \frac{n}{2}$$

For $n = 1$, $\sin\theta = \frac{1}{2}$

$$\Rightarrow \quad \theta = 30°$$

For $n = -1$, $\sin\theta = -\frac{1}{2}$

$$\Rightarrow \quad \theta = -30°$$

$$\therefore \quad \theta = \pm 30°$$

9. $\lambda = \frac{v}{f} = \frac{360}{180} = 2$ m

Path difference between the reflected wave and the direct wave,

$$\Delta x = 2\sqrt{2^2 + \left(\frac{x}{2}\right)^2} - x$$

For maxima, $\quad \Delta x = n\lambda$

$$\Rightarrow \quad 2\sqrt{2^2 + \left(\frac{x}{2}\right)^2} - x = (1)2$$

[$\because n = 1$ for minimum value of x]

$$\Rightarrow \quad x = 3 \text{ m}$$

10.6 Equation of Stationary Sound waves

1. (a) $\lambda = \frac{2\pi}{k} = \frac{2\pi}{10\pi} = 0.2$ m

$$f = \frac{\omega}{2\pi} = \frac{100\pi}{2\pi} = 50 \text{ Hz}$$

$$v = \frac{\omega}{k} = \frac{100\pi}{10\pi} = 10 \text{ m/s}$$

(b) $B = \rho v^2 = (10^{-3} \times 10^3)(10)^2 = 100 \text{ N/m}^2$

$$\Delta p_m = BAk = 100 \times (20 \times 10^{-3}) \times 10\pi$$

$$= 20\pi \text{ N/m}^2 = 62.8 \text{ N/m}^2$$

(c) $\frac{\lambda}{4} = \frac{0.2}{4} = 0.05$ m

2. $v = \sqrt{\frac{Y}{\rho}} = \sqrt{\frac{2 \times 10^{11}}{8000}} = 5000$ m/s

Since, the end points are clamped, they will be displacement nodes. There are 5 antinodes of displacement wave. Hence, the rod will oscillate in 5 loops of displacement wave.

$$5\left(\frac{\lambda}{2}\right)=1 \Rightarrow \lambda = 0.4 \text{ m/s}$$

$$k=\frac{2\pi}{\lambda}=\frac{2\pi}{0.4}=5\pi \text{ rad/m}$$

$$\omega = kv = 5\pi(5000) = 25000\pi$$

Equation of stationary wave,

$$y = A \sin kx \cos(\omega t + \phi)$$

$$\Rightarrow \quad y = (2\times 10^{-6} \text{ m}) \sin 5\pi x \cos(25000\pi t + \phi)$$

10.7 Organ Pipes

1. Distance between adjacent nodes $= \frac{\lambda}{2} = 4$

$$\Rightarrow \quad \lambda = 8 \text{ cm}$$

$$f = \frac{v}{\lambda} = \frac{336}{8\times 10^{-2}} = 4.2 \text{ kHz}$$

2. (a) Fundamental frequency $= \frac{v}{2L} = \frac{320}{2(0.8)} = 200$ Hz

First overtone frequency $= 2\left(\frac{v}{2L}\right) = 400$ Hz

Second overtone frequency $= 3\left(\frac{v}{2L}\right) = 600$ Hz

(b) Fundamental frequency $= \frac{v}{4L} = \frac{320}{4(0.8)} = 100$ Hz

First overtone frequency $= \frac{3v}{4L} = 300$ Hz

Second overtone frequency $= \frac{5v}{4L} = 500$ Hz

3. $(2n-1)\frac{v}{4L} = 1250$

$$\Rightarrow \quad (2n-1)\frac{(340}{4(0.85)} = 1250$$

$$\Rightarrow \quad n = 6.75$$

So, possible values of n are 1, 2, 3, 4, 5 and 6.

4.

$$\frac{nv}{2L} = 1800 \quad \text{...(i)}$$

$$\frac{(n+1)v}{2L} = 2100 \quad \text{...(ii)}$$

From Eqs. (i) and (ii), we get

$$n = 6$$

$$\therefore \quad \frac{6(330)}{2L} = 1800$$

$$\Rightarrow \quad L = 0.55 \text{ m} = 55 \text{ cm}$$

5. (a) $425 : 595 : 765 = 5 : 7 : 9$

Since, even harmonics are missing, pipe will be closed at one end.

(b) $5f = 425 \Rightarrow f = 85$ Hz

$$f = \frac{v}{4L} = 85$$

$$\Rightarrow \quad \frac{340}{4(L)} = 85 \Rightarrow L = 1 \text{ m}$$

6. 3rd harmonic of P_1 = Ist overtone of P_2

$$\Rightarrow \quad 3\left(\frac{v}{4L_1}\right) = 2\left(\frac{v}{2L_2}\right)$$

$$\Rightarrow \quad L_2 = \frac{4L_1}{3} = 40 \text{ cm}$$

7. For open pipe, $f = \frac{v}{2L}$

When half of the pipe is dipped in water, it will become closed pipe of length $L/2$.

$$f' = \frac{v}{4(L/2)} = \frac{v}{2L} = f$$

8.

$$f_1 = f_2$$

$$\Rightarrow \quad \frac{v}{4x} = 2\left(\frac{v}{2(100-x)}\right)$$

$$\Rightarrow \quad x = 20 \text{ cm}$$

$\therefore$ Length of closed pipe piece = 20 cm

Length of open pipe piece = 80 cm

For open pipe piece, $f = \frac{v}{2l} = \frac{320}{2(0.8)} = 200$ Hz

9. Second overtone $\Rightarrow$ 3rd harmonic $\Rightarrow$ 3 loops

$$3\left(\frac{\lambda}{2}\right) = L \Rightarrow \lambda = \frac{2L}{3}$$

Distance between consecutive displacement node and pressure node $= \frac{\lambda}{4} = \frac{1}{4}\left(\frac{2L}{3}\right) = \frac{L}{6}$

10. 3rd overtone $\Rightarrow$ 3 full loops + 1 half loop

$$3\left(\frac{\lambda}{2}\right) + 1\left(\frac{\lambda}{4}\right) = L \Rightarrow \lambda = \frac{4L}{7}$$

The closed end is displacement node. At a distance $\frac{L}{7} = \frac{\lambda}{4}$, there will displacement antinode. So, the amplitude will be equal to maximum amplitude a.

11. For wire, $\mu = \frac{m}{L_1} = \frac{5\times 10^{-3}}{0.5} = 0.01$ kg/m

Second overtone frequency $= \frac{5v_1}{4L_1}$

For closed pipe,

Fundamental frequency $= \frac{v_2}{4L_2} = \frac{320}{4(1)} = 80$ Hz

For resonance, $\frac{5v_1}{4(0.5)} = 80$

$$\Rightarrow \quad v_1 = 32 \text{ m/s}$$

$$T = \mu v^2 = 0.01(32)^2 = 10.24 \text{ N}$$

10.8 End Correction

1. $f = \frac{v}{2L'} \Rightarrow 320 = \frac{320}{2L'}$

$\Rightarrow \quad L' = 0.5\,\text{m} = 50\,\text{cm}$

$L' = L + 2(0.3D)$

$\Rightarrow \quad 50 = 48 + 0.6D \Rightarrow D = 3.33\,\text{cm}$

2. For open pipe, $f_1 = \frac{v}{40 + 2e}$

For closed pipe, $f_2 = \frac{3v}{4(31 + e)}$

$f_1 = f_2$

$\Rightarrow \quad \frac{v}{40 + 2e} = \frac{3v}{4(31 + e)} \Rightarrow e = 2\,\text{cm}$

10.9 Resonance Tube

1. $\lambda = 2(l_2 - l_1) = 2(31.25 - 9.75) = 43\,\text{cm}$

$v = \lambda f = 0.43 \times 800 = 344\,\text{m/s}$

2. $\lambda = 2(l_2 - l_1) = 2(38 - 12) = 52\,\text{cm}$

$f = \frac{v}{\lambda} = \frac{312}{0.52} = 600\,\text{Hz}$

3. $\lambda = 2(l_2 - l_1) = 2(100 - 32) = 136\,\text{cm}$

For first resonance, $\frac{\lambda}{4} = 32 + e$

$\Rightarrow \quad \frac{136}{4} = 32 + e$

$\Rightarrow \quad e = 2\,\text{cm}$

4. $\lambda = 2(l_2 - l_1) = 2(122 - 40) = 164\,\text{cm}$

$l_3 = l_2 + \frac{\lambda}{2} = 122 + \frac{164}{2} = 204\,\text{cm}$

5. $\lambda = \frac{v}{f} = \frac{340}{340} = 1\,\text{m} = 100\,\text{cm}$

Length of air column $= \frac{\lambda}{4}, \frac{3\lambda}{4}, \frac{5\lambda}{4}, \ldots$

$= 25\,\text{cm}, 75\,\text{cm}, 125\,\text{cm}, \ldots$

$\therefore$ Maximum length of air column possible = 75 cm

$\Rightarrow$ Minimum height of water = 120 − 75 = 45 cm

10.10 Vibration in Rods

1. $v = \sqrt{\frac{Y}{\rho}} = \sqrt{\frac{2 \times 10^{11}}{8 \times 10^3}} = 5000\,\text{m/s}$

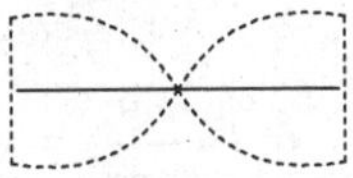

Fundamental mode

Fundamental frequency $= \frac{v}{2L} = 2.5\,\text{kHz}$

First overtone frequency $= \frac{3v}{2L} = \frac{3(5000)}{2(1)} = 7.5\,\text{kHz}$

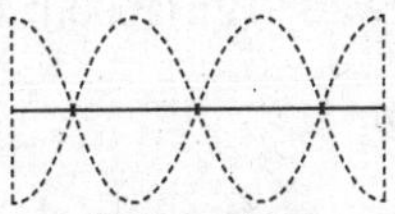

First overtone

2. Since, points A and B are clamped, therefore, nodes are formed at these points or rod oscillates with integer number of loops in the middle part. Let, the number of these loops be m.

$\therefore \quad m\left(\frac{\lambda}{2}\right) = l - 2a = 40$

$\Rightarrow \quad m\lambda = 80\,\text{cm}$ ...(i)

Since, the ends of the rod are free, therefore, antinodes are formed at each end of the rod or at one end of each end part is an antinode and at the other end is a node. It means that number of loops in each end part will be an odd multiple of half.

Let, these be $\frac{2n-1}{2}$, where n is an integer

$\therefore \quad \left(\frac{2n-1}{2}\right)\left(\frac{\lambda}{2}\right) = a$

$\Rightarrow \quad (2n-1)\lambda = 120\,\text{cm}$ ...(ii)

Dividing Eq. (i) by Eq. (ii),

$\frac{m}{2n-1} = \frac{2}{3}$

For minimum frequency, $m = 2, n = 2$

$\therefore \quad \lambda = 40\,\text{cm}$

$v = \sqrt{\frac{Y}{\rho}} = \sqrt{\frac{144 \times 10^9}{9000}} = 4000\,\text{m/s}$

$f_1 = \frac{v}{\lambda} = \frac{4000}{0.4} = 10\,\text{kHz}$

For next higher frequency, $m = 6, n = 5$

Substituting $m = 6$ in Eq. (i),

$\lambda = \frac{40}{3}\,\text{cm}$

$f_2 = \frac{v}{\lambda} = \frac{4000}{(0.4/3)} = 30\,\text{kHz}$

10.11 Beats

1. $f_{beat} = f_1 - f_2$

$\Rightarrow \quad 6 = \frac{v}{1.0} - \frac{v}{1.02} \Rightarrow v = 306\,\text{m/s}$

2. (a) $f_{beat} = |f_1 - f_2| = |300 - 305| = 5\,\text{Hz}$

Number of beats in 5 s $= f_{beat} \times t = 5 \times 5 = 25$

(b) $T = \frac{1}{f_{beat}} = \frac{1}{5} = 0.2\,\text{s}$

Required time $= \frac{T}{2} = 0.1\,\text{s}$

3. Since, the beat frequency is 5 per second, the possible frequencies of A before loading are

(480 + 5) Hz or (480 − 5) Hz

i.e., 485 Hz or 475 Hz

Due to wax, frequency of A will decrease. Since, beat frequency also decreases, frequency of A before loading must be 485 Hz.

After loading, $f_{beat} = |f_A - 480|$

$\Rightarrow 3 = |f_A - 480|$

$\Rightarrow f_A = 483$ Hz or 477 Hz

4. $f_{beat} = |f_A - f_B| \Rightarrow 3 = |158 - f_B|$

$\Rightarrow f_B = 155$ Hz or 161 Hz

As B is filed, its frequency increases. Since, beat frequency increases to 7 per second, frequency of B before filing can be either 155 Hz or 161 Hz which after filing will become 165 Hz.

5. $\beta = |f_X - f_Y|$

$\Rightarrow 4 = |300 - f_Y|$

$\Rightarrow f_Y = 304$ Hz or 296 Hz

When the tension of string Y is slightly increased, f_Y also increases. Since, the beat frequency decreases, f_Y must be 296 Hz.

6. Let, the frequency of tuning fork $= f$

Frequency of sonometer,

$$f' = \frac{1}{2L}\sqrt{\frac{T}{\mu}}$$

$$\therefore \quad f + 4 = \frac{1}{2(95)}\sqrt{\frac{T}{\mu}}$$

and $$f - 4 = \frac{1}{2(100)}\sqrt{\frac{T}{\mu}}$$

$$\Rightarrow \frac{f+4}{f-4} = \frac{100}{95} \Rightarrow f = 156 \text{ Hz}$$

7. Let, the frequency of the tuning fork $= f$

For sonometer, $f' = \frac{1}{2L}\sqrt{\frac{T}{\mu}}$

Since, beat frequency is 5 Hz, f' will be either $f + 5$ or $f - 5$.

$$f + 5 = \frac{1}{2L}\sqrt{\frac{100}{\mu}} \quad \text{...(i)}$$

$$f - 5 = \frac{1}{2L}\sqrt{\frac{81}{\mu}} \quad \text{...(ii)}$$

Dividing Eq. (i) by Eq. (ii), we get

$$\frac{f+5}{f-5} = \frac{10}{9} \Rightarrow f = 95 \text{ Hz}$$

8. $$f = \frac{1}{2L}\sqrt{\frac{T}{\mu}}$$

$$\Rightarrow \frac{\Delta f}{f} = \frac{1}{2}\frac{\Delta T}{T} \Rightarrow \frac{6}{600} = \frac{1}{2}\left(\frac{\Delta T}{T}\right)$$

$$\Rightarrow \frac{\Delta T}{T} = 0.02 \text{ or } 2\%$$

9. $$\mu = \frac{m}{L} = \frac{2.5 \times 10^{-3}}{25 \times 10^{-2}} = 0.01 \text{ kg/m}$$

Fundamental frequency of closed pipe,

$$f_1 = \frac{v_1}{4L} = \frac{320}{4(0.4)} = 200 \text{ Hz}$$

As beat frequency is 8 Hz, frequency of string can be either 192 Hz or 208 Hz. Since, decreasing the tension, decreases the beat frequency, frequency of string must be 208 Hz.

First overtone of string, $f = \frac{v}{L}$

$$\Rightarrow 208 = \frac{v}{(0.25)}$$

$$\Rightarrow v = 52 \text{ m/s}$$

$$T = \mu v^2 = 0.01(52)^2 = 27.04 \text{ N}$$

Level 02

Single Choice Correct Questions

1. $\Delta p = -B\frac{\partial s}{\partial x} = -B$ (slope of s-x graph)

2. $v \propto \sqrt{T} \Rightarrow \frac{v_1}{v_2} = \sqrt{\frac{T_1}{T_2}}$

$$\Rightarrow \frac{v}{2v} = \sqrt{\frac{300}{T_2}}$$

$$\Rightarrow T_2 = 1200 \text{ K} = 927^\circ \text{C}$$

3. $$v_1 = v_2$$

$$\Rightarrow \sqrt{\frac{\gamma R T_1}{32}} = \sqrt{\frac{\gamma R(273+15)}{28}}$$

$$\Rightarrow T_1 = 288 \times \frac{32}{28} = 329 \text{ K} = 56^\circ \text{C}$$

4. $$M_{mix} = \frac{n_1 M_1 + n_2 M_2}{n_1 + n_2} = \frac{3(2) + 2(32)}{3+2} = 14$$

$$v = \sqrt{\frac{\gamma RT}{M}}$$

$$\Rightarrow \frac{v_1}{v_2} = \sqrt{\frac{M_2}{M_1}}$$

$$\Rightarrow \frac{v}{v_2} = \sqrt{\frac{14}{2}}$$

$$\Rightarrow v_2 = \frac{v}{\sqrt{7}}$$

5. $$I = \frac{1}{2}\rho v \omega^2 A^2$$

$$\therefore \frac{I_1}{I_2} = \left(\frac{\omega_1 A_1}{\omega_2 A_2}\right)^2 = \left(\frac{200\pi \times 2}{150\pi \times 5}\right)^2 = \frac{64}{225}$$

6. $$I = \frac{P}{4\pi r^2} = \frac{10}{4\pi(10)^2} = \frac{1}{40\pi} \text{ W/m}^2$$

$$I = \frac{1}{2}\rho v \omega^2 A^2$$

$$\Rightarrow \frac{1}{40\pi} = \frac{1}{2} \times 1.29 \times 340[2\pi(1000)]^2 A^2$$

$$\Rightarrow A = 0.96 \,\mu\text{m}$$

7. $$I = \frac{\Delta p_m^2}{2\rho v}$$

$$\Rightarrow \quad 10^{-10} = \frac{\Delta p_m^2}{2 \times 1.3 \times 330}$$

$$\Rightarrow \quad \Delta p_m = 3 \times 10^{-4}\ \text{N/m}^2$$

8. $$L = 10\log_{10}\left(\frac{I}{I_0}\right)$$

$$\Rightarrow \quad 40 = 10\log_{10}\left(\frac{I}{10^{-12}}\right)$$

$$\Rightarrow \quad I = 10^{-8}\ \text{W/m}^2$$

$$P = IA = 10^{-8} \times 10^{-6} = 10^{-14}\ \text{W}$$

$$P = \frac{E}{t} \quad \Rightarrow \quad 10^{-14} = \frac{1}{t}$$

$$\Rightarrow \quad t = 10^{14}\ \text{s}$$

9. $\Delta L = 10\log_{10}\left(\frac{I_2}{I_1}\right) = 10\log_{10}\left(\frac{400}{20}\right) = 13\ \text{dB}$

10. $$I \propto \frac{1}{r^2}$$

$$\therefore \quad \Delta L = 10\log_{10}\left(\frac{I_2}{I_1}\right) = 10\log_{10}\left(\frac{r_1}{r_2}\right)^2$$

$$\Rightarrow \quad L_2 - 50 = 10\log_{10}\left(\frac{1}{10}\right)^2$$

$$\Rightarrow \quad L_2 = 30\ \text{dB}$$

11. $$\Delta L = 10\log_{10}\left(\frac{I_2}{I_1}\right)$$

$$\Rightarrow \quad L_2 - 60 = 10\log_{10}\left(\frac{8I}{I}\right)$$

$$\Rightarrow \quad L_2 = 69\ \text{dB}$$

12. Let the number of years taken is n.

$$\Delta L = 10\log_{10}\left(\frac{I_2}{I_1}\right)$$

$$\Rightarrow \quad n \times 1 = 10\log_{10}\left(\frac{2I}{I}\right)$$

$$\Rightarrow \quad n = 3$$

13. $$\frac{I_{max}}{I_{min}} = \left(\frac{\sqrt{I_1}+\sqrt{I_2}}{\sqrt{I_1}-\sqrt{I_2}}\right)^2 = \left(\frac{\sqrt{4}+\sqrt{1}}{\sqrt{4}-\sqrt{1}}\right)^2 = 9$$

$$\Delta L = 10\log_{10}\left(\frac{I_{max}}{I_{min}}\right) = 10\log_{10} 9 = 20\log_{10} 3$$

14. $I = I_1 + I_2 + 2\sqrt{I_1}\sqrt{I_2}\cos\Delta\phi$

$$I_A = I + 4I + 2\sqrt{I}\sqrt{4I}\cos\left(\frac{\pi}{2}\right) = 5I$$

$$I_B = I + 4I + 2\sqrt{I}\sqrt{4I}\cos\pi = I$$

$$\therefore \quad I_A - I_B = 5I - I = 4I$$

15. $$\phi_P = kr_1 - \omega t + \frac{\pi}{2}$$

$$\phi_Q = kr_2 - \omega t$$

$$\phi_P - \phi_Q = k(r_1 - r_2) + \frac{\pi}{2} = \frac{2\pi}{200} \times 50 + \frac{\pi}{2} = \pi$$

16. For maxima, $\Delta x = n\lambda$

$$\Rightarrow \quad \pi r - 2r = n\left(\frac{v}{f}\right)$$

$$\Rightarrow \quad f = \frac{nv}{r(\pi - 2)}$$

17. $\frac{\lambda}{2} = 24 - 12 \Rightarrow \lambda = 24\ \text{cm}$

$$f = \frac{v}{\lambda} = \frac{330}{0.24} = 1375\ \text{Hz}$$

18. 3 maxima corresponding to $\Delta x = \lambda, 2\lambda$ and 3λ..

19. At the ends of the major axis, path difference is 2.7λ.

At the ends of the minor axis, path difference is zero which means 2 maxima will be on the minor axis.

In each quadrant, path difference varies between 0 and 2.7λ.

So, there will be 2 maxima in each quadrant corresponding to path differences λ and 2λ.

Total number of maxima $= 4 \times 2 + 2 = 10$

20. For maxima, $\Delta\phi = 2n\pi$

$$\Rightarrow \quad -\frac{\pi}{2} + \frac{2\pi}{\lambda}(d\sin\theta) = 2n\pi$$

$$\Rightarrow \quad \sin\theta = \left(2n + \frac{1}{2}\right)\frac{\lambda}{2d}$$

$$\Rightarrow \quad \frac{y}{\sqrt{(100\lambda)^2 + y^2}} = \frac{1}{2}\frac{\lambda}{2(3\lambda)}$$

[$\because n = 0$ for minimum value of y]

$$\Rightarrow \quad \frac{y}{100\lambda} = \frac{1}{12}$$

$$\Rightarrow \quad y = \frac{25\lambda}{3}$$

21. $\Delta x = 2\sqrt{(60)^2 + (25)^2} - 120 = 10\ \text{m}$

For constructive interference,

$$\Delta x = n\lambda$$

$$\Rightarrow \quad 10 = n\lambda$$

$$\Rightarrow \quad \lambda = \frac{10}{n}$$

$$\Rightarrow \quad \lambda = \frac{10}{1}, \frac{10}{2}, \frac{10}{3}, \frac{10}{4}, \ldots$$

22. $\Delta x = 2 \times 5 = 10\lambda$

$$\Rightarrow \quad \lambda = 1\ \text{cm}$$

23. $f = \frac{v}{4L}, \frac{3v}{4L}, \frac{5v}{4L}$ = 425 Hz, 1275 Hz, 2125 Hz

24. $f_n = (2n+1)\frac{v}{4L} \le 20000$

$\Rightarrow (2n+1)(1400) \leq 20000$

$\Rightarrow \quad n \leq 6.67$

$\therefore \quad n_{max} = 6$

25. $\dfrac{v}{4L_1} = 2\left(\dfrac{v}{2L_2}\right)$

$\Rightarrow \quad L_1 = \dfrac{L_2}{4} = 12.5 \text{ cm}$

26. Ist overtone of P_1 = 3rd overtone of P_2

$\Rightarrow \quad \dfrac{3v}{4L_1} = 4\left(\dfrac{v}{2L_2}\right)$

$\Rightarrow \quad \dfrac{L_1}{L_2} = \dfrac{3}{8}$

27. $3\left(\dfrac{v}{4L}\right) = 100 + \left(\dfrac{v}{2L}\right)$

$\Rightarrow \dfrac{v}{2L} = 200$

$\therefore$ Fundamental frequency of the open pipe = 200 Hz

28. $f = \dfrac{v}{2L}, \quad f' = \dfrac{v}{4(2L/3)} = \dfrac{3f}{4}$

29. $\dfrac{v}{2L_1} = 100 \Rightarrow L_1 = \dfrac{v}{200}$

$\dfrac{v}{4L_2} = 50 \Rightarrow L_2 = \dfrac{v}{200}$

When they are joined,

$$f = \frac{v}{4(L_1 + L_2)} = 25 \text{ Hz}$$

30. $f_C = \dfrac{v_3}{2(2l/3)} = \dfrac{3}{4l}\sqrt{\dfrac{(7/5)RT}{28}}$

$f_D = \dfrac{v_4}{2(l/3)} = \dfrac{3}{2l}\sqrt{\dfrac{(7/5)RT}{44}}$

$\therefore \quad \dfrac{f_C}{f_D} = \sqrt{\dfrac{11}{28}}$

31. 50 : 150 : 250 = 1 : 3 : 5

Since, even harmonics are missing, it will be a closed pipe with fundamental frequency of 50 Hz.

$$f = \frac{v}{4L} = 50$$

$\Rightarrow \quad \dfrac{340}{4L} = 50 \Rightarrow L = 1.7 \text{ m}$

32. $10 \text{ cm} = \dfrac{\lambda}{4}$

Open end is displacement antinode. So, the point at a distance $\dfrac{\lambda}{4}$ from the open end will be displacement node.

33. Taking the closed end as origin,

$y = 2A \sin\left(\dfrac{2\pi}{\lambda} x\right) \cos \omega t$

$\therefore$ Displacement amplitude $= 2A \sin\left(\dfrac{2\pi}{\lambda} x\right)$

Second overtone $\Rightarrow$ 2.5 loops

$\therefore \quad 2.5\left(\dfrac{\lambda}{2}\right) = 10$

$\Rightarrow \quad \lambda = 8 \text{ cm}$

At a point 9 cm from open end or 1 cm from closed end

Displacement amplitude $= 2 \sin\left[\dfrac{2\pi}{8}(1)\right] = \sqrt{2}$ mm

34. Ist overtone $\Rightarrow$ 1.5 loops

$\therefore \quad 1.5\left(\dfrac{\lambda}{2}\right) = 1.2$

$\Rightarrow \quad \lambda = 1.6 \text{ m}$

Open end is pressure node. So, pressure antinode will be $\dfrac{\lambda}{4} = 0.4$ m from the open end.

35. $f = \dfrac{1}{2L}\sqrt{\dfrac{T}{\mu}}$ ...(i)

$3f = \dfrac{1}{2L}\sqrt{\dfrac{T+8}{\mu}}$ ...(ii)

Dividing Eq. (i) by Eq. (ii), we get

$T = 1 \text{ N}$

36. $\dfrac{3v}{4(2-x)} = 170$

$\Rightarrow \quad \dfrac{3 \times 340}{4(2-x)} = 170 \Rightarrow x = 0.5 \text{ m}$

37. $f = \dfrac{v}{2L'}$

$\Rightarrow \quad 660 = \dfrac{330}{2L'} \Rightarrow L' = 25 \text{ cm}$

$L' = L + 2(0.6r)$

$\Rightarrow \quad 25 = 24 + 1.2r \Rightarrow r = 0.83 \text{ cm}$

38. For closed pipe,

$\dfrac{\lambda}{4} = L + 0.6r_1$ ...(i)

For open pipe,

$2\left(\dfrac{\lambda}{2}\right) = L + 2(0.6r_2)$ ...(ii)

Dividing Eq. (i) by Eq. (ii), we get

$\dfrac{1}{4} = \dfrac{L + 0.6r_1}{L + 1.2r_2}$

$\Rightarrow \quad r_2 - 2r_1 = 2.5L$

39. $\lambda = \dfrac{v}{f} = \dfrac{340}{680} = 0.5 \text{ m}$

$x = \dfrac{\lambda}{2} = 0.25 \text{ m} = 25 \text{ cm}$

40. $\lambda = 2(l_2 - l_1) = 2(46 - 16) = 60 \text{ cm}$

$v = \lambda f = 0.6 \times 500 = 300 \text{ m/s}$

41. $\lambda = \frac{v}{f} = \frac{340}{850} = 0.4\,\text{m} = 40\,\text{cm}$

Air column length

$= \frac{\lambda}{4}, \frac{3\lambda}{4}, \frac{5\lambda}{4}, \frac{7\lambda}{4}, \frac{9\lambda}{4}, \ldots$

= 10 cm, 30 cm, 50 cm, 70 cm, 90 cm, 100 cm, ...

Minimum level of water = 100 − 90 = 10 cm

42. $\lambda = 2(l_2 - l_1) = 2(74.1 - 24.1) = 100\,\text{cm}$

For first resonance,

$$\frac{\lambda}{4} = l_1 + e$$

$$\Rightarrow \frac{100}{4} = 24.1 + e$$

$$\Rightarrow e = 0.9\,\text{cm}$$

$$e = 0.3d \Rightarrow 0.9 = 0.3d$$

$$\Rightarrow d = 3\,\text{cm}$$

43. $\lambda = 2(l_2 - l_1) = 2(29.5 - 10.5) = 38\,\text{cm}$

$l_3 = l_2 + \frac{\lambda}{2} = 29.5 + \frac{38}{2} = 48.5\,\text{cm}$

44. $\lambda = \frac{v}{f} = \frac{330}{500} = 0.66\,\text{m} = 66\,\text{cm}$

Possible length of air column

$= \frac{\lambda}{4}, \frac{3\lambda}{4}, \frac{5\lambda}{4}, \frac{7\lambda}{4}$

= 16.5 cm, 49.5 cm, 82.5 cm, 115.5 cm

Since, tube is of length 1 m, total number of resonances obtained will be 3.

45. $\lambda = \frac{v}{f} = \frac{340}{170} = 2\,\text{m}$

Water height reduced in consecutive resonances

$= \frac{\lambda}{2} = 100\,\text{cm}$

Volume drained $= \pi r^2 h = \frac{22}{7} \times (2.5)^2 \times 100 = \frac{13750}{7}\,\text{cm}^3$

Time passed $= \frac{\text{Volume drained}}{\text{Draining rate}} = \frac{13750/7}{55} = \frac{250}{7}\,\text{s}$

46. $\lambda = 2(L_2 - L_1)$

For first resonance, $\frac{\lambda}{4} = L_1 + e$

$$\Rightarrow e = \frac{L_2 - 3L_1}{2}$$

Distance of the displacement antinode from the top end of the tube is equal to the end correction.

47. $\lambda = 2(l_2 - l_1) = 2(63.2 - 30.7) = 65\,\text{cm}$

$v = \lambda f = (65 \times 512)\,\text{cm/s}$

Total error in measurement of $\lambda = 2 \times$ least count

$= 2 \times 0.1 = 0.2\,\text{cm}$

$$\frac{\Delta v}{v} = \frac{\Delta\lambda}{\lambda}$$

$$\Rightarrow \frac{\Delta v}{65 \times 512} = \frac{0.2}{65}$$

$$\Rightarrow \Delta v = 102.4\,\text{cm/s}$$

48. $v = \sqrt{\frac{Y}{\rho}} = \sqrt{\frac{10^{11}}{10 \times 10^4}} = 1000\,\text{m/s}$

$t = \frac{2L}{v} = \frac{2(100)}{1000} = 0.2\,\text{s}$

49. $\frac{\lambda}{2} = L \Rightarrow \lambda = 2L = 2 \times 1 = 2\,\text{m}$

$v = \lambda f = 2 \times 2500 = 5000\,\text{m/s}$

50. $f_1 - f_2 = (2 \times 1)\,\text{Hz}$

$$\Rightarrow \frac{v}{1} - \frac{v}{(165/164)} = 2$$

$$\Rightarrow v = 330\,\text{m/s}$$

51. $f_1 = \frac{500\pi}{2\pi} = 250\,\text{Hz},\ f_2 = \frac{506\pi}{2\pi} = 253\,\text{Hz}$

$\beta = f_2 - f_1 = 253 - 250 = 3$ beats per second

Number of beats per minute $= 3 \times 60 = 180$

52. (a)

53.

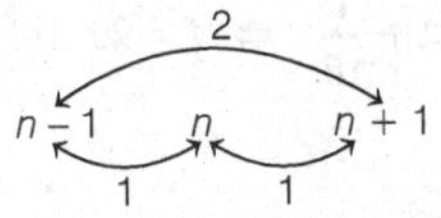

Now, divide 1 second into number of beats between two frequencies

$\left(\frac{1}{1}\right)$

$\left(\left(\frac{1}{2}\right)\right) \quad \left(\frac{2}{2}\right)$

Total number of beats = 2

54. $T = \frac{1}{|f_1 - f_2|} = \frac{1}{6}\,\text{s}$

Time interval between maximum and minimum sound

$= \frac{T}{2} = \frac{1}{12}\,\text{s}$

55. Let the unknown frequency be f.

$$|262 - f| = 2|256 - f|$$

$$\Rightarrow 262 - f = \pm 2(256 - f)$$

$$\Rightarrow f = 250\,\text{Hz or } 258\,\text{Hz}$$

56. $|f_A - f_B| = 4$

$$\Rightarrow |256 - f_B| = 4$$

$$\Rightarrow f_B = 252\,\text{Hz or } 260\,\text{Hz}$$

When B is loaded with wax, f_B will decrease. Since, beat frequency decreases, f_B must be 260 Hz.

57. $l_1 + l_2 = 100\,\text{cm},\ l_1 - l_2 = 0.2\,\text{cm}$

$\therefore\ l_1 = 50.1\,\text{cm}, l_2 = 49.9\,\text{cm}$

$$f = \frac{1}{2l}\sqrt{\frac{T}{\mu}}$$

$$\Rightarrow fl = \text{constant}$$

$$\therefore f_1 l_1 = f_2 l_2$$

$\Rightarrow \quad f_1(50.1) = (f_1 + 1)(49.9)$

$\Rightarrow \quad f_1 = 249.5 \text{ Hz}$

$\therefore \quad f_2 = f_1 + 1 = 250.5 \text{ Hz}$

58. $f = \dfrac{1}{2l}\sqrt{\dfrac{T}{\mu}}$

$\Rightarrow \quad \dfrac{\Delta f}{f} = \dfrac{1}{2}\dfrac{\Delta T}{T}$

$\Rightarrow \quad \dfrac{3/2}{f} = \dfrac{1}{2}\left(\dfrac{1}{100}\right) \Rightarrow f = 300 \text{ Hz}$

59. Let the frequency of tuning fork be f. Therefore, frequency of air column at $27°C = f + 5$.

As no beats are heard at $-3°C$, frequency of air column at $-3°C$ will be f.

$f \propto v \Rightarrow \dfrac{f+5}{f} = \dfrac{v_1}{v_2}$

$\Rightarrow \quad \dfrac{f+5}{f} = \sqrt{\dfrac{300}{270}} \Rightarrow 1 + \dfrac{5}{f} = \left(1 + \dfrac{1}{9}\right)^{1/2}$

$\Rightarrow \quad 1 + \dfrac{5}{f} = 1 + \dfrac{1}{18} \Rightarrow f = 90 \text{ Hz}$

60. (c)

Numerical Value Questions

1. $I_{max} = 4I_0$

$\Delta L = 10\log_{10}\left(\dfrac{I_{max}}{I_0}\right) = 10\log_{10} 4 = 6 \text{ dB}$

2. $I = \dfrac{P}{4\pi r^2}$

$\Rightarrow \quad \dfrac{I_1}{I_2} = \left(\dfrac{r_2}{r_1}\right)^2 \Rightarrow \dfrac{I_1}{25} = \left(\dfrac{4}{5}\right)^2$

$\Rightarrow \quad I_1 = 16 \text{ W/m}^2$

$\Delta x = \sqrt{3^2 + 4^2} - 4 = 1 \text{ km} = 1000 \text{ m}$

$\Delta\phi = \dfrac{2\pi}{\lambda}\Delta x = \dfrac{2\pi}{(48/5)} \times 1000 = \dfrac{625\pi}{3} \text{ or } \dfrac{\pi}{3}$

$I = I_1 + I_2 + 2\sqrt{I_1}\sqrt{I_2}\cos\Delta\phi$

$= 16 + 25 + 2\sqrt{16}\sqrt{25}\cos\left(\dfrac{\pi}{3}\right) = 61 \text{ W/m}^2$

3. Let the cardboard be moved upwards by a distance x.

Initial path difference,

$\Delta x = 2\sqrt{12^2 + 5^2} - 24 = \dfrac{\lambda}{3} \Rightarrow \lambda = 6 \text{ cm}$

New path difference,

$\Delta x' = 2\sqrt{12^2 + (5+x)^2} - 24$

For both waves to be in phase,

$\Delta x' = \lambda$

$\Rightarrow \quad 2\sqrt{12^2 + (5+x)^2} - 24 = 6$

$\Rightarrow \quad x = 4 \text{ cm}$

4. Ist overtone of closed pipe = Ist overtone of open pipe

$\Rightarrow \quad \dfrac{3v}{4L_1} = 2\left(\dfrac{v}{2L_2}\right) \Rightarrow L_2 = \dfrac{4L_1}{3}$

nth harmonic of closed pipe = mth harmonic of open pipe

$\Rightarrow \quad n\left(\dfrac{v}{4L_1}\right) = m\left(\dfrac{v}{2L_2}\right)$

$\Rightarrow \quad n = \dfrac{3m}{2} = \dfrac{3 \times 6}{2} = 9$

5. Let the liquid column in arm A be depressed by a distance y.

$p_1 = p_2$

$\Rightarrow \quad \rho_2 g h_2 = \rho_1 g(2y)$

$\Rightarrow \quad \left(\dfrac{\rho_1}{2}\right)h_2 = \rho_1(2y)$

$\Rightarrow \quad h_2 = 4y$

2nd overtone of A = Ist harmonic of B

$\Rightarrow \quad \dfrac{5v}{4(70 - h_2 + y)} = \dfrac{v}{4(20 - y)}$

$\Rightarrow \quad 6y - h_2 = 30$

$\Rightarrow \quad 6y - 4y = 30$

$\Rightarrow \quad y = 15 \text{ cm}$

$\therefore \quad h_2 = 4y = 60 \text{ cm}$

6. $\dfrac{\lambda}{4} = L \Rightarrow \lambda = 4L$

$p = p_0\cos\left(\dfrac{2\pi}{\lambda}x\right)$

$\Rightarrow \quad \dfrac{\sqrt{3}}{2}p_0 = p_0\cos\left(\dfrac{2\pi}{4L}x\right)$

$\Rightarrow \quad \dfrac{\pi x}{2L} = \dfrac{\pi}{6} \Rightarrow x = \dfrac{L}{3}$

$\therefore \quad n = 3$

7. Let water column goes down by distance y on the left side when the beaker is filled upto brim.

$\pi(2)^2 \times y = \pi(4)^2 \times 10$

$\Rightarrow \quad y = 40 \text{ cm}$

$l_2 - l_1 = y = \dfrac{\lambda}{2}$

$\Rightarrow \quad \lambda = 80 \text{ cm} = 0.8 \text{ m}$

$v = \lambda f = 420 \times 0.8 = 336 \text{ m/s}$

8. $f, f+4, f+8, \ldots, (f + 55 \times 4)$

$f_{56} = 2f_1 \Rightarrow f + 220 = 2f$

$\Rightarrow \quad f = 220 \text{ Hz}$

$\therefore \quad f_3 = f + (3-1)4 = 228 \text{ Hz}$

9. $f = f_1 - f_2$

$\Rightarrow \quad 2 = \dfrac{v}{2L} - \dfrac{v}{4L} \Rightarrow \dfrac{v}{L} = 8$

$f' = f_1' - f_2' = \dfrac{v}{2(L/2)} - \dfrac{v}{4(2L)} = \dfrac{7v}{8L} = 7 \text{ Hz}$

10. Fundamental frequency of pipe $= \frac{v}{4L} = \frac{320}{4(0.4)} = 200$ Hz

Since, beat frequency is 8 Hz, frequency of string will be either 208 Hz or 192 Hz.

Decreasing the tension will decrease frequency of string. As beat frequency decreases, frequency of string must be 208 Hz.

First overtone of string $= \frac{v}{L} = 208$

$$\Rightarrow \quad v = 208 \times 0.25 = 52 \text{ m/s}$$

$$T = \mu v^2 = \frac{0.25 \times 10^{-3}}{1 \times 10^{-2}}(52)^2 = 67.6 \text{ N}$$

Level-03

Single Choice Correct Questions

1. Time for one loop $= \frac{30}{36} = \frac{5}{6}$ s

Speed of sound, $v = \frac{\text{distance}}{\text{time}} = \frac{2 \times 130}{(5/6)} = 312$ m/s

2. $dp = -B\left(\frac{\partial y}{\partial x}\right) = -\gamma p\left(\frac{\partial y}{\partial x}\right) \Rightarrow \frac{dp}{p} = \gamma\left(\frac{u}{c}\right)$

3.
$$T = \left(\frac{T_2 - T_1}{l}\right)x + T_1$$

$$\Rightarrow \frac{dT}{dt} = \left(\frac{T_2 - T_1}{l}\right)\frac{dx}{dt}$$

$$\Rightarrow \frac{dT}{dt} = \left(\frac{T_2 - T_1}{l}\right)\alpha\sqrt{T}$$

$$\Rightarrow \int dt = \frac{l}{\alpha(T_2 - T_1)}\int_{T_1}^{T_2}\frac{dT}{\sqrt{T}}$$

$$\Rightarrow t = \frac{2l(\sqrt{T_2} - \sqrt{T_1})}{\alpha(T_2 - T_1)}$$

$$\Rightarrow t = \frac{2l}{\alpha(\sqrt{T_2} + \sqrt{T_1})}$$

4.
$$\lambda = \frac{v}{f} = \frac{320}{160} = 2 \text{ m}$$

$$\Delta\phi = \mathbf{K}\cdot\mathbf{r} = \frac{2\pi}{2}\left(\frac{3\hat{i} + 4\hat{j}}{5}\right)\cdot(2\hat{i} + \hat{j} + 2\hat{k}) = \frac{\pi}{5}(6 + 4) = 2\pi$$

5. $\Delta p = -B\left(\frac{\partial y}{\partial x}\right) = -B \times \text{Slope}$

Slope is most negative at point R. So, Δp is most positive at point R. Hence, pressure will be maximum at R.

6. $p_0 = BkS_0 = B\left(\frac{2\pi}{\lambda}\right)S_0 \Rightarrow p_0 \propto \frac{1}{\lambda}$

Thus, pressure amplitude is highest for minimum wavelength, other parameters B and S_0 being same for all.

$\because \quad \lambda_1 > \lambda_2 > \lambda_3 \Rightarrow p_3 > p_2 > p_1$

7.
$$I = \frac{\Delta p_m^2}{2\rho v}$$

$$\Rightarrow 10^{-10} = \frac{(2 \times 10^{-4})^2}{2 \times 1 \times v}$$

$$\Rightarrow v = 200 \text{ m/s}$$

$$k = \frac{\omega}{v} = \frac{1000}{200} = 5 \text{ rad/m}$$

$$B = \rho v^2 = 1 \times (200)^2 = 4 \times 10^4 \text{ N/m}^2$$

$$\Delta p_m = BAk$$

$$\Rightarrow 2 \times 10^{-4} = 4 \times 10^4 \times A \times 5$$

$$\Rightarrow A = 10^{-9} \text{ m}$$

$$y = A\sin(\omega t + kx + \phi)$$

$$= 10^{-9}\sin\left(1000t + 5x + \frac{\pi}{2}\right)$$

$$= 10^{-9}\cos(1000t + 5x)$$

8.
$$\rho = \frac{m}{V}$$

$$\Rightarrow \frac{\Delta\rho}{\rho} = -\frac{\Delta V}{V} = -\frac{A\Delta S}{A\Delta x}$$

$$\Rightarrow \Delta\rho = -\rho\left(\frac{\partial S}{\partial x}\right)$$

$$S = S_0\sin(\omega t - kx)$$

$$\Rightarrow \Delta\rho = \rho S_0 k\cos(\omega t - kx)$$

At $t = \frac{T}{4}$,

$$\Delta\rho = \rho S_0 k\cos\left(\frac{2\pi}{T}\left(\frac{T}{4}\right) - kx\right) = \rho S_0 k\sin kx$$

9.
$$I = \frac{\Delta p_m^2}{2\rho v}$$

$$\Rightarrow \frac{I_1}{I_2} = \left(\frac{\Delta p_{m_1}}{\Delta p_{m_2}}\right)^2\left(\frac{\rho_2}{\rho_1}\right)\left(\frac{v_2}{v_1}\right)$$

$$= \left(\frac{4 \times 10^{-2}}{3 \times 10^{-2}}\right)^2\left(\frac{3}{1.5}\right)\left(\frac{1200}{400}\right) = \frac{32}{3}$$

10.
$$I \propto \frac{1}{r^2}$$

$$\Delta L = 10\log_{10}\left(\frac{I_2}{I_1}\right) = 10\log_{10}\left(\frac{r_1}{r_2}\right)^2$$

$$\Rightarrow 20 = 10\log_{10}\left(\frac{r}{r_2}\right)^2 \Rightarrow r_2 = \frac{r}{10}$$

Displacement of man $= r_1 - r_2 = r - \frac{r}{10} = \frac{9r}{10}$

11.
$$\Delta L = 10\log_{10}\left(\frac{I_2}{I_1}\right)$$

$$\Rightarrow L_2 - 60 = 10\log_{10}\left(\frac{50I}{200I}\right) \Rightarrow L_2 = 54 \text{ dB}$$

12. $$L = 10\log_{10}\left(\frac{I}{I_0}\right)$$

$$\Rightarrow \quad 60 = 10\log_{10}\left(\frac{I}{10^{-12}}\right)$$

$$\Rightarrow \quad I = 10^{-6}\ \text{W/m}^2$$

$$I = \frac{\Delta p_m^2}{2\rho v}$$

$$\Rightarrow \quad 10^{-6} = \frac{\Delta p_m^2}{2(15/11)330} \quad \Rightarrow \Delta p_m = 0.03\ \text{N/m}^2$$

13. $$SL = 10\log_{10}\left(\frac{I}{I_0}\right) = 10\log\left(\frac{P/4\pi r^2}{I_0}\right)$$

$$\Rightarrow \quad SL = 10\log\left(\frac{P}{4\pi I_0}\right) + 10\log\left(\frac{1}{r^2}\right)$$

$$\Rightarrow \quad SL = 10\log\left(\frac{P}{4\pi I_0}\right) - 20\log r$$

$$\therefore \quad SL = a - b\log r$$

14. $$\Delta\phi = \frac{2\pi}{\lambda}\Delta x = \frac{2\pi}{\lambda}\times 100.25\lambda = 200.5\pi$$

At point A,

$$\Delta\phi_A = 200.5\pi + 0.5\pi = 201\pi \text{ or } \pi$$

At point B,

$$\Delta\phi_B = 200.5\pi - 0.5\pi = 200\pi \text{ or } 0$$

$$I \propto A^2 \quad \Rightarrow \quad I_1 : I_2 = 1:4$$

$$\frac{I_A}{I_B} = \frac{(\sqrt{I_1}-\sqrt{I_2})^2}{(\sqrt{I_1}+\sqrt{I_2})^2} = \left(\frac{1-2}{1+2}\right)^2 = \frac{1}{9}$$

15. When a sound wave gets reflected from a rigid boundary, the particles at the boundary are unable to vibrate. Thus, a reflected wave is generated which interferes with the oncoming wave to produce zero displacement at the rigid boundary. At these points (zero displacement), the pressure variation is maximum. Thus, the reflected pressure wave has the same phase as the incident wave.

16. $$\Delta x = (2n-1)\frac{\lambda}{2}$$

$$\Rightarrow \quad 0.5 = \left(\frac{2n-1}{2}\right)\left(\frac{300}{f}\right)$$

$$\Rightarrow \quad f = (2n-1)300$$

$$\Rightarrow \quad f = 300, 900, 1500, 2100, 2700, \ldots \text{ Hz}$$

17.

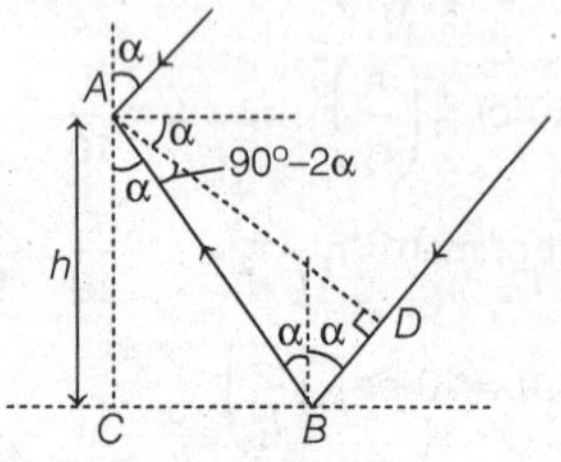

$$\frac{h}{AB} = \cos\alpha$$

$$\Rightarrow \quad AB = \frac{h}{\cos\alpha}$$

$$\frac{BD}{AB} = \cos 2\alpha$$

$$\Rightarrow \quad BD = AB\cos 2\alpha = \frac{h\cos 2\alpha}{\cos\alpha}$$

$$\Delta x = AB + BD + \frac{\lambda}{2} = \lambda$$

$$\Rightarrow \quad \frac{h}{\cos\alpha} + \frac{h\cos 2\alpha}{\cos\alpha} = \frac{\lambda}{2}$$

$$\Rightarrow \quad h = \frac{\lambda}{4\cos\alpha}$$

18. Initial path difference = 0

Final path difference = 2m

$$\Delta x = 5\lambda \Rightarrow 2 = 5\lambda$$

$$\Rightarrow \quad \lambda = 0.4\ \text{m}$$

19. Path difference between the direct wave and the reflected wave detected by the detector,

$$\Delta x = 2S = (2n-1)\frac{\lambda}{2}$$

$$\Rightarrow \quad 2\times 2 = (2(10)-1)\frac{\lambda}{2}$$

$$\Rightarrow \quad \lambda = \frac{8}{19}\ \text{m}$$

$$v = \lambda f = \frac{8}{19}\times 1000 = 421\ \text{m/s}$$

20. For open pipe, $f = (n+1)\frac{v}{2L}$

For closed pipe, $f' = (2n+1)\frac{v}{4L}$

$$\therefore \quad \frac{f}{f'} = \frac{2(n+1)}{2n+1}$$

21. $f_1 = \frac{v}{2L_1}, \quad f_2 = \frac{v}{4L_2}$

When they are joined, $f = \frac{v}{4(L_1+L_2)}$

$$= \frac{v}{4\left(\frac{v}{2f_1}+\frac{v}{4f_2}\right)} = \frac{f_1 f_2}{2f_2 + f_1}$$

22. $$f_1 = f_2$$

$$\Rightarrow \quad \frac{3v_1}{4L} = \frac{v_2}{L_2}$$

$$\Rightarrow \quad \frac{3}{4L}\sqrt{\frac{\gamma p}{\rho_1}} = \frac{1}{L_2}\sqrt{\frac{\gamma p}{\rho_2}} \quad \Rightarrow \quad L_2 = \frac{4L}{3}\left(\frac{\rho_1}{\rho_2}\right)^{1/2}$$

23. $$f = \frac{c}{4l}$$

$$\Rightarrow \quad \frac{df}{dt} = \frac{c}{4}\left(-\frac{1}{l^2}\right)\frac{dl}{dt} = \frac{cv}{4l^2}$$

24. 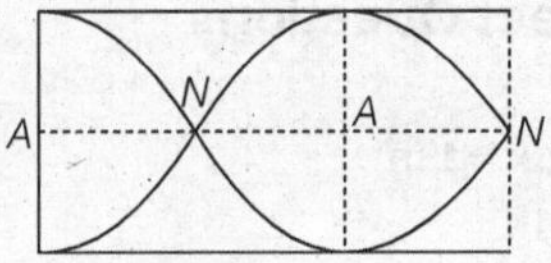

First overtone of pressure wave

25. $\lambda = \dfrac{2\pi}{k} = \dfrac{2\pi}{\pi/2} = 4$ m

Second overtone $\Rightarrow$ 2.5 loops

$\therefore \quad L = 2.5\left(\dfrac{\lambda}{2}\right) = 5$ m

26. At $x = 0$ and $x = 2$, pressure amplitude is maximum.
So, it will be pipe of length 2 m closed at both ends.

27. 11 consecutive nodes $\Rightarrow$ 10 loops

$$10\left(\frac{\lambda_1}{2}\right) = 1 \Rightarrow \lambda_1 = 0.2 \text{ m}$$

$$v_1 = \lambda_1 f = 0.2 \times 800 = 160 \text{ m/s}$$

$$v \propto \sqrt{T} \Rightarrow \frac{v_1}{v_2} = \sqrt{\frac{T_1}{T_2}}$$

$$\Rightarrow \frac{160}{v_2} = \sqrt{\frac{(352+273)}{(127+273)}}$$

$$\Rightarrow v_2 = 128 \text{ m/s}$$

$$v_2 = \lambda_2 f \Rightarrow 128 = \lambda_2 \times 800$$

$$\Rightarrow \lambda_2 = 0.16 \text{ m}$$

Distance between consecutive nodes $= \dfrac{\lambda_2}{2} = 0.08$ m

28. First overtone $\Rightarrow$ 1.5 loops

$$1.5\left(\frac{\lambda}{2}\right) = L \Rightarrow \lambda = \frac{4L}{3}$$

$$k = \frac{2\pi}{\lambda} = \frac{2\pi}{(4L/3)} = \frac{3\pi}{2L}$$

Pressure amplitude, $p = p_0 \sin kx = p_0 \sin\left(\dfrac{3\pi}{2L}x\right)$

At point Q, $p = p_0 \sin\left(\dfrac{3\pi}{2L}\left(\dfrac{7L}{9}\right)\right) = \dfrac{p_0}{2}$

$$\therefore \quad \frac{p}{p_0} = \frac{1}{2}$$

29. As ends A and B are set in vibrations, so displacement antinodes are formed at these ends.

$$f_1 = \frac{v_1}{4L} = \frac{1100}{4(0.5)} = 550 \text{ Hz}$$

$$f_2 = \frac{v_2}{4L} = \frac{300}{4(0.5)} = 150 \text{ Hz}$$

As the fundamental frequencies of the two columns are different, they are not vibrating in the fundamental mode. The close column of gas vibrates only in odd harmonics with frequencies in the ratio 1 : 3 : 5 : 7 ...

$$\frac{f_1}{f_2} = \frac{550}{150} = \frac{11}{3}, \frac{22}{6}, \frac{33}{9}, \ldots$$

For minimum frequency, $3f_1 = 11f_2$

$$\therefore \quad f_{min} = 3f_1 = 3(550) = 1650 \text{ Hz}$$

30. $$\frac{\lambda}{4} = 7 + e \quad \text{...(i)}$$

$$(2n+1)\frac{\lambda}{4} = 39 + e \quad \text{...(ii)}$$

Dividing Eq. (i) by Eq. (ii),

$$\frac{1}{2n+1} = \frac{7+e}{39+e}$$

$\Rightarrow n(7+e) = 16$

If $n = 1 \Rightarrow e = 9$ cm

$n = 2 \Rightarrow e = 1$ cm

$\because e < l \Rightarrow e = 1$ cm

$\therefore \quad \dfrac{\lambda}{4} = 7 + 1 = 8$ cm

and $\quad \dfrac{5\lambda}{4} = 39 + 1 = 40$ cm

$$\frac{3\lambda}{4} = l + e$$

$\Rightarrow \quad 3(8) = l + 1 \Rightarrow l = 23$ cm

31. $\lambda = \dfrac{v}{f} = \dfrac{330}{440} = \dfrac{3}{4}$ m

Height of air column in pipe $= \dfrac{\lambda}{4} = \dfrac{3}{16}$ m

$\therefore$ Height of water $= 0.4 - \dfrac{3}{16} = \dfrac{17}{80}$ m

Mass of water $= \dfrac{17}{80} \times 0.1 \times 1000 = 21.25$ kg

32. $f = \dfrac{v}{2(l+2e)}$, where $e = 0.6r$

$$\therefore \quad f = \frac{v}{2(l+1.2r)}$$

$$\frac{\Delta f}{f} \times 100 = \left(\frac{\Delta l + 1.2\Delta r}{l + 1.2r}\right) \times 100$$

$$= \left(\frac{0.1 + 1.2(0.05)}{94 + 1.2 \times 5}\right) \times 100 = 0.16\%$$

33. For rod, $\dfrac{\lambda}{4} = l \Rightarrow \lambda = 4l$

$$v_r = \lambda f = 4lf$$

For air column, $v_a = (2\Delta l) f$

$$\therefore \quad \frac{v_r}{v_a} = \frac{2l}{\Delta l}$$

$$\Rightarrow \quad \frac{v_r}{330} = \frac{2 \times 1}{0.6}$$

$$\Rightarrow \quad v_r = 1100 \text{ m/s}$$

34. For not hearing the echo, the time interval between the beats of drum must be equal to the time of echo.

$$t_1 = \frac{2d}{v} = \frac{1}{(40/60)}$$

$$\Rightarrow \qquad \frac{2d}{v} = \frac{3}{2} \qquad \text{...(i)}$$

$$t_2 = \frac{2(d-90)}{v} = \frac{1}{(60/60)}$$

$$\Rightarrow \qquad 2d - 180 = v \qquad \text{...(ii)}$$

Solving Eqs. (i) and (ii), we get

$$d = 270 \text{ m}$$

35. $f_A - f_B = 8$

$$\Rightarrow \qquad \frac{v}{4(37.5)} - \frac{v}{4(38.5)} = 8$$

$$\Rightarrow \qquad v = (8 \times 4 \times 37.5 \times 38.5) \text{ cm/s}$$

$$\therefore \qquad f_A = \frac{v}{4(37.5)} = 308 \text{ Hz}$$

$$f_B = \frac{v}{4(38.5)} = 300 \text{ Hz}$$

36. $f_1 - f_2 = 5$

When f_2 is waxed,

$$f_1 - f_2' = 6 \qquad \text{...(i)}$$

When f_1 is filed,

$$f' - f_2 = 7 \qquad \text{...(ii)}$$

Adding eqs. (i) and (ii), we get

$$(f_1' - f_2') + (f_1 - f_2) = 13$$

$$\Rightarrow \qquad f_1' - f_2' = 8$$

37. $n_0 = \frac{v}{2l} \quad \Rightarrow \quad v = 2ln_0$

$$f = f_1 - f_2 = \frac{v}{2\left(\frac{l}{2} - \Delta l\right)} - \frac{v}{2\left(\frac{l}{2} + \Delta l\right)} = \frac{4v\Delta l}{l^2} = \frac{8n_0\Delta l}{l}$$

38.

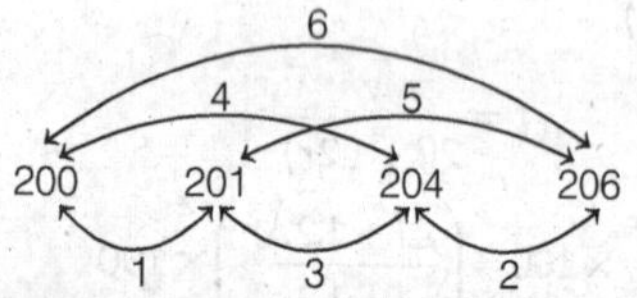

Now divide 1 s into number of beats between two frequencies

$\left(\frac{1}{1}\right)$

$\left(\left(\frac{1}{2}\right)\right)$ $\left(\frac{2}{2}\right)$

$\left\{\frac{1}{3}\right\}$ $\left[\frac{2}{3}\right]$ $\left(\frac{3}{3}\right)$

$\frac{1}{4}$ $\left(\left(\frac{2}{4}\right)\right)$ $\frac{3}{4}$ $\left(\frac{4}{4}\right)$

$\frac{1}{5}$ $\frac{2}{5}$ $\frac{3}{5}$ $\frac{4}{5}$ $\left(\frac{5}{5}\right)$

$\frac{1}{6}$ $\left\{\frac{2}{6}\right\}$ $\left(\left(\frac{3}{6}\right)\right)$ $\left[\frac{4}{6}\right]$ $\frac{5}{6}$ $\left(\frac{6}{6}\right)$

Total number of beats $= 8 + 4 = 12$

Multiple Choice(s) Correct Questions

1. $\Delta\phi = k\Delta x$

$$\Rightarrow \qquad \pi = \pi(\Delta x) \quad \Rightarrow \quad \Delta x = 1 \text{ m}$$

$$f = \frac{\omega}{2\pi} = \frac{4\pi}{2\pi} = 2 \text{ Hz}$$

The wave travels along positive X-axis.

$$v_P = \frac{\partial S}{\partial x} = -(0.15)\,\pi\cos(4\pi t - \pi x)$$

At $t = 4$ s and $x = 0.2$ m,

$$v_P = -0.15\pi\cos[4\pi(4) - \pi(0.2)] = 0$$

2.

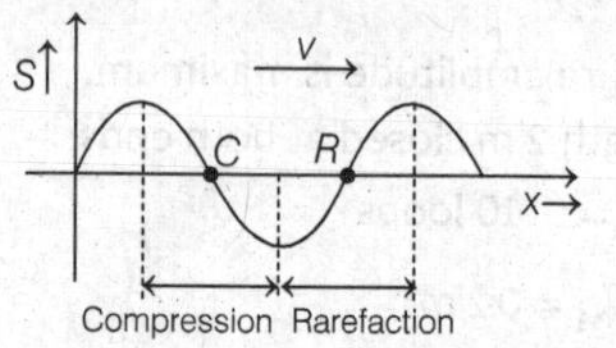

(a) $\left|\frac{\partial S}{\partial x}\right|_C = \left|\frac{\partial S}{\partial x}\right|_R$ = magnitude of slope of S-x graph

(b) Particle velocity is maximum at C and R.

(c) $\Delta p = -B\left(\frac{\partial S}{\partial x}\right)$

$$p_C = p_0 + B\left|\frac{\partial S}{\partial x}\right|_C$$

$$p_R = p_0 - B\left|\frac{\partial S}{\partial x}\right|_R$$

$$\therefore \qquad p_C - p_R = 2B\left|\frac{\partial S}{\partial x}\right|_C$$

(d) At extreme position, velocity is zero.

3. $I = \frac{\Delta p_m^2}{2\rho v}$

ρ and v are constant for a given medium.

Since, pressure amplitudes are given equal,

$$I_1 = I_2 \quad \Rightarrow \quad p_1 = p_2$$

$$\Delta p_m = BS\left(\frac{2\pi}{\lambda}\right) \quad \Rightarrow \quad S \propto \lambda$$

$$\therefore \qquad \frac{S_1}{S_2} = \frac{\lambda_1}{\lambda_2} = 2$$

4. (a, c, d)

5. Let intensity of each source be I.

When they interfere in phase,

$$I_0 = (\sqrt{I} + \sqrt{I})^2 = 4I$$

$$\Rightarrow \qquad I = \frac{I_0}{4}$$

$$I_{max} = (\sqrt{0.36I} + \sqrt{I})^2 = 2.56I = 2.56\left(\frac{I_0}{4}\right) = 0.64I_0$$

$$I_{min} = (\sqrt{0.36I} - \sqrt{I})^2 = 0.16I = 0.16\left(\frac{I_0}{4}\right) = 0.04I_0$$

$$\frac{I_{max}}{I_{min}} = 16$$

6. At B, $\Delta\phi_B = \frac{\pi}{2} + \frac{2\pi}{\lambda}\Delta x = \frac{\pi}{2} + \frac{2\pi}{20}(5) = \pi$ or $180°$

At A, $\Delta\phi_A = \frac{\pi}{2} - \frac{2\pi}{\lambda}\Delta x = 0$

At C, $\Delta\phi_C = \frac{\pi}{2}$

$$I = I_1 + I_2 + 2\sqrt{I_1}\sqrt{I_2}\cos\Delta\phi$$

$\therefore \quad I_A = 4I, \quad I_B = 0, \quad I_C = 2I$

$\Rightarrow \quad I_A : I_B : I_C = 2:0:1$

7. $\Delta x = 2\sqrt{60^2 + 25^2} - 120 = 10$ m

For constructive interference, $\Delta x = n\lambda$

$\Rightarrow \quad \lambda = \frac{\Delta x}{n} = \frac{10}{n}$

$\Rightarrow \quad \lambda = \frac{10}{1}, \frac{10}{2}, \frac{10}{3}, \frac{10}{4}, \ldots$ m

8. $\lambda = \frac{v}{f} = \frac{340}{850} = 0.4\,\text{m} = 40$ cm

nth overtone $\Rightarrow \left(n + \frac{1}{2}\right)$ loops

$\therefore \quad \left(n + \frac{1}{2}\right)\frac{\lambda}{2} = 28 + e$

$\Rightarrow \quad e = 20n - 18$

If $n = 1$, $e = 2$ cm

9. (a)

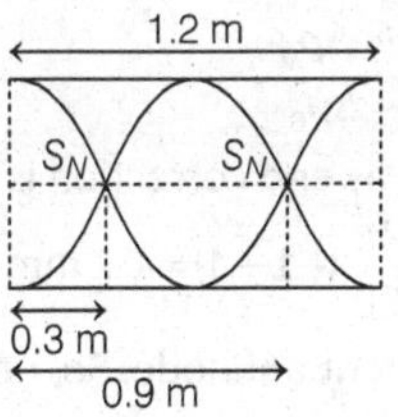

(b)

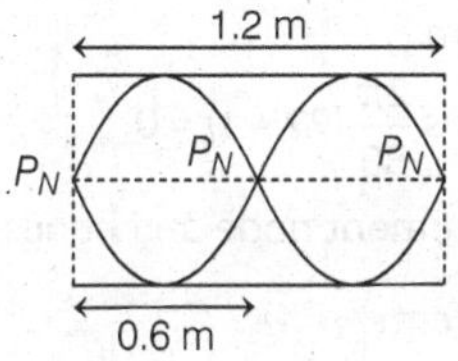

(c)

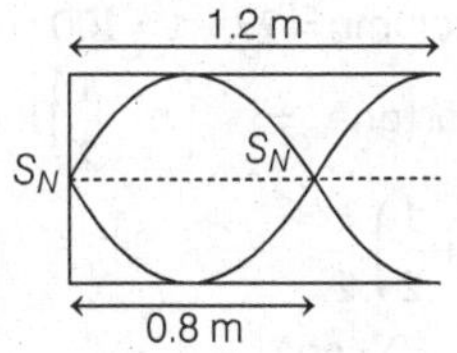

(d)

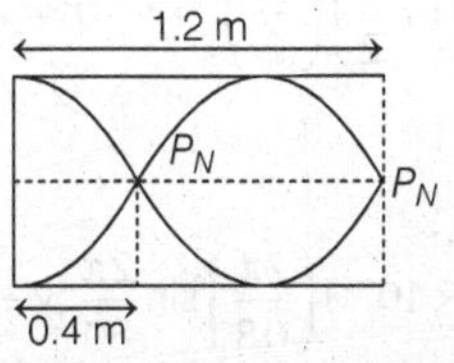

10. $f_A = f_B$

$\Rightarrow \quad 3\left(\frac{v}{2L_A}\right) = 5\left(\frac{v}{4L_B}\right)$

$\Rightarrow \quad L_B : L_A = 5:6$

Ratio of fundamental frequencies $= \left(\frac{v}{2L_A}\right) : \left(\frac{v}{4L_B}\right) = 5:3$

Ratio of first overtones $= \left(\frac{v}{L_A}\right) : \left(\frac{3v}{4L_B}\right) = 10:9$

11. 3rd harmonic of open pipe = 5th harmonic of closed pipe

$\Rightarrow \quad 3\left(\frac{v}{2L_1}\right) = 5\left(\frac{v}{4L_2}\right) \quad \Rightarrow \quad 5L_1 = 6L_2$

12. When sound wave is reflected from rigid end, displacement wave gets extra phase of π and pressure wave gets no extra phase.

13. $f = \frac{v}{4L} = \frac{1}{4L}\sqrt{\frac{\gamma RT}{M}}$

$\Rightarrow \quad f \propto \sqrt{T}$ and $f \propto \frac{1}{\sqrt{M}}$

f is independent of pressure.

First overtone frequency $= \frac{3v}{4L} = 3(300) = 900$ Hz

14. $\lambda = \frac{v}{f} = \frac{340}{340} = 1\,\text{m} = 100$ cm

Distance between successive nodes $= \frac{\lambda}{2} = 50$ cm

Length of air column $= \frac{\lambda}{4}, \frac{3\lambda}{4}, \frac{5\lambda}{4} = 25$ cm, 75 cm, 125 cm

Minimum height of water = 120 – 75 = 45 cm

Maximum height of water = 120 – 25 = 95 cm

15. $T_1 > T_2 \quad \Rightarrow \quad f_1 > f_2$

$\therefore \quad f_1 - f_2 = 6$

If T_1 is increased, f_1 will increase and hence, beat frequency will increase.

If T_1 is decreased, f_1 will decrease and it may be possible that now, $f_2 - f_1 = 6$ Hz.

Similarly, when T_2 is increased, f_2 will increase and again $f_2 - f_1$ may become equal to 6 Hz.

Comprehension Based Questions

1. $v_P = -v \times$ slope

Here, v is negative as the wave is travelling along negative X-axis. So, v_P will be negative where slope of y-x graph will be negative. Such points are b, c, d, j and k.

2. For v_P to be positive, slope should be positive. Such points are f, g and h.

3. Slope is zero at a, e and i. So, v_P is zero at these points.

4. Points at extreme are a, e and i.

5. $\Delta p = -B\left(\frac{\partial y}{\partial x}\right) = -B \times$ slope

Slope is most negative at c and k. So, Δp will be most positive at these points.

6. Slope is most positive at g. So, Δp will be most negative at g.

7. $$\Delta x = n\lambda \Rightarrow \frac{3\pi R}{2} - \frac{\pi R}{2} = n\lambda$$

$$\Rightarrow \quad \lambda = \frac{\pi R}{n} \Rightarrow \lambda = \pi R, \frac{\pi R}{2}, \frac{\pi R}{3}, \frac{\pi R}{4}, \ldots$$

8. $$\Delta x = (2n-1)\frac{\lambda}{2} \Rightarrow \pi R = (2n-1)\frac{\lambda}{2}$$

$$\Rightarrow \quad \lambda = \frac{2\pi R}{2n-1} \Rightarrow \lambda = 2\pi R, \frac{2\pi R}{3}, \frac{2\pi R}{5}, \ldots$$

9. $I_{max} = \left(\sqrt{\frac{I_0}{2}} + \sqrt{\frac{I_0}{2}}\right)^2 = 2I_0$

10. $\lambda_{max} = \pi R$

11. $\lambda_{max} = 2\pi R$

12.

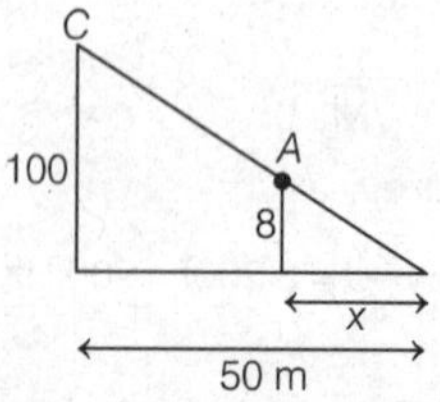

When point A reaches the wall, pressure will become 16 Pa, beyond that detector will work.

$$\frac{100}{50} = \frac{8}{x} \Rightarrow x = 4\text{ m}$$

Distance travelled $= 80 + 4 = 84$ m

$$t = \frac{84}{400} = 21 \times 10^{-2}\text{ s}$$

13.

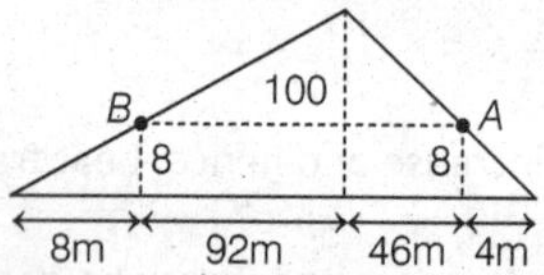

$$t = \frac{92+46}{400} = 34.5 \times 10^{-2}\text{ s}$$

14. $F_{max} = p_{max}A = (2\times 100)(2\times 2) = 800$ N

15. $I = \int F\,dt = \int (2pA)\left(\frac{dx}{v}\right) = \frac{2A}{v}\int p\,dx$

$$\int p\,dx = \text{Area of pulse} = \frac{1}{2}\times 150 \times 100 = 7500$$

$$\therefore \quad I = \frac{2\times(2\times 2)}{400}\times 7500 = 150\text{ N-s}$$

16. $\frac{\lambda_1}{2} = 10 \Rightarrow \lambda_1 = 20$ cm

$$\frac{\lambda_2}{2} = \frac{50}{\sqrt{42}} \Rightarrow \lambda_2 = \frac{100}{\sqrt{42}}\text{ cm}$$

$$f_1 = f_2 \Rightarrow \frac{v_1}{\lambda_1} = \frac{v_2}{\lambda_2}$$

$$\Rightarrow \quad \frac{1}{\lambda_1}\sqrt{\frac{\gamma_1 RT}{M_1}} = \frac{1}{\lambda_2}\sqrt{\frac{\gamma_2 RT}{M_2}}$$

$$\Rightarrow \quad \frac{1}{20}\sqrt{\frac{7/5}{M_1}} = \frac{\sqrt{42}}{100}\sqrt{\frac{5/3}{4}}$$

$$\Rightarrow \quad M_1 = 2\text{ g}$$

17. $$\frac{v_a}{\lambda_a} = \frac{v_r}{\lambda_r}$$

$$\Rightarrow \quad \lambda_r = \left(\frac{v_r}{v_a}\right)\lambda_a = 10 \times 20 = 200\text{ cm}$$

$$L = \frac{\lambda_r}{2} = 100\text{ cm} = 1\text{ m}$$

18. 2nd overtone $\Rightarrow$ 2.5 loops

$$\therefore \quad L = 2.5\left(\frac{\lambda}{2}\right) = \frac{5\lambda}{4}$$

$$\Rightarrow \quad \lambda = \frac{4L}{5}$$

$$\Delta p = \Delta p_0 \sin\left(\frac{2\pi}{\lambda}x\right)$$

At the middle of pipe,

$$\Delta p = \Delta p_0 \left|\sin\left(\frac{2\pi}{(4L/5)}\times\frac{L}{2}\right)\right| = \frac{\Delta p_0}{\sqrt{2}}$$

19. Open end is a pressure node. So, pressure amplitude is zero at the open end.

20. Closed end is a pressure antinode. So, pressure amplitude is maximum at the closed end.

$$p_{max} = p_0 + \Delta p_0$$
$$p_{min} = p_0 - \Delta p_0$$

21. For upper end, $y = -1$ cm as end correction is 1 cm.

$$\xi = (0.1\text{ mm})\cos\frac{2\pi}{80}(-1+1) = 0.1\text{ mm}$$

$\Rightarrow$ Upper end is displacement antinode. So, upper end is open.

For lower end, $y = 99$ cm

$$\xi = (0.1\text{ mm})\cos\frac{2\pi}{80}(99+1) = 0$$

$\Rightarrow$ Upper end is displacement node and hence closed.

22. $\frac{2\pi}{\lambda} = \frac{2\pi}{80} \Rightarrow \lambda = 80$ cm

Effective length of air column $= 99 + 1 = 100$ cm

For closed pipe, nth overtone $\Rightarrow \left(n + \frac{1}{2}\right)$ loops

$$\therefore \quad L = \left(n+\frac{1}{2}\right)\frac{\lambda}{2}$$

$$\Rightarrow \quad 100 = \left(n+\frac{1}{2}\right)\left(\frac{80}{2}\right) \Rightarrow n = 2$$

23. $p_{ex} = -B\left(\frac{\partial \xi}{\partial x}\right)$

$$= (5\times 10^5)\times(0.1\times 10^{-3})\left(\frac{2\pi}{0.8}\right)\sin\frac{2\pi}{80}(y+1)\cos 2\pi(400)t$$

$$= (125\pi\, N/m^2) \sin \frac{2\pi}{80} (y + 1 \text{ cm}) \cos 2\pi (400t)$$

24. $v = \sqrt{\frac{Y}{\rho}} = \sqrt{\frac{6.4 \times 10^{10}}{4 \times 10^3}} = 4000 \text{ m/s}$

6 antinodes $\Rightarrow$ 5.5 loops

$\therefore \quad L = 5.5 \left(\frac{\lambda}{2}\right)$

$\Rightarrow \quad \lambda = \frac{4L}{11} = \frac{4}{11} \text{ m}$

$k = \frac{2\pi}{\lambda} = \frac{11\pi}{2} \text{ rad/m}$

$\omega = kv = 22\pi \times 10^3 \text{ rad/s}$

At $x = 0, t = 0, S = A$

Equation of standing wave,

$S = A \cos kx \cos \omega t$

$\Rightarrow \quad S = (4 \times 10^{-6} \text{ m}) \cos \left(\frac{11\pi}{2} x\right) \cos (22\pi \times 10^3 t)$

25. Strain $= \frac{\partial S}{\partial x}$

$$= -\left(\frac{11\pi}{2}\right)(4 \times 10^{-6}) \sin \left(\frac{11\pi}{2} x\right) \cos (22\pi \times 10^3 t)$$

Stress $= Y \times$ Strain

$$= (140.8\pi \times 10^4) \sin \left(\frac{11\pi}{2} x\right) \cos (22\pi \times 10^3 t)$$

26. Strain $= (22\pi \times 10^{-6}) \sin \left(\frac{11\pi}{2} x\right) \cos (22\pi \times 10^3 t)$

At $x = 0.5$ m and $t = 1$ s,

$$\text{Strain} = (22\pi \times 10^{-6}) \sin \left(\frac{11\pi}{2} \times 0.5\right) \cos (22\pi \times 10^3)$$

$$= 11\sqrt{2}\, \pi \times 10^{-6}$$

Match the Columns Questions

1. $v_P = -v \times \left(\frac{\partial y}{\partial x}\right)$ ...(i)

$\Delta p = -B \times \left(\frac{\partial y}{\partial x}\right)$ ...(ii)

From Eqs. (i) and (ii), we get

$$v_P = \Delta p \left(\frac{v}{B}\right)$$

(A) $v_P > 0 \Rightarrow \Delta p > 0 \Rightarrow$ Point P

(B) $v_P < 0 \Rightarrow \Delta p < 0 \Rightarrow$ Points R and S

(C) $v_P = 0 \Rightarrow \Delta p = 0 \Rightarrow$ Points Q and T

(D) v_P is maximum $\Rightarrow \Delta p$ is maximum $\Rightarrow$ Points P and R

2. A→ T, B→ PQT, C→ RS, D→ RS

3. A→ S, B→ P, C→ R, D→ Q

4. In A and B, point B is a pressure antinode and hence displacement node. So, potential energy will be maximum at point B.

In C, point B is displacement node and hence potential energy will be maximum.

In D, point B is displacement antinode. At extreme position, velocity is zero and acceleration is maximum.

5. A→ PS, B→ PRS, C→ Q, D→ QR

Numerical Value Questions

1. $I \propto \frac{1}{r^2} \Rightarrow \frac{I_2}{I_1} = \left(\frac{r_1}{r_2}\right)^2$

$$\Delta L = 10 \log_{10} \left(\frac{I_2}{I_1}\right) = 10 \log_{10} \left(\frac{r_1}{r_2}\right)^2$$

$\Rightarrow \quad 10 - 70 = 10 \log_{10} \left(\frac{4}{r_2}\right)^2$

$\Rightarrow \quad r_2 = 4000 \text{ m} = 4 \text{ km}$

2. $L = 10 \log_{10} \left(\frac{I}{I_0}\right)$

$\Rightarrow \quad 20 = 10 \log_{10} \left(\frac{I}{10^{-12}}\right)$

$\Rightarrow \quad I = 10^{-10} \text{ W/m}^2$

$v = \sqrt{\frac{B}{\rho}} = \sqrt{\frac{4 \times 10^4}{1}} = 200 \text{ m/s}$

$I = \frac{\Delta p_m^2}{2\rho v}$

$\Rightarrow \quad 10^{-10} = \frac{\Delta p_m^2}{2 \times 1 \times 200}$

$\Rightarrow \quad \Delta p_m = 2 \times 10^{-4} \text{ N/m}^2$

$\therefore \quad \alpha = 2$

3. For S_1 and S_2,

$\Delta x = \sqrt{3^2 + 4^2} - 4 = 1 \text{ m}$

$\Delta\phi = \frac{2\pi}{\lambda} \Delta x = \frac{2\pi}{(340/170)} \times 1 = \pi$

Resultant intensity due to S_1 and S_2 at P,

$I'_R = I + I + 2\sqrt{I}\sqrt{I} \cos \pi = 0$

$\therefore$ Resultant intensity due to S_1, S_2 and S_3 at $P = I_R = I$

$\Rightarrow \quad \frac{I_R}{I} = 1$

4. $I_1 = \frac{P_1}{4\pi d_1^2} = \frac{8\pi}{4\pi (1)^2} = 2 \text{ W/m}^2$

$I_2 = \frac{P_2}{4\pi d_2^2} = \frac{18\pi}{4\pi (1.5)^2} = 2 \text{ W/m}^2$

$\lambda = \frac{v}{f} = \frac{300}{100} = 3 \text{ m}$

$\Delta x = d_2 - d_1 = 1.5 - 1 = 0.5 \text{ m}$

$\Delta\phi = \frac{2\pi}{\lambda} \Delta x = \frac{2\pi}{3} (0.5) = \frac{\pi}{3}$

$$I = I_1 + I_2 + 2\sqrt{I_1}\sqrt{I_2}\cos\Delta\phi$$

$$= 2 + 2 + 2\sqrt{2}\sqrt{2}\cos\left(\frac{\pi}{3}\right) = 6\,\text{W/m}^2$$

5. Equation of standing wave,

$$\Delta p = 2\Delta p_0 \sin kx \cos \omega t$$

$\therefore$ Maximum pressure amplitude $= 2\Delta p_0$

$$f_L = (2\Delta p_0)A = (2\times 2\times 10^3)5\times 10^{-4} = 2\,\text{N}$$

6. $$f = \frac{v}{2L} = \frac{1}{2L}\sqrt{\frac{\gamma RT}{M}}$$

$$\therefore \quad \frac{\Delta f}{f} = -\frac{\Delta L}{L} + \frac{1}{2}\frac{\Delta T}{T}$$

$$\Rightarrow \quad 0 = -\alpha\Delta T + \frac{1}{2}\frac{\Delta T}{T_0} \Rightarrow T_0 = \frac{1}{2\alpha}$$

$$\therefore \quad \eta = 7$$

7. $$\frac{\lambda}{4} = 20 + e \quad \text{...(i)}$$

$$\frac{5\lambda}{4} = 108 + e \quad \text{...(ii)}$$

Subtracting Eq. (i) from Eq. (ii), we get

$$\lambda = 88\,\text{cm} \quad \text{and} \quad e = 2\,\text{cm}$$

Possible air column length

$$= \frac{\lambda}{4}, \frac{3\lambda}{4}, \frac{5\lambda}{4}, \frac{7\lambda}{4}, \frac{9\lambda}{4}, \frac{11\lambda}{4}, \ldots$$

= 22, 66, 110, 154, 198, 242, ...

Since, pipe is of length 2 m, total number of resonances possible will be 5.

8. Change in height of water in successive resonances

$$= \frac{\lambda}{2} = \frac{v}{2f}$$

$$t = \frac{\text{Volume change}}{\text{Volume flow rate}} = \frac{\pi r^2\left(\frac{v}{2f}\right)}{R} = \frac{\pi r^2 v}{2Rf}$$

$$\therefore \quad \alpha = 2$$

9. $y_1 = A\sin 200\pi t$, $y_2 = A\sin 204\pi t$

$y = y_1 + y_2 = 2A\cos 2\pi t \sin 202\pi t$

Resultant amplitude $= 2A|\cos 2\pi t|$

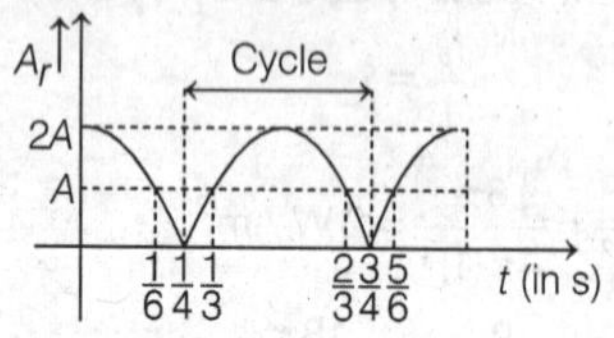

$$2A\cos 2\pi t = A$$

$$\Rightarrow \quad 2\pi t = \frac{\pi}{3} \quad \Rightarrow \quad t = \frac{1}{6}\,\text{s}$$

In one cycle of interval $\frac{1}{2}$ s, the detector remains idle for

$$2\left(\frac{1}{4} - \frac{1}{6}\right) = \frac{1}{6}\,\text{s}$$

$$\therefore \text{ Active time} = \frac{1}{2} - \frac{1}{6} = \frac{1}{3}\,\text{s}$$

In 12 s interval, active time $= 12 \times \frac{(1/3)}{(1/2)} = 8\,\text{s}$

10. $$f = \frac{1}{2L}\sqrt{\frac{T}{\mu}}$$

$$\Rightarrow \quad \frac{\Delta f}{f}\times 100 = \frac{1}{2}\left(\frac{\Delta T}{T}\times 100\right)$$

$$\Rightarrow \quad \frac{3}{100}\times 100 = \frac{1}{2}\left(\frac{\Delta T}{T}\times 100\right)$$

$$\Rightarrow \quad \frac{\Delta T}{T}\times 100 = 6\%$$

Previous Year's Questions

JEE Main

1. Fundamental frequency of closed organ pipe is,

$$f_1 = \frac{v}{4L_1},\ v = \text{Speed of sound}$$

L_1 = Length of closed organ pipe

First overtone of open organ pipe has frequency,

$$f_2 = 2\cdot\frac{v}{2L_2},$$

L_2 = Length of open organ pipe

Given, $f_1 = f_2$ and $L_2 = 60$ cm

$$\therefore \quad \frac{v}{4L_1} = 2\cdot\frac{v}{2L_2} \Rightarrow L_1 = \frac{L_2}{4} = \frac{60}{4} = 15\,\text{cm}$$

2. As intensity of sound is inversely proportional to square of distance;

$$I \propto \frac{1}{r^2} \quad \text{or} \quad I_1 r_1^2 = I_2 r_2^2$$

So, Intensity at 2m distance

$$I_1 = \frac{16\times 10^{-8}}{2^2} = 4\times 10^{-8}\,\frac{\text{W}}{\text{m}^2}$$

Intensity at 4 m distance

$$I_2 = \frac{16\times 10^{-8}}{4^2} = 1\times 10^{-8}\,\frac{\text{W}}{\text{m}^2}$$

So, difference is,

$$I_1 - I_2 = (4-1)\times 10^{-8}\,\frac{\text{W}}{\text{m}^2} = 3\times 10^{-8}\,\frac{\text{W}}{\text{m}^2}$$

3. Given,

For closed organ pipe fundamental frequency, $f = 30$ Hz

Let, length of closed organ pipe $= L$

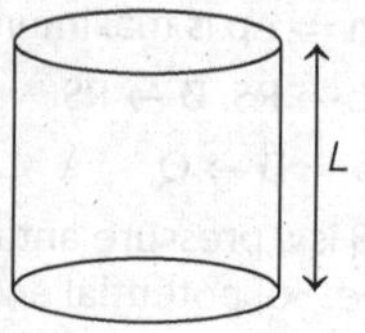

We know that,

Fundamental frequency $f = \frac{v}{4L}$

$$30 = \frac{330}{4L} \quad (v = 330 \text{ m/s given})$$

$$L = \frac{330}{30 \times 4} = \frac{11}{4} = 2.75 \text{ m}$$

Now, x g of water is added

Water filled upto height h.

New frequency $f' = 110$ Hz

Again using formula Eq.(i)

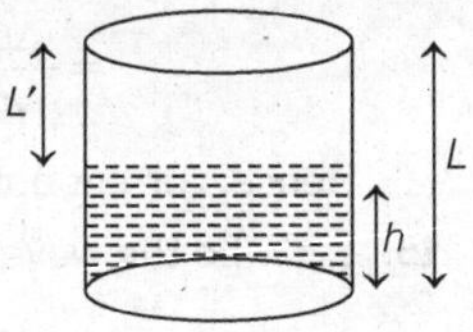

$$f' = \frac{v}{4L'} \quad [L' = L - h]$$

$$110 = \frac{330}{4L'}$$

$$\Rightarrow \quad L' = \frac{330}{110 \times 4} = 0.75 \text{ cm}$$

$$h = L - L'$$

$$\Rightarrow \quad h = 2.75 - 0.75 = 2 \text{ m}$$

Volume of liquid (water) filled = area × height

$$V = 2 \times 200 \text{ cm}^3 \quad (a = 2 \text{ cm}^2 \text{ given})$$

$$= 400 \text{ cm}^3$$

Amount of water (mass) = Volume × density of water

$$= 400 \times 1 = 400 \text{ g}$$

4.

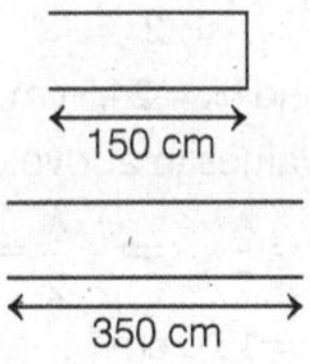

$$f_1 = \frac{v}{4l_1}, f_2 = \frac{v}{2l_2}$$

$$f_1 = \frac{v \times 100}{4 \times 150}, f_2 = \frac{v \times 100}{2 \times 350}$$

$$f_1 = \frac{v}{6} \Rightarrow f_2 = \frac{v}{7}$$

$$\frac{v}{6} - \frac{v}{7} = 7 \Rightarrow \frac{v}{42} = 7$$

$$v = 7 \times 42 \Rightarrow v = 294 \text{ m/s}$$

5. For an open tube in second harmonic,

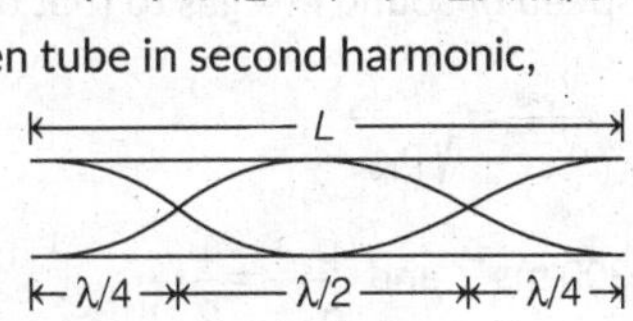

Wavelength of sound produced,

$$\lambda = L$$

L = Length of tube

As, $\quad f \cdot \lambda = v$

(f = frequency, v = Speed of sound)

$$\Rightarrow \quad f = \frac{v}{\lambda} = \frac{v}{L} = \frac{360}{40 \times 10^{-2}} = 900 \text{ Hz}$$

6. Given,

$$l_1 = 20.0 \text{ cm}$$
$$v = 336 \text{ m/s}$$
$$f = 400 \text{ Hz}$$

For Ist resonance

$$l_1 + e = \frac{\lambda}{4}$$

$$20 + e = \frac{336}{400} \times 100 \text{ cm} \times \frac{1}{4}$$

$$20 + e = \frac{84}{4}$$

$$e = 21 - 20 = 1 \text{ cm}$$

For IIIrd resonance

$$l_2 + 3 = \frac{5\lambda}{4}$$

$$\Rightarrow \quad l_2 + 1 = 5 \times 21$$

$$\Rightarrow \quad l_2 = 105 - 1 = 104 \text{ cm}$$

7. In a closed organ tube, frequency of resonance of air column is

$$f = \frac{nv}{4L}$$

(where $n = 1, 3, 5, 7$ .....)

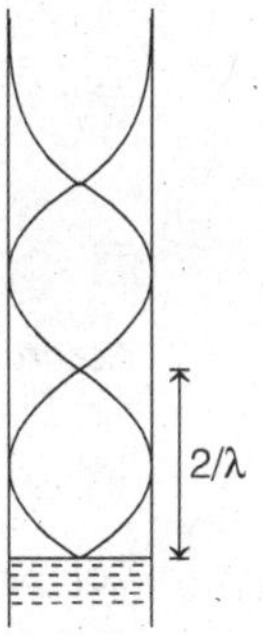

Here, $f = 340$ Hz, $v = 340$ m/s

$$L = 1.25 \text{ m}$$

$$\text{So, } 340 = \frac{n \times 340}{4 \times 1.25}$$

$\Rightarrow n = 5$ (This is 3rd mode of vibration)

Hence, wavelength associated with this frequency,

$$\lambda = \frac{44}{5} = \frac{4 \times 1.25}{5}$$

$$= 1 \text{ m}$$

or $\lambda = 100$ cm

Next mode of vibration occurs at a distance of half wavelength,

$$\text{So, } h = \frac{100}{2} = 50 \text{ cm}$$

8. As we know that, $f \times \lambda = v$

And beat frequency $= f_2 - f_1$

We have, $f_2 - f_1 = \frac{40}{12}$ [Given]

$$\Rightarrow \quad \frac{v}{4.08} - \frac{v}{4.16} = \frac{40}{12}$$

$$\Rightarrow \quad v = \frac{40 \times 4.08 \times 4.16}{12 \times (4.16 - 4.08)}$$

$$\Rightarrow \quad v = 707.2 \text{ m/s}$$

9. Let f be frequency of first tuning fork.

According to given situation, $\quad f_1 = f$

Frequency of second tuning fork, $f_2 = f + 4$

Frequency of third tuning fork,

$$f_3 = f + 2 \times 4$$
$$\vdots$$
$$f_{20} = f + (19 \times 4)$$

Since given that, $f_{20} = 2f_1$

$$\Rightarrow \quad f + (19 \times 4) = 2f$$

$$\Rightarrow \quad f = 76 \text{ Hz}$$

$\therefore$ Frequency of last tuning fork $= 2f = 2 \times 76 = 152$ Hz

10. We know that, $f = \dfrac{nv}{4L}$

For L to be minimum, $n = 1$

$$\therefore \quad 250 = \frac{v}{4L} \Rightarrow 250 = \frac{340}{4L}$$

$$\Rightarrow \quad L = \frac{34}{4 \times 25} = 0.34 \text{ m}$$

$$\Rightarrow \quad L = 34 \text{ cm}$$

11. First overtone of open pipe $= v_2 / L_2$

First overtone of closed pipe at one end $= \dfrac{3v}{4L_2}$

As per question, $\dfrac{3v}{4L} = \dfrac{v_2}{L_2}$

$$\Rightarrow \quad \sqrt{\frac{B}{\rho_1}} \cdot \frac{3}{4L} = \sqrt{\frac{B}{\rho_2}} \cdot \frac{1}{L_2} \qquad \left(\because V = \sqrt{\frac{B}{\rho}}\right)$$

$$\Rightarrow \quad L_2 = \frac{4L}{3}\sqrt{\frac{\rho_1}{\rho_2}} \qquad \text{...(i)}$$

According to question, the length of the open pipe is

$$L_2 = \frac{x}{3} L \sqrt{\frac{\rho_1}{\rho_2}} \qquad \text{... (ii)}$$

Comparing Eqs. (i) and (ii), we get

$$x = 4$$

12. Given, $f = 340$ Hz

Let beat frequency of tuning fork A be f_A

and f_A' be the frequency of tuning fork A after filling.

In first case, beat frequency $= 5$

$$\Rightarrow \quad f_A = 340 \pm 5$$

$$\Rightarrow \quad f_A = 345 \text{ Hz} \quad \text{or} \quad 335 \text{ Hz}$$

After filling tuning fork A,

$$f_A' = 340 \pm 2$$

$$\Rightarrow \quad f_A' = 342 \text{ or } 338 \text{ Hz}$$

As on filling, frequency of A increases.

Hence, original frequency of tuning fork A is 335 Hz.

13. $\lambda = \dfrac{v}{f} = \dfrac{336}{504} \text{ m} = \dfrac{2}{3} \text{ m}$

For end correction,

$$\therefore \quad \frac{\lambda}{4} = l + e = l + 0.3d \qquad (d = \text{diameter of column})$$

$$\Rightarrow \frac{\frac{2}{3} \times 100}{4} = l + 0.3 \times 6 \Rightarrow 16.66 = l + 1.8$$

$$\therefore \quad l = 14.8 \text{ cm}$$

14. The pressure difference is given by,

$$\Delta p = \frac{B\omega}{v} \times s$$

$\therefore$ Displacement of air,

$$s = \frac{\Delta p \times v}{B\omega} = \frac{\Delta p v}{\rho v^2 \omega}$$

$$= \frac{\Delta p}{\rho v \omega} = \frac{10}{1 \times 300 \times 1000} \approx \frac{3}{100} \text{ mm}$$

Hence, correct option is (d).

15. Let λ be the wavelength, L be the length of the tube.

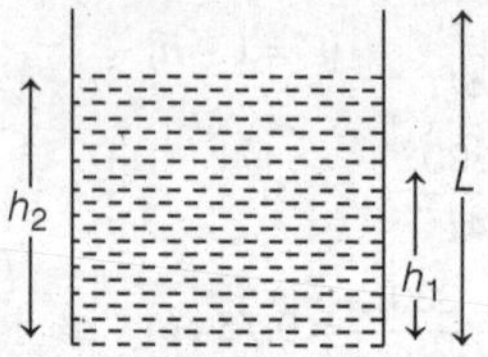

The resonance conditions for the given two cases are:

$$L - h_1 = \frac{n\lambda}{2} + \frac{\lambda}{4} \qquad \text{...(i)}$$

$$L - h_2 = (n-1)\frac{\lambda}{2} + \frac{\lambda}{4} \qquad \text{...(ii)}$$

Subtracting Eq. (ii) from Eq. (i), we get

$$(L - h_1) - (L - h_2) = \frac{n\lambda}{2} + \frac{\lambda}{4} - (n-1)\frac{\lambda}{2} - \frac{\lambda}{4}$$

$$h_2 - h_1 = \frac{\lambda}{2}$$

Here, $h_1 = 17.0$ cm and $h_2 = 24.5$ cm

Substituting these values in above equation, we get

$$24.5 - 17.0 = \frac{\lambda}{2} \Rightarrow \frac{\lambda}{2} = 7.5 \text{ cm}$$

$$\Rightarrow \quad \lambda = 15.0 \text{ cm}$$

Now, the tuning fork frequency,

$$f = \frac{v}{\lambda} = \frac{330}{15 \times 10^{-2}} = 2200 \text{ Hz}$$

Hence, correct option is (c).

16. Speed of sound in air by Laplace formula,

$$v = \sqrt{\frac{\gamma p}{\rho}}$$

So, ratio of speed of sound in a gas to that of air,

$$\frac{v_{gas}}{v_{air}} = \sqrt{\frac{\rho_{air}}{\rho_{gas}}}$$

Here, $v_{air} = 300 \text{ ms}^{-1}$ and $\dfrac{\rho_{air}}{\rho_{gas}} = \dfrac{1}{2}$

So, we have $\dfrac{v_{gas}}{300} = \dfrac{1}{\sqrt{2}}$

$$\Rightarrow \quad v_{gas} = \frac{300}{\sqrt{2}} = 150\sqrt{2} \text{ ms}^{-1}$$

Now, for a tube open at both ends.

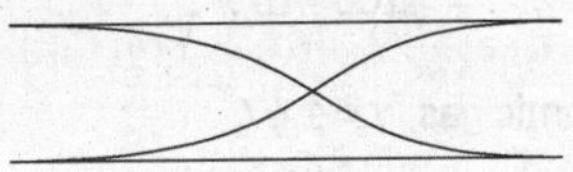

$L = \lambda/2$

$\therefore$ Fundamental frequency,

$$f_1 = \frac{v}{\lambda} = \frac{v}{2L}$$

Second harmonic frequency f_2 in tube,

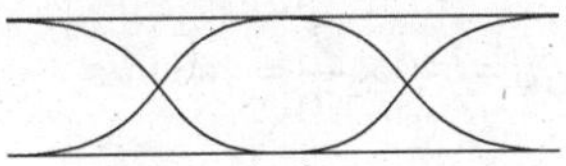

$L = \lambda$

$$f_2 = \frac{v}{\lambda}, f_2 = v / L$$

So, frequency difference,

$$\Delta f = f_2 - f_1 = \frac{v}{L} - \frac{v}{2L}$$

$$= \frac{v}{2L} = \frac{150\sqrt{2}}{2 \times 1} \quad (\because L = 1\,\text{m})$$

$$= 75\sqrt{2} = 106.06 \text{ Hz}$$

17. In a resonance tube apparatus, first and second resonance occur as shown below.

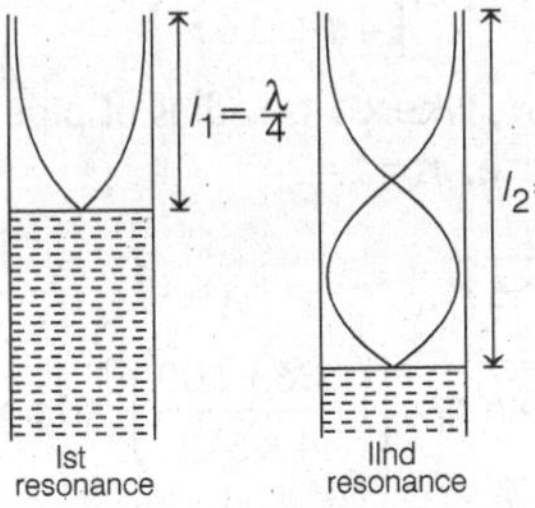

As in a stationary wave, distance between two successive nodes is $\frac{\lambda}{2}$ and distance of a node and an antinode is $\frac{\lambda}{4}$.

$$l_2 - l_1 = \frac{3\lambda}{4} - \frac{\lambda}{4} = \frac{\lambda}{2}$$

So, speed of sound, $v = f\lambda = f \times 2(l_2 - l_1)$

$$= 480 \times 2 \times (70 - 30) \times 10^{-2} = 384 \text{ ms}^{-1}$$

18. Given,

$$p = 0.01 \sin(1000t - 3x) \text{ N/m}^2$$

Comparing with the general equation of pressure wave of sound, i.e.

$$p_0 \sin(\omega t - kx),$$

we get $\quad \omega = 1000$ and $k = 3$

Also, $\quad k = \frac{\omega}{v} \Rightarrow v = \omega / k$

$\therefore$ Velocity of sound is $|v_1| = \frac{1000}{3}$

Now, relation between velocity of sound and temperature is

$$v = \sqrt{\frac{\gamma RT}{m}} \Rightarrow v \propto \sqrt{T}$$

or $\quad \frac{v_2}{v_1} = \sqrt{\frac{T_2}{T_1}} \Rightarrow T_2 = \frac{v_2^2}{v_1^2} \cdot T_1$

Here, $v_2 = 336$ m/s, $v_1 = 1000/3$ m/s, $T_1 = 0°\text{C} = 273$ K

$$\therefore \quad T_2 = \frac{(336)^2}{(1000/3)^2} \times 273 = 277.38 \text{ K}$$

$$\therefore \quad T_2 = 4.38°\text{C} \simeq 4°\text{C}$$

19. In first resonance,

length of air coloumn $= \frac{\lambda}{4}$.

So, $\quad l_1 + e = \frac{\lambda}{4}$

or $\quad 11 \times 4 + 4e = \lambda$

So, speed of sound is

$$\Rightarrow \quad v = f_1\lambda = 512(44 + 4e) \quad \text{...(i)}$$

And in second case,

$$l_1' + e = \frac{\lambda'}{4}$$

or $\quad 27 \times 4 + 4e = \lambda'$

$$\Rightarrow \quad v = f_2\lambda' = 256(108 + 4e) \quad \text{...(ii)}$$

Dividing both Eqs. (i) and (ii), we get

$$1 = \frac{512(44 + 4e)}{256(108 + 4e)}$$

$$\Rightarrow \quad e = 5 \text{ cm}$$

Substituting value of e in Eq. (i), we get

Speed of sound, $v = 512(44 + 4e)$

$$= 512(44 + 4 \times 5)$$

$$= 512 \times 64 \text{ cm s}^{-1}$$

$$= 327.68 \text{ ms}^{-1} \approx 328 \text{ ms}^{-1}$$

JEE Advanced

1. $\quad f \propto \frac{1}{l_1}$

$$\Rightarrow \quad f = \frac{k}{l_1} \quad \text{... (i)}$$

(where, $l_1 \Rightarrow$ initial length of pipe)

$$\left(\frac{v}{v - v_T}\right) f = \frac{k}{l_1} \quad \text{... (ii)}$$

(where, v_T = speed of tuning fork, l_2 = new length of pipe)

Dividing Eq. (i) by Eq. (ii), we get

$$\frac{v - v_T}{c} = \frac{l_2}{l_1}$$

$$\frac{l_2}{l_1} - 1 = \frac{v - v_T}{v} - 1 \Rightarrow \frac{l_2 - l_1}{l_1} = \frac{-v_T}{v}$$

$$\frac{l_2 - l_1}{l_1} \times 100 = \frac{-2}{320} \times 100 = -0.625$$

Therefore, smallest value of percentage change required in the length of pipe is 0.625.

2. Let nth harmonic is corresponding to 50.7 cm and $(n+1)$th harmonic is corresponding 83.9 cm.

$\therefore$ Their difference is $\frac{\lambda}{2}$.

$\therefore \quad \frac{\lambda}{2} = (83.9 - 50.7)$ cm

or $\quad \lambda = 66.4$ cm

$\therefore \quad \frac{\lambda}{4} = 16.6$ cm

Length corresponding to fundamental mode must be close to $\frac{\lambda}{4}$ and 50.7 cm must be an odd multiple of this length.

$16.6 \times 3 = 49.8$ cm. Therefore, 50.7 cm is 3rd harmonic.

If end correction is e, then

$$e + 50.7 = \frac{3\lambda}{4}$$

$$e = 49.8 - 50.7 = -0.9 \text{ cm}$$

$\therefore$ Speed of sound, $v = f\lambda$

$$\Rightarrow \quad v = 500 \times 66.4 \text{ cm/s} = 332 \text{ m/s}$$

3. Let individual amplitudes are A_0 each. Amplitudes can be added by vector method.

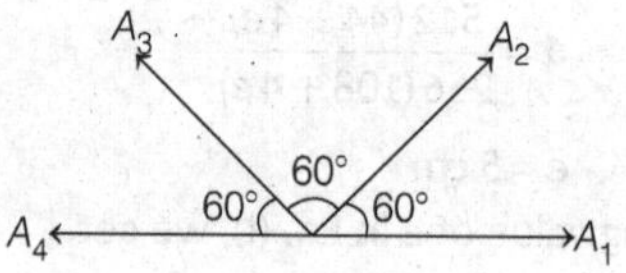

$$A_1 = A_2 = A_3 = A_4 = A_0$$

Resultant of A_1 and A_4 is zero. Resultant of A_2 and A_3 is

$$A = \sqrt{A_0^2 + A_0^2 + 2A_0A_0\cos 60°} = \sqrt{3}A_0$$

This is also the resultant amplitude.

Now, $\quad I \propto A^2$

$\therefore$ Net intensity will become $3I_0$.

$\therefore$ Answer is 3.

4. Minimum length $= \frac{\lambda}{4}$

$$\lambda = 4l$$

Now, $\quad v = f\lambda = (244) \times 4 \times l$

as $\quad l = 0.350 \pm 0.005$

$\Rightarrow v$ lies between 336.7 m/s to 346.5 m/s

Now, $v = \sqrt{\frac{\gamma RT}{M \times 10^{-3}}}$, here M is molecular mass in gram

$$= \sqrt{100\gamma RT} \times \sqrt{\frac{10}{M}}.$$

For monoatomic gas, $\gamma = 1.67$

$$\Rightarrow \quad v = 640 \times \sqrt{\frac{10}{M}}$$

For diatomic gas, $\gamma = 1.4$

$$\Rightarrow \quad v = 590 \times \sqrt{\frac{10}{M}}$$

$$\Rightarrow \quad v_{Ne} = 640 \times \frac{7}{10} = 448 \text{ m/s}$$

$$\Rightarrow \quad v_{Ar} = 640 \times \frac{17}{32} = 340 \text{ m/s}$$

$$\Rightarrow \quad v_{O_2} = 590 \times \frac{9}{16} = 331.8 \text{ m/s}$$

$$\Rightarrow \quad v_{N_2} = 590 \times \frac{3}{5} = 354 \text{ m/s}$$

$\therefore$ Only possible answer is Argon.

5. With end correction,

$$f = n\left[\frac{v}{4(l+e)}\right] \quad \text{(where, } n = 1, 3, \ldots)$$

$$= n\left[\frac{v}{4(l+0.6r)}\right]$$

Because, $e = 0.6r$, where r is radius of pipe.

For first resonance, $n = 1$

$$\therefore \quad f = \frac{v}{4(l+0.6r)}$$

or $\quad l = \frac{v}{4f} - 0.6r = \left[\left(\frac{336 \times 100}{4 \times 512}\right) - 0.6 \times 2\right]$ cm

$$= 15.2 \text{ cm}$$

6. At open end phase of pressure wave changes by 180°. So, compression returns as rarefaction. At closed end there is no phase change. So, compression returns as compression and rarefaction as rarefaction.

7. In organ pipes, longitudinal waves are formed.

In string, transverse waves are formed. Open end of pipe is displacement antinode and closed end is displacement node. In case of string fixed end of a string is node.

Further, least distance between a node and an antinode is $\lambda/4$ and between two nodes is $\lambda/2$. Keeping these points in mind answer to this question is as under ;

(A) $\rightarrow$ (P, T); (B) $\rightarrow$ (P, S); (C) $\rightarrow$ (Q, S); (D) $\rightarrow$ (Q, R)

CHAPTER~11

DOPPLER EFFECT

LEVEL 01 Starter Level

11.1 Stationary Source and Moving Observer

1. A car moving at 30 m/s is approaching a factory whistle that has a frequency of 500 Hz. If the speed of sound in air is 340 m/s, then find the apparent frequency and the apparent wavelength as recorded by the driver.
2. A person is sitting in a car which is moving with a velocity of 50 m/s away from a source which is emitting a sound of frequency 600 Hz. What frequency would be heard by person sitting in car if speed of sound is 340 m/s?
3. A fixed source of sound emitting a certain frequency appears as f_a when the observer is approaching the source with speed v and frequency f_r when the observer recedes from the source with the same speed. Find the frequency of the source.
4. Two identical tuning forks vibrating at the same frequency 256 Hz are kept fixed at some distance apart. A listener runs between the forks at a speed of 3.0 m/s, so that he approaches one tuning fork and recedes from the other. Find the beat frequency observed by the listener. Speed of sound in air = 332 m/s.

11.2 Moving Source and Stationary Observer

1. A person riding a car moving at 20 m/s sounds a whistle emitting a wave of frequency 1250 Hz. What frequency will be heard by another person standing on the road
   (a) in front of the car? (b) behind the car?
   Speed of sound in air = 340 m/s.
2. A source of sound produces waves of wavelength 60 cm when it is stationary. If the speed of sound in air is 320 m/s and the source moves with speed 20 m/s, what will be the wavelengths of sound in the forward and backward drections, respectively?
3. A source of sound is moving with a velocity 50 m/s towards a stationary observer. He measures the frequency of the source as 1000 Hz. What will be the apparent frequency of the sound when it is moving away from the observer after crossing him? The velocity of the sound in the medium is 350 m/s.
4. A bullet passes past a person at a speed of 220 m/s. Find the fractional change in the frequency of the whistling sound heard by the person as the bullet crosses the person. Speed of sound in air = 330 m/s.
5. The apparent frequency of the whistle of an engine changes in the ratio of 6 : 5 as the engine passes a stationary observer. If the velocity of sound is 330 m/s, then what is the velocity of the engine?
6. Figure shows a person standings somewhere in between two identical tuning forks, each vibrating at 128 Hz. If both the tuning forks move towards right at a speed of 10 m/s, find the number of beats heard by the listener. Speed of sound in air = 330 m/s.

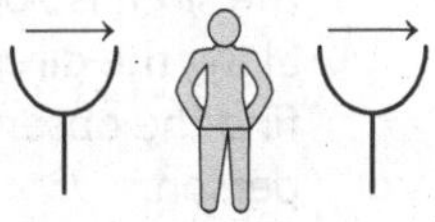

7. A violin player riding on a slow train plays a 440 Hz note. Another violin player standing near the track plays the same note. When the two are close by and the train approaches the person on the ground, he hears 4.0 beats per second. The speed of sound in air = 340 m/s.
   (a) Calculate the speed of the train.
   (b) What beat frequency is heard by the player in the train?

11.3 Both Source and Observer in Motion

1. Two trains are moving towards each other at a speed of 72 km/h and 54 km/h relative to the ground. The velocity of sound is 320 m/s. The first train sounds a whistle of frequency 900 Hz, find the frequency of whistle heard by
   (a) the passenger sitting in the first train
   (b) the passenger sitting in the second train

2. Two cars *A* and *B* are moving in the same direction with velocities 30 m/s and 10 m/s, respectively. Car *B* is behind from car *A*. Car *A* blows a horn of frequency 450 Hz. The velocity of sound is 330 m/s. What will be the apparent frequency heard by the driver in car *B*?

3. Two cars *A* and *B* are travelling in opposite directions at 30 m/s each, cross each other while car *A* is whistling. The apparent frequency as heard by the driver of car *B* before they cross each other is 4320 Hz. What will be the apparent frequency as heard by the driver of car *B* after they have crossed each other? The velocity of sound is 330 m/s.

11.4 Effect of Wind in Doppler Effect

1. A person going away from a factory on his scooter at a speed of 36 km/h listens to the siren of the factory. If the actual frequency of the siren is 700 Hz and a wind is blowing along the direction of the scooter is 36 km/h, find the observed frequency heard by the person.
   (Given speed of sound = 340 m/s)

2. A stationary source emits sound of $n = 1200$ Hz. Speed of the sound is 300 m/s. If a wind blows at the speed of 30 m/s, find the wavelength and frequency for a stationary observer on the wind-side of the source.

3. Two tuning forks *A* and *B* having a frequency of 500 Hz each are placed with *B* to the right of *A*. An observer in between the forks is moving towards *B* with a speed of 25 m/s. The speed of sound is 345 m/s and the wind speed is 5 m/s from *A* to *B*. Calculate the difference in the two frequencies heard by observer.

11.5 Doppler Effect in Reflected Sound

1. A siren emitting a sound of frequency 2000 Hz moves away from you towards a cliff at a speed of 8 m/s.
   (a) What is the frequency of the sound you hear coming directly from the siren?
   (b) What is the frequency of sound you hear reflected off the cliff ? Speed of sound in air is 330 m/s.

2. An engine driver moving towards a wall with velocity of 50 ms^{-1} emits a note of frequency 1.2 kHz. What willl be the frequency of note after reflection from the wall as heard by the engine driver when speed of sound in air is 350 ms^{-1}?

3. A SONAR system fixed in a submarine operates at a frequency 40.0 kHz. An enemy submarine moves towards the SONAR with a speed of 360 km h^{-1}. What is the frequency of sound reflected by the submarine? Take the speed of sound in water to be 1450 ms^{-1}.

4. A car is moving towards a huge wall with a speed $= c/10$, where $c =$ speed of sound in still air. A wind is also blowing parallel to the velocity of the car in the same direction and with the same speed. If the car sounds a horn of frequency *f*, then what is the frequency of the reflected sound of the horn heard by driver of the car ?

5. A train approaching a hill at a speed of 40 km/h sounds a whistle of frequency 600 Hz when it is at a distance of 1 km from a hill. A wind with a speed of 40 km/h is blowing in the direction of motion of the train. Find the distance from the hill at which the echo from the hill is heard by the driver and its frequency. (Velocity of sound in air = 1200 km/h)

6. A source emits sound waves of frequency 1000 Hz. The source moves to the right with a speed of 32 m/s relative to ground. On the right, a reflecting surface moves towards left with a speed of 64 m/s relative to the ground. The speed of sound in air is 332 m/s. Find
   (a) the wavelength of sound in air incident on reflecting surface
   (b) the number of waves arriving per second which meet the reflecting surface.
   (c) the speed of reflected waves.
   (d) the wavelength of reflected waves.

7. *S* is source, *R* is receiver. *R* and *S* are at rest. The reflecting surface is moving away with velocity *u*. Frequency of sound from *S* is *f*. Find the beat frequency registered by *R*. Velocity of sound is *v*.

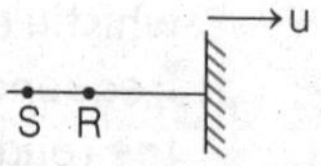

8. A boy is walking away from a wall at a speed of 1.0 m/s in a direction at right angles to the wall. The boy blows a whistle steadily. A stationary observer towards whom the boy is moving hears 4 beat/s. If the speed of sound is 340 m/s, what is the frequency of the whistle?

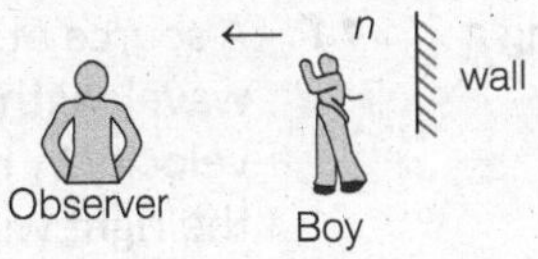

11.6 Source and Observer Moving along Different Lines

1. A train approaching a railway crossing at a speed of 120 km/h sounds a short whislte at frequency $f_0 = 640$ Hz when it is 300 m away from the crossing. The speed of sound in air is 340 m/s. What is the frequency heard by a person standing on a road perpendicular to the track at a distance 400 m from the crossing?

2. At $t = 0$, a source of sonic oscillations S and an observer O start moving along X and Y axes with 5 m/s and 10 m/s. The figure shows their positions at $t = 0$. If frequency of source is 1000 Hz, find the frequency of signals received by the observer after 5 s. $v_{sound} = 330$ m/s

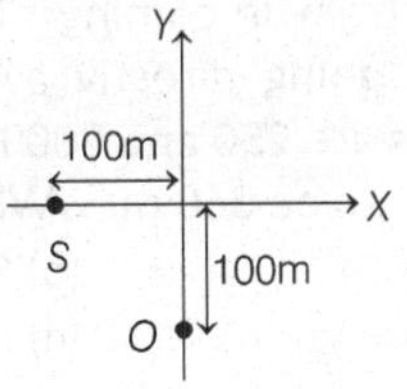

3. A source emitting sound at frequency 4000 Hz, is moving along the Y-axis with a speed of 33 m/s. A listener is situated on the ground at the position (600 m, 0). Find the frequency of the sound received by the listener at the instant the source crosses the origin. Speed of sound in air = 330 m/s.

4. A source of sound with natural frequency $f_0 = 1.8$ kHz moves uniformly along a straight line separated from a stationary observer by a distance $d = 250$ m. The velocity of the source is equal to $\eta = 0.80$ fraction of the velocity of sound. Find
   (a) the frequency of sound received by the observer at the moment when the source gets closest to him,
   (b) the distance between the source and the observer at the moment when the observer receives a frequency $f = f_0$.

5. A sonic source of frequency $n_0 = 272$ Hz is moving along a horizontal circle of radius $R = 3$ m with a speed $u = 10$ m/s. A stationary receiver lies in the same plane at a distance $d = 5$ m from centre of the circle. Speed of sound in air $v = 330$ m/s.
   (a) Calculate minimum and maximum frequencies received by the receiver.
   (b) If at $t = 0$ receiver receives minimum frequency, calculate minimum value of time t when it receives maximum frequency.

LEVEL 02 JEE Advanced Level

Single Choice Correct Questions

1. An observer moves towards a stationary source of sound with a speed (1/5)th of the speed of sound. The wavelength and frequency of the source emitted are λ and f, respectively. The apparent frequency and wavelength recorded by the observer are, respectively.
   (a) $1.2f$ and λ (b) f and 1.2λ
   (c) $0.8f$ and 0.8λ (d) $1.2f$ and 1.2λ

2. If an observer moving with velocity v crosses a stationary source of frequency n, then the change in the frequency would be (speed of sound = V)
   (a) $\dfrac{2n(V^2 + v^2)}{Vv}$ (b) $\dfrac{2n(V^2 - v^2)}{Vv}$
   (c) $\dfrac{2nV}{v}$ (d) $\dfrac{2nv}{V}$

3. A siren placed at a railway platform is emitting sound of frequency 5 kHz. A passenger sitting in a moving train A records a frequency of 5.5 kHz, while the train approaches the siren. During his return journey in a different train B he records a frequency of 6.0 kHz while approaching the same siren. The ratio of the velocity of train B to that train A is
   (a) $\dfrac{242}{252}$ (b) 2 (c) $\dfrac{5}{6}$ (d) $\dfrac{11}{6}$

4. Two sources A and B are sounding notes of frequency 680 Hz. A listener moves from A to B with a constant velocity u. If the speed of sound is 340 m/s what must be the value of u, so that he hears 10 beats per second?
   (a) 2.0 m/s (b) 2.5 m/s
   (c) 3.0 m/s (d) 3.5 m/s

5. A motorcycle starts from rest and accelerates along a straight line at 2.2 m/s^2. The speed of sound is 330 m/s. A siren at the starting point remains stationary. When the driver hears the frequency of the siren at 90% of its value when the motorcycle is stationary, the distance travelled by the motorcyclist is

(a) 123.75 m (b) 247.5 m (c) 495 m (d) 990 m

6. A detector is released from rest over a source of sound of frequency $f_0 = 10^3$ Hz. The frequency observed by the detector at time t is plotted in the graph. The speed of sound in air is $(g = 10\ m/s^2)$

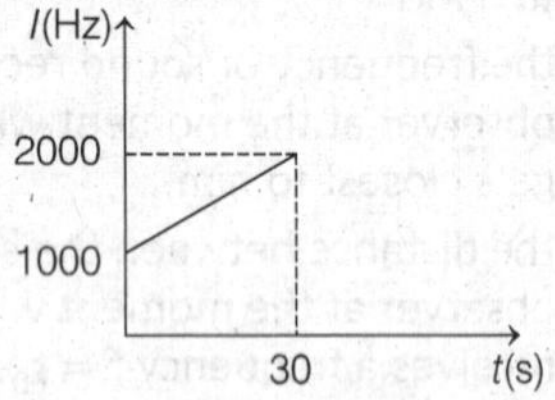

(a) 330 m/s (b) 350 m/s
(c) 300 m/s (d) 310 m/s

7. A train moving at 25 m/s emits a whistle of frequency 200 Hz. If the speed of sound in air is 340 m/s, find the frequency observed by a stationary observer

(i) if the observer is in front of the train
(ii) if the observer is behind the train

(a) 186 Hz, 216 Hz (b) 216 Hz, 186 Hz
(c) 172 Hz, 220 Hz (d) 220 Hz, 172 Hz

8. A man standing on a platform hears the sound of frequency 605 Hz coming from a frequency 550 Hz from a train whistle moving towards the platform. If the velocity of sound is 330 m/s, then what is the speed of train?

(a) 30 m/s (b) 35 m/s (c) 40 m/s (d) 45 m/s

9. When a source moves away from a stationary observer, the frequency is 6/7 times the original frequency. Given, speed of sound = 330 m/s. The speed of the source is

(a) 40 m/s (b) 55 m/s
(c) 330 m/s (d) 165 m/s

10. The frequency of a car horn is 400 Hz. If the horn is honked as the car moves with a speed $v_s = 34$ m/s through still air towards a stationary receiver, the wavelength of the sound passing the receiver is [velocity of sound is 340 m/s]

(a) 0.765 m (b) 0.850 m
(c) 0.935 m (d) 0.425 m

11. A source at rest emits waves with wavelength λ in a medium with velocity V. If the source moves to the right with velocity V_s (see figure), the distance between adjacent crest λ' directly behind the source is

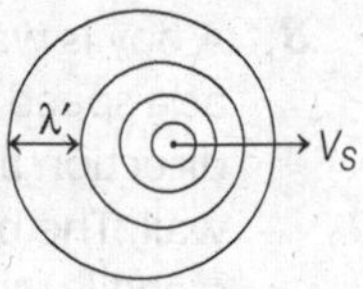

(a) $\dfrac{\lambda V}{V + V_s}$ (b) $\dfrac{\lambda V}{V - V_s}$

(c) $\lambda\left(1 + \dfrac{V_s}{V}\right)$ (d) $\lambda\left(1 + \dfrac{V}{V_s}\right)$

12. A train moves towards a stationary observer with speed 34 m/s. The train sounds a whistle and its frequency recorded by the observer is f_1. If the train's speed is reduced to 17 m/s, the frequency registered is f_2. If the speed of sound is 340 m/s, then the ratio $\dfrac{f_1}{f_2}$ is

(a) $\dfrac{18}{19}$ (b) $\dfrac{1}{2}$

(c) 2 (d) $\dfrac{19}{18}$

13. A student near a railroad track hears a train's whistle when the train is coming directly toward him and when it is going directly away. The two observed frequencies are 250 and 200 Hz. Assume the speed of sound in air to be 360 m/s. What is the train's speed?

(a) 20 m/s (b) 30 m/s
(c) 40 m/s (d) 50 m/s

14. A source of sound attached to the bob of a simple pendulum executes SHM. The difference between the apparent frequency of sound as received by an observer during its approach and recession at the mean position of the SHM motion is 2% of the natural frequency of the source. The velocity of the source at the mean positon is (velocity of sound in the air is 340 m/s)
[Assume velocity of sound source << velocity of sound in air]

(a) 1.4 m/s (b) 3.4 m/s (c) 1.7 m/s (d) 2.1 m/s

15. When a train approaches a stationary observer, the apparent frequency of the whistle is n' and when the same train recedes away from the observer, the apparent frequency is n''. Then, the apparent frequency n when the observer sitting in the train is

(a) $n = \dfrac{n' + n''}{2}$ (b) $n = \sqrt{n'n''}$

(c) $n = \dfrac{2n'n''}{n' + n''}$ (d) $n = \dfrac{2n'n''}{n' - n''}$

16. An engine whistling at a constant frequency n_0 and moving with a constant velocity goes past a stationary observer. As the engine crosses him, the frequency of the sound heard by him changes by a factor f ($f_{after} = f \times f_{before}$). The actual difference in the frequencies of the sound heard by him before and after the engine crosses him is

(a) $\frac{1}{2} n_0 (1 - f^2)$
(b) $\frac{1}{2} n_0 \left(\frac{1-f^2}{f}\right)$
(c) $n_0 \left(\frac{1-f}{1+f}\right)$
(d) $\frac{1}{2} n_0 \left(\frac{1-f}{1+f}\right)$

17. A man is watching two trains, one leaving and the other coming in with equal speed of 4 m/s. Velocity of sound in air is 320 m/s. If they sound their whistles, each of frequency 240 Hz, the number of beats heard per second by the man will be equal to

(a) 6
(b) 3
(c) 0
(d) 12

18. Two sound sources are moving in opposite directions with velocities v_1 and v_2 ($v_1 > v_2$). Both are moving away from a stationary observer. The frequency of both the source is 900 Hz. What is the value of $v_1 - v_2$, so that the beat frequency observed by the observer is 6 Hz? Speed of sound $v = 300$ m/s. Given that v_1 and $v_2 << v$

(a) 1 m/s
(b) 2 m/s
(c) 3 m/s
(d) 4 m/s

19. A source emitting a sound of frequency f is placed at a large distance from an observer. The source starts moving towards the observer with uniform acceleration a. Find frequency heard by the observer corresponding to the wave emitted just after the source starts. The speed of sound in medium is v

(a) $\frac{vf^2}{2vf - a}$
(b) $\frac{2vf^2}{2vf + a}$
(c) $\frac{2vf^2}{3vf - a}$
(d) $\frac{2vf^2}{2vf - a}$

20. A train blowing its whistle moves with a constant velocity v away from an observer on the ground. The ratio of the natural frequency of the whistle to that measured by the observer is found to be 1.2. If the trains is at rest and the observer moves away from it at the same velocity, this ratio would be given by

(a) 0.51
(b) 1.25
(c) 1.52
(d) 2.05

21. A source and a detector move away from each other, each with a speed of 10 m/s with respect to the ground with no wind. If the detector detects a frequency 1980 Hz of the sound coming from the source, what is the original frequency of the source? Speed of sound in air = 340 m/s

(a) 1867 Hz
(b) 2007 Hz
(c) 2100 Hz
(d) 2170 Hz

22. A source S of frequency f_0 and an observer O, moving with speeds v_1 and v_2 respectively, are moving away from each other. When they are separated by distance a (at $t = 0$), a pulse is emitted by the source. This pulse is received by O at time t_1, then t_1 is equal to

(a) $\frac{a}{v_s + v_2}$
(b) $\frac{a}{v_1 + v_s}$
(c) $\frac{a}{v_s - v_2}$
(d) $\frac{a}{v_1 + v_2 + v_s}$

23. A source of sound S is moving with velocity $u/2$ and two observers A and B are moving with velocity u as shown. Find the ratio of wavelength received by A and B. Given that velocity of sound is 10 u.

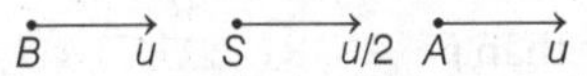

(a) $\frac{19}{21}$
(b) $\frac{17}{21}$
(c) $\frac{21}{23}$
(d) $\frac{17}{23}$

24. Bullets are fired at regular intervals of 10 s from a car moving with a speed of 30 ms^{-1} towards another car approaching with a speed of 60 ms^{-1}. The interval at which the sound of bullet firing can be reported by second car is
(speed of sound = 330 ms^{-1})

(a) 7.7 s
(b) 8.32 s
(c) 6.7 s
(d) 12 s

25. A police car moving at 22 m/s chases a motorcyclist. The police man sounds his horn at 176 Hz, while both of them move towards a stationary siren of frequency 165 Hz. If the motorcyclist does not observe any beats, the speed of motor cycle is (velocity of sound is 330 m/s)

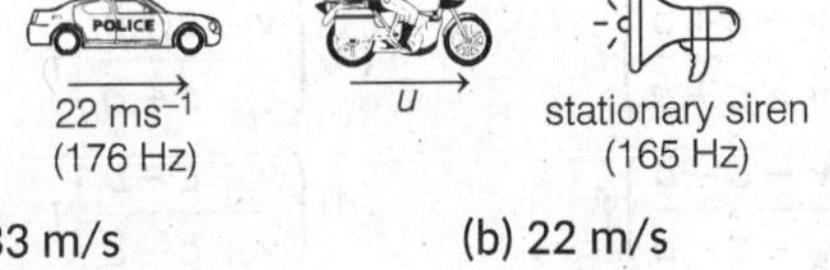

(a) 33 m/s
(b) 22 m/s
(c) zero
(d) 11 m/s

26. A sounding body of negligible dimension emitting a frequency of 150 Hz is dropped from a height. During its fall under gravity it passes near a balloon moving up with a constant velocity of 2 m/s, one second after it stated to fall. The difference in the frequency observed by the man in balloon just before and just after crossing the body will be, (Given that velocity of sound = 300 m/s; $g = 10\ m/s^2$)

(a) 12 Hz (b) 6 Hz
(c) 8 Hz (d) 4 Hz

27. A whistle of frequency $f_0 = 1300$ Hz is dropped from a height $H = 505$ m above the ground. At the same time, a detector is projected upwards with velocity $v = 50$ m/s along the same line. If the velocity of sound is $V = 300\ ms^{-1}$, the frequency detected by the detector after $t = 5$ s is ($g = 10\ ms^{-2}$)

(a) 1600 Hz (b) 1500 Hz
(c) 1700 Hz (d) 1800 Hz

28. The frequency of a car horn is f. What frequency is observed if both the car and the observer are at rest, but a wind is blowing from the car toward the observer?

(a) f
(b) greater than f
(c) less than f
(d) either greater or less than f

29. In the case of sound waves, wind is blowing from source to receiver with speed U_W. Both source and receiver are stationary. If λ_0 is the original wavelength with no wind and V is speed of sound in air, then wavelength as received by the receiver is given by

(a) λ_0 (b) $\left(\frac{V+U_W}{V}\right)\lambda_0$
(c) $\left(\frac{V-U_W}{V}\right)\lambda_0$ (d) $\left(\frac{V}{V+V_W}\right)\lambda_0$

30. A source of frequency f and an observer are moving on a straight line with velocities a and b respectively, if the source is ahead of the observer and if the medium is also moving in the direction of their motion with velocity c (the velocity of sound being v), then the apparent frequency of sound heard by the observer would be

(a) $\left(\frac{v+c+b}{v+c+a}\right)f$ (b) $\left(\frac{v-c+b}{v-c+a}\right)f$
(c) $\left(\frac{v-c-b}{v-c-a}\right)f$ (d) $\left(\frac{v+c-b}{v+c-a}\right)f$

31. A police car with a siren of frequency 8 kHz is moving with uniform velocity 36 km/h towards a tall building which reflects the sound waves. The speed of sound in air is 320 m/s. The frequency of the siren heard by the car driver is

(a) 8.5 kHz (b) 8.25 kHz
(c) 7.25 kHz (d) 7.5 kHz

32. A racing car moving towards a cliff sounds its horn. The driver observed that the sound reflected from the cliff has a pitch one octave higher than the actual sound of the horn. If v = the velocity of sound, the velocity of the car is

(a) $v/\sqrt{2}$ (b) $v/2$ (c) $v/3$ (d) $v/4$

33. A sound wave of frequency f propagating through air with a velocity c, is reflected from a surface which is moving away from the source with a constant speed v. Find the frequency of the refelcted wave, measured by the observer at the position of the source.

(a) $\left(\frac{c+v}{c-v}\right)f$ (b) $\left(\frac{c-v}{c+v}\right)f$
(c) $\left(\frac{c-v}{c}\right)f$ (d) $\left(\frac{c}{c+v}\right)f$

34. A wall is moving with velocity u and a source of sound moves with velocity $u/2$ in the same direction as shown in the figure.

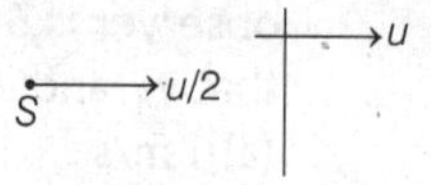

Assuming that the sound travels with velocity $10u$. The ratio of incident sound wavelength on the wall to the reflected sound wavelength by the wall, is equal to

(a) 9 : 11 (b) 11 : 9 (c) 4 : 5 (d) 5 : 4

35. A train moving towards a tunnel in a huge mountain with a speed of 12 m/s sounds its whistle. Sound is reflected from the mountain. If the driver hears 6 beats per second and speed of sound in air is 332 m/s, the frequency of the whistle is

(a) 80 Hz (b) 120 Hz (c) 160 Hz (d) 240 Hz

36. An ultrasonic burglar alarm in still air transmits a signal at a frequency of 4.5×10^4 Hz, part of which is reflected by the burglar to receiver along side the transmitter. The alarm is triggered by any beat frequency greater than 5 Hz. Velocity of sound in air is 340 m/s. The minimum velocity of approach of the burglar to activate the alarm, will be

(a) 0.2 m/s (b) 4 cm/s
(c) 2 m/s (d) 20 mm/s

37. A band playing music at frequency *f* is moving towards a wall at a speed of v_b. A motorist is following the band with a speed v_m. If *v* is the speed of sound, the expression for the beat frequency heard by the motorist is

(a) $\left(\dfrac{v+v_m}{v+v_b}\right)f$ (b) $\left(\dfrac{v+v_m}{v-v_b}\right)f$

(c) $\left(\dfrac{2v_b(v+v_m)}{v^2-v_b^2}\right)f$ (d) $\left(\dfrac{2v_m(v+v_b)}{v^2-v_m^2}\right)f$

38. A stationary source is emitting sound at a fixed frequency f_0, which is reflected by two cars approaching the source. The difference between the frequencies of sound reflected from the car is 1.2% of f_0. What is the difference in the speed of the cars? The cars are moving at constant speeds much smaller than the speed of sound which is 330 m/s.

(a) 7.128 km/h (b) 4.236 km/h
(c) 8.128 km/h (d) 5.236 km/h

39. A tuning fork of frequency 380 Hz is moving towards a wall with a velocity of 4 m/s, then the number of beats heard by a stationary listener between direct and reflected sounds will be (velocity of sound in air is 340 m/s)

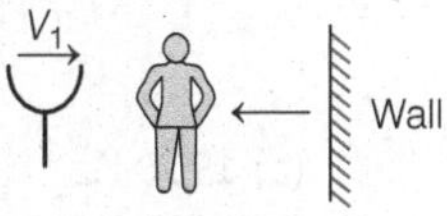

(a) 0 (b) 5 (c)7 (d) 10

40. A car is approaching a railway crossing at a speed of 72 km/h. It sounds a horn, when it is 800 m away, at 600 Hz. If velocity of sound in air is 330 ms^{-1}, the apparent frequency as received by a man at rest near the railway track perpendicular to the road at a distance of 600 m from the crossing is

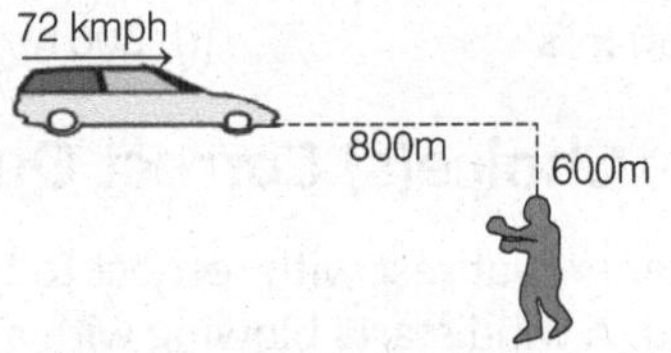

(a) 653 Hz (b) 365.5 Hz
(c) 630.5 Hz (d) 563.5 Hz

41. Two cars are moving on two perpendicular roads towards a crossing with uniform speeds of 72 km/h and 36 km/h. If second car blows horn of frequency 280 Hz, then the frequency of horn heard by the driver of first car when the line joining the cars makes angle of 45° with the roads, will be (velocity of sound is 330 m/s)

(a) 321 Hz (b) 298 Hz
(c) 289 Hz (d) 280 Hz

42. In the figure shown a source of sound of frequency 510 Hz moves with constant velocity $v_s = 20$ m/s in the direction shown. The wind is blowing at a constant velocity $v_w = 20$ m/s towards an observer who is at rest at point *B*. The frequency detected by the observer corresponding to the sound emitted by the source at initial position A, will be (speed of sound relative to air = 330 m/s)

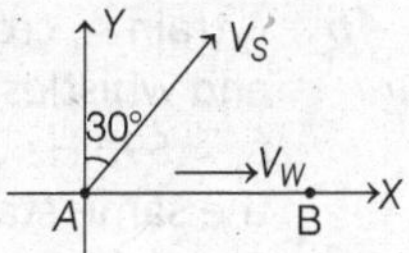

(a) 485 Hz (b) 500 Hz
(c) 512 Hz (d) 525 Hz

43. The figure shows the location of a source and detector at time *t* = 0. The source and detector are moving with velocities $v_S = 5\hat{i}$ m/s and $v_D = 10\hat{j}$ m/s respectively. The frequency of source is 100 Hz. The frequency of signals received by the detector at the moment when the source crosses the origin is (velocity of sound 330 m/s)

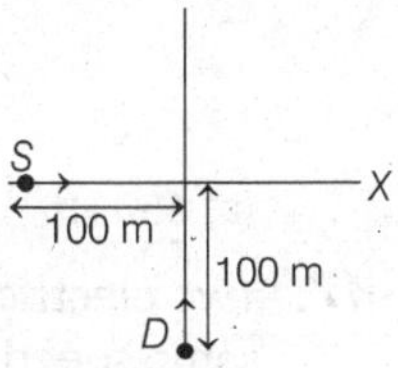

(a) 97 Hz (b) 47 Hz (c) 90 Hz (d) 60 Hz

44. In the figure shown *S* is a source of constant frequency and *O* is an observer moving with constant velocity. The graph of frequency detected by observer v/s time is

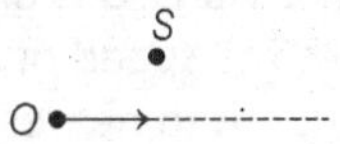

(a) 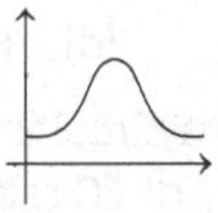 (b) 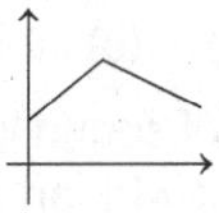

(c) 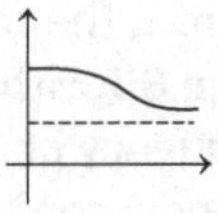 (d) 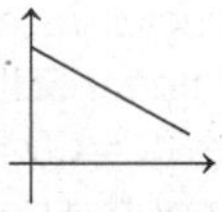

45. Source and observer both start moving simultaneously from origin, one along *x*-axis and the other along *y*-axis with speed of source = twice the speed of observer. The graph between the apparent frequency observed by observer *f* and time *t* would approximately be

(a) 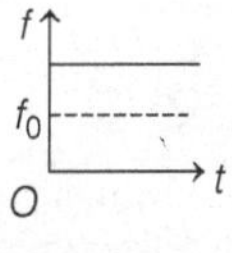

(b) 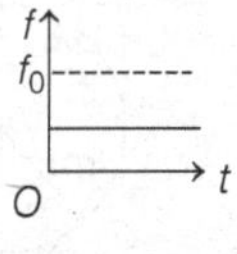

(c) 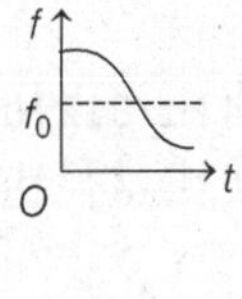

(d) 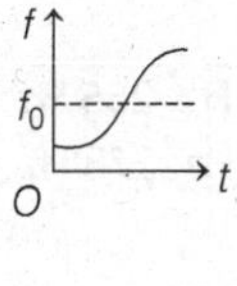

46. A train A, crosses a station with a speed of 40 m/s and whistles a short pulse of natural frequency $f_0 = 596$ Hz. Another train B is approaching towards the same station with the same speed along a parallel track. Two tracks are separated by a distance $d = 99$ m. When train A whistles, train B is 152 m away from the station as shown in figure. If velocity of sound in air is $v = 330$ m/s, the frequency of the pulse heard by driver of train B is

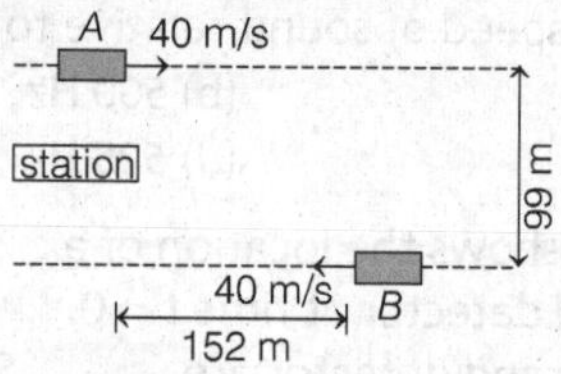

(a) 650 Hz (b) 724 Hz (c) 778 Hz (d) 850 Hz

47. Two electric trains run at the same speed of $v = 90$ km/h along a straight track one after the other with an interval of $l = 2.0$ km between them. At the instant when they are located symmetrically relative to point A at a distance of $b = 1.0$ km from the track (figure) both trains give a brief sound signal of the same frequency of $f = 50$ Hz. What will be the number of beats heard per second at point A when the vibrations produced by the signals arrive at it? The speed of sound is $v = 350$ m/s. Round off to nearest integer.

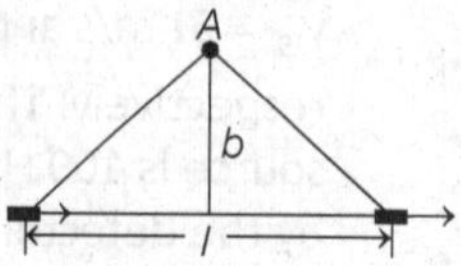

(a) 5 Hz (b) 6 Hz (c) 7 Hz (d) 8 Hz

48. A source of sound is moving along a circular orbit of radius 3 m with an angular velocity of 10 rad/s. A sound detector located far away from the source is executing linear SHM along the line BD with an amplitude $BC = CD = 6$ m. The frequency of oscillation of the detector is $5/\pi$ per second. The source is at the point A when the detector is at the point B. If the source emits a continuous sound wave of frequency 340 Hz, the maximum and minimum frequencies recorded by the detector, respectively are ($V_{sound} = 330$ m/s)

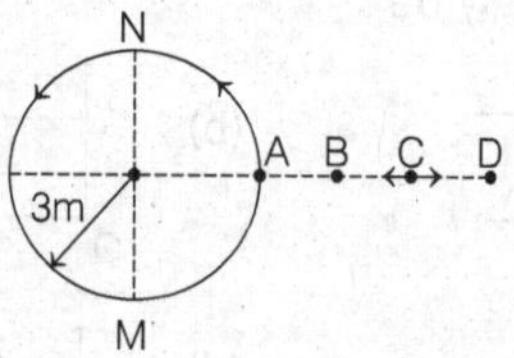

(a) 442 Hz, 255 Hz (b) 374 Hz, 312 Hz
(c) 402 Hz, 278 Hz (d) 475 Hz, 225 Hz

49. A whistle revolves in a circle with angular speed $\omega = 20$ rad/s using a string of length 50 cm. If the frequency of sound from the whistle is 385 Hz, then what is the minimum frequency heard by an observer which is far away from the centre? ($v_{sound} = 340$ m/s)

(a) 385 Hz (b) 374 Hz
(c) 394 Hz (d) 333 Hz

50. A train is moving in an elliptical orbit in anti-clockwise sense with a speed of 110 m/s. Guard is also moving in the given direction with same speed as that of train. The ratio of the length of major and minor axis is 4/3. Driver blows a whistle of 1900 Hz at P, which is received by guard at S. The frequency received by guard is (velocity of sound $v = 330$ m/s)

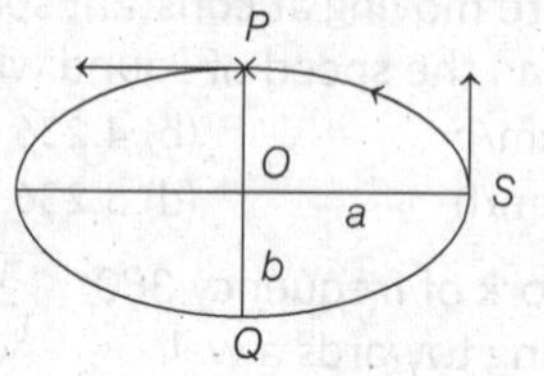

(a) 1900 Hz (b) 1800 Hz
(c) 2000 Hz (d) 1500 Hz

51. A fighter plane is moving in a vertical loop with constant speed of radius R. The centre of the loop is at a height $2R$ directly overhead of an observer standing on the ground. The observer receives maximum frequency of the sound produced by the plane when it is nearest to him. Find the speed of the plane. Velocity of sound in air is $v = \frac{600\sqrt{3}}{\pi}$ ms^{-1}.

(a) 150 m/s (b) 200 m/s
(c) 250 m/s (d) 300 m/s

Multiple Choice(s) Correct Questions

1. A listener is at rest with respect to the source of sound. A wind starts blowing with a constant velocity along the line joining the source and the observer. Which of the folowing quantities do not change?

(a) Wavelength
(b) Frequency
(c) Time period
(d) Velocity of sound

2. A stationary observer receives a sound of frequency $f_0 = 2000$ Hz. The apparent frequency f varies with time as shown in figure. Speed of sound = 300 m/s. Choose the correct alternative(s)

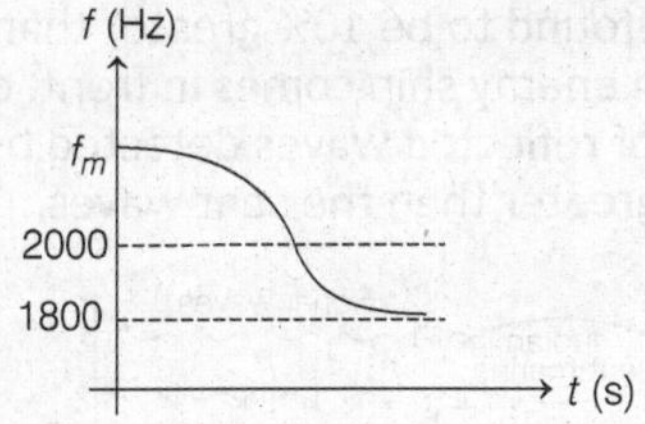

(a) Speed of source is 66.7 m/s
(b) f_m shown in figure cannot be greater than 2500 Hz
(c) Speed of source is 33.33 m/s
(d) f_m shown in figure cannot be greater than 2250 Hz

3. A sound wave of frequency f travels horizontallly to the right. It is reflected from a large vertical plane surface movng to left with a speed u. The speed of sound in medium is c.

(a) The number of waves striking the surface per second is $\frac{(c+u)}{c}f$

(b) The wavelength of reflected wave is $\frac{c(c-u)}{f(c+u)}$

(c) The frequency of the reflected wave as observed by the stationary observer is $f\frac{(c+u)}{(c-u)}$

(d) The number of beats heard by a stationary listener to the left of the reflecting surface is $\frac{uf}{c-u}$

4. In the figure shown an observer O_1 floats (static) on water surface with ears in air while another observer O_2 is moving upwards with constant velocity $V_1 = V/5$ in water. The source moves down with constant velocity $V_s = V/5$ and emits sound of frequency f. The velocity of sound in air is V and that in water is $4V$. For the situation shown in figure

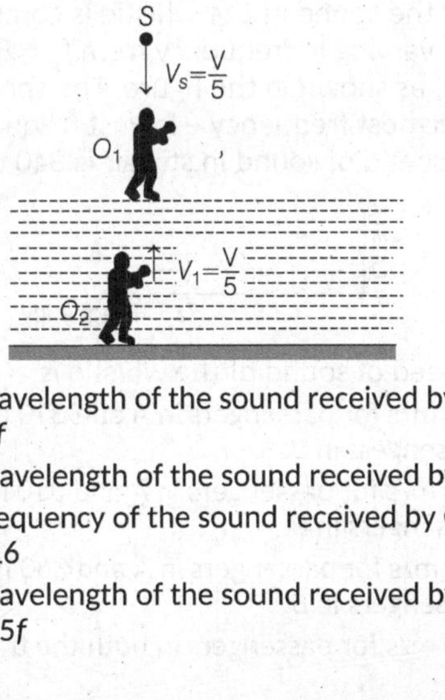

(a) The wavelength of the sound received by O_1 is $4V/5f$
(b) The wavelength of the sound received by O_1 is V/f
(c) The frequency of the sound received by O_2 is $21f/16$
(d) The wavelength of the sound received by O_2 is $16V/5f$

5. A source is moving across a circle given by the equation $x^{2} + y^2 = R^2$, with constant speed $\frac{330\pi}{6\sqrt{3}}$ m/s, in anti-clockwise sense. A detector is at rest at point $(2R, 0)$ w.r.t the centre of the circle. If the frequency emitted by the source is f and the speed of sound, $C = 330$ m/s. Then,

(a) the position of the source when the detector records the maximum frequency $\left(+\frac{\sqrt{3}}{2}R, -\frac{R}{2}\right)$

(b) the co-ordinate of the source when the detector records minimum frequency is $(0, R)$

(c) the maximum frequency recorded by the detector is $\frac{6\sqrt{3}}{\pi + 6\sqrt{3}}f$

(d) the minimum frequency recorded by the detector is $\frac{6\sqrt{3}}{6\sqrt{3} - \pi}f$

Comprehension Based Questions

Comprehension-1

A source emitting a sound wave at a certain frequency moves with constant speed along the X-axis as shown in figure (a). The source moves directly towards a stationary detector A and directly away from another stationary detector B. The superimposed three plots as shown in figure (b) indicate the pressure function $P(x)$ of the sound wave as measured by detector A, by detector B, and by someone (C) in the rest frame of the source.

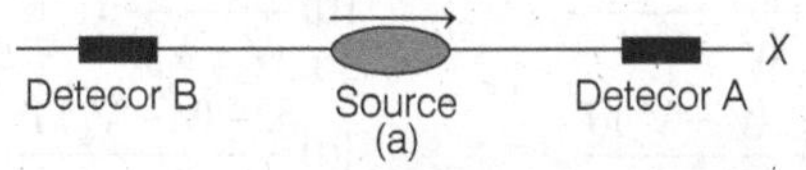

(a)

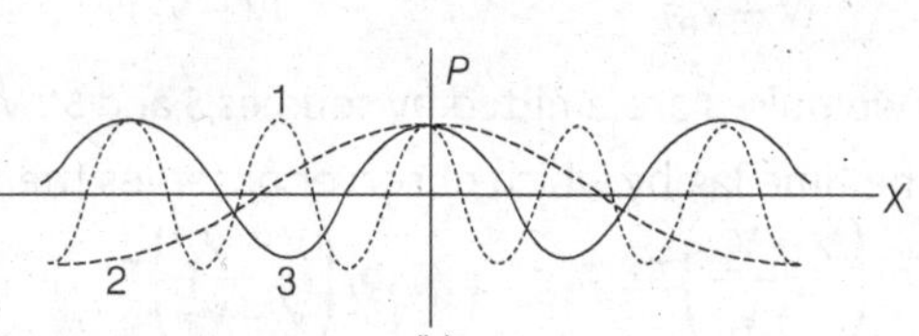

(b)

1. Which of the following plot corresponds to the measurement done by detector A?
(a) 1
(b) 2
(c) 3
(d) These plots are not possible

2. The plot corresponding to the measurement done by detector B is
(a) 1
(b) 2
(c) 3
(d) These plots are not possible

3. The plot corresponding to the measurement done by the detector C is
(a) 1
(b) 2
(c) 3
(d) These plots are not possible

4. Now the source stops and begins to move along Y-axis with same speed, the plot which corresponds to the measurement of B now is
(a) 1 (b) 2
(c) 3 (d) None of these

Comprehension-2

Observe O is ahead by L from source S which are moving along same line with velocities V_0 and V_S respectively. The speed of sound is V. The source emits a wave pulse that reaches the observer in time t_1. At time $t = T$, the source reaches at S'. It is obvious that the observer will not be at O this time. The source emits a wave pulse at this time to reach the observer in time t_2, which is measured from $t = 0$.

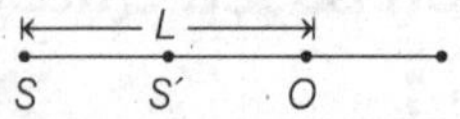

5. Find the time t_1
(a) $\dfrac{L}{V+V_0}$ (b) $\dfrac{VL}{(V-V_0)V_0}$
(c) $\dfrac{V_0 L}{(V-V_0)V_0}$ (d) $\dfrac{L}{(V-V_0)}$

6. Find the time t_2
(a) $\dfrac{L+(V-V_0)T}{(V-V_s)}$ (b) $\dfrac{(V-V_s)}{(V-V_0)}T$
(c) $\dfrac{L+(V-V_s)T}{(V-V_0)}$ (d) $\dfrac{L-(V-V_s)T}{(V-V_0)}$

7. Two pulses are emitted by sources S and S'. What is the time lag by which observer observes them?
(a) $\left(\dfrac{V-V_s}{V+V_0}\right)T$ (b) $\left(\dfrac{V+V_s}{V-V_0}\right)T$
(c) $\left(\dfrac{V+V_s}{V+V_0}\right)T$ (d) $\left(\dfrac{V-V_s}{V-V_0}\right)T$

Comprehension-3

An Indian submarine is moving in "Arab Sagar" with a constant velocity. To detect enemy, it sends out sonar waves which travel with velocity 1050 m/s in water. Initially the waves are getting reflected from a fixed island and the reflected waves are coming back to submarine. The frequency of reflected waves are detected by the submarine and found to be 10% greater than the sent waves. Now, an enemy ship comes in front, due to which the frequency of reflected waves detected by submarine becomes 21% greater than the sent waves.

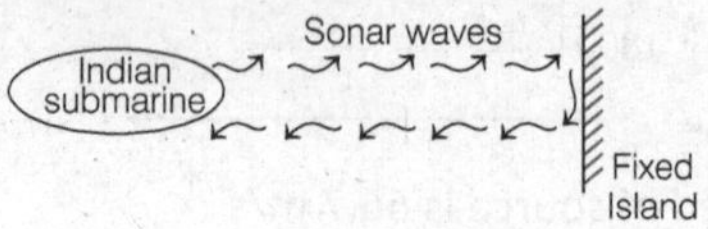

8. The speed of Indian submarine is
(a) 10 m/s (b) 50 m/s
(c) 100 m/s (d) 20 m/s

9. The velocity of enemy ship should be
(a) 50 m/s towards Indian submarine
(b) 50 m/s away from Indian submarine
(c) 100 m/s towards Indian submarine
(d) 100 m/s away from Indian submarine

10. If the wavelength received by enemy ship is λ_1 and wavelength of reflected waves received by submarine is λ_2, then $\left(\dfrac{\lambda_1}{\lambda_2}\right)$ equals
(a) 1 (b) 1.1
(c) 1.2 (d) 2

11. Bulk modulus of sea water should be approximately ($\rho_{water} = 1000\ \text{kg/m}^3$)
(a) $10^8\ \text{N/m}^2$ (b) $10^9\ \text{N/m}^2$
(c) $10^{10}\ \text{N/m}^2$ (d) $10^{11}\ \text{N/m}^2$

Comprehension-4

Two trains A and B are moving with speeds 20 m/s and 30 m/s respectively in the same direction on the same straight track, with B ahead of A. The engines are at the front ends. The engine of train A blows a long whistle. Assume that the sound of the whistle is composed of components varying in frequency from $f_1 = 800$ Hz to $f_2 = 1120$ Hz, as shown in the figure. The spread in the frequency (highest frequency – lowest frequency) is thus, 320 Hz. The speed of sound in still air is 340 m/s.

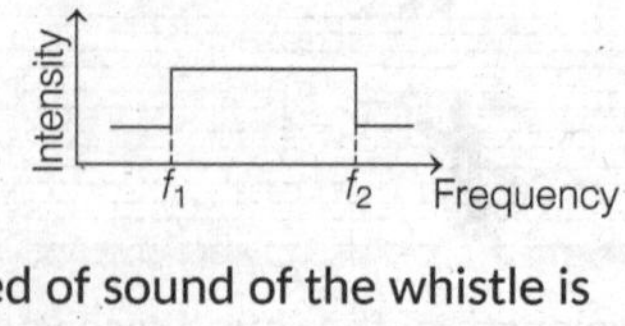

12. The speed of sound of the whistle is
(a) 340 m/s for passengers in A and 310 m/s for passengers in B.
(b) 360 m/s for passengers in A and 310 m/s for passengers in B.
(c) 310 m/s for passengers in A and 360 m/s for passengers in B.
(d) 340 m/s for passengers in both the trains.

13. The distribution of the sound intensity of the whistle as observed by the passengers in train A is best represented by

(a) 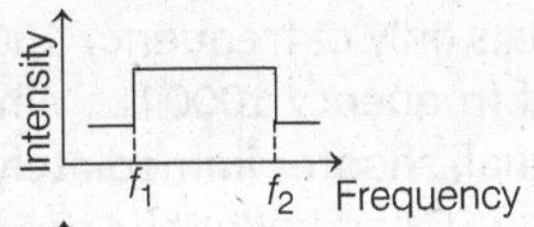

(b) 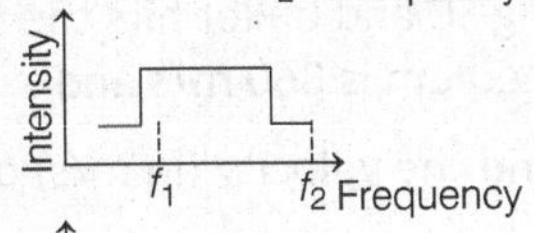

(c) 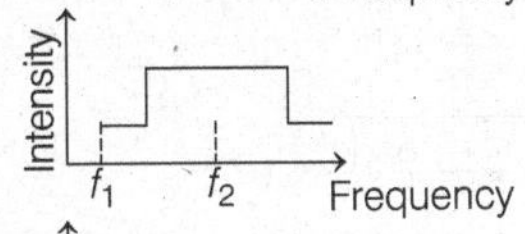

(d) 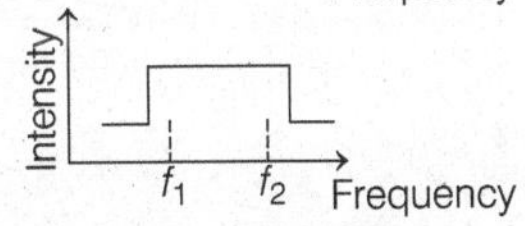

14. The spread of frequency as observed by the passengers in train B is

(a) 310 Hz (b) 330 Hz (c) 350 Hz (d) 290 Hz

Match the Columns Questions

1. A sound source emits a sound wave of wavelength 2 m when stationary. The velocity of sound with respect to the medium is 330 m/s. Column I indicates a situation and Column II indicates the possible values of wavelength and frequency recorded by recorder. Speeds of source recorder and wind are subsonic.

	Column I		Column II
(A)	[Source] $\xrightarrow{\text{wind blowing}}$ [Recorder] Source and recorder stationary	(P)	$\lambda = 2.5$ m, $f = 165$ Hz
(B)	[Source] $\rightarrow$ [Recorder] Source moving as shown, wind and recorder stationary	(Q)	$\lambda = 2$ m, $f = 170$ Hz
(C)	[Source] $\leftarrow$ [Recorder] Source and wind stationary, recorder moving as shown.	(R)	$\lambda = 1.5$ m, $f = 220$ Hz
(D)	[Source] $\rightarrow$ $\leftarrow$ [Recorder], wind $\rightarrow$ Source, wind and recorder moving in direction shown.	(S)	$\lambda = 2$ m, $f = 160$ Hz
		(T)	$\lambda = 2.5$ m, $f = 180$ Hz

2. 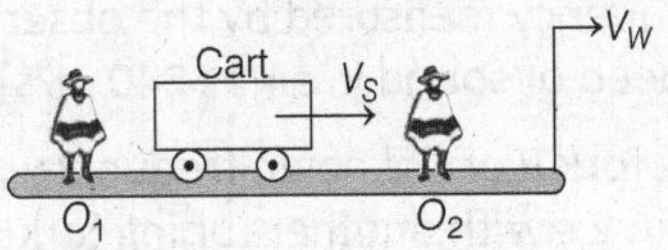

Observer O_1 and O_2 are at rest and wall is moving with velocity V_W. Cart is moving with constant velocity towards wall. The source of sound is in the cart, the original frequency of the wave is f. Sound has velocity C w.r.t ground (medium is stationary). Then, match the column I with column II

	Column I		Column II
(A)	Wavelength received by O_1 directly from cart	(P)	$\left(\frac{C - V_W}{C + V_W}\right)\frac{(C - V_S)}{f}$
(B)	Wavelength received by O_2 directly from cart	(Q)	$\frac{C + V_S}{f}$
(C)	Wavelength received by driver of the cart after reflection from wall	(R)	$\left(\frac{C + V_W}{C - V_W}\right)\frac{(C - V_S)}{f}$
(D)	Wavelength received by O_1 after reflection from wall	(S)	$\frac{C - V_S}{f}$
		(T)	None of these

Numerical Value Questions

1. A source of sound starts receding away from a stationary listener at $t = 0$, such that its distance from the listener at any later time t is $x = 10t(t+6)$, where x is in m and t in s. Further the frequency of the source is decreasing with time and is given by, $\nu = \frac{525 \text{ Hz}}{t}$, where t is in s. Find the frequency (in Hz) of the sound heard by the listener when the source is 212.5 m away from him. Speed of sound = 320 m/s.

2. An observer standing at a railway crossing receives frequency of 2.2 kHz and 1.8 kHz when the train approaches and recedes from the observer. What is the velocity (in m/s) of the train?
The speed of the sound in air is 300 m/s.

3. Two tuning forks A and B each of natural frequency 85 Hz move with velocity 10 m/s relative to stationary observer O. Fork A moves away from the observer while the fork B moves towards him as shown in the figure. A wind with a speed 10 m/s is blowing in the direction of motion of fork A. Find the

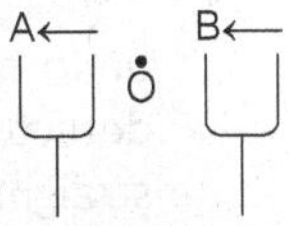

beat frequency measured by the observer in Hz. [Take speed of sound in air as 340 m/s]

4. A tuning fork P of unknown frequency given 7 beats in 2 s with another tuning fork Q. When Q runs towards the wall with a speed of 5 m/s, it gives 5 beats per second with its echo. On loading wax on P, it gives 5 beats per second with Q. What is the original frequency (in Hz) of P? Assume speed of sound = 332 m/s.

5. A motor car moving away from a cliff with a velocity of 324 km/h sounds the horn and the echo is heard after 30 s. Wind is blowing towards the cliff with speed 50 m/s. Assuming the velocity of sound in air to be 350 m/s, find the distance (in km) between the car and cliff when the horn is sounded.

6. Two buses X and Y are moving towards each other with same speed 50 km h^{-1}. They blow horns of the same frequency 690 Hz. Wind is blowing at speed 25 km h^{-1} in the direction of motion of X. The driver of the bux X hears the sound of horn blown by bus Y and the sound of horn of his own bus after reflection from the bus Y. Find the difference between the two frequencies (in Hz). [v_{sound} = 1225 km/h]

7. At particular instant a source of sound of frequency 100 Hz is at (2 m, 1 m) and an observer is at (5 m, 5 m). The velocity of source and observer are $15(2\hat{i} + \hat{j})$ m/s and $5(\hat{i} + 3\hat{j})$ m/s, respectively at this instant. The velocity of sound in air is 330 m/s. Find the frequency (in Hz) of sound received by the observer.

8. A road passes at some distance from a standing man. A truck is coming on the road with some acceleration. The truck driver blows a whistle of frequency 500 Hz when the line joining the truck and the man makes an angle $x°$ with the road. The man hears a note having a frequency of 600 Hz when the truck is closest to him. Also the speed of truck has got doubled during this time. Find the value of x.

9. A source of sound with natural frequency f_0 moves uniformly along a straight line. A stationary sound detector is located at a distance of 300 m from the straight line. When the source is closest to the detector, it records a frequency of $3f_0$ as received from the source. If the distance of the source from the detector at the instant when it records natural frequency f_0 of the source is $100\sqrt{n}$ m, then find n.

10. A bus is moving with a velocity v_B, along positive X-axis along a road as shown in the figure. A shooter S is at a distance l from the road. He has a detector which can detect signals only of frequency 1500 Hz. The bus blows horn of frequency 1000 Hz. When detector detects a signal, shooter immediately shoots towards the road along SC and bullet hits the bus. If velocity of sound in medium is 360 m/s and $\frac{v_{bus}}{v_{sound}} = \frac{2}{3\sqrt{3}}$, then find the velocity (in m/s) of the bullet.

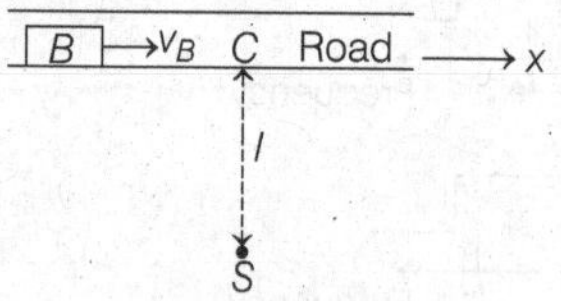

Previous Year's Questions

JEE Main

1 The engine of a train moving with speed 10 ms^{-1} towards a platform sounds a whistle at frequency 400 Hz. The frequency heard by a passenger inside the train is (neglect air speed. Speed of sound in air = 330 ms^{-1}) **[2023, 8 April, Shift-I]**

(a) 400 Hz (b) 388 Hz (c) 412 Hz (d) 200 Hz

2 A car P travelling at 20 ms^{-1} sounds its horn at a frequency of 400 Hz. Another car Q is travelling behind the first car in the same direction with a velocity 40 ms^{-1}. The frequency heard by the passenger of the car Q is approximately (Take, velocity of sound = 360 ms^{-1}) **[2023, 11April, Shift-II]**

(a) 471 Hz (b) 421 Hz
(c) 485 Hz (d) 514 Hz

3 A person observes two moving trains, A reaching the station and B leaving the station with equal speed of 30 m/s. If both trains emit sounds with frequency 300 Hz, (Speed of sound: 330 m/s) approximate difference of frequencies heard by the person will be **[2023, 29 Jan, Shift-I]**

(a) 55 Hz (b) 10 Hz
(c) 80 Hz (d) 33 Hz

4 A person driving car at a constant speed of 15 m/s is approaching a vertical wall. The person notices a change of 40 Hz in the frequency of his car's horn upon reflection from the wall. The frequency of horn is .... Hz.

(Given, Speed of sound : 330 m/s) **[2023, 6 April Shift-I]**

5 A train blowing a whistle of frequency 320 Hz approaches an observer standing on the platform at a speed of 66 m/s. The frequency observed by the observer will be .... Hz.
(Given, speed of sound = 330 ms^{-1})
[2023, 25 Jan Shift-II]

6 An observer moves towards a stationary source of sound with a velocity equal to one-fifth of the velocity of sound. The percentage change in the frequency will be **[2022, 27 June Shift I]**
(a) 20% (b) 10%
(c) 5% (d) zero

7 An employee of a factory moving away from his workplace by a car listens to the siren of the factory. He drives the car at the speed of 72 kmh^{-1} in the direction of wind which is blowing at 72 kmh^{-1} speed. Frequency of siren is 720 Hz. The employee hears an apparent frequency of .... Hz. (Assume speed of sound to be 340 ms^{-1}) **[2022, 30 June, Shift-I]**

8 The frequency of echo will be .... Hz if the train blowing a whistle of frequency 320 Hz is moving with a velocity of 36 km/h towards a hill from which an echo is heard by the train driver. (Velocity of sound in air is 330 m/s). **[2022, 28 July Shift-I]**

9 When a car is approaching the observer, the frequency of horn is 100 Hz. After passing the observer, it is 50 Hz. If the observer moves with the car, the frequency will be $x/3$ Hz where x = ...
[2022, 26 July Shift-I]

10 An observer is riding on a bicycle and moving towards a hill at 18 kmh^{-1}. He hears a sound from a source at some distance behind him directly as well as after its reflection from the hill. If the original frequency of the sound as emitted by source is 640 Hz and velocity of the sound in air is 320 m/s, the beat frequency between the two sounds heard by observer will be .... Hz. **[2022, 25 July Shift-I**

JEE Advanced

S_1 and S_2 are two identical sound sources of frequency 656 Hz. The source S_1 is located at O and S_2 moves anti-clockwise with a uniform speed $4\sqrt{2}$ ms^{-1} on a circular path around O, as shown in the figure. There are three points P, Q and R on this path such that P and R are diametrically opposite while Q is equidistant from them,. A sound detector is placed at point P. The source S_1 can move along direction OP.
(Given : The speed of sound in air is 324 ms^{-1})

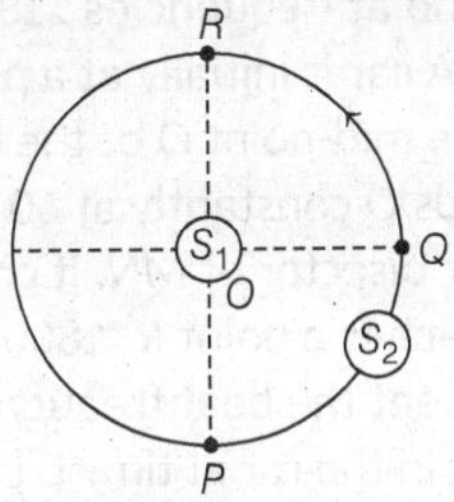

1 When only S_2 in emitting sound and it is at Q, the frequency of sound measured by the detector in Hz is .... **(2023 Adv.)**

2 Consider both sources emitting sound. When S_2 is at R and S_1 approaches the detector with a speed 4 ms^{-1}, the beat frequency measured by the detector is ...... Hz. **(2023 Adv.)**

3 A source, approaching with speed u towards the open end of a stationary pipe of length L, is emitting a sound of frequency f_s. The farther end of the pipe is closed. The speed of sound in air is v and f_0 is the fundamental frequency of the pipe. For which of the following combination(s) of u and f_s, will the sound reaching the pipe lead to a resonance? **(2021 Adv.)**
(a) $u = 0.8v$ and $f_s = f_0$
(b) $u = 0.8v$ and $f_s = 2f_0$
(c) $u = 0.8v$ and $f_s = 0.5f_0$
(d) $u = 0.5v$ and $f_s = 1.5f_0$

4 Two men are walking along a horizontal straight line in the same direction. The man in front walks at a speed 1.0 ms^{-1} and the man behind walks at a speed 2.0 ms^{-1}. A third man is standing at a height 12 m above the same horizontal line such that all three men are in a vertical plane. The two walking men are blowing identical whistles which emit a sound of frequency 1430 Hz. The speed of sound in air 330 ms^{-1}. At the instant, when the moving men are 10 m apart, the stationary man is equidistant from them. The frequency of beats in Hz, heard by the stationary man at this instant, is .... **(2018 Adv.)**

5 A stationary source emits sound of frequency $f_0 = 492$ Hz. The sound is reflected by a large car approaching the source with a speed of 2 ms^{-1}. The reflected signal is received by the source and superposed with the original. What will be the beat frequency of the resulting signal in Hz? (Given that the speed of sound in air is 330 ms^{-1} and the car reflects the sound at the frequency it has received). **(2017 Adv.)**

6 Two loudspeakers M and N are located 20m apart and emit sound at frequencies 118 Hz and 121 Hz, respectively. A car is initially at a point P, 1800 m away from the mid-point Q of the line MN and moves towards Q constantly at 60 km/h along the perpendicular bisector of MN. It crosses Q and eventually reaches a point R, 1800 m away from Q. Let $\nu(t)$ represent the beat frequency measured by a person sitting in the car at time t. Let ν_P, ν_Q and ν_R be the beat frequencies measured at locations P, Q and R respectively. The speed of sound in air is 330 ms^{-1}. Which of the following statement(s) is (are) true regarding the sound heard by the person? **(2016 Adv.)**

(a) The plot below represents schematically the variation of beat frequency with time

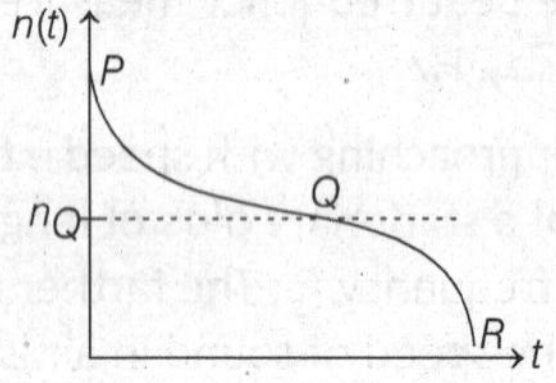

(b) The rate of change in beat frequency is maximum when the car passes through Q

(c) $\nu_P + \nu_R = 2\nu_Q$

(d) The plot below represents schematically the variations of beat frequency with time

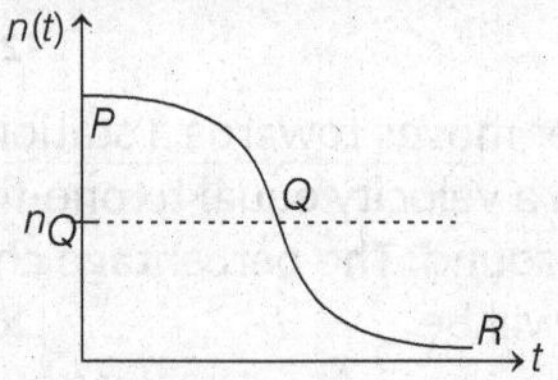

7 A police car with a siren of frequency 8 kHz is moving with uniform velocity 36 km/h towards a tall building which reflects the sound waves. The speed of sound in air is 320 m/s. The frequency of the siren heard by the car driver is **(2011 Adv.)**

(a) 8.50 kHz

(b) 8.25 kHz

(c) 7.75 kHz

(d) 7.50 kHz

Answer Key

Level 1

11.1 Stationary Source and Moving Observer

1. 544.1 Hz, 0.68 m **2.** 511.8 Hz **3.** $(f_a + f_r)/2$ **4.** 4.6 Hz

11.2 Moving Source and Stationary Observer

1. (a) 1328.1 Hz, (b) 1180.6 Hz

2. 56.25 cm, 63.75 cm

3. 750 Hz **4.** 0.8 **5.** 30 m/s

6. 8 Hz **7.** (a) 11 km/h (b) 4 Hz

11.3 Both Source and Observer in Motion

1. (a) 900 Hz (b) 1005 Hz **2.** 425 Hz **3.** 3000 Hz

11.4 Effect of Wind in Doppler Effect

1. 680 Hz **2.** 0.275 m, 1200 Hz **3.** 72.5 Hz

11.5 Dopper Effect in Reflected Sound

1. (a) 1953 Hz (b) 2050 Hz **2.** 1.6 kHz **3.** 45.93 kHz

4. $11f/9$ **5.** 0.935 km, 643 Hz

6. (a) 0.3 m, (b) 1320, (c) 332 m/s, (d) 0.2 m

7. $\frac{2uf}{v+u}$ **8.** 680 Hz

11.6 Source and Observer Moving along Different Lines

1. 680 Hz **2.** 1030 Hz **3.** 4040 Hz

4. (a) 5 kHz (b) 320 m

5. (a) 264 Hz, 280.5 Hz (b) $127\pi/300$ s

Level 2

Single Choice Correct Questions

1. (a)	2. (d)	3. (b)	4. (b)	5. (b)
6. (c)	7. (b)	8. (a)	9. (b)	10. (a)
11. (c)	12. (d)	13. (c)	14. (b)	15. (c)
16. (b)	17. (a)	18. (b)	19. (d)	20. (b)
21. (c)	22. (c)	23. (a)	24. (a)	25. (b)
26. (a)	27. (b)	28. (a)	29. (b)	30. (b)
31. (a)	32. (c)	33. (b)	34. (a)	35. (a)
36. (d)	37. (c)	38. (a)	39. (a)	40. (c)
41. (b)	42. (d)	43. (a)	44. (c)	45. (b)
46. (b)	47. (a)	48. (a)	49. (b)	50. (b)
51. (b)				

Multiple Choice(s) Correct Questions

1. (b,c)	2. (c,d)	3. (a,b,c)	4. (a,c,d)
5. (a,b)			

Comprehension Based Questions

1. (a)	2. (b)	3. (c)	4. (d)	5. (d)
6. (c)	7. (d)	8. (b)	9. (a)	10. (b)
11. (b)	12. (b)	13. (a)	14. (a)	

Match the Columns Questions

1. (A)-P, (B)-R, (C)-Q, (D)-QT

2. (A)-Q, (B)-S, (C)-R, (D)-R

Numrical Value Questions

1. 200	2. 30	3. 5	4. 160	5. 3.6
6. 62.5	7. 105	8. 60	9. 15	10. 144

Previous Year's Questions

JEE Main

1. (a)	2. (b)	3. (a)	4. (420)	5. (400)
6. (a)	7. (680)	8. (340)	9. (200)	10. (20)

JEE Advanced

1. (648)	2. (8.2)	3. (a,d)	4. (5.00)	5. (6)
6. (b,c,d)	7. (a)			

SOLUTIONS

Level-01

11.1 Stationary Source and Moving Observer

1. $f_{app} = \left(\frac{v + v_O}{v}\right) f = \left(\frac{340 + 30}{340}\right) 500 = 544.1\text{ Hz}$

Motion of observer does not affect the wavelength reaching the observer.

$$\therefore \quad \lambda_{app} = \lambda = \frac{v}{f} = \frac{340}{500} = 0.68\text{ m}$$

2. $f_{app} = \left(\frac{v - v_O}{v}\right) f = \left(\frac{340 - 50}{340}\right) 600 = 511.8\text{ Hz}$

3. $f_a = \left(\frac{v_{sound} + v}{v_{sound}}\right) f \quad \text{...(i)}$

$f_r = \left(\frac{v_{sound} - v}{v_{sound}}\right) f \quad \text{...(ii)}$

Adding eqs. (i) and (ii), we get

$$f = \frac{f_a + f_r}{2}$$

4. When he is approaching A,

$$f_{app} = \left(\frac{v + v_O}{v}\right) f$$

$$\Rightarrow \quad f_A = \left(\frac{332 + 3}{332}\right) 256$$

When he is receding from B,

$$f_{app} = \left(\frac{v - v_O}{v}\right) f$$

$$\Rightarrow \quad f_B = \left(\frac{332 - 3}{332}\right) 256$$

Beat frequency $= f_A - f_B = 4.6\text{ Hz}$

11.2 Moving Source and Stationary Observer

1. In front of the car,

$$f_{app} = \left(\frac{v}{v - v_s}\right) f = \left(\frac{340}{340 - 20}\right) 1250 = 1328.1\text{ Hz}$$

Behind the car,

$$f_{app} = \left(\frac{v}{v + v_s}\right) f = \left(\frac{340}{340 + 20}\right) 1250 = 1180.6\text{ Hz}$$

2. In the forward direction,

$$\lambda_{app} = \left(\frac{v - v_s}{v}\right) \lambda = \left(\frac{320 - 20}{320}\right) 60 = 56.25\text{ cm}$$

In the backward direction,

$$\lambda_{app} = \left(\frac{v + v_s}{v}\right) \lambda = \left(\frac{320 + 20}{320}\right) 60 = 63.75\text{ cm}$$

3. When the source is moving towards the observer,

$$f_{app} = \left(\frac{v}{v - v_s}\right) f$$

$$\Rightarrow \quad 1000 = \left(\frac{350}{350 - 50}\right) f$$

$$\Rightarrow \quad f = \frac{6000}{7}\text{ Hz}$$

When the source is moving away from the observer,

$$f_{app} = \left(\frac{v}{v + v_s}\right) f = \left(\frac{350}{350 + 50}\right)\left(\frac{6000}{7}\right) = 750\text{ Hz}$$

4. When the bullet is approaching the person,

$$f_1 = \left(\frac{v}{v - v_s}\right) f = \left(\frac{330}{330 - 220}\right) f = 3f$$

When the bullet has crossed the person,

$$f_2 = \left(\frac{v}{v + v_s}\right) f = \left(\frac{330}{330 + 220}\right) f = 0.6f$$

Fractional change in frequency $= \frac{f_1 - f_2}{f_1} = 0.8$

5. When the engine approaches the observer,

$$f_{app} = \left(\frac{v}{v - v_s}\right) f$$

$$\Rightarrow \quad f_1 = \left(\frac{v}{330 - v}\right) f$$

When the engine is receding from the observer,

$$f_{app} = \left(\frac{v}{v + v_s}\right) f$$

$$\Rightarrow \quad f_2 = \left(\frac{v}{330 + v}\right) f$$

$$\frac{f_1}{f_2} = \frac{6}{5} \Rightarrow \frac{330 + v}{330 - v} = \frac{6}{5} \Rightarrow v = 30\text{ m/s}$$

6. For the left tuning fork,

$$f_{app} = \left(\frac{v}{v - v_s}\right) f$$

$$\Rightarrow \quad f_1 = \left(\frac{330}{330 - 10}\right) 128 = 132\text{ Hz}$$

For the right tuning fork,

$$f_{app} = \left(\frac{v}{v + v_s}\right) f$$

$$\Rightarrow \quad f_2 = \left(\frac{330}{330 + 10}\right) 128 = 124\text{ Hz}$$

Beat frequency $= f_1 - f_2 = 8\text{ Hz}$

7. (a) The apparent frequency heard by the standing person will be more than 440 Hz due to Doppler's effect. Since, he hears 4 beats per second, the apparent frequency heard by him will be 440 + 4 = 444 Hz.

$$f_{app} = \left(\frac{v}{v - v_s}\right) f$$

$$\Rightarrow \quad 444 = \left(\frac{340}{340 - v_s}\right) 440$$

$$\Rightarrow \quad v_s = 3.06 \text{ m/s or } 11 \text{ km/h}$$

(b) For the person in the train, the source on the ground is stationary and observer approaches.

$$f_{app} = \left(\frac{v + v_O}{v}\right) f = \left(\frac{340 + 3.06}{340}\right) 440 = 443.96 \text{ Hz}$$

Beat frequency = 443.96 − 440 = 3.96 Hz ≈ 4 Hz

11.3 Both Source and Observer in Motion

1. (a) Since, there is no relative motion, frequency will not change.

(b) $v_A = 72$ km/h = 20 m/s,
$v_B = 54$ km/h = 15 m/s

$$f_{app} = \left(\frac{v + v_B}{v - v_A}\right) f = \left(\frac{320 + 15}{320 - 20}\right) 900 = 1005 \text{ Hz}$$

2. $f_{app} = \left(\frac{v + v_B}{v + v_A}\right) f = \left(\frac{330 + 10}{330 + 30}\right) 450 = 425 \text{ Hz}$

3. Before they cross each other,

$$f_{app} = \left(\frac{v + v_B}{v - v_A}\right) f \quad \Rightarrow \quad 4320 = \left(\frac{330 + 30}{330 - 30}\right) f$$

$$\Rightarrow \quad f = 3600 \text{ Hz}$$

After they have crossed each other,

$$f_{app} = \left(\frac{v - v_B}{v + v_A}\right) f = \left(\frac{330 - 30}{330 + 30}\right) 3600 = 3000 \text{ Hz}$$

11.4 Effect of Wind in Doppler Effect

1. $v_O = 36$ km/h = 10 m/s, $v_W = 36$ km/h = 10 m/s

$$f_{app} = \left(\frac{v + v_W + v_O}{v + v_W}\right) f = \left(\frac{340 + 10 - 10}{340 + 10}\right) 700 = 680 \text{ Hz}$$

2. $\lambda = \frac{v + v_W}{f} = \frac{300 + 30}{1200} = 0.275 \text{ m}$

Since, both the source and the observer are stationary, frequency will not change.

3. For the sound from A,

$$f_{app} = \left(\frac{v + v_W - v_O}{v + v_W}\right) f = \left(\frac{345 + 5 - 25}{345 + 5}\right) 500 = 464.3 \text{ Hz}$$

For the sound from B,

$$f'_{app} = \left(\frac{v - v_W + v_O}{v - v_W}\right) f = \left(\frac{345 - 5 + 25}{345 - 5}\right) 500 = 536.8 \text{ Hz}$$

$$\Delta f = 536.8 - 464.3 = 72.5 \text{ Hz}$$

11.5 Doppler Effect in Reflected Sound

1. (a) $f_{app} = \left(\frac{v}{v + v_s}\right) f = \left(\frac{330}{330 + 8}\right) 2000 = 1953 \text{ Hz}$

(b) First the cliff acts as a stationary observer,

$$f_1 = \left(\frac{v}{v - v_s}\right) f = \left(\frac{330}{330 - 8}\right) 2000 = 2050 \text{ Hz}$$

Now, the cliff acts as a stationary source. Since, the observer is also stationary,

$$f_{app} = 2050 \text{ Hz}$$

2. First the wall acts as a stationary observer,

$$f_1 = \left(\frac{v}{v - v_s}\right) f = \left(\frac{350}{350 - 50}\right) 1.2 = 1.4 \text{ kHz}$$

Now, the wall acts as a stationary source of sound,

$$f_2 = \left(\frac{v + v_O}{v}\right) f_1 = \left(\frac{350 + 50}{350}\right) 1.4 = 1.6 \text{ kHz}$$

3. Speed of enemy submarine $= 360 \times \frac{5}{18} = 100$ m/s

First the source is at rest and the observer (enemy submarine) is moving toward it.

$$f_1 = \left(\frac{v + v_O}{v}\right) f = \left(\frac{1450 + 100}{1450}\right) 40 = 42.76 \text{ kHz}$$

For the reflected sound, enemy submarine acts as a moving source of sound,

$$f_2 = \left(\frac{v}{v - v_s}\right) f_1 = \left(\frac{1450}{1450 - 100}\right) 42.76 = 45.93 \text{ kHz}$$

4. First the wall acts as a stationary observer and the source is moving towards it,

$$f_1 = \left(\frac{v + v_W}{v + v_W - v_s}\right) f = \left(\frac{c + 0.1\,c}{c + 0.1c - 0.1\,c}\right) f = 1.1f$$

Now, the wall acts as a stationary source and the observer (driver) is moving towards it,

$$f_2 = \left(\frac{v - v_W + v_O}{v - v_W}\right) f = \left(\frac{c - 0.1\,c + 0.1\,c}{c - 0.1\,c}\right) (1.1f) = \frac{11f}{9}$$

5.

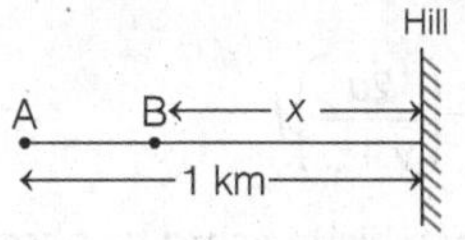

Let the echo from the hill is heard by the driver at point B which is at a distance x from the hill.

Time taken by the driver to reach from A to B,

$$t_1 = \frac{1 - x}{40}$$

Time taken by sound, $t_2 = \frac{1}{1200 + 40} + \frac{x}{1200 - 40}$

$$t_1 = t_2$$

$$\Rightarrow \quad \frac{1 - x}{40} = \frac{1}{1240} + \frac{x}{1160}$$

$$\Rightarrow \quad x = 0.935 \text{ km}$$

The frequency of echo as heard by the driver can be calculated by considering that the source is the acoustic image.

$$f_{app} = \left(\frac{v - v_w + v_s}{v - v_w - v_0}\right) f = \left(\frac{1200 - 40 + 40}{1200 - 40 - 40}\right) 600 = 643 \text{ Hz}$$

6.

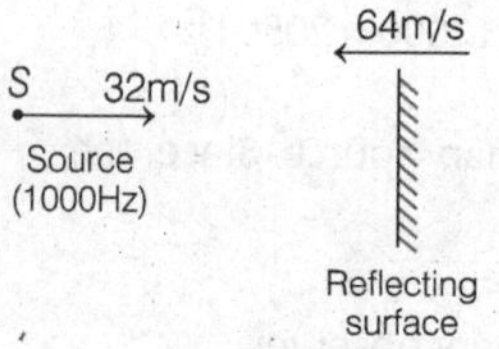

(a) Wavelength in front of source,

$$\lambda = (v - v_s)T = \frac{v - v_s}{f} = \frac{332 - 32}{1000} = 0.3 \text{ m}$$

(b) Here the reflecting surface acts as an observer moving towards the source,

$$f_{app} = \left(\frac{v + v_0}{v - v_s}\right) f = \left(\frac{332 + 64}{332 - 32}\right) 100 = 1320 \text{ Hz}$$

(c) Reflected waves will travel with the speed of sound.

(d) For the reflected waves, the reflecting surface acts as a moving source.

Wavelength in front of source,

$$\lambda = \frac{(v - v_s)}{f_{app}} = \frac{332 - 64}{1320} = 0.2 \text{ m}$$

7. Frequency of sound directly received by R from source S,

$$f_1 = f$$

For the reflected sound,

First the reflecting surface acts as an observer moving away from the stationary source,

$$f_{app} = \left(\frac{v - v_0}{v}\right) f = \left(\frac{v - u}{v}\right) f$$

Now, the reflecting surface acts as a source moving away from the stationary observer,

$$f_2 = \left(\frac{v}{v + v_s}\right) f_{app} = \left(\frac{v}{v + u}\right)\left(\frac{v - u}{v}\right) = \left(\frac{v - u}{v + u}\right) f$$

Beat frequency $= f_1 - f_2$

$$= f - \left(\frac{v - u}{v + u}\right) f = \left(\frac{2u}{v + u}\right) f$$

8. The frequency of direct sound of whistle heard by observer,

$$f_1 = \left(\frac{v}{v - v_s}\right) f = \left(\frac{340}{340 - 1}\right) f = \left(\frac{340}{339}\right) f$$

The frequency of sound of whistle reflected by wall,

$$f_2 = \left(\frac{v}{v + v_s}\right) f = \left(\frac{340}{340 + 1}\right) f = \left(\frac{340}{341}\right) f$$

Given, $\qquad f_1 - f_2 = 4$

$$\Rightarrow \quad \left(\frac{340}{339}\right) f - \left(\frac{340}{341}\right) f = 4$$

$$\Rightarrow \quad f = 680 \text{ Hz}$$

11.6 Source and Observer Moving along Different Lines

1. $v_T = 120 \text{ km/h} = \frac{100}{3} \text{ m/s}$

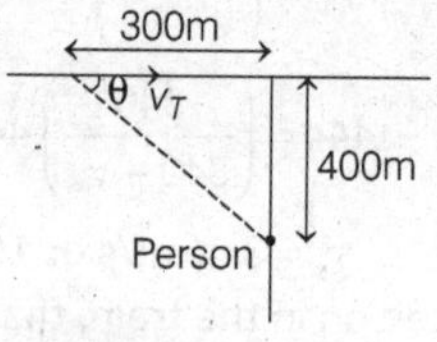

$$\cos\theta = \frac{300}{\sqrt{(300)^2 + (400)^2}} = \frac{3}{5}$$

$$f_{app} = \left(\frac{v}{v - v_s \cos\theta}\right) f$$

$$= \left(\frac{340}{340 - \left(\frac{100}{3} \times \frac{3}{5}\right)}\right) 640 = 680 \text{ Hz}$$

2.

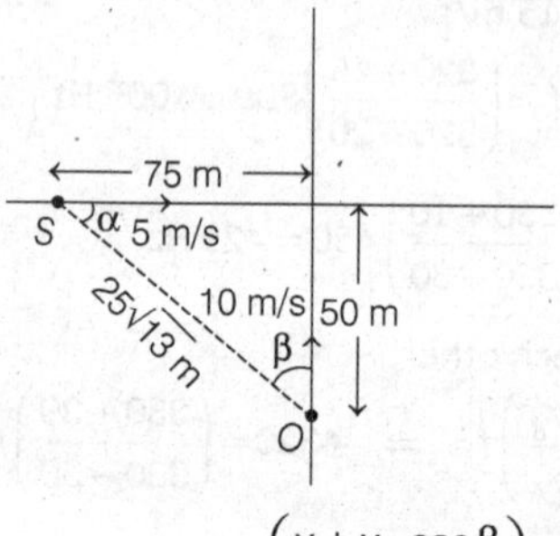

$$f_{app} = \left(\frac{v + v_0 \cos\beta}{v - v_s \cos\alpha}\right) f$$

$$= \left(\frac{330 + 10\left(\frac{50}{25\sqrt{13}}\right)}{330 - 5\left(\frac{75}{25\sqrt{13}}\right)}\right) 1000 = 1030 \text{ Hz}$$

3.

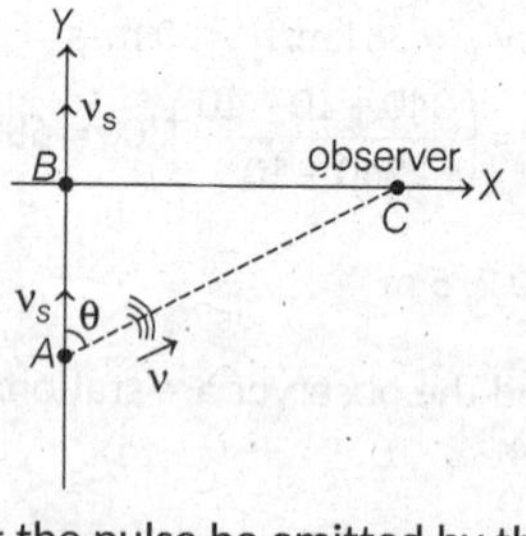

Let the pulse be emitted by the source at point A which is received by the observer when the source crosses the origin. If time taken is t, then

$$AB = v_s t, \; AC = vt$$

$$\therefore \quad \cos\theta = \frac{AB}{AC} = \frac{v_s}{v}$$

$$\Rightarrow \quad \cos\theta = \frac{33}{330} = \frac{1}{10}$$

$$f_{app} = \left(\frac{v}{v - v_s \cos\theta}\right) f$$

$$= \left(\frac{330}{330 - 33(0.1)}\right) 4000 = 4040 \text{ Hz}$$

4. (a)

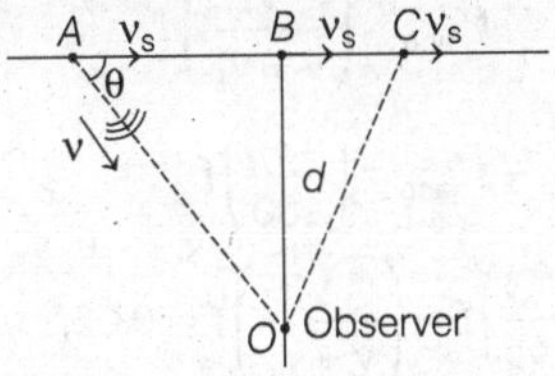

Let the pulse be emitted by the source at point *A* which will be received by the observer when the source reaches point *B*. If time taken is *t*, then

$$AB = v_s t, \; AO = vt$$

$$\cos\theta = \frac{AB}{AO} = \frac{v_s}{v} = \eta$$

$$f_{app} = \left(\frac{v}{v - v_s \cos\theta}\right) f_0$$

$$= \left(\frac{v}{v - \eta v(\eta)}\right) f_0 = \frac{f_0}{1 - \eta^2}$$

Substituting numerical values, we get $f_{app} = 5$ kHz

(b) $f_{app} = \left(\frac{v}{v - v_s \cos\theta}\right) f_0 = f_0 \Rightarrow \theta = 90°$

So, the source will be at point *B*. By the time sound reaches the observer, the source has moved to point *C*.

Time taken by sound to reach the observer $= \frac{d}{v}$

Distance moved by the source in this time $= v_s\left(\frac{d}{v}\right) = \eta d$

$$\therefore \quad OC = \sqrt{d^2 + (\eta d)^2} = d\sqrt{1 + \eta^2}$$

$$= 250\sqrt{1 + (0.8)^2} = 320 \text{ m}$$

5. (a)

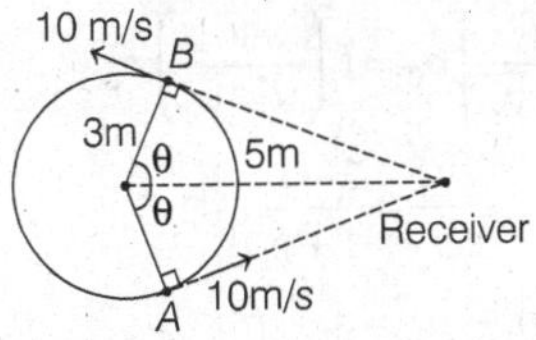

Pulse emitted from position *A* will be received as maximum frequency and pulse emitted from position *B* will be received as minimum frequency.

$$f_{max} = \left(\frac{v}{v - v_s}\right) f = \left(\frac{330}{330 - 10}\right) 272 = 280.5 \text{ Hz}$$

$$f_{min} = \left(\frac{v}{v + v_s}\right) f = \left(\frac{330}{330 + 10}\right) 272 = 264 \text{ Hz}$$

(b) $\cos\theta = \frac{3}{5} \Rightarrow \theta = 53°$

For minimum time taken to go from *B* to *A*,

$$\theta = \omega t$$

$$\Rightarrow \quad 2\pi - (2 \times 53°)\frac{\pi}{180°} = \left(\frac{10}{3}\right) t$$

$$\Rightarrow \quad t = \frac{127\pi}{300} \text{ s}$$

Level-02

Single Choice Correct Questions

1. $f_{app} = \left(\frac{v + v_0}{v}\right) f = \left(\frac{v + (v/5)}{v}\right) f = 1.2f$

Motion of observer does not affect the wavelength reaching the observer.

$$\therefore \quad \lambda_{app} = \lambda$$

2. When the observer is approaching the source,

$$f_1 = \left(\frac{V + v}{V}\right) n$$

When the observer has crossed the source,

$$f_2 = \left(\frac{V - v}{V}\right) n$$

$$\therefore \quad f_1 - f_2 = \frac{2nv}{V}$$

3. $f_{app} = \left(\frac{v + v_0}{v}\right) f$

For train *A*,

$$5.5 = \left(\frac{v + v_A}{v}\right) 5 \Rightarrow v_A = 0.1v$$

For train *B*,

$$6 = \left(\frac{v + v_B}{v}\right) 5 \Rightarrow v_B = 0.2v$$

$$\therefore \quad \frac{v_B}{v_A} = 2$$

4. When the listener is receding from *A*,

$$f_1 = \left(\frac{340 - u}{340}\right) 680$$

When the listener is approaching *B*,

$$f_2 = \left(\frac{340 + u}{340}\right) 680$$

Given, $\quad f_2 - f_1 = 10$

$$\Rightarrow \quad \frac{(2u)(680)}{340} = 10 \Rightarrow u = 2.5 \text{ m/s}$$

5. $f_{app} = \left(\frac{v - v_0}{v}\right) f$

$$\Rightarrow \quad 0.9f = \left(\frac{330 - v_0}{330}\right) f$$

$$\Rightarrow \quad v_0 = 33 \text{ m/s}$$

For motorcycle,

$$v^2 = u^2 + 2as \Rightarrow (33)^2 = 0^2 + 2(2.2)s$$

$$\Rightarrow \quad s = 247.5 \text{ m}$$

6. At $t = 30$ s,

$v = u + at = 0 + 10(30) = 300$ m/s

$$f_{app} = \left(\frac{v + v_O}{v}\right) f$$

$$\Rightarrow \quad 2000 = \left(\frac{v + 300}{v}\right) 1000$$

$$\Rightarrow \quad v = 300 \text{ m/s}$$

7. When the observer is in front of the train,

$$f_{app} = \left(\frac{v}{v - v_s}\right) f = \left(\frac{340}{340 - 25}\right) 200 = 216 \text{ Hz}$$

When the observer is behind the train,

$$f_{app} = \left(\frac{v}{v + v_s}\right) f = \left(\frac{340}{340 + 25}\right) 200 = 186 \text{ Hz}$$

8. $f_{app} = \left(\frac{v}{v - v_s}\right) f$

$$\Rightarrow \quad 605 = \left(\frac{330}{330 - v_s}\right) 550$$

$$\Rightarrow \quad v_s = 30 \text{ m/s}$$

9. $f_{app} = \left(\frac{v}{v + v_s}\right) f$

$$\Rightarrow \quad \frac{6f}{7} = \left(\frac{330}{330 + v_s}\right) f \quad \Rightarrow v_s = 55 \text{ m/s}$$

10. $\lambda_{app} = \frac{v - v_s}{f_s} = \frac{340 - 34}{400} = 0.765$ m

11. $\lambda' = (v + v_s)T = (v + v_s)\left(\frac{\lambda}{v}\right) = \lambda\left(1 + \frac{v_s}{v}\right)$

12. $f_{app} = \left(\frac{v}{v - v_s}\right) f \qquad \Rightarrow f_{app} \propto \frac{1}{v - v_s}$

$$\therefore \quad \frac{f_1}{f_2} = \frac{v - v_2}{v - v_1} = \frac{340 - 17}{340 - 34} = \frac{19}{18}$$

13. When the train is coming directly towards him,

$$f_{app} = \left(\frac{v}{v - v_s}\right) f$$

$$\Rightarrow \quad 250 = \left(\frac{360}{360 - v_s}\right) f \qquad \text{...(i)}$$

When the train is going directly away from him,

$$f_{app} = \left(\frac{v}{v + v_s}\right) f$$

$$\Rightarrow \quad 200 = \left(\frac{360}{360 + v_s}\right) f \qquad \text{...(ii)}$$

Dividing Eqs. (i) by (ii), we get

$$\frac{360 + v_s}{360 - v_s} = \frac{250}{200}$$

$$\Rightarrow \quad v_s = 40 \text{ m/s}$$

14. When the source is approaching the observer,

$$f_{app} = \left(\frac{v}{v - v_s}\right) f$$

When the source is receding from the observer,

$$f'_{app} = \left(\frac{v}{v + v_s}\right) f$$

Given, $\quad f_{app} - f'_{app} = \left(\frac{2}{100}\right) f$

$$\Rightarrow \quad \left(\frac{v}{v - v_s}\right) f - \left(\frac{v}{v + v_s}\right) f = 0.02f$$

$$\Rightarrow \quad \frac{2vv_s}{v^2 - v_s^2} = 0.02$$

$$\Rightarrow \quad \frac{2vv_s}{v^2} = 0.02 \qquad [\because v_s << v]$$

$$\Rightarrow \quad v_s = 0.01v = 3.4 \text{ m/s}$$

15. $n' = \left(\frac{v}{v - v_s}\right) n$

$$\Rightarrow \quad \frac{n}{n'} = \frac{v - v_s}{v} \qquad \text{...(i)}$$

$$n'' = \left(\frac{v}{v + v_s}\right) n$$

$$\Rightarrow \quad \frac{n}{n''} = \frac{v + v_s}{v} \qquad \text{...(ii)}$$

Adding Eqs. (i) and (ii), we get

$$\frac{n}{n'} + \frac{n}{n''} = 2$$

$$\Rightarrow \quad n = \frac{2n'n''}{n' + n''}$$

16. $n_1 = \left(\frac{v}{v - v_s}\right) n_O, \quad n_2 = \left(\frac{v}{v + v_s}\right) n_O$

$n_2 = fn_1$

$$\Rightarrow \quad \left(\frac{v}{v + v_s}\right) n_O = f\left(\frac{v}{v - v_s}\right) n_O$$

$$\Rightarrow \quad \frac{v_s}{v} = \frac{1 - f}{1 + f}$$

$$\therefore \quad n_1 - n_2 = n_1 - fn_1$$

$$= (1 - f)\, n_1 = (1 - f)\left(\frac{n_O}{1 - \frac{1 - f}{1 + f}}\right)$$

$$= \frac{n_O(1 - f^2)}{2f}$$

17. $f_1 = \left(\frac{320}{320 - 4}\right) 240 = 243$ Hz

$$f_2 = \left(\frac{320}{320 + 4}\right) 240 = 237 \text{ Hz}$$

Beat frequency $= f_1 - f_2 = 6$ Hz

18. $f_2 - f_1 = 6$

$$\Rightarrow \quad \left(\frac{300}{300+v_2}\right)900 - \left(\frac{300}{300+v_1}\right)900 = 6$$

$$\Rightarrow \quad \frac{(v_1 - v_2)(300 \times 900)}{(300)^2} = 6$$

$$[\because v_1 \text{ and } v_2 << 300]$$

$$\Rightarrow \quad v_1 - v_2 = 2 \text{ m/s}$$

19. The first pulse emitted (at $t = 0$) by the source at A reaches the observer at O in time $t_1 = \frac{d}{v}$.

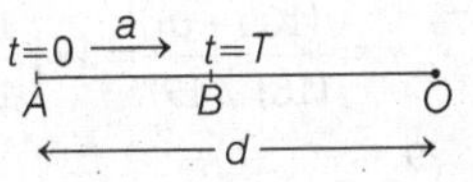

Let the second pulse be emitted by the source at time $t = T$. In this time, the source moves a distance

$$s = ut + \frac{1}{2}at^2 = 0 + \frac{1}{2}aT^2 = \frac{1}{2}aT^2$$

Time taken by the second pulse to reach the observer,

$$t_2 = \frac{d - \frac{1}{2}aT^2}{v}$$

Time between two consecutive pulses heard by the observer,

$$T' = (t_2 + T) - t_1 = T - \frac{aT^2}{2v} = \frac{1}{f} - \frac{a}{2vf^2}$$

$$\therefore \quad f' = \frac{1}{T'} = \frac{2vf^2}{2vf - a}$$

20. When the train moves away from the stationary observer,

$$f_{app} = \left(\frac{v}{v + v_s}\right)f$$

$$\Rightarrow \quad \frac{f}{f_{app}} = 1 + \frac{v_s}{v} = 1.2$$

$$\Rightarrow \quad \frac{v_s}{v} = 0.2$$

When the observer moves away from the stationary train,

$$f_{app} = \left(\frac{v - v_o}{v}\right)f$$

$$\Rightarrow \quad \frac{f}{f_{app}} = \frac{1}{1 - \frac{v_o}{v}} = \frac{1}{1 - 0.2} = 1.25$$

21. $f_{app} = \left(\frac{v - v_o}{v + v_s}\right)f$

$$\Rightarrow \quad 1980 = \left(\frac{340 - 10}{340 + 10}\right)f$$

$$\Rightarrow \quad f = 2100 \text{ Hz}$$

22. $t_1 = \frac{a}{v_{rel}} = \frac{a}{v_s - v_2}$

23. Motion of observer does not affect the wavelength reaching the observer.

In front of source, $\lambda_A = (v - v_s)T$

$$= \left(10u - \frac{u}{2}\right)T = \frac{19uT}{2}$$

Behind the source, $\lambda_B = (v + v_s)T$

$$= \left(10u + \frac{u}{2}\right)T = \frac{21uT}{2}$$

$$\therefore \quad \frac{\lambda_A}{\lambda_B} = \frac{19}{21}$$

24. $T_{app} = \left(\frac{v - v_s}{v + v_o}\right)T = \left(\frac{330 - 30}{330 + 60}\right)10 = 7.7 \text{ s}$

25. Frequency of sound heard by the motorcyclist from the stationary horn,

$$f_1 = \left(\frac{v + v_o}{v}\right)f = \left(\frac{330 + u}{330}\right)165$$

Frequency of sound heard by the motorcyclist from the car horn,

$$f_2 = \left(\frac{v - v_o}{v - v_s}\right)f = \left(\frac{330 - u}{330 - 22}\right)176$$

For no beats observed, $f_1 = f_2$

$$\Rightarrow \quad \left(\frac{330 + u}{330}\right)165 = \left(\frac{330 - u}{308}\right)176$$

$$\Rightarrow \quad u = 22 \text{ m/s}$$

26. Velocity of body at $t = 1$ s,

$$v = u + at = 0 + 10(1) = 10 \text{ m/s}$$

Just before crossing,

$$f_{app} = \left(\frac{v + v_o}{v - v_s}\right)f$$

$$\Rightarrow \quad f_1 = \left(\frac{300 + 2}{300 - 10}\right)150 = 156 \text{ Hz}$$

Just after crossing,

$$f_{app} = \left(\frac{v - v_o}{v + v_s}\right)f$$

$$\Rightarrow \quad f_2 = \left(\frac{300 - 2}{300 + 10}\right)150 = 144 \text{ Hz}$$

$$\Delta f = f_1 - f_2 = 12 \text{ Hz}$$

27. Sound wave received at $t = 5$ s must be emitted earlier. Let t_1 is the time at which the source emits a sound wave which is detected at $t = 5$ s. Then, the time for which sound moves is $t - t_1$.

Distance travelled by the sound wave $= v(t - t_1)$

Let the distance moved by the detector be h, then

$$h = ut - \frac{1}{2}gt^2$$

Distance moved by the source in t_1 time,

$$h_1 = \frac{1}{2}gt_1^2$$

$\therefore \quad H - \frac{1}{2}gt_1^2 - h = v(t - t_1)$

Substituting numerical values,

$$t = 5\text{ s}, g = 10\text{ m/s}^2 \text{ and } v = 300\text{ m/s}$$

$$505 - 5t_1^2 - 125 = 300(5 - t_1)$$

$$\Rightarrow \quad t_1^2 - 60t_1 + 224 = 0$$

$$\Rightarrow \quad t_1 = 4\text{ s}$$

At $t = 4$ s, $v_s = gt_1 = 40$ m/s

At $t = 5$ s, $v_0 = 50 - 10(5) = 0$

$$f_{app} = \left(\frac{v + v_0}{v - v_s}\right) f = \left(\frac{300 + 0}{300 - 40}\right) 1300 = 1500\text{ Hz}$$

28. Since, there is no relative motion between the source and the observer, frequency will remain the same.

29. $\lambda = \frac{V + U_W}{f} = \left(\frac{V + U_W}{V}\right)\lambda_0$

30. $f_{app} = \left(\frac{v - v_W + v_0}{v - v_W + v_s}\right) f = \left(\frac{v - c + b}{v - c + a}\right) f$

31. Frequency received by wall,

$$f_1 = \left(\frac{v}{v - v_c}\right) f$$

Frequency received by wall will be reflected back and now wall will behave as a fixed source and the car will behave as an observer approaching the source.

$$f_{app} = \left(\frac{v + v_c}{v}\right) f_1 = \left(\frac{v + v_c}{v - v_c}\right) f$$

$$\therefore \quad f_{app} = \left(\frac{320 + 10}{320 - 10}\right) 8 = 8.5\text{ kHz}$$

32. One octave higher means frequency gets doubled.

$$f_{app} = \left(\frac{v + v_c}{v - v_c}\right) f = 2f$$

$$\Rightarrow \quad v_c = \frac{v}{3}$$

33. First the wall acts as an observer moving away from the stationary source.

$$f_1 = \left(\frac{v - v_0}{v}\right) f = \left(\frac{c - v}{c}\right) f$$

Now, the wall acts as a source moving away from the stationary observer.

$$f_{app} = \left(\frac{v}{v + v_s}\right) f_1 = \left(\frac{c}{c + v}\right)\left(\frac{c - v}{c}\right) f$$

$$\Rightarrow \quad f_{app} = \left(\frac{c - v}{c + v}\right) f$$

34. For incident sound,

wavelength in front of source,

$$\lambda_i = (v - v_s)T = \left(10u - \frac{u}{2}\right)\frac{1}{f} = \frac{19u}{2f}$$

For reflected wave,

$$f_{app} = \left(\frac{v - v_0}{v - v_s}\right) f$$

$$= \left(\frac{10u - u}{10u - \frac{u}{2}}\right) f = \frac{18f}{19}$$

Now, the wall will act as a source moving towards right. Wavelength behind the source,

$$\lambda_r = (v + v_s)T_{app}$$

$$= \frac{(10u + u)}{(18f/19)} = 19\left(\frac{11u}{18f}\right)$$

$$\therefore \quad \frac{\lambda_i}{\lambda_r} = \frac{9}{11}$$

35. $f_{app} = \left(\frac{v + v_T}{v - v_T}\right) f = \left(\frac{332 + 12}{332 - 12}\right) f = \left(\frac{43}{40}\right) f$

$$f_{beat} = f_{app} - f = 6$$

$$\Rightarrow \quad \left(\frac{43}{40}\right) f - f = 6$$

$$\Rightarrow \quad f = 80\text{ Hz}$$

36. $f_{app} = \left(\frac{v + v_b}{v - v_b}\right) f$

$$f_{beat} = f_{app} - f = 5$$

$$\Rightarrow \quad \left(\frac{v + v_b}{v - v_b}\right) f - f = 5$$

$$\Rightarrow \quad \left(\frac{2v_b}{v - v_b}\right) f = 5$$

$$\Rightarrow \quad v_b = \frac{5v}{2f} \qquad [\because v_b << v]$$

$$\Rightarrow \quad v_b = \frac{5 \times 340}{2(4.5 \times 10^4)} = 18.9 \times 10^{-3}\text{ m/s}$$

$$\simeq 20\text{ mm/s}$$

37.

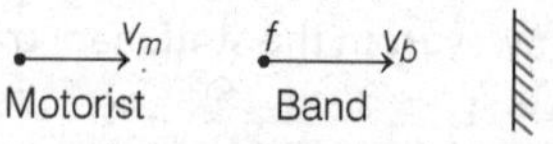

Frequency heard by motorist directly from the band,

$$f_1 = \left(\frac{v + v_0}{v + v_s}\right) f = \left(\frac{v + v_m}{v + v_b}\right) f$$

Frequency received by the wall,

$$f' = \left(\frac{v}{v - v_s}\right) f = \left(\frac{v}{v - v_b}\right) f$$

For the reflected sound, the wall acts as a stationary source and the observer (motorist) is moving towards it.

$$f_2 = \left(\frac{v + v_m}{v}\right) f' = \left(\frac{v + v_m}{v - v_b}\right) f$$

$$f_{beat} = f_2 - f_1 = \frac{2v_b(v + v_m)f}{v^2 - v_b^2}$$

38. Frequency of sound reflected by a car,

$$f = \left(\frac{v + v_c}{v - v_c}\right) f_0$$

As $v_c << v$

$$\Rightarrow \quad f = \left(\frac{1 + \frac{v_c}{v}}{1 - \frac{v_c}{v}}\right) f_0 = \left(1 + \frac{2v_c}{v}\right) f_0$$

$$\Rightarrow \quad \Delta f = \left(\frac{2f_0}{v}\right) \Delta v_c$$

$$\Rightarrow \quad \frac{1.2f_0}{100} = \frac{2f_0}{330} \Delta v_c$$

$$\Rightarrow \quad \Delta v_c = 1.98 \text{ m/s or } 7.128 \text{ km/h}$$

39. Beat frequency will be zero, since frequency of directed sound and reflected sound heard by the stationary observer will be same.

40. $$\cos\theta = \frac{800}{\sqrt{(600)^2 + (800)^2}} = 0.8$$

$$v_s = 72 \text{ km/h} = 20 \text{ m/s}$$

$$f_{app} = \left(\frac{v}{v - v_s \cos\theta}\right) f$$

$$= \left(\frac{330}{330 - 20(0.8)}\right) 600 = 630.5 \text{ Hz}$$

41. $v_1 = 72$ km/h = 20 m/s,
$v_2 = 36$ km/h = 10 m/s

$$f_{app} = \left(\frac{v + v_1 \cos\alpha}{v - v_2 \cos\beta}\right) f$$

$$= \left(\frac{330 + 20 \cos 45°}{330 - 10 \cos 45°}\right) 280 = 298 \text{ Hz}$$

42. $$f_{app} = \left(\frac{v + v_w}{v + v_w - v_s \sin 30°}\right) f$$

$$= \left(\frac{330 + 20}{330 + 20 - 20 \sin 30°}\right) 510 = 525 \text{ Hz}$$

43. Time taken by the source to reach the origin $= \frac{100}{5} = 20$ s

Distance moved by the detector in this time $= 10 \times 20 = 200$ m

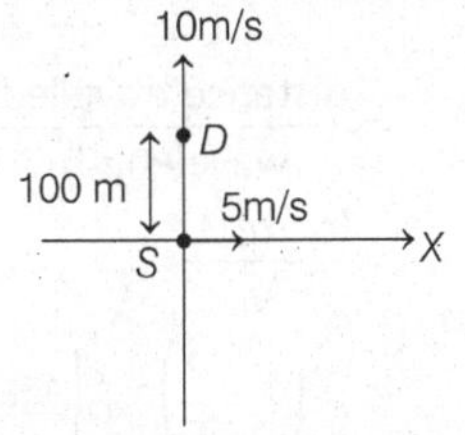

$$f_{app} = \left(\frac{v - v_0 \cos\alpha}{v - v_s \cos\beta}\right) f$$

$$= \left(\frac{330 - 10 \cos 0°}{330 - 5 \cos 90°}\right) 100 = 97 \text{ Hz}$$

44.

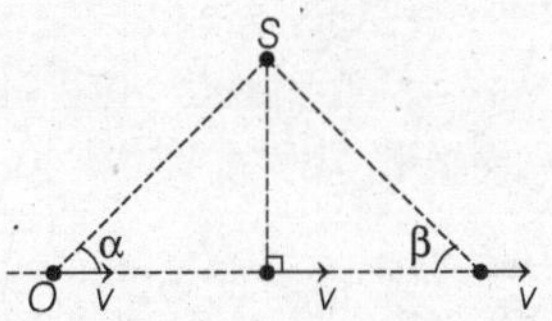

From figure, velocity of approach ($v \cos\alpha$) decreases as the observer comes closer (as α increases). And the velocity of separation also increases as β decreases. Hence, frequency detected by the observer will go on decreasing.

45. $$\tan\alpha = \frac{OA}{SA} = \frac{v_0 t}{v_s t} = \frac{1}{2}$$

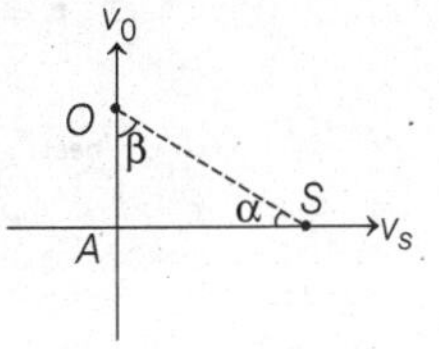

$$\therefore \quad \cos\alpha = \frac{2}{\sqrt{5}}, \cos\beta = \frac{1}{\sqrt{5}}$$

$$f_{app} = \left(\frac{v - v_0 \cos\beta}{v + v_s \cos\alpha}\right) f_0$$

$$= \left(\frac{v - v_0\left(\frac{1}{\sqrt{5}}\right)}{v + 2v_0\left(\frac{2}{\sqrt{5}}\right)}\right) f_0$$

$\therefore$ f_{app} will be less than f_0 and constant with time.

46. When train *A* whistles, sound pulse starts to travel in air from train *A* to train *B*. During this interval, train *B* moves some distance towards the station. Let sound pulse takes time *t* to travel from train *A* to train *B*. Distance moved by train *B* during this interval is 40*t*. Therefore, the distance of train *B* from station when its driver hears the pulse is 152 – 40*t*. Hence, the distance travelled by the pulse is

$$\sqrt{(152 - 40t)^2 + (99)^2}$$

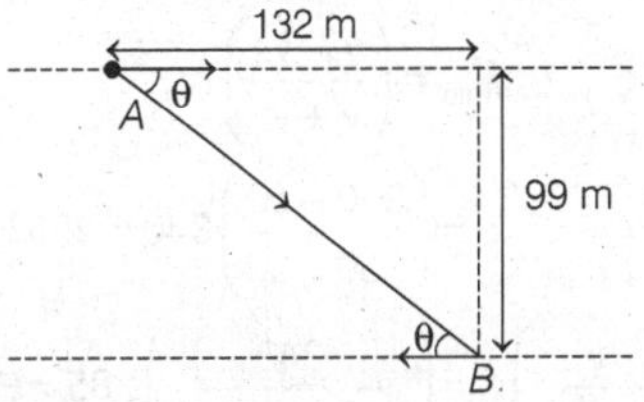

But it is equal to $vt = 330t$

$$\therefore \quad \sqrt{(152 - 40t)^2 + (99)^2} = 330t$$

$$\Rightarrow \quad t = 0.5 \text{ s}$$

Therefore, driver of train *B* hears the pulse when his train is $152 - 40t = 132$ m from the station.

$$\tan\theta = \frac{99}{132} \quad \Rightarrow \theta = 37°$$

Velocity component of train *A* along the path of the pulse,

$$v_s = 40 \cos 37° = 32 \text{ m/s}$$

Velocity component of train *B* along the path of the pulse,

$$v_0 = 40 \cos 37° = 32 \text{ m/s}$$

$$f_{app} = \left(\frac{v + v_0}{v - v_s}\right) f_0$$

$$= \left(\frac{330 + 32}{330 - 32}\right) 596 = 724 \text{ Hz}$$

47.

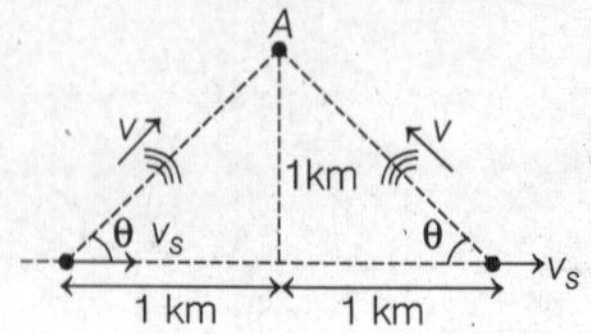

$$\tan\theta = \frac{1}{1} \Rightarrow \theta = 45°$$

$$v_s = 90 \text{ km/h} = 25 \text{ m/s}$$

$$f_1 = \left(\frac{v}{v - v_s \cos\theta}\right) f, \; f_2 = \left(\frac{v}{v + v_s \cos\theta}\right) f$$

$$f_{\text{beat}} = f_1 - f_2$$

$$= \frac{2fvv_s \cos\theta}{v^2 - (v_s \cos\theta)^2} \simeq 5 \text{ Hz}$$

48. Time period of source $= \frac{2\pi}{\omega} = \frac{\pi}{5}$ s

The time periods for the circular motion and SHM are the same. Thus, when the source is at *N*, the detector is at *C* (they are moving away from each other) and the apparent frequency is minimum.

When the source is at *M*, the detector is at *C* (they are moving towards each other) and the apparent frequency is maximum.

The velocity of detector at $C = A\omega$

$$= 6 \times 2\pi\left(\frac{5}{\pi}\right) = 60 \text{ m/s}$$

Velocity of source $= \omega R = 10 \times 3 = 30$ m/s

$$f_{\max} = \left(\frac{v + v_0}{v - v_s}\right) f = \left(\frac{330 + 60}{330 - 30}\right) 340 = 442 \text{ Hz}$$

$$f_{\min} = \left(\frac{v - v_0}{v + v_s}\right) f$$

$$= \left(\frac{330 - 60}{330 + 30}\right) 340 = 255 \text{ Hz}$$

49. $f_{\min} = \left(\frac{v}{v + v_s}\right) f = \left(\frac{340}{340 + 20(0.5)}\right) 385 = 374$ Hz

50.

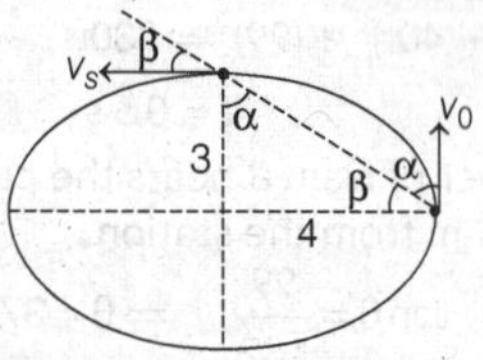

$$f_{\text{app}} = \left(\frac{v + v_0 \cos\alpha}{v + v_s \cos\beta}\right) f$$

$$= \left(\frac{330 + 110\left(\frac{3}{5}\right)}{330 + 110\left(\frac{4}{5}\right)}\right) 1900$$

$$= 1800 \text{ Hz}$$

51. $\cos\theta = \frac{R}{2R} = \frac{1}{2}$

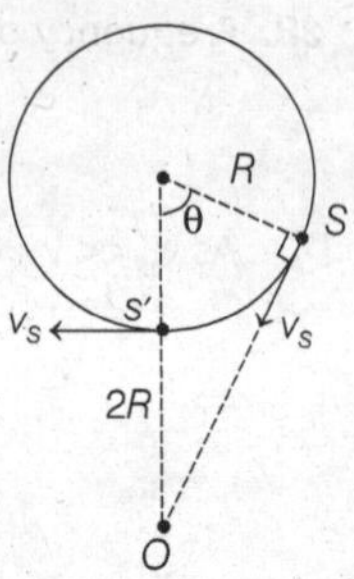

$$\Rightarrow \quad \theta = \frac{\pi}{3}$$

The pulse of maximum frequency will be emitted as *S*, where v_s is directed towards *O*. The observer receives maximum frequency when the plane is nearest to him i.e. at *S'*.

So, by the time the pulse reaches from *S* to *O* with speed *v*, the plane reaches from *S* to *S'* with speed v_s.

$$t = \frac{SO}{v} = \frac{SS'}{v_s}$$

$$\Rightarrow \quad \frac{\sqrt{3}R}{v} = \frac{\left(\frac{\pi}{3}\right)R}{v_s}$$

$$\Rightarrow \quad v_s = \left(\frac{\pi}{3\sqrt{3}}\right) v = 200 \text{ m/s}$$

Multiple Choice(s) Correct Questions

1. Frequency (No. of pulses per second) is the property of the source. So, the frequency and time period are not affected by the wind. However, particles of the medium will move faster due to wind. Hence, velocity of sound will increase. Frequency remaining same, wavelength changes proportional to the sound velocity.

2. $f_{\min} = \left(\frac{v}{v + v_s}\right) f_0$

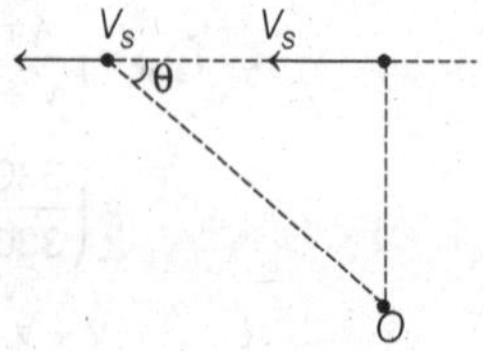

$$\Rightarrow \quad 1800 = \left(\frac{300}{300 + v_s}\right) 2000$$

$$\Rightarrow \quad v_s = \frac{100}{3} \text{ m/s}$$

$$f_{\max} = \left(\frac{v}{v - v_s}\right) f_0$$

$$= \left(\frac{300}{300 - \frac{100}{3}}\right) 2000 = 2250 \text{ Hz}$$

3. Number of waves encountered by the moving plane per unit time

$$= \frac{\text{distance travelled}}{\text{wavelength}}$$

$$= \frac{(c + u)(1)}{\lambda}$$

$$= \frac{c}{\lambda}\left(1 + \frac{u}{c}\right) = f\left(1 + \frac{u}{c}\right)$$

First the vertical plane acts on observer moving towards the stationary source.

$$f_1 = \left(\frac{v + v_0}{v}\right) f = \left(\frac{c + u}{c}\right) f$$

Now, for the reflected sound frequency, the vertical plane acts a source moving towards the stationary observer.

$$f_2 = \left(\frac{v}{v - v_s}\right) f_1 = \left(\frac{c}{c-u}\right)\left(\frac{c+u}{c}\right) f = \left(\frac{c+u}{c-u}\right) f$$

Wavelength of reflected wave $= \dfrac{c}{f_2} = \dfrac{c}{f}\left(\dfrac{c-u}{c+u}\right)$

$$f_{beat} = f_2 - f = \left(\frac{c+u}{c-u}\right) f - f = \frac{2uf}{c-u}$$

4. For observer O_1,

$$\lambda_a = \frac{V - V_s}{f} = \frac{V - (V/5)}{f} = \frac{4V}{5f}$$

When sound enters water, frequency will remain unchanged.

$$\therefore \quad \frac{V}{\lambda_a} = \frac{4V}{\lambda_w}$$

$$\Rightarrow \quad \lambda_w = 4\lambda_a = \frac{16V}{5f}$$

Frequency received by O_2,

$$f_2 = \frac{\text{velocity of wave w.r.t. observer}}{\lambda_w}$$

$$= \frac{4V + \frac{V}{5}}{(16V/5f)} = \frac{21f}{16}$$

5.

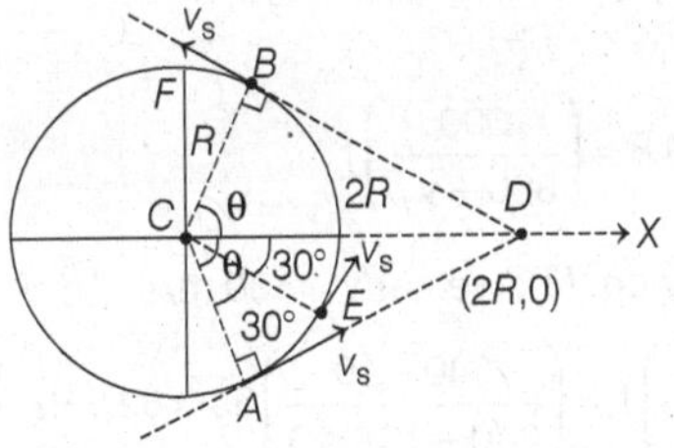

$$\cos\theta = \frac{R}{2R} = \frac{1}{2} \quad \Rightarrow \theta = \frac{\pi}{3}$$

Pulse corresponding to maximum frequency will be emitted at point A.

Time taken by the pulse to reach detector $= \dfrac{AD}{v} = \dfrac{\sqrt{3}R}{v}$

Distance travelled by the source within this time

$$= \frac{330\pi}{6\sqrt{3}}\left(\frac{\sqrt{3}R}{330}\right) = \frac{\pi R}{6}$$

Angle rotated $= \dfrac{\pi R/6}{R} = \dfrac{\pi}{6}$

So, the source will reach point E.

Co-ordinates of $E = (R\cos 30°, -R\sin 30°)$

$$= \left(\frac{\sqrt{3}R}{2}, -\frac{R}{2}\right)$$

For minimum frequency, co-ordinates of $F = (0, R)$

$$f_{max} = \left(\frac{v}{v - v_s}\right) f$$

$$= \left(\frac{330}{330 - \frac{330\pi}{6\sqrt{3}}}\right) f = \frac{6\sqrt{3}f}{6\sqrt{3} - \pi}$$

$$f_{min} = \left(\frac{v}{v + v_s}\right) f = \frac{6\sqrt{3}f}{6\sqrt{3} + \pi}$$

Comprehension Based Questions

1. $f_A = \dfrac{vf}{v - v_s}, \quad f_B = \dfrac{vf}{v + v_s}, \quad f_C = f$

$\therefore \quad f_A > f_C > f_B \quad \Rightarrow \lambda_B > \lambda_C > \lambda_A$

Since A has the least wavelength, A corresponds to plot 1.

2. Since B has the largest wavelength, B corresponds to plot 2.
3. C corresponds to plot 3.
4. Frequency will not be constant. So, none of the given plots.
5. $t_1 = \dfrac{S}{v_{rel}} = \dfrac{L}{V - V_0}$
6. Separation between the source and the observer at $t = T$,

$$d = L + (V_0 - V_s)T$$

$$t_2 = T + \frac{d}{v_{rel}} = T + \frac{L + (V_0 - V_s)T}{V - V_0} = \frac{L + (V - V_s)T}{V - V_0}$$

7. $t = t_2 - t_1 = \dfrac{(V - V_s)T}{V - V_0}$
8. $f' = \left(\dfrac{v + v_1}{v - v_1}\right) f_0 = 1.1 f_0$

$$\Rightarrow \frac{1050 + v_1}{1050 - v_1} = 1.1$$

$$\Rightarrow v_1 = 50 \text{ m/s}$$

9.

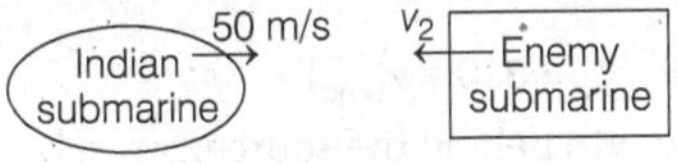

$$f_1 = \left(\frac{v + v_2}{v - 50}\right) f_0$$

$$f_2 = \left(\frac{v + 50}{v - v_2}\right) f_1 = \left(\frac{v + 50}{v - 50}\right)\left(\frac{v + v_2}{v - v_2}\right) f_0$$

$$= \frac{11}{10}\left(\frac{1050 + v_2}{1050 - v_2}\right) f_0$$

Given, $f_2 = 1.21 f_0$

$$\Rightarrow \quad \frac{11}{10}\left(\frac{1050 + v_2}{1050 - v_2}\right) f_0 = 1.21 f_0$$

$\Rightarrow v_2 = 50$ m/s, towards Indian Submarine

10. $\lambda_1 = \dfrac{\text{velocity of wave w.r.t. observer}}{f_1}$

$$= \frac{v+v_2}{\left(\dfrac{v+v_2}{v-50}\right)f_0} = \frac{v-50}{f_0}$$

$$\lambda_2 = \frac{v+50}{f_2} = \frac{(v-v_2)(v-50)}{(v+v_2)f_0}$$

$\therefore$ $$\frac{\lambda_1}{\lambda_2} = \frac{v+v_2}{v-v_2} = \frac{1050+50}{1050-50} = 1.1$$

11. $B = \rho v^2 = 1000 \times (1050)^2 \simeq 10^9 \ \text{N/m}^2$

12.

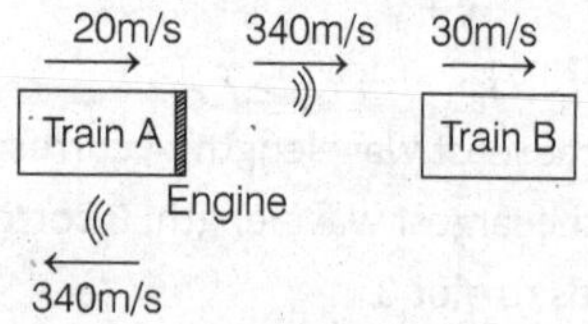

For passenger in *A*,

$$v_{sound} = 340 + 20 = 360 \text{ m/s}$$

For passenger in *B*,

$$v_{sound} = 340 - 30 = 310 \text{ m/s}$$

13. Since, there is no relative motion between the source and the observer, the frequency spread will remain the same.

14. $f_B = \left(\dfrac{v-v_O}{v-v_s}\right) f_A = \left(\dfrac{340-30}{340-20}\right) f_A = \dfrac{31}{32} f_A$

$\therefore$ $$\Delta f_B = \frac{31}{32}\Delta f_A = \frac{31}{32} \times 320 = 310 \text{ Hz}$$

Match the Columns Questions

1. $f = \dfrac{v}{\lambda} = \dfrac{330}{2} = 165 \text{ Hz}$

$$f_{recorder} = \left(\frac{v_{sound} \pm v_R}{v_{sound} \pm v_S}\right) 165$$

$$\lambda_{recorder} = \frac{v_{sound} \pm v_S}{f}$$

$$v_{sound} = 330 + v_{wind}$$

2. (A) Wavelength behind the source,

$$\lambda = (C + V_s)T = \frac{C+V_s}{f}$$

(B) Wavelength in front of the source,

$$\lambda = (C - V_s)T = \frac{C-V_s}{T}$$

(C) $f_1 = \left(\dfrac{C-V_W}{C-V_s}\right) f$

$$f_2 = \left(\frac{C+V_s}{C+V_W}\right) f_1 = \left(\frac{C-V_W}{C+V_W}\right)\left(\frac{C+V_s}{C-V_s}\right) f$$

$$\lambda = \frac{C+V_s}{f_2} = \left(\frac{C+V_W}{C-V_W}\right)\frac{(C-V_s)}{f}$$

(D) $f_1 = \left(\dfrac{C-V_W}{C-V_s}\right) f$

$$f_2 = \left(\frac{C}{C+V_W}\right) f_1 = \left(\frac{C-V_W}{C+V_W}\right)\left(\frac{C}{C-V_s}\right) f$$

$$\lambda = \frac{C}{f_2} = \left(\frac{C+V_W}{C-V_W}\right)\frac{(C-V_s)}{f}$$

Numerical Value Questions

1. $x = 10t(t+6) = 10t^2 + 60t$

$\Rightarrow$ $$v = 20t + 60$$

$$10t^2 + 60t = 212.5 \quad \Rightarrow t = 2.5 \text{ s}$$

But the pulse which is received by the listener at $t = 2.5$ s must have been emitted at a earlier time lets say t_1.

Distance travelled by sound $= 320(2.5 - t_1)$

$\therefore$ $$10t_1^2 + 60t_1 = 320(2.5 - t_1)$$

$\Rightarrow$ $$t_1^2 + 38t_1 - 80 = 0$$

$\Rightarrow$ $$t_1 = 2 \text{ s}$$

At $t = 2$ s, $v_s = 20(2) + 60 = 100$ m/s

$$f_{app} = \left(\frac{v}{v+v_s}\right) f = \left(\frac{320}{320+100}\right)\left(\frac{525}{2}\right) = 200 \text{ Hz}$$

2. $2.2 = \left(\dfrac{300}{300 - v_T}\right) f$ ...(i)

$$1.8 = \left(\frac{300}{300+v_T}\right) f \quad \text{...(ii)}$$

Dividing eq. (i) by eq. (ii), we get $v_T = 30$ m/s

3. $f_A = \left(\dfrac{v - v_w}{v - v_w + v_s}\right) f = \left(\dfrac{340-10}{340-10+10}\right) 85 = 82.5 \text{ Hz}$

$$f_B = \left(\frac{v+v_w}{v+v_w-v_s}\right) f = \left(\frac{340+10}{340+10-10}\right) 85 = 87.5 \text{ Hz}$$

$$f_{beat} = f_B - f_A = 5 \text{ Hz}$$

4. $|f_P - f_Q| = \dfrac{7}{2}$

Frequency of echo,

$$f_Q + 5 = \left(\frac{332+5}{332-5}\right) f_Q$$

$\Rightarrow$ $$f_Q = 163.5 \text{ Hz}$$

On loading wax on P, f_P will decrease. As beat frequency increases, $f_Q > f_P$

$\Rightarrow$ $$f_Q - f_P = 3.5$$

$\Rightarrow$ $$f_P = 160 \text{ Hz}$$

5. Let the initial distance between the car and cliff be *x*.

Velocity of car $= 324$ km/h $= 90$ m/s

Distance travelled by car in 30 s

$$= 90 \times 30 = 2700 \text{ m}$$

Time taken by sound,

$$\frac{x}{350+50}+\frac{x+2700}{350-50}=30$$

$\Rightarrow$ $x = 3600\,\text{m} = 3.6\text{ km}$

6.

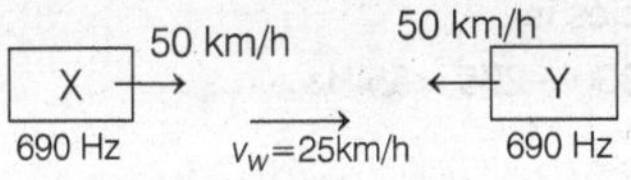

For direct sound,

$$f_1=\left(\frac{1225-25+50}{1225-25-50}\right)690=750\text{ Hz}$$

For reflected sound,

$$f'=\left(\frac{1225+25+50}{1225+25-50}\right)690=747.5\text{ Hz}$$

$$f_2=\left(\frac{1225-25+50}{1225-25-50}\right)747.5=812.5\text{ Hz}$$

$\therefore$ $\Delta f = f_2 - f_1 = 62.5\text{ Hz}$

7. $\mathbf{r}_{SO}=(5\hat{\mathbf{i}}+5\hat{\mathbf{j}})-(2\hat{\mathbf{i}}+\hat{\mathbf{j}})=3\hat{\mathbf{i}}+4\hat{\mathbf{j}}$

Component of velocity of source along line *SO*,

$$v_s=\frac{15(2\hat{\mathbf{i}}+\hat{\mathbf{j}})\cdot(3\hat{\mathbf{i}}+4\hat{\mathbf{j}})}{5}=30\text{ m/s}$$

Component of velocity of observer along line *SO*,

$$v_0=\frac{5(\hat{\mathbf{i}}+3\hat{\mathbf{j}})\cdot(3\hat{\mathbf{i}}+4\hat{\mathbf{j}})}{5}=15\text{ m/s}$$

$$f_{app}=\left(\frac{v-v_0}{v-v_s}\right)f=\left(\frac{330-15}{330-30}\right)100=105\text{ Hz}$$

8. Let the truck velocity be v_s.

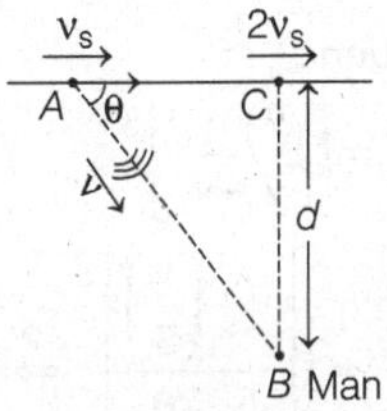

$$600=\left(\frac{v}{v-v_s\cos\theta}\right)500 \qquad \text{...(i)}$$

$v = u + at \quad \Rightarrow 2v_s = v_s + at$

$\Rightarrow$ $v_s = at$ ...(ii)

Distance travelled by sound, $AB = vt$

Distance travelled by truck,

$$AC = ut + \frac{1}{2}at^2$$

$\Rightarrow$ $AC = v_s t + \frac{1}{2}at^2$

$\Rightarrow$ $AC = (at)t + \frac{1}{2}at^2 = \frac{3}{2}at^2$

$$\cos\theta = \frac{AC}{AB} \quad \Rightarrow \quad \cos\theta = \frac{(3/2)\,at^2}{vt}$$

$\Rightarrow$ $at = \left(\frac{2\cos\theta}{3}\right)v$

$\Rightarrow$ $v_s = \frac{2v\cos\theta}{3}$

Substituting value of v_s in eq. (i),

$$600=\left(\frac{v}{v-\left(\frac{2v\cos\theta}{3}\right)\cos\theta}\right)500$$

$\Rightarrow$ $\cos\theta = \frac{1}{2}$

$\Rightarrow$ $\theta = 60°$

9.

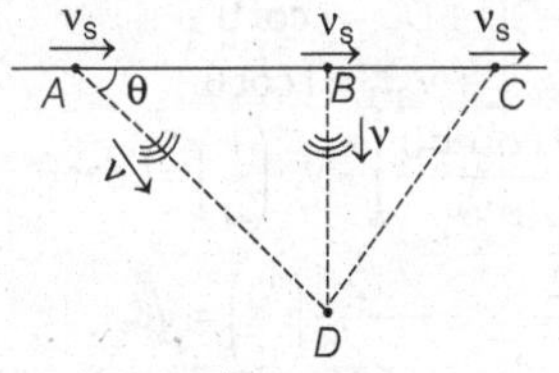

$$\cos\theta=\frac{AB}{AD}=\frac{v_s t_1}{vt_1}=\frac{v_s}{v}$$

$$f_{app}=\left(\frac{v}{v-v_s\cos\theta}\right)f$$

$\Rightarrow$ $3f_0=\left(\frac{v}{v-v_s\left(\frac{v_s}{v}\right)}\right)f_0$

$\Rightarrow$ $\frac{v_s}{v}=\sqrt{\frac{2}{3}}$

$$t_2=\frac{BD}{v}=\frac{BC}{v_s}$$

$\Rightarrow$ $BC=\left(\frac{v_s}{v}\right)BD=\left(\sqrt{\frac{2}{3}}\right)300$

$$CD=\sqrt{(BC)^2+(BD)^2}=100\sqrt{15}\text{ m}$$

$\therefore$ $n = 15$

10. Let the bus be at *O* when it sends a signal that is detected by the detector.

$$f_{app}=\left(\frac{v}{v-v_s\cos\theta}\right)f$$

$\Rightarrow$ $1500=\left(\frac{v}{v-\left(\frac{2v}{3\sqrt{3}}\right)\cos\theta}\right)1000$

$\Rightarrow$ $\cos\theta=\frac{\sqrt{3}}{2}$

$\Rightarrow$ $\theta = 30°$

By the time, signal reaches at *S*, the bus reaches at *D*. Let this time be t_0.

$\therefore \quad t_0 = \frac{OS}{v} = \frac{l \operatorname{cosec} \theta}{v}$

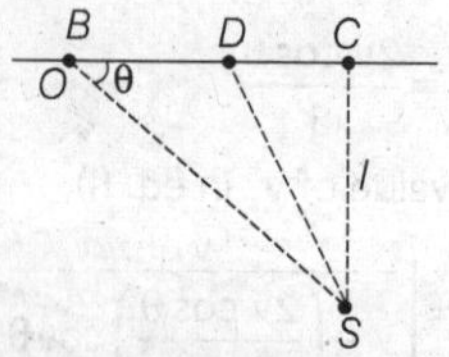

Now, man fires and the bullet reaches C in time t_1 (say). In the same time, bus moves from D to C.

$\therefore \quad t_1 = \frac{l}{u}$ where u = speed of bullet

Also, $\quad OD + DC = l \cot \theta$

$\Rightarrow \quad v_B t_0 + v_B t_1 = l \cot \theta$

$\Rightarrow \quad v_B \left(\frac{l \operatorname{cosec} \theta}{v} \right) + v_B \left(\frac{l}{u} \right) = l \cot \theta$

$\Rightarrow \quad \frac{2}{3\sqrt{3}} \times 2 + \frac{2}{3\sqrt{3}} \left(\frac{v}{u} \right) = \sqrt{3}$

$\Rightarrow \quad u = \frac{2}{5} v = \frac{2}{5} \times 360 = 144 \text{ m/s}$

Previous Year's Questions

JEE Main

1. As passenger inside train has no relative speed relative to engine of train, so frequency heard by passenger is same as that of true frequency.

$\therefore$ Frequency heard by passenger

$= 400 \text{ Hz}$

2. $\boxed{Q} \rightarrow 40$ m/s, $\boxed{P} \rightarrow 20$ m/s

Using doppler's effect,

$$f' = f_0 \left(\frac{v_w + v_D}{v_w + v_s} \right)$$

$$f' = 400 \left(\frac{360 + 40}{360 + 20} \right) = 400 \times \frac{400}{380}$$

$$= 400 \times \frac{400}{380} = \frac{160000}{380}$$

$$f = 421 \text{ Hz}$$

3. Given,

Given; Frequency of horn,

$f_A = 300$ Hz

Speed of sound, $v = 330$ m/s

Speed of trains, $v_s = 30$ m/s

In case of train A, source is moving towards an stationary observer.

So, frequency of sound heard will be

$$f_A' = f_A \left(\frac{v}{v - v_s} \right) = 300 \left(\frac{330}{330 - 30} \right) = 330 \text{ Hz}$$

For train B, source is moving away from a stationary observer.

So, $f_B' = f_B \left(\frac{v}{v + v_s} \right) = \frac{300 \times 330}{(330 + 30)} = 275 \text{ Hz}$

Difference of frequencies is

$$f_A' - f_B' = 330 - 275 = 55 \text{ Hz}$$

4. $f' = f_0 + 40$

$\Rightarrow \quad f_0 \left(\frac{330 + 15}{330 - 15} \right) = f_0 + 40$

$$f_0 \times \frac{345}{315} = f_0 + 40$$

$$f_0 \times \frac{345}{315} - f_0 = 40$$

$$f_0 \times \frac{30}{315} = 40$$

$$f_0 = \frac{40 \times 315}{30}$$

$$f_0 = 420 \text{ Hz}$$

5. Frequency of whistle blowing by train, $f = 320$ Hz

Speed of train, $v_s = 66$ m/s

Speed of sound, $v = 330 \text{ ms}^{-1}$

Frequency observed by the observer,

$$f' = f \left(\frac{v}{v - v_s} \right) = 320 \left(\frac{330}{330 - 66} \right) = 320 \times \frac{330}{264} = 400 \text{ Hz}$$

6. When source is at rest,

$$v_s = 0$$

Velocity of an observer, $v_o = \frac{v}{5}$

Apparent frequency,

$$f' = f \left[\frac{v + v_o}{v - v_s} \right]$$

$$f' = f \left[\frac{v + \left(\frac{v}{5} \right)}{v - 0} \right] \Rightarrow f' = \frac{6f}{5}$$

$\therefore$ % Change in frequency,

$$\frac{f' - f}{f} \times 100\% = \frac{6 - 5}{5} \times 100\% = 20\%$$

7. Given, $v = 340 \text{ ms}^{-1}$

$$v_0 = 72 \text{ km/h} = 20 \text{ m/s}$$

$$v_m = 20 \text{ m/s}$$

$$f = 720 \text{ Hz}$$

Here, $f' = f \left(\frac{v - v_0}{v + v_s} \right) = 720 \left(\frac{(340 + 20) - 20}{(340 + 20) - 0} \right)$

$$= \frac{720 \times 340}{360} = 680 \text{ Hz}$$

8. Given, frequency of whistle,

$$f = 320 \text{ Hz}$$